Nineteenth-Century Literature Criticism

Guide to Gale Literary Criticism Series

For criticism on	Consult these Gale series
Authors now living or who died after December 31, 1959	**CONTEMPORARY LITERARY CRITICISM (CLC)**
Authors who died between 1900 and 1959	**TWENTIETH-CENTURY LITERARY CRITICISM (TCLC)**
Authors who died between 1800 and 1899	**NINETEENTH-CENTURY LITERATURE CRITICISM (NCLC)**
Authors who died between 1400 and 1799	**LITERATURE CRITICISM FROM 1400 TO 1800 (LC)** **SHAKESPEAREAN CRITICISM (SC)**
Authors who died before 1400	**CLASSICAL AND MEDIEVAL LITERATURE CRITICISM (CMLC)**
Black writers of the past two hundred years	**BLACK LITERATURE CRITICISM (BLC)**
Authors of books for children and young adults	**CHILDREN'S LITERATURE REVIEW (CLR)**
Dramatists	**DRAMA CRITICISM (DC)**
Hispanic writers of the late nineteenth and twentieth centuries	**HISPANIC LITERATURE CRITICISM (HLC)**
Native North American writers and orators of the eighteenth, nineteenth, and twentieth centuries	**NATIVE NORTH AMERICAN LITERATURE (NNAL)**
Poets	**POETRY CRITICISM (PC)**
Short story writers	**SHORT STORY CRITICISM (SSC)**
Major authors from the Renaissance to the present	**WORLD LITERATURE CRITICISM, 1500 TO THE PRESENT (WLC)**

Volume 66

Nineteenth-Century Literature Criticism

Excerpts from Criticism of the Works of Novelists, Poets, Playwrights, Short Story Writers, Philosophers, and Other Creative Writers Who Died between 1800 and 1899, from the First Published Critical Appraisals to Current Evaluations

**Gerald R. Barterian
Denise Evans**
Editors

DETROIT • NEW YORK • LONDON

STAFF

Gerald R. Barterian and Denise Evans, *Editors*

Dana Barnes, Dan Marowski, *Contributing Editors*
Amy Crook, *Associate Editor*
Ira Mark Milne, *Assistant Editor*

Aarti D. Stephens, *Managing Editor*

Susan M. Trosky, *Permissions Manager*
Kimberly F. Smilay, *Permissions Specialist*
Sarah Chesney, Steve Cusack, Kelly A. Quin, *Permissions Associates*

Victoria B. Cariappa, *Research Manager*
Julia C. Daniel, Jeff Daniels, Tamara C. Nott,
Tracie A. Richardson, Cheryl L. Warnock, *Research Associates*
Phyllis Blackman, Corrine Stocker, *Research Assistants*

Mary Beth Trimper, *Production Director*
Deborah L. Milliken, *Production Assistant*

Gary Leach, *Macintosh Artist*
Randy Bassett, *Image Database Supervisor*
Robert Duncan, Michael Logusz, *Imaging Specialists*
Pamela A. Reed, *Imaging Coordinator*

Since this page cannot legibly accommodate all copyright notices, the acknowledgments constitute an extension of the copyright notice.

While every effort has been made to secure permission to reprint material and to ensure the reliability of the information presented in this publication, Gale Research neither guarantees the accuracy of the data contained herein nor assumes any responsibility for errors, omissions or discrepancies. Gale accepts no payment for listing; and inclusion in the publication of any organization, agency, institution, publication, service, or individual does not imply endorsement of the editors or publisher. Errors brought to the attention of the publisher and verified to the satisfaction of the publisher will be corrected in future editions.

This publication is a creative work fully protected by all applicable copyright laws, as well as by misappropriation, trade secret, unfair competition, and other applicable laws. The authors and editors of this work have added value to the underlying factual material herein through one or more of the following: unique and original selection, coordination, expression, arrangement, and classification of the information.

All rights to this publication will be vigorously defended.

Copyright © 1998
Gale Research
835 Penobscot Building
Detroit, MI 48226-4094

All rights reserved including the right of reproduction in whole or in part in any form.

This book is printed on acid-free paper that meets the minimum requirements of American National Standard for Information Sciences—Permanence Paper for Printed Library Materials, ANSI Z39.48-1984.

Library of Congress Catalog Card Number 84-643008
ISBN 0-7876-1905-1
ISSN 0732-1864
Printed in the United States of America

10 9 8 7 6 5 4 3 2 1

Contents

Preface vii

Acknowledgments xi

Elizabeth Barrett Browning 1806-1861 1
English poet and translator; entry devoted to Aurora Leigh.

Isabelle de Charrière 1740-1805 119
Dutch-born Swiss novelist, essayist, dramatist, short story writer, librettist, and poet.

Mary Moody Emerson 1774-1863 185
American intellectual.

Gustave Flaubert 1821-1880 233
French novelist, short story writer, and playwright; entry devoted to Madame Bovary.

Christina Georgina Rossetti 1830-1894 297
English poet, short story writer, and prose writer; entry devoted to Goblin Market.

Literary Criticism Series Cumulative Author Index 393

Literary Criticism Series Topic Index 457

NCLC Cumulative Nationality Index 467

NCLC-66 Title Index 471

Preface

Since its inception in 1981, *Nineteenth-Century Literature Criticism* has been a valuable resource for students and librarians seeking critical commentary on writers of this transitional period in world history. Designated an "Outstanding Reference Source" by the American Library Association with the publication of its first volume, *NCLC* has since been purchased by over 6,000 school, public, and university libraries. The series has covered more than 400 authors representing 30 nationalities and over 18,000 titles. No other reference source has surveyed the critical reaction to nineteenth-century authors and literature as thoroughly as *NCLC*.

Scope of the Series

NCLC is designed to introduce students and advanced readers to the authors of the nineteenth century, and to the most significant interpretations of these authors' works. The great poets, novelists, short story writers, playwrights, and philosophers of this period are frequently studied in high school and college literature courses. By organizing and reprinting commentary written on these authors, *NCLC* helps students develop valuable insight into literary history, promotes a better understanding of the texts, and sparks ideas for papers and assignments. Each entry in *NCLC* presents a comprehensive survey of an author's career or an individual work of literature and provides the user with a multiplicity of interpretations and assessments. Such variety allows students to pursue their own interests; furthermore, it fosters an awareness that literature is dynamic and responsive to many different opinions.

Every fourth volume of *NCLC* is devoted to literary topics that cannot be covered under the author approach used in the rest of the series. Such topics include literary movements, prominent themes in nineteenth-century literature, literary reaction to political and historical events, significant eras in literary history, prominent literary anniversaries, and the literatures of cultures that are often overlooked by English-speaking readers.

NCLC continues the survey of criticism of world literature begun by Gale's *Contemporary Literary Criticism (CLC)* and *Twentieth-Century Literary Criticism (TCLC)*, both of which excerpt and reprint commentary on authors of the twentieth century. For additional information about *TCLC, CLC,* and Gale's other criticism series, users should consult the Guide to Gale Literary Criticism Series preceding the title page in this volume.

Coverage

Each volume of *NCLC* is carefully compiled to present:

- criticism of authors, or literary topics, representing a variety of genres and nationalities

- both major and lesser-known writers and literary works of the period

- 5-8 authors or 4-6 topics per volume

- individual entries that survey critical response to an author's work or a topic in literary history, including early criticism to reflect initial reactions, later criticism to represent any rise or decline in reputation, and current retrospective analyses.

Organization

An author entry consists of the following elements: author heading, biographical and critical introduction, list of principal works, excerpts of criticism (each preceded by a bibliographic citation and an annotation), and a bibliography of further reading.

- The **Author Heading** consists of the name under which the author most commonly wrote, followed by birth and death dates. If an author wrote consistently under a pseudonym, the pseudonym will be listed in the author heading and the real name given in parentheses on the first line of the biographical and critical introduction. Also located at the beginning of the introduction to the author entry are any name variations under which an author wrote, including transliterated forms for an author whose language uses a nonroman alphabet.

- The **Biographical and Critical Introduction** outlines the author's life and career, as well as the critical issues surrounding his or her work. References are provided to past volumes of *NCLC* in which further information about the author may be found.

- Most *NCLC* entries include a **Portrait** of the author. Many entries also contain reproductions of materials pertinent to an author's career, including manuscript pages, title pages, dust jackets, letters, and drawings, as well as photographs of important people, places, and events in an author's life.

- The list of **Principal Works** is chronological by date of first publication and identifies the genre of each work. In the case of foreign authors with both foreign-language publications and English translations, the English-language version is given in brackets. Unless otherwise indicated, dramas are dated by first performance, not first publication.

- **Criticism** in each author entry is arranged chronologically to provide a perspective on changes in critical evaluation over the years. All titles of works by the author featured in the entry are printed in boldface type to enable the user to easily locate discussion of particular works. Also for purposes of easier identification, the critic's name and the publication date of the essay are given at the beginning of each piece of criticism. Unsigned criticism is preceded by the title of the journal in which it appeared. Publication information (such as publisher names and book prices) and some parenthetical numerical references (such as page and line references to specific editions of works) have been deleted at the editors' discretion to provide smoother reading of the text. Footnotes that appear with previously published pieces of criticism are reprinted at the end of each essay or excerpt. In the case of excerpted criticism, only those footnotes that pertain to the excerpted text are included.

- A complete **Bibliographic Citation** provides original publication information for each piece of criticism.

- Critical excerpts are prefaced by **Annotations** providing the reader with a summary of the critical intent of the piece. Also included, when appropriate, is information about the critic's reputation, individual approach to literary criticism, and particular expertise in an author's works, as well as information about the relative importance of the critical excerpt. In some cases, the annotations cross-reference excerpts by critics who discuss each other's commentary.

- An annotated list of **Further Reading** appearing at the end of each entry suggests secondary sources on the author. In some cases it includes essays for which the editors could not obtain reprint rights.

Cumulative Indexes

- Each volume of *NCLC* contains a cumulative **Author Index** listing all authors who have appeared in Gale's Literary Criticism Series, along with cross-references to such biographical series as *Contemporary Authors* and *Dictionary of Literary Biography*. Useful for locating authors within the various series, this index is particularly valuable for those authors who are identified with a certain period but who, because of their death dates, are placed in another, or for those authors whose careers span two periods. For example, Fyodor Dostoevsky is found in *NCLC*, yet Leo Tolstoy, another major nineteenth-century Russian novelist, is found in *TCLC* because he died after 1899.

- Each *NCLC* volume includes a cumulative **Nationality Index** which lists all authors who have appeared in *NCLC*, arranged alphabetically under their respective nationalities.

- Each new volume in Gale's Literary Criticism Series includes a cumulative **Topic Index**, which lists all literary topics treated in *NCLC, TCLC, LC 1400-1800*, and the *CLC* Yearbook.

- Each new volume of *NCLC*, with the exception of the Topics volumes, contains a **Title Index** listing the titles of all literary works discussed in the volume. In response to numerous suggestions from librarians, Gale has also produced a **Special Paperbound Edition** of the *NCLC* title index. This annual cumulation lists all titles discussed in the series since its inception. Additional copies of the index are available on request. Librarians and patrons have welcomed this separate index: it saves shelf space, is easy to use, and is recyclable upon receipt of the following year's cumulation. Titles discussed in the Topics volume entries are not included in the *NCLC* cumulative index.

Citing *Nineteenth-Century Literature Criticism*

When writing papers, students who quote directly from any volume in Gale's Literary Criticism Series may use the following general forms to footnote reprinted criticism. The first example pertains to material drawn from periodicals, the second to material reprinted from books:

[1]T.S. Eliot, "John Donne," *The Nation and Athenaeum*, 33 (9 June 1923), 321-32; excerpted and reprinted in *Literature Criticism from 1400-1800,* Vol. 10, ed. James E. Person, Jr. (Detroit: Gale Research, 1989), pp. 28-9.

[2]Clara G. Stillman, *Samuel Butler: A Mid-Victorian Modern* (Viking Press, 1932); excerpted and reprinted in *Twentieth-Century Literary Criticism,* Vol. 33, ed. Paula Kepos (Detroit: Gale Research, 1989), pp. 43-5.

Suggestions Are Welcome

In response to suggestions, several features have been added to *NCLC* since the series began, including annotations to excerpted criticism, a cumulative index to authors in all Gale literary criticism series, entries devoted to criticism on a single work by a major author, more illustrations, and a title index listing all literary works discussed in the series.

Readers who wish to suggest authors, single works, or topics to appear in future volumes, or who have other suggestions, are cordially invited to write: The Editors, *Nineteenth-Century Literature Criticism*, 835 Penobscot Bldg., 645 Griswold St., Detroit, MI 48226-4094; call toll-free at 1-800-347-GALE; or fax to 1-313-961-6599.

Acknowledgments

The editors wish to thank the copyright holders of the excerpted criticism included in this volume and the permissions managers of many book and magazine publishing companies for assisting us in securing reproduction rights. We are also grateful to the staffs of the Detroit Public Library, the Library of Congress, the University of Detroit Mercy Library, Wayne State University Purdy/Kresge Library Complex, and the University of Michigan Libraries for making their resources available to us. Following is a list of the copyright holders who have granted us permission to reproduce material in this volume of *NCLC*. Every effort has been made to trace copyright, but if omissions have been made, please let us know.

COPYRIGHTED EXCERPTS IN *NCLC*, VOLUME 66, WERE REPRODUCED FROM THE FOLLOWING PERIODICALS:

Children's Literature, v. 12, 1984. Reproduced by permission.—*Eighteenth-Century Life,* v. 13, February, 1989. (c) 1989. Reproduced by permission of The Johns Hopkins University Press.—*ELH,* v. 58, Winter, 1991. Copyright (c) 1991 by The Johns Hopkins University Press. All rights reserved. Reproduced by permission.—*The Explicator,* v. 51, Fall, 1992. Copyright (c) Helen Dwight Reid Educational Foundation. Reproduced with permission of the Helen Dwight Reid Educational Foundation, published by Heldref Publications, 1319 18th Street, NW, Washington, DC 20036-1802.—*Forum for Modern Language Studies,* Vol. XXVIII, April, 1992. (c) *Forum for Modern Language Studies,* 1992. Reproduced by permission.—*French Forum,* v. 11, September, 1986. Copyright (c) by French Forum Publishers, Inc. Reproduced by permission.—*French Studies,* v. XLIX, July, 1995. (c) The Society for French Studies 1995. Reproduced by permission.—*International Journal of Women's Studies,* v. 3, September/October, 1980 for "New Yet Orthodox: Female Characters in *Aurora Leigh*" by Kathleen K. Hickok. Reproduced by permission.—*Nineteenth-Century Literature,* v. 51, December, 1996. (c) 1996 by The Regents of the University of California. Reproduced by permission of the publisher and the author.—*PMLA,* v. 93, October, 1978. Copyright (c) 1978 by the Modern Language Association of America. Reproduced by permission of the Modern Language Association of America.—*Studies in Eighteenth-Century Culture,* v. 14, 1985; v. 21, 1991. Copyright (c) 1985, 1991 American Society for Eighteenth-Century Studies. All rights reserved. Both reproduced by permission of the University of Wisconsin Press.—*Studies in the American Renaissance,* 1986, 1993. Both reproduced by permission.—*The Victorian Newsletter,* Spring, 1986 for "Genre and Gender in *Aurora Leigh*" by Dorothy Mermin. Reproduced by permission of *The Victorian Newsletter* and the author.—*Victorian Poetry,* v. 19, Spring, 1981 for "*Aurora Leigh*: The Vocation of The Woman Poet," by Barbara Charlesworth Gelpi/ v. 21, Summer, 1983 for "Heroic Sisterhood in *Goblin Market,*" by Dorothy Mermin/ v. 22, Winter, 1984 for "'Speaking Likenesses': Language and Repetition in Christina Rossetti's *Goblin Market,*" by Steven Conner/ v. 29, Spring, 1991 for "The Potential of Sisterhood: Christina Rossetti's *Goblin Market,*" by Janet Galligani Casey/ v. 29, Winter, 1991 for "'Eat Me, Drink Me, Love Me,': The Consumable Female Body in Christina Rossetti's *Goblin Market,*" by Mary Wilson Carpenter. All reproduced by permission of the authors.

COPYRIGHTED EXCERPTS IN *NCLC*, VOLUME 66, WERE REPRODUCED FROM THE FOLLOWING BOOKS:

Allison, Jenene J. From *Revealing Difference: The Fiction of Isabelle de Charrière.* Associated University Presses, 1995. (c) 1995 by Associated University Presses, Inc. All rights reserved. Reproduced by permission.—Barish, Evelyn. From *Mothering the Mind: Twelve Studies of Writers and Their Silent Partners.* Edited by Ruth Perry and Martine Watson Brownley. Holmes & Meier, 1984. Copyright (c) 1984 by Ruth Perry and Martine Watson Brownley. All rights reserved. Reproduced by permission.—Cole, Phyllis. From *Emerson: Prospect and Retrospect.* Edited by Joel Porte. Harvard University Press, 1982. Copyright (c) 1982 by the President and Fellows of Harvard College. All rights reserved. Reproduced by permission.—Festa-McCormick, Diana. From *Gender and Literary Voice.* Edited by Janet Todd. Holmes & Meier Publishers, Inc., 1980. Copyright (c) 1980 by Holmes & Meier Publishers, Inc. All rights reserved. Reproduced by permission.—Gilbert, Sandra M. and Susan Gubar. From *The Madwoman in the Attic: The*

Woman Writer and the Nineteenth-Century Literary Imagination. Yale University Press, 1979. Copyright (c) 1979 Yale University Press. All rights reserved. Reproduced by permission.—Ginsburg, Michal Peled. From *Flaubert Writing: A Study in Narrative Strategies.* Stanford University Press, 1986. Copyright (c) 1986 by the Board of Trustees of Leland Stanford Junior University. Reproduced with the permission of the publishers, Stanford University Press.—Hodder, Alan D. From *Emerson's Rhetoric of Revelation: Nature, the Reader, and the Apocalypse Within.* The Pennsylvania State University Press, 1989. Copyright 1989 by The Pennsylvania State University. Reproduced by permission of the publisher.—Jaeger, Kathleen M. From *Male and Female Roles in the Eighteenth Century: The Challenge to Replacement and Displacement in the Novels of Isabelle de Charrière.* Peter Lang, 1994. (c) Peter Lang Publishing, Inc., New York. All rights reserved. Reproduced by permission.—Kaplan, Cora. From *Women Writing and Writing About Women.* Edited by Mary Jacobus. Croom Helm, 1979. (c) 1979 Gillian Beer, Inga-Stina Ewbank, Elaine Feinstein, John Goode, Mary Jacobus, Cora Kaplan, Laura Mulvey, Elaine Showalter, Anne Stevenson. Reproduced by permission of Routledge.—LaCapra, Dominick. From *Madame Bovary on Trial.* Cornell University Press, 1982. Copyright (c) 1982 Cornell University Press. All rights reserved. Reproduced by permission of the publisher, Cornell University Press. All additional uses of this material—including, but not limited to, photocopying and reprinting—are prohibited without the prior written approval of Cornell University Press.—Leighton, Angela. From *Elizabeth Barrett Browning.* The Harvester Press, 1986. (c) Angela Leighton. All rights reserved. Reproduced by permission.—Moers, Ellen. From *Literary Women.* Doubleday & Company, Inc., 1976. Copyright (c) 1963, 1972, 1973, 1974, 1975, 1976 by (c) Ellen Moers. Reproduced by permission of Doubleday, a division of Bantam Doubleday Dell Publishing Group, Inc. and Curtis Brown, New York.—Porter, Dennis. From *Flaubert and Postmodernism.* Edited by Naomi Schor and Henry F. Majewski. University of Nebraska Press, 1984. Copyright (c) The University of Nebraska Press 1984. Reproduced by permission.—Reynolds, Margaret. From an introduction to *Aurora Leigh,* by Elizabeth Barrett Browning. Edited by Margaret Reynolds. Ohio University Press, 1992. Introduction and Notes (c) copyright 1992 by Margaret Reynolds. All rights reserved. Reproduced by permission.—Simmons, Nancy Craig. From *The Selected Writings of Mary Moody Emerson.* Edited by Nancy Craig Simmons. The University of Georgia Press, 1993. (c) 1993 by the University of Georgia Press. All rights reserved. Reproduced by permission.—Stewart, Joan Hinde. From *A New History of French Literature.* Edited by Denis Hollier. Harvard University Press, 1989. Copyright (c) 1989 by the President and Fellows of Harvard College. All rights reserved. Reproduced by permission of the publishers.—Tanner, Tony. From *Adultery in the Novel: Contract and Transgression.* The Johns Hopkins University Press, 1979. Copyright (c) 1979 by The Johns Hopkins University Press. All rights reserved. Reproduced by permission.—Wing, Nathaniel. From *The Limits of the Narrative: Essays on Baudelaire, Flaubert, Rimbaud and Mallarmé.* Cambridge University Press, 1986. (c) 1986 Cambridge University Press. Reproduced with the permission of Cambridge University Press and the author.

PHOTOGRAPHS AND ILLUSTRATIONS APPEARING IN *NCLC*, VOLUME 66, WERE RECEIVED FROM THE FOLLOWING SOURCES:

Browning, Elizabeth Barrett (wearing dark, hooded cape, ringlets), engraving. Corbis-Bettman. Reproduced by permission.—*Browning, Elizabeth Barrett* (seated, in dark dress with lace collar), print. Archive Photos, Inc. Reproduced by permission.—*Barrett, Edward,* painting by H. W. Pickersgill.—*Browning, Elizabeth Barrett,* drawing by her mother, 1823.—*Browning, Elizabeth Barrett,* tomb in the English Cemetery, Florence, photograph.—*Charrière, Isabelle de,* pastel by Maurice Quentin de la Tour. The Granger Collection, New York. Reproduced by permission.—*Emerson, Ralph W.* (wearing bow tie), engraving by S. A. Choff c. 1878. The Library of Congress.—*Flaubert, Gustave,* photograph. Library of Congress.—A title page for *Madame Bovary* by Gustave Flaubert, 1857, photograph. Corbis-Bettmann. Reproduced by permission.—A scene from *Madame Bovary* by Gustave Flaubert, Monsieur Bovary opens desk, photograph. Corbis-Bettmann. Reproduced by permission.—A drawing by Hernan Roundtree for *Madame Bovary* by Gustave Flaubert, of Emma Bovary, photograph. Corbis-Bettmann. Reproduced by permission.—An illustration for *Madame Bovary* by Gustave Flaubert, the death of Emma Bovary, photograph. Corbis-Bettmann. Reproduced by permission.—Illustration for the 1885 scene for *Madame Bovary* by Gustave Flaubert, Emma and the Abbey Bournisien, photograph. Corbis-Bettmann. Reproduced by permission.—Illustration for *Madame Bovary* by Gustave Flaubert, the death of Emma Bovary, photograph. Corbis-Bettmann. Reproduced by permission.—*Rossetti, Christina* (seated at wooden table), illustration. Corbis. Reproduced by permission.—*Rossetti, Christina,* 1863, photograph by Lewis Carroll. UPI/Bettmann. Reproduced by permission.

Aurora Leigh

Elizabeth Barrett Browning

The following entry presents criticism of Browning's poem *Aurora Leigh* (1857). For further information on Browning's complete career, see *NCLC*, Volumes 1 and 61; for discussion of the poetry collection *Sonnets from the Portuguese*, see *NCLC*, Volume 16.

INTRODUCTION

Regarded by contemporary and recent critics as one of the most notable female poets in Western literature, Elizabeth Barrett Browning wrote *Aurora Leigh* at the height of her literary career, and the poem is deemed her masterwork in terms of poetics and narrative. Part autobiography and part social criticism, the poem traces the life of an Englishwoman and poet, Aurora Leigh, and is frequently cited as a proto-feminist treatise for its portrayal of difficulties arising for female characters from traditional values and practices of English society. Browning's innovative use of genre, self-reference, and feminine perspective make *Aurora Leigh* a landmark of nineteenth-century literature.

Biographical Information

Browning had planned to write a novel in blank verse as early as 1845, and had proposed that the subject would be a critical narrative of ordinary English life. At the time of *Aurora Leigh*'s publication in 1857, Browning, supported by her friendship and eventual marriage to Robert Browning in September of 1846, had recovered from a long period of poor health, family catastrophes, and isolation. In 1850, *Sonnets from the Portuguese*, written during her courtship with Browning, had been published to popular acclaim, and her reputation as a poet, especially of sentimental works, had grown. A son, Robert Wiedemann Barrett Browning, had been born to the couple in 1849, and this seems to have rejuvenated Browning's artistic endeavors. The Brownings began to travel extensively and became involved in politics on the Continent; Barrett Browning subsequently expressed in *Aurora Leigh* a concern with social issues, particularly the rights of women and the poor, and revealed her familiarity with European and classical literature as well. *Aurora Leigh*, published in 1857, was the most successful of Browning's works from a commercial standpoint: the book had gone through nineteen editions by 1885.

Plot and Major Characters

A "novel in verse," as Coventry Patmore called it, *Aurora Leigh* follows the life of its heroine through

her birth and childhood in Italy, intellectual development, literary career, and personal relationships. At a young age, Aurora Leigh resists the conventional and complacent English values imposed on her by a maiden aunt who cares for her after the death of her parents, and she discovers the pleasures of literature. Her early creative compositions stir her ambitions to support herself through a poetic career, and in time she becomes moderately successful in London literary circles. In the process of accomplishing this, Aurora rejects a marriage proposal from her cousin Romney Leigh, a wealthy philanthropist and owner of the family estate, who soon rescues a young woman named Marian Erle from poverty. The growing attachment between Romney and Marian is severed, however, by the unscrupulous Lady Waldemar, who is herself in love with Romney. Lady Waldemar contributes to Marian's disappearance from London and her reappearance in a Paris brothel, where Marian is sexually assaulted and bears a child. Aurora, on her way to Italy, recognizes Marian in Paris and takes her and her child to Florence. When Romney's socialist utopian community disastrously fails, he acknowledges the emptiness and hypocrisy of conventional methods of philanthropy, and travels to Florence. After a series of misunderstandings in which Aurora believes Romney has already wed Lady Waldemar, Romney once again asks Aurora to marry him. This she does, recognizing that art needs to be aided by love and partnership in the process of self-realization.

Major Themes

Browning addressed several major social issues in the narrative of *Aurora Leigh*—the relationship between art and individual self-fulfillment, the issue of class politics, and the issue of gender roles. The work suggests that individual freedom, regardless of class or gender, allows for inner development and the cultivation of creativity and inspiration. However, the novel-poem shows sensitivity to other aspects of the creative process, such as the background to the production of any artistic work and the source of creativity in turmoil and conflict. Furthermore, *Aurora Leigh* intricately weaves the political implications of Browning's own strong individualism and her emphasis on the actualization of one's life's work into Aurora Leigh's struggle to find her place, as a woman poet, in the traditional social order found in the poem. In addition, the work focuses on the institutionalized sexism and classicism of the Victorian age, and directs its severest criticism at conventional philanthropy as hypocritical and paternalistic. Also, *Aurora Leigh* depicts, through the character of Marian Erle, the horrific consequences of the abuse and neglect suffered by the poor—particularly poor women. The subplot of Marian and her child also censures the Victorian tendency to reject those who have been sexually attacked, and argues for greater concern for and treatment of the innocent victims.

Critical Reception

Despite its tremendous popular success, *Aurora Leigh* received mixed reactions from contemporary critics. Many, in addition to calling it immoral, found fault with its characterization, plot, and language; others, however, found the work proof of Browning's "poetic genius." The poem was largely neglected by subsequent critics until the early 1930s, when Virginia Woolf's enthusiastic article on the poem was published. The emergence of feminist criticism helped spark renewed interest in the work, although *Aurora Leigh* is not unanimously accepted as a precursor to modern feminism. Commenting on the poem's conclusion in particular, many feminist critics have regarded Aurora's acceptance of marriage as the beginning of her loss of independence. Others have found in the ending a radical deviation from traditional nineteenth-century thought—instead of losing her independence through marriage, Aurora gains a rewarding and satisfying life through the blending of her artistic achievement with the love and partnership of another. According to several twentieth-century critics, this innovation is echoed in Browning's style: although contemporary reviewers criticized her unconventional poetic tendencies, more recent scholars consider her style to be innovative. Altogether, *Aurora Leigh* illuminates both Browning's artistic strengths and her weaknesses: she is praised for her ability to express passionate emotion, yet she is criticized for choosing such an abstract topic for *Aurora Leigh* as her "highest convictions upon Life and Art." She is commended for her lyrical tone and innovative use of imagery, yet she is criticized for her verbose style, improbable plot, and unrealistic characters. In light of fervent endorsements of the poem by such literary figures as Emily Dickinson and Virginia Woolf, *Aurora Leigh* is generally judged to be a masterwork with noticeable flaws and remains highly significant to contemporary literary historians and critics.

CRITICISM

Henry Fothergill Chorley (review date 1856)

SOURCE: Review of *Aurora Leigh*, in *The Athenaeum*, No. 1517, November 22, 1856, pp. 1425-7.

[*In this review, Chorley praises Browning's style and intent but claims that the plot of* Aurora Leigh *is "in its argument unnatural, and in its form infelicitous."*]

Our best living English poetess—our greatest English poetess of any time—has essayed in *Aurora Leigh* to blend the epic with the didactic novel. The medium in which the story floats is that impassioned language—spotted and flowered with the imagery suggested by fancy or stored up by learning,—which has given the verse of Mrs. Browning a more fiery acceptance from the young and spiritual, and her name a higher renown than any woman has heretofore gained.

We dwell on the sex of the author of *Aurora Leigh* in no disrespectful spirit of comparison, but simply because to overlook it is rendered impossible by the poetess herself. *Aurora Leigh,* into which she says "have entered her highest convictions upon Life and Art," is her contribution to the chorus of protest and mutual exhortation, which Woman is now raising, in hope of gaining the due place and sympathy which, it is held, have been denied to her since the days when Man was created, the first of the pair in Eden. Who can quarrel with the intent? Who would silence any struggle made by those who fancy themselves desolate, oppressed, undervalued,—to unlock the prison-doors,—to melt the heart of injustice? Mrs. Browning is never unwomanly in her passionate pleadings for women: unwomanly she could not be, after having wrought out that beautiful and tender conception of Eve, which gives such peculiar grace to her '**Drama of Exile.**' Her Confession (for like all works of its class, *Aurora Leigh* has in it a tone of confession,) amounts to an admission of failure: its conclusion is that indicated from another point of view by Mrs. Hemans, in her 'Properzia Rossi.' The moral is the insufficiency of Fame and Ambition, be either ever so generous, to make up for the absence of Love:—a class-vindication wound up by an appeal against class-separation. Thus, as in all the works of its kind, which women have so freely poured out from their full hearts during late years, we see the agony more clearly than the remedy. We are shown, at first, restlessness disdaining quiet; till, fevered and forlorn, as time and grief do their work, the restless heart ends in courting the very repose it so scorned when first tendered. But while Truth closes the tale, in its progress Imagination has been strained beyond permissible freedom. In brief, we regret to declare that Mrs. Browning's longest and most matured effort, jewelled though it be with rich thought and rare fancies, is in its argument unnatural, and in its form infelicitous.

Aurora Leigh is a born poetess, the child of an English father and an Italian mother,—on the father's side connected with wealth and old name. She is sent over to England, when an orphan, to be cared for and educated by a maiden aunt,—that well-worn spectral apparition of convention in buckram, without which no tale of woman's aspirings, it seems, can be told. Such persons, whose narrow capacities bring on limited views of duty, have been long abused; but their time, it appears, has not yet come. Meanwhile, they serve their turn with those who make fantastic panoramas of life. Without such aunts (grim substitute for the stepmother of ancient romance!) no woman of genius could be cradled into poetry through wrong; and Mrs. Browning only adopts a convention in denouncing convention. Aurora is wooed by her cousin, Romney Leigh, a rich, high-hearted philanthropist, to whom her heart is not disinclined. But he is too big in the consciousness of his own philanthropy; and waywardly she conceives the idea that she is asked to become his wife in a strain of persuasion unworthy the ear of a great and gifted woman,—that she is sought from low motives, (as, indeed, are most wives,) and that her career, as an unassisted and independent woman of genius, will be brighter if she retains her heart in her own keeping. Accordingly Aurora rejects Romney as a husband,—spurns his generous attempts to smooth the path of life for her by tendering a share of the family fortune. Putting on poverty as a singing robe, she adopts authorship in London, becomes famous and admired, and dwells like a star apart. Foiled of his object, Romney Leigh embraces his plans of social reforms with an earnestness, in which there is the intoxication of a wounded spirit as much as the conviction of one called to the priest's office. He opens a phalanstery, affects only the society of the sick, sorrowful, or guilty, and, willing to attest his superiority to class prejudice by the most solemn act a man can do, prepares to marry one Marian Erle, a milliner's apprentice,—who is humble, ignorant, but as devoted and as noble in her way as either Romney or Aurora. The latter (in spite of her having begun to discover that she had made a mistake in rejecting her cousin, and in fancying that fame could supply the place of love) seeks out Marian. The girl's story is powerfully told, but is unreal in the poetry and holiness of nature it reveals in one nurtured, tortured, and beset as she has been. Such resistance as hers must have hardened the victim in the struggle,—whereas Marian is soft as a briar-rose, besides being pure as the dew-bead on it. Aurora welcomes and embraces her with enthusiastic devotion. Not so other of Romney's female friends. A wicked influence is at work against the poor sempstress:—a woman of fashion, one Lady Waldemar, who has fallen in love with Romney Leigh, (and for his sake, with Christian socialism) so practises upon Marian, that on the appointed wedding-day, when St. Giles and St. James are bidden to church to see the Socialist gentleman married (a parade somewhat insolent in its condescension), the bride is not forthcoming, but in her place a mysterious letter. Instead of the bridal revel, where Rank and Rags were to sit at the same board, there is a brawl in the church:—Marian is gone—no one knows whither.

As years roll on, Aurora's authorship prospers. She is praised in the reviews—she is a lion in London *soirées;* and from not any of the most common-place and frivolous of these transactions, with all their train of prosaic and poverty-stricken adjuncts, does *our* artist shrink as a subject for art. Nevertheless, Aurora finds out that she is alone in spirit after all; and more stung than she cares to own, by a rumour in the *coteries* that Cousin Romney is about to marry this evil Lady Waldemar, she resolves to give up England for a time, and go home to Italy. On her way—in Paris—she lights on Marian, now the unwedded mother of a beautiful boy, and learns from her the sequel to her story: how Lady Waldemar had not only detached her from the noble gentleman who would have married her; had not only, as we have seen, prevailed on her to give up Cousin Romney; but, under pretext of sending her out to the Colonies, had allowed her to fall into the hands of an infamous woman, by whom Marian—herself innocent—was forced into ruin. In this hideous page of the romance Mrs. Browning puts forth all her power. Aurora at once takes the outraged Marian to her heart, carries her off with her child to Italy, and writes home her disclosure of Lady Waldemar's machinations—in order that it may reach Romney. After them, in due course of time, he arrives. By the old trick, well worn in novels and plays, Aurora receives him, under the misapprehension that he is Lady Waldemar's husband; but he presently assures her that, so far from being so, he has come to Italy still to marry Marian, and to adopt the child of violence and misery as his own. Once more, however, and this time unprompted by all except her own nature, Marian refuses to marry Romney;—assuring him that she does not love him now; that indeed she never did love him as he deserved to be loved; that she will live for her child, and no creature else: and it is in this crisis that Aurora and Romney at last come to an understanding. The artist has found the hollowness of Art to fill and to satisfy; and the philanthropist's experiences are drearier still. He has been rewarded for his care for the vile and the humble by having his father's house burnt over his head—in the catastrophe having lost his sight, it is hinted, owing to the vengeance of Marian's reprobate father.

Such is a brief sketch of the argument of *Aurora Leigh;* and not a few who read it will be tempted to say, This looks not like a poem, but a novel, belonging to the period which has produced 'Ruth,' and 'Villette,' and 'The Blithedale Romance.' We will not stop to ask how far the invention be true to life and to art; since the form of its presentment may be pleaded in excuse for anything unreal in character, false in sentiment, or exaggerated in incident, which exists in the plot and the persons working it out. But what are we to say if we waive purpose—if we do not discuss the wisdom of the form selected (large concessions these, yet due to one so gifted and so passionately in earnest as Mrs. Browning)—if we treat *Aurora Leigh* as a poetical romance? Simply, that we have no experience of such a mingling of what is precious with what is mean—of the voice of clarion and the lyric cadence of harp with the cracked school-room spinet—of tears and small-talk—of eloquent apostrophe and adust speculation—of the grandeur of passion and the pettiness of modes and manners—as we find in these nine books of blank verse. Milton's organ is put by Mrs. Browning to play polkas in May-Fair drawing-rooms, and fitted out by her with its *Æsthetic Review* stop, which drones out lengths and strains of a strange quality. But it yields, too, beneath her fingers those glorious chords and melodies, which (musicians have fancied) are the real occupation and utterance of that instrument. Is this severe? Let any one that thinks so take the following commencement of the scene in the church at Romney's interrupted wedding as a passage from a poem:

> We waited. It was early: there was time
> For greeting, and the morning's compliment;
> And gradually a ripple of women's talk
> Arose and fell, and tossed about a spray
> Of English *ss,* soft as a silent hush,
> And, notwithstanding, quite as audible
> As louder phrases thrown out by the men.
> —"Yes, really, if we've need to wait in church,
> We've need to talk there."—"She? 'Tis Lady Ayr,
> In blue—not purple! that's the dowager."
> —"She looks as young."—"She flirts as young, you mean!
> Why if you had seen her upon Thursday night,
> You'd call Miss Norris modest."—"*You* again!
> I waltzed with you three hours back. Up at six,
> Up still at ten: scarce time to change one's shoes.
> I feel as white and sulky as a ghost,
> So pray don't speak to me, Lord Belcher."—
> "No,
> I'll look at you instead, and it's enough
> While you have that face."—"In church, my lord! fle, fle!"
> —"Adair, you stayed for the Division?"—"Lost
> By one."—"The devil it is! I'm sorry for't.
> And if I had not promised Mistress Grove". .
> —"You might have kept your word to Liverpool."
> "Constituents must remember, after all,
> We're mortal."—"We remind them of it."
> "Hark,
> The bride comes! Here she comes, in a stream of milk!"
> —"There? Dear, you are asleep still; don't you know
> The five Miss Granvilles? always dressed in white
> To show they're ready to be married."—"Lower!
> The aunt is at your elbow."—"Lady Maud,
> Did Lady Waldemar tell you she had seen
> This girl of Leigh's?"—"No—wait! 'twas Mrs. Brookes,
> Who told me Lady Waldemar told her—
> No, 'twasn't Mrs. Brookes."—"She's pretty?"—"Who?
> Mrs. Brookes? Lady Waldemar?"—"How hot!
> Pray is't the law to-day we're not to breathe?
> You're treading on my shawl—I thank you, sir,"
> —"They say the bride's a mere child, who can't read,
> But knows the things she shouldn't, with wide-awake
> Great eyes. I'd go through fire to look at her."
> —"You do, I think."—"And Lady Waldemar
> (You see her, sitting close to Romney Leigh;
> How beautiful she looks, a little flushed!)
> Has taken up the girl, and organized
> Leigh's folly. Should I have come here, you suppose,
> Except she'd asked me?"—"She'd have served him more
> By marrying him herself."—
> "Ah—there she comes,
> The bride, at last!"
> "Indeed, no. Past eleven.
> She puts off her patched petticoat to-day
> And puts on May-fair manners, so begins
> By setting us to wait."

Surely the above is in the step of Mrs. Gore's prose, without its pungency. Or is the following more poetical?

> Five acts to make a play.
> And why not fifteen? why not ten? or seven?
> What matter for the number of the leaves,
> Supposing the tree lives and grows? exact
> The literal unities of time and place,
> When 'tis the essence of passion to ignore
> Both time and place? Absurd. Keep up the fire,
> And leave the generous flames to shape themselves.

Aurora Leigh contains too many pages as perversely trivial, too many passages as carelessly dry, as the above. We cannot forgive either the flippancy or the dreary disquisition from one like Mrs. Browning, when her theme, too, is of art and artists. Such are affectations, not discoveries. There is humanity even in May-Fair babble; there may be thought in criticism, be it ever so clear; but to bring *Mr. Yellowplush,* with his powder and calves, into a serious poem of grief and aspiration;—and when we would see *Corinna* to come upon a Gifford or Conder nibbing his pen for a succinct paragraph,—these things, we repeat, are novelties to which no diffusion of the new light will reconcile serious readers.

Why these fopperies and mistakes grieve us in Mrs. Browning we will show forthwith; for not one of her former works is richer in passages of power and beauty, in noble lines and lofty thoughts than *Aurora Leigh*. The following is full of a half-severe, half-humorous observation, not exceeded by Cowper's most terse and true character in verse. Here is the being to whom the Italy-born Poetess was confided when arriving as a child in England.—

> I think I see my father's sister stand
> Upon the hall-step of her country-house
> To give me welcome. She stood straight and calm,
> Her somewhat narrow forehead braided tight
> As if for taming accidental thoughts
> From possible pulses; brown hair pricked with grey
> By frigid use of life (she was not old,
> Although my father's elder by a year),
> A nose drawn sharply, yet in delicate lines;
> A close mild mouth, a little soured about
> The ends, through speaking unrequited loves,
> Or peradventure niggardly half-truths;
> Eyes of no colour,—once they might have smiled,
> But never, never have forgot themselves
> In smiling; cheeks, in which was yet a rose
> Of perished summers, like a rose in a book,
> Kept more for ruth than pleasure,—if past bloom,
> Past fading also.

Next comes an apology, too (to use the word in its secondary sense), made by the artist for the direction of her studies, which is very graceful and tender.—

> I read much. What my father taught before
> From many a volume, Love re-emphasised
> Upon the self-same pages: Theophrast
> Grew tender with the memory of his eyes,
> And Ælian made mine wet. The trick of Greek
> And Latin, he had taught me, as he would
> Have taught me wrestling or the game of fives
> If such he had known,—most like a shipwrecked man
> Who heaps his single platter with goats' cheese
> And scarlet berries; or like any man
> Who loves but one, and so gives all at once,
> Because he has it, rather than because
> He counts it worthy. Thus, my father gave;
> And thus, as did the women formerly
> By young Achilles, when they pinned the veil
> Across the boy's audacious front, and swept
> With tuneful laughs the silver-fretted rocks,
> He wrapt his little daughter in his large
> Man's doublet, careless did it fit or no.
>
> But, after I had read for memory,
> I read for hope. The path my father's foot
> Had trod me out, which suddenly broke off,
> (What time he dropped the wallet of the flesh
> And passed) alone I carried on, and set
> My child-heart 'gainst the thorny underwood,
> To reach the grassy shelter of the trees.
> Ah, babe i' the wood, without a brother-babe!
> My own self-pity, like the red-breast bird,
> Flies back to cover all that past with leaves.

This, again, is charming.—

> Many fervent souls
> Strike rhyme on rhyme, who would strike steel on steel
> If steel had offered, in a restless heat
> Of doing something. Many tender souls
> Have strung their losses on a rhyming thread,
> As children, cowslips:—the more pains they take,
> The work more withers. Young men, ay, and maids,
> Too often sow their wild oats in tame verse,
> Before they sit down under their own vine
> And live for use. Alas, near all the birds
> Will sing at dawn,—and yet we do not take
> The chaffering swallow for the holy lark.

Here is a true strain of the poetry of London, taken from a later book of the poet's confessions.

So, happy and unafraid of solitude,
I worked the short days out,—and watched the sun
On lurid morns or monstrous afternoons,
Like some Druidic idol's fiery brass,
With fixed unflickering outline of dead heat,
In which the blood of wretches pent inside
Seemed oozing forth to incarnadine the air,—
Push out through fog with his dilated disk,
And startle the slant roofs and chimney-pots
With splashes of fierce colour. Or I saw
Fog only, the great tawny weltering fog,
Involve the passive city, strangle it
Alive, and draw it off into the void,
Spires, bridges, streets, and squares, as if a spunge
Had wiped out London,—or as noon and night
Had clapped together and utterly struck out
The intermediate time, undoing themselves
In the act. Your city poets see such things,
Not despicable. Mountains of the south,
When, drunk and mad with elemental wines,
They rend the seamless mist and stand up bare,
Make fewer singers, haply. No one sings,
Descending Sinai: on Parnassus mount,
You take a mule to climb, and not a muse,
Except in fable and figure: forests chant
Their anthems to themselves, and leave you dumb.
But sit in London, at the day's decline,
And view the city perish in the mist
Like Pharaoh's armaments in the deep Red Sea,—
The chariots, horsemen, footmen, all the host,
Sucked down and choked to silence—then, surprised
By a sudden sense of vision and of tune,
You feel as conquerors though you did not fight,
And you and Israel's other singing girls,
Ay, Miriam with them, sing the song you choose.

The following, too, is eloquent in its sarcasm.

Distrust that word.
"There is none good save God," said Jesus Christ.
If He once, in the first creation-week,
Called creatures good,—for ever, afterward,
The Devil only has done it, and his heirs,
The knaves who win so, and the fools who lose;
The word's grown dangerous. In the middle age,
I think they called malignant fays and imps
Good people. A good neighbour, even in this,
Is fatal sometimes,—cuts your morning up
To mince-meat of the very smallest talk,
Then helps to sugar her bohea at night
With your reputation. I have known good wives,
As chaste, or nearly so, as Potiphar's;
And good, good mothers, who would use a child
To better an intrigue; good friends, beside,
(Very good) who hung succinctly round your neck
And sucked your breath, as cats are fabled to do
By sleeping infants. And we all have known
Good critics, who have stamped out poet's hopes;
Good statesmen, who pulled ruin on the state;
Good patriots, who, for a theory, risked a cause;
Good kings, who disembowelled for a tax;
Good popes, who brought all good to jeopardy;
Good Christians, who sate still in easy chairs,
And damned the general world for standing up.—
Now, may the good God pardon all good men!

How bitterly I speak,—how certainly
The innocent white milk in us is turned,
By much persistent shining of the sun!—
Shake up the sweetest in us long enough
With men, it drops to foolish curd, too sour
To feed the most untender of Christ's lambs.

We have spoken of the passion thrown into the frightful story of Marian Erle. What we now cite will explain itself.—

"And you call it being lost,
That down came next day's noon and caught me there
Half gibbering and half raving on the floor,
And wondering what had happened up in heaven,
That suns should dare to shine when God himself
Was certainly abolished.
"I was mad,—
How many weeks, I know not,—many weeks.
I think they let me go, when I was mad,
They feared my eyes and loosed me, as boys might
A mad dog which they had tortured. Up and down
I went by road and village, over tracts
Of open foreign country, large and strange,
Crossed everywhere by long thin poplar-lines
Like fingers of some ghastly skeleton Hand
Through sunlight and through moonlight evermore
Pushed out from hell itself to pluck me back,
And resolute to get me, slow and sure;

> While every roadside Christ upon his cross
> Hung reddening through his gory wounds at
> me,
> And shook his nails in anger, and came down
> To follow a mile after, wading up
> The low vines and green wheat, crying, 'Take
> the girl!
> She's none of mine from henceforth.' Then, I
> knew,
> (But this is somewhat dimmer than the rest)
> The charitable peasants gave me bread
> And leave to sleep in straw: and twice they
> tied,
> At parting, Mary's image round my neck—
> How heavy it seemed! as heavy as a stone;
> A woman has been strangled with less weight:
> I threw it in a ditch to keep it clean
> And ease my breath a little, when none
> looked;
> I did not need such safeguards:—brutal men
> Stopped short, Miss Leigh, in insult, when
> they had seen
> My face,—I must have had an awful look."

Two Florentine pictures; the first in the open air.—

> I rode once to the little mountain-house
> As fast as if to find my father there,
> But, when in sight of't, within fifty yards,
> I dropped my horse's bridle on his neck
> And paused upon his flank. The house's front
> Was cased with lingots of ripe Indian corn
> In tesselated order, and device
> Of golden patterns: not a stone of wall
> Uncovered,—not an inch of room to grow
> A vine-leaf. The old porch had disappeared;
> And, in the open doorway, sate a girl
> At plaiting straws,—her black hair strained
> away
> To a scarlet kerchief caught beneath her chin
> In Tuscan fashion,—her full ebon eyes,
> Which looked too heavy to be lifted so,
> Still dropt and lifted toward the mulberry-tree
> On which the lads were busy with their staves
> In shout and laughter, stripping all the boughs
> As bare as winter, of those summer leaves
> My father had not changed for all the silk
> In which the ugly silkworms hide themselves.
> Enough. My horse recoiled before my heart—
> I turned the rein abruptly. Back we went
> As fast, to Florence.

The second an interior.—

> Musing so,
> I walked the narrow unrecognizing streets,
> Where many a palace-front peers gloomily
> Through stony vizors iron-barred, (prepared
> Alike, should foe or lover pass that way,
> For guest or victim,) and came wandering out
> Upon the churches with mild open doors
> And plaintive wail of vespers, where a few,
> Those chiefly women, sprinkled round in blots
> Upon the dusky pavement, knelt and prayed
> Toward the altar's silver glory. Oft a ray
> (I liked to sit and watch) would tremble out,
> Just touch some face more lifted, more in need,
> Of course a woman's—while I dreamed a tale
> To fit its fortunes. There was one who looked
> As if the earth had suddenly grown too large
> For such a little humpbacked thing as she;
> The pitiful black kerchief round her neck
> Sole proof she had a mother. One, again,
> Looked sick for love,—seemed praying some
> soft saint
> To put more virtue in the new fine scarf
> She spent a fortnight's meals on, yesterday,
> That cruel Gigi might return his eyes
> From Giuliana. There was one, so old,
> So old, to kneel grew easier than to stand,—
> So solitary, she accepts at last
> Our Lady for her gossip, and frets on
> Against the sinful world which goes its rounds
> In marrying and being married, just the same
> As when 'twas almost good and had the right,
> (Her Gian alive, and she herself eighteen).
> And yet, now even, if Madonna willed,
> She'd win a tern in Thursday's lottery,
> And better all things.

Ere we close it we will show a few of the happy touches with which this book is full.—

> For even prosaic men, who wear grief long,
> Will get to wear it as a hat aside
> With a flower stuck in't.

. . . . .

> I used him for a friend
> Before I ever knew him for a friend.
> 'Twas better, 'twas worse also, afterward:
> We came so close, we saw our differences
> Too intimately.

. . . . .

> But I could not hide
> My quickening inner life from those at watch.
> They saw a light at a window now and then
> They had not set there. Who had set it there?

. . . . .

> We talked on fast, while every common word
> Seemed tangled with the thunder at one end,
> And ready to pull down upon our heads
> A terror out of sight. And yet to pause

> Were surelier mortal: we tore greedily up
> All silence, all the innocent breathing-points,
> As if, like pale conspirators in haste,
> We tore up papers where our signatures
> Imperilled us to an ugly shame or death.

The last of all our quotations are taken almost from the last pages—from the last explosion of long-pent passion, when the Poetess confesses that her life has been a failure, and lays her love in the arms of him who has been hungering and thirsting for it so many a weary day.—

> Could I see his face,
> I wept so? Did I drop against his breast,
> Or did his arms constrain me? Were my cheeks
> Hot, overflooded, with my tears, or his?
> And which of our two large explosive hearts
> So shook me? That, I know not.
>
> . . . . .
>
> What he said,
> I fain would write. But if an angel spoke
> In thunder, should we, haply, know much more
> Than that it thundered? If a cloud came down
> And wrapt us wholly, could we draw its shape,
> As if on the outside, and not overcome?
>
> . . . . .
>
> But oh, the night! oh, bitter-sweet! oh, sweet!
> O dark, O moon and stars, O ecstasy
> Of darkness! O great mystery of love,—
> In which absorbed, loss, anguish, treason's self
> Enlarges rapture,—as a pebble dropt
> In some full wine-cup, over-brims the wine!
> While we two sate together, leaned that night
> So close, my very garments crept and thrilled
> With strange electric life; and both my cheeks
> Grew red, then pale, with touches from my hair
> In which his breath was; while the golden moon
> Was hung before our faces as the badge
> Of some sublime inherited despair,
> Since ever to be seen by only one.

Here we must hand over *Aurora Leigh* to those who will wonder at, or decry, or enthusiastically commend, or pass over the differences and discords of the tale; for it will have readers of all the four classes. To some it will be so much rank foolishness,—to others almost a scriptural revelation. The huge mistake of its plan, the disdain of selectness in its details, could not be exhausted were we to write for column and column,—nor would page on page suffice to contain the high thoughts, the deep feelings, the fantastic images showered over the tale with the authority of a prophetess, the grace of a muse, the prodigality of a queen. Such a poem, we dare aver, has never before been written by woman; and if our apprehension of its discords and discrepancies has been keen and expressed without measure, it is because our admiration of its writer's genius, and our sympathy with the nobility of her purpose, are also keen and without measure.

Coventry Patmore (review date 1856/57)

SOURCE: "Mrs. Browning's *Poems*," in *North British Review*, Vol. XXVI, No. LII, November 1856—February 1857, pp. 443-62.

[*In the following excerpt, Patmore gives a mixed review of* Aurora Leigh, *summarizing the "novel in verse" and assessing the poetic imagery as it advances Browning's opinions on life and art.*]

Aurora Leigh is the latest, and Mrs. Browning tells us, in the dedication, "the most mature" of her works; the one into which her "highest convictions upon Life and Art have entered." It was not well judged to prejudice the reader, at the very outset, with the inevitable doubt, "Is a poem the right place for 'highest convictions upon Life and Art?'" This poem is two thousand lines longer than "Paradise Lost." We do not know how to describe it better than by saying that it is a novel in verse,—a novel of the modern didactic species, written chiefly for the advocacy of distinct "convictions upon Life and Art." If poetry ought to consist only of "thoughts that voluntary move harmonious numbers," a very large portion of this work ought unquestionably to have been in prose. But the question seems open to discussion, and we give Mrs. Browning the benefit of the doubt. Perhaps the chief misfortune for the poem is, that there may always be two opinions on all "convictions upon Life and Art." For example, we ourselves dissent altogether from certain of the views advocated. We think that "conventions," which are society's unwritten laws, are condemned in too sweeping and unexamining a style; that the importance of an ordinary education in the formation of character is too emphatically denied by the example of Marian Erle, whom we regard as an impossible person, under her circumstances; that Art is not the highest power in the world; and so forth. *Aurora Leigh* would assuredly have been a more *poetical* work if it had made the question, "Do you agree with it?" an absurd one, and had only allowed of the question, "Do you or do you not understand it?" The safest way of speaking of this poem, which, expressly or by implication, has so considerable a polemic element in it, is to place a simple analysis of it before our readers. Concerning the great beauty and subtlety of some of the extracts we shall give, there fortunately cannot be two opinions.

The father of Aurora Leigh "was an austere Englishman, who, after a dry lifetime, spent at home in college-learning, law, and parish talk," went to Italy, and fell suddenly in love with an Italian girl who passed him in a procession.

> Her face flashed like a cymbal on his face,
> And shook with silent clangours brain and heart,
> Transfiguring him to music.

Mr. Leigh gained the hand of the fair Florentine, and Aurora was born; but before the child was four years old, her mother died, having changed the nature of her husband, and made the "austere Englishman" into a man of sentiment.

> There's a verse he set
> In Santa Croce to her memory:
> '*Weep for an infant, too young to weep much
> When death removed this mother*'—stops the mirth
> To-day on women's faces, when they walk
> With rosy children hanging on their gowns.

Mr. Leigh left Florence, and lived in almost entire solitude, with his child and one servant, "among the mountains above Pelago," and there he

> Who through love had suddenly
> Thrown off the old conventions, broken loose
> From chinbands of the soul, like Lazarus,

taught his child "what he had learned best," grief and love, and, as it afterwards appears, Latin and Greek; also, "the ignorance of men," how

> A Fool will pass for such through one mistake,
> While a Philosopher will pass for such
> Through said mistakes being ventured in the gross,
> And heaped up to a system.

So nine years passed, and Aurora Leigh thus describes herself at thirteen:—

> 'I am like,
> They tell me, my dear father; broader brows,
> Howbeit, upon a slenderer undergrowth
> Of delicate features; paler, near as grave—
> But then my mother's smile breaks up the whole,
> And makes it sometimes better than itself.'

At this time Mr. Leigh suddenly died. The child was soon torn from her nurse, now her only companion, by "a stranger with authority," from England, who conducted her to the house of her father's sister. This lady is thus described:—

> She stood straight and calm,
> Her somewhat narrow forehead braided tight,
> As if for taming accidental thoughts
> From possible pulses; brown hair, pricked with grey,
> By frigid use of life (she was not old,
> Although my father's elder by a year);
> A nose drawn sharply, yet in delicate lines;
> A close, mild mouth, a little soured about
> The ends, through speaking unrequited loves,
> Or, peradventure, niggardly half-truths;
> Eyes of no colour, once they might have smiled,
> But never, never have forgot themselves
> In smiling; cheeks in which was yet a rose
> Of perished summers, like a rose in a book,
> Kept more for ruth than pleasure, if past bloom.
> Past fading also.
> . . . . .
>
> She, my aunt,
> Had loved my father truly, as she could,
> And hated, with the gall of gentle souls,
> My Tuscan mother, who had fooled away
> A wise man from wise courses, a good man
> From obvious duties, and, depriving her,
> His sister, of the household precedence,
> Had wronged his tenants, robbed his native land,
> And made him mad, alike by life and death,
> In love and sorrow. She had pored for years
> What sort of woman could be suitable
> To her sort of hate, to entertain it with;
> And so, her very curiosity
> Became hate too, and all the idealism
> She ever used in life was used for hate,
> Till hate, so nourished, did exceed at last
> The love from which it grew, in strength and heat,
> And wrinkled her smooth conscience with a sense
> Of disputable virtue (say not sin)
> When Christian doctrine was enforced at church.

Miss Leigh's notions of female education differed widely from her brother's. She seems to have thought both love and grief were weeds of flowers that need no cultivating, but spring up readily enough in every woman's heart. Here is Aurora's English school programme, which, with many hundreds of lines like them, have certainly no right to be called verse:—

> I learnt the collects and the catechism,
>
> . . . . .
>
> And various popular synopses of
> Inhuman doctrines never taught by John,

> Because she liked instructed piety.
> I learnt my complement of classic French
> (Kept pure of Balzac and neologism),
> And German also, since she liked a range
> Of liberal education,—tongues, not books.
> I learnt a little algebra, a little
> Of the mathematics; brushed with extreme
>   flounce
> The circle of the sciences, because
> She misliked women who were frivolous.
> I learnt the royal genealogies
> Of Oviedo, the internal laws
> Of the Burmese empire, by how many feet
> Mount Chimborazo outsoars Himmeleh,
> What navigable river joins itself
> To Lara, and what census of the year five
> Was taken at Klagenfurt.

Aurora had a cousin, Romney Leigh, the owner of the family estate, Leigh Hall. The two children saw much of each other, but were of dispositions and tastes so opposite, that their intercourse consisted chiefly of disputes. As they grew up they diverged further from one another. Romney became a philanthropic socialist, bent on utilitarian plans of action, and pondering on the dregs of humanity; while Aurora grew into a poetess, for ever musing on the ideal and beautiful. She discovered, in an attic, piles of books marked with her father's name, and from this sanctuary would steal spiritual food, unknown to her aunt. She read "books good and bad;" and makes the following admirable remarks upon the perils of such a course of study:—

>   You cheer him on
> As if the worst could happen were to rest
> Too long beside a fountain. Yet behold,
> Behold!—the world of books is still the world;
> And worldlings in it are less merciful
> And more puissant. For the wicked there
> Are winged like angels. Every knife that strikes
> Is edged from elemental fire to assail
> A spiritual life. The beautiful seems right
> By force of beauty, and the feeble wrong
> Because of weakness. Power is justified
> Though armed against St. Michael.
>
> . . . . .
>
> True, many a prophet teaches in the roads;
> True, many a seer pulls down the flaming
>   heavens
> Upon his own head in strong martyrdom,
> In order to light men a moment's space.
> But stay!—who judges?—who distinguishes?
> 'Twixt Saul and Nahash justly, at first sight,
> And leaves King Saul precisely at the sin,
> To serve King David? Who discerns at once
> The sound of the trumpets, when the trumpets
>   blow
> For Alaric as well as Charlemagne?
> Who judges prophets, and can tell true seers
> From conjurors?

The delineation of her mind at this period gives occasion to the following remarkable passage:—

> The cygnet finds the water, but the man
> Is born in ignorance of his element,
> And feels out blind at first, disorganized
> By sin i' the blood,—his spirit-insight dull'd
> And crossed by his sensations. Presently
> We feel it quicken in the dark sometimes;
> Then mark, be reverent, be obedient—
> For those dumb motions of imperfect life
> Are oracles of vital Deity
> Attesting the Hereafter. Let who says
> 'The soul's a clean white paper,' rather say,
> A palimpsest, a prophet's holograph
> Defiled, erased and covered by a monk's,—
> The Apocalypse, by a Longus! poring on
> Which obscene text, we may discern perhaps
> Some fair, fine trace of what was written once,
> Some upstroke of an alpha and omega
> Expressing the old scripture.

From reading poetry, she became a writer of it, and gives us scores of pages of "her highest convictions upon art," all more or less acute, and worth considering, but which would be more in place in a review than an epic. The development of her powers as a poetess is elaborately depicted; but as Mrs. Browning is herself almost the only modern example of such development, the story is uninteresting from its very singularity.

Aurora wrote and read on in secret, her aunt only half suspecting this development, of which she would have disapproved with all her might.

> She said, sometimes, 'Aurora, have you done
> Your task this morning—have you read that
>   book,
> And are you ready for the crochet here?'
> As if she said, I know there's something
>   wrong;
> I know I have not ground you down enough
> To flatten and bake you to a wholesome crust
> For household uses and proprieties.

The poetess did her work meekly, her "soul singing at a work apart," and all went on without let or hindrance, till one June morning, when Aurora arose upon her twentieth birthday. She got up early, and left the house, "brushing a green track along the grass," and finding that the world would not, or rather could not, crown her, seeing that she was a poetess only in secret, she took a sudden fancy to crown herself; and after hesitating between bay, myrtle, verbena, and guelder roses, she turned to a wreath of ivy, and twisted it round her head. At this moment she beheld her cousin beside her,

> With a mouth
> Twice graver than his eyes.

Romney had found her manuscript poems, with "Greek upon the margin." A conversation ensued on the subjects of art and philanthropy, the cousins espousing different sides. The burden of Aurora's argument was this:—

> You will not compass your poor ends
> Of barley feeding and material ease
> Without the Poet's individualism
> To work your universal. It takes a soul
> To move a body,—it takes a high-souled man
> To move the masses—even to a cleaner stye:
> It takes the ideal, to blow an inch inside
> The dust of the actual: and your Fouriers failed,
> Because not poets enough to understand
> That life develops from within.

And, as she eloquently says, in another place:—

> the thrushes sang
> And shook my pulses and the elm's new leaves,—
> And then I turned, and held my finger up,
> And bade him mark, that howsoe'er the world
> Went ill, as he related, certainly
> The thrushes still sang in it.—At which word
> His brow would soften,—and he bore with me
> In melancholy patience, not unkind,
> While breaking into voluble ecstacy,
> I flattered all the beauteous country round,
> As poet's use . . . the skies, the clouds, the fields,
> The happy violets, hiding from the roads
> The primroses run down to, carrying gold,—
> The tangled hedgerows, where the cows push out
> Their tolerant horns and patient churning mouths
> 'Twixt dripping ash boughs,—hedgerows all alive,
> With birds, and gnats, and large white butterflies,
> Which look as if the May-flower had caught life
> And palpitated forth upon the wind,—
> Hills, vales, woods, netted in a silver mist;
> Farms, granges, doubled up among the hills,
> And cattle grazing in the watered vales,
> And cottage chimneys smoking from the woods,
> And cottage gardens smelling everywhere,
> Confused with smell of orchards. 'See,' I said,
> 'And see, is God not with us on the earth?
> And shall we put Him down by aught we do?
> Who says there's nothing for the poor and vile,
> Save poverty and wickedness? behold!'
> And ankle-deep in English grass I leaped,
> And clapped my hands, and called all very fair.

The burden of Romney's argument was, that women write at best but such poetry as gains for highest eulogy, comparison to a man's; that poetry, unless of the very best, is frivolous work; that there is earnest work to do, for him to do, and for her to do, if she will become his helper and his wife.

The young poetess, indignant at being sought as a mere helpmate, refuses the offer. Her aunt, on hearing of Romney's offer and rejection, expresses great grief, and tells Aurora that she will inherit no money, all her father's and all her aunt's being settled on Romney, by a clause in a former deed, excluding offspring by a foreign wife. She told her further, that Romney's father had wished that the cousins should marry, in order to repair this injustice, and that her own father had known and approved the wish, all of which strengthened Aurora in her determination to adhere to her refusal.

Soon after this, the aunt was found dead by her bedside, with an unopened letter in her hand. On the reading of the will, it was found that she had left Aurora three hundred pounds, "and all other monies of which she died possessed." Romney, who, as heir, attended the funeral, told Aurora that the old lady died possessed of £30,000, of which no mention was made in the will; but Aurora, suspecting that her cousin was by some means bestowing upon her this money, insisted on seeing deeds to prove her aunt's possession of it. A little inquiry showed that Romney had presented this sum to his aunt, and that the unopened letter found in her hand, contained the deed of gift, which, though made, had never been accepted. Aurora tore the deed in shreds and went to lodgings in London.

Seven years later, we find her an established authoress, with piles of literary letters; solitary and poor, hard-worked, but uncomplaining. One day a stranger enters, and announces herself as Lady Waldemar. With little prelude, she declared herself to be a widow, and in love with Romney Leigh. She told Aurora that her cousin was on the point of espousing a beggar's daughter from St. Giles's, and asked her help in breaking off, or at any rate, postponing the marriage. Aurora ascertained that Lady Waldemar was commissioned by Romney to tell her the news, and introduce her to his bride-elect, and to get her countenance to the marriage, which marriage Lady Waldemar to him appeared to approve and promote. She would have nothing to say to this double dealing on the part of Lady

Waldemar, to whom she plainly says as much, in not very courteous terms. Aurora then hastened to St. Margaret's Court to see the woman whom her cousin was to marry. "An ineffable face" met her on the threshold of a wretched room, and being soon assured by Aurora's friendly manner, its owner, Marian Erle, told her story.

She was the daughter of a drunken poaching tramper, who beat her mother, her mother turning in anger to beat her:—

> Her first cry in our strange and strangling air,
> When cast in spasms out from the shuddering womb,
> Was wrong against the social code, forced wrong.
> What business had the baby to cry there?

She grew up neglected and ill-used, till some ladies got her to a Sunday-school. There she learned to read and write, also to understand the wickedness of her parents, but little else. She found, however, a more profitable school in "Heaven's high blue," which she would steal away to gaze at; and in sundry fragments of the English poets which chanced to come into her hands: thus, we are to suppose, she learned the high code of morality and virtue which she afterwards adhered to, for no one taught or spoke to her but her brutish parents, and the unprofitable Sunday teacher. When she reached early womanhood, her mother attempted to betray her to a drunken squire, from whom she fled in terror. Swooning, she was picked up and taken to an hospital. She had a long illness, and it was on her recovery that she first saw Romney Leigh, who was visiting the sick people, and on hearing that she was about to leave, inquired what her future plans were, and by degrees learned her history. "He sent her to a famous sempstress house far off in London," and there she worked well till one of her companions fell sick. Marian then left the house to nurse her, and after the death of the girl, stayed to watch and nurse the crazy mother who was now alone. Romney found her at this work. "He was not angry that she had left the house wherein he placed her." "He did not say 'twas well, yet Marian thought he did not take it ill,"—and on the day her last patient died, Romney asked her to be his helpmate and wife.

Aurora was charmed by the girl's manner, and embraced her as her future cousin. Romney came in while they were still talking, and Aurora expressed a wish that the wedding should be from her home, but her cousin refused:—

> I take my wife
> Directly from the people, and she comes,
> As Austria's daughter, to imperial France,
> Betwixt her eagles, blinking not her race,
> From Margaret's Court, at garret height, to meet
> And wed me at St. James's, nor put off
> Her gown of serge for that. The things we do,
> We do: we'll wear no mask, as if we blushed.

The marriage-day arrived, and

> Half St. Giles in frieze
> Was bidden to meet St. James in cloth of gold;
> And, after contract at the altar, pass
> To eat a marriage-feast on Hampstead Heath.

The congregation assembled early, and chatted long, expecting the bride, but she came not; and at the last moment, a letter is delivered to Romney in Marian's hand. In this letter, Marian states her conviction that she best shows her love to Romney by saving him the unhappiness that must follow a union with her:

> It would be dreadful for a friend of yours
> To see all England thrust you out of doors,
> And mock you from the windows.

She hints at there being some one else whom Romney loves:

> You might say,
> Or think, (that worse,) 'There's some one in the house,
> I miss and love still!' Dreadful!

She then goes on to say she shall go where no one can find her:—

> I never could be happy as your wife,—
> I never could be harmless as your friend:
> I never will look more into your face
> Till God says 'Look.'—I charge you seek me not,
> Nor vex yourself with lamentable thoughts,
> That, peradventure, I am come to grief:
> Be sure I'm well, I'm merry, I'm at ease!
> But such a long way, long way, long way off,
> I think you'll find me sooner in my grave.

Inexplicable as the mystery was to Romney, it was still more so to the congregated hundreds of St. Giles's who did not read the letter, and were too much exasperated at their missed triumph to listen to Romney, who wished to address them. "Pull him down, strike him, kill him!" was called out from the crowd, some of whom suggested foul play on the part of the bridegroom; and it was not till the police were called in, that the church could be cleared, and order restored.

Romney made long search for Marian, but could find no trace of her. He then left London, and Aurora again lost sight of him. On his return to the country, Romney became more than ever engrossed in his schemes of philanthropy. He turned his family seat into a Phalanstery, and devoted himself to the reformation of the thieves and poachers, who took up their abode there.

Aurora now wrote a great poem, in which, after long feeling dissatisfied with her productions, she at last had a consciousness of having in some degree conveyed in words, the things she had thought and felt. She went soon after to a party, and refused an offer from a man of birth and fortune, and heard that Romney was engaged to Lady Waldemar. Almost immediately after this, she left her new poem with a publisher, and set out for Florence.

On her way, Aurora was detained a few days in Paris; and walking one day in the flower market, she met Marian Erle. Marian has a child, and would gladly avoid Aurora, but Aurora persists in going to her home, and succeeds at last in learning the mystery of Marian's flight, and present condition.

Lady Waldemar had been often to her, and had contrived to make her believe that misery would follow her marriage with Romney; that Romney had loved her, Lady Waldemar, and she him; that his offer to Marian was prompted by principle only, and would be followed up in a spirit of martyrdom. Lady Waldemar then offered to send her in the charge of a respectable person, who had formerly been her maid, to Australia. Marian gladly accepted the offer, and went with the woman, who, instead of taking her to Australia, had brought her to an infamous house in Paris, where drugs and force were used to accomplish her ruin. She had fled from this place in delirium, was taken in by a farmer's wife; obtained employment, but lost it on its appearing that she was about to become a mother; and had, since then, supported herself and her child, now a year old, by needlework.

Aurora took both mother and child to her own home; and, after long debate, wrote two letters, one to a mutual friend of her's and Romney's, telling him all, and asking him only to communicate this story to her cousin should he not be married to Lady Waldemar; and the other to that lady, reproaching her for having

> Tricked poor Marian Erle,
> And set her own love digging her own grave,
> Within her green hope's pretty garden ground:
> Ay, sent her forth with some one of your sort,
> To a wicked house in France.

She adds that, if Lady Waldemar is Romney's wife, and will

> Keep warm his heart, and clean his board, and when
> He speaks, be ready with obedience . . .

If she will attend to all this, she is "safe from Marian and Aurora;" but if she "fail a point," they will

> Open mouth,
> And such a noise will follow, the last trump's
> Will scarcely seem more dreadful, even to her.

These letters sent, Aurora proceeded with Marian and her child to Florence. A letter from a friend tells her that her poem has won all suffrages, and is doing the work of an evangelist; and then speaks of Romney in words which Aurora misunderstands into conveying news of his marriage with Lady Waldemar. The natural effect of the first news is counterbalanced by the second, and Aurora sinks into a state of melancholy, which lasts till the concluding scene.

On looking up one evening, as she is sitting alone in the garden, she sees Romney standing before her. By this time, it is clear to every one but Aurora herself, and perhaps to her, that she loves him deeply. She is too much agitated to notice, either from his manner of greeting her or sitting down, that he is blind. Romney believes that she has heard of his misfortune, for it was indeed an allusion to it that she had misunderstood for a notice of his marriage; they, therefore, talk for some time at cross purposes. Romney, however, says one thing in a straightforward way:—

> I have read your book,
>
> . . . . .
>
> The book is in my heart;
> Lives in me, wakes in me, and dreams with me:
> My daily bread tastes of it, and my wine
> Which has no smack of it, I pour it out;
> It seems unnatural drinking,—

and refers to their old argument on Aurora's birthday, confessing himself a convert to all she then urged. He also tells her of the failure of his labours at Leigh Hall, where the people had risen up and burnt the old house to the ground; of an illness which had attacked him afterwards; and speaks so plainly, in the course of his narrative, of his unchanged love to Aurora, that she, believing him to be the husband of another woman, rebukes him. All this misunderstanding and beating about the bush, is tedious, though it gives occasion to a magnificent simile—Aurora, bidding her cousin look at the stars,—

> I signed above, where all the stars were out,
> As if an urgent heat had started there
> A secret writing from a sombre page,
> A blank last moment, crowded suddenly
> With hurrying splendours.

The *éclaircissement* comes at last. Aurora, mentioning Lady Waldemar as her cousin's wife,—

>   Are ye mad?
> He echoed—'Wife! mine! Lady Waldemar!'

and this half of the mistake is rectified; and Romney gives a letter from Lady Waldemar to Aurora, in which that lady repudiates the charge of having sent Marian "to a wicked house in France." She explains that Marian's conductor was an old servant who had lived "five months" in her house, and had money for the voyage to Australia, the embezzlement of which had probably tempted her to stop short on the way. Having finished the letter, which related also how all was broken off between Romney and its writer, Aurora exclaims,—

>   Ah, not married!
>   'You mistake,' he said,
> 'I'm married,—Is not Marian Erle my wife?
> As God sees things, I have a wife and child;
> And I, as I'm a man who honours God,
> Am here to claim them as my wife and
>   child.'
>
> I felt it hard to breathe, much less to speak.
> Nor word of mine was needed. Some one else
> Was there for answering. 'Romney,' she began,
> 'My great good angel, Romney.'
>   Then at first
> I knew that Marian Erle was beautiful.
> She stood there still and pallid as a saint,
> Dilated, like a saint in ecstacy,
> As if the floating moonshine interposed
> Betwixt her foot and the earth, and raised her
>   up,
> To float upon it. 'I had left my child,
> Who sleeps,' she said, 'and having drawn this
>   way
> I heard you speaking . . . friend, confirm me
>   now.
> You take this Marian, such as wicked men
> Have made her, for your honourable wife?'
>
> The thrilling, solemn, proud, pathetic voice!
> He stretched his arms out toward the thrilling
>   voice,
> As if to draw it on to his embrace.
> 'I take her as God made her, and as men
> Must fail to unmake her, for my honoured
>   wife.'
>
> She never raised her eyes nor took a step,
> But stood there in her place and spoke again—
> 'You take this Marian's child which is her
>   shame,
> In sight of men and women, for your child,
> Of whom you will not ever feel ashamed?'
>
> The thrilling, tender, proud, pathetic voice!
> He stepped on toward it, still with outstretched
>   arms,
> As if to quench upon his breast that voice.
> 'May God so father me, as I do him,
> And so forsake me, as I let him feel
> He's orphaned haply. Here I take the child
> To share my cup, to slumber on my knee,
> To play his loudest gambol at my foot,
> To hold my finger in the public ways,
> Till none shall need inquire, 'Whose child is
>   this?'
> The gesture saying so tenderly, 'My own.'

This is all Marian required. She would fain have her own consciousness of innocence ratified by such proof from the man she most revered; but sorrow has driven love from her heart; she cannot re-awaken in herself an interest for any but her child; she gratefully but firmly refuses to marry Romney, who believing his love to Aurora unreturned, is taking his leave, when on her alluding again to the stars, he tells her of his blindness, and relates how the illness which produced it, was caused by an assault from Marian Erle's father, whom Romney had endeavoured to save from justice, at the time of the riots at Leigh Hall: he then again says, farewell, but is stopped by Aurora, who confesses her love to him; and so the story ends—considerably to the vexation, we should think, of those readers, who may be such thorough-going haters of "conventions" as to wish to have had Romney actually married to Marian Erle.

The command of imagery shown by Mrs. Browning, in this poem, is really surprising, even in this day when every poetaster seems to be endowed with a more or less startling amount of that power; but Mrs. Browning seldom goes out of her way for an image, as nearly all our other versifiers are in the habit of doing continually. There is a vital continuity, through the whole of this immensely long work, which is thus remarkably, and most favourably distinguished from the sand-weaving of so many of her contemporaries. The earnestness of the authoress is, also, plainly without affectation, and her enthusiasm for truth and beauty, as she apprehends them, unbounded. A work upon such a scale, and with such a scope, had it been faultless, would have been the greatest work of the age; but unhappily there are faults, and very serious ones, over and above those which we have already hinted. The poem has evidently been written in a very small proportion of the time which a work so very ambitiously conceived ought to have taken. The language which in passionate scenes is simple and real, in other parts becomes very turgid and unpoetical; for example:—

>   What if even God
> Were chiefly God by working out himself
> To an individualism of the Infinite,

> Eterne, intense, profuse,—still throwing up
> The golden spray of multitudinous worlds
> In measure to the proclive weight and rush
> Of his inner nature,—the spontaneous love
> Still proof and outflow of spontaneous life?

Or, in a different style, the style, unfortunately, of hundreds of lines:—

> In those days, though, I never analyzed
> Myself even: all analysis comes late.

Or again:—

> Those faces! 'twas as if you had stirred up hell
> To heave its lowest dreg-fiends uppermost
> In fiery swirls of slime,—such strangled fronts,
> Such obdurate jaws were thrown up constantly.

These, and other artistic defects, detract somewhat from the general effect of the poem; but no one who reads it, with true poetic sympathy, can withhold his tribute of admiration from a work possessing so many of the highest excellencies.

William Edmondstoune Aytoun (review date 1857)

SOURCE: "Mrs. Barrett Browning—*Aurora Leigh*," in *Blackwood's Edinburgh Magazine,* Vol. LXXXI, No. CCCCXCV, January, 1857, pp. 23-41.

[*In the following excerpt, Aytoun summarizes the plot of* Aurora Leigh *and gives it a mixed assessment; he criticizes some of the book's themes while admiring Browning's poetic style.*]

For the application of his gifts, every author is responsible. He may exercise them well and usefully, or he may apply them to ignoble purposes. He may, by the aid of art, exhibit them in the most attractive form, or his execution may be mean and slovenly. In the one case he is deserving of praise; in the other he is liable to censure. Keeping this principle in view, we shall proceed to the consideration of this new volume from the pen of Mrs. Browning,—a lady whose rare genius has already won for her an exalted place among the poets of the age. Endowed with a powerful intellect, she at least has no reason to anticipate the treatment prophesied for her literary heroine, Aurora:—

> You never can be satisfied with praise
> Which men give women when they judge a book
> Not as men's work, but as mere woman's work,
> Expressing the comparative respect
> Which means the absolute scorn. 'Oh, excellent!
> What grace! what facile turns! what fluent sweeps!
> What delicate discernment—almost thought!
> The book does honour to the sex, we hold.
> Among our female authors we make room
> For this fair writer, and congratulate
> The country that produces in these times
> Such women, competent to—spell.'

Mrs. Browning takes the field like Britomart or Joan of Arc, and declares that she will not accept courtesy or forbearance from the critics on account of her sex. She challenges a truthful opinion, and that opinion she shall have.

Aurora Leigh is a story of the present time in nine books. When we say a story, it must not be understood in the sense of a continuous narrative or rather poem of action, for a great portion of the work is reflective. Still there is a story which we shall trace for the information of the reader, abstaining in the mean time from comment, and not making more quotations than are necessary for its elucidation. The poem is a monologue, and the opening scene is laid in Tuscany.

The father of Aurora Leigh, an Englishman of fortune and a scholar, fell in love with a young Florentine girl, whom he first saw bearing a taper in a religious procession. They were married; but the wife died shortly after she had given birth to her sole daughter, Aurora. The widower, in a frenzy of grief, withdrew to a cottage among the mountains, and there occupied his time in the education of his child, who soon became a proficient in the classics.

> The trick of Greek
> And Latin he had taught me, as he would
> Have taught me wrestling or the game of fives,
> If such he had known,—most like a shipwrecked man
> Who heaps his single platter with goats' cheese
> And scarlet berries; or like any man
> Who loves but one, and so gives all at once,
> Because he has it, rather than because
> He counts it worthy. Thus my father gave;
> And thus, as did the woman formerly
> By young Achilles, when they pinned the veil
> Across the boy's audacious front, and swept
> With tuneful laughs the silver-fretted rocks.
> He wrapt his little daughter in his large
> Man's doublet, careless did it fit or no.

This mode of tuition—the same, by the way, which Dominie Sampson proposed for the mental culture of Lucy Bertram—had a strong effect upon the character of Aurora, who throughout the poem discourses in a most learned manner. When she was only thirteen her father died, and she was brought away, most reluctantly, from her pleasant Italy, to dwell in foggy England with a virgin aunt, who is thus described:—

> I think I see my father's sister stand
> Upon the hall-step of her country-house
> To give me welcome. She stood straight and calm,
> Her somewhat narrow forehead braided tight
> As if for taming accidental thoughts
> From possible pulses; brown hair pricked with grey
> By frigid use of life (she was not old,
> Although my father's elder by a year),
> A nose drawn sharply, yet in delicate lines;
> A close mild mouth, a little soured about
> The ends, through speaking unrequited loves,
> Or peradventure niggardly half-truths;
> Eyes of no colour,—once they might have smiled,
> But never, never have forgot themselves
> In smiling; cheeks, in which was yet a rose
> Of perished summers, like a rose in a book,
> Kept more for ruth than pleasure,—if past bloom,
> Past fading also.
>   She had lived, we'll say,
> A harmless life, she called a virtuous life,
> A quiet life, which was not life at all,
> (But that, she had not lived enough to know),
> Between the vicar and the county squires,
> The lord-lieutenant looking down sometimes
> From the empyreal, to assure their souls
> Against chance - Vulgarisms, and, in the abyss,
> The apothecary looked on once a-year,
> To prove their soundness of humility.
> The poor-club exercised her Christian gifts
> Of knitting stockings, stitching petticoats,
> Because we are of one flesh after all,
> And need one flannel (with a proper sense
> Of difference in the quality)—and still
> The book-club, guarded from your modern trick
> Of shaking dangerous questions from the crease,
> Preserved her intellectual. She had lived
> A sort of cage-bird life, born in a cage,
> Accounting that to leap from perch to perch
> Was act and joy enough for any bird.
> Dear heaven, how silly are the things that live
> In thickets, and eat berries!
>   I, alas,
> A wild bird scarcely fledged, was brought to her cage,
> And she was there to meet me. Very kind.
> Bring the clean water; give out the fresh seed.

This prim old lady was not exactly to Miss Aurora's mind; indeed, there was not much love lost between them, for Aunt Marjory had been sorely incensed, and with good reason, as will presently appear, at her brother's marriage with a foreigner, and never thoroughly forgave the daughter. However, she did her duty by her in her own fashion, supplementing her education by giving her instruction in such things as are usually taught to English girls, an intellectual regimen which excited the profoundest disgust in Aurora. However, she had strength enough to stand the trial, though occasionally threatening to die; and her patience was at length rewarded by finding her father's books in a garret. These she devoured furtively, and lighting upon the poets, at once perceived her vocation.

>   At last, because the time was ripe,
>   chanced upon the poets.
>   As the earth
> Plunges in fury, when the internal fires
> Have reached and pricked her heart, and, throwing flat
> The marts and tempels, the triumphal gates
> And towers of observation, clears herself
> To elemental freedom—thus, my soul,
> At poetry's divine first finger-touch,
> Let go conventions and sprang up surprised,
> Convicted of the great eternities
> Before two worlds.

So Aurora began to make verses, and found herself all the better for the exercise. But there were more Leighs in the world than Aurora. She had a cousin, Romney Leigh, the proprietor of Leigh Hall, who, even as a youth, exhibited queer tendencies:—

>   Romney, Romney Leigh.
> I have not named my cousin hitherto,
> And yet I used him as a sort of friend:
> My elder by few years, but cold and shy
> And absent—tender, when he thought of it,
> Which scarcely was imperative, grave betimes,
> As well as early master of Leigh Hall,
> Whereof the nightmare, sate upon his youth
> Repressing all its seasonable delights,
> And agonising with a ghastly sense
> Of universal hideous want and wrong
> To incriminate possession. When he came
> From college to the country, very oft
> He crossed the hills on visits to my aunt,
> With gifts of blue grapes from the hothouses,
> A book in one hand,—mere statistics (if
> I chanced to lift the cover), count of all
> The goats whose beards are sprouting down toward hell,
> Against God's separating judgment-hour.
> And she, she almost loved him,—even allowed
> That sometimes he should seem to sigh my way;

It made him easier to be pitiful,
And sighing was his gift.

This young gentleman, after his own odd fashion, has conceived an attachment for Aurora; nor is he an object of total indifference to her, though her mind is more occupied with versification than with love. The two characters, male and female, are meant to stand in strong contrast to each other. Romney is a Socialist, bent on devoting himself to the regeneration of mankind, and the improvement of the condition of the working classes, by carrying into effect the schemes of Fourier and Owen—the aim of Aurora is, through Art, to raise the aspirations of the people. The man is physical, the woman metaphysical. The one is for increasing bodily comfort, the other for stimulating the mind. Both are enthusiasts, and both are intolerably dogmatic. Now it so happens that, on the morning of the twentieth anniversary of her birthday, Miss Aurora sallies forth early, with the laudable purpose of crowning herself after the manner of Corinna, and is surprised by Romney in the act of placing an ivy wreath upon her brows. Romney has picked up a volume of her manuscript poems, which he returns, not, however, with any complimentary phrase, but rather sneeringly, and forthwith begins to read her a lecture, in a high puritanical strain, upon the vanity of her pursuits. This, of course, rouses the ire of Aurora, who retorts with great spirit on his materialistic tendencies. In the midst of this discussion he has the bad taste to propose, not so much, as he puts it, through love, but because he wants a helpmate to assist him in the erection of public washing-houses, soupkitchens, and hospitals; whereupon our high-souled poetess flies off at a tangent:—

> 'What you love,
> Is not a woman, Romney, but a cause:
> You want a helpmate, not a mistress, sir—
> A wife to help your ends—in her no end!
> Your cause is noble, your ends excellent,
> But I, being most unworthy of these and that,
> Do otherwise conceive of love. Farewell.'
>
> 'Farewell, Aurora? you reject me thus?'
> He said.
>
> 'Why, sir, you are married long ago.
> You have a wife already whom you love,
> Your social theory. Bless you both, I say.
> For my part, I am scarcely meek enough
> To be the handmaid of a lawful spouse.
> Do I look a Hagar, think you?'

Aunt Marjory, when she hears of this refusal, is frantic, and rates Aurora soundly for rejecting a fortune laid at her feet. She explains that by a special clause in the Leigh entail, offspring by a foreign wife were cut off from succession—that no sooner was Aurora born than the next heir, Romney Leigh's father, pro-

Elizabeth Barrett Browning.

posed that a marriage should be arranged between his son and the child, so that the penalties of disinherison might be avoided—and that Romney, by asking her to marry him, was in fact carrying out that intention. Otherwise Aurora is a beggar, for her aunt has no fortune to leave her. Such suggestions as these, when they occur in romance and poetry, always prove arguments in favour of obstinacy; and Aurora, even though she likes Romney, fixes upon them as insuperable obstacles to the marriage:—

> Romney now was turned
> To a benefactor, to a generous man,
> Who had tied himself to marry—me, instead
> Of such a woman, with low timorous lids
> He lifted with a sudden word one day,
> And left, perhaps, for my sake.—Ah, self-tied
> By a contract,—male Iphigenia, bound
> At a fatal Aulis, for the winds to change,
> (But loose him—they'll not change); he well might seem
> A little cold and dominant in love!
> He had a right to be dogmatical,
> This poor, good Romney. Love, to him, was made
> A simple law-clause. If I married him,
> I would not dare to call my soul my own,

>   Which so he had bought and paid for: every thought
>   And every heart-beat down there in the bill,—
>   Not one found honestly deductible
>   From any use that pleased him! He might cut
>   My body into coins to give away
>   Among his other paupers; change my sons,
>   While I stood dumb as Griseld, for black babes
>   Or piteous foundings; might unquestioned set
>   My right hand teaching in the Ragged Schools,
>   My left hand washing in the Public Baths,
>   What time my angel of the Ideal stretched
>   Both his to me in vain! I could not claim
>   The poor right of a mouse in a trap, to squeal,
>   And take so much as pity, from myself.

In short, she will be her own mistress, and work out her own independence. Her aunt dies, leaving Aurora about three hundred pounds. She peremptorily rejects a large sum of money which Romney, with delicate generosity, had attempted to place at her disposal, without allowing her to incur the sense of obligation, and starts for the metropolis:—

>   'I go hence
>   To London, to the gathering-place of souls,
>   To live mine straight out, vocally, in books;
>   Harmoniously for others, if indeed
>   A woman's soul, like man's, be wide enough
>   To carry the whole octave (that's to prove),
>   Or if I fall, still, purely for myself.

Locating herself at Kensington, she begins her literary career, and achieves distinction. One day she is waited on by a certain Lady Waldemar, who gives her the astounding information that her cousin Romney, whom she had not seen for three years, is on the eve of marriage—

>   To a girl of doubtful life, undoubtful birth.
>   Starved out in, London, till her coarse-grained hands
>   Are whiter than her morals.

This Lady Waldemar is personally in love with Romney Leigh, and comes to ask the aid of Aurora in breaking off the ill-assorted marriage. Aurora, however, having conceived a disgust to her visitor (which is not surprising, seeing that her conversation is so flavoured with allusions to garlic, that even the Lady of Shallot would have recoiled from her whispers), refuses to have any participation in the matter, but resolves immediately to see this girl, Marian Erle, who resides in a garret somewhere in the purlieus of St. Giles. After passing through the abominations of that quarter, and receiving the maledictions of thief and prostitute, the poetess discovers the object of her search, and hears her story. Marian Erle, the selected bride of Romney Leigh, was the daughter of a tramp and squatter on the Malvern Hills, and her education was essentially a hedge one. Her father drank and beat his wife, and the wife in turn beat her child. When Marian arrived at the age of puberty, her unnatural mother was about to sell her as a victim to the lusts of "a squire," when the girl, in horror, ran away, burst a blood-vessel in her flight, was found senseless on the road by a waggoner, and conveyed to an hospital in a neighbouring town, where Romney Leigh was a visitor. Finding that she was friendless and homeless, he procured her a place in a sowing establishment in London, which she quitted to attend the deathbed of a poor consumptive companion, who had sunk under the pressure of overwork. Here Romney Leigh again appeared, and after the death of her friend, proposed to marry her, fashioning his proposal thus:—

>   'Dear Marian, of one clay God made us all,
>   And though men push and poke and paddle in't
>   (As children play at fashioning dirt-pies),
>   And call their fancies by the name of facts,
>   Assuming difference, lordship, privilege,
>   When all's plain dirt,—they come back to it at last;
>   The first grave-digger proves it with a spade,
>   And pats all even. Need we wait for this,
>   You, Marian, and I, Romney?
>   She, at that,
>   Looked blindly in his face, as when one looks
>   Through driving autumn-rains to find the sky.
>   He went on speaking.
>   Marian, I being born
>   What men call noble, and you, issued from
>   The noble people,—though the tyrannous sword
>   Which pierced Christ's heart, has cleft the world in twain
>   'Twixt class and class, opposing rich to poor,—
>   Shall *we* keep parted? Not so. Let us lean
>   And strain together rather, each to each,
>   Compress the red lips of this gaping wound,
>   As far as two souls can,—ay, lean and league,
>   I, from my superabundance,—from your want,
>   You,—joining in a protest 'gainst the wrong
>   On both sides!'

While Marian is telling her story to Aurora, Romney comes in, looks certainly a little surprised at finding his cousin there, but is by no means disconcerted. Naturally enough Aurora supposes that he must be influenced by a very strong passion for the girl whom he is about to make his wife, and congratulates him, with what sincerity we need not inquire, on having made choice of so fair and gentle a creature. Romney, however, utterly denies the soft impeachment, in so far as it implies that his affections were any way engaged. Ordinary men contract marriages from love—*he* is influenced by a far higher principle. He says:—

> 'You did not, do not, cannot comprehend
> My choice, my ends, my motives, nor myself:
> No matter now—we'll let it pass, you say.
> I thank you for your generous cousinship
> Which helps this present; I accept for her
> Your favourable thoughts. We're fallen on
>   days,
> We two, who are not poets, when to wed
> Requires less mutual love than common love,
> For two together to bear out at once
> Upon the loveless many. Work in pairs,
> In galley-couplings or in marriage-rings,
> The difference lies in the honour, not the
>   work,—
> And such we're bound to, I and she. But love,
> (You poets are benighted in this age;
> The hour's too late for catching even moths,
> You're gnats instead), love!—love's fool-
>   paradise
> Is out of date, like Adam's. Set a swan
> To swim the Trenton, rather than true love
> To float its fabulous plumage safely down
> The cataracts of this loud transition-time,
> Whose roar, for ever henceforth, in my ears,
> Must keep me deaf to music.

In short, the man has not an atom of love for the girl, whom he proposes to wed entirely from motives of general philanthropy! At this Aurora is somewhat disgusted; but, wishing to show kindness to her cousin—perhaps to testify her own indifference, which, however, is rather feigned than real—she suggests that the marriage should take place at her house. But Master Romney will not hear of such an arrangement, as it might weaken the effect of the grand moral lesson which he intends to convey to society:—

> He answered, 'But it is:—I take my wife
> Directly from the people,—and she comes,
> As Austria's daughter to imperial France,
> Betwixt her eagles, blinking not her race,
> From Margaret's Court, at garret-height, to
>   meet
> And wed me at St. James's, nor put off
> Her gown of serge for that. The things we do,
> We do: we'll wear no mask, as if we blushed.

The following sketch of the company assembled to witness the marriage ceremony is too racy and rich to be omitted here. As the union was to be typical of the inpending abolition of all class distinctions, Romney determined that it should be celebrated in the presence of high and low, and issued cards accordingly.

>   Well,
> A month passed so, and then the notice came;
> On such a day the marriage at the church.
> I was not backward.
>   Half St. Giles in frieze
> Was bidden to meet St. James in cloth of gold,
> And after contract at the altar, pass
> To eat a marriage-feast on Hampstead Heath.
> Of course the people came in uncompelled,
> Lame, blind, and worse—sick, sorrowful, and
>   worse,
> The humours of the peccant social wound
> All pressed out, poured out upon Pimlico,
> Exasperating the unaccustomed air
> With hideous interfusion: you'd suppose
> A finished generation, dead of plague,
> Swept outward from their graves into the sun,
> The moil of death upon them. What a sight!
> A holiday of miserable men
> Is sadder than a burial-day of kings.
>
> They clogged the streets, they oozed into the
>   church
> In a dark, slow stream, like blood. To see that
>   sight,
> The noble ladiess tood up in their pews,
> Some pale for fear, a few as red for hate,
> Some simply curious, some just insolent,
> And some in wondering scorn,—'What next?
>   what next?'
> These crushed; their delicate rose-lips from the
>   smile
> That misbecame them in a holy place,
> With broidered hems of perfumed hand-
>   kerchiefs;
> Those passed the salts with confidence of eyes
> And simultaneous shiver of moire silk;
> While all the aisles, alive and black with heads,
> Crawled slowly toward the altar from the street,
> As bruised snakes crawl and hiss out of a hole
> With shuddering involutions, swaying slow
> From right to left, and then from left to right,
> In pants and pauses. What an ugly crest
> Of faces rose upon you everywhere
> From that crammed mass! you did not usually
> See faces like them in the open day:
> They hide in cellars, not to make you mad
> As Romney Leigh is.—Faces! O my God,
> We call those, faces? men's and women's—
>   ay,
> And children's;—babies, hanging like a rag
> Forgotten on their mother's neck,—poor
>   mouths,
> Wiped clean of mother's milk by mother's
>   blow,
> Before they are taught her cursing. Faces!—
>   phew,
> We'll call them vices festering to despairs,
> Or sorrows petrifying to vices: not

A finger-touch of God left whole on them;
All ruined, lost—the countenance worn out
As the garments, the will dissolute as the acts,
The passions loose and draggling in the dirt
To trip the foot up at the first free step!—
Those faces! 'twas as if you had stirred up hell
To heave its lowest dreg-flends uppermost
In fiery swirls of slime,—such strangled fronts.
Such obdurate jaws were thrown up constantly,
To twit you with your race, corrupt your blood,
And grind to devilish colours all your dreams
Henceforth,—though, haply, you should drop asleep
By clink of silver waters, in a muse
On Raffael's mild Madonna of the Bird.

So there they wait—that strangely assorted company—the denizens of St. Giles thronging on the inhabitants of St. James—both parties curious to behold the marriage which is to inaugurate the future revolution and fusion of society. Romney Leigh appears to do the honours; but time rolls on, and still the bride comes not. The fashionables stare and talk gossip; the vulgar murmur, and desire a smoke—until a rumour to the effect that something is amiss, pervades the throng.

A murmur and a movement drew around;
A naked whisper touched us. Something wrong!
What's wrong? The black crowd, as an overstrained
Cord, quivered in vibrations, and I saw—
Was that *his* face I saw?—his—Romney Leigh's—
Which tossed a sudden horror like a sponge
Into all eyes,—while himself stood white upon
The topmost altar-stair, and tried to speak,
And failed, and lifted higher above his head
A letter,—as a man who drowns and gasps.

'My brothers, bear with me! I am very weak.
I meant but only good. Perhaps I meant
Too proudly,—and God snatched the circumstance,
And changed it therefore. There's no marriage—none.
She leaves me,—she departs,—she disappears,—
I lose her. Yet I never forced her "ay,"
To have her "no" so cast into my teeth,
In manner of an accusation, thus.
My friends, you are all dismissed, Go, eat and drink
According to the programme,—and farewell!'

At this St. Giles' rises in insurrection, cursing Romney as a seducer, and accusing him of having made away with the girl. There is a superb row, with threats of violence and arson, until the police enter and clear the church.

Beyond an engimatical letter of leave-taking, which gives no explanation of her avoiding the marriage ceremony, we hear nothing of Marian for a long time. Romney retires to Leigh Hall, which he has turned into a "phalanstery," by which term, we presume, is meant an Owenite community. Miss Aurora continues her devotion to the muses, and becomes more notable day by day; but a horrid suspicion crosses her that Lady Waldemar has found the weak side of her wealthy cousin. For, at a conversazione at the house of a certain Lord Howe she learns that the fair and intriguing Waldemar is commonly considered as Romney's pet disciple—nay, that she is considered as his bride intended. In the words of Mrs. Browning, which we give without the metrical divisions,—

You may find her name on all his missions and commissions, schools, asylums, hospitals. He has had her down with other ladies, whom her starry lead persuaded from other spheres, to his country-place in Shropshire, in the famed phalanstery at Leigh Hall, christianised from Fourior's own, in which he has planted out his sapling stocks of knowledge into social bursaries; and there, they say, she has tarried half a week, and milked the cows, and churned, and pressed the curd, and said 'my sister' to the lowest drab of all the assembled castaways. Such girls! Ay, sided with them at the washing-tub.

Lady Waldemar, in a very spiteful speech, confirms this impression; and Miss Aurora, who all this time has had a secret hankering for her cousin, determines to square her balances with her publisher, and to depart for Italy.

In Paris she encounters Marian, and finds her a mother. The explanation is, that Lady Waldemar had tampered with the girl; and by representing to her that her marriage with Romney would be his social ruin, induced her to take flight on the day preceding that which had been arranged for the nuptials. The place of her future destiny was Australia, but her ladyship had confided her to the charge of an unprincipled *soubrette,* who, whether or not by design of her mistress, took Marian over to France, conveyed her to an infamous house, and sold her, while under the influence of drugs, to violation. On awakening to a sense of her situation and wrongs, the unfortunate girl became mad, and was allowed to make her escape, underwent various adventures and vicissitudes, and finnally brought into the world a male child, in whom her whole existence was wrapt up, and for whom alone she lived, when she was recognised and challenged by Aurora in the streets of Paris. The sequel may be easily imagined. Miss Leigh, convinced of Marian's innocence, insists that she, with her child, shall accompany her to Florence; and there are some letters and cross purposes, into which, for the mere sake of the story, it is not necessary to enter. In fine, Aurora, in the full belief that Lady Waldemar, to whom she has sent a most insulting letter, is now the wife of her cousin, becomes melancholy and heart-sick, and time drags wearily on, until one night, watching the stars from her terrace, she is startled by the sudden apparition of Romney by her side. Gentler than in his early youth, and far more humble, Romney first pays homage to her genius, and then confesses that his social schemes have proved an utter failure.

> 'My vain phalanstery dissolved itself;
> My men and women of disordered lives,
> I brought in orderly to dine and sleep,
> Broke up those waxen masks I made them wear,
> With fierce contortions of the natural face;
> And cursed me for my tyrannous constraint
> In forcing crooked creatures to live straight;
> And set the country hounds upon my back
> To bite and tear me for my wicked deed
> Of trying to do good without the church
> Or even the squires, Aurora. Do you mind
> Your ancient neighbours? The great book-club teems
> With "sketches," "summaries," and "last tracts" but twelve,
> On socialistic troublers of close bonds
> Betwixt the generous rich and grateful poor.
> The vicar preached from "Revelations" (till
> The doctor woke) and found me with "the frogs"
> On three successive Sundays; ay, and stopped
> To weep a little (for he's getting old)
> That such perdition should o'ertake a man
> Of such fair acres,—in the parish, too!
> He printed his discourses "by request;"
> And if your book shall sell as his did, then
> Your verses are less good than I suppose.
> The women of the neighbourhood subscribed,
> And sent me a copy bound in scarlet silk,
> Tooled edges, blazoned with the arms of Leigh:
> I own that touched me.'
>   'What, the pretty ones?
> Poor Romney!'
>   'Otherwise the effect was small.
> I had my windows broken once or twice
> By liberal peasants, naturally incensed
> At such a vexer of Arcadian peace,
> Who would not let men call their wives their own
> To kick like Britons,—and made obstacles
> When things went smoothly as a baby drugged,
> Toward freedom and starvation; bringing down
> The wicked London tavern-thieves and drabs,
> To affront the blessed hill-side drabs and thieves
> With mended morals, quotha,—fine new lives!—
> My windows paid for't. I was shot at, once,
> By an active poacher who had hit a hare
> From the other barrel, tired of springeing game
> So long upon my acres, undisturbed,
> And restless for the country's virtue (yet
> He missed me)—ay, and pelted very oft
> In riding through the village. "There he goes,
> Who'd drive away our Christian gentlefolks,
> To catch us undefended in the trap
> He baits with poisonous cheese, and lock us up
> In that pernicious prison of Leigh Hall
> With all his murderers! Give another name,
> And say Leigh Hell, and burn it with fire.
> And so they did, at last, Aurora.

The worst of it was, that the garrotters, ticket-of-leave men, and street-walkers, with whom he had filled his house, thought the proceeding rare fun, and joined in the incendiarism; and Will Erle, Marian's father, "tramp and poacher," whom he had attempted to reclaim, struck Romney on the head with a burning brand as he was leaving the house, inflicting an injury which brought him nearly to the verge of the grave. In the course of conversation Romney undeceives Aurora as to his connection with Lady Waldemar, but declares that he considers himself bound, notwithstanding her misfortune, to wed Marian, and to adopt her child. Marian, who has overheard this, comes forward, and after a passionate scene of great beauty, rejects the offer. Here we cannot resist a quotation.

> 'I have not so much life that I should love
> —Except the child. Ah God! I could not bear
> To see my darling on a good man's knees,
> And know by such a look, or such a sigh,
> Or such a silence, that he thought sometimes,
> "This child was fathered by some cursed wretch"—
> For, Romney,—angels are less tender-wise
> Than God and mothers; even *you* would think
> What *we* think never. He is ours, the child;
> And we would sooner vex a soul in heaven
> By coupling with it the dead body's thought,
> It left behind it in a last month's grave,
> Than, in my child, see other than—my child.
> We only, never call him fatherless
> Who has God and his mother. O my babe,
> My pretty, pretty blossom, an ill-wind
> Once blew upon my breast! can any think
> I'd have another,—one called happier,
> A fathered child, with father's love and race
> That's worn as bold and open as a smile,
> To vex my darling when he's asked his name,
> And has no answer? What! a happier child
> Than mine, my best,—who laughed so loud to-night

> He could not sleep for pastime? Nay, I sware
> By life and love, that, if I lived like some,
> And loved like—*some*—ay, loved you,
>   Romney Leigh,
> As some love (eyes that have wept so much,
>   see clear),
> I've room for no more children in my arms;
> My kisses are all melted on one mouth;
> I would not push my darling to a stool
> To dandle babies. Here's a hand, shall keep
> For ever clean without a marriage-ring,
> To tend my boy, until he cease to need
> One steadying finger of it, and desert
> (Not miss) his mother's lap, to sit with men.
> And when I miss him (not he me) I'll come
> And say, "Now give me some of Romney's
>   work,
> To help our outcast orphans of the world,
> And comfort grief with grief." For you,
>   meantime,
> Most noble Romney, wed a noble wife,
> And open on each other your great souls,—
> I need not farther bless you. If I dared
> But strain and touch her in her upper sphere,
> And say, "Come down to Romney—pay my
>   debt!"
> I should be joyful with the stream of joy
> Sent through me. But the moon is in my
>   face—
> I dare not,—though I guess the name he loves;
> I'm learned with my studies of old days,
> Remembering how he crush'd his under-lip
> When some one came and spoke, or did not
>   come:
> Aurora, I could touch her with my hand,
> And fly, because I dare not.'
>   She was gone.

And so Marian departs. But now comes an awful disclosure—Romney is blind. The blow struck by the poacher had destroyed the visual nerves; and for that unfortunate Lord of Leigh, the glory of the sun, moon, and stars, was but a remembrance. So Aurora, who had always loved him, even though she would not allow it to herself—and whom he had never ceased to love amidst his perverted dreams of duty—gives her whole woman's heart to the helpless; and the poem closes with the interchange of vows and aspirations.

Such is the story, which no admirer of Mrs. Browning's genius ought in prudence to defend. In our opinion it is fantastic, unnatural, exaggerated; and all the worse, because it professes to be a tale of our own times. No one who understands of how much value probability is to a tale, can read the foregoing sketch, or indeed peruse the poem, without a painful feeling that Mrs. Browning has been perpetrating, in essentials, an extravaganza or caricature, instead of giving to the public a real lifelike picture; for who can accept, as truthful representation, Romney's proposal of marriage to an ignorant uneducated girl whom he does not love; or that scene in the church, which is absolutely of Rabelaisian conception? We must not be seduced by beauty and power of execution from entering our protest against this radical error, which appears more glaring as we pass from the story to the next point, which is the delineation of character. Aurora Leigh is not an attractive character. After making the most liberal allowance for pride, and fanaticism for art, and inflexible independence, she is incongruous and contradictory both in her sentiments and in her actions. She is not a genuine woman; one half of her heart seems bounding with the beat of humanity, while the other half is ossified. What we miss in her is instinctiveness, which is the greatest charm of women. No doubt she displays it now and then, and sometimes very conspicuously, but it is not made the general attribute of her nature; and in her dealings with Romney Leigh, instinct disappears altogether. For we hold it absolutely impossible that a woman, gifted as she is represented to be, would have countenanced a kinsman, whom she respected only, in the desperate folly of wedding an uneducated girl from the lowest grade of society, whom he did not love, simply for the sake of a theory, thereby making himself a public laughing-stock, without the least chance of advancing the progress of his own preposterous opinions. There is nothing heroic in this; there is nothing reconcilable with duty. The part which Aurora takes in the transaction, degrades rather than raises her in our eyes; nor is she otherwise thoroughly amiable; for, with all deference to Mrs. Browning, and with ideas of our own perhaps more chivalric than are commonly promulgated, we must maintain that woman was created to be dependent on the man, and not in the primary sense his lady and his mistress. The extreme independence of Aurora detracts from the feminine charm, and mars the interest which we otherwise might have felt in so intellectual a heroine. In fact, she is made to resemble too closely some of the female portraits of George Sand, which never were to our liking. In Romney we fail to take any kind of interest. Though honour-able and generous, he is such a very decided noodle that we grudge him his prominence in the poem, do not feel much sympathy for his misfortunes, and cannot help wondering that Aurora should have entertained one spark of affection for so deplorable a milksop. Excess of enthusiasm we can allow; and folly, affecting to talk the words of wisdom, meets us at every turning: but Romney is a walking hyperbole. The character of Marian is very beautifully drawn and well sustained, but her thoughts and language are not those of a girl reared in the midst of sordid poverty, vice, and ignorance. This is an error in art which we are sure Mrs. Browning, upon mature consideration, will acknowledge; and it might easily have been avoided by the simple expedient of making Marian's origin and antecedents a few shades more respectable, which still would have left enough disparity between her and

Romney to produce the effect which Mrs. Browning desires. Lady Waldemar is a disgusting character. Mrs. Browning intended her to appear as despicable; but it was not therefore necessary to make her talk coarse and revolting. As an example let us cite the following passage:—

> Of a truth, Miss Leigh,
> I have not, without struggle, come to this.
> I took a master in the German tongue,
> I gamed a little, went to Paris twice;
> But, after all, this love!—you eat of love,
> And do as vile a thing as if you eat
> Of garlic—which, whatever else you eat,
> Tastes uniformly acrid, till your peach
> Reminds you of your onion. Am I coarse?
> Well, love's coarse, nature's coarse—ah,
>   there's the rub!
> We fair fine ladies, who park out our lives
> From common sheep-paths, cannot help the
>   crows
> From flying over,—we're as natural still
> As Blowsalinda. Drape us perfectly
> In Lyons velvet,—we are not, for that,
> Lay-figures, look you! we have hearts within,
> Warm, live, improvident, indecent hearts,
> As ready for distracted ends and acts
> As any distressed sempstress of them all
> That Romney groans and toils for. We catch
>   love
> And other fevers, in the vulgar way.
> Love will not be outwitted by our wit,
> Not outrun by our equipages:—mine
> Persisted, spite of efforts. All my cards
> Turned up but Romney Leigh; my German
>   stopped
> At germane Wertherism; my Paris rounds
> Returned me from the Champs Elysées just
> A ghost, and sighing like Dido's. I came
>   home
> Uncured,—convicted rather to myself
> Of being in love—in love! That's coarse
>   you'll say.
> I'm talking garlic.

In this there is neither truth, power, nor humour. The offence against taste is so rank that it cannot easily be forgiven.

In poetry passages such as that which we have quoted are intolerable, because by juxtaposition with others exquisite in themselves, they impair our capacity for enjoyment. Anything very hideous or revolting taints the air around it, and produces a sensation of loathing, from which we do not immediately recover. Hence poets, even when their situations are of the most tragic nature—even when they are dealing with subjects questionable in morality—do, for the most part, sedulously avoid anything like coarseness of expression, and frame their language so as to convey the general idea without presenting special images which are calculated to disgust. Indeed, whilst reading this poem, which abounds in references to art, we have been impressed with a doubt whether, with all her genius, accomplishment, and experience, Mrs. Browning has ever thought seriously of the principles upon which art is founded. For genius, as we all know, or ought to know, is not of itself sufficient for the construction of a great poem. Artists, like architects, must work by rule—not slavishly indeed, but ever keeping in mind that there are certain principles which experience has tested and approved, and that to deviate from these is literally to court defeat. Not that we should implicitly receive the doctrines laid down by critics, scholiasts, or commentators, or pin our faith to the formula of Longinus; but we should regard the works of the great masters, both ancient and modern, as profitable for instruction as well as for delight, and be cautious how we innovate. We may consider it almost as a certainty that every leading principle of art has been weighed and sifted by our predecessors; and that most of the theories, which are paraded as discoveries, were deliberately examined by them, and rejected because they were false or impracticable. In the fifth book of this poem there is a dissertation upon poetry, in which Mrs. Browning very plainly indicates her opinion that the chief aim of a poet should be to illustrate the age in which he lives.

> But poets should
> Exert a double vision; should have eyes
> To see near things as comprehensively
> As if afar they took their point of sight,
> And distant things, as intimately deep,
> As if they touched them. Let us strive for this.
> I do distrust the poet who discerns
> No character or glory in his times,
> And trundles back his soul five hundred years,
> Past moat and drawbridge, into a castle-court,
> Oh not to sing of lizards or of toads
> Alive i' the ditch there!—'twere excusable;
> But of some black chief, half knight, half
>   sheep-lifter,
> Some beauteous dame, half chattel and half
>   queen;
> As dead as must be for the greater part,
> The poems made on their chivalric bones.
> And that's no wonder: death inherits death.
>
> Nay, if there's room for poets in the world
> A little overgrown (I think there is),
> Their sole work is to represent the age,
> Their age, not Charlemagne's,—this live
>   throbbing age,
> That brawls, cheats, maddens, calculates,
>   aspires,
> And spends more passion, more heroic heat,
> Betwixt the mirrors of its drawing-rooms,

> Than Roland with his knights, at Roncesvalles.
> To flinch from modern varnish, coat or flounce
> Cry out for togas and the picturesque,
> Is fatal,—foolish too. King Arthur's self
> Was commonplace to Lady Guenever;
> And Camelot to minstrels seemed as flat
> As Regent Street to poets.
>
>   Never flinch,
> But still, unscrupulously epic, catch
> Upon the burning lava of a song,
> The full-veined, heaving, double-breasted Age:
> That, when the next shall come, the men of that
> May touch the impress with reverent hand, and say,
> 'Behold,—behold the paps we have all sucked!'
> That bosom seems to beat still, or at least
> It sets ours beating. This is living art,
> Which thus presents, and thus records true life.'

This, in our apprehension, would lead to a total sacrifice of the ideal. It is not the province of the poet to depict things as they are, but so to refine and purify as to purge out the grosser matter; and this he cannot do if he attempts to give a faithful picture of his own times. For in order to be faithful, he must necessarily include much which is abhorrent to art, and revolting to the taste, for which no exactness of delineation will be accepted as a proper excuse. All poetical characters, all poetical situations must be idealised. The language is not that of common life, which belongs essentially to the domain of prose. Therein lies the distinction between a novel and a poem. In the first, we expect that the language employed by the characters shall be strictly natural, not excluding even imperfections, and that their sentiments shall not be too elevated or extravagant for the occasion. In the second, we expect idealisation—language more refined, more adorned, and more forcible than that which is ordinarily employed; and sentiments purer and loftier than find utterance in our daily speech. Whilst dealing with a remote subject the poet can easily effect this, but not so when he brings forward characters of his own age. We have been told that both the late John Kemble and his sister Mrs. Siddons had become so accustomed to the flow of blank verse that they carried the trick of it into private life, and used sorely to try the risible faculties of the company by demanding beef or beer in tragic tones and rhythm. That which would have sounded magnificently on the stage was ludicrous at a modern table. Mrs. Browning has evidently felt the difficulty, but she cannot conquer it. In this poem she has wilfully alternated passages of sorry prose with bursts of splendid poetry; and her prose is all the worse because she has been compelled to dislocate its joints in order to make it read like blank verse. Let us again revert to the experiment of exhibiting one or two of these passages printed in the usual form:—

> We are sad to-night. I saw—(goodnight, Sir Blaise! ah Smith—he has slipped away) I saw you across the room, and stayed, Miss Leigh, to keep a crowd of lion-hunters off, with faces toward your jungle. There were three; a spacious lady five feet ten, and fat, who has the devil in her (and there's room) for walking to and fro upon the earth from Chippewa to China; she requires your autograph upon a tinted leaf 'twixt Queen Pomare's and Emperor Soulouque's; pray give it; she has energies, though fat; for me, I'd rather see a rick on fire than such a woman angry. Then a youth fresh from the back-woods, green as the underboughs, asks modestly, Miss Leigh, to kiss your shoe, and adds, he has an epic in twelve parts, which when you've read, you'll do it for his boot,—all which I saved you, and absorb next week both manuscript and man.

Is that poetry? Assuredly not. Is it prose? If so, it is as poor and faulty a specimen as ever was presented to our notice. It would not pass muster even in a third-rate novel, where sense is an element of minor consideration, and style is habitually disregarded. Here is an extract from an epistle by Lady Waldemar:—

> Parted. Face no more, voice no more, love no more! wiped wholly out like some ill scholar's scrawl from heart and slate—ay, spit on, and so wiped out utterly by some coarse scholar. I have been too coarse, too human. Have we business in our rank with blood in the veins? I will have henceforth none; not even to keep the colour at my lip. A rose is pink and pretty without blood,—why not a woman? When we've played in vain the game, to adore,—who have resources still, and can play on at leisure, being adored: here's Smith already swearing at my feet that I'm the typic She. Away with Smith!—Smith smacks of Leigh, and henceforth, I'll admit no Socialist within three crinolines to live and have his being. But for you, though insolent your letter and absurd, and though I hate you frankly, take my Smith! For when you have seen this famous marriage tied, a most unspotted Earl to a noble Leigh (his love astray on one he should not love), howbeit you should not want his love, beware, you'll want some comfort. So I leave you Smith; take Smith!

What a rare specimen of a rhythmical fashionable letter! Still more singular is the effect when the mob becomes articulate:—

> Then spoke a man, 'Now look to it, coves, that all the beef and drink be not filched from us like the other fun; for beer's spilt easier than a woman is. This gentry is not honest with the poor; they bring us up to trick us.' 'Go it, Jim,' a woman screamed back. 'I'm a tender soul; I never banged a child at two years old, and drew blood from him, but I sobbed for it next moment—and I've had a plague of seven. I'm tender: I've no stomach even for beef, until I know about the girl that's lost—that's killed, mayhap. I did misdoubt, at first, the fine lord meant

no good by her or us. He maybe got the upper hand of her by holding up a wedding-ring, and then . . a choking finger on her throat last night, and just a clever take to keep us still, as she is, poor lost innocent!'

Reading such passages as these—so flat, distorted, and unworthy—shall we not exclaim with Mrs. Browning herself,

> Weep, my Æschylus,
> But low and far, upon Sicilian shores?

It is not the part of critics to strain their vision so as to detect spots on the disc of the sun; but it is their duty to mark the appearance of even a partial eclipse. It is far easier, as it is more pleasant, to praise than to condemn; but praise, injudiciously or indiscriminately bestowed, cannot be commended, since it leads to the perpetuation of error. In dealing with the works of authors of high name and established repute, it is of the utmost importance that the judgment should be clear and calm; for we know by experience that the aberrations or eccentricities of a distinguished artist are immediately copied by a crew of imitators, who, unable to vie with their original in beauties, can at least rival him in his faults. We doubt not that, before a year is over, many poems on the model of *Aurora Leigh* will be written and published; and that conversations in the pot-house, casino, and even worse places, will be reduced to blank verse, and exhibited as specimens of high art. To dignify the mean, is not the province of poetry—let us rather say that there are atmospheres so tainted that in them poetry cannot live. Its course is in the empyrean or in the fresh wholesome air, but if it attempts to descend to pits and charnel-vaults, it is stifled by the noxious exhalations. We by no means confound the humble with the mean. The most sanctified affections, the purest thoughts, the holiest aspirations, are as likely to be found in the cottage as in the castle. Wherever there is a flower, however lowly, beauty may be seen; the prayer of a monarch is not more heeded in heaven than the supplication of an outcast; the cry of a mother is as plaintive from the dungeon as though it sounded from the halls of a palace. This very poem which we are reviewing affords a remarkable illustration of the æsthetical point which we are anxious to enforce. We have already said that the character of Marian Erle is beautifully drawn and well sustained, and yet it is the humblest of them all. But in depicting her, Mrs. Browning has abstained from all meanness. If she errs at all, it is by making the girl appear more refined in thought and expression than is justified by her previous history, but that is an error on the safe side, and one which may be readily excused. Marian, little better than a pariah-girl, does undoubtedly attract our sympathies more than the polished and high-minded Aurora, the daughter of a noble race—not certainly as the bride of Romney, but as the mother of a hapless child. There, indeed, Mrs. Browning has achieved a triumph; for never yet—no, not in her **"Cry of the Children,"** one of the most pathetic and tear-stirring poems in the English language—has she written anything comparable to the passages which refer to Marian and her babe. Take for example this description:—

> I saw the whole room, I and Marian there
> Alone.
>   Alone? She threw her bonnet off,
> Then sighing as 'twere sighing the last time,
> Approached the bed, and drew a shawl away:
> You could not peel a fruit you fear to bruise
> More calmly and more carefully than so,—
> Nor would you find within, a rosier flushed
> Pomegranate—
>   There he lay, upon his back,
> The yearling creature, warm and moist with life
> To the bottom of his dimples,—to the ends
> Of the lovely tumbled curls about his face;
> For since he had been covered over-much
> To keep him from the light-glare, both his cheeks
> Were hot and scarlet as the first live rose
> The shepherd's heart-blood ebbed away into,
> The faster for his love. And love, was here
> As instant! in the pretty baby-mouth,
> Shut close as if for dreaming that it sucked;
> The little naked feet drawn up the way
> Of nestled birdlings; everything so soft
> And tender,—to the little holdfast hands,
> Which, closing on a finger into sleep,
> Had kept the mould of't.
>   While we stood there dumb,—
> For oh, that it should take such innocence
> To prove just guilt, I thought, and stood there dumb;
> The light upon his eyelids pricked them wide,
> And, staring out at us with all their blue,
> As half perplexed between the angelhood
> He had been away to visit in his sleep,
> And our most mortal presence,—gradually
> He saw his mother's face, accepting it
> In change for heaven itself, with such a smile
> As might have well been learnt there,—never moved,
> But smiled on, in a drowse of ectasy,
> So happy (half with her and half with heaven)
> He could not have the trouble to be stirred,
> But smiled and lay there. Like a rose, I said:
> As red and still indeed as any rose,
> That blows in all the silence of its leaves,
> Content, in blowing, to fulfil its life.

Now contrast that with, the stuff, which we have put into the form of prose, and then tell us, good reader, if we are not justified in feeling annoyed, and even incensed, that a lady capable of producing so exquisite a picture, should condescend to fashion into verse what is essentially mean, gross, and puerile? We must have no evasions here, for this is an important question of art. We may be told that Shakespeare, in his highest tragedies, has introduced the comic element; and his example, so distinguished as almost to amount to an unimpeachable authority, may be cited in defence of Mrs. Browning. But, on examination, we shall find that there is no analogy. In the first place, whenever Shakespeare descends to low comedy, he makes his characters discourse in prose, thereby marking broadly the elevation of sentiment and dignity which belongs to verse, and he does so even when low comedy is excluded. When Hamlet is familiar, as with the players, Polonius, the gravediggers, or Osric, he speaks in prose; and the rhythmical periods are reserved for the higher and more impassioned situations. So in *Othello*, in the scenes between Iago, Cassio, and Roderigo. So in *Julius Cæsar* (in which, being a classical play, the temptation lay towards stateliness), whenever the citizens or the cynical Casca are introduced; and in *Henry V.*, in the night-scene before Agincourt, there is even a more remarkable instance of this. It was evidently the view of Shakespeare that verse is the proper vehicle for poetry alone: he would not dignify ignoble thoughts or common sentiments by admitting them to that lofty chariot. Mrs. Browning follows the march of modern improvement. She makes no distinction between her first and her third class passengers, but rattles them along at the same speed upon her rhythmical railway.

There is no instance of a poem of considerable length which is free from faults and blemishes; and whatever may be said to the contrary, the detection of existing faults is the real business of the critic. He either is, or is supposed to be, the holder of the touchstone, by means of which true metal is distinguished from that which is base, and he is bound in duty to declare the result of his investigation. In the present instance, while dealing with ***Aurora Leigh,*** we have been at some pains to arrive at the metal. Our task has been rather that of an Australian or Californian gold-seeker, who puts into his cradle or his pan a spadeful of doubtful material. From the first shaking there emerges mud—from the second, pebbles—but, after clearance, the pure gold is found at the bottom, and in no inconsiderable quantities.

If we have not been able conscientiously to praise the story, either as regards conception or execution, no such restriction is laid upon us while dealing with isolated passages. Mrs. Browning possesses in a very high degree the faculty of description, presenting us often with the most brilliantly coloured pictures. In this respect, if we may be allowed to institute such a comparison, she resembles Turner, being sometimes even extravagant in the vividness of her tints. By this we mean that she has a decided tendency, not only to multiply, but to intensify images, and occasionally carries this so far as to bewilder the reader. The following sketch of London is drawn in her most florid manner:—

> So, happy and unafraid of solitude,
> I worked the short days out,—and watched the sun
> On lurid morns or monstrous afternoons,
> Like some Druidic idol's fiery brass,
> With fixed unflickering outline of dead heat,
> In which the blood of wretches pent inside
> Seemed oozing forth to incarnadine the air,—
> Push out through fog with his dilated disk,
> And startle the slant roofs and chimneypots
> With splashes of fierce colour. Or I saw
> Fog only, the great tawny weltering fog,
> Involve the passive city, strangle it
> Alive, and draw it off into the void,
> Spires, bridges, streets, and squares, as if a sponge
> Had wiped out London,—or as noon and night
> Had clapped together and utterly struck out
> The intermediate time, undoing themselves
> In the act. Your city poets see such things,
> Not despicable. Mountains of the south,
> When, drunk and mad with elemental wines,
> They rend the seamless mist and stand up bare,
> Make fewer singers, haply. No one sings,
> Descending Sinai: on Parnassus mount,
> You take a mule to climb, and not a muse,
> Except in fable and figure: forests chant
> Their anthems to themselves, and leave you dumb.
> But sit in London, at the day's decline,
> And view the city perish in the mist,
> Like Pharaoh's armaments in the deep Red Sea,—
> The chariots, horsemen, footmen, all the host,
> Sucked down and choked to silence—then, surprised
> By a sudden sense of vision and of tune,
> You feel as conquerors though you did not fight,
> And you and Israel's other singing girls,
> Ay, Miriam with them, sing the song you choose.

There can be no doubt as to the power which is here exhibited, but in our opinion the passage is overwrought. There is a prodigality of illustration which mars the general effect by creating confusion. In marked contrast to it is our next extract. Aurora, returning to Italy, is watching on deck for the first glimpse of her native land.

> That night we spent between the purple heaven
> And purple water: I think Marian slept;
> But I, as a dog a-watch for his master's foot,
> Who cannot sleep or eat before he hears,

> I sate upon the deck and watched all night,
> And listened through the stars for Italy.
>
> . . . . .
>
> I felt the wind soft from the land of souls;
> The old miraculous mountains heaved in sight,
> One straining past another along the shore,
> The way of grand dull Odyssean ghosts
> Athirst to drink the cool blue wine of seas
> And stare on voyagers. Peak pushing peak
> They stood: I watched beyond that Tyrian belt
> Of intense sea betwixt them and the ship,
> Down all their sides the misty olive-woods
> Dissolving in the weak congenial moon,
> And still disclosing some brown convent-tower
> That seems as if it grew from some brown rock,—
> Or many a little lighted village, dropt
> Like a fallen star, upon so high a point,
> You wonder what can keep it in its place
> From sliding headlong with the waterfalls
> Which drop and powder all the myrtle-groves
> With spray of silver. Thus my Italy
> Was stealing on us. Genoa broke with day;
> The Doria's long pale palace striking out,
> From green hills in advance of the white town.
> A marble finger dominant to ships,
> Seen glimmering through the uncertain grey of dawn.

That is poetry—splendid, magnificent poetry—without intermixture of conceits or far-fetched images. Our younger poets, who, as a class, aspire to dazzle rather than to please, might derive a very useful lesson from the study of these extracts. The first is undoubtedly gorgeous, but it is so overlaid with ornament that it leaves no distinct impression on the mind; the second is a perfect picture, which once seen can never be forgotten. To these we are tempted to add a third, descriptive of Florence:—

> I found a house, at Florence, on the hill
> Of Bellosguardo. 'Tis a tower that keeps
> A post of double-observation o'er
> The valley of Arno (holding as a hand
> The outspread city) straight toward Ficsole
> And Mount Morello and the setting sun,—
> The Vallombrosan mountains to the right,
> Which sunrise fills as full as crystal cups
> Wine-filled, and red to the brim because it's red.
> No sun could die, nor yet be born, unseen
> By dwellers at my villa: morn and eve
> Were magnified before us in the pure
> Illimitable space and pause of sky,
> Intense as angels' garments blanched with God,
> Less blue than radiant. From the outer wall
> Of the garden, dropped the mystic floating grey
> Of olive-trees (with interruptions green
> From maize and vine) until it was caught and torn
> On that abrupt black line of cypresses
> Which signed the way to Florence. Beautiful
> The city lay along the ample vale,
> Cathedral, tower and palace, piazza and street;
> The river trailing like a silver cord
> Through all, and curling loosely, both before
> And after, over the whole stretch of land
> Sown whitely up and down its opposite slopes,
> With farms and villas.

The reader will find in the volume itself descriptions almost as vivid and charming as the above of English scenery; for Mrs. Browning, when her palette is not overcharged with carmine, can paint such things as perfectly as Morland, Gainsborough, or Constable. Witness the few following lines, which we cannot deny ourselves the pleasure of extracting:—

> I flattered all the beauteous country round,
> As poets use . . the skies, the clouds, the fields,
> The happy violets hiding from the roads
> The primroses run down to, carrying gold—
> The tangled hedgerows, where the cows push out
> Impatient horns and tolerant churning mouths,
> 'Twixt dripping ash-boughs,—hedgerows all alive
> With birds and gnats *and large white butterflies,*
> *Which look as if the May-flower had caught life*
> *And palpitated forth upon the wind,—*
> Hills, vales, woods, netted in a silver mist,
> Farms, granges, doubled up among the hills,
> And cattle grazing in the watered vales,
> And cottage-chimneys smoking from the woods,
> And cottage-gardens smelling everywhere,
> Confused with smell of orchards. 'See,' I said,
> 'And see! is God not with us on the earth?
> And shall we put Him down by aught we do?
> Who says there's nothing for the poor and vile
> Save poverty and wickedness? behold!'
> And ankle-deep in English grass I leaped,
> And clapped my hands, and called all very fair.

Nor is the great genius of Mrs. Browning less conspicuous in other portions of the poem which relate to the natural affections. Once and again, whilst perusing this volume, have we experienced a sensation of regret that one so admirably gifted should have wasted much of her power upon what are, after all, mere artistic experiments, when by adhering throughout to natural sentiment and natural expression, she might have produced a work so noble as to leave no room for cavilling or reproach. The tendency to experiment, which is simply a token of a morbid craving for originality, has been the bane of many poets. Their first victory being won, they think it incumbent on them to shift their campaigning-ground, and alter their strategy, forgetful that the method which has brought them success, and which they intuitively adopted because it was most suited to their powers, is precisely that most likely to insure them a future triumph. For ourselves, we are free to confess that we have not much faith in new theories of art; we are rather inclined to class them in the same category with schemes for the regeneration of society. Mrs. Browning, beyond all modern poets, has no need of resorting to fantasias for the sake of attracting an audience. For whenever she deserts her theories, and touches a natural chord, we acknowledge her as a mistress of song. In proof of which we cite the description of Marian Erle, the outcast girl, when waking from her trance in the hospital:—

> She stirred;—the place seemed new and strange as death.
> The white strait bed, with others strait and white,
> Like graves dug side by side at measured lengths,
> And quiet people walking in and out,
> With wonderful low voices and soft steps,
> And apparitional equal care for each,
> Astonished her with order, silence, law:
> And when a gentle hand held out a cup,
> She took it, as you do at sacrament,
> Half awed, half melted,—not being used, indeed,
> To so much love as makes the form of love
> And courtesy of manners. Delicate drinks
> And rare white bread, to which some dying eyes
> Were turned in observation. O my God,
> How sick we must be ere we make men just!
> I think it frets the saints in heaven to see
> How many desolate creatures on the earth
> Have learnt the simple dues of fellowship
> And social comfort, in a hospital,
> As Marian did. She lay there stunned, half tranced,
> And wished, at intervals of growing sense,
> She might be sicker yet, if sickness made
> The world so marvellous kind, the air so hushed,
> And all her wake-time quiet as a sleep;
> For now she understood (as such things were)
> How sickness ended very oft in heaven,
> Among the unspoken raptures. Yet more sick,
> And surelier happy. Then she dropped her lids,
> And, folding up her hands as flowers at night,
> Would lose no moment of the blessed time.

One more quotation, and we have done with extracts. We have thought it our duty to point out what seemed to us egregious faults; but not, on that account, are we blind to the many beauties of the poem. We envy the imagination that can conceive a sweeter picture than this:—

> Marian's good,
> Gentle and loving,—lets me hold the child,
> Or drags him up the hills to find me flowers,
> And fill those vases, ere I'm quite awake,—
> The grandiose red tulips, which grow wild,
> Or else my purple lilies, Dante blew
> To a larger bubble with his prophet-breath;
> Or one of those tall flowering reeds which stand
> In Arno like a sheaf of sceptres, left
> By some remote dynasty of dead gods,
> To suck the stream for ages and get green,
> And blossom wheresoe'er a hand divine
> Had warmed the place with ichor. Such I've found
> At early morning, laid across my bed,
> And woke up pelted with a childish laugh
> Which even Marian's low precipitous 'hush'
> Had vainly interposed to put away,—
> While I, with shut eyes, smile and motion for
> The dewy kiss that's very sure to come
> From mouth and cheeks, the whole child's face at once
> Dissolved on mine—as if a nosegay burst
> Its string with the weight of roses overblown,
> And dropt upon me. Surely I should be glad.
> The little creature almost loves me now,
> And calls my name . . 'Alola,' stripping off
> The *r*s like thorns, to make it smooth enough
> To take between his dainty, milk-fed lips,
> God love him!

It has been well remarked that the chief defect of modern British poems consists in the carelessness of their construction. Plot, arrangement, and even probability, are regarded as things of minor moment; and the whole attention of the artist is lavished upon expression. This, if we are to judge from antecedents, is a symptom of literary decadence. The same tendency is observable in the later literature of Greece and Rome; nay, it may be remarked within a narrower sphere—as, for example, in the writings of Euripides—the last of the great Hellenic triumvirate. Æschylus excelled in energy and masculine strength; Sophocles in his development of the passions; Euripides in expression—but, with Euripides, Athenian tragedy declined. It is ever an evil sign when mere talk is considered by a nation as something preferable to action, for it shows that sound and pretension are becoming more esteemed than sense and deliberate purpose. We might, upon this text, say something the reverse of complimentary to a large body of politicians; but we refrain from mingling the political with the poetical element. It is however, impossible to deny the fact that, by many, brilliant writing, or writing which seems brilliant, is esteemed as of the highest kind, without regard to congruity or design. This is a grievous error, which cannot be exposed too broadly; and to it we trace the almost total extinction, in our own day, of the British drama. Our great dramatists, with Shakespeare at their head, succeeded in gaining the attention of the public by the interest of their plots, far more than by the felicity of their diction; and until that truth is again recognised and acted on, we need not expect a resuscitation of the drama. Also be it remembered, that a plot—that is, a theme—well-considered, developed, and divided, must, to make it effective, be adequately and naturally expressed. Adequate expression is no more than the proper language of emotion; and emotion must be tracable to some evident and intelligible cause. All this is disregarded by our "new poets," as they love to style themselves, who come upon their imaginary stage, tearing their hair, proclaiming their inward wretchedness, and spouting sorry metaphysics in still sorrier verse, for no imaginable reason whatever. One of them has the curse of genius upon him, and seems to think that delirium is the normal state of the human mind. Another rails at Providence because he has not been placed in a situation which he supposes commensurate to his merits. A third, when he sets his characters in motion, pulls the strings so violently as to make them leap like fantoccini. A fourth is a mere crowder, and spins merciless rigmaroles about the "heart of the coming age." Now with the exception of the crowder, each of these men has some intellect and power; but they do not know how to apply it. They think that the public will be content to receive their crude thoughts as genuine notes of issue from the Bank of Genius, if so be that they are dressed up in a gaudy, glittering, and hyperbolical form; and they ransack, not only earth and sea, but heaven itself for ornaments. All this while they forget that there is no meaning in their talk; that people who are desirous to hear a story, do not call the minstrel in for the purpose of listening to his disappointed aspirations, or the bleatings of his individual woes, but because they require of him, as a professed member of the greatest craft since the prophets disappeared, a tale of energy or emotion that shall stir the heart, or open one of the many fountains of our common sympathy.

We could wish—though wishes avail not for the past—that Mrs. Browning had selected a more natural and intelligible theme which would have given full scope for the display of her extraordinary powers; and we trust that she will yet reconsider her opinion as to the abstract fitness for poetical use of a subject illustrative of the times in which we live. It may be that there is no difficulty which genius cannot conquer; at the same time, we cannot commend the wisdom of those who go out of their way on purpose to search for difficulties. It is curious to observe that poets in all ages have shrunk from the task of chronicling contemporaneous deeds. These are first confined to the tutelage of the muse of history; nor is it until time has done its consecrating office, that poetry ventures to approach them. The bards of old touched their harps, not for the glorification of their compatriots, but in memory of the deeds of their ancestors. No one supposes that the time has yet arrived when the Peninsular War or the sea-victories of Britain can be taken up as proper epical themes, though Nelson and Wellington have both entered into the famous mansions of the dead. This universal repugnance to the adoption of immediate subjects for poetical treatment, seems to us a very strong argument against its propriety; and certainly Mrs. Browning has not succeeded, by practice, in establishing her theory. There is sound truth in the observation that no man ever yet was a hero in the eyes of his valet, and the remark is equally just if we extend it from individuals to the masses. We select our demigods from the dead, not from the living. We cannot allow fancy to be trammelled in its work by perpetual reference to realities.

Still, with all its faults, this is a remarkable poem; strong in energy, rich in thought, abundant in beauty; and it more than sustains that high reputation which, by her previous efforts, Mrs. Browning has so honourably won.

George Eliot (review date 1857)

SOURCE: Review of *Aurora Leigh*, in *Westminster and Foreign Quarterly Review*, Vol. XI, No. 1, January, 1857, pp. 306-10.

[*In the following excerpt, Eliot praises* Aurora Leigh's *emotive power, claiming that it is Browning's infusion of "genuine thought and feeling" that distinguishes the work from those of her contemporaries.*]

Foster, the essayist, has somewhere said that the person who interests us most is the one that most gives us the idea of *ample being*. Applying this remark to books, which are but persons in a transmigrated form, we discern one grand source of the profound impression produced in us by ***Aurora Leigh***[1]. Other poems of our own day may have higher finish, or a higher degree of certain poetic qualities; but no poem embraces so wide a range of thought and emotion, or takes such complete possession of our nature. Mrs. Browning is, perhaps, the first woman who has produced a work which exhibits all the peculiar powers without the negations of her sex; which superadds to masculine vigour, breadth, and culture, feminine subtlety of perception, feminine quickness of sensibility, and feminine tenderness. It is difficult to point to a woman of genius who is not either too little feminine, or too exclusively so. But in this, her longest and greatest poem, Mrs. Browning has shown herself all the greater poet because she is intensely a poetess.

The *story* of *Aurora Leigh* has no other merit than that of offering certain elements of life, and certain situations which are peculiarly fitted to call forth the writer's rich thought and experience. It has nothing either fresh or felicitous in structure or incident; and we are especially sorry that Mrs. Browning has added one more to the imitations of the catastrophe in "Jane Eyre," by smiting her hero with blindness before he is made happy in the love of Aurora. Life has sadness and bitterness enough for a disappointed philanthropist like Romney Leigh, short of maiming or blindness; and the outflow of love and compassion towards physical ills is less rare in woman than complete sympathy with mental sorrows. Hence we think the lavish mutilation of heroes' bodies, which has become the habit of novelists, while it happily does not represent probabilities in the present state of things, weakens instead of strengthening tragic effect; and, as we said, we regret that Mrs. Browning has given this habit her strong sanction. Other criticisms might be passed on *Aurora Leigh,* considered as a representation of incident and dialogue, but we are little inclined to spend our small space in pointing out faults which will be very slightly felt by any one who has heart and mind enough to respond to all the beautiful feeling, the large thought, and the rich melodious song of this rare poem. "Quel grand homme est le seigneur Pococuronte! rien ne peut lui plaire!" is a kind of praise to which we do not in the least aspire. We would rather be suspected of obtuseness to many faults than fail in giving the due tribute of reverence and admiration to a single great merit.

The most striking characteristic of *Aurora Leigh,* distinguishing it from the larger proportion of that contemporary poetry which wins the applause of reviewers, is, that its melody, fancy, and imagination—what we may call its poetical *body*—is everywhere informed by a *soul,* namely, by genuine thought and feeling. There is no petty striving after special effects, no heaping up of images for their own sake, no trivial play of fancy run quite astray from the control of deeper sensibility; there is simply a full mind pouring itself out in song as its natural and easiest medium. This mind has its far-stretching thoughts, its abundant treasure of well-digested learning, its acute observation of life, its yearning sympathy with multiform human sorrow, its store of personal domestic love and joy; and these are given out in a delightful alternation of pathos, reflection, satire playful or pungent, and picturesque description, which carries us with swifter pulses than usual through four hundred pages, and makes us sorry to find ourselves at the end. . . .

Notes

[1] *Aurora Leigh.* By Elizabeth Barrett Browning. London: Chapman and Hall. 1856.

W. C. Roscoe (review date 1857)

SOURCE: "*Aurora Leigh,*" in *The National Review,* Vol. 4, No. VIII, April, 1857, pp. 239-67.

[*In the following excerpt, Roscoe claims that* Aurora Leigh *shows great poetic promise, but faults its excessive length, finding the work filled with unnecessary detail and its characters vague and indistinct.*]

If we rightly understand her, [Elizabeth Parrett Browning] tells us that *Aurora Leigh* is her attempt in a poem "unscrupulously epic" to "represent the age" in which she lives. She admits that to most men their own age, being too close, is as ill-discerned, as would be the lineaments of that colossal statue into which Xerxes proposed to carve Mount Athos to the peasants "gathering brushwood in his ear." But, she says,

> Poets should
> Exert a double vision; should have eyes
> To see near things as comprehensively
> As if after they took their point of sight,
> And distant things as intimately deep
> As if they touched them.

She tells us, that if there is any room for poets in the world, their sole work is to represent their own times. And she seems to think that in a single poem a poet can condense a sort of distillation of his age; and this she has attempted in *Aurora Leigh*. Such, at least, is what we gather from the poem itself.

Now there is no doubt that every great poet must more or less give expression to the times in which he lives. No man can be a great poet whose power and knowledge are not derived from an insight into the actual life which surrounds him; and it is impossible that the conditions under which he has lived, and the things which he has most familiarly known, should not leave their impress upon him, and through him, upon his work. As Wordsworth's poetry is haunted by the influences of the lakes and mountains; as the nature of the Scottish peasant underlies the genius of Burns; as a self-willed worldly spirit clings to the highest flights of Byron; as Milton cannot shake off the Puritan, and even Shakespeare has some flavour of the courtier,—so it is idle to suppose every poet and every man does not carry the impress of the less close but more universal influences of the social conditions which surround him. It does not follow, however, that he is the greatest poet who most fully and most immediately reproduces these influences in the gross; still less that it is the highest effort of the poet consciously to devote himself to this task. Man is greater and more interesting than the life he lives, and it is greater to paint him simply under the conditions of his own nature than under any restricted conditions of circumstances; it is profounder and more lasting to use the special surroundings in which men exist (and without using which they cannot be painted at all) to body forth the men themselves than to attempt to reproduce an abstract whole of men and their lives as they live at a given time,—a higher task to use the age to show a man than to use men to show an age. When it was said of the greatest poet that he was of no age, it was no idle compliment; it was not meant that he wrote of things abstract and disconnected from the realities of every age; but that he pierced to those deeper realities which underlie all the ages of men, which are what the root and springing sap of the tree are to the fleeting generations of its leaves. He used the special as a body for the universal. It is true, a poet may legitimately take a lower flight than this; he may choose to embody the leading ideas and characteristics of the period of time in which he lives; and this, no doubt, is a higher artistic effort than to attempt to embody those of any other particular age,—if for no other reason, because he is dealing with things more real, more familiar, and in all probability of a deeper interest. It does not follow, however, even if this be his direct object, that his events and his characters must be chosen from those which immediately surround him. He may select in the past, or invent for himself, the framework of his poem of modern ideas; or he may deal with the ideas of the past for the sake of some bearing they have, either by contrast or analogy, on the ideas of the present. Kingsley's *Saint's Tragedy,* and Tennyson's *Princess,* are cases in point. Mrs. Browning, however, holds,—and the idea is a common one at the present day,—that it is higher effort to represent modern ideas in their actual modern dress. Perhaps it is. Certainly it is a much more difficult one. Perhaps the poet ought to be able to see his own times at the same moment with the eyes of one removed from them and one near to them; but we know no poet who has ever done so. It is obvious enough to cite Homer; but even granting that "Wolff's an atheist," it is not easy to believe that "the tale of Troy divine" was written in the actual times it deals with. The Homeric poems give us our knowledge of the Homeric age; but whether they are a true description of the times of Achilles, or a story cast in those times, and an incidentally true delineation of the manners and thoughts of a later time in which they were written, is, to say the least of it, an open question. Even the satirist paints his times, not as they are, but in their relation to a special preconceived idea of his own. No doubt it is easy to clothe some of the simpler elements of the present life in the dress of the time; but the deeper and more searching the knowledge of a poet of the great and fundamental characteristics of the life which surrounds him, the more difficult and intricate a task does it become to reproduce these things in their actual context with the thousand crossing and entangled details through which he has pierced to and gathered up their real significance. His instinct,—and we think it is a true one,—is, to take what he has gained quite away from these complications; and crystallize it in some new form, in which it may shine in fuller clearness and simplicity.

However this may be, Mrs. Browning has undertaken to build a poem purely from modern materials. She has produced a work which, in completeness of form and artistic execution, falls far short of many of her previous efforts; but which in matter far surpasses the best of them. A wider experience, a profounder philosophy, a more real and human knowledge, attempt to find a voice in language more removed than that of any of her other poems from the adequacy of genuine simplicity, and are couched in a semi-dramatic form, which is one the author's genius least qualifies her to deal successfully with. As is natural, nay, inevitable, from the conformation of Mrs. Browning's mind, her poem deals primarily with ideas of her own; and all the narrative and dramatic elements in the book are but the constituent materials in the erection of an edifice of thought. We cannot help thinking, that where this is the case, care should be taken that these elements should preserve the same secondary place in the poem that they do in the matter. Mrs. Browning has unfortunately given a most undue prominence to the least valuable and most defective part of her work. Unpossessed, as we have before said, of that pliancy and mobility of mind which qualifies a poet to deal with details of external life, she selects a poem to which such details are indispensable, and even then overlays her matter with a mass of them totally unnecessary. Minuteness of incident receives the utmost redundancy of expression; and the real thread of her meaning runs through the whole like a golden wire strung thick with beads, and obscured from all but special research. Perhaps one reader in a thousand can master Mrs. Browning's poem at a single reading; though, indeed, some parts of it are so contrived as that it shall be impossible to understand them on a first perusal (as in that behaviour and those allusions of Romney, in his interview with Aurora, which result from his blindness, of which we are ignorant). The poem is worth reading once, twice, thrice, oftener, till you do understand the full force and significance of all it contains: but it is a long poem, a very long poem; and we fear Mrs. Browning would not be pleased with a statistical return of those who have received from it only confused impressions and a brief excitement of the imagination and feelings. It would have been a greater, a simpler, a truer, and a more valuable poem, if it had been compressed within one-fourth of its present limits. Nor is its author unwise only in her excess of detail and exuberance of secondary matter. It was necessary that she should deal with human beings; but it was not necessary that she should display them by dramatic forms, and so conduct her story as to lay bare the most prominent defect of her poetic genius in its most undisguised nakedness.

There are many persons in the poem who are made to express themselves in the first person; but characters, except in brief description, there are none,—nothing but vague hazy embodiments given to certain contrasted sets of ideas. They do not deceive us for an instant. We never think of them as individuals who have, or ever have had, life, as we do of Agamemnon, or Hamlet, or Cuddie Headrigg; we see them at once to be only some other person's notion of a person;—phantoms which may have had flesh-and-blood antecedents, but now walk only in books, and whose vaporous unsubstantial forms betray them to be but reveries of the poet, simulating speech and motion. Aurora Leigh, the poetess, tells her own story; and yet even with her you never feel that you know her personally, or have pierced beyond one or two of the marked and prominent characteristics of her nature. You are conscious that she is but the representative of the real poet behind; and that she comes forward only to give a voice to the inner convictions, the intellectual questionings and problems, and the heart's solutions of the artist who employs her. The poetess, the philanthropist, the woman of fashion, and the vagrant child, all express themselves in exactly the same language, use the same tropes, the same recondite imagery, and are on the same high level of intellectual cultivation and vigorous thought. The child of brutal parents, kept pure by the instincts of her own nature, but owing her only intellectual discipline to stray half-torn volumes, picked up from wandering pedlars, does not scruple to talk of "madrepores," and invariably employs more recondite forms of expression than would be used by one woman in a hundred of the educated classes of England.

The characters were meant to be distinct, nay, were no doubt conceived as distinct; but in passing through the author's mind, they have retained so much of her, and lost so much of what is distinctive, that they seem only like shadows of herself in various attitudes and different lights. In actually describing what she has seen, however, whether in nature or in human character, Mrs. Browning is often very successful. Lord Howe is well touched:

>   Let me draw Lord Howe;
> A born aristocrat, bred radical,
> And educated socialist, who still
> Goes floating, on traditions of his kind,
> Across the theoretic flood from France,—
> Though, like a drenched Noah on a rotten deck,
> Scarce safer for his place there. He, at least,
> Will never land on Ararat, he knows,
> To recommence the world on the old plan:
> Indeed, he thinks, said world had better end:
> He sympathises rather with the fish
> Outside, than with the drowned paired beasts within
> Who cannot couple again or multiply:
> And that's the sort of Noah he is, Lord Howe.
> He never could be any thing complete,
> Except a loyal, upright gentleman,
> A liberal landlord, graceful diner-out,
> And entertainer more than hospitable,
> Whom authors dine with and forget the port.
> Whatever he believes, and it is much,
> But no-wise certain . . now here and now there, . .
> He still has sympathies beyond his creed,
> Diverting him from action. In the House,
> No party counts upon him, and all praise
> All like his books too, (he has written books)
> Which, good to lie beside a bishop's chair,
> So oft outreach themselves with jets of fire
> At which the foremost of the progressists
> May warm audacious hands in passing by,
> —Of stature over-tall, lounging for ease;
> Light hair, that seems to carry a wind in it,
> And eyes that, when they look on you, will lean
> Their whole weight half in indolence, and half
> In wishing you unmitigated good,
> Until you know not if to flinch from him
> Or thank him—'Tis Lord Howe.

Marian, too, the daughter of the people, is admirably described,—rather, we should say, admirably conceived; and the fine and most truthful and delicate conception glimmers through the brief description. But, unfortunately, Mrs. Browning will not rely on description; and when Marian comes to speak for herself we are utterly thrown out, and a nondescript confused image of a somewhat affected young woman, of vast powers of poetical expression, usurps the place of that true idea we in vain attempt to hold steadily before us. Thus she paints the personal appearance of Marian:

>   No wise beautiful
> Was Marian Erle. She was not white nor brown,
> But could look either, like a mist that changed
> According to being shone on more or less.
> The hair, too, ran its opulence of curls
> In doubt 'twixt dark and bright, nor left you clear
> To name the colour. Too much hair perhaps
> (I'll name a fault here) for so small a head,
> Which seemed to droop on that side and on this,
> As a full-blown rose uneasy with its weight,
> Though not a breath should trouble it. Again,
> The dimple in the cheek had better gone
> With redder, fuller rounds: and somewhat large
> The mouth was, though the milky little teeth

> Dissolved it to so infantine a smile!
> For soon it smiled at me; the eyes smiled too,
> But 'twas as if remembering they had wept,
> And knowing they should, some day, weep again.

It seems strange, that one who can both observe and describe so accurately, should stand always at arm's length from other minds, and should be powerless to paint people as they appear to themselves, or to make them paint themselves as they appear to others. The only trace of dramatic power occurs now and then in some brief flash, which is, indeed, only the shining of a spark of accurate observation, and makes the surrounding dimness more noticeable; as when, in Marian's letter, she says:

> I'm poor at writing at the best,—and yet
> I tried to make my *g*s the way you showed.

Aurora Leigh is the daughter of an English gentleman and an Italian mother, born in Italy, early orphaned, and brought back to be educated in England by a maiden-aunt. Under all the repressions and exactions of a young lady's education more recondite than we have elsewhere heard of, she leads an inner life of her own, familiar with nature and the books of her dead father's collecting; and at the age of twenty years, walking in the dewy garden on the morning of her birthday, she crowns herself with an ivy-wreath—a poet by anticipation. Mrs. Browning describes the child let loose in the world of books in some lines replete with that wealth of thought, and that rich and vivid imagination, which, with all its shortcomings and sins against true keeping, make *Aurora Leigh* a great poem. But our space for quotation is limited, and we turn rather to those lovely verses in which she describes the young poetic girl rejoicing in the external beauty around her:

> I flattered all the beauteous country round,
> As poets use . . the skies, the clouds, the fields,
> The happy violets hiding from the roads
> The primroses run down to, carrying gold,—
> The tangled hedgerows, where the cows push out
> Impatient horns and tolerant churning mouths
> 'Twixt dripping ash-boughs,—hedgerows all alive
> With birds and gnats and large white butterflies
> Which look as if the May-flower had caught life
> And palpitated forth upon the wind,—
> Hills, vales, woods, netted in a silver mist,
> Farms, granges, doubled up among the hills,
> And cattle grazing in the watered vales,
> And cottage-chimneys smoking from the woods,
> And cottage-gardens smelling every where,
> Confused with smell of orchards. 'See,' I said,
> 'And see! is God not with us on the earth?
> And shall we put Him down by aught we do?
> Who says there's nothing for the poor and vile
> Save poverty and wickedness? behold!'
> And ankle-deep in English grass I leaped,
> And clapped my hands, and called all very fair.

Standing with her ivy-wreath on her head, and her arms raised to bind it on, she is startled by her cousin Romney Leigh. Romney is a philanthropist, as she is a poet. The physical distress and pain of the universe, the misery of his fellow-men, have weighed so deeply on his spirit, that, in the violence of a sort of despair, he has dedicated his whole life and being to the effort of lightening their toil, and satisfying at least the cravings of the illfed multitude for the supply of their bodily wants. He comes to ask her to be his wife. He has found a volume of her poems. He warns her against playing with art, which he assumes is all a woman can do, and bids her choose the nobler work, to seek some cure for the social strait; he asks her to help him with love and fellowship through bitter duties. She turns on him sharply enough with the retort, that she who, he says, is not competent to stand alone, or to sing even like a blackbird, can never be competent to uphold him and to love. "Any thing does for a wife," she tells him. And when he replies, that though her sex is weak in art, it is strong for life and duty, and still urges their common task, she retorts upon him, that he loves a cause and not a woman, and wants not a mistress but a helpmate,—to bear about with him a wife, a sister, like the apostle. Like a man, she says, he talks of woman as only the complement of his own sex; but

> That every creature, female as the male,
> Stands single in responsible act and thought,
> As also in birth and death.

That the work proposed must be not only *his* best, but *her* best work, the best she was ordained to, before she can love and work with him. That she too has her vocation; and though the world were twice as wretched, no less necessary work than his, nay, more so; for that his best success would be but failure, if man,—all his physical wants supplied, and the best socialistic union and plenty prevailing,—should not have the poet to keep open the pathways to and from the unseen world which surrounds them. Nay, she tells him he cannot attain his own poor limits of material ease without the poet's aid:

> It takes a sail
> To move a body; it takes a high-souled man
> To move the masses, even to a clearer stage;
> It takes the ideal to blow a hair's breadth off
> The dust of the actual. Ah, your Fouriers failed,
> Because not poets enough to understand
> That life develops from within.

For herself, she says, perhaps she is not worthy of work like this, perhaps a woman's soul aspires and not creates; yet she will try out these perhapses, and, at any rate, will love her art, and not wish it lower to suit her own stature. So they part; yet a shadow passes over her, as if it were hard to refuse even the mere potentiality of love. But when her somewhat grim and straightlaced aunt declares she loves Romney, in spite of her refusal, she indignantly repudiates the charge, and is naturally confirmed in her feelings by finding that Romney had motives of generosity for marrying her, and might possibly, therefore, not be prompted by love alone, or even, if so, might oppress her with too resistless an obligation. Aurora's aunt dies, and she and Romney go out on their several paths into the world. After years, and at the end of the book, they meet again in Italy. She is somewhat worn with her work, supporting herself with one hand, and labouring for her art with the other. She has tasted the emptiness of reputation, the disgusts of shallow applause and false criticism, the painful sense of her own shortcomings. She has bent the whole force of her energy and life to one great task, and accomplished it; but still her ideal lies unreached before her. She thinks the artist may be childless like the man; and when she gathers fame, though it be the love of all, her woman's heart is troubled with the absence of the love of one. Thus wearied, she goes to her native Italy to rest. Romney's failure has been more complete. A Lady Waldemar,—drawn in colours more coarse and repulsive than there seems occasion for, and whose character seems to be somewhat sacrificed to Mrs. Browning's taste for high-pressure writing,—falls in love with him. He, on the other hand, has resolved to marry the Marian of whom we have spoken, with the view of establishing a sort of matrimonial suspension-bridge over the gulf which separates English classes. Lady Waldemar spirits Marian away on the very wedding-day, and she is decoyed into some den of infamy in France, where she falls a victim to violence. All Romney's schemes for the reconstruction of the world fail. He turns Leigh Hall into a phalanstery, and brings all the country about his ears. The very wretches he had brought in "cursed him for his tyrannous constraint, in forcing crooked creatures to live straight;" and they and the scandalised peasantry unite together and burn the Hall down, Romney himself losing his eyesight by the malice of one whom he was saving. In France, Aurora has found Marian; and has taken her and her boy, the offspring of her misery, with her to Italy. Thither comes Romney too, who has learned her miserable history, to redeem his old obligations, and make her his wife. He finds Aurora; and has a long conversation with her, in which they confess and compare their several failures and shortcomings. Their colloquy is full of noble poetry; and wants but compression, and the greater closeness, strength, and simplicity, which compression gives, to make it entirely worthy of the great powers of the author. The blind Romney, whose aspiring reconstructive schemes God has defeated, and put himself aside like a broken tool, confesses the truth of the words Aurora had spoken on that June-day which parted their youth. He sees now that his ends were too low, that his despair of the world, and his harassing desire to reconstruct it, as if he alone could do it and were needful to success, betrayed a want of faith, and merited the lesson of humility he had received. He speaks with bitter scorn of his presumptuous endeavour.

> to stand and claim to have a life
> Beyond the bounds of the individual man,
> And raze all personal cloisters of the soul
> To build up public stores and magazines,
> As if God's creatures otherwise were lost,
> The builder surely saved by any means!
> To think,—I have a pattern on my nail,
> And I will carve the world new after it,
> And solve so, these hard social questions,—nay,
> Impossible social questions,—since their roots
> Strike deep in Evil's own existence here,
> Which God permits because the question's hard
> To abolish evil nor attaint free-will.
> Ay, hard to God, but not to Romney Leigh!
> For Romney has a pattern on his nail,
> (Whatever may be lacking on the Mount)
> And not being overnice to separate
> What's element from what's convention, hastes
> By line on line, to draw you out a world,
> Without your help indeed, unless you take
> His yoke upon you and will learn of him,—
> So much he has to teach; so good a world!
> The same the whole creation's groaning for!
> No rich nor poor, no gain nor loss nor stint,
> No potage in it able to exclude
> A brother's birthright, and no right of birth,
> The potage,—both secured to every man;
> And perfect virtue dealt out like the rest,
> Gratuitously, with the soup at six,
> To whoso does not seek it.

And it needs Aurora to remind him that

> If he strained too wide,
> It was not to take honour, but give help;
> The gesture was heroic. If his hand
> Accomplished nothing . . (well, it is not proved)
> That empty hand thrown impotently out
> Were sooner caught, I think, by One in heaven,
> Than many a hand that reaped a harvest in
> And keeps the scythe's glow on it.

She too confesses,

> We both were wrong that June-day,—both as wrong
> As an east wind had been. I who talked of art,

And you who grieved for all men's griefs . .
    what then?
We surely made too small a part for God
In these things. What we are, imports us more
Than what we eat; and life, you've granted me,
Develops from within. But innermost
Of the inmost, most interior of the interne,
God claims his own, Divine humanity
Renewing nature,—or the piercingest verse,
Prest in by subtlest poet, still must keep
As much upon the outside of a man,
As the very bowl in which he dips his beard.
—And then, . . the rest. I cannot surely speak.
Perhaps I doubt more than you doubted then,
If I, the poet's veritable charge,
Have borne upon my forehead. If I have,
It might feel somewhat liker to a crown,
The foolish green one even.—Ah, I think,
And chiefly when the sun shines, that I've
    failed.
But what then, Romney? Though we fail
    indeed,
You . . I . . a score of such weak workers, . .
    He
Fails never. If He cannot work by us,
He will work over us. Does He want a man,
Much less a woman, think you? Every time
The star winks there, so many souls are born,
Who all shall work too. Let our own be calm:
We should be ashamed to sit beneath those
    stars,
Impatient that we're nothing.

Aurora has supposed Romney married to Lady Waldemar; and as he amazedly vindicates himself from the charge, as involving an incredible degradation, and reminds her of the claim that Marian Erle has on him, she herself appears between them, and the poem deepens to the pathos of her renunciation of him; for her love for him (if it was not always worship rather than love) is lost in her passion for her child; and thence the strain rebounds and scales the highest heaven of joy as the secret of Aurora's heart is wrung from her by the sudden knowledge of Romney's blindness, and her passionate and capacious nature finds in his love its full contentment. The barriers of her pride fall away, and she learns the error of her life,—that she had striven to be an artist instead of a woman, rather than been content to be a simple woman, and let her art spring from that true basis; and the truth, which is the deepest moral of the work, overwhelms her with its sudden conviction, that great as is art, greater is the human life of the artist; and greatest, love, which is the centre of that life and of all life—

    Art symbolises heaven, but Love is God
    And makes heaven.

As the theme deepens, and the faulty artist forgets herself in the true poet, the verse runs smooth and clear; the startling, jarring metaphors are subdued to the element in which they move, and the verse is no unfit medium for the lofty matter. Our brief argument of the poem is not for the purpose of conveying any adequate idea of its varied contents; but only preserves the sequence of incident and follows the main clue of thought sufficiently to enable us to quote some of the later passages, which give the best idea of the best parts of the work:

    'Ah!—not married.'

        'You mistake,' he said;
'I'm married. Is not Marian Erle my wife?
As God sees things, I have a wife and child;
And I, as I'm a man who honours God,
Am here to claim them as my child and wife.'

I felt it hard to breathe, much less to speak.
Nor word of mine was needed. Some one else
Was there for answering. 'Romney,' she began,
'My great good angel, Romney.'
        Then at first,
I knew that Marian Erle was beautiful.
She stood there, still and pallid as a saint,
Dilated like a saint in ecstasy,
As if the floating moonshine interposed
Betwixt her foot and the earth, and raised her
    up
To float upon it. 'I had left my child,
Who sleeps,' she said, 'and, having drawn this
    way,
I heard you speaking, . . friend!—Confirm me
    now.
You take this Marian, such as wicked men
Have made her, for your honourable wife?'

The thrilling, solemn, proud, pathetic voice.
He stretched his arms out toward the thrilling
    voice,
As if to draw it on to his embrace.
—'I take her as God made her, and as men
Must fail to unmake her, for my honoured
    wife.'

She never raised her eyes, nor took a step,
But stood there in her place, and spoke again.
—'You take this Marian's child, which is her
    shame
In sight of men and women, for your child,
Of whom you will not ever feel ashamed?'

The thrilling, tender, proud, pathetic voice.
He stepped on toward it, still with outstretched
    arms,
As if to quench upon his breast that voice.
—'May God so father me, as I do him,
And so forsake me as I let him feel
He's orphaned haply. Here I take the child

> To share my cup, to slumber on my knee,
> To play his loudest gambol at my foot,
> To hold my finger in the public ways,
> Till none shall need inquire, 'Whose child is this,'
> The gesture saying so tenderly, 'My own.'

She appeals to Aurora; and she too gives her verdict:

> That Romney Leigh is honoured in his choice,
> Who choses Marian for his honoured wife.
>
> Her broad wild woodland eyes shot out a light;
> Her smile was wonderful for rapture. 'Thanks,
> My great Aurora.' Forward then she sprang,
> And dropping her impassioned spaniel head
> With all its brown abandonment of curls
> On Romney's feet, we heard the kisses drawn
> Through sobs upon the foot, upon the ground—
> 'O Romney! O my angel! O unchanged
> Though, since we've parted, I have past the grave!
> But Death itself could only better *thee,*
> Not change thee!—*Thee* I do not thank at all:
> I but thank God who made thee what thou art,
> So wholly godlike.'
>   When he tried in vain
> To raise her to his embrace, escaping thence
> As any leaping fawn from a huntsman's grasp,
> She bounded off and 'lighted beyond reach,
> Before him, with a staglike majesty
> Of soft, serene defiance,—as she knew
> He could not touch her, so was tolerant
> He had cared to try. She stood there with her great
> Drowned eyes, and dripping cheeks, and strange sweet smile
> That lived through all, as if one held a light
> Across a waste of waters,—shook her head
> To keep some thoughts down deeper in her soul,—
> Then, white and tranquil as a summer-cloud
> Which, having rained itself to a tardy peace,
> Stands still in heaven as if it ruled the day,
> Spoke out again.

She renounces him on the grounds we have indicated; and we move on to where, after learning Romney's never-failing love and the greatness of his calamity, the floodgates of Aurora's passion are broken down:

>   No matter: let the truth
> Stand high; Aurora must be humble: no,
> My love's not pity merely. Obviously
> I'm not a generous woman, never was,
> Or else, of old, I had not looked so near
> To weights and measures, grudging you the power
> To give, as first I scorned your power to judge
> For me, Aurora: I would have no gifts
> Forsooth, but God's—and I would use *them,* too,
> According to my pleasure and my choice,
> As he and I were equals,—you, below,
> Excluded from that level of interchange
> Admitting benefaction. You were wrong
> In much? you said so. I was wrong in most.
> Oh, most! You only thought to rescue men
> By half-means, half-way, seeing half their wants,
> While thinking nothing of your personal gain.
> But I who saw the human nature broad,
> At both sides, comprehending, too, the soul's,
> And all the high necessities of Art,
> Betrayed the thing I saw, and wronged my own life
> For which I pleaded. Passioned to exalt
> The artist's instinct in me at the cost
> Of putting down the woman's,—I forgot
> No perfect artist is developed here
> From any imperfect woman. Flower from root,
> And spiritual from natural, grade by grade
> In all our life. A handful of the earth
> To make God's image! the despised poor earth,
> The healthy odorous earth,—I missed, with it,
> The divine breath that blows the nostrils out
> To ineffable inflatus: ay, the breath
> Which love is. Art is much, but love is more.
> O Art, my Art, thou'rt much, but Love is more!
> Art symbolises heaven, but Love is God
> And makes heaven. I, Aurora, fell from mine:
> I would not be a woman like the rest,
> A simple woman who believes in love,
> And owns the right of love because she loves,
> And, hearing she's beloved, is satisfied
> With what contents God: I must analyse,
> Confront, and question; just as if a fly
> Refused to warm itself in any sun
> Till such was *in leone:* I must fret
> Forsooth, because the month was only May;
> Be faithless of the kind of proffered love,
> And captious, lest it miss my dignity,
> And scornful, that my lover sought a wife
> To use . . to use! O Romney, O my love,
> I am changed since then, changed wholly,—for indeed,
> If now you'd stoop so low to take my love,
> And use it roughly, without stint or spare,
> As men use common things with more behind,
> (And, in this, ever would be more behind)
> To any mean and ordinary end,—
> The joy would set me like a star, in heaven,
> So high up, I should shine because of height
> And not of virtue. Yet in one respect,
> Just one, beloved, I am in nowise changed:

> I love you, loved you . . loved you first and last,
> And love you on for ever. Now I know
> I loved you always, Romney. She who died
> Knew that, and said so; Lady Waldemar
> Knows that; . . and Marian: I had known the same
> Except that I was prouder than I knew,
> And not so honest. Ay, and, as I live
> I should have died so, crushing in my hand
> This rose of love, the wasp inside and all,—
> Ignoring ever to my soul and you
> Both rose and pain,—except for this great loss,
> This great despair,—to stand before your face
> And know I cannot win a look of yours.
> You think, perhaps, I am not changed from pride,
> And that I chiefly bear to say such words,
> Because you cannot shame me with your eyes?
> O calm, grand eyes, extinguished in a storm,
> Blown out like lights o'er melancholy seas,
> Though shrieked for by the shipwrecked,—O my Dark,
> My Cloud,—to go before me every day
> While I go ever toward the wilderness,—
> I would that you could see me bare to the soul!—
> If this be pity, 'tis so for myself,
> And not for Romney: *he* can stand alone;
> A man like *him* is never overcome:
> No woman like me, counts him pitiable
> While saints applaud him. He mistook the world:
> But I mistook my own heart,—and that slip
> Was fatal. Romney,—will you leave me here?
> So wrong, so proud, so weak, so unconsoled,
> So mere a woman!—and I love you so,—
> I love you, Romney.'
>   Could I see his face,
> I wept so? Did I drop against his breast,
> Or did his arms constrain me? Were my cheeks
> Hot, overflooded, with my tears, or his?
> And which of our two large explosive hearts
> So shook me? That, I know not. There were words
> That broke in utterance . . melted, in the fire;
> Embrace, that was convulsion, . . then a kiss . .
> As long and silent as the ecstatic night,—
> And deep, deep, shuddering breaths, which meant beyond
> Whatever could be told by word or kiss.

She learns how he had ever loved her, since he,

> A boy still, had been told the tale
> Of how a fairy-bride from Italy,
> With smells of oleanders in her hair,
> Was coming through the vines to touch his hand;

and how the very strength of his devotion, and the greatness of his worship, had made him feel, too, that she must be made part of his "dedication to the human need," and "prove he kept back nothing, not his soul." And again the tide of joy rolls up, and gives a fuller voice than any other poet has ever done to the intensity of love's rapture in a woman's heart:

> But oh, the night! oh, bitter-sweet! oh, sweet!
> O dark, O moon and stars, O ecstasy
> Of darkness! O great mystery of love,—
> In which absorbed, loss, anguish, treason's self
> Enlarges rapture,—as a pebble dropt
> In some full wine-cup, over-brims the wine!
> While we two sate together, leaned that night
> So close, my very garments crept and thrilled
> With strange electric life; and both my cheeks
> Grew red, then pale, with touches from my hair
> In which his breath was; while the golden moon
> Was hung before our faces as the badge
> Of some sublime inherited despair,
> Since ever to be seen by only one,—
> A voice said, low and rapid as a sigh,
> Yet breaking, I felt conscious, from a smile,—
> 'Thank God, who made me blind, to make me see!
> Shine on, Aurora, dearest light of souls,
> Which rul'st for evermore both day and night!
> I am happy.'
>   I flung closer to his breast,
> As sword that, after battle, flings to sheath;
> And, in that hurtle of united souls,
> The mystic motions which in common moods
> Are shut beyond our sense, broke in on us,
> And, as we sate, we felt the old earth spin,
> And all the starry turbulence of worlds
> Swing round us in their audient circles, till
> If that some golden moon were overhead
> Or if beneath our feet, we did not know.

He accepts the limits that have been assigned him through his calamity, and bids the artist assume her true functions, nor cease from her labour on the earth; and together they turn their faces to the East, to await God's great coming day of final restoration.

A noble poem, and every where throughout it the poet shows greater than her work. Indeed, given a poem of certain excellence, and the degree in which it shows defectiveness in the interpretive faculty (in which we have described Mrs. Browning as wanting) is but a measure of the higher order of personal qualities necessarily present in the poet; who by that very defectiveness is thrown back more than another on the resources of his own mind and nature. Mrs. Browning is conscientiously devoted to her art; it is no by-work to her, but the deliberately undertaken business of her life. There is no reason why she should not gain a much higher degree of artistic unity and simplicity than she now possesses. The fountains of her genius show an unfailing freshness and force; and high as *Aurora Leigh* stands, its author may live to look back on it as only a stepping-stone to the highest things of which she is capable.

C. C. Everett (review date 1857)

SOURCE: "Elizabeth Barrett Browning," in *North American Review,* Vol. LXXXV, No. 177, October, 1857, pp. 415-41.

[*In the excerpt that follows, Everett finds fault with several stylistic elements of* Aurora Leigh, *but finds that it succeeds primarily as a spiritual autobiography, tracing, as it does, the development and maturation of a woman and a poet.*]

[Elizabeth Barrett Browning's] poem, *Aurora Leigh,* contains some faults of a very different description; which appear to be caused, to a great degree, by carelessness. The style is at times diffuse; a fault, to which the freedom of blank verse can easily entice one of Mrs. Browning's ardent temperament. It is difficult to conjecture at what epoch of the story the book purports to have been written. It does not seem to have been written in the form of a journal, while the events were taking place; nor yet after the story was completed. It opens, indeed, as if this latter were the case. The heroine begins by saying,

> I . . .
> Will write my story for my better self;

and the reader supposes that she had it all in her mind at that moment. When she says, therefore, in regard to Romney Leigh,

> I attest
> The conscious skies and all their daily suns,
> I think I loved him not . . nor then, nor
>   since . .
> Nor ever,

the reader believes it.

In the third book we find her sitting, a maiden lady and an authoress, reading letters and commenting upon them, in a manner that puts us very much in mind of Ruth Hall; and the reader thinks that that is where the story must have left her; and though it looks very much as if she were in love with her cousin, yet he must be mistaken about it. Notwithstanding all this, she says in the last book:

> I love you, loved you . . loved you first and
>   last,
> And love you on for ever. Now I know
> I loved you always, Romney.

This contradiction confuses the reader, and he feels almost as if he were trifled with.

Besides this confusion in the point of view from which the heroine regards the story she is telling, we find the same figures repeated, in a manner scarcely to be accounted for, except on the ground of carelessness. It is related that, when the works of Jean Paul were revised, it was found that, notwithstanding the abundance, we might almost say the super-abundance, of figures with which they are crowded, scarcely one had been repeated. A similar examination of the *Aurora Leigh* would furnish a very different result; thus we read:

> Sweet heaven, she takes me up
> As if she had fingered me and *dog-eared* me
> And spelled me by the fireside, half a life!

This Aurora says of Lady Waldemar. We afterwards find Romney saying to Aurora:

> You thought to have shut a tedious book
> And farewell. Ah, you *dog-eared* such a page,
> And here you find me.

Other examples might be adduced of the same kind. So long as these are gathered from pleasing objects, or at least from objects that are not unpleasing, they simply mar the artistic beauty of the work; but when they are taken from objects which excite our repugnance, this repetition becomes almost offensive. Thus one of Mrs. Browning's favorite figures is taken from the "*chin band.*" This expression suggests, not the repose of death, but its powerlessness and its ghastliness, and, if used at all, should be employed only when the strongest effects are to be produced.

Another peculiarity of the *Aurora Leigh* is suggested by the example just cited. Mrs. Browning seems, as some one has said, to have adopted some realistic theory in regard to art. Thus she compares Romney, devoting his life to purposes of philanthropy, after his disappointment in love, to a man drowning a dog. Through the whole poem, truth of description is never yielded to taste, even though this truth may excite our loathing. Examples of this might be given, but it would be a thankless task to select from a work so full of beauty that which is fitted only to excite feelings of repulsion. . . .

Here [in *Aurora Leigh,* Barrett Browning's] whole past life, with its many griefs and disappointments, with its aspirations and its failures, and with its final crown of love and joy, is placed before us. In it we have the substance of the earlier and that of the later poems, each of which had been before incomplete without the other, made the elements of a new and more perfect work, their union mediated by deeper views of art and of life than she had before expressed. We do not mean that it is, in the common sense of the word, an autobiography, like the earlier and the later sonnets. That which before had gushed directly from her heart is now treated as something entirely outside of herself. Yet so far as the spiritual development is concerned, it may be called an autobiography. It appears to express the complete development of the life of a woman and of an artist. The child of English and Italian birth begins her life in Italy. The lonely father does the best he can for her, and cradles her among the mountains, that the gentle influences of nature may supply, as far as possible, the want of a mother's care. She says, he taught her what he had learned the best, "Grief and Love," and we see that he cared for her with more than a mother's tenderness, though without a mother's gladness. So the unconscious childhood passed, and the child awoke

> To full life and its needs and agonies.
> His last word was 'Love,'
>
> . . . . .
>
> And none was left to love in all the world.

Now comes the transition from the poetry of childhood to the prose of life, from Italy to England. Torn from every influence which had lent its aid to her earlier years, she was committed to the care of her father's sister, who lived

> A harmless life, she called a virtuous life,
> A quiet life, which was not life at all,
> (But that she had not lived enough to
>   know).

This well-meaning kinswoman made the utmost effort to engraft her own prosaic nature upon the child, and to fashion her according to her own notion of a woman; that is, she taught her to sit with her back to the window, that she might not see the trees, to read nice books upon womanhood, to brush "with extreme flounce the sciences," and if ever she caught her "soul agaze in her eyes," she knew how to bring it back to crochet, cross-stitch, or some other stupid task. Aurora seems to have been docile and compliant; yet she found a way to let the sunshine and the lime-tree in; she read the poets too when "the time was ripe," and while "the patient needle spilt the thread," she says she was not sad.

> My soul was singing at a work apart
> Behind the wall of sense.

So her girlhood was fashioned, and the crisis came, on that June morning when she stood

> Woman and artist,—either incomplete.

She laid the poet's crown from off her brow to receive from her cousin Romney that offering of love, which we find afterwards she did not take too coldly. There was a conflict for her then, a sacrifice to be made; she had the strength to choose the sterner part, and replaced the crown of ivy. So the two separated, and were left alone with their ideals. We follow their respective courses, and see how nobly they pursued them, how faithfully they always kept them pure above the dust, in all things striving for their fulfilment. We never have to tremble lest either will stoop too low; we trust them through all perplexities, sure that each carries a consecrated aim. But when all is done, when each has found the desired success, disappointment comes with it. The work has been accomplished, the ideal has been embodied; but the very success of their plans involves the most terrible failure of them. They do not gain satisfaction; they only have opened before them a larger vision.

With this self-depression comes the true mutual recognition, when each beholds the other's purpose pure and high, when each sees the imperfection of the aim which has been pursued; and though the June morning lost nothing of its nobleness, another morning rose to crown that day.

Let us now examine more closely the objects they sought, and the cause of their failure.

Romney was a mere reformer of the outward evils of society. He says of himself:

> My soul is gray
> With poring over the long sum of ill;
> So much for vice, so much for discontent,
> So much for the necessities of power,
> So much for the connivances of fear,—
> Coherent in statistical despairs,
> With such a total of distracted life, . .
> To see it down in figures on a page,
> Plain, silent, clear . . as God sees through the
>   earth
> The sense of all the graves! . . that's terrible
> For one who is not God, and cannot right
> The wrong he looks on.

That there was hope in the future did not satisfy him.

> Observe,—it had not much
> Consoled the race of mastodons to know
> Before they went to fossil, that anon
> Their place should quicken with the elephant;
> They were not elephants but mastodons.

He saw only the physical evils of life, and attempted to remedy them by physical means.

> I beheld the world
> As one great famishing carnivorous mouth,—
> A huge, deserted, callow, black, bird Thing,
> With piteous open beak, that hurt my heart,
> Till down upon the filthy ground I dropped,
> And tore the violets up to get the worms.
> Worms, worms, was all my cry: an open mouth,
> A gross want, bread to fill it to the lips,
> No more!

Romney established a phalanstery in his paternal hall on socialistic principles. Society tends more and more to become a mere machine; the reformers seek too often to complete the process. But the individual makes himself felt more strongly for the constraint. It is too often thought, that men have naturally only the principle of love within them; it is forgotten that the principle of hate is no less one of the original elements of the soul; or rather, that principle of opposition and negation which, when stimulated, grows to hate. Thus every atom contains the twofold element of attraction and repulsion; let the power of attraction have undue force for one moment, that of repulsion will make itself felt more powerfully in the next. Love and hate thus sleep together in the human breast; hate has the quicker senses of the two, and he who would make love must be careful not to move too harshly, or the sterner brother will start up before the gentler. Attraction or love is the principle which binds society together; the principle of repulsion is that by which the individual preserves his identity. Neither of these principles is to be sacrificed to the other. The surrender of our will must be a *voluntary* surrender; thus does the individual preserve his rights by the very act of yielding them. In the words of Tennyson, in the hymn with which the "In Memoriam" opens,

> Our wills are ours, we know not how;
> Our wills are ours, to make them thine.

This fact was overlooked by our reformer. He won the hate instead of the love of those he sought to save. With jeering shouts they burned his hall, and he himself was made blind among its ruins. Not only did he seek to distort the nature of others, but his own. Even his love he attempted to make merely a co-worker. He even endeavored to force it into still greater opposition to its true nature. He saw his error later, and exclaims:

> Distort our nature never, for our work,
> Nor count our right hands stronger for being hoofs.
> The man most man, with tenderest human hands,
> Works best for men,—as God in Nazareth.

. . . . .

> Fewer programmes; we who have no prescience.
> Fewer systems; we who are held and do not hold.
> Less mapping out of masses, to be saved,
> By nations or by sexes. Fourier's void,
> And Compte is dwarfed,—and Cabet, puerile.
> Subsists no law of life outside of life;
> No perfect manners, without Christian souls.
> The Christ himself had been no Lawgiver,
> Unless He had given the life, too, with the law.

He had felt that the world was to be renewed by his own labors alone, and, failing in his plans, he doubts of all things.

> I was wrong,
> I've sorely failed; I've slipped the ends of life,
> I yield; you have conquered.

This he says sadly to Aurora; but she answers:

> Stay, ...
> I've something for your hearing also. I
> Have failed too. . . .
> I've surely failed, I know; if failure means
> To look back sadly on work gladly done.

She sees more clearly than he the great fault in all their plans. She says:

> We both were wrong that June-day,—both as wrong
> As an east wind had been. I who talked of art,
> And you who grieved for all men's griefs . . . what then?
> We surely made too small a part for God
> In these things.

In alternating speech they paint the true life. It is Aurora who speaks first:

> 'The man, most man,
> Works best for men: and, if most man indeed,
> He gets his manhood plainest from his soul:
> While, obviously, this stringent soul itself
> Obeys our old rules of development;
> The Spirit ever witnessing in ours,
> And Love, the soul of soul, within the soul,
> Evolving it sublimely. First, God's love.'

> 'And next,' he smiled, 'the love of wedded souls,
> Which still presents that mystery's counterpart.
> Sweet shadow-rose, upon the water of life,
> Of such a mystic substance, Sharon gave
> A name to! human, vital, fructuous rose,
> Whose calyx holds the multitude of leaves.—
> Loves filial, loves fraternal, neighbor-loves,

And civic, . . all fair petals, all good scents,
All reddened, sweetened from one central
    Heart!'

We cannot follow further this closing scene, which glows with love and promise. They sit talking of the past and of the future, looking forward with a joyous faith, until the night has passed and the redness of the dawn gleams upon them. In the flaming jasper clouds is imaged the glory of which they speak. They stand together, hand in hand, their faces turned towards the brightness of the morning; she, the singer, the representative of the spiritual life, gazing with her clear vision into the heavens, yet no longer spurning the worker by her side; he blinded in his struggle with vice and suffering, and wearied with his labors upon the earth, yet his face catching something of the glory of the coming day: the two, in their loving union, imaging the time when the singer and the worker, the spiritual and the blind material, having accomplished their separate missions, shall be blended into one. Thus they stand, and see the new heaven descending amid the clouds.

> My Romney!—Lifting up my hand in his,
> As wheeled by Seeing spirits towards the east,
> He turned instinctively,—where, faint and
>   fair,
> Along the tingling desert of the sky,
> Beyond the circle of the conscious hills,
> Were laid in jasper-stone as clear as glass
> The first foundations of that new, near Day
> Which should be builded out of heaven, to
>   God.
> He stood a moment with erected brows,
> In silence, as a creature might, who gazed:
> Stood calm, and fed his blind, majestic eyes
> Upon the thought of perfect noon. And when
> I saw his soul saw,—'Jasper first,' I said,
> 'And second, sapphire; third, chalcedony;
> The rest in order, . . last, an amethyst.'

Besides the relation in which the *Aurora Leigh* stands to the great question of life in general, it has a particular application to the questions which have been started in regard to the nature and position of woman. It is often thought that a large mental culture tends to unfit her for the more tender and domestic relations of life. Here is illustrated the reverse of this. Aurora and Romney could not meet in the highest union of love until they had each attained to the highest development of which they were separately capable. When this was accomplished, they became united in a love as much more noble than that of common lovers, as their individual development was more perfect than that of ordinary individuals. This view is entitled to great consideration, as coming from one who has herself passed through both stages, that of the lonely struggle and of the reward.

Coventry Patmore, in a letter to poet William Allingham, February 18, 1857:

Aurora Leigh is a strange book for a modest sensible little woman like Mrs. Browning to have written. It is full of "fine things" of course; but I am inexpressibly sick of such under such conditions. . . .

Coventry Patmore, in Memoirs and Correspondence of Coventry Patmore, *by Basil Champneys,* Vol. II, *George Bell and Sons, 1900.*

Algernon Charles Swinburne (essay date 1898)

SOURCE: A Prefatory Note to *Aurora Leigh,* by Elizabeth Barrett Browning, William Heinemann, Ltd., 1898, pp. 3-8.

[*In the following essay, Swinburne recalls his first reading of* Aurora Leigh, *and claims that the book pays adequate tribute to the genius of its author.*]

The hardest task to which a man can set his judgment is the application of its critical faculty to the estimate of work neither classical nor contemporary. It is not now of the present, and as yet it is not of the past. We may be unable to forget the impression it made on our boyhood when fresh from the maker's hand, and we cannot be sure that something too much of unconscious reaction from the crudity of juvenile enthusiasm may not now interfere with the impartial temperance of a maturer estimate. But if there is any real element of eternal life, any touch of greatness in the work, no man whose opinion is worth the record will fail to recognise that there was more of truth, of justice, of sound sense and right instinct, in the enthusiasm which saw no spots on the sun than in the criticism which allowed them to obscure it. The magnificent work of Mrs. Browning is exceptionally certain to evoke such enthusiasm, to provoke such reaction, and to receive such ultimate, if far from unqualified, homage. No English contemporary poet by profession has left us work so full of living fire. Fire is the element in which her genius lives and breathes; it has less hold on earth than Tennyson's or Browning's or Miss Ingelow's, and less aerial impulse, less fantastic or spiritual aspiration, than Miss Rossetti's. But all these noble poets seem to play with life and passion like actors or like students if compared with her. The devout and undevout imaginations which caught hold on her passionate fancy and her sensitive conscience flew up at once into utterance, and became as Marlowe's—'all air and fire'; which by no means always 'made her verses clear' as those of that prince of poets. Nor was the fine madness of her inspiration always such as 'rightly should possess a poet's brain.' But in moral ardour and ethical energy it is unlike any other woman's; and the peculiar passion which it gave to her very finest work, the rush and glow and ardour of aspiring and palpitating life, cannot properly be compared with the dominant or distinctive quality of any other poet. Such poems as **Confessions** and **The Cry of the Children** could only have been written by a woman, and could have been written by one woman alone: the cruel injuries inflicted on them by revision and alteration of the original text can only serve to show how utterly the power and the glory of her genius depended on the first confident impulse of lyric emotion. It is no dispraise to her intelligence to say so—unless it be dispraise to say or imply that she was a great woman and a great poet.

The advent of **Aurora Leigh** can never be forgotten by any lover of poetry who was old enough at the time to read it. Of one thing they may all be sure—they were right in the impression that they never had read, and never would read, anything in any way comparable with that unique work of audaciously feminine and ambitiously impulsive genius. It is one of the longest poems in the world, and there is not a dead line in it. The noble passion and the noble pathos of its greater parts are alike indiscussible and irresistible. And even if we allow that it might not irrationally be defined as a lyrical poem in nine books of blank verse, we must admit that it contains some really admirable sketches and outlines of lifelike and acceptable figures. Lord Howe is excellent; but I must needs express my wonder that his painter should have given, or been permitted to give, the name of a hero to the image of a dilettante. The career of Aurora in London is rather too eccentric a vision to impose itself upon the most juvenile credulity: a young lady of family who lodges by herself in Grub Street, preserves her reputation, lives on her pen, and dines out in Mayfair, is hardly a figure for serious fiction.

Genius cannot do everything: the great Dumas, to whom Mrs. Browning paid so handsome and creditable a tribute in this very book, was hardly well advised when he set his name to a pathetic and tragic work of fiction—a 'scene of clerical life' in England—which appealed to the reader's sympathetic compassion for the sorrows of a humble vicar, expelled from his modest vicarage by the merciless tyranny of his proud and unscrupulous curate, whose lawless love had been rejected, despite its dazzling offers, by the vicar's virtuous daughter and her equally virtuous family; which is doubtless difficult to believe. Mrs. Browning's pictures of English life and society are, of course, less delicious than this: at times she hits off most accurately, with the admirable intuition or instinct of genius, certain notable types and certain undeniable characteristics of her countrymen; but her point of view, if compared with that of such a realist in fiction as here she would fain have shown herself, is not less obviously that of an outsider.

This is a secondary if a serious matter: the treatment of character and conduct, the handling of passion and principle, is a more important subject for critical consideration. Aurora is, of course, in all essentials a conscious and intentional portrait of the author by herself—a study from the life after her own spiritual and intellectual likeness, set in the frame of an utterly and obviously imaginary experience: and, as such, this figure has an absolutely unique interest. No equally great genius, no equally noble nature, ever set itself, as far as I know, with the same strenuous and conscientious ardour, to the discharge of a task so nearly comparable to that which was naturally undertaken by such egoists, if not egomaniacs, as Rousseau, St. Augustine, and George Sand. In her there is nothing of autolatry, veiled or barefaced, conscious or unconscious; the absolute purity of her selfless and dauntless and infinite sincerity, her passionate and single-hearted and headstrong devotion to whatever great cause might attract or whatever great illusion might allure her sympathy, is too childlike and heroic for any comparison to be possible with these. To this great and glorious Englishwoman, who was never more obviously and more regrettably English and womanish than when decrying or denouncing her country, the modest and wholesome scepticism which keeps fast and firm hold on principle and honour, but feels itself bound to test and examine the articles of the faith which may reassure and the details of the evidence which may convince it, was as impossible as the submissive and implicit infidelity which makes cardinals of men who do not even believe in the existence or understand the nature of belief in anything whatsoever.

The heroic and feminine enthusiasm which can never for an instant see more than one thing at a time, or see more than one side of a question at any time, succeeds in making the figure of Aurora as naturally as it fails in making the figure of Romney real and vital, conceivable and credible. The close of the poem is so magnificent in the passion and exaltation of its grave and profound rapture that no reader not unworthy to read anything so noble and so great will ever be able to remember at the moment whether the man is or is not as living a figure as the woman whom we see made one with him for ever in the light of imagination and of love. But no reader not given over to sentimental or hysterical hallucination will afterwards fail to realise and recollect the too evident fact that many a woman whom no one would name in the same day with Mrs. Browning has succeeded as thoroughly as she has failed in painting at full length—under the modern conditions and restrictions of literary fidelity—a recognisable and acceptable portrait of a man. Marian, if not more credible, is much more conceivable than Romney. A noble lady of exceptional character and genius who attempts to imagine the emotions of a poor good girl under almost unimaginable afflictions will at least succeed in representing something of a real woman's emotions, even though the form they take in her imagination, the excess and the expression of them, may be obviously and obtrusively impossible; for we can hardly believe that an Isabella could have been begotten by Barnardine on Mrs. Overdone. But when such allowance as is only due to genius has duly been made for improbabilities and incredibilities of detail, there is but one view possible to any eye but that of a Fitzdottrel. The piercing and terrible pathos of the story is as incomparable and as irresistible as the divine expression of womanly and motherly rapture which seems to suffuse and imbue the very page, the very print, with the radiance and the fragrance of babyhood. There never was, and there never will be, such another baby in type as that. Other poets, even of the inferior sex, have paid immortal tribute to the immortal Godhead incarnate in the mortal and transitory presence of infancy; the homage of one or two among them, a Homer or a Hugo, may have been worthy to be mistaken for a mother's; but here is a mother's indeed; and 'the yearlong creature' so divinely described, must live in sight of all her readers as long as human nature or as English poetry survives. No words can ever be adequate to give thanks for such a gift as this.

Martha Hale Shackford (essay date 1935)

SOURCE: "E. B. Browning: *Aurora Leigh*," in *E. B. Browning; R. H. Horne: Two Studies*, The Wellesley Press, Inc., 1935, pp. 5-27.

[*In the following essay, Shackford discusses* Aurora Leigh *in the context of Browning's other works and her literary interests, as well as in relation to other narrative poems.*]

The manuscript of *Aurora Leigh* is a green-bound octavo notebook of about four hundred pages, written in a small, cramped, delicate hand. A reader needs a magnifying glass in order to decipher the text, where corrections, emendations, and amplifications, written at various angles, give many pages some resemblance to a literary spider's web. In this first draft the heroine's name was Aurora Vane; minor differences between the manuscript and the printed versions offer an interesting study of Mrs. Browning's critical judgment. *Aurora Leigh* was first published early in January, 1857, by Chapman and Hall; a fortnight later, a second edition was issued; between 1857 and 1884 eighteen printings were made necessary by the demand for the book. Probably the most enthusiastic reader (except Robert Browning) was John Ruskin who in a long letter to the author said, in part:

> I think *Aurora Leigh* the greatest poem in the English language, unsurpassed by anything but Shakespeare—not surpassed by Shakespeare's Sonnets—and therefore the greatest poem in the language. I write this, you see, very deliberately.

At the other extreme is the opinion of a distinguished modern critic who wrote of *Aurora Leigh*: "the work will probably survive the exaggerated contempt which its undeniable faults have called down upon it in our day."

Although Mrs. Browning herself had high hopes for the lasting success of *Aurora Leigh,* she was not guilty of self-laudation, being a cool and sane critic of pretentiousness on the part of authors, and she touched merrily the weakness of those who had delusions of greatness. A note written August 12, 1846 to Robert Browning is illustrative:

> Here is a letter from a lady in a remote district... who sends me lyrical specimens, and desires to know if *this be Genius*. She does not desire to publish; at any rate for an indefinite number of years; but for her own private and personal satisfaction, she would be glad to be informed whether she is a Sappho or George Sand or anything of that kind.

Furthermore, Mrs. Browning was aware that her own widely extended reputation was based partly upon the fact of her femininity rather than upon her artistic merit. The hero of *Aurora Leigh* said to the heroine:

> You never can be satisfied with praise
> Which men give women when they judge a book
> Not as mere work but as mere woman's work,
> Expressing the comparative respect
> Which means the absolute scorn: "Oh, excellent!
> What grace, what facile turns, what fluent sweeps,
> What delicate discernment . . . . . almost thought!
> The book does honor to the sex, we hold,
> Among our female authors we make room
> For this fair writer, and congratulate
> The country that produces in these times
> Such women, competent to. . . . spell."

Regarding the future rank of *Aurora Leigh* it is safest not to offer prophecy; yet the work may be judged, today, in comparison with other narrative poems of the nineteenth century and, with some justice, may be given a comparative position. It stands below *The Prelude, Hyperion, Childe Harold, The Ring and the Book,* but certainly far above certain works that had a vogue in their time. What is the reputation, to-day, of Southey's long epics which so fascinated and influenced young Shelley, *Thalaba* particularly? What is the fate of *Lallah*

Rookh for which Moore was paid £3000 upon its publication? Who now reads *Gertrude of Wyoming? The Princess* to-day seems sentimental and mawkish, not even required reading for our defenceless high-school students, though it must be remembered that Tennyson by this gilded poem helped somewhat to reconcile the Age to academic women. Surely **Aurora Leigh,** despite any and all faults, holds a secure place among nineteenth-century poems, for its theme has perennial appeal, its scope is wide, its drama realistic, its tone liberal, its manner distinguished, and its wisdom that of a sound and acute thinker. **Aurora Leigh** does not propound the views of a cult; it is not bent on mere description or on local color; it has no such record of intimate personal experiences as appears in Patmore's *The Angel in the House,* nor is it the expression of emotional bias as is *The City of Dreadful Night.* Moreover, it is free from many of the blemishes which disfigure Mrs. Browning's earlier poems, **The Romance of the Swan's Nest, The Lay of the Brown Rosary, Lady Geraldine's Courtship,** and that over-ambitious experiment in the circle of the supernatural, **The Seraphim,** in all of which poems appear themes tenuous, sentimental, egotistical, developed by a technique often faulty, with too much "scope" for rimes that "droop." These poems are notably amateurish in execution, weakened by a hovering, uncertain stroke, and an equally tremulous sentiment that falls short of genuine lyric emotion. Moreover, the learned lady is dominant. One critic, favorably inclined toward Mrs. Browning's verse, spoke harshly of her "abstruse wanderings of thought" and "terrible phalanxes of Greek and German expressions."

On the other hand, in looking over the works of the many women poets of the century, especially such popular authors as L. E. L., Mrs. Norton, Mary Howitt, Mrs. Barbauld, Mrs. Hemans, Jean Ingelow, we must be aware that Mrs. Browning grapples with ideas more frequently than do these other women poets. She gradually grew away from plaintive ballads and naive reveries. In such poems as **Crowned and Buried, Cowper's Grave, The Dead Pan, A Drama of Exile, The Cry of the Children,** the sonnets, **Work,** and **Cheerfulness taught by Reason,** she welded thought and feeling in imaginative phrases. **Sonnets from the Portuguese** is a series of lyrics, incontestably one of the great works of the nineteenth century, and also one of the most spiritual epithalamia ever written. Even if in individual sonnets there appear inferior lines, feeble or fanciful, the sequence as a whole is a melodious, intense, stately expression of "essential passions of the heart." The imaginative elements are impressively individual, not imitative; the figures of speech have a freshness, an appropriateness, a force due to the fact that they are shaped out of the heart of experience. **Casa Guidi Windows** may be not a poem but a document on the problems that underlie political unity, yet as a document it will be read along with other famous passages on civil liberty.

Not only because of her ardor and sensibility, her love of nature, her profound interest in questions, social or individual, ethical or more distinctly religious and mystical, did Mrs. Browning win a place in the annals of nineteenth century poetry; she was much more than a cultured, sympathetic woman, she was a student and an independent thinker. She read the Greek text of the tragedies of Æschylus, Sophocles, Euripides, all of the dialogues of Plato, besides many other works of Hellas. Already, in the juvenile poems published by her proud father, **The Battle of Marathon** and **An Essay on Mind,** she showed both wide reading and speculative intelligence, though these poems are absurdly priggish and pedantic, bristling with countless learned allusions. **An Essay on Mind,** in well-pointed Popian couplets, so neatly epitomizes the history of philosophy and literature that it would be profitable reading for candidates for the doctor's degree. She was not a trained systematic thinker, she had too much of the acquisitive, too much of the quickly intuitive in her mental habit. Maturer works, in prose, that show learning more discreetly are: **Some Account of the Greek Christian Poets,** which appeared first as papers in *The Athenaeum,* 1842, as did also **The Book of the Poets,** a critique sparkling with piquant, penetrating comments on English poets from Chaucer to Wordsworth. **Prometheus Bound,** published anonymously in 1833, revised and republished in 1850, gives a comprehensive illustration of Mrs. Browning's powers. It is one of the most vivid and most idiomatic translations from Æschylus, and even if specialists may demur about an interpretation here or there, Mrs. Browning's translation is a remarkable piece of work, showing finely imaginative sympathy with the dramatist's spirit of rebellion against tyranny. Especially successful is her rendering of those complexly woven double-epithets which give the pages of Æschylus such fire, glamour, subtlety of thought, and such deep, overflowing melody.

All these aspects of her reading and study are seen reflected in **Aurora Leigh,** and other influences, too, appear as a result of her unexpected freedom of adventure in her father's library. The story has frequently been told of her father's command that she should not read the books "on this side," but apparent permission was granted for all others; so the young poetess read with ardor Tom Paine's *The Age of Reason,* Voltaire's *Philosophical Dictionary,* Hume's *Essays, Werther,* Rousseau, and Mary Wollstonecraft. Throughout her life Mrs. Browning read widely in various fields, as will be shown later. In March, 1853, for example, she wrote to Mrs. Jameson: "We have been meditating Socialism and mysticism of various kinds, deep in Louis Blanc and Prudhon, deeper in the German spiritualists, added to which I have by no means given up my French novels." . . . More, however, than anything else **Aurora Leigh** was inspired by and influenced by Mrs. Browning's devotion to prose fiction.

Fiction she read assiduously. Her letters to Robert Browning and to Miss Mitford are full of mention of her invalid's solace and her artist's pleasure in the novels of Scott, Thackeray, Dickens, Kingsley, Disraeli, Ainsworth, Bulwer-Lytton, the Brontës, Mrs. Gaskell, Mrs. Stowe, Jane Porter, Mrs. Radcliffe, Jane Austen, Mrs. Shelley and many other English or American writers. More directly influential upon *Aurora Leigh* were novels by the French writers: Dumas, Balzac, Madame de Staël, George Sand, and dramas by Dumas *fils,* Scribe and others. We should picture Mrs. Browning in *Casa Guidi* reading in the long warm afternoons, or in the winter evenings beside the fire, novels and yet more novels. Robert's catholicity of taste did not equal hers, for his critical faculty was much more active, and, too, he evidently did not need the physical or mental relaxation gained from fiction.

Aurora Leigh is the inevitable result of this reading of many novels. Writing to her cousin, John Kenyon, in October, 1844, Miss Barrett had said:

> I have a great fancy for writing some day a longer poem, [than *Lady Geraldine's Courtship*].... a poem comprehending the aspect and manners of modern life, and flinching at nothing of the conventional.... Now I do think that a true poetical novel—modern and on the level of the manners of the day—might be as good a poem as any other, and much more popular besides. Do you not think so?

A glance at the story element of *Aurora Leigh* will show how, in nine books, not quite eleven thousand lines in all, the author developed a plot. Aurora Leigh, daughter of an English father and an Italian mother, was transferred from Italy to England when as a child she was left an orphan. Under the strict care of her father's spinster sister, she lived in rural England, loving nature and books, but fiercely opposed to becoming a proper Victorian young lady. Having refused to marry her cousin Romney, heir to the Leigh estate, because she found him too laggard a lover, too absorbed in philanthropic projects, she went to London, and there in an incredibly short time achieved success in literature. One day she was visited by Lady Waldemar and told that Romney was about to marry, out of humanitarian motives, a daughter of the people, Marian Earle, a *mésalliance* for various reasons, but opposed by Lady Waldemar because she was seeking to marry him herself. Rapidly events marched. Aurora made very friendly overtures to Marian, the wedding day arrived, but no bride came to church to wed magnanimous Romney. During the following months Aurora sought tirelessly for Marian and at last discovered the fugitive in Paris supporting herself and her, nameless, son. The story of Marian's flight because of Lady Waldemar's jealous and unscrupulous interference; the account of her being drugged and betrayed, victim of greed and lust; the recital of her efforts to find work for herself before and after the child's birth; the brief suggestion of her sufferings at the hands of employers who penalized her for her misfortune, occupy many spirited and sympathetic pages. Aurora carried Marian and the child to Florence where all three were happily established in a villa on the hillside. Meanwhile Romney solaced himself by supervising the work of conducting Leigh Hall, his ancestral home, as a retreat for poverty-stricken and otherwise wretched men and women of the lower classes, initiating thus an experiment after the ideas of certain French socialists. It is evident, though not a very effectively managed element of the story, that Aurora had always loved Romney, therefore, when he appeared in her garden in Florence on a beautiful summer evening, readers are not surprised to discover that after two books of ardent argument between Romney and Aurora, regarding social problems and their own personal problems, the two confessed their love, but not before Romney had in knightly fashion offered to wed Marian Earle. She, intuitively aware of Aurora's feeling for Romney, sacrificed her own happiness. The conclusion came when Romney, just before his departure, revealed the fact that he had lost his sight as a consequence of the fire which destroyed Leigh Hall, and Aurora with a passionate access of tenderness dedicated herself to him. The poem ends in a symbolic dawn in which the true Aurora is seen at last.

The story is a readable and fairly well-sustained narrative, though delayed by frequent digressions on artistic or social topics. Told in the form of an autobiography, with some elements that are obviously drawn from Mrs. Browning's own life, this would-be novel has not sufficient projection and artistic escape from the author's controlling hand; she did not show adequate skill in developing either situation or characters. Moreover, the plot has a tendency toward melodrama in its exaggeration of both good and evil and in the suddenness of certain events. Thus, the death of Aurora's aunt, the quick success of Aurora the author, the extreme perfidy of Lady Waldemar, the unnecessary blinding of Romney undermine the naturalness of the tale.

However, if digressions and over-stimulation take turns in bewildering the seeker for a story, they are balanced for the more tolerant reader by elements that do not appear in some excellent narratives. A turn for epigram, sometimes philosophical truth, sometimes a satiric thrust, gives *Aurora Leigh* a challenging tone. There is an almost constant liveliness, a play of humor in the poem giving it a lightness of touch which redeems the work from being a novel with a purpose. Mrs. Browning had read to good purpose Dryden, Pope, Byron, the best of Chaucer in *The Canterbury Tales,* and, early in her life, *Piers Plowman,* because of her residence in the Malvern Hills. Her instinctive humor, developed and trained by her reading, served as an effective aid in *Aurora Leigh*. Mrs. Browning's humor has been too much ignored in the solemn efforts to appreciate her sensibility and her spirituelle exaltation. She has been sentimentalized as a spectacle, on her invalid's couch; her dog, her husband, her son, have been made melodramatic properties, and she has been robbed of her real personality and vigor. Few letters of the nineteenth century are comparable with hers in lambent flashing appreciation of little incongruities, such shrewd and piercing thrusts at weakness, or hypocrisy, or mistaken opinion. Her letters to Robert Browning are delightfully full of little flippancies and tart, well-directed shafts at books or persons deserving a bit of ridicule. And many of the more personal passages have playful, teasing elements, passages which show how a poetess in love may be whimsical, tender, irreverent, and bewildering to her more ceremonious and intensely serious lover.

Almost every page of *Aurora Leigh* gleams with some humorously turned comment, some piquant phrase, some pointed satire, charmingly urbane. The smugness of the Victorian, or, as she dubbed it, "the Pewter Age," is exposed, and illusions of various sorts are mercilessly pilloried in a neat style. Detached samples of her humor will serve no purpose, for it is always the context which sets off the flash, but one or two specimens will serve, such as the gibe at Romney's preöccupation with the lower classes:

> Had I any chance
> With Mister Leigh, who am Lady Waldemar
> And never committed felony?

or, more objectively:

> The world's male chivalry has perished out,
> But women are knights-errant to the last;
> And if Cervantes had been Shakespeare too,
> He had made his Don a Donna.

or a brief generalization:

> Humility's so good
> When pride's impossible.

or an ironic thrust at vague idealists:

> Recipes for . . . . . .
> . . . . . . acting heroism without a scratch. . . . .

or, even more pictorially:

> He sets his virtues on so raised a shelf,
> To keep them at the grand millennial height,
> He has to mount a stool to get at them.

Contrasted with her playful humor, the overflow of her own happy, full, and thoughtful days in Florence, is the high stern note of an idealism, artistic, social, religious. A certain sympathy with the mood of Victorian Evangelicalism turned her into a presumptive teacher and preacher. In a letter to Ruskin about Miss Mitford, Mrs. Browning wrote, November, 1855:

> She never taught *me* anything but a very limited admiration of Miss Austen, whose people struck me as wanting souls, even more than is necessary for men and women of the world. The novels are perfect as far as they go—that's certain. Only they don't go far enough, I think. It may be my fault.

There is perhaps too much soul in *Aurora Leigh,* too much accent on abstract issues when more concrete details are needed for the reader's imagination to work upon, if he is to get pleasure in a work of fiction.

There is abundant concreteness of detail in the setting of the poem, for Mrs. Browning's acquaintance with England, Italy, and France were such as to make it possible for her to place her story in scenes faithfully described,—rural England and London, Paris, Northern Italy, and Florence. The following passage, describing the approach to Genoa, by sea, shows the nature artist's power in word and phrase and image, catching the very look of the Italian shore, in a description, charming and memorable:

> Peak pushing peak
> They stood. I watched, beyond that Tyrian belt
> Of intense sea betwixt them and the ship,
> Down all their sides the misty olive-woods
> Dissolving in the weak, congenial moon,
> And still disclosing some brown convent-tower
> That seems as if it grew from some brown rock,
> Or many a little lighted village, dropt
> Like a fallen star upon so high a point,
> You wonder what can keep it in its place
> From sliding headlong with the waterfalls
> Which powder all the myrtle and orange groves
> With spray of silver. Thus my Italy
> Was stealing on us. Genoa broke with day,
> The Doria's long pale palace striking out,
> From green hills in advance of the white town,
> A marble finger dominant to ships,
> Seen glimmering through the uncertain grey of dawn.

The better known description of the Florentine villa, in part Villa Briochion on Bellosguardo, where Isa Blagden, the Brownings' friend, lived, need not be quoted in full, though a few lines demand acknowledgment— such as the vignette of Florence, seen from Bellosguardo:

> I found a house at Florence on the hill
> Of Bellosguardo. 'Tis a tower which keeps
> A post of double-observation o'er
> That valley of Arno (holding as a hand
> The outspread city) straight towards Fiesole.
> And Mount Morello and the setting sun,
> The Vallombrosan mountains opposite,
>
> . . . . .
>
> From the outer wall
> Of the garden drops the mystic floating grey
> Of olive trees (with interruptions green
> From maize and vine), until 'tis caught and torn
> Upon the abrupt black line of cypresses
> Which signs the way to Florence. Beautiful
> The city lies along the ample vale,
> Cathedral, tower and palace, piazza and street,
> The river trailing like a silver cord
> Through all, and curling loosely, both before
> And after, over the whole stretch of land
> Sown whitely up and down its opposite slopes
> With farms and villas.

The setting is made very real, both in *locale* and in general conditions of social background, adding to the realism of the *dramatis personae*. The author pictured Victorian life in the drawing-room, in the studio, in the slums of London, and in the beautiful Florentine villa; we see class distinctions and prejudices sharply contrasted, we hear the soft drawl of the sophisticated gentleman as well as the harsh voice of poverty and squalor. Moreover, she presented both sides of the Victorian era, emphasizing its humanitarianism, its simplicity, its essential efforts after justice and happiness for all, its untiring zeal for finding truth in science and religion; but she also exposed the irresponsibility of many well-fed, over-dressed persons, inclined to fatuous trust in a Providence that had, for all time, created a distinction between rich and poor, a Providence that relieves the pious from any need of struggle to defeat chaos and chance in economic life.

Mrs. Browning was essentially a Romantic, and also, hers was one of the clearest voices crying out in the second half of the nineteenth century for liberty, equality, and fraternity, continuing and echoing strains she had heard in the works of the great Revolutionary poets. But her special plea was for the liberty of women, a plea particularized in the histories of Aurora Leigh and Marian Earle who from different classes of society, one the leader, the other, led, illustrate many (but not all!) of Mrs. Browning's doctrines in regard to women's rights, women's duties, women's sufferings, and women's potential capabilities. This passionate desire for the liberation of womankind and the equally passionate sympathy with victims of injustice and tyranny must have been defined very early in Mrs. Browning's life, or she would not have chosen, from all the Greek tragedies, ***Prometheus Bound,*** for translation. Here in the work of Æschylus, she found portrayed two chief figures who illustrate the bitterness and almost helpless pain of bondage and persecution,—Prometheus and Io. Io is one of the most interesting characters in Greek myth, the prototype of helpless womanhood victimized by masculine power. Is there not a direct relationship between Marian Earle's fate and wanderings and Io's? The innocence, the helplessness, the prolonged and bitter suffering of Marian Earle, treacherously betrayed through the greed of Lady Waldemar's maid-servant to "carniverous" man, are depicted by a courageous, sympathetic woman, a champion of the defenceless. Moreover, Mrs. Browning lived in an era when gifted women were winning high regard. Not only Mary Wollstonecraft, Madame de Staël, and George Sand, pioneers, but lesser persons well-known and admired by her: Miss Mitford, with whom Mrs. Browning had been long associated in an intimate friendship; Mrs. Jameson, the "Mona Nina" addressed in many letters; Harriet Martineau, Margaret Fuller, Harriet Beecher Stowe, Harriet Hosmer, sculptress; Fanny Kemble, the actress, Mrs. Siddon's niece; Frances Power Cobbe, social reformer, and, slightly, Florence Nightingale.

With high-hearted enthusiasm and genuine knowledge of her subject Mrs. Browning portrayed Aurora Leigh, succeeding in that portrait much better than in those of the other *dramatis personae* of the poem. The girl, Aurora, ardent, generous, intellectual, and painfully lonely, rebelled against her conventional aunt's efforts to instil into the young mind the ideals proper for a Victorian woman, namely, a weak and timid view of life, a deference to rank and money, a distinctly "fugitive and cloistered virtue," and an acquiescent will. Bent on self-expression, eager for life and for the world of ideal values, she found expression and satisfaction in Art, spurning marriage as proposed by Romney and interpreted by her Aunt. She pictured wifehood in lurid colors, but, fortunately for her, only in soliloquy!

> Love, to him, was made
> A simple law-clause. If I married him.
> I should not dare to call my soul my own
> Which so he had bought and paid for: every thought
> And every heart-beat down there in the bill;
> Not one found honestly deductible
> From any use that pleased him! He might cut
> My body into coins to give away
> Among his other paupers; change my sons,
> While I stood dumb as Griseld, for black babes
> Or piteous foundlings; might unquestioned set
> My right hand teaching in the Ragged Schools,
> My left hand washing in the Public Baths,
> What time my angel of the Ideal stretched
> Both his to me in vain.

Certain dangers, certain tendencies in the feminine attitude towards life are suggested in one early debate between Aurora and Romney, when Romney's spontaneous scepticism about her "art" is an irritant to the ambitious and self-confident Aurora. With a frankness almost suicidal in a writer, Mrs. Browning expounds the fact that women, as artists, and as individuals, take things too personally, lack the generous objectivity of the large, free, tolerant and genuinely artistic imagination:

> The human race
> To you means, such a child, or such a man,
> You saw one morning waiting in the cold,
> Beside that gate, perhaps. You gather up
> A few such cases, and when strong sometimes
> Will write of factories and of slaves, as if
> Your father were a negro, and your son
> A spinner in the mills. All's yours and you,
> All, colored with your blood, or otherwise
> Just nothing to you. Why, I call you hard
> To general suffering.

It is obvious that Aurora's compassion for Marian Earle is in part prompted by the unrealized, unconfessed love of Aurora for Romney, though unselfish, untiring energy are shown in Aurora's search for the lost Marian, and in Aurora's beautiful and successful efforts to atone to Marian for evils wrought by the lustful cruelty of man, by the indifference of society to such outrages, and by persecution on the part of self-righteous virtue. Little by little Aurora approaches a state where she begins to reject worldly, egotistical success, and dreams of life made perfect by love.

The portrait of Romney is not as vivid as is that of Aurora; it is too earnest a tract. We see him unquestionably kind, wholly virtuous, intelligent, and almost mechanically self-sacrificing. But like the characters in the dramas of Joanna Baillie (regarded by Mrs. Browning "as the first female poet in all senses in England"), Romney is characterized too entirely by one "passion,"—philanthropy. He is a sort of humanitarian chimera, bloodless, it would seem, and one wonders why Lady Waldemar sought his love:

> Have you heard of Romney Leigh,
> Beyond what's said of him in newspapers,
> His phalansteries there, his speeches here,
> His pamphlets, pleas, and statements,
>   everywhere?

Beginning badly in his too abstract wooing of Aurora, he went on to worse by planning a marriage with Marian Earle, based on a desire to solve a social problem rather than on a legitimate desire for love and congenial companionship. But he had courage, stubborn tenacity of purpose, for in this project of marriage he defied a society with deep-rooted, archaic ideas regarding the inviolability of class. When, after her tragedy, he again asked Marian to marry him he was sincerely performing an atonement to one of the many victims of evil, ground down to tragedy by misfortunes of birth, economic forces, and the brutal rapacity of certain individuals.

Founding a "phalanstery" in Leigh Hall, he tested theories promulgated in France and in England by philosophical socialists. In the middle of that century there was much study of the doctrines of Fourier, Comte, Proudhon, Le Blanc, and Cabet. Romney's hostelry was modeled after Fourier's *phalanstère*, founded in 1830, at Condé-sur-Vire. A *phalanstère*, technically the residence of a phalange or about 1,800 persons, was "to include all aspects of human capacity, to give life either common or solitary." This institution was planned by a "thinker" who recognized in man "twelve radical passions out of whose free play harmony would be educed." Romney, however, gathered together poor and broken spirits suffering from various forms of ignorance and sin, and he regulated his establishment by autocratic fiat, seeking to coerce his men and women to redemption and happiness. By "trying to do good without the church or even the squire" he offended the county; the peasants were vaguely displeased by his innovations and by his reception of London thieves and dissolutes. Finally between the peasants and the joyous help of the ungrateful inmates of the phalanstery Leigh Hall was set on fire and thoroughly destroyed.

The fire which ended this social experiment brought a blinding flash of light to Romney, showing him how priggish and arbitrary he had been, in a situation where only the brotherhood and humor of a Saint Francis could really prevail. The story was slowly unfolded, in that Florentine garden, by Romney who, with caustic irony, at his own expense, exposed his futile efforts to predate the millennium, bestowing liberty, equality, fraternity, soup, and virtue by a careful schedule. His terse summary and neat anti-climax in the following verses, present in miniature the fine ideals and the faulty methods of his program:

> So much he has to teach! so good a world!
> The same the whole creation's groaning for!
> No rich nor poor, no gain nor loss nor stint;
> No pottage in it able to exclude
> A brother's birthright, and no right of birth
> The pottage—both secured to every man,
> And perfect virtue dealt out like the rest
> Gratuitously, with the soup at six,
> To whoso does not seek it.

Relentlessly he pointed out the poetic justice which rewarded his patronizing, theoretical, yet autocratic methods:

> My men and women of disordered lives,
> I brought in orderly to dine and sleep,
> Broke up those waxen masks I made them wear,
> With fierce contortions of the natural face,—
> And cursed me for my tyrannous constraint
> In forcing crooked creatures to live straight.

In a debate, growing more and more dramatic, drawing more and more to harmony of opinion, these two persons, Aurora and Romney, discussed the causes of his failure and, inclusively, the failures of many socialistic theories, fashioning a somewhat Platonic dialogue, in which Mrs. Browning had a chance to express her ideas on certain social problems. Romney, penitent, satirized the materialism, the mechanical and mathematical program to which he had subscribed:

> We talk by aggregates,
> And think by systems, and, being used to face
> Our evils in statistics, are inclined
> To cap them with unreal remedies
> Drawn out in haste on the other side of the slate.

Aurora added:

> If we give,
> Our cup of water is not tendered till
> We lay down pipes and found a Company
> With Branches.

The conclusion reached by Romney was that:

> ... men who work can only work for men,
> And, not to work in vain, must comprehend
> Humanity and so work humanly,
> And raise men's bodies still by raising souls,
> As God did first.

Romney stands for many good men and women of the Age, who had inherited Rousseau's doctrines regarding Return to Nature, innate virtue, instinctive love, and good will, but who had failed to understand Rousseau's plea for individualism. These people expected to see evil traits translated into virtue by waving the magician's wand called "good will." Romney found to his surprise and pain that the passions of the crafty, mean, and cruel have a terrible tenacity. Aurora, the artist, had been wiser than he, and had warned him long before, against externalism in reforms:

> I hold you will not compass your poor ends
> Of barley-feeding and material ease,
> Without a poet's individualism
> To work your universal. It takes a soul
> To move a body: It takes a high-souled man
> To move the masses, even to a cleaner stye:
> It takes the ideal, to blow a hair's breadth off
> The dust of the actual.—Ah, your Fouriers failed,
> Because not poets enough to understand
> That life develops from within.

Shaken by his failure, sardonically distrustful of the single individual's effort, Romney tended to lapse into a sort of *laissez-faire* mood:

> I stood myself there worthier of contempt,
> Self-rated in disastrous arrogance,
> As competent to sorrow for mankind,
> And even their odds. A man may well despair,
> Who counts himself so needful to success.

To this Aurora:

> And yet take heed, I answered, lest we lean
> Too dangerously on the other side,
> And so fail twice. Be sure, no earnest work
> Of any honest creature, however weak,
> Imperfect, ill-adapted, fails so much,
> It is not gathered as a grain of sand
> To enlarge the sum of human action used
> For carrying out God's end. No creature works
> So ill, observe, that therefore he's cashiered.

Later, in a happy mood, Romney formulated his new faith:

> Fewer programmes, we who have no prescience.
> Fewer systems, we who are held and do not hold.
> Less mapping out of masses to be saved,
> By nations or by sexes. Fourier's void,
> And Comte absurd, and Cabet, puerile.
> Subsist no rules of life outside of life,
> No perfect manners, without Christian souls;
> The Christ Himself had been no Lawgiver
> Unless he had given the life, too, with the law.

But Aurora added one deeper idea, growth through love:

> The man, most man,
> Works best for men, and, if most man indeed,
> He gets his manhood plainest from his soul:
> While obviously this stringent soul itself
> Obeys the old law of development,
> The Spirit ever witnessing in ours,
> And Love, the soul of soul, within the soul,
> Evolving it sublimely.

This pronouncement of Aurora is the key to Mrs. Browning's belief, and is the theme of the poem,—growth through love, a doctrine enunciated by many thinkers, especially by Plato, Christ, Dante, Shakespeare, Wordsworth, Shelley, and Browning, in *Paracelsus*. Steadfastly holding to this doctrine she had tested by it certain modern schemes and found them wanting. Reading, pondering and often discussing with her husband the progress of various moderns she had arrived at very clear cut judgments regarding Socialism. Her *Letters* offer keen comments on the subject. About 1850, she wrote to Isa Blagden (*Letters,* I: 467):

> Christian Socialists are by no means a new sect, the Moravians representing the theory with as little offence and absurdity as may be. What is it, after all, but an out-of-door extension of the monastic system? The religious principle, more or less apprehended, may bind men together so, absorbing their individualities, and presenting an aim *beyond the world;* but upon merely human and earthly principles no system can stand, I feel persuaded, and I thank God for it. If Fourierism could be realized (which it surely cannot) out of a dream, the destinies of our race would shrivel up under the unnatural heat, and human nature would, to my mind, be desecrated and dishonored—because I do not believe in purification without suffering, in progress without struggle, in virtue without temptation. Least of all do I consider happiness the end of man's life. We look to higher things, have nobler ambitions.
>
> Also, in every advancement of the world hitherto, the individual has led the masses. Thus, to elicit individuality has been the object of the best political institutions and governments. Now, in these new theories, the individual is ground down to the multitude, and society must be "moving all together if it moves at all"—restricting the very possibility of progress by the use of the lights of genius. Genius is *always individual.*

Possibly her stand was based somewhat upon Margaret Fuller's reports of the failure of the American experiment at Brook Farm, for it was in 1848 and 1849 that Margaret Fuller, after her marriage to Count D'Ossoli, saw much of the Brownings. In 1852 Mrs. Browning wrote to Mrs. Martin: (*Letters,* II: 61):

> As for the socialists, I quite agree with you that various of them, yes, and some of their chief men, are full of pure and noble aspiration, the most virtuous of men, the most benevolent. Still, they hold in their hands, in their clean hands, ideas that kill, ideas which defile, ideas which, if carried out, would be the worst and most crushing kind of despotism. I would rather live under the feet of the Czar than in those stages of perfectibility imagined by Fourier and Cabet, if I might choose my "pis aller"! All these speculators (even Louis Blanc, who is one of the most rational) would revolutionize, not merely countries, but the elemental conditions of humanity, it seems to me; none of them seeing that antagonism is necessary to all progress. A man in walking, must set one foot before another, and in climbing (as Dante observed long ago) the foot behind "é sempre il piu basso." Only the gods (Plato tells us) keep both feet joined together in moving onward. It is not so, and cannot be so, with men.

Mrs. Browning's conception of good included liberty for the masses as well as for the classes, not merely political enfranchisement but the liberty to grow through individual effort, error, blunder. What Mrs. Browning thought important for the future of the race is,—freedom from the consciousness of being directed, supervised from above, in a fashion which implied authority rather than persuasion, suggestion, guidance. Leaders she did believe in, most certainly, but such leaders as will coöperate, not coerce. Progress comes through strange, miserable, passionate experience, often through mistakes, or through a driving need for understanding; there must be some lure held out to each person, some desire awakened, some power quickened, some motive crystallized whereby self activity may be stirred to more and more complete self-guidance.

Her attitude towards these social questions is an application of Mrs. Browning's theory of Art, involving her philosophy of the beautiful, whether in specific creation of poem or painting, or in the harmonies achieved by human souls in their mortal lives. There are many discussions short and long in *Aurora Leigh* regarding art, all of which help us to understand better her conceptions of "the principle of beauty," her idealistic faith that in life as in art man can

> feel
>
> . . . . .
>
> The spiritual significance burn through
> The hieroglyphic of material shows.

The following quotation summarizes very well the composite nature of her sources, and enunciates her ideas regarding the origin, the method, the purpose, and the influence of poetry as one of the several arts. Aristotle and Plato, Wordsworth, Coleridge, and Shelley are surely remembered here:

> Art's the witness of what is
> Behind this show. If this world's show were all,
> Then imitation would be all in art;
> There, Jove's hand gripes us!—For we stand here, we,
> —If genuine artists, witnessing for God's
> Complete, consummate, undivided work;
> —That every natural flower which grows on earth
> Implies a flower upon the spiritual side,
> Substantial, archetypal, all a-glow
> With blossoming causes,—not so far away,
> But we, whose spirit-sense is somewhat cleared,

> May catch at something of the bloom and
>   breath,—
> Too vaguely apprehended, though indeed
> Still apprehended, consciously or not,
> And still transferred to picture, music, verse,
> For thrilling audient and beholding souls
> By signs and touches which are known to souls.

Social science should be an art, and the construction of a social cosmos should be an imaginative achievement, a harmony. In the passage by this "memorable lady" referred to in Meredith's sonnet, *The World's Advance,* she had made Aurora say:

> What is art
> But life upon the larger scale, the higher,
> When, graduating up in a spiral line
> Of still expanding and ascending gyres,
> It pushes toward the intense significance
> Of all things, hungry for the Infinite?
> Art's life,—and where we live, we suffer and
>   toil.

Among the influences noted in **Aurora Leigh** three seem to be of chief importance: Madame de Staël, George Sand, Robert Browning, influences affecting both thought and form. Little has been said regarding Madame de Staël's place in Mrs. Browning's pantheon. Surely this cosmopolitan woman's life and prestige affected the portrait of Aurora, and the novel *Corinne* seems to have contributed to the plot. Corinne half English and half Italian was born in Italy and brought up by an Aunt, until Corinne was taken to England to spend a lonely girlhood under the guardianship of a frigid unsympathetic English step-mother. Escaping at length, Corinne went to Italy where she became famous as an *improvisatrice,* possessing brilliant poetic gifts, scholarship, and great personal charm. By her beauty she won the love of Lord Nevil, a cold English noble. Though Aurora Leigh is the most decorous of rebels she seems to be kin to the intense Corinne whose letter (Book XIV) to Lord Nevil has some interesting ideas in common with Aurora. Between Romney and Albert, the hero of George Sand's *Consuelo* and *The Countess of Rudolstadt* there are some parallels, also, for the two men are similar in their priggish virtue, in their absorbed devotion to humanitarian causes, in their inability to take life joyously. Both are deeply concerned with schemes carefully thought out for a social Utopia.

More than suggestions for plot and characters came from Madame de Staël and George Sand; certain attitudes and opinions were probably deepened, especially by careful reading of the works of George Sand. I do not know if anyone has suggested that George Sand's name, Aurore Dudevant, may have influenced the christening of Mrs. Browning's ardent heroine, Aurora Leigh. The admiration Mrs. Browning felt for George Sand was of early growth, vividly and often expressed. Two sonnets (1844) as well as various allusions in her letters show her unbounded and daring enthusiasm for the Frenchwoman's gifts. To Mr. Chorley, of *The Athenaeum,* she wrote, in 1845:

> I am more of a latitudinarian in literature than it is generally thought expedient for women to be; and I have that admiration for *genius* which dear Mr. Kenyon calls my "immoral sympathy with power"; and if Madame Dudevant is not the first female genius of any country or age, I really do not know who is. And then she has certain noblenesses—granting all the evil and "perilous stuff"—noblenesses and royalnesses which make me loyal.

In spite of George Sand's defiance of moral and civil law, Mrs. Browning was able to admire the humanitarian and the artist, and to agree with Matthew Arnold in tribute to George Sand's intense feeling for nature, and for humble life, her passionate plea for greater naturalness and sincerity in social life, her desire for justice, her faith in individualism as opposed to the rule of class or creed. But Robert, less fascinated by the robust, not to say wilful and passionate, woman, had not his wife's tolerance, and some of Mrs. Browning's **Letters** give playful glimpses of Robert's stiff efforts to be courteous to this lady whose "terrestrial lavendars and supercelestial blues," were symbolically offensive to him. Mrs. Browning, however, far outstripped both George Sand and Madame de Staël in her conception of the depth and potential power of character, in her conception of the fundamental significances of life and death. She has a far steadier, saner, more understandable view of humanity than do these other two women who present too exalted and impossible portraits of feminine character.

The most dominant influence—felt all through the poem in technique of verse as well as in thought and feeling—was, as we know, that of Robert Browning. One or two selected instances may stand for several. *Fra Lippo Lippi* had expressed the doctrine in the last two verses:

> The rising painter, Vincent Carrington,
> Whom men judge hardly as bee-bonneted,
> Because he holds that, paint a body well,
> You paint a soul by implication.

Many lines from Browning come to mind as one reads the following on "success and failure":

> All success
> Proves partial failure: all advance implies
> What's left behind; all triumph, something
>   crushed
> At the chariot wheels, all government
>   something wrong.

And rich men make the poor, who curse the rich.

Possibly she recalled in **One Word More**:

> Where the heart lies let the brain lie also;
>
> . . . . .
>
> Life means, be sure,
> Both heart and head,—both active, both complete
> And both in earnest.

And here is a glowingly frank tribute to her husband, the author of *Pippa Passes* and of *Saul*:

> "There's nothing great
> Nor small," has said a poet of our day,
> Whose voice will ring beyond the curfew of eve,
> And not be thrown out by the matin's bell:
> And truly, I reiterate, nothing's small!
> No lily-muffled hum of a summer-bee,
> But finds some coupling with the spinning stars;
> No pebble at your foot, but proves a sphere.

Inevitably **Aurora Leigh** (1857) must be paralleled with *The Ring and the Book* (1868), for each represents its author's most mature thought and art. Both poems have Italian settings, both present the problem of the dependent woman, in one case Marian Earle, in the other, Pompilia, and we see the rescue of each one, her evolution of soul under stress. Romney a highly magnanimous but professional philanthropist is an interesting contrast to Caponsacchi, a priest suddenly become a liberator and a soldier saint. The development of each of these characters out of immaturity into a strong and sensitive understanding of the purpose of life is traced with compelling power. Aurora Leigh herself epitomizes the ideas of Mrs. Browning regarding love and marriage, who draws her romantic tale to a close with a happy marriage. *The Ring and the Book* is of sterner import, it is a tragedy wherein the chief characters suffer irrevocably, but possess forever, Browning says, the principle of love and life. A deeper knowledge of *The Ring and the Book* can be gained through study of **Aurora Leigh** written a dozen years earlier in the complete happiness of the **Casa Guidi**. The unanimity of thought and feeling between husband and wife is evident, and evident also are the differences in their imaginative power, their conceptions of feeling. Because Mrs. Browning had a more trusting, simpler faith in divine providence she sometimes begs the question regarding evil and sorrow, being able to endure all things, through religious fervor. Browning's faith equally convinced, threw upon man a greater burden of responsibility, and also a greater need of initiative, of speculation and experiment and defiance of convention. An interesting comparison may be made between the Pope's monologue in *The Ring and the Book* and the dialogue between Aurora and Romney in the last two books of *Aurora Leigh*.

The following passage, presenting liberal views, social and deeply religious, expresses the philosophy of progress, shared by Elizabeth and Robert Browning:

> What height we know not,—but the way we know,
> And how by mounting ever, we attain,
> And so climb on. It is the hour for souls,
> That bodies, leavened by the will and love,
> Be lightened to redemption. The world's old,
> But the old world waits the time to be renewed,
> Toward which, new hearts in individual growth
> Must quicken, and increase to multitude
> In new dynasties of the race of men;
> Developed whence, shall grow spontaneously
> New churches, new economies, new laws,
> Admitting freedom, new societies
> Excluding falsehood: He shall make all new.

Ellen Moers on *Aurora Leigh*:

Aurora Leigh is in fact a pretty good novel—not the best Victorian novel you have ever read, not quite on the level where Woolf placed it (with Trollope and Gaskell); but its heroine interests, its love story moves, its melodrama agitates, its settings and conversations and human vignettes amuse, interest, and inform the reader. "As we rush through page after page of narrative in which a dozen scenes that the novelist would smooth out separately are pressed into one, in which pages of description are fused into a single line, we cannot help feeling," Woolf went on, "that the poet has outpaced the prose writer. Her page is packed twice as full as his." But that is exactly the problem. The reader is likely to forget that Mrs. Browning was a poet first of all, and that the reason to read *Aurora Leigh* is not for the good second-rate novel in it, but for the poetry. We want to read it slowly, as Emily Dickinson did, for lines like "I too sat quiet, satisfied with death"; or phrases—remarkably Dickinsonian phrases—like "forgot herself in grief" or "changes backward rang" or "each emerging sense." We need to slow down, to stop running up against conventions and rushing into drawing rooms, to avert our face for a moment from Humanity and plain truth. We want to retreat into solitude, silence, decorum, and rhymed obscurity with Emily Dickinson. . . .

Ellen Moers, in Literary Women, *Anchor Books, 1977.*

Sandra M. Gilbert and Susan Gubar (essay date 1979)

SOURCE: "The Aesthetics of Renunciation," in *The Madwoman in the Attic: The Woman Writer and the Nineteenth-Century Literary Imagination,* Yale University Press, 1979, pp. 539-80.

[*In the excerpt that follows, Gilbert and Gubar claim that* Aurora Leigh *"may well have been the most reasonable compromise between assertion and submission that a sane and worldly woman poet could achieve in the nineteenth century."*]

Elizabeth Barrett Browning also made most of her finest poetry out of her reconciliation to that graceful or passionate self-abnegation which, for a nineteenth-century woman, was necessity's highest virtue. But because she had little natural taste for the drastic asceticism [Christina] Rossetti's temperament and background seem to have fostered, Barrett Browning ultimately substituted a more familiar Victorian aesthetic of service for the younger woman's somewhat idiosyncratic aesthetic of pain. Her masterpiece, *Aurora Leigh* (1856), develops this aesthetic most fully, though it is also in part an epic of feminist self-affirmation. *Aurora Leigh* is too long to analyze here in the kind of detail we have devoted to "Goblin Market," but it certainly deserves some comment, not only because (as Virginia Woolf reports having discovered to her delight)[69] it is so much better than most of its nonreaders realize, but also because it embodies what may well have been the most reasonable compromise between assertion and submission that a sane and worldly woman poet could achieve in the nineteenth century. Indeed, as we shall see, Emily Dickinson's implicit rejection of Barrett Browning's compromise no doubt indicates just how "mad" and unworldly the "myth" of Amherst was.

Briefly, *Aurora Leigh* is a *Künstlerroman* in blank verse about the growth of a woman poet and the education of her heart through pride, sympathy, love, and suffering. Born in Florence to an Englishman and the Italian bride he has been disinherited for marrying, its heroine comes to England as a thirteen-year-old orphan, to be initiated into the torments of feminine gentility by her censorious maiden aunt, an ungentle spinster who acts (like so many women in novels by women) as patriarchy's agent in "breeding" young ladies for decorous domesticity. Partly perhaps because of her un-English and therefore unconventional childhood, Aurora refuses to submit to her aunt's strictures; early, studying her dead father's books, she decides to become a poet. When her highminded, politically ambitious cousin Romney Leigh—a sort of reincarnated St. John Rivers—asks her to become his wife and helpmate, she proudly declines his offer, explaining that she has her vocation, too: art, which is at least as necessary as social service.[70]

Here, although the specific polarities of self-developing art and self-abnegating "work" recall the prototypical Victorian polarities Tennyson described in, say, "The Palace of Art," Barrett Browning gives the girl's self-justifying speech a feminist dimension that sets her rejection of Romney into precisely the tradition of rebellious self-affirmation that Jane Eyre so notoriously pioneered when she rejected St. John's marriage proposal. Repudiating Romney's patronizing insinuation that women "play at art as children play at swords, / To show a pretty spirit, chiefly admired / Because true action is impossible," she refuses also his invitation to "love and work with me," to work "for uses, not / For such sleek fringes (do you call them ends, / Still less God's glory?) as we sew ourselves / Upon the velvet of those baldoquins / Held 'twixt us and the sun." As passionately assertive as Jane, she insists that "every creature, female as the male, / Stands single in responsible act and thought . . . [and] I, too, have my vocation,—work to do, . . . Most serious work, most necessary work."[71] At this point in the book, she is "all glittering with the dawn-dew, all erect" and, in a metaphor Dickinson was later to convert to her own uses, "famished for the noon." For this reason, it seems to her, as with masculine aggressiveness she seeks "empire and much tribute," that it is both contemptible and contemptuous for someone to say "I have some worthy work for thee below. / Come, sweep my barns, and keep my hospitals, / And I will pay thee with a current coin / Which men give women."

Significantly, however, *Aurora Leigh* begins where *Jane Eyre* leaves off. Jane rejects St. John's invitation to a life of self-denying work, and enters instead a self-gratifying earthly paradise about which Brontë is unable to give us many details; but Aurora has a whole career ahead of her, and a career—poetry—whose perils are precisely those dangers of hyperbolic self-aggrandizement associated with the prideful "it" that she revealingly calls "the devil of my youth." Thus where Jane's assertion was the product of a long struggle for identity, Aurora's is the postulate with which a long renunciation (or repression) of identity must begin. Jane had to learn to be herself. Aurora has to learn not to be herself.

The particular agent of Aurora's education is Marian Erle, a "woman of the people" who functions as a sisterly double, showing her the way to act and suffer, first by loving and serving Romney, and then by (not quite intentionally) sacrificing her virginity for him. Romney is about to marry Marian Erle as a political gesture toward social equality but Marian is persuaded to renounce him by Lady Waldemar, a self-indulgent and "bitchy" aristocrat who is in love with him herself. Packed off to France under the care of one of this "lady's" servants, Marian—in properly Richardsonian fashion—is trapped in a whorehouse, drugged, raped, impregnated, and driven temporarily mad. What Aurora has to learn from all this is, first, sympathy, and then service. Tormented by her belief that Romney (whom she really loves) plans to marry Lady Waldemar, Aurora goes to Paris, where she encounters the abused Marian and her illegitimate child. By this time Aurora Leigh is a famous and quite formidable poet. But she quickly decides to make a home in her "motherland" of Florence for Marian and the child, a decision that does seem to strike a happy feminist balance between service and "selfishness." Aurora will continue to write her ambitious poems, yet Marian and her child will be secure.

Watching Marian tend the baby, however, the proud poet has learned more than the pleasures of humility. She has learned to envy that "extremity of love" in which a woman is "self-forgot, cast out of self." At this point, Romney appears in Florence and reveals that he has no intention of marrying Lady Waldemar, and moreover that he has been blinded while attempting to rescue Marian's drunken father from a conflagration that destroyed the Leighs' ancestral mansion. On the surface, therefore, he seems to have metamorphosed from a stonily righteous St. John Rivers to a seductively vulnerable Rochester. Softened by her affection for Marian and chastened by this news, Aurora finally concedes to her Victorian audience that "Art is much; but love is more," especially for a woman.

> Art symbolizes heaven; but love is God
> And makes heaven. I, Aurora, fell from mine,
> I would not be a woman like the rest,
> A simple woman who believes in love,
> And owns the right of love because she loves,
> And, hearing she's beloved, is satisfied
> With what contents God: I must analyze,
> Confront, and question, just as if a fly
> Refused to warm itself in any sun
> Till such was *in leone*. . . .[72]

The imagery of her confession is significant, suggesting that in her love Aurora is as unlike Jane Eyre as Romney, despite his blindness, is unlike Rochester. For a woman not to love is to "fall" from heaven like Satan or Eve; to love, on the other hand, is to be like a contented fly, basking in the noontide sun without rivalrously seeking to displace it.

Married to blind Romney, Aurora will be both as wife and as artist her husband's helpmeet. She will not so much desire the sun (the way she did when younger) as she will study it, harvest it, benefit from it. "Gaze on, with inscient vision, toward the sun," Romney admonishes her, "And from his visceral heat pluck out the roots of light beyond him," for "Art's a service, mark: / A silver key is given to thy clasp, / And thou shalt stand unwearied, night and day, / And fix it in the hard, slow-turning wards."[73] In other words, the artist, and specifically the woman poet, is neither a glittering and inspired figure nor a passionately self-assertive Jane Eyre. Rather, she is a modest bride of Apollo who labors for her glorious blind master—and for humanity too—in an "unwearied" trance of self-abnegation almost as intense as the silent agony Rossetti's dream queen endured in "From House to Home."

As her name indicates, therefore, Aurora becomes the dawn goddess who ministers to the god Dickinson was to call "the man of noon" by laying "the first foundations" of *his* reconstructed house. As Romney feeds his "blind majestic eyes / Upon the thought of perfect noon," his artist-wife describes the biblical stones of light she sees in the east—jasper, sapphire, chalcedony, amethyst—from which the visionary walls are being built. Like Dorothea ministering to Casaubon, she enacts Milton's daughter's idealized role: the role of dutiful handmaiden to a blind but powerful master. And just as sightless but still severely patriarchal Romney now seems to be half Rochester and half St. John Rivers, she and her author appear to have achieved a perfect compromise between the docility required by Victorian marriage and the energy demanded by poetry. They have redefined the relationship between the poet's "inspiration" and the poet herself so that it reflects the relationship of a Victorian sage and his submissive helpmeet.

At the same time, however, just as George Eliot's allusion to Milton's daughters hints at secret fantasies of rebellion even while ostensibly articulating a patriarchal doctrine of female servitude, Barrett Browning's compromise aesthetic of service conceals (but does not obliterate) Aurora Leigh's revolutionary impulses. For though the chastened Aurora vows to work *for* Romney, the work Barrett Browning imagines her doing is violent and visionary. As if to mute the shock value of her imaginings, Barrett Browning has Romney rather than Aurora describe Aurora's task. Part of this poet's compromise consists in her diplomatic recognition that Victorian readers might be more likely to accept millenarian utterances from a male character. But the millenarian program Romney outlines is not, of course, his own; it is the revolutionary fantasy of his author—and of her heroine, his wife-to-be—discreetly transferred from female to male lips. He himself concedes this point, though he also elaborates upon the tactful notion that a loving Victorian marriage will sanctify even revolution.

> Now press the clarion on thy woman's lip,
> (Love's holy kiss shall still keep consecrate)
> And breathe thy fine keen breath along the brass,
> And blow all class-walls level as Jericho's . . .

he cries, adding, so there should be no mistake about the sweeping nature of his program, that

> . . . the old world waits the time to be
>   renewed,
> Toward which new hearts in individual growth
> Must quicken, and increase to multitude
> In new dynasties of the race of men,
> Developed whence shall grow spontaneously
> New churches, new economies, new laws
> Admitting freedom, new societies
> Excluding falsehood: HE shall make all new.[74]

The fact that a divine patriarch, aided by a human patriarch and his helpmeet, shall "make all new" does not, finally, conceal the more startling fact that all must and shall, in Barrett Browning's scheme, be *made new*.

Emily Dickinson, who wrote that she experienced a "Conversion of the Mind" when she first read "that Foreign Lady" Elizabeth Barrett Browning, must have perceived the Romantic rage for social transformation concealed behind the veil of self-abnegating servitude with which *Aurora Leigh* concludes.[75] She must have noticed, too, that the celestial city Aurora sees in the sunrise at the end of the poem is, after all, Aurora's and not blind Romney's to see, perhaps because it is that shining capital, the *new* Jerusalem. If the "heat and violence" of Aurora Leigh's heart have been tamed, then, at least her dawn-fires have not been entirely extinguished. It is for this reason, no doubt, that Barrett Browning, while looking everywhere for "grandmothers," became herself the grand mother of all modern women poets in England and America. Certainly she was the spiritual mother of Emily Dickinson who, as we shall see, rejected her compromises but was perpetually inspired by the "inscient vision" with which she solved the vexing "problem" of poetry by women.

Notes

[69] See Woolf, *Aurora Leigh*, in *The Second Common Reader* [New York: Harcourt, Brace and Company, 1932].

[70] The hint of incest in the courtship of the lovers, together with the striking parallelism of Aurora Leigh's name with the name of Byron's half-sister Augusta Leigh, suggests that Barrett Browning may be simultaneously retelling and "purifying" the legendary story of Byron's shocking romance with Augusta. It has also been suggested that Mrs. Gaskell's *Ruth* was the source for the Marian Erle story.

[71] *Aurora Leigh*, [in *The Poetical Works of Elizabeth Barrett Browning* (New York: Crowell, 1891)], pp. 22-27.

[72] Ibid., p. 173.

[73] Ibid., p. 177.

[74] Ibid., p. 178.

[75] See J. 593, "I think I was enchanted / When first a sombre Girl— / I read that Foreign Lady— / The Dark—felt beautiful—" . . .

Kathleen K. Hickok (essay date 1980)

SOURCE: "New Yet Orthodox: Female Characters in *Aurora Leigh*," in *International Journal of Women's Studies*, Vol. 3, No. 5, September/October, 1980, pp. 479-89.

[*In the following essay, Hickok explores Browning's feminist inversion of conventional literary and social norms in* Aurora Leigh.]

I

Interest in *Aurora Leigh*, by Elizabeth Barrett Browning, has revived during the last few years, chiefly because of the feminist perspective from which this remarkable "verse novel" examines nineteenth-century England. In turn, renewed interest in *Aurora Leigh* has led to re-evaluation of Barrett Browning's[1] other poems, especially those depicting female figures, a process rewarded with rediscoveries of numerous of her poems long ago allowed to disappear from the literary canon of Victorian poetry.[2] We must not forget, however, that just as *Aurora Leigh* exists in the context of Barrett Browning's other poetry, her other poetry itself exists in the context of the nineteenth-century feminine poetic tradition in England—a tradition exemplified by such poets as Felicia Hemans, Letitia Landon, Mary Howitt, and Caroline Norton; a tradition with which Elizabeth Barrett Browning was demonstrably familiar.[3]

Under this microscope, her poems appear not as *sui generis*, but as part of a field of established poetic figures, themes, and purposes shared by her feminine peers. To name several, these included, first, stereotypical female figures such as the lovelorn pining maiden, the fallen woman, the self-sacrificing wife, and the bereaved mother; second, critical examination of the Victorian ideology of love and marriage—especially criticism of the marriage ideal, of the presumed differences between woman's love and man's, and of the tension in gifted women's lives between love and fame; and, finally, the aim of social protest—concerning English seamstresses, child labor, prostitution, the American slave trade, and the miserable condition of the British poor. For each of these traditions there were established poetic norms of imagery, plot, theme, point of view, and tone.

Of course, it is true that an imaginative difference, a twist of plot, or a mastery of imagery usually saved Barrett Browning's poems from the tedium of most giftbook verse. In Book III of *Aurora Leigh*, Aurora remarks upon the difficulty of simultaneously observing and transcending conventionality in her work:

> My critic Belfair wants another book
> Entirely different, which will sell (and live?)
> A striking book, yet not a startling book,
> The public blames originalities. . . .
> Good things, not subtle, new yet orthodox,
> As easy reading as the dog-eared page
> That's fingered by said public fifty years,
> Since first taught spelling by its grandmother,
> And yet a revelation in some sort:
> That's hard, my critic Belfair.[4]

Barrett Browning accomplished this task to some extent in popular poems like **"The Poet's Vow"** (1836), **"The Romaunt of the Page"** (1839), and **"Lady Geraldine's Courtship"** (1844). By and large, however (as I have shown elsewhere[5]) her early poetry fell well within conventional expectations and traditional forms.

However, *Aurora Leigh* is another matter entirely. In *Aurora Leigh,* Barrett Browning departed from the feminine traditions of the century with sufficient force to impress many, alarm some, and startle nearly all of her readers.[6] Years later Swinburne remembered, "The advent of *Aurora Leigh* [in 1856] can never be forgotten by any lover of poetry who was old enough at the time to read it . . . they never had read, and never would read anything in any way comparable with that unique work of audaciously feminine and ambitiously impulsive genius."[7] Swinburne was right: *Aurora Leigh* was a courageous, thorough-going exposition of feminist beliefs about nineteenth-century women. Yet Barrett Browning conveyed her socially advanced ideas in a vehicle which—despite its claim to singularity as a verse novel—represented well known female characters involved in specifically female predicaments, all of which were already quite familiar to the reading public. The audacity and the achievement of *Aurora Leigh* resided in its confrontation all at once of so many social and personal facts of nineteenth-century English life and in its challenge to the validity of the conventions which customarily concealed those facts.

Barrett Browning realized, of course, just what she had dared to do; consequently, she was astonished by the poem's sensational popular success. She had fully expected, she said, "to be put in the stocks" for it "as a disorderly woman and free-thinking poet."[8] Yet she also believed it to be "nearer the mark . . . fuller, stronger, more sustained" than any of her previous poems.[9] Apparently, the technique of presenting radical ideas within a familiar context—"new yet orthodox"—constituted a camouflage sufficient to get the poem past the reading public's barricades of self-defensive disapprobation.

Of course, there *were* objections from some quarters to the immorality and impurity of the situations and the shamelessness and coarseness of the language in the poem. Furthermore, *Aurora Leigh* was not, finally, a critical success. In addition to their other reservations, reviewers were nearly unanimous in finding the poem's characterizations weak and its major figures unattractive. Since, with the exceptions of Romney Leigh and Aurora's father, all these characters are female, it is most illuminating to approach the poem's relationship to its social and literary context by examining Barrett Browning's various representations of English womanhood within it.

II

In *Aurora Leigh,* Barrett Browning focuses on female characters in each of the three social classes in England. Lady Waldemar, of course, represents the upper class. She is an idle aristocratic lady, who dabbles somewhat carelessly in philanthropy and affairs of the heart. Aurora Leigh, despite an aristocratic heritage from her father, is essentially a middle-class professional woman, who depends upon her own earnings as a writer for support. Marian Erle comes from the lower class. The daughter of a "tramp," she has become (with the help of Romney Leigh) a seamstress, in order to avoid a life of prostitution. Until she and her illegitimate child are rescued by Aurora, she lives a life of abject poverty which constantly borders upon outright destitution. From the poem's glorification of Marian Erle and vilification of Lady Waldemar, we might conclude that Barrett Browning's sympathies lay with the oppressed lower classes of England.

However, that would be an oversimplification. Marian's father is an unsavory character who drinks, beats his wife, and evades employment; in turn, her mother abuses Marian and tries to barter her virginity for favors from a neighboring squire. Lady Waldemar's servant later succeeds where Marian's mother failed, by selling Marian into sexual slavery. Furthermore, the throngs of angry poor people who threaten and finally maim the generous, if misguided, aristocrat Romney Leigh are nasty, brutish, and ungrateful mobs. Romney himself is a gentleman in the best sense of the word, and though his social peers are sometimes snobbish and hypocritical, they also include admirable men like Vincent Carrington, the painter, and Lord Howe, Aurora's faithful friend and correspondent. Despite the novelistic way in which characters of diverse social classes are made to rub elbows throughout the poem, class consciousness does not supply its unity of perspective. Feminist consciousness does.[10]

In *Aurora Leigh,* Elizabeth Barrett Browning explored virtually all the women's roles with which the public was familiar in mid-nineteenth-century England. By considering the poem's female characters in terms of their social roles and in light of the continual feminist commentary upon women in general which Aurora provides, we can discover the full force of the poem: *Aurora Leigh* rejects the conventional wisdom about women at virtually every point.

The interaction between Aurora and the three women who were significant figures in her childhood immediately illustrates some of the poem's departures from tradition. To begin with, Aurora's mother was not an Englishwoman at all, but a foreigner, a Florentine, whose southern charms won the heart of Aurora's austere English father "after a dry lifetime spent at home / In college-learning, law, and parish talk" (I. 66-67). Through love of her, he "had suddenly / Thrown off the old conventions, broken loose / From chin-bands of the soul . . ." (I. 176-178). Unfortunately, this woman was so weakened by the birth of Aurora that she died when the child was only four years old. Aurora's recollection of her sense of loss owes something, perhaps, to many popular women poets' descriptions of maternal death, as well as to Barrett Browning's own bereavement at age twenty-two.

> I felt a mother-want about the world,
> And still went seeking, like a bleating lamb
> Left out at night in shutting up the fold,—
> As restless as a nest-deserted bird . . .
> (I. 40-43)

Yet her dead mother's portrait on the wall stirs the child not simply to adoration but also to terror.

> And as I grew
> In years, I mixed, confused, unconsciously,
> Whatever I last read or heard or dreamed,
> Abhorrent, admirable, beautiful,
> Pathetical, or ghastly, or grotesque,
> With that still face . . .
> (I. 146-151)

The mother figure becomes for Aurora a kind of Lamia, alternately benign and malignant, according to the child's own fantasies and fears. This unsentimental depiction of childhood bereavement is much more psychologically sound than the treatment of the subject in most popular women's poetry.

In her natural mother's stead, Aurora has Assunta, an Italian servant whose devotion to the child is quite touching. Assunta cares for Aurora until she is thirteen, when the English father suddenly dies and his relatives send for Aurora to come to England. Once again, Aurora is separated from maternal love; both she and the faithful servant are devastated with grief.

> I do remember clearly how there came
> A stranger with authority, not right
> (I thought not), who commanded, caught me up
> From old Assunta's neck; how, with a shriek,
> She let me go,—while I, with ears too full
> Of my father's silence to shriek back a word,
> In all a child's astonishment at grief
> Stared at the wharf-edge where she stood and moaned . . .
> (I. 223-230)

The demands of English laws and customs separate the child and her surrogate mother—who is, after all, only a servant and thus beyond consideration; we feel both the injustice and the inevitability of this outcome. By the time Aurora, as a grown woman, returns to Italy, her beloved Assunta is dead. The longlasting affection between Barrett Browning and her own maid-servant Wilson may have contributed to the representation of this female servant in *Aurora Leigh*. In any case, its sympathetic depiction of Assunta is extraordinary, considering that women's poetry in the nineteenth century generally failed to characterize female domestics at all; and the recognition of a genuine love between mistress and servant shows unusual sensitivity on Barrett Browning's part to the humanity of the serving class.

Reaching England, Aurora is turned over to the care and tutelage of her maiden aunt, whom Barrett Browning approached with neither of the prevailing attitudes—sentimentality or ridicule—but with a degree of individuality which distinguishes this particular spinster from the current poetical stereotype.

> She stood straight and calm,
> Her somewhat narrow forehead braided tight
> As if for taming accidental thoughts
> From possible pulses; brown hair pricked with grey
> By frigid use of life . . .
> Eyes of no colour,—once they might have smiled,
> But never, never have forgot themselves
> In smiling; cheeks, in which was yet a rose
> Of perished summers, like a rose in a book,
> Kept more for ruth than pleasure,—if past bloom,
> Past fading also.
> (I. 272-276, 282-287)

This physical description of Aunt Leigh emphasizes the repression and rigidity of a single woman who found herself consigned to "A harmless life, she called a virtuous life, / A quiet life, which was not life at all" (I. 288-289). She fills her days with the poor-club, the book-club, obligatory calls from the neighbors, and hatred for her brother's wife, Aurora's mother. When she dies, some seven years after Aurora's arrival in England, she is found sitting "Bolt upright in the chair beside her bed" (II. 925) with blank open eyes and an unbudging posture that aptly reflect her living personality.

Looking back, Aurora recognizes the essential difference between her aunt and herself, and expresses this difference in a classic image from women's poetry—that of the caged bird.

> She had lived
> A sort of caged-bird life, born in a cage,
> Accounting that to leap from perch to perch
> Was act and joy enough for any bird.
> . . . I, alas,
> A wild bird scarcely fledged, was brought to her cage,
> And she was there to meet me. Very kind.
> Bring the clean water, give out the fresh seed.
> (I. 304-307, 309-312)

Aurora was not an ideal English girl when she came to Aunt Leigh, but a natural, undisciplined, Italian child, and the spinster determined to take her in hand and mold her into the courtesy-book ideal of English maidenhood. Consequently, Aurora, who had been tutored by her father from his own store of genuine knowledge, is now set to the task of absorbing the English girl's customary mix of trivial information, accomplishment, and conventionality. Only her communings with nature and her clandestine reading from her father's library enable her spirit to survive. The long passage in which Aurora describes the struggle (I. 372-481) is classic in its denunciation of both the process and the product of women's education. Aunt Leigh fails in her attempts to quench the spark of independence and intellectuality which Aurora brought within herself from her Italian girlhood. "Certain of your feebler souls," Aurora conceded, "Go out in such a process; many pine / To a sick inodorous light" of English womanhood. "My own," she thanks God, "endured" (I. 470-472).

The character of Aurora is the most fully delineated in the poem, which traces her growth and maturation, the cultivation of her talents, and the education of her heart. After her successful defiance of the conventional demands of English girlhood, Aurora continues to reject current social ideas which pertain to her own situation and to the condition of women in general. She refuses to marry her cousin Romney and subordinate or abandon her artistic pursuits in order to participate in his own vocation of social work. "You want a helpmate, not a mistress, sir," she accuses, "A wife to help your ends,—in her no end" (II. 402-403). Mistakenly, she believes their match would be loveless, utilitarian, and she chooses instead to award her devotion to her art. "You'll grant that even a woman may love art, / Seeing that to waste true love on anything / Is womanly, past question" (II. 495-497). Aurora's objections to marriage are undeniably feminist and, in light of English law and custom, justifiable. Yet she misunderstands her own emotional needs, and we the readers recognize from the beginning what it takes Aurora many lonely years to perceive: her own need for intimacy and her love for her cousin Romney.

So deep are these emotions that Aurora, in absence of any other opportunity, acts them out by playing husband and father to Romney's affianced Marian Erle and her illegitimate child. All through Book VII of the poem, Aurora takes on an androgyny of character," dismissing her feminine tears and fears and letting the man inside her (VII. 212, 230)[11] predominate over the woman. "It is very good for strength," she learns, "To know that someone needs you to be strong" (VII. 414-415). She takes full responsibility for Marian and her baby, conveying them to Italy and safety in her own dead father's house, where the three form a tight little family group. Aurora soon discovers, through putting on the masculine role, that male-female personality distinctions are artificial, and that there is no magic in masculinity after all:

> Note men!—They are but women after all,
> As women are but Auroras!—there are men
> Born tender, apt to pale at a trodden worm . . .
> (VII. 1017-1019).

This new-found sympathy with men as human beings like herself is part of what softens Aurora toward Romney and enables her in the poem's conclusion to recognize and declare her love for him. Of course, the fact of his blindness is significant also. His handicap finally equalizes them, in a way, and allows Aurora to exercise both her sympathy and her strength. The marriage they now contemplate will be passionate, mystical, mature—a union of separate souls each bringing its own capacities to the joint endeavor humbly to do God's work. If this is an idealized version of marriage, it is at least more egalitarian than the conventional marriage ideal of complementary male-female roles. Furthermore, Barrett Browning manages here to do something that even the most critical of her contemporary women poets failed to do: she not only criticizes the existing structure of marriage, but she boldly envisions a joyful alternative.

In thus viewing Aurora in relationship to her man, we must not neglect her other great passion: her art. Ellen Moers has rightly called *Aurora Leigh* the "epic of the literary woman"[12] Despite Swinburne's protest that Aurora's life as a professional writer was "too eccentric" to be believed,[13] it is quite convincingly presented. We see her struggling with the double standard of literary criticism which frustrated so many women writers (II. 232-243), opening her fan mail (III. 210-232), and experiencing doubts about the quality of her work (I. 881-895). Aurora is constantly aware of financial pressures, writing for cyclopedias, magazines, and weekly papers, just to buy a little time to pursue her poetry (III. 306-328). She is her own most severe critic, always unsatisfied with her completed work and striving to make the next poem better than the last. Barrett Browning does not shrink from admitting the diligent work and punishing schedule Aurora's artist's life requires:

> I worked on, on.
> Through all the bristling fence of nights and days
> Which hedges time in from the eternities,
> I struggled,—never stopped to note the stakes
> Which hurt me in my course. The midnight oil
> Would stink sometimes; there came some vulgar needs;
> I had to live that therefore I might work,
> And, being poor, I was constrained, for life,
> To work with one hand for the booksellers
> While working with the other for myself
> And art.
>
> (III. 295-305)

Aurora has a high conception of her calling and a determination to maintain her integrity as a poet. When, in the story's conclusion, she tells Romney, "Art is much, but Love is more" (IX. 656), it is not as a repudiation of Art but as a greater testimony to the joy of love. "O Art, my Art, thou'rt much," she continues, "but love is more! / Art symbolises heaven, but Love is God / And makes heaven" (IX. 657-659). The pursuit of artistic excellence and public fame is not wrong in itself, but only insofar as it necessitates the sacrifice of human love. Elizabeth Barrett Browning was herself living proof that this sacrifice was avoidable, even in nineteenth-century England.

Lady Waldemar, the villain of the poem, twits Aurora on their first meeting with the contemporary stereotype of the literary woman:

> You stand outside,
> You artist women, of the common sex;
> You share not with us, and exceed us so
> Perhaps by what you're mulcted in, your hearts
> Being starved to make your heads: so run the old
> Traditions of you.
>
> (III. 406-411)

Yet in her arrogance of speech, she reveals not a truth about women artists, but rather a hint of her own potential for cruelty. Some critics have felt that Lady Waldemar is made to appear worse than she actually is, by being presented only through the eyes of the jealous Aurora, and that judged impartially, she would seem less a *femme fatale*.[14] Others have dismissed her as a mere adventuress,[15] a stereotypical "Wicked Lady of Quality."[16] Certainly there is something of the *femme fatale* in Lady Waldemar's deceptiveness and her sexual appetite, but she can perhaps be judged most accurately by observing in her the dilemma of the post-Regency aristocrat, the bored lady of leisure. Both her coarseness of language and her sophistication of manner can be seen as attributes of Regency society. Now that a different era is upon her, she attempts to take on the colors of the "modest women" (III. 580) of the present day, but succeeds only in achieving hypocrisy. In this result, she resembles Lady Howe, whose air of condescension is her most natural attitude (V. 582-607).[17]

Lady Waldemar's chief crime is that she does not take life as seriously as a proper Victorian woman ought to do. She unintentionally mocks Romney's attempts to do good by playing at philanthropy as a sort of lovers' game, and she offends Aurora Leigh by the frankness and physicality of her feelings for Romney.

> Am I coarse?
> Well, love's coarse, nature's coarse—ah, there's the rub.
> We fair fine ladies, who park out our lives,
> From common sheep-paths, cannot help the crows
> From flying over,—we're as natural still
> As Blowsalinda.
>
> (III. 454-459)

Outrageous though she may be, Lady Waldemar's earthiness and cynicism are attractive in their own colorful way—to the modern reader—at least, if not to the like of Romney, Aurora, and their peers. The callous way in which she dispatches Marian Erle to the colonies is reprehensible, of course. But the blame for Marian's abduction and rape lies with the unscrupulous servant, not with Lady Waldemar directly. Probably she is sincere when she expresses her regrets about the incident and writes to "thank" Aurora Leigh "For proving to myself that there are things / I would not do—not for my life, nor him" (IX. 19-20). She is not merely a conventional villain, nor yet a careless aristocrat. She seems rather to be an anachronism, a vital, energetic woman vexed by the century's continuing encroachments upon her freedom to express those qualities. Her attachment to Romney Leigh, invested though it is with pride, represents a genuine attempt to find a niche. "I cannot choose but think," she writes Aurora, "That, with him, I were virtuouser than you / Without him" (IX. 167-169), and the statement has a ring of truth.

The well known case of Marian Erle must be considered in light of both existing social conditions and the mid-century literary tradition of the fallen woman. The primitive life-styles among the lowest classes of England were definitely conducive to the type of casual immorality epitomized in Marian's mother's attempt to sell her daughter to a local squire. Marian's frantic flight into the city, the hopelessness of her life as a seamstress (like Lucy Gresham), and the squalor of her living quarters are accurately presented. Furthermore, the horrifying circumstances of her abduction, rape, and imprisonment in a Paris brothel were not unrealistic, as W.T. Stead's series of articles on the white slave trade would later attest.[18] Neither is Marian's reintegration into society unlikely; had she married a respectable man and settled into a bland domesticity, it would not have violated probability, but only literary and social conventions.

In **"A Year's Spinning"** (1846), Barrett Browning had depicted the fallen woman in an entirely conventional manner: seduction, abandonment, illegitimate motherhood, infant death, and the grave. In *Aurora Leigh,* Marian's childhood friend Rose Bell, who apparently has become a prostitute of the sort later interviewed by sociologist Bracebridge Hemyng,[19] seems to be irrevocably lost to sin. Even Marian pities Rose: "I heard her laugh last night in Oxford Street, / I'd pour out half my blood to stop that laugh, / Poor Rose, poor Rose!" (III. 927-929). Barrett Browning, of course, knew, and on occasion adhered to, the literary stereotype of the harlot's inevitable progress to the grave or to perdition.

In depicting Marian Erle, however, she rejected those familiar patterns entirely. Marian's story is in consonance with the reality, not the myth, of the "great social evil" of England. She is not seduced, but raped; she is not abandoned by a faithless lover, but flees from sexual captivity. Her devotion to her illegitimate infant son is rewarded by smiles and affection, not by bereavement. The child cannot even be properly said to "redeem" his mother, for, though despoiled, she has never sinned. When Marian is offered the incredible option of honorable marriage, she refuses; nor does she then sink into a premature grave, but lives peacefully on, for the sake of her son. It is only as a mother, and not as a ruined woman, that Marian approaches conventionality. In declining Romney's offer of marriage, she replies, "Here's a hand shall keep / For ever clean without a marriage-ring, / To tend my boy . . ." (IX. 431-433). No doubt the story of Marian Erle owed something to Mrs. Gaskell's *Ruth* (1853), but Barrett Browning's fallen heroine's fate far exceeds Mrs. Gaskell's for social realism and for sheer audacity. Furthermore, the astonishing facts are that *Aurora Leigh* appeared one year before William Acton's ground-breaking study *Prostitution,*[20] six years before Henry Mayhew's *London Labour and the London Poor,*[21] and almost thirty years before Stead's "The Maiden Tribute of Modern Babylon." Her literary representation of Marian Erle was far ahead of its time.

Contemporary critics who disliked the characters of Aurora Leigh and Lady Waldemar adored Marian Erle, although they found her idealistic beliefs and elegant language to be out of synchrony with her lower-class background.[22] The sentimental appeal of the guiltless sexual victim was perhaps irresistible. However, the unrelenting realism with which Barrett Browning articulated Marian's wrongs and alluded to the extent and horrors of English prostitution raised eyebrows among most conservative English readers. In describing these tabooed subjects in the most explicit language, Barrett Browning purposely defied both literary and social conventions. In her own defense, she explained, "If a woman ignores these wrongs, then may women as a sex continue to suffer them; there is no help for any of us—let us be dumb and die."[23]

III

Aurora Leigh believed in performance, rather than argument, as the way to prove the validity of women's God-given abilities and prerogatives (VIII. 813-846). Elizabeth Barrett Browning obviously shared this opinion, for *Aurora Leigh* was an incredibly wide-ranging and intense poetical production, for a poet of either sex. After *Aurora Leigh,* no subsequent poem of hers ever "caught the crowd"[24] in quite the same way. The poetry she published between 1856 and her death in 1861 reached a certain level of sophistication appropriate to her age and experience, but by and large, it also lapsed back into tradition and conventionality in its characterization of women. With the achievement of *Aurora Leigh,* however, the continuing significance of her contribution to the literature of women was assured. The risk she had dared to take in defense of nineteenth-century womanhood was justified by the popular impact, if not by the critical reception, of her longest poem. Today, without even a hint of condescension, we may pronounce *Aurora Leigh* the nineteenth-century masterpiece among English poems written by and about women.

Notes

[1] "Barrett Browning" seems to be the most respectful shorthand version of Elizabeth Barrett Browning's name which will at the same time distinguish her from her husband.

[2] See, for example, Helen Cooper, "Working into Light: Elizabeth Barrett Browning," in *Shakespeare's Sisters: Feminist Essays on Women Poets,* ed. Sandra M. Gilbert and Susan Gubar (Bloomington: Indiana University Press, 1979), pp. 65-81.

[3] Barrett Browning published poetry in various ladies' giftbooks and annuals, as did most popular women writers of her day. Among these were *Findens' Tableaux, Keepsake, The Amaranth,* and *The English Bijou Almanack.* She wrote thoughtful poems upon the deaths of Felicia Hemans and Letitia Landon. In his biography of Barrett Browning, Gardner B. Taplin notes that she knew the writings of Mary Howitt and Caroline Norton; he also records an instance of her satisfaction with a copy of the *Literary Souvenir,* in 1826. See Gardner B. Taplin, *The Life of Elizabeth Barrett Browning* (New Haven: Yale University Press, 1957), pp. 128, 237, 411.

[4] Elizabeth Barrett Browning, *The Complete Works,* ed. Charlotte Porter and Helen A. Clarke (New York:

Thomas Y. Crowell, 1900), IV, 80-81, Book III, lines 68-79. Further citations from the poem will be from this edition and will be referred to by book and line number.

[5] See my doctoral dissertation, "Representations of Women in the Work of Nineteenth-Century British Women Poets," Chapter X (University of Maryland, 1977).

[6] See Taplin, pp. 310-13, 337-47, on the reception of *Aurora Leigh*.

[7] Algernon C. Swinburne, "Introduction," *Aurora Leigh* (London, 1898), p. ix, quoted in Taplin, p. 310.

[8] *The Letters of Elizabeth Barrett Browning*, ed. Frederic G. Kenyon (New York: Macmillan, 1898), II, 252.

[9] Ibid., II, 253.

[10] For a provocative Marxist-Feminist analysis of the poem, see Marxist-Feminist Literature Collective, "Women's Writing: 'Jane Eyre,' 'Shirley,' 'Villette,' 'Aurora Leigh'," in *Eighteen-Forty-Eight: The Sociology of Literature,* ed. Francis Barker, John Coombes, et. al., Proceedings of the Essex Conference on the Sociology of Literature, July 1977, pp. 185-206.

[11] Barrett Browning had recognized and, to some extent, applauded this aspect of the character of George Sand, whom she very much admired. See the 1844 sonnets, "To George Sand: A Desire" and "To George Sand: A Recognition." The former opens, "Thou large-brained woman and large-hearted man, / Self-called George Sand!" (II, 239). George Sand's novels are generally acknowledged as sources for *Aurora Leigh*.

[12] Ellen Moers, *Literary Women: The Great Writers* (New York: Doubleday, 1977), p. 60.

[13] Quoted in Moers, p. 310.

[14] J. M. S. Tompkins, *"Aurora Leigh,"* The Fawcett Lecture, 1961-62 (London: Bedford College, 1961); reviewed in *Modern Language Review,* 58 (October, 1963), 625-26.

[15] Taplin, p. 320.

[16] Alethea Hayter, *Mrs. Browning: A Poet's Work and Its Setting* (New York: Barnes and Noble, 1963), p. 171.

[17] For this observation on Lady Howe, I am indebted to Elaine Ruth Harrington, "A Study of the Poetry of Elizabeth Barrett Browning," doctoral dissertation, New York University, 1977, p. 338.

[18] W. T. Stead, "The Maiden Tribute of Modern Babylon," a series of articles in the *Pall Mall Gazette* during July, 1885.

[19] For *London Labour and the London Poor,* Vol. IV (see note 21 below).

[20] William Acton, *Prostitution* (1857), ed. Peter Fryer (New York: Praeger, 1969).

[21] Henry Mayhew, *London Labour and the London Poor* (1862); Vol. IV rpt. as *London's Underworld,* ed. Peter Quennell (London: Spring Books, 1957).

[22] See Taplin, p. 341.

[23] Barrett Browning, *Letters,* II, 254.

[24] Ibid., II, 242.

Barbara Charlesworth Gelpi (essay date 1981)

SOURCE: "*Aurora Leigh*: The Vocation of the Woman Poet," in *Victorian Poetry*, Vol. 19, No. 1, Spring, 1981, pp. 35-48.

[*In the essay that follows, Gelpi sees* Aurora Leigh *as a metaphorical investigation of Browning's changing attitudes toward herself, her profession, and womanhood in general.*]

In recent years Elizabeth Barrett Browning's *Aurora Leigh* has reemerged, after more than half a century of neglect, as a strikingly important Victorian poem, historically significant in its interaction with the works of other Victorian writers and immediately relevant in its depiction of a feminist consciousness. Cora Kaplan's essay on the poem uses the earlier insights of Ellen Moers and Patricia Thomson to bring both these aspects of the poem together.[1] She demonstrates that the plot of *Aurora Leigh,* far from being a pastiche of those scenes and characters from other writers which had caught Barrett Browning's fancy, is in fact "an overlapping sequence of dialogues" with other texts. The borrowings from Madame de Staël, George Sand, Charlotte Brontë, Alfred Tennyson, and others give Barrett Browning the opportunity to comment, positively and negatively, on the responses of these writers to various aspects of Victorian society, including "the woman question," and to define her own ideas—coming in the process to feminist insights applicable and significant today.

Barrett Browning's witty and broad-ranging treatment of her society is marred only, Kaplan points out, by the intellectual and imaginative constriction in her presentation of the working class, particularly of working-class women. Her sentimental depiction of the poor seamstress Marian Earle shows Barrett Browning to be limited by class values which she accepts without question, even while questioning so much else in her society. The effectiveness of her feminist vision is thereby hampered both for her own day and for ours.

Except in terms of this social consciousness, Kaplan's excellent analysis only glances at *Aurora Leigh* as a reflection of Barrett Browning's sensibility. Yet the poem is a bildungsroman as well as a novel/poem of social concern: "I have put much of myself in it—I mean to say, of my soul, my thoughts, emotions, opinions; in other respects, there is not a personal line, of course," Barrett Browning wrote.[2] Although no personal line comes through the plot, the *images* of the poem tell a separate story: not the public story of a woman poet living in Victorian society but the inner story of such a woman's feelings about herself, particularly about her femininity. In her concern for the poor, Barrett Browning seems to have been unaware of how much her thinking was narrowed by the presuppositions of her class, but when thinking about women, whether poor or affluent, she recognized very clearly the influence of a similar conditioning. That is, she saw women's central problem as the antifeminine biases they had themselves internalized. While telling Aurora's story, then, Barrett Browning is also describing the process by which she herself threw off those "mind-forg'd manacles," an underplot which unfolds primarily through the metaphorical language of the poem.

When *Aurora Leigh* was widely and enthusiastically read, its imagery was in the accepted judgment its chief drawback: "Mrs. Browning's greatest failure is her metaphors: some of them are excellent, but when they are bad—and they are often bad—they are very bad"[3] ran the 1857 criticism of the *Westminster Review*. The critic then went on to give as his chief and best example of "a perfect shoal of mangled and pompous similes" a passage from Book I which describes a portrait of Aurora Leigh's mother. The portrait, Aurora explains, was painted after her Italian mother's death, which occurred when Aurora was four. In place of the shroud customary in such funerary portraits the mother was, at the insistence of her grieving maidservant, robed in her best red brocade. The resulting picture was a source of fascination yet also of terror to Aurora as she was growing up:

> I mixed, confused, unconsciously,
> Whatever I last read or heard or dreamed,
> Abhorrent, admirable, beautiful,
> Pathetical, or ghastly, or grotesque,
> With still that face . . . which did not therefore change,
> But kept the mystic level of all forms,
> Hates, fears, and admirations, was by turns
> Ghost, fiend, and angel, fairy, witch, and sprite,
> A dauntless Muse who eyes a dreadful Fate,
> A loving Psyche who loses sight of Love,
> A still Medusa with mild milky brows
> All curdled and all clothed upon with snakes
> Whose slime falls fast as sweat will; or anon
> Our Lady of the Passion, stabbed with swords
> Where the Babe sucked; or Lamia in her first
> Moonlighted pallor, ere she shrunk and blinked
> And shuddering wriggled down to the unclean;
> Or my own mother, leaving her last smile
> In her last kiss upon the baby-mouth
> My father pushed down on the bed for that,—
> Or my dead mother, without smile or kiss,
> Buried at Florence.
>
> (I. 147-168)[4]

Nothing that we learn about Aurora's mother either before or after this passage justifies the association with her of such negative figures as the Medusa or a Lamia. She is described as deeply and passionately loved by both her English husband and their child, a love just as deeply returned. One might consider the possibility that, ahead of her time, Barrett Browning realized the depths of irrational anger which a child—or even we adult, older children—have for a loved one who by dying has, as it were, abandoned us and so left us feeling as Aurora did:

> I felt a mother-want about the world,
> And still went seeking, like a bleating lamb
> Left out at night in shutting up the fold.
>
> (I. 40-42)

The images in these lines themselves suggest such a sense of betrayal on the lamb's part from the mother-shepherd who has, seemingly, deserted it. However, such an image contains none of the ferocity present in the Medusa passage. If Barrett Browning meant to argue for feelings as violent as those in the child's heart, she would be artistically obliged to explain them.

Nor can the Medusa passage be considered an eruptive autobiographical digression expressing Barrett Browning's feelings toward her own mother. Perhaps the most negative comment ever made by her about her mother was the description to Robert Browning of her mother's nature as "harrowed up into some furrows by the pressure of circumstances," and that seems more a comment on the unhappy effects of her father's dominating spirit than on the mother's hurt and narrowed one.[5] Beside it too must be set these lines from Barrett Browning's personal diary, written when she was twenty-five, three years after her mother's death. They begin with what appears to be a remembrance of something said by Mrs. Barrett herself:

> *"You will never find another person who will love you as I love you"*—And how I felt that to hear

again the sound of those beloved, those ever ever beloved lips, I wd. barter all other sound & sights—that I wd. in joy & gratitude lay down before her my tastes & feelings each & all, in sacrifice for the love, the exceeding love which I never, in truth, can find again. Have I not tried this, & know this & felt this: & do I not feel *now,* bitterly, dessolately, that human love like her's, I never can find again!⁶

Thinking of the description of the portrait as applicable either to Aurora's fictional mother or Barrett Browning's real one only confuses interpretation. This strange piling up of ambivalent and paradoxical images—"angel" and "witch"; "loving Psyche" and "still Medusa"; Lamia as she "wriggled down to the unclean" and "my own mother, leaving her last smile / In her last kiss upon the baby-mouth"—*is* explicable within the context of the whole poem if we think of the portrait before which the young Aurora sits brooding not as the image of her mother but as the image to her of womanhood itself.⁷ The phrases thus interpreted describe the deep ambivalence she feels about being a woman. Central to their paradoxes is the thought that if as woman she is to be an artist, she will betray her role as mother; yet the mother in her will also in turn betray and transfix the artist. So the artist's "dauntless Muse" and "loving Psyche" will never find fulfillment, turned to stone by the "mild milky brows" of her mothering role. At the same time, the mother's reward for having suckled babes will be the swords of her unfulfilled artistic ambitions.

It is noteworthy that with the exception of Aurora's mother and of the faithful servant Assunta, whose appearances are very brief and early, and of Marian Earle, whose significance will appear later, there are no attractive women in ***Aurora Leigh***. There is even something emulative, sycophantic, and untrustworthy about Aurora's worshipping admirer Kate Ward, who "desires the model of my cloak, / And signs 'Elisha to you'" (III. 53-54). Aurora's difficulty in finding the companionship of women congenial may be the result in part of her mother's absence. From her mother, Aurora says explicitly, she might have imbibed a loving openness of spirit which her father's earnest concern for her could not replace: "Fathers love as well [as mothers] / —Mine did, I know,—but still with heavier brains, / . . . So mothers have God's license to be missed" (I. 60-64). Then also, the English aunt who takes over Aurora's education after her father's death is a cold, unloving woman, much concerned with Aurora's acquisition of "feminine" accomplishments yet harsh in her feelings towards women. "My father's sister was to me / My mother's hater," says Aurora (I. 359-360).

These apparently coincidental circumstances begin to seem part of a pattern when we realize that there are no other more appealing mothers or mother-surrogates in the poem. No matter what their social class, mothers are presented as cold, self-centered, and destructive. Marian Earle's father is a drunken wastrel and a wife-beater, but the child's experience of beating is from her mother: when beaten by her husband, "she turned / (The worm), and beat her baby in revenge" (III. 868-869). Even a mother-surrogate who makes a "cameo" appearance adds, in what seems to be her only function in the poem, yet another instance of womanly hardness of spirit toward other women. Marian goes to the aid of another seamstress, Lucy Gresham, dying of consumption. Aurora's cousin, Romney Leigh, enters the room after Lucy has died, at which Lucy's bedridden grandmother, taking him for the undertaker and fearing lest she be confused with the corpse, speaks these words of grief:

If Lucy here . . . sir, Lucy is the corpse . . .
Had worked more properly to buy me wine;
But Lucy, sir, was always slow at work,
I shan't lose much by Lucy.
(IV. 71-74)

One further quick example: Marian says of a woman who makes a white slave of her, selling her to French brothel-keepers, "('Twas only what my mother would have done) / A motherly, right damnable good turn" (VII. 9-10).

Lady Waldemar, the most significant villainess of the poem though not herself a mother, provides us with the most important further clues to the meaning behind the images describing Aurora's mother's portrait. The latter was in physical appearance made up of sharply contrasted red and white:

That swan-like supernatural white life
Just sailing upward from the red stiff silk
Which seemed to have no part in it nor power
To keep it from quite breaking out of bounds.
(I. 139-142)

Several books later, without alluding to the grotesque resemblance-in-difference, Aurora thus describes Lady Waldemar at a soirée:

The woman looked immortal. How they told,
Those alabaster shoulders and bare breasts,
On which the pearls, drowned out of sight in milk,
Were lost, excepting for the ruby clasp!
They split the amaranth velvet-bodice down
To the waist or nearly, with the audacious press
Of full-breathed beauty.
(V. 618-624)

In one description the white breast rising from the crimson bodice becomes an image of heavenly aspira-

An 1823 drawing of Elizabeth Barrett Browning by her mother.

tion, in the other of worldly enfleshment; yet the images, just as images, are striking in their similarity.

Again, when Aurora hears from Marian Earle of Lady Waldemar's role in preventing Marian's marriage to Romney Leigh, the epithets with which Aurora mentally describes her dwell continually, obsessively, on the image of a Lamia: "that woman-serpent" (VI. 1103); "The Lamia-woman" (VII. 152); "Lamia! shut the shutters, bar the doors / From every glimmer on thy serpent-skin!" (VII. 170-171). These are only a few examples; they recur with virtually every allusion to Lady Waldemar from this point in the story.

Indeed, Aurora "over-reacts" to Lady Waldemar's villainy, taking it for granted, for instance, that Lady Waldemar planned for Marian a journey which would end not in Australia but in a brothel—a suspicion later shown to be untrue (IX. 84-92). Her vehemence betrays Aurora as being in what C. G. Jung would call a "shadow relationship"[8] with Lady Waldemar: that is, some of Lady Waldemar's attitudes and reactions are uncomfortably and unadmittably close to Aurora's own. When she blames Lady Waldemar for persuading Marian Earle to flee from marriage, she seems to have forgotten the words of Marian's farewell letter to Romney. In it Marian mentions Lady Waldemar's nine or ten visits but makes even more significant the single visit from Aurora: "ever since / I've pondered much a certain thing she asked . . . / 'He loves you, Marian?'" (IV. 944-946). Thinking of Lady Waldemar as the "shadow" aspect of Aurora's own psyche gives added significance to Lady Waldemar's parting words. In her farewell letter to Aurora she sneers at women poets as capable of scattered fine thoughts but wanting "string to tie our flowers" (IX. 59). She continues, "Male poets are preferable, straining less / And teaching more" (IX. 65-66). Hers is the voice of Aurora's own self-distrust, the disabling faithlessness of the inner oppressor.[9]

To recapitulate then: The portrait of Aurora's mother, not as it looks in fact (that, of course, is unknowable) but as in Aurora's imagination it appears, mirrors her ambivalence toward femininity itself. This ambivalence means that as a woman she "but slenderly knows herself," thus unwittingly causing both herself and others great pain and leading her to share, albeit unconsciously, in the very circle of woman-evil she wishes to avoid.

Because of her divided attitude toward being a woman, Aurora cannot recognize her own love for Romney—although other women in the poem, good and bad, know her feelings (IX. 685-687). Instead, she turns away from painful ambivalence by becoming identified with masculinity, a process in which Romney figures with importance yet with another kind of ambivalence. We must take it as highly significant not only that Romney is a first cousin who bears the same name but that he looks like Aurora: "Your droop of eyelid is the same as his," writes Lady Waldemar contemptuously (IX. 163); "Your cousin!—ah, most like you!" (IV. 939) is Marian's comment. Remembering Barrett Browning's love for her younger brother Edward, we might take the counsinship to be both vehicle for and bar to fantasies of incest. Without discounting that actual relationship as the creative source for Aurora's imagined one, I would suggest that the resemblance and relationship between them are significant in that they make of Romney Aurora's "alter ego," the brother in her soul. That thought was expressed as long ago as 1861 by J. Challen in the *National Quarterly Review,* who noted that "The whole of the interest of the story consists in the intellectual and moral development of two personages, both of whom are projections of Mrs. Browning's own nature" (*Works,* IV, 231), but the idea has had little subsequent exploration. Seeing Romney and Aurora in this way, as the dual expression of a single though ambivalent mind, provides a different, interiorized plot to the poem.

On Aurora's twentieth birthday Romney catches her as she is crowning herself with ivy leaves in a daydream of poetic success. He teases her and makes light of her capabilities, not only because he thinks little of the worth of poetry but because he believes that she as a woman can never write poetry of the first order. Then (with the worst possible sense of timing) he asks that she devote her life instead to helping him, as his wife, in the philanthropical works he thinks truly significant. In the verbal sparring between them which surrounds Romney's clumsy proposal, her subsequent refusal, and her departure for London, the metaphors used clearly show Aurora's identification with the masculine. Yet because her womanhood can never be completely denied or forgotten, the metaphors also blend and blur masculinity and femininity.

In thinking about herself as a poet, for instance, Aurora imagines herself as the effeminately beautiful young Trojan prince, Ganymede, whom Zeus's eagle carried up to Olympus to serve as cup-bearer. The cup of her poetry becomes in the image a masculine not a feminine instrument giving pleasure to the effeminized mouths of the gods, as she keeps "the mouths of all the godheads moist / For everlasting laughters" (I. 924-925).

Again, belief in herself as a poet leads Aurora to escape when possible from her conventional life as an English young lady and see herself as a deer—but a stag, not a doe: "I threw my hunters off and plunged myself / Among the deep hills, as a hunted stag / Will take the waters" (I. 1071-73). There are too many such examples to cite them all, but consider the complex image with which Aurora describes her father's instruction to her in the classic languages. She compares her situation to that of the young Achilles when his mother, Thetis the sea-nymph, hid him in women's clothing among the maidens at the court of Lycomedes so that he might not be called to serve in the Trojan War. He was wrapped in women's garments through a mother's agency, Aurora in man's through a father's:

> And thus, as did the women formerly
> By young Achilles, when they pinned a veil
> Across the boy's audacious front, and swept
> With tuneful laughs the silver-fretted rocks,
> He wrapt his little daughter in his large
> Man's doublet, careless did it fit or no.
>   (I. 723-728)

The poor "fit" of the doublet creates two problems. First of all, dividing as it does her sense of a self which is learned, poetic, and masculine from a self that is social, visible, and feminine, the masculine identification tends to exacerbate the very ambivalence toward the feminine which it promised to circumvent. Worse still, the doublet becomes a shirt of Nessus (if I may myself be allowed a metaphor) since it involves identification not only with learning and poetic power seen as male prerogatives but with all male attitudes, including male derogation of the feminine. So the sense of herself as masculine, which she feels she needs in order to think seriously of herself as a poet, becomes the sense also which eats into the flesh of her self-esteem. She is manlike (according to the culture's associations with masculinity) in some respects but not, after all, a man, just as Achilles was not a woman. Yet through cultural conditioning she shares men's feelings that men are inherently superior to women.

Thus in their first quarrel Romney's questioning of her powers is in fact only an expression, a projection of her own divided feelings about herself. We know Romney only through Aurora's consciousness of him, and at this point in their relationship he functions for her as the intellectual Charles Tansley does for Lily Briscoe in Virginia Woolf's *To the Lighthouse:* a voice in her head repeating, "Women can't write. Women can't paint." Or, to phrase the thought in Romney's image: "When Egypt's slain, I say, let Miriam sing! / Before—where's Moses?" (II. 171-172). A few lines later he repeats the idea more explicitly:

> Women as you are,
> Mere women, personal and passionate,
> You give us doating mothers, and perfect wives,
> Sublime Madonnas, and enduring saints!
> We get no Christ from you,—and verily
> We shall not get a poet, in my mind.
>   (II. 220-225)

To the Aurora who, as we have seen in the images just discussed, passionately identifies with male power and male leadership, and turns shuddering away from "doating mothers" and "perfect wives," Romney could find no bitterer terms than those which deny her any likeness to a Moses or a Christ. Her answering strategy is to use images that sneeringly feminize him. When she learns from her aunt after she has rejected Romney's proposal that in fact Romney agreed to an arrangement made years before between her father and his that the cousins marry in order to preserve for Aurora a share in the family fortune, she feels no gratitude. She enjoys instead seeing him in the situation of one of the most helpless women in mythology, the maiden Iphigenia sacrificed at Aulis so that the winds might blow her father's ships to Troy. Aurora herself becomes powerful and dominant (and therefore male), contemptuously ordering not death but release:

> Ah, self-tied
> By a contract, male Iphigenia bound
> At a fatal Aulis for the winds to change
> (But loose him, they'll not change).
>   (II. 778-781)

As she leaves for London, Romney writes one last appeal, bungling matters as hopelessly—or as stubbornly—as ever by seeing her still as his feminine "angel in the house":

> Write woman's verses and dream woman's
>   dreams;
> But let me feel your perfume in my home
> To make my sabbath after working-days.
>   (II. 831-833)

The Keatsian synesthesia of his "let me feel your perfume" gives her the retort she needs. In an image reminiscent of that which describes the virginal Madeline of "The Eve of St. Agnes"—"Clasp'd like a missal where swart Paynims pray"—Aurora writes back to Romney:

> I know your heart,
> And shut it like the holy book it is,
> Reserved for mild-eyed saints to pore upon
> Betwixt their prayers at vespers.
>
> (II. 836-839)

Her image makes him one in spirit and kind with the angel-wife he has described and transforms her into a Byronic worldling with a heart of gold who resists attempting the angel's seduction.

In the short run this reversal of roles is a satisfying vent for anger. The difficulty at its center lies in the fact that by feeling the lofty kindness mixed with contempt typical of a masculine cavalier toward a Romney whom she has made feminine and passive, she shares in the very derogation of the feminine which she justly resents. She cannot really win that way either. By the end of the second book of the poem, in fact, we can see—and the images underline the fact—that her male identification has led her to scorn women and has cut her off as well from the possibility of loving a man.

The plot of this verse novel is blocked out in the traditional form of introduction, rising action, turning point or crisis, falling action, climax, and resolution. Near the center of the poem comes the critical insight which will show her the way through the psychic impasse just described. At what was to be his wedding, as Romney lamely attempts to explain Marian's nonappearance to an angry mob of paupers and instead rouses them to attack him, Aurora suddenly "sees":

> with a cry
> I struggled to precipitate myself
> Head-foremost to the rescue of my soul
> In that white face.
>
> (IV. 873-876)

Interestingly, just before that moment, Romney is described for the first time in strongly masculine terms as standing his ground "with his masterful pale face,— / As huntsmen throw the ration to the pack" (IV. 850-851). The image, coming where it does, suggests that the conscious recognition of how deeply she is identified with Romney, how much, that is, she has internalized masculine values, makes it possible for Aurora to return his masculinity to him as something which, so to speak, they share. The same consciousness, though, brings the first glimmering sense of how much her femininity suffers from this identification, an awareness which will make eventually possible her reconciliation with her own womanhood. But first the glimmer must grow. She must see how negative a force the "Romney-in-her-mind" is to her poetic gift. In the long meditation on art which begins the fifth book, Aurora chides herself as "womanish" for her dependence on Romney's good opinion of her and comes in the process to see that her image of her poetic power as a masculine figure is the source also of her self-doubt. She describes that image with the word used earlier of Romney, "my soul":

> But I am sad:
> I cannot thoroughly love a work of mine,
> Since none seems worthy of my thought and hope
> More highly mated. He has shot them down,
> My Phoebus Apollo, soul within my soul,
> Who judges, by the attempted, what's attained,
> And with the silver arrow from his height
> Has struck down all my works before my face
> While I said nothing. Is there aught to say?
> I called the artist but a greatened man.
> He may be childless also, like a man.
>
> (V. 410-420)

"Epipsychidion"—"soul within my soul"—the phrase which for Shelley signified union with a feminine Muse leading to the rapturous artistic fertility which is the concluding vision of his poem—is for Aurora a sterile union because she can think of any artist, herself included, only as a man. Her first use of the word "man" in the lines just quoted seems generic, but the second, emphasizing as it does the humanly biological, shifts its meaning subtly to give the impression that *real* poets are in fact *men*. That niggling thought sterilizes her imagination.

The next important stage in Aurora's process of self-understanding is described not through images but in overt action and statement, consistent with the increasing clarification she experiences. After she has heard Marian's pathetic story of being sold to a brothel and there raped, angry at herself for the mental judgments she has been making about Marian's illegitimate child, Aurora embraces her. She uses a significant phrase to describe the moment: "I . . . / *With woman's passion* clung about her waist / And kissed her hair and eyes" (VI. 778-780, my italics). And as she asks Marian to accompany her to Italy, she calls her a friend. Together they will be "two mothers" to the child (VII. 124). Thus, her identification with Marian as woman both in the sexual humiliation Marian has endured and in the ecstatic joy of motherhood she has experienced reconciles Aurora more than ever before in the poem to her own womanhood. The incident has another significance as well in what Barrett Browning calls the "double action" of the poem.[10] It is the first instance in which we see the imaginative Aurora involved in the physical care of a fellow human being, while just at this time, we learn later, the actively charitable Romney lies quiet for the first time, listening to and deeply moved by Aurora's poetry. The split between "masculine" activity and "feminine" spiritual insight is disappearing.

The new advance in Aurora's acceptance of womanhood brings with it a virtually simultaneous recognition of her true feeling for Romney, but a recognition mingled with despair at the belief that she has lost him to the villainous Lady Waldemar. Broken in spirit, she is still enough the old Aurora to despise her tears as womanish; yet even this thought brings with it a sudden understanding of the problem described earlier with so many obscure images: "It seems as if I had a man in me, / Despising such a woman" (VII. 212-213). Previously her sense of this internal man's contempt had made all her struggles to act creatively seem petty and useless. Open recognition of his presence makes it possible for her to use him—in this case to act in making Marian's true history known to Romney:

> If, as I have just now said,
> A man's within me,—let him act himself,
> Ignoring the poor conscious trouble of blood
> That's called the woman merely.
> (VII. 229-232)

It remains for these new insights to permeate, inform, and metamorphose her sense of herself as an artist, yeast in the loaf. Their effects become visible in Aurora's culminating meditations in Book VII on the meaning of art. The terms of her ideas themselves are deeply neoplatonic, but explication of them, while important to any consideration of Barrett Browning's aesthetic theory, is not relevant to the theme I have been tracing. What is significant in that connection, however, is the image Aurora associates with the artist both at the beginning and at the end of the passage on artistic endeavor. She sees the artist, she sees herself as an artist, no longer as boyish Ganymede plucked up by Jove's eagle, but as Io, the young girl whom Jove transformed into a heifer to hide her from a suspicious Juno. The myth usually describes Juno, not fooled for a moment, as the deity who sends a gadfly to pursue Io. Aurora, interestingly, associates the gadfly instead with Jove as another version of the tormenting yet activating "man within." The artist's sense of truth hounds her, she says:

> As Jove did Io; and, until that Hand
> Shall overtake me wholly and on my head
> Lay down its large unfluctuating peace,
> The feverish gad-fly pricks me up and down.
> (VII. 830-833)

The final reconciliation with her womanhood comes in a Florentine church as she watches the women—of course they are women, she notes—praying. A detached observer, male or at least asexual in that she *is* detached from these women worshippers, she sees a hunchbacked spinster, a young girl, an old woman. Out of the confused and drab lives of these "poor blind souls," she muses, God must somehow bring salvation. Then a sudden jolting recognition interrupts these thoughts in which she as artist hobnobs with God, as it were, about the spiritual condition of beings very different from herself. She has described the women as young ravens who "cry for carrion." There comes a break in the line, and she exclaims:

> O my God,
> And we, who make excuses for the rest,
> We do it in our measure. Then I knelt,
> And dropped my head upon the pavement too,
> And prayed, since I was foolish in desire
> Like other creatures, craving offal-food,
> That He would stop His ears to what I said,
> And only listen to the run and beat
> Of this poor, passionate, helpless blood
>   And then
> I lay, and spoke not: but He heard in heaven.
> (VII. 1263-72)

If I may skip ahead for a moment, I believe that these lines offer the true explication for the famous statement near the conclusion, "Art is much, but Love is more!" (IX. 656), which is often interpreted as Aurora's utter capitulation and retreat into Victorian domesticity as the angel in Romney's house. I believe Barrett Browning's point rather is that although the artist—here the literary artist—uses words and forms them into images, "the deep truth is imageless," and her response to that truth as a human can only be wordless. Her thought is one put in other terms by T. S. Eliot when he writes in *Four Quartets:* "The poetry does not matter." Neither Eliot nor Barrett Browning, of course, is denying the worth of the struggle to express artistically the vision of life which each holds true, but they both believe that vision to transcend any possible expression of it.

The silence of the moment in the church lengthens out, becomes a period for which Jungians could use the alchemical term "nigredo"—a blackening, a deliquescence and decomposition of materials in the alembic whose conclusion seems annihilation but is actually metamorphosis. Barrett Browning's image carries the same thought as she describes "quickening glooms" in which Aurora sits, not reading, writing, or even thinking, "Most like some passive broken lump of salt / Dropped in by chance to a bowl of oenomel" (VII. 1308-09).

In that state of dissolution, the speck of salt drowned in the honey-drink, she gazes out one evening on what in one sense is the city of Florence spread out beneath her but is more truly the vision of her own inner depths, seeing "some drowned city in some enchanted sea, / Cut off from nature" (VIII. 38-39). There her quickening imagination spies "the man within" but in a new form:

> a sea-king with a voice of waves,
> And treacherous soft eyes, and slippery locks
> You cannot kiss but you shall bring away
> Their salt upon your lips.
>
> (VIII. 41-44)

Not Phoebus Apollo now with his arrow of judgment to annihilate her work, nor Jove to goad yet mock her with unfulfillable fantasies of power, but a force through which she can explore her own inner deeps—that is what he has become. All his negative qualities seem to have vanished save for the treachery in his "soft eyes" and the slipperiness of a presence no sooner promised than withdrawn.

Then Romney Leigh appears on her balcony: "the sea king! In my ears / The sound of waters. There he stood, my king!" (VIII. 60-61). He is hers, and he is blind.

But why? Why did Barrett Browning feel that Romney must be blinded? An exhaustive answer to that question would demand an essay of its own, involving as it does a number of fictitious Victorian gentlemen blinded and often maimed as well by their feminine creators to the unease of Victorian reviewers and the horror of later Freudian critics.[11] Barrett Browning's ladylike but implacable response to remonstrance on the subject, "He had to be blinded, observe, to be made to see . . . I am sorry, but indeed it seemed necessary,"[12] is not a particularly enlightening answer, since Aurora too comes to "see" herself and others very much better in the course of the poem but is physically unscathed in the process.

Many difficulties involving the justice meted out to Romney as a fictional personality become irrelevant, however, if we continue to think of him as a projection of the man within Aurora and thus a vehicle for Barrett Browning's extended meditation on the experience of being both woman and artist. In these terms, the answer to why the sea-king's soft eyes are "treacherous" will also explain why Romney must be blinded. And surely that answer lies in an association between the sea-king's eyes and the eyes of Phoebus Apollo which aim his "silver arrow" of judgmental criticism. Blinded, the sea-king/Romney is not castrated or weakened; on the contrary, he is a far more effective because an undivided source of poetic power.

Up to this point in the poem the "man within" had been essentially Aurora's critic and thus an aspect of that self-distrust which Barrett Browning sees as the principal barrier to women's achievement.[13] When she has Aurora complain of the prating about "women's rights" and "women's mission," she is speaking to this point, not rebuking feminist effort; a woman's lack of faith in herself—"she must prove what she can do / Before she does it" (VIII. 818-819)—makes her talk rather than act, stultifying her creative élan.

As Aurora comes to love and trust her own womanhood, Romney, no longer a critic, becomes a Muse. As such he is the dramatic projection of that faith in self—blind faith if you will—and self-acceptance which underlie all true creativity, whether in the arts, in social endeavor, or in human interaction. Aurora's creative gift and Romney's belief in it form "Love, the soul of soul, within the soul, / Evolving it sublimely" (IX. 880-881). Their reunion on the starlit balcony is not a prelude to a life of Victorian domesticity with the roles amusingly reversed, she the worker, Romney the loving helpmate; much less is it an idealized version of the Brownings' romance. "They," Aurora and Romney, are the united spirit of a creative woman at last trustful of her power.

Notes

[1] Ellen Moers, *Literary Women* (Garden City, N. J., 1976), pp. 55-62; Patricia Thomson, *George Sand and the Victorians* (London, 1977), pp. 54-60; Cora Kaplan, "Introduction," *Aurora Leigh and Other Poems* (London, 1978), pp. 5-36.

[2] *The Letters of Elizabeth Barrett Browning*, ed. Frederic G. Kenyon (London, 1897), II, 228.

[3] Rpt. in *The Complete Works of Mrs. E. B. Browning*, Arno edition, ed. Charlotte Porter and Helen A. Clarke (New York, 1901), IV, 206. Ellen Moers compares the "jumble of metaphors in *Aurora Leigh*" to "the clutter of objects on a Victorian table top" (*Literary Women*, p. 62).

[4] All citations from *Aurora Leigh* are taken from Volumes IV and V of the Arno edition, hereafter cited as *Works*. Roman numerals refer to the nine books of the poem, Arabic to the line numbers.

[5] Barrett's words are "Scarcely was I woman when I lost *my* mother—dearest as she was & very tender, . . . but of a nature harrowed up into some furrows by the pressure of circumstances. . . . A sweet, gentle nature, which the thunder a little turned from its sweetness—as when it turns milk—One of those women who never can resist,—but, in submitting & bowing on themselves, make a mark, a plait, within, . . . a sign of suffering" (*The Letters of Robert Browning and Elizabeth Barrett Barrett 1845-1846*, ed. Elvan Kintner [Harvard Univ. Press, 1969], II, 1012).

[6] *The Barretts at Hope End: The Early Diary of Elizabeth Barrett Browning,* ed. Elizabeth Berridge (London, 1974), p. 137.

[7] Kaplan has a similar thought when she describes the portrait as "the representation of women in western culture" (*Aurora Leigh,* p. 20), but does not explain the ambivalent images.

[8] C. G. Jung, "The Shadow," *Aion: Researches into the Phenomenology of the Self* (Princeton Univ. Press, 1959), pp. 8-10.

[9] The thought is close to Barrett Browning's "secret profession of faith" made to Robert Browning in July, 1845, but is not, given my interpretation of *Aurora Leigh,* to be taken as her final opinion: "There *is* a natural inferiority of mind in women—of the intellect ... not by any means, of the moral nature" (*Letters,* ed. Kintner, I, 113).

[10] *Letters,* ed. Kenyon, II, 243.

[11] One of her reviewers, for instance, murmured, "We think the lavish mutilation of heroes' bodies, which has become the habit of novelists, while it happily does not represent probabilities in the present state of things, weakens instead of strengthening tragic effect" (*Works,* IV, 204). The best-known modern statement of distress over the Victorian literary women's imaginary violence toward their heroes is Richard Chase's essay, "The Brontës, or Myth Domesticated," in *Forms of Modern Fiction,* ed. William Van O'Connor (Univ. of Minnesota Press, 1948), pp. 102-119. For a reconsideration of the meaning of the motif, cf. Elaine Showalter, *A Literature of Their Own: British Women Novelists from Brontë to Lessing* (Princeton Univ. Press, 1977), p. 150.

[12] *Letters,* ed. Kenyon, II, 242.

[13] I am grateful to Sandra Donaldson, whose comments on an earlier version of this essay helped me to clarify this point. *The Madwoman in the Attic* (Yale Univ. Press, 1979) was published while this paper was in press, and so I could not incorporate the fine ideas of Sandra Gilbert and Susan Gubar about *Aurora Leigh.*

Dorothy Mermin (essay date 1986)

SOURCE: "Genre and Gender in *Aurora Leigh*, in *The Victorian Newsletter,* No. 69, Spring, 1986, pp. 7-11.

[*In this essay, Mermin contends that* Aurora Leigh *transgresses the distinction between poetry and fiction, and between males and females, claiming that the "novel in verse" ends "with an assertion of the primacy of poetry's world and values over the novel's, and of women over men."*]

Elizabeth Barrett Browning devoured novels voraciously and indiscriminately, especially French ones of a kind that a respectable Englishwoman could hardly admit to knowing. In novels she found some of the experience of life that her sex and seclusion had denied her, and that she felt she needed to give color and reality both to her life and to her art. She was thinking of prose fiction in these terms in 1845 when she described the project that was to issue twelve years later as ***Aurora Leigh***. "My chief *intention* just now," she said, "is the writing of a sort of novel-poem . . . running into the midst of our conventions, & rushing into drawing-rooms & the like, 'where angels fear to tread'; & so, meeting face to face & without mask the Humanity of the age, & speaking the truth as I conceive of it, out plainly" (***Letters,*** ed. Kintner, 1:31).

Of all the important Victorian long poems, ***Aurora Leigh*** is the only "novel-poem," or novel in verse. Arthur Hugh Clough in exuberant youth and Robert Browning late in his career wrote what might be called long short stories—*The Bothie of Tober-na-Vuolich, Red-Cotton Night-Cap Country, The Inn Album*—but these are not really much like novels. Unlike other long Victorian poems, ***Aurora Leigh*** is a continuous story told retrospectively by a single speaker, with a contemporary setting and a thoroughly novelistic plot—that of the *bildungsroman,* or more specifically the *kunstlerroman*—much of which in fact is borrowed from other novels. Like a Victorian novel, it is deeply attentive to characterization and to the development of character and of relationships through time; it is analytic and satirical in its presentation of society, rushing not only into drawing-rooms but into slums and brothels as well, and running more fearlessly than an angel into immediate questions of political philosophy and social reform with which contemporary novelists were also very much concerned. But its heightened feeling and language, especially its elaborate metaphors and ostentatious epic similes, are deeply and often obtrusively "poetical."

Aurora herself insists that genre—or form—does not matter:

> What form is best for poems? Let me think
> Of forms less, and the external. Trust the spirit,
> As sovran nature does, to make the form;
> For otherwise we only imprison spirit
> And not embody. Inward evermore
> To outward,—so in life, and so in art
> Which still is life.
>
> (V. 223-229)

A play, she says, should have as many acts as it needs—fifteen, perhaps, or ten, or seven (V. 229-239). She would not think the work in which she herself appears disqualified for epic status by having only nine books. Such disdain for genre rules was common in the nineteenth century: the Victorians wrote poems in all sorts of strange and nameless forms without worrying about how to define them. Generically, *Aurora Leigh* was only one anomaly among many, but it was a peculiarly bold one.

Early readers of *Aurora Leigh,* like many later ones, were deeply struck and also, often, profoundly disturbed by its transgressions, in particular by its apparent violations of *two* boundaries: between poetry and fiction, and between masculine and feminine—the boundaries, that is, of genre, and of gender. Reviewers distinguished between poetic and novelistic aspects, regardless of whether or not they approved of the mixture or of which parts they preferred; some admired the intensely poetical sections which others found strained and excessive, while some liked the pathos, or the social satire. Many found large parts of it beneath the dignity of verse. *The Athenaeum* sympathetically recognized it as something difficult to assess, because unprecedented: "we have no experience of such a mingling of what is precious with what is mean—of the voice of clarion and the lyric cadence of harp with the cracked schoolroom spinet—of tears and small-talk—of eloquent apostrophe and adust speculation—of the grandeur of passion and the pettiness of modes and manners—as we find in these nine books of blank verse. Milton's organ is put by Mrs. Browning to play polkas in May-Fair drawing-rooms" (1425).

Milton's organ (by which expressive phrase the reviewer means, of course, that exclusively male form the epic) in a lady's drawing-room—transgressions of genre and gender go together, as Tennyson showed when he symbolized the relations of men and women in *The Princess* by the juxtaposition of narrative and lyric. (In *The Princess,* however, the two elements meet but do not mingle.) The blurring of sexual boundaries in *Aurora Leigh* was remarked by reviewers with varying degrees of pleasure or distress. It was a matter not just of plot or setting or character, but of the gender characteristics of the poem as a whole. Leigh Hunt saw a wonderful mixture of "masculine power and feminine tenderness' in it (739), and George Eliot made the same point more fully: Mrs. Browning, she said, "is, perhaps, the first woman who has produced a work which exhibits all the peculiar powers without the negations of her sex; which superadds to masculine vigour, breadth, and culture, feminine subtlety of perception, feminine quickness of sensibility, and feminine tenderness" (306). Others, however, while equally excited, were less pleased. A reviewer for the *Westminster Review* complained that the poet used to "prove her manhood" by the coarseness of her language and an "ostentation of strength" (401, 400). Several thought Aurora herself disagreeably unwomanly. They found transgressions of other boundaries, too: between the "universal element" and "the peculiarities of our time," and between the beautiful and the repulsive (Everett 441, 423) as well as in mixed metaphors, in lines written by a woman not fit for women to read, and, in general, in sins against taste and decorum that crossed the boundary between literature and parts of life that could not be written about. (There are others, too: the fact that Aurora's name after marriage to Romney Leigh will still be Aurora Leigh, for instance, eradicates the line between daughter and wife; Marian is sexually violated and yet remains pure, mother and maid at once; and Virginia Woolf heard the author's voice too clearly in the poem and found, as one might with many poets of mid-century, that her life impinges too much on her art (222).

Transgressions of genre and of gender in *Aurora Leigh,* along with the lesser transgressions that these subsume, are linked as interrelated parts of Barrett Browning's attempt to remake the structures she had inherited from male predecessors in order to create a place for herself. Victorian women poets tended to use narrative or a narrative frame whenever they wanted to express feelings, ideas, or relationships that did not fit the conventions and implied narrative contexts of poetic tradition. Emily Brontë's strange and violent lyrics spring from the Gondal story and are often inexplicable without it. Christina Rossetti seems in her religious and amatory short lyrics to be expressing only the kinds of experience—yearning, resignation, renunciation, self-repression, and so on in that dreary litany of sorrow—appropriate to female figures in nineteenth-century poetry; she put her rebellious or radically unconventional feelings about sexuality and the relations between the sexes into narratives like "Goblin Market" and "The Prince's Progress," which give quite unexpected contexts and meanings to the feelings expressed in the lyrics. Barrett Browning's early explorations of woman's lot and of her own unconscious feelings come mostly in the form of ballads or strange, dream-like narratives: lyric would not accommodate them. She expresses a mother's murderous ambivalence towards her baby, for instance, not in lyric—simply as lyric, it would have been incomprehensible and shocking, and therefore inexpressible—but in a long dramatic monologue that justifies the feeling with a narrative context of slavery, rape, and racial difference. By turning not just to narrative but to the novel, furthermore, she could escape the dominance of male forerunners and place herself in a powerful female tradition. Once she had said of the English poets, "I look everywhere for grandmothers and see none" (*Letters,* ed. Kenyon, 1: 232): but the family resemblances between Aurora Leigh and Corinne, Consuelo, and Jane Eyre, or between Marian Erle and Mrs. Gaskell's Ruth—aunts and cousins at least, if not grandmothers—suggests similar relationships among their authors, even if Barrett Browning herself did not care to acknowledge them.

The contemporary life in which the poem is set, furthermore, offered Barrett Browning a world that seemed uniquely rich in opportunities for a woman poet. Her male contemporaries, oppressed by a sense of belatedness, did not find it so. Arthur Hallam, for instance, thought the nineteenth century a late and tired time for poetry—the nation was hostile to "the poetic impulse," he said, and so poets were inevitably melancholy and withdrawn (189, 190). Matthew Arnold exhorted his friend Clough to reflect on "how deeply *unpoetical* the age and all one's surroundings are. Not unprofound, not ungrand, not unmoving:—but *unpoetical*" (99). Dante Gabriel Rossetti told William Morris that it was better to paint pictures than write poems, because the poetry "'has all been said and written'" (Mackail 1: 110). Romney Leigh (whose function is to represent the male viewpoint, although not a poet's) speaks in a similar vein of "the world we've come to late," "swollen hard / With generations perished of their sins" (II. 160, 263). *The Idylls of the King* and *The Ring and the Book* are set far in the past, well away from Victorian England. *Maud, Modern Love* and *Amours de Voyage* uneasily test out poetic attitudes in contemporary, novelistic settings which make them look ineffectual and silly—unlike ***Aurora Leigh***, in which juxtapositions of lyric intensity and modern daily life are not *intended* (whatever their effect may be) to play off against or diminish each other. But for women poets there was no lost heroic age to be regretted, no female tradition that could make a modern women's poetry look inadequate or out of place. On the contrary: when Elizabeth Barrett was a child she intended to become (as she put it later) "the feminine of Homer" (*The Brownings' Correspondence* 1: 361), the first and greatest of women poets—and although she soon learned to moderate this ambition, it seemed to many people even before ***Aurora Leigh*** was published, and still more afterwards, that she had achieved it. Aurora herself sets out to prove that women can be poets (II. 1181-1187), and before the poem ends she has done so. She is Aurora, the *dawn* of a new era.

Elizabeth Barrett's problem from the very beginning had been to find an epic subject that would accommodate a female hero, and this too led her to value her own times. While male poets were finding heroes, if at all, in the past (Thackeray wrote his great novel of nineteenth-century England explicitly without one), Elizabeth Barrett had looked backwards and seen no more female heroes than poetic grandmothers. ***The Battle of Marathon***, published when she was fourteen, is an Homeric epic about male warriors, with no women in it except goddesses and a few Athenian "matrons" who only get in the way of the action and are quickly disposed of. Her next long poem, ***The Seraphim***, evades the issue by having no human characters at all, dramatizing the crucifixion through the conversation of a couple of angels. *A Drama of Exile* does find a heroine, but only by going through and beyond Milton all the way back to the first woman and presenting the fall and its aftermath from the point of view of Eve—who can be heroic, unfortunately only through her repentance and her ability to suffer. Barrett Browning also wrote ballad-narratives, but Aurora Leigh scornfully describes women in the ballad world as "half chattel and half queen" (as they are in her author's ballads and also, we might add, in the poems by Tennyson and Browning that are set in a similar world: despite Browning's poetical woman-worship and exemplary behavior to his wife, or Tennyson's somewhat feminized heroes, their poems—even *The Princess,* in the end—rigidly adhere to conventional gender roles for women; imagine a female knight in Tennyson's Camelot, where "work" is represented only as fighting battles, or a Pompilia who can write). There are no happy endings for women—no attainment of power, work, or even love—in Barrett Browning's narratives until **"Lady Geraldine's Courtship,"** when she finally arrives (and she was almost forty years old by then) in modern times.

Male poets resisted with varying degrees of firmness critics' frequent injunctions to write on modern subjects. Matthew Arnold in sheer perverseness went so far as to compose a shamelessly ersatz Greek tragedy. Browning wrote two long narratives with contemporary settings, *Red Cotton Night-Cap Country* and *The Inn Album,* but they show a world in which all attempts at heroism turn out to be foolish, useless, and perverse. But Aurora Leigh joyfully declares that poetry is still possible, that even Homer's heroes were only men, that all men (by which word, as usual, she means women) are possible heroes, and that every age can be heroic (V. 146-153). Poets'

> sole work is to represent the age,
> Their age, not Charlemagne's,—this live, throbbing age,
> That brawls, cheats, maddens, calculates, aspires,
> And spends more passion, more heroic heat,
> Betwixt the mirrors of its drawing-rooms,
> Than Roland with his knights at Roncesvalles.
> (V. 202-207)

In drawing rooms, of course, there are women. ***Aurora Leigh*** is the "unscrupulously epic" (in Aurora's words [V.214]—"unscrupulous" because it does not respect prescribed boundaries) culmination of Barrett Browning's epic ambitions.

The novelistic form did more than replace the epic structures that had excluded women. It offered a way to explore a woman poet's place both in the world and—a more subtle, interesting, and important matter—in poems. As poet, Aurora is conceived by herself and others in various discrepant ways: as the Muse (III.363; V.796) and antithetically as Danae impregnated by Jove, as the mother of works which have died in embryo (III.247-248) or been killed like Niobe's children. But muses don't write, and mothers as nineteenth-century women poets see them don't either. In a gloomy moment she thinks of herself as Niobe (in contradistinction to Pygmalion): her poems are not separate creations like Pygmalion's Galatea but are born like a woman's children from her own flesh—her children, parts of herself—and unlike Pygmalion she cannot satisfy with art her need for love. Often she is thought of (in the common Victorian habit, railed at by some poets, practiced by almost all) as herself a work of art: a book that others "dog-ear" (V. 1054) or refuse to read. She both speaks and *is* the poem whose name is also her own, and she spends a lot of time trying to distinguish between her poems and herself.

Barrett Browning works out the question of a woman poet's place *within* poems, however—as informing intelligence and speaking subject rather than object and other—mostly in terms of Aurora's relations with the kinds of female figures who normally appear in nineteenth-century poems by men but could not themselves be poets or epic protagonists. There is no natural place in a poem for a woman like Aurora unless she chooses either to exist simply as the object of male desire, essentially speechless (which is what Romney proposes early on), or—if she wants to speak—to speak only her unapparently unrequited love. She refuses to take those places: she sends Romney away and doesn't acknowledge her love—that is, doesn't speak it except by indirection—until nearly the end of the story. *Her* predecessors come from novels, not poems; they are Corinne and Jane Eyre. And yet she is in a poem, not in a novel, and like her creator she is a poet. What, then, is her relation to the kind of women who *do* inhabit poems, appearing in them as erotic object, or mysterious Other? This is perhaps the central problem that the poem has to work out, and her relations to women are therefore exceptionally intense.

Are they possible selves, since she's a woman too? Or objects of desire, since she's the poet? She experiences men as belonging to the world of what Myra Jehlen calls exteriority (596, 598) and describes them coolly, usually satirically—even her father, even Romney; but the female characters have an almost mythic depth and intensity and arouse her strongest, most complex feelings. Aurora is looking for a mother in relation to whom she might find her place and her identity: in the tradition of women's *bildungsromanen*, the poem traces the heroine's attempt to return to the pre-Oedipal maternal world figured by nature. Of her own dead mother she has only the recollection of a few words spoken to her—"Hush, hush—here's too much noise" ([I.17] a legacy that would preclude for a girl who wants to write any simple possibility of identification with her mother); and a deeply ambiguous portrait in which she appears as the composite of woman in her various roles as literary object, "Ghost, fiend, and angel, fairy, witch, and sprite" (I.154), Lamia and Our Lady of the Passion, a portrait onto which Aurora projects her fantasies and her experiences of women in literature. This is woman as mysterious Other; Aurora can neither become her—for then she would cease to be the speaking subject, nor—because she is a woman herself—establish a relationship with her.

And so the image splits into two somewhat more realistic, novelized figures; virtuous Marian Erle and wicked Lady Waldemar, the victimized innocent and the predatory sophisticate, the good mother and the bad. They bear in their names, however, the traces of the mythicized female figures of the preternatural and of nature from whom they spring: *Marian Erle,* virgin mother and fairy, Lady *Waldemar* (wald-e-mar) of the forest and the sea. The original image also spills over onto other figures that are female for male poets, turning what is safely metaphorical in men's writings into something disturbingly literal. The Romantic poets' maternal Nature turns into the explicitly breast-like hills of Italy; and the image of the "Mother-Age," which is almost inert when Tennyson uses it in "Locksley Hall," has the power to shock even now in Barrett Browning's version. "Hide me from my deep emotion, O thou wondrous Mother-Age," Tennyson's hero innocuously cries (line 108); but Aurora Leigh, astonishingly, says:

> Never flinch,
> Eat still, unscrupulously epic, catch
> Upon the burning lava of a song
> The full-veined, heaving, double-breasted Age:
> That, when the next shall come, the men of that
> May touch the impress with reverent hand, and say
> "Behold,—behold the paps we all have sucked!
> This bosom seems to beat still. . . .
> (V. 213-220)

What Aurora learns from her intense relations with these various figures, who together represent the normal female population of poetry, is first, that she isn't one of them; and second, that she doesn't, after all, have to define herself as a poet in terms of her relation to them. That is, she is neither the female object of a male poem, nor the male subject for whom these figures are objects of desire. This is figured in her detachment at last from Lady Waldemar and Marian, in her changing relation to Romney, and in the diminishing of her uncomfortable awareness of herself as a physical object, something to be seen. The first effect of Romney's declaration of love is that everybody seems to be looking at her all the time—even the servants, even the dog; her aunt dies, in effect, as a result of such looking: as soon as Aurora wishes that her aunt would "'sleep, / And spare [her] yet the burden of [her] eyes'" (II.909-910), she discovers that the offending eyes are sightless in death. She accepts Romney's love only when he too is blind, his blindness signaling the crucial reversal of roles and power between them. His arrival at the end of the story is heralded by her image of him as her "sea-king"—a male version of the mysterious, half natural half human erotic Other that men have figured as a mermaid. When she rejected his love, early in the story, she spoke of his heart as a book that she would not read any more (II.836-837); now, accepting his place as text or object rather than beholder, he describes himself as a book that she has "dog-eared" (VIII.77) and asks her to reopen it. She can look, with or without desire, as she pleases, at him, but he can't look at her. She is no longer the object; she has defined a new space for a woman: as epic protagonist, as speaking subject.

But this is not simply a matter of reversing roles, which can only be done in very limited ways, at least in nineteenth-century poems. Barrett Browning retains the identification of woman with the inner, spiritual, emotional, and subjective sphere that she found everywhere, in poetry, in fiction, and in the fictions of life itself, which identifies women with poems. She doesn't switch gender roles; instead, she switches the locus of power within them. She asserts that power resides only in the inner life: in poetry, that is, and in women, and so in the woman poet most of all. Romney is forced to acknowledge that social change will be brought about not by politicians, philosophers, or philanthropists, but by poets. In the story's final and decisive transgression of the lines of gender, Romney asserts that when they marry, Aurora will "work for two"—real "work" having been defined as writing poems—and he "for two, shall love" (IX.911-912). The novelistic story concludes, that is, with an assertion of the primacy of poetry's world and values over the novel's, and of women over men.

Perhaps the oddest thing of all about *Aurora Leigh* is the thoroughly happy ending—happy for the heroine, at any rate, if not for her disempowered and humiliated lover. *The Idylls of the King, The Ring and Book, Empedocles on Etna, Modern Love, Amours de Voyage*—all the great long Victorian poems end in failure or loss (except, perhaps, *In Memoriam,* which begins there). Heroines of novels don't do much better: even Jane Eyre has no real independence, no vocation comparable to Brontë's or Barrett Browning's. Maggie Tulliver dies, and Dorothea Brooke exerts a quiet and unacknowledged influence as the wife of a political reformer, settling into precisely the sort of life that Aurora indignantly rejects when Romney offers it to her. It has often been remarked that women novelists do not imagine lives for their heroines that are as successful, in terms of achievment or scope for achievement, as their own (see Heilbrun 71-92). But in her strange mix of genres, Barrett Browning did what women novelists had not done, and perhaps could not do. Alone among heroines of *bildungsromanen* in the nineteenth century, Aurora follows the central part of the male pattern of development as Jerome Hamilton Buckley describes it: she leaves the provinces, goes to the city, and has (in effect) two love-affairs, one debasing and one ennobling (Lady Waldemar, that is, and Marian Erle [17-18]).[1] The novelistic context and elaboration of plot allows Aurora to work her way out of the passive position of erotic object to which women in *poems* had been relegated; and at the same time the poetry establishes a context in which freedom and the heroic triumph of the spirit feel not only appropriate but possible and which (if the poem is successful for us) proves, in the very texture of the work, its energy, zest, and self-confidence, the heroine's vocation. By transgressing the boundaries of genre—by appealing not from literature to life, but from one genre to another, and back again—*Aurora Leigh* goes farther than any other poem or novel of the Victorian period towards transcending the limits imposed on literature by gender.

Notes

[1] The pattern of the female *bildungsroman,* which differs notably from the male version, is analyzed by Abel, Hirsch, and Langland. *Aurora Leigh* has many of the characteristics of both kinds.

Works Cited

Abel, Elizabeth, Marianne Hirsch, and Elizabeth Langland. *The Voyage In: Fictions of Female Development.* Hanover, N. H.: UP of New England, 1983.

Arnold, Matthew. *The Letters of Matthew Arnold to Arthur Hugh Clough.* Ed. Howard Foster Lowry. Oxford: Clarendon Press, 1932.

Rev. of *Aurora Leigh. The Athenaeum* 1517 (Nov. 22, 1856): 1425-1427.

Rev. of *Aurora Leigh. Westminster Review* 68, n. s. 12 (1857): 399-415.

Barrett, Elizabeth Barrett and Robert Browning. *The Letters of Robert Browning and Elizabeth Barrett Barrett 1845-1846.* Ed. Elvan Kintner. 2 vols. Cambridge, Mass: Harvard UP, 1969.

Browning, Elizabeth Barrett. *The Complete Works of Elizabeth Barrett Browning.* Ed. Charlotte Porter and Helen A. Clarke, 6 vols. 1900. Rpt. ed. New York: AMS, 1973.

———. *The Letters of Elizabeth Barrett Browning.* Ed. Frederic G. Kenyon. 4th ed. 2 vols. London: Smith Elder, 1898.

———, and Robert Browning. *The Brownings' Correspondence.* Ed. Philip Kelley and Ronald Hudson. 2 vols. to date, Winfield, KS: Wedgestone Press, 1984–.

Buckley, Jerome Hamilton, *Season of Youth: The Bildungsroman from Dickens to Golding.* Cambridge, Mass.: Harvard UP, 1974.

[Eliot, George.] Rev. of *Aurora Leigh. Westminster Review* 67, n.s. 11 (1857): 306-310.

[Everett, Charles Carroll.] "Elizabeth Barrett Browning." *North American Review* 85 (1857): 415-441.

Hallam, Arthur, "On Some of the Characteristics of Modern Poetry, and on the Lyrical Poems of Alfred Tennyson." *The Writings of Arthur Hallam.* Ed. T. H. Vail Motter. New York: Modern Language Association of America, 1943. 182-198.

Heilbrun, Carolyn. "Women Writers and Female Characters: The Failure of Imagination." *Reinventing Womanhood.* New York: W. W. Norton, 1979. 71-92.

[Hunt, Leigh.] "*Aurora Leigh:* an Unpublished Letter from Leigh Hunt." *Cornhill Magazine* n. s. 3 (1897): 738-749.

Jehlen, Myra. "Archimedes and the Paradox of Feminist Criticism." *Signs* 6 (1981): 575-601.

Mackail, J. W. *The Life of William Morris.* 2 vols. London: Longmans, Green, 1899.

Tennyson, Alfred. *The Poems of Tennyson.* Ed. Christopher Ricks. London: Longman's, 1969.

Woolf, Virginia. "*Aurora Leigh.*" *The Second Common Reader.* New York: Harcourt Brace, 1932.

Angela Leighton (essay date 1986)

SOURCE: "'If orphaned, we are disinherited': The Making of the Poet," in *Elizabeth Barrett Browning,* The Harvester Press, 1986, pp. 114-40.

[*In the following essay, Leighton claims that in* Aurora Leigh *Browning traces the liberation of her own creative abilities through Aurora's "failed quest" for her father and her subsequent acceptance of her "disinherited state."*]

Barrett Browning first projected the composition of *Aurora Leigh* as early as 1844. She wrote to her cousin and friend, John Kenyon, of her wish to write another poem like **'Lady Geraldine's Courtship'**. Such a poem would be longer and more ambitious, but similarly 'comprehending the aspect and manners of modern life, and flinching at nothing of the conventional' (*Kenyon,* I, 204). Some months later, she embellished this first description in a letter to Miss Mitford: 'And now tell me,—where is the obstacle to making as interesting a story of a poem as of a prose work . . . Conversations & events, why may they not be given as rapidly & passionately & lucidly in verse as in prose—'. Her main intention in such a work, she stresses, is 'to go on, & touch this real everyday life of our age, & hold it with my two hands'. She adds, confidently: 'I want to write a poem of a new class' (*MRM,* III, 49).

A year later, she had not yet begun this poem but was still contemplating its composition. She informed Robert that 'my chief *intention* just now is the writing of a sort of novel-poem . . . running into the midst of our conventions, & rushing into drawing-rooms & the like "where angels fear to tread"; & so, meeting face to face & without mask the Humanity of the age' (*Letters: 1845-1846,* I, 31). The poem she outlines will be crusadingly modern, iconoclastic and outspoken, and it will contain, as well as philosophical digressions on the age, the popular interest of a story. Barrett Browning did not begin to write ***Aurora Leigh*** until after her marriage and the birth of Pen. It belongs, therefore, to some of the happiest years of her life—years in which she became a wife, mother, cosmopolitan traveller and tireless observer of the revolutionary events in Europe after 1848. It was published in 1856, a few months before the death of Mr Barrett.

In its exuberant and fierce commitment to the present, ***Aurora Leigh*** indeed succeeds in being 'a poem of a new class'. Not only does Barrett Browning unflinchingly relate a story of modern life, highly charged and melodramatic as it is; she also successfully promulgates a message of literary contemporaneity which other writers of the time enthusiastically welcomed. She repudiates the habit of nostalgia which tempts the Victorian poet with the glamour of the past, and from this new sense of the present she develops a crusadingly female poetics. The heroine of the work is a poet herself, who writes the story of her life and literary success as one example of the general cause of women's emancipation and independence. The 'real everyday life of our age' which Barrett Browning confronts in ***Aurora Leigh*** is mainly the 'real everyday life' of women, in all its small domestic detail; and it is from this specific bias that she derives a theory of women's writing as contemporary, combative and self-sufficient. However, it is one of the strengths and merits of the work that it also traces the hidden personal cost of this achievement.

Between 1846, the year of Elizabeth's marriage, and 1857, the year of Mr Barrett's death, there was no word from him. Although Elizabeth wrote many pleading letters to the father who might once have bound her to him 'hand and foot' (*Kenyon,* I, 291), his silence was unremitting. On one visit to England, in 1851, her continuing hopes for reconciliation must have been finally dashed by his abrupt return of all her past letters, unopened. Yet, in spite of this characteristically unsparing rigidity, the cherished ideal of her father continued to haunt his daughter, and all the rich compensations of her new life continued to be measured, in a sense, against the fact of his silence. 'All her life [the daughter] may longingly seek that lost state of plenitude and peace',[1] de Beauvoir writes.

In *Aurora Leigh,* Barrett Browning builds her hopeful political message of independence and equality for women upon a hidden last quest for the father. That quest is mapped in the sub-plot of the story, and its end is realised in Aurora's final knowledge and acceptance of her 'orphaned' and 'disinherited' state. Thus, it is not only a literary, but also a personal nostalgia for the past which this poet must repudiate in order to fulfil her own high specifications for poetry. In order to write 'a poem of a new class' which touches the 'real everyday life of our age', Barrett Browning finally dispossesses herself of the powerful figure of the father, both in fact and in imagination. The 'feminist' conviction of *Aurora Leigh* grows out of this harsh emotional and imaginative loss.

There are three interrelated stories in the work. First, there is the story of Aurora's life. Born of an Italian mother and English father, Aurora is early orphaned of them both, and is reared by an English aunt. She comes in time to reject the oppressive, puritanical education of this aunt, as well as the more insidiously oppressive offer of marriage by her rich cousin, Romney. She chooses instead to live alone in London and to earn her living by writing. Finally, through a series of novelistic detours, she returns to Italy to find that literary success and love are not irreconcilable after all. Secondly, there is the story of Marian Erle, the working-class girl to whom Romney also proposes, in a high-minded attempt to match his practice to his socialistic theories. Marian comes under the evil influence of the aristocratic Lady Waldemar, who persuades her to desert Romney on the very day of the wedding and to escape to France. Here she is raped in a brothel, gives birth to a child, and is finally discovered by Aurora, with whom she goes to Italy to live in an alternative liaison of women. It is there that Romney finds them both, when, defeated and broken by the practice of his misplaced philanthropical ideals, he too arrives in Italy. Thirdly, there is the underlying story of Aurora the poet, who is a scarcely disguised representative of Barrett Browning herself. This is an autobiography of literary development, which takes the form of a poetic quest for two figures whose presences shape Aurora's growth as a poet. It is this third story which holds the key to Barrett Browning's purpose and achievement in *Aurora Leigh.*

The main plot of the work is that of an improbable melodramatic romance interlaced with long philosophical digressions on the art and spirit of the age. In its general references and outline, this plot is indebted, as Cora Kaplan has shown,[2] to a large number of other nineteenth-century works, among which the most prominent are Madame de Staël's *Corinne* and Charlotte Brontë's *Jane Eyre*. The sub-plot, however, remains characteristically and underivatively Barrett Browning's own. It traces Aurora's quest for two figures, whom she seeks with the lover-like urgency of a poet seeking her muse. The first of these is the father, whose presence is movingly and anxiously solicited, as if in a last appeal by the daughter whose strong consciousness of disinheritance had come cruelly true in life. It is this appeal to the past which the poem ultimately rejects and supersedes, in order to free Aurora for her second quest—for a sister.

> Of writing many books there is no end;
> And I who have written much in prose and verse
> For others' uses, will write now for mine,—
> Will write my story for my better self . . .
> (I, 1-4)

Aurora Leigh begins with a declaration of literary purpose which the whole poem then supports. Aurora has already 'written much in prose and verse', but this, her latest book, will be a different story, which answers to the requirements of her 'better self'. The fact that the poem opens with a fanfare on the theme of writing reveals the extent to which this is the story of that self's writing. Beneath its flamboyant plot, *Aurora Leigh* is a woman's 'Prelude', which is concerned to chart the origins and development of the woman poet's mind. These origins are not, however, nurturing Wordsworthian presences of nature, but, true to Barrett Browning's Victorian and daughterly preoccupations, they are the heroine's actual parents. It is these whom she invokes at the start: 'But still I catch my mother at her post / Beside the nursery door' (I, 15-16), and then, more intimately: 'Still I sit and feel / My father's slow hand, when she had left us both' (I, 19-20). These presences are so vivid to the speaker's imagination that the writing slips into a present tense of strongly nostalgic recuperation.

However, the very vividness of these memories of mother and father betrays the curiously apprehensive foreboding which prompts them. Aurora does not simply commemorate those first powerful influences on her life; she also thinks, in the present tense:

> O my father's hand,
> Stroke heavily, heavily the poor hair down,
> Draw, press the child's head closer to thy knee!
> I'm still too young, too young, to sit alone.
> (I, 25-8)

'His hand would not lie so heavily,' Elizabeth once wrote of her own father, 'without a pulse in it' (*Letters: 1845-1846,* II, 882). The image of the father's hand in her poetry is one which, as Virginia Steinmetz points out,[3] often links strong human love and hard, God-like authority. This first description of the father in *Aurora Leigh* clearly draws on the contradictions in the character of that real father. His hand is a comfort to the child, but it is also unthinkingly heavy.

However, this description of the father is already loaded with intimations of change. The generalised present tense of these first passages subtly mixes fact and memory, event and premonition. The child who thinks, 'I'm still too young, too young, to sit alone', does so in the same grammatical time as Aurora who writes it many years later, and this trick of perspective carries an emotional and imaginative significance which the whole poem confirms. The sense of impending death comes earlier in the speaker's consciousness than it does in the poem's narrative, and thus it impresses the adult's foreboding on the chronology of events. Furthermore, it suggests a connection which will recur, with striking frequency, throughout the work. Although, in the plot, Aurora's father dies when she is thirteen, in Barrett Browning's consciousness he dies as soon as she begins to write.

This connection is evident in the apposition of lines which follows:

> I'm still too young, too young, to sit alone.
> I write.
>
> (I, 28-9)

The declaration 'I write' interrupts the sequence of events in a way that is highly suggestive. In the poet's imagination, the idea of losing her father and of having, therefore, 'to sit alone', leads by some swift association of ideas to the act of writing. Barrett Browning's insistence on the verb 'to write' in these first paragraphs of *Aurora Leigh*[4] goes with a premonition of being dispossessed of a mother and a father. The very break between the first and second paragraphs, like the famous 'awkward break'[5] noted by Virginia Woolf in *Jane Eyre,* is resonant with possible connections. The one connection which so much of Barrett Browning's work corroborates is that between the fear of being 'orphaned' and the confidence of being able to write.

After this richly revealing confusion of ideas in the first passages of *Aurora Leigh,* Book I relates in a more orderly way the deaths of Aurora's mother and father, and the child's subsequent exile from her homeland, Italy, to her father's land, England. The mother dies first. 'She was weak and frail' (I, 33), Aurora tells, in words which recall Barrett Browning's descriptions of her real mother in her letters. This death is then obscurely linked with the mothering role: 'The mother's rapture slew her' (I, 35). It is not a literal death in childbirth which is referred to here, but some vague excess of motherly experience. All Elizabeth Barrett's old distrust and antagonism towards the figure of the mother is then vented in Aurora's confused, horrified attitude to her mother's portrait. As Barbara Gelpi has shown, this portrait becomes the focus of all the child's wild and frightened imaginings about 'womanhood itself'.[6] In the firelight, the white of the woman's skin and the red of her ballroom gown contrast luridly: 'That swan-like supernatural white life / Just sailing upward from the red stiff silk' (I, 139-40). The portrait then draws the child's thoughts into a region of shifting and uncertain images of woman: it is 'by turns / Ghost, fiend, and angel, fairy, witch, and sprite' (I, 153-4), or else a 'Muse' (155), a 'Psyche' (156), a 'Medusa' (157), 'Our Lady of the Passion' (160), a 'Lamia' (161). These are all either threatening or tragically defeated figures of womanhood. Even the 'Muse' is not one to inspire poems, for she is about to be overcome by 'a dreadful Fate' (155). The Gothicism of this whole passage recalls the younger poet's profound anxiety of womanliness—an anxiety which, in her early ballads, turned the figure of the ghostly mother into a sometimes grotesque object of suspicion and fear.

Predictably, *Aurora Leigh* confirms that it is the father whose image dominates and inspires the daughter poet. Aurora relates that, after her mother's death:

> He left our Florence and made haste to hide
> Himself, his prattling child, and silent grief,
> Among the mountains above Pelago . . .
>
> (I, 109-11)

The 'prattling child' and the austerely 'silent' father make a strange company in the little mountain house. Their touchingly incongruous intimacy is not only, however, an authentic fact of the narrative; it is also a sign of what is to come. The idea of the father's 'silence' is one which soon acquires, not only the harsh authority of subsequent events, but also the subtle, guilty authority of an imaginative need.

Aurora tells:

> I was just thirteen,
> Still growing like the plants from unseen roots
> In tongue-tied Springs,—and suddenly awoke
> To full life and life's needs and agonies
> With an intense, strong, struggling heart beside
> A stone-dead father. Life, struck sharp on death,
> Makes awful lightning.
>
> (I, 205-11)

As has been pointed out, 'Aurora loses her mother at the Oedipal moment—age four—and her father as she attains the menarch.'⁷ This timing of the father's death has an eerie deliberateness about it. It happens suddenly and inexplicably, without narrative justification; but it retains, nonetheless, some hidden connection with Aurora's awakening to 'full life'. The juxtaposition is cruel, but apposite. It may be that Elizabeth's own experience of her father's tyrannical opinions about 'the iniquity of love-affairs' (***Letters: 1845-1846,*** II, 1072) lies behind this carefully timed literary death. Certainly, the passage strongly reinforces the connection made many years before in the ballads: it is the daughter's growth into womanhood, with all its wider physical and emotional needs, which signifies the loss of the father to her; she has ceased to be to him 'as if . . . a child'.

But there is another connection in the passage. It is not only the daughter's emotional development, but also her literary development which coincides with the father's death. The imagery of the passage confuses the two. Aurora grows as if from 'roots / In tongue-tied Springs' to find, beside the fact of her 'stone-dead father', her own 'intense, strong, struggling heart'. Such language recalls the early drama of 'The Tempest'. There is the same sudde juxtaposition of the 'struggling' protagonist and the dead man, and the same contrast between the desired self-expression of the one and the silence of the other. The very strength of life in Aurora provides a cruel contrast to, but also a subtle reason for, the father's death. 'Life, struck sharp on death, / Makes awful lightning,' Barrett Browning writes. Such imagery carries an irresistible suggestion, not only of emotional violence, but also of literary exhilaration. Just as the daughter wakes to womanhood and self-expression, so the father, by some ruthless logic of the imagination, appears 'stone-dead'. So sharp is the clash between daughter and father that it seems like life won at the cost of death; like speech won from some profound subsconscious crime against that father, the 'familiar'. Out of this clash, however, comes poetry: 'lightning'.

But it is characteristic of ***Aurora Leigh,*** as of all Barrett Browning's work, to feel the loss behind its power, and to go on hearing the silence behind its speech. This is the legacy of the father muse. Aurora claims that the last word of her dying father was to '"Love, my child, love, love!"' (I, 212). However, the rest of the poem makes clear that the real legacy of the father to his poet daughter is a legacy to hear, behind all the new and varied sounds of her life, his powerful silence. It is that silence which fills her imagination with its harshly formative strength of contradiction. Thus, when the child Aurora is torn away from her Italian home and Nanny, it is 'with ears too full / Of my father's silence to shriek back a word' (I, 227-8). It is not her father's last word to '"love"' which rings in her ears, but his last 'silence'.

Sandra Gilbert has argued that Aurora's subsequent struggle to survive is a struggle between 'two *paysages moralisés,* her mother country of Italy and her fatherland of England';⁸ and she concludes that Aurora chooses the generous nurture and eroticism of Italy and rejects the 'patriarchal history'⁹ represented by the father's tongue and country. But this ideological alignment fails to take into account the poem's movingly persistent quest for the lost father in the landscapes of *both* England and Italy. The significance of each of those places is a significance provided by the father's absence from them. Aurora's real choice is not so much one of motherland or fatherland, as it is the choice to survive in a world which, because of the father's absence, is all a desert. The story of her development and eventual independence as a woman and as a poet is a story wrung out of the emotionally and imaginatively realised fact that 'If orphaned, we are disinherited'.

Aurora first feels the meaning of her new orphaned state in the boat which takes her to England. She finds that 'the very sky' (I, 244) is

> Bedraggled with the desolating salt,
> Until it seemed no more that holy heaven
> To which my father went. All new and strange;
> The universe turned stranger, for a child.
> (I, 247-50)

The estranged and bewildered child finds that, with the loss of her father, the mark of the whole 'universe' is to be strange and bewildering. The sense of a 'holy heaven' which contains the presence of that father quickly fades before the literal 'desolating' grey of the real sky. Not only is there a new emptiness at the heart of things in Aurora's consciousness; there is also a new pressing and oppressive fullness. The obstructing reality of the actual sky takes the place of the 'holy heaven' of her child's faith. Just as in the grieving sonnets of 1844, the visionariness of 'stars and sun' is denied to the true mourners in the desert, so here, any consoling vision of 'heaven' is slowly usurped by the ordinary, separating fact of the sky. Skies, for Barrett Browning, are only a consolation to those whose loss is redeemable.

This contrast between poetic vision and ordinary sight is made again when Aurora describes her reluctant survival in England:

> I did not die. But slowly, as one in swoon,
> To whom life creeps back in the form of death,
> With a sense of separation, a blind pain
> Of blank obstruction, and a roar i' the ears
> Of visionary chariots which retreat
> As earth grows clearer . . . slowly, by degrees;
> I woke . . .
> (I, 559-65)

Elizabeth Barrett Browning's father, Edward Barrett, from a painting by H. W. Pickersgill.

As she becomes accustomed to life again, the 'visionary chariots' seem to retreat with their beloved company of dead. They leave her with a form of sensory deprivation which is more like death than life, however: 'a blind pain / Of blank obstruction, and a roar i' the ears'. All the new sights and sounds of the world to which Aurora once again awakes merely obtrude senselessly upon her imagination's desire for the other lost visions. Because she cannot see or hear her father in this world, its clarity is an oppression: an 'obstruction' of things and a 'roar' of sounds. With the father, the very imaginative resources of poetry seem to have been lost.

However, this exchange, which seems at first to be an exchange of life for death, of vision for dull sight, will become the principle of Barrett Browning's poetics. Aurora's gradual realisation of her 'orphaned' state is one which comes by finding that the salty, grey sky takes the place of the 'holy heaven', and that the clear 'earth' takes the place of 'visionary chariots'. The substitution of something loveless, hard and literal for the inspiring presence of the father is one on which the daughter's poetry must grow.

This principle of an exchange is suggested again in Book II. Aurora, now become a woman, encounters her cousin Romney in the garden in June, and there rejects his humiliating proposal of marriage. She accuses him of merely desiring a helpmate in his philanthropical projects, and of belittling her own different vocation of writing. Her description of that vocation, however, is one which still calls upon the memory of her father. She tells Romney:

> I too have my vocation,—work to do,
> The heavens and earth have set me since I changed
> My father's face for theirs . . .
>
> (II, 455-7)

The public message of **Aurora Leigh** is that the poet's work is as socially and politically beneficial as the philanthropist's. However, its private message is much less assured, and concerns the difficult, nearly unprecedented struggle of the woman poet to define her creativity. Barrett Browning's new poetics of contemporary commitment to the age is one which the woman achieves only through a principle of exchange or choice. Thus, Aurora admits that she has 'changed' her 'father's face' for a view of 'heavens and earth'. Although this new view is large and full, the father's absence makes it seem empty. 'Fatherlessness,' writes André Bleikasten, 'is not so much the absence of a relationship as a relationship to absence.'[10] The exchange of a father for the whole world, Barrett Browning knew, is in some ways an exchange of something for nothing. Nonetheless, it is that nothing which must nourish her imagination, and prepare it to meet 'this real everyday life of our age'. It is not her 'father's face' but the estranging 'heavens and earth' which have set Aurora to write poetry.

It is interesting that, at one point, Aurora distinguishes her bad early verses from her mature poems in terms of two different attitudes to the muse and of two different landscapes. In the first, she generalises:

> We call the Muse,—'O Muse benignant Muse,'—
> As if we had seen her purple-braided head,
> With the eyes in it, start between the boughs . . .
>
> (I, 980-2)

This easy confidence of finding the muse, like the lovely ladies of old, in a wood, is the mark of false poetry. True creativity, she knows now, comes in a very different place:

> In order to discover the Muse-Sphinx,
> The melancholy desert must sweep round,
> Behind you as before.—
>
> (I, 1020-2)

It is only in the 'melancholy desert', in the saddening and confusing plains that sweep, significantly, 'Behind' as well as 'before', that the muse is to be found. It is in the 'desert' of a world that harbours no beloved spirits of the past that Barrett Browning eventually discovers the muse of her contemporary 'feminist' epic.

But first, her quest for the lost father is pursued to its end. That the death of her father is not just a narrative strategy to liberate the heroine for life and love, as it is in many Victorian novels, is shown by the reluctance with which Aurora's imagination consents to that death. Her struggle with the figure of the dead, forsaking father is one which rivals in its emotional and poetic intensity the struggle between herself and Romney. Thus, for instance, at the moment when she rejects Romney's proposal of marriage and asserts her own vocation to be a poet, her thoughts turn to the presence which might have rivalled Romney for love:

> I had a father! yes, but long ago—
> How long it seemed that moment. Oh, how far,
> How far and safe, God, dost thou keep thy saints
> When once gone from us! We may call against
> The lighted windows of thy fair June-heaven
> Where all the souls are happy,—and not one,
> Not even my father, look from work or play
> To ask, 'Who is it that cries after us,
> Below there, in the dusk?' Yet formerly
> He turned his face upon me quick enough,
> If I said 'Father.' Now I might cry loud;
> The little lark reached higher with his song
> Than I with crying. Oh, alone, alone,—
> Not troubling any in heaven, nor any on earth,
> I stood there in the garden, and looked up
> The deaf blue sky that brings the roses out
> On such June mornings.
> (II, 734-50)

Having defended her different vocation of writing, Aurora is left to savour her loneliness. At the moment of her triumphant self-assertion as a poet, she looks for her father and finds him absent: 'Oh, alone, alone'.

This cry of despair is poignantly placed. Aurora has just crowned herself, as if in imitation of Corinne, poet laureate of the garden, and she has just proved to herself, and to Romney, that her ambition is strong and self-sufficient. But it is not so much from Romney's love that her self-sufficiency must be won, as from her father's. When she looks, the scene of her victory seems desolate and unresponsive. The 'fair June-heaven' is no different from the first heavy skies which the child saw on her journey to England. Both intrude themselves in place of the father's 'face'. For all its 'lighted windows', there is nothing to be seen in this summer sky; no one looks down through it, 'Not even my father'. The very transparency of the sunlit atmosphere is another form of 'blank obstruction'.

Once again, this Victorian daughter poet finds that the routes of vision, which might lead to the beloved dead, are blocked. Her imagination finds only the literal, spiritless spaces of the real sky, and remains 'alone, alone'. This moment in the garden is a crucial and symbolic one. 'June' is not just a time of year, but the sign of Aurora's poetic success. When Romney returns at the end of the poem to make a very different proposal of marriage, the memory of this day in June provides the *leitmotif* of his recognition of Aurora's superiority over himself. He greets her, for instance, as the 'same Aurora of the bright June-day' (VIII, 320), and as his unfailing 'June-day friend' (VIII, 609). June is the summer and high noon of her poetic ambition, and it is the June in her which proves, at the end, resilient and triumphant.

However, at the time, the June-day also has another connotation. Aurora finds that the cost of her ambition is not only the loss of Romney, but the loss, in her imagination, of the figure of her father. The windows of the 'June-heaven' are empty and its light is 'deaf'. The place where the daughter poet realises her vocation, and ambitiously crowns herself poet, is the place where she must also realise her desolation and her disinheritance. Aurora's imagination finds that the place, for all its sun and roses, is still, to her, a desert:

> Oh, alone, alone,—
> Not troubling any in heaven, nor any on earth,
> I stood there in the garden . . .

It is interesting that a little earlier, when Aurora crowns herself a poet with audacious but premature self-confidence, she crowns herself not with bay or myrtle, but with 'ivy' (II, 50); which is, she tells, 'as good to grow on graves / As twist about a thyrsus' (II, 51-2). She chooses as the symbol of her new-found power, one that will remind her of 'graves'. The association lies at the heart of Barrett Browning's poetics. Although the sunny stage-set of Aurora's poetic triumph is a garden in June, the true landscape of her poetic consciousness is still that of 'a desert place' full of 'tombs'.

The extent to which the quest for the father in *Aurora Leigh* is also an intensely personal one is suggested by a passage in Book V, where Aurora admits she envies other poets, not their work, but their appreciative families. She therefore envies Mark Gage his mother, on whose knee he 'lays his last book's prodigal review' (V, 525). It is clearly Barrett Browning herself who speaks so feelingly here of the other poet's mother. Parents are still, in her imagination, the inspiration and the goal of writing, and it is in the knowledge of what she herself has lost that she then invokes their once powerful names:

>   Dearest father,—mother sweet,—
> I speak the names out sometimes by myself,
> And make the silence shiver. They sound strange,
> As Hindostanee to an Ind-born man
> Accustomed many years to English speech;
> Or lovely poet-words grown obsolete,
> Which will not leave off singing. Up in heaven
> I have my father,—with my mother's face
> Beside him in a blotch of heavenly light;
> No more for earth's familiar, household use,
> No more. The best verse written by this hand
> Can never reach them where they sit, to seem
> Well done to *them*.
>
>   (V, 540-52)

Just as once the 'prattling child' kept company with the 'silent' father, and just as the girl struggled for self-expression beside his 'stone-dead' body, so here the poet still tests her words, her 'lovely poet-words', against the fact of father's and mother's absence. But against that absence they ring false. 'They sound strange' and 'obsolete'. The names which serve at the start as an invocation of the daughter's beloved first muses become, for lack of any response, a mere poeticism—a tired routine. 'Dearest father,—mother sweet' is a nostalgic and redundant call. To go on invoking presences which do not reply, and which may not be attending any more, is to indulge in a mere incantation of sweet names. '"O Muse, benignant Muse"' is the rashly confident summons of the immature poet. The mature poet no longer calls, but stands alone in 'the melancholy desert'.

Once again, Aurora finds that the actual sky mocks her nostalgic imaginative aspirations. 'Up in heaven / I have my father,' she thinks. But the religious and Romantic possibilities of that 'heaven' have also 'grown obsolete'. The best she can imagine is 'a blotch of heavenly light' where her mother's face might be. The larger visionary scope of skies is denied to this Victorian daughter, and in their place she confronts only the ordinary, empty atmosphere. Her imagination thus begins to learn its disinheritance even from 'the Dead'. These are increasingly distant and irrecoverable figures, who do not answer to their own dear names, and whose presences are gradually lost behind the bare literalness of the contemporary world.

The story of Aurora's development as a woman poet is thus one which depends on a characteristic poetics of the 'disinherited' daughter. But it also depends on a poetics of the 'disinherited' Victorian. The two are linked. Aurora finds, not only that the spirit of the one particular father is absent from the new landscapes of her life, but also that the spirit of the literary 'grandfathers' has gone. Even Italy, for all the erotic and maternal splendour of her hills, remains an alien and empty landscape which repudiates the mythopoeic yearnings of this belated poet. When Aurora approaches the Italian border, she needily invokes some sentient spirit of the place:

>   My own hills! Are you 'ware of me, my hills,
> How I burn toward you? do you feel to-night
> The urgency and yearning of my soul,
> As sleeping mothers feel the sucking babe
> And smile?
>
>   (V, 1266-71)

But she is too honest to grant her own wishes, and the answer she supplies is negative: 'Still ye go / Your own determined, calm, indifferent way' (V, 1273-4). Her retrogressive desire for a mother, or at least for some mothering spirit of Nature, is denied, and she confronts a landscape which is merely 'determined, calm, indifferent'. Aurora must learn, even in Italy, to stand alone in the desert, and to write without mythologies and without muses. Orphaned of both father and 'grandfathers', this Victorian daughter stands alone in the literal, indifferent and unhaunted landscapes of the world, and finds in these desert plains the place of poetry.

However, it is not till nearly the end of *Aurora Leigh* that this literalism of the imagination is accepted without regret. When Aurora first reaches Italy, her thoughts are still moved by nostalgia for the past. She writes:

>   And then I did not think, 'My Italy,'
> I thought 'My father!' O my father's house,
> Without his presence!
>
>   (VII, 490-2)

Italy cannot yet make up for what Aurora has lost. The place is still, in her consciousness, only an outer shell of something that has fled: the father's 'presence'. It is that father who might have given significance to the place, like some presiding *genius loci,* or answering muse. But there is only the place, without its spirit; the house without the father in it.

The connection between the fact of fatherlessness and poetic creativity is made a few lines later, when Aurora moralises on the sense of loss which the beauty of Italy does not alleviate but merely reinforces. The idea of her father's empty house reminds her of the fate of being without dreams in an alien world. She writes:

>   'Tis only good to be or here or there,
> Because we had a dream on such a stone,
> Or this or that,—but, once being wholly waked
> And come back to the stone without the dream,
> We trip upon't,—alas, and hurt ourselves;
> Or else it falls on us and grinds us flat,
> The heaviest gravestone on this burying earth.
>
>   (VII, 497-503)

To wake altogether from dreams, this Victorian poet declares, is to find the place forlorn and literal and full of graves. Without the spirit of things, the earth is a place which seems to kill the dreaming spirit of the poet with the weight of its gravestones. Yet, to *wake* from dreams has been the long and repeated experience of this 'orphaned' poet. She woke first to 'full life' beside her 'stone-dead father'. Later, she woke 'slowly, by degrees' from dreams of 'visionary chariots'. Now, she wakes again among 'stones' which, because of the failure of her father's 'presence', are all like gravestones. The 'burying earth' is the cruel but authentic landscape of her waking poetic consciousness.

Thus, in spite of her declared individualistic and Christian world-view, Barrett Browning's imagination is in fact shaped by a different and more pessimistic creed. That imagination rejects any mystical encounter with the dead, and it rejects any poetic mythologising of the landscape. Having lost the smile of her beloved father so absolutely, it is the absence of his spirit which characterises the world of the daughter. She must survive without dreams of him in the modern, urbane, materialistic age which is her own. Having been 'disinherited' of the father, she is 'disinherited' also of the past, and the world comes bare and literal to her imagination.

But the sense of graves remains strong in Aurora's consciousness, and they continue to underlie her new perceptions of Italy. 'My graves are calm, / And do not too much hurt me' (VII, 929-30), she tells at one point, revealing how far 'graves' are something carried in the soul, as well as found in the landscape. A little later, she thinks she might be able to forget the dead altogether, and in a fine simile imagines how she might 'be a man' (VII, 985) and seal off the past from her consciousness:

> I'm not too much
> A woman, not to be a man for once
> And bury all my Dead like Alaric,
> Depositing the treasures of my soul
> In this drained watercourse, then letting flow
> The river of life again with commerce-ships
> And pleasure-barges full of silks and songs.
> (VII, 984-90).

Nonetheless, the language works against the intentions of the speaker. However much she may bury them again, the 'Dead' are still 'the treasures' of her 'soul', and all the richest 'silks and songs' of the river of life are poor by comparison. Below this brilliant, commercial, busy world of 'silks and songs', the sense of 'graves' remains strong and seductive. All the other riches her imagination has gained continue to be measured against their preciousness, and in the end, the passage betrays the fact that this poet is still indeed 'too much / A woman' to repress the dead so successfully. The high enterprise of her life and poetry, of her 'silks and songs', will retain this difference from that of men.

After this movingly reluctant attempt to bury the past, Aurora makes one last bid to find her father. The woman cannot yet relinquish what the man might bury with ease. In Florence, Aurora begins to discover her independence as a woman and her success as a poet, but she discovers them, at first, only in sad contrast to the past:

> How I heard
> My father's step on that deserted ground,
> His voice along that silence, as he told
> The names of bird and insect, tree and
>   flower,
> And all the presentations of the stars
> Across Valdarno, interposing still
> 'My child,' 'my child.' When fathers say 'my
>   child,'
> 'Tis easier to conceive the universe,
> And life's transitions down the steps of law.
> (VII, 1110-18)

This touchingly heartfelt memory of the father's authoritative presence in childhood is one which connects that presence with the child's whole conception of 'the universe'. It is the father who gives, not only the 'names' of things, like Adam in the garden, but the meaning of things as well: 'the steps of law'. However, the woman is no longer a child, and the father is no longer there, to be her authority and her guide. To have power to walk alone and to be one's own namer of the world is to have lost for certain that first dependent companionship in the Eden of childhood. As a result, the woman who has become a namer and a poet in her own right walks on a 'deserted ground'. Even Valdarno, with all its birds and flowers and stars, seems, in the daughter's 'orphaned' consciousness, but a desert plain. In such a place she must 'conceive the universe' alone.

Aurora's life in Italy is thus one of gradually learned resignation and independence. It is not the realisation that she has loved and lost Romney, but that she has loved and lost her father, which tests and educates her imagination. It is this loss which turns the landscapes even of Italy into a 'melancholy desert'. She then makes one last attempt to break this mental solitude when she returns to visit the house in which she lived alone with him, as a child. The episode marks the last stage of Barrett Browning's long, hard quest for her beloved first muse. 'I rode once to the little mountain-house / As fast as if to find my father there' (VII, 1119-20), she writes.

What Aurora finds, however, is something else:

> The house's front
> Was cased with lingots of ripe Indian corn
> In tessellated order and device
> Of golden patterns, not a stone of wall
> Uncovered,—not an inch of room to grow
> A vine-leaf.
>
> (VII, 1123-8)

Not only is the place barely recognisable, but Aurora is forced to witness the actual destruction of her father's bowers of vines: 'the lads were busy with their staves / In shout and laughter, stripping every bough / As bare as winter' (VII, 1135-7). This is reminiscent of Wordsworth's 'Nutting', and by implication of Barrett Browning's early quest poems, which went in search of 'a spirit in the woods'. But if it is this old hope which drives Aurora back to the landscape of her childhood, the reality which confronts her is very different, and her reaction is a sign of it: 'Enough. My horse recoiled before my heart; / I turned the rein abruptly' (VII, 1140-1).

The horror of this literal devastation of the father's garden is unmistakable. To interpret the episode as an ideological statement about the patriarchal house being taken over by 'female fertility symbols',[11] as Sandra Gilbert does, is to miss the emotional point. Aurora is appalled and stunned by what she sees. But she is also harshly educated by it. The father's absence is finally experienced for what it is: the total failure of an old, idyllic world of childhood and of natural abundance and of Romantic hauntings. The bower has been lost, the garden deserted, all over again, and in their place Aurora finds the crudely utilitarian rule of trade and wealth: the 'tessellated order and device / Of golden patterns'.

The episode not only signifies at last the daughter's complete 'disinheritance' by the past; it also expresses something of the nature of the present in which she must live and write. The garden was always a place of lost childhood gladness in Barrett Browning's early poems. But in *Aurora Leigh* this loss has a new point. Aurora's nostalgic expedition to 'the little mountain-house' turns into a necessary confrontation with the remorseless order of the contemporary world. Aurora finds, not the ghostly spirits of the past, but the 'real everyday life of our age'. The father's Romantic garden has been ruined and overrun by a new order of things. The implication, not only of this one passage but of the whole poem, is that the new order is Barrett Browning's own. The pain of Aurora's discovery is the pain of the poet in her, at meeting 'face to face & without mask the Humanity of the age'. That this 'Humanity' is discovered at the expense of her beloved father's face is something the poem has predicted from its very first lines.

This episode represents the end of the quest. After the journey to her father's house, Aurora is resigned to be alone. She writes:

> That was trial enough
> Of graves. I would not visit, if I could,
> My father's, or my mother's any more . . .
>
> (VII, 1142-4)

The whole poem has been, till now, a 'trial' of 'graves'. Aurora has carried the sense of them, and the sense of one in particular, in her soul and in her imagination's eye. Those 'graves' came to mark and underlie the landscapes of the whole world. Whether the place was England or Italy, it was, to the 'orphaned' daughter, a burial ground, a place of stones, a desert plain.

However, after the expedition to the father's house, Aurora is changed. She is no longer nostalgic, lonely and haunted. She no longer searches out the spirits of her childhood's past, or calls the names of her 'Dearest father,—mother sweet'. Instead, she is content with the present. In the state of sudden creative exhilaration which ensues, the world around her acquires a new sufficiency and brilliance. She declares:

> I'm happy. It's sublime,
> This perfect solitude of foreign lands!
> To be, as if you had not been till then,
> And were then, simply that you chose to be . . .
> . . . possess, yourself,
> A new world all alive with creatures new,
> New sun, new moon, new flowers, new
>   people—ah,
> And be possessed by none of them!
>
> (VII, 1193-6, 1200-3)

Here, Aurora greets a world which is no longer a substitute for her father's face and her father's presence. For the first time, her loneliness does not stem from a sense of his lack and absence, but is a 'perfect solitude', desired and willed. This is not the 'solitude' of the desert, in which objects seemed to be only more burial-stones on her consciousness; it is the 'solitude of foreign lands' that are full of new, live, ordinary things: 'New sun, new moon, new flowers, new people'. No longer 'possessed' by the figure of the absent father, Aurora gains a whole world for poetry instead, and gains it, suddenly, for free. There is no exchange in this acceptance of a 'new world all alive'. The last journey to the father's devastated garden, for all its horror, finally releases her from the burden of the past, and from the burden of her disinheritance. Self-sufficient and self-possessed, she at last knows her emancipation, as a woman and as a poet, from the long shadow of the father muse.

Aurora Leigh thus maps, in its sub-plot, the progress of Barrett Browning's own last quest for the father, whose silence in real life she was to hear in her imagination for so many years after she had 'disinherited' herself in actuality from his affection. Throughout the poem she registers that silence, she appeals against it and even hopes to break it, until, finally, she dispossesses herself of the memory of it in a 'new world all alive with creatures new'. In the end, the daughter poet who has been 'orphaned' and 'disinherited', both in her life and in her poetic consciousness, realises that she has also therefore been freed—freed to make her loss and her loneliness creative. It is over the daughter's failed quest for the absent father that the other quest of the poem—the quest for a sister—can proceed.

Abbreviations

Kenyon: The Letters of Elizabeth Barret Browning, 2 vols, ed. Frederic G. Kenyon (London, 1897).

Letters: 1845-1846: The Letters of Robert Browning and Elizabeth Barrett 1845-1846, 2 vols, ed. Elvan Kintner (Cambridge, Mass., Harvard University Press, 1969).

MRM: The Letters of Elizabeth Barrett Browning to Mary Russell Mitford: 1860-1854, 3 vols, ed. Meredith B. Raymond and Mary Rose Sullivan (The Browning Institute and Wellesley College, 1983).

References to *Aurora Leigh* are by volume and line number only, and are from *Aurora Leigh and Other Poems*, introduced by Cora Kaplan (London, The Women's Press, 1978). All other published poems are from *The Complete Works of Elizabeth Barrett Browning*, 6 vols, ed. Charlotte Porter and Helen A. Clarke (New York, Thomas Y. Crowell, 1900).

Notes

[1] Simone de Beauvoir, *The Second Sex* (1949; Harmondsworth, Women's Press, 1983), pp. 17–35.

[2] Cora Kaplan, Introduction to *Aurora Leigh* (London, The Women's Press, 1983), pp. 17–35.

[3] Virginia Steinmetz, 'Beyond the Sun: Patriarchal Images in *Aurora Leigh*', *Studies in Browning and His Circle*, 9 (1981), 18-41, p. 28.

[4] Kaplan, op. cit., p. 10.

[5] Virginia Woolf, *A Room of One's Own*, new edition (London, The Hogarth Press, 1931), p. 104.

[6] Barbara Charlesworth Gelpi, '*Aurora Leigh*: The Vocation of the Woman Poet', *Victorian Poetry*, 19 (1981), 35-48, p. 38.

[7] Marxist Feminist Literature Collective, 'Women's Writing: *Jane Eyre, Shirley, Villette, Aurora Leigh*', in *1848: The Sociology of Literature,* Proceedings of the Essex conference July 1977 (Colchester, University of Essex, 1978), p. 203.

[8] Sandra M. Gilbert, 'From *Patria* to *Matria:* Elizabeth Barrett Browning's Risorgimento', *PMLA,* 99 (1984), 194-209, p. 200.

[9] Ibid., p. 202.

[10] André Bleikasten, 'Fathers in Faulkner', in *The Fictional Father: Lacanian Readings of the Text,* ed. Robert Con Davis (Amherst, Mass., The University of Massachusetts Press, 1981), p. 117.

[11] Gilbert, op. cit., p. 205.

Margaret Reynolds (essay date 1992)

SOURCE: An introduction to *Aurora Leigh*, by Elizabeth Barrett Browning, edited by Margaret Reynolds, Ohio University Press, 1992, pp. 1-77.

[*In the following excerpt, Reynolds discusses the politics and literary influences that shaped Browning's* Aurora Leigh. *She also summarizes the poem and discusses its approach to issues of femininity.*]

II

"Of course you are self-conscious—How c^d. you be a poet otherwise? Tell me."[41]

The readily retained (and easily caricatured) picture of Elizabeth Barrett Browning which is liable to overshadow interpretation of **Aurora Leigh** is, in part, the product of the memorable circumstances of her life, well documented through her own inveterate letter writing and well covered because of ideological assumptions about women and poetry. But it is also due, in large part, to Barrett Browning's own seriously held Romantic view of the significant worth of the individual and of the uniqueness of personal experience.

Barrett Browning is usually given a literary critical place in a mid-nineteenth-century context where she is compared either to her contemporaries among Victorian women novelists or else to mid-Victorian poets, particularly Alfred Tennyson and Robert Browning. These alignments, though significant and probably valid in that her distinctive voice is not heard until the publication of **The Seraphim and Other Poems** in 1838, nevertheless obscure the formative influences of Barrett Browning's historical context. Born in 1806, Elizabeth Barrett's formative reading years fell circa 1816-1830 and make her, in that sense, not Victorian at all. The burdens for women poets of a Romantic (or specifically Wordsworthian) conception of the function of women in poetry (as Mother Nature who provides subjects for her poet son; as the mistress/Muse who is the silent subject of men's poetry) have been set out by Margaret Homans, but only a small amount of attention has been given to the effects of Barrett Browning's inherited Romanticism.[42]

At fourteen, Barrett Browning endorsed the liberal politics of self-consciousness and intellectual independence which characterized the tenets of Romanticism:

> My mind is naturally independant and spurns that subserviency of opinion which is generally considered necessary to feminine softness. But this is a subject on which I must always feel strongly for I feel within me an almost proud consciousness of independence which prompts me to defend my own opinions and yield them only to conviction!!!!!!!
>
> Better oh how much better to be the ridicule of mankind, the scoff of society than lose that self respect which tho' this heart [were] bursting yet would elevate me above misery—above wretchedness and above abasement!!! These principles are irrevocable! It is not I feel it is not vanity that dictates them! it is not I know it is not an encroachment on masculine prerogative but it is a proud sentiment which will never allow me to be humbled in my own eyes!!!

As far as poetry was concerned, Elizabeth Barrett accepted the notions of (divine) inspiration, the subjective character of poetry, and the role of the poet as a prophet for the time.[43] During the 1820s, in her earliest expression of poetic theory, Barrett Browning emphasized the imperatives of the poet's task as mediator between God and man, joining "in mysterious union, the natural and spiritual, the mortal and the eternal, the creature and the Creator."[44] In her articles published in *The Athenaeum* (1842),[45] she described the "poetic temperament" as existing "half way between the light of the ideal and the darkness of the real," and she disclosed her poetic affiliations by evaluating the work of certain poets in subjective terms. Thus, for example, she attributed to Philip Sidney: "the completest 'Ars poetica' extant,—'Foole, sayde my Muse to mee, looke in thine heart, and write'".[46]

In 1842 Elizabeth Barrett's view on the real seemed to her to have shrunk to a very small compass, but the sources of the ideal, on the other hand, were readily accessible. Like Shelley's mysterious creative power arising from within,[47] Elizabeth Barrett sought truth in her own mind.[48] Contemporary poetic theory confirmed and sanctioned an inclination to introspection and the long habit (and prescription) of seclusion. At the same time the private processes of study, translation, reading, and criticism provided her with an internal world of reference made up exclusively of texts. Consequently, much of Barrett Browning's work then presents itself not as autobiography, but rather as an intellectual patchwork, "a discourse about society composed from other discourses."[49]

Eventually a thorough self-knowledge, supported by the observation gained through extended study, presented itself to Barrett Browning as an acceptable, albeit regrettable, substitute for the knowledge of a wider social world and an adequate apparatus for her function as a poet: "I have had much of the inner life—and from the habit of selfconsciousness of selfanalysis, I make great guesses at Human Nature in the main."[50] There remains discernable in this remark, and in other letters (especially to Robert Browning), a tentativeness hinting at the anxiety which characterizes Barrett Browning's claims to the poet's role. To be a poet was for her enabling, but to be a woman (and eventually an invalid woman) introduced a difficulty which had to be negotiated.

Wordsworth remained an important presence in Elizabeth Barrett's work, but a still earlier and more immediate influence was the work of Mary Wollstonecraft. The first documented allusion to Elizabeth Barrett's adherence to Wollstonecraft occurs, interestingly, in a letter from her mother written in September 1821. Referring to a forthcoming marriage in the family, she speaks of her hopes for the bride's happiness: "tho' I hope she has no visionary hopes of finding it upon your & M^rs. Wolstonecrafts system; if so, it may *at best* be anticipated that she will *oftener* find herself wrong than *right:* however it may do very well for an *old maids singleness* of *will &c.* I would not put you out of conceit with it, as long as it is y^r. intention to belong to the sisterhood." Elizabeth Barrett's juvenile autobiographical essays echo the argument and tone of Wollstonecraft's *Vindication,*[51] and although she was later to assert, apparently without any trace of irony that "I am *not,* as you are perhaps aware, a very strong partizan on the Rights-of-Woman-side of the argument—at least I have not been, since I was twelve years old," the name of Wollstonecraft occurs a number of times in Barrett Browning's correspondence, and her ideas still more frequently.[52]

Competent in contemporary (proto-)feminist theory as in contemporary poetics, the fourteen-year-old Elizabeth Barrett recognized that when she claimed her right to independent thought and expression, she was denying the conventions of female acquiescence ("My mind is naturally independant and spurns that subserviency of opinion which is generally considered necessary to feminine softness"); her claims *were* an annexation of "masculine prerogative." So Barrett Browning found herself at once within the positions of Romantic self-determination, yet simultaneously excluded, "alien and critical."[53]

As in other areas, the woman who claimed the part of the poet challenged (however unwillingly) man's primacy as the conventional repository of authority.[54] And yet it was her allegiance to the literary discourses of "high Art" in poetry which yielded her a strategy for negotiating the terms of her own transgression. As a young woman living in a household which revolved around the patriarch[55] and quite cut off from the masculine worlds of politics and study, Elizabeth Barrett found that without venturing too far into the rebellion marked out by Wollstonecraft, she could adopt an occupation which offered her a claim to existence and identity. The current character of poetic theory, where the poet functioned as an inspired prophet, offered Elizabeth Barrett a means of self-aggrandizement which did not affront too directly the common notion of female passivity.[56]

But there was a price. The gift of inspiration is an ambiguous one, for while it elevates the individual to the authoritative rank of prophet, it simultaneously debases her to the status of unconsenting instrument. Although of course limited by her specific cultural horizons, Barrett Browning acknowledged this paradox, and she seems to have been especially aware of its dangerous implications for the poet who was also a woman. The double aspects of the poet/prophet's role are respectively documented in two of Barrett Browning's best known poems, **"The Soul's Expression"** (1844) and **"A Musical Instrument"** (1860),[57] and the ambiguities appear also in *Aurora Leigh*. In a notable passage, the poet is compared to the priestess of Apollo who, possessed by the god, is only able to utter the "oracular shriek" (5.945). Yet notwithstanding this, Aurora maintains throughout a proud consciousness of her role as one of the "truth-tellers" left to God (1.859).

Barrett Browning's published Dedications to her volumes of poetry betray the same combination of subservience and self-assertion and can be read as ironic commentaries on the restricted liberties of the female poet in the nineteenth century. In 1844, while insisting that poetry was an "earnest object" with her, she still cast herself as a child, appealing to her father for protection and conjuring "your beloved image between myself and the public."[58] Similarly, the Dedication to *Aurora Leigh,* while boldly describing the poem as "the most mature of my works, and the one into which my highest convictions upon Life and Art have entered," invokes the generosity of her male cousin and friend as an intermediary.

The juxtaposition of Wordsworth and Wollstonecraft as formative influences on Barrett Browning does not just point up the poet's ambivalent relation to the traditions of poetry. Two central political issues dealt with in *Aurora Leigh*—the efficacy of nineteenth-century socialism and the "woman-question"—are both approached and resolved as problems related to the ideals and difficulties of individual freedom. Consistent in her commitment to personal development, certain discrepancies, or what might appear at first sight to be discrepancies, arise in Barrett Browning's political commentary and in her poetry. Cora Kaplan proposes that the sources of feminist humanism can be traced to the "separate but linked responses to the transforming results of the French Revolution" contained in two key texts, Mary Wollstonecraft's *Vindication of the Rights of Woman* (1792) and Wordsworth's Prefaces to *Lyrical Ballads* (1800, 1802). Kaplan further suggests that those two discourses of feminism and Romanticism were related to, and contradicted by, the demands of democratic politics—thus opening the way for an explanation of the divergence often found in modern criticism between the principles of feminism and the principles of socialism.[59] Elizabeth Barrett's particular cultural context places her at this confluence of Romantic and feminist ideology, and her intellectual life plotted a course between their contradictions which led her into a class conflict of "gifted" versus "other" and a condemnation of socialist endeavor which can be an embarrassment to some twentieth-century readers.

Barrett Browning's emphasis upon, and self-consciousness of, the individual will meant that she endorsed the arguments of Thomas Carlyle, especially his *Heroes and Hero-Worship and the Heroic in History* (1840). She saw Carlyle himself as a hero, an inspired prose poet, fulfilling the office of the poet by "analysing humanity back into its elements, to the destruction of the conventions of the hour." Carlylean arguments in favor of individual development (and the collateral supremacy of the man of genius) are cited in book 2 and throughout *Aurora Leigh* where individual genius is opposed to and preferred to the socialist doctrine of collectivity.[60]

Yet Barrett Browning did undoubtedly look forward to reform, both social and feminist. She criticized the forces and conventions which gave rise to and permitted the continuance of child labor, slavery, prostitution, the sexual double standard, and class inequality. She argued vehemently in favor of woman's right to useful occupation,[61] and, perhaps more unusually, she deplored the rigid allocation of character by gender which propriety demanded.[62] Given that the theories of the early nineteenth-century socialists, Owen and Fourier for instance, had their origins in Romanticism and typically included a promise of relief for the oppressed and a challenge to the conventions of class and gender, they might for those reasons have appeared attractive to Barrett Browning's conscience. Fourier himself, so abused in *Aurora Leigh,* saw the state and status of women in any society as the measure of that society's progress, proposing that "the degree of emancipation of women is the natural measure of general emancipation." And yet Elizabeth Barrett Browning consistently criticized socialist principles because, in her view, in furthering the general good, they denied the exercise of individual will—an exercise already severely limited in the case of individual women.[63]

Barrett Browning's feminism very obviously grows out of her overriding perspective on individual freedom. Less obvious is the way in which some of her remarks, occasionally read today as antifeminist, result from the same priority. Thus, she argues against the oppressive channeling of the unique female talent into sanctioned activities, refuting Anna Jameson's suggestion that Florence Nightingale's ministry in the Crimea (however proper it may have been for her) could be accounted a step gained for her sex as a whole.[64] Recalling her argument that individual talent requires an individual and not necessarily approved course of development, Barrett Browning dramatized the proposition in book 2 of *Aurora Leigh* where Aurora refuses to accept a marriage which would reduce her to the feminine role of social worker and purveyor of domestic balm for the refreshment of an embattled husband. But when, after nine books of self-sufficiency, Aurora finds love and marriage in a conventionally happy ending, some critics have read this, rather crudely, as a failure of principle,[65] or an acquiescence in patriarchy's version of a mild general reform.[66] But Barrett Browning hinges her plot on the growth of individual personality—and for the character Aurora, as she was conceived by her author, the completest freedom and self-recognition is to be found in the liberated expression of desire combined with the recognition of poetic originality and power.

Barrett Browning's letters suggest that she was unwilling to commit herself on the politics of *Aurora Leigh*. Certainly her self-conscious analysis of her position as a woman poet equipped her with the background for polemic, and in her private correspondence at the time she acknowledged that she was entering an area of contemporary debate and showed herself to have been acutely aware that her principal opponents in that debate, Tennyson (*The Princess*, 1847),[67] and Coventry Patmore (*The Angel in the House*, 1854 and 1856),[68] were likely to be afforded the public space in which to quarrel with her views. In October 1856, while she was still correcting proof for *Aurora Leigh,* Barrett Browning commented on the state of the woman question:

> Bessie Parkes is writing very vigorous articles on the woman question, in opposition to Mr. Patmore, poet & husband, who expounds infamous doctrines on the same subject—see 'National Review',—& send {thus} them "with the author's regards" to Mrs. Browning—Oh if you heard Bessie Parkes!—she & the rest of us militant, foam with rage—But he'll have the best of it as far as I am concerned: inasmuch as I hear he is to Review in the North British my poor **'Aurora Leigh,'** who has the unfeminine impropriety to express her opinion on various "abstract subjects,"—which Mr. Patmore cant abide, he says.[69]

Yet, in spite of this declaration, after the publication of *Aurora Leigh* Barrett Browning is to be found writing (admittedly to a friend who was not for the "rights of woman") that she was surprised that the public associated her work with the woman question: "Did you see in the list of Lectures to be delivered by Gerald Massey, (advertised in the *Athenaeum*) one on "*Aurora Leigh,* and the womans question?" . . . I did not fancy that this poem would be so identified as it has been, with that question, which was only a collateral object with my intentions in writing."[70]

In *Aurora Leigh* the woman question and the discussion concerning socialism are both made subservient to the reiterated arguments for individual liberty and self-recognition. Each of the three main characters enacts a learning process which is essentially private, and each one adopts to this end a subjective or self-conscious view which parallels (but does not mimic) Barrett Browning's own reliance upon "selfconsciousness of selfanalysis." But, a question remains as to how whole the idealized self, constructed and valued by a Romantic and liberal position, can ever be, when the subject is a woman.[71] Barrett Browning's poetics were conceived within contemporary cultural structures which included a discrepancy between the elevated status accorded by the poetic inheritance and her oppressed place as a woman within that culture. The poet's political position was equally ambivalent: the promotion of a concept of individuality valorized her (female and therefore subversive) self-will, while it permitted exercise of power on the part of authorized genius, excusing social obligation and even forbidding general social reform. Just as her poetic theory was always in crisis and cannot be nearly labeled as consistently one, so her political views were similarly unsettled. In spite of a reiterated emphasis upon the idea of the unified psyche growing along an undeviating line leading to wisdom and integration, Barrett Browning's own politics, poetics, and personal needs were often in conflict, preventing the wholeness to which she apparently aspired. However, if for Barrett Browning, this fragmentation/conflict represented a problem to be controlled, for the twentieth-century reader it is clear that those very contradictions provided the impetus which engendered and empowered the ideas, both poetic and political, which shaped *Aurora Leigh*.

III

"You have in your vision two worlds . . ."[72]

"But poets should
Exert a double vision;"[73]

The presence of contradiction and revision in Barrett Browning's poetry is acknowledged in recent criticism, but how to describe and pinpoint those changes still presents a problem. It is too simple to argue, as some critics have done, for a change from solipsistic lyric to concerned commitment at a moment neatly fixed by a marriage which offered regeneration and social engagement.[74] Barrett Browning did not abandon lyricism in 1846, nor was she suddenly motivated by social conscience. Her certainty of the mediating character of the poet remained constant, but her perception of how that mediation was best to be effected evolved with the years.

Barrett Browning's articles in *The Athenaeum* (1842) expressed her belief in the divinity of the poet's inspiration and in the necessity of subjectivity in poetic creation. But the consideration to which Elizabeth Barrett repeatedly turned in her articles did not content itself with an affirmation of the isolated role of the subject, but rather went on to speculate upon the relationship between the ideal and the real, and the poet's part in interpreting (and enacting) that relationship. She suggested that the poet who simultaneously perceives both ideal and real must adopt some means tending to their reconciliation, either by concentrating exclusively upon the spiritual ("subjectivity perfected"), or by endowing objective things with symbolic reference ("objectivity transfigured") or, "by attaining to the highest vision of the idealist, which is subjectivity turned outward into an actual objectivity."[75] Concerned to define and substantiate her notion of the parts played by subject and object in the poet's work, Elizabeth Barrett cited Shakespeare as both a "natural genius" capable of rendering both the objective surfaces of the visible world and an artist able to expound the subjective significances of the spiritual world beyond.[76] With this notional fusion in mind Elizabeth Barrett reiterated her idealist vision by adding that he who is "wise in nature"—an apparently objective exercise concerned with looking outward rather than in—is necessarily wise in self-knowledge and the subjective.[77]

At the end of her series of articles on the anthology *The Book of the Poets*, Elizabeth Barrett repeated her views on the close alliance of Nature and Art to argue for the poet's prerogative to seek the object of poetry in any chosen sphere: "Let a poet never write the words 'tree,' 'hill,' 'river,' and he may still be true to nature." Poetry is to be found wherever the poet sees an object susceptible of interpretation.[78]

The poetic function of enlarging the subject in such a way as to transform, and effectively absorb, the external objects (whatever their character) upon which the poet focuses, was further explored in Barrett Browning's review of Wordsworth's volume. The poet is described as one who envelops the objects of his contemplation with his own self, thus producing not simple mimetic description, but poetry which is realized intellectual insight.[79]

More than two years before her first exchanges with Robert Browning, Elizabeth Barrett had begun to formulate a theory of poetry which, trying to reconcile two differing poetic philosophies, extended her certainty of the value of subjectivity to incorporate and interpret the natural and social world in a multiple poetic view. Commentators have given little attention to Barrett Browning's *Athenaeum* articles, but critics have recently pointed to a presence in Elizabeth Barrett's early poetry which is concomitant with her view of poetry's double application. In general, nineteenth-century critics appreciated Barrett Browning's early work, her "Romaunts" and ballads, because they were sentimental, moral, often (debasedly) romantic or mock-medieval. Twentieth-century critics, for the most part, found them embarrassing. But those ballads, in spite of their defusing sentiment, often contain a condemnation of gender stereotypes, an anxiety about the demands of conventional feminine virtue, and a complaint against sexual inequality and the abuses of patriarchy.[80] Although these poems appear at first sight to be what could be loosely termed subjective and feminine, being ostensibly concerned with art, emotion, and other "eternal verities," they prove on closer inspection to be objective—that is politicized, realistic, contemporary, confrontational—and consequently "masculine."

Elizabeth Barrett's closest literary confidante from 1836 to 1845 was Mary Russell Mitford, and the relationship between these two writers included an irresolvable difference of "poetical principle"; Mary Russell Mitford championed the cause of realism in art, in direct opposition to what she termed Barrett's "mysticism." When Elizabeth Barrett put aside her more usual metaphorical and visionary stance to write a story of contemporary life in **"Lady Geraldine's Courtship"** (1844), Mitford approved a defection which Barrett herself admitted: "Yes—I confess that **'Geraldine's Courtship'** is on your principle rather than mine."[81]

By the time she wrote this, Elizabeth Barrett had, some months since, formed the idea (which was to inform *Aurora Leigh*) of "writing some day a longer poem of a like class—a poem comprehending the aspect and manners of modern life and flinching at nothing of the conventional," and she confided her maturing plan to Mary Russell Mitford: "And I mean to write a poem of length on your principle—a sort of novel-poem! I am looking about for a story—Something not too complex, and admitting of high application."[82]

When Mitford suggested Napoleon as an appropriate subject for the work, Barrett was forced to clarify her intentions and, in particular, to make clear that even while planning to write a realistic and modern poem, she had no wish to abandon her long-held conviction of poetry's spiritual aspect:

> No—I am afraid of Napoleon for a subject: & also it w^d. not I fancy, suit me. If I had a story of my own

I might be as wild as I liked, & I sh^d. have a chance besides of interesting other people by it in a way I could not do with known story. And I dont want to have to do with masses of men,—I sh^d. make dull work of it so. A few characters—a simple story—& plenty of room for passion & thought—*that* is what I want . . & am not likely to find easily . . without your inspiration. Oh yes, my dearest friend,—I wrote **"Lady Geraldine"** on your principles, I admit: but still you shall grant to me that **"Lady Geraldine's Courtship"** has more mysticism (or what is called mysticism) in it,—hid in the story . . than all the other ballad-poems of the two volumes. I hold *that*. But people care for a story—there's the truth! And I who care so much for stories, am not to find fault with them. And now tell me,—where is the obstacle to making as interesting a story of a poem as of a prose work—Echo answers *where*. Conversations & events, why may they not be given as rapidly & passionately & lucidly in verse as in prose—echo answers *why*. You see nobody is offended by my approach to the conventions of vulgar life in **"Lady Geraldine"**—and it gives me courage to go on, and touch this real everyday life of our age, and hold it with my two hands. I want to write a poem of a new class, in a measure—a Don Juan, without the mockery & impurity, . . under one aspect,—& having unity, as a work of art,—& admitting of as much philosophical dreaming & digression (which is in fact a characteristic of the age) as I like to use. Might it not be done, even if I could not do it? & I think of trying at any rate.[83]

In this early summary of the plan for the work which was to become *Aurora Leigh,* Barrett Browning emphasizes the blend of everyday life (the objective and real) with discursive philosophy (the subjective and mystic). The problem of finding a form enabling this amalgam preoccupied the poet and soon spilled into her correspondence with Robert Browning. Unlike Mitford, Browning endorsed many of Barrett's views on the purpose of poetry, and their literary exchanges from 1845 were to refine and extend the theoretical address of both poets. Early in their correspondence, even before the project for "a sort of novel-poem" was confided to Robert, the poets embarked with some polite competition for terms of commendation, upon a discussion concerning their artistic ideals and ambitions. Browning compared what he saw as Elizabeth Barrett's achievement with his own aspiration: "you *do* what I always wanted to do, hoped to do, and only seem now likely to do for the first time. You speak out, *you,*—I only make men & women speak—give you truth broken into prismatic hues, and fear the pure white light, even if it is in me . . ." Browning stressed Elizabeth Barrett's ability to express her own self in writing—"You speak out, *you*"—but while he declared himself to value that capacity for self-expression,[84] he classified Elizabeth Barrett as a subjective poet, and he may have conceived her confessional style as private, autobiographical, and, in that way, feminine.[85]

Returning the compliment using the "language of the schools of the day," Elizabeth Barrett confessed to admiring in Browning's work his capacity for using not only the subjective, which permitted him an area of "abstract thought," but also the objective view, which allowed him to deal most intimately with "human passion."[86] Her congratulatory description is followed by a telling comparison: "Then you are 'masculine' to the height—& I, as a woman, have studied some of your gestures of language and intonation wistfully, as a thing beyond me far! & the more admirable for being beyond." This remark (disregarding social motives) reveals Barrett Browning's theorized association of the masculine with the objective, and implies the analogous association of feminine and subjective. It also suggests her sense of gender definitions for appropriate subject and form ("I am afraid of Napoleon for a subject: & also it w^d. not I fancy, suit me"; "a Don Juan, without the mockery & impurity").[87]

When the germ of the poem was first described to Robert Browning in February 1845, Elizabeth Barrett emphasized the character of her projected poem as one composed of varieties or oppositions fused. So the work was to be a novel but was also to be a poem; it was to encompass the real and the modern, but it was also to include an idealistic vision by "speaking the truth as I conceive of it." Because her intention included the introduction of the objective view of the real in modern life, she classed her enterprize as one specifically challenging the conventions appropriate to feminine poetry—"rushing into drawing-rooms and the like, 'where angels fear to tread.'"[88]

The literary exchange begun in 1845 did not end with the poets' marriage. In his "Essay on Shelley," an introduction to a volume of (forged) Shelley letters, written just over a year before Barrett Browning began work on *Aurora Leigh,* Robert Browning described the "subjective poet of modern classification" as one typically reaching toward a supreme intelligence through the route of his own soul's instincts:

> Not what man sees, but what God sees—the *Ideas* of Plato, seeds of creation lying burningly on the Divine Hand—it is toward these that he struggles. Not with the combination of humanity in action, but with the primal elements of humanity he has to do; and he digs where he stands,—preferring to seek them in his own soul as the nearest reflex of that absolute Mind, according to the intuitions of which he desires to perceive and speak.

The objective poet by contrast, looked outward, endeavoring "to reproduce things external (whether the phenomena of the scenic universe, or the manifested action of the human heart and brain) with an immediate reference, in every case, to the common eye and apprehension of his fellow men."[89] The specific quality which distinguished this second poet was discriminated as his "double faculty" of seeing more clearly than the average mind while minutely apprehending the capacity of his audience and tailoring his expression to the limits of their comprehension.

That Barrett Browning approved of these definitions is made clear in *Aurora Leigh* when she borrows Browning's metaphors (the seeds of creation and the double vision) to identify the aspirations of her poet-heroine. In book 3 Aurora assures herself of her genuine (if temporarily latent) poetic faculty:

> "And yet I felt it in me where it burnt,
> Like those hot fire-seeds of creation held
> In Jove's clenched palm before the worlds were sown,—
> But I—I was not Juno even!
>
> (3.251-54)

The Aurora Leigh we meet in book 3 is a naturally subjective poet, because of her sex, and yet is threatened, by the fact of her gender, with exclusion from her poetic inheritance. In the pivotal book 5, which includes the longest and most sustained arguments on the appropriate character and function of poetry, the heroine argues that the poet should adopt a masculine and objective manner in order to represent and reproduce the external world of the modern age. Thus, as an aspiring objective poet, she proposes that it is the poet's (and her own) duty to "exert a double vision," able to perceive at once broadly and intimately (5,183-88).

For her poet-character, Barrett Browning conceived a blend of both poetic models, not abandoning the subjective (and more recognizably feminine) inward view but expanding the capacity of seeing to include the objective faculties of mimesis, drama, and realism which reflected the contemporary scene and its urgent social concerns, to make them an integral part of Aurora's vision.

Here Barrett Browning encountered, and overcame, a significant and demanding problem. The work which purports to be the autobiography of such a poet must necessarily enact the fusion of the artist's view of subject and object, must actively display and live out in the poetry itself the very qualities described as distinguishing the works written by the poet-heroine. To achieve such "living form"[90] in verse required a new approach to form and narrative treatment.

IV

"Education against development
System against instinct"[91]

When describing her plans for a verse-novel to Mary Russell Mitford and Robert Browning in 1844 and 1845, Elizabeth Barrett made particular reference to the necessity of seeking a "new story" for the purpose. One of her objections to Napoleon as a subject was that his was "a known story," for she wished to interest her readers in "a new way," not possible with a known story. To Browning also she reiterated the importance of originality, saying that only with a new story could she "take liberties" with the treatment.[92] This concern suggests very clearly that, as initially conceived, part of the novelty of Barrett Browning's poem depended upon her being able to use elements of surprise and challenge which would not be open to her if her audience were able to anticipate her story. Knowledge in the reader, or expectations based on experience of conventional literary form, brought constriction in Barrett Browning's view. Familiar narratives and conventional forms were to be rejected in favor of a new story enabling a language and form which forced the poem into a lived existence by emphasizing its process of making.[93] Her project, formal as well as political, was to privilege instinct and development as process, over the ordering limits of education and system.[94]

"Lady Geraldine's Courtship" (*Poems* 1844), a poem closely related to the genesis of *Aurora Leigh,* offers an early model for Barrett Browning's experiment with narrative treatment. Like the later verse-novel, the ballad is a first-person narrative, but it is also a curtailed autobiography in the form of a letter written (though not sent) by a male poet, Bertram, to an unnamed (male) friend and "fellow-student." The presence of the friend is conjured at the beginning of the poem to provide the impetus for self-revelation which inspires the ensuing work. The act of telling the story is presented as an act of appropriation as the poet-speaker attempts to exert some control over the events he narrates by organizing his story into a proper shape.[95] This act of control on the poet's part is particularly desirable to the speaker—and potentially misleading for both speaker and reader—because the events which the poet would narrate are not yet resolved and their consequences still unknown.

As the poem unfolds the reader learns, through a retrospective summary, that the poet is staying at Wycombe Hall, that he was invited there by the owner of the estate, Lady Geraldine, and that his time there has been passed in her intellectual company. The narrative then approaches the present time at stanza 57 where the events of "this morning" are related, partly in dramatic dialogue. A break occurs when the poet-narrator faints before Lady Geraldine (stanzas 87-88), and the narrative finally catches up with the present as the speaker describes himself alone in his room in the act of writing his letter—the poem itself.[96]

For the conclusion, the narrative method changes from first to third person as it describes the resolution of Geraldine's approach to Bertram. The conversion of narrative method from first to third person is awkward and distracting; it suggests a degree of discomfort with this fantasy of reconciliation, especially as Lady Geraldine is still barely permitted any speech.[97] Indeed, the change in narrative method, the emphasis upon Bertram's vision, Lady Geraldine's silence, the sense of trance, and chanting repetition, might all imply that these events are not real but a fantastic delusion. The possibility of such a reading challenges any notion of this poem's simple recommendation of cross-class marriage and the recognition of poetry's nobility as a cure for social ills.

The employment of a first person narrative, written in the midst of events, as opposed to comfortable retrospect, and liable consequently to error which is communicated to the reader as truth,[98] as well as the change to third person immediate narrative, make **"Lady Geraldine's Courtship"** a potentially unsettling poem, capable of a subversive questioning of order and expectation through the use of an unknown story.

As some of Elizabeth Barrett's early ballads and romances included a doubleness through the juxtaposition of a sentimental surface with a condemnation of current values, so Barrett Browning's later poems often exhibited similar balancing acts through the use of more specifically technical literary devices. Such devices included reversal of conventional expectation, narrative unreliability; repetition and revision, dual time-scales allowing readjustment, and narratives split between speakers or rhetorically adjusted for particular listeners. The presence of these techniques promotes the involvement of the reader, as well as inserting a challenge to her perspectives on literature and on social issues (e.g., **"Lord Walter's Wife"**). The later poems also suggest an increasing exploitation of the idea of immediacy. Far from allowing her poems to rise from "emotion recollected in tranquillity," Barrett Browning's longer poems (e.g., *Sonnets from the Portuguese, Casa Guidi Windows,* and *Aurora Leigh*) claim to express the emotion of the moment, complete with misapprehension and error.

Casa Guidi Windows, the first of Barrett Browning's "Italian" poems, and one of those written during the eight-year interval between the conception and the composition of *Aurora Leigh,* drew on a known story. But it nonetheless presented a discomforting ambivalence through its reliance upon the poet's personal view. In *Casa Guidi Windows* the real political events of 1847-1849 were described in the manner of the objective poet; but the subjective is also employed as Barrett Browning makes herself the viewer and narrator of the tale. She is the actor who interprets the manner of Leopold II as he appears on the balcony of the Palazzo Pitti in 1847; she witnesses the arrival of the Austrian army of occupation and offers the bitterness of her own reaction as a measure of general opinion; she frankly owns her attitudes to political events and personalities to be influenced by her personal life, even including her own pregnancy; and in the smile of her own son, her Florentine, the poet sees a general hope for Italian freedom and rebirth. The work is presented as an intensely personal view which—and this is where the poem claims an originality of form—thereby obtains power as an authentic fragment of experience. What is revolutionary about the sexual politics of the poem is that the central voice which carries the weight of this truth through subjectivity, is clearly identified as that of a woman. With apparent subjectivity comes an actual objectivity; the conventional margin (the female self watching from a window) is translated to the actual center.

Barrett Browning certainly conceived of the value of *Casa Guidi Windows* as lying with its sincere presentation of a personal view, consciously including all her own errors of judgment as a measure of her developing perception. In the **"Advertisement to the First Edition,"** the poet chose to point to the disparity between the optimistic opinion of Duke Leopold expressed in part 1 and the disillusionment recounted in part 2, as a means of proving the writer's honesty and thus adding to the work's authority and value. Barrett Browning's "confession of error"—"Absolve me, patriots, of my woman's fault / That ever I believed the man was true"—and the subjective view acknowledged in the **"Advertisement,"** have been the evidence invoked to charge Barrett Browning's political poetry with naiveté. But such criticism completely fails to take account of the poet's arguments for the value of the personal view as the true measure of the universal. Her "confession" of her "woman's fault" is extraordinary, both for its own irony (it was a fault to believe a man and a ruler true) and for the simple way in which it has been misread by critics (only a woman could be so stupid—the critic forgetting what it is that she has been stupid about). Significantly, in the **"Advertisement"** Barrett Browning endorsed subjective error as representing, in itself, a form of truth: "But such discrepancies we are called upon to accept at every hour by the conditions of our nature, implying the interval between aspiration and performance, between faith and disillusion, between hope and fact."[99]

But subjective error in *Casa Guidi Windows* is recognizably that. Because Barrett Browning was dealing with recent events, her readers had access to a measure which enabled them to discern the degree of error included in her version. In 1851 any reader with an interest in European affairs might have known the eventual outcome of the historical events Barrett Browning was describing, and she or he might have been able to appreciate the irony of part 1 where the poet expresses the trust invested in the Grand Duke by witnesses to the scenes of 1847. *Aurora Leigh,* like *Casa Guidi Windows,* fused a description of the modern world with a private focus for observation and interpretation. But

Aurora Leigh, unlike *Casa Guidi Windows,* told a new and unknown story where the reader was not to be permitted any indication which should help her to assess the partiality of its narrator by reference to historically verifiable fact.

Aurora Leigh displays the changing perceptions of one consciousness—explicitly female—in a given set of situations. But while in *Sonnets from the Portuguese* and *Casa Guidi Windows* the protagonist was (more or less) frankly Elizabeth Barrett Browning's self, in *Aurora Leigh* that prominence is given to a fictional character. The events which make up the plot of the verse-novel are not so much of interest for themselves as for the opportunities which they allow that character to raise, to ponder, and to resolve a variety of intellectual, cultural, and social questions. Carrying through her notion of the subjective view as the nearest approach to a genuinely objective view, Barrett Browning offers the reader intimate access to the consciousness of only one character, that one character being both actor and narrator—and a woman.

As the narrative progresses, certain problems arise out of this dependence upon the one consciousness. Like the poet-narrators of **"Lady Geraldine's Courtship"** and *Casa Guidi Windows,* Aurora writes her autobiography while living in the midst of the events she describes. Moreover, as her autobiography is also a record of Aurora's intellectual life, supposedly written while it is still being carried forward and before she reaches any resolved understanding of her personality and potential, the narrative must include error, misapprehension, modification, and revision. The reader is asked to share all the fluctuating opinions of the actor-narrator enacted before her, not to demand consistency but to experience each step toward a notional growth as and when Aurora herself experiences it. These are the liberties which appear in the story used for Barrett Browning's verse-novel, and yet few contemporary critics attended to that enterprise, inclining rather to view the narrative as "chaotic."[100] The form of fictional autobiography allowed space to chart the conflicting processes of modification and reassessment. And crucial to this enacted experience is a chronological structure which gives the narrative a past, present, and future.[101]

Aurora Leigh's story covers a period of thirty years, by which time she is an acclaimed poet living in Florence. But Aurora does not tell her story from this vantage point, nor is the verse-novel constructed upon principles of retrospect and linear time. The narrative of *Aurora Leigh* begins in the midst of the period which spans the events described, and the Aurora who resolves to embark upon her autobiography at the beginning of book 1 is twenty-six or twenty-seven, a writer of only moderate repute, living alone in London.[102] That it is this character (Aurora in her mid-twenties) whose narrative voice is intermittently encountered in books 1-4 of the work is implied at the opening of book 3, but that character herself is only fully explained to the reader at book 5.[103]

The initial pages of the first draft manuscript of *Aurora Leigh* throw light on this feature of the work, showing the opening of the chronological and narrative scheme and employing the confessional tone which colors the published version.[104] In draft the poem commences with three passages: the first contemplates the discrepancy between the aspirations of youth and the realities of unfolding life; the second looks back upon the childhood of the narrator and begins "God help me—I am <young> still—<twenty six>"; and the third, returning to the present situation of the speaker, discloses her intention to write (something) that very evening:

> "Leave the lamp, Agnes, & go up to bed—
> This hair does very well—I have to write
> Beyond the stroke of midnight—."

Only on the fifth page of the draft does the heroine embark upon a retrospective autobiography. All three of the draft opening passages appeared in modified form in the published versions, but the first and the third of these were removed, apparently early in the composition process, to form the beginning of book 3. Thus, the evidence of the original version for the opening of *Aurora Leigh* indicates that the beginning of book 3 is related to the opening scene of the entire verse-novel. Moreover, it suggests that the work which Aurora sits down to write in book 3 is her autobiography. In revision Barrett Browning made the age and condition of her actor/narrator less explicit, but Aurora is still described as a woman living alone (1.28) and supporting herself by writing (1.2-3).

At 1.29 Aurora Leigh begins her story in the conventional way with an account of her parents, her birth, and childhood. Books 1 and 2 give a retrospective account of her youth and education, her developing vocation, and Romney's proposal, all the events being described as past, although many conversations are related in the present tense.

In the opening passage of book 3 (1-156) the present Aurora (living in London as a writer aged twenty-six or twenty-seven) is discovered. As at 1.1-9 the present tense is adopted for the initial reverie (3.1-24) and the immediacy of the scene is further emphasised by Aurora's address to her maid (3.25-35). It is seven years since Aurora's twentieth birthday (2.1238 and 3.146), and Aurora has not seen Romney Leigh for some eighteen months (as we discover at 5.572-73). This passage is actually written after the events described in books 3 and 4 have taken place: thus Carrington's letter refers to Romney's "phalansteries"

Elizabeth Barrett Browning's tomb in the English Cemetery, Florence.

(3.108) although Romney apparently did not found the Fourierist community at Leigh Hall until after the loss of Marian Erle (5.574-75). Also, Aurora opens her account of the failed wedding by confessing her own contribution by default to the events of that day (4.438-39, 445-50, 464-67) revealing that she knows of that failure before she begins writing. At 3.156 Aurora breaks off her present tense meditation in order to resume the retrospect on her past history: "No matter; I bear on my broken tale."

As in the first two books, books 3 and 4 are set in the past, though many scenes are related dramatically in the present tense. At book 5 the narrative catches up with the chronological development of the story and thereafter the retrospective narrative is discarded in favor of a series of "journal entries," each entry including a summary of events in the recent past but beginning and ending in the present tense. The first of these entries (5.579-1278) tells of the party at Lord Howe's which has taken place on the day upon which Aurora is writing (5.580, 1037) and ends with Aurora's decision to leave England for Italy (5.1261). The second journal entry shows Aurora in Paris, includes her sighting Marian Erle, and ends with her extended but futile search for the girl (6.1-411). The illusion of a diary is maintained with the immediacy of the next entry:

—I thank God I have found her! I must say
"Thank God," for finding her, although 'tis true
I find the world more sad and wicked for't.
But she—
    I'll write about her, presently.
My hand's a-tremble, as I had just caught up
My heart to write with, in the place of it.
At least you'd take these letters to be writ
At sea, in storm!—wait now . .
                                    (6.412-19)

The large block of narrative which follows, dealing with the discovery of Marian, her story, and agreement to travel to Italy, is related in the present tense though it takes place in the past. As the entry comes to a close in the present, Aurora reproduces the letters she has just written to Lord Howe and Lady Waldemar and carries the reader into her present as she speaks in soliloquy while watching over Marian and her child (7.391-94).

The following journal entry (7.395-1039) is written some time after Aurora's establishment in Florence and catches up with Aurora's present on the day when she receives the letter from Vincent Carrington. The verse moves through the past to the present tense to bring the reader into Aurora's present (7.661-62, 668-69, 672, 675, 696-97). The final entry (7.1040-311) covers a considerable period of time (7.1040, 1273) though no new incidents occur to advance the plot.

In books 8 and 9, a third narrative method is adopted. The action covered by these two books takes place on the one night, and yet no lapse of time is included which might allow Aurora the opportunity of formally recording the events. Instead, the living Aurora overlaps with the narrating Aurora at the moment of experience. Discussion with Romney is related in quotation marks (e.g., 8.71-78, 80-123, 129-35) while Aurora's thoughts in reaction are presented as responses to specific words, formulated at the moment of reaction, and uninfluenced by any later knowledge, including knowledge acquired on that same evening (8.78-80, 123-29, 136-40, 159-69). The formally realistic methods of simple retrospect (books 1-4) and journal entries (books 5-7) are displaced in the concluding books (books 8-9) in favor of a purely literary narrative approach which transgresses the rules of narrative order to record events while in progress.[105]

This narrative experiment takes up from **"Lady Geraldine's Courtship"**: in that poem the difficulties of a narrative conclusion without mature retrospect are side-stepped by the resort to an omniscient third person. In the concluding books of *Aurora Leigh* however, the accessibility of strict representation is exploited by retaining the objective and realistic characteristics of the novel part of the verse-novel formula—that is, the colloquial language, the use of dialogue, and the device of the introduced letter. But at the same time the unrealistic narrative method of an immediate recording of events allows scope for the poetic and subjective elements of philosophic and prophetic digression.

The verse-novel does have a form, but it is one which is defined either by its opposition to—and evasion of—conventional forms (not novel, not epic, not lyric, not ballad, not drama),[106] or else as an innovative and self-consciously literary form. In its chronology, the poem has a precise pattern, the main action covering the ten years between Aurora's twentieth and thirtieth birthdays, but within that shape is a contrived pattern of repetitions which promote the possibilities for revision and comparison. In book 2, Aurora and Romney argue about poetry, the woman question, philanthropy, and independence; in book 8, Romney and Aurora's debate is resurrected and revised. Over books 3-5, Marian tells her story of isolation and humiliation; in books 6-7, her second story repeats and modifies her first.[107]

Just as events are repeated, so each of the three secondary characters reflect or parallel Aurora's experience. Similar techniques of repetition, inversion, and modification are employed for metaphors, images, ideas, and dialogues set up to be recalled and redefined at a later stage. Thus, for example, Marian twice refers to the painfully dazzling quality of Lady Waldemar's beauty (4.937-38 and 6.1007-10); the portrait of Aurora's mother is obliquely recalled on more than one occasion; and Romney's weak eyesight is remarked (4.976-77) foreshadowing his blinding.[108] The image of the book, or the muse, the question of an ideal education, the influence of father and mother, are all repeated and reexamined without any resolving summary. Thus the very length of the verse-novel gives the work a figurative past, but that past is a shifting history and subject to constant revision.

V

"The artist's part is both to be and do"[109]

"subjectivity turned outward into an actual objectivity"[110]

As the narrative pattern of *Aurora Leigh* includes the doubling processes of repetition and revision, so the same procedure of fragmentation is evoked in the poem's employment of a multiplicity of voices. Aurora's is the overriding voice, but stories other than Aurora's are told: the histories of Aurora's parents (1.29-214 and 2.606-31); Marian's two stories (3.827-4.150 and 6.900-7.113); the homilies of Romney (2.129-324) or Lord Howe (5.922-51); Lady Waldemar's tale (3.344-737). The numerous letters included in the text (Romney to Aurora and vice-versa in book 2; Aurora to Lady Waldemar in books 5 and 7, and Lady Waldemar to Aurora in book 9; Vincent Carrington to Aurora in books 3 and 7) also create stories and texts other than Aurora's own. But those alternative versions are always mediated by Aurora's authoritative narrating voice as she takes over to repeat and reinterpret, offering those other stories with a double focus.[111] More important and more striking still is the duality of Aurora's own voice as both actor and poet. Aurora Leigh describes the poet's art in terms of an amputation of experience on the one hand and of song on the other,[112] and in her autobiographical narrative she acts out both parts, suffering and recording.

Barrett Browning's own literary creed recognized her ambivalent position as a woman poet on the margins of a tradition which enabled and excluded her, so that her accounts of the importance of poetry in her life are always couched in terms of a division between the natural and physical life and the truer life attainable in the practice of composition.[113] And to Aurora, also a woman poet, Barrett Browning lends the same sense of the poetic as an alternative to nature and experience.

The metaphor which announces Aurora's autobiographical enterprise to the reader points to the split between the protagonist's role as actor and her role as self-regarding narrator:

> Of writing many books there is no end;
> And I who have written much in prose and verse
> For others' uses, will write now for mine,—
> Will write my story for my better self
> As when you paint your portrait for a friend,
> Who keeps it in a drawer and looks at it
> Long after he has ceased to love you, just
> To hold together what he was and is
>
> (1.4-8)

It also declares the exploratory nature of the ensuing narrative, which will craft the experience of the protagonist into poetic shape and which, through that very act of writing, will enable Aurora to construct and analyze her self. In the early books of the verse-novel, Aurora, as narrator, shows herself to be aware of the various attempts foisted upon her as an individual—and a woman—to write her story for her. Her aunt tells of the compact made between Aurora's father and Romney's, Vane Leigh, thus inscribing a plot for Aurora which is apparently foreordained (2.582-655). When Aurora tears up Romney's letter to her aunt—significantly unread—she escapes the "cruel springe" (2.1095) of the preordained story and the plotted self written for her by others.[114] Only with the destruction of that text is she released into the possibility of self-construction which initiates the composition of her autobiography. At the beginning of the verse-novel "I write" is reiterated, bringing those two projects together,[115] and the act of writing, in numerous forms, is emphasized and incorporated into the text. Autobiography, the private journal, and correspondence, as well as the professional acts of composing poetry and writing for the journals, are all represented within the verse-novel. In addition, the processes of writing and reading are recalled in elaborate metaphors usually relating to self-knowledge and knowledge of others (1.1-8; 824-32; 2.74-80, 369, 836-37; 5.39-41; 7.1232-35; 8.475-77).

The first four books of Aurora's story present to the reader Aurora the actor, the events of whose life are retailed, and Aurora the narrator, who comments upon those events from the point of view of her apparent maturity.[116] The brooding presence of the narrating Aurora overshadows the early books of *Aurora Leigh,* where she examines the dialogue and interrupts the (apparently) precise account with a commentary upon the action which interprets the scenes and characters with retrospective knowledge and with seeming candor.[117] The irony of this narrative method relies upon the ability of the reader to recognize the discrepancies between the versions which Aurora chooses to tell at any given time.

In these early books, the two roles of the protagonist, as actor and narrator/writer, are clearly distinguished both in chronological terms and also in terms of personality. At the same time, the two strains of literary form which make up the fabric of the poem—objective fiction and subjective lyric—are similarly aligned: the relation of events and conversations—the novelistic element—belongs largely to the past, and the heroine of that tale is the youthful Aurora characterized by enthusiasm and aspiration; the philosophical exposition and digression—the poetic element—is presented as retrospective commentary delivered in the present tense, and originates with the narrator, the Aurora of book 5 who is older, and as we are led to believe, wiser.

As from book 5 however, the narrative method comprising the journal entry sequence lessens the divide between actor and narrator, the interval between experience and expression is correspondingly curtailed, and the Aurora who both suffers and speaks is no longer temporally divided. The novelistic and poetic elements of the work are segregated still, but Aurora's lyrical reveries are no longer presented as a commentary on past events but take on a new, more urgently self-analytical character. Each aside or discursive passage is dedicated to testing and questioning, to exercises in self-recognition and self-definition; and it is the very act of writing up her journal entries which becomes the instrument of that process. For instance, concluding her account of the party at Lord Howe's with Lady Waldemar's spiteful speech, Aurora writes in her journal noting, "This reckoning up and writing down her talk / Affects me singularly" (5.1042-43) and then goes on to analyze the reasons for this reaction. In book 6, it is only while writing down the circumstances of her brief sighting of Marian some time after that event that Aurora recalls a facet of the memory of that encounter which she had attempted to suppress—the sight of the child in Marian's arms:

> . . . can I keep my own soul blind
> To the other half, . . the worse? What are our souls,
> If still, to run on straight a sober pace
> Nor start at every pebble or dead leaf,

They must wear blinkers, ignore facts, suppress
Six tenths of the road? Confront the truth, my
    soul!

(6.337-42)

The writing up of the story of Marian's rape is also used as a means of revealing to the narrator new aspects of her own character as, in the process of writing, Aurora relives the emotions engendered by the tale which she would now retell. Aurora records all her own temporary errors and misunderstandings (6.582-83, 612-17) without reference to the knowledge she has acquired before beginning to write, and so she leads up to a confrontation with her error, effected in the process of "writing up."

Aurora goes on attempting to "write herself"[118] and to inscribe her own story, both through the choices which she makes in her life (for instance, the move from England to Italy; see 7.1193-96, 1200-1203), and through the writing of the text-within-the-text, the book which Aurora Leigh writes and publishes during the period of action covered in the verse-novel. Through the presence of that book in the poem, the work proposes a swerve away from its reiterated emphasis upon subjectivity and the construction of the identity of the female self and outward into an actual objectivity. Once Aurora has written herself clearly into contemporary history and culture by "publishing herself," she can be read and even be more accurately interpreted by the (masculine) public world from which her (feminine) private subjectivity should otherwise exclude her. Romney, Vincent Carrington, and Kate Ward all read Aurora's book, and, in different ways, endorse its general and political, as opposed to its private and personal, significance.[119] Thus, as in Barrett Browning's *Casa Guidi Windows,* the feminine margin with its valorization of the subjective and personal is presented as the true account of the central, general, and political masculine world.

Cora Kaplan notes that *Aurora Leigh,* as an attempt "to discuss the relationship between women's experience, politics and creativity" stands behind other novels centering on women's writing, notably Doris Lessing's *The Golden Notebook* (1962).[120] In fact, the two works are also remarkably similar in their strategy of initial disintegration, segregating prose narrative of events (Lessing's "Free Women" novel-within-novel; Barrett Browning's relation of the conventions of contemporary life in the plot of the verse-novel) and lyrical exposition and expansion upon politics, philosophy, and art (in Lessing's novel, the notebooks; in *Aurora Leigh,* the interspersed subjective commentary). Furthermore, in both cases, the emphasis in the philosophical and subjective discursive narrative is placed upon the construction of an individualized self to be analyzed and explored there. In this way, *Aurora Leigh* is recognizably an ancestor, not only to *The Golden Notebook* but also to all those experimental works which cross the boundaries between the genres of fiction and criticism to employ the digressions of history, or philosophy, or fantasy, as narrative tools. Thus firstly enabling the analysis of woman's subjectivity and secondly permitting a more overtly political project which confronts conventional restrictions upon the expression of that female self.[121]

Aurora's book, the text-within-the-text of *Aurora Leigh,* is an idealized projection of Barrett Browning's own verse-novel. Aurora's poetic theories, expounded in book 5, indicate that the book which she produces is composed on the same principles as those which inspired Barrett Browning.[122] And it is not only the theory of poetry proposed and displayed in *Aurora Leigh* but even the actual circumstances of its publication which are mirrored with Aurora's own work; in 1856 Barrett Browning, like Aurora, left her poem in the hands of her publisher as she departed for Italy to await its publication and reception. In addition, Barrett Browning included in *Aurora Leigh* the two fantasies of a group of ideal readers and a welcoming public reception to her literary and political messages. In fact, as it turned out, Barrett Browning's model for the public reception accorded her poem remained only a fantasy, for the contemporary critical attention given to the actual verse-novel focused on the personal and not on the theoretical. And in the verse-novel itself, the conclusion is the place where Barrett Browning faces the possibility that her optimistic projections for the construction of an autonomous and written self might be exposed as fables of desire.

After she has written her book, Aurora's scope for action, both as actor and narrator, shrinks into a smaller sphere (7.1296-1311). This silencing and absence of text appears for the first time in a work which insists upon its self-consciousness as a text-in-process. When the verse-novel reaches its resolution with the union of Romney and Aurora, Aurora herself comments upon the transference of her written text into lived emotion:

I have written day by day,
With somewhat even writing. Did I think
That such a passionate rain would intercept
And dash this last page?

(9.725-28)

Aurora seems, at the end, to accept a limit on the poet's narrating capacity and confesses herself unable to articulate:

What he said, indeed,
I fain would write it down here like the rest,

. . . . .

    What he said,
I fain would write. But if an angel spoke

> In thunder, should we haply know much more
> Than that it thundered? If a cloud came down
> And wrapt us wholly, could we draw its shape,
> As if on the outside and not overcome?
>
> (9.728-29, 737-42)

The clue to the reason for this new silence on Aurora's part is suggested by the late introduction of the feminizing elements pressurizing Aurora: Marian as natural woman, Italy as motherland, her identification with other women. One possible resolution of Aurora's story, a resolution which Aurora is unable to articulate, is proposed by Romney.

A passage from book 7 prefigures this moment in the poem in arguing that "Love strikes higher with his lambent flame / Than Art can pile the faggots."[123] As has long been recognized, Aurora's life-argument seems to rest, in the end, upon a love versus art opposition. Less immediately obvious is the fact that these two ideas are only relevantly opposed when the poet/artist under discussion is also a woman. Aurora (and, to some extent, Barrett Browning—like other women poets of the nineteenth century) internalizes the ideology of the woman's sphere where, as a *woman,* she can only be fully *human* with the fulfillment of romantic love and a sexual relation.[124]

Aurora Leigh is a narrative which involves a quest, but it is a heroine's quest for the whole self and, as such, requires a resolution which includes successful marriage as the conventionally defining characteristic of feminine completeness. But by accepting this part of the ideology of patriarchy, Aurora might be courting a self-silencing; once she is complete as a woman—and resolved as a story—she will not be able to go on with the speaking/writing of the self but will be authored by conventional expectations (as in Romney's account of an ending), losing those imperatives of self-determination which were the incentive to narrative in the first place."[125] Yet as the poem concludes, Aurora resists that ending to insist that she will go on with her professional career. The poem's perspective on the nature of woman and the place of romantic expectation in that nature suggests the character of the assumptions which require that Aurora negotiate, and avoid, a potentially negative resolution.

VI

> "I'm a woman, sir,
> I use the woman's figures naturally"[126]

From the opening account of the conventionally feminine career of Aurora's mother (youth, marriage, childbirth, death), Barrett Browning initiates a discussion of the traditional, the natural, and the actual in the female character.[127] Aurora's mother, associated with an other prearticulate world (a Wordsworthian "outer Infinite" where the only word she speaks is "Hush") and a foreign and sensuous land, is given priority in the introduction to her autobiography (1.1-19). The figure of the mother as the embodiment of Aurora's "anxiety of womanliness"[128] is then powerfully represented in the portrait which haunts Aurora's childhood (1.128-75).

But in opposition to this womanly heritage is placed the image of Aurora's father, who embodies the masculine principle as intellectual, articulate, cold, conventional, and English—and his presence is invoked by Aurora as she begins to write:

> O my father's hand,
> Stroke heavily, heavily the poor hair down,
> Draw, press the child's head closer to thy knee!
> I'm still too young, too young, to sit alone.
>
> I write.
>
> (1.25-29)

When Aurora begins to write her autobiography, at the age of twenty-six and while the self-construction enacted in the autobiographical process is still going forward, she perceives her mother as representing a feminine ideal which enjoins her to silence and offers a role model restricted to that of object to be viewed. Through her father, by contrast, Aurora envisions herself as empowered to speak as he gives her the qualifications which will allow her to enter literary discourse otherwise closed to her because of her sex. He provides a traditionally masculine education in the classics ("He wrapt his little daughter in his large / Man's doublet," 1.727-28), and encourages independent thought (1.189-90). Thus, when Aurora looks for literary models, it is to father-poets that she turns (1.1003-15). With this background Aurora cannot conform to the feminine mould which her aunt prescribes; she ridicules the trivial program of an orthodox female education (1.392-426),[129] and incongruously embroiders her shepherdess with pink eyes (1.451). Aurora declares herself self-sufficient (1.470-80, 1026-66), and, claiming a vocation as a poet, she regrets the necessity of gender for any poet (2.90-91).

As Aurora reaches adulthood, she learns that it is not possible to reject altogether the imperatives of gender construction. Because of her alien mother, and, in effect, her own very femaleness which places her outside masculine traditions, she will be denied her rightful patrimony (1.606-13) and be forced to a position of dependency. In the proposal scene where Romney and Aurora dispute the area and scale of female achievement, Romney's conventional perspective can offer Aurora only two appropriate female roles; charity worker under his lead (2.350-77) or domestic solace and inspiration (2.832-33). Rejecting the abdication of power implicit in both these parts, Aurora accepts that by exchanging the heart for the head and becoming a writer, she must inevitably obtain an unsexed or transsexual condition (3.406-11 and 5.805-11). Thus Aurora's feminine inheritance is discarded and all her achievement as a poet is effected in her father's land and in his language.[130] Associating the power of writing and the right to self-expression with the masculine, Aurora goes on with her search for the father, which is also a quest for her own literary authority.[131]

During this period of alienation from the traditional values associated with the feminine, Aurora Leigh has a great deal to say about women and the female character. And most of it is platitudinous and derogatory: the emotional life of woman is illogical, irrational, and not susceptible of control (2.701-6, 7.200-202, 966-67); it is the nature of woman to crave the approbation of some one certain man in all she attempts (5.43-44) and to find herself incapable of tolerating loneliness even though she may have chosen an independent life (5.439-41); women will, for love, submit to self-sacrifice (7.222-23) and yet persist in attention-seeking overreaction in trivial matters (8.188-92).[132] But an inspection of these and similar passages reveals that each one follows directly on some penetrating realization on Aurora's part which almost (but not quite) forces her to confront her long-suppressed desire for her cousin. Associating her unnamed, indissoluble, and disruptive passion with her female nature, Aurora condemns that female character as weak, irresolute, and changeable, and values the masculine in her character as the site of reason and order:

> Poor mixed rags
> Forsooth we're made of, like those other dolls
> That lean with pretty faces into fairs.
> It seems as if I had a man in me,
> Despising such a woman . . .
>
> . . . . .
>
> Put away
> This weakness. If, as I have just now said,
> A man's within me,—let him act himself,
> Ignoring the poor conscious trouble of blood
> That's called the woman merely.
> (7.210-14, 228-32)

Nonetheless, when occasion arises, Aurora is shown to be not unwilling to play the traditionally feminine part. Sharing Romney's distress after the disappearance of Marian Erle, Aurora attempts to comfort him and to the task she brings a technique which she recognizes as typical of conventional female skills: "And I, instinctively, as women use" (4.1088-1108). Here Aurora gives up her self-consciously intellectual stance to relinquish reason for instinct (4.1088), her claim to speech for inarticulateness ("humming" and "murmuring" 4.1090, 1095), and her knowledge for "ignorance" (4.1091).[133] Aurora might seem here to have established her identity sufficiently securely to be able to afford some concession to the old-fashioned values of her sex. But this murmuring and ignorance is far removed from Aurora's intelligent capacity for speech. To gain, momentarily, Romney's approval, Aurora indulges in a masquerade of womanliness,[134] which she soon has to abandon for her old antagonistic asexuality (5.32-72) in the face of Romney's condescending evaluation of her poetry (4.1111-17). Testing out feminine roles in the first half of the verse-novel, Aurora can find none compatible with her professional life. Not, however, because woman and art are essentially incompatible but because Aurora's idea of the repertoire of the feminine is constricted by the stereotyped models available to her.

Because Aurora believes in the poet's (and her own) special capacity to see the truth, she is seduced into pronouncing the half-truths and generalizations which her private needs dictate as if they were absolutes. Yet the poem does not propose that Aurora's credos on womanhood be taken seriously, for the narrative includes a reconciliation with her sex in its account of Aurora's intellectual progress. This reconciliation is eventually effected through the mediation of Marian Erle.[135] The trajectory described by Marian Erle's career inverts the pattern of Aurora's[136] to demonstrate the essential need of the individual (woman) to establish a security of self-recognition. Marian is a natural woman: she "springs up" like a "nettle" (3.854-58) and begins life as an outcast (3.836-46), much as Aurora's feminine side is formulated in the foreignness of her mother. But where the middle-class Aurora is inducted into conventional social order by her father's education and her aunt's function as "patriarchy's paradigmatic housekeeper,"[137] Marian, partly as a result of her class, remains altogether unsocialized, naturally female—a nettle and not an artifically selected pink (3.853).[138]

The comparison is an important one, for it clearly shows the way in which Barrett Browning employs and questions a conventional idea of woman as "undevelopt man." She draws on contemporary biological theories which, extrapolating from such facts as brain weight (which is theorized into an opposition of feminine intuition versus masculine reason and mentioned in Aurora Leigh at 1.60-63), argued that woman, like earlier forms of human development in the evolutionary chain, represented a lower form of life than that higher stage represented by man.[139] From her first introduction, Marian is associated closely with natural images which suggest both her untroubled femininity—markedly unlike Aurora's—and the consequent exploitation which she suffers in common with all the natural world used by the higher order of civilized man. Even the description of Marian's birth affirms her alliance with a generalized Mother Nature who brings her forth in defiance of "man's law" and "the social code" (3.841-46).

Marian remains an outcast educated by looking at the sky (3.881-901), by reading the book of the earth (3.950-52), and through studying scraps of texts which she gleans to make "a nosegay of the sweet and good / To fold within her breast" (3.991-92). Without social power, she is bodily subject to exploitation: her parents regard her as a meal-ticket and her mother (whose own wretched experience Marian's life seems set to repeat) attempts to sell her, forcing her to flee from the hills and dwell in the town. There, too, Marian finds no companionship with her worldly fellow seamstresses, until one of them requires her womanly assistance in her illness.[140]

When Romney offers Marian marriage he also offers her the feminine role of assistant in philanthropic enterprise for which she is naturally suited. But in describing the scene of Romney's proposal, Barrett Browning uses a metaphor which suggests that here, too, Marian suffers the rapacious (though natural) physical exploitation of the weak by the strong and is more Romney's victim than his willing bride:

> All the rest, he held her hand
> In speaking, which confused the sense of much.
> Her heart against his words beat out so thick,
> They might as well be written on the dust
> Where some poor bird, escaping from hawk's beak,
> Has dropped and beats its shuddering wings,—
> the lines
> Are rubbed so, . . .
>   (4.131-37)

Marian is willing, but blindly so, not recognizing any conditions which she herself might require of such a union. When Aurora questions Romney's love for Marian, the girl, puzzled at first that any woman might make demands (4.168-202), later realizes the significance of the question (4.944-49). In book 2, Aurora had refused Romney's offer of marriage because it reduced her to the status of a slave, denying her vocation and identity. Marian, we learn eventually, was prepared to accept the same reductive offer because she acquiesced in the necessity of female sacrifice:[141]

> She felt his
> For just his uses, not her own at all,
>
> . . . . .
>
>   . . . let him write
> His name upon her . . it seemed natural;
>   (6.906-7, 911-12)

In Marian's second story, the notional rape expressed by this formula is translated into actual experience of the extremes of sexual humiliation ("Do wolves seduce a wandering fawn in France? / Do eagles, who have pinched a lamb with claws, / Seduce it into carrion?" 6.767-69), and Marian does, literally, lose her identity and sense of self. She is deranged for some time (6.1230-68) and describes herself thereafter as changed, tortured into a different form as the sea marks a stone (6.809-12) or altered as death reshapes body and spirit (6.812-31). The evolutionary character of those passages is also rendered clear by the introduction of the "madrepores" passage in book 6 (804-12). As in a similar (though more extended) passage in Charles Kingsley's *Alton Locke*,[142] Marian hallucinates an accelerated process of biological development from the lowest form of life where she loses all sense of a civilized individual self and becomes nothing but a body. That this process is figuratively applied to the "use-value"[143] experience of women in the nineteenth century is made explicit later in the verse-novel when Aurora refers to the prevalence of prostitution in the "civilized" cities of Europe as the marketing of daughters as "offal" (7.864-66).

As a mother, too, Marian continues her role as natural (and subservient) woman. At first, she declares that it is only for the sake of her (male) child that she continues to live, and in that relation she remains unaware of any personal need:

> She leaned above him (drinking him as wine)
>
> . . . . .
>
>   . . . Self-forgot, cast out of self,
> And drowning in the transport of the sight
>   (7.599, 604-5)

However, when Romney later comes to claim Marian, urged on by the apparent requirement of protection for the social exile, he finds that Marian (through Aurora's example) has learnt a new sense of her own worth which confers an independence:

> . . . I, who felt myself unworthy once
> Of virtuous Romney and his high-born race,
> Have come to learn,—a woman, poor or rich,
> Despised or honoured, is a human soul,
> And what her soul is, that, she is herself,
> Although she should be spit upon of men
>   (9.326-31)

Furthermore, after refusing Romney's offer of protective marriage, Marian can envisage a life without her son, which makes practical use of her female experience of suffering (9.436-39).

That Marian's career should examine a progression from a natural femininity of sacrifice to a learned self-respect and identity is endorsed by the replies which Barrett Browning gave to friends who complained of the violence meted out to the character. To Sarianna Browning she wrote, "Marian had to be dragged through the uttermost debasement of circumstances to arrive at the sentiment of personal dignity": Marian's progress is woman's evolution in little. In a lengthy unpublished letter, Barrett Browning compared Marian to Richardson's Clarissa, noting that Marian should be permitted dignity and purity and that she should "triumph" over Clarissa in being allowed to live.[144]

In contrast to Marian, Aurora Leigh begins her story with too much of the naturally masculine in her psychological character, and consequently she devalues the feminine. Although sufficiently sure of her special perception to defend Marian against Romney's suspicions "As I'm a woman and know womanhood" (4.1067), she nonetheless assumes the worst of the female character upon finding Marian in France with an illegitimate baby and accuses Marian of weakness in succumbing to a seducer and of complacency in contemplating the child, the fruit of her "sin" (6.612-17, 742-47). Marian's vindicating disclosure of the violent circumstances of her impregnation forces Aurora, and for the first time, to recognize her own fallibility. That acknowledgment is linked to her reconciliation to her nature as a woman, sharing in Marian's suffering:

> But I, convicted, broken utterly,
> With woman's passion clung about her waist
> And kissed her hair and eyes,—"I have been wrong,
> Sweet Marian" . . (weeping in a tender rage)
>
> . . . . .
>
> . . . Innocent,
> My sister!
> (6.778-81, 787-88)

Aurora begins by showing Marian the way to independence, but then Marian takes over to show Aurora the way toward an integrated female self. The point is emphasized in the rhetoric of the poem when Aurora leads Marian "As if . . . by a narrow plank / Across devouring waters" (6.482-83) but subsequently follows Marian: "Then she led / The way, and I, as by a narrow plank / Across devouring waters, followed her" (6.500-502).

Through the second part of the verse-novel, Aurora moves into a feminized environment in her mother's native land (5.1266-71) where she shares her household with Marian and her child and learns to appreciate the healing qualities of mutual support (7.409-416, 426-28, 504-14) and to involve herself actively in Marian's mothering (6.120-25, 930-57). Her newly discovered sympathy embraces women other than Marian, as Aurora revisits the city and the landmarks associated with her mother's life (7.1223-56). By the time Romney arrives, apparently intruding on this female world, Aurora can assert with new dignity a fact which has been obvious to the reader of the poem for some time: "I'm a woman, sir, / I use the woman's figures naturally" (8.1130-31). For throughout her narrative, even while condemning the feminine nature, Aurora has employed imagery explicitly female in its concerns—suckling, weaning, sewing, cooking, manipulating trailing skirts, and cumbersome arrangements of hair. From the beginning, Aurora's feminine perspective has yielded her an enriched poetic vocabulary, but it is only at the conclusion, once a "correct" balance between womanly and manly attributes has been achieved, that the value of that perspective can be acknowledged.

It should be noted here that Barrett Browning gave Marian Erle, and not Aurora, a personal appearance which very closely resembled her own (3.809-26; 6.399-401; 9.277-78). That Marian should be depicted as her author's physical self, while the character of Aurora portrayed her intellectual self-construction in writing, suggests again the inevitable duality which Barrett Browning conceived as necessary to the writing woman, a crossbreed, evolving out of a feminine nature and a masculine order.

But to have Aurora arrive at a correct balance between womanly and manly is not the whole solution to the questions which *Aurora Leigh* raises. Aurora begins with a stereotyped idea of what is possible for, and appropriate to, female achievement, and even after she has accepted Marian's "lesson" of reconciliation, she still retains the conventional notions which force women's lives into an opposition between love and art. Once arrived in Italy, and fully reintegrated into the feminine, Aurora finds that she is a "ghost" of herself (7.1158-64). She cannot act or write (7.1296-1311)—she has, after all, left behind her father's country and language and with it, apparently, all claim to action and to speech. She chooses not to revisit her mother's grave, partly because the tombstone can only be a false trace of the real existence it represents so inadequately and partly because even that "inscription" itself will soon be obliterated (7.1142-55). But now Aurora seems to be following her mother's pattern, and she is threatened with being wiped out as a text and as a producer of texts. With other ordinary women Aurora resigns herself to an apparently inevitable passivity and resolves not to ask but to wait for something to be given to her (7.1265-72).

At this point in the verse-novel, the acceptance of the feminine reinforces the imperative of silence proposed by the contemporary conventions of femininity and endorsed in *Aurora Leigh* by Marian and Aurora's mother. The only feminine element missing is romantic love and successful marriage which, according to the codes of the nineteenth-century feminine, should conclude the poem because only then will Aurora fully realize her human potential. Thus, if Aurora continued to integrate herself into the stereotypes of cultural history by accepting the earthy passivity which responds but does not act,[145] then she would indeed dissolve her self (7.1308-11). But in fact, Aurora reaches this archetypal negative of femininity *before* the end of the poem, so that those critics who see her marriage as capitulation are taking too gloomy a view of the possibilities Barrett Browning proposed for her heroine.[146]

The ending of *Aurora Leigh* imagines a radical break from the traditions of the nineteenth-century feminine by proposing that a woman's life might contain both love and work and that each might reinforce, rather than contradict, the other. Aurora is threatened with the loss of her work well before the conclusion of the verse-novel; she is reduced to passivity at the end of book 7 but recovers her voice in books 8 and 9. Furthermore, before Aurora finally reaches a union with Romney she is faced with the prospect of having to give him up to Marian, and the image which she uses to describe that act of sisterly self-sacrifice includes the suggestion that she may also, thereby, give up poetry. Her robe as a poet is that of Aaron the prophet, embroidered with bells and pomegranates (7.1302-3). In her part as the feminine negative at the end of book 7 she still wears the robe, though she cannot "jingle bells upon [her] robe" or write. But when Aurora advises Marian to accept Romney, she describes her regret as the doffing of the poet/prophet's robe in preparation for death (9.251-54). Marian rejects Romney's offer and, as she has once already reversed roles with Aurora, "gives" Romney to Aurora (9.424-26, 439-52), permitting, not through law, but from a feminine and a specifically outcast position, Aurora's desire and marriage.

Marian Erle as natural woman functions as a mirror of possibilities for Aurora. But it is the figure of Romney Leigh which functions in the major part of the narrative as her most significant mirror. One contemporary reviewer of *Aurora Leigh* complained of Romney as a "noodle" who did not deserve his prominence in the poem.[147] But it is that very prominence in itself which presents a problem, for Romney rarely appears before the reader without the bias of Aurora's vision. He enters the action of the plot only thrice (in books 2, 4, and 8-9), and yet his name is constantly repeated as all Aurora's musings are refined down to the two points of "Romney and me." Aurora thus reverses the tradition of the silent woman used by the male poet and lover to define himself: like the male sonneteer, Aurora does not recognize her lover's individual or independent life but reduces him to a cipher used as mirror for the personal purpose of self-construction.[148] On Romney's first extended appearance in book 2, he *is* Aurora's "public" (2.59) and for him she will "perform" (2.253-55).

In an effort to justify herself and construct her own sense of a valued identity, Aurora continues to harp on Romney's early errors and earnest pomposity. Her resentment gradually leads her to give an increasingly wayward account of Romney's character. Believing him capable of self-deceit, Aurora grows disgusted—"How vile must all men be, since *he's* a man" (8.138). In the end she can believe not only that Romney is married to Lady Waldemar but that he nonetheless enviously wishes himself married to a girl (Kate Ward) whom he has never seen (8.123-37). At the conclusion of book 8, Romney laughs scornfully at Aurora's supposition that he is married to Lady Waldemar and accuses her of "forgery" (8.1231-35).[149] Thus Aurora's impudent and disruptive intrusion into conventionally masculine traditions and texts has betrayed her into falsehood. The methods Aurora has hitherto used to create her identity are based only on the old traditions but with an added gender reversal. As a result, they still produce misreadings.

While Aurora creates Romney, her retrospective view of the image of Romney's face haunts her memory (2.510-11, 1172-73, 1237-38; 3.233-34), provokingly wielding an apparently inexplicable power (2.1238-42).[150] The reiterated emphasis upon Romney's face, Romney's look, Romney's eyes, so disturbing, and for most of the narrative, so unintelligible to Aurora, prepares the way for a conclusion which deprives Romney of his sight. Romney's looking at Aurora is constructed in her imagination as a narcissistic self-reflection. He functions as the "other" by which she is defined, offering an absolute against which she can assert her distinction.

Barrett Browning justified depriving Romney of his sight by an argument related to Milton's blindness.[151] Romney has to be blind to the material world in order to learn to see the spiritual truths of Aurora's argument—and Aurora herself.[152] But once Romney is blind, Aurora loses the gaze which created her difference of opposition and resistance—a difference which constructed her self, certainly, but constructed that self as a negative term.[153] With Romney's gaze removed, Aurora can start with new terms, new forms of language. Having accepted a valuing of her female identity, Aurora needs to shed ideas of hierarchy and value in male and female—and one way that reeducation takes place is through the abolition of the systems of difference and measurement which Aurora had used to "make" a self.[154]

With the discovery of Romney's blindness comes release into autonomous action. No longer waiting to be given a resolution but inspired by desire and uninhibited by correct behaviour or proper form, Aurora declares herself unreservedly, and does not even mention marriage (though it is assumed). This conclusion, where Aurora is the active partner, is an explicit improvement upon the concluding scene of **"Lady Geraldine's Courtship"** where Geraldine appears as a silent statue whose desire has to be expressed and authorized by the male poet.

The end of the poem also affirms that Aurora will write again, working "for two" (9.911).[155] She offers concrete evidence of renewed creativity with both a lyrical hymn (9.814-42) and an epic of revision (9.843-964) written into her text. Now, instead of masquerading as a woman, Aurora can express herself independently both of conventional prescription for the feminine and of the defining systems which gave her an identity through resistance. She is not complete or whole in the strictly conventional sense where the "undisciplined heart" learns its lesson—which is why she declines to write Romney's version of their resolving union. But Aurora is triumphant in that, having recognized difference, contradiction, opposition, and process, she can incorporate all of those failures and errors without needing a seamless truth—or even a neat pattern. She goes on polishing, adding, revising to the end, offering even at this late stage yet another, and different, version of the whole story of the verse-novel with her summary of Romney's version of the past (9.760-813). These constantly renewed attempts at repetition, variety, and revision suggest the inadequacy of any absolute conclusion. But they also indicate the potential for an approximation to vision through this legible, if fragmented, text.

The final lines of the poem acknowledge that the verse-novel itself is only a hieroglyph for a significance beyond its own formal "material" literary show (7.861); Aurora and Romney look out at the dawn—but what she imagines, and what he sees with his new spiritual vision, is the idea of "perfect noon" (9.961). Aurora herself, named for the promise of a new day, shadows out that dawn.

VII

"I am inclined to think that we want new *forms,* as well as thoughts. The old gods are dethroned. Why should we go back to the antique moulds .. classical moulds, as they are so improperly called? . . . Let us all aspire rather to *Life* . . ."[156]

"What form is best for poems? Let me think Of forms less, and the external. Trust the spirit, As sovran nature does, to make the form";[157]

One of the most striking characteristics of *Aurora Leigh,* an aspect of the verse-novel much overlooked, largely because of a critical focus upon the supposed autobiographical and experiential nature of the poem, is the *literariness* of the work. When the poem opens with the announcement of Aurora's intention to write she not only claims a right to speak as a woman, but she draws attention to the character of the verse-novel as a self-conscious text which examines the processes of writing and reading. That the work itself was conceived (as was the ideal book which Aurora writes) as a crossbreed verse-novel, androgynous in its appropriation of the feminine subjective and the masculine objective, is one reason for its obsessive artfulness and introspection, but the ways in which that literary enterprise of textual self-examination are effected are diverse in character.

One result of this formal enterprise is an intertextuality which uses allusion to widen its scope of reference. That *Aurora Leigh* employs allusion as a formal device promoting "philosophical dreaming and digression"[158] is a fact ignored by critics who (often unwittingly) downgrade the achievement of poetry written by women. Since the poem's first appearance, the story which was created for *Aurora Leigh* has been condemned by some as a patchwork of plagiarism, George Sand and Charlotte Brontë being the most regularly noticed influences.[159] Other sources have been variously listed as Eugene Sue (especially his *Mystères de Paris*), Balzac, Charles Kingsley, Elizabeth Gaskell's *Ruth,* Clough's *Bothie of Tober-na-Vuolich* and, most persuasively, Germaine de Stael's *Corinne, or Italy*.[160] If reductive source-hunting is the end, then the constituents of the plot of *Aurora Leigh* are an easy target for criticism. But this approach to the techniques of allusion betrays a critical doublethink, which essentially trivializes the reading process where the reader is a woman: novel-reading for her is a vice or a relaxation and the woman reader is excessively susceptible of influence because of her imitative nature.[161]

Cora Kaplan offered a positive description of the plot as "an elaborate collage of typical themes or motifs of the novels and long poems of the 1840's and 1850's," and much has been made since of the fact that *Aurora Leigh* is a dense work of textual and cultural reference, offering telling reinterpretations of familiar tropes, archetypes, myths, and literary texts.[162] Thus *Aurora Leigh* becomes not a plagiarized would-be novel, but a poetic framework for suggestion and reference which foreshadows the constructive uses of fragmentation found in such later productions as Virginia Woolf's *Between the Acts,* or Angela Carter's art of *bricolage*.[163] And this magpie form, which steals fragments of a tradition or language from which women have been alienated, to rewrite or invert them, can be defined in itself (though practiced in modernist and postmodernist works by both women and men[164]) as culturally feminine.[165]

Yet while the very form of the bastard verse-novel might express, in its diffuseness, the sense of female exclusion and marginalization both in and from a patriarchal culture, the example of *Aurora Leigh* shows how secret that femaleness has to be—in part, precisely because of the nineteenth-century woman author's acceptance of the ideology which excludes her. The most significant sources forming an allusive background to the poem were the works of Sand, Brontë and de Stael. Yet in *Aurora Leigh,* while the list of names or works cited include those of Aeschylus, Wordsworth, Carlyle, Keats, Browning, and Rousseau, not one woman author is named or quoted directly.[166] Barrett Browning's experience of a personal anxiety of influence or rather, authority, meant that while allusions to the works of male writers are explicit, those to the works of female writers are implicit.[167]

As the techniques of allusion break up formal constrictions, responding to the challenge of a new form, so the verse-novel recommends a program of exchange between text and reader which similarly breaks up conventional literary order. The very length of the verse-novel, the changing narrative methods, the palindrome of the plot, the repetition and modification of dominant images, the use of "round" time and the shuffling of tenses, provide scope for reflection and revision in the reader's experience of the poem—and the narrative form of *Aurora Leigh* insists that the reader participate in that process. A model for this procedure is included in the account of an ideal poetics as Aurora imagines an active reader-response which would allow her to convey ideas to "thrilling audient and beholding souls / By signs and touches which are known to souls" (7.849-50).[168]

Barrett Browning's acknowledged aim in adopting formal methods which demanded the participation of the reader was related to her belief that the poet's art should live; taking God as the ultimate model for the artist, and God's art as the living world (5.434-35). Thus Aurora lives before the reader, all mistakes and confusions included, and we are expected to adjust assessment and judgment accordingly. In 1845 Robert Browning and Elizabeth Barrett had agreed that the dramatic poet should realize fictional characters before the eyes of the reader,[169] and Barrett Browning included this necessity in her exposition of Aurora's poetic theory, "The rulers of our art" (5.307):

> . . . conceive, command,
> And, from the imagination's crucial heat,
> Catch up their men and women all a-flame
> For action, all alive and forced to prove
> Their life by living out heart, brain, and
>   nerve . . .
>
> (5.309-13)

It is of course the metaphor of writing which provides the first and most fully realized range of allegories on the theme of reader participation. In the central reverie of *Aurora Leigh* (book 5) the author presents, through her poet-heroine, the principles of poetry which have motivated both the book composed by the fictional author (5.352, 1213, 1263-64) and *Aurora Leigh* itself. The circumstances of production are the same for both books, and at the conclusion of the verse-novel Romney Leigh acts as the incarnation of Barrett Browning's ideal reader, able to read and comprehend all Aurora's poem, delivered though it is in shadowing "signs and touches" (8.265-69, 283-88, 605-13). Thus, a circular displacement is enacted as Barrett Browning writes a verse-novel which dramatizes the autobiography of a fictional woman writer who herself, within the poem, writes a verse-novel which mirrors the form, scope, and proposed achievement of the actual poem, *Aurora Leigh* itself. And this very circularity suggests the living quality of the vision Barrett Browning's work attempts, which is not static and clearly seen but subject to interference and variety—as in Aurora's own vision at the climax of the poem:

> His breath against my face
> Confused his words, yet made them more
>   intense,
> (As when the sudden finger of the wind
> Will wipe a row of single city-lamps
> To a pure white line of flame, more luminous
> Because of obliteration)
>
> (9.743-48)[170]

In addition to writing/reading images, *Aurora Leigh* employs a number of images where visual art, particularly the portrait,[171] is invoked as an artifact powerfully suggestive to the viewer (or reader). Thus the narrator declares her intention to write her story in these terms (1.4-8), and each of the many portraits cited in the work is used, through the reactions of the viewer (usually Aurora herself), to reflect or emphasize some aspect of Aurora's personal narrative. The portrait of Aurora's mother is the medium which the child invests with capacity to represent all forms of feminine incarnation (1.145-63), and the reflexive suggestion of the portrait is developed as each incarnation is reenacted through the female characters in the poem: Aurora plays the part of the "dauntless Muse who eyes a dreadful Fate" (1.155) and the "loving Psyche who loses sight of Love" (1.156); her aunt, repressed and damaging, whose eyes are imaged as knives (1.327-330) represents Medusa; Marian, suffering virgin and mother, merges with "Our Lady of the Passion, stabbed with swords / Where the Babe sucked" (7.126-32); while Lady Waldemar becomes, in Aurora's imagination, the "woman-serpent" Lamia (6.1100-1101; 7.144-74).[172]

In book 3, Aurora's status as a poet, alternately aspiring and quiescent awaiting inspiration, is mirrored in the two pictures of Danae which the artist Vincent Carrington sends to her (3.122-35), and in which Aurora recognizes an implied application to her own situation (3.135-42).[173] The irony of Carrington's portrait of Kate Ward, which shows her in a cloak of Aurora's pattern, holding in complimentary reverence the poet's latest book, is not lost upon Aurora, who at that point has lost all faith in her own literary capability (7.705-7). Even Romney's decisive attachment to the portrait of their shared ancestor Lady Maud (8.955-59), is not so much a device for facilitating Romney's tragedy as another mirror of Aurora's destiny—for the picture resembles Aurora herself, and Romney's rescuing it leads obliquely to their reunion.

Like the process of allusion, which steals a language appropriate to the woman author (both Aurora and Barrett Browning) who at once accepts and resists her marginalization, the metaphoric emphasis upon images derived from writing/reading and painting/being viewed suggest the besieged ambivalences of the nineteenth-century woman writer. Aurora shows herself (like Barrett Browning) to be conscious always of her dual role as active subject and passive object (artist/woman, writer/text, individual/portrait), and she takes that self-consciousness into her text by introducing other objects (literary texts, the idea of the book and the picture, mirror characters), against which to measure herself as subject. Her poetic language, a woman's language growing out of her oblique relation to cultural and literary order, cannot employ any positive terms but works, initially at least, through resistance and difference while it attempts a new language and form. Using this language, the woman poet (Aurora/Barrett Browning) adopts a poetic method which returns continually to herself and her difference, playing endlessly between the two—thus her experience of cultural marginalization (rather than any biological essence or authenticity) yields her both a subject and a form.[174]

To read Barrett Browning's verse-novel in the light of feminist theory is to acknowledge that there can be no jubilant and whole recovery of women's writing of the nineteenth century. When Barrett Browning looked for "grandmothers" and found only "poetesses," when she admired Robert Browning's masculine and objective method over her own subjective manner, when she attempted a synthesis of the two in the experimental form of the verse-novel, when she marshaled there metaphors, mirrors, and narrative procedures which relied upon difference and opposition, then Barrett Browning revealed her beleaguered position as a disinherited or bastard girl-child of the culture which fathered her. Her own awareness of that position was obvious to her only fitfully, but its effects can be clearly read from our perspective[175]—and the results of that potential for disintegration can be positive.

Barrett Browning's (conscious and unconscious) recognition of difference promoted the strengths of experiment, subversion, and challenge both in the subjects tackled in *Aurora Leigh* and in the narrative and literary forms adopted there. And even when Aurora achieves the full integration into the nineteenth-century ideal of human individuality (that is, through marriage), she attempts strenuously to escape the (conventional platitudes of the) feminine which would lead to resolution/dissolution and silence. Instead of accepting the stereotype that to be a woman writer is to be unsexed and to be forced to make a choice between love and art, Aurora forcefully claims both.

Aurora Leigh is a woman's book; as the story of a woman poet told by a woman poet, its subjects and their treatment, its narrative and poetic form, are all dictated by that fact. Too frequently, however, that fact has been read not in relation to the historical context and cultural assumptions which produced the verse-novel but in the light of other, unexamined, ideological assumptions about what constitutes a woman's book. In these repeated, but diverse, erroneous readings lies the reason for the variety of critical reaction to *Aurora Leigh*. Always perceived as a woman's book, it was consequently valued—as a gospel by sympathetic nineteenth-century readers, as an authentic record of female experience by twentieth-century feminist readers—and dismissed—as shrill and unwomanly by nineteenth-century reviewers, as chaotic, uncontrolled, and sloppy by twentieth-century humanist critics.

Aurora Leigh has never been admitted to the canon of literature; women's texts are only permitted to appear there provided they are not read as women's texts.[176] When *Aurora Leigh* can be included in the canon, recognized as of human and therefore generally significant interest *because* of its overriding address to the theoretical (and practical) questions of the cultural and literary formation, exclusion, and prohibition of women in writing, then its significance as a primary text of the nineteenth century might be acknowledged.

Notes

...[41] EBB to RB, commenting on his account of John Stuart Mill's marginal notes to *Pauline,* 27 Feb. 1845, *RB/EBB Letters* 1:31.

[42] Homans, *Women Writers,* 12-40; Leighton locates her immediate literary influences in the Romantic poets, particularly Wordsworth. *Elizabeth Barrett Browning,* 12-13. Kathleen Blake shows how that influence is translated into the work of the woman poet. "Elizabeth Barrett Browning and Wordsworth: The Romantic Poet as Woman." *Victorian Poetry,* vol. 24, no. 4, (Winter 1986): 387-98. Helen Cooper reads Barrett Browning's "The Poet's Vow" (from *The Seraphim*) as the reinterpretation by the "daughter poet" of the female presence of Nature in Romantic poetry. *Elizabeth Barrett Browning, Woman and Artist* (Chapel Hill and London, 1988), 37-43.

[43] "In Romantic poetry, the self and the imagination are primary." Homans, *Women Writers*, 12; "Glimpses into my own life and literary character" (1820); ed. W. S. Peterson, *BIS* 2 (1974) 121-33 and *The Brownings' Correspondence:* 1:348-56; "I quite believe as you do that what is called the 'creative process' in works of Art, is just inspiration & no less.' *RB/EBB Letters* 1:96; in her articles for *The Athenaeum* (1842) she speaks of Wordsworth as the "poet-hero" and "poet-prophet." See also her references to the role of the poet in *Aurora Leigh* 1.858-69 and 5.1-343.

[44] Preface to *An Essay on Mind* (London, 1826), xii. A comprehensive account (though as yet incomplete) of Barrett Browning's poetic theory is contained in Meredith B. Raymond's three articles in *BSN* vol. 8, no. 3 (1978): 3-7; vol. 9, no. 1 (1979): 5-9; vol. 11, no. 2 (1981): 1-11.

[45] *The Athenaeum*, 4, 11, 25 June and 6, 13, 27 August 1842. Five articles were devoted to reviewing an anthology, *The Book of the Poets*, and one to Wordsworth's *Poems Chiefly of Early and Late Years, including the Borderers, a tragedy*. Although the two reviews stand as separate pieces, together they form a coherent exposition of Barrett Browning's views on literature from Chaucer to Wordsworth.

[46] Review of *The Book of the Poets*, *The Athenaeum* (11 June 1842): 521, 522.

[47] ". . . the mind in creation is as a fading coal, which some invisible influence, like an inconstant wind, awakens to transitory brightness; this power arises from within, like the colour of a flower which fades and changes as it is developed, and the conscious portions of our nature are unprophetic either of its approach or its departure." Percy Bysshe Shelley, "A Defence of Poetry," *Essays, Letters from Abroad, Translations and Fragments* ed. by Mrs. Shelley (London, 1840) 1:47-48.

[48] She was, of course, not exceptional in this. Compare J. S. Mill on the characteristics of contemporary poetry: "The truth of poetry is to paint the human soul truly: . . . Great poets are often proverbially ignorant of life. What they know has come by observation of themselves; they have found *there* one highly delicate, and sensitive, and refined specimen of human nature, on which the laws of human emotion are written in large characters." (1833), *Mill's Essays on Literature and Society* ed. J. B. Schneewind (New York and London, 1965), 106. See also Robert Browning *Paracelsus* (1835) 1:726-29: "Truth is within ourselves; it takes no rise / From outward things, whate'er you may believe. / There is an inmost centre in us all, / Where truth abides in fulness." *The Poetical Works of Robert Browning*, ed. Ian Jack and Margaret Smith (Oxford, 1983), 1:195. Nonetheless, as a woman claiming to find the sources of truth in her own soul, she was peculiarly vulnerable to the critics who found the self-conscious stance of the (woman) poet/prophet unattractive and ridiculous: "She had persuaded herself that she had a message from the Infinite to deliver, and to discover this she had only to dive deep enough into the depths of her own unassisted internal consciousness." William Stigand, "The Works of Elizabeth Barrett Browning," *The Edinburgh Review*, no. 232 (Oct. 1861): 519-20.

[49] Deirdre David so describes *Aurora Leigh*. See *Intellectual Women and Victorian Patriarchy* (London, 1987), 105.

[50] EBB to RB, 20 Mar. 1845, *RB/EBB Letters* 1:41. This theme was to be taken up and reforged in *Aurora Leigh* on more than one level: there the poet who needs must practice self-examination, contemplating her own mind as the nearest reflection of the spiritual ideal, is in this way tempted not to look around her but to rely instead upon "great guesses at Human Nature."

[51] Mary Moulton Barrett to EBB, [c. Sept. 1821], *The Browning's Correspondence* 1:132; see "My own character" (1818), "Glimpses into my own life and literary character" (1820-21), "My character and Bro's compared" (1821), and the two untitled essays (1827 and c. early 1840s) in *The Brownings' Correspondence* 1:347-62. The manuscript fragment of an "Essay on Woman" ("Man's noble powers, the Poets pen sustains") now in the collection of the University of Pennsylvania, may have been influenced by Elizabeth Barrett's reading of Wollstonecraft, but the attribution of the fragment is questionable, as the handwriting has not been identified as certainly EBB's. See *Reconstruction* D308.

[52] [19] Feb. 1845, *EBB to MRM* 3:81. It may be significant that this was written at the time of the beginning of EBB's correspondence with RB; "Yes—I know Mary Wolstonecraft. I was a great admirer at thirteen of the Rights of women. I know too certain letters published under her name; but Godwin's Life of her I never saw & sh^d. like much to do so." 28-29 [27-28] Mar. 1842, *EBB to MRM* 1:379. ". . . and I read Mary Wolstonecraft when I was thirteen: no, twelve! . . and, through the whole course of my childhood, I had a steady indignation against nature who made me a woman, & a determinate resolution to dress up in men's clothes as soon as ever I was free of the nursery, & go into the world "to seek my fortune." "*How,*" was not decided; but I rather leant towards being poor Lord Byron's PAGE." 22 July [1842], *EBB to MRM* 2:7. "Mary Wolstonecraft!—yes. I used to read Mary Wolstonecraft,—(the 'Rights of woman,') . . when I was twelve years old, & "quite agree with her." Her eloquence & her doctrine were equally dear to me at that time, when I was inconsoleable for not being born a man. Ah—if I had thought that I sh^d. have lived all my life without leaving my petticoats, both in the ac-

53 "Again if one is a woman one is often surprised by a sudden splitting off of consciousness, say in walking down Whitehall, when from being the natural inheritor of that civilization, she becomes on the contrary, outside of it, alien and critical." Virginia Woolf, *A Room of One's Own* (Harmondsworth, Middlesex, 1973), 96.

54 Indeed, the woman poet's first anxieties often lie within the contradictions inherent in that challenge which sets up a conflict "between the romantic notion of the poet as the transcendant speaker of a unified culture and the dependant and oppressed place of women within that culture." Kaplan, "Language and Gender" in *Sea Changes,* 70. In Barrett Browning's case, Deirdre David sees her self-mythologizing into a member of the privileged elite and her affiliation with her male precursors and the male poets of her own generation as a compromise to her feminism. David, *Intellectual Women,* 97-98. However, this point of view takes no account of the fact that historical perspectives must give feminism different meanings at different times for different women. See Janet Todd *Feminist Literary History* (Oxford, 1988), 137.

55 It would appear that in the Moulton Barrett household women were "relative." Only sons were counted when Edward Moulton Barrett named his youngest children Septimus and Octavius. In 1810, after the birth of EBB's sister Mary (who died in infancy), Mary Trepsack, a close associate of the Moulton Barrett family, wrote to Elizabeth Barrett Williams, "Mary has had another Girl to the great disappointment of every one...." *The Brownings' Correspondence* 1:311.

56 In her *Intellectual Women,* David offers an account of the ways in which Barrett Browning, as with other women writers of the period, negotiated a literary strategy which was both "resistant to" and "complicit with" the culture that simultaneously encouraged and demeaned them. The duality of elevation and debasement in the prophet/poet's role is one of these strategies.

57 Dorothy Mermin's reading of "A Musical Instrument" puts gender (and the woman poet's anxieties) back into the poem by referring to the legend of Pan and Syrinx. See "Barrett Browning's Stories," *BIS* 13 (1985): 99-112.

58 "Somewhat more faint-hearted than I used to be, it is my fancy thus to seem to return to a visible personal dependence on you, as if indeed I were a child again; to conjure your beloved image between myself and the public, so as to be sure of one smile,—and to satisfy my heart while I sanctify my ambition, by association with the great pursuit of my life, its tenderest and holiest affection." EBB, Dedication "To My Father," *Poems* (1844).

59 Cora Kaplan, "Pandora's Box: Subjectivity, Class and Sexuality in Socialist Feminist Criticism," in *Making a Difference: Feminist Literary Criticism,* ed. Gayle Greene and Coppélia Kahn. (London, 1985), 149-51.

60 See EBB's contribution to the essay on Carlyle in R. H. Horne's *New Spirit of the Age* (1844). W. Robertson Nicoll and Thomas J. Wise, *Literary Anecdotes of the Nineteenth Century* (London, 1895-96), 2:115-18; EBB to RB, 27 Feb. 1845, *RB/EBB Letters* 1:29; although *Aurora Leigh* exhibits some consciousness of the irony of Aurora's role as a hero (when she is clearly excluded from all exercise of strength by the fact of her sex), the text reveals a measure of acceptance of the contemporary cultural hierarchy even while it assumes the possibility of usurping the roles more usually assigned to men. In effect this case provides an example of the early procedures of feminist history which Elaine Showalter labels as "feminine." "Toward a Feminist Poetics" in *The New Feminist Criticism,* ed. Elaine Showalter (London, 1986), 137-38.

61 Her most powerful statement on this is contained in a letter of advice to Mary Hunter: "How good it is to have a thing to do,—for women especially .. if women are to be distinguished from human beings; and for single women, most especially. It seems to me that the cry for work does not come from a <desire for restlessness> [restless ambition] but from a yearning for rest—In the very old times, women had less accomplishment & more occupation with an end = if they made pies & worked with their maids, it was a work, to order their homes aright—an end, if a low end. But when the fashion of refinement came up, & young ladies were to be taught to draw & play & read foreign verses, with no real artistic end>(mind?), but as poor puny amateurs, then corruption and misery fell upon women at once. Oh, if I had a daughter, she would be educated to stand by herself and work; she should learn nothing that she could not turn to use. I would rather have her a good housekeeper & cheapener in the market, than a fritterer away of time at the piano & painting & reading .. in an amateur fashion. Our fore>Grand fathers were wiser than we in some things—but I trust that our sons will be wiser than our grandfathers. For women now-a-days (taking the mass) are educated for the intellectual seraglio, no otherwise; & when the time for seraglios is past, & they remain unmarried, or with too small families of children to fill up their whole time, they are miserable, they cease to grow in their souls, the time hangs on them till it crushes them, .. there is no bright colour for them in the world.

If the injury were only in this world it would signify less. But I believe in a necessary relation between the natural & the spiritual. Every attitude & action of ours here involves a corresponding counterpart there. Therefore I cry & will cry to all who (hear?) {the page is torn} me & loudest to those whom I best . . . (love?) {torn page} work, work—any kind of work . . . (nothing?) {torn page} degrades except empty hands." EBB to Mary Hunter, 9 Jan. 1859. Berg Collection, New York Public Library. See *Checklist* 59:72.

[62] Her proposition that men should be permitted more so-called feminine characteristics is less familiar than her arguments in favor of women's adoption of masculine roles. Examples are to be found in her letters—see for instance, her rejection of the word "manly" as an appropriate adjective to describe Charles Kingsley (*Letters of EBB* 2:134); her approving remarks on Tennyson's reaction to paternity—"I do like men who are not ashamed to be happy beside a cradle" (*Letters of EBB* 2:84), and her pleasure in her son's possessing a component of "girl-nature" (*EBB to Mrs. Ogilvy*, 100). In her poetry, see particularly the "good parenting" which Aurora receives at her father's hands.

[63] Charles Fourier, *Théorie des Quatre Mouvements, Oeuvres Complètes* (Paris, 1841-1845), 43. Quoted by Barbara Taylor in *Eve and the New Jerusalem: Socialism and Feminism in the Nineteenth Century* (London, 1983), x; "I would have the government educate the people absolutely, and *then* give room for the individual to develop himself into life freely. Nothing can be more hateful to me than this communist idea of quenching individualities in the mass. As if the hope of the world did not always consist in the eliciting of the individual man from the background of the masses, in the evolvement of individual genius, virtue, magnanimity." EBB to John Kenyon, 1 May 1848, *Letters of EBB* 1:363.

[64] "Since the siege of Troy and earlier, we have had princesses binding wounds with their hands; it's strictly the woman's part, and men understand it so. . . . Every man is on his knees before ladies carrying lint, calling them 'angelic she's,' whereas, if they stir an inch as thinkers or artists from the beaten line (involving more good to general humanity than is involved in lint), the very same men would curse the impudence of the very same woman and stop there. . . . I acknowledge to you that I do not consider the best use to which we can put a gifted and accomplished woman is to *make her a hospital nurse*. If it is, why then woe to us all who are artists! The woman's question is at an end. The men's 'noes' carry it." EBB to Anna Jameson, 24 Feb. 1855, *Letters of EBB* 2:189.

[65] "Mrs. Browning's heroine cannot, in justice to the species, be considered a career woman at heart. . . . She may scribble till midnight in her attic, review books, write a masterpiece and become famous, but all that makes her none the less ready to admit to Romney, whenever she is given a second chance, that ". . . Art is much, but love is more. / O Art, my Art, thou art much, but Love is more!" It is difficult to feel that, by her defection, the structure of women's employment lost one of its sturdier props." Patricia Thomson, *The Victorian Heroine: A Changing Ideal 1837-1873* (London, 1956), 78.

[66] Deirdre David sees concession in the conclusion of *Aurora Leigh* where woman's art is only to be used to bring about the erection of the conventional "New Jerusalem." See "'Art's a Service': Social Wound, Sexual Politics and *Aurora Leigh*," *BIS* 13 (1985): 113-36.

[67] "At last we have caught sight of Tennyson's Princess & I may or must profess to be a good deal disappointed. What woman will tell the great poet that Mary Wolstonecraft herself never dreamt of setting up collegiate states, proctordoms & the rest, . . which is a worn-out plaything in the hands of one sex already, & need not be *transferred* in order to be proved ridiculous? . . ." 28 May [1848], *EBB to MRM* 3:240. Marjorie Stone compares the two poems in their alliance of gender discussion with genre experiment. "Genre Subversion and Gender Inversion: *The Princess* and *Aurora Leigh*." *Victorian Poetry*, vol. 25, no. 2 (Summer 1987): 101-27.

[68] For the relation between *Aurora Leigh* and *The Angel in The House*, and between Barrett Browning and Patmore, see explanatory annotation to 1:427-42.

[69] EBB to Isa Blagden, [20 Oct. 1856], unpublished letter in the Fitzwilliam Museum. See *Checklist* 56:162. Two days earlier EBB had written to her sister on the same subject: "He [Coventry Patmore] has just written (& forwarded to *me* meanwhile) an article upon *women*, putting us all in our places most dogmatically. Fine mincemeat he will make of me in the North British! He *must* if he's consistent." EBB to Arabel, 18 Oct. 1856, unpublished letter in the collection of Ronald A. Moulton-Barrett and Myrtle Moulton-Barrett (hereafter cited as Moulton-Barrett Collection). See *Checklist* 56:160. Patmore's article appeared in the *National Review* 6 (Oct. 1856): 317-42.

[70] EBB to Julia Martin, [14 May 1858], quoted from Kenyon Typescript (and dated therein 14 May 1857). See *Checklist* 58:54.

[71] "for liberal humanism, feminist versions included, the possibility of a unified self and an integrated consciousness that can transcend material circumstance is represented as the fulfilment of desire, the happy closure at the end of the story. . . . As a result, the struggle for an integrated female subjectivity in nineteenth-century texts is never interrogated as ideology or fantasy, but seen as a demand that can actually be met, if not in 1848, then later." Kaplan, "Pandora's Box," in

Making a Difference, 152. "Traditional humanism . . . is in effect part of patriarchal ideology. At its centre is the seamlessly unified self—either individual or collective—which is commonly called 'Man'. . . . Gloriously autonomous, it banishes from itself all conflict, contradiction and ambiguity. . . ." Toril Moi, *Sexual/Textual Politics: Feminist Literary Theory* (London, 1985), 8.

72 EBB to RB, 15 Jan. 1845, *RB/EBB Letters* 1:9.

73 *Aurora Leigh* 5:183-88.

74 For instance, "Elizabeth Barrett was a lyric poet with an interest in political and social questions; Elizabeth Barrett Browning was primarily a political poet.". . . Kaplan, Introduction to *Aurora Leigh,* 6. See also Gilbert, "From *Patria* to *Matria,* 194-211. It is even more simple—and more incorrect—to suggest that a change in EBB's poetry occurred because of her contact with Robert Browning—in the C20th, though not in the mid-C19th, regarded as the superior poet. That view was once a commonplace but, increasingly in the face of the elevation of Barrett Browning's literary status, the critical trend is to find 'Barrett Browning influences' in Robert Browning's poetry. See Nina Auerbach, "Robert Browning's Last Word," *Victorian Poetry* 22 (Summer, 1984): 161-73; U. C. Knoepflmacher, "Projection and the Female Other: Romanticism, Browning and the Victorian Dramatic Monologue," *Victorian Poetry* 22 (1984): 139-59; Adrienne Auslander Munich, "Robert Browning's Poetics of Appropriation," *BIS* 15 (1985): 69-78; James McNally, "Touches of *Aurora Leigh* in *The Ring and the Book,*" *Studies in Browning and His Circle* 14 (1986): 85-90; and George M. Ridenour "Robert Browning and *Aurora Leigh,*" *Victorian Newsletter,* no. 67 (Spring 1987): 26-32.

75 *The Athenaeum* (11 June 1842): 521.

76 "That he was a great natural genius nobody, we believe, has doubted— . . . but that he was a great artist the majority has doubted. Yet Nature and Art cannot be reasoned apart into antagonistic principles. Nature is God's art—the accomplishment of a spiritual significance hidden in a sensible symbol. Poetic art (man's) looks past the symbol with a divine guess and reach of soul into the mystery of the significance,—disclosing from the analysis of the visible things, the synthesis or unity of the ideal,—and expounds like symbol and like significance out of the infinite of God's doing into the finite of man's comprehending. Art lives by Nature, and not the bare mimetic life generally attributed to Art: she does not imitate, she expounds. *Interpres naturae*—is the poet-artist; and the poet wisest in nature is the most artistic poet!" *The Athenaeum* (25 June 1842): 559.

77 "Every being is his own centre to the universe, and in himself must one foot of the compasses be fixed to attain to any measurement—nay, every being is his own mirror to the universe. Shakspeare wrote from within—the beautiful; and we recognise from within—the true. He is universal, because he is individual." *The Athenaeum* (25 June 1842): 559.

78 "Poetry is where God is! Can you go up or down or around and not find Him? In the loudest hum of your machinery, in the dunnest volume of your steam, in the foulest street of your city,—there, as surely as in the Brocken pinewoods, and the watery thunders of Niagara,—there, as surely as He is above all, lie Nature and Poetry in full life." *The Athenaeum* (13 Aug. 1842): 729.

79 "He is eminently and humanly expansive; and spreading his infinite egotism over all the objects of his contemplation, reiterates the love, life and poetry of his peculiat being in transcribing and chanting the material universe, and so sinks a broad gulf between his descriptive poetry and that of the Darwinian painter-poet school. Darwin was, as we have intimated all optic nerve, Wordsworth's eye is in his soul. He does not see that which he does not intellectually discern, and he beholds his own cloud-capped Helvellyn under the same conditions with which he would contemplate a grand spiritual abstraction." *The Athenaeum* (27 Aug. 1842): 757. Compare EBB's description of Wordsworth's expansiveness, "spreading his infinite egotism over all the objects of his contemplation," with the sense of expansion which the poet Aurora Leigh describes. See 1. 910-15, 5.1-30.

80 See Leighton's readings of "A Romance of the Ganges" (1838), "The Lay of the Brown Rosary" (1844), "The Romaunt of Margret" (1838), "Bertha in the Lane" (1844), and "The Romance of the Swan's Nest" (1844). Leighton, *Elizabeth Barrett Browning,* 32-39, 62-66, and 95-97. See also Mermin's readings of some of these poems and also of "The Romaunt of the Page" (1844). Mermin, "Barrett Browning's Stories," *BIS* 13 (1985): 99-112 and "The Damsel, the Knight and the Victorian Woman Poet," *Critical Inquiry,* vol. 13, no. 1 (Autumn 1986): 64-80.

81 Meredith B. Raymond and Mary Rose Sullivan, *EBB to MRM,* 1:xxxvi-vii; 24 Dec. 1844; *EBB to MRM* 3:42.

82 EBB to John Kenyon, 8 Oct. 1844, *Letters of EBB* 1:204; 24 Dec. 1844, *EBB to MRM* 3:42.

83 30 Dec. 1844, *EBB to MRM* 3:49.

84 27 Feb. 1845, *RB/EBB Letters* 1:31; 13 Jan. 1845, ibid., 1:7. And he does express a similar creed in his work. Compare *Pauline* 268-76, *Paracelsus* 1:726-37, and the "Essay on Shelley," passim.

⁸⁵ Karlin suggests that RB saw EBB as a subjective poet because the terms of Browning's compliment are essentially personal, revealing that he perceives of Barrett's poetry as first of all *private* in its uses. Contrastingly, he suggests that EBB saw RB as an objective poet because Elizabeth Barrett's compliment to him is couched in public terms, connecting his work to the arena in which it is conducted—that is, within the received "schools of the day." See Karlin, *Courtship*, 64.

⁸⁶ "You have in your vision two worlds—or to use the language of the schools of the day, you are both subjective and objective in the habits of your mind. You can deal both with abstract thought & with human passion in the most passionate sense. Thus, you have an immense grasp in Art...." 15 Jan. 1845, *RB/EBB Letters* 1:9.

⁸⁷ 15 Jan. 1845, *RB/EBB Letters* 1:9; 30 Dec. 1844, *EBB to MRM* 3:49.

⁸⁸ "But my chief *intention* just now is the writing of a sort of novel-poem—a poem as completely modern as 'Geraldine's Courtship,' running into the midst of our conventions, and rushing into drawing-rooms and the like, 'where angels fear to tread'; and so, meeting face to face and without mask the Humanity of the age, and speaking the truth as I conceive of it out plainly. I am waiting for a story, and I won't take one, because I want to make one, and I like to make my own stories, because then I can take liberties with them in the treatment." 27 Feb. 1845, *RB/EBB Letters* 1:31.

⁸⁹ See Robert Browning's introductory essay to *Letters of Percy Bysshe Shelley* (London, 1852), 7, 2.

⁹⁰ "the language and structure of nineteenth-century poetry . . . aspires to 'Living Form,' to make, not to copy. What kind of language is chosen, what kind of organisation occurs, and what kind of difficulties are encountered, when the poem asserts that it 'Makes'?". See Isobel Armstrong, *Language as Living Form in Nineteenth Century Poetry* (Brighton, 1982), xi.

⁹¹ From EBB's notes on the plot, at Dartmouth College, New Hampshire. See descriptions of manuscripts below.

⁹² 30 Dec. 1844, *EBB to MRM*, 3:49; 27 Feb. 1845, *RB/EBB Letters* 1:31.

⁹³ See Armstrong's reading of Robert Browning's *Sordello*. "The language behaves as if the poem is always in the making, just at the point of being brought into being, always becoming, maintained by fiats and acts of mental and physical bravado which deliberately draw attention to the *display* of making fiction...." *Language as Living Form*, 141.

⁹⁴ EBB's fragmentary notes on the plot (at Dartmouth College, New Hampshire) include these definitions. Compare the oppositions set out in her notes with her expressed reasons for objecting to contemporary socialist thought (see section 3 above). EBB's resistance to conventions of order in education and system anticipates the insights of feminist theory. Compare, for instance, Hélène Cixous: "It is impossible to *define* a feminine practice of writing . . . for this practice can never be theorized, enclosed, coded." "The Laugh of the Medusa," in *New French Feminisms,* ed. Elaine Marks and Isabelle de Courtivron (Brighton, 1980), 253.

⁹⁵ "Lady Geraldine's Courtship," 1:1-4; "Dear my friend and fellow-student, I would lean my spirit o'er you / Down the purple of this chamber *tears should scarcely run at will*" ibid., 1:1-2 (my emphasis).

⁹⁶ Attention is drawn to the immediacy of the poet's process of writing: "but that "Bertram"—why, it lies there on the paper" and "But for me—you now are conscious why, my friend, I write this letter, / How my life is read all backward, and the charm of life undone," ibid., 84.1, 90.1-2.

⁹⁷ Lady Geraldine appears in the conclusion as a vision, a statue ("Shining eyes, like antique jewels set in Parian statue-stone," conclusion, 3.2), and the fact of her silence is reiterated in stanzas 5-8 and 10.

⁹⁸ E.g., Bertram's misreading of Geraldine's remarks in stanza 66.

⁹⁹ *Casa Guidi Windows* (London, 1851), v-vii and *Casa Guidi Windows,* ed. Julia Markus (Washington, D.C., 1977), xli, 2. 64-65, xvii-xix, xli.

¹⁰⁰ In 1856 W. E. Aytoun complained that *Aurora Leigh*, in common with most British poetry, was carelessly constructed. See W. E. Aytoun, "Mrs. Barrett Browning—*Aurora Leigh*," *Blackwood's Edinburgh Magazine* 81 (Jan. 1857): 40. EBB was unperturbed; the review "coming from the camp of the enemy (artistically and socially) cannot be considered other than generous." *Letters of EBB*, 2:255. For an account of W. E. Aytoun's attack on *Aurora Leigh*, a review he made the occasion for castigating all the "Spasmodic" school, see Mark Weinstein, *William Edmondstoune Aytoun and the Spasmodic Controversy, Yale Studies in English,* 165 (Yale, 1968): 187-90. In *The Victorian Temper* (London, 1952), 61-63, Jerome H. Buckley briefly considers *Aurora Leigh* as a "Spasmodic" poem.

¹⁰¹ Those writers who have commented on the chronology and narrative structure of *Aurora Leigh* are Tompkins, *"Aurora Leigh"*; Michael L. Magie, "The Verse-Novel: Bastard Child of the Nineteenth Century," (Ph.D. diss. University of California, 1971); C. Castan, "Structural Problems in the Poetry of *Aurora Leigh*,"

[102] The narrative organization of *Aurora Leigh* resembles that of Emily Brontë's *Wuthering Heights* with part of the story delivered in retrospect before the conventional resolution of the tale (marriage/death of the protagonists) is reached.

[103] When *Aurora Leigh* was first published, reviewers did not attempt to disentangle the difficulties of the chronology. The writer in the *North American Review*, who came closest to addressing the question, professed himself puzzled: "It is difficult to conjecture at what epoch of the story the book purports to have been written. It does not seem to have been written in the form of a journal, while the events were taking place; nor yet after the story was completed...." C. C. Everett, "Poems by Elizabeth Barrett Browning," 421–22.

[104] See transcription in the Appendix.

[105] Castan finds the form of books 8 and 9 unsatisfactory: "... Mrs. Browning had sacrificed realism in the method of narration in order to keep the final Aurora—fully informed and grown sound in judgement—out of the poem till the last minute. This gives the poem a highly dramatic conclusion.... To achieve this dramatic climax, however, Mrs. Browning cheated. This lessens for me its impact, for I am annoyed that knowledge has been withheld which, according to the epic situation, should have been given." "Structural Problems," 77. However, this complaint suggests the experimental strengths of the poem's departures from the dictates of realism, genre, order, and law.

[106] "Five acts to make a play. / And why not fifteen? why not ten? or seven? / What matter for the number of the leaves, / Supposing the tree lives and grows?" *Aurora Leigh* 5:229-32.

[107] Cooper offers a diagram of the poem's "palindromic" correspondences. See *Elizabeth Barrett Browning*, 153-54.

[108] See *Letters of EBB* 2:246 where, writing to Anna Jameson about Romney's blindness, EBB makes it clear that she expected her reader to make the connection.

[109] *Aurora Leigh* 5.367.

[110] EBB, *The Athenaeum* (11 June 1842): 521.

[111] See, for instance, Aurora's account of how Marian's stories are retold in her narrative: "She told me all her story out, / Which I'll re-tell with fuller utterance,/ As coloured and confirmed in aftertimes / By others and herself too" (3.827-30) and "She told the tale with simple, rustic turns,—/ . . . I have rather writ / The thing I understood so, than the thing / I heard so" (4.151, 154-56). See also Aurora's reading of Lady Waldemar's letter: "I tore the meaning out with passionate haste / Much rather than I read it. Thus it ran. / Even thus. I pause to write it out at length" (8.1252-9.1).

[112] "The artist's part is both to be and do, / Transfixing with a special, central power / The flat experience of the common man, / And turning outward, with a sudden wrench, / Half agony, half ecstasy, the thing / He feels the inmost,—never felt the less / Because he sings it." *Aurora Leigh* 5.367-73.

[113] "What pleasure is like the pleasure of pen & ink work—when you are in the heat of it? Is it not the intense consciousness of Being—twenty senses instead of the natural complement—a doubling & tripling of the powers of life? And then, the great priviledge of throwing WORK between Life & its shadow: between yourself & all natural trouble & sense of frailty, Art & its ideal!" 6 July 1843, *EBB to MRM* 2:263. "And, for happiness . . why my only idea of happiness, as far as my personal enjoyment is concerned, . . . lies deep in poetry & its associations. And then, the escape from pangs of heart & bodily weakness . . when you throw off *yourself* . . what you feel to be *yourself,* . . into another atmosphere & into other relations, where your life may spread its wings out new, & gather on every <feather> separate plume a brightness from the sun of the sun!" EBB to RB, 3 Feb. 1845, *RB/EBB Letters* 1:15. "Like to write? Of course, of course I do. I seem to live while I write—it is life, for me. Why what is to live? Not to eat & drink & breathe, . . but to feel the life in you down all the fibres of being, passionately & joyfully. And thus, one lives in composition surely...." EBB to RB, 20 Mar. 1845, *RB/EBB Letters* 1:42. "If my poetry is worth anything to any eye,—it is the flower of me. I have lived most & been most happy in it, & so it has all my colours; the rest of me is nothing but a root, fit for the ground & the dark." EBB to RB, 15 May 1845, *RB/EBB Letters* 1:65. "I . . . so weary of my own being that to take interest in my very poems I had to lift them up by an effort & separate them from myself & cast them out from me into the sunshine where I was not . . . making indeed a sort of pleasure & interest about that factitious personality associated with them . . but knowing it to be far on the outside of *me . . myself* . . not seeming to touch it with the end of my finger . . & receiving it as a mockery & a bitterness when people persisted in confounding one with another." EBB to RB, 31 Oct. 1845, *RB/EBB Letters* 1:255.

[114] That one escape however, does not represent the last attempt at an unauthorized version of Aurora's story, each of which she has to explicitly reject and reverse: for instance, Lady Waldemar offers a story of the isolated and unsexed Sibyl based on "the old / Traditions of you" (3.406-24), and Lord Howe advises

acquiescence to the stereotyped proposals of John Eglinton (5.863-971).

[115] "Public writing and public speech, closely allied, were both real and symbolic acts of self-determination for women. Barrett Browning uses the phrase "I write" four times in the first two stanzas of book 1, emphasizing the connection between the first person narrative and the "act" of women's speech...." Kaplan, Introduction to *Aurora Leigh,* 10.

[116] For instance the reader is shown both the intolerance which the youthful Aurora felt for her aunt and her pedantic scheme of education (1.297-309, 442-46) and the contrasting understanding which the "grown up" Aurora can feel for her aunt's predicament (1.337-58; 2.893-95). Another contradiction is embodied in the presentation of Aurora's childish enthusiasm for life, books, and poetry which is juxtaposed with her more tentative commentary in retelling her story (1.798-801, 954-55).

[117] A candor most misleading, of course, where she records her denial of love in the scene of Romney's proposal (2.497-98, 501-6) only later to deny this account of her indifference (9.681-83). Other characters in the poem recognize the existence of Aurora's desire for Romney (2.687-688; 3.731-33; 9.425-27), so that the reader is not left wholly without a guide. However, one contemporary reviewer complained, quoting these passages, of the poem's confusion: Everett, "Poems by Elizabeth Barrett Browning," 422. The reviewer in *Blackwood's* declared Aurora to be "incongruous and contradictory both in her sentiments and in her actions." Aytoun, *"Aurora Leigh,"* 32. In a convincing article, published since this introduction was written, Alison Case also makes the point that Elizabeth Barrett Browning's special narrative technique in *Aurora Leigh* is designed to allow for the enactment of Aurora's processes of self-discovery. See Alison Case, "Gender and Narration in *Aurora Leigh*," *Victorian Poetry* (Spring 1991): 17-32.

[118] "Woman must write herself: must write about women and bring women to writing, from which they have been driven away ... woman must put herself into the text—as into the world and into history—by her own movement." Cixous, "Laugh of the Medusa," in *New French Feminisms,* 245.

[119] Romney's philosophy of public philanthropy and social change is overturned by Aurora's published insistence on the significance of the private and individual perspective (8.323-35); Carrington records the public recognition of the book as on a level with "our masculine white heats" (7.562-71); Kate Ward makes of the book an emblem of female achievement to be used "against" her lover and symbolically included in her portrait, thereby turning Carrington's "reading" of her in the painting into a self-dictated construction (7.603-8).

[120] Kaplan, Introduction to *Aurora Leigh,* 35-36.

[121] Such "daughter texts" might include George Eliot's *Middlemarch,* Virginia Woolf's *Orlando,* and *A Room of One's Own,* Cixous's "The Laugh of the Medusa," Rachel Blau DuPlessis's "For the Etruscans," Angela Carter's *Nights at the Circus,* (1984), and Jeanette Winterson's *The Passion* (1987).

[122] Aurora's extended discussion on the nature of and the appropriate form for poetry includes these conclusions: that poetry should expound the relation between the spiritual and natural worlds (5.120-27); that the era proper to poetry includes the modern age (5.139-88); and that the poet should dispense with traditional forms if she is to forge a new shape appropriate to the living impulse of her work (5.223-39).

[123] "Art itself, / We've called the larger life, must feel the soul / Live past it. For more's felt than is perceived, / And more's perceived than can be interpreted, / And Love strikes higher with his lambent flame / Than Art can pile the faggots" (7.889-94).

[124] In drawing on this juxtaposition *Aurora Leigh* can be placed in that peculiarly female subgenre in nineteenth-century poetry where the claims of home are weighed against the claims of art: e.g., Felicia Hemans's "Corinne at the Capitol" and "Woman and Fame," and Caroline Norton's "Obscurity of Women's Worth." That Barrett Browning was not wholly unaware of the "woman's sphere" proposition as a cultural platitude, is suggested by the fact that she puts the assertion of love's necessity to women into the mouth of a man, when Vincent Carrington tells Aurora of his engagement because "Most women (of your height even) counting love / Life's only serious business" (7.575-76).

[125] "In nineteenth-century narrative, where women heroes were concerned, quest and love plots were intertwined, simultaneous discourses, but at the resolution of the work, the energies of the *Bildung* were incompatible with the closure in successful courtship or marriage. Quest for women was thus finite...." Rachel Blau DuPlessis, *Writing Beyond the Ending: Narrative Strategies of Twentieth Century Women Writers* (Bloomington, Indiana, 1985), 6.

[126] *Aurora Leigh* 8.1130-31.

[127] As Barrett Browning's letters do make clear, she was a product of her context in believing in a difference between a masculine and feminine intellect, each of those characterized in stereotypical terms. Where she is unusual is in her belief that men and women

[128] need not possess one or the other category of characteristics straightforwardly as a result of biology but that a woman can possess a masculine intellect (and vice versa). 22 Sept. 1850, *EBB to Mrs. Ogilvy*, 32.

[128] Leighton, *Elizabeth Barrett Browning*, 121. See also Gelpi, "Vocation of the Woman Poet," 35-48. Dorothy Mermin offers a discerning review of the various 'mother' images and guests which the poem presents. See *Elizabeth Barrett Browning: The Origins of a New Poetry*, 190-208.

[129] Compare EBB's remarks on the conventional education offered to middle class girls in her letter to Mary Hunter, 9 Jan. 1859, Berg Collection. See *Checklist* 59:72, quoted above in text.

[130] "The girl then has to suppress or devalue that fullness of recognition [of the maternal body] in order to line up within the order of the phallic term" Jacqueline Rose, "Introduction II," in *Feminine Sexuality: Jacques Lacan and the École Freudienne*, ed. Juliet Mitchell and Jacqueline Rose (London, 1982), 54; Gilbert, "From *Patria* to *Matria*" 194-209. It is, of course, a significant move when Aurora sells her father's books (5.1211-71) in order to return to her "mother country."

[131] Leighton, *Elizabeth Barrett Browning*, 114-40.

[132] Taking Aurora's pronouncements on women's failings at face value, David sees them as evidence of Barrett Browning's internalization of patriarchal values. See *Intellectual Women*, 145-52. But these exaggerated statements rather demonstrate Barrett Browning's ironic recognition of the difficulties that result through Aurora's temporary annexation of those values.

[133] As Aurora's mother's nonverbal expressivity is defined by its association with the primitive essential which is prior to the order of Symbolic law obtaining in the social world (the Wordsworthian "outer Infinite" derived from the "Intimations" ode), Aurora, at this point, can only imagine a version of the feminine which is pre-linguistic and pre-thought. See Rose, "Introduction II" in *Feminine Sexuality*, 54.

[134] See Joan Riviere, "Womanliness as a Masquerade" (1929) in *Formations of Fantasy*, ed. Victor Burgin, James Donald, and Cora Kaplan (London, 1986), 35-37.

[135] Leighton balances Aurora's initial search for the "father" as exhibited in her early traditional poetic practice against her championing of the fallen "sister" in an experimental poetics appropriate to the modern age. See Leighton, *Elizabeth Barrett Browning*, 141-57.

[136] Lady Waldemar (like Marian) represents a reflection and exaggeration of certain aspects of Aurora's character. She is a version of the socially constructed woman who fails to rebel, unlike Aurora, against the trivialities of female education and socialization.

[137] "... Nelly Dean is patriarchy's paradigmatic housekeeper, the man's woman who has traditionally been hired to keep men's houses in order by straightening out their parlors, their daughters, and their stories." "Looking Oppositely: Emily Brontë's Bible of Hell" in Sandra Gilbert and Susan Gubar, *The Madwoman in the Attic: The Woman Writer and the Nineteenth Century Literary Imagination* (New Haven and London, 1979), 291-92.

[138] In Marian's accounts of herself (and Lady Waldemar's argument concerning her unfitness for class translation), the processes of natural selection are opposed to the civilized processes of artificial selection. "You take a kid you like, and turn it out / In some fair garden: though the creature's fond / And gentle, it will leap upon the beds / And break your tulips, bite your tender trees; / The wonder would be if such innocence / Spoiled less" (6.932-37), and "'You take a pink, / 'You dig about its roots and water it / 'And so improve it to a garden-pink, / 'But will not change it to a heliotrope, / 'The kind remains'" (6.1044-48).

[139] Alfred Tennyson, *The Princess* (1847), 7.259; compare Charles Darwin (whose *Origin of the Species* was not published until 1859 but whose propositions were common to other theorists in the 1850s): "It is generally admitted that with woman the powers of intuition, of rapid perception, and perhaps of imitation, are more strongly marked than in man; but some, at least, of these faculties are characteristic of the lower races, and therefore of a past and lower state of civilization." *The Descent of Man, and Selection in Relation to Sex* (London, 1871) 2:326-27.

[140] In the manuscript, Lucy Gresham was initially described as a "sistersoul." See textual notes to 4.36-37. The revised reading extends the inevitability of Marian's isolation until her eventual alliance with Aurora.

[141] Again, the comparison of developed civilization with the primitive is made through Aurora's analogy of Western bourgeois marriage (and the consequent legal annihilation of the woman) with the Hindu practice of suttee (4.176-202).

[142] See explanatory annotation to 6.808.

[143] The manuscript includes a deleted reference to the loss of "individual life." See textual notes to 6.808; "woman is traditionally use-value for man, exchange-value among men. Merchandise, then." Luce Irigaray, "Ce sexe qui n'en pas un" in *New French Feminisms*, 105.

[144] EBB to Sarianna Browning, Nov. 1856, *Letters of EBB* 2:242; EBB to Arabel, 4 Oct. 1856, Moulton-Barrett Collection. See *Checklist* 56:142.

[145] See Irigaray, "Ce sexe qui n'en est pas un" in *New French Feminisms,* 99-101, and Hélène Cixous's diagram of oppositions in "Sorties" in ibid., 90-91.

[146] See particularly DuPlessis, *Writing Beyond the Ending* and David, *Intellectual Women*. See also Christine Sutphin's rejection of the "negative" ending in "Revising Old Scripts: The Fusion of Independence and Intimacy in *Aurora Leigh*," *BIS* 15 (1987): 43-54. Joyce Zanona argues that this passivity in book 7 is the point when Aurora begins to listen to her 'blood' and make herself into her own Muse; see "The Embodied Muse: Elizabeth Barrett Browning's *Aurora Leigh* and Feminist Poetics," *Tulsa Studies in Women's Literature,* 8 (1989): 240-262.

[147] W. E. Aytoun said Romney was "such a very decided noodle that we grudge him his prominence in the poem, do not feel much sympathy for his misfortunes, and cannot help wondering that Aurora should have entertained one spark of affection for so deplorable a milksop." "*Aurora Leigh,*" 33.

[148] Tompkins, "*Aurora Leigh,*" 12; Jan Montefiore, "Two-Way Mirrors: Psychoanalysis and the Love Sonnet" in *Feminism and Poetry,* 97-134. Dorothy Mermin also makes this point in ". . . the blindness seems consequent on her needs rather than his." See *Elizabeth Barrett Browning: The Origins of a New Poetry* (1989): 214.

[149] In some discarded lines in the draft manuscript at Wellesley, he also remarks on Aurora's inability to "read" him. See textual notes to 9.512.

[150] Romney's voice, like his face, haunts Aurora, his words echoing as accusations to be refuted or assessments to be conceded. See 3.237-41; 5.56-58, 487, 1076-77; 7.750-52; and 7.880-82.

[151] When defending herself against the charge of plagiarizing *Jane Eyre,* Barrett Browning argued that his blindness rather resembled Milton's than Rochester's and added "For it was necessary, I thought, to the bringing out of my thought, that Romney should be mulcted in his natural sight." EBB to Anna Jameson, 26 Dec. 1856, *Letters of EBB* 2:246.

[152] Karlin links Romney's blinding to the extended metaphors linking seeing and loving in the 1845-46 correspondence. Referring to two letters (EBB to RB, 1 May 1846 and 15 July 1846) Karlin suggests that in Elizabeth Barrett's view love "does without" true sight precisely because its transfiguration prevents clear seeing. *Courtship,* 136.

[153] "the 'feminine' is constituted as a division in language, a division which produces the feminine as a negative term. If a woman is defined as other it is because the definition produces her as other and not because she has another essence." Rose, "Introduction II" in *Feminine Sexuality,* 55-56.

[154] In fact, Aurora's difference from Romney is a dubious fact, for the cousins share the same name—and appearance (4.939;9.163).

[155] Romney, by contrast, takes on the "woman's part" of doing the loving for two (9.912). See Sutphin, "Revising Old Scripts," *BIS* 15 (1987): 43-54.

[156] EBB to RB, 20 Mar. 1845, *RB/EBB Letters* 1:42.

[157] *Aurora Leigh* 5.223-25.

[158] 30 Dec. 1844, *EBB to MRM* 3:49.

[159] "It is only a novel á la *Jane Eyre,* a little tainted by Sand." William Bell Scott to William Michael Rossetti, 22 Dec. 1856, *Ruskin: Rossetti: Pre-Raphaelitism Papers 1854-1862,* ed. William Michael Rossetti (London, 1899) 147. Anna Jameson accused EBB of borrowing the catastrophe which caused Romney's blindness from *Jane Eyre*. See EBB to Anna Jameson, 26 Dec. 1856, *Letters of EBB,* 2:245-46. Other similarities have been noted since then. See Julia Bolton Holloway, "*Aurora Leigh* and *Jane Eyre,*" *Brontë Society Transactions* 17 (1977): 126-32. The influence of George Sand's novels in supplying character types and melodramatic incident has been documented by Alethea Hayter, *Mrs. Browning: A Poet's Work and Its Setting* (London, 1962), 160-62 and Patricia Thomson, *George Sand and the Victorians: Her Influence and Reputation in Nineteenth Century England* (London, 1977), 54-60.

[160] The best accounts of the influence of *Corinne* are to be found in Moers's *Literary Women,* 173-210 and passim, and in Kaplan's Introduction to *Aurora Leigh,* 17-22.

[161] William Irvine satirizes the plot of *Aurora Leigh* as one "drawn from the teeming recollections of twenty years' compulsive novel-reading." Irvine and Honan, *The Book, the Ring and the Poet,* 349; this attitude to woman's reading is, of course, rooted in the nineteenth century, but its rudiment remains a common critical notion. See Kate Flint, "Reading the New Woman," *BSN* vol. 17, nos. 1-3 (1987-88): 55-57.

[162] Kaplan, Introduction to *Aurora Leigh,* 14; see Kathleen Hickok, "'New Yet Orthodox': The Female Characters in *Aurora Leigh,*" *International Journal of Women's Studies,* vol. 3, no. 5 (Sept./Oct. 1980): 479-89; Dolores Rosenblum, "Face to Face: Elizabeth Barrett Browning's *Aurora Leigh* and Nineteenth Cen-

[163] tury Poetry," *Victorian Studies,* vol. 26, no. 3 (Spring 1983): 321-38; Blake, "Elizabeth Barrett Browning and Wordsworth," *Victorian Poetry* 24 (Winter 1986): 387-98; David, *Intellectual Women,* 143-58; Sutphin "Revising Old Scripts," *BIS* 15 (1987): 43-54; Cooper, *Elizabeth Barrett Browning,* 145-88.

[163] "I have always used a very wide number of references because of tending to regard all of western Europe as a great scrap-yard from which you can assemble all sorts of new vehicles . . . *bricolage.*" Angela Carter in John Haffenden, *Novelists in Interview* (London, 1985), 92; 'stealing the language' is a term derived from Claudine Herrmann's *Les Voleuses de Langue* (Paris, 1979).

[164] Carol Christ sees a direct precedent for Modernist poetry in Victorian experiments with pluralism of form and historical relativism, especially as exhibited in the long poem. See *Victorian and Modern Poetics* (Chicago and London, 1984), 115.

[165] See, for instance, Cixous: "Woman un-thinks the unifying, regulating history that homogenizes and channels forces, herding contradictions into a single battlefield. In woman, personal history blends together with the history of all women, as well as national and world history"—and, of course, literary history. "Laugh of the Medusa" in *New French Feminisms* 250. See also Alicia Suskin Ostriker, "Thieves of Language: Women Poets and Revisionist Mythology" in *Stealing the Language: The Emergence of Womens' Poetry in America* (London, 1987), 210-38.

[166] With the possible exceptions of Helen Sheridan's (Lady Dufferin's) poem "The Charming Woman" (see note to 5.1041) and Emily Brontë's *Wuthering Heights* (see note to 5.1097-1105).

[167] Compare this self-censoring process with Irigaray on the psychoanalytic marginalization of woman's sexuality. "The rejection, the exclusion of a female imaginary undoubtedly places woman in a position where she can experience herself only fragmentarily as waste or excess in the little structured margins of a dominant ideology. . . . The role of "femininity" is prescribed moreover . . . and corresponds only slightly to woman's desire, which is recuperated only secretly, in hiding, and in a disturbing and unpardonable manner." "Ce sexe" in *New French Feminisms,* 104.

[168] Compare Robert Browning's requirement that his reader allow him "licences" which would permit him to "make shift with touches and bits of outlines which succeed if they bear the conception from me to you." Robert Browning to John Ruskin, 10 Dec. 1855, *The Works of John Ruskin* 36:xxxiv.

[169] "And what easy work these novelists have of it! a Dramatic poet has to *make* you love or admire his men and women,—they must *do* and *say* all that you are to see and hear—really do it in your face, say it in your ears, and it is wholly for *you,* in *your* power, to *name,* characterize and so praise or blame, *what* is so said and done . . if you don't perceive of yourself, there is no standing by, for the Author, and telling you: but with these novelists, a scrape of the pen—out blurting of a phrase, and the miracle is achieved—'Consuelo possessed to perfection this and the other gift'—what would you more" RB to EBB, 10 Aug. 1845, *RB/EBB Letters* 1:150. EBB replied "there can be no disagreeing with you about the comparative difficulty of novel-writing & drama-writing." EBB to RB, 13 Aug. 1845, *RB/EBB Letters* 1:155.

[170] Virginia Woolf's well-known image in "Modern Fiction" is reminiscent of this passage. "Life is not a series of gig lamps symmetrically arranged; life is a luminous halo, a semi-transparent envelope surrounding us from the beginning of consciousness to the end." *The Common Reader* 1:189. Certainly, the similarity of the two images provides a useful juxtaposition in arguing for the experiments of *Aurora Leigh* as ancestors of Modernist (and feminist) practice.

[171] Antique sculpture is also used in this way: see explanatory annotation to 3.513-14; 517-19, 706; 5.798-99; and 7.666-67, 787.

[172] Compare 1.139-142 and 5.618-624. See Tompkins, "*Aurora Leigh,*" 14 for an account of Lady Waldemar's transformation into "woman-serpent," and see Gelpi, "Vocation of the Woman Poet," 39-40 for a comparison of the portrait with Lady Waldemar's appearance in book 5. All the snake images associated with Lady Waldemar derive from Aurora, with the one exception of that image at 9.112-13 where Lady Waldemar says of herself, "I shot my tongue against my fly / And struck him." In draft, however, the image was first applied to Lady Waldemar by Aurora. See textual notes to 7.312.

[173] The first draft manuscript at Wellesley includes some discarded lines which refer to another picture (of Daphne) by Vincent Carrington which also applies to Aurora as poet. See textual notes to 7.562.

[174] See Irigaray, "Ce sexe" in *New French Feminisms,* 99-106, and Montefiore, *Feminism and Poetry,* 147-52.

[175] "at the pole of difficulty we have the construction of female subjects as speakers presented with a taboo against public speech, the price of and effects of that repression, a male centred linguistic tradition which, in an extreme form, is their female (and therefore human) identity. At the other pole is the field of language itself, open to invasion and subversion by female speakers. The overt and hidden subject of women's poetry is often a dialectic between those two poles." Kaplan, "Language and Gender" in *Sea Changes,* 92.

[176] Terry Lovell, *Consuming Fiction* (London, 1987), 139.

Short Titles

BIS: Browning Institute Studies

BSN: Browning Society Notes

Reconstruction: The Browning Collections: A Reconstruction with Other Memorabilia, comp. Philip Kelley and Betty A. Coley (Winfield, Kansas, and London, 1984).

Checklist: The Brownings' Correspondence: A Checklist, comp. Philip Kelley and Ronald Hudson (The Browning Institute, 1978).

EBB to MRM: The Letters of Elizabeth Barrett Browning to Mary Russell Mitford 1836-1854, ed. Meredith B. Raymond and Mary Rose Sullivan. 3 vols. (Winfield, Kansas, 1983).

EBB to Mrs. Ogilvy: Elizabeth Barrett Browning's Letters to Mrs. David Ogilvy 1849-1861, ed. Peter N. Heydon and Philip Kelley (London, 1974).

Letters of EBB: The Letters of Elizabeth Barrett Browning, ed. Frederic G. Kenyon. 2 vols. (London, 1897).

RB/EBB Letters: The Letters of Robert Browning and Elizabeth Barrett Barrett 1845-1846, ed. Elvan Kintner. 2 vols. (Cambridge, Massachusetts, 1969).

Bibliography

Editions of Aurora Leigh

Aurora Leigh. 1857.

Aurora Leigh. New York and Boston, 1857.

Aurora Leigh. 1857. "Second edition."

Aurora Leigh. 1857. "Third edition."

Aurora Leigh. 1859. "Fourth edition," revised.

Aurora Leigh. 1860. "Fifth edition."

Aurora Leigh. Leipzig, 1872.

Aurora Leigh, prefatory note by Algernon Swinburne. 1898.

Aurora Leigh, ed. H. Buxton Forman. 1899.

Aurora Leigh, with an introduction by E. Wingate Rinder. 1899.

Aurora Leigh, traduit de l'anglais (by "A.B."). Paris, 1890.

Aurora Leigh, with an introduction by Charlotte Porter and Helen A. Clarke. 1902.

Aurora Leigh and Other Poems, introduced by Cora Kaplan. 1978. Women's Press facsimile reprint.

Aurora Leigh, introduced by Gardner B. Taplin. Chicago, 1979. Facsimile reprint.

Other works by Elizabeth Barrett Browning

An Essay on Mind. 1826.

"The Book of the Poets." *The Athenaeum* (4, 11, 25 June; 6, 13 August 1842). . . .

Poems by Elizabeth Barrett Barrett. 2 Vols. 1844.

Casa Guidi Windows. 1851. . . .

Casa Guidi Windows. Edited by Julia Markus. New York, 1977. . . .

Letters of Elizabeth Barrett Browning and Robert Browning

Heydon, Peter N., and Kelley, Philip, eds. *Elizabeth Barrett Browning's Letters to Mrs. David Ogilvy 1849-1861.* 1974. . . .

Kelley, Philip, and Hudson, Ronald, eds. *The Brownings' Correspondence.* 1809-43. vols. 1-8 Winfield, Kansas, 1984-90.

Kenyon, Frederic, ed. *The Letters of Elizabeth Barrett Browning.* 2 vols. 1897. . . .

Kintner, Elvan, ed. *The Letters of Elizabeth Barrett Barrett and Robert Browning.* 1845-46. 2 vols. Cambridge, Mass., 1969. . . .

Raymond, Meredith B., and Sullivan, Mary Rose, eds. *The Letters of Elizabeth Barrett Browning and Mary Russell Mitford 1836-1854.* 3 vols. Winfield, Kansas, 1983. . . .

Contemporary reviews of Aurora Leigh

Aytoun, William Edmondstoune. "Mrs. Barrett Browning. *Aurora Leigh.*" *Blackwood's Edinburgh Magazine* 81 (January 1857): 23-41. . . .

Everett, C. C. "Poems by Elizabeth Barrett Browning." *The North American Review* (October 1857): 415-41. . . .

Patmore, Coventry. "Mrs. Browning's *Poems* and *Aurora Leigh*." *The North British Review*, vol. 26, no. 52 (February 1857): 443-62. . . .

Stigand, William. "The Works of Elizabeth Barrett Browning." *The Edinburgh Review*, no. 232, (October 1861): 513-34. . . .

SECONDARY SOURCES:

Armstrong, Isobel. *Language as Living Form in Nineteenth-Century Poetry*. Brighton, 1982. . . .

[Auerbach, Nina]. "Robert Browning's Last Word." *Victorian Poetry* 22 (Summer 1984): 161-73. . . .

[Blake, Kathleen]. "Elizabeth Barrett Browning and Wordsworth: The Romantic Poet as Woman." *Victorian Poetry* 24 (Winter 1986): 387-98. . . .

Browning, Robert. Introductory essay to *Letters of Percy Bysshe Shelley*. 1852. . . .

———. *The Poetical Works of Robert Browning*, edited by Ian Jack and Margaret Smith. Vols. 1 and 2. Oxford, 1983-1984.

Buckley, Jerome H. *The Victorian Temper*. 1952. . . .

Case, Alison. "Gender and Narration in *Aurora Leigh*." *Victorian Poetry* (Spring 1991): 17-32.

Castan, C. "Structural Problems in the Poetry of *Aurora Leigh*." *Browning Society Notes* 7 (December 1977): 73-81. . . .

[Christ, Carol T]. *Victorian and Modern Poetics*. Chicago and London, 1984.

Cixous, Hélène. "The Laugh of the Medusa." In *New French Feminisms*, edited by Elaine Marks and Isabelle de Courtivron, 245-64. Brighton, 1980. . . .

[Cooper, Helen]. *Elizabeth Barrett Browning, Woman and Artist*. Chapel Hill and London, 1988. . . .

David, Deirdre. "'Art's a Service.': Social Wound, Sexual Politics and *Aurora Leigh*." *Browning Institute Studies* 13 (1985): 113-36.

———. *Intellectual Women and Victorian Patriarchy: Harriet Martineau, Elizabeth Barrett Browning and George Eliot*. 1987. . . .

DuPlessis, Rachel Blau. *Writing Beyond the Ending: Narrative Strategies of Twentieth Century Women Writers*. Bloomington, Indiana, 1985.

———. "For the Etruscans." In *The New Feminist Criticism: Essays on Women, Literature and Theory*, edited by Elaine Showalter, 271-91. 1986. . . .

Flint, Kate. "Reading the New Woman." *Browning Society Notes*, Vol. 17, nos. 1-3 (1987-88): 55-63. . . .

Gelpi, Barbara Charlesworth. "*Aurora Leigh*: The Vocation of the Woman Poet." *Victorian Poetry* 19 (Spring 1981): 35-48.

Gilbert, Sandra M., and Gubar, Susan. *The Madwoman in the Attic: The Woman Writer and the Nineteenth Century Literary Imagination*. New Haven and London, 1979. . . .

Gilbert, Sandra M. "From *Patria* to *Matria*: Elizabeth Barrett Browning's Risorgimento." *PMLA* 99 (March 1984): 194-211. . . .

Hayter, Alethea. *Mrs. Browning: A Poet's Work and Its Setting*. 1962. . . .

Hickok, Kathleen. "'New Yet Orthodox': The Female Characters in *Aurora Leigh*." *International Journal of Women's Studies*. 3 (September/October 1980): 479-89. . . .

Holloway, Julia Bolton. "*Aurora Leigh* and *Jane Eyre*." *Bronte Society Transactions* 17, (1977): 126-32. . . .

Homans, Margaret. *Women Writers and Poetic Identity: Dorothy Wordsworth, Emily Brontë and Emily Dickinson*. Princeton, New Jersey, 1980.

Horne, R. H. *A New Spirit of the Age*. 2 vols. 1844. . . .

Irigaray, Luce. "Ce sexe qui n'en pas un." In *New French Feminisms*, ed. Elaine Marks and Isabelle de Courtivron, 99-106. Brighton, 1980.

Irvine, William, and Honan, Park. *The Book, the Ring, and the Poet: A Biography of Robert Browning*. 1974. . . .

Jameson, Anna Brownell. *Anna Jameson: Letters and Friendships: 1812-1860*, edited by Mrs. Stuart Erskine. 1915. . . .

Kaplan, Cora. "Pandora's Box: Subjectivity, Class, and Sexuality in Socialist Feminist Criticism." In *Making a Difference: Feminist Literary Criticism*, edited by Gayle Greene and Coppélia Kahn, 149-51. 1985.

———. *Sea Changes: Culture and Feminism*. 1986.

Karlin, Daniel. *The Courtship of Robert Browning and Elizabeth Barrett*. Oxford, 1985.

Kelley, Philip, and Hudson, Ronald. *The Brownings' Correspondence: A Checklist.* New York: The Browning Institute, 1978.

Kelley, Philip, and Coley, Betty A. *The Browning Collections: A Reconstruction with Other Memorabilia.* Winfield, Kansas, and London, 1984. . . .

Leighton, Angela. *Elizabeth Barrett Browning.* Brighton, 1986. . . .

Lovell, Terry. *Consuming Fiction.* 1987. . . .

McNally, James. "Touches of *Aurora Leigh* in *The Ring and the Book.*" *Studies in Browning and His Circle* 14 (1986): 85-90. . . .

Magie, Michael L. "The Verse-Novel: Bastard Child of the Nineteenth Century" (Ph.D. diss., University of California, 1971). . . .

[Mermin, Dorothy]. "Barrett Browning's Stories." *Browning Institute Studies* 13 (1985): 99-112. . . .

———. "The Damsel, the Knight and the Victorian Woman Poet." *Critical Inquiry* 13 (Autumn 1986): 64-80. . . .

———. *Elizabeth Barrett Browning: The Origins of a New Poetry.* Chicago, 1989. . . .

Mill, John Stuart. "What is Poetry?" and "The Truth of Poetry." *The Monthly Repository* (1833), revised and amalgamated in "Thoughts on Poetry and Its Varieties" in *Dissertations and Discussions: Political, Philosophical and Historical* (London, 1867). . . .

Moers, Ellen. *Literary Women: The Great Writers.* New York, 1977.

Moi, Toril. *Sexual/Textual Politics: Feminist Literary Theory.* 1985.

Montefiore, Jan. *Feminism and Poetry: Language, Experience and Identity in Women's Writing.* 1987. . . .

Munich, Adrienne Auslander. "Robert Browning's Poetics of Appropriation." *Browning Institute Studies* 15 (1985): 69-78.

Nicoll, W. Robertson, and Wise, Thomas J., eds. *Literary Anecdotes of the Nineteenth Century.* 1895-96. . . .

Ostriker, Alicia Suskin. *Stealing the Language: The Emergence of Women's Poetry in America.* 1987. . . .

Raymond, Meredith B. "Elizabeth Barrett's Early Poetics: The 1820's; 'The Bird Pecks Through the Shell.'" *Browning Society Notes* 8 (1978): 3-7.

———. "Elizabeth Barrett Browning's Poetics 1830-1844: 'The Seraph and the Early Piper.'" *Browning Society Notes* 9 (1979): 5-9.

———. "Elizabeth Barrett Browning's Poetics 1845-1846: 'The Ascending Gyre.'" *Browning Society Notes* 11 (1981): 1-11. . . .

Ridenour, George M. "Robert Browning and *Aurora Leigh.*" *Victorian Newsletter,* no. 67 (Spring 1987): 26-32. . . .

Riviere, Joan. "Womanliness as Masquerade." 1929. Reprint in *Formations of Fantasy,* edited by Victor Burgin, James Donald, and Cora Kaplan, 35-44, 1986. . . .

Rose, Jacqueline. In *Feminine Sexuality: Jacques Lacan and the École Freudienne,* edited by Juliet Mitchell and Jacqueline Rose, 1982. . . .

Rosenblum, Dolores. "Face to Face: Elizabeth Barrett Browning's *Aurora Leigh* and Nineteenth Century Poetry." *Victorian Studies* 26 (Spring 1983): 321-38. . . .

Rossetti, William Michael, ed. *Ruskin: Rossetti: Pre-Raphaelitism, Papers 1854-1862.* 1899. . . .

Ruskin, John. *The Works of John Ruskin,* edited by E. T. Cook and Alexander Wedderburn. 36 vols. 1903-12. . . .

Shelley, Percy Bysshe. "A Defence of Poetry." In *Essays, Letters from Abroad, Translations and Fragments,* edited by Mrs. Shelley. 2 vols. 1840. . . .

[Showalter, Elaine], ed. *The New Feminist Criticism: Essays on Women, Literature and Theory.* 1986. . . .

[Stone, Marjorie]. "Genre Subversion and Gender Inversion: *The Princess* and *Aurora Leigh.*" *Victorian Poetry* 25 (Summer 1987): 101-27.

Sutphin, Christine. "Revising Old Scripts: The Fusion of Independence and Intimacy in *Aurora Leigh.*" *Browning Institute Studies* 15 (1987): 43-54. . . .

Taylor, Barbara. *Eve and the New Jerusalem: Socialism and Feminism in the Nineteenth Century.* 1983. . . .

Thomson, Patricia. *The Victorian Heroine: A Changing Ideal 1837-1873.* 1956.

———. *George Sand and the Victorians: Her Influence and Reputation in Nineteenth Century England.* 1977. . . .

Tompkins, J. M. S. *"Aurora Leigh".* The Fawcett Lecture, 1961. Bedford College, 1962.

Todd, Janet. *Feminist Literary History.* Oxford. 1988. . . .

Weinstein, Mark. *W. E. Aytoun and the Spasmodic Controversy.* Yale Studies in English, 165 (Yale, 1968)....

Woolf, Virginia, *A Room of One's Own.* Harmondsworth, Middlesex. 1973.

———. "Aurora Leigh." *The Common Reader.* 2nd ser. 1932, reprinted 1975....

Zanona, Joyce. "The Embodied Muse: Elizabeth Barrett Browning's *Aurora Leigh* and Feminist Poetics." *Tulsa Studies in Women's Literature* 8 (1989): 240-262.

FURTHER READING

Case, Alison. "Gender and Narration in *Aurora Leigh*." *Victorian Poetry* 29, No. 1 (Spring 1991): 17-32.
   Contends that in *Aurora Leigh* Browning transgressed the conventions of the novel.

Castan, C. "Structural Problems and the Poetry of *Aurora Leigh*." *Browning Society Notes* 7, No. 3 (December 1977): 73-81.
   Considers the development of Aurora from an unreliable narrator into a fully informed and mature character.

Cooper, Helen. "Woman and Artist, Both Complete." In *Elizabeth Barrett Browning: Woman and Artist*, pp. 145-88. Chapel Hill: University of North Carolina Press, 1988.
   Emphasizes the confluence of poetic authority and feminine emotion in *Aurora Leigh*.

David, Deirdre. "Woman's Art as Servant of Patriarchy: The Vision of *Aurora Leigh*." In *Intellectual Women and Victorian Patriarchy: Harriet Martineau, Elizabeth Barrett Browning, George Eliot*, pp. 143-58. Ithaca, N.Y.: Cornell University Press, 1987.
   Contends that, despite feminist interpretations to the contrary, *Aurora Leigh* engages in a traditional and conservative endorsement of patriarchal politics.

Freiwald, Bina. "'The praise which men give women': Elizabeth Barrett Browning's *Aurora Leigh* and the Critics." *Dalhousie Review* 66, No. 3 (Fall 1986): 311-36.
   Surveys the reception of *Aurora Leigh* by Browning's contemporaries as well as by modern critics, claiming that female critics such as Virginia Woolf have served as correctives to those who interpret the poem as mere autobiography.

Gilbert, Sandra M. "From *Patria* to *Matria*: Elizabeth Barrett Browning's Risorgimento." *PMLA* 99, No. 2 (March 1984): 194-211.
   Parallels Browning's attitude toward Italy's developing national identity with the struggle of the female poet for creative autonomy.

Holloway, Julia Bolton. "*Aurora Leigh* and *Jane Eyre*." *Brontë Society Transactions* 17, No. 2 (1977): 126-32.
   Considers the influence of *Jane Eyre* on Browning's *Aurora Leigh*, focusing specifically on the blinding of Romney.

Leighton, Angela. "'Because men made the laws': The Fallen Woman and the Woman Poet." *Victorian Poetry* 27, No. 2 (Summer 1989): 109-27.
   Contends that Browning assumed the voice of the fallen woman in order to undermine the stereotype that women are "either types of 'vice' or types of 'virtue'."

Radley, Virginia L. "*Aurora Leigh*: The Artist as Woman." In *Elizabeth Barrett Browning*, pp. 120-5. New York: Twayne Publishers, 1972.
   Summarizes and evaluates *Aurora Leigh* against a backdrop of primarily negative reviews.

Reynolds, Margaret. "*Aurora Leigh*: 'Writing her story for her better self'." *Browning Society Notes* 17, Nos. 1-3 (1987-88): 5-11.
   Uses the relationship between Aurora and Romney to illustrate that love and sex underlie the creative impulse.

Ridenour, George M. "Robert Browning and *Aurora Leigh*." *The Victorian Newsletter* No. 67 (Spring 1985): 26-31.
   Compares the philosophies of art, characterization, and themes of *Aurora Leigh* with Robert Browning's *The Ring and the Book*.

Rosenblum, Dolores. "Face to Face: Elizabeth Barrett Browning's *Aurora Leigh* and Nineteenth-Century Poetry." *Victorian Studies* 26, No. 3 (Spring 1983): 321-38.
   Discusses the female face in *Aurora Leigh* as a mirror of humanity, situating Browning in a larger "Romantic visionary aesthetics."

Steinmetz, Virginia. "Beyond the Sun: Patriarchal Images in *Aurora Leigh*." *Studies in Browning and His Circle* 9, No. 2 (Fall 1981): 18-41.
   Contends that Barrett Browning's symbolic use of hands and the sun in *Aurora Leigh* elucidates the poet's relationship with male authority figures, particularly with her father.

———. "Images of 'Mother-Want' in Elizabeth Barrett Browning's *Aurora Leigh*." *Victorian Poetry* 21, No. 4 (Winter 1983): 351-67.
   Discusses *Aurora Leigh*'s maternal imagery and Aurora's search for her origins, primarily her search for a mother-figure.

Stephenson, Glennis. "Love and Life: The Expansion of Boundaries in *Aurora Leigh*." In *Elizabeth Barrett Browning and the Poetry of Love*, pp. 91-116. Ann Arbor, Mich.: UMI Research Press, 1989.

Examines Barrett Browning's exploration of the social definition of love, and how this is specifically played out in the relationship between Aurora and Romney.

Sutphin, Christine. "Revising Old Scripts: The Fusion of Independence and Intimacy in *Aurora Leigh*." *Browning Institute Studies* 15 (1987): 43-54.

Argues that the ending of *Aurora Leigh* represents a non-traditional and feminist approach to marriage when studied in relation to its nineteenth-century social context.

Taplin, Gardner B. "*Aurora Leigh*." In *The Life of Elizabeth Barrett Browning*, pp. 310-47. New Haven: Yale University Press, 1957.

Closely summarizes the plot and provides a historical overview of the critical opinions of *Aurora Leigh*.

Tompkins, J. M. S. *Aurora Leigh: The Fawcett Lecture, 1961-62*. London: Bedford College (University of London), 1961, 21 p.

Discusses *Aurora Leigh* as Browning's exploration of the physical and moral, individual and social position of a woman writer. (Reprint of Tompkins' 1961 lecture.)

Tucker, Herbert F. "*Aurora Leigh*: Epic Solutions to Novel Ends." In *Famous Last Words: Changes in Gender and Narrative Closure*, edited by Alison Booth, pp. 62-85. Charlottesville: University Press of Virginia, 1993.

Considers the epic conventions used in the poem as Browning's "means for loosening the realist novel's grip on Victorian narrative as a shaper of women's lives."

Wilsey, Mildred. "Elizabeth Barrett Browning's Heroine." *College English* 6, No. 2 (November 1944): 75-81.

Contends that the title character of *Aurora Leigh* redefines the role of marriage, paradoxically, as liberating for the wife's independent nature.

Zonana, Joyce. "The Embodied Muse: Elizabeth Barrett Browning's *Aurora Leigh* and Feminist Poetics." *Tulsa Studies in Women's Literature* 8, No. 2 (Fall 1989): 241-62.

Portrays the title character as a muse who inspires poetic achievement but resists traditional idealization and objectification.

Additional coverage of Browning's life and career can be found in the following sources published by Gale Research: *Nineteenth-Century Literature Criticism*, Vols. 1, 16, and 61; *DISCovering Authors*; *Poetry Criticism*, Vol. 6; *World Literature Criticism, 1500 to the Present*; and *Dictionary of Literary Biography*, Vol. 32.

Isabelle de Charrière

1740-1805

(Born Isabelle-Agnès-Elisabeth van Tuyll van Serookskerken van Zuylen) Dutch-born Swiss novelist, essayist, dramatist, short story writer, librettist, and poet.

INTRODUCTION

Part of the French feminine literary tradition of Marie de Sévigné, Germaine de Staël, and George Sand, Charrière is noted for the originality and boldness of her work, specifically in her challenge to the traditionally female roles of eighteenth-century society. Identified by some critics as one of the subtlest and most compelling novelists of the century, Charrière has been praised for her innovation in both theme and form, and has attained prominence as an early advocate of gender equality.

Biographical Information

Charrière was born into Dutch nobility and raised in aristocratic fashion at the family castle outside Utrecht. The first of seven children, she was educated both at home and abroad, studying in both Geneva and Paris under the tutelage of her Swiss governess, Jeanne-Louise Prevost, learning several languages and studying the writings and philosophies of numerous thinkers, developing a fierce independence of mind and spirit. In 1760 she met and began a relationship with a married Swiss colonel serving in the Netherlands, Baron Constant d'Hermenches. Although the two rarely saw each other, their affair lasted nearly fifteen years. The same year Charrière met the baron she also wrote her first novel, *Le Noble* (*The Nobleman*), a scathing satire of the aristocracy. When it was published in 1763, the novel caused immediate scandal, and Charrière's parents withdrew it from publication almost as soon as it appeared. Realizing the futility of attempting to publish her work on a wide scale, Charrière turned her literary talent to letter-writing and small self-circulated publications. In the meantime, she was courted by Scottish author James Boswell, to whom she responded curtly in a letter dated 17 January 1768: "I have sufficient mental ability to manage without a husband and without a household; I do not need, as they say, to be looked after." In 1771 Charrière did marry Charles-Emmanuel de Charrière, her brothers' governor, and a man who promised her the wide range of freedom within marriage she demanded. They moved to his manor in Switzerland, Isabelle bringing her two unmarried sisters to live with her. By 1783 she resumed writing and began traveling around Switzerland as well as to Paris and London, where she was presented at the royal court and was the guest of philosopher David Hume. The publication of her novel *Lettres neuchâteloises* in 1784 marked the beginning of an immense literary outpouring which characterized the later part of her life. In 1787 Charrière began a relationship with nineteen-year-old Benjamin Constant, nephew of Baron d'Hermenches and son of author Samuel Constant, to whose *Le mari sentimental* she had responded directly in her own *Lettres de Mistriss Henley* (*Mistriss Henley*, 1784). Despite a later break, the two remained in close correspondence until Charrière's death in 1805.

Major Works

Charrière is best known for her epistolary novels of the 1780s. *Lettres neuchâteloises* weaves a chance encounter, an accidental pregnancy, and the interaction of a poor seamstress, a merchant's son, and the daughter of a noble French family into a commentary on the social costs of privilege. *Mistress Henley* takes the stifling marriage relationship described by Constant and interprets it from the woman's point of view. The principal action takes place as a pregnant Mrs. Henley faces admonishment by her husband for her independent actions, and the silencing of her voice in the matter of the child's upbringing. Notably, it is in this work that Charrière first used an intentionally ambiguous ending, with Mrs. Henley saying, "In a year, in two years, you will learn, I hope, that I am reasonable and happy, or that I am no more." In *Lettres écrites de Lausanne* (*Letters from Lausanne*, 1785), a widow writes of the pleasures and difficulties of raising a daughter on her own and seeking a suitable marriage for the girl that would allow her the freedom she so values. Importantly, the daughter recognizes this difficulty as well, and, in the end, matrimony and society living are rejected. And in what was to become her most popular work, *Caliste, ou suite des Lettres écrites de Lausanne* (*Caliste*, 1787), Charrière describes a relationship ruined by humility, complacency, and cowardice. While the work, which was published in her final years, is not as well known, it is notable for its variety and depth. During 1787 and 1788, Charrière published *Observations et conjectures politiques,* a series of political writings considering the respective causes of the French royalists and revolutionaries. She also examined the themes of the Revolution in a play, *L'émigré,* and another epistolary novel, *Lettres trouvées dans des portefeuilles d'émigré* (both 1793). Additionally, Charrière produced a study on Immanuel Kant's notion of duty in her 1796 novel, *Trois femmes,* and explored philosophies of education in works such as *Les Ruines d'Yedburg* (1799) and *Sir Walter Finch et son fils William* (published posthumously in 1806). Independent of her published work, Charrière was a prodigious letter-writer; collected, her correspondence comprises most of her ten-volume *Oeuvre complètes* (1979-84).

Critical Reception

Widely published and translated, even in her own time, Charrière's work has received a great deal of critical attention. Early studies included two extensive efforts by noted nineteenth-century critic C. A. Sainte-Beuve. Her first biographer, Philippe Godet, in his *Madame de Charrière et ses amis* (1906), attributed much of her writing to biographical experience rather than literary skill; and this perception was seconded in the first English-language biography of Charrière, Geoffrey Scott's *The Portrait of Zélide* (1926), a study based largely on Godet's account. More recent biographies, however, have recognized her importance as both a literary figure and as an early advocate of gender equality. Critic Joan Hinde Stewart calls her work "powerfully seductive" in both form and style, and Susan Jackson adds that Charrière "provides a shining example of feminist revisionism already at work in the eighteenth century." Stewart describes her writing as "a delicate weave of inconspicuous circumstances and almost infinitesimal occurrences." This same characteristic critics such as Susan Lanser contrast with the larger, more general issues that figure prominently in the work of her contemporaries. While some critics praise the originality of her characters and themes, others, such as Jenene Allison, claim otherwise: "Relative to conventional figures, Charrière's heroines seem at first glance quite innovative. Considered more closely, they are better described as refutations of the conventional." Despite continuing debate over her literary reputation, critics generally commend Charrière's boldness and recognize her importance to the feminist literary tradition.

PRINCIPAL WORKS

Le noble [*The Nobleman*] (novel) 1763
Lettres neuchâteloises (novel) 1784
Lettres de Mistriss Henley publiées par son amie [*Mistriss Henley*] (novel) 1784
Lettres écrites de Lausanne [*Letters from Lausanne*] (novel) 1785
Caliste, ou suite des Lettres écrites de Lausanne [*Caliste*] (novel) 1787
Observations et conjectures politiques (essays) 1787-88
L'émigré (drama) 1793
Lettres trouvées dans des portefeuilles d'émigrés (novel) 1793
Trois femmes (novel) 1796
Les Ruines d'Yedburg (novel) 1799
Sainte-Anne (short story) 1799
Sir Walter Finch et son fils William (novel) 1806
Oeuvres complètes 10 vols. (novels, drama, essays, short stories, letters, and poetry) 1979-84

CRITICISM

Geoffrey Scott (essay date 1926)

SOURCE: An Introduction to *Four Tales,* by Isabella A. (Van Tuyll) de Charrière, translated by Sybil Marjorie Scott, Books for Libraries Press, 1926, reprinted 1970, pp. xi-xxvii.

[*In the following essay—a 1970 reprint of a work originally published in 1926—Scott connects numerous events in the author's life to those which appear in her fiction.*]

The four tales here translated [*The Nobleman, Mistress Henley, Letters from Lausanne,* and *Letters from Lausanne—Caliste*] have, I think, a dual interest. As literature they possess a quiet but genuine merit, and fill a graceful if inconspicuous niche in the cold temple of eighteenth-century romance. But, also, to an unusual extent they throw light upon their author, and help to complete the picture of Madame de Charrière, whose story, brought to light by the late Prof. [Philippe] Godet, [In his *Madame de Charrière et ses amis, d'après de nombreux documents inédits* (1740-1805), Geneva: Jullien, 1906] is briefly told in *The Portrait of Zélide*.

Madame de Charrière had many considerable literary gifts, but invention was not one of them. She drew directly on her own experience. The background of her stories is the background of her own life; the opinions of her heroines are her opinions; their misfits her misfits. In life she was proud and reserved; yet in her novels she told out her secrets without compunction. Her fictions stood like a transparent screen between her and the world.

Madame de Charrière was born in 1740 of one of the oldest families in Holland, a van Tuyll of Zuylen. The first thirty years of her life were spent in the towered and moated castle of Zuylen or in the grave family house by a quiet canal in Utrecht. Endowed by nature with a simple heart, a sensuous temperament, and a mind of amazing alacrity, she was confined by the circumstances of her birth in a society that was slow, stifling, and heraldic. The rumour of her wit, her learning, and her unconventionality—qualities which were viewed at home with critical apprehension or affectionate dismay—spread beyond Holland, where dowagers tossed their heads in disapproval, to Voltaire at Ferney and the King of Prussia at Potsdam, who both desired to attract her to their courts. Alone by candlelight in the still room at Zuylen she had her own occupations, writing satires on Dutch society, studying Plutarch, battling with physics and carrying on, for twelve years, a clandestine correspondence with a rake. Suitors were proposed to her: Dutch gentlemen of breeding; she refused them. Some, who would have served her turn, took flight. She turned down Boswell, and rejected Lord Wemyss. And at last she married her brother's Swiss tutor, a timid, phlegmatic, stammering, and mathematical man.

From the cold dignity of Zuylen she found herself transplanted to the sleep of Neuchâtel. It was her own choice. Disdainful alike of worldly advantage and intellectual display, she had reasoned herself, under the influence of Rousseau, into the simple life. It proved less simple than vacant. The society on the shores of the lake feared her and starved her mind. A husband who proved as chilly as a fish disappointed, no less, her human and simple proclivities. Two sisters-in-law, one peevish and one pious, remained with her till her death, dividing between them the care of the house. Madame de Charrière lived, gallantly, in a perpetual void. Stoically, she sought to fill it by a ceaseless activity of the mind and pen. For a stretch of fifteen years she never took a walk outside the walls of her garden. A deep Dutch orderliness in her, which neither she nor others had suspected, attuned her habits, without reconciling her heart, to the circumstances of this life.

The distance between her and her punctilious husband widened, as the years passed, to a gulf. Childless, Madame de Charrière lived on at Colombier, a small band of dependents at her feet. She preferred to remain shut in her bedroom, playing the harpsichord, teaching Locke on the Human Understanding to her maid, writing and writing. The dream of literary fame that had haunted her girlhood was realized in *Caliste*. But the disillusion of life stole like a dry rot over her later books, "the bric-à-brac of her disenchanted mind."

Twice after her marriage she sought an outlet for the locked riches of her nature. She fell disastrously in love with an insignificant and handsome individual at Geneva, an episode which ended in humiliation and despair. Later, she centred her life on Benjamin Constant. This relation, perilous from a wide disparity in their ages, was made not less so by the excessive likeness of their natures. Eight years of an intimacy that was sometimes a torture had given her affection for Constant its most vital hold, when she saw him reft from her by Madame de Staël. Her life closed in. She wrote on, dryly, dead books, and died.

> "But for whom can one write nowadays?" asked the Abbé de la Tour.
>
> "For me," answered the young Baroness de Brenghen. . . .
>
> "Lord, Madam! if only I could—"
>
> "You could," interrupted the Baroness.
>
> "No; I could not," said the Abbé. "My style would appear too insipid compared to that of the writers of today. Do people pause to observe a man who is merely walking when they are accustomed to seeing only mountebank tricks or acrobatic leaps?"
>
> "Yes," said the Baroness, "people *do* pause to observe anyone who walks with sufficient grace and rapidity to a point of interest."
>
> "Well! I will do my best," said the Abbé.
>
> . . . . .

This little preamble to one of the later (and duller) of Zélide's novels would serve equally as a preface, or apology, for all of them. One must not look, in these leisurely and urbane trifles of the eighteenth century, for any originality of method, for sweep or speed in the action, or medical zest in the psychology. But Madame de Charrière was always able to cause the personages of her novels to "walk with sufficient grace" to some point of interest in their lives. And there she usually leaves them: and we may speculate as we will on the issue of Cécile's romance, the end of Mistress Henley's marriage, or the future of Caliste's unhappy love. The society has been described, the problem posed, the characters made clear; how it will all work out remains almost as uncertain in literature as in life.

For literature, at any rate the literature she made, was hardly a thing in itself, hardly an art or a vocation, but just a part of Zélide's life, an extension of herself—beyond the moat at Zuylen, beyond the *potager* at Colombier.

Family portraits and scutcheons, family genealogies, family parties, if one had to be serious about such things in company, at least one must laugh at them when alone. So, behind her locked door at Zuylen, she wrote **"Le Noble."** The trifling satire—it is no more than a scenario—had a *succès de scandale*. Its authorship was not divulged, but it was more than suspected; and eyebrows were raised higher than ever when Zélide merrily entered the sedate drawing-rooms of Utrecht and The Hague. *Une demoiselle . . . cela!* And indeed, for a girl imprisoned in the stiffest Dutch society of the eighteenth century the satire was extremely audacious. The theme—that kind hearts are more than coronets—was less threadbare, it is only fair to remember, in 1760 than today. Its author would have been the last person to claim for this tale a serious literary merit; it is told with zest, and the figure of Baron d'Arnonville is rendered with a youthful and brilliant absurdity. But the interest of this first tale is frankly biographical rather than literary. **"Le Noble"** was an episode in—and an escape from—Belle de Zuylen's early life.

And then she escaped in earnest, by marrying the tutor. She was her own mistress at last, freed from the blank painted gaze of those framed ancestors, and the gaze, traditionally blank, of her living (but were they living?) relations. Rousseau's Switzerland proved disappointing, the vintage unclassical, the tasks of Nausicaa monotonous, the games of cards tedious, the gossip more tedious still. But to observe and note with skill and malice, until a work of delicate realism—the **Lettres Neuchâteloises**—had taken shape, that was to use all this tedium to good effect. What matter if the publication of this sketch made the gossip more spiteful, and narrowed the available society yet more? To be bored alone was always, Belle thought, better than being bored in company.

But she was not alone; there was always Monsieur de Charrière to reckon with. Blameless, hesitating, pedantic, and unruffled, there he was. And would be, to the end of the world; ever so close, beside her. And Madame de Charrière, shrinking from that cold ceaseless contact, from those conventional maxims uttered with such remorseless deliberation, from that tightness, that impeccability, once more took refuge in a book. She wrote *Mistress Henley*.

This novel was ostensibly an answer to a story called "The Sentimental Husband" written by Samuel Constant, the uncle of Benjamin, which exhibited the misfortunes of a middle-aged husband unequally yoked with a gay young wife. In *Mistress Henley* we are given the other side of the picture. Although the book was published anonymously, its authorship was an open secret. And though the scene is laid in England and the circumstances are disguised, no one at Neuchâtel had any doubt as to the identity of the protagonists.

Some books are like shutters inadvertently left ajar; they reveal, we are uncomfortably aware, the author's private foible in a degree he does not measure or intend. In *Mistress Henley* the doors are flung wide. The writer lifts the curtains with the most disarming gesture, and "here," she says, "you may see just what happens—not through my husband's fault, certainly, nor wholly through my own—if a man of his character live with a woman of mine." What happens—what must inevitably happen: Madame de Charrière's attention dwells always on the rules of the human comedy, seeks impartially to discover them, delights in expressing them tersely, justly, without exaggeration or adjustment to her own case. If in her letters, or in this novel, she seems absorbed in her own reactions it is because these present themselves most readily and most fully for analysis. Her subject is human nature; she watches it in herself.

The story is "a pack of little things." Very deftly Madame de Charrière puts her heroine always in the wrong. Mr. Henley is credited only with one offence: that of being always and consciously and sadly in the right. "And all this for a cat to whom I have done no hurt!" said Mr. Henley, with a sad and gentle look, a look of resignation; and he went away. "No," I cried after him, "it is *not* the cat. . . ." But he was already far away. The story abounds with touches that Miss Austen would not have despised.

"Mistress Henley," wrote Zélide to a friend in Holland, "caused a schism in Geneva society. All the husbands were on Mr. Henley's side, many of the women on his wife's, while the girls did not dare to say what they thought. Never had fictitious personages seemed so much alive." Monsieur de Charrière read the book "with a sad and gentle look." Very carefully he read it, and tried to understand. But he could not apprehend that it was not the cat.

And in consequence of this crucial misapprehension he saw Madame de Charrière fall in love with a young gentleman at Geneva.

Mistress Henley was published in 1784, and in the same year Madame de Charrière printed the ***Lettres de Lausanne***. The one deals with an actual, perhaps an indecently actual situation; the other with an imaginary one. In both she herself is speaking. And both are, like herself, refreshingly impersonal.

In the ***Lettres de Lausanne*** the scene is delineated with the same irony that in her first book caused such offence, to the citizens of Neuchâtel. Madame de Charrière never paid but the briefest visits to Lausanne. The tea-parties where Gibbon strutted and the clients of Dr. Tissot compared their ailments in all the tongues of Europe were not to her taste; and she watched with aloof amusement the efforts of the Swiss provincials to imitate the habits of a horde of French financiers, German princes with the colic, and English noblemen on the Grand Tour.

The story cast against this background is the tale of an inconclusive love affair between the *ingénue* Cecilia and a little English lord upon his travels, told in a series of letters from the girl's mother. The latter is, admittedly, Madame de Charrière herself. She advises her child with a directness and honesty which, we are told, shocked the prudish and sentimental ladies of the day, much as it might have offended Victorian mothers. Was it necessary, they asked, that a young girl should know that a suitor might sigh for her charms at the Governor's reception and yet embrace, that same evening, a woman of another sort? But the mind revealed in these letters is one of remarkable wisdom and charm; and Cecilia's dignity at the defection of the little Englishman to whom she had lost her heart is so unaffected, that we cannot be altogether unmoved when she is left to console herself in true romantic fashion with a pianoforte, a portfolio of prints, the care of a sick negro—the inevitable eighteenth-century negro—and of a starving dog. As in the ***Lettres Neuchâteloises***, the provincial setting of the story is a truthful piece of *genre;* and the quiet light reflected on the writer may redeem the slender construction.

Cecilia—so the author told Monsieur de Salgas—was drawn, in her physical traits at any rate, from a certain Mademoiselle Röell. We must accept this statement; yet here too, I am convinced, there is an element of self-portraiture. If the mother is Madame de Charrière with her mature knowledge of human nature, Cecilia, by many touches, is Belle at the castle of Zuylen two years before the correspondence with d'Hermenches, when the candour and simplicity, so naively present beneath the brilliant surface of those letters, were still childish: wondering and waiting for life while the poplars flecked the unrippled moat with the slow sun.

Be that as it may, the relation between mother and daughter is drawn with an equally firm touch on both. It was a relation for which, as Monsieur de Salgas said, she had a born gift; and had the marriage with Charrière been fruitful, had there been a Cecilia at Colombier as well as a too real Mr. Henley, the tragic development of Madame de Charrière's nature would never have been played out.

The faith in education, characteristic of Rousseau's period, was hers to an almost pathetic degree. As a girl at Zuylen she had brought up her young brothers, teaching Plutarch to Vincent and life to the wide-eyed and romantic Dietrich. At Colombier we find her giving lessons in Locke to her maid Henriette, and some dim lights on Latin; the lifelong devotion of this unlikely pupil is a proof that her efforts, if misplaced, were not resented. Moreover, this Socratic energy, for ever goading the dormant minds around her to life, was coupled with a vigorous instinct of protection; and when Henriette, unregenerated by Locke, was compelled to concentrate her mind on an illegitimate baby, Madame de Charrière rose up with fine spirit as her champion against the persecution of the Calvinist community. In later years this protective instinct grew more masterful and pronounced; and Colombier became the centre of a strange band of curious dependents, exiles and eccentrics, whose wayward fortunes she guided and tolerated with a wise patience. But this, the richest vein in her nature, never found its obvious outlet.

There was no daughter to educate at Colombier; no one could educate Monsieur de Charrière. Inside the case which contained him his regulated mind irreproachably ticked. His clear complacency was without a crack. There was no Cecilia—and we have ***Caliste***.

Here the effort to disguise the personal confession is far more sustained than it was in ***Mistress Henley***. But we have it from Benjamin Constant that the inspiration of this tale—the only tragic tale she wrote—was drawn from that mysterious episode at Geneva; and Madame de Charrière herself remarked, "I have never re-read ***Caliste:*** it cost me too many tears to write."

Zélide saw herself as Caliste; and Benjamin Constant, the most penetrating and critical of all her friends, has written, "To her who created Caliste and who resembles her." And yet nothing could well be more different from Madame de Charrière, as she presented herself to the world—a masterful, caustic blue-stocking, than the gentle heroine of this tale.

> Caliste is Madame de Charrière's hidden self: or, if you will, her anti-self. Caliste is made up, singly

and limpidly, of all those emotions she knew she would have lived by, and had not. Zélide, at Zuylen, had sometimes revealed them ('But if I love . . . if I love,' she had written to Hermenches, the words starting like a jet from a smooth rock); but she had lost herself in the maze of her own mind: her sceptical and mocking reason. Yet, in the Portrait of Zélide, the features of Caliste are there behind the mask she was resolved to wear, and wore till the mask stiffened upon the face. Here, for once, she told it out. Caliste dies: it is the only one of her tales that can be said to have a conclusion. She wrote *Caliste,* and never re-read it. (Geoffrey Scott, *The Portrait of Zélide,* 1926.)

The book had an immediate success. Madame de Staël owns that but for it *Corinne* might never have been written. It was translated into English: it was the rage in Paris. Madame de Charrière had achieved her literary fame.

Yet in certain respects *Caliste* has stood the test of time less well than the earlier volumes. We shall look in it in vain for those truthfully observed details—those pieces of provincial *genre*—which give the **Lettres Neuchâteloises** and the **Lettres de Lausanne** their charm for any student of eighteenth-century life and manners who is willing to endure slowness of pace and slightness of incident for the sake of so entirely genuine a picture. *Caliste,* on the contrary, is a pure product of the Romantic Movement. It has all the improbable machinery and much of the high-flown sentiment which delighted the last years of the eighteenth century. Two infants are jumbled at birth; and the uncertainty as to which is the elder twin inspires in both of them a lifelong fraternal devotion with vows of perpetual celibacy in order that the rights of property may never be called in question. This is a bad beginning; or a good one, according to whether we are looking for a serious plot or prepared to enjoy an excellent "specimen" in the history of taste.

And, if the motive of literary curiosity is strong enough to carry us through the conventional romantic stock-in-trade which surrounds the story, we shall be rewarded by the genuine pathos and humanity of the central figure. For here Madame de Charrière is writing once more of what she knows. She never deceived herself, never falsified her own emotions; and it is not difficult to distinguish, beneath the occasional conventionality of the language of her time, the reality of Caliste's tragedy.

And if her lover, with his endless vacillations and Werther-like vapours remains unconvincing to the end, the father, stupid, obstinate, upright, and benevolent is old Monsieur de Tuyll to the life. He cannot be made to act against his convictions, and Caliste has no feelings of bitterness against him for his firmness. Indeed, she has no bitterness at all. Society is thus; facts are so. Is not this Zélide herself? Ardent, seeking diligently for a happiness that escapes her, never deceived by convention, often mocking it, sometimes revolted by it; yet in the bottom of her Dutch soul *ordentlyk* to the last?

So she lived on at Colombier; writing, reasoning, protecting, and pretending that it was life. Proudly reserved and scornfully resigned, she hid all of her that was Caliste from the eyes of the world and from her own. Pastor Chaillet, her peering, inquisitive guest, divined it; Monsieur de Charrière dumbly apprehended it. But only Benjamin Constant was permitted to penetrate that screen, and scarcely forgiven for having done so.

When, after eight years, came the rupture with Benjamin, she sought in a first impulse of devotion to hold him at least by a literary sympathy. "I thought I would write new *Calistes* simply for your entertainment"—new romances shorn of "that bare style which you have blamed," romances in the manner of Madame de Staël. She returned to her books; but she never sought to make literature out of her broken friendship with Constant. Her books, thenceforward, are filled with theories, inspired by theories, not by life—her own, or anyone else's. They are Rousseau's theories in *Sir Walter Finch,* her own theories of democracy in *Les Trois Femmes,* political theories in *Les Emigrés* and half a dozen pamphlets. But never anything the least like life again. Her novels were only the extension of Zélide's personal life; and that, with the disappearance of Benjamin, was ended. Only her mind lived on, still seeking scornfully to follow the thread of Reason. Madame de Charrière's service of the eighteenth-century goddess was stoical to the last. Reason in books. Reason in human affairs. Was it enough? Had not the flame of her existence, the spark of it which endures in these few tales, been lent not by reason, but by something less logical, more humorous, more tragic, subtler—by life itself, which she had ardently longed for, and studied, and mistrusted, and renounced?

Susan K. Jackson (essay date 1985)

SOURCE: "The Novels of Isabelle de Charrière, or, A Woman's Work is Never Done," in *Studies in Eighteenth-Century Culture*, Vol. XIV, 1985, pp. 299-306.

[*In the following essay, Jackson discusses the theme of women's work in Charrière's novels, noting that her conveying of "Everywoman's experience of everyday life . . . provides a shining example of feminist revisionism already at work in the eighteenth century."*]

If, as popular wisdom would have it, a woman's work is never done, then the eighteenth century witnessed no more womanly works than the novels of Isabelle de

Charrière. In his *Portrait of Zélide,* Geoffrey Scott singles out **Caliste,** where the heroine dies, as "the only one of her tales that can be said to have a conclusion."[1] Caliste aside, Charrière's protagonists are routinely abandoned, whether at a crossroads or simply en route, before their fates can be decided once and for all. The typical Charrière novel eschews comic and tragic denouements alike, in favor of a murky middle ground between death and the happily ever after. A particularly telling example is provided by the **Lettres de Mistriss Henley,** Charrière's recasting from the woman's point of view of Samuel de Constant's *Le Mari sentimental.* Whereas Constant's henpecked husband had been made to "end it all," Charrière's equally desperate wife declares herself incapable of suicide, and wonders whether she will have changed "dans un an, dans deux ans." As if to symbolize her own uncertain future, she alludes in her last letter to the baby which, contrary to conventional novelistic wisdom, she has *not* yet miscarried, though the perfect opportunity has just presented itself, and may again.[2] More inconclusive still are the several later novels: **Lettres écrites de Lausanne, Lettres trouvées dans des porte-feuilles d'émigrés, Trois femmes,** and **Sir Walter Finch et son fils William,** for which Charrière provided sequels, only to thicken her plots with new characters and complications.

Feeling themselves to have been left in the lurch, contemporary readers, from her own sisters-in-law to erstwhile rival Germaine de Staël, repeatedly cajoled and challenged Charrière to produce what Christabel Braunrot has called a "dénouement en bonne et due forme."[3] But it was to no avail that Staël declared "rien de plus pénible que votre manière de commencer sans finir," and likened withdrawal pains suffered by readers of the **Lettres neuchâteloises** to those occasioned by the interruption of actual mail service from Paris. And it was only a matter of time before Charrière's alleged hard-heartedness would work to the detriment of her reputation as a writer of novels other than **Caliste,** that perennial favorite and, not incidentally, anomaly of completeness. At the hands of the critical establishment, she who *would* not became she who *could* not finish; the corpus became easy to dismiss as technically flawed, and seemingly impossible to rehabilitate without serious attention to the by now inevitable "charge of incompleteness often cast upon these novels."[4]

In her own defense, Charrière offers increasingly little direct testimony. Her purported reasons for failure to follow through are most often circumstantial and valid only for the particular novel in question, rather than suggestive of an overall philosophy or strategy. One early novel must be abandoned because, the author's identity having been discovered, she can no longer hide behind her fictional correspondents; another, because events in her own life have so soured her on men and marriage that she can summon no enthusiasm to write about them, even in negative terms. Or so she confesses to Benjamin Constant. For Chambrier d'Oleyres, she reserves the more impersonal claim that there can be no thought whatsoever of novels at a time when *le romanesque* pales in comparison with the reality of Revolution.[5] Three novels of Revolution and emigration later, she would seem to have changed her mind.

However sincerely proffered at the moment, these excuses are finally less intriguing than one which comes closer to endowing Charrière's chronic incompleteness with an underlying purposiveness. Writing near the outset of her career on denouements in general, she confides: "j'aurois peut-être encore moins de talent pour les dénouemens que pour le reste. Les tristes sont tristes et les heureux sont fort sujets à être plats."[6] Made under cover of modesty, the rhetorical attack on endings is nonetheless sudden, swift, and incisive. One, the tautological formulation "les tristes sont tristes" magically condemns the tragic denouement to absolute and absolutely sterile finality. Two, with the refusal to balance the period rhythmically or semantically, *les heureux* trail off appropriately into terminal insipidity. Three, by assuming the right to classify all possible endings as either *tristes* or *heureux,* a practice taken over from that most conventional of all genres, the classical theater, Charrière places a curse of conventionality on the ending per se. Nowhere is the theoretical irony more cleverly translated into practice than in the one novel, **Saint Anne,** whose loose ends would seem to have been tied up as neatly as those of any Corneille comedy or Gilbert and Sullivan operetta. Having duly unmixed and matched her young lovers, Charrière then undermines their happy ending by dispatching the title character and his new bride in search of two nameless friends whose only prior function in this novel has been to discourse on the implausibility of novels in general.[7] Rather than work within the system to refurbish old denouements or even invent new ones, Charrière has chosen, once and for all, to concentrate on *le reste.*

For want of imagination? So saying, the critical chorus has neglected, I think, to recognize that Charrière's unfinished novels perform an important illustrative function. I would suggest here that, through their very form or formlessness, these novels ultimately show what their content has been telling all along: namely, that a woman's work is unique in nature, and more precisely, never done.

By women's work, I mean not only the generalized business of living as a woman, but the specific womanly activities encompassed by the dictionary term *ouvrages de dames:* sewing, embroidery, knitting, and weaving. The latter *ouvrages* can be counted on to figure in each of Charrière's novels; linked to a female subject, the verb *travailler* invariably means nothing more than "to work with a needle." The corpus abounds in accomplished seamstresses, beginning with Julianne, the *Lettres neuchâteloises*' professional *tailleuse*, whose dress-making assignments provide the sole occasion of her coming into contact with the two more socially prominent members of the novel's central triangle. Hers, though, turns out to be an isolated case, insofar as *les ouvrages de dames* gradually retreat, in the ensuing novels, from the actual and plot economies. Amateurs all, Cécile works in her mother's drawing room; Geneviève, in the solitude of her own apartment; groups of women, in the latter-day gynecea of both *La Nature et l'art* and *Le Roman de Charles Cecil*.[8]

This increasing isolation of the female workplace parallels Charrière's growing skepticism about the possibility of true interaction and intuitive understanding between the sexes. Whatever steps are undertaken to bridge the gender gap become the sole responsibility of her ever more enterprising heroines, who, for example, almost always initiate correspondence with their absent lovers. For their part, Charrière's men take no interest in the world or work of women. Time and again, Charrière peoples her drawing rooms with a symbolic dyad, the woman with her *ouvrage,* the man absorbed in his book.[9] Even when treated to the spectacle of women's work, men do not see it. Sir Walter Finch promotes the invisibility of women's work to the status of an ideal, by repeated allegorical reference to the single scrawny cat who works behind the scenes to rid the household of rats so that her brother fat cats may thrive. Women's work is a sight fit only for the downcast eyes of the worker, as when Cécile hides her embarrassment at untoward advances in the *ouvrage* at hand.[10]

For Charrière's heroines, their *ouvrage* is, in fact, always at hand, ready at a moment's notice to serve as a diversion from what male-dominated society would call the real business of living. No need to mention Cécile's sewing prior to her availing herself thereof if, as Charrière suggests, sewing is less an economic activity than a natural biological function, less an autonomous piece of work than an always available appendage of the female body. Only an unnatural woman like the Marquise of *Trois femmes* would, by her perverse preoccupation with *toilette* and *vapeurs,* neglect the one end to which her hands were created.[11] Is it any wonder that Caliste and Bianca, the novels' two quintessential *femmes fatales,* are *said* to possess extraordinary aptitude for "tous les ouvrages de femme," Bianca to the exclusion of all other talents? Or that neither is ever *shown* in the act of sewing?[12] Women's work is always there, but never done. There is no credit given for women's work; it is certainly not the stuff of which lives—or novels—are made. Charrière thus exposes the assumption on which her predecessors had merely proceeded.

Nor is women's work ever done in the sense of "finished." What ever became of the purse in progress by which Henriette intended to spin a web communication between herself and the absent Richard? No sooner has it served one evening as a receptacle for her tears than the purse disappears from the reader's sight once and for all.[13] In keeping with the dictates of French grammar, what women do—not "ouvrages" (works), but "de l'ouvrage" (*some work*)—remains a single, interminable process, devoid of product. It cannot count in part because it cannot be counted.

There is, of course, a sense in which the unfinished nature of *les ouvrages de dames* provides a safe and comforting alternative to forays into the domain of real life. The inaction of sewing serves Julie d'Arnonville well as a mirror and pretext for the inaction of relatively harmless reverie. Likewise, when tempted to unleash her tart tongue in after-dinner conversation, Henriette turns to her work as a defense against saying something she might always regret.[14] What Charrière's heroines fear more than anything else is the irrevocable word or deed by which their fate would be sealed once and for all. They recognize, as does their creator, that attempting to act would involve a trade-off: more *lauriers* perhaps, but more *souffrance* as well.[15] In this respect, they hardly differ from their counterparts throughout the eighteenth-century corpus, all those Julies and Clarissas whose missteps had proven fatal. Except that Charrière would dispense with the prevailing notion of female destiny as absolutely grounded in biology. Even in *Caliste,* death is no longer the inevitable long-term result of sexual relations per se. Rather, the heroine's mortal despair emanates from a series of trifling incidents which to her make all the difference: a door slammed and not reopened, a letter never sent, an apology tendered too late, and so forth. Even here, the infamous fatal moment is displaced and disseminated throughout the life.

In fact, Caliste long outlives her unworthy lover's first assumption that she must be dead by now. Has he read too many novels? Charrière suggests as much when she recasts heroines from novels past in the role of survivors. Where Rousseau's Baronne d'Etange had taken to her deathbed on discovering evidence of Julie's fall, Cécile's mother vows that, should history repeat itself, *she* would not die of chagrin. "Non," she continues, "je vivrois, je tâcherois de vivre, de prolonger ma vie pour adoucir les malheurs de la vôtre."[16] No longer, in Charrière's hands, is female life possessed of but a single shape. Rather, it is rendered shapeless, open-ended, subject to change for better or worse, perhaps tedious, even trivial, but at least not necessarily or uniformly tragic, in close conformity with the model provided by female *ouvrage*. Survivors all, Charrière's heroines are, like her heroes, entitled to contend, each in her own way, with the never finished business of living. In the process, the female novelist's work has been made to consist, not so much in doing, as in *un*doing, stitch by careful stitch, the ever-so-tightly woven tapestry of novelistic convention.

But if her own labor derives less from Hercules' than from Penelope's, so too, implies Charrière, does every woman's. It is fitting that Charrière should have given voice in the lyric opera **Pénélope** to the mythological figure who presides in silence over the whole of the novelistic production. Though only a brief opening fragment of the opera remains, the extant text makes clear the librettist's intention to focus on Penelope the weaver, rather than on Penelope the much-maligned mother or even on Penelope the faithful and long-suffering wife. Charrière's heroine is immediately shown in the act of unweaving which the Homeric material had relegated to flashback, albeit on three separate occasions.[17] A devotee of Fénelon's *Télémaque*, Charrière nonetheless confesses in her correspondence never to have read the original *Odyssey* because of deep-seated antipathy for *le prudent*, that is, *le trop prudent Ulysse*.[18] No wonder that, in her opera, the goal of fidelity to Ulysses is all but forgotten in favor of Penelope's chosen stratagem, unweaving by night what she has woven by day, so as never to complete Laertes' burial shroud.

Fashioning a coherent narrative out of the novels' scattered strands, the seven-page operatic fragment succeeds in telling the whole truth and nothing but the truth about women's work. An initial chorus for drunken suitors, supposed rivals now united in their adoration of Bacchus, dramatizes the solitude of the working woman in a world where real work is defined in masculine terms.[19] Though Telemachus does not figure in Charrière's scenario, one can almost hear his Homeric counterpart dispatching his mother to her room, commanding as follows: "Look to your own province, distaff and loom, and tell your women to ply their own task; public speech shall be men's concern, and my concern most of all; authority in this house is mine."[20] Meanwhile, addressed to no one but herself, Pénélope's own repeated imperatives: "Défaisons . . . Défaisons . . . Défaisons . . . Défaisons . . . Travaillons, . . ." eloquently declare the incompatibility, even the antonymy for her sex of "working" and "doing." Turning process into a finished product is likewise out of the question: "c'est un si long ouvrage."[21]

Suddenly caught in the act of unweaving by apparently sympathetic suitor Eurimaque, who here replaces Homer's traitorous handmaidens, Pénélope insists that she cannot work with someone watching.[22] Has it not already been written that women's work must remain, if not literally nocturnal, at least invisible to men? Pénélope is drawn to Eurimaque, so *séduisant* and *attendrissant* in his protestations of undying love, so different from the other suitors and, by implication, from Ulysse, whose *billets-doux* all date from *before* their marriage.[23] Yet she dares not speak, nor even avert her gaze from the fragile *ouvrage* which alone stands between her and total vulnerability. His advances, her retreat, are resumed in the counterpoint of their respective refrains: "Regardez-moi" and "Ah laissez-moi."[24] Pénélope feels her defenses to be weakening. If only, having seen her work, Eurimaque could read her mind and thus, embody the heretofore unattainable ideal of intuitive manhood. Alas! It only remains for the drunken chorus to thrust Pénélope's loom aside, with the mocking announcement that, prior bargains to the contrary, they will *play* for her hand, with dice no less. The opera itself may not be complete; its dismissal of women's work as "ce chien d'ouvrage" most certainly is.[25]

But Penelope's story need not end on such a gloomy note. In the *Odyssey*'s third, possibly apocryphal version, the burial robe is, for the first time, presented as a finished product: "With the weaving over, she washed the great web and then displayed it; it shone out like the sun and moon."[26] Likewise, Isabelle de Charrière finished—at least, according to her own lights—carefully edited, and published the majority of her novels. And yet, in making her escape into the literary world of discrete *ouvrages* (masculine plural), Charrière never failed to look back with subtle intelligence and subversive charm on the gyneceum of endless female *ouvrage*. Granted, she did not invent the possibility of interchanging needles and pens; the metaphor was already moribund, if not dead on arrival. Nor did she lack for models of incompleteness in an age which celebrated the open book as a passport to reflection, debate, and social change. In her hands, however, the metaphor lends new and particular meaning to the structure, which, in turn, rescues the metaphor from innocuous banality, and makes it a useful tool for understanding Everywoman's experience of everyday life. Forever undoing the complete novels of her fellow writers, Charrière provides a shining example of feminist revisionism already at work in the eighteenth century.

Notes

[1] Geoffrey Scott, *The Portrait of Zélide* (New York: Charles Scribner's Sons, 1926), p. 94.

[2] Isabelle de Charrière, *Lettres de Mistriss Henley,* in *Oeuvres complètes,* ed. Jean-Daniel Candaux et al. (Amsterdam: G. A. van Oorschot, 1979—), 8:122. All references to Charrière's works are to this edition.

[3] Christabel Braunrot's Introduction to *Lettres neuchâteloises,* in *Oeuvres,* 8:43. Braunrot cites Staël on the same page. For the sisters-in-law's entreaties, see Charrière's *Correspondance*, specifically, "De son frère Vincent," seconde quinzaine d'août 1784, Letter 533,

in *Oeuvres,* 2:636. See also: "De sa belle-soeur Johanna Catharina van Tuyll van Serooskerken-Fagel," 24 juillet 1787, Letter 590; and "De sa belle-soeur Johanna Catharina van Tuyll van Serooskerken-Fagel," entre mi-juin et mi-juillet 1790, Letter 720, both in *Oeuvres,* 3:27, 226.

[4] Sigyn C. Minier-Birk, "L'Oeuvre romanesque de Madame de Charrière: Réflexion systématique et création dans les *Lettres neuchâteloises, Mistriss Henley,* et les *Lettres écrites de Lausanne,*" *Dissertation Abstracts International* 38 (1978): 4871A.

[5] "A Jean-Pierre de Chambrier d'Oleyres," 1 février 1785, Letter 549, in *Oeuvres,* 2:454; "A Benjamin Constant," 31 août 1790, Letter 726, in *Oeuvres,* 3:231; "A Jean-Pierre de Chambrier d'Oleyres," 17 avril 1790, Letter 703, in *Oeuvres,* 3:200-201.

[6] Charrière, Letter 549, in *Oeuvres,* 2:454.

[7] Charrière, *Saint Anne,* in *Oeuvres,* 9:310.

[8] Charrière, *Lettres écrites de Lausanne,* in *Oeuvres,* 8:164, 192; *Henriette et Richard,* in *Oeuvres,* 8:321; *La Nature et l'art,* in *Oeuvres,* 8:601; *Le Roman de Charles Cecil,* in *Oeuvres,* 9:642.

[9] See, for example: Charrière, *Henriette et Richard,* p. 320; *Louise et Albert, ou Le Danger d'être trop exigeant,* in *Oeuvres,* 9:425.

[10] Charrière, *Sir Walter Finch et son fils William,* in *Oeuvres,* 9:533, 535-36, 592; *Lettres écrites de Lausanne,* p. 169.

[11] Charrière, *Trois femmes,* in *Oeuvres,* 9:47.

[12] Charrière, *Lettres écrites de Lausanne,* p. 192; *Trois femmes,* p. 147.

[13] Charrière, *Henriette et Richard,* pp. 325, 336.

[14] Charrière, *Le Noble,* in *Oeuvres,* 8:25; *Henriette et Richard,* p. 335.

[15] "Au baron Constant d'Hermenches," 22 novembre 1768, Letter 326, in *Oeuvres,* 2:133.

[16] Charrière, *Lettres écrites de Lausanne,* p. 164.

[17] Charrière, *Pénélope,* in *Oeuvres,* 7:103; Homer, *The Odyssey,* trans. Walter Shewring (Oxford: Oxford University Press, 1980), pp. 14, 231, 288-89.

[18] "A Jean-Pierre de Chambrier d'Oleyres," 30 mars 1789, Letter 645, in *Oeuvres,* 3:133.

[19] Charrière, *Pénélope,* p. 103.

[20] Homer, *Odyssey,* trans. Shewring, p. 9.

[21] Charrière, *Pénélope,* p. 106.

[22] Ibid., p. 103.

[23] Ibid., pp. 105-6.

[24] Ibid., pp. 106-7.

[25] Ibid., p. 108.

[26] Homer, *Odyssey,* trans. Shewring, pp. 288-89.

Marie-Paule Laden (essay date 1986)

SOURCE: " 'Quel Aimable et Cruel Petit Livre': Madame de Charrière's *Mistriss Henley,*" in *French Forum,* Vol. XI, No. 3, September, 1986, pp. 289-99.

[*In the essay that follows, Laden discusses* Mistriss Henley *as an epistolary autobiography in which Charrière provides a detailed account of living in a male-dominated society.*]

The socio-literary issues surrounding the status of women writers in the 18th century come together in the epistolary works of Madame de Charrière.[1] Born in Holland, Mme de Charrière spent most of her life in Switzerland and wrote in French. Her literary reputation is as ambiguous as the nature of her literary form; she is well-known to literary historians because of her correspondence with various celebrities of the period (Constant d'Hermenches and James Boswell as well as Benjamin Constant), but apart from *Caliste* her works are seldom read in their own right.[2] Her life and personality, on the other hand, have been described by numerous biographers.[3] The neglect that has been the fate of her literary work seems somewhat hard to explain, in view of the fact that her novels are endowed with considerably more literary substance and merit than those of the better-known Mme de Graffigny or Mme Riccoboni.

What makes Mme de Charrière's case so interesting is not just that her life has eclipsed her work, but that this occultation may be construed as an identifiable socio-literary phenomenon, a common reaction to the way she handles her subject matter. Her short epistolary novel, *Mistriss Henley,* manages to explore the problems of identity inherent in the letter and also in the status of women at the time. *Mistriss Henley* was published in 1784, shortly after the publication of another novel by Samuel de Constant, *Le Mari sentimental,* a misogynous tale in which a decent and sensitive husband is driven to suicide by the shrewishness of his self-centered wife. One way of reading *Mistriss Henley* is thus as a polemical novel, Mme de Charrière's feminist riposte to Constant. The first paragraph of the novel invites such a reading: "Quel aimable et cruel petit livre que celui qui nous est arrivé de votre pays il y a quelques semaines. . . . On vient de le traduire, et je suis sûre que le *Sentimental Husband* va être entre les mains de tout le monde" (101).[4] More commonly, the book has tended to be dismissed as a story about "incompatible personalities," as it was by Mme de Charrière's main biographer, Philippe Godet,[5] or else taken as a disguised autobiography, which is what Mme de Charrière's contemporaries invariably took it to be. These interpretations are by no means devoid of interest, particularly the latter: since Mme de Charrière's fiction falls chronologically between two important bodies of correspondence—with Constant d'Hermenches, which ends in 1775, and subsequently with his nephew Benjamin Constant, whom she met during a trip to Paris in 1786—it is as if her fictional output relieved her need to confide in her friends. But the book itself has a much greater dimension, as I hope to show.

On the surface, **Mistriss Henley** is characteristic of the writing of women novelists in the 18th century. Like those of Mme Riccoboni, Mme de Graffigny, and Fanny Burney, to mention but the best known women novelists of the period, it is epistolary.[6] Although the genre enjoyed broad popularity—which reached an apogee in the second half of the century after the resounding success of Richardson's *Pamela*—it had an extraordinary appeal for women writers, and the epistolary novel is inevitably referred to as their primary vehicle of literary expression. François Jost remarks that "non seulement la femme est presque toujours—sauf dans la tradition Werther—l'héroïne principale: le roman épistolaire devient encore le genre favori des dames entrant dans la carrière des lettres" (115). Laurent Versini also emphasizes the important role played by women in the diffusion of the epistolary novel.[7] Even Pierre Fauchery, who devotes a mere 20 pages to women writers out of his important 895-page study of the European novel in the 18th century, admits that, although women did not create the epistolary novel, it is nonetheless a genre "qu'elles adoptent avec ferveur et dont elles prolongeront la maturité bien au-delà de sa période la plus féconde, [un genre] auquel elles ont imposé leur marque et dont elles ont fait le roman 'féminin' par excellence."[8] Although Fauchery considers that the works of women writers of the 18th century do not merit particular attention (93), he underscores the profound affinity existing between epistolary fiction and the 18th-century conception of femininity: "Epistolière de foundation, la femme passe pour ainsi dire insensiblement de la lettre spontanée à la lettre imaginée. . . . Le roman par lettre assure à la femme ce support étranger à la contemplation de soi-même, ce *tu* indispensable au Narcisse féminin; le présent s'y transmue aussitôt en 'présenté' " (111).

Indeed a large number of the novels written by women are composed of letters written by a female character and addressed to a female friend, a relationship which accounts for its confessional and autobiographical quality.[9] *Mistriss Henley* is composed of six letters written by Mrs. Henley, in which, if we take the book at face value, she tells a woman friend about the circumstances and outcome of her unsuccessful marriage to an extremely reasonable and virtuous man. As she points out, the letters are full of the "petites choses," the little things which make up everyday life: "Ce sont de petites choses qui m'affligent, m'impatientent, et me font avoir tort. Ecoutez donc encore un tas de petites choses" (112).

Characteristically, the heroine does not presume to write her autobiography. Mrs. Henley is impelled to write not in order to complain about her lot but to confess her failings: she is guilty of not making her husband happy, a capital sin for a woman of the period. Yet, at the same time, she informs her friend of her wish to teach husbands a lesson, "sinon corriger, du moins avertir les maris; je voudrais remettre les choses à leur place, et que chacun se rendît justice" (102). In order to do so she asks her friend to publish her letters if they have "quelque *justesse* et vous paraissent propres à exciter quelque intérêt" (102). Her concern with rightness and truth, with "justesse" and "justice," naturally suggests that, for her, justice has not yet been done. It implies that she suffers from a feeling of injustice, of bruised and tarnished innocence.

What she writes must therefore be construed both as an apology and as an apologia. The doubleness of purpose, the duplicity of this opening letter is emblematic of what Fauchery calls the "ambiguity" of feminine first-person writing in the 18th century.[10] What induces Mrs. Henley to write her friend is her lack of self-assurance, her feeling of inadequacy. The result of this feeling is a further ambiguity or paradox. On the one hand, the sense of failure that marks her letters indicates that she has passed judgment on herself and has found herself guilty—a situation so traumatic, so fraught with tension that she must find solace in writing, purging herself of tension, expiating her sin in the act of confession and repentence. Yet, at the same time, she declares herself incompetent to judge and, not trusting her own vision, her own judgment of her actions, she looks to her friend as an arbiter.

Her feeling of inferiority is further reflected in the fairy-tale portrait she traces of Mr. Henley in her first letter. She calls him "a true story-book husband" ("un vrai mari de roman," 103) whose moral as well as physical qualities leave nothing to be desired: he has the noblest figure, he is tall, has the softest blue eyes, the most beautiful teeth, the sweetest smile, he has "de la raison, de l'instruction, de l'équité, une égalité d'âme parfaite." The implication clearly is that Mrs. Henley is not worthy of such a man. Typically, when she marries him, Mrs. Henley has no doubt that she can only improve in the company of this paragon of virtue and that it will be particularly easy for her to fulfill all the duties of a perfect wife:

> Je me flattais que la société d'un homme que j'admirais tant, me rendrait comme lui, et je partis pour sa terre au commencement du printemps, remplie des meilleures intentions, et persuadée que j'allais être la meilleure femme, la plus tendre belle-mère, la plus digne maîtresse de maison que l'on eût jamais vue. (104)

The following letters, however, relate the shattering of Mrs. Henley's great expectations. Her least impulse meets with disapproval, and certain of her innocent initiatives have truly catastrophic results. She showers presents on Mr. Henley's daughter, but Mr. Henley tells her that she is spoiling the girl. When she wants to teach the child some of La Fontaine's fables, her husband's response is that she will not be able to understand them. She chases the dog out of the dining room, but the sulking animal thereafter refuses to leave the servants' quarters, and Mr. Henley is saddened by the absence of his pet. She buys an angora cat, but Mr. Henley, fearful of what the cat will do to his heirloom furniture, is displeased; Mrs. Henley thereupon takes it upon herself to replace the furniture with sturdier pieces, but during the redecoration the cat escapes and is presumed dead, leaving Mrs. Henley to blame herself for the creature's demise. Not heeding Mr. Henley's warning, she takes her chambermaid with her to the country. One of the servants falls in love with the maid, causing the jilted girl to whom he was betrothed to flee to London, where she ends up as a prostitute; meanwhile, her mother, long a faithful servant, leaves the château, while the father of the young man involved disowns his son. When Mrs. Henley sends the maid away, Mr. Henley observes that she is punishing an innocent girl without rectifying any of the harm already done. No matter how tortuous and unforeseeable the chain of circumstances, Mrs. Henley knows that she herself is to blame.

The full list of her misfortunes is so extraordinary that it would move even the most stoic of philosophers to helpless laughter. But the unfortunate consequences of her actions arouse in the heroine an almost pathological sense of guilt. An obsessive insistance on her wrongdoings or faults, her "torts," runs through her enumeration of her blunders: "J'avais tort, je le sais bien; c'est moi qui avais tort" (105), "je déplore mes torts" (107), "là j'ai déploré amèrement . . . tout le mal dont j'étais cause" (110), "Aurait-il raison, ma chère amie, aurais-je eu encore tort, toujours tort, tort en tout?" (111). This series of catastrophes arises from the fact that Mrs. Henley tries too hard and does too much, instead of being satisfied with the role of a passive spectator that society offers her.

She is, in short, too alive, and the current of pure energy emanating from the heroine is invariably arrested by her husband's admonitions: " 'Pourquoi cette impatience' reprit doucement Mr. Henley" (105); " 'Comment une personne raisonnable peut-elle s'affecter!'" (107); " 'Je souhaite que la raison et la décence vous gouvernent, et non que vous cédiez à mes préventions' " (115). After one particular episode, Mrs. Henley sums up the difference between herself and her husband as follows: "Il est étonné que nous autres gens passionnés soyons les dupes des saillies et des exagérations les uns des autres. Nous devrions savoir, à son avis, combien il y a à rabattre de ce que la passion nous fait imaginer et dire" (111).

We should not lose sight of the fact that Mrs. Henley is speaking to a friend. She is not writing her diary, but rather a series of letters which afford her the opportunity of talking about herself, and by so doing, of defining herself, using the relationship with her friend to help her arrive at her own sense of identity.[11] The privacy of confession enables her to sort out her truth or truths: the ambiguities or multiple hypotheses which her account of her life offers her friend. But we may well wonder just what role the recipient of these letters is designed to play.[12] Is Mrs. Henley's friend a comforting presence, an image of herself? Or is she, on the contrary, an agent of repression, an extension of the societal norm? The answer, I believe, lies in what I have termed the "duplicity" of the initial letters: Mrs. Henley's friend has a twofold function.[13] She is both the confidante, the person with whom Mrs. Henley can let her hair down, so to speak, and relate the series of blunders she has committed; and she is also the Other, the outside world, the custodian of the public image to whom Mrs. Henley entrusts her letters, asking her to publish them and thereby take them out of their original context of intimacy.[14]

The ambivalent part played by the recipient of Mrs. Henley's letters illustrates—and perhaps implicitly explains—why what we might call "epistolary autobiography" enjoyed such special favor as a vehicle for female expression in the 18th century. The no less ambivalent nature of the letter itself, simultaneously coherent and fragmented, provides the same sort of mirror as the letter's addressee for the 18th-century woman's place in society. Letters, as we have seen, betray a curious duality and even duplicity, since their existence designates an absence or a lack, yet they try to substitute a presence which will either fill or disguise the void.[15] Letters, furthermore, are inescapably fragmentary, reminding us not only of the physical separation between the author of the letter and the intended recipient, but also of the temporal divisions which mark the time at which the narrated events occurred, the time at which they are transcribed, and the time when the message is read, if the letter reaches the intended recipient (which it may not). Such fragmentation mirrors the position of the woman in 18th-century society. She must live this ambivalence, torn between her public image and her private vision of herself. As Eagleton remarks in his discussion of the function of writing in *Clarissa,* "The problem of writing is . . . the problem of the woman: how is she to be at once decorous and spontaneous, translucently candid yet subdued to social pressure? Writing, like women, marks a frontier between public and private, at once agonized outpouring and prudent stratagem" (46; see also 49-52). The tension of this dual role has its corollary within Mrs. Henley's writing: her description of her model husband, of the hopes and dreams of the new bride, her recounting of the mistakes and minor disasters that ensue, and particularly her own feeling of failure are all imbued with and propagate the literary conformism of the era; they demonstrate how ready Mrs. Henley is to let masculine authority dictate her own myth for her, formulate for her what she is supposed to signify. As her choice of the expression "a true story-book husband" ("un vrai mari de roman," 103) suggests, her perception of her husband is shaped by a stereotype, a societal ideal. So too are the heroine's aspirations a product of prior conditioning rather than a true reflection of her inner feelings. Any acceptance of their authenticity has to reckon with the appalling conclusion of the second letter:

> Chacun admire Mr. Henley et me félicite de mon bonheur; je réponds: 'C'est vrai, vous avez raison . . . Quelle différence avec les autres hommes de son rang, de son âge! quelle différence entre mon sort et celui de Madame une telle, de Milady une telle!' Je le dis, je le pense, et mon cœur ne le sent point; il se gonfle ou se serre, et souvent je me retire pour pleurer en liberté. (107-08)

Such a passage unmistakably points out the discordance between what Mrs. Henley should feel and what she actually does feel, and the novel is in fact punctuated by similar expressions of how hard it is to reconcile the private self with a woman's public image. "Ai-je eu tort, ma chère amie, autrement que par la forme?" she asks her friend. And shortly thereafter she writes, "Je dis vrai mais j'ai tort car je lui fais de la peine" (106-07). Such instances help to reinforce the contradictory impulses of the first letter—the need to confess her sins at the same time as she is demanding justice and redress. Such a structure is carried forward by the following letters as well, since they are built around a litany of oppositions between good and evil, reason and emotion, spontaneity and the fear of failure, reality and fiction, patience and impatience, action and passivity. As a couple, the Henleys incarnate these polarities. Her spontaneity is constantly thwarted by his rationality, in a contrast curiously reminiscent of the quarrel between the Ancients and the Moderns, as witness the following exchange: " 'Autrefois on trouvait ceci fort beau . . .' 'Oui, autrefois,' ai-je répliqué; 'mais je vis à présent' " (106).

By the obsessive binary construction of the letters and by its manifold contradictions Mme de Charrière's text holds out the possibility of another interpretation: a reading opposed to the confessional tone which seems to dominate the book, and which manages to subvert it. To state it succinctly, despite the many wrongs of which the heroine accuses herself, the fault really lies not with her but with the society in which she is forced to live. Evidence for such an interpretation becomes more apparent in the second part of the novel. The gentle condescension and imperturbable irony that characterizes Mr. Henley's attitude toward his wife—an attitude perfectly in keeping with the period, displayed in remarks such as "Je vois avec plaisir que ma chère femme est aussi jeune que sa coiffure, et aussi légère que ses plumes" (115)—gradually takes on overtones of unconscious cruelty in the heroine's account. When Mrs. Henley, trying to decide whether to nurse the child she is expecting (and torn between conflicting feelings in this as in so many matters) asks her husband's advice, Mr. Henley coolly replies that "son intention était de consulter le docteur M. son ami, pour savoir si mon extrême vivacité et mes fréquentes impatiences devaient faire préférer une étrangère" (120).

In light of the last letter, it can be argued that the pseudo-confession of the heroine is, in fact, a total rejection of that world symbolized by her husband's perfection. Though she is profuse in her admiration of her husband—"jamais je ne l'avais tant admiré; plus il me coûtait, plus je l'admirais; jamais je n'avais vu si distinctement sa supériorité" (122)—even this worship is strangely ambivalent. The irrepressible tension of this ambivalence, and its effect on the heroine, is readily visible in the following passage: "j'étais tellement combattue entre l'estime que m'arrachait tant de modération, de raison, de droiture dans mon mari, et l'horreur de me voir si étrangère à ses sentiments, si fort exclue de ses pensées, si inutile, si isolée, que je n'ai pu parler. Fatiguée de tant d'efforts, ma tête s'est embarrassée, je me suis évanouie" (122).

What is once again underlined here, reaching in this case a paroxysm of despair, is the heroine's inability to reconcile what she should be with that authentic self she cannot forever deny. The anxiety behind such expressions as "excluded from his thoughts" ("exclue de ses pensées") and "so useless" ("si inutile") is double; it reflects both her sense of failure in her socially appointed role and a disguised rejection of that role, indirect in that it can only take the form of an implicit subversion. Her fainting suggests the impossibility of living in a world in which her sex bars her from participating: a forced paralysis. The same perception emerges from her description of her husband's estate: "Ce séjour est comme son maître, tout y est trop bien; il n'y a rien à changer, rien qui demande mon activité ni mes soins" (118). It is probably no accident that Mme de Charrière elected to name the estate "Hollowpark." Amid such perfection, the heroine's blunders are invariably a consequence of her misguided energy, her inability to acquiesce to the role of a passive spectator which society prescribes for her sex. Mrs. Henley's temperament might let us see in her a curious foreshadowing—a sort of elder sister—of the Comtesse de Ségur's Sophie, also described as "trop vive," too lively or spirited, i.e., too alive. Unlike Sophie, however, Mme de Charrière's heroine does not yield, and her text ends on a parting remark as ambiguous and elliptical as that which began it. "Le chagrin tue aussi," she writes. "Dans un an, dans deux ans, vous apprendrez, je l'espère, que je suis raisonnable et heureuse, ou que je ne suis plus" (122). What are we to make of this phrase "I hope" ("je l'espère")? Does it express a sincere desire, and if so, what logic lies behind it? Does Mrs. Henley really wish for a settled and tranquil existence, for reason and happiness, those notions which are, for most writers of the time, inextricably entwined? Is she ready to pay the price to achieve a happiness described by Marmontel as residing "in the silence of the passions, in stability and repose," or by Buffon as consisting ideally "in one's inner harmony"?[16] More to the point, does she really have a choice? For Mrs. Henley, and for women in the 18th century in general, are the two alternatives actually distinct? Is there not, in fact, more similarity than difference between being "happy and reasonable" and ceasing to be, and is not the very ambition to become happy and reasonable a renunciation of one's authentic being, a wish equivalent to suicide?

Mrs. Henley's letters are strewn with signs that lead to such a pessimistic conclusion. The end of the fourth letter, for example, hints at an ultimate repudiation of the self. Speaking of nature stirring in the springtime, as she sees it from her window, she writes:

> Je ne me connais à rien, je n'approfondis rien, mais je contemple et j'admire cet univers si rempli, si animé. Je me perds dans ce vaste tout si étonnant, je ne dirai pas si sage, je suis trop ignorante: J'ignore les fins, je ne connais ni les moyens ni le but, je ne sais pas pourquoi tant de moucherons sont donnés à manager à cette vorace araignée; mais je regarde, et des heures se passent sans que j'aie pensé à moi ni à mes puérils chagrins. (118)

The preceding quotation is built around a series of contrasts between Mrs. Henley's ignorance and the emptiness of her life, on the one hand, and the vitality and animation of a world closed off to her by reason of her sex, on the other. This contemplative mood, tending toward a surrender of the self, follows the overall movement of Mrs. Henley's writing and is recapitulated by the ambiguous conclusion of the novel. But it always appears in counterpoise with a rejection, an ironic *reductio ad absurdum* or veiled challenge to that very rationality and deliberation which the heroine claims to admire in her husband: here, for instance, in her implicit identification with the helpless gnat devoured by the spider. Or, as she says elsewhere, "Tout ce que je sens est donc absurde, ou bien M. Henley est insensible et dur" (120), and her best efforts or impulses make no dent whatsoever in her husband's wall of rationality. Although the novel may be read on one level as a hymn to reason, in total conformity with the values of its time, this superficial faith in reason is gradually and subtly eroded by our consciousness of the heroine's predicament. Her initial distress and alienation—"Je suis seule, personne ne sent avec moi" (107), she says—slowly evolve into direct accusation, as in her remark "car si vous étiez jaloux, je vous verrais au moins sentir quelque chose" (116), occasionally interrupting the litany of her blunders and misdeeds.

This transmutation of the first letter's effusive praise unmasks Mr. Henley's rationality as an aloof and uncaring insensitivity to others. In this light, the reaction to the novel of Pastor Chaillet, one of Mme de Charrière's friends, is hardly surprising: "Je ne sais si je ne parlerai point quelque jour de cet *aimable cruel petit livre,* excellent en littérature, mais selon moi dangereux en morale à divers égards."[17] Pastor Chaillet fails to specify who is the object of the book's cruelty or precisely why he considers it dangerous, but his statement demonstrates that on some level he has grasped the import of the book's irony and realized that all of the societal norms and presuppositions initially adopted are undermined and upset by the heroine's plight. Mrs. Henley's text constitutes a radical departure from the 18th-century exaltation of reason; it implies that to this firm faith in reason corresponds a no less firm distrust of the feminine, automatically associated with instability and passion, not to mention hysteria.[18]

In the eyes of all the Pastor Chaillets of France, Switzerland, and Navarre, Belle de Charrière's heroine is guilty not so much because of the long list of wrongs to which she confesses, but because she perceived, in writing her letters, what lay through the looking-glass: a different, if not a topsy-turvy, system of values. Her writing moves from self-accusation to justification, in an evolution that includes first a questioning and then a rejection of its initial framework. In so doing, it usurps the position of authority and judgment that belongs to society. Yet, it does not simply occupy the position of authority; rather, it undermines it, transforms its discourse by inserting it within another text, a different vision of things. What I have called the double character of the letter—simultaneously reflexive and referential—lends itself perfectly to such subversion. Like a typical subject of a colonial master, Mrs. Henley does not dare strike out directly at her oppressor, for such is the power of her social conditioning that her image of her role will not let her do so. Instead, her revolt takes the more circuitous path of the letter, a kind of guerilla maneuver that perhaps explains, in its furtiveness, why even after finishing the novel the reader is still not absolutely sure who Mrs. Henley really is.

One impression that nevertheless leaps out at the reader is of Mrs. Henley as a sort of pure energy, but we might think of this energy as kinetic, and of the heroine as a movement constantly impeded or confined by form and stability, that is, by the values Mr. Henley incarnates. But can this energy ever find a destination, a form of its own in which to appear, or must it by its very impulsive nature remain abstract? The paradox of a movement betrayed by any form that represents it is in fact that of writing itself: its outpouring is lost in the linguistic gap between the act of enunciation and what is enunciated. Epistolary writing makes us acutely conscious of this gap by adding to it that which separates the author of the letter from the receiver. Furthermore, the same gap, the same impossibility of finding its destination, also characterizes the fate of feminine writing in the 18th century: always a prisoner of another's discourse, it can never achieve its complete realization or expression. As Mme de Charrière demonstrates, the problem for the 18th-century woman is that she can only produce her own text to the extent that she can use parasitically that which is offered to or imposed upon her; only parasitically can she arrive at her own sense of self.

Notes

[1] *Oeuvres complètes,* ed. Jean-Daniel Candaux, et al., 10 vols. (Amsterdam: Van Oorschot; Geneva: Slatkine, 1979-81). See *Lettres écrites de Lausanne* and *Lettres neuchâteloises.*

[2] For studies of *Caliste,* see Jean Starobinski's excellent essay, "Les Lettres écrites de Lausanne de Madame de Charrière: Inhibition psychique et interdit social," in *Romans et Lumières au XVIIIe siècle* (Paris: Editions Sociales, 1970), 130-51, and Janine Rossard, "Le Désir de mort romantique dans *Caliste,*" *PMLA* 87 (1972), 492-98.

[3] See in particular Philippe Godet, *Madame de Charrière et ses amis, d'après de nombreux documents inédits,* 2 vols. (Geneva: Jullien, 1906), and also Sainte-Beuve, "Benjamin Constant et Madame de Charrière," *Revue des Deux-Mondes,* April 15, 1844, in *Oeuvres complètes,* ed. Maxime Leroy (Paris: Gallimard, 1951) 2:677-760; Geoffrey Scott, *Portrait of Zelide* (London: Constable, 1925), and Anthony West, *Mortal Wounds* (New York: McGraw-Hill, 1973), among others.

[4] *Oeuvres complètes* 8: 91-122. All quotations are from this edition.

[5] See *Madame de Charrière et ses amis* 1: 257-74.

[6] For a bibliography on epistolary fiction, see François Jost, *Essais de littérature comparée* (Fribourg: Editions Universitaires; Champaign: U of Illinois P, 1968), 380-402.

[7] *Le Roman épistolaire* (Paris: PUF, 1979): "consacré aux femmes, composé très souvent par des femmes, le roman par lettres a pour premier public les femmes" (59-60).

[8] *La Destinée féminine dans le roman européen du dix-huitième siècle 1713-1807* (Paris: Colin, 1972) 11; see also 93-95. For an attempt to explain why women writers were so attracted to epistolary fiction, see Ruth Perry, *Women, Letters and the Novel* (New York: AMS, 1980).

[9] See Mme Riccoboni's *Lettres de Milady Juliette Catesby à Milady Henriette Campley, son amie* (1759), and *Lettres d'Elizabeth-Sophie de Vallière à Louise-Hortence de Canteliers, son amie* (1771).

[10] "Il y a une ambiguïté, et comme une duplicité foncière de la romancière au XVIIIe siècle. Le territoire sur lequel s'aventurent alors les femmes de lettres est un des plus dangereux qu'une femme puisse affronter: dans l'activité romanesque, la femme se 'découvre,' et l'aventure qu'elle court alors rappelle par plus d'un trait celle de l'héroïne qui se risque sur la scène du monde" (93).

[11] Ruth Perry expresses a somewhat similar view in her *Women, Letters, and the Novel:* "Letters were the perfect vehicle for women's highly developed art of pleasing, for in writing letters it is possible to tailor a self on paper to suit the expectations and desires of the audience" (69).

[12] In her study on the epistolary novel, Janet Altman emphasizes the recurrence in French epistolary fiction of the themes of *confiance* and *confidence:* "The confidant who inspires, wins, or loses trust is an essential figure in epistolary literature, called into existence by the need of every letter writer to have a 'friendly bosom' into which he can 'disburden his cares,' as Smollett's Lydia Milford so often expresses it to her friend Laetitia Willis." *Epistolarity: Approaches to a Form* (Columbus: Ohio State UP, 1982) 50. Although Altman distinguishes between "active" and "passive" confidants, she is mainly concerned with the former category.

[13] Although Mrs. Henley's confidante never intervenes directly in the novel, her role is twofold like that of

Anna Howe in *Clarissa*. It is through her correspondence with Anna that Clarissa's female autonomy is maintained, but Anna Howe is also part of the patriarchal system which Clarissa opposes. The similarity to *Pamela* is even more obvious since Pamela confides in her parents and asks them to keep her letters so that she—and as it turns out in the second part of the novel, a larger audience—may read them.

[14] See the obsessive use of terms relating to judgment in the work: the word *tort* appears 18 times, and *raison* 17 in 30 pages. Mrs. Henley shows a great deal of concern for the opinion of her friend (101), and thus of all her readers since she wants the letters to be published. She asks her friend to judge her actions first by her standards and then in terms of society's interest (102).

[15] Richardson was already aware of this ambiguity: "Who then shall decline the converse of the pen? The pen that makes distance, presence; and brings back to sweet remembrance all the delights of presence, which makes even presence but body, while absence becomes the soul." *Selected Letters* 65, as quoted by Terry Eagleton in *The Rape of Clarissa* (Oxford: Blackwell, 1982) 43-44.

[16] "Le bonheur est dans le silence des passions, dans l'équilibre et le repos." Marmontel, *Contes moraux*. "Le bonheur de l'homme consiste dans l'unité de son intérieur." Buffon, *Discours sur la nature des animaux*. As quoted by Robert Mauzi in *L'Idée du bonheur au 18e siècle* (Paris: Colin, 1960) 124.

[17] Cited by Philippe Godet in *Madame de Charrière et ses amis* 1: 260. Note that Pastor Chaillet quotes the very words Mme de Charrière's heroine uses to qualify Constant's work in the opening paragraph of the novel.

[18] In such a system of thought, women are regarded as they are by Diderot in *Sur les femmes* or as Voltaire defines them in his *Dictionnaire philosophique:* as at once incomplete and dangerously excessive versions of men.

Alix S. Deguise (essay date 1989)

SOURCE: "Mme de Charrière: Travel and Uprooting," in *Eighteenth-Century Life*, Vol. XIII, No. 1, February, 1989, pp. 42-8.

[*In the essay below, Deguise traces the themes of travel and displacement—important literary devices for the epistolary novel—throughout Charrière's oeuvre.*]

The valuable introduction to the ten-volume edition of Isabelle de Charrière's ***Oeuvres complètes*** reveals that the author traveled more in reality and in spirit than had been previously thought. At the age of ten she spent several months in France and Geneva with her governess, Mlle Prévost. Many of the letters she wrote during her six-month stay in England in 1767 have long been available, and we know that she went to Paris several times, at one point remaining there for eighteen months. She spent more than half this time without her husband. For several subsequent years after her marriage, she returned home to Zuylen, and for an extended period spent summers in Spa with members of her family, as members of the gentry often did. She also took the cure in watering places in the unfulfilled hope of becoming pregnant and, later in life, in search of better health. This last wish even led her in 1783 to consult Cagliostro in Strasbourg. There were also long winters spent in Geneva, and summers when Belle left Colombier for the Pays de Vaud in Chexbres or Payerne.

After 1787 she hardly left her residence, but then she had always traveled by proxy as well and continued to do so in many ways, first through the literature she read[1] and the literature she wrote, then through her numerous acquaintances from England, France, Germany, and elsewhere who visited and wrote her. Some of them had colonial experiences that may have influenced her as source material. Her friend Du Peyrou, for instance, had been raised in Surinam; during one of her Parisian stays she met a M. de Caritan from Martinique; and she must have heard about the voyages of Captain Cook from her friend Thérèse Huber, whose husband, Georg Forster, accompanied Cook.

At the time, travel could be hazardous and unpredictable, even in Switzerland. A letter from M. de Charrière written to his wife in 1785 complains about the terrible roads and inns he found on his way to Lucerne, and of being charged exorbitant prices for eggs, the only available food in one place. During this eventful trip, his sick coachman lost his way at nightfall while the horses were exhausted. An innkeeper offered him a room where, it turned out, two men were already sound asleep. Fearing a fire hazard, the innkeeper refused a suggestion to put hay on the floor (***O.c.***, 2:485). Isabelle, who never traveled without her favorite French books, mentions in her novel ***Trois femmes*** the importance of undertaking a journey well-equipped: "Toutes les précautions contre le froid, la faim, l'ennui étant prises. . . . ils partirent" (***O.c.***, 9:130).

Some travels signified important undertakings. Her marriage at the age of thirty-one meant uprooting, but it was not unwelcome; life at home had become difficult since her mother's death and she was going to live in Switzerland, a country she knew and felt comfortable with, and which was the home of her longtime correspondent, Constant d'Hermenches. The Protestant moral ethic in Switzerland was not so different from the one in which Isabelle had been raised in the Netherlands. Her travels during the first years of her marriage were to relieve the monotony of life in Colombier, and were those of a leisurely class that could afford to stay away, often in one place, for months at a time.

Isabelle was a good observer and recorder. Her letters from England in 1767 reveal an alert mind, avidly taking in politics, the stage, and the Court. She reported customs that seemed alien to her, such as extramarital affairs and the love of the English for landscape gardening. Her pen, gossipy and gently ironical, amusingly describes the foibles of English high society. Many of her observations would later find their way into her "English" novels.

A stay in Paris in 1786 brought enrichment of a different kind. Isabelle composed a great deal of music and had her sonatas for the harpsichord engraved, and she wrote some plays and had several novels reviewed in Parisian papers. She went to the theatre, met a few first-class minds, including Benjamin Constant, whose acquaintance was to play such an important part in both of their lives.

Later, she became an armchair traveler who lived the lives of her faraway friends. Her most striking vicarious travel was to Corsica. She was unusually well-acquainted with the Mediterranean island, first through Boswell's enthusiastic and famous *Account of Corsica*,[2] and later through the disparaging letters of Constant d'Hermenches who, also in 1768, had told a very different story. Boswell had been received as a friend in Corsica, partly because he was a British subject with important connections—Britain professed sympathy for the islanders—and because he considered Corsica's leader, Paoli, a hero and wise legislator steeped in classical culture, comparing him to Lycurgus. D'Hermenches, on the other hand, arrived as an officer serving the king of France; his task was to pacify the island. He was involved in numerous battles and skirmishes, which he dutifully recorded in great detail in his long letters to Agnès, as he called Isabelle.[3] She had at first been convinced by Boswell's observations to the point of wanting to translate his *Account,* and she could, as she wrote D'Hermenches, name every village on the map, report what crops grew and where, and give many useful indications about the mountainous regions; but she would not relay this information to D'Hermenches out of loyalty to Paoli (*O.c.,* 2:92). D'Hermenches considered Paoli an ambitious coward and plunderer, and the Corsicans as savages who were far worse off under their leader than under the French (*O.c.,* 2:145). Some of his letters to Belle, while dispelling perhaps a certain myth, cannot hide the feelings of jealousy toward a former rival,[4] but their content seemed reasonable and was enhanced by the prestige of military exploits told in a lively fashion. Isabelle began to think that Boswell had indeed been carried away by his enthusiasm, and another book on Corsica read in the meantime convinced her of the truth of D'Hermenches's observations. It was finally his letters, with their detailed narratives of his campaign, that she adapted for publication in a newspaper in the Hague.

Other travels by proxy later took her to England and Scotland during Benjamin Constant's escapade, and to Brunswick, from where Constant described at great length his boredom at the court where he held the official post of chamberlain. Isabelle also became acquainted with the courts of Berlin and Potsdam when her young friend, Henriette L'Hardy, became a companion to King Frederick Wilhelm II's common law wife, Countess Dönhoff. Charrière followed their flight from Berlin and, as an older friend and wise counselor, was always able to offer advice and models of behavior for places she had never visited.

Travel occupies a large part of eighteenth-century novels, and Charrière's characters move about a great deal, whether their fate brings them to cities she was familiar with or to faraway places she had only read about. She was interested in differences in the character and behavior of people when transplanted to foreign countries. Geographical descriptions have little place in her work, and women rarely wrote travel books at the time;[5] but travel itself became an important literary device useful to any *bildungsroman,* and the separation of characters—as by travel—was necessary for the epistolary novel so dear to Charrière.

The Grand Tour inspired many travelogues as well as works of fiction (including one of Charrière's favorites, Sterne's *Sentimental Journey* [*O.c.,* 2:133]). It is an integral part of the action of **Lettres écrites de Lausanne,** as of *Clarissa Harlowe.* After all, it was Lovelace's previous experiences on the Continent that gave Clarissa an excuse to write to him,[6] and Cécile falls in love with a young English aristocrat traveling in Europe with his tutor. Boswell had undertaken such an extended voyage, though Corsica had been an unusual addition to the Grand Tour. Like the young English lord of **Lettres écrites de Lausanne,** who leaves without asking for Cécile's hand, Boswell had hesitated to marry Zélide, as he called Isabelle. Like the novelistic character who is entertained in the best circles of Lausanne's Rue de Bourg, Boswell had letters of introduction to the highest society abroad. Charrière's protagonist is en route to England after a long voyage to Portugal and a year's stay in Italy—the author is very precise about it in **Caliste.** He conquers the heart of Cécile, a well-bred young woman of the Lausanne Protestant establishment, and, no doubt, like many other young Englishmen in Switzerland at the time, moves on without proposing marriage.[7] In the end, Cécile and her mother undertake a trip to Languedoc to visit a French cousin who is the mother's correspondent in this epistolary novel. This branch of the family had remained in France after the revocation of the Edict of Nantes because a grandfather had converted to Catholicism, while another branch had emigrated to Lausanne. Cécile is in need of a change after her romantic disappointment, and travel is the classic remedy.

In the ***Lettres neuchâteloises,*** Julianne, a young apprentice, finds herself pregnant, in danger of being ostracized and driven out of town. The culprit, who we understand cannot marry her because of class barriers, arranges with the help of a young woman friend and kind relatives to send Julianne to Germany, where his family will care for her and the baby. An embarrassing problem is solved by moving away.

For Charrière, travel in France is deemed indispensable to perfect one's education. French literature had nourished her mind since childhood. Through three of her eponymous characters it becomes apparent that, to her, France is the epitome of culture: Caliste spends a year in a Parisian convent until the money of her protector runs out; before her marriage, Mistriss Henley perfects her knowledge of French and music in Montpellier, while living with a relative; and Sir Walter Finch spends a year in Paris, where he learns to admire some of the qualities of French society while his young son acquires polish. These events take place before and after the French Revolution.

The great French political upheaval generated a different breed of traveler who was not seeking enlightenment and culture, but was simply avoiding the guillotine. Many passed through Neuchâtel, and some became Charrière's friends. No longer the frivolous temporary pastime of an idle society, a panacea for love's disappointments, or expatriation for professional reasons, travel became uprooting and an experience in precarious survival. Most of the ceaseless flow of émigrés through Switzerland were not allowed to settle there. Some émigrés behaved admirably, adapted to their reduced circumstances, and earned their keep modestly and with dignity. Others, unable to adjust, remained arrogant. Isabelle's letters about these refugees may seem unfeeling at times. She had been uprooted, but it was by choice and in different circumstances. A Belle de Zuylen arriving in Colombier as a new bride of an old and honorable family enjoyed the consideration awarded to the descendant of an illustrious and still powerful family, whereas a continuous stream of often penniless refugees, boasting of their lost privileges, was considered a strain on the economy and a source of irritation.

Charrière's writing at this time became political; she could no longer write lighthearted comedies. Instead she used contemporary events and the émigrés' predicaments, familial separations, and diverse political beliefs for dramatic effect, as in her play ***L'émigré.*** To some who roamed the roads of Europe separated from their families, and even served in adverse armies, the forced uprooting unwittingly became a positive experience. It brought maturity, a more balanced view of the world, and a lesson in tolerance. In ***Lettres trouvées dans des porte-feuilles d'émigrés,*** the vicomte des Fossés cheerfully earns his living upon arrival in England: he gardens, works in the fields, and gives lessons to the local minister's sons. And in exile an equality of a sort is created between his servant and himself. During the same time, Laurent Fontbrune, a wounded officer of the French Republic, discovers great humane qualities—and love—in the aristocratic family that nurses him back to health in its chateau. Laurent writes to his friend Alphonse, who, though a nobleman, refuses to bear arms against France, that he now reads only "des relations de voyage" for entertainment, as all novels appear superficial and dishonest to him at this stage. The author shared this belief. Travel literature, at any rate "des relations de voyage," was popular throughout the late eighteenth century, partially because it satisfied readers' curiosity during a time of restricted movement, and provided an escape during troubled times.

Evasion and escapism are not found in Charrière's novels. People are on the move for practical reasons and learn from their travels, as Télémaque learns from his peregrinations. Fénelon's work was a favorite with Isabelle who was always interested in pedagogical experiences.[8] In ***Lettres trouvées dans des porte-feuilles d'émigrés,*** all the good characters separated by circumstance recognize the virtue, courage, and disinterestedness of their adversaries. Forced separation and forced travels produce letters filled with feeling and nobility. The most striking example takes place at the end, with a land and sea voyage in which Fontbrune, the Republican officer, escorts the young noblewoman he has fallen in love with to a harbor. She embarks on a ship bound for Holland to join her father, a fiercely Royalist marquis who fights for his beliefs against the French Republic.

Uprooting is an important theme for the transplanted Charrière, who had adopted her husband's country. She clearly saw the problems it created for people of all conditions and ages and its possible use in dramatic and novelistic plots. The differing behaviors and fates of three young émigré women constitute the plot of ***Trois femmes*** (1795). These three learn to adapt to new surroundings in a Westphalian village in Germany. Such a theme has attracted other writers, and the *Memoirs* of the Marquise de la Tour du Pin come to mind, but they were written late in the Marquise's life, and tell us also that she eventually left America to return to France during the Directoire period. The reader of ***Trois femmes,*** gifted with hindsight, can easily surmise that the protagonists, two of whom have married Germans, will return for visits to their homeland after the convulsions of the French Revolution are over (this is hinted at in the novel); but, unable to predict the future, Charrière ends her story with a flight to escape advancing armies, and imagines a *Suite* in which "L'histoire de Constance" antedates the events described in ***Trois femmes***. This flashback offers an eventful sea crossing to Martinique, which, once more, reflects the taste of the eighteenth century for exotic travels. Authors who had never seen them used as settings faraway countries they had read about in the accounts of explorers, scientists, and diarists.[9] The *Suite* presents us with the weaknesses and errors of an uprooted colonial society whose prosperity rests on slavery. The successful establishment of Constance's family in Martinique becomes a calamity that causes its untimely disappearance and the death of innocent people. This, incidentally, does not mean that Charrière rejected the idea of dynamic young men going abroad in search of fortune—the Dutch as well as the Swiss had a long tradition of expatriation for economic reasons—and she seemed to have had an enterprising spirit about it.

The less Isabelle traveled, the more her protagonists seemed to do so, and notably to faraway places. Sir William Finch, having completed his education but failing in love, is encouraged by his father (who will visit America) to join the expedition of Admiral Sir William Sidney Smith[10] to Turkey and Egypt, a situation not without parallel to that of Rousseau's St-Preux leaving Europe on Admiral Anson's expedition around the world. Here Charrière inserts a clever intertextuality, as she so often does, mingling real people with her own protagonists. To have joined Smith's adventurous career served three purposes: it gave veracity to the ending, finished the education of the young man, which was after all, the subject of ***Sir Walter Finch et son fils William,*** and at the same time allowed him to forget his disappointment in love. One can surmise that William will return to England a mature young man, ready to accept the responsibilities of a useful country squire.

If travel in Charrière's works reflects the taste and events of the period, it is not an idle addition to a plot, or an adventure for the sake of adventure. The search for happiness does not lie elsewhere, although the characters may move away to escape an intolerable situation. The purpose of travel is education or necessity. The characters are on the go; they have just arrived or are going somewhere, whether of their own free will or not. While conveying a dynamic quality to Charrière's works, travel also expresses—and this is at its truest sense during the French Revolution when it became displacement—a feeling of restlessness and instability better discussed elsewhere. This impression is of the kind that is also apparent to any reader of *Manon Lescaut,* which Belle considered one of the two greatest French novels.

Isabelle de Charrière's lifelong interest in people, books, ideas, and contemporary events had made her metaphorically "un port, un marché, où il arrive et d'où il part des idées" (*O.c.,* 6:62). Years after leaving the Netherlands, the seafaring country where she was born and whose prosperity was based on trade, the author compared herself in a letter to a busy port, suggesting arrival, departure, exchange, and motion. Such an image signifies awareness of travel as a means of communication and enrichment.

Notes

[1] Throughout her life she kept in touch with French and English literature, and later with German writings. In her youth she had read Lady Mary Wortley Montagu's *Letters,* which began to appear in 1763 and described her journey to Constantinople. Isabelle read Bougainville's *Voyage autour du monde* (1771) with much pleasure (*Oeuvres complètes,* 10 vols. [Amsterdam: G. A. van Oorschot; Geneva: Slatkine, 1979-84], 2:293; subsequently abbreviated as *O.c.*), probably read Abbé Raynal's *Histoire philosophique et politique des établissements et du commerce des Européens dans les deux Indes* (1781), and loved Fénelon's *Aventures de Télémaque.*

[2] *An Account of Corsica, The Journal of a Tour to that Island: and Memoirs of Pascal Paoli,* Feb. 1768. Belle-Zélide wanted to shorten it for publication, but Boswell was opposed to it.

[3] For the correspondence with D'Hermenches about Corsica, see *O.c.,* vol. 2: letters 306, 307, 309, 310, 313-19, 322, 323, 326, 327, 333, 335-37, 339, 340.

[4] "et votre Mr Boswell en veut faire des Héros, et vous vouliez le traduire! et vous souhaitez du malheur à nos armes! c'est pour l'honneur de l'humanité qu'il faut exterminer ou transplanter cette abominable race" (*O.c.,* 2:94). D'Hermenches finds low flattery, bad taste, and historical errors in Boswell's *Account* and concludes: "Ah ma chère Agnès que je vous aime, que j'augmente d'estime pour votre bon goût, de n'avoir voulu ni traduire, ni épouser, le fou qui ose faire imprimer *where shall I find a man greater than Paoli*" (*O.c.,* 2:109 [spelling and punctuation modernized]).

[5] There are exceptions, of course. Mrs. Radcliffe and Mme de Graffigny relied heavily, however, on secondary sources.

[6] Clarissa writes to Miss Howe: "You have seen some of his letters and have been pleased with his account of persons, places, and things; and we have both agreed that he was no common observer upon what he had seen ... my father who had been abroad in his youth, said that his remarks were curious, and showed him to be a person of reading, judgment and taste" (Samuel

Richardson, *Clarissa* [N.Y.: Henry Holt, 1930], p. 7). In the *Suite* of *Trois femmes,* the author discusses the inevitability of Clarissa's fate (*O.c.,* 9:135).

[7] Gibbon had fallen in love with Suzanne Curchod in Lausanne. After his return to England, his family's wishes prevailed and he did not marry the young woman who later became Necker's wife and the mother of Mme de Staël. He had, however, proposed.

[8] For Charrière's affinities with Fénelon, see Alix Deguise, "Trois Femmes et Fénelon," in *Trois Femmes: Le monde de Mme de Charrière* (Geneva: Slatkine, 1981), pp. 212-16.

[9] See Percy G. Adams, *Travel Literature and the Evolution of the Novel* (Lexington: Univ. of Kentucky, 1983), chaps. entitled "The Truth-Lie Dichotomy" and "Realism and Romanticism."

[10] Sir William Sidney Smith (1764-1840) advised the king of Sweden in his war against Russia (1790-92), tried to set fire to the French fleet at Toulon (1793), was sent as ambassador to Constantinople, and defended Acre against Bonaparte (1799).

Susan S. Lanser (essay date 1989)

SOURCE: "Courting Death: Roman, romantisme, and *Mistress Henley*'s Narrative Practices," in *Eighteenth-Century Life*, Vol XIII, No. 1, February, 1989, pp. 49-59.

[*In the following essay, Lanser discusses* Mistriss Henley *in relation to Samuel de Constant's novel of 1783,* Le Mari sentimental, *contrasting the triviality of Charrière's domestic detail with the larger questions of adultery and death found in Constant's work.*]

In 1972, when *PMLA* was still publishing in foreign languages, Janine Rossard's "Le Désir de mort romantique dans *Caliste*"[1] inaugurated on this side of the Atlantic what has become a steadily growing interest in Isabelle de Charrière. Rossard evoked that interest by associating Charrière with the ethos of early romanticism and particularly with the presence in Caliste—both the novel and the character—of a longing for death. The "désir de mort" in *Caliste,* Rossard implies, is a crystallization of Charrière's own pessimism, which cannot be accounted for simply by "une hérédité calviniste et un stoïcisme classique mêlés de raison voltairienne" (p. 492), but is rather "werthérien, car il trouve sa source dans trois découvertes inéluctables de Belle de Charrière: l'inanité de la philosophie du bonheur à la fin du dix-huitième siècle; la vanité de la lutte stoïque dans une pareille société, et l'impotence de la raison" (p. 492). *Caliste* does not reconcile "la raison et le sentiment, l'état de nature et l'état social, le relatif et l'absolu, l'égoïsme et l'interêt du groupe, le devoir et le plaisir," but demonstrates "par l'absurde—la mort—leurs contradictions insurmontables" (p. 493).

I want to look more closely at Rossard's notion of a "désir de mort" in Charrière, using it as a frame through which to read the ***Lettres de Mistriss Henley publiées par son amie*** (1784). Charrière published this short novel just before the two-part ***Lettres écrites de Lausanne*** (1785, 1787), the second and subordinate portion of which, *Caliste,* is now commonly taken for the whole. At the end of this essay I will come back to the implications of that inverted title and to the question of a "désir de mort romantique" in ***Caliste*** itself. But I want to come there by way of the particular "désir de mort" in ***Mistriss Henley,*** which I will call a "désir de mort *romanesque*" and which, I believe, asks us to read in the light of gender the phenomena that Rossard's 1972 essay associates with a more general *mal du siècle*.

Charrière's novels of the 1780s, all epistolary in form, locate themselves within a particular and gender-specific form of the "romanesque": the tradition Nancy Miller has labeled the "heroine's text."[2] As Rachel Brownstein describes it, in this tradition a young woman "moves toward her inevitable end, death or marriage, along lines her body generates." That is, "one of two courses of action is possible: she will either get virtue's earthly reward, a rich husband, or be seduced and die of it."[3] These "absurdly simple" alternatives, as Brownstein calls them, become the conventional frame that each text is asked to interpret, evade, or redefine. Most novels complicate the courtship plot itself, as Charrière does in her first novel, the ***Lettres neuchâteloises*** (1784).[4] In contrast, Charrière's next published work, the ***Lettres de Mistriss Henley,*** begins where the heroine's tale usually ends—after what Charlotte Perkins Gilman once called "a ceaseless repetition of the Preliminaries," which is hardly "any sort of picture of a woman's life"[5]—and determines to recount the "tas de petites choses"[6] that constitute the aftermath to the presumably eternal happiness of those heroines whose stories end in the nuptial event.

The immediate pretext for ***Mistriss Henley*** was the publication in 1783 of Samuel de Constant's *Le Mari sentimental,*[7] in which a contented bachelor marries in middle age and is made miserable by a wife who takes control of his household and destroys everything he cherishes, including his good name. Abandoned and disgraced, completely "subjugé sous l'empire d'une femme,"[8] M. Bompré finally sees no choice but suicide. Charrière apparently found the book so distressing in its misogyny that immediately after its publication she set aside other projects, probably including the ***Lettres écrites de Lausanne,*** and drafted her own fictional response.[9] Disturbed by the injustices that *Le*

Mari sentimental might generate, Charrière's epistolary narrator, Mistriss Henley, sets out explicitly to counterpose a wife's story to a husband's, to tell not only her correspondent but the public "l'histoire de mon mariage" and to portray "ma vie telle qu'elle est aujourd'hui." But it is not only her own life that Mistriss Henley hopes to represent; she is motivated explicitly by the conviction that "beaucoup de femmes sont dans le même cas que moi" (8:102).[10] In effecting the transformation from the husband's story to the wife's, **Mistriss Henley** begins by rewriting the small domestic episodes in Constant's novel; but whereas *Le Mari sentimental* soon moved to "large" questions such as adultery and death, Charrière's novel undertakes an innovative refusal of the conventional, large-gestured plot in favor of an exclusive focus on "trivial" domestic detail.

Mistriss Henley's tale begins, however, with the event that forms the entire preoccupation of the conventional heroine's plot. Educated and accomplished but orphaned and without means, Mistriss Henley must marry; she has already been abandoned by the one man she truly loved and has refused several others whom she considered her intellectual inferiors. At twenty-five, her heart "triste et vide" (8:103), faced finally with the choice between a pleasure- and art-loving, world-traveling sophisticate and a titled country widower of incomparable character, she sets aside her attraction to the sophisticate as originating in "la partie vile de mon coeur" (8:103) and accepts the public consensus that Mr. Henley is the perfect spouse: "spirituel, élégant, décent, délicat, affectueux" (8:104), a man with "de la raison, de l'instruction, de l'équité, une égalité d'âme parfaite" (8:103). In this way, Mistriss Henley gets herself the heroine's proper husband, a "mari de roman" (8:104). But these qualities that make Mr. Henley a "mari de roman" will become precisely the source of the narrator's misery.

While Constant's Bompré gave over his estate into the inept and dangerous hands of a henpecking wife, Charrière's Mistriss Henley learns almost immediately that despite her husband's rhetoric she is mistress of nothing at all. Life in the aptly-named Hollowpark is a life over which she has little control; custom, law, and his own temperament all designate Mr. Henley her master and superior. Although Henley "m'avait dit que j'étais la maîtresse" (8:106), he opposes virtually all her preferences and desires, so that to choose herself is invariably to choose against him, to reject both traditional marital authority and the public estimation of Mr. Henley's personal superiority. From the first negative incident, when the narrator decorates her five-year-old stepdaughter with baubles and Mr. Henley disapproves, the structure of dominance is made clear: "*vous avez raison*, Monsieur . . . *j'ai eu tort*" (8:104; emphasis mine). As the novel continues and small episodes pile up, the words "raison" and "tort" become an insistent refrain in which Mistriss Henley deplores her "torts," which are even worse than she believed (8:108), and tells her husband over and over, "vous avez raison."

In shaping her response to Constant's portrait of the cruel and capricious Mme Bompré, Charrière does not, then, simply reverse gender stereotypes in order to criticize the age-old opposition of irrational woman to rational man. That is, rather than creating in the Henleys an irrational husband and a rational wife, she makes a gesture at once more subtle and more radical: she challenges the linguistic and moral coupling of "reason" and "right." While Mme Bompré epitomized the irrational, Mr. Henley fails by being too reasonable: he is "un peu trop parfait; mes fantaisies, mes humeurs, mes impatiences trouvaient toujours sa raison et sa modération en leur chemin" (8:104). Although she seems at first to accept his "raison" and her "tort," the very repetition of this opposition dialogizes the discourse, eventually subverting these oppositions so that they are exposed as less a matter of truth or fault than of power and complicity; as Mistriss Henley writes to her confidante after admitting that she has told Mr. Henley her honest estimation of some of his relatives, "Je dis vrai; mais j'ai tort" (8:107). Finally Mrs. Henley lets herself openly question so many "wrongs": "Aurait-il raison, ma chère amie? Aurais-je eu encore tort, toujours tort, tort en tout? Non, je ne veux pas le croire" (8:111). If she is not to be wrong, reason must be acknowledged not always to be right, and indeed she suggests that "des coups de poing me seraient mois fâcheux que toute cette raison" (8:107).

Mistriss Henley's critique of reason cannot in itself, however, undermine the balance of marital power; the Henleys' differences in personal value and taste assume the character of moral absolutes in a situation of social dominance. That is, as Mistriss Henley struggles to assert herself in small matters of domestic life, she finds that Mr. Henley *is* right after all, simply because both power and its attendant self-assurance are his. The novel's challenge to the linguistic coupling of "right" and "reason" becomes, therefore, a challenge as well to the coupling of "woman" and "wife" in *"femme."*

The first open conflict is worth describing for its revelation of the narrator's efforts to "right" her double identity as "femme." Disapproving a costume she has chosen for a ball, Mr. Henley argues that "une femme de vingt-six ans ne doit pas être habillée comme une fille de quinze, ni une femme comme il faut comme une comédienne" (8:112). Yet later, when his own sister appears in a similar dress, he expresses no disapproval because "Elle n'est pas ma femme" (8:115). *Woman* can dress this way; his *wife* may not. Furious, Mistriss Henley tries to retaliate by flirting at the ball; when she fails to arouse his jealousy, she resorts to a cruelly frank display of "honesty" in their carriage on the way home:

si vous étiez jaloux, je vous verrais au moins sentir quelque chose; je serais flattée; je croirais vous être précieuse; je croirais que vous craignez de me perdre, que je vous plais encore; que, du moins, vous pensez que je puis encore plaire. Oui! . . . les injustices d'un jaloux, les emportements d'un brutal, seraient moins fâcheux que le flegme et l'aridité d'un sage. (8:116)

This outburst generates an equally dramatic, almost groveling apology as Mrs. Henley realizes she has spoken in front of his child:

Vous avez raison. . . . Pardon, Monsieur! pardon, cher enfant! . . . Je vous donne un mauvais exemple. . . . Je devrais vous tenir lieu de mère: je vous l'avais promis, et je n'ai aucun soin de vous, et je dis devant vous des choses que vous êtes heureuse de ne pas bien entendre! (8:116)

This extreme movement from rebellion to self-effacement depicts the divided self that the novel is beginning to represent as the heroine's fate: one must cease to be a woman as one becomes a wife. "Femme" becomes a split identity, representable only through a split subjectivity and hence a double voice.

Faced with her own subordination, which is as much psychological as social and legal, Mistriss Henley resorts to the desperate strategy of the powerless: the aggressive display of self-erasure, the performance of martyrdom in a final effort to be rescued and redeemed.[11] Mistriss Henley attempts to resolve her self-division by courting death, actively asserting the annihilation of woman beneath the role of wife. Immediately after the episode of the ball, she drafts a letter to her husband, a palimpsest that screams self-censorship, with "presqu'autant de mots éffacés que de mots laissés" (8:117). On the surface it embraces a caricature of Mr. Henley's notion of wifehood and reconstitutes the wife on the basis of the husband's identity. From this position of willed submission Mistriss Henley lets herself turn the opposition "raison" and "tort" against her husband at last: proclaiming his superiority, she can also hold him accountable. He is accused of two wrongs: "vous m'avez fait trop d'honneur en m'épousant"; and having chosen her, he has opted to "dédaigner tout ce que je savais et tout ce que j'étais," making her a kind of generic "wife," when he might well have found the qualities he now insists upon "chez mille autres femmes" (8:117). But if this recognition of his wrongs gives her a certain right, she will not realign right with reason: "une femme raisonnable ne pouvait manquer d'être heureuse," but "je ne suis pas une femme raisonnable."

Even as Mistriss Henley accuses her husband, however, in an aggressive double gesture, she makes a pledge of unity and obedience that recalls the old feminist adage that in marriage two are one, and that one is the man:[12] she asks him to become her conscience so that she will commit no further "torts." Together they can attempt to "arranger ma conduite de manière à réparer les plus grands de mes torts" (8:117). She, in turn, will try to understand what he wants without his having to tell her so: "je ne vous demande pas de me tracer un plan; je tâcherai de deviner vos idées pour m'y soumettre." If she fails, he is to "me dire ce que vous voudrez que je fasse à la place de ce que je fais" (8:118). In substituting his values and desires, his sense of right and wrong for her own, Mrs. Henley will finally be the "femme" her husband wants. In this way the narrator and the text enact a grotesque exaggeration of wifely submission as if to make clear the price of marriage—to the readers, if not to Mr. Henley himself. For clearly this is a bitter and ironic submission in name alone, indeed in *his* name alone, since the narrator signs only "S Henley," as if her given name no longer matters or exists.

Such self-erasure in the name of marriage means that **Lettres de Mistriss Henley** has collapsed the oppositions of marriage and death that structure the heroine's text: in this novel it is not a question of marriage *or* death, but of marriage *as* death, a death underscored when Mr. Henley fails even to mention receiving this painfully crafted letter of surrender from his wife. Indeed, if Mistriss Henley's performance of self-erasure is a desperate plea for a restored subjectivity, Mr. Henley's failure to respond to her letter makes her gesture of (aggressive) submission seem wholly gratuitous and suggests the impotence of private communication that will end in Mistriss Henley's abandonment of her correspondence with her confidante. The final episodes that seal the wife in silent domestic privacy occur, indeed, soon after she discovers she is pregnant. Whether the excitement of new life makes her careless or motherhood makes her feel more beholden to her husband, she begins to reassert her own, clearly irrepressible desires. First she seeks out Mr. Henley's opinion about nursing and finds, of course, that "De moi, de ma santé, de mon plaisir, pas un mot: il n'était question que de cet enfant qui n'existait pas encore" (8:120). Then she blurts to him her fantasies of a daughter whose "brillants talents, cultivés par la plus étonnante éducation, exciteraient l'admiration de tout le pays ou même de l'Europe entière" (8:120) and is devastated when Henley (again predictably) insists that he wants his daughters trained for domesticity: "modestes, douces, raisonnables, femmes complaisantes et mères vigilantes" (8:121)—*Hen*-ley girls indeed.

It is just after Mr. Henley has dashed his wife's hopes for a daughter who could have the life she herself has been denied, that he delivers his next and final blow: the news that he has turned down a seat in Parliament and an appointment at court—hence the opportunity for her to live in London and escape the isolation and boredom of Hollowpark. When she asks, "lentement avec une voix que je m'efforçais de rendre naturelle" (8:121), why he has made such a choice, he claims that his reasons are moral ones: politics might corrupt him or incite dissatisfaction when he returns to private life. He is only telling her about his refusal, in fact, for the sake of marital appearances, the matter having become, "pour ainsi dire, publique" (8:122). Had she heard the news from others, he fears, she might "en être trop affectée, et trop montrer au public, par un premier mouvement de chagrin, que le mari et la femme n'ont pas une seule âme entre eux, ni une même façon de penser et de sentir" (8:121). It is not her "chagrin" but its public display that he wants to avoid; without any doubt, she must now recognize, she is not person but position, not woman but wife.

This confirmation of his dispassionate and impersonal control over her destiny, and the degree to which Mrs. Henley now courts her own death, are both evident in her response to this news. In the moment of her deepest despair, she does not even protest; she can only confirm his authority: " 'Je vous admire, Monsieur,' lui ai-je dit, 'et en effet jamais je ne l'avais tant admiré; plus il m'en coûtait, plus je l'admirais, jamais je n'avais vu si distinctement sa supériorité' " (8:121). Beyond this puppet-gesture, she cannot speak at all:

> J'ai voulu dire quelque chose, mais j'avais été si attentive, j'étais tellement combattue entre l'estimate que m'arrachait tant de modération, de raison, de droiture dans mon mari [this the first time she has used the word "mari" in the entire narrative] et l'horreur de me voir si étrangère à ses sentiments, si fort exclue de ses pensées, si inutile, si isolée, que je n'ai pu parler. (8:122)

The effort erases consciousness itself, and Mistriss Henley faints.

As I suggested, this annihilation as character leads Mistriss Henley to a parallel annihilation as narrating voice. The sixth letter begins with the announcement that it will be her last. While Constant's Bompré chose suicide, however, Mrs. Henley says she "ne m'ôterai pas la vie, je n'en aurai pas le courage" (8:122), because "je ne suis qu'une femme"—only a woman? only a wife? The two words have collapsed entirely now that even her body is not her own. Insisting, however, that "le chagrin tue aussi," she concludes with the equivocation that "dans un an, dans deux ans, vous apprendrez, je l'espère, que je suis raisonnable et heureuse, ou que je ne suis plus" (8:122). Since it is clear that this is no "reasonable" woman, that any "happiness" she could show would be nothing but a masquerade, there is no question that one way or the other, Mrs. Henley dies. In this sense the apparently "open" ending is not open at all. Mistriss Henley the character, and **Mistriss Henley** the text, court death in order to make utterly clear that marriage in Mr. Henley's patriarchal terms—the terms of the heroine's text—is no life at all. Mistriss Henley's refusal to continue her letters, and Charrière's refusal to close the text with even an epilogue, marks the silence, the living death, which is the heroine's fate, the unwritten sequel to the *romanesque* tradition of the eighteenth century.

In order to make this representation of marriage as death, however, Charrière has engaged in a fairly radical narrative act by taking literary risks considerably larger than Constant's. The plot in *Le Mari sentimental* builds quickly from small domestic quarrels to large matters such as the charge of adultery and finally to suicide. In the eighteenth century, plot is, of course, generally constructed from such large events: adultery, abandonment, seduction, abuse, financial ruin, rape, kidnapping, illness, and death. But **Mistress Henley** builds its narrative structure with subtler and more "minor" materials, with "choses bien peu intéressantes," "petites choses qui m'affligent ou m'impatientent" (8:112), refusing even the large gesture of physical death. As Virginia Woolf put it much later, "this is an important book, the critic assumes, because it deals with war. This is an insignificant book because it deals with the feelings of women in a drawing room."[13] Taking Woolf's word "war" as metaphor, *Le Mari sentimental* is a war novel, along with *Clarissa, La Religieuse,* and *Les Liaisons dangereuses,* while **Mistriss Henley** is only about a woman's feelings in a drawing room. As Mistriss Henley and Virginia Woolf make clear from vantage points two centuries apart, there is a hierarchy of literary subjects, and the stuff of women's ordinary lives has until very recently been considered trivial. Above all, as the contemporary writer Mary Gordon comments, it is the domestic that gets devalued or purged: "Men could write about their fears of dying by exposure in the forest; we could not write about our fears of being suffocated in the kitchen. Our desire to write about these things only revealed our shallowness."[14] Gordon evokes a critical establishment that would echo Mr. Henley's smiling, patronizing, "Qu'importe!" When Mistriss Henley goes beyond "Il m'importe à moi!" (8:115) to suggest that her experience matters to other women as well—"beaucoup de femmes sont dans le même cas"—we have the beginnings of a new and threatening fictional form. For beneath the trivializing of domestic detail is surely a profound reluctance to confront the oppressive dimensions of women's lives.

It is perhaps to be expected, then, that early reaction to the **Lettres de Mistriss Henley** was divided primarily along lines of sex; Charrière reported that it "causa un schisme dans la société de Genève. Tous les maris étaient pour Monsieur Henley; beaucoup de femmes pour Madame; et les jeunes filles n'osaient dire ce qu'elles en pensaient" (*O.c.*, 6:559). A reviewer named

Chaillet may have been speaking for many men when he judged the novel an " 'aimable cruel petit livre excellent en littérature mais selon moi dangereux en morale à divers égards' " (*O.c.,* 2:420).[15] Just as predictable, this novel, born in rebuttal, spawned a rebuttal of its own: in 1785 there appeared a *Justification de M. Henley* that continued the debate begun by *Le Mari sentimental.* Thus a novel like **Mistriss Henley,** written explicitly against the patriarchal text, could only embroil Charrière—and fiction—in an endless oppositional struggle for which there was as yet no solution (textual, biographical, or political), nor much support from the canonizers of Literature. This is why going "beyond the Preliminaries" to make a truer "picture of a woman's life" was likely to end in narrative death.

There is, however, a crucial positivity to Mistriss Henley's display of narrative paralysis, for the "death" of Mistriss Henley and her private voice is also the condition for the publication of Charrière's text. In her very first letter, Mistriss Henley had imagined that her story might benefit other women and had licensed her confidante to publish the letters if they seemed to have some general validity. It is the cessation of Mistriss Henley's correspondence, then, that forms the precondition for the friend's act of putting them into print, making them a public document—indeed a novel, for the identities of the *dramatis personae* are to be changed and the text translated and edited—intended explicitly to "sinon corriger, du moins avertir les maris" and "remettre les choses à leur place" (8:102). The silencing of the private text, the "death" of both Mistriss Henley and her letters, makes possible the public protest that hopes to effect social change.

I want to suggest that this "mort romanesque" lurks behind the "mort romantique" that Janine Rossard finds in Charrière generally and in *Caliste* in particular. The "death" of Mistriss Henley may help to fill in the transition from the first (1785) section of the *Lettres écrites de Lausanne,* a fiction squarely in the tradition of the "heroine's text," to the early Romantic 1787 section known as *Caliste.* Especially since the first half of the *Lettres écrites de Lausannne* was conceived and probably begun before Charrière wrote *Mistriss Henley,* it is possible to read *Mistriss Henley* as the illuminating link that helps to explain the sharp movement from *comédie romanesque* to *tragédie romantique* that characterizes the *Lettres écrites de Lausanne.*

The 1785 portion of the *Lettres écrites de Lausanne* is an eighteenth-century heroine's text in which the epistolary narrator, mother of a young woman of marriageable age and limited resources (as Mistriss Henley had been) writes about her daughter's fortunes in courtship. Narrated not by the heroine but by an older woman, wise in the politics of sexual-economic exchange, the *Lettres écrites de Lausanne* makes its heroine's situation the basis for a feminist analysis that exposes sexual double standards and projects alternative social ideals. But the story of Cécile's courtship is never resolved; in a gesture of truncation even sharper than Charrière's typical refusals of closure,[16] Mme de C's letters simply leave off, yielding to a narrative sharply different in content and tone: the story of Caliste told by William, who loves her but is unable to surmount paternal pressure in order to marry a woman whose reputation has been compromised. Sold by her mother first to the theatre and then to a man's keeping, having thereby become an unacceptable spouse for the man she loves, Caliste is clearly a victim of gender oppression, an exceptional woman whose fate has been determined by a sexual-political economy and indeed by the sexual double standards that Cécile's mother, in the first part of the *Lettres écrites de Lausanne,* exposes and condemns. But Charrière does not allow Caliste's story to become an overt feminist morality tale like Mistriss Henley's and Cécile's; when William tells Caliste's story along with his own, the emphasis is on sensibility in an insensible world, on the classic conflict between desire and duty, passion and propriety. The gender-specific problems that have created this plot dissolve along with William's own culpability beneath the twinning of William and Caliste as Romantic suicides.

What Rossard speaks of as a Romantic death wish in *Caliste,* then, is at least in part an evasion or mystification of a sexual politics. I agree that Charrière recognized the "emptiness of the philosophy of happiness at the end of the eighteenth century; the futility of heroic struggle in this same society; and the impotence of reason" (Rossard, p. 492), but I suggest that Charrière realized and experienced these failures, as did Mistriss Henley and Caliste, as gendered phenomena. That is, there is both a sharpness and a specificity to the despair that stems from the particular contradictions, futilities, and irrationalities of women's lives, even privileged women's lives, as the "age of reason" draws to a close. For what could happiness mean if a woman had to marry or be "kept" by a man—that is, engage in prostitution—in order to survive at all? What kind of social struggle was possible for a woman isolated geographically in Hollowpark or socially in a sexual double standard? And how could reason succeed if Mr. Henley and William's father were to epitomize the rational man? Certainly in biographical terms, and whatever the differences and similarities between Mr. Henley and M. de Charrière, Charrière's own malaise was as specifically the product of her imprisonment in female expectations and necessities as was the malaise of her characters.[17]

I have suggested, however, that **Mistriss Henley** courts death because the conventions of the novel were not amenable to these feminist questions, that Charrière could not easily have written what counted for Literature if she kept telling this tale. On the other hand, a

Wertherian *mal du siécle* offered a newly conventional shape for a "désir de mort" in which questions of gender were subordinated to a more general distress. One can see this muting of sexual politics not only in Charrière's complete abandonment of Cécile's story,[18] but also in the choice of a suffering, Romantic male narrator who emphasizes those aspects of Caliste's story that denote a shared and bisexual plight. What Charrière actually helped to inaugurate in this gesture was a tradition of Romantic narratives in which subjectivity, and hence narrative voice, becomes almost exclusively male. Almost fifty years later, at the other end of this movement, George Sand would have to work out of this male-centeredness of Romantic discourse and its subsumption of sexual politics by building questions of gender back into novels like *Indiana* and *Lélia*.

Finally, I want to observe that this Romantic mystification is repeated in the critical reception of Charrière's work, beginning with the disappearance of the *Lettres écrites de Lausanne* beneath its second part, *Caliste*. Elizabeth J. MacArthur describes this erasure as a "virtual suppression" of the "dangerous half of the *Lettres écrites de Lausanne*" and claims that in reducing not only the *Lettres écrites de Lausanne* but Charrière's entire *oeuvre* to *Caliste*, critics have "privileged the most conventional, least threatening of her works."[19] I mentioned that Rossard's essay was probably the first contemporary piece on Charrière that reached a wide scholarly audience, at least in America. In 1972, *PMLA* would have been fairly receptive to an essay about a "forgotten" woman writer when that writer's work could be located squarely within the existing values of literary scholarship; *PMLA* would not have been eager in 1972 to publish an essay on the "trivial" matters of Mrs. Henley's domestic life or on the feminist implications of Charrière's discontent. Indeed, Rossard's strategy is precisely to relocate *Caliste* in a textual field that includes *Clarissa, La Nouvelle Héloïse, Werther,* and *Madame Bovary* as well as the philosophies of Lessing and Herder, Kant and Voltaire; likewise, the concept of a Romantic "désir de mort" blurs the differences between Charrière's values and those of eighteenth-century men.

I have been suggesting, however, that *Caliste* too is feminist discourse in Romantic code, and that the more openly political *Lettres de Mistriss Henley,* which imagines a less exotic fate for the fictional heroine, exposes the source of *Caliste*'s "désir de mort" as a despair as specific to late eighteenth-century upper-class women's experience as a Wertherian anguish was to upper-class men's. Certainly the French publishing house, Editions des femmes, recognized the political resonance of *Caliste* when, in 1979, it brought back into print both parts of the *Lettres écrites de Lausanne*. It will be up to contemporary critics to continue exploring the complex intersections of gender and genre in all of Charrière's work that make her writings not only *romanesque* or *romantique* but *féministe*.

Notes

[1] *PMLA* 87 (1972): 492-98.

[2] *The Heroine's Text: Readings in the French and English Novel 1722-1782* (N.Y.: Columbia Univ., 1980).

[3] *Becoming a Heroine: Reading About Women in Novels* (N.Y.: Viking, 1982), p. 81.

[4] There are many differences between the conventional courtship novel and the *Lettres neuchâteloises,* not the least of which are the economic and class issues it raises and the refusal of definitive closure that, as I will discuss later, characterizes most of Charrière's works. See Joan Stewart's essay in this volume for an excellent analysis of these unconventional aspects of the *Lettres neuchâteloises*.

[5] *The Man-Made World or, Our Androcentric Culture* (N.Y.: Charlton, 1911), pp. 96, 102.

[6] *Oeuvres complètes* (Amsterdam: G. A. van Oorschot; Geneva: Slatkine, 1980), 8:112. Both *Lettres de Mistriss Henley* and *Lettres écrites de Lausanne* appear in vol. 8. Charrière's voluminous correspondence occupies vols. 1-6. Spelling modernized (ed.).

[7] Samuel de Constant should not be confused either with Benjamin Constant, with whom Charrière was deeply and stormily involved for many years, or with Charrière's dear friend and confidant, Constant d'Hermenches. Charrière did not meet Benjamin Constant until 1787.

[8] *Le Mari sentimental ou le mariage comme il y en a quelques-uns* (1783; rep. Milano: Cesalpino-Galiardica, 1975), p. 182.

[9] In a letter of 1804 to the Baron Gerard Godard Taetsvan Amerongen van Schalkwijjk, Charrière suggests that she wrote *Mistriss Henley,* "ce très petit ouvrage," between the first and second parts of the *Lettres écrites de Lausanne* (*O.c.,* 6:559).

[10] One could argue, indeed, that Charrière intends her portrait of marriage to be even more representative than Constant's: while the subtitle of *Le Mari sentimental* is "le mariage comme il y en a *quelques-uns,*" the epigraph to *Mistriss Henley,* "j'ai vu beaucoup d'hymens, &c.," has as its (elided) second clause, "*aucuns* d'eux ne me tentent" (LaFontaine, *Fables,* Livre 7:2; emphases mine).

[11] This aggressive martyrdom gets mystified when we speak of it as masochism.

[12] Such a gesture has already been ironized when, in response to a request from his wife, Henley claimed marriage to be a union in which giving is precluded: "Donner! ma très-chère vie! . . . donne-t-on à soi-même?" (8:106).

[13] *A Room of One's Own* (N.Y.: Harcourt Brace, 1929), p. 77.

[14] "The Parable of the Cave or: In Praise of Watercolors," in *The Writer on Her Work,* ed. Janet Sternburg (N.Y.: Norton, 1980), pp. 29-30.

[15] This comment is written to Charrière in a letter from her husband dated 14 July 1784.

[16] The open-endedness of Charrière's novels was the subject of disgruntled comment in her own day, as for example, in this complaint from Mme de Staël: "je ne sais rien de plus pénible que votre manière de commencer sans finir, ce sont des amis dont vous nous séparez, et la cessation de toute correspondance avec eux me donne contre vous un peu de l'humeur que je ressens contre le comité des postes de Paris" (27 Aug. 1793 [4:162]). Contemporary analyses have suggested a feminist or feminine strategy in the refusal of closure; see especially Susan K. Jackson, "The Novels of Isabelle de Charrière, Or, A Woman's Work is Never Done," *Studies in Eighteenth-Century Culture* 14 (1985): 299-306; Elizabeth MacArthur, "Devious Narratives: Refusal of Closure in Two Eighteenth-Century Epistolary Novels," *Eighteenth-Century Studies* 21 (Fall 1987): 1-20; and Lanser, *Fictions of Authority: Women Writers and Narrative Voice* (forthcoming).

[17] There is a certain degree of scholarly disagreement over the extent to which the Henleys resemble the Charrières. There is no question, however, that Isabelle de Charrière's ambitions and desires far exceeded the conventional expectations for her sex and class and that she married of necessity into dull domesticity.

[18] Charrière did draft two brief scraps of a "suite," each only a letter in length. In one version, Cécile's marriage to Edouard (William's cousin) still seems a viable possibility; in the other she has clearly married someone else.

[19] MacArthur, p. 17.

Joan Hinde Stewart (essay date 1989)

SOURCE: "Isabelle de Charrière Publishes *Caliste*," in *A History of New French Literature,* edited by Denis Hollier, Harvard University Press, 1989, pp. 553-7.

[*In the essay below, Stewart lauds Charrière's form and style, and observes specifically that her novel* Caliste *"glosses the most urgent concerns of the female novel of the late 18th century."*]

The 18th century—and especially its last few decades—saw the publication of a surprising number of novels by women, most of which have been excluded from the canon. Although students of French literature can usually identify Marie-Madeleine de La Fayette, who wrote in the 17th century, and Germaine de Staël and George Sand, who wrote in the 19th, few have heard of 18th-century writers such as Françoise de Graffigny, Marie-Jeanne Riccoboni, Marie Leprince de Beaumont, or Anne-Louise Elie de Beaumont. Whereas Staël, by the force of her personality and politics and the sheer volume of her writing, represents the woman writer and intellectual of the early 19th century, the 18th century is characterized instead by scores of women who frequently wrote in obscurity and signed pseudonymously or not at all, and whose works are basic commentaries on the social debates of the era and on woman's place in it. Their experiments with epistolarity, sentimentality, and the figure of the heroine helped shape the emerging novel and establish a public for a genre that was still often disparaged by critics.

Among the period's female writers was Isabelle de Charriére, one of the century's subtlest and most compelling novelists, who has been excluded from the French canon by reason of both her sex and her nationality. Born Isabella van Tuyll van Serooskerken in 1740 to an aristocratic Dutch family (and known as Belle de Zuylen from the name of the family castle), she never belonged to the Parisian intellectual or social milieu. She counted among her lovers Benjamin Constant, and her hand was at one time sought by James Boswell. Her marriage at the age of thirty to Charles-Emmanuel de Charrière, an obscure Swiss citizen, took her from Holland to Switzerland, where she lived until her death in 1805. There she produced in French a voluminous oeuvre that includes novels, essays, verse, plays, and music. Her correspondence reveals her as provocative and sometimes grim, and her novels resemble her personality. She does not conform to the stereotype of the 18th-century female novelist as someone who wrote casually for lack of anything better to do. Like Riccoboni, Graffigny, Isabelle de Montolieu, and countless other women, Charrière worked hard and wrote to sell, and the financial and material arrangements of her publications were of paramount importance to her.

Her best-known novels are written in the epistolary form, which attained its greatest popularity during this period, especially from the pens of women writers such as Graffigny and Riccoboni. With Charrière, the epistolary novel demonstrates its intrinsic suitability to the evocation of woman's life. Where woman's access to the public domain is problematic, the letter form conceals and compensates for her exclusion from history while it gives full play to her lifespace and her private experience of time. It stresses private relations—secrets, confessions, the act of confiding—in short, woman's traditional sphere. Some of Charrière's novels involve an exchange among several correspondents; in others, a single protagonist writes. Unlike many 18th-century novels, Charrière's major works contain no cases of mistaken identity or disfigurement by smallpox; nor a single duel, rape, purloined letter, secret marriage, or lost will. Her writing is a delicate weave of inconspicuous circumstances and almost infinitesimal occurrences whose accumulated weight nonetheless determines the heroines' destinies. For all the careful psychology of its investigation of seduction and betrayal, Riccoboni's *Lettres de Mistriss Fanni Butlerd* (1757; *Letters of Mistress Fanni Butlerd*) appears coarse when compared to the fine texture of Charrière's novels. Charrière, who has been rightly compared to Jane Austen, also dramatizes the domestic, intertwining psychological, aesthetic, and economic concerns and exploring a carefully delimited and vividly depicted interior space where the dropping of a sheet of music, the closing of a door, or a half-muted reproach can resound like thunder. But the situations and destinies the letters narrate gain an exemplary emancipatory strength from this very restrictiveness. By the breadth of her concerns and the finesse of her analyses, Charrière may be considered as epitomizing a group of women who reigned over the novel. But she is simultaneously distinguished by her very foreignness and by the qualities that account for her continuing readability: her economy of means, the psychological distinctness of her work, and the way she uses novelistic conventions such as closure. Coming late in a long tradition of women's epistolary writing, Charrière draws on that tradition while implicitly rejecting the exaggerations often associated with the novel.

Charrière's best work includes *Lettres écrites de Lausanne* (1785; *Letters Written from Lausanne*) and its sequel, *Caliste, ou suite des lettres écrites de Lausanne* (1787; *Caliste, or the Sequel to Letters Written from Lausanne*). The themes of both—woman's marginality, her social and financial vulnerability—eloquently translate the patterns of life into fiction. The first half is the story of seventeen-year-old Cécile, told by her enlightened mother in letters to a friend in France. Without a fortune, Cécile has poor marriage prospects. She has a few viable suitors but loves Edward, a young English lord who is beguiled but insufficiently motivated to propose marriage. When Cécile begins to languish, her mother takes her away for a change of air. And so the story ends—or fails to end.

The sequel, **Caliste,** is an extraordinarily powerful piece and also, like Charrière's other novels, quite short: less than fifty pages. William, Lord Edward's melancholy companion, writes for Cécile's mother his own story and that of the brilliant, artistic Caliste. Caliste is made a child actress by her impoverished mother; then she is more or less bought by an English nobleman who takes her as his mistress but also gives her an impeccable education. After his death, she meets and falls in love with William, bereaved by the death of his twin brother. William never musters the courage either to marry her despite his father's interdiction or to take her as mistress despite her craving for respectability. He finally marries instead a trifling widow of his father's choosing, while Caliste weds a country gentleman. She dies in England in an aura of sainthood (during a performance of Pergolesi's *Stabat Mater*), while back in Lausanne William wallows in self-reproach.

Differences in tone and events do little to undermine similarities between the two stories: *Caliste* is the tragic version of Cécile's story—tragic because William, like Edward, manifests a fatal inertia. Jean Starobinski has noted that William's compulsive abdication of decisive action is accompanied by discreet but insistent suggestions of latent homosexuality. They include, for example, his attachments to a twin brother (during their military service, they spend their free hours studying and making music, while other soldiers "wasted their time on gambling and women") and to a young stepson who resembles the deceased brother. In fact this ten-year-old child accompanies William on a trip (honeymoon?) after William's marriage, while the bride stays at home with her father-in-law. Finally, of course, William attaches himself to Edward. When William falls in love with Caliste, he feels instinctively unfaithful to his brother and, despite his realization of Caliste's passion, shrinks from physical love. He is willing to be treated like a "sister" by Caliste and is indifferent to his own wife's infidelities. Although there is no explicit indication that William feels threatened by Caliste's ardor, this is subtly suggested by his irresolution, his tendency to yield rather than persevere. In most sentimental novels, by contrast, male aggressiveness is a fundamental fact: the men tirelessly strategize to get the women into bed. Here, too, William says he wants to sleep with Caliste, and she says no; but her underlying passion and his passivity, like his virginity and her sexual experience, in effect constitute a reversal of roles. *Caliste* does not die because she has engaged in illicit sex; instead, she withers away for lack of it. Her death, caused largely by the jealous force of a male bond, is also a commentary on the power of a patriarchal system to exclude a woman who is not "normal."

In their utter social dependence on male initiative, Cécile and Caliste are the victims of a system that makes autonomy almost impossible for women. They are oppressed by habits of mind engraved in a sociological landscape defined by a religion, a culture, and the slow pace of time. While men act, women are obliged to wait and practice female "virtue." In

Charrière's work, chastity is motivated by practical considerations. The abstinence that Caliste obsessively practices after the death of her first lover is designed to be rewarded by rehabilitation: because she can aspire to become William's wife only by refusing to become his mistress, she mounts a campaign of intellectual and moral resistance. Although she thereby proves herself "worthy" of William, his own lethargy guarantees that her worth will go unrewarded by sex or marriage, and her obstinate, virtuous victory over desire weakens and ultimately kills her.

Cécile, too, has to resist the physical: her story suggests a new definition of virtuous behavior, which her mother attempts to motivate less with religious arguments than with a more concrete inducement: it helps find a husband. Cécile must therefore artfully conceal the attraction she feels toward the English lord if she is to induce him to marry her. Here virtue functions as imposture—the concealment of what Charrière calls one's *sensibilité,* and what we understand as both sentiment and the sexual urge.

The possibility of domestic happiness is one of Charrière's main concerns. Neither Cécile, nor Caliste, nor most of her other heroines have access to other than domestic satisfactions: their thoughts range restlessly within a cage constructed and reinforced by patriarchal concepts. Yet even the domestic sphere excludes or thwarts them. Conjugal and domestic structures are seen as constituting the principal mode of fulfillment for women, yet such structures are also progressively revealed as the chief obstacle to their happiness. The case of the protagonist of Charrière's ***Lettres de Mistress Henley*** (1784; ***Letters of Mrs. Henley***) is the clearest: her decision (like the author's own) to marry a man of solid and retiring virtue rather than one of ambition and eminence is a choice of the domestic over the worldly. Delimited by the parameters of her spouse's mind and home, Mrs. Henley's fate is wretched, just as Charrière's own life in the village of her stolid Swiss husband was stifling. Is Charrière not suggesting that the male version of happiness for women is a verbal fabrication? Are women not alienated by the complicity of moralizing, rationalizing men with empty words? We are reminded of Louise d'Epinay's remark that "reason" means following the advice you are given.

Just as Edward and William are characterized by an appalling passivity, so Cécile's story is fragmented, its inscription strangely incomplete, except insofar as Caliste's tragic end represents Cécile's. Just as these plots anatomize the critical junctures arising out of the minute incidents of daily life, the ending refuses to transcend the quotidian. This indeterminacy itself mimics the heroines' contingency, their social, economic, or affective estrangement. These very domestic representations of individuality reveal and represent patterns of the literary and the social, especially as they figure in novels by female writers throughout the century. They are dialogues with the late 18th-century European culture in which Charrière lived and worked, a culture in which there seemed to be little salvation for a woman outside of marriage and, as her own experience demonstrated, little hope of personal satisfaction for an exceptional woman within it. In Charrière's world, there exists no recipe for marrying or for marital success, biological and economic imperative though marriage is, and men may lack even the mettle to make love.

Caliste has an unusually rich literary posterity, both in works such as Germaine de Staël's *Corinne* (1807) and Benjamin Constant's *Adolphe* (wr. 1806-07, pub. 1816) and in the real-life connections among their authors. Charrière, who as a young woman had a long (mostly epistolary) relationship with a Swiss officer eighteen years her elder, Baron Auguste Constant d'Hermenches, later counted among her intimates his nephew Benjamin, whom she met when she was in her late forties and he not yet twenty. His tumultuous affair with Germaine de Staël, which began a few years later, embittered Charrière, although she and Benjamin Constant remained in correspondence until her death. Staël, for her part, esteemed her older rival (although she complained about her annoying habit of leaving her novels unfinished) and specifically prized ***Caliste:*** "How I wish I hadn't read ***Caliste*** ten times!" she wrote to Charrière during the Terror. "I would have before me the certain prospect of an hour's respite from all my troubles" (31 December 1793, in Charrière, ***Oeuvres complètes,*** 4:299).

Like William in ***Caliste,*** Staël's hero (Corinne's lover) irresolutely forsakes the woman who fascinates him to marry the woman of his father's choosing, cementing the paternal bond through the conjugal. *Adolphe* is a male version of the story: here the heroine who dies of despair is rather less genius and more harpy, and the courage that the man lacks is not so much courage to marry as courage to leave. Lovers and (writing) rivals in a triangular relation curiously skewed by their chonological ages and by the historical passage from Revolution to Empire, Charrière, Constant, and Staël each translated a personal drama into a masterpiece of fiction and an essential myth about patriarchy. In each case a novel about female passion and marginality and male impotence is curiously configured by the role of the father/brother for whom the hero feels the profoundest bond, the most inviolable desire.

Caliste glosses the most urgent concerns of the female novel of the late 18th century: love, of course, and marriage, without which vulnerable female protagonists recognize that survival is difficult. The author herself had reason to understand this. The drama of the problematic marriageability of the modestly dowered and too brilliant Belle de Zuylen with her motley band of mostly lukewarm suitors, her dubious decision to accept the hand of the man who promised (and proved) least fit to be her husband—this drama has been amply evoked by her biographers. Her novels also epitomize women's complicated relation to 18th-century sensibility. It was in the wake of Richardson and Rousseau that the notion of *sensibilité* reached its apogee in the French novel and that the novel itself (and especially the epistolary form) became increasingly recognized as an effective means of representing not just morality and sentiment but also complex social realities. Novels by women during this era mediate social conditions and literary conventions: women helped enthrone sensibility, which enthroned women, but they also explored its connections with oppression. Charrière and other women used the novel to write about themselves in a century that saw fewer autobiographies and memoirs than works of fiction. The extent to which sentimentality and apparent morality mask revolt in fiction, and the play between conformism and questioning, help account for the subversions they wrought. By their use of form and by the force of style, Charrière's stories are powerfully seductive. The meaning she invests in morality, domesticity, sensibility, reason, and virtue connects her to a tradition of women's writing. It also suggests the relation of her work to woman's domestic culture and indicates the extent to which a close reading of fictional conventions in the century's female novel may reveal the currents beneath a seemly, seamless surface.

Nadine Bérenguier (essay date 1991)

SOURCE: "From *Clarens* to *Hollow Park*, Isabelle de Charrière's Quiet Revolution," in *Studies in Eighteenth-Century Culture*, Vol. XXI, 1991, pp. 219-43.

[*In the following essay, Bérenguier compares* Mistriss Henley *with Jean-Jacques Rousseau's 1761 work* Julie; ou la Nouvelle Héloïse, *contrasting Charrière's narrative innovation with Rousseau's more traditional approach.*]

"Love is more pleasant than marriage for the reason that novels are more amusing than history."[1] In this lapidary maxim, Chamfort effectively captures what characterizes the plots of eighteenth-century novels. By placing novels on the side of love, this observer of eighteenth-century mores reminds us of the age-old dichotomy between love and marriage and underlines that, unlike love and the novel, the novel and marriage do not make a good match. What happens, then, when such a golden rule is transgressed and the intruder, that is, marriage, becomes the major topic of a novel? What is the impact of such a break with tradition on the ideological content of the novel? Such questions are raised by **Lettres de Mistriss Henley**, initially published in 1784, in which Isabelle de Charrière departs radically from the novelistic tradition of her time.[2] This break did not escape the attention of the first public reviewers who gave a critical reading of **Lettres de Mistriss Henley** with Samuel de Constant's *Le mari sentimental*, published together (anonymously) in the 1785 Paris edition.[3] In *Le Mercure de France,* the review began thus: "Le fond de ce double roman, dont la forme est assez singulière, a le mérite d'être absolument neuf."[4] [The content of this double novel, whose form is quite remarkable, has the advantage of being absolutely new.] It pointed out that the authors had left the beaten tracks of French prose-fiction by omitting "aventure merveilleuse, amants persécutés, dispersés, réunis; . . . ces intrigues filées, promenées d'obstacles en obstacles . . . Amants, passions amoureuses" (186) [unreal adventure, persecuted, separated, and reunited lovers; . . . these endless plots meandering from obstacles to obstacles . . . Lovers, amorous passions]. These remarks were echoed by the *Année littéraire:*

> Ce roman, monsieur a une marche différente de celle des autres. La plupart renferment des intrigues amoureuses qui se terminent par le mariage; celui-ci, ou ceux-ci (car il y en a deux) commencent là où les autres finissent. On n'imagine guère que deux personnes mariées soient capables d'exciter un intérêt bien vif.[5]

> [This novel, Sir, takes a different path from the others. Most of them have amorous plots which end in marriage. This one (or these for they are two) begins where the others end. It is difficult to imagine that two married persons can arouse such great interest.]

It seems that even at the end of the century Chamfort's remark was still accurate. Nevertheless, both reviewers praised this attempt to provide insight into a matter previously ignored by novels: the (mal)functioning of conjugal unions. The *Mercure de France* in particular displayed an unambiguous enthusiasm:

> Cette tentative a déjà été faite au théâtre; mais nous croyons que c'est la première fois qu'elle ait été risquée dans un roman: il nous semble cependant qu'elle pourrait être répétée avec succès, et même infiniment étendue (186).

> [Such an attempt has already been made in the theater; but we believe that it is the first time that it has been risked in a novel: it seems nonetheless that it could be repeated successfully, and even infinitely extended.]

Novels, in order to fulfill their edifying mission, should not leave any aspect of life unexplored but should rather "tracer les tableaux de la vie, afin que parmi ceux qui se rapprochent le plus des circonstances qui nous entourent, nous choisissions la route que nous devons suivre, les écueils que nous devons éviter" (187) [draw pictures of life, so that among those which are closest to the circumstances familiar to us, we can choose the path that we must follow and the obstacles that we must avoid]. As suggested by the format of the 1785 Parisian edition, the two novels were perceived as inseparable parts of a diptych. In *Le mari sentimental*, M. Bompré is led to commit suicide by the selfish behavior and insensitivity of his wife, while in **Mistriss Henley**, Mrs. Henley is disenchanted by the excessively rational attitude of her husband.[6] In their haste to acclaim the uniqueness of this double plot, both reviewers privileged the issues raised by the controversy between *Le mari sentimental* and **Mistriss Henley** and forgot to mention a prior attempt to include married life in a novel: Jean-Jacques Rousseau's *Julie ou la Nouvelle Héloïse* (1761).

Le mari sentimental is explicitly inscribed (as we shall see) in **Mistriss Henley,** but the dialogue does not stop with the companion text. Too many allusions to be ignored point, in **Mistress Henley,** to *Julie*. It is unnecessary to recall at length the impact of *Julie* on the public of the period or to document the fact that Charrière had read Rousseau's work.[7] In the Second Preface to *Julie,* Rousseau, an ardent detractor of contemporary novels, proposes to break with the literary conventions of his day and to revolutionize prose-fiction in France by focusing on married life and domestic concerns.[8] Charrière does not voice her own claims in such an outspoken way, but her deliberate choice to deal exclusively with the bare matter of married life and domesticity constitutes in itself another radical departure. Unlike Mary Wollstonecraft, who very explicitly responds to Rousseau in her *Vindication of the Rights of Woman,* Charrière answers implicitly but in fictional terms; she offers a serious and significant contribution to discussions about marriage and the family through a critical rewriting of the marriage ideology displayed in *Julie*.

I suggest with Nancy K. Miller that "Learning to read women's writing entails not only a particular attentiveness to the marks of signature that [she has] called 'overreading'; it also involves 'reading in pairs (or, in Naomi Schor's coinage, 'intersexually'). By this [Miller] mean[s] looking at the literature of men's and women's writing side by side to perceive at their points of intersection the differentiated lines of a 'bi-cultural' production of the novel—Persian *and* Peruvian—more complicated than the familiar, national history of its tropes.'"[9] I do not propose **Mistriss Henley** for an exercise in overreading, but for "reading in pairs," taking *Julie* as a grid through which to read **Mistriss Henley,** and vice versa. This method does not mean that I will look at the influence of Rousseau on Charrière. Rather, I will examine Charrière's fictional treatment of Rousseau's marriage narrative and of its consequences for women. **Mistriss Henley** fully explores the new paths opened by *Julie* and, I will argue, more radically than *Julie*. Charrière's novel departs from narrative tradition in areas where Rousseau fell short of doing so. In fact, Rousseau preserved major rules of the genre he despised so much, a feature of *Julie* widely acknowledged by scholars studying his fiction.[10] For her part, in **Mistriss Henley,** Charrière abandons all the conventions still favored by Rousseau and simultaneously provides a veiled ironic comment on *Julie* by giving a very different outlook on marriage as an institution, marital relationships, and domestic affairs (e. g., running a household, education and child-rearing, social functions).

Why did the first reviewers and later critics ignore a precedent as well-known as *Julie?* On the one hand, Rousseau's status and legacy might explain this silence. Rousseau was not considered merely a novelist, but rather a *philosophe* (in the general sense), concerned with various political and social issues (such as the passage from a state of nature to civil society, the birth of property, the role of arts and sciences in society). Therefore, the characters, relationships, and situations in Rousseau's successful novel could be perceived as part of a wider system representative of his opinions and principles. The "didactic" side of *Julie* was commented upon by Rousseau's contemporaries, such as Duclos, d'Alembert, and Madame Necker, and has been examined by more recent critics, such as Jean-Louis Lecercle: "He could not avoid entrusting his characters with themes which obsessed him, to the extent that this book has been called a synthesis of his thought."[11] The short and bare format of the *Mari sentimental*/***Mistriss Henley*** duet seems far removed from the all-encompassing project of *Julie*. Because of their focus on the severed relationship between two spouses, the critics perceived the new novels as very topical works whose perspective was limited to the psychoemotional and the private. Such a view could conveniently accommodate the biographical reading of **Mistriss Henley** initiated by Philippe Godet, Charrière's first major biographer, who qualified it as "insignificant" despite its interest as a reflection of "the moral state of the author during this period of her life.[12] Though an autobiographical view is historically justified, it is regrettably likely to hide other possible implications of her departure from novelistic convention.[13] Both the polemic and the autobiographical approaches reduce Charrière's innovation to a mere emotional reaction, be it to another novel, or to her own experience. In short, the difference of status between *Julie* and **Mistriss Henley** can account for the failure of literary critics to establish a connection between them.

Both the polemic and autobiographical elements that have prevailed among the novel's readers are actually embedded in the first page of **Mistriss Henley**. The reader is immediately invited by the protagonist to see her writing as a response to a "cruel et charmant petit livre" [cruel and charming little book] (*Le mari sentimental*) that has tormented her ever since she read it. A reading of the novel to her husband and his reaction to it are decisive in prompting her "confessions" to a silent "confidante." Hoping that her husband will perceive differences between their situation and that of Bompré in *Le mari*, she is distressed to sense his perception of similarities and his tendency to identify with the unfortunate husband:

> Quand j'ai lu tout cela à mon mari, au lieu de sentir encore mieux que moi ces différences, comme je m'en étais flattée en commençant la lecture, ou de ne point sentir du tout cette manière de ressemblance, je l'ai vu tantôt sourire, tantôt soupirer; il a dit quelques mots, il a caressé son chien et regardé l'ancienne place du portrait. Ma chère amie, ils se croiront tous des MM. Bompré, et seront surpris d'avoir pu supporter si patiemment la vie (101). [When I read all of this to my husband, instead of feeling these differences more than I did, as I had flattered myself he would when I started, or not feeling this sort of resemblance at all, I saw him sometimes smile, sometimes sigh; he said a few words, petted his dog and looked at the former place of the portrait. My dear friend, they will all think themselves Bomprés, and are surprised that they have been able to endure life so patiently.]

Besides identifying itself as a party in a controversy, the novel introduces the question of the influence of fiction on "real" life. By affording them a comparison with their own experience, *Le mari sentimental* becomes part and parcel of the conjugal difficulties encountered by the Henleys. After interpreting Constant's novel according to her own experience, Mrs. Henley tries to decipher its negative impact on her husband's behavior:

> Il vivait et me jugeait, pour ainsi dire, au jour la journée, jusqu'à ce que M. et Mme Bompré le soient venus rendre plus content de lui et plus mécontent de moi. J'ai eu bien du chagrin depuis ma dernière lettre (108). [He was living and judging me, so to speak, on a day-by-day basis, until Mr. and Mrs. Bompré made him more content with himself and less satisfied with me. I have had much sorrow since I last wrote to you.]

Fiction and personal experience fuse and become confused, as fiction becomes so palpable that it intensifies the pain inflicted by life.

The well-established belief that novels had an impact on readers' taste and behavior was central to the debate that raged in the eighteenth century regarding this relatively new genre.[14] Because of the preeminence of love in their plots, novels were accused of corrupting the morals of their readers, especially of young women. In **Mistriss Henley,** Charrière reformulates the relationship between the effects of fiction and its content and gives it a completely new turn. Even when fiction promotes a "serious" topic—and marriage is one—it can be harmful. Even "good" models—devoid of seduction, adultery, abduction, disobedience, and life-threatening conflicts—do not guarantee a beneficial effect of fiction on readers who might still have to pay an emotional price, contrary to what one might deduce from *Julie*'s Second Preface:

> Si les romans n'offraient à leurs lecteurs que des tableaux d'objets qui les environnent, que des devoirs qu'ils peuvent remplir, que des plaisirs de leur condition, les romans ne les rendraient point fous, ils les rendraient sages (22). [If novels offered to their readers only depictions of objects that surround them, duties that can be fulfilled, the pleasures of their conditions, novels would not render them insane, they would render them reasonable.]

As it refutes this point, Charrière's "insignificant" novel begins to take a radical stand.

A comparison of prefatory remarks in the Second Preface of *Julie* and the first letter of **Mistriss Henley** illustrates a novel's possible effects on readers who identify with their characters. Both novelists innovate by targeting not individuals, but married couples. However, each sheds a very different light on this enterprise. In *Julie*'s Second Preface, in the dialogue between R and N, R attributes to the depiction of a domestic life the power to reform mores in general and regenerate conjugal relations in particular:

> J'aime à me figurer deux époux lisant ce recueil ensemble, y puisant un nouveau courage pour supporter leurs travaux communs, et peut-être de nouvelles vues pour les rendre utiles. Comment pourraient-ils y contempler le tableau d'un ménage heureux, sans vouloir imiter un si doux modèle? Comment s'attendriront-ils sur le charme de l'union conjugale, même privé de celui de l'amour, sans que la leur se resserre et s'affermisse? (23) [I like to imagine husband and wife reading this collection of letters together, drawing from it new courage to endure their common tasks, and perhaps gaining new views to render these tasks useful. How could they contemplate the picture of this happy household, without wishing to imitate such a pleasing model? How can they be moved by the charm of the conjugal bond, even deprived of the charm of love, without seeing their own union tightened and strengthened?]

In this passage, Rousseau presents his novel as a conduct-book that prescribes a new way of life (centered upon the home and the family) and that should inspire married readers to have more harmonious unions.

In the first page of *Mistriss Henley,* we see Mrs. Henley practicing what R advocates: that is, reading novels with her husband; ironically, however, she reads not *Julie,* but *Le mari sentimental.* Far from providing a model to be imitated by both spouses (like *Julie,* in Rousseau's opinion), this novel creates a split between husband and wife, who read it very differently. The lack of harmony between them is underscored by the purpose suggested by Mrs. Henley for the publication of her own letters. From a reader she turns into a writer:

> Si ma lettre ou mes lettres ont quelque justesse et vous paraissent propres à exciter quelque intérêt, seulement assez pour se faire lire, traduisez-les en changeant les noms, en omettant ce qui vous paraîtra ennuyeux ou inutile. Je crois que beaucoup de femmes sont dans le même cas que moi. Je voudrais, sinon corriger, du moins avertir les maris (102). [If my letter or my letters are in any way correct and seem to you likely to trigger any interest, if only enough to be read, translate them, changing the names and suppressing whatever seems to you boring or useless. I believe that many women are in a situation similar to mine. I would like, if not to reform, at least to alert husbands.]

If Charrière makes her (male) readers reconsider their own attitudes, it is through a warning and not through a positive model. The prefatory material built into the novel's body bears witness to the urgency of the situation and finds itself in stern contrast with *Julie*'s elaborate dialogued preface (also entitled "Ecrit sur les romans") in which Rousseau indicates the objectives of his novel and debates the laws of the genre. Both novelists, eager to see reforms implemented in the mores of their contemporaries, are innovative in aiming at married readers, but this common effort reveals opposite attitudes on their part: on Rousseau's, a propensity to idealize situations; on Charrière's an attempt to scrutinize them as lucidly as possible, and lay them as bare as possible.[15] This contrast emerges through their use (or neglect) of certain traditional plot elements. In what follows, I will compare Julie's and Mrs. Henley's fates as married heroines and mention a few aspects of Rousseau's fidelity to novelistic tradition, not in order to lessen the impact of his enterprise, but to highlight more clearly Charrière's narrative boldness in *Mistriss Henley.*

In eighteenth-century France, marriage, as social historians Jean-Louis Flandrin and James Traer have documented, was central to strategies of alliances ensuring the transmission, redistribution or acquisition of property, the continuation of a lineage, and the improvement of social status.[16] Such conclusions, based on the study of family documents, are also found in the writings of social critics of the period, who claimed that as long as marriages were based on transactions between families rather than on individual agreements, no personal satisfaction could come from married life. Montesquieu, Diderot, collaborators in the *Encyclopédie,* as well as Rousseau himself, did not question the institution of marriage so much as the custom of arranged marriages, and they favored freedom in the choice of a partner, combined with the right to divorce (except Rousseau), as the solution to conjugal misery.[17] In turn, fiction often dealt with obligatory arranged marriage; *Julie* was no exception. Like many other novels of the period, the first half of *Julie* stages an amorous passion between two young protagonists (Julie and Saint-Preux) and the stubborn opposition of Julie's father to their union. Under such circumstances, marriage is treated as a transaction upsetting the familial stability and as a source of conflict between generations. Family relationships crystallize and intensify around the prohibition of Julie's union with Saint-Preux and then, around the arrangement of Julie's marriage to Wolmar. Seen from this angle, Julie's situation resembles that of other novels' heroines, adolescents who have reached a marriageable age and struggle with the difficulties generated by the critical transition from childhood to adulthood. Thus marriage becomes a source of conflict between generations and the focus of parent/child power dynamics.[18]

In *Mistriss Henley,* the period directly preceding marriage, central to many eighteenth-century novels, is practically discarded. Mrs. Henley does not use any pretext to linger on her past. When she announces to her correspondent in a rhetorical question: "Voulez-vous, ma chère amie, que je vous fasse l'histoire de mon mariage, du temps qui l'a précédé, et que je vous peigne ma vie telle qu'elle est aujourd'hui?" (102) [Do you want, my dear friend, to hear the story of my marriage, of the time which preceded it, do you want me to describe my life as it is nowadays?], one would expect her to focus on "the time that preceded it," as is customary in a fair number of eighteenth-century novels.[19] Instead, Mrs. Henley briefly summarizes those years: an orphan raised by a loving aunt who treated her like a daughter, she was promised to Lord Alesford (the heir of her aunt's husband) at a very young age, and both quietly waited for their future union. Sent on a tour of Europe, the young lord died in Italy after being unfaithful to his beloved.[20] This period is narrated very hastily, her sorrow remembered in a few lines: "Je ne vous dirai point tout ce que je souffris alors, tout ce que j'avais déjà souffert pendant plusieurs mois. Vous vîtes à Montpellier les traces que le chagrin avait laissées dans mon humeur" (102). [I shall not tell you how much I suffered then, how much I had already suffered for several months. You saw in Montpellier the traces that my sorrow had left in my temper.] The ellipsis, underscored by the "I shall not tell you," supposes the reader well enough equipped to fill in the gaps of the narrative. Of course, no more details are necessary for a correspondent whom she met at the time of her affliction, just as they are superfluous for any reader familiar with the deceived lovers populating the fiction of the time. She can thus concentrate on her "life as it is nowadays"; this focus is signalled by the absence of her maiden name, which precludes any other identity.

The circumstances more directly surrounding their marriages also create a contrast between Julie and Mrs. Henley. Given by her authoritative father to an aging husband, Julie is again submitted to the fate of many heroines who are denied a say in the choice of a spouse and must marry according to family interests (or not marry at all and enter a convent). Fundamentally, in regard to their situation as women, both Julie and Mrs. Henley have an obligation to marry, and no other option is offered to either of them (as non-Catholics, not even the convent). Julie, whose brother is dead, is responsible, among other things, for continuing the family blood-line, which is threatened with extinction. As she will inherit very little money from her aunt, the future Mrs. Henley must find a husband in order to enjoy financial security. However, in contrast to Julie, Charrière's heroine is given a choice of possible partners, which she perceives as extreme freedom.[21] Far from from rejoicing over this widely praised freedom, Mrs. Henley expresses ambivalent feelings toward it and in retrospect she regrets having been given the right to prefer Mr. Henley, a man of the gentry, over a merchant returned rich from India (whom she calls the "Nabab"):

> Si un père tyrannique m'eût obligée à épouser le Nabab, je me serais fait peut-être un devoir d'obéir; et m'étourdissant sur l'origine de ma fortune par l'usage que je me serais promis d'en faire, "les bénédictions des indigents d'Europe détourneront," me serais-je dit, "les malédictions de l'Inde." En un mot, forcée d'être heureuse d'une manière vulgaire, je le serais devenue sans honte et peut-être avec plaisir; mais me donner moi-même de mon choix, contre des diamants, des perles, des tapis, des parfums, des mousselines brodées d'or, des soupers, des fêtes, je ne pouvais m'y résoudre, et je promis ma main à Mr. Henley (103-104). [If a tyrannical father had obliged me to marry the Nabob, I probably would have made a point of obeying; and in an attempt to forget the origin of my fortune through the use I made of it, "the blessings of the needy of Europe will divert," I would have told myself, "the maledictions of India." In a word, forced to be happy in a vulgar manner, I would have become so shamelessly and perhaps with pleasure; but I could not decide on my own to exchange myself freely for diamonds, pearls, carpets, perfumes, gold embroidered muslins, suppers, feasts, and I promised my hand to Mr. Henley.]

Irony pervades this passage, in which the character is creating her own fiction on the basis of traditional narratives and providing a defense of forced marriages. This ironic tone fits the paradox of her situation: she perceives her relative freedom as an unbearable burden and regrets the absence of a severe and impervious father who would have imposed his will (as Julie's father did). She could have been sold by her father (or her aunt, for that matter), but does not feel entitled to be herself the performer of the exchange as well as its object. This passage lucidly analyzes the unexpected consequences of the freedom to choose a husband. As Elisabeth de Fontenay argues in an article on the invention of "ménage" by Rousseau, "companionate marriage, [on the other hand], subjects the woman because it transforms the patriarchal contract between families into a conjugal and inter-individual bond deprived of any socio-political dimension. In making this bond private, one excludes women from public life and one condemns them exclusively to domestic life."[22] In refusing to marry primarily for money (she does not marry for love either), Mrs. Henley seals an inter-personal agreement with the man whom she has elected as her husband.

This type of conjugal bond introduces the protagonist into a private and enclosed world, limited to the family and domestic duties. The absence of a father's strong coercion is symptomatic of the absence of external causes for the failed relationship: "Je suis d'autant plus malheureuse qu'il n'y a rien à quoi je puisse m'en prendre, que je n'ai aucun changement à demander, aucun reproche à faire, que je me blâme et me méprise d'être malheureuse" (107). [I am all the more unhappy that there is nothing which I can blame, no change I can request, no reproach I can make, and that I blame myself and despise myself for being unhappy.] Again, this predicament is linked to the double role that she has had to perform: as a woman giving herself, she does not feel entitled to place responsibility outside herself. The focus on marriage as a private relationship between two individuals rather than as a function of external principles, as in *Julie,* is a revolt against **Mistriss Henley's** predecessor. The married couple, exposed as an internally fragile unit when stripped of external threats, becomes a newly-constituted literary character through Charrière's innovation.

While in other novels of the period, married life eludes narration as if its privacy had to be kept from indiscreet readers, or rather, as if it were unlikely to provide an acceptable plot line, in *Julie* as in **Mistriss Henley,** the marriage ceremony does not constitute a happy and hasty conclusion.[23] In both novels, marriage opens a new era for the protagonists, and married life is the object of much attention. *Julie,* one might add, is the first novel published in France in which the heroine leads her married life in the country, cares about the success of her marriage, has children and is involved in their education. The "révolution soudaine" [sudden revolution] that strikes her during the wedding ceremony constitutes the best symbol of the power of marriage, inaugurating simultaneously a new life for the character and a new theme for novelistic fiction. However, Julie's wedding is powerfully described as a sacrifice through which she undoes the violation of her sexual integrity: "Je fus menée au temple comme une victime impure qui souille le sacrifice où l'on va l'immoler" (353; III, 18). [I was brought to the temple as an impure victim that sullies the sacrifice where she is going to be immolated.] Her devotion to married life appears as a way to expiate her premature loss of virginity: "Douce et consolante vertu, je la [la vie] recommence pour toi; c'est toi qui me la rendras chère; c'est à toi que je la veux consacrer" (355; III, 18). [Sweet and consoling virtue, I recommence it (my life) for you; you will make it dear to me; I want to devote it to you.] Julie's past and her "fault" justify her mystical devotion to domesticity and give her marriage to Wolmar all the characteristics of an expiation for her illicit relationship with Saint-Preux. This suffices to make the Wolmars an exception to the rule asserted by the reviewer of the *Année littéraire* ("It is difficult to imagine that two married persons can arouse such great interest"); they are likely to interest readers greatly.

Only a brief sentence inaugurates Mrs. Henley's career as a wife, her wedding being the object of no detailed description. "Nos noces furent charmantes" (104) [Our wedding was charming] says it all, because the frustrated wife wants to introduce without any further delay the central issue of the novel, that is, her relationship with her husband. She portrays him thus:

> Spirituel, élégant, décent, délicat, affectueux, M. Henley enchantait tout le monde; c'était un mari de roman; il me semblait quelquefois un peu trop parfait; mes fantaisies, mes humeurs, mes impatiences trouvaient toujours *sa raison et sa modération* en leur chemin (104; my emphasis). [Witty, elegant, decent, delicate, affectionate, Mr. Henley enchanted everyone; he looked like a story-book husband and sometimes appeared too perfect; my fancies, my moods, my irritations always found his reason and his temperance in their way.]

Strangely enough, though, the expression "mari de roman" can hardly mean "husbands as novels portray them," since husbands are rarely given a positive role in the plot of French novels.[24] "Mari de roman," thus, might refer to prospective husbands, "prince charmings" who fight abusive fathers and (sometimes) defeat them at the end of the story. However, there is one exception to this rule, the perfect "mari de roman" identified in *Julie:* M. de Wolmar.

Mr. Henley is a younger and more seductive version of M. de Wolmar. Describing their husbands, both wives mention reason and moderation as the men's fundamental traits. Julie introduces him to Saint-Preux:

> Sa physionomie est noble et prévenante, son abord simple et ouvert, ses manières sont plus honnêtes qu'empressées; il parle peu et d'un grand sens, mais sans affecter ni précision ni sentence. Il est le même pour tout le monde, ne cherche et ne fuit personne, et *n'a jamais d'autres préférences que celles de la raison* (369; III, 20; my emphasis). [His physiognomy is noble and welcoming, his demeanor simple and open, his manners more honest than zealous; he talks little and with logic, but does not pretend to precision or sententiousness. He is the same for everybody, seeks nobody and avoids nobody, and has no other preferences than those dictated by reason.]

Henley's position as Wolmar's heir is all the more interesting in that their reasonable behaviors have very different outcomes. Wolmar is a "mari de roman" of a new kind. Like any other novelistic husband he has not been chosen, but unlike most of them, he is highly praised and admired by his young wife. Unlike Mrs. Henley, Julie does not hint at the difficulties likely to result from daily intercourse with such a controlled personality. This reign of reason in their relationship, executed by Wolmar, is yet another manifestation of Julie's urge to expiate her passionate past. The perfection that Julie claims for her union with M. de Wolmar is best explained by her attempt to compensate for her haunting love of Saint-Preux. When Wolmar invites Saint-Preux to join them at Clarens, the past illicit love is reenforced by its possible resurgence under the guise of adultery. In that respect, Rousseau remains faithful to the tradition according to which married life serves as a background for the analysis of illicit love, and more precisely of the feminine struggle against adultery or its temptation.[25] Wolmar's initiative regarding Saint-Preux, moreover, shows the limits of his reasonable behavior as he takes perverse pleasure at the triangular situation with which he experiments and tests his wife: "Il prend plaisir à la confiance qu'il me témoigne" (498; IV, 12) [He takes pleasure in the trust that he shows me], Julie comments to Claire.[26] Their relationship is shaped by a mediation which allows Rousseau to glorify simultaneously a married couple and an irresistible illicit passion, as if he made his innovations more admissible through the pervasive use of more traditional novelistic elements. This is at the same time the strength of his project and possibly the limit of his transgressive fiction.

Such traditional elements, though suggested briefly, are never carried out in ***Mistriss Henley,*** and no underlying passion counterbalances the reason incarnated by Mr. Henley. Mrs. Henley fantasizes about adultery as a device to arouse her husband's jealousy and modify his cool behavior towards her. At a ball, she has made the acquaintance of a young woman and her brother whom she has invited to dinner. She makes a point of telling her husband of this man's resemblance to her first fiancé, Lord Alesford, but to no avail. No titillating effect is obtained. Her attempt is immediately dismissed as irrelevant by Mr. Henley who declares, smiling: "Heureusement je ne suis pas jaloux" (116). [Fortunately, I am not jealous.] Reacting vehemently to what she perceives as indifference, she draws the portrait of a paradoxical "husband of her dreams": " 'Oui!' ai-je ajouté, excité à la fois par ma propre vivacité et par son sang-froid inaltérable, 'les injustices d'un jaloux, les emportements d'un brutal, seraient moins fâcheux que le flegme et l'aridité d'un sage' " (116). ['Yes!' I added, irritated as much by my own outburst of temper as by his unfailing self-control, 'the injustice of a jealous man, the anger of a brute would be less of a nuisance than the phlegm and the dullness of a wise man.'] Not only does she allude once more to another possible novelistic institution (the abusive husband), but she also reveals her mistrust of rationality and her delusion regarding the ability of reasonable behavior to operate in all realms of human endeavor. In a letter written after this outburst, she addresses her husband in these terms:

> Vous avez pourtant eu un tort: vous m'avez fait trop d'honneur en m'épousant. Vous avez cru—et qui ne l'aurait cru?—que trouvant dans son mari tout ce qui peut rendre un homme aimable et estimable, et dans sa situation tous les plaisirs honnêtes, l'opulence et la considération, une femme raisonnable ne pouvait manquer d'être heureuse. Mais je ne suis pas une femme raisonnable, vous et moi l'avons vu trop tard (117). [You are however wrong on one account: you honored me too much by marrying me. You believed—and who would not have believed it?—that, finding in her husband all that can make a man lovable and estimable, and in her situation all honest pleasures, opulence and consideration, a reasonable woman could not fail to be happy: but I am no reasonable woman; you and I have realized it too late.]

The link established between marriage and happiness corresponds to a modern notion of the married couple. In her striving to perfection, Mrs. Henley is a very modern wife. Just before leaving London to settle with her husband in the country, she had dreamed of becoming "la meilleure femme, la plus tendre belle-mère, la plus digne maîtresse de maison que l'on eût jamais vue" (104) [the best wife, the most tender step-mother, the most worthy housewife that was ever seen]. Because this marriage is of her own doing, she sees it not only as the functional association of two persons in order to procreate, to continue the lineage, and to transmit wealth, but also as a strong affective bond, with its own dynamics that suppose a dedicated contribution of the individual to the benefit of the relationship. As a consequence, Mrs. Henley's affective energy is centered on her rapport with her husband. As the young Mrs. Henley has placed high expectations on married life as a source of personal success and happiness, she perceives its failure as a traumatic experience, all the more poignant in that no external factor (such as arranged marriage or love for another man still found in *Julie*) can be held accountable for it. While Rousseau still uses external elements to undermine the Wolmar couple, Charrière demystifies Rousseau's ideal pair by planting the seeds of its destruction inside the private conjugal walls.

Since no paternal constraint, no past illicit passion, no jealousy, no threat of adultery endangers their relationship, what exactly imperils the Henleys' marriage? Mrs. Henley indirectly answers this question at the beginning of her fourth letter:

> Je vous entretiens ma chère amie, de choses bien peu intéressantes, et avec une longueur, un détail!—mais c'est comme cela qu'elles sont dans ma tête; et je croirais ne vous rien dire, si je ne vous disais pas tout. Ce sont de petites choses qui m'affligent ou m'impatientent, et me font avoir tort. Ecoutez donc encore un tas de petites choses (112). [I talk to you, my dear friend, about things without interest, at too great a length and with too many details!—but so they are in my head; and I would feel as if I said nothing if I did not tell you everything. It is small things which afflict or irritate me, and put me in the wrong. Listen then to a heap of small things.]

Their relationship is endangered by "a heap of small things." Aware of the lack of diversion in her life, she admits to focusing too much on domestic affairs, such as the education of her step-daughter, the replacement of wallpaper and furniture, the unfortunate acquisition of a cat, the affair of her chambermaid with a neighboring farmer, the argument about a dress that she wears at a ball. With regard to Mrs. Henley's personal story, these incidents illustrate her incompatibility with Mr. Henley, and their accumulation expresses the emptiness of her life. More importantly for my purpose, these episodes engage problems of education and mothering that greatly preoccupied Rousseau. In order to complete the assessment of Charrière's critique of *Julie*'s seemingly perfect world, I shall consider not so much the filiation of ideas as the way these issues are incorporated into **Mistriss Henley**'s plot.

While Rousseau makes education and parenting the topic of a single enlightened conversation among Julie, Wolmar and Saint-Preux (who narrates it in letter 3 of part V), Charrière stages the issue in a series of short quarrels between husband and wife, concerning the clothes suited for her step-daughter, the teaching of La Fontaine fables, their diverging views on the future of their unborn child, and maternal breast-feeding. In *Julie*, the pages devoted to education are didactic and summarize major principles developed at length in *Emile*. Consequently, Julie's and Wolmar's ideas on the education of their sons are in full harmony. She will take care of them until they reach the age to leave the "gynécée" and come under the guidance of their father and Saint-Preux, their future tutor. Regarding the education of Henriette (Claire's daughter, whom Julie considers her daughter), Wolmar has nothing to say, since men cannot be involved in girls' education, and this discussion is absent from *Julie* insofar as "les principes en sont si différents qu'ils méritent un entretien à part" (585; V, 3). [Its principles are so different that they deserve a separate discussion.] In *Julie,* education is a segregated activity according to the children's age and sex, while in **Mistriss Henley,** all aspects of child-rearing (of male and female children) concern both parents, and constitute a potentially problematic endeavor as a source of conflict between them.[27]

What unifies the Wolmars divides the Henleys. A case in point is provided by La Fontaine's *Fables*. On this topic, Julie peacefully expresses ideas that have Wolmar's full approbation:

> Et convaincue que les fables sont faites pour les hommes, mais qu'il faut toujours dire la vérité nue aux enfants, je supprimai La Fontaine. . . . Je veux aussi l'habituer de bonne heure à nourrir sa tête d'idées et non de mots: c'est pourquoi je ne lui fais rien apprendre par cœur (581-82; V, 3). [And convinced that fables are meant for adults but that one must always tell the naked truth to children, I suppressed La Fontaine. . . . I also want to get him into the habit of feeding his mind with ideas and not with words: this is why I never have him learn anything by heart.][28]

In **Mistriss Henley,** the same topic is the pretext for a dispute between Mrs. Henley and her husband. As a good Rousseauian father (although he does not strictly go by the book on Rousseau's principles regarding geography and history), Mr. Henley condemns the teaching of the fable "Le Chêne et le Roseau": " 'Elle récite à merveille,' dit M. Henley; 'mais comprend-elle ce qu'elle dit? Il vaudrait mieux peut-être mettre dans sa tête des vérités avant d'y mettre des fictions: l'histoire, la géographie . . . ' " (105). ['She recites beautifully,' said Mr. Henley, 'but does she understand what she is saying? Maybe it would be better to teach her truths before teaching her fictions: history, geography. . . .'] The short exchange that ensues so baffles Mrs. Henley that she leaves the room in tears. Unlike M. de Wolmar, who considers Julie as a disciple,[29] Mr. Henley does not share his philosophical maxims with his wife and instead utters snap judgments at specific moments. Such patterns govern all their discussions, including those on education, in which he preaches modesty and simplicity in realms as disparate as clothing suited for girls and moral principles instilled in children. These animated confrontations are a far cry from the Wolmars' serene tone in their hour-long conversation, during which they appear to be less than literary characters, mere conduits for the philosophy of their author. In contrast, by weaving the topic of education into the plot of the novel, Charrière not only gives an account of how a couple comes to grip with new concerns, but also denounces the possible shortcomings of the models presented by Rousseau in his didactic novel.

As spokesmen of reason and philosophy, both Wolmar and Mr. Henley show interest in the pregnancy of their wives. Talking about her first pregnancy, Julie valorizes the *philosophe* in her husband:

> Durant ma première grossesse, effrayée de tous mes devoirs et des soins que j'aurais bientôt à remplir, j'en parlais souvent à M. de Wolmar avec inquiétude. Quel meilleur guide pouvais-je prendre en cela qu'un observateur éclairé qui joignait à l'intérêt d'un père le sang-froid d'un *philosophe?* (561; V, 3). [During my first pregnancy, in fear of all the duties I would have to fulfill and of all the care I would have to give, I often imparted my worries to M. de Wolmar. What better guide could I take for this matter than an enlightened observer who reconciled the concern of a father with the controlled attitude of a *philosophe?*]

As a disciple of her husband, Julie harmonizes both roles (husband and *philosophe*) and attributes to the *philosophe* the ability to know what is best for women. Pregnancy, as a particular moment in the life of a woman, is not discussed, but rather what follows it. At stake is the larger issue of the rearing of men, and not the specific preoccupations and needs of the expectant mother. Her concerns—maternal "duties" and "care" for the infant—reflect those of male *philosophes* and their thoughts on the role to be played by women in the educational process. Mrs. Henley has a very different position on the question, as illustrated by the discussion on breast-feeding.

During her pregnancy, ridden by anxieties about nursing, Mrs. Henley focuses on female physicality, and especially on the physicality of motherhood, to address sexuality and reproduction from the woman's point of view. She debates within herself whether or not to breastfeed her child and (rationally) considers the pros and cons: against it, the burden and fatigue involved and the damage to a woman's figure, and in its favor, the pleasure of bonding with the child and above all, her sense of duty joined to the "humiliation d'être regardée comme incapable et indigne de remplir ce devoir" (119) [humiliation of being considered unable and unworthy to fulfill this duty]. She feels that her body escapes her control through the moral pressure placed on mothers for the well-being of their children. Her attempt to hold a dialogue with her husband leads to a sermon, which once more reinforces her fears and hurts her more than it comforts her:

> A son avis, rien au monde ne pouvait dispenser une mère du premier et du plus sacré de ses devoirs, que le danger de nuire à son enfant par un vice de

tempérament ou des défauts de caractère, et il me dit que son intention était de consulter le docteur M. son ami, pour savoir si mon extrême vivacité et mes fréquentes impatiences devaient faire préférer une étrangère. De moi, de ma santé, de mon plaisir, pas un mot. (120) [According to him nothing in the world could excuse a mother from the first and most sacred of her duties, except the danger of harm to her child through a defect in her temperament or in her personality, and he told me that his intention was to take the advice of his friend, doctor M., in order to know whether my extreme liveliness and my frequent impatience would justify choosing a wet-nurse. Not a single word about me, about my health, about my pleasure.]

As physiocrats and *philosophes* warned against a decline in the population, a new valorization of children's lives (also preached by doctors[30]) engendered in large part the doctrine of motherhood that prevailed in the second half of the eighteenth century. Rousseau made it readily available to those reading literature, particularly in passages of *Emile*.[31] Mrs. Henley fully measures the consequences of the double-edged argument borrowed from Rousseau, who valorized motherhood at the expense of the woman's other needs (emotional, physical, etc.). It is precisely because her role was seen as so crucial that a woman was considered unable to fulfill it alone and had to be placed under a competent authority.[32] Mrs. Henley's new responsibility as the mother of a priceless child, so well delineated by her husband, is accompanied by a loss of self-esteem. In correlating Mr. Henley with a *philosophe* who seeks the advice of his ally, the doctor, Charrière expresses serious doubts regarding the benefits for women of these recently introduced educational principles that deprived them of control over their own bodies. Such discussions, in presenting the Rousseauian model as a possible source of anxiety for women and of tension in a family, make the harmony of Clarens suspect and unveil its dark side. Ultimately, what threatens the Henleys' relationship is the Rousseauian philosophy.

Through its terrifying perfection, Hollow Park appears as a territory of strangeness that underscores Mrs. Henley's alienation: "Je ne vous parlerai pas non plus de tout ce que je fais pour me rendre la campagne intéressante. Ce séjour est comme son maître, tout y est trop bien; il n'y a rien à changer, rien qui demande mon activité ni mes soins" (118). [I will not talk to you any more about everything I did to make the country interesting for me. This dwelling is like its master, everything is too nice; there is nothing to change, nothing requiring my activity or my care.] As a woman from the city, she is a stranger in a rural environment which she does not understand and where she feels out of place. Any attempt on her part to contribute to her new environment leads to unfortunate events. Even her chambermaid disturbs the status quo by attracting the attention of a young farmer and breaking up his marriage to the daughter of Hollow Park's housekeeper. The moving about of old furniture and the removal of the portrait of the first Mrs. Henley from her room bear witness to her effort not to be a stranger any more in what should be her house: "Je ne dois pas être une étrangère jusque dans ma chambre" (106). [I must not be a stranger in my own room.] She fails in this endeavor, and in her last letter, concedes that her estrangement from her husband has reached its apex. After another excruciating conversation during which he announces his refusal of a prestigious position at court and in the parliament, Mrs. Henley admits to being torn between "l'estime que m'arrachait tant de modération, de raison, de droiture dans mon mari et l'horreur de me voir étrangère à ses sentiments, si fort exclue de ses pensées, si inutile, si isolée" (122) [the esteem forced from me by so much moderation, reason, right-mindedness in my husband and the horror of feeling so estranged from his feelings, so excluded from his thoughts, so useless, so isolated]. The destructive power of their marriage leads to the dissolution of her self, inscribed in the fainting fit that follows this moment of unbearable internal tension.

Her growing awareness of being a stranger is paralleled by her inability to secure a stable position in the privacy of her home. Her correspondence opens with a fear of being identified by her husband with *Le mari sentimental*'s selfish Mme Bompré, a sign that her self-image rests on very unstable grounds. Subsequently, she becomes haunted by images of other women with whom she compares herself, only to reinforce her sense of failure and displacement. In the privacy of her home, she replaces Mr. Henley's first wife, whose portrait hangs in her bedroom, and is very conscious of her inadequacy as a substitute mother. In her social circle, she feels an absolute misfit in the presence of Lady Bridgewater, magnificent through her elegance and simplicity, and of Miss Clairville, a young and modest country woman to whom her husband pays much attention. Their seemingly superior company subjects her to a vertigo of comparison which casts her into a well of self-loathing. The ball scene, during which Mr. Henley criticizes the dress her aunt sent from London, attests to her identity crisis: "Je me déplaisais, j'étais mal à mon aise" (115). [I disliked myself, I felt uneasy.]

Under these circumstances, Mrs. Henley's correspondence appears as the only means to break her solitude and her silence while scrutinizing the causes of her alienation. The confession of absolute loneliness, "Je suis seule, personne ne sent avec moi" (107) [I am alone, nobody feels with me], echoes Claire's situation at the end of *Julie*: "Je suis seule au milieu de tout le monde" (744; VI, 13) [I am alone amid everyone], allowing "a glimpse [here] of the unspeakable solitude at the heart of all relationships that every other page of the book has worked to transcend or conceal or deny," to quote Tony Tanner.[33] Through this line written from Claire to Saint-Preux after Julie's death, Tanner explicates a fundamental component of Rousseau's novel: idealization. In Charrière's novel, denial and concealment (through idealized situations and characters) give way to a lucid confrontation with the belief that only family life will bring back order and happiness. The utopia of the perfect husband in the perfect home is replaced by a rigorous observation of the cruel absence of communication in the family. She achieves this through a plot that leaves no room for complacency, and by the same token, is deprived of a major characteristic used (by men) to describe women's fiction: the use of imagination. Repeating a truism about women's talents in fiction writing, Choderlos de Laclos writes in a famous epistolary exchange with Marie-Jeanne Riccoboni:

> Peut-être alors, conviendront-ils [les lecteurs] que c'est aux femmes seules qu'appartiennent cette sensibilité précieuse, cette imagination facile et riante qui embellit tout ce qu'elle touche, et crée les objets tels qu'ils devraient être; mais que les hommes condamnés à un travail plus sévère, ont toujours suffisamment bien fait quand ils ont rendu la nature avec exactitude et fidélité. [Perhaps then, will they agree that women alone possess this precious sensibility, this easy and cheerful imagination that embellishes everything it touches, and creates objects as they should be; but men, who are condemned to a harsher labor, have always acquitted themselves when they have rendered nature exactly and faithfully.][34]

On the contrary, Charrière refuses to play with imagination or to embellish her story. It is not fortuitous that Clarens crumbles to give way to Hollow Park. Testing Rousseau's ideals in a hypothetical marriage, Charrière cannot protect the woman against the negative impact of doctrinaire self-control. After all, being human involves uncontrollable emotions.[35] In contrast to Rousseau, who idealizes reason and self control in *Julie*'s marriage narrative while creating imaginary models and situations, Charrière condemns reason by paradoxically discarding from her novel's plot anything that would cater to readers' imaginations.

Even Mrs. Henley's attempt to dissect and question her lack of control—her correspondence—comes to an end. Witness to her deep identity crisis, her last letter simultaneously announces her prospect of giving life and repeatedly hints at her possible death. As an apparently open-ended conclusion to the novel, this ultimate message leaves us with the bitter-sweet taste of a puzzling alternative:

> Je ne suis qu'une femme, je ne m'ôterai pas la vie, je n'en aurai pas le courage; si je deviens mère, je souhaite de n'en avoir jamais la volonté; mais le chagrin tue aussi. Dans un an, dans deux ans, vous apprendrez, je l'espère que je suis raisonnable et heureuse, ou que je ne suis plus (122). [I am only a woman and I will not take my life, I will not be courageous enough; if I become a mother, I hope not to want death; but sorrow also kills. In one year, in two years, you will hear, I hope, that I am reasonable and happy, or that I am no more.]

If the alternative to death is happiness (based on reason), happiness becomes a simulacre, and acquires a macabre flavor. This is not surprising since the novel emphasizes the inadequacy of reasonable behavior and its inability to secure satisfactory relationships, particularly in the private realm of the family. Mrs. Henley's acceptance of self-control, through the permanent suppression of affects and emotions, will only confirm the erasure of her self, by annihilating her ability to quietly challenge her husband's order. In *Mistriss Henley*, neither disease nor accident nor deathbed scene is necessary to signify the death of a woman. Charrière resorts to no external devices, and relies on the internal dynamics of the Henley family. Susan Lanser is right to state that the alternative "marriage *or* death" gives way to the collusion "marriage *as* death" (53) and that "*Mistriss Henley*'s apparent 'open' ending is not open at all. Mistriss Henley the character and *Mistriss Henley* the text, court death in order to make utterly clear that marriage in Mr. Henley's patriarchal terms—the terms of the heroine's text—is no life at all" (54).[36] Mrs. Henley's death—symbolic or "real"—prepared in the quiet, confined, and smothering atmosphere of Hollow Park sparks fundamental questions regarding what might be gained by women from the reforms suggested by Rousseau and other men in the preceding decades of the century. Heiress of Enlightenment ideas and ideals, Charrière participates in the ongoing debate about such issues as the extent of freedom in the choice of a spouse, the conditions of a harmonious married life, and the education of children: regarding marriage matters, freedom of choice is no panacea, and in domestic affairs "reason" surely cannot claim victory.

As a polemical novel, **Mistriss Henley** entered a much wider debate than its framing publication (*Le mari sentimental*) suggests. Reading in pairs (through a parallel with Julie's marriage narrative) proves rewarding as it highlights the far-reaching implications of the novel. In taking readers into a field of scrutiny that French novels (by women and men) had neglected until Rousseau and in radicalizing this new option (through the centrality of marriage as a personal relationship between two individuals and the integration of issues dear to Rousseau in this "trivial" plot), Charrière denounces the pretense of happiness implied by Julie's conjugal practices and shows the possible fallacies of Julie's idealized model of private relationships. The price exerted by idealization is tragic: the sacrifice of the woman's self. Remarkably, though confined to the domestic realm, the novel opens outward on a public debate concerning women's private role and status. Far from being limiting, Charrière's choice of such an intimate plot in **Letters de Mistriss Henley** vindicates the right of the private woman to enact a quiet, but pervasive, revolution.

Notes

[1] Nicolas Sébastien Roch de Chamfort, *Products of Perfected Civilization,* trans. W. S. Merwin (San Francisco: North Point Press, 1984).

[2] Isabelle de Charrière, *Lettres de Mistriss Henley, œuvres complètes* 8 (Amsterdam: Van Oorschot; Genève: Slatkine Reprints, 1980). All references in the text come from this edition. Except where otherwise indicated, translations are mine. The term "tradition" refers not so much to the novel's form (epistolary and "monovocal," quite frequent in the period) as to its plot.

[3] A history of its publication can be found in the introduction to the above edition. Following a first publication in Geneva in 1784, the Parisian edition appeared without her authorization in 1785 and, in the *Journal de Paris* of May 1786, she disavowed more particularly the apocryphal "Justification de M. Henley," in which Mr. Henley expresses remorse about the death of his wife subsequent to childbirth. The Parisian edition is anonymous and none of the reviewers seems very much concerned with the identity of the author(s). The *Année littéraire* does not raise the question. In the *Mercure de France,* the novelists are differentiated, since the reviewer refers to the author of *Le mari sentimental* as the author of *Camille, ou Lettres de deux filles de ce siècle* (without mentioning any name) and attributes *Lettres de Mistriss Henley* to Mme de C. . . . de Z. Even recently, the confusion about authorship has led Béatrice Didier to attribute both novels to Isabelle de Charrière in *L'écriture-femme* (Paris: P. U. F., 1981).

[4] *Mercure de France,* no. 16 (22 avril 1786), 186 (republished by Slatkine Reprints, 1974).

[5] *Année littéraire* 8, lettre VII (1785): 270.

[6] The polemical aspect of the relationship between the two novels recalls legal briefs called "factums" written by lawyers in defense of their clients. They were usually presented in pairs to the judge, since each, representing a different party, gave a very different version of the facts. The judicial metaphor is also suggested by Marie-Paule Laden, who sees *Mistriss Henley* as a self trial: " 'Quel aimable et cruel petit livre': Madame de Charrière's *Mistriss Henley,*" *French Forum* 11 (September, 1986): 287-99.

[7] In 1790, Charrière published an *Eloge de Jean-Jacques Rousseau* that was first written for a literary competition organized by the Académie française; she was involved with her friend DuPeyrou in the polemic surrounding the publication of the second part of *The Confessions.* Throughout her correspondence there are numerous references to Rousseau's works.

[8] "Les gens du bel air, les femmes à la mode, les grands, les militaires: voilà les acteurs de tous vos romans. Le raffinement du goût des villes, les maximes de la cour, l'appareil du luxe, la morale épicurienne: voilà les leçons qu'ils prêchent, et les préceptes qu'ils donnent." *Julie ou la Nouvelle Héloïse,* Seconde Préface (Paris: Bibl. de la Pléiade, Gallimard, 1961), 2:19. All references in the text come from this edition. [People of high rank, fashionable women, nobility, military men: here are the protagonists of all your novels. The affectedness of city taste, maxims of the court, luxury, epicurian morals: here are the lessons that they preach and the precepts that they convey.] All translations of *Julie* are mine. The only modern translation is abridged: *Julie or the New Eloise,* trans, and abridged by Judith H. McDowell (University Park: Pennsylvania State University Press, 1968).

[9] Nancy K. Miller, "Men's Reading, Women's Writing: Gender and the Rise of the Novel," *Yale French Studies* 75 (1988): 48-49. In this article, Nancy Miller discusses canon formation using Françoise de Graffigny's *Lettres d'une Péruvienne* as a paradigm for the way literary historians have treated women's writing.

[10] Among others, Gagnebin and Raymond, in notes of the Pléiade edition of Rousseau's œuvres complètes, Joseph Boone in *Tradition Counter Tradition* (Chicago: University of Chicago Press, 1987), 43-45, and Jean-Louis Lecercle in *Rousseau et l'art du roman* (Paris: Armand Colin, 1969), chapter 3.

[11] "Il n'a pas pu éviter de confier à ses personnages les thèmes qui l'obsédaient, à tel point que ce livre a pu être qualifié de synthèse de sa pensée." *Rousseau et l'art du roman,* 73, with a reference to M. B. Ellis, *Julie or La Nouvelle Héloïse: A Synthesis of Rousseau's Thought* (Toronto: University of Toronto Press, 1949). For reactions of Rousseau's contemporaries to *Julie,* see Lecercle, 72.

[12] "Quant à l'autre roman [*Mistriss Henley*], insignifiant comme peinture de mœurs et comme intrigue, il reflète d'une façon intéressante l'état moral de l'auteur à cette époque de sa vie. *Mistriss Henley ou la femme sentimentale* n'est guère autre chose que la plainte de son âme endolorie. On ne peut comprendre *Mistriss Henley* que si l'on a lu le *Mari sentimental* de Samuel de Constant, dont elle est en quelque sorte la contrepartie." *Madame de Charrière et ses amis,* abridged

edition (Paris: Attinger, 1927), 149 (two-volume original 1905). Other perspectives have been offered more recently in doctoral dissertations by Teresa Lluch Myintoo (Berkeley, 1980), Christable Braunrot (Yale, 1973), and Sigyn Minier-Birk (Connecticut, 1977), and most recently by Susan S. Lanser in "Courting Death: *Roman, romantisme*, and *Mistress Henley*'s Narrative Practices," *Eighteenth Century Life* 13, n.s. 1 (February 1989). Lanser's article, which reads *Mistriss Henley* in relation to Charrière's *Caliste ou lettres écrites de Lausanne*, provides an excellent reading of both novels.

[13] Laden points out that "Charrière's fiction falls chronologically between two important bodies of correspondence—with Constant d'Hermenches, which ends in 1775, and subsequently with his nephew Benjamin Constant, whom she met during a trip in Paris in 1786—it is as if her fictional output relieved her need to confide in her friends" (290).

[14] The most thorough treatment of this question can be found in Georges May's *Le dilemme du roman au dix-huitième siècle* (Paris: P. U. F., 1963).

[15] This aspect of Charrière's prose-fiction has been widely recognized, as is clear from the titles of articles such as: Suzanne Muhlemann, "Madame de Charrière ou un regard lucide," *Documentatieblad* 27-29 (June 1975): 141-57, or S. Dresden, "Madame de Charrière et le goût du témoin," *Neophilologus* 45 (October 1961): 261-78.

[16] Jean-Louis Flandrin, *Familles. Parenté, maison, sexualité dans l'ancienne société* (1976; reprint, Paris: Seuil, 1984); James Traer, *Marriage and the Family in Eighteenth-Century France* (Ithaca: Cornell University Press, 1980).

[17] In spite of slight divergences, the freedom of choice of a partner remains one of the major claims of male Enlightenment thinkers regarding marriage.

[18] Numerous variations on themes such as the absolute and abusive authority of parents opposed to their daughter's marriage with the man of her choice, as well as the arranged and forced marriage with a man of their choice and consequential illicit love, are discussed in Pierre Fauchery's monumental thesis, *La destinée féminine dans le roman européen du dix-huitième siècle 1713-1807. Essai de gynécomythie romanesque* (Paris: Armand Colin, 1972), 132-38.

[19] Marivaux's *Vie de Marianne* constitutes an extreme example, since the narrative is interrupted as soon as a suitor proposes marriage to Marianne.

[20] She compares the traveling lord with Rousseau's Lord John from *Emile*, Book V (Pléiade, 4:853-54; Bloom translation, 470-71). This explicit reference in the early pages of the novel substantiates Charrière's unnoticed dialogue with the *philosophe*.

[21] The fact that the novel is set in England may not be fortuitous, since continental observers contended that the English enjoyed more freedom in marriage matters. Lawrence Stone points out that "foreign visitors in the mid- and late eighteenth century were unanimous in their conviction that the English enjoyed a greater freedom of choice of a marriage partner and greater companionship in marriage than on the Continent." *The Family, Sex, and Marriage in England 1500-1800*, abridged ed. (New York: Harper and Row, 1979), 214.

[22] "Le mariage de convenance, en revanche, assujettit la femme puisqu'il transforme le contrat entre familles, de type patriarcal, en un lien conjugal interindividuel, et dénué de toute dimension socio-politique. En privatisant ce lien, on rejette la femme hors de la vie publique et on la condamne exclusivement à la vie domestique"—Elisabeth de Fontenay, "Pour Emile et par Emile, Sophie ou l'invention du ménage," *Les temps modernes* 358 (1976): 1792. Erica Harth, in "The Virtue of Love: Lord Hardwicke's Marriage Act," similarly questions the progressive status of love-based marriage and concludes that it entails dependency for the woman. *Cultural Critique* 9 (Spring 1988): 3123-54.

[23] In *Lettres de Madame de Sancerre*, despite many comments on unsuccessful unions, Marie-Jeanne Riccoboni summarizes the happy ending of her novel in one sentence: "Malgré la différence de leurs caractères, ces deux aimables femmes rendirent leurs maris également heureux"—*Œuvres complètes* (Paris: 1786), 6:338. [In spite of their different personalities, these two lovable women made their husbands equally happy.]

[24] See Fauchery, 378-396.

[25] In the section "Le mariage dix-huitième siècle" (368-69), Fauchery presents adultery as a French specialty in fiction. Madame de Clèves in Lafayette's *La princesse de Clèves*, the Marquise in Crébillon fils' *Lettres de la marquise de M*****, the Presidente de Tourvel in *Liaisons dangereuses* all provide vivid examples of attempts to resist adultery.

[26] Put differently by Jean Starobinski: "*La Nouvelle Héloïse* is an 'ideological' novel. Happily for the work, however, the quest for a moral synthesis does not prevent constant slippage into passional ambivalence. It is highly significant that the success of Wolmar, the novel's rational character, is threatened by psychological ambiguities that Rousseau constantly finds in himself and that are represented in the novel by Saint-Preux and Julie. Thus the enticement of failure coun-

terbalances the aspiration to happiness, and desire for punishment coexists with the will to justification"—*Jean-Jacques Rousseau. Transparency and Obstruction,* trans. Arthur Goldhammer (Chicago and London: University of Chicago Press, 1988), 115.

[27] From the outset, we know that Mr. Henley is looking for a mother for his five-year-old daughter: "Il me parla de sa fille et du désir qu'il avait de lui donner, non une gouvernante, non une belle-mère, mais une mère" (103). [He told me about his daughter and about his desire to give her not a governess, not a stepmother, but a mother.]

[28] This issue is treated extensively in *Emile,* Book II (Pléiade, 4: 351-57; Bloom's translation, 112-16).

[29] In the letter on education, Julie insists that "je ne fais que suivre de point en point le système de M. de Wolmar; et plus j'avance, plus j'éprouve combien il est excellent et juste, et combien il s'accorde avec le mien" (437; V, 3). [I only follow scrupulously M. de Wolmar's system; and the further I go, the more I feel how excellent and just it is, and how much it matches my own system.]

[30] Tissot in *Avis au peuple sur la santé* (1761), Raulin in *De la conservation des enfants* (1767), and Buchan in *Médecine domestique* (1775) combined medical and hygienic advice with educational principles. Much information can be found in the chapter "The Preservation of Children" in Jacques Donzelot's *The Policing of Families* (New York: Pantheon Books, 1979).

[31] In the first book of *Emile,* Rousseau contributes to the age-old debate about the advantages and drawbacks of maternal breast-feeding. He defends the old idea that milk can transmit passions to the child and therefore prefers a healthy nurse to a spoiled mother (4:257; Bloom, 45). But from a moral point of view, however, no hesitation is possible: "Mais que les mères dignent nourrir leurs enfants, les mœurs vont se réformer d'elles-mèmes, les sentiments de la nature se réveiller dans tous les cœurs, l'Etat va se repeupler; ce premier point, ce point seul va tout réunir" (4:258). [But let mothers deign to nurse their children, morals will reform themselves, nature's sentiments will be awakened in every heart, the state will be repeopled. This first point, this point alone will bring everything back together (Bloom, 46).]

[32] In *Emile,* the competent authority is not a doctor but the narrator-governor: "Au nouveau-né il faut une nourrice. Si la mère consent à remplir son devoir, à la bonne heure; on lui donnera ses directions par écrit: car cet avantage a son contrepoids et tient le gouverneur un peu plus éloigné de son élève (4:272). [For the newly born a nurse is required. If the mother consents to perform her duty, very well. She will be given written instructions, for this advantage has its counterpoise and keeps the governor at something more of a distance from his pupil (Bloom, 56).]

[33] *Adultery in the Novel. Contract and Transgression* (Baltimore: The Johns Hopkins University Press, 1979), 178.

[34] "Correspondance entre Mme Ricconboni et M. de Laclos," *Œuvres complètes* (Paris: Bibl. de la Pléiade, Gallimard, 1951), 759. I use Nancy Miller's translation of this passage (50).

[35] In *Emile,* Rousseau's approval of the rational husband is spelled out in the governor's stand on virtue through self-control: "Qu'est-ce donc que l'homme vertueux? C'est celui qui sait vaincre ses affections. Car alors il suit sa raison, sa conscience, il fait son devoir, il se tient dans l'ordre et rien ne l'en peut écarter. . . . Maintenant sois libre en effet; apprends à devenir ton propre maître; commande à ton cœur, ô Emile, et tu seras vertueux" (4:818). [Who then is the virtuous man? It is he who knows how to conquer his affections; for then he follows his reason and his conscience; he does his duty; he keeps himself in order, and nothing can make him deviate from it. . . . Now be really free. Learn to become your own master. Command your heart, Emile, and you will be virtuous (Bloom, 445).]

[36] In the alternative death/marriage one can recognize the categories "dysphoric"/"euphoric" used by Nancy Miller in *The Heroine's Text* to characterize female destinies in eighteenth-century male fiction. Charrière's "unfinished" novels were criticized by Germaine de Stael in a letter to Charrière dated "27 août 1793" (*OEuvres complètes* 4:162-63). The "openness" of her novels and tales has been reassessed by feminist critics who have challenged the idea that open-ended narratives fail. See Susan K. Jackson, "The Novels of Isabelle de Charrière, or, a Woman's Work is Never Done," *Studies in Eighteenth-Century Culture* 14 (1985): 299-306, and Elizabeth MacArthur, "Devious Narratives: Refusal of Closure in Two Eighteenth-Century Epistolary Novels," *Eighteenth Century Studies* 21 (1987): 1-20.

Kathleen M. Jaeger (essay date 1994)

SOURCE: "Charrière and the Androgynous Ideal," in *Male and Female Roles in the Eighteenth Century: The Challenge to Replacement and Displacement in the Novels of Isabelle de Charrière,* Peter Lang Publishing, Inc., 1994, pp. 197-218.

[*In the essay below, Jaeger argues that Charrière strives for the equality of male and female voices in her work, rejecting the notion of sex-based difference, and advocating instead the full development of androgynous individual potential.*]

In her introduction to the feminist edition of **Caliste ou Lettres écrites de Lausanne** [Paris: Editions des Femmes, 1979] Claudine Herrmann states the following:

> L'une des idées intéressantes me paraît être que Caliste soit aimée *en remplacement* du frère, que la cousine soit épousée *à cause de son fils* et que la consolation finale soit trouvée dans une promenade touristique *avec le jeune lord*. On ne peut pas dire mieux que la femme occupe dans la société une position de remplacement où l'amour ne peut être qu'un accident fâcheux (9).

This pronouncement, that the woman occupies a position of replacement, is valid for certain social situations in Charrière's novel such as that of the captain's wife in Lausanne and that of William's wife, Lady Betty, in Bath. It also applies to the marriage between Sir Walter Finch and his wife, and the marriage of Mr. and Mistriss Henley. However, in the case of other Charrière heroines, one can "say better." Marianne de la Prise, Julie, Mme Melvill, Cécile, even Caliste, all possess in varying degrees the aggressiveness and the tenderness which, together, help to constitute the androgynous individual. Henri Meyer and William possess varying degrees of tenderness and aggressiveness as well. . . . [I wish] to illustrate that Charrière suggests, through her female and male models of representation, an androgynous ideal which approaches the definition of androgyny proposed by Carolyn Heilbrun.[1] The three areas in which Charrière anticipates Heilbrun's thinking are: 1) the androgynous individual; 2) the concept of the woman hero; and 3) the androgynous novel. In the introduction to her text Heilbrun offers the following:

> Androgyny suggests a spirit of reconciliation between the sexes; it suggests, further, *a full range of experience open to individuals* who may, as women, be aggressive, as men, tender; it suggests *a spectrum upon which human beings choose their places without regard to propriety or custom* (x, my emphasis).

Charrière's quest to achieve balance between the sexes and to permit development of the full potential of the individual is amply demonstrated in the novelistic universe she creates, and which encompasses the totality of her *oeuvre*. She presents the woman as an individual human being, capable and willing to fashion, even at great risk, a place for herself in society, although society itself may be incapable of even visualizing such a place. Marianne de la Prise possesses and admits to a knowledge of sexual matters which goes far beyond the popular conception of that to which a young, aristocratic French-Swiss woman of the times should admit. She exhibits a masculine aggressiveness by not being content merely to imagine secretly a new role for herself, but by actively actualizing that new role in order to determine her own happiness. Just as George Sand "was an individual who invented a role for herself in a world which could find no place in which such a role might be played," (Heilbrun, 87), and despite the fact that her novels demonstrate this to a much lesser degree, so, ironically, Charrière constitutes a reversal of Sand in that *her life illustrates perhaps less than her works* the successful realization of a movement toward androgyny. Marianne de la Prise's unique position, the place of the *ami,* as she defines it (and this power to define is accorded to the *male* under patriarchy), or, as I propose to define Marianne and her newly acquired space, the place of the *femme-ami,* suggests the openness of the range of experience to which Marianne has full access. The *femme-ami,* feminine in the biological sense, for Marianne remains Marianne, and yet masculine in the function she assumes in her new relationship with Henri Meyer and Julianne (she assumes a dominant position and engages in a subject not considered "feminine"), allows for a harmonious blending leading to a richer synthesis, and not the reductive division typical of a rigid gendering system that ignores talent, inclination or attribute. As the *femme-ami,* Marianne's feminine attributes are complemented by an aggressive demeanor (her lack of "réserve" and "timidité," her "moments d'extravagance" [**Lettres neuchâteloises,** Bibliothèque romande, 1971, p. 52]) which permits her to act, to intervene in Henri Meyer's life: "Je suis au fait de ses affaires; j'agis pour lui" (84). The duality of the *femme-ami* undermines the patriarchal concept of "woman's place" and anticipates the duality of the androgynous heroine, or Heilbrun's "woman hero."[2]

Activity or aggressiveness is also present in Charrière's female characters, Julie d'Arnonville and Mme Melvill. Julie's passions are not to be held within the limits of a narrow norm, i.e., within the limits of *ancienneté;* she is, rather, aggressively inventive when it comes to determining her own life, and therefore exercises her option of removing the portraits and utilizing them to achieve her own ends. In so doing she becomes, not the woman the hero pursues or loves, marries or doesn't marry, but rather the protagonist who carries the weight of the action. Her role is not determined by her "femaleness." Thus she fulfills Heilbrun's definition of the woman hero.

Mme Melvill is equally active. By refusing to define her sense of obligation in accordance with the definition demanded by society, which assumes that she will demur to Mr. Delaware's suggestion and *refuse to act* upon his proposal of marriage (this is the "feminine behavior," or the sense of modesty or self-sacrifice which Mr. Delaware believes he knows and can predict), she fulfills an obligation to her self by refusing, instead, to remain in the place in which God or fate had put her. As Sir Harry Raleigh acknowledges, "... elle était malheureuse et pauvre *par accident* et fort contre son gré, la voici riche et contente de son plein gré" (*Sir Walter Finch,* vol. 9 in *Oeuvres complètes,* Amsterdam: G.A. Van Oorschot, 1979—, p. 605, my emphasis), and *through her own activity.*

Mme Melvill is not a "héroïne de roman," a Manon Lescaut or a Julie d'Étanges, for they represent patriarchy's "answer" to the active or self-determining woman. Both Julie d'Arnonville and Mme Melvill appropriate masculine power in the sense that they exceed their feminine boundaries and perform acts uncharacteristic of their biological sex and of the image patriarchy has painted of them. More importantly, they perform these acts without retribution. Julie usurps the power of the paternal figure by dominating the Baron and essentially ridiculing his authority. Mme Melvill appropriates masculine power by determining herself Mr. Delaware's marital fate. With the possession, then, of masculine and feminine qualities Julie and Mme Melvill represent the balance of sexual characteristics and power inherent in the androgynous ideal.[3] In the successful translation of these qualities into revolutionary actions, both of Charrière's female characters can be said to illustrate a *feminist* ideal as well.[4] . . . [We] will look at other Charrière heroines who, although perhaps less feminist than those mentioned above, can yet be perceived within the context of Heilbrun's androgyny.

The Lettres écrites de Lausanne *and* Caliste: *Interchangeability as a Power Move*

The women represented in the **Lettres écrites de Lausanne** and **Caliste**—Cécile, the mother, Caliste herself—are less radically "feminist" than Mme Melvill or Julie d'Arnonville or Marianne de la Prise. The successful accomplishment of their particular revolutionary actions is less tangible, or is overshadowed by a sense of waste or loss—the curiously deformed world characterized by the "gel des énergies vitales" of which Starobinski speaks ("Présentation," in, Introduction à l'édition de *Julie ou la Nouvelle Héloïse, Lettres écrites de Lausanne,* Lausanne: Editions Rencontre, 1970, p. 66). However, each is uniquely aggressive in her determination to circumvent the male power structure, to choose her place "without regard to propriety or custom," and therefore conforms to Heilbrun's definition of the androgynous individual.[5]

Charrière observes that the strategy of replacement, or the interchangeability of women, emphasizes the prerequisites of place. When one wealthy young woman is considered as suitable as another in a marriage arrangement, the external attributes of the one are designated as equal to those of the other and therefore dominate, the individual qualities and traits thereby being reduced or eliminated. Isabelle de Charrière distances herself from this particular strategy when constructing her novelistic universe, and proposes instead a different kind of interchangeability. The Charrière universe employs an interchangeability of male and female voices, of male and female beings, and, because interchangeability continues to imply equality, this exchange of female for male, of feminine for masculine, establishes a new and additional source of power. This newly attained power can be interpreted in certain instances by what I propose to call a "power move," for it grants, in the exchange, equal yet different power to the woman that she does not otherwise possess.

The Lettres écrites de Lausanne

An example of the sliding and shifting boundaries which permit the feminine voice to articulate its desire as something other than the authorized "feminine" can be observed in the *Lettres écrites de Lausanne.* The mother's expression of her social and political views in her third letter eventually gives her access to the masculine realm in her fifth letter by enabling her to take on her cousin's husband in a direct confrontation. Rather than merely ignoring or subtly reversing her feminine challenge to the status quo as Mr. Henley might have done, the husband ". . . s'est donné la peine de faire une liste des inconvénients de mon project" (39). In so doing the *cousin* (masculine) is granting a certain power to the *cousine* (feminine) by crossing, ever so slightly, that frontier separating male and female as rational and irrational beings. By taking her voice *seriously enough* to warrant a written rebuttal on his part, he is according the mother her own portion of masculine rationality, which she justly deserves, and ignoring momentarily her biological femininity. In short, he acknowledges her androgynous nature. And, the elimination of definition by gender is precisely what the mother is seeking: "Ecoutez mon cousin: la première fois qu'un souverain me demandera l'explication de mon projet, dans l'intention d'en faire quelque chose, je l'expliquerai et le détaillerai de mon mieux . . ." (40). Implicit in her declaration is the desire to have someone/anyone/a *male* question her about the feasibility or practicality of her idea while yet forgetting or ignoring the fact that *he,* the interrogator, is a *man* and that *she,* the visualizer of a new order, is a *woman.* If biological difference, which declares that, automatically, being the product of a woman, her project is "mal imaginé" and "impracticable" (40), is denied, the mother's idea can be heard objectively and seriously and, if necessary, rejected on its own lack of merit and not on the basis of the gender of its initiator. Although the *cousin* states, apparently, "Il est bien d'une femme," when drawing up his list of objections, we can legitimately question whether his negative assessment is founded on "l'examen" ("s'il se trouve *à l'examen* aussi mal imaginé et aussi impracticable que vous le croyez, je l'abandonnerai courageusement" [40]), or on the loss of male (patriarchal) power which the mother's vision obviously assumes. His fear, therefore his complaint, derives from Charrière's hypothetical modification of existing reality. To those who would interpret Charrière's and the mother's vision as a feminist one, I point to the following statement by Heilbrun: "If the argument on behalf of androgyny sounds more often than not, like a feminist or "women's lib" cry, that is because of the power men now hold, and because of the political weakness of women" (xii-xix). That the *cousin* rejects the new social structure visualized by the *cousine* is evidence of the strength of patriarchy; that the *cousine* is willing and able to engage the *cousin* on his own political ground and force him to act by putting his objections into written form is a power move born of the mother's own androgynous nature.

The full range of experience and the ability to choose without regard to custom or propriety (the core of Heilbrun's definition of androgyny) describe the Lausanne mother's philosophy of education insofar as it pertains to Cécile's education. Again, there is no sense of obligation on the mother's part to adhere to the established norm for a young girl's education if individual circumstances demand substitution or improvisation. There exists a greater range of possibilities for Cécile than solely harp or dance lessons, the study of English or Italian. She experiences a freedom of choice in many respects, for the mother admits that, apart from a little math and sewing, Latin and religion, she has "laissé tout le reste au hasard" (42).

Charrière's undermining of society's displaced effort to achieve a balanced human experience, in the sense of a balance of power and obligation on the part of each sex, is clearly illustrated by the mother's discussion of male and female roles in society. Faced with Cécile's query concerning the possibility that the male sex may have happily escaped adherence to the law of virtue ("Mais, maman, les hommes n'ont-ils pas reçu les mêmes lois?" [63]), the mother replies:

> Ce que je puis vous dire, c'est que la société, qui dispense les hommes et ne dispense pas les femmes d'une loi [la loi de la vertu] que la religion paraît avoir donnée également à tous, impose aux hommes d'autres lois qui ne sont peut-être pas d'une observation plus facile (63).

The recognition of androgyny is inherent ideally in religious law which makes no gender distinction, demanding equally from male and female in terms of their equal status as human beings. Social law, however, and in the eyes of the mother, attempts to achieve its own balance through a philosophy of "separate but equal" based on the separation of the sexes. The mother continues:

> Je ne trouve pas . . . que la condition des hommes soit . . . si extrêmement différente de celle des femmes . . . Croyez-vous, par exemple, que, si la guerre se déclare, il soit bien agréable à votre cousin de nous quitter au mois de mars pour aller s'exposer à être tué ou estropié, à prendre, couché sur la terre humide et vivant parmi des prisonniers malades, les germes d'une maladie dont il ne guérira peut-être jamais? (63-64).

A fictitious balance is realized between the sexes by patriarchal decree: because men are "aggressive," they will fight the wars, and because women must live up to a "virginal" image, they will practice virtue. This is fiction, nonetheless, and not the "balanced human experience" of androgyny (Heilbrun, x), for these human beings, male and female alike, *do not choose* these places which they occupy. As the mother insists, ". . . c'est le devoir, c'est la profession de toute femme que d'être sage. *Elle ne se l'est pas choisie, mais la plupart des hommes n'ont pas choisi la leur*" (64, my emphasis). Charrière subtly subverts the "fictitious" balance achieved by societal or patriarchal authority by implying that the only "balanced human experience"[6] which the sexes enjoy is their *equally imposed lack of freedom to choose* according to talent or inclination alone.

Further justification for androgyny as represented by Cécile and the mother lies in their appropriation of mobility. Mobility is a recognized masculine prerogative, for it is an overt expression of the power accorded to the male under patriarchy. Both women, mother and daughter, exercise options of mobility, however, in an effort to obtain a share of the power necessary to determine their own destiny. Cécile is aggressive in her thinking: her masculine capacity to reason permits her to evaluate her situation with the young English lord and realize that she and her mother must change their life style by becoming more "masculinely" mobile. We do not need to go so far as to say that Cécile is a calculating or devious young woman. There is, however, a definite period of reflection during which she ponders her circumstances and appears to arrive at a conclusion via some manner of deductive reasoning:

> Ce matin vous savez que nous n'avons presque parlé. Eh bien! je me suis occupée pendant notre silence de la manière dont il me conviendrait que vous voulussiez vivre pendant quelque temps . . . Il me semble qu'il faudrait moins rester chez nous, et que ces trois ou quatre hommes nous trouvassent moins souvent seules . . . Il vaudra mieux, au risque de s'ennuyer, aller chercher le monde (79).

The mother and daughter refuse to be bound by the physical limits of their own home and by the unnecessary and self-imposed obligation to receive passively the visits of the various young gentlemen. Cécile's desire to frequent Lausanne society, to exercise mobility by socializing in one home and then another in a constant round of activity, imitates the mobility of the foreigners themselves who come and go, passing in and through Lausanne, which itself acts the role of passive female awaiting *their* determination of *her* (her female inhabitants') destiny.

The androgynous nature of Cécile is also evident in her pleasure in anticipating a world of work—a masculine option—in Holland or England. In these countries her ambition and individual talents might very well permit her to enlarge upon the strictly "feminine" role of wife which Swiss or Lausanne society has assigned to her. Cécile is open to a far wider range of experience—a career or an occupation, a female (mother's) friendship, as opposed to the constrained existence imposed by a society that chooses her role for her by telling her she must marry and have children in order to be happy. With multiple options Cécile would have numerous routes by which to achieve happiness; with only a narrow norm to which to conform happiness is reduced to a single path which, if not followed, signifies the absence of happiness, or unavoidable despair. Cécile herself states: ". . . si je n'avais rien à faire que d'être demoiselle au milieu de gens qui auraient des maris, des amants, des femmes, des maîtresses, des enfants, je pourrais trouver cela bien triste . . ." (90).

Finally, the mother builds upon Cécile's initiative of mobility by initiating, herself, a move destined to restore some sense of autonomy to her daughter's life. The anticipated sojourn in Provence and the south of France and the preliminary move to the country house outside Lausanne are steps taken which record the passage from a passive or feminine position, remaining within the limits of the Lausanne home, to an active or masculine position, i.e., they demonstrate the shifting of the subject from one gender position to another, or the free play typical of the androgynous subject.

The quest for a balance of power between the feminine and the masculine, or the "moves" of Cécile and the mother in response to the "moves" of the young lord and his companion, William, seems to be inspiration for Charrière's structuration of plot. (The young lord and *l'Anglais* have also accomplished "moves" within Lausanne as well, from one residence to another.) Indeed, these "moves" and the struggle for power, or equal accessibility to the power structure, which they represent, have already been symbolically suggested by Cécile's and the young lord's moves on the chessboard in their frequent matches. The "marche des échecs" and the "mouvements de l'âme," or the simultaneous movement of game pieces and emotions, reflects a particular balance attained, if only momen-

tarily, between the two opponents in their chess game and in the emotional game in which both are investing their desire. The mother describes this balance, one emotion for another or emotions equally experienced, that is at first achieved in the match:

> Assise entre les deux tables, je travaillais et regardais jouer . . . ces deux enfants, qui ce soir-là avaient l'air d'enfants beaucoup plus qu'à l'ordinaire; car ma fille se méprenant sans cesse sur le nom et la marche des échecs, cela donnait lieu à des plaisanteries aussi gaies que peu spirituelles. *Une fois le petit lord s'impatienta de son inattention, et Cécile se fâcha de son impatience. Je tournai la tête. Je vis qu'ils boudaient l'un et l'autre* (60, my emphasis).

The emotion Cécile experiences immediately following this moment—the young lord takes and kisses her hand as she is about to pick up a fallen pawn—demands to be acknowledged as equal to his own gesture, just as her anger was the counterbalance to his impatience. When, within the prescribed code for feminine behavior, this emotion *cannot* be acknowledged ("Ignorez-vous, ma chère Cécile . . . combien les hommes sont enclins à mal penser et à mal parler des femmes?" [61]), it is Cécile's *androgynous cry for a more balanced human experience* which resounds: "Mais, dit Cécile, s'il y a ici de quoi penser et dire du mal, *il ne pourrait m'accuser sans s'accuser encore plus lui-même. N'a-t-il pas baisé ma main, et n'a-t-il pas été aussi troublé que moi?*" (61, my emphasis).

Caliste

Caliste is perhaps Isabelle de Charrière's most androgynous work if we consider Heilbrun's two definitions of the androgynous novel: 1) in androgynous novels "the reader identifies with the male and female characters equally;" and, 2) in the androgynous novel "the sense of waste, of lost spiritual and sexual power, of equality of worth between the two sexes, is presented with no specific cry for revolution, but with a sense of a world deformed" (58, 59). The reader's equal identification with Caliste and with William,[7] and the spirit of reconciliation which appears between Caliste and William, between William and his father, and between the father and Caliste, although at the bitter cost of great potential for love and happiness, appear to satisfy Heilbrun's definitions.

Nonetheless, the balance of power inherent in androgyny also requires that Caliste realize a power move if we are to consider her as truly androgynous, and not merely a victim of society's authority.[8] The interchangeability of male and female, or the male being "replaced" by the female, although only in the sense that the female acquires a *new, different, and yet equal* position of power, can be illustrated by the relationship between William, Caliste, and William's deceased brother. Caliste does not wish to appropriate that space belonging to the departed brother and constituting a bond even death cannot sever. She wishes simply to effect a transfer of energy or impulse from the brother to herself by means of establishing a new position which is powerful in itself and unique to her. Her words, "heureuse la femme qui remplacera ce frère chéri" (119), imply the shift in power from a brother who signifies absence and the sacrifice of present for past to a woman who signifies presence and the fulfillment of the needs of self. That the two, Caliste and the brother, represent differing, yet equally powerful, positions can be construed from Caliste's continuing remarks: "Vous n'aimerez pas une femme autant que vous l'aimiez; mais si vous aviez seulement cette tendresse que vous pouvez encore avoir, si on se croyait ce que vous aimez le mieux à présent que vous n'avez plus votre frère . . ." (119). What Caliste loses to the deceased brother, or to the male sex—a greater degree of emotional attachment (the woman will be loved less)—she regains via the fact that she is a living being able to give and receive love, i.e., her inferiority in terms of gender is adequately balanced by her superiority in terms of presence. Therefore, her positionality is one of equality or interchangeability despite its difference as a source of power. Achieving this position is a victory, a power move for Caliste's feminine voice whose presence speaks, as opposed to the masculine voice of the brother whose absence imposes eternal silence.

The displacement, or re-direction of desire, which Caliste's and William's situation is obliged to produce under the conditions meted out by eighteenth-century society, can also be interpreted as a power move. The void created in William by the necessity of withdrawing from Caliste is partially filled by the addition of a new and mutual attachment to the young Sir Harry. This fact illustrates, certainly, the ability of the masculine voice to be interchangeable, in turn, with the feminine voice. In other words a series of exchanges is being choreographed by Charrière: the deceased brother is replaced, in terms of a power shift, by Caliste, and Caliste is then replaced, in terms of a second power shift, by Sir Harry. With the masculine voice of Sir Harry eventually achieving what would seem to be the final position of power, the series of exchanges, while yet demonstrating the process of androgyny at work, appears to wrest power from the female once more. However, if we are to view the relationship of Caliste and William as one yielding fulfillment of individual desire *and* societal approval—it constitutes a heterosexual relationship in accord with norms prescribing marriage and the perpetuation of the species—then we must also view the displacement William achieves through his marriage to Lady Betty as a power move for Caliste.[9] What William can achieve with Caliste—at once desire or love *and* the configuration of the authorized heterosexual couple—must, without Caliste, be achieved by the establishment of two separate relationships: the emotional union with Sir Harry and the socially approved, marital union with Lady Betty. Charrière, by inventing the double configuration of William/Sir Harry and William/Lady Betty as the "solution" to the absence of Caliste, undermines patriarchal authority which demands her absence and accords Caliste a significant power move: simply put, it requires *two* people to "replace" *one* Caliste.[10]

Novelistic Structure as a Power Move

Finally, it is through structuration of plot that one can single out yet another power move in Caliste's repertoire by noting the miscarriage she suffers upon the shock of learning that William has married Lady Betty. Let us look at Mme de Lafayette's *La Princesse de Clèves* in terms of the princess's significance as a "final daughter." By choosing an existence divided between home and convent, following the death of the Prince de Clèves, and which excludes the possibility of a life, marriage, and children with the Duc de Nemours, the Princess, and Mme de Lafayette, effectively end the perpetuation of the traditional female plot.[11] Charrière establishes a similar "final daughter" image in *Caliste* through her development of plot. Whereas the birth of a child, particularly a daughter, to Caliste would have appeared to perpetuate the unhappy destiny of the heroine—a marriage signifying the sacrifice of self—Charrière manipulates events in such a way that the pregnant Caliste loses her child when William's marriage is disclosed in sudden and startling fashion.

In *Sir Walter Finch,* as well as in *Caliste,* Charrière's development of plot is a power move in itself which acts to eliminate displacement. We recall that in *Finch* young William's sister, Felicia, represents a displacement of Sir Harry Raleigh's desire for William himself when he (Sir Harry) has lost Molly Melvill. To allow a marriage to take place between Sir Harry and Felicia would obviously continue this strategy. However, by situating Felicia in a distant America and announcing Sir Walter's intention to marry her to John Lee, if they appear to be compatible, Charrière effectively rules out this possibility. Likewise, in *Caliste* the baby daughter born to Lady Betty and William is destined to serve Caliste as a compensation for William himself by virtue of her resemblance to her father. Charrière states, nonetheless, that "quoi qu'elle n'ait que dix-huit mois, on voit déjà qu'elle ressemblera à sa mère" (176). In choosing to deny a resemblance to William in the case of the child, or proximity in the case of Felicia, Charrière puts an end to displacement and realizes a variation on the "final daughter" image. Each of these "new" females, Felicia and William's baby daughter, by *not* serving to compensate for the absence of another desired and unobtainable individual, becomes a "final daughter": she terminates the practice of displacement and maintains at least the possibility of some autonomy over her own life.[12] Caliste, also, exhibits a degree of autonomy through her miscarriage, and this is the power move to which I refer: Charrière, in novelistically "commanding," through her narration, Caliste's body to reject the baby who represents the continuation of society's restrictions on woman's life, denies that which the dominant male culture would desire.

Charrière's development of plot in the **Letters écrites de Lausanne** reveals the fundamentally androgynous structure of her novelistic universe. The mother from Lausanne, by virtue of her status as widow, slips quite easily into a dominant or masculine role wherein her voice assumes authority. It is the mother/narrator/correspondent who appropriates language and the control which language grants. Her epistolary role permits her voice to dominate all other voices through the power of her pen, and it is she alone who determines what the reader will know. It is the mother to whom Cécile looks for guidance, the one in whom she confides her fears, her questions, and her strategies to achieve autonomy. It is the mother who concerns herself with her daughter's marriage situation and her lack of fortune, who determines rationally the advantages and disadvantages attached to each of the young men who appear as suitors for Cécile's hand, and who concludes, finally, that "dans ces quatre amants, il n'y a pas un mari" (34).[13] Such conclusions traditionally result from the exercise of paternal option; however, they are appropriated here by the maternal—they illustrate the shift in positionality characteristic of androgyny, and which is made possible by Charrière's choice of the widow and simultaneous elimination of the father figure.

The blending or harmonizing of masculine and feminine qualities that allows the individual to move easily back and forth within a wide spectrum of male/female roles and positions is most notably evident in Charrière's narrative options. I have alluded above to her female narrating voice, the feminine voice of the mother in Lausanne. As the novel progresses to the narrative in retrospect which is **Caliste,** the female narrating voice slips into silence and permits Charrière's male narrator, William, to assume the position of authority with regard to events, individuals, and the reader. The two voices illustrate the androgyny of which Charrière is capable.[14] Each discourse likewise illustrates the blend of the masculine and feminine with which each narrator is endowed. Charrière, as the voice of William, in fact breaks with tradition, with Didier's noted "style de l'affectivité" wherein "sous les plumes féminines [on trouve] une sorte de licence à l'épanchement sans mesure, parce que la répartition traditionnelle accorde la sensibilité à la femme et l'intelligence à l'homme ("La femme à la recherche . . . ," 1988). Whereas Didier finds Charrière "plus intéressante" in her ability to suggest the female body, including its "deformities" (Cécile's "gros cou"), I find that the interest also lies in the blend or "mélange" of the mother's "feminine" qualities—her tendency to pour out her feelings, to reveal her dreams, to employ liberally the question mark and the exclamation point as a means of conveying her emotion—in harmony with her "masculine" display of reason, intelligence and foresight. This blend constitutes clearly an androgynous nature, as opposed to the traditional gender divisions. Although Rousseau's Julie and Prévost's Manon exhibit similar androgynous natures, what is of interest in Charrière vis-à-vis these male novelists is the juxtaposition of reward to retribution: Julie and Manon are punished for their challenge to patriarchal authority, made possible by their androgyny, but Charrière's mother is, on the contrary, rewarded through her pleasure in seeing Cécile become an individual, and not an imitation of herself. In the same manner William, through the "feminine" emotion he exhibits in the telling of his tragic history with Caliste ("O femmes! femmes! que vous êtes malheureuses, quand celui que vous aimez . . ." [124]), in harmony with his simple, direct, "masculine" style of narrating, represents the same blend of sentiment and expression, of emotion and intelligence, which characterizes the androgynous individual.

Let us return briefly, for the sake of comparison, to the **Lettres neuchâteloises**. In her letters to Mlle de Ville and to Henri Meyer Marianne de la Prise manifests an ability to shift from the feminine to the masculine in her discourse which is strikingly similar to that of Charrière in her movement from the narrating position of the mother to the narrating position of William. Marianne's letter to Eugénie bursts with "feminine" intuition: ". . . il m'aime. Il ne me l'a pas dit; mais il me l'aurait dit mille fois que je ne le saurais pas mieux" (84). Her response to Henri Meyer, acknowledging his declaration of love, exemplifies brief, concise, and intelligent understatement, the true litote: "Si vous vous étiez trompé, Monsieur, je serais fort embarrassée; mais pourtant je vous détromperais" (89). Marianne's gesture to Meyer is that of the masculine "friend," and to Eugénie, that of the romantically inclined and feminine "young woman" (the "femme-ami"). And, Meyer's own feminine or submissive qualities are nicely complemented by Marianne's masculine or aggressive traits. Thus, it is possible, with the balance attained, for Marianne to take charge, to intervene in Meyer's affairs and to lead him and herself, to lead *them* as a couple, or the two halves which constitute a harmonious whole, to the brink of pleasant possibilities that otherwise would never be.

Opposite-sex twins are a unique androgynous symbol because they are viewed as an original unit divided by circumstance, yet destined to be reunited by sexual love.[15] William and his brother, although not opposite-sex twins, nonetheless complement each other by virtue of their differing, individual natures, much as the natures of Henri Meyer and Marianne complement each other. Caliste remarks to William during the early stages of their relationship: "Vos courses, vos jeux, vos exercices avec votre frère vous ont rendu robuste et adroit, et *avec lui votre coeur naturellement sensible est devenu délicat et tendre*" (119, my emphasis). It is not necessary for William to have been born biologically a female in order to possess a feminine sensitivity, as Caliste observes. This sensitivity, in harmony with the more masculine nature and influence of his brother, as evidenced by the brother's authorization of "masculine" activities such as riding, games, and physical exercise, has produced an androgynous being. As Caliste acknowledges, "Je vois . . . pourquoi vous êtes tendre, doux, et pourtant un homme" (118). In her ability to create a new space, an intense yet *differing* relationship with William born of a resemblance which is metaphysical (she is capable of evoking emotions within William as the brother had done) and a difference which is biological, and which therefore promises a unique combination of sexual and emotional love and fulfillment, Caliste becomes the opposite-sex twin. Caliste and William represent Charrière's novelistically interpreted view of the original unit which has split and is destined to be reunited by sexual love: William and his brother are the unit which has been divided by the brother's death; they will be (re)united by Caliste's androgynous capacity to be interchangeable with the brother, yet individually distinct—there is resemblance but no equality—and to assure her own unique irreplaceability. Caliste's power move allows her to intercept William's lost male "half" as *female* and establish her own place as the unrepeatable combination of each.

William and the mal du siècle *hero*

Margaret Waller [in her "Cherchez la Femme: Male Malady and Narrative Politics in the French Romantic Novel," *PMLA* 104 (1989): 141-149] discusses the *mal du siècle* hero, particularly Chateaubriand's René, and the feminization of his character that is both incapacitating and empowering (142). Although Waller speaks of the "male power and prowess in eighteenth-century libertinism, which established conventions of male impunity and favored the heroine as exclusive victim" (141), it is possible arguably to state that Charrière's William, in opposition to this portrait of the libertine, bears characteristics of an early *eighteenth-century mal du siècle* hero. William's indecisiveness is an incapacitating quality. His inability to act, whether it be to refute verbally or in writing his father's letter, or to marry Caliste, is perhaps an unconscious imitation of the paternal model. This inability to "faire la moindre tentative" (*Caliste,* 126), evident in both father and son where Caliste is concerned, is comparable to what Waller describes as René's "emotional bondage" (142).

William can be said to embody the "vague des passions" attributed to René (142), not in his travels with Sir Harry or the young lord, but in the description of the total emptiness, the void he experiences following the death of his brother. It is Caliste, the woman, who restores William to physical and emotional health in Bath by restoring to a state of balance the imbalance in emotions which the brother's death had precipitated. The *vague des passions* characteristic of William is most precisely ascertained in the father's enunciation prior to William's marriage to Lady Betty. Speaking of his desire for grandchildren who might replace his lost loved ones, who might replace *William himself,* the father declares: ". . . vous n'avez jamais été et ne serez peut-être jamais à vous, à moi, ni à la raison" (*Caliste,* 153).

The narcissism that Waller finds in René's ability to take pleasure in the depth of his grief at Amélie's death can also be observed in William's despair upon receiving Caliste's final letter and the eventual news of her death. William closes his letter to the mother from Lausanne with the following words: "Me voici donc seul sur la terre. Ce qui m'aimait n'est plus. J'ai été sans courage pour prévenir cette perte; je suis sans force pour la supporter" (180). His enunciation shows a similar mixture of grief, pain, *and* a sense of superiority. The "seul" distinguishes William from other males. His tragedy is profound, yet the feminine sensitivity he displays in his grief is also empowering, for it not only "sets him apart from—but also *above*—his fellow men" (Waller, 145).

Nonetheless, there are aspects of William's narration which contradict Waller's description of René or the typical *mal du siècle* hero. Whereas the "*mal du siècle* hero is incapable of social production" and the "[*mal du siècle*] novel's plot revolves around his inability to carry on society's reproduction" (Waller, 141), both statements can be countered in *Caliste*. William's marriage to Lady Betty, although a strange affair, is yet proof of William's ability to fulfill his social role as husband. Likewise, the birth of their daughter verifies that he does indeed carry on society's reproduction. (However, if the daughter, as the image of Lady Betty, represents the continuation of society and its established order, i.e., if the daughter's destiny is to be that of the mother, then Charrière's vision is indeed an ironic one.) We would have to concede that William's relationship with the young lord is a *productive* one, and not the unproductive one more typical of the *mal du siècle* hero. He accepts the role of traveling companion to the young man, not to escape Caliste or fate (their situation is basically resolved), nor to lose himself in his emotions, but to *render a service*. The young lord's father states explicitly: "Voyons si vous pourrez, si vous voudrez me rendre un grand service . . . mon fils est très jeune; cependant j'aime encore mieux l'envoyer voyager tout seul, que de le confier à qui que ce soit d'autre que vous" (169-70).

Another characteristic of the sensitive and vulnerable *mal du siècle* protagonist, according to Waller, is his inability to adapt to conventional male roles as they have been established by society: "If the hero is unable to be a man in a man's world, the reason is in part that, according to the novel's premises and early nineteenth-century notions of gender difference, he is like a woman" (142). This is refuted by William's narration. He recounts, on the contrary, his easy and pleasurable re-entry into the masculine world represented by his father's home, and the positive acknowledgement he receives from his father's friends and from society, male and female, which constitute this microcosm. Referring to the male society of "amis" and "voisins" (***Caliste***, 138), William states: "Je chassai et courus avec eux, et *j'eus le bonheur de ne leur être pas désagréable*" (138, my emphasis). William is not, therefore, the alienated or "socially emasculated" individual whom Waller finds in René (144).

Another divergence can also be noted in the two heroes. Waller suggests that René's alienation from male society derives, in part, from his marginalized position as a second son. William, on the contrary, in Charrière's structuration of plot, is not marginalized with respect to his brother: not only are the brothers twins, but, as narrator, he declares that "on n'a jamais su lequel de nous deux était l'aîné" (***Caliste***, 110).

Both novels, ***Caliste*** and *René*, are first-person narratives which constitute a specific type of literature. Waller speaks of the confession narrative, exemplified by *René*, in which

> the power that literally and figuratively frames the hero's disclosure is paternal authority. As in later mal du siècle novels, *telling a story in the first person is a rite of confession—more often than not between men* (143, my emphasis).

If we look at William's narrative in terms of the "rite of confession," we must observe, however, that he chooses to direct his confession of ***Caliste*** to the mother in Lausanne, and not to another male. It is the mother as interlocutor or correspondent who holds the power to judge and to condemn or forgive. Therefore, the bonding between confessor and interlocutor or correspondent, between William and the mother, is a bonding between male and female which anticipates androgyny.

At this point I would like to confront my conception of William as an androgynous hero with Waller's definition of the *mal du siècle* hero. The balance inherent in androgyny, to which the passages from Heilbrun's text attest, is exemplified by the male/female, confessor/interlocutor relationship that exists in ***Caliste***. In addition, the ease with which William moves back and forth between the masculine world of the father—the *maison paternelle*—and the feminine world of Caliste (in fact, throughout his narrative he is continually moving back and forth between the two), suggests the fluidity of the androgynous being who can shift from one gender position to another.

René and Amélie, according to Waller, are ideal mates. The sister is the "mirror of the self" which René desires, and "the feminine qualities which they share draw them close" (Waller, 146, 144). In the case of William and Caliste, the "ideal mates" are those who, in Charrière's universe, do *not* share similar qualities, but possess *opposing* natures, masculine and feminine qualities which complement and balance each other positively. This suggests why, as a couple, Caliste and William function successfully when Caliste is in the dominant (masculine) position and William is in the submissive (feminine) position.

In short, William appears to vacillate between a *mal du siècle* hero and an androgynous hero, depending on the circumstances. When an equilibrium can be maintained with the presence of more dominant masculine qualities to offset the proportionally more dominant feminine qualities in William's nature, i.e., when there is an overshadowing presence of a brother or male companions who enjoy riding and hunting, for example, or of a Caliste who can regulate and therefore dominate their relationship, William manifests the balance signified by the androgynous individual. However, in the absence of complementing qualities, in the absence of the brother and of Caliste, William's sensitivity predominates, and he is "feminized" in an environment that fails to offer him the "masculine." With a woman in the mold of René's Amélie, William would indeed become another René, he would indeed become, in the presence of feminizing influences, "vaporeux" and "pusillanime" (***Caliste***, 119), as Caliste clearly perceives.

The Woman Hero

Marriage in the eighteenth century, says Charrière, is most often patriarchy's overdetermination of woman's life ("woman" signifying the collective, and not the individual). For Charrière, marriage as novelistic closure is, on the contrary, reduced to possibility or circumstance, and is not each woman's ultimate destiny. Marriage depends on desire and the capacity to realize that desire. Compatibility in Charrière's novels resides in the recognition of the individual and in the specific recognition of the androgynous individual. The ability to maintain a balance between the sexes is paramount. Therefore, regardless of Cécile's inability to promise a fortune equal to that of the young lord, the mother from Lausanne can state: "Le jeune Anglais est en homme ce que ma fille est en femme" (29). This does not mean, however, in Charrière's vision of things, that marriage will provide the conclusion to the history of the young English lord and the exceptional *Lausannoise*. Marianne de la Prise in Neuchâtel reveals, rather, Charrière's philosophy on marriage as novelistic closure. Referring to her own situation with Henri Meyer, she declares: "Nous étions certainement nés l'un pour l'autre: *non pas peut-être pour vivre ensemble, c'est ce que je ne puis savoir; mais pour nous aimer*" (**Lettres neuchâteloises,** 85, my emphasis). What is implicit in Marianne's declaration is Charrière's conviction that complementary characteristics of the male and of the female, including the androgynous possibilities of the aggressive woman or the tender man, are greatly responsible for a mutual attraction which can indeed become love. *They are not sufficient, however, to produce a happy marriage.* Marianne must make a concerted effort to ensure that love, even being "born to love each other," does in fact lead to marriage. Heilbrun recognizes that the woman hero "is sustained by some sense of her own autonomy as she contemplates and searches for a destiny; she does not wait to be swept up by life as a girl is swept up in a waltz" (92). Marianne de la Prise is the modern woman hero. Her remarkable activity at the second Neuchâtel *assemblée*, with regard to Henri Meyer, is far removed from the passive attitude of a typical young, eighteenth-century *Neuchâteloise* waiting to be swept up, figuratively and literally, in the *contre-danse* of feminine destiny.

Cécile in Lausanne also fits this particular definition of the woman hero, for she both contemplates and searches, outside Lausanne, in far-off Provence, in England or Holland, for a destiny. She and the young lord appear, like Marianne and Henri Meyer, to be "made for each other," according to the mother. Why, then, is she unsuccessful, when compared to Marianne, in achieving her desire? The same transition is apparent—the transition from passive girl to active woman hero. Cécile's activity is, nevertheless, newly emerging (she is only seventeen) in comparison to that of Marianne. One might also sense that the proportion of masculine qualities (aggressiveness) to feminine qualities appears greater in Marianne than in Cécile. Likewise, the maturity seen in Henri Meyer appears considerably more significant than that of the young lord, for we recall the latter's own testimony that he is "too young" to anticipate marriage.

Caliste is a woman hero as well. Her early conduct of the relationship with William, her "regulation" of his coming and going, her efforts to communicate with the father, her trips to London and Whitehall, her acceptance of the "rival," M.M***, and her preparation of the little "drama" which climaxes in the *"C'est fait"* are not indicative of a woman waiting "for a man to come that way and furnish [her] with a destiny" (Heilbrun, 92). (This "drama" corresponds, in a less "aggressive" manner, to Cécile's strategy to force the young lord to reveal his feelings, and to Marianne's intervention in the Henri Meyer-Julianne affair.) Indeed, William alludes to Caliste's aggressiveness when he himself fails to pursue the opening furnished by Sir Harry's praise of "mistriss Calixta," a moment which could have altered the father's opinion:

> Oh! Caliste, combien vous auriez été plus courageuse que moi! Vous auriez profité de cette occasion précieuse; vous auriez tenté et réussi, et nous aurions passé ensemble une vie que nous n'avons pu apprendre à passer l'un sans l'autre (145).

What William is proposing here is that Caliste should have been the "man" and he should have been the "woman" in order for their happiness to have been realized. But, Caliste, the woman, is also unsuccessful in achieving her desire. These Charrière heroines, Marianne, Cécile, Caliste, are wonderfully diverse,[16] and it is diversity, the "mélange" which is life, that determines Caliste's failure as much as it determines Marianne's success. The uniqueness, the unrepeatable combination which signifies the *individual,* male *or* female, derives from the proportion of qualities, one to another, the particular balance of masculine and feminine, as opposed to a perfect equilibrium which Charrière defines as mediocrity. And, in regard to this proportion, the words of the mother from Lausanne are of immeasurable significance: "Changez quelque chose, vous changez tout" (**Letters écrites de Lausanne,** 88). If Marianne were less masculinely aggressive, or if Henri Meyer were less femininely sensitive, let us say, to the needs of Julianne, their constitution as a couple would perhaps be less likely or even impossible. If the young lord were something other than what he is—less young, perhaps?—his and Cécile's destiny might well be joined. And, finally, if Caliste were a little more aggressive, or William less tender and therefore less easily manipulated by society, by the father, by Caliste herself, their union might have been achieved. There is much to admire in Marianne, much to criticize in William, but each represents in Charrière's construct a unique combination, and further proof that the "revers de la médaille est de son essence aussi bien que le beau côté" (**Lettres écrites de Lausanne,** 88).

From another perspective this "shift in proportion," in addition to creating, hypothetically, different individuals in each of the above cases, would possibly result in novelistic closure: Cécile would become a euphoric heroine whose destiny would be, ultimately, a conventionally acceptable "happy marriage" with the young lord, and Marianne would possibly find happiness with the more socially suitable Count Max. Through the manner in which Charrière prefers to leave her heroines, however, Cécile and Marianne both appear to avoid a destiny *which will not be of their own making.* Caliste, although she succumbs eventually to death, does not in reality exemplify the dysphoric heroine: death is not the means to prevent her union with William as it is in the case of Manon and Des Grieux, for she has exercised independently a different option—her marriage to M.M.***—and the union with William has already been realized in their (re)union in Saint-James Park. In a manner of speaking Charrière rewrites Mistriss Henley in Caliste: rather than experiences "marriage *as* death," to use Lanser's expression [in her "Courting Death: *Roman, romantisme,* and *Mistriss Henley's* Narrative Practices," *Eighteenth Century Life* Vol. 13 n.s.1 (February 1989): 49-59], Caliste experiences "marriage *and* death." Thus Charrière preserves, even for Caliste, more than a single option.

For Charrière, androgyny itself has a "revers de la médaille." On one hand it grants power to the woman who is otherwise politically weak. This is why

> ... in an age of great sexual polarization, and great patriarchal power, where women have no life without husbands and no identity with them[17] the androgynous impulse and the feminist impulse must appear, or even, be, for a time identical (Heilbrun, 58).

Androgyny permits the establishment of a new and unique source of power for Caliste when it allows her to effect a transfer of emotion from William's deceased brother to herself, when her voice assumes an authority that was formerly held by the brother. But, the shifting boundaries between feminine and masculine, characteristic of androgyny, produce an ambivalence in Caliste's status. Whereas she is at first able to appropriate power by dominating William in the absence of his brother, she is later subject to a reversal of that same power she had enjoyed when Sir Harry's presence becomes dominant. In other words Charrière makes no "feminist" assertion through her representation of Caliste; rather, she insists upon the androgynous ideal, the balance between the sexes which mandates that, although the feminine voice is not restricted, but able to occupy traditionally masculine territory, the masculine voice, likewise, is free and able to occupy feminine territory: by virtue of their emotional capacities which exceed their definition by gender the male brother, the female Caliste, and the male nephew, Sir Harry, are all equally capable of establishing unique and differing relationships with William.

Although living within the boundaries and structures of a patriarchal society, Isabelle de Charrière succeeds nevertheless in constructing a new universe that challenges significantly the concept of separation or definition by sex. In Lausanne, Cécile and the mother are not simply two females whose options are reduced for reasons of gender and role. They constitute instead a "couple idéal" (Didier, *L'écriture-femme,* 101), individuals whose natures complement each other, and who could happily fulfill each other in a society which would offer them a broader range of possibilities, and not a constricting norm narrowly defining the "feminine" and the "maternal."

The balanced human experience of androgyny underlines Charrière's discourse, masculine and feminine alike. The mother from Lausanne cautions Cécile:

> ... il ne vous faut pas faire illusion: un homme cherche à inspirer, pour lui seul, à chaque femme un sentiment qu'il n'a le plus souvent que pour l'espèce ... ce qui est trop souvent la grande affaire de notre vie n'est presque rien pour lui (*Letters écrites de Lausanne,* 62).

And William states similarly: "Je crus que toutes les femmes aimaient, et que le hasard, plus qu'aucune autre chose, déterminait l'objet d'une passion à laquelle toutes étaient disposées d'avance" (142). I choose these particular passages to illustrate not only that the recognition of the individual is incontrovertibly at risk in such discourse, but also that, *enunciated equally from both the masculine and feminine positions,* their discourse becomes a balanced and thus androgynous one.[18]

Charrière invents not only new discourse, but new options as well. Lack of fortune, immature or irresponsible behavior—their own or that of others—do not limit women's possibilities. They serve, rather, to *extend* those possibilities by forcing women to use capacities and resources which they possess, regardless of whether these are a part of the traditional or authorized female *persona.* Even Caliste uses the resource which her servant, James, provides—the carriage which he summons—in order to challenge society's power to define the sexes (to define the "marriageable woman" and thereby separate her from William) by realizing the moment of (re)union in Saint-James Park. Are not Caliste and William variations, shifts in proportion, of Julie d'Arnonville and Valaincourt, who meet to flee the Baron's and patriarchal society's resounding *non*? (Julie and Valaincourt make use of a carriage also!) These are Charrière's imaginative challenges to eighteenth-century conventions and to feminine destiny.

If a rigid and constricting sexual identity characterizes patriarchy, Isabelle de Charrière, through her texts and subtexts, through her novelistic inventions, can be said to imagine something indeed beyond, something which is ... toward androgyny. What is intriguing, fundamentally, is not simply Charrière's use of androgyny, but the purpose which lies behind it: to permit the woman to move freely between the two poles, which are the limits established by gender, according to her own individual talents and inclinations, in order to achieve a balance with the man. I refer once again to Claudine Herrmann's introduction to *Caliste ou Letters écrites de Lausanne,* which contains the following quotation from Charrière: "L'imagination se dessèche en voyant tout ce qui est, ou bien on se croit fou quand on s'est ému quelques instants pour ce qu'on croyait qui pouvait être" (13).[19] It is Charrière's remarkable "moments of madness' which give twentieth-century readers not only a sense of proximity to the eighteenth century, but also a feeling of optimism that imagination, that an androgynous ideal, like hope, "springs eternal in the human breast."

Notes

[1] Carolyn G. Heilbrun, *Toward a Recognition of Androgyny* (New York: Alfred A. Knopf, 1973). All references to Heilbrun's text are taken from this edition.

[2] Marianne corresponds quite well to Heilbrun's definition of an androgynous ideal: ". . . an appealing individual whose expression of her own obligations and passions are not strictly held within the limits of a narrow 'norm' . . . 'Active' is the operative word" (27). See Heilbrun's discussion of the woman hero in Part 2 of her text. Rousseau's Julie could also be described, therefore, as a "woman hero" if she were not to surrender eventually to paternal authority and ultimately to death.

[3] In her essay on Friedrich Schlegel's novel *Lucinde,* Margaret Higonnet refers to Schlegel's theory of individual development through sexual balance and states: "True balance is that of the androgynous individual." See Higonnet's "Writing from the feminine: *Lucinde* and *Adolphe*" in the *Annales Benjamin Constant* (Lausanne: Institut Benjamin Constant, 1980]. No. 1 *Cahiers Vilfredo Pareto* No. 50 vol. 5 (1985) p.17.

[4] Heilbrun indicates that ". . . in an age of great sexual polarization and great patriarchal power . . . the androgynous impulse and the feminist impulse must appear, or even be, for a time, identical" (58).

[5] I suggest that Caliste, in choosing to meet with William in Saint-James Park, for example, is also choosing her place, as Heilbrun states, "without regard to propriety or custom." Caliste's evolving lack of regard for society's "laws" or conventions climaxes in her declaration to M. M.***: "Mes juges ne sont . . . que des hommes et des femmes, c'est-à-dire ce que je suis moi-même, et je me connais bien mieux qu'ils ne me connaissent" (184).

[6] I quote Heilbrun's statement that "The cry within literary works for more balanced human experience . . . has largely been the cry of women" (xvi).

[7] It is difficult to justify Heilbrun's choice of terminology here when she refers to the "reader's identification" with the characters. According to Wolfgang Iser (*The Act of Reading*) there is no such person as the "reader." There is, instead, the construct of the "implied reader," a role the reader is invited to play by responding to structures presented by the author. The interaction between his responses and the textual signals then produce a "meaning" which the reader himself has constructed. I would interpret Heilbrun's statement to mean that narrating voice and narrating time, to which the reader has full access, appear to be "equally divided" between the female and male characters.

[8] Society governs Caliste's existence in two ways: 1) it defines her as an immoral woman; and 2) it separates or categorizes her according to that limited definition.

[9] I refer *only* to the fact that Caliste is a woman, a female, biologically, and therefore an appropriate marriage partner for William, and not to the reasons of immorality for which society would condemn her and deem her an inappropriate partner.

[10] I use "replace" in quotations because Caliste can never be replaced. We recall that William, on his "honeymoon" with Sir Harry, searches for Caliste's face and yearns to discuss his impressions of sights and sounds with her.

[11] See Nancy K. Miller's *Subject to Change,* (New York: Columbia University Press, 1988, p. 222). Miller states that female plot limits the heroine's development to those possibilities which culture inscribes for her based on her sex (208). Rousseau, for example, perpetuates similarly woman's inscribed existence by "continuing" Julie in Claire's daughter, Henriette, so that Julie cannot, in fact, serve as a "final daughter."

[12] Does the baby's resemblance to her mother anticipate, however, the perpetuation of Lady Betty's own unhappy destiny?

[13] Although the mother assumes paternal authority in seeking an appropriate husband for Cécile, she does not display the usual paternal or parental ambition in making her choices. Whereas the typical literary father figure might hasten to approve and even urge a marriage between Cécile and her cousin for financial reasons, the mother exhibits rational thinking of a different order that perceives the incompatibility of the two young people: "Quoiqu'il soit fils unique de riches parents, et qu'il doive hériter de cinq ou six tantes, Cécile n'épousera pas son cousin le ministre; ce serait Agnès et le corps mort: mais au lieu de ressusciter, il pourrait devenir plus mort" (30).

[14] Referring to Charrière's male narrating voice of William, Béatrice Didier [in *SVEC* 193 (1980): 1981-88] states: "Ce n'est pas là le moindre paradoxe de l'aliénation, qu'une romancière des dernières années du dix-huitième siècle n'ait pu trouver véritablement

son style que par ce détour qui l'amenait à employer la voix de l'autre pour découvrir sa propre identité" ("La femme à la recherche de son image: Mme de Charrière et l'écriture féminine dans la seconde moitié du XVIIIe siècle," 1987).

[15] Heilbrun states that opposite-sex twins are "complementary, different in heredity and sex but identical in birth experience" and that "the two are always seen as an original unit which has split, a unit destined to be reunited by sexual love, the ultimate symbol of human conjoining" (34).

[16] See Béatrice Didier's discussion of Charrière in her text, *L'écriture-femme* (Paris: Presses Universitaires de France, 1981). She acknowledges that "Mme de Charrière a su créer des héroïnes extrêmement diverses. Cécile. Caliste, Mistriss Henley, l'épouse du mari sentimental sont toutes très individualisées, et ne sortent absolument pas d'un moule unique" (108-09). Didier is in error here, however, in her reference to "l'épouse du mari sentimental," because she attributes authorship of *Le Mari sentimental* to Charrière rather than to Samuel de Constant.

[17] This statement summarizes quite succinctly the difficult situations of Cécile in Lausanne and Mistriss Henley in Hollowpark.

[18] Another example of how Charrière converts patriarchal discourse into androgynous discourse can be illustrated through William. I refer to Eve Sedgwick, who utilizes Gayle Rubin's assessment of women in patriarchy, to represent patriarchal discourse. According to Sedgwick [in her *Between Men: English Literature and Mate Homosocial Desire,* New York: Columbia University Press, 1985], Rubin states that patriarchal heterosexuality implies a traffic in women, that women are used as "exchangeable, perhaps symbolic property for the primary purpose of cementing the bonds of men with men" (25-26). On the other hand, Charrière's William states: "Il faut que dans le fond, quoiqu'il n'y paraisse pas toujours, les femmes aient une grande confiance au jugement et au goût les unes des autres. *Un homme est une marchandise qui, en circulant entre leurs mains, hausse quelque temps de prix, jusqu'à ce qu'elle tombe tout-à-coup dans un aécri total, qui n'est d'ordinaire que trop juste*" (159, my emphasis). Charrière thus balances the patriarchal discourse.

[19] Herrmann gives no indication of the precise source of Charrière's statement.

Jenene J. Allison (essay date 1995)

SOURCE: "New Heroines: Countering Women's Fiction(s)," in *Revealing Difference: The Fiction of Isabelle de Charrière*, University of Delaware Press, 1995, pp. 19-39.

[*In the following essay, Allison compares Charrière's work to other eighteenth-century fiction, noting that she not only condemns the existing stereotypes of women but also challenges the very force of stereotyping itself.*]

The success of *Lettres portugaises* [The letters of a Portuguese nun] (1669), probably authored by Gabriel de Guilleragues (d. 1685), illustrates well the way in which representations of women can serve to perpetuate a stereotype of woman.[1] This brief, monophonic epistolary novel presents the letters of an abandoned Portuguese nun to the French officer who seduced her. So great was the appeal of the novel *Lettres portugaises* that the term "une portugaise" came to designate the standard abandoned-woman's passionate letter. That the title should be so readily adapted for current usage in seventeenth-century France reflects a receptivity to the image of woman implied by such a form.[2] The novel itself, in part because of the question of authorship, has been the focus of debates concerning the idea of a female voice.[3] The woman pouring her emotions into a letter was a woman in thrall to her passion, and this image reflected the notion that women, being closer to nature, were less able than men to repress passion. The literary form that received the name "une portugaise," and the image of woman that informed it, are intimately linked; indeed they are "entangled," to use Nancy K. Miller's metaphor. Speaking of our need to rewrite the history of the novel, she proposes "look[ing] . . . at the sites where the intersecting discourses on femininity (as the inflected term of the masculine-feminine couple) and fiction become—like the recklessly heterosexual couples of the social text they also articulate—permanently and dangerously entangled."[4] The complexity of this relationship between femininity and fiction structures the heroine in the eighteenth-century novel.[5] Relative to these conventional figures, Charrière's heroines seem at first glance quite innovative. Considered more closely, they are better described as refutations of the conventional.

Miller's *The Heroine's Text: Readings in the French and English Novel, 1722-1782* has become a point of reference for eighteenth-century fiction, although she has moved beyond the critical approach employed in this survey.[6] She sorts the eight canonical novels she examines into two categories: "euphoric" plots, in which the female protagonist rises gloriously to "integration into society" through marriage, and "dysphoric" plots, in which she falls tragically into the abyss of death or exile. "The heroine's text is plotted within this ideologically delimited space of an either/or closure, within the conventional rhetoric of the sociolect."[7] The literary convention of such plots parallels the social forces confining women to one type of role—that of spouse, a role that was itself confining. Reflecting on this, Margaret Higonnet wonders if the distinction between the two types of plots is not perhaps paradoxical since "a marriage without describable future" may well be "more static and fatal to its heroine" than the more obviously tragic conclusion in a dysphoric plot.[8] In the three texts I discuss here, Charrière plots her protagonists along the euphoric line leading to marriage. However, by the conclusion of each novel, the conventional plot has been modified because it has been articulated so that a stereotypical image of woman is first presented and then undermined.

Not only does the euphoric plot undergo a subtle alteration, the heroines themselves are described with atypical attributes.[9] Pierre Fauchery's monumental *La Destinée féminine dans le roman européen du dixhuitième siècle: 1713-1807* catalogues female protagonists, and among all the variants and possibilities that he lists, there are certain attributes that appear consistently. The common denominator, according to Fauchery, is that woman "remains an eternal minor," the fictional heroines reflecting the "original vice of *being a woman*."[10] While he does include Charrière in his monumental survey, the sheer number of characters considered causes him to assimilate her characters into a model that is oversimplified.[11] To free these characters from such a reductive classification, I compare three versions of the same type (the heroine progressing according to a euphoric plot). The heroines in "**Le Noble**" (1763), ***Lettres trouvées dans des porte-feuilles d'émigrés*** (1793), and ***Sainte Anne*** (1799) are all of this type yet significantly different from this type. These three novels also feature the device of a letter that is either not written or not read. This device is of particular interest because of the cultural implications of the association between women and letter writing in the eighteenth century. Letter writing was not authoritative; as Elizabeth J. MacArthur notes, "Women could write letters without considering themselves, and without being considered by others, as authors."[12] In addition, letter writing was confined, like women, to the private sphere. [I will] pursue the various facets of the link between women and letter writing as it is represented in Charrière's fiction.[13] Through a close reading of a letter-writing scene in each novel, we will see that the representation of an apparently conventional heroine may serve to weaken the force of literary convention itself.

Countering the Wrong Image

The first work by the then unmarried Isabelle van Tuyll is "**Le Noble**" [(8:19-34) Unless otherwise stated, the work of Isabelle de Charrière is quoted from her ***Oeuvres Complètes,*** ed. Jean-Daniel Candaux et. al., 10 Vols. (Amsterdam: G.A. van Oorschot, 1979-84). References to the Volume and page number of this work will be given parenthetically in the text.]. Like Voltaire's "Candide" (1959) it is often ironical and consistently sharp in its criticism of the old nobility. The problem presented in "**Le Noble**" is a classic one: Julie loves Valaincourt, but her father, the Baron d'Arnonville, prohibits the marriage because the young man's family has been noble for only one generation. The characters are clearly delineated in terms of good and bad: those who oppose the young lovers are incarnations of blind prejudice; the lovers are complex, appealing individuals. The Baron d'Arnonville, for example, is an idiot, "ne pensant pas que la parfaite inutilité fût indigne de la haute naissance, ni que ce fût déroger que n'être bon à rien" (22) [not believing that absolute uselessness was unworthy of high birth, nor that it was ignoble to be good for nothing].[14] Both Julie and Valaincourt have the necessary attributes of physical beauty, but in addition to this quality, their relationship is described with the sort of titillating innuendo that was so frequently condemned in the novel of the eighteenth century. While visiting Valaincourt's family, Julie bumps into him one evening in the dark hallway and they kiss for the first time: "Alors Valaincourt prit un baiser à Julie, & Julie qui n'aimoit pas à refuser ce qu'elle pouvoit donner sans peine, le laissa prendre" (23) [Then Valaincourt took a kiss from Julie, and Julie, who didn't like to refuse what she could easily give away, let it be taken]. The way in which the characters are drawn, and the fact that it is the joys of young love that are threatened by aristocratic prejudice, all seem to make of "**Le Noble**" an indictment of the aristocracy.

On the other hand, a more attentive reading of "**Le Noble**" makes classifying it as pure antiaristocratic propaganda problematic. The quotation Charrière placed on the title page is: "On ne suit pas toujours ses aïeux ni son père" [One does not always follow one's ancestors or one's father] from "L'Education" by La Fontaine (one of her favorite authors).[15] The fable is important, for the moral is that unless one cultivates both one's talents and skills, a well-born person can easily degenerate into a despicable being. In "**Le Noble**," then, Charrière, would not so much be condemning the aristocracy in the figure of the Baron d'Arnonville as using him to suggest that the aristocracy needs renewal and fresh blood. This is confirmed by the description of how Valaincourt's father, through his conduct and his good deeds, became noble: "Les Sages diroient que quand c'est de cette façon qu'on a acquis la noblesse, la plus nouvelle est la meilleure, que le premier noble de sa race doit être le plus glorieux d'un titre dont il est l'auteur" (23) [Wise men would say that when it is in this manner that one has acquired nobility, the most recent is the best, that the first nobleman of his line ought to be the most proud of a title of which he is the author]. Such an interpretation can be further supported by the argument that Charrière makes in ***Lettres ècrites de Lausanne,*** written twenty-three years after "**Le Noble.**" In this novel, the female narrator digresses at one point to elaborate on her idea for what might be termed an aristocratic meritocracy. While maintaining the basic structure of three distinct classes, she would ennoble the children of all the members of the governing council so as to replace noble families on the verge of extinction (8:142).[16]

Given this concern for the perpetuation and even amelioration of aristocratic bloodlines, **"Le Noble"** might represent a plea that the aristocracy be preserved. After all, Charrière does have Julie return to her father. When he arranges for Julie's brother to marry a loathsome but eminently noble woman, there is a wedding celebration; Julie and Valaincourt sneak in and are forgiven by her father, "lorsque le vin commençoit à confondre dans sa tête l'ancienne, & la nouvelle Noblesse" (34) [when the wine began to muddle up the ancient and the recent nobility in his mind]. In this conclusion, we see that Charrière's explicit condemnation of the aristocracy in **"Le Noble"** is attenuated by her belief in some aspects of it. However, her rejection of a typical feminine destiny for her protagonist is not similarly attenuated. With her choice of a standard eighteenth-century plot based on a daughter's rebellion against her father's authority, Charrière set up her female protagonist in a situation that could easily lend itself to the euphoric/dysphoric alternative. Although the author does resolve Julie's dilemma with marriage, the conclusion is atypical because it involves a loss of status for her. As Fauchery explains, the eighteenth-century novel tends towards *invraisemblance* by consistently returning one or both young lovers to their original social rank.[17] In the case of **"Le Noble,"** the concluding moral of the story—"Julie fut heureuse et ses Fils ne furent point Chevaliers" (34) [Julie was happy and her sons were not knights]—places the focus on the simultaneity of the woman's happiness and her violation of social conventions.[18]

To appreciate the subversive nature of this text, we need to ask, How does Julie escape the typical feminine destiny? How does Charrière plot her heroine's escape from the physical and social structures oppressing her? In her description of Julie's evolution from "daughter oppressed by her father" to "woman married to the man of her choice," Charrière presents two possible solutions to the dilemma of her protagonist: the first one involves a fake genealogy, the second one an elopement. Julie will accede to the freedom to marry against her father's wishes only after the wrong solution has been rejected. By setting up and rejecting this wrong solution—a solution that, by the terms of the plot alone might have led to the same conclusion—**"Le Noble"** devalues a stereotype of woman.

The first attempt at solving Julie's dilemma has a catastrophic result: her incarceration. Upon being asked by the Baron the all-important question about Valaincourt's ancestry, Julie had improvised and claimed that he was descended from ancient and impeccable bloodlines (26). Realizing that her father's discovery of her lie would imperil her chances to wed Valaincourt, Julie resolves to write to the young man so that together they could forge a fake genealogy to implant (or transplant) him firmly into the aristocratic order. This letter-writing scene is crucial to the assessment of Charrière's female protagonist because it so clearly represents the stereotypical image of woman that is countered in the conclusion to **"Le Noble."**

> Elle prit l'écritoire, les plumes, & le papier; elle imagina le moyen de faire parvenir sa lettre, & je jurerois qu'elle auroit écrit si elle eût été sure de son stile, & de son ortographe; mais Julie passa légèrement sur ses véritables motifs de ne point écrire; elle se persuada en remettant tout cet attirail que la prudence, la réserve, la modestie, le respect des bienséances, l'arrêtoient, & elle s'applaudit des vertus qu'elle n'avoit pas. (27)

> [She took the writing desk, the quills, and the paper; she imagined the means by which to have her letter delivered, and I swear she would have written if she had been sure of her style and of her spelling; but Julie glossed over her real motives for not writing. She persuaded herself, while putting away all this equipment, that caution, reserve, modesty, respect for good behavior, were stopping her and she congratulated herself on virtues she didn't have.]

Julie's action here hardly qualifies as an event since it turns into a nonevent: after the precise description of her preparations for writing, Julie fails to do so. The value of the scene is as an image rather than as an element advancing the plot. The image presented is of the stereotypical woman, and the details given here describe with accuracy this stereotype. First and foremost, woman is superficial, a creature of appearances. In the eighteenth century, as Landes explains, femininity was taken to be the opposite of reason; it was "pleasure, play, eroticism, artifice, style, politesse, refined facades, and particularity."[19] This is reflected in Julie's primary concern about her letter: its style and spelling as opposed to its content. Secondly, woman is incapable of moral conduct. In the words of one authority on "the woman question," Diderot, one must never forget that because of women's lack of intellectual capacity, they have no profound comprehension of anything, and "les idées de justice, de vertu, de vice, de bonté, de méchanceté nagent à la superficie de leur âme" [the ideas of justice, virtue, vice, good, and evil hover at the furthest reaches of their soul].[20] Thus, even in the privacy of her own thoughts, Julie lies about her motivation for not writing, attributing this motivation to morality (spelled out, rather to excess, in a lengthy list) so that she may proudly congratulate herself on "virtues she didn't have." That it is the narrator who, in juridical terms, authenticates Julie's duplicity ("I swear") further reinforces it; truth can only come from outside the innermost thoughts of the woman presented in this image.[21]

The letter-writing scene acquires a negative quality by the result it generates: Julie's incarceration. The image of Julie at her writing desk, an image that concretizes the stereotype of woman, leads to a betrayal scene duplicating this image. Not knowing that Julie had concocted a magnificent bloodline for him, the lovesick Valaincourt, when confronted by the Baron, blurted out the truth about his ancestry in the course of a hyperbolic protestation of his love for the young noblewoman (28). Valancourt's description of what he had done wrong is significant. He did not blame himself for being honest but for betraying Julie's *dis*honesty. His error was in failing to assume that a woman would, naturally, lie: "Je devois deviner, je devois me taire.... Ah! c'est pour moi que vous êtes coupable, & c'est moi qui vous trahis!" [I ought to have guessed, I ought to have kept quiet.... Ah! It's for me that you're guilty and it's me who is betraying you!] Upon learning from Valaincourt of Julie's duplicity, the Baron imprisons her in the castle.

A different solution to her dilemma must be found. Unlike the fake genealogy, the solution involving an elopement reverses the type of deceptive speech act that led to Julie's confinement, and it will successfully solve her dilemma. Having persuaded the gardener's daughter to carry messages to his loved one, Valaincourt plans Julie's escape from the castle so that they may elope. However, in contrast to the betrayal scene, where Julie appeared in her role as a stereotype—a superficial, duplicitous creature—here she will be made to appear as a woman of her word, and this is what will precipitate her freedom. An integral component of the plan for her physical escape is Valaincourt's decision to take Julie at her word. He concludes the letter planning their elopement, "Je ne demande point de réponse, vous m'avés dit que vous m'aimiés, c'étoit tout me promettre" (31) [I am not asking for an answer, you told me that you loved me, that was to promise me all]. Julie, for her part, reiterates Valaincourt's confidence that she will be true to her word. The idea that she could be true to her word presents a different image than that in the letter-writing scene, where the narrator drew the reader's attention to Julie's dishonest assessment of her reasons for not writing ("virtues she didn't have"). In **"Le Noble,"** then, a pernicious stereotype of woman is undermined in the course of what appears to be an antiaristocratic satire. An apt metaphor for the text is provided by the basket that concealed Valaincourt's letter. The letter, in which he takes Julie at her word, had been delivered in a basket that eluded the vigilance of Julie's guardian because the guardian assumed it was innocuous; the old woman failed to suspect "la vertu secrete de la corbeille" (30) [the secret virtue of the basket]. This image of a woman as true to her word is "the secret virtue" of the text.

Furthermore, Charrière's protagonist frees herself not just from a physical prison but from the patriarchal structure that legitimated her confinement. To escape from her father's castle, Julie must cross the moat, and she uses portraits of her grandfathers, not of her grandmothers, to do so.[22]

Le Grand-pere fut jetté dans la boue, & celui-là ... fut suivi d'un second, & puis d'un troisieme. Jamais Julie n'avoit cru qu'on pût tirer si bon parti des Grands-peres.... [L]e visage d'un de ses Ancêtres ... se romp sous ses pieds. (32-33)

[The grandfather was thrown in the mud and that one ... was followed by a second and then a third. Never had Julie believed one could profit so well from grandfathers.... (T)he face of one of her ancestors ... cracks under her feet.][23]

Jean Starobinski sees in this blasphemous act what he terms a symbolic murder of the father.[24] Another scholar is more critical of Charrière's audacious treatment of grandfathers, pointing to the poor taste and lack of respect in the moat-crossing scene.[25] I read the destruction of these portraits, icons of her confinement, as a way to distance Julie from all that is implied by the image of woman as a solitary letter writer. This heroine, in exceeding the limits of the stereotypical woman, both overcomes her father's opposition to the young man of her choice and symbolically steps outside the patriarchal order to create an identity of her own making.[26]

The wrong solution to Julie's dilemma—one that would have reinforced the patriarchal order by supplying a genealogy for Valaincourt and by determining Julie's identity within this order—has been rejected. We should read her father's condemnation of her accordingly: "Vous mérités bien peu d'être née ce que vous êtes!" (29) [How little you merit having been born what you are!]. In the context of a satire on the aristocracy, we would understand her to have been "born" an aristocrat, but in the context of a feminocentric parable, she was "born" a woman. Through the subversive reimaging of Charrière's protagonist, a way out of the social structure that limits woman to being what she was born is delineated. The key difference between Charrière's text and novels featuring heroines in their role as "eternal minor[s]" is the presence of a challenge to the image of woman that elicited oppressive customs and laws.

In **"Le Noble,"** the plot not only presents a successful heroine but counters a repressive stereotype of woman. The next text under consideration, ***Lettres trouvées dans des porte-feuilles d'émigrés***, features a female protagonist who will be as successful as Julie. Here, however, Charrière sets up two heroines in the daughter-versus-father power struggle, and the effect is to undermine the stereotype of woman in a different way: namely, through the suppression of one protagonist in favor of another.

Privileging the Right Heroine

Lettres trouvées is a two-part, polyphonic epistolary novel set in both the London of the French aristocrats who had fled from the threat of the guillotine, the émigrés, and the battlegrounds where the revolutionary and counterrevolutionary armies faced each other. Under the entry for "Charrière" in the *Bloomsbury Guide to Women's Literature,* the work is classified as a text in which Charrière "looks at the causes of the Revolution, and includes a project for a Constitution."27 In this novel, Charrière permits herself to give vent to her political opinions, and so it is not surprising to find that the fierceness with which she consistently blamed both sides for their equal share in the suffering appears in the novel as an insistence on depicting in detail the pain proper to both. She describes the dismay felt by the lower class in confronting a weak, useless, needlessly cruel aristocracy, as well as the horror of the upper class in facing an irrational, greedy, destructive mob. In addition to the two fighting parties, Charrière focuses on the émigrés in exile, although with less compassion, due no doubt to her well-known impatience with them. Living in Neuchâtel, one of the passageways of the emigration, she was exposed to too many self-pitying, displaced aristocrats to have much sympathy for them.28 However, an attentive reading of this novel will show that, as with **"Le Noble,"** where the apparent satire of the aristocracy coexists with a more subversive topic, the theme of the war between the various political factions in no way exhausts **Lettres trouvées**. The flux in political hierarchy triggered by the Revolution leads ultimately to posing the question, at the end of the novel, What can the status of woman be now?

The love story in this text is structured like that in **"Le Noble,"** but this one involves two sets of lovers. The Marquis de *** has safely tucked away one daughter, Germaine, in London with some other émigrés so that he may do battle against the revolutionaries. Pauline, another daughter (from a different marriage), remains in their besieged castle in France. Predictably, both young women have formed alliances that are unsuitable because of the political situation. Germaine loves Alphonse, an aristocrat who has refused to join the war on behalf of "la Royauté, la noblesse, & la foi" (8:437) [royalty, nobility, and the faith] as her father defines it. Alphonse is described as so horrified by the inhuman violence of the Revolution that he could not close his eyes to the bloodshed long enough to view it as a political conflict in which one faction might be philosophically superior to the other (439). For her part, Pauline falls in love with L. B. Fonbrune, a republican on the wrong side of "royalty, nobility, and the faith."

The focus of the novel is largely on Germaine's love story; she faces her father's disapproval of her inappropriate choice of spouse whereas Pauline is not shown in this situation. In addition, while Germaine is featured in **Lettres trouvées** both as a character and as an author of letters (in fact, the first letter is hers), Pauline is featured as a character only: she is represented through description and reported dialogue in the letters of Fonbrune and later, in the sequel (**Lettres trouvées dans des porte-feuilles d'émigrés, suite**), in a remarkable letter from a servant in Holland that concludes the novel. Because the sequel has only six letters compared to the twenty-four of the previous section, and because it seems to end *in medias res,* the text might be deemed unfinished. On the contrary, an inherent coherence emerges from a focus on the heroines, making **Lettres trouvées** conclusive as it stands. Over the course of the novel, Germaine recedes into the background after having been the heroine of the first part, and Pauline, previously a background figure, comes to occupy the center of attention. As Germaine is progressively silenced while Pauline acquires more and more a voice of her own, a new image of woman comes to efface an older, more stereotypical one.

Germaine's letters serve primarily to describe the dizzying idleness of the dispossessed émigrés until the occurrence of the event that forces her to address her father's disapproval of Alphonse; at this point, the topic of woman displaces that of revolutionary turmoil. The duchess in charge of Germaine is an arrogant busybody who feels she must not only protect but also control the ward entrusted to her (440). Intercepting a letter from Alphonse, the duchess officiously forwards it to the marquis. Germaine's reaction to this theft is significant because it makes of her the stereotype of woman. Upon discovering what the duchess has done, and in fear of her father's reprisals, Germaine writes a letter to Alphonse, and once again we see the heroine in a letter-writing scene. In fact, this letter-writing scene, occurring as it does within a letter, is even more overdetermined by the association of women with letter writing. Furthermore, as in **"Le Noble,"** no actual letter results from the scene, making the scene's value more visual than narrative. In **Lettres trouvées,** however, the heroine is not seen making the preparations to write but instead is seen imagining a letter—namely, her own version of the real one from Alphonse. Germaine endows this imaginary letter of hers with great power.

> C'était l'heure de faire ma toilette. Victoire m'a habillée comme on habillerait une figure de bois; & sans que je m'apperçusse seulement de ce qu'elle faisait. Je cherchai à me rappeller *tout ce que je*

> *vous avais écrit, & à m'imaginer tout ce que vous aviez pu me répondre, & après m'être fait une Lettre de vous, dont je voyais distinctement le pli, les marges, l'écriture, la signature; je voyais mon pere l'ouvrir, se fâcher, lire, rêver & s'appaiser peu-à-peu. . . . La poupée habillée, on l'a fait descendre & se mettre à table. Il y avait beaucoup de monde.* (446-47; emphasis added)

> [It was time for my toilette. Victoire dressed me as one would a stick figure and without my even noticing what she was doing. I tried to remember *everything I had written to you* and to imagine every way that you could have answered me. After having *made myself* a letter from you, a letter whose fold, margins, handwriting, and signature I saw distinctly, I saw my father open it, become angry, read on, daydream, and little by little calm down. . . . The doll having been dressed, she was made to go downstairs and to be seated at the table. There were a lot of people.]

Germaine specifies that the basis of her letter is "everything I had written to you," and that the resulting letter is one she "made myself." This means that although she is imagining a letter from a man, this letter is not a man's; it is her own creation. Indeed, it must be, since she has never laid eyes on the letter from Alphonse that was sent off on a detour to Germaine's father by the duchess.

It seems that the expression of her father's power over Germaine, manifested through the duchess's capacity to appropriate what belongs rightfully to her ward, brings out Germaine's status as mere object; the labels "stick figure" and "doll" frame the letter-writing scene. The scene with the young woman imagining a letter, like the scene with Julie not writing one, draws on and contributes to a certain image of woman. The passivity with which Germaine confronts the crisis, taking no action except to fantasize, while stereotypically feminine, can in no way serve to free her from the constraint under which she lives. Her passivity is brought out in the contrast between the list she uses to describe her imagined letter and the one she uses to describe the effect of this letter. While she emphasizes the concrete or physical attributes of her imagined letter, the "fold, margins, handwriting, and signature," the list of actions she attributes to her father ranges from his opening the letter to his having a change of heart after he daydreams about it. The progression from concrete details to daydreaming, which together add up to Germaine's formula for obtaining what she wants, completes the picture of her reaction as feminine. By the way in which she reacts to a threat to her freedom—with passivity, evident in the decision to imagine rather than to act, and the valorization of daydreaming, as opposed to logical argumentation, for example—she acts out a stereotype of woman prevalent in the eighteenth-century novel.

Clearly such a stick figure/doll could not be expected to liberate herself. Instead of achieving the freedom to marry the man of her choice, Germaine has it given to her without having to smash any graven images of her male ancestors. A way she can both conform to her father's wishes and marry the man she loves is developed when her father undergoes precisely the change of heart about which she had fantasized. In fact, if we follow the letter intercepted by the duchess, we will find that the father's response to this real letter from Alphonse is remarkably close to Germaine's fantasy. What is significant is that he makes a comment about the intercepted letter that serves to mock the conceit underlying the novel itself.

Forgiving his daughter for her clandestine correspondence with a man of whom he disapproved, the marquis graciously admits the letter is from a nice young man. Instead of punishing her, he grants her a voice: "*Dans le choix d'un époux comme dans toute autre chose, il faut voir par vos propres yeux, & puis ne prendre un parti qu'avec mon consentement*" (452) [In the choice of a spouse, as in all other matters, you must see through your own eyes and then follow a course of action only with my consent]. However, the marquis also refers to what was done by Germaine's guardian in London: "*Je ne sais comment remercier la Duchesse de son zèle; intercepter une Lettre, la détourner de son chemin & lui en faire prendre un si différent, ne m'entrerait jamais dans l'esprit*" (451) [I do not know how to thank the duchess for her zeal. To intercept a letter, to divert it from its route and make it take such a different one, would never enter my mind]. And yet, is this not the very conceit upon which is based the eighteenth-century convention of epistolary novels presented as found letters? Of all Charrière's epistolary novels (***Lettres neuchâteloises, Lettres écrites de Lausanne, Lettres de Mistriss Henley***), none makes so blatant a reference to this conceit: the title ***Lettres trouvées dans des porte-feuilles d'émigrés*** evokes a scene in which an editor accidentally finds a satchel of letters, probably in his attic or in an old trunk. When the marquis mocks what the duchess did with Alphonse's letter, his comment serves to mock the conceit inherent in the title of Charrière's novel. Through the irony in the marquis's comment, the conformity of ***Lettres trouvées*** to a literary convention is implied. It is pertinent that the heroine simultaneously acquires the freedom to marry as she wishes. The formulation of the heroine's success in this text differs sharply from that presented in **"Le Noble."** Where Julie found a way to bypass her father's power, Germaine remains at the disposal of her father. Where **"Le Noble"** undermined the stereotype of woman, this first part of ***Lettres trouvées*** confirms it. The most important difference is the addition in the latter of a reference that may direct the reader's attention to what is purely conventional in the text, a category into which the heroine falls. Although a successful heroine, Germaine is not an unconventional one: she is just a woman who does what her father tells her to do.

In the course of the transition from the first part to the sequel, Germaine recedes into the background as Pauline becomes more important. The first part ends with the discussion of the marquis's efforts to acquire safe passage for his wife and Pauline out of France. *Lettres trouvées dans des porte-feuilles d'émigrés, suite* begins with what will be Germaine's last letter, a letter that is superficial at best. Germaine writes from the countryside to inform Alphonse that she is in "la plus noble, la plus grave, la plus solitaire des retraites" [the most noble, the most solemn, the most solitary of retreats] but that she will not offer him a description because it would be "trop semblable aux descriptions de Romans" (475) [too similar to descriptions found in novels]. She then describes it. Her character seems to fade away in the void of this verbiage, and she will not appear again. The extreme difference between Germaine and Pauline is brought out by the sequel, and the effect of switching from one rather colorless character to a more compelling one is to privilege the latter as heroine. In order to appreciate this contrast, it is necessary to trace the evolution of Pauline.

The best introduction to Pauline is to show what she is not and what she becomes.[29] A German friend was planning a sequel to *Lettres trouvées,* and Charrière foresaw that an author other than herself would pervert the character of Pauline: "Je vois que cela deviendra un roman tragique, Laurent [Fonbrune] poura bien être guillotiné. a la bonne heure. Pauline peut-être se noyera, soit" (412) [I see that it will become a tragic novel. Laurent (Fonbrune) might well be guillotined; why not. Perhaps Pauline will drown herself; so be it]. In fact, the Pauline that Charrière created is a far cry from the sad but beautiful descendants of Ophelia. When Fonbrune states that Pauline is in love with him, he does so by explaining that because she *cannot* see herself as a character in a novel, she does not realize she is in love (469). As for what she becomes, it must be considered one of the most audacious representations of a woman in eighteenth-century French fiction. In the conclusion to the novel, a letter from a servant reports that Pauline has safely escaped from France. To do so, she disguised herself as a man, an action her mother refused to take. The mother is recognized and detained while Pauline makes good her escape.[30] About halfway through the letter, it becomes a record of a conversation with Pauline. Thus Pauline ends *Lettres trouvées* and in such a way as to make Germaine, who began it, seem even more of a stereotype. The servant wants to know what to call her, but this audacious young woman has trouble answering him.

> Pauline tout court. Ni Madame ni Mademoiselle. . . . Mais qu'etes vous? je suis Mademoiselle, Mais j'aimerois mieux qu'on me crut Madame. . . . Disons donc Madame Pauline Madame Pauline ne va pas trop bien . . . auriez vous dans votre famille quelque terre dont vous pussiez prendre le nom. Sans doute mais il ne nous est plus permis de porter de ces noms là. En Hollande cela n'a pas d'inconvenient. . . . [E]h bien donc je m'apellerai Madame Pauline de. non je ne puis m'y resoudre cela pouroit faire quelque tort à mes parens & deplaire à un homme à qui je veux toujours plaire. (482)

> [Just Pauline. Neither Mrs. nor Miss. . . . But which are you? I am "Miss" but I would prefer to be thought a "Mrs." Let us say, then, Mrs. Pauline. Mrs. Pauline will not do very well. Would you have in your family some estate whose name you could take? No doubt, but it is no longer permitted to bear those names. In Holland there is no problem with that. . . . Very well, I will be called Mrs. Pauline of. . . . No, I cannot commit to it, it could harm in some way my relatives and displease a man whom I wish to always please.]

This novel about the Revolution concludes with a woman's search for an identity properly her own in the context of both the social flux then underway and of her desire to be named in such a way as to embody her choice of marital status. Such a conclusion illustrates the acuity with which *Lettres trouvées* raises the issue of woman's status.

The significance of Pauline may be confirmed if we consider her place in the narrative. With two exceptions, she is never spoken about but only to, and when spoken to she serves to disrupt a discussion between men. Her first appearance in the novel is representative of this. In a letter that Fonbrune writes to Alphonse about the war and politics, he digresses without warning into an apostrophe to "Beautiful Pauline," whom he has not yet even mentioned to Alphonse (421). This digression recurs on the following page and even interrupts his condemnation of counter-revolutionary armies: "Mais où m'entraîne mon saint patriotisme? Belle Pauline je vous oubliais" [But how far is my blessed patriotism taking me? Beautiful Pauline, I was forgetting you].[31] Pauline first appears in *Lettres trouvées,* then, as a figure serving to direct an epistolary exchange between men away from the Revolution and toward a woman. When words are attributed to Pauline we find they are not of the typically feminine variety. She speaks to warn Laurent in a skirmish that takes place inside the castle (465) and then to accept his marriage proposal, aggressively stipulating, however, that they must commit never to divorce (466).[32] This is not the stick figure/doll Germaine who was pictured sitting in her boudoir fantasizing about a letter.

Given a figure such as Pauline, it is not surprising to find that she serves to conclude the novel in a provocative way. In *Lettres trouvées,* we see represented first the stereotype of woman and then, in a more sketchy form, a radical new type of woman. As with Germaine, although the desired wedding is not set, it seems that it is not out of the heroine's reach. The text ends with Pauline only seeking, not finding, a new name, illustrating well the difficulty of representing female subjectivity in the novel of the eighteenth century. For the woman Charrière is outlining, even if the old names are set aside, there cannot yet be a name. There can only be an ellipsis: "Very well, I will be called Mrs. Pauline of. . . ." It is as if Charrière, having come to focus on Pauline, could go no further in her analysis of this character. Given the framework of the epistolary novel, it would be logical to have Pauline become a letter writer at this point. As it stands, she never appears in this role.[33] Any incompleteness that we see in this text attests to its originality.[34] Pauline is an even more exceptional figure if we take into account the consistency with which Fauchery finds instead of such an unusual figure, the "eternal minor" punished time and time again for the sin of being woman.

The switch from one female protagonist to another effaces the stereotype represented by the first one, replacing it with the outline of a new image of woman. In the next text under consideration, a novel about the repatriation of the émigrés, the way in which the stereotype of woman served the purposes of oppression is manifest at a more profound level.

Questioning the Authority of Reading

Unlike Julie, Germaine, or Pauline, the heroine in *Sainte Anne* is not an aristocrat. She is the result of a liaison between a nobleman and the daughter of his gardener, a liaison he hastily legitimated before going off to war, where he was killed (9:267). What is most particular about Mlle d'Estival is that she is illiterate. The novel begins with, "Elle ne sait pas lire!" [She can't read!], and Charrière referred to *Sainte Anne* by that tag (257). At first glance it might seem that she is foregrounding this character's illiteracy in order to make a point about the way in which illiteracy (then affecting twice as many women as men) disempowers women. For example, in the case of novels featuring exotic heroines, Julia Douthwaite finds that "access to education and learned language form the central obstacles to [their] full participation in society."[35] In *Sainte Anne* we do not have an exotic heroine, and illiteracy functions differently. Mlle d'Estival's inability to read triggers a series of plot developments that will articulate a challenge to our ability to read. Charrière's innovation in this novel is more far reaching than in the novels previously considered.

As with "Le Noble" and *Lettres trouvées,* the plot here involves an obstacle to the union of two young lovers. In this instance, there is no disapproving father to overcome. The obstacle to their union is constituted in part by the heroine, who condemns the institution of marriage, and in part by a conspiracy to marry her off to a different man. The man she loves will have to propose twice before their marriage can take place. A comparison of the two scenes where she is shown responding to a proposal of marriage from him reveals how the illiteracy of the female protagonist is used to make a comment on our reading of the novel.

The man whom Mlle d'Estival loves is Sainte Anne, an émigré called home to France by his mother after the threat of the guillotine had passed. Setting the historical context for the novel, the details of his homecoming also evoke the passing of ancien régime society. The day Sainte Anne returned to his ancestral home, he found that his mother had assembled his female relatives. "Leurs peres, leurs maris, leurs fils avoient péri, ou vivoient encore dans cet exil auquel s'étoit condamné une partie de la noblesse françoise" (265) [Their fathers, their husbands, their sons had died, or lived still in that exile to which a part of the French nobility had condemned itself]. The noblewomen relentlessly recount to Sainte Anne lugubrious accounts of death and mayhem. Under these circumstances, the young nobleman falls in love with Mlle d'Estival, a woman who would have been, under the old social order, an unthinkable choice.

When Sainte Anne first proposes to Mlle d'Estival, she refuses him. This first proposal scene is striking because of the setting in which it occurs and the form Mlle d'Estival's refusal takes. Sainte Anne walks her home one night and takes a route past the cemetery. This setting results predictably enough in a formulaic description, including the fear of ghosts, the appearance of "petites flammes bleuâtres sortant de dessous terre" [little bluish flames coming out from underneath the ground], and the spooky hooting of owls, not to mention the fearfulness of the superstitious young girl, daunted by the proximity of those who are buried there (272). The dead in this scene are linked metonymically to the dead whose absence set the historical context for this novel. That the tutor of Sainte Anne is also buried in this graveyard, and that the young man stops kissing Mlle d'Estival when the voices of the dead cry out at his blasphemy, delimits the presence of patriarchal authority. It is no surprise that a union as improper as one between a nobleman and a gardener's granddaughter should not be furthered by what takes place in such a location. For the reader, this scene seems like a gothic cliché; indeed, it is telegraphically summed up, in the words of one character, as "cet endroit lugubre cette fille craintive" (276) [that lugubrious place, that fearful girl].[36] The form of Mlle d'Estival's rejection of Sainte Anne's proposal creates a shocking contrast to the literary convention of the graveyard setting. Mlle d'Estival could have accepted Sainte Anne's proposal or at least turned him down in an appropriate feminine manner. Instead, she turns down the man she loves by systematically enumerating a catalogue of married couples she has known, including her parents, and analyzing the various ways that the institution of marriage made them unhappy (273-74). As it stands, this first proposal scene embodies the incompatibility between a scene (the spooky graveyard) whose meaning is given by a literary convention, and a social establishment for woman (marriage) whose meaning is given by Mlle d'Estival's all too realistic facts. With her perspicacious commentary on marriage, she debunks the myth that being a wife makes women happy. By so doing, her character exercises a right for which women had to fight: the right not to be married. However, the text articulates an even more radical statement about women when Mlle d'Estival finally does accept Sainte Anne's proposal. This may seem contradictory, since it would appear to endorse the myth that being a wife does make women happy. The implications of the second proposal scene, however, far exceed this myth.

A brief digression is in order before consideration of this second scene. In between the two proposals of marriage, a conspiracy is hatched that might preclude the desired marriage—a plot that serves to raise the issue of who has power over the seemingly autonomous young woman. Sainte Anne's mother absolutely disapproves of this young woman, and she conspires to marry off Mlle d'Estival to another man. For Mme de Sainte Anne, Mlle d'Estival threatens both her sense of family honor, representing the danger of a shocking union that "donneroit pour aïeul à mes petits-fils le jardinier de Monsieur d'Estival" (279) [would give my grandsons the gardener of Mr. d'Estival as ancestor], and her desire to have her son marry Mlle Rhedon, the daughter of the man that she wishes she had married after she became a widow (280). While Mlle Rhedon is delighted at the prospect, Sainte Anne adamantly opposes the arrangement, pointing out to his mother that Mlle Rhedon is as much the daughter of her mother as she is of her father. His mother is inflexible and resolute. Unfortunately, Mlle d'Estival represents such an improper match for a nobleman that he would have to be his own master (287) to manage it against the wishes of his sole surviving parent. Furthermore, the power Mme de Sainte Anne has over Mlle d'Estival is considerable. When Sainte Anne leaves to go visit one of their abandoned castles, his mother takes steps to force the young woman into a marriage with Sainte Anne's best friend, Tonquedec.

It is a letter and its reading that will set the stage for the second proposal scene, although this proposal will not be made by Sainte Anne. The scheme of Mme de Sainte Anne is halted at the very party celebrating the success of this scheme. All the characters, except Sainte Anne, are gathered for a dinner party in honor of Mlle d'Estival's imminent marriage to Tonquedec. However, Mme de Sainte Anne's jubilation at having prevented her son from marrying someone other than Mlle Rhedon is troubled by an incident suggesting the young people around her are not as much under her thumb as she had assumed. "Je m'aperçois, dit-elle, que personne n'a chez moi moins d'autorité que moi" (304) [I notice, she said, that no one has less authority in my house than I do]. Her pique is caused by the way in which a mysterious letter is handled. This letter is one that Mlle d'Estival pulls out of her purse while everyone is seated at the dinner table. Being illiterate, she cannot read it, and so she passes it on to Mlle Rhedon, her rival for Sainte Anne, asking her to read it. Mlle Rhedon reads the letter but then passes it on to Tonquedec, despite Mme de Sainte Anne's efforts to take possession of it. Tonquedec reads the letter but then passes on to Mlle d'Estival not the letter but the right to decide what it means. The letter is from Sainte Anne's manservant, and in it, he tells Mlle d'Estival that if she marries anyone other than his master, Sainte Anne will die. Both the readers of the letter, Mlle de Rhedon and Tonquedec, could have held the letter and used it to further their own desires: for Mlle de Rhedon, this would mean marriage to Sainte Anne; for Tonquedec, marriage to Mlle d'Estival. Both the readers choose to pass on the letter, causing Mlle d'Estival to receive her second marriage proposal indirectly from Sainte Anne. Right in front of Mme de Sainte Anne, Tonquedec asks Mlle d'Estival whether she prefers him or Sainte Anne (306). The young woman chooses Sainte Anne because she loves him. The sequence of readings that brings about the happy ending reflects a lateral, not hierarchical, power structure, so that mutual trust and sacrifice are the determining factors, not any sort of dominance.[37]

I have considered this scene with the manservant's letter as the second proposal scene in the novel, even though Sainte Anne is not present to do the proposing. His physical absence confirms the freedom that is given to the woman: the ability to choose her husband on her own. Furthermore, having the movement of the letter serve to redistribute the authority for who will dispose of Mlle d'Estival's hand in marriage provides a striking contrast with the first proposal scene. To appreciate the nature of this conclusion, we need only consider how Madame de Sainte Anne is disarmed. The oppositional parent is reconciled to her son's marriage when one of the guests makes her read a letter from Sainte Anne in which he presents as a fact his attachment to Mlle d'Estival: "Mademoiselle de Kerber, en éclairant Madame de Ste. Anne, *l'avoit forcée* à souscrire de bonne grace à ce qu'elle ne pouvoit empêcher" (306; emphasis added) [Miss de Kerber, by enlightening Mrs. Sainte Anne, *had forced* her to endorse what she could not prevent]. The gothic graveyard scene, whose reading is predetermined, has vanished, to be replaced by a scene in which reading can contest the dominant power structure.

Once the d'Estival/Sainte Anne wedding is set, the other dinner guests manifest a fever for nuptials, and within the space of two pages no fewer than four marriages are set. Such a plethora of weddings in a conclusion, unless it is a comedy by Molière or Marivaux, seems out of place, and the narrator, anticipating some resistance on the part of the reader, intervenes at this point to defend the plausibility of the conclusion:

> C'est bien assez que les lectures soient inutiles; elles seroient très-nuisibles, si d'après de romanesques folies qui n'ont rien coûté à l'auteur, on sacrifioit des sentimens plus vrais, plus naturels, et qui sont parfaitement honnêtes. Laissons quelques admirateurs de Werther se tuer, et quelques folles pleurer toute leur vie ce qu'elles n'ont peut-être jamais eu sujet d'aimer. Il ne faut pas dans la vie véritable imiter un invraisemblable roman. (308)

[It's already enough that reading is useless. It would be very harmful if, after novelistic flights of fancy that cost the author nothing, one sacrificed feelings that are more true, more natural, and in fact perfectly honest. Let a few admirers of Werther kill themselves, and a few madwomen cry their whole life over never perhaps having had a reason to love. One must not in real life imitate an unrealistic novel.]

It seems as if the narrator is defying the reader to find the wedding-prone characters of the conclusion deficient in feelings that are "true . . . natural, and . . . perfectly honest"; to find, in other words, that the conclusion is "unrealistic." And yet, the conclusion is precisely that.[38]

Faced with such a confrontation between a cliché that, in the context of this novel, is bound to seem *invraisemblable,* and an imperative from the narrator to accept the cliché as *vraisemblable,* the reader may be led to question this category. We know that this category has a repressive function: "What a particular society judges to be logical or probable is always bound up with a prior determination of what is deemed proper."[39] Charrière's conclusion contests what society deems proper by asking the question, Who is to say what is and is not *vraisemblable?*[40] Is it *invraisemblable* for a woman's freedom to choose her spouse to be coded as desirable by appending to it the many-happy-marriages conclusion, a literary sign for "All's well that ends well"? In provoking from us these questions, she recreates the act of reading inscribed in the route taken by the manservant's letter. Passing on the crucial letter, the fictional readers staged the question, Who will have power over Mlle d'Estival? Daring the reader to see an *invraisemblable* conclusion as *vraisemblable,* **Sainte Anne** stages the question, Who will have power over what is proper?

In the three novels considered here, there is a progression in Charrière's innovation with regard to the figure of the heroine. Undermining specific stereotypes of women leads finally to contesting the force of stereotyping itself, as expressed in the constraint of *vraisemblance*. In this, her fiction has a political content and possibly more. Hypothesizing that "an impotent feminine sensibility is a basic structure of the novel, representing one of the important ways that the novel embodies the basic structures of this society," Myra Jehlen proposes that "the achievement of female autonomy must have radical implications not only politically but also for the very forms and categories of all our thinking."[41] The heroines considered here are all the more distinctive because the autonomy they attain is represented in a text which itself challenges ways of thinking about women. Their distinctiveness is well illustrated in a novel of which we have only one sentence, **Camille ou le nouveau roman** (1796). Through this novel, she proposed to create a radically new heroine: "Mon plan . . . a été de changer ce que les romans font toujours c'est de faire l'heroine belle comme le jour, je la ferai ici laide comme la nuit" (9:355) [My plan . . . was to change what novels always do: namely, to make the heroine as pretty as a picture. Here I will make her as ugly as sin]. In fact, Charrière did create such a radically new heroine: her names are Julie, Germaine/Pauline, and Mlle d'Estival.

Notes

[1] *Lettres portugaises, Lettres d'une péruvienne et d'autres romans d'amour par lettres,* ed. Bernard Bray and Isabelle Landy-Houillon (Paris: Flammarion, 1983).

[2] In Isabelle Landy-Houillon's introduction to this novel, she cites the correspondence of Mme du Deffand and Horace Walpole and their use of it to threaten each other. (*Lettres portugaises,* 23.) Similarly, Linda Kauffman cites Mme de Sévigné's use of "une portugaise" to describe the type of letter that she will not write in response to an overly tender correspondent. (Linda S. Kauffman, *Discourses of Desire: Gender, Genre and Epistolary Fictions* [Ithaca, N.Y.: Cornell University Press, 1986], 95.) As an example of the force that a particular representation of woman can acquire, *Lettres portugaises* is perhaps overdetermined, but it denotes well the symbiotic relationship between social perceptions of women and the literary texts that both draw on and sustain them.

[3] See, for example, Elizabeth L. Berg, "Iconoclastic Moments: Reading the *Sonnets for Helene,* Writing the *Portuguese Letters,*" in *Poetics of Gender,* ed. Nancy K. Miller (New York: Columbia University Press, 1986), and Peggy Kamuf, "Writing like a Woman," in *Women and Language in Literature and Society,* ed. Sally McConnell-Ginet, Ruth Borker, and Nelly Furmen (New York: Praeger Publishers, 1980).

[4] Nancy K. Miller, "Men's Reading, Women's Writing: Gender and the Rise of the Novel," in *Displacements: Women, Tradition, Literatures in French*, ed. Joan DeJean and Nancy K. Miller (Baltimore: The Johns Hopkins University Press, 1991), 41.

[5] For example, images of women in both literature and art share a common ground in the eighteenth century. Thus, Gutwirth looks at revolutionary-era images of beautiful women drowning. With regard to paintings and novels, she emphasizes the force of these images which were so compelling because they "mirror[ed] men's desire." (Madelyn Gutwirth, "The Engulfed Beloved: Representations of Dead and Dying Women in the Art and Literature of the Revolutionary Era," in *Rebel Daughters: Women and the French Revolution*, ed. Sara E. Melzer and Leslie W. Rabine [New York: Oxford University Press, 1992], 212.) My own concern is with less extreme images which nonetheless convey an equivalent force.

[6] *The Heroine's Text* is an early work by Miller. Her more recent essays on eighteenth-century woman-authored texts—for example, in *Subject to Change: Reading Feminist Writing* (New York: Columbia University Press, 1988)—draw on the methods of feminist literary criticism. Note Miller's qualification of the theoretical framework of *The Heroine's Text* in the version of "Men's Reading, Women's Writing: Gender and the Rise of the Novel" that was first printed in a special issue of *Yale French Studies* (75 [1988]: 47 n. 11). This note does not appear in the version of "Men's Reading" reprinted in 1991.

[7] Miller, *The Heroine's Text,* ix.

[8] Margaret Higonnet, "Speaking Silences: Women's Suicide," in *The Female Body in Western Culture: Contemporary Perspectives,* ed. Susan Rubin Suleiman (Cambridge, Mass.: Harvard University Press, 1985), 74.

[9] The insistence on presenting an archetypal heroine causes eighteenth-century novelists sometimes to stretch the limits of the believable, according to Vivienne Mylne. For example, she defines the dangerous boating trip in Jean-Jacques Rousseau's *Julie ou la Nouvelle Héloïse* which almost results in a shipwreck as "non-literal" because of the description he gives of Julie's actions during the crisis. Mylne asserts that Rousseau's "interest is concentrated on the notion of Julie as . . . fulfilling the universal rôle of Woman when her menfolk are in danger." (Vivienne Mylne, *The Eighteenth-Century French Novel: Techniques of Illusion* [Cambridge, Mass.: Cambridge University Press, 1981], 171.) Whatever the plot, the heroine's actions are dictated less by the particulars of their predicament and more by the stereotypes that both create and sustain such heroines.

[10] Fauchery, *La Destinée féminine,* 516, 653 (emphasis in the original; translation mine). Miller's review of this book is itself an excellent take on the problem of the heroine. (Nancy K. Miller, "The Exquisite Cadavers: Women in Eighteenth-Century Fiction," review of *La Destinée féminine,* by Pierre Fauchery, *Diacritics* 5 [1975]: 37-43.)

[11] Fauchery classifies Charrière as one of those European women writers who represent woman's superiority in the form of their heroines' greater capacity for emotion and of their heros' inadequacy in this area. (*La Destinée féminine,* 581.) Thus, for him, the death of the loving but unloved Caliste in Charrière's *Lettres écrites de Lausanne* is ennobling (101). It is true that the male characters in Charrière's fiction often seem as if they are not quite able to cope with love. However, her female characters are more than just human beings endowed with extreme emotions; they function at several different levels. This is especially true of Caliste, a character who must be situated in the larger context of this two-part novel to be understood.

[12] Elizabeth J. MacArthur, "Devious Narratives: Refusal of Closure in Two Eighteenth-Century Epistolary Novels," *Eighteenth-Century Studies* 21, no. 1 (Fall 1987): 19 n. 29.

[13] For a discussion of the epistolary form and its relationship to gender with particular regard to the image of woman, see Linda S. Kauffman, *Discourses of Desire: Gender, Genre and Epistolary Fictions* (Ithaca, N.Y.: Cornell University Press, 1986). For a telling example of this relationship, see Nancy K. Miller's analysis of a scene from a Jane Austen novel (*Persuasion*) in which it is not a woman but a man writing a love letter. Miller qualifies this scene, because of its allegorical value, as a "staging of the scene of reading, writing, and sexual difference." ("Rereading as a Woman: the Body in Practice," in *The Female Body in Western Culture: Contemporary Perspectives,* ed. Susan Rubin Suleiman [Cambridge, Mass.: Harvard University Press, 1985], 360.)

[14] A figure such as Julie's brother, who laughs at her dilemma, appears to be a cardboard character. Although he boasts of how he has just cheated a fellow gambler, his crime appears not as a product of his personal vice but as a symptom of the degeneration of the aristocracy. Thus, Julie's reaction to his boast is to dream of escaping with Valaincourt so that she can go far away from representatives, like her brother, of what she ironically calls "cette aimable Noblesse" (32) [this worthy nobility].

[15] La Fontaine, *Oeuvres complètes* (Paris: Editions du Seuil, 1965), 137. Translation mine.

[16] Charrière makes a similar suggestion in an undated political parable, "Les deux familles" (9:617-20).

[17] Fauchery, *La Destinée féminine*, 298.

[18] We need to remember how unsuitable this marriage is. Michèle Mat-Hasquin comments on an even more unsuitable marriage in Charrière's play *L'Inconsolable* [*The Unconsolable*], a marriage that ties an aristocrat to a peasant girl. Mat-Hasquin emphasizes that the plot is organized so that this marriage is understood to have been authorized two years prior to the action shown on stage, as if to forestall criticism of such an outrageous match by virtue of its being a given within the fictional context presented. (Michèle Mat-Hasquin, "Dramaturgie et démistification dans les comédies d'Isabelle de Charrière," *Etudes sur le XVIIIe siècle* 8 [1981]: 63.)

[19] Landes, *Women and the Public Sphere*, 46.

[20] Denis Diderot, "Sur les femmes" [On women], in *Qu'est-ce qu'une femme?* [What is a woman?], ed. Elisabeth Badinter (Paris: P. O. L., 1989), 179. Translation mine.

[21] Fauchery writes that the epistolary novel is founded on "attention à soi" [attention to oneself], but that this does not imply "clairvoyance." He suggests that part of the reader's pleasure depends on understanding the heroine better than she understands herself. (*La Destinée féminine*, 646 n. 6; translation mine.) From this point of view, the narrator's comment on Julie's dishonesty makes her even more disempowered, as it opposes the knowing narrator/reader to the unknowing heroine.

[22] We know she has such portraits when she modestly remarks to Valaincourt, "Mes Grandes-meres ne sont pas belles, mais cela ne fait rien, elles sont anciennes" (25) [My grandmothers are not pretty, but that doesn't matter: they're ancient].

[23] This is comparable to what happens in Françoise de Graffigny's *Lettres d'une péruvienne* (1747) when the kidnapped Zilia achieves financial independence as a result of the stolen Peruvian gold throne that is melted down for her. In Julia Douthwaite's study of the novel, she describes this sacrilege with an exclamation: "The Peruvian icon, symbol of a patriarchal cult, is melted down and becomes the foundation for a woman's independent life!" (Julia Douthwaite, *Exotic Heroines: Literary Heroines and Cultural Strategies in Ancien Régime France* [Philadelphia: University of Pennsylvania Press, 1992], 124.) Julie's grandfatherly portraits are destroyed and not, one assumes, reworked (or even retrieved) to fulfill some new function. Furthermore, it was not Zilia herself who caused the gold to be melted down, whereas it is Julie who, on her own, destines the portraits for the murky moat. In this, the destruction of the portraits in Charrière's text seems a more aggressive gesture, although the end result, Julie's marriage to the man she loves, is less unconventional than Zilia's choice of an independent life.

[24] Jean Starobinski, "Les *Lettres écrites de Lausanne* de Madame de Charrière: inhibition psychique et interdit social," in *Roman et lumières au XVIIIe siècle* (Paris: Editions Sociales, 1970), 147.

[25] S. Dresden, "Madame de Charrière et le goût du témoin," *Neophilologus* 45 (1961): 266-67.

[26] Julie's cry when, having crossed the moat by trampling on the graven images of her grandfathers, she finds that the door to the outside of the castle is locked, represents well this stepping outside the old structure: "Dieux! que deviendrai-je . . . si je ne trouve point d'issue!" (33) [Heavens! What will I become . . . if I can't find a way out!]. Indeed, it is as much a question of what she "will become" as it is a question of simply rejoining Valaincourt.

[27] "Charrière, Isabelle-Agnès-Elisabeth van Tuyll van Serooskerken van Zuylen de (1740-1805)," in *Bloomsbury Guide to Women's Literature*, ed. Claire Buck (London: Bloomsbury, 1992), 410. *Lettres trouvées* was preceded by another text in a political vein, *Lettres trouvées dans la neige* [Letters found in the snow], also published in 1793 (10:226-54). The latter is more overtly political. Written in direct response to the unrest that the French Revolution had inspired in the area around Neuchâtel, it consists of commentary on social issues with no development of the two male characters who write to each other.

[28] A letter she wrote in 1792 reveals just how unfeeling she must have seemed: "Depuis quelque tems je recommande l'étude de la logique à toutes les femmes que je rencontre. Les émigrées m'ont surtout persuadé qu'il faloit s'être accoutumé à raisonner avec une stricte justesse pour ne pas deraisonner grossierement dès que la douleur ou le desir, ou le ressentiment nous y invitent" (letter to Henriette L'Hardy, 5 April 1792; 3:352) [For some time now, I have been recommending the study of logic to all the women that I meet. The women émigrés especially have convinced me that one has to be accustomed to reasoning with strict exactitude in order not to miscalculate grossly once pain, desire, or resentment incite us to it].

[29] In contrast to my interpretation, one of the editors of the *Oeuvres complètes* sees Pauline as unimportant. Jerome Vercruyesse's essay concerning the impact of the Revolution on Charrière's theater assimilates *Lettres trouvées* to her political writings. This means that for him the significance of Pauline is purely symbolic and does not make of *Lettres trouvées* a novel. (Jerome Vercruyesse, "Histoire et théâtre chez Isabelle de Charrière," *Revue d'histoire littéraire de la France* 85, no. 6 [1985]: 979-80.)

[30] Pauline's mother had been afraid of being embarrassed: "Si on venoit à me reconnoitre malgré mon

deguisement quelle risée! quel esclandre! Les railleries les plus insultantes feroient rougir ma respectable Mere & parviendroient jusqu'à Mon Mari" (480) [If I came to be recognized despite my disguise, what a big joke! What a brouhaha! The most insulting teasing would make my respectable mother blush and would reach even my husband].

31 Fonbrune met Pauline as a result of being wounded and then being housed in her castle. In a subsequent letter concerning his screaming nightmares, he once again addresses her in a letter to Alphonse: "Elle . . . envoy[a] quelqu'un, qui . . . demanda si c'était ma blessure qui me causait de si violentes douleurs . . . C'est pis que cela, compâtissante Pauline; ce sont des spectres, ce sont de sanglans cadavres" (430) [She . . . sent someone who . . . asked if it was my wound that was causing me such violent pain . . . It is worse than that, compassionate Pauline; it is specters, it is bloody cadavers].

32 Similarly, when she agrees to accept a ring from him, she formulates her acceptance as an imperative: "Oui, je le veux, donnez" (466) [Yes, I want it. Give it to me].

33 Stewart has described Charrière's use of the letter-novel as being "to describe the fleeting and the inconclusive," asserting that this genre "realizes its potential as the form best suited to writing the life of a woman and to exploring the unacknowledged control exercised by domestic concerns over female psychology." (Stewart, *Gynographs,* 97.) I agree, but I also find in Charrière's fiction evidence of an understanding of what may be implied by the affiliation between women and the letter-novel or letter writing itself.

34 In Isabelle Vissière's anthology of Charrière's works concerning the Revolution, she suggests that the author may have stopped here with *Lettres trouvées* because the magnitude of the changes taking place in the aftermath of 1789 made her hesitate to go too far with her own representation of these changes. Vissière describes *Lettres trouvées* as a little story written in the shadow of the Revolution. (*Isabelle de Charrière: Une aristocrate révolutionnaire. Ecrits 1788-1794* [Paris: Des Femmes, 1988], 368.) The focus of such an interpretation tends to obscure the evolution from one heroine to the next, and in no way accounts for the striking qualities of Pauline.

35 Douthwaite, *Exotic Heroines,* 13.

36 By gothic, I mean the literary genre first popularized in England by the success of Horace Walpole's *The Castle of Otranto* (1764). In George E. Haggerty's analysis of the gothic, he emphasizes that "from its first literary appearance [the term] implied not just a particular setting but a particular *use* of setting."

(George E. Haggerty, *Gothic Fiction/Gothic Form* [University Park: The Pennsylvania State University Press, 1989], 11.) The description of the graveyard in *Sainte Anne* is clearly organized around such a use—namely, creating an emotional effect rather than conveying geographical details. In Alice M. Killen's study of the French reception of the gothic, she describes the origins of the genre by citing British poets who first began to "promener leurs lecteurs dans de noirs cimetières, hantés par les ombres de la mort" [walk their readers through black cemeteries haunted by the shadows of death]. (Alice M. Killen, *Le Roman terrifiant ou roman noir de Walpole à Anne Radcliffe et son influence sur la littérature française jusqu'en 1840* [Geneva: Slatkine Reprints, 1984], ix; translation mine.) Killen shows that the gothic reached French literary circles later, long after its start in England, having become more appealing in Anne Radcliffe's work, giving 1797 as the significant date (77). In a letter Charrière wrote the following year, she reassured her correspondent about the collection of which *Sainte Anne* was a part: "Ne craignez ou n'esperez pas que ce soyent des ruines à Spectres ni même à Hiboux. Je ne donne pas dans le genre de Mrs Ratcliffe [sic]" (letter to Dudley Ryder, 5:443) [Do not fear or hope that there should be any ruins with specters or even with owls. I do not lean toward the Mrs. Ratcliffe genre]. The choice to include the graveyard scene in *Sainte Anne* must be understood not as giving into what was fashionable but as including, in a parodic manner, a genre she regarded as trivial. Later in 1802, Charrière writes to a friend that she regrets not having read a certain novel by Madame de Staël because "bon ou mauvais il m'auroit amusée. Elle y donnoit à ce qu'on m'a dit dans les spectres & les apparitions" (letter to Isabelle Morel-de Gélieu, 6:514) [good or bad it would have amused me. According to what I've heard, she leans toward specters and apparitions]. Charrière qualifies this style as "à la Ratcliffe" and then goes on to complain about the paucity of invention in contemporary literature.

37 In her interpretation of *Sainte Anne,* Whatley also emphasizes the development of a new type of reading. Her conclusion is supported by a consideration of a letter Charrière wrote to her nephew. According to Whatley, the author suggests through both her letter and her novel that "learning to read" represents learning how to negotiate a place for oneself within a society in transition. (Whatley, "Isabelle de Charrière," 42.)

38 The hyperbolic description of the resolution—"jamais on n'avoit montré tant d'amitié de générosité. Tonquedec étoit le meilleur des amis, Mademoiselle de Rhedon la plus généreuse des rivales" (9:306) [never had so much generosity, so much friendship been shown. Tonquedec was the best of friends, Miss Rhedon the most generous of rivals]—is similar to a description of a real situation Charrière described in a letter

in 1762: "jamais on ne vit de parens plus delicats, d'amant plu honnête ni de fille plus irresolue" (letter to the Baron Constant d'Hermenches; 1:147) [never did one see parents more delicate, a lover more honest, nor a girl so irresolute].

[39] Kamuf, "Writing like a Woman," 293.

[40] In an undated fragment catalogued by the editors of the *Oeuvres complètes* as *Le Roman de Charles Cecil*, we find the following eloquent formulation: "N'est-il pas etrange, que le jugement même que l'on porte de la figure, que chacun voit, depende d'une opinion préalable, & qu'il faille à la plupart des gens l'autorité de la voix publique pour juger de ce qu'ils ont devant les yeux" (9:641-42) [Is it not strange that the judgment one passes on the person we all see depends on a preexisting opinion, and that most people need the authority of the public voice in order to judge what they have before their eyes]. Due to the uncertain status of the text, I do not treat it in the present study; however, it is hard to conceive of a statement that could describe so well the type of force exercised by *vraisemblance*.

[41] Myra Jehlen, "Archimedes and the Paradox of Feminist Criticism," in *Feminisms: An Anthology of Literary Theory and Criticism*, ed. Robyn R. Warhol and Diane Price Herndl (New Brunswick, N.J.: Rutgers University Press, 1991), 95.

FURTHER READING

Biography

Dubois, Pierre H. "'An Utrecht Lady's Charms': Belle van Zuylen/Isabelle de Charrière." In *The Low Countries: Arts and Society in Flanders and the Netherlands, A Yearbook: 1994-97*, pp. 125-30. N.p.: Flemish-Netherlands Foundation "Stichting Ons Erfdeel," 1995.

Offers a brief overview of Charrière's life and response to her work.

Fink, Beatrice. "Isabelle de Charrière: Correspondent, Novelist, and Woman of Independent Mind." *Eighteenth-Century Life* 13, No. 1 (February 1989): 1-3.

Provides an introduction to a series of articles concerning the life and work of Charrière.

Lacy, Margriet Bruyn. "Madame de Charrière and the Constant Family." *Romance Notes* XXIII, No. 2 (Winter 1982): 154-58.

Examines the relationships between Charrière and both David Constant d'Hermenches and his nephew, Benjamin Constant.

———. "Belle van Zuylen/Isabelle de Charrière (1740-1805), Tradition and Defiance." *Canadian Journal of Netherlandic Studies* XI, No. ii (Fall 1990): 33-6.

Gives an overview of Charrière's life and work, with English translations.

Scott, Geoffrey. *The Portrait of Zélide*. New York: Charles Scribner's Sons, 1926, 216 p.

First comprehensive biography of Charrière in English, based largely on Philippe Godet's detailed 1906 account *Madame de Charrière et ses amis*.

West, Anthony. "Madame de Charrière." In his *Mortal Wounds*, pp. 183-221. New York: McGraw-Hill Book Co., 1973.

Biographical account placed in the context of "behavioral studies of three women writers," in which West compares Charrière with Madame de Staël and George Sand. The essay includes English translations of numerous letters.

Whatley, Janet. "Isabelle de Charrière (1740-1805)." In *French Women Writers: A Bio-Bibliographical Source Book*, edited by Eva Martin Sartori and Dorothy Wynne Zimmerman, pp. 35-46. New York: Greenwood Press, 1991.

Surveys Charrière's life, oeuvre, and the major themes manifested in her work.

Criticism

Courtney, C. P. "Isabelle de Charrière and the 'Character of H. B. Constant': A False Attribution." *French Studies* XXXVI, No. 3 (July 1982): 282-89.

Disputes the attribution of a short character-sketch of Benjamin Constant to Charrière, ascribing it instead to John Wilde, a fellow student of Constant's at Edinburgh.

Jackson, Susan Klem. "Disengaging Isabelle: Professional Rhetoric and Female Friendship in the Correspondence of Mme de Charrière and Mlle de Gélieu." *Eighteenth-Century Life* 13, No. 1 (February 1989): 26-41.

Traces the lifelong friendship between "the two Isabelles," and the mediating circumstances generated both by eighteenth-century society and the two women themselves.

MacArthur, Elizabeth J. "Devious Narratives: Refusal of Closure in Two Eighteenth-Century Epistolary Novels." *Eighteenth-Century Studies* 21, No. 1 (1987): 1-20.

Discusses Charrière's *Mistriss Henley* and Françoise de Graffigny's *Lettre d'una Peruviana* as eighteenth-century works which takes up female identity at a formal level, rejecting the closed narrative of the male literary model.

Mary Moody Emerson

1774-1863

American intellectual.

INTRODUCTION

Although Mary Moody Emerson has generally been overshadowed by the renown of her nephew, Ralph Waldo Emerson (1803-1882), the originality of her ideas has recently earned her a reputation in her own right, as a unique American woman and scholar. Not only was she an important precursor of transcendentalism, but she was also an inheritor of Calvinist tendencies; her intellectual position between early and modern America was a deeply significant amalgamation of individualism, stoicism, and faith.

Biographical Information

Emerson was born in Concord, Massachusetts, where she was to spend much of her life, into a family of ministers. She took great pride in this heritage of Puritan spirituality and remained fiercely pious throughout her life. When she was two years old, and upon the death of her father, she was sent away from her family to be raised on an isolated farm in Malden with her paternal grandmother. Although Emerson spent many of her early years in relative poverty and solitude in the wake of the American Revolution, she managed to familiarize herself with the works of Shakespeare and several English poets as well as with religious texts. After 1811, when her brother William died, she supervised the moral, spiritual, and intellectual education of her nephews. This led to a long and close relationship with Ralph Waldo Emerson—although she reviled his decision to leave the ministry in 1832 and was disturbed for many years over his controversial "Divinity School Address," delivered at Harvard in 1838, in which he renounced the tenets of historical Christianity and defined Transcendental philosophy in terms of the "impersoneity" of God. Throughout her adulthood, she spent her time journeying around New England, visiting friends and relatives, although from 1807 to 1850 she co-owned a farm in Waterford, Maine. Toward the end of her life, she became known in Concord as an eccentric who spent much time anticipating her own death and engaging in theological debates.

Major Works

Although Emerson was a voracious reader, her writing is limited to a multitude of letters and *Almanacks*—what she called her journals—in which she recorded daily events from about 1802 to 1855. Her letters reflect a life steeped in religious thought and self-sufficiency; her harsh assessments of "human pretensions" lie in stark contrast to her celebrations of the wonder of God's creations. Her interpretation of Calvinism emphasized the importance of solitary reflection, and what she called "alchemy": the transformation of suffering into creative and spiritual energy, which leads to atonement and "access to divinity." This very personal relationship with God and the divine order led to an interest in natural phenomena, which she recorded in her *Almanacks*. The *Almanacks* are only a marginal example of the woman's diary, as they document events much less personal than cosmic. Emerson called the journals "a letter to me"; her musings there retain the intellectual focus of her letters to others. She was an ardent and prolific correspondent; her letters were a primary mode of communication during her travels around New England, and reflect the strength of her commitment to spiritual purification through duty and compassion, as well as her disgust at the degeneration of religious influences in nineteenth-century America.

Textual History

Emerson's surviving letters, which scholar Nancy Craig Simmons estimates to be "half or less" of the original number, were preserved by many of her correspondents and are now collected in several libraries around New England. Her missives to her most intimate friends—including Ralph Waldo Emerson—are among those that have not survived in their original form. Ralph Waldo Emerson kept and transcribed long passages from both the *Almanacks* and the letters, but the original manuscript of the *Almanacks* was damaged in an 1872 fire at his residence. George Tolman, a Concord historian who (in 1902) presented the first full account of Emerson's life and work, also generated a transcription that has become the authoritative version of the *Almanacks*, which runs to almost one thousand pages.

Critical Reception

While popular opinion in Concord labeled Emerson an unconventional and grim woman preoccupied with the spiritual decay of the nation, the recipients of her letters respected her intellectual agility and keen understanding of theology. The most prominent of the American transcendentalists—Henry David Thoreau and Ralph Waldo Emerson—considered her to be a stimulating and demanding correspondent; Ralph Waldo Emerson called her his "muse." More recent critics have emphasized the unique position of Mary Moody Emerson as a woman who strove to fulfill an inheritance of scholarly and spiritual ability and thus rejected conventional values. Her letters and *Almanacks* document the transition that brought the nation politically from the earliest years of the nineteenth century to the brink of the Civil War, and intellectually from the rule of Puritan faith to the contemplative movement of transcendentalism.

PRINCIPAL WORKS

**Almanacks (journals) 1902
†*The Selected Letters of Mary Moody Emerson* (letters) 1993

*Written approximately 1802-1855.
†Written 1793-1862.

CRITICISM

Phyllis Cole (essay date 1982)

SOURCE: "The Advantage of Loneliness: Mary Moody Emerson's *Almanacks*, 1802-1855," in *Emerson: Prospect and Retrospect,* edited by Joel Porte, Harvard University Press, 1982, pp. 1-32.

[*In the following essay, Cole examines Emerson's spiritual beliefs, derived from early American Puritanism and romanticism, as expressed in her* Almanacks *and letters.*]

> Were the genius of the Xian religion painted, her form would be full of majesty, her mien solemn, her aspect benign, and strongly impressed with joy & hope, her eyes raised to Heaven with tears for Zion and rays of glory descending to illuminate the earth at her intreaties![1]

In 1804, when Mary Moody Emerson described this emblematic female "genius" in the pages of her *Almanack,* she was thirty years old and clearly hopeful of living out the ideal she imagined. It is an impressively strong figure. A single female form—unaccompanied by parents or husband or children, friends or congregation—raises its eyes directly to Heaven, without the intercession of priest or even redeeming Christ. In fact she hopes herself to intercede for others. She weeps for Zion, the fallen city and apostate people, and at the same time she conveys heavenly glory and hope back to earth. She seems a New England Rachel or Virgin Mary, but also a Jeremiah.[2] An explicitly female figure, she nonetheless goes beyond the conventional piety of New England women in her separation from the domestic sphere and her unfeminine prophetic power.[3]

Such an idealization of the solitary self was radical for both its gender and its time: indeed a significant anticipation of the self-reliance that Mary's nephew Ralph Waldo Emerson would articulate as the primarily masculine romantic vision of the next generation. Waldo later acknowledged Mary's importance as an influence on his vision and a "representative life" of New England in her own time. When in the 1820s he recalled the aunt who had taken on the intermittent role of spiritual instructor to his fatherless childhood, he saw her as a "genius" from whom "rained . . . influences of ancestral religion" upon his soul and thus saved it from the arid forms of Cambridge Unitarianism. After Mary's death in 1863, when he fully memorialized her in a biographical lecture, Waldo again characterized his aunt as a figure mediating between "ancestral religion" and Transcendentalism: her life marked "the precise moment when the power of the old creed yielded to the influence of modern science and humanity." Further, he specified the quality of this transitional life as solitary, unladylike, and prophetic. A woman who "could keep step with no human being," Mary was "our Delphian"—"Cassandra domesticated in a lady's house" and as such a "troublesome boarder."[4] Waldo's portrait of Mary was both sympathetic and astute.

But it was also a portrait made from very close perspective, and one that to a considerable extent possessed and controlled its troublesome subject as "*our* Delphian" aunt. Both in historical sequence and in her own priority of values, Mary was herself before she was Waldo's aunt. Whether for the study of Emerson or for the broader histories of women and religion in America, it is time that Mary be disengaged from Waldo's memory of her, seen within her own generation, and more fully represented by her own words. Waldo revered these words: he quoted at length from both her *Almanacks* and letters in the biographical sketch, and he transcribed an even more extensive selection of passages into journals as he prepared his study. But Waldo's transcriptions are only a fraction of the manuscript record available to modern scholars. Believing Waldo's testimony to the "representative" value of Mary's solitude, we need to construct a sense of it that is ours and not his.

Mary's *Almanacks* are her fullest exploration of solitude: this journal she called "a letter to me when unable to think . . . Private" (22, 1), a "conversation with my chamber" (17, A), and a prayer from "my soul to its author" (22, 3). Its earliest extant entry (28, 2) is undated but was probably written in 1802,[5] its last (broken off in mid-sentence) dated 1855, eight years before Mary's death at nearly eighty-nine. The journal began, that is, just before Waldo was born, his father

William took on the job of editing Federalist Boston's *Monthly Anthology,* and the New England Way split permanently into orthodox and Unitarian factions; it ended the year Whitman sent *Leaves of Grass* to Emerson, who was by then the aging mentor of the American Renaissance. The *Almanacks* are a major text, possibly New England's longest as well as last Puritan diary by a woman.[6] In them the full life of Mary Moody Emerson is in fact not evident; her voluminous correspondence, which Evelyn Barish has for several years been studying, offers the better sense of her life with and influence on family and friends.[7] But the *Almanacks* express her central, even obsessive, theme: "My life I would occupy only in the study of its wonders—in arranging my ideas of its real character" (7, 6).

In the essay that follows I will try to suggest the terms of this self-study: first, Mary's sense of her own position in the post-Revolutionary generation of Emersons; second, her religious temperament and theological position in the earliest part (1802-1807) of the *Almanacks;* third, her preoccupation with and exercise of memory, especially memory of childhood; and finally, her intellectual position between Jonathan Edwards and Ralph Waldo Emerson.

Mary was always more concerned with eternity than time: she seems to have called her journal an *Almanack* because she was consciously projecting herself into the heavens, chronicling "sun and moon's rising" as a "horologue" in time of the timeless God she sought (20, 12; 24, D.)[8] The "wonders" she wished to study were moments of apprehending divine, not social, relationship. But of course this unworldly consciousness is itself one expression of time and place, of a woman's opportunities and exclusions in the years of the early Republic.[9]

Mary's sense of herself as an Emerson dictated the terms in which she experienced both opportunities and exclusions. Born in Concord's ministerial manse in 1774, less than a year before the battle at North Bridge, Mary as an adult laid hold of the double heritage of Puritan clerical status and Revolutionary fervor. The Emersons were an eminent clerical dynasty, one whose position and theological leaning were often reinforced by marriage: Mary's grandfather the Reverend Joseph Emerson of Malden had married Mary Moody, daughter of the Reverend Samuel Moody of York, Maine; their twelfth child, the Reverend William Emerson, had settled in Concord and married Phebe Bliss, daughter of his predecessor the Reverend Samuel Bliss. All the Emerson, Moody, and Bliss clergy had actively supported Jonathan Edwards and George Whitfield in the 1740s, and by the 1770s, as chaplain to the Concord Minutemen, William was redirecting this Great Awakening piety into pro-Revolutionary politics.[10] For Mary, the center of the Revolution—indeed of all America— was the heroism and martyrdom of her father, William. It was his privilege to hear "the toskin of early war— of glorious freedom!" (7, 6). Yet not much more than a year after the battle in Concord he died of camp fever on his way home through Vermont from Fort Ticonderoga. In her own elder years, regarding an America compromised to materialism and slavery, Mary wished that she could take "the dust of my father from the Green Mountains" back to England (15, 11).

For in her view the glory both of America and of her own life had only declined since that early moment: "Soul of man made for immortal races sickens at possession. Ah it was the possession of headless families—of poverty—of protracted sufferings wh quench the light even of such a noble struggle—wh doom the helpless orphan to find liberty & all that makes life valuable sunk in the beloved grave" (7, 6). The grandiose self-pity of this statement should not keep us from recognizing its hard truth: William anticipated the Revolution as millennial glory; his daughter inherited the Revolution as social chaos, deprivation, orphanhood. Either when William departed from Concord or when he died, Phebe (with five children under the age of eight) sent Mary to be raised by her widowed grandmother Mary Moody Emerson in Malden. In 1779 grandmother Mary died of smallpox,[11] and mother Phebe married the Reverend Ezra Ripley, next in the line of Concord ministers; but Mary stayed in Malden, now as ward of her childless and economically struggling aunt Ruth Emerson Sargent (later Waite). When Mary eventually rejoined her siblings and mother, she did so as a young adult and domestic helper, one only half socialized into the genteel ways of clerical households. Malden was still her primary home in 1804 as she described her Christian "genius."

Throughout the *Almanacks* Mary sees herself, with resentment and defiance, as a have-not in a world of American and Emersonian haves. "Hail happy day," she writes on the fiftieth anniversary of Independence, "—tho' the revolution gave me to slavery of poverty & ignorance & long orphanship,—yet it gave my fellow men liberty" (6, 5). She prays in 1802 that God will "remember thy favor, thy covenant with my ancestors—their faith their holiness were eminent. *Why not mine!*" (28, 7). Her life, she adds three decades later, has been an exile from that ancestry: "I have wandered, from [the] cradle—and in the apartments of social affection . . . all say—*forbear to enter the pales of the initiated by birth wealth talents & patronage!*" (12, 16). But Mary proudly claims the covenant in exile, in fact implies that only have-nots will be its inheritors. "I submit with delight," she continues, "— for it is the echo of a decree from above—and from highway hedges where I get lodging . . . I get a passing vision wh is an earnest of the interminable skies where the mansions are prepared for the poor" (12,

16). Exclusion allows her to appropriate for herself what is best from a compromised but holy past.

Mary's piety-in-exile was the source of a strong if exaggerated minority view at a time when most children of the Revolution were consecrating their religious faith to the secular Republic and to internally divisive sectarian dispute.[12] Among Mary's male contemporaries in the New England church, the orthodox (including some of her Emerson cousins) were fostering group revival that ended in group conformity, the liberals (like her brother William) helping to create the Athens of America in Boston.[13] In 1827 Mary looked back at William's career at First Church Boston, ended early by his death in 1811, and found him the victim of "the imitations & competition wh alas attend City ministers" (7, 3). About ten years later she listed the thirty-one Emerson ancestors and relatives who had graduated from Harvard, using the Latin names that symbolized their (but not her) status as male scholars; and she asked, "How much of poetry in this catalogue of Cambridge Emersons?" (16, A). In her experience poetry, like the covenant, could not be had by the institutional accesses of Cambridge and Boston.

As a female lay scholar—formally educated only to bare literacy but abreast of all the theological writing of the competing seminaries—Mary could dwell everywhere and nowhere in sectarian New England. In her itinerant life she moved constantly in and out of Cambridge and Andover, Concord and the Connecticut Valley, and all the religious allegiances past and present that these places represented, able personally to resist both the fragmentation and the secularization of their joint tradition. By 1809 she had found a retreat on the upcountry frontier of Waterford, Maine, sharing land with two sisters and their husbands. But the frontier only accelerated fragmentation: Mary watched as one sister and brother-in-law lost their liberal parish before a multiplication of new sects, and as another sister and brother-in-law joined the "scamp millerites" (25, 6) in awaiting Christ's imminent Second Coming. The children of Chaplain William Emerson went many ways, and among them Mary held closest to the heart of the faith.

To a certain extent Mary's sex helped her to play this role. Puritan women had always enjoyed the freedom of privacy as well as suffered its restrictions; though required to "keep silence in the churches,"[14] they were considered to have special access to grace. But Mary sought visionary power in her private devotionalism, and this search required her to reject her generation's conventional womanhood as she rejected its secular Republic and its diminishing Church. Puritan women had traditionally found the chief end of private holiness to be the creation of a pious home, not a free self, and after the Revolution such domesticity took on ideological, patriotic meaning too. Within both the orthodox and liberal cultures of New England, women were considered Republicans: they exercised their authority in the home to encourage civic virtue in their husbands and sons, and eventually they edged into the public sphere themselves through association for benevolent reform. Mary consciously, vehemently, rejected domesticity and chose for herself a "moral grandeur" that was by implication both celibate and androgynous: "Alass," she exclaimed in 1817, "with low timid females or vulgar domestics how apt is this [grandeur] to lose its power when the nerves are weak. . . . But give me that oh God—it is holy independence—it is honor & immortality—dearer than friends wealth & influence. . . . I bless thee for giving me to see the advantage of loneliness" (38, 5). Loneliness gave her an access to divinity unavailable to either the competitive clergymen or their "low timid" wives.

Neither of the major theological views of the contemporary New England church, Calvinism or Arminianism, entirely contained Mary's independent holiness. Her inner life partook of both—of the humility, self-loathing, and fatalism of Calvinism and the willfulness and aspiration of Arminianism—just as her outer life provided social and intellectual contact with both of the increasingly separate sects defined by those theologies. The first five years of the *Almanacks,* from 1802 to 1807, express that complex temperament in the personal terms of life in Malden, just at the moment of the cultural and theological divide between Arminian Cambridge and Calvinist Andover.[15]

These were Mary's last years in her childhood home, and though she was already in her late twenties and early thirties, they appear to mark as well the end of her youth and the occasion for decisions that would be binding for life. By this time she is part owner of the house in Malden that was first her grandmother's and then her Aunt Ruth's, still sharing it with Ruth and Ruth's second husband, Samuel Waite. In January of 1807 this period ends, because Mary and Samuel jointly sell the house, and Mary leaves Malden to seek "better company" (2, 10) and greater freedom in which to perfect her mind and spirit. But these years of early adulthood serve as a continuing touchstone for Mary: sadly, she feels later in life that she has never again achieved the sustained holiness of "the years between 27 & 30, when in entire solitude I asked not books or [?] but the quietism of faith & obedience" (21, 3). Retrospectively, the very privations of Malden increase its aura of holiness. But in fact, as Mary records the immediate experience of those years, she is hungry for books, she has to fight for solitude, and she finds obedience and quietism difficult virtues.

In these early *Almanacks,* Mary uses the traditional language of Puritan sainthood with ease and immediacy. "I feel assured from the experience of years and various trials that I am a deciple," she writes in 1802

(28, 4). She never refers to an experience of conversion or recalls a time when she was unconverted, but she records the pursuit of a "sanctification" that "God willeth . . . [and] I will" (28, 7). But Mary's belief in God's "incontrovertible . . . elections" is fraught with tension, for she never forgets that they "gave to the glowing Seraph his joys & to me my vile imprisonment" (3, 5). And while she tries to believe that imprisonment will itself bring holiness, through the patience of "*waiting*—for more grace knowledge" (28, 4)— she in fact beats on her prison walls and wants immediate perfection. "Away with devout prayers—faith in a Mediator's responsibility—delight at tho't of death, & assurance of salvation because of the leading feature of Xianity. Nothing short of standing *Complete & perfect*—of imitating Jesus Christ in every part of his inimitable & sacred character shall henceforth be my object" (2, 9). Even in heaven nothing must get in the way: "The first question I shall ask after droping the flesh, if I behold any created being more immediately than my Father, *where is the throne?*" (28, 4). Mary's God is alternately her jailer and the goal of her liberation, the enthroned Being to which her freed soul will seek absolute access.

The prison that Mary decides by turns to endure and to escape is mortality itself, but it is also the actual house in Malden, surely the originating scene of her radical antidomesticity. This is a house tolerable only when her "poor old folks" and their "care and clamour" have gone elsewhere (1, 1, 4); otherwise she seems to get along by fleeing to solitude in the Malden woods or the roads to nearby towns. Ruth, the woman who primarily raised her, appears only as a negative entity: Mary assures herself that not losing her temper with her aunt will give her the "glee of virtue," provide humbling means to sanctification (1, 10; 1, 4). Such virtue, however, is merely negative, as is all domestic "duty." Mary hardly dismisses the value of humble domesticity; she is pleased, for instance, with a "week of duty" that has made room for washing, carding, housecleaning, and baking as well as for reading Butler, Cicero, Shakespeare, and the Scriptures. But even here she gives away her spiritual elitism: "There is a sweet pleasure in bending to our circumstance while superior to others" (1, 4). Domesticity is not itself a vehicle of the spirit, but a privation and punishment that prepares one to deserve the spirit: "scenes of dirt, vulgarity, misery, & unqualified ignorance" embraced as "the safest, speediest passage to the worlds of light" (1, 4).

And Mary feels that she needs such punishment. If her ideal self would storm heaven, her actual being is small, passive, polluted, female, analogous to the scenes of dirt around her. "God beholds something abhorrent to his pure nature in my heart—Oh could I see it—could I tear it away" (28, 8). Not only is "negative existence" (3, 4) a sin itself, but in addition her pride and anger and resistance to negativity become a worse sin, reason for God's special wounds. She laments her high "animal spirits" and fears that, even when expressed in religious rapture, they are more "gross" than "etherial" (2, 1). "I want humility by nature & lately by habit . . . Merciful God . . . afflict me, crush me into the lowest cavern of the earth . . . Let my body be sunk into the depths of the sea or dispersed by the vultures of the desert" (2, 7). Because she wants to rise from her vile prison she must be lowered, torn asunder, driven back to female passivity; and only after such humbling can she again seek "passage to the worlds of light."

Caring for the sick—in Mary's eyes, woman's dirtiest and most holy duty—brings out in Mary her strongest gestures of duty and avoidance, self-punishment and cosmic arrogance. Ruth's sister Rebecca Brintnall, brought home to Malden insane in 1802, is to Mary a "mortifying sight" of instinct undetained by reason or the wish of others. But attending her needs "alarms me not. I shall delight to return to God" (28, 3). And similarly the call by Newburyport in-laws to come nurse her sister Hannah is to Mary "no matter—it will not retard my glory in the skies a moment"; a single view of the heavens will instead give her, in a phrase from Milton's "Il Penseroso," " 'the spirit of Plato to unfold' " (2, 3). Mary constantly juxtaposes the sickroom and the heavens, and when she becomes her "Penseroso" self, she leaves female identity behind as well as duty. "I should have soared like the eagle & basked in the rays of light joy and serenity," Mary writes after a day of petty anger in Newburyport (3, 7). Soaring is masculine, clean, and free; the sickroom is feminine, dirty, and constricted. "I took care of my weak folks with pleasure," she writes in Malden, "but there are some [?] with bodies of ladies so disgusting to reason & refinement that to shrink is not anti-benevolent" (2, 10). Clearly the most personally acceptable way to shrink is to soar.

Mary's psychological being, then, embraces extreme and apparently disjunctive feelings: God has imprisoned her but wills her straight ascent to His throne; she is "abhorrent," deserving to be torn apart by vultures, and "superior," deserving to fly like an eagle. If I have begun this essay emphasizing the visionary strength of Mary's isolation, I would not want to disregard its deeply neurotic, even potentially suicidal, personal origins. There is much in her that is not life-affirming. But "sanctification" does provide Mary with a language for understanding and (somewhat precariously) bringing together her extremes. Her solution is a highly personal reading of the contemporary religious culture. Like the liberal Arminians of Cambridge she wishes for a self-initiated and self-affirming knowledge of God. But her sense of personal fallenness is much greater than theirs, and at the same time her eagle-self aspires to more inward and ecstatic experience than their socially oriented sainthood of good works. The

Calvinist orthodoxy of Andover more fully comprehends these paradoxical depths of sin and heights of sanctity. But Calvinism too must be reworked so as more fully and radically to affirm the individual ego.

It is the Calvinists' atoning Christ who both meets Mary's depravity and allows her exaltation. Personal power, in her experience, comes only and absolutely as salvation by Christ. "Had I my deserts what shame & pain would involve me! Blessed & adorable Jesus— thy attonement how rich how adapted to my condition" (2, 7). For Mary, this is an implicitly feminine condition. Christ is a glorious "portion," a dowry in her life of poverty; Christ is "my high Priest" (2, 7; 2, 8). "With what rapture must the thief have received the promise of life—and the unnamed woman at the feet of Jesus her pardon!" (2, 7). Mary's portrayal of union with Christ is physically immediate on both her side and His. "*Blood of Christ*. How I cling to that" (28, 4). Even an unnamed "poor deformed soul" that Mary cannot tolerate—probably insane Aunt Brintnall—can be a "member of his body" (28, 4). Bodies are transformed by His body.

But Mary's Christ is a means, not an end; here she departs most drastically from Andover theology, appropriating and extending something of Cambridge. Later in life she would specify her belief as "Arian," that is, belief in Christ as a secondary, divine-human "influx" from God the "one infinite *consciousness*" rather than fully and originally divine (20, 4).[16] In the earlier years she does not use this conceptual language, but the experience that would lead to Arian belief is already present. That is, though she claims selfhood only as part of the body of Christ, she is in her moments of ecstasy alone before the one God rather than within Christ's body. It is in her desire for such moments that she can wish to do "away with . . . faith in a Mediator's responsibility" and stand *"complete and perfect"*—like Christ, "imitating . . . his inimitable & sacred character," but not in Him, not stopping short of the throne with any mere "created being." In being thus Arian but not Arminian, Mary preserves both her humility and her "moral grandeur": atonement is central to her belief, but she receives it as entitlement to God's absolute presence.

Mary's spiritual life, following from her intense desire for this transformation, is both more ascetic and more self-exalting than the traditional Puritan ways of sanctification. The occasion for her prayer that God would remember His covenant with her ancestors, which I quoted earlier, is a vow not to allow herself "one indulgence of sleep food drink raiment shelter labour friends fame or life" (28, 7). Her ancestors would recognize such vows. But they, despite a strong denial of the body, also married, sanctioning family life rather than celibacy as the holier way. Mary was a celibate by conscious decision as well as temperament. And what surprises us about this is less her denial of sexuality than her ability to act upon her feelings and to choose a condition of life that had essentially no context or precedent in her family or community. Her celibacy is in this sense more a self-declaration than a self-denial. As Waldo wrote in his biographical essay on Mary, she could have married if she chose. "I walked to Capt Dexter's," she records early in 1807, "—sick— promised never to put that ring on" (3, 5). And a few weeks later, "Henceforth the picture I'll image shall be girded loins, a bright lamp, fervent devotion" (3, 11). With no other company to join, she "images" herself among the faithful maidens of the Biblical parable who light their lamps to await the heavenly bridegroom. But she is a more active and masculine maiden than most: as well as lighting her lamp she girds her loins to prepare for work, like the *men* who await the kingdom in another version of the parable.[17]

Even asceticism for Mary has this quality of energetic individualism in it. And her moments of positive vision are joyfully transcending and self-affirming. Her sanctified life is still attuned to the rhythms of the Puritan church: "Sabbath" is always marked as such at the head of a journal entry, often with a response to church that day. But she mentions taking communion—traditional sign of belonging to Christ and the church—only once in the entire record of the *Almanacks* (28, 3). And church services are valuable only insofar as they arouse her own "fervid emotions" (2, 7). The hearing of sermons is a central part of her life, but often in the opportunity thus provided for dismissing the preacher as "poor" or "frivolous" (1, 1; 1, 2). One day before describing the female "genius" in her *Almanack* she records this experience: "I could not be reverent tonight with poor Mr. G's preaching—I sympathized with the joys of the vulgar—I trod on air—I danced to the musick of my own imajanation—it is well no one knows the frolick of my fancy, for they w^d think me wild unless they knew me" (1, 4).[18] Mary may misspell Imagination, that crucial term of Transcendentalism, but she understands, when Waldo is only a year old, how its music can overwhelm mediocrity in the pulpit. In Mary's religious life authority, community, and sacrament have already started to disappear before a dance of the inner self in direct contact with divinity.

And the setting for this dance before God is as often Nature as church. When Mary flees home to view the heavens, she encounters as well as avoids, finds rapture and assurance in the "regular radiant orbs" of the stars (28, 5). On the occasion of a complete solar eclipse in June of 1806, Mary escapes "to the woods to get beyond the din of human tongues." The sun starts to emerge before she can get to the "most sequestered spot," so she fails to capture quite the fullness of "the sublime in perception" (2, 13). Yet this is one of the highest moments in her Malden years: "The appearance was unexpected so exquisite a light I cannot describe—winds were hushed as if in awe—birds screamed—stars glowed—with what rapt devotion did I view my Maker's hand" (2, 13). Here is a recognizably Emersonian scene: flight to solitude, and solitude as close to the perfect center of things as possible; aesthetic savoring of sublime light and sound that brings a freely perceiving soul to "rapt devotion" of the Maker. "In communion with trees, with streams and stars and suns, man finds his own glory inscribed on every flower and sparkling on every beam," concludes Mary two days later (2, 13).

Moreover, Mary approaches Waldo's Transcendentalism not only in her reverence for the God of nature, but in the temporal pattern of her regenerate life. Even though she looks for slow growth on the model of Puritan sanctification, she instead experiences isolated "moments" (17, 7)—whether in church or in the woods—that are absolute as revelations of eternity but permanent only in their value for memory. It seems to have been only after her Malden years that Mary started calling her journals *Almanacks* in ironic recognition that she was recording a calendar of constant changes in time and weather. But again these earliest years of the *Almanacks* show her new sanctification of momentary consciousness taking shape, if she has not yet recognized it as such.

Both Mary's stated desire for progressive holiness and her actual experience of briefer inspiration are present in the entry for December 26, 1806: "Never was a date issued from the hand of royalty more important than the above. It is related to days and ages beyond this sphere. It is the record of virtue—the beginning of a portion of the history of a soul—struggling with weakness & ignorance & opposite appetites to the pure state of Heaven! God of infinite power & love, aid the being before thee to honor thee & herself in this little history. Bless her with no common & ordinary portion of thy wisdom—all else is dust & ashes! This day so dark—so incumbered hath been filled—yes filled with devotion & zeal—patience & joy" (3, 1). Mary hopes to experience (and record) a continuing "history" that, though "little," compared to the history of kings, will take her beyond kings to the purity of heaven. Yet all she is sure of is that *this* day has been filled by God's spirit. And she looks ahead for more fullness in terms that are absolute and subjective, unmediated by Christ or Christian community: either she will experience an inward wisdom beyond the "common & ordinary" or she will be left to "dust & ashes."

Such inwardness is Mary's triumph, her self-reliance when New England's intellectual centers had not yet imagined self-reliance. But it also begs for failure of fulfillment, for long periods of drought and few high moments. Mary can dare hope for such a life of inner wisdom at the end of 1806 because she knows that she is about to leave Malden behind. Just a week later she writes that she is bargaining for her estate, jointly selling the Malden house with Uncle Samuel Waite and angry that he is "loth to let me have my money" (3, 2). Clearly she knows that her independence is at stake in these transactions and shows all her feistiest qualities. "There is an awfull—a sublime and unspeakable duty of self-preservation in the constitution of man," she comments; and, when the bargaining ends, "My dear self has done well" (3, 2; 3, 4). Leaving Malden in February of 1807 she writes, with characteristic absolutism, "I begin a new life—free—oh merciful God—from levity, pride, flattery, folly & weakness" (3, 6). This is an "awful moment wh divides the polluted past from the spotless, the tremendous future" (3, 5).

There is a tragic absence of personal realism in this division of experience between the polluted and the spotless, as well as the insistence on projecting pollution outward and backward to Malden. Mary would never find a suitably tremendous future for her dear self. As good a symbol as any of this reality is that, as she speaks of her "new life," Mary is moving from Malden not to a new place of freedom but at least temporarily back to her sister's sickroom in Newburyport.

In fact, given Mary's own absolutism and the social constraints around her, she did well. The *Almanack* is disappointingly uninformative about Mary's plans at this important juncture of her life, simply breaking off after May, 1807. But when her record begins again it is dated "Waterford, 1809" and immediately plunges into a reflection on Calvinist theology (4, 1-2). It was near the White Mountains in Waterford, Maine that she settled to read and contemplate, again as part owner (with her brother-in-law Robert Haskins) of a farm that she always called "Elm Vale." This was another shared family home, eventually full of Haskins children, but it was also the setting for moments of high privacy both of "feasting in books" (22, 11) and of rapture in sublime nature. Mary's experiment in "holy independance" was far from a failure.

But she was too self-accusing to take full satisfaction in either freedom or intellectual pursuit. She would eventually remember Malden not for its pollution but for the quietism of faith that "asked not books." And even during her early years in Waterford she seems to have needed frequent returns to the domestic duties from which she had fled. "After a day of crying babes" in widowed Ruth Emerson's Boston house in 1813, she sits in "rich . . . tranquillity" and takes rather grim satisfaction that the "defeated pursuit of knowledge" has been replaced by "return to labour—to service to cares instead of ease & reading & sentiment & hope" (34, 7). If eventually Ruth Emerson's children would inherit richly from Mary's solitary spirit, they first appear in the *Almanacks* as a "labour" that serves Mary's own needs by off-setting the feared selfishness of solitude.

Mary anticipated mortal perfection only in her youth; as her comment on the day of crying babes suggests, she was already in 1813 beset by an unshakable sense of defeat. She still looked for transformation, but only through release by death from a "dreaming polluted life" (30, 15). The death-longing that had always been implicit in her sensibility now became a litany: "alas no progress and no death!" (32, 16).

But Mary's egoistic power is expressed even here: she sees death as the ultimate "tremendous future" where she will be able to vindicate, not escape from, her life. Reaching her fiftieth birthday in 1824, Mary reflects on years of tedium, weakness, miscalculation, and stupidity, but then decides that even such a life can "thro' the divine alchymy be remembered with joy," because "it may bear an amaranthine bloom in other soil," in paradise (26, 4). The "divine alchymy" is itself a capacity to remember: human memory is "an emblem, at least, of the infinite view" of God, and "reminiscence will be natural when we void our clay" (14, 11; 7, 4). Once she even imagines sharpening her wits against Spinoza's in heaven, the two of them together "taking sketches of the long & weary barren & briery roads of life" (14, 9). She seeks "individuation" (20, 8) with God, not obliteration, and that means never letting go of the details of her own being.

If her early perfectionism itself anticipates romanticism in New England, this exercise of memory is her own full-fledged romanticism and most complex frame of mind. And memory, though a proper function of heaven, need not await heaven; Mary's retrospective capacity is exercised too in the writing of the *Almanacks,* especially in her middle and old age. Earlier she had experienced holiness only in isolated days of sublimity and fullness; now she learns how to draw sustenance from those days. Memory itself, she writes in 1828, is a book whose "blank & blotted pages" the soul can turn until "it comes to the leaf turned down on a luminous hour" (8, 4). Such a luminous hour, she adds elsewhere, is a "notch" in her prison, a chink of open sky (19, 2). Recollection of holiness in youth, then, does not always serve to condemn the present. Mary's more characteristic and often-repeated thought is that though her youthful vow to rejoice in God's will "has never been equalled," still it "returns in the long life of destitution, like an Angel" (10, 4). When Mary writes in late middle age that she wishes to occupy her life "only in the study of its wonders," she refers to such angelic visitations.

Stages of life converge in this exercise of memory: if middle or old age is its actual setting, and heaven its fulfillment, childhood is its favorite subject. And the childhood thus revealed is complex rather than sentimental, both painful and holy. Heaven, Mary writes in 1817, "may well resemble our infancy" in that it is "under the gov't and care & design of God," yet it will maintain at least "all the powers of mind" characteristic of adulthood, rather than infancy's "darkness & ignorance" (38, 3). Since infancy for Mary is orphanhood, she is incapable of remembering it untroubled; and as far as "powers of mind" are concerned, she sees adulthood as a growth, not a lapse, from childhood.

Yet Mary clearly traces her own personal power back to troubled childhood. George Tolman wrote that she claimed in old age to remember her father riding away from Concord to the Revolution.[19] Her *Almanacks* do not make that claim to recollection from the age of two. But they do reveal a comparable effort to recall earliest—and surely traumatic—memories, memories at the heart of Mary's psychological and religious life. Two such passages, widely spaced in time of composition and quite different in content, are best seen together:

> South Conway June [27, 1841] Sab. at Hotel. How well this huming fly brings back emotions of a certain Sab. Morn, when I was perhaps 4 years old and every chair & old bit of furniture on wh the sun glanced thro' a small eastern window. That consciousness of sober rich tranquility has never been lost to memory, & returns when the contented vagrant serenades my lonely chamber—not more alone than in childhood & youth and after all of effort here I am thinking it well to note a few moments wh stand connected with nothing before them or afterward, only the formation of modes of feeling. Alas the blank of mortal existence. But not to be deprecated if the infant (uninstructed at those times) soul can imbibe so rich a pleasure within itself. What a prototype may it be of its immortality; and would the childhood of age but give a succession of these emotions. They have recurred—richly endowed with the sense of divinity—of hereafter. But they will love old haunts—and this journeying for health—'twill pay me in the glorious Autumn. I already see the cold beams of the sun glowing thro' the leafless arms of the trees on my grandmother's portrait—and feel the still nameless tone of feeling wh will unite the infinite to the finite—tho' no chain of dialectics will be the medium. Ah where has that carried the inquirer at times! (17, 17)

> Mr. Sears Jan 7 [18]55. My early remembrance at 5 respecting trouble continued till at 17 I entered refined society at N.[ewbury] Port. After that I was obliged to go to Concord & learn duties wh tried me. But the first sermon I heard with attention, *probably,* was to prove the divine goodness. It surprised & pained! the impossibility of the reverse. This "theodicy" depresses. The knowledge of children in mines & all the modes of slavery & suffering of history (wh I avoid) brings up a mystery, a "cloud," but I never doubted the perfection of perfect *benevolence* & justice. I *knew* that righteousness "was the habitation of his existence." (22, 1)

Interestingly, neither of these powerfully evocative memories concerns her "exile" from Concord, but both take off from a sense of her Malden home a few years later. It was when Mary was five that her grandmother died, and both passages are at least indirectly reflections on that loss, the second (and actually remembered) "orphanhood" in her life. "Trouble" (with Aunt Ruth?) began then and continued through adolescence, we learn in the 1855 passage, but trouble was preceded by its opposite, "sober rich tranquility," says the 1841 passage. And both trouble and tranquillity are given theological meaning in memory; the first necessitates Mary's intuitive "theodicy," the second offers a "prototype of immortality." Together they give us the basic rhythm of Mary's inner life.

The essential mystery of Christian faith, she says, is that children suffer—suffer "in mines & all the modes of slavery." Mary always sympathized with slaves—abolitionism was the one public cause that deeply moved her—and here we have a brief glimpse of Malden as plantation and dark Satanic mill. The adult mind tries to "avoid" such suffering. And yet, most strikingly, the mind is always active even during the slavery of childhood: children not only suffer, but have "knowledge" in that suffering. Knowledge in part, surely, of injury done them; resentment lurks not far from the surface of this memory. Yet the knowledge explicitly claimed is quite different, the grandly compensatory awareness of God's "perfect *benevolence & justice.*" Searching for "the agency of God," Mary says again and again in the *Almanacks,* has been her aim since "afflicted childhood" (31, 16). "I never need meta[physic]s for the first thought at orphanship or sorrow was God's will" (20, 1).

The metaphysics that she knew before she read are of course Calvinist, Edwardian: human suffering as the will of and for the greater glory of a creating and providing God whose ways cannot be known. Mary speaks as though such metaphysical insight was quite simply her own "first thought." Elsewhere she pays her true debt to the Calvinist culture of her Malden home: Aunt Ruth "early impressed [her] . . . that Providence and Prayer were all in all."[20] But Aunt Ruth's version of the faith emphasized the self-denial of Calvinism; Mary saw its glory as well. "Tho' [in] childhood was taught & received the full terrors of Calvinism, yet never terrified," Mary once had to "most humbly confess" (8, 9). Mary the child-Edwardian could accept earthly affliction, but only with the confidence that "divine goodness" would reward her. It was just during these years, of course, that Calvinist ministers and theologians were hinging their arguments for the "full terrors" of the faith on a sovereign God's right to damn innocent infants.[21] Mary's Calvinism was unorthodox from childhood: the mystery of her suffering was a thing of earth not heaven; in God's "habitation" would come the compensation of benevolence and justice.

Mary seems to have had an unshakable faith in the heavenly value of her own individual being as well as the benevolence of God. Amid all her orphanhood and trouble, an early affirmation must have occurred, or else she could not have felt this inner power to transcend them. It is the "huming fly" reverie that most fully suggests such affirming experience of nurture, nurture not by Aunt Ruth but by Grandmother Mary.

"Nurture" is a term to be used cautiously in describing this recollection: in it Mary, both child and adult, is alone. But she is alone with a benignly humming fly, worn furniture, and winter sunshine in her grandmother's house. In all of the *Almanacks,* this is Mary's only pleasant evocation of a domestic interior. It is a Sabbath scene, both immediately and retrospectively: holy but not churchly, interior and private. Most of all, though, the grandmother is oddly distanced as she presides over her house. Sun shines coldly "thro' the leafless arms of the trees" on her *portrait,* which in turn overlooks the tranquil room. And the "infant . . . soul" is able to "imbibe" rich pleasure from this scene, as though it were a nursing mother, yet the infant imbibes "within itself," not from grandmother or portrait or room. Mary seems to be recalling her grandmother both as present, nurturing, and as absent, dead. It is as though she remembers an experience of love and tranquillity in early childhood but cannot attach an actual face to it, only the face of the portrait that survived death. Thus it is both a "rich" scene and a "cold," wintry one; and it evokes a "nameless tone of feeling," a feeling of loss as well as pleasure, in the remembering adult.

But in the very ambiguity of this "nameless tone" also lies its power in forming permanent "modes of feeling"—that is, the series of visionary "moments" in Mary's otherwise blank existence. The quality of the feeling and the moment is that it "will unite the infinite to the finite"; it will restore the finite, mourning child to contact with the infinite, lost parent-figure. "Sober rich tranquility" is, then, not only a primal experience of Mary's childhood but, after its loss, a feeling to "imbibe . . . within" and a "prototype" of the afterlife.

This memory-circuit from early childhood to heaven is Mary's most fundamental alchemy, one that converts loss to imaginative power and access to divinity. Inveighing against the danger of accommodating the divine idea to the present age, she writes on one occasion that "our utilities & our enjoyments resemble the mirth of [the?] ideot, who ran about the house of mourning saying '*she* was not dead' " (11, 30). Surely this explicitly female "ideot" is the heedless figure that Mary, child or adult, would never allow herself to be. Instead of granting herself a happy survival in the house of mourning, Mary seeks to join the Calvinist God who has created her orphanhood and thus become her only enduring parent: "Decrees—predestination—place—purpose by whatever name I love thee in *secret*—the faith has been my father mother prized house & home" (11, 4).

Whether in the explicit meditation of the "huming fly" passage or the submerged memory of evocative language concerning "house & home," Mary is capable of powerfully expressing the sources and results of her holy orphanhood. She perceives her solitude not as deprivation of parenting so much as displacement to heaven of father, mother, grandmother. Father turns out to matter most, despite Mary's evocation of her distantly benign grandmother. What is of most value in motherhood—security and nurture—is finally subsumed into the figure of a God who is transpersonal and androgynous, yet still on balance paternal. Heaven will "resemble our infancy" in that it is "under the gov't and care & design of God." Such an infancy will be safer than the first, because "gov't"—necessarily by a father—will not have disappeared.

Femininity is finally more to be repudiated than embraced in this ascent to a parental heaven. In a recollection triggered by the sight of fireflies in 1828, one perhaps related in source and feeling to the later passage on the humming fly, Mary affirms that she cannot "doubt mental identity when the dim eye of age recognises the same tranquil hues—the same bright visions which soothed the sorrows of childhood and youth." But then she breaks off and adds that only "to poetry we owe the charms of the glow-worm's lamp"; "science" has revealed them as "little harlots, who shine to capture the lover. Ill omen of my ill-fated sex" (8, 4). This is Mary's most explicit comment on her sex in the whole of the *Almanacks;* and one suspects that it is not science alone, but also repugnant and submerged personal memory, that makes her turn against the female reproductive cycle as harlotry. Her almost complete silence about her real mother and her aunt in this writing can only appear as avoidance of "trouble," trouble surely having to do with women in families. She identifies her own position in relation to mothers—one she cannot admit in autobiographical terms—when she says that "the [spiritual] man himself . . . is disengaged & disinterred from tangible substance as really as the embryo man from his mother's womb—who as little touches his destiny in this life where he swims, as the foetus its habitation" (6, 5). Mary speaks within Christian tradition in identifying earthly nature as a female vessel from which the aspiring soul must break free,[22] but her refusal to imagine the fetus even touching its mother's womb is a disturbingly personal intensification of the inherited idea.

Mary's self-proclaimed Arianism is entirely of a piece with her intense need for divine paternity. Lacking any real memory of her father, she freely identifies him with the ideal on heaven and earth, the "first & highest relation" from which she has been "estranged" (20, 3). The goal of her masculine child-soul—once "disinterred" from the mother—is to seek reunion with that father. "And it is the personal ever active Substance—God!—on whom his infant child would ever fix an eye with a holy carelessness of all beside one operation of conscience, wh is his own possession by natural right from God" (16, 12). Directly from God comes the infant's capacity directly to contemplate and return to God: a cycle requiring no mother, no siblings, no intermediate realities. Even when recalling her debt to the incarnated Christ, Mary pauses for "one inquiry beyond. Will this Being so exalted by God not be ashamed of me? Whence the thought—oh stranger be gone—that my soul in such case would naturally recurr to the Omniscient—the first Cause . . . [for] the spirit instinctively hugs—seeks—hungers after the Absolute" (20, 2-3). Christ, being grandly human as well as grandly divine, may turn away from Mary's defective self like a brother of superior education and status;[23] "the Absolute" will not. Mary seeks absolute reunion with a father-God not only in confidence, but also in estrangement and exile. Her religious life contains such radical egotism and such extreme vulnerability because it is, through the work of conscious and unconscious memory, a constant reversion to the conditions of childhood.

Mary Moody Emerson's *Almanacks* record a private religious awareness that proceeds from uniquely personal and even disturbed sources; her Calvinism and her Arianism both reflect the same inner need for a paternal deity of absolute reliability and providential wisdom. Hers is "the faith that at some moment of His existence I was present—that tho' cast from Him—my sorrows, my ignorance & meanness were a part of His plan" (8, 6). Nevertheless, in her faith Mary is not merely a private and passive receiver of cultural circumstance but also an analyst of culture. I have pointed out that Mary was, both by family position and personal temperament, heir to the Edwardian tradition at the start of the nineteenth century and at the same time attracted to some aspects of its liberal opposition. It remains to say that she realized and explored this situation; in the theological and devotional language of the *Almanacks* she brings Edwards and the First Awakening straight across the intervening generations into the nascent romantic culture of nineteenth-century Massachusetts. She is consciously and intellectually a "representative life" of her time.

Mary knew the Awakening from its own polemic literature, not just its latter-day traditions. And, typically, she defined her own faith from elements of both sides of the controversy. The *Almanacks* confirm what Waldo later wrote, that Mary's most important early reading included, as well as Milton and the Bible and the eighteenth-century poets, the theological writing of Samuel Clarke and Jonathan Edwards. Waldo did not add, though, that these most respected authorities opposed each other, Edwards writing his *Freedom of the Will* as rebuttal of the rationalist Arminianism held by Anglican Clarke and his disciples. In Mary's own lifetime Clarke's argument for free will had become the property of Cambridge, and Edwards' determinism of Andover and Yale.[24] But Mary's interest in their writing is not limited to the issue that divided them; in fact she more often brings them together.

Clarke early opened to Mary the possibility of "natural religion," the witness "within and without" that she saw to underlie all possibility of more formalized revelation (19, 1). "Dear immortal Clarke," Mary writes, argued that the Newtonian concepts of Space and Time lead directly to the "substances" Space and Time as "attributes of a Being who is necessarily immense and eternal" (12, 15). Mary never forgets Clarke's sense of cosmic "design" or his "glorious intuition . . . [that] God's non-existence is inconceivable & therefore impossible" (11, 31). Clarke shows her with airtight certainty the existence of that "necessary source" which she has always known as her true father (11, 18), and he goes on to show that all true moral virtues are really "fitnesses," harmonious responses, to this knowably benevolent and harmonious divinity (17, 5). Here is a God of "plan," and plan that the human mind can become "part of."

It is surely the goal of Mary's contemplative sainthood to move into such a relation of "fitness" to God. But she begins from and constantly lapses back into a radical sense of unfitness, original sin, that can be overcome only by God's will. And so the divine plan that speaks most deeply to her need is not Clarke's design but Edwards' determinism, a plan affirming human freedom only within dependence "for every mode of existence on the Absolute" (17, 3). It was Edwards' *Freedom of the Will* that, through a lifetime, spoke to Mary's central need of reconciling human helplessness and glory. She read it "early," probably long before she started writing the **Almanacks;** reread it with care in 1810 at Waterford; kept abreast of orthodox revisions of its doctrine into the 1840s; declared in 1838 that, while Michelangelo's beautiful forms would perish, "the dry arid work of Edwards on 'Will' . . . will outlive time" (17, 3; 5, 3; 18, 5; 31, 11). Mary, unlike some of her orthodox contemporaries, really finds freedom in Edwards' treatise; for her the paradox of personal agency and divine Providence is so emotionally ingrained that she cannot quite see the need for metaphysical argument. "For myself, I never remember to have met with that difficulty in the scriptures in a way to perplex. When the Eternal declares his sovereignty and electing conduct, I see and rejoice in the security of such a Governor." It is only with such an Absolute Governor that she can feel "beyond the possibility of doubt, *an agent*—one on whom he will pour the riches of his grace" (5, 3).

But in the moments and days when Mary has experienced this outpouring of grace, she lives a "natural religion" of sublime perception that genuinely synthesizes Clarke and Edwards. She joins both in admiring Newton and the God of Newton, a divinity acting through the aesthetic harmonies of motion in time and space: "He who fills all space exists in every particle" (6, 14). This God is more Edwards' than Clarke's, an "indwelling" presence in the universe (11, 15) and not just a designer: " 'the end of creation,' " Mary quotes from Edwards, " 'was God's glory—to manifest himself' " (17, 4). And likewise Mary's highest activity of mind is closer to Edwards than to Clarke: she values Clarke's reason but considers it a variety of intuition, the "proteus capability of revelation" that elsewhere produces a silent Quaker or a fiery Calvinist (12, 30). Her most frequent term for such intuition—a pejorative term in Edwards' time but certainly not for Mary—is "enthusiasm": a "light of the soul," "a heavenly gift, the receptacle of knowledge" (39, 3; 38, 6). But the goal of Mary's contemplative "enthusiasm" brings Clarke and Edwards together: a virtue of harmony with absolute Benevolence, a "love of being universally" (17, 5).

To Mary, Clarke and Edwards were metaphysical adventurers of the early eighteenth century both compromised to "common sense" by their followers: the true enemy, the one possibility she systematically repudiates, is empiricism. "Poor Dr. Reid," says Mary, found Clarke's affirmation of Space and Time as divine substances mere " 'sublime speculations, whether the wanderings of imaja.[nation] beyond the limits of human und.[erstanding] or not he was unable to determine.' " Thomas Reid's problem, Mary implies, was his lofty intellectual separation from the real voice of the self: "So far from uncertainty and negative conceptions nothing of clear mental conception is more positive to ordinary ones" (11, 15). Further, Mary "can't see . . . why I. Taylor in reviewing Edwards 'on will' should flout met[aphysics] . . . He says we have no notation to render them sure. *Notation!* who needs arithmetic to be conscious of existence—thought is the best" (18, 5). To Mary nothing has less true "common sense" in it that this late eighteenth-century "arithmetic"; true sense, available to all "ordinary ones," is a consciousness that penetrates to its source in God.

It was in the 1830s and 40s that Mary defended the possibility of Clarke's and Edwards' sublime speculations, and she was explicitly Coleridgean in so doing—at once, then, an eighteenth-century pietist and a nineteenth-century romantic. On the same page as her defense of Clarke, in fact, she quotes Coleridge's dictum that *"there is nothing the absolute ground of which is not a mystery."* "For how," Mary asks along with Coleridge, "can that wh is to explain all things be susceptible of explanation?" (11, 15). Mary had probed the mystery of her own source and ground long before she encountered Coleridge in 1829 (10, 4). But, though she balked at his "topsy-turvy phraseology" (10, 12) and once simply "went to sleep in [God's] arms" while the philosopher "mazed away with his clearings & notes" (15, 11), she found her "old face all in smiles" (11, 9) over his new philosophy.

Mary read Coleridge's work along with and under the influence of Waldo, who was in these same years living out his great discoveries. But Mary's Coleridge is not Waldo's, despite a deep emotional and intellectual bond between aunt and nephew. Rather Coleridge is a new defender of the old faith, the old faith seen as always for its possibilities of radical self-transformation. " 'Is not the creating of a new heart . . . the one essential miracle?' " Mary quotes from Coleridge. " 'Is it not emphatically that leading of the Father without wh none can come to Christ?' " (10, 3). This Father is recognizably Mary's own lost "first and highest relation." "In this excluded world whose inmates were foundering in idolatry & guilt, to have God send his son! A being who knew of the Infinite—to tell of His will— . . . The intangible incomprehensible I AM to reveal himself so mercifully!" (15, 11). Waldo, Mary recounts, agreed with Coleridge that prayer was difficult because it was addressed from individual to universal Reason. But Mary differed from both, though modestly admitting that she spoke "in haste" and partial understanding: "I . . . only answered that we were so distinct from this universal Reason, as to need prayer, so intimate with it as to be heard & answered." Waldo "praised the remark" (14, 13): the instincts of the old piety lurked in him too.[25]

But Mary belonged to the eighteenth century as Waldo did not because she always remained a "Realist in faith of God & spirit & matter"—"notwithstanding Coleridge's and Wordsworth's affectation of sublimer truths" (10, 8). If empirical philosophy leaves one imprisoned in space and time, the romantics and their American "ultra trans[cendental]ist" followers, she writes, pretend to "get rid of" time and space (17, 6). She has no patience with post-Kantian subjectivism, but finds the romantic celebrators of consciousness "idolaters—making to themselves images instead of Plato's ideas" (10, 13). Even though she discovers God through her private consciousness, she needs to discover and know Him absolutely.

And if Mary differs from Waldo in her epistemological realism, she does so even more vehemently in her moral realism, her insistence on the stubborn fact of human woe: the "spontaneous reason" of the "dear transcendentalist" is fine but incomplete, she comments, for "it points you to a standard of perfection wh your capacity leaves unattained" and thus the need for "an expiatory religion" (17, 2). Mary judges Waldo's lectures harshly by the same standard of personal experience that she has brought to all her wide intellectual life: "to me their power neither diminishes nor adds to the weight wh oppresses me . . . His theory is not based on the real nature of man, corresponds neither with history, experience nor revelation" (31, 5). Only redemption can lift that weight. "What an inspiration is in the words—'The Lord will perfect that wh concerneth me; thy mercy, oh Lord, *endureth forever;* foresake not the work of thy own hands![']. Here be sanctuary for the miseries wh crowd our world of prisons, plantations, Siberias & gibbets—wars of sword & wars of statesmen" (17, 6). Mary's list of woes sounds like one Melville might fling at Emerson. Her "sanctuary," though, reflects both the troubles and the faith of an older generation than theirs.

Mary knew that her sanctuary was a lonely place, no Awakening and no Revolution. Edwards had talked "much of duty & effort in the future," but her own life round "fruition [only] in rest & worship," in "an absorbing reliance on Him . . . purer than action may be" (31, A). The social, millennial impulse of her father's Edwardian piety found no comparable exercise in her own world. In fact even when she imagines a "dying patriot" she provides him no war, no cause, no enemies, but only the vertical relationship of divine inspiration: "when one glance of his eye is raised in stern enthusiasm to the skies—how futile are creeds of faith & formulas of worship—the infinite stirs within—surrounds—absorbs" (31, 22). But Mary's absorption in infinity is surely a significant development out of eighteenth-century Awakening religion: one remarkably different from Andover orthodoxy or Cambridge liberalism, ultimately central not peripheral to New England culture in its anticipation of the private voices of the next generation.

Moreover, Mary's writing is of interest not only in that it anticipates what will be culturally influential—the self-reliance of Ralph Waldo Emerson—but also in its own voice, its very sense of exile from influence. For, however obscure and private her life, Mary never really repudiates the interest in prophetic power characteristic of the New England clerical-intellectual tradition. This impulse emerges most often in her sense of failure to find means of communicating her religious vision to others: "Oh that I . . . could have been an innocent instrument of the life-breathing-giving consciousness," she laments in 1842 (43, 1). If not inclined to a public priestly role comparable to Anne Hutchinson's or Ann Lee's, she admits that she would "gladly . . . missionize from house to house . . . to speak of the mercies of God in the simpel language of these [rustic] people. . . . I know not what to do oftentimes—offer my every sense & faculty to God—trusting Him for their disposal, waiting for His sending for me" (38, 10). Public authorship never offers Mary the substitute form of religious vocation that it would soon offer to other women, despite a clear pull in that direction too: "At reading the lives of women eminent for piety learning influence &c I feel a secret exulting that I am eminent for non-advantages in this life. . . . I am glad I have nothing, as I can't have much" (28, 1).

Insofar as Mary finds a vehicle of authorship and influence, it is the private authorship of the *Almanacks* and letters and the private influence of educating her nephews. But even here, significantly, she does not see the extent to which she has been the "instrument of . . . consciousness": she finds Waldo, though her most precious society, still "lost" to her tutelage as of 1835, giving lectures like the "fleeting flowers of a summer day" rather than voicing the abolitionist zeal that would let her "rejoice like Simeon of old" (10, 5; 15, 9, 5). She is exactly this, Simeon to the coming Emersonian Christ, but if she rejoices in him she does so grudgingly, and from within her private sanctuary.

In that sanctuary, however, she does not just admit her failure of influence, but also exercises an awareness that must be called prophetic. "I have found no one to sympathise with—," Mary admits, "tho' I sympathise in general benevolence from the President to the Cat" (7, 6). Her qualification is a major one: this sympathy of general benevolence that extends from the leader of the Republic to the creatures of nature is a significant—and in its self-deprecating irony significantly female—part of the continuing tradition from Edwards to Emerson. Perhaps, Mary offers with diffidence, "the mental exercises of piety and benevolence go to make up a part of the universe—are themselves a part of the divine will & agency." At any rate she cannot agree with those who say that "nothing is added to the wealth of a nation but what is dug out of the earth" (6, 11). Clearly she hopes to add to the wealth of America, at least through her private supplications for Zion.

Notes

[1] Ms. transcription of the *Almanacks* by George Tolman, Houghton Library, Harvard University; folder 1, page 3. Hereafter all citations will be to the Tolman transcription and will be given in the text of the essay by folder and page number or letter.

Waldo's notebooks transcribing passages from Mary's *Almanacks* and letters have for some time been in the Emerson collection at Houghton. But now available for the first time are also both the extant original manuscripts of the *Almanacks* and a full (946-page) transcription of them by Concord antiquarian George Tolman (1836-1909). The originals are of many sizes and shapes, often in loose sheets; the paper is brittle, faded, and singed around the edges by the 1872 fire in Emerson's house. We cannot know how many pages were lost in the fire, but I have found almost no passages in Waldo's pre-fire notebooks not also represented in the damaged originals. The originals, however, are very hard to work with: time and fire have rendered Mary's handwriting, always a challenge to scholarly patience, nearly indecipherable. In this situation George Tolman's transcriptions, prepared only thirty years after the fire with editorial precision and blessedly readable hand, offer our best way into the text short of the eventual definitive edition that the *Almanacks* deserve. In quoting Mary's words I have followed Tolman's practice of exactly reproducing her eccentric spelling and punctuation. Since the cataloguing of these manuscripts is still in progress as I write, and the Tolman folder and page numbers will soon be replaced by a new ordering system, I will deposit a copy of this essay at Houghton annotated with the new numbers for the use of future Mary Moody Emerson scholars.

[2] My sense of the New England prophetic tradition is shaped most immediately by Sacvan Bercovitch, *The American Jeremiad* (Madison: Wisconsin University Press, 1978); by the teaching of Alan Heimert and his *Religion and the American Mind: From the Great Awakening to the Revolution* (Cambridge, Mass.: Harvard University Press, 1966); and by Perry Miller, "From Edwards to Emerson," in his *Errand into the Wilderness* (Cambridge, Mass.: Harvard University Press, 1956), pp. 184-203.

[3] For the place of women in the New England religious tradition, see Margaret W. Masson, "The Typology of the Female as a Model for the Regenerate: Puritan Preaching, 1690-1730," *Signs*, 2 (Winter 1976), 304-315; Laurel Thatcher Ulrich, "Vertuous Women Found: New England Ministerial Literature, 1668-1735," *American Quarterly*, 28 (Spring 1976), 20-40; and Mary Maples Dunn, "Saints and Sisters: Congregational and Quaker Women in the Early Colonial Period," *American Quarterly*, 30 (Winter 1978), 582-601. I have learned about the larger issues of married and celibate women in Christian patriarchy both from *AQ*'s "Special Issue: Women and Religion" (Winter 1978) and from Rosemary Ruether and Eleanor McLoughlin, eds., *Women of Spirit: Female Leadership in the Jewish and Christian Tradition* (New York: Simon and Schuster, 1979), especially the introduction. In the vast reaches of Emerson scholarship, only Erik Thurin has seriously considered gender as an analytic idea, in his brilliant study *The Universal Autobiography of Ralph Waldo Emerson* (Lund: C. W. K. Gleerup, 1974). Arguing, however, for a spiritual "marriage of heaven and earth" (p. 8) as Emerson's (failed) vision, he approaches Mary's unmarried, celibate-clerical role rather dismissively (for example, pp. 65-66, 81). He works, of course, only from Emerson's sense of her, not from her own writing.

[4] *The Journals and Miscellaneous Notebooks of Ralph Waldo Emerson*, ed. William H. Gilman et al. (Cambridge, Mass.: Harvard University Press, 1960-), V, 323; *The Complete Works of Ralph Waldo Emerson*, ed. Edward Waldo Emerson, Centenary Edition (Boston: Houghton Mifflin, 1903-1904), X, 373, 381, 404

(hereafter cited as *Works,* followed by volume and page numbers).

[5] Here and throughout my construction of the text I have, wherever possible, attached years to unspecified entries through Mary's frequent habit of heading an entry "Sabbath." For example, "Sep . . . 12 Sab morn" (28, 4): September 12 was a Sunday in 1802, and not again until 1813, an unlikely date to fit the entry's content. In this method I am following Tolman.

[6] I judge from a survey of William Matthews, *American Diaries: An Annotated Bibliography* (Boston: J. S. Canner, 1959); Matthews, *American Diaries in Manuscript, 1580-1954: A Descriptive Bibliography* (Athens, Ga., University of Georgia Press, 1974); and Andrea Hinding et al., eds., *Women's History Sources: A Guide to Archives and Manuscript Collections in the United States* (New York and London: R. R. Bowker, 1979). But Mary's *Almanacks* are not themselves listed in any of these bibliographies; it is possible that other major New England women's religious diaries are still to be discovered.

[7] See "Emerson and the Angel of Midnight: The Legacy of Mary Moody Emerson" in *Mothering the Mind,* ed. Ruth Perry and Martine Brownley (Athens, Ga.: University of Georgia Press, 1982, forthcoming). Barish has also nearly completed a book-length study of Waldo's early life, *Emerson and the Roots of Prophecy,* focusing significantly on his relation to Mary. Two earlier studies based upon an actual reading of Mary Moody Emerson manuscripts are George Tolman's insightful essay *Mary Moody Emerson* (n. p., 1929), a private reprinting of his 1902 address to the Concord Antiquarian Society; and Louise Hasting's summary of a paper, "Transcendentalism and the *Almanacks* of Mary Moody Emerson," in *Emerson Society Quarterly,* 6 (I Quarter, 1957), p. 9. Rosalie Feltenstein, in "Mary Moody Emerson: The Gadfly of Concord," *American Quarterly,* 5 (Fall 1953), 231-246, makes a useful synthesis of available second-hand impressions of Mary. Brief biographies of Mary are included both in the *Dictionary of American Biography* (New York: Scribner, 1931), VI, 130-131, and in *Notable American Women* (Cambridge, Mass.: Harvard University Press, 1971), I, 580-581, a remarkable fact given her lack of public voice or activity.

[8] An almanac is also a kind of diary, a brief register of daily events interleaved between pages of the popular printed almanacs serving as astronomical and weather charts of the year. Mary's father William kept such a diary in his *Ames Almanack* (the ms. is in the Houghton Library), and Mary quite likely had seen it. But her own writing in no way resembles that terse listing of events, and her title thus seems metaphoric, an allusion to her charting of astronomical time and space. For an account of the almanac-diary, see Lawrence Rosenwald, "Three Early American Diarists" (Ph.D. diss., Columbia University, 1979), chap. 3; for the printed almanac, Clarence S. Brigham, *An Account of American Almanacs and Their Value for Historical Study* (Worcester, Mass.: American Antiquarian Society, 1925).

[9] There are two excellent recent studies of "Republican Motherhood," both focusing on conflicts and syntheses of domestic and political roles, but not on the particular place of religious culture in either home or nation: Mary Beth Norton, *Liberty's Daughters: The Revolutionary Experience of American Women, 1750-1800* (Boston: Little, Brown, 1980); and Linda K. Kerber, *Women of the Republic: Intellect and Ideology in Revolutionary America* (Chapel Hill: North Carolina University Press, 1980). Nancy Cott speaks of the difficulties of women's role-formation at this time in "Young Women in the Second Great Awakening in New England," *Feminist Studies* 3 (Fall 1975), 15-29. Mary's holy individualism stands as a strong counter to the alliance of "sentimental" women and ministers described in Ann Douglas, *The Femininization of American Culture* (New York: Knopf, 1977).

[10] Benjamin Kendall Emerson, *The Ipswich Emersons* (Boston: D. Clapp, 1900); Whitfield, *Journals* (London: Banner of Truth, 1960), especially pp. 466, 468, 474, 519, 533; "An Account of the Late Assembly of Pastors . . . to Bear Their Testimony to the Wondrous Work of His Power and Grace in the Late Revival of Religion," in *The Christian History . . . for the Year 1743* (Boston: Kneeland and Green, 1744), pp. 155-166 (Emerson, Moody, and Bliss all signed this pro-Awakening testimony); Amelia Forbes Emerson, ed., *The Diaries and Letters of William Emerson, 1743-1776* (Concord: privately printed, 1972); Robert Gross, *The Minutemen and Their World* (New York: Hill and Wang, 1976), esp. chap. 1 and pp. 71-74.

[11] Benjamin Kendall Emerson incorrectly lists her date of death as 1799; 1779 is the date listed in the Malden *Vital Records* and in Deloraine Corey, *The History of Malden, Mass., 1633-1785* (Malden: privately printed, 1899), pp. 648-649n.

[12] For the major church groups, see Conrad Wright, *The Beginnings of Unitarianism in America* (Boston: Starr King, 1955); Joseph Haroutunian, *Piety vs. Moralism: The Passing of the New England Theology* (New York: Henry Holt, 1932); and Daniel Walker Howe, *The Unitarian Conscience: The Harvard Moral Philosophy, 1805-61* (Cambridge, Mass.: Harvard University Press, 1970); for private devotionalist responses to the age, Richard I. Rabinowitz, "Soul, Character, and Personality: The Transformation of Personal Religious Experience in New England, 1790-1860" (Ph.D. diss., Harvard University, 1977), part III; and Stephen Marini, *The Revolution of the Spirit: Religious Sects in Rural*

New England (Cambridge, Mass.: Harvard University Press, 1982). Marini also analyzes the sectarian complexion of the post-Revolutionary settlements (like Waterford) of inland and northern New England (chaps. 2-3).

[13] The orthodox cousins were descended from father William's older sister Hannah and younger brother John: see Benjamin Kendall Emerson, *The Ipswich Emersons*, on Joseph Emerson of Beverly, Mass., author of *The Evangelical Primer* (pp. 219-220); Ralph Emerson of Andover Seminary (pp. 220-221); Samuel Moody Emerson of Manchester, Mass. (pp. 484-485). For William Emerson of Boston, see Benjamin Kendall Emerson (pp. 176-179); Ralph Rusk, *The Life of Ralph Waldo Emerson* (New York: Scribner's, 1949), chap. 1; and Lewis P. Simpson, *The Federalist Literary Mind: Selections from the "Monthly Anthology" and "Boston Review," 1803-11* (Baton Rouge: Louisiana State University Press, 1962).

[14] I Corinthians 14:34.

[15] See Wright, *Beginnings of Unitarianism*, chap. 4, and Haroutunian, *Piety vs. Moralism*, chap. 9, for the doctrinal positions; and for a more psychological and developmental analysis of will and will-lessness, Philip Greven, *The Protestant Temperament: Patterns of Child-Rearing, Religious Experience, and the Self in Early America* (New York: Knopf, 1977), esp. sec. I. Greven's sense of the evangelical's lack of self-worth, hatred of the body, and need for rebirth (pp. 12, 62, 65) all inform the sense of Mary described in the middle sections of my essay. But Mary's sense of her own power—both in childhood and in the new childhood of sanctity—makes her something other than a colonial evangelical by Greven's definition, and places her in close relation instead to the self-affirmations of nineteenth-century American romanticism.

[16] Cf. Wright's sense of "Arian" (ending with a quotation from William Emerson), chap. 9, *Beginnings of Unitarianism;* Mary is explicitly *not* a "Socinian" (13, 5; 25, 8; 28, 6).

[17] On asceticism and the family, cf. Greven, *Protestant Temperament*, sec. I, and Edmund Morgan, *The Puritan Family: Essays on Religion and Domestic Relations in Seventeenth Century New England* (Boston: Trustees of the Public Library, 1944). *Works*, X, 389. The two versions of the parable are Matthew 25:1-13 and Luke 12:35-40.

[18] Probably the Rev. Aaron Green, the Arminian heir of Mary's grandfather's church in Malden. See Joshua W. Wellman, *The Ecclesiastical History of Malden*, in D. Hamilton Hurd, *History of Middlesex County* (Philadelphia: J. W. Lewis, 1890), pp. 500-505.

[19] Tolman, *Mary Moody Emerson*, p. 3.

[20] *Works*, X, 387.

[21] Cf. Haroutunian, *Piety vs. Moralism*, pp. 25-30, on the argument about infant damnation, and all of chap. 2 on the liberalizing impulse to interpret sin and suffering as preparation for beatitude by a benevolent God.

[22] See, for instance, Thurin, *The Universal Biography*, chap. 2.

[23] I would not want to push too hard the analogy between such a Christ and Mary's clerical brother William. But she does speak of him (7, 3) as "my only first natural protector" and one at whose death she "could not grieve." Human protectors, she implies, are all too unreliable.

[24] *Works*, X, 376. Haroutunian speaks of the Edwardian legacy throughout *Piety vs. Moralism;* Wright of Clarke on pp. 98-99 and 140-143 of *Beginnings of Unitarianism*. Other testimonies to Mary's devotion to Clarke are her letter to Ezra Ripley of April 6, 1830 (Houghton ms.) and F. B. Sanborn's anecdote about her facing down Henry James, Sr. in Clarke's name, though Sanborn incorrectly identifies Mary's authority as Dr. *Adam* Clarke ("The Women of Concord," *The Critic*, 48 [1906], 150).

[25] On the introduction of Coleridge to America, see Perry Miller, ed., *The Transcendentalists: An Anthology* (Cambridge, Mass., Harvard University Press, 1967), pp. 34-39; and my "The Purity of Puritanism: Transcendentalist Readings of Milton," *Studies in Romanticism*, 17 (Spring 1978), 129-148.

Evelyn Barish (essay date 1984)

SOURCE: "Emerson and the Angel of Midnight: The Legacy of Mary Moody Emerson," in *Mothering the Mind: Twelve Studies of Writers and Their Silent Partners*, edited by Ruth Perry and Martine Watson Brownley, Holmes and Meier, 1984, pp. 219-37.

[*In the essay that follows, Barish studies the intellectual interactions of Mary Moody Emerson and Ralph Waldo Emerson, and focuses particularly on how the title character of Ralph Waldo Emerson's early gothic story "Uilsa" resembles his aunt.*]

> All your letters are valuable to me; those most so I think which you esteem the least. I grow more avaricious of this kind of property like other misers with age, and like expecting heirs would be glad to put my fingers into the chest of "old almanacks" before they are a legacy.
>
> —Emerson, age twenty-four, to his aunt

For most of his life, Ralph Waldo Emerson had a passion for the ideas and language of his aunt, Mary Moody Emerson. His admiration for her, though sometimes ambivalent, was remarkable; even as a mature man he regarded her in her prime as the best writer in Massachusetts, and named her as the deepest early influence on his own religious voice and language.[1]

Numerous aunts in literary history have influenced their talented younger relatives. What makes Waldo Emerson's nephewhood different is the intellectual quality of the sister of his dead father, the intellectual intimacy between them, and the complexities and ambivalence of their interaction. During Emerson's formative years he probably had no other literary contact who so shaped his mind or who posed so useful a challenge against which to test his own continuing growth. For her part, Mary Moody Emerson, regarded as eccentric as well as brilliant even by those who loved her, never found elsewhere so generous, subtle, or appreciative an audience. To him, as he wrote a friend, she was "alone among women"; she was his "muse" and the mediator of an intensely individualistic, romantic stance, which he was, with modifications, to make his own. To her he was from his adolescence at once "genius," "deer play Mate," a fellow student, and finally, a doctrinal opponent.[2]

Little, however, is known today about these dynamics, for the two or three commentators who have been interested in Mary have largely focused their interpretations as Emerson himself did in his late essay, which is reverential and entertaining, but does not express the nature of their interaction.[3] His conclusion, that her meaning was essentially expressed as "Faith alone, Faith alone," is considerably less than half the story, for a subject so intimately involved with his own development almost half a century earlier was inevitably elusive. Their relationship is contained largely in two insufficiently explored sources: Waldo's letters to his aunt, letters which appeared partly in the early *Journals* but which were omitted in part from Rusk's later *Letters* and in toto from the newer *Journals and Miscellaneous Notebooks;* and Mary's own letters, still almost entirely unpublished.[4] These sources, together with "Uilsa" itself, provide a double picture of a brilliant if uncertain young writer, intent on shaping a unique self, significant elements of which he had first glimpsed through the mediatory vision of the aunt he justly named his muse, who was herself a seeker, knower, and perhaps artist as well.

One of the literary practices he absorbed from her was the keeping of a voluminous journal. He began his when he was sixteen, naming it "Wide World," and liking to exchange it for her own productions, called "almanacks." It was against this background in 1822 that she wrote him when he was nineteen, telling him tartly that she had shared one of his writings, "the sorry tale of the old hag," with a young woman who "was so glad to read something new" that it had "amused her." "I promised something better," Mary noted, and then entreated further installments of the journals from which this "sorry tale" had been taken: "Send the wide or narrow *world* . . . be sure to send many pages to one who ever loves you."[5] The mixture of reproof and love in Mary's tone seems understandable—even restrained—when we realize that the "old hag" of the "sorry tale," known in the family as "Uilsa," contained central elements of a portrait of Mary herself, recognizable within the family if not beyond it.[6] It says something about the forty-eight-year-old aunt's sense of humor and detachment about her peculiarities that she could thus publicize this early example of Waldo's fictions. ("My taste was formed in romance," she once wrote, "and I knew I was not destined to please.")[7]

We may share Mary's interest, however begrudging, for "Uilsa," though a youthful tale of gothic terror rather than a work of filial piety, represents a significant new stage in Emerson's development both as a writer and in relation to his aunt. He began it just after graduating from Harvard at age eighteen, when questions of personal and vocational identity were beginning to press hard upon him, and he worked on it in four separate stages between August 1821 and February 1822. Still embedded in the journals and never printed together as a separate unit, each of the four sections halts so abruptly that I have called these breaks stammers, a characteristic which may give the impression that "Uilsa" is fragmentary. On the contrary, however, the narrative structure and language are complete, coherent, and often powerful.[8] The manuscript contains few corrections and seems to have flowed easily from Emerson's pen.

Part I begins without preamble:

> Her habits were very singular; she would come to the neighbouring village and while a family were warmly seated about their evening fire they encountered her bright eye and frightful face at the window, where she would remain motionless a moment and suddenly start away and reenter the wood. If pursued she would be found perhaps squatted on the heath near her hut twisting a string out of the dead grass and muttering to herself."
> [*JMN* I, 266-67]

Uilsa has lived there about thirty years when the narrator arrives at the town and inevitably hears of her from the "peasants." After secretly watching her, he finally seeks her, sitting down near a pile of leaves, and is soon "shocked—to see a bare arm outstretched" and to hear her "screaming to the woods and the sky"—evidently out of the leaf pile. Her words reveal her magnificent sense both of self and of great loss:

> **An excerpt from Edward Emerson's biography of his father (1889):**
>
> And it would be hard to overestimate the effect upon these young minds [Ralph Waldo Emerson and his brothers] of this same proud, pious, eccentric, exacting, inspiring Aunt Mary Moody Emerson. . . . Though exacting in her standards of conduct, and often exasperatingly frank in her criticisms of her friends, her pride in and real affection for her young relations, and interests not only lofty but broad, commanded their loyal affection. Their mother was a serene and ennobling presence in the house; their aunt a spur, or, better, a ferment in their young lives, and one that was never inert, for she made frequent visits to her relations, and, in whatever remote part of New England she might be boarding, her letters, by every opportunity of travelling minister or friend, incited her nephews to the search for wisdom or pursuit of virtue, and required of them an account of their progress. She guided their reading and made them think about it. She stimulated them by discussion, rallied them on their young vanities, and by this very correspondence trained them in reasoning and expression. Of her, her nephew wrote thus: "She gave high counsels. It was the privilege of certain boys to have this immeasurably high standard indicated to their childhood, a blessing which nothing else in education could supply." "Lift your aims;" "Always do what you are afraid to do;" "Scorn trifles;"—such were the maxims she gave her nephews, and which they made their own.
>
> *Edward, Waldo Emerson, in*
> Emerson in Concord: A Memoir,
> *Houghton, Mifflin and Company, 1889.*

"Fall, fall, scarlet leaves! The trees are my servants to cover me with a royal crimson mantle. And am not I a queen of the woods? I scared the wild eagle at the dawn, for the eye of my mother's daughter was fiercer than his. And who is he," she said, turning suddenly upon me, "who comes to the Cave of the Grey Queen? Is the spoon or the doublet . . . or the gold stolen . . . or is the magistrate come up that they have hunted out Uilsa again?"

When he asks if she can offer guidance for his life, Uilsa replies that although she is despised by the crowd as a "decrepit worm" and has "lived in a land which is hateful [,] I did not come from the vulgar dust—Uilsa is highly and proudly descended from an hundred weird women [,] fatal and feared daughters of Odin" (*JMN* I, 268). The youth mentally acknowledges her claim of having "supernatural light" as the sibyl, looking north "as if expecting a sign in the firmament . . . stood up between two blasted oaks [,] glaring on me." There suddenly the narrative breaks off.

It will resume in midsentence later, but the next entry, a variant opening, also begins in the middle of things: "By the time Wilfred had reached the heath the north wind which had before been resounding faintly in the glens began to flow fiercely and [,] while it rapidly separated the clouds [,] gave indication of a cold night. The sun had set and the stars shone with increased brilliancy through the purified atmosphere." He stops to listen to the wind, but as the gale dies, he hears "an articulate sound which no ear could mistake for the breeze" (*JMN* I, 273-74). And here, once again, the piece breaks off.

In this haunting passage of chilly beauty, an isolated figure without patronym or earthly tie moves through the empty terrain of the frozen North, avoiding the coal pits "which were supposed to make a nocturnal path dangerous." In these negations, as in their broken landscapes and even the sounds of their names, Wilfred and Uilsa are cognate figures; Emerson probably realized this, for he quickly returned to the main story, in which Uilsa's "fiery eyes and perturbed countenance" seize the narrator's attention until "I forgot the world I had left and saw nothing but the Spirit of Prophecy" (*JMN* I, 284). She speaks, Uilsa says, as "a voice from the sepulchres and caves [,] a voice from the wrinkled rottenness which the earth spurns from her bosom." In earlier years, she relates, she had borne a son who was seized from her by a "gold caravan with galloping horses and tasseled elephants from Birmah." In reply to her screams, "Odin knew me and thundered." Her violent language emphasizes the capacity for tearing and eating alive possessed by Odin's wolves, who defend her and in some sense are identified with her:

> A thousand wolves ran down by the mountain scared by the hideous lightning and baring the tooth to kill; they rushed after the cumbrous host. I saw when the pale faces glared back in terror as the black wolf pounced on his victim. I saw them as he dashed his tooth into the Indian's throat and mangled his bones in the sand. They died, and the wild thunder crashed the wolves but one escaped with mine infant son to the cave of the forest, and nourished him from her dugs. I made my bed in the cavern, my feast with the whelp of a wolf. . . .

The distinction between Uilsa herself and the wolves who both defend and betray her has faded: a wolf suckles Uilsa's son while Uilsa feasts with a wolf whelp in a cavern. The sadistic, almost cannibalistic elements of the tale expand further, as the boy grows up to reject and hate her:

> My son commanded the snows of the pole. Who is he now but Vahn, the Master of Magicians? But the proud magician forgot the mother that bore him, and the circle of enchantments which he drew was a ring of fiend-dogs to bay at me,—to scare me over the snowdrift in the cold starless night. [*JMN* I, 285]

Ralph Waldo Emerson, nephew of Mary Moody Emerson.

This is the only reference in the story to Vahn (Vain? Wan?), who is clearly meant to be the magician of the title, but never actually appears. Uilsa herself does not speak again until the very end; the focus on her seems to shift, as she becomes larger, more mythic, and more strange. The narrator, from a more distant point of view, now calls her a "barbarian," and her animality in sex and eating (two linked taboos for Emerson)[9] associates her with wild, dangerous terrain. That setting is to become metaphoric of her moral extremity: To be as Uilsa (Else?) is to be Other, not human.

The tale now moves vaguely forward in time, with the speaker no longer a youth, but a rather protective gentleman. He shows a literary attitude toward nature and self-consciously appreciates it—unlike Uilsa, who lives in a cave, erupts out of a leaf pile, and seems almost a part of nature, auctocthynous. He seeks her out among "those fine shades which never failed to elevate the imagination" (*JMN* I, 286), but she is not there. Instead, his attention is caught by a strange young boy, who calls him to follow to "dangerous places . . . in the midst of the coal mines" where sudden abysses open to unfathomable depths.

But the narrative breaks off for a third time. When Emerson resumes it four months later, the seeker moves on, now accompanied not by a child but by a villager who wants to warn Uilsa that a large "ottar-snake" lies among the rocks. They pursue her, though she outruns them until they suddenly see the "immense folds" of a serpent coiled on the edge of a chasm. The now speechless narrator sees every detail of the scene as Uilsa with "majestic gait" advances consciously toward the monster, looking north toward dark clouds:

> She came within a few yards of the snake, and stopping abruptly, raising both arms to the sky, stood like a giantess and cried aloud, "Art thou come, Minister!" The next moment that terrible animal was wound around her, tightening his terrific folds while his victim seemed struggling with superhuman strength and her hand grappled with the head of her destroyer. Suddenly they sunk and I rushed to the mouth of the abyss and listened, as there murmured up from its depths a loud cry to Odin from the suffocating gripe of the Serpent. THE END. [*JMN* I, 302-303.]

It is a terrifying dénouement, for we must now see into the abyss that had earlier threatened Wilfred. There are hints here also of the primal scene, as it is perceived ambiguously on the one hand by an adult and his companion—who in a previous metamorphosis had been an oddly knowledgeable child—and on the other by two uncomprehending persons who are childlike beside the giant Uilsa.

Inherent in the structure of the tale is a criticism of moral extremity and violent emotion. Uilsa never articulates an answer to the young man's question about how to guide his steps in life; her flow of language describing her violent personal history is followed only by silence and then a dreadful metamorphosis. But her real message is clear through the transparent paradox of her silence, for she acts out a terrifying animalism that in fact "guides his steps" literally to the brink of destruction. The narrator holds back from the abyss, but he has learned that the way she points is one he cannot take.

There are parallels between Mary Moody Emerson and this gothic portrait. She was the daughter of a minister who went off to the Revolution as a chaplain but inexplicably first removed his child from his wife's care and gave her to his mother and sister to be raised. Mary grew up on the farm of these relatives, taught by poverty to shift for herself and others, out of contact with her mother, siblings, and almost all society. Not until she was around twenty did she gain some freedom and begin to see more of her relatives. Despite her unusual intellectual gifts, she was almost entirely self-educated. Emerson tellingly reported that one of her few early books was a volume of poetry she found on the farm without cover or title page, which she learned intimately; only in later years did she learn that the author was Milton, the poem *Paradise Lost*.[10]

After the death of Waldo's father in 1811, Mary—who had refused a respectable offer of marriage and now had a small income of her own—helped Ruth Emerson to bring up the five boys by running a series of boarding houses. Mary's interests, however, were not domestic. With a passionate interest in religion and an equally passionate attachment to solitude, nature, and writing, she oscillated between life in Boston with her relatives and retreats to her country farm, where she read, wrote her journals, and meditated. Sometimes she had visionary experiences. Brilliant, difficult, a self-acknowledged "scourge" with a sharp wit, she could be deliberately cruel and had difficulties in dealing with other people. Nevertheless, she sought out gifted persons and took a great interest in certain young people, particularly her nephews, who could respond to her eccentric magnetism and to whom her appearance was a "holiday."[11]

The points of similarity between her and Uilsa are numerous. Both women have been in the neighborhood for about thirty years when they come into the lives of their observers, and both live, by preference, in a condition marginal to society, deep in the woods. Uilsa inhabits a cave or a leaf pile, while Mary, harbinger to Waldo of the romantic, preferred to dwell on a remote farm deep in the woods of central Maine, from which she preached the spiritual benefits of communion with nature. But although both women choose to live outside society, they also insist that they are a kind of royalty. Uilsa is the "Grey Queen," while Mary, in a family given to jocular grandiloquence, was typically referred to by her nephews as "Your proud ladyship," "Abbess," and even "Dr. Moody."[12] Uilsa is directly descended from Odin, greatest of the Norse gods. Mary, for her part, never ceased to remind her nephews that they came from six generations of New England's aristocracy, God's ministers on earth. "The kind Aunt whose cares instructed my youth," Emerson wrote a few years later, "told me oft the virtues of her and mine ancestors." He added significantly that "the dead sleep in their moonless night; my business is with the living" (*JMN* I, 316). Uilsa is also an outlaw, the mother of an illegitimate child, who is hunted down by her son and the magistrate alike. Mary Moody Emerson traveled from town to town in New England in search of enlightenment, health cures, and, most probably, new experience, but she frequently quarreled with her fellow boarders, her hosts, and the ministers she sought out. On two occasions she borrowed men's horses. Though these acts were more joyrides than thefts, the antisocial quality preserved them in her relatives' memories.[13]

Both figures speak darkly, like sibyls—a term Waldo applies to both. Thus Uilsa's language is said to be "severe and abrupt and always mingled with unintelligible terms" (*JMN* I, 267), while Mary's language is often so difficult to construe (one reason that she remains unstudied) that she demands closer reading than anyone but her nephew has been willing to grant. Uilsa and Mary, moreover, are equally associated with death, and specifically with worms. Uilsa seeks her own death in the embrace of a "worm," while Mary was literally obsessed by death. She rode around in public draped in her shroud, until it wore out and had to be replaced—several times. She also had her bed made in the shape of a coffin.[14] Her letters emphasized her longing for death, and one of her oddities was her well-known fascination with snakes, worms, and reptiles, which stood, supposedly, for that yearning. "There are many," she wrote Waldo, "who are forced to creep thro' the entrails of reptiles . . . to find an infinite Designer. Never dislike their little lobes and [livers]" (*JMN* I, 380). And he might end a letter to her by saying, "Your imagination is fond of recurring to the poor reptiles and I give you joy of the worm!"[15]

One of the most interesting verbal parallels between the two is Waldo's use of the term "weird women" for both of them. Uilsa claims that she is "proudly descended from an hundred weird women, feared and fatal daughters of Odin."[16] In his journals some months before composing his tale, he described Mary as "the Weird-woman of her religion" (*JMN* I, 49). "Weird," of course, means gifted with second sight, and he was then thinking of religious vision, but in the context of "Uilsa" and the poem by Thomas Gray to which he alludes, a weird woman is also one who is capable of almost any kind of perversity and destruction. It may have been these resonances, in addition to the unwelcome compliment of the tale itself, which led Mary, weary of the joke, to write four years later to Charles, Waldo's younger brother: "Pardon the whim, if such it be, to ask you not to compare me to any weird woman. I who lived so as to try never to offend by one singular word, whose whole time is devoted to one and the same object, pray you spare my age and vocation."[17]

No characteristic shared by Uilsa and Mary is more important than their supernatural powers and capacity for prophecy, for with these they name their followers and endow them with their identity and genius. In the tale the narrator asks the Grey Queen "how to guide his steps in life" because she is the "Spirit of Prophecy" and has supernatural powers, and she relates how she has passed these on to her son Vahn, "the Master of Magicians" (*JMN* I, 268, 285). Mary apparently purported at some indefinite time to have something like second sight, and her letters reveal her in the posture of the Watcher, straining after ethereal revelation. At times she prophesies—though refusing coyly to do so—for her nephews, while at others she urges the boys to develop their own visionary powers: "I won't prophesy half the good things I know." Waldo called her "Cassandra" and wanted to share her knowledge,[18] undoubtedly encouraged by the fact that from his early teens she had named him as one with magical powers; he was the "Magician maker" and the "magician of nature and art."[19] Most striking is the letter she wrote to him in some excitement when he went off to Harvard at fourteen:

> What dull Prosaic Muse [herself] would venture from the humble dell of an unlettered District to address a son of Harvard? Son . . . of poetry of genius—ah were it so and I destined to stand in near consanguinity to this magical possessor. Age itself would throw off its gravity for a moment and dream that there is a vestige of fame to attach it to earth—that a name so dear was one day to leave some memorial. Vain wish . . . A name on this flying planet . . . is not matter of sin when viewed by the celestial light of faith. . . . In that great assembly, where human nature is purified from its native dross and ignorance, may the name of my dear Waldo be inrolled.[20]

Did Emerson, by age seventeen, feel a need like Vahn's to keep such a sibyl at some distance? Whether they are tangible or "such stuff as dreams are made on," great gifts, like identity and "genius," mean great debts for the recipient. Despite the depth of Emerson's obligation, it is important to distinguish between the significance and meaning of "Uilsa" and the ongoing relationship of Waldo and Mary Moody Emerson. Obviously the structure of the story expresses distrust of its protagonist's mode of life, ending as it does on a note of gothic terror and seeming defeat. But if Emerson were rejecting the psychic presence of an overwhelming parent, or parent surrogate, as Vahn does, we should expect Emerson's contact with this aunt to have diminished over the next five years. Such distancing, after all, would only have been normal for a young person in his early twenties. In reality, however, the opposite was true. Between his graduation from Harvard in 1821 and his being licensed to preach in 1826, he turned to her above all other correspondents.

It was a period in his life when Emerson had little helpful family contact. When he graduated in 1821, Charles was only thirteen, and Edward at sixteen was already chronically ill with the tubercular symptoms that required three extended absences by 1825.[21] Emerson was on a more equal footing with William, with whom he jointly kept a school, but this older brother left to study in Germany late in 1823 and stayed almost two years.[22] Waldo's brothers were either too young or too far away to discuss ideas with. His classmates had scattered, and he was left to himself, burning with ambition but trapped in schoolteaching and poverty. He reached out to two or three contemporary correspondents for intellectual contact, but the letters of one left him, as he complained, "hungering and thirsting"; like Mary, who wished to receive only "treatise[s]," he wanted real thought, not gossip or news.[23] His well-known contact with Dr. Channing was actually, as he told Oliver Wendell Holmes, comparatively superficial. It did not begin until 1823, and consisted of Dr. Channing's giving Waldo a reading list but refusing to "undertake the direction" of his studies. They talked "from time to time," but their temperaments were equally remote, and although Emerson revered the older man's sermons, the two "never really came together."[24]

More significantly, almost immediately after entering Harvard Divinity School in early 1825, Waldo lost the use of his eyes for reading and retired to work on a country farm, thus entering an even more lonely period. Undoubtedly this and subsequent episodes of disease, which culminated in the breakdown of his health in 1826-1827, were related to Waldo's sense of personal and intellectual stress.[25] Since he had no other guide or mentor during the difficult years when he was forging his vocational and personal sense of self, his contacts with Mary were central.

The literary nature of this interaction must be stressed, for they saw little of each other. "*We* can only commune by pen," Mary once wrote him after a tiff, exaggerating perhaps only a little.[26] Their relationship in some ways is less a personal one than that between two texts, hers having a privileged status won by her style and her long concentration on and insight into her "sole object," while his writings from an early stage received from her flattering respect and serious criticism.

His intellectual and personal isolation encouraged, though it could not have produced, the intense interest Waldo felt in his aunt's ideas, style, and, above all, her visionary stance. He gave direct testimony to this fascination frequently, both to her and to others. Emerson read widely and continually throughout this period, and even without Mary he would have become acquainted with the religious controversies and the romantic, visionary stance she made her own. But he felt that he could not unravel these controversies alone. "I ramble among doubts," he wrote her, imploring her answer to puzzles prompted by skeptical philosophy. "My reason offers no solution. Books are old and dull and unsatisfactory; the pen of a living witness and faithful lover of these mysteries of Providence is worth all the volumes of all the centuries." That pen worth "all the volumes" of "all . . . centuries" was hers not only because of her faith but because of her interest in "the connexions existing between this world and the next." He valued in her precisely that capacity which he was to develop highly in himself: the ability to draw analogies between the real world and the transcendent world of moral order and to see "the marvellous moral phenomena" which Providence daily exhibited.[27]

He valued equally her example as a writer, with a true writer's obsessive commitment to her task. In later years he reflected that there could be "no strong performance without a little fanaticism in the performers"; only that could account for the "fervid work in M.M.E.'s journals . . . the vehement religion which would not let her sleep nor sit, but write, night and day, year after year."[28] Interestingly, Emerson by then had long since become a writer whose practices, as the seemingly endless journals and notebooks show, were very similar.

He also testified that she had provided the model for his use of religious language. "Religion was her occupation," he noted, and he said that he had learned as a youth the very nature and sound of religious language from repeating hers. When he later came to write sermons, "I could not find any examples or treasuries of piety so high-toned, so profound, or promising such rich influence as my remembrances of her conversations and letters" (*JMN* I, 323-24). Sometimes he might be jocular on the subject of his aunt and her prophetic stance, as when he wrote a contemporary that by comparison with his aunt, "of whom . . . you have heard before and who is alone among women," he felt like a "coarse, thrifty cit [who] profanes the grove [of Nature] by his presence." In her view, he went on, Nature was a temple " . . . where the fiery soul can begin a premature communication with other worlds."[29] But while he might joke, he shared that yearning to know the unknowable, desiring, in passages that parallel this essay's epigraph, to "know what living wit . . . has . . . concluded upon the dark sayings and sphinx riddles of philosophy and life; I do beseech your charity not to withhold your pen," and requesting "the legacy of all your recorded thought."[30]

The language Emerson desired so avidly has proved difficult for other readers, as he finally acknowledged.[31] She wrote all her life either for no reader or for only one; this lack of audience undoubtedly increased the densely allusive tendencies of her language. Hurried and elliptical, she often carelessly dropped words or whole phrases. She also liked to experiment with style, pushing meaning into wild, baroque structures. For all its difficulties, however, her writing, as Emerson said, is always spontaneous, unexpected, and sometimes brilliant.

Her fundamental theme, which later was to become in some degree Emerson's, was to see in nature, as eighteenth-century divines had done, a perpetual allegory of God's provenance. Her interest in nature was less theological than literary and aesthetic; where eighteenth-century philosophers had used metaphors drawn from the material world heuristically to strengthen the argument from design, Mary's practice was to dwell on her experience of the natural world, like a brooding poet, until it led her almost ecstatically with baroque syntactic twists to the visionary stance she sought. "Do we love poetry . . . ," she asked rhetorically one evening after a night walk, "as we do the flowers of the field—because they supply not the necessaries, but the luxuries of life and give presentiments to the soul so rich, of an existence where all cares and labours cease."[32] She watched a cloud, then thought about "éclat of name—of fame" and the relation of these to the movement of the cloud "as it . . . climbs the sides of the mountain over bog and brake and tree and suddenly disappears at the instant of arriving at its summit." Just as "shadows add to the beauty of fleeting scenes," so does "the aspirant of other mounts to the interest of life." She did not have to add that the "éclat of name" was of course to be Waldo's, and his future was to mount—fleeting, like clouds and all human wishes—the peaks of human renown and disappear perhaps in some apotheosis. "This richly laden season," she went on that September day, "when every leaf begins its own mystic story, which soothes the soul and dwells upon the soul and blends itself into the soul, derives a zest . . . from prophecy of those who are rising into honor."[33] She embroiders on the idea that "there does appear a soul in nature. And when we clothe it in a human form, its head is lost amongst clouds—we behold—we live only in her skirts. . . ."[34] The subject, the soul of nature, may have been suggested by Waldo, but the figure of nature as a giant, its head in the upper atmosphere, its feet on the ground, dwarfing tiny humanity, may well be a source of Emerson's later use of this trope.

Waldo could learn not only from the emphasis Mary as a romantic gave to natural theology, but from her emotional posture as well. As one who cultivated religious enthusiasm, rather than a "frigid" rational faith, she was identified in the Emerson family with the term "sentiment," which became her byword and a family joke. When her nephew asked her for some "facts or news," she replied in a phrase he later adopted in "History": "What indeed are *facts* to me?"[35] To one who understood intuitively, facts *per se* were irrelevant, except for their analogical meaning. Alluding probably to Jonathan Edwards and the treatise he wrote at the age of twelve on spiders, she went on to say that some might study spiders or the petals of a flower, "and say they are finding the way to a designing Cause." Similarly, a friend has shown her the "peculiar dandelion . . . in each petal or blade hung a perfect flower itself. The little children will soon amuse themselves with seeing its downy leaves fly away. Now my dear Waldo," she commented, archly denying her role, "if your imagination wanders into regions of *sentiment,* don't blame me. I will keep to fact."[36]

Mary could tease him the more freely because Waldo was known to be her disciple in this, advocating to his brothers the "sentimental" or even the "flashy sentimental" style as a way of looking at nature, shaking off depression, and finding food for thought. He asked how the ten-year-old Edward could "read a letter of Aunt Mary's, an enthusiast in rural pleasures, and yet want a subject?" Ten years later, now encouraging Charles, Waldo used several of Mary's figures of speech: "Is it not a better inquiry than hunting new minerals or dissecting spiders or counting lobes and petals of flowers to explore observe the obscure birth of sentiment at the frugal board perhaps of a poor wise man and see how slowly it struggles into fame."[37] The dissection of spiders, the counting of "lobes," insects, and petals of flowers, the slow growth of "sentiment" into "fame" and glory—these figures were not only identified with Mary, but were her very language and thought itself. If she had provided his "treasuries" of religious language, as he wrote in 1837, Waldo became at times her moral treasurer, coining that gold and issuing it.

In addition to Mary's sharply observant eye for natural details, her imagination loved to soar from them to cosmic and supernal imagery: Angels, stars, and the light night skies are favorite tropes for the crescendo passages of her letters. As stylists and eventually doctrinal opponents, she and Waldo often interchanged imagery. When Waldo after his return from the South wrote in late 1827 that he had determined not to be guided by any mysticism or sentiment that his reason condemned, he added that he would not "surrender to the casual and morbid exercise of the sentiment of a midnight hour the steady light of all my days, my most vigorous and approved thoughts [and] barter the sun for the waning moon."[38] This new departure stung Mary to extend and elevate the metaphor, dramatizing it almost into a scenario: "The lover of beauty," she replied, "will not desire to analyse the mystic mistress of his heart . . . its source is God. . . . If the Angel of 'midnight' who is commissioned to turn the starry mirror of reflection has oftener visited him—it may be that truth is more clearly discerned then [than] in the sunny influence of vigorous thoughts and business."[39] The image of the angel of midnight (who in some sense must be Mary herself) turning the mirror of reflection so that Emerson might see into his soul is effective, equal to the offhand scorn she feels for his "approved thoughts" and sunny, businesslike days.

A lover of poetry who was almost as eager for her nephew to be a poet as a preacher, she was certain these great gifts could not be practiced within society's purview. She, more than any other influence, undoubtedly taught Emerson the necessity of solitude for the growth of individual talent. Emerson tended "to talk with the most apparent simplicity of the sympathies of society—they are needed, it is true, to form the 'common mind' to principles of action"—but not minds, clearly, such as their own. She would prefer that poetry, "my young favorite," as Mary called her, much as she might a protegée-niece, "would wander wild among the flowers and lairs of nature—would scale the 'tempel where the Genius of the Universe resides' [and] view herself in the rays of distant stars, while you are getting her a home more permanent."[40] In later years Emerson had a wonderful dream in which "I floated at will in the great ether, and I saw this world floating also not far off, but diminished to the size of an apple. Then an angel took it in his hand and brought it to me and said, 'This thou must eat'—and I ate the world," he wrote (*JMN* VII, 525). To see the world "in the light of distant stars" or "to get beyond the precincts of this earth" was a shared urge, but such a vision could not be pursued in society.

Emerson asked his aunt the difficult religious questions, especially about the afterlife. When her ideas of "the posthumous" were requested, Mary was at first coy, questioning the advantage of parting with such ideas, "that portion of one's soul." Then she responded by conjuring up the shade of the intellectual, religious, and yet worldly Madame de Staël, a contemporary and a heroine of Mary's, evoking that lady's performing a similar sacrifice: "Think of a De Staël . . . treasuring up sentiments and ideas for a Son—abandoning her own publick existence that he might be 'decked with unfading honors!' " Madame de Staël in fact had had no son, but this was irrelevant; since she had *not* so renounced public glory, "*Never,* oh no not one leaf of amaranthine will deck the brow of mere genius like hers. The humblest example of meekness will shine in light when the meteors are gone . . . Good night. Oh for that 'long and moonless night' to shadow my dust, tho' I have nothing to leave but my carcase to fatten the earth—it is for my own sake I long to go."[41] That "humblest example of meekness" is again clearly Mary herself in this grotesquerie.

Emerson's own early writings often link death with magical prophecy, as "Uilsa" does.[42] These themes are also often linked in his aunt's letters: "Before I ever knew you, I did not ask even a dirge. I invoked nature with rapture to sweep over my grave with her roughest elements: for there would be the voice of a strange spirit, and there might be a strange light to guide the icy worm to his riot." Once he asked her to play Cassandra for him. "Were I a seer," she rejoined, the failure of certain of his writings on drama would "bode good. . . . I do ask the favour to be remembered rather as a dead Cassandra, not prophesying but praying for thy welfare."[43] In her fantasy, death and salvation meant translation to a more romantic realm, where, lit by "strange light," she, the "icy worm," would yet pulse with consuming and immortal energy. Similarly, in portraying herself as a dead but prayerful Cassandra, Mary improved on the Greek model, Christianizing the pagan seer and transmuting classical power into protestant witness. Implicit in her rebuff of Emerson's critical writings was the idea that, like Mary, he ought to turn from the pagan to the Christian world, from drama to theology. Using her gift for rapid, dense, and allusive language, she never lost an opportunity to evoke models of spiritual progress, even in this wayward example of what one might call *imitatio rinascimento*.

But for all her pursuit of the visionary gleam and her willingness to involve Waldo in it, Mary Emerson was sharp and hardheaded in sniffing not heresy but the kind of ambivalence that could lead to half-hearted professions and subsequent disappointment. When her nephew had publicly joined his congregation, an ancient custom requisite for a budding minister, she inquired sharply, *"What mean you by this rite?"* hinting at a suspicion that it might be "the *key* to a profession."[44] Her criticism was as consistent as her admiration. Emerson had complained that his muse had become " 'faint and mean.' " "Ah well she may," Mary replied, "and better oh far better leave you . . . [if he were to be] one whose destiny tends to lead him to sensation rather than sentiment, whose intervals of mentality seem to be rather spent in collecting facts than energising itself. . . . Oh would the Muse forever leave you, till you had prepared for her a celestial abode. . . . You are not inspired in heart, with a gift for immortality, because you are the Nursling of surrounding circumstances—you become yourself a part of the events which make up ordinary life." She wanted him, in short, to be as self-reliant as she was. But she went on to prophesy more happily the "approaching period I dread worse than this sweet stagnation—when your Muse shall be dragged into éclat—tho' like Cicero['s] perhaps, your poetry will not be valued because your prose is so much better." Emerson later wrote on the bottom of this page, "this letter is a most beautiful monument of kindness and highminded but partial affection. Would I were worthy of it."[45]

Emerson went through a period of skepticism and especially took an interest in the writings of David Hume, but only to Mary did Waldo dare voice speculations deriving from Hume's ideas in any significant way. She, however, secure in her faith, was scornful of the philosopher whom she called "that bloated old scotsman" and whose influence she alone—and accurately—saw as pervading her nephew's thought and style. Hume's arguments against intuitive knowledge left her unmoved, for to her even "walking and riding before breakfast . . . so cloudy, so exquisitely cloudy," made her sure that "we are more certain of this beauty than if it were real." "Old Hume," she snorted, "was a morbid hermit in the nest of being" and his impoverished mind could have drawn no such inferences. But as late as 1828, while praising writing by Waldo, she commented, "Your reading Hume when young has rendered you, I cannot but think, so imbued with his manner of thinking, that you cannot shake him off. There seems or I am stupid, so much of his *manner,* tho' better, in this letter that I feel as I do when reading him. But to *my old* frame his arguments, if such they can be called, make no more impression than the spray of a child's squirt."[46] To Emerson the problems of skepticism could not be erased so easily, and he and Mary began to draw apart in later years over his gradual resolution of these issues. That separation, however, was intellectual rather than personal; Mary lived more consistently, although not permanently, in Concord after he moved there in the 1830s, and their mutual respect continued.

Given the multiple and dense connections and parallels between the thinking of the two Emersons, any reduction of this relationship or of Mary to the plot or protagonist of "Uilsa" would be uninteresting. Mary was rueful about the story of "Uilsa" because in her own mind she had played the part of a Madame de Staël, not of an "old hag," to the only person whose "mind" had met hers "in sympathy."[47] Emerson, for his part, knew Mary to be no destructive witch, but a "seeker," like himself—though one who knew answers, as well as asked questions.[48] Mary was not Uilsa, but she provided Waldo with a model of the pilgrim, the self-reliant seeker in whom romantic individualism was uneasily yoked with a neo-Calvinist desire to subsume earthly to spiritual glory. Uilsa is intensely an invention of the romantic literary tradition, especially that of Scott, but she is also a figure in search of transcendent experience, which when it comes has spiritual as well as demonic and sexual connotations. The young Emerson liked to attribute to his aunt quasi-magical powers desired by but denied to himself, because he imagined that they enabled one to stand romantically and heroically outside society and grapple with dangerous knowledge. For several years after writing this tale he prepared himself for that role by a variety of means, not least of which was coming to grips with Mary herself in their protracted and frequently argumentative correspondence. He moved from but did not need to struggle to throw off her influence; on the contrary, even in childhood he seems to have known instinctively the right distance from which to maintain the good humor of their game. Rather he made it his task to internalize Mary's voice, her daring, her faith, and her sense of the grandeur of her pursuit, while establishing for himself a more stable relation to society than hers. More than a decade later he began in Concord to carve out for himself a position that was deliberately marginal to the established church and Boston's intellectual life, a place from which he exercised the privileges of the critic's stance during his productive years. He managed to live there, in a sense, on the edge of the abyss, a "stink in the nostrils" of the Brahmin class, to quote his friend Clough, without moving over its edge into the virtually complete isolation of his aunt.[49] It was to be years before he could establish that balance, however, and the writing of "Uilsa" may have been to some extent a first project toward that end, a stage in the process of inventing himself and shaping the space he needed around him in which to evolve myths of human beings engaged in far more nurturant relations with nature than he had once been able to dream. Mary is not Uilsa, but without the model of his aunt's peculiar combination of literary and personal daring and reserve, he could never have invented the great myths with which he conjured a young nation to imagine itself free of history and able to cross the abyss of nonentity, as he called it, into personhood. "Uilsa" as a juvenile fiction has been justifiably forgotten, but Mary Moody Emerson deserves recognition for her own contribution toward those strange dreams.

Notes

[1] Franklin Benjamin Sanborn, "A Concord Notebook: Sixth Paper: The Women of Concord—I," *The Critic* 48 (February 1906), 157; Ralph Waldo Emerson, *The Journals and Miscellaneous Notebooks of Ralph Waldo Emerson,* ed. Merton M. Sealts, Jr. (Cambridge: Harvard University Press, 1965), V, 324. Further references to this text will be abbreviated *JMN* and included in the text.

[2] Ralph L. Rusk, ed. *The Letters of Ralph Waldo Emerson* (New York: Columbia University Press, 1939) I, 133 (cited hereafter as *L*); Emerson MSS., Houghton Library, Harvard University, bMS Am 1280 226.18 [?], 1820. All quotations from the Emerson family manuscripts come from this source, which will be abbreviated as H. MS. and distinguished by year. For clarity, I have regularized the punctuation but kept Mary's idiosyncratic spelling and capitalization; I render the ampersand used by her and her nephew as "and." All other emendations are indicated by square brackets and ellipses.

[3] Van Wyck Brooks, "The Cassandra of New England," *Scribner's Magazine* 81 (February 1927), 125-29; Rosalie Feltenstein, "Mary Moody Emerson: The Gadfly of Concord," *American Quarterly* 5, No. 3 (Fall 1953), 231-46; Ralph Waldo Emerson, "Mary Moody Emerson," in *The Complete Works of Ralph Waldo Emerson,* ed. Edward W. Emerson (Cambridge, Mass.: Riverside Press, 1904), X, 433 (cited hereafter as *Works*). The privately printed monograph by George Tolman, *Mary Moody Emerson,* ed. Edward Emerson Forbes (Cambridge, Mass., 1929), was not widely circulated. See also my earlier studies: Evelyn Barish Greenberger, "Emersonian Gothic: The Misprision of an Aunt," Bunting Institute Working Paper, Radcliffe College (Cambridge, Mass., 1979); and Evelyn Barish, "Emerson and 'The Magician': An Early Prose Fantasy," *American Transcendental Quarterly,* No. 31, pt. 1 (Summer 1976), 13-18, parts of which have been incorporated in the present paper. Phyllis Cole's "The Advantage of Loneliness: Mary Moody Emerson's Almanacks," in Joel Porte, ed., *Emerson: Prospect and Retrospect,* (Cambridge: Harvard University Press, 1982), pp. 1-32, came to my attention only after the present paper had been prepared for publication.

[4] *Journals of Ralph Waldo Emerson: 1820-1876,* Edward Waldo Emerson and W. E. Forbes, eds., 10 vols. (Cambridge, Mass.: Riverside Press, 1909-1914); cited hereafter as *J.* See *JMN* I, xxxviii. The omission of Emerson's draft letters from *JMN* tends to obscure the relationship, as the large majority of these were to Mary, and many of the final versions are not available elsewhere, since the *Journals,* which printed excerpts, is out of print. The revised edition of the *Letters* being prepared by Professor Eleanor Tilton should remedy this problem.

[5] H. MS. 1822.

[6] My first discussion of this previously unknown tale in 1976 (see note 3 above) referred to it as "The Magician," but later research suggests that it was known in the family as "Uilsa" (Charles Chauncy Emerson, letter to his brother, H. MS. 1827).

[7] *Works* X, 404.

[8] *JMN* I, 266-68, 273-74, 284-86, 302-303.

[9] Evelyn Barish Greenberger, "The Phoenix on the Wall: Consciousness in Emerson's Early and Late Journals," *American Transcendental Quarterly,* No. 21, Pt. 1 (Winter 1974), 45-46.

[10] *Works* X, 411.

[11] *Works* X, 403, 402.

[12] H. MS. 1824; *L* I, 22.

[13] Edward Waldo Emerson, *Emerson in Concord: A Memoir* (Boston: Houghton Mifflin, 1889), pp. 52-53.

[14] *Works* X, 428-29.

[15] *L* I, 105.

[16] The allusion here is not primarily to Shakespeare, but to Thomas Gray, who wrote two so-called "Norse poems," one named "The Weird Sisters" (an alternative title for "The Fatal Sisters"), and the other entitled "The Descent of Odin" (A. L. Poole, ed., *The Poetical Works of Gray and Collins,* 2nd rev. ed. [London: Oxford University Press, 1926], pp. 65-79). In these grisly works, the hundred weird women are valkyrie-like creatures of evil who clank and flit over battlefields after a war, gathering up the dismembered parts of slain warriors to use in their horrible tapestries. We know that Emerson alludes to Gray for two reasons, the first being that he makes Uilsa the daughter of these children of Odin, who are Gray's invention. Second, Emerson twice mentions Gray's companion poem, in which Odin visits the underworld to coax his estranged wife, Hela, to do his bidding, although her only reply is "Now my weary lips I close, / Leave me, leave me, to repose." Emerson teased Mary when he was trying to get her to answer his letters by telling her she was like "those weird women" who uttered this line; he

echoed it also in "Uilsa" when he remarked, "At one time, her only answer to all who approached her was Avoid, avoid" (*L* I, 197).

[17] H. MS. 1826.

[18] *L* I, 104-105.

[19] H. MS. 1827, 1828, 1823.

[20] H. MS. 1817 [?].

[21] H. MS. 1820, 1822, 1825.

[22] *L*, p. 141n.; Ralph L. Rusk, *The Life of Ralph Waldo Emerson* (New York: Columbia University Press, 1949), pp. 113, 518n.

[23] *L* I, 132; H. MS. 1823; *L* I, 171.

[24] Oliver Wendell Holmes, *Ralph Waldo Emerson* (Boston: Houghton Mifflin, 1885), p. 102.

[25] Evelyn Barish, "The Moonless Night: Emerson's Crisis of Health, 1825-27," in Joel Meyerson, ed., *Emerson Centenary Essays* (Carbondale: Southern Illinois University Press, 1982), pp. 1-16.

[26] H. MS. 1826.

[27] H. MS. 1823; *L* I, 137.

[28] E. W. Emerson, *Emerson in Concord*, p. 95.

[29] *L* I, 133.

[30] *J* I, 357.

[31] *Works* X, 601n.

[32] H. MS. 1821.

[33] H. MS. 1824.

[34] H. MS. 1821.

[35] *Works* II, 32-33; H. MS. 1822 [?].

[36] H. MS. 1821.

[37] *L* I, 66, 62, 246.

[38] *J* II, 222-23.

[39] H. MS. 1828.

[40] H. MS. 1821.

[41] H. MS. 1821.

[42] Barish, "The Birth of Merlin: Emerson, Magic, and Death," in Saul N. Brody and Harold Schecter, eds., *CUNY English Studies 1979* (New York: AMS Press, forthcoming).

[43] H. MS. 1821.

[44] H. MS. 1822.

[45] H. MS. 1822.

[46] H. MS. 1827, 1828.

[47] H. MS. [1825].

[48] *L* I, 208, 205.

[49] Frederick L. Mulhauser, ed., *The Correspondence of Arthur Hugh Clough* (Oxford: Clarendon Press, 1957), II, 340.

David R. Williams (essay date 1986)

SOURCE: "The Wilderness Rapture of Mary Moody Emerson," in *Studies in the American Renaissance*, 1986, pp. 1-16.

[*In the following essay, Williams analyzes the influences of Calvinism and early transcendentalism on R. W. Emerson's thought, which are reflected in the pervasive symbol of the spiritual wilderness.*]

Even at its most refulgent, Emersonian Transcendentalism owed a debt to New England's native Calvinism. Certainly, the Transcendental plant was nourished by European Romanticism, but it had native roots and these were anchored solidly in the local soil. Ralph Waldo Emerson's return to nature, in particular, grew from a literal misreading of an originally theological metaphor preached to him by his Calvinist aunt, Mary Moody Emerson, who urged him to enter into the wilderness of his soul and there experience the terror and the ecstacy of conversion.

The first Calvinist settlers had brought to New England an ancient tradition in which the Children of Israel's crossing the Sinai and entering Canaan prefigured the crucifixion and resurrection of Christ. Through an association of this typological interpretation with the call for conversion, the wilderness came to represent the location of the conversion experience, the human psyche. From the Old Testament use of the wilderness as a symbol of primordial chaos and "therapeutic punishment," to John the Baptist's crying in the wilderness, to medieval mysticism's "interiorization of the wilderness," to Calvin's conception of the wilderness as the hell of self-knowledge, to Hooker's use of the wilderness as a type of redemptive madness, to

Edwards' insistence that sinners, before they could be converted, had first to be "led into a wilderness . . . and made to see their own helplessness and absolute dependence on God's power and grace," the wilderness became the symbolic location both of damnation and salvation. Consciousness was pictured by Calvin and his followers as a thin layer of conditioned rationality suspended over a "howling wilderness" of fear within the soul. According to this "wilderness tradition," it was in the soul, in what today would be called the wilderness of the subconscious, that sinners were expected to face their internal fears, experience the ego-destroying chaos of subconscious terror, and there yield themselves to divine sovereignty. This traditional, typological use of wilderness imagery underlay much of the Transcendentalists' mystic belief in the redemptive power of nature.[1]

The Transcendental debt to European Romanticism, thus, should not be allowed to obscure the extent to which much of Transcendentalism was, in Stephen Whicher's words, "essentially 'reminiscent Puritanism' thinly disguised as philosophy." The foreign ideas, as Perry Miller has argued, merely "stirred native propensities" by providing a new language with which the Transcendental revivalists could disguise their regression—even from themselves—to the spirit of the Great Awakening and the Antinomian crisis. Coleridge and Kant, Carlyle and Cousin did not introduce romanticism into America. They simply provided the language with which the heirs of Edwards could "rephrase the ancient religious pre-occupations of New England." In *Freedom of the Will,* Edwards had argued that the "inclinations of the heart" precede the "speculative notions" of the mind, that the loves and hates of youth determine the intellectual decisions of maturity. Certainly, the European Romantics were important sources of the specific ideas with which the Transcendentalists articulated their new beliefs, but the attitudes, the inclinations, that prepared the way for those new ideas were the effects of closer causes.[2]

Nor should the optimistic emphasis of romanticism be thought of as a foreign import altogether alien to the gloomy native temperament. Calvinism, after all, did have an enthusiastic side. The Calvinist image of wilderness was never just a symbol of darkness and sin, but combined both terror and joy, crucifixion and resurrection, the sojourn through the desert and entrance into Canaan. New England Calvinists had always held that the beneficiaries of the conversion experience received a heightened perception of beauty, a new appreciation of divine truth, and an intuitive love of moral excellency. Ralph Waldo Emerson's "divine light of Reason" was but a distant reflection of Edwards' "Divine and Supernatural Light Immediately Imparted to the Soul by the Spirit of God." Edwards' grandfather, Solomon Stoddard, had said quite clearly that saints know their election "by intuition, or seeing of grace in their own hearts. It is by consciousness." Edwards had "seen" the immediate presence of Christ in the beauties of the woods and fields. The Transcendentalists, according to Octavius Brooks Frothingham, could not deny their ancestry: "Indeed, whenever orthodoxy spread its wings and rose into the region of faith, it lost itself in the sphere where the human soul and the divine were in full concurrence. Transcendentalism simply claimed for all men what Protestant Christianity claimed for its own elect."[3]

This much is not new. The parallels between Edwards and R. W. Emerson, their love of the natural world, their philosophical idealism, their symbolic consciousness, are well known. Long before Perry Miller published his famous essay "From Edwards to Emerson," Harriet Beecher Stowe had noted that "Waldo Emerson and Theodore Parker were the last results of the current set in motion by Jonathan Edwards." Henry Bamford Parkes, in the year Miller's essay was published, went even further than Miller dared go and claimed that almost "all the ideas of Transcendentalism can be found in Edwards." Miller's essay, like much of this other criticism, merely pointed out to those who were looking elsewhere the true mountain source of the mighty stream that was American Romanticism. Most critics have been content with little more than a repetition of the news of his discovery, for Miller left no map, and there are no obvious paths up the mountain from Emerson back to Edwards.[4]

Had Waldo studied Edwards more carefully than he did, and left clearer records of his borrowings, there would be little problem.[5] If Waldo had been brought up by Calvinist parents, the job would be simpler. But without such specific trails to follow, the argument would have to be made in terms of general cultural inheritances, that Waldo, as Parkes argued, "seems to have absorbed ideas which Edwards put into circulation rather than to have studied Edwards himself."[6] This could be done, but there is at least one trail, one clear Calvinist influence on Waldo, that largely has been ignored: his aunt, Mary Moody Emerson.[7]

A true mystic and a true New England Calvinist, Mary Moody Emerson was one of her nephews' most influential teachers. She did not define her faith by creed or catechism, she lived it. To her "the fiery depths of Calvinism, its high and mysterious elections to eternal bliss, beyond angels, and all its attendant wonders" was not dogma. It was an attitude that knew man to be but flesh, a wind that passeth away and cometh not again. She held human endeavor to be worthless, human pretensions absurd. Whatever point of view anyone put forward she took delight in destroying. She never denied the vain satisfaction this gave her, but she also insisted on a serious intent, to prove to the worldly that all human speculations fall short of the ultimate, that the glory of God forever stands above and against all human idolatry, that despite all pretensions Israel remained in the wilderness. "If she found anything that was dear or sacred to you," wrote Van Wyck Brooks, "she instantly flung broken crockery at it."[8]

Waldo was well acquainted with his aunt's eccentricities. No one reading his letters to her, or his essay commemorating her life, can deny that he loved her. When William Emerson died in 1811, Aunt Mary, as she was always known, was asked to come to Concord. She agreed, as long as she could take over not just the household chores but the spiritual education of the four boys. When she arrived, it was to make sure, as Waldo himself put it, that her nephews should be "bred to purify the old faith of what error and narrowness adhered to it, and import all its fire into the new age." She was determined that her nephews should rekindle the spiritual flame and set their generation afire with the faith once delivered to the saints.[9]

Born in 1774, the heir of "six generations of a sovereign priesthood," Mary was, as she later told Lafayette, "in arms" at the battle of Lexington and Concord. Her father had died of a fever while serving as Chaplain to the army at Ticonderoga, and her widowed mother had sent the infant to Malden to be raised by an aging uncle and aunt. Tried by harsh poverty and ill-tempered guardians, forced to care for a second "insane" aunt, she found solace during her hours of lonely drudgery in the doctrines of self-denial and divine sovereignty. Later, when she had access to books, she gave herself to study. Her earliest reading, according to Waldo, was "Milton, Young, Akenside, Samuel Clarke, Jonathan Edwards, and always the Bible." Her treasured copy of *Paradise Lost* lacked a title page and not until years later did she learn who its author was. In this setting, she saturated herself with the moods and the language of orthodox Calvinist piety. In time she passed these on to her nephews. There can be little doubt that Waldo not only heard but himself spoke and prayed with the heavily symbolic language of New England Calvinism. "In my childhood," recalled Waldo, "Aunt Mary herself wrote the prayers which first my brother William, and when he went to college, I read aloud morning and evening at the family devotions, and they still sound in my ear with their prophetic and apocalyptic ejaculations." Throughout his life he continued to consult her letters for inspiration. "In reading these letters of M. M. E.,' he wrote in 1841, "I acknowledge (with suprise that I could ever forget it) the debt of myself & my brothers to that old religion."[10]

Scholars have not found it easy to characterize Mary Moody Emerson's faith. She was far too imaginative and lively for those who know only the literal and legal side of Calvinism. She was certainly no Transcendentalist. And she scorned the negations of Unitarianism. Phyllis Cole defines her as "Arian but not Arminian." She did have her intellectual heroes, but she followed no earthly leader. Even her favorite Calvinists felt the sting of her tongue. Her God stood beyond the horizon of human speculation. Many a pompous balloon (and there were many in Concord) was punctured by a shard of her broken crockery.

Edwards had preached the necessity of men's crucifying their innate self-love in the typological wilderness before they could hope to enter Canaan. Calvinism had always held that human beings must crucify their self-love and accept in its place what Edwards had called love for "being in general, or the great system of universal existence." This was Mary's faith, a willingness to be damned for the glory of God. If God should cast her off, she wrote, she would cling to her faith that "at some moment of His existence, I was present: that, though cast from Him, my sorrows, my ignorance, my meanness were a part of His plan." If God required crucifixion, then the never-ending crucifixion of her life put her in touch with God.[11]

One of Calvinism's highest attractions was the meaning that it gave to human suffering. By denying the necessity of the emotional pain of conversion, by preaching that Canaan could be gained without a sojourn in the wilderness, the Unitarians and their sentimental allies had taken away that cosmic sense of purpose that Calvinism had claimed for the sufferings of humanity. Mary valued her own despair because it assured her of the existence of God. Being in the wilderness put her on the road to Canaan and gave her life an eternal, Biblical context. Hers was the paradoxical spirit of Calvinism that found in the darkest despair the most arrogant presumption of holiness, that embraced rejection and turned it into an identification with Eternity. For her, the wilderness and Canaan, suffering and ecstacy, the shabby real and the cosmic ideal, were all bound up in the bundle of life together.

This dualistic desire for self-denial and for the substitution of God in place of self was what defined her Calvinism. In one of her earliest journal entries, Mary resolved to forgo self and lie in the dust: "Alive with God is enough—'tis rapture." To suffer was to be crucified unto Christ: "Oh let my miseries be arguments with God to bless me!" And she made a vow, at the age of twenty-five, "of contrition, submission,—(oh how sweet) to His will, wherever recognized, of joyful silence that has nothing to utter before Him." Years later in Maine, at her farm "Elmvale," she held to her original insight, embracing suffering as her one tangible connection to God: "The problem still the same, how one soul cast out from all books, society, & health, sicken of its own follies & narrow limits, can love to adore the creation, rejoice in His infinite joy, and ask nothing but the conviction that pain is immediate from Him as His decree."[12]

Proud as she was of her trials in the wilderness, Mary was able to confess herself "a striking specimen of egotism." She regretted it, but she was not about to deny it. She did it for God. And she accepted the moments of regenerating grace as a free gift not to be questioned or denied. Here was the other side of the cross. There was the wilderness, but there was also the vision of the heavenly bridegroom coming into the wilderness:

> The rapture of feeling I would part from, for days more devoted to higher discipline. But when Nature beams with such excess of beauty, when the heart thrills with hope in its Author . . . it exults—too fondly perhaps for a state of trial. But in dead of night, nearer morning, when the eastern stars glow, or appear to glow, with more indescribable lustre, a lustre which penetrates the spirits with wonder and curiosity,—then, however awed, who can fear? . . . I shall delight to return to God. His name my fullest confidence. His sole presence ineffable pleasure.

The presumption of assuming oneself a recipient of grace was a dangerous thing. Mary was a good enough Calvinist to know that enthusiasm can be a snare and a delusion. She thought of herself as a sojourner in the wilderness, but like Moses she had climbed Pisgah and had visions of paradise to come.[13]

Nevertheless, the dominant note in her writings continued to be one of self-denial. Believing life to be futile, knowing herself unable to reach God, she prayed constantly that she might lose herself in Eternity. She took to wearing a shroud and complained bitterly of death's delay. Irritated by the daily frustrations of being human, she could not wait to lose her individual existence in Universal Existence, her idea of what it meant to be one with the blowing clover: "There is such an abyss of capacity to live; of falling short of the plainest duty, that I could live all *without,* that is, in God's agency—lose myself. O wise and sublime theology of the ancient Hindoos who sought to lose themselves!" But if life was futile and full of pain, still there was a God, an Existence, a universal Being-In-General whose acts and thoughts were not futile. For His sake, she endured: "I keep going round and round like the squirrel on a wheel, but I revolve about the center of infinity."[14]

This was her goal: "the desire of being absorbed in God, retaining consciousness" seemed to her more real than the vaunted "usefulness" of "action." This was the vision at once of her own damnation and of Christ's glorification. This was the point of balance between Canaan and the wilderness, the joy rescued from despair, the Bridegroom discovered in the desert. For the Calvinist, the human being in the lonely depths of despair who turns to the heavens to accept the justice of God's judgement and thereby receives grace, is the complete human being, fully damned, fully justified, and on fire with the vision of Christ. "Never," wrote Mary, "do the feelings of the Infinite and the consciousness of finite frailty and ignorance harmonize so well as at this mystic session in the deserts of life." Like Augustine, she rejoiced Not I, but Thou, Oh Lord, "Away with knowledge;—God alone."[15]

Mary Moody Emerson believed that life was a dance to an unheard tune, all striving and exertion spinning endless circles around infinity. She believed that a person desiring to hear the divine music could only return to the wilderness where, after forty years of self-denial, the soul might be led out of chaos to Pisgah to view the promised land. She certainly believed the metaphor to be spiritual, that the wilderness was of the soul, in consciousness. But she was not immune from the temptation to believe that the physical creation was more than just a symbol of the invisible world, that the presence of the body in a literal wilderness, while not the same thing as conversion, might be a helpful prerequisite for conversion. From her wilderness Pisgah, she had her visions of Canaan. The feeling of being lost in God came to her most frequently, she claimed, at Elmvale, her farm in Maine, where the Divinity was felt as seldom elsewhere. She valued her "years of privation . . . in the beautiful wilderness." Time, she wrote, is but "an image of Eternity," and "in the stillness of the wilderness where God hath built at midnight—it thus becomes undefiled."[16]

Her sojourn in the wilderness, in silent waiting on God, held out the hope that despite her intellect and her pride God might make use of her. His Aunt, wrote Waldo, is "the weird-woman of her religion & conceives herself always bound to walk in narrow but exalted paths which lead onward to interminable regions of rapturous and sublime glory." To be made use of, with all one's sins, was the only way Calvinists could hope to obtain any participation in glory. Mary rejoiced when she remembered that there can be no contingencies, in "the nature and origin of things none but all that to us and by us is so, was foreseen and met by weaving all the blunders and sins into a web of gathering beauty & happiness, like as the flower grows from . . . the dunghill." Thus she allowed herself to flow with the rhythms of the universe waiting and praying for God to call on her to serve creation and lead her onward to "regions of rapturous and sublime glory." When she first received a request to assist in the education of her nephews, surely she entertained the hope that finally her call had come.[17]

Mary Moody Emerson began and ended her attempt to persuade her nephew, Waldo, of the benefits of Calvinism with the wilderness tradition, literally and figuratively, urging him both to leave the city for the solitude of nature and to lose his ego in the psychic wilderness for the hope of divine perception. It was during his years at Harvard that Waldo's correspondence with his aunt was most intense. Having failed to instill in him when he was young her own love of self-denial, Mary now appealed to his intellect. But the very fact that his intellect had become the judge showed how far from self-denial Waldo was.

Mere philosophical contemplation, his aunt wrote to him in 1821, "cannot long actuate the mind." To endure life, "we must have some method of affecting the senses and imagination and must embrace some *historical* as well as *philosophical* account of the divinity." Fearing she might lose him to the pale speculations of Harvard's rational religion, Mary forcefully argued for the necessity not just of thought but of feeling. As had Edwards in *Religious Affections*, she argued that the emotions and not just the intellect must be part of the worship of God. Emotional responses, she insisted, cannot be gained by reading books about philosophy. They come as the result of a process of self-examination, self-denial, and regeneration, of a crossing of the inner wilderness to the promised land of vision:

> Those who paint the primitive state of man's creation are sweet poets—those who represent human nature as sublimed by religion are better adapted to our feelings and situation; but those who point the path to the attainment of moral perfection are the guardian angels. But this is no easy poetic task. The lowly vale of penitence and humility must be crossed before the mount of vision—the heights of virtue are gained. Therefore we so often hear the warning voice of high-toned morality against the seductions of the vagrant flower-clad muse. May yours if she should continue and prune her wings be sanctified by piety.[18]

Mary hammered away at her theme that "superficial science & false philosophy" cannot lead to God. "Away with your offerings at his shrine," she scolded him, "if they come not like the emblem of those laid up in the ancient ark pure gold & polished without & celestial manna within." Surrounded by the latest from the advocates of rational and natural theology, Waldo valued the letters he received from his aunt. They breathed a spirit that he did not find at Unitarian Harvard. But he was unable to give intellectual assent to the doctrines they contained. He resisted their attraction and held himself aloof. Mary reacted to his continuing rationalism by accusing him of "collecting facts," or preferring "sensation" to "sentiment" when he should be "energising" his soul. She prophecied his fall but prayed that "your fall may call down some uncommon effort of mercy and you may rise from the love of deceitful good to that of [the] real."[19]

At this point, Mary's efforts were directed toward saving her nephew from philosophy and winning him for the religion of the heart. As Joel Porte has shown, it was his aunt who introduced Waldo to the Moral Sense philosophers, and she used their arguments to convince him to trust his moral intuition.[20] Although they used philosophical arguments as their means, these philosophers emphasized the priority of intuition, of felt sense, over intellect. As Waldo strove to externalize and objectify his understanding, Mary fought to bring it back to the heart: "As to words or language being so important—I'll have none of it. The images, the sweet immortal images are within us—born there, our native right, and sometimes one kind of sounding word or syllable awakens the instruments of our souls, and sometimes another. But we are not slaves to sense any more than to political usurpers, but by fashion and imbecility." Thus with support from the philosophers of the moral sense, Mary tried to save her nephew from Lockean rationalism, but there were dangers on the other side. One could, by not diving deep enough into and beyond the wilderness, become a slave to a merely superficial "sense." By saying that "the sweet immortal images are within us," she had unwittingly played into the hands of the Romantics.[21]

In 1824, responding to Waldo's growing interest in the rhetoric of European Romanticism, Mary argued the benefits of Calvinist spirituality over those of the "flower-clad muse": "This deep and high theology," she proclaimed, "will prevail & German madness may be cured—The public ear[,] weary of the artifices of eloquence[,] will ask for the wants of the soul to be satisfied. May you . . . be among others who will prove a Pharos to your country & times."[22] But Mary was not able to persuade her nephew to look still deeper beyond the superficial "sensations" of his heart and surrender to the fear that she knew was there. Convinced of the errors of Lockean rationalism, unconvinced of the glories of Calvinism, Waldo found in Romanticism an alternative that allowed him to sing the praises of heart religion and retain his ego too. As Edwards had and as Freud would, Waldo used his intellect to construct a rational defense of irrationality, a romantic affirmation of the "all" in which the self remained distinct and in control.

Mary blamed herself for Waldo's stubborn defense of his own capacity: "It was pretty, it seemed best, to tell children how good they were,—the time of illusion and childhood is past, and you will find mysteries in man which baffle genius." But Waldo's nature rebelled at the notion of self-denial; he could not see any benefit in yielding his intellect, and he was determined to remain comfortably sane. He was intrigued and revolted, fascinated and repelled:

> I am blind, I fear, to the truth of a theology which I can't but respect for the eloquence it begets and for the heroic life of its modern, and the heroic death of its ancient defenders. I acknowledge it tempts the imagination with an epic (and better than epic) magnificence; but it sounds like mysticism in the ear of understanding. Paley's deity and Calvin's

deity are plainly two beings, both sublime existences, but one a friend and the other a foe to that capacity of order and right, to that understanding which is made in us arbiter of things seen, the prophet of things unseen. . . . I can not help revolting from the double deity, gross Gothic offspring of some Genevan school.

By making his own "capacity" and "understanding" the ultimate criteria, of course Waldo could not see the benefits of a deity who would cast those central idols into chaos.[23]

But Mary Moody Emerson was not one to give up easily. If Waldo would only keep his mind open, he might yet experience the truth of his understanding's depravity and accept the sovereignty of God over man's feeble "capacity." The Holy Ghost, she reminded him, comes not from human effort but is "the reward of prayer, agony, self-immolation!" And she added bitterly, "Dost not like the faith and the means? Take thy own—or rather the dictates of fashion.—" but still she held out hope that he might yet experience the truth of Calvinist doctrine and reject the authority of man's feeble, determined, depraved understanding: "You have not had time to feel that this huge globe was but a web drawn round about us that the light the skies the mountains are but the painted vicissitudes of the soul." When he did realize this, Waldo embraced not Calvinism but the doctrine of correspondence. He did not lose himself but saw himself in "the light the skies the mountains."[24]

When Waldo became ill in 1825, Mary saw his sickness as an opportunity for him to be held over the pit and forced to confess the folly of his dangerous self-confidence. But he recovered and her disappointment was bitter and unrestrained: "I say you are getting well too soon before you have seen the mystic visions which visit the sick;—before *thought* (O wonderful mysterious power which allies us to Him who passes wonder) has dispelled those mists which rested on some of your speculations." She complained that he had not suffered enough. "Never mind," she consoled him, "you will, if you are destined to future eminence." And still she hoped that he might be brought over to the cause of God in time. "I rejoice," she wrote to him, "that you have been kept from launching till your anchor is stronger than I suspect it is, till the tide which you imagine is sweeping away old beliefs will ebb & return with full bearings of truth."[25]

To all this Waldo responded by agreeing, intellectually, with much of the thought but never by giving himself to the deed. "I agree," he wrote from his sickbed at St. Augustine, Florida, "to the sentiment of your letter that I shall be a wiser and a better man. He has seen but half of the universe who never has been shown the house of pain." He even acknowledged "a principle in human nature . . . that suggests and sanctions the crucifixion of the flesh before the mighty image of god within the soul." Nevertheless, he added, "we are not bound by suggestions of sentiment, which our reason not only does not sanction, but also condemns." Waldo's reason remained firmly in control. But he was tempted. He found it pleasant, he admitted to his aunt, "to hover on the verge of worlds we cannot enter, and explore the bearings of piled mists I cannot penetrate." He would hover but never enter. He was not ready to sacrifice his reason for the sake of mystic promises he could not trust. Would it not be a crime, he asked, to "surrender to the casual and morbid exercise of the sentiment of a midnight hour the steady light of all my days, my most vigorous and approved thoughts, barter the sun for the waning moon?"[26]

If sickness could not force Waldo into the wilderness of his mind, there was always the possibility that a sojourn in the literal wilderness might be the needed catalyst. To this end, Mary continually urged her nephew to leave the city and return to nature. Apparently, at this stage of his life, Waldo was not altogether enamored of the country life. After a hike through central Massachusetts in 1822, he had written to his aunt expressing his doubts about her enthusiasm for the wilds. He had found much of nature enjoyable but not somehow divine.

> I cannot tell but it seemed to me that Cambridge would be a better place to study than the woodlands. I thought I understood a little of that *intoxication*, which you have spoken of; but its tendency was directly opposed to the slightest effort of mind or body; it was a soft animal luxury, the combined result of the beauty which fed the eye; the exhilarating Paradise *air*, which fanned and dilated the sense; the novel melody which warbled from the trees. Its first charm passed away rapidly. . . . Perhaps in the Autumn, which I hold to be the finest season in the year, and in a longer abode the mind might, as you term it, return upon itself.

Mary had convinced her nephew that there was some spiritual benefit to be gained from going to nature, but he did not know what it was. In a letter to his friend John Boynton Hill, Waldo expressed his frustration:

> My aunt, (of whom I think you have heard before & who is alone among women,) has spent a great part of her life in the country, is an idolater of Nature, & counts but a small number who merit the privilege of dwelling among the mtns. The coarse thrifty cit profanes the grove by his presence—& she was anxious that her nephew might hold high and reverential notions regarding it (as) the temple where God & the Mind are to be studied & adored & where the fiery soul can begin a premature communication with the world. When I took my book therefore to the woods—I found nature not half poetical, not half visionary enough.

Waldo understood that there was something sacred to be discovered in nature, but what it was and how to obtain it remained mysteries.[27]

Mary did not try to argue the benefits of the pastoral life. She stuck closely to her central concern, the need to lose oneself in the wilderness. It was to this end that she urged her nephew to leave the city, not to improve his reading ability but to plunge him into the darkness of the solitude of his soul: "Then you find no necessary sacredness in the country, nor did Milton; but his mind & his spirits were their own place, & came when he called them in the solitude of darkness. Solitude . . . is to learning & genius the only sure labyrinth, tho' sometimes gloomy, to form the eagle wing that will bear one farther than suns & stars. . . . Would to Providence your unfoldings might be there." But her efforts were to no avail. Waldo agreed that the wilderness was pretty, that it perhaps had a supernatural beauty in which the will of God could be discerned, but even that cold analysis was made from his civilized study. When she went to the woods, she enticed him, "I shall not think . . . only feel pleasantly abroad." But she also confronted him demanding, "But why are you in the city? They will buzz to you of music, of literature, of chemistry, of everything that will disturb the culture of your character, everything averse to that enthusiasm of piety,—of extensive benevolence of highminded principle which can alone support devotion to God and love to the race." But Waldo never did see the wilderness, not in the Calvinist sense. His own strict self-control kept his intellect away from the chaotic depths. Even in the woods, he saw, not wildness, but order: "nothing done at random, No accidents in nature . . . Never get out of God's city, Order, order everywhere." For Waldo the wilderness had become Canaan.[28]

Mary Moody Emerson soon wearied of her nephew's inability to understand her. When he tried to explain to her his belief that nature itself was the voice of God, she shot back angrily, "if this withering Lucifer doctrine of Pantheism be true what mortal truth can you preach or by what authority should you feel it?" He did not comprehend how his going to the woods differed from her sojourn in the wilderness, and he complained of her "always fighting in conversation against the very principles which governed & govern her." In 1832 she wrote to his brother, Charles, that Waldo "is lost in the halo of his own imagination." She also wrote, "As to Waldo's letter, say nothing to him. It is time he should leave me. His sublime negations, his non-informations I have no right in the world to complain of. His letters are always elegantly spiced with flattery, which I love. What he thinks sound, or intends, time and report may unfold." Time and report brought Mary news of *Nature* in 1836 and of the Divinity School Address in 1838. It was as bad as she had feared. She had, she believed, introduced him to nature but he had learned the wrong lesson there. She accepted defeat but she was not defeated. Her spirit remained to the end as fiery as it had ever been: "The yesterday does never smile, as I would, Yet in the name of the Sheperd of mankind, I defy tomorrow. God himself cannot withdraw himself. Health feeble alone, most alone, but I defy tomorrow."[29]

Ralph Waldo Emerson's rejection of his aunt's Calvinism was at heart a refusal to yield his ego to the untrodden wilderness of introspective terror. It was a defense of the rational self against the deeper terrors of the soul. The philosophy of romanticism was part of the fortress that Waldo's intellect built, the rampart or parapet with which he protected himself:

> I dare not peer over this parapet
> To gauge with glance the roaring gulf below,
> The depths of sin to which I had descended,
> Had not these me against myself defended.[30]

Having enthroned his self and fortressed it, he was by 1838 able to proclaim the self so near to God that every human being should be able to partake of the Godhead. Yet he was unable to break out of the prison of his own intellectuality. He wanted "Aunt" Mary's mysticism, he wanted grace, but he was unwilling to go through her ordeal to get it. He wanted God without having to sacrifice the self. He wanted Canaan without the wilderness. The question was, "How?"

In *Nature,* in 1836, he described one time when he had "enjoyed a perfect exhilaration." But he did not know how to reproduce this experience. "[T]he power to produce this delight," he equivocated, "does not reside in nature, but in man, or in a harmony of both." Later he instructed his readers to "conform your life to the pure idea in your mind." He did not say how to do this. In "The Poet," he suggested that it was "some obstruction or some excess of phlegm in our constitution which does not suffer them to yield the due effect." It was to try to attain this experience, he suggested, that bards love "wine, mead, narcotics, coffee, tea, opium, . . . or whatever other procurers of animal exhilaration." But he knew that this was the wrong approach. Instead he suggested that the poet put himself in touch with this "new energy . . . by unlocking, at all risks, his human doors, and suffering the ethereal tides to roll and circulate through him"; the answer seemed to have something to do with taking risks. But every time he urges his readers—and implicitly himself—to "break off your association with your personality, and identify yourself with the universe," the frustrated reader can only cry out, "How?"[31]

Waldo did of course have one answer. It is hard to avoid the conclusion that while he was unwilling to accept the spiritual meaning of the sojourn in the wilderness, he was ready to embrace the literal, in the hope that somehow in nature he would find the experience he sought.

> He who frequents those scenes, where nature discloses her magnificence to silence and solitude, will have his mind occupied by trains of thought of a peculiarly solemn tone, which never interrupt the profligacy of libertines, the money-getting of the miser, or the glory-getting of the ambitious. In the depths of the forest, where the noon comes like twilight, on the cliff in the cavern, and by the lonely lake, where the sound of man's mirth and of man's sorrow were never heard . . . is a shrine which few visit in vain.

Waldo went with his aunt only as far as the trees. Although he asserted that "Nature is the symbol of the spirit," he went only to the literal woods, not to the symbolic wilderness.[32]

The Puritan typologists of the seventeenth century had also forgotten the spiritual meaning of the sojourn in the wilderness and by the end of the century had confused the type with the antitype, the symbol with the substance, mistaking their sojourn in the literal wilderness for true conversion. So Mary Moody Emerson herself, while urging her nephew to lose himself, stressed the solitude of the wilderness and the woods as the locale of this transformation. So Waldo, remembering his aunt's insistence that he return to the wilderness to see God, went to the woods and sat on a log and wondered why the mystic visions never came. Because he refused to accept the separation of the real and the ideal, of this world and the heavenly Canaan, he imagined himself reborn in Canaan without having crossed the wilderness, and he elevated his worldly imaginings to the status of the divine.

The Unitarians, by denying in effect that this world is merely symbolic, denied that there was anything higher beyond the veil. Waldo knew better, but his attempt to embrace the antitype brought the Transcendent down to earth and led to a denial of the duality of symbol and substance. If symbol and substance are one, then there is no symbolism. The end result must be a materialism as cold and sterile as any tea the Unitarians served.

Ralph Waldo Emerson's attraction to nature, then, came not only from the influence of European Romanticism but also from his own New England heritage, and more directly from his aunt, Mary Moody Emerson. The typological association of the wilderness crossing with the experience of conversion in the wilderness of the soul was much in the minds of the Emersons' Puritan ancestors when they came to New England, and this wilderness tradition was carried to Waldo through the agency of his aunt. That he forgot the spiritual meaning of the metaphor and confused the literal woods with the spiritual wilderness does not weaken the connection between the Transcendental religion of nature and the Calvinist wilderness tradition. The Transcendentalists may have looked to nature to bring the self in touch with God while the Calvinists looked to the wilderness to destroy the self in favor of God. But both looked to the wilderness as a means of grace however different these means may have been. The Transcendental love of nature was thus a product of a cultural fascination with the wilderness as a type of the wilderness of the soul, of an unconscious projection of the antitype onto the type, of the spiritual onto the literal. Ralph Waldo Emerson sought an easy way to Canaan, but in the back of his mind were Mary Moody Emerson's "prophetic and apocalyptic ejaculations" and her warning that the "lowly vale of penitence and humility must be crossed before the mount of vision—the heights of virtue are gained."

Notes

[1] See my book, *Wilderness Lost: The Religious Origins of the American Mind* (Rutherford, N.J.: Susquehanna University Press, 1987). See also John King, *The Iron of Melancholy* (Middletown, Conn.: Wesleyan University Press, 1983), particularly the first chapter, in which a similar interpretation of "wilderness" in Puritan thought is presented.

[2] *Selections from Ralph Waldo Emerson*, ed. Stephen E. Whicher (Boston: Houghton Mifflin, 1957), p. xvii; Perry Miller, "New England's Transcendentalism: Native or Imported?" in *Literary Views*, ed. Carroll Camden (Chicago: University of Chicago Press, 1964), p. 121; *The Transcendentalists: An Anthology,* ed. Perry Miller (Cambridge: Harvard University Press, 1950), p. 10.

[3] Solomon Stoddard, *A Treatise Concerning Conversion* (Boston: Henchman, 1719), p. 86; Jonathan Edwards, "The Excellency of Christ," in *Jonathan Edwards: Representative Selections*, rev. ed., ed. Clarence H. Faust and Thomas H. Johnson (New York: Hill and Wang, 1962), p. 373; Octavius Brooks Frothingham, *Transcendentalism in New England* (New York: Putnams, 1876), p. 108.

[4] "From Edwards to Emerson" can be found in Perry Miller, *Errand into the Wilderness* (Cambridge: Harvard University Press, 1956), pp. 184-203; Harriet Beecher Stowe, *Old Town Folks* (Cambridge: Harvard University Press, 1966), p. 260; Henry Bamford Parkes, *The Pragmatic Test* (San Francisco: Colt Press, 1941), p. 34. In Joel Porte's *Emerson: Prospect and Retrospect* (Cambridge: Harvard University Press, 1982), Phyllis Cole, in the most recent contribution, discusses MME's "intellectual position between Jonathan Edwards and Ralph Waldo Emerson."

[5] RWE did read Edwards. In his journal for 1823, he wrote: "Oct. 5. Milord W. from Andover let me into his mystery about Edwards on the will & told me withal that the object of the piece was to prove that President E. has not advanced human knowledge one step. . . . the subject which, though so intricate before as to have ever been debateable ground, is made so plain by the able & skillful statements of Edwards, that we are made to see the truth, & wonder that it ever was disputed. Waldo E. will please consult upon this topic" (*The Journals and Miscellaneous Notebooks of Ralph Waldo Emerson*, ed. William H. Gilman, Ralph H. Orth, et. al., 16 vols. [Cambridge: Harvard University Press, 1960-82], 2:159; hereafter cited as *JMN*). In addition, the *Treatise on Religious Affections* later became a part of RWE's personal library (Walter Harding, *Emerson's Library* [Charlottesville: University Press of Virginia, 1967], p. 87).

[6] Parkes, *The Pragmatic Test*, p. 34.

[7] Considering the amount of published literature devoted to all the Transcendentalists, it is suprising how little has been written about MME. There are no biographies of her and her enormously influential letters are only now being prepared for publication. RWE's own recollections, "Mary Moody Emerson," in *Lectures and Biographical Sketches* (Boston: Houghton, Mifflin, 1884), pp. 371-404, remains the major source. MME is dealt with in passing in most of the critical and biographical works on RWE, but rarely do the critics go beyond Waldo's own anecdotes. The list of scholary articles on her is quite short: George Tolman, "Mary Moody Emerson," a paper read before the Concord Antiquarian Society and privately printed in 1902, later republished in Cambridge in 1929; Van Wyck Brooks, "The Cassandra of New England," *Scribner's Magazine*, 81 (February 1927): 125-29; Rosalie Feltenstein, "Mary Moody Emerson: The Gadfly of Concord," *American Quarterly*, 5 (Fall 1953): 231-46; and Nancy Barcus, "Emerson, Calvinism, and Aunt Mary Moody: An Irrepressable Defender of New England Orthodoxy," *Christian Scholar's Review*, 7 (1977): 146-52. See also the biographical sketch in *Notable American Women*. Two recent additions to this scholarship are Phyllis Cole, "The Advantage of Loneliness: Mary Moody Emerson's *Almanacks*, 1802-1855," in *Emerson: Prospect and Retrospect*, ed. Porte, pp. 1-32, and Evelyn Barish, "Emerson and the Angel of Midnight," in *Mothering the Mind*, ed. Ruth Perry and Martina Brownley (forthcoming).

[8] RWE, "Mary Moody Emerson," p. 403; Brooks, "Cassandra," 125.

[9] *JMN*, 7:446.

[10] Brooks, "Cassandra," 125; RWE, "Mary Moody Emerson," pp. 400-402; *JMN*, 5: 323-324; *JMN*, 7:445. In his journal, RWE used the anagram "Tnamurya," sometimes shortened to "Tnam," to identify his aunt.

[11] Edwards, "The Nature of True Virtue," *Selections*, p. 351; RWE, "Mary Moody Emerson," p. 427.

[12] RWE, "Mary Moody Emerson," p. 415; RWE, "Notebook MME," 3:3, MH; "Notebook MME," 2:27. In the Emerson Collection at MH are four notebooks into which Waldo apparently copied portions of his aunt's letters and journal entries. They are quoted here by permission of the Ralph Waldo Emerson Memorial Association and of the Houghton Library. Phyllis Cole (see note 7) reveals the recent discovery of Tolman's transcript of MME's "Almanack," which, she writes, is now placed in MH.

[13] RWE, "Mary Moody Emerson," pp. 412-13.

[14] "Notebook MME," 3:70-71; "Notebook MME," 4:129.

[15] RWE, "Mary Moody Emerson," pp. 426-27.

[16] "Notebook MME," 2:39, 49.

[17] *JMN*, 1:49; "Notebook MME," 2:29-30.

[18] MME to RWE, 1821, *JMN*, 1:336; MME to RWE, 1821, *JMN*, 1:333.

[19] MME to RWE, 1821, *JMN*, 1:196; MME to RWE, 1822, *JMN*, 2:373-74.

[20] Joel Porte, *Emerson and Thoreau: Transcendentalists in Conflict* (Middletown, Conn.: Wesleyan University Press, 1965), pp. 69-70.

[21] MME to RWE, 1822, *JMN*, 2:375.

[22] MME to RWE, 1824, *JMN*, 2:383.

[23] MME to RWE, 1824, *JMN*, 2:384; RWE to MME, 1824, *Journals of Ralph Waldo Emerson*, ed. Edward Waldo Emerson and Waldo Emerson Forbes, 10 vols. (Boston: Houghton Mifflin, 1909-14), 2:32-33; hereafter cited as *Journals*.

[24] MME to RWE, 1824, *JMN*, 2:382, 385.

[25] MME to RWE, 1825, "Notebook MME," 1:61; MME to RWE, 21 February 1826, MH; MME to RWE, 1826, "Notebook MME," 1:130.

[26] RWE to MME, 1827, *Journals*, 2:180, 221-22, 212, 222-23.

[27] RWE to MME, 1822, *The Letters of Ralph Waldo Emerson*, ed. Ralph L. Rusk, 6 vols. (New York: Columbia University Press, 1939), 1:115; RWE to Hill, 1823, *Letters*, 1:133.

[28] MME to RWE, 1824, *JMN*, 2:380; MME to RWE, 1827, *JMN*, 2:392-93; MME to RWE, 1829, "Notebook MME," 1:153; 1831, *Journals*, 2:437.

[29] MME, quoted in Tolman, *Mary Moody Emerson*, p. 23; 1835, *JMN*, 7:64; Tolman, *Mary Mood Emerson*, p. 24; MME to Charles Chauncy Emerson, 1832, "Notebook MME," 1:23; "Notebook MME," 2:7.

[30] "Grace," *The Complete Works of Ralph Waldo Emerson*, ed. Edward Waldo Emerson, 12 vols. (Boston: Houghton, Mifflin, 1903-1904), vol. 9, *Poems* (1904), p. 359.

[31] "Nature," *The Collected Works of Ralph Waldo Emerson*, ed. Alfred R. Ferguson, Joseph Slater, et al., 3 vols. to date (Cambridge: Harvard University Press, 1971-), pp. 10, 45; "The Poet," *Collected Works*, vol. 2, *Essays: First Series* (1979), ed. Ferguson and Jean Ferguson Carr, pp. 4, 16; *JMN*, 5;391.

[32] *Journals*, 1824, 1:354-55; "Nature," *Collected Works*, 1:17.

Ralph Waldo Emerson's biographer, Ralph L. Rusk, on Mary Moody Emerson:

She escaped wealth and was glad, for she believed it would have spoiled her. After due consideration she refused an offer of marriage from "a man of talents, education and good social position, whom she respected." She liked solitude and long found a kind of mystical delight in nature. Nature had taught her to say, "Alive with God is enough,—'t is rapture." But she was a bundle of contradictions. Whatever her mysticism amounted to, she continued to be both a fiery Calvinist and a liberal daughter of the Enlightenment. For many years she longed for death and was prepared for it, even to her shroud. But in spite of her secession from the world, she managed to keep open the one outlet to it through which she was able to exert the whole force of her character. Few had patience with her bad taste, her clownish defiance of proprieties, her cryptic style of speech and writing, and her cruel self-torment. But Ralph and one or two of her other nephews were among the exceptions to the rule and were richly repaid for their trouble.

Ralph L. Rusk, in *The Life of Ralph Waldo Emerson*, *Charles Scribner's Sons, 1949.*

Alan D. Hodder (essay date 1989)

SOURCE: "*Kenosis* and Creation," in *Emerson's Rhetoric of Revelation: Nature, the Reader, and the Apocalypse Within*, Pennsylvania State University Press, 1989, pp. 33-68.

[In the excerpt that follows, Hodder claims that Emerson's interpretation of Calvinism was an important precursor of the apocalyptic strand in Ralph Waldo Emerson's work.]

When reading over [Ralph Waldo] Emerson's earliest journals, the ones he called his "Wide World," it is hard not to be struck, and a little surprised, by the prevalence of doomsday rhetoric one encounters there. New England had come a long way since the days of the Great Awakening, but this is difficult to tell from these journals. The sermons he was hearing were evidently still filled with echoes of the old apocalyptic themes, if not exactly fire and brimstone. During the month of December in 1820, he seems to have been nearly obsessed with his visions of the end of time. He recorded one entry that begins, "The human soul, the world, the universe are labouring on to their magnificent consummation," and ends with this excited exhortation:

> Roll on then thou stupendous Universe in sublime incomprehensible solitude, in an unbeheld but sure path. The finger of God is pointing out your way. And when ages shall have elapsed and time is no more, while the stars shall fall from heaven and the Sun become darkness and the Moon blood, human intellect purified and sublimed shall mount from perfection to perfection of unmeasured and ineffable enjoyment of knowledge and glory.

A few days later, Emerson began another entry with the comment: "I am going to set apart a page or two of this variety-shop for unconnected reflections or allusions to the day of retribution to the human race. Teeming with such importance so universal and so intense, it cannot be named too often or pressed with too much force." The heading of the long entry which follows is simply "The Day of Judgement" ([*The Journals and Miscellaneous Notebooks of Ralph Waldo Emerson*, ed. William H. Gilman, Alfred R. Ferguson, et al. 16 vols. 1960-82; hereafter JMN], I, 46-48). In the "Wide World" journal of 1822 we are presented with an entry which has a direct bearing on *Nature*: "Without, there is an Order of the Universe—broken, if the Arm which sustains it be withdrawn; and the forerunner of this dissolution, the Angel of Prophecy has already published the day.—Watch, for the Time is at hand—when the heavens shall be rolled together as a scroll and the elements shall melt with fervent heat. What then is Nature?—it is the transitory pleasure of the Divine Mind" (JMN, I, 81)[8]

It is fairly clear that the person principally responsible for nursing Waldo to this feverish apocalyptic pitch was his aunt, Mary Moody Emerson.[9] In a eulogy delivered in 1869, six years after her death, Emerson described with veneration and some humor his aunt's hard, lonely, and at times eccentric life. It was, he said, a "representative life"—one distinguished above all by the passion of her religious genius. To her more than anyone else, he owed his earliest lessons in fortitude, humility, and prayer. The single-mindedness of her own preoccupation with death and the world beyond is evidenced in his facetious recounting of how, as old age approached, she took to wearing her burial shroud as a robe ([*The Complete Works of Ralph Waldo Emerson*, Centenary Edition. 14 vols. Houghton Mifflin, 1903-4], X, 371-404). But the fervency and perseverance of her conservative religious feeling and the high esteem in which she was held by her nephews suggest that such practices could not be dismissed as symptoms of religious pathology. As Stephen Whicher aptly puts it, she showed Emerson "something of the white-hot core of the original Calvinistic piety."[10]

For the young Emerson there seems to have been no influence as consequential as that of Mary Moody Emerson. She was his earliest and, for long stretches of time, his primary correspondent and mentor. He studiously copied long extracts of her letters into his journals. The standard view is that she was mainly Emerson's representative apologist for the old Calvinist faith. She was partly this, but as Phyllis Cole suggests, she was also young Emerson's co-explorer in the area of new ideas and perhaps at times even the main instigator of some of the centrifugal tendencies which, in the end, would lead to apostasy and his irreconcilable break with organized religion and with her.[11] In any case, there can be no doubt of the love and admiration he felt for his charismatic aunt:

> The religion of my Aunt is the purest and most sublime of any I can conceive. It appears to be based on broad and deep and remote principles of expediency and adequateness to an end—principles which few can comprehend and fewer feel. It labours to reconcile the apparent insignificance of the field to the surpassing grandeur of the Operator and founds the benignity and Mercy of the Scheme on adventurous but probable comparisons of the Condition of other orders of being. Although it is an intellectual offspring of beauty and splendour, if that were all, it breathes a practical spirit of rigid and austere devotion. It is independent of forms and ceremonies and its ethereal nature gives a glow of soul to her whole life. She is the Weird-woman of her religion and conceives herself always bound to walk in narrow but exalted paths which lead onward to interminable regions of rapturous and sublime glory. (JMN, I, 49)

Though Mary may have unwittingly conspired with the enemies that would soon bring her age to an end, when she did recognize in Transcendentalism a monster she had helped breed, she quickly showed her true diehard loyalties. What she despised most about the new views her nephew was falling prey to was that they had foolishly left out the Judgment Day and the "consummation of this passing world."[12] But throughout her long correspondence with Waldo, and especially during the period of the early twenties, her letters are rife with allusions to apocalypse and the Book of Revelation. "Ask the Genius assigned to some incalculable period of time, if he does not foresee the moment when the whole history of this world will pass through the hand of some ancient librarian of Heaven as a scroll!" (transcribed in JMN, I, 199). The most suggestive bit of evidence for Mary's influence on Emerson's apocalyptic leanings comes in a retrospective entry he made in his journal in 1837:

> I cannot hear the young men whose theological instruction is exclusively owed to Cambridge and to public institution, without feeling how much happier was my star which rained on me influences of ancestral religion. The depth of the religious sentiment which I knew in my Aunt Mary imbuing all her genius and derived to her from such hoarded family traditions, from so many godly lives and godly deaths of sainted kindred at Concord, Malden, York, was itself a culture, an education.... In my childhood Aunt Mary herself wrote the prayers which first my brother William and when he went to college I read aloud morning and evening at the family devotions, and they still sound in my ear with their prophetic and apocalyptic ejaculations. Religion was her occupation, and when years after, I came to write sermons for my own church I could not find any examples or treasuries of piety so high-toned, so profound, or promising such rich influence as my remembrances of her conversation and letters. (JMN, V, 323-24) . . .

Notes

. . .[8] It is possible to multiply these instances. For another striking early example, see JMN, II, 45, which begins: "The sublimest scene which ever opened on the thought of man, is the Judgement of the World, in the partial representations of the sacred writers."

[9] I am indebted to Phyllis Cole, who has kindly helped to support and clarify my intuitions about the importance of this relationship. See Cole, ["The Advantage of Loneliness: Mary Moody Emerson's Almanacks, 1802-1855," in *Emerson: Prospect and Retrospect*, ed. Joel Porte, Harvard English Studies 10 (Cambridge: Harvard University Press, 1982)].

[10] [Stephen E. Whicher, *Freedom and Fate: An Inner Life of Ralph Waldo Emerson* (Philadelphia: University of Pennsylvania Press, 1953)], p. 8.

[11] In a letter of 1824 which Emerson transcribed into his journal, Mary seems to voice some regret at the boosterism she showed to her young nephews. Here she blames "the atmosphere of theology," her own "speculation," and above all "the sore of human nature" for any harm her early permissiveness may have caused (J, II, 31).

[12] [Ralph L. Rusk, *The Life of Ralph Waldo Emerson* (New York: Columbia University Press, 1949)], p. 230.

Nancy Craig Simmons (essay date 1993)

SOURCE: "A Calendar of the Letters of Mary Moody Emerson," in *Studies in the American Renaissance*, 1993, pp. 1-41.

[*In the following excerpt, Simmons briefly recounts what is known of the life and character of Emerson, with a primary focus on the style and content of her letters.*]

In the midst of her intense correspondence with Waldo Emerson in the 1820s, Mary Moody Emerson (1774-1863) dated one of her letters "Space & time." This Calendar, which lists in chronological order all of the located letters of this prolific writer, traces her wandering path through New England over a period of seventy years, between 1793 and 1862. It helps to map the life of a woman whose biography has still not been published, to provide a framework for her thoughts.

Her letters provide, however, more than biographical information. They record a lifelong spiritual and intellectual quest conducted in the primary arena available to a woman in the early years of the American republic. Late in his life, her nephew Waldo tried to sum up what these letters represented:

> M. M. E.'s style is that of letters,—an immense advantage—admits of all the force of colloquial domestic words, & breaks, & parenthesis, & petulance—has the luck & inspiration of that,—has humor, affection, & a range from the rapture of prayer down to details of farm & barn & *help*.
>
> All her language in writing was happy but inimitable as if caught from some dream.[1]

As Waldo Emerson suggests, Mary's letters set a standard for letter-writing as a genre—one that she practiced and that he emulated. They demonstrate the power and range of the letter form.

Many of Mary Emerson's correspondents commented on the style, quality, richness, variety, and stimulation of her letters. The fact that so many letters survive in manuscript also indicates their value to her correspondents. Circumstances conspired to make Mary Emerson a great letter writer. She did not live a rooted life. Essentially orphaned during the American Revolutionary War and sent to live with relatives outside her immediate family, as a young woman she moved from one family to another before deciding to settle in Maine, far from her childhood haunts; later she boarded in homes all over New England between visits to various relatives. Because she moved around a great deal, she was constantly in the position of the letter-writer: removed from the ordinary and relating her experiences in distant or unfamiliar places.

Mary's Federalist sense of family as the source of values also drove her epistolary urge: despite her ease of movement among "strangers," they remained somewhat outside her family circle. She was proud of the Emerson name and the traditions associated with it. Frequently absent from her family's physical center, she kept the circle tight through her letters. When she was in Newburyport, she wrote back to her family at Concord and Harvard, Mass.; when she was in Boston or Concord or Waltham, she had her Waterford connection to keep up; when at Waterford, she corresponded with her Boston relatives. Letters were her way of maintaining connections.

Mary's letter-writing also reflects her position as a single woman in the early years of the American republic. Although she had imbibed a lot of ideas about liberty from the Revolution and lived in an era of great change and speculation, she found only limited opportunities to practice these ideas within the culture she inherited. Having been denied or having refused all other avenues of expression (such as preaching, teaching, publishing, and especially the one open to women, marriage and mothering), Mary exploited the field she found open to her. In her letters, she preaches, teaches, criticizes, debates, converses—and mothers. Possessed of a vivid pictorial imagination, but with no skill at drawing or sketching (none of her letters contain even doodles) Mary Emerson poured her intellectual and imaginative talents into her writing. There she could describe the outer landscape of sights and experiences, events, reading, weathers and seasons—but most of all the inner landscape of her thoughts and being.

Letters were Mary Emerson's major form of communication, used both to keep in touch with the family and friends from whom she was frequently separated, and to explore the big questions that interested her, concerning free will, destiny, agency, death, and a host of other metaphysical subjects. Scholars interested in her life, her relationship with her nephew Ralph Waldo Emerson, the situation of women in the early years of the republic, theological issues, Emerson family questions, nineteenth-century female friendships and epistolary correspondence, and other matters will find these letters a rich source of information. On the whole, her letters contain more metaphysical speculation than local details; however, many of her shorter notes as well as portions of her longer letters reveal her interest in the hodiernal, physical world in which she lived.

When writing to people in distant places, Mary Moody Emerson usually wrote on large sheets of paper, somewhat larger than today's "legal" page, folded to make four sides. She wrote before envelopes were in use; instead, before mailing, she again folded the completed letter, wrote the address in a space left on the fourth side, and, using her thimble for a seal, sealed it with wax. Such letters would be carried by post or by a "bearer"—someone travelling in the right direction. Other letters are actually considerably briefer notes, often written to people nearby. Most of her longer, more formal, letters can be securely dated, but for various reasons many others present problems. Some have been torn away from the whole letter and others were probably enclosed with another letter that contained the outside address, date, or postmark. Some notes were scrawled on the backs of used pages and delivered by hand. Her datelines sometimes contain only a month or day of the month, or sometimes just the day of the week—frequently abbreviated to "Sab." for "Sabbath," reflecting her habit of saving Sunday for writing. Continuations may be dated "11" or "Thurs. Eve." . . .

The surviving letters are addressed to more than fifty correspondents; references in various sources suggest these letters represent perhaps a half or less of what she probably wrote. No letters remain from her correspondences with the aunts who raised her, friends Ann Bromfield and perhaps Mrs. Dexter, her brother Daniel, Louisa and Orville Dewey, other important nieces and nephews; Unitarian preacher Thomas Treadwell Stone and perhaps William Ellery Channing; former "hosts" such as Dr. Parrish at Byfield, Griswold at Fryeburg, and Frothingham at Belfast, Maine, and their families; younger women like the "Misses Searle" and Sally J. Gardner, anti-slavery friends such as Mary Merrick Brooks and Lydia Maria Child, and many others. She probably wrote frequently to people like her mother, step-uncle and brother-in-law Lincoln Ripley, sisters, and brother Samuel Ripley, as well as Elizabeth Peabody, Henry Thoreau, Mary Wilder White, Ruth Hurd, George Barrell Emerson, Martha Bradford, other nieces and nephews—but very few letters to these correspondents have turned up. It is clear that still other letters to her principal correspondents—her brother William, his wife Ruth, her Emerson nephews William, Waldo, Edward, and Charles, Lidian Emerson, Sarah Bradford Ripley, Elizabeth Hoar, and Ann Gage—have been lost. . . .

Notes

[1] "MME Notebook 3," quoted by permission of the Houghton Library, Harvard University.

Nancy Craig Simmons (essay date 1993)

SOURCE: "Mary Moody Emerson: Woman Writing," in *The Selected Letters of Mary Moody Emerson*, edited by Nancy Craig Simmons, University of Georgia Press, 1993, pp. xxvii-xliii.

[*In the following introduction to* The Selected Letters of Mary Moody Emerson, *Simmons discusses the distinctive characteristics of Emerson's correspondence, which, the critic states, "set a standard for letter-writing as a genre."*]

"Where does a woman write, what does she look like writing, what is my image, your image, of a woman writing?"[1] Ursula Le Guin's questions haunt me as I think about how to introduce this selection of the letters of Mary Moody Emerson. They are an extraordinary record of woman writing. We know, of course, that she wrote: thousands of pages of manuscript letters and spiritual diaries survive, along with numerous comments about her in print, even passages from her writing published in connection with the life and work of her well-known nephew Ralph Waldo Emerson. But the image of her as woman writing is obscured by the more familiar emphasis on her stern Calvinism, her role as a father figure for her Emerson nephews, her eccentricities, her great "velocity." The letters here, most of them published for the first time, reveal, instead, a woman of great intelligence, a woman challenged and excited by intellectual questions, passionately engaged with her subjects and her audience, using language to express the great truths that were the object of her life's pilgrimage. They also show us a woman negotiating the difficulties created by "single blessedness" in a culture that viewed wife- and motherhood as woman's vocation.

The question of where she wrote is complicated, because the setting was always changing: like the old pilgrims, Mary liked to point out, she rarely stayed "but a month at a place" (MWA). The datelines of her letters often identify towns in which she was staying—Boston, Concord, Waterford, Waltham, Hartford, Newburyport, Ashfield, Belfast—but the houses must often be inferred. Her life as a single woman and a boarder gave her one advantage often denied the woman writer, a room of her own, and at times she mentions writing after midnight, perhaps in moonlight, in the quiet after the family has gone to sleep. Nevertheless, lack of a warm fire or a good lamp, or the desire for company, often led her to the common parlor, where the noise of conversations and family activities interrupted her. Still, she wrote and wrote: letters, her ***Almanack,*** mini-reviews, metaphysical speculations.

Often she began letters on Sunday afternoons (abbreviated "Sab. PM") and wrote on into the evening, until, as she would note, "bad light" precluded writing clearly. "You must pardon this scrool," she would explain. At other times she wrote from hotels or stagecoach stops. Her letters inform about other adverse conditions: poor pens; a shortage of writing paper; her inability to locate the letter she is responding to or the book she wants to quote from; the sound of the stagecoach or the arrival of the bearer for the letter, both of which necessitated a hasty close.

Trying to form an image of her writing is also complicated by a paucity of visual representations of her: no painting exists, no daguerreotype survives to help us see this woman (whom contemporaries often described as a small whirlwind). It is hard to see her seated, engaged in her work. Did she write at a table? Did she use a lap desk (she refers at times to her secretary)? Did she sit on a settee, with papers and books strewn about her? The one surviving pictorial representation made during her lifetime is a paper silhouette, cut before 1810 and reproduced as the frontispiece of this edition, which suggests a rather elegant and delicate young woman, frozen in profile. Only N. C. Wyeth, in his painting *Thoreau and Miss Mary Emerson*, has attempted to construct a visual image for us, and he imagines a sweet-faced, elderly woman wearing an old-fashioned bonnet, seated in a large wing chair, and knitting, while a handsome, young Henry Thoreau leans forward from his rocking chair to look intently into her eyes.[2] But Mary Emerson did not knit; she was neither adept at nor interested in the usual domestic occupations performed by women. Reading, writing, and conversing were her vocations.

Once, when she had experienced "favored omens" of her imminent departure from earthly life, Mary Emerson wrote to her friend Ann Gage about the disposition of her manuscripts, which she hoped might provide "sympathy" to others in "age & solitude"—but, she added, "Not a scrap is to see print as many deceased persons have had their papers." Yet she also indulged in the thought of being remembered through her writings, at the same time that "the love or the esteem or censure of others" seemed irrelevant in the face of immortality (MWA).[3] A great deal of this literary estate survives: almost 900 letters written between 1793 and 1862 to more than fifty people, as well as over one thousand pages of her *Almanack,* the spiritual diary she kept for fifty years.[4] This edition prints 334 of the letters, selected to reveal the range of her voice and correspondence over this seventy-year span. Although Waldo Emerson thought of using some of them to tell the "interior & spiritual history of New England" (*JMN* 7:446), his single product was the essay "Mary Moody Emerson," published posthumously from the fragmentary lecture read to the New England Women's Club in 1869.[5] Embedded in his essay are numerous extracts from her letters and *Almanack*.

Until now, the only other printed primary materials available to scholars interested in her writing have been extracts included in George Tolman's monograph, *Mary Moody Emerson* (1929); twenty-three excerpts or whole letters printed as part of Emerson's journal (1909-14, 1961-82); and passages quoted in James Elliot Cabot's memoir of Emerson, by Ralph L. Rusk in Emerson's *Letters* (1939) and *Life* (1949), and by a few other editors of works that are less well known. Eleanor Tilton's recently published volumes of additional Emerson letters have finally made Waldo's side of this correspondence available in accurate and accessible texts, and, in her notes, Tilton also prints some extensive extracts from Miss Emerson's letters. Before the computer simplified word processing, the sheer volume and complexity of these letters daunted several would-be editors, and only recently have a few intrepid scholars begun to use the manuscript sources in new ways.[6]

As Waldo Emerson recognized, these letters provide a unique source of information about a remarkable woman in a remarkable age. During the crucial period spanned by Mary Emerson's life—from the American Revolution to the Civil War—a young United States struggled to define itself, federalism yielded to more democratic values, religious orthodoxy came into conflict with Unitarianism and then Transcendentalism, and the great shadow of slavery loomed over the democratic experiment. In this volume, students of R. W. Emerson will find much concerning his relationship with his aunt and her formative influences on him. Moreover, Mary Emerson's writing testifies to what Jean Baker Miller has called "the variety of ways of being in the world that different women have constructed" and the vast "storehouse of creativity" that new scholarship on women has revealed. The work of Phyllis Cole, in particular, has begun to place this writing in the context of feminist scholarship, which seeks to "rethink the larger network of cultural traditions and social structures."[7] Here we find a woman negotiating her freedom beyond marriage, practicing a vocation that is closest to theology, and transforming the minor genre of letter writing into a major vehicle for free discussion.

Our portrait of Mary Moody Emerson—eccentric, demanding, rigid, Calvinistic, always in old age—comes largely from a younger generation, who did not know her until she was in her forties. In one frequently cited account, Frank Sanborn claimed her full height was only four feet, three inches; but she was eighty-one years old when he met her for the first time, in 1856, and, according to an earlier piece by Sanborn, she was about five feet tall. She was a woman of incredible energy: according to Waldo, she spun faster than the other tops. He also called her the "representative" figure of an older New England. Many are the reports that she always dressed in white (though references to dress fabrics in her letters dispel that notion), wore out several "shrouds," slept in a bed shaped like a coffin, and dwelt on death and the worm. Her disregard for social conventions is legendary: anecdotes stress her vagabond life, outspoken directness and obtuse questions, preference for the conversation of men, ability to say the most disagreeable things in the least time, strange eating habits, demanding nature, inability to manage finances, and quarrels with her landladies.

Like all round characters, Mary Emerson combined seemingly contradictory qualities: despite her emphasis on humility, she admitted she possessed the "cardinal virtue of *pride*" (MH: 834); contemning honor and ambition, she was supremely aware of the distinction attached to the Emerson name, which she traded on frequently. Her reputed distress at her most famous nephew's apostasy was countered by her excitement in engaging in the theological debate he stimulated. And she was a very youthful Sibyl: Elizabeth Hoar described her as having steely blue eyes, as always fair, with rosy skin that never wrinkled, and bobbed yellow hair that never grayed—and never quite stayed confined in its old-fashioned mobcap. Elizabeth Palmer Peabody told Mary in 1845, "You do not exhibit any of this death-in-life which I complain of—but coquette with life like a girl of fifteen—who knows herself sovereign and can afford to play with *All*" (MWA). In 1855 Henry Thoreau described her as, at age eighty-one, the "youngest person in Concord." When she reached her forties she began to use glasses for reading, and in her eighties, she was still riding horseback for exercise.[8]

Among Mary Emerson's "eccentricities" was her decision not to marry or become dependent on anyone. Instead, she turned a small inheritance into a living arrangement designed to serve her well—as it would have, had she not lived so much longer than she had anticipated. Unmarried, refusing to live as a poor relation, and unequipped for any other occupation, the Aunt Mary the younger generation knew moved about New England as she pleased, turning up to visit for weeks or months at a time, boarding at distant places, always searching for the excitement offered by solitude, society, and intellectual exercise.

The plain facts of her life are quickly told. Born in Concord on 25 August 1774, the fourth child and third daughter of Phebe Bliss and William Emerson (another daughter was born before Mary was two years old), Mary was, as she later punned, "in arms"—her mother's—during the battle of Concord, fought at the bridge close by the family home, the "Manse" built by her father in 1769. Her mother, the daughter and wife of Concord ministers, was (in Sanborn's terms) a "stately and cultivated lady" whose life was drastically changed by the American Revolution. Mary was less than two years old when her father—minister at Concord, son of the minister at Malden, and grandson of ministers who served at Concord, York, and Newbury—marched off as a chaplain with the Continental army. William's death at Rutland, Vermont, a few months later, in October 1776, deprived the child of father, mother, siblings, and home.

An excerpt from Henry David Thoreau's *Journal*, dated 13 November 1851:

Just spent a couple of hours (eight to ten) with Miss Mary Emerson at Holbrook's. The wittiest and most vivacious woman that I know, certainly that woman among my acquaintance whom it is most profitable to meet, the least frivolous, who will most surely provoke to good conversation and the expression of what is in you. She is singular, among women at least, in being really and perseveringly interested to know what thinkers think. She relates herself surely to the intellectual where she goes. It is perhaps her greatest praise and peculiarity that she, more surely than any other woman, gives her companion occasion to utter his best thought. In spite of her own biases, she can entertain a large thought with hospitality, and is not prevented by any intellectuality in it, as women commonly are. In short, she is a genius, as woman seldom is, reminding you less often of her sex than any woman whom I know. In that sense she is capable of a masculine appreciation of poetry and philosophy. I never talked with any other woman who I thought accompanied me so far in describing a poetic experience....

Henry David Thoreau, in
The Journal of Henry D. Thoreau,
edited by Bradford Torrey and Francis H. Allen, Houghton Mifflin Company, 1906.

Instead of the Manse at Concord, Mary grew up in Malden, where she alone was sent to stay with widowed grandmother Mary Moody Emerson; after her grandmother's death in 1779, she remained in Malden with her childless aunt and uncle, Ruth Emerson and Nathan Sargeant (or Sargent). In 1780 her mother married Ezra Ripley, the new Concord minister, and they produced a second family, while Mary was unofficially adopted by the Sargeants—with the provision, it seems, that Aunt Ruth's portion of the grandmother's estate should come to Mary. (As one of five daughters, Mary's monetary prospects were extremely slim.) Also living in Malden was another aunt, Rebecca Emerson Brintnall, who was considered "insane" by the early 1780s. Thus, Mary spent her early "orphanship" (as she called this period of her life)[9] with genteel women in straitened circumstances. Mary was excluded from all that her brother inherited, and in this her life epitomized woman's situation in a patriarchal culture. But she was not the tragic victim that writers such as Phillips Russell have created, with his description of her wandering "desolately from one house to another," cursed with a "mind which found no companionship, lacking any normal outlet or channel for her energies." Mary's solution to the problem of being a woman in this culture was both unique and personally satisfying.

In 1791, when she was seventeen, Mary went to live in fashionable Newburyport with her sister Hannah, who had recently married William Farnham, a bookseller from a liberal and cultured family; after less than two years in Newburyport she returned to Concord to help out in the home of her mother, an invalid who was "confined to her chamber most of her life,"[10] and stepfather. Thus Mary spent her early adulthood caring for the Farnham family (Hannah left ten living children when she died in 1807) and three generations of Blisses, Emersons, and Ripleys in Concord. Probably it was during these years that she eagerly listened to her brother and his friends from Harvard discuss Milton and discovered that the untitled poem she had found in her aunt's house and loved was *Paradise Lost*.[11] Her grandmother Bliss died in 1797, and when her aunt Ruth (widowed in 1798) remarried in 1802, Mary returned to Malden to live with new uncle Samuel Waite and Aunt Ruth. This six years was a delightfully happy period in her life; though she felt profoundly ignorant on the theological topics that her aunt and uncle frequently debated, finally, as she approached her thirtieth birthday, she had her first opportunity to develop her own knowledge.

Despite her apparently meager formal education[12] and heavy responsibilities for the young and the sick (she was an excellent nurse), Mary Emerson also managed to read, visit, converse—to enjoy, in other words, an intellectual and social life. She began friendships and correspondences with the elegant Mary Wilder Van Schalkwyck of Concord (whose marriage to Daniel White of Newburyport in 1807 resulted from Mary's matchmaking), Ann Bromfield of Newburyport, Sarah Hurd of Concord, and other young women (very few of these letters survive), and in 1804 and 1805 she wrote, as "Constance," to Mary Van Schalkwyck's "Cornelia" in a fictional epistolary conversation published in the *Monthly Anthology and Boston Review*.[13] In 1807 she turned down a proposal of marriage.

Perhaps the most important event in this outer life occurred between 1807 and 1813, when, through a complicated legal and financial maneuver, Miss Emerson invested her legacy from Aunt Ruth (who died in 1808) in a farm at Waterford, Maine, that she called Elm Vale. She shared the property with Rebecca and Robert Haskins, her sister and brother-in-law, in a secret arrangement that was the source of much rancor between Mary and her relations. For almost forty years, her home was this secluded farmhouse nestled among Waterford's gentle mountains and thirteen ponds or lakes, and close to Mutiny Brook and the cemetery—even though disputes over the property, mortgages, and rents and her own desire for mental stimulation often prompted her to spend long periods, from a month to several years, visiting and boarding elsewhere. (Less than half of the period from 1810 to 1850 was actually lived at Waterford.) Part of almost every year she spent with her family in Boston, Concord, and Waltham, with the remainder lived in towns all over New England. At times she writes pitifully of saying good-bye, of passing Vale for the last time—only to return later. When she could not return to the Vale, she might board in Waterford with friends or relatives: another sister, Phebe, was married to Waterford's first Congregational minister, Lincoln Ripley (brother of their stepfather Ezra), the first link to Waterford.

The attractions of Vale, her early experiences as nurse or nanny, her hardwon independence from marriage and the ties that bind—all must have contributed to Mary Emerson's attempt to refuse the part for which she seemed to be destined: as maiden aunt or surrogate father for the children of her brother, William, who died in 1811, leaving a Boston-bred widow and six children under the age of ten. Despite sister-in-law Ruth's urging that she make her home with them (and help not only with the children but also with the boarders Ruth hoped would support them), for six years after her brother's death Mary Emerson divided her time among the families at Boston and Concord, even returning to Waterford (with five-year-old Charles) for much of 1813. The War of 1812 brought her back to Boston in 1814, and soon after celebrating peace in February 1815, she moved with the Emersons for the fourth time in sixteen months. By the fall of 1817—when Ralph Waldo left home for Cambridge—Mary believed Ruth could do without her. Now forty-three years old, she returned to Vale, the place she chose to call home.

But Vale was never to be a permanent home. The letters after 1817 give us some sense of her wanderings, preserving the rhythms of visits and encounters, journeys forth from and returns to the farm. These moves chronicle her outer life for four decades; the inner life is the subject of her writing. (Writing to Waldo in 1830, she exclaimed, "I send you and **Almanack!** 'Catch me'—Soberly—I will not till you return the others. They are my *home*—the only images of having existed.") For this reason, I have not attempted to print a chronology of her life, for, beyond a few serious illnesses and her moves, such a list would have chronicled events—the marriages, births, deaths, accomplishments, and publications—in the lives of others, not in her own. Instead, the Calendar of Residences at the beginning of each section after part 1 tracks her movement from one address to the next; in the six introductions, I suggest how her life intersects with the lives of her correspondents.

In 1850, Elm Vale was sold. Now in her late seventies and eighties, Mary Emerson became a full-time "pilgrim," unsuccessfully seeking the "home for life" of which she dreamed. She boarded frequently in Concord and other New England towns until her final move in 1859 to Williamsburgh (Brooklyn), New York, where she lived her last, increasingly enfeebled, years under the care of niece Hannah Haskins Parsons. She died on

1 May 1863, a few months before her eighty-ninth birthday.

Those of Mary Emerson's letters that have survived (probably less than half of those she must have written) record her continuing conversation with the people in this world she crisscrossed for so many years.[14] In 1832 her nephew Charles tried to explain how their conversation affected him:

> How often I think of your sister Hannah's critique on you—"There's Mary—Death, Judgment, & Eternity, nothing else will do for her". I think of it, because when I sit down to write to you, I involuntarily go through a mental process that answers to what Cousin talks about—"finding one's East"—I poise myself on my principles—& undertake simply to tell what is going on in the inner soul, after all the gates of disguise & deceit are passed. What is it to you, how I flutter or creep, through this day's show, or that day's drudgery? And how cold would you feel the style which should affect the Epicurean, & skim over the top of things, as if there were no depths to sound, & no wounds of the spirit to probe. (MT/MH)

Waldo—who reread her letters frequently—felt this power throughout his life, especially when experiencing doubts about his own creative powers and his profession. *"How rich the world is!* I said on reading a letter of M. M. E.," he exclaimed in 1839 (*JMN* 7:220). Rereading Mary's letters in 1843, he wrote, "Never any gave higher counsels . . . nor played with all the household incidents with more wit & humor" (*JMN* 8:391). Two years earlier, he had appreciated her letters as the work of "Genius always new, frolicsome, musical, unpredictable." He went on to describe their style and effect: "What liberal, joyful architecture, liberal & manifold as the vegetation from the earth's bosom, or the creations of frost work on the window! Nothing can excel the freedom & felicity of her letters,—such nobility is in this self rule, this absence of all reference to style or standard: it is the march of the mountain winds, the waving of flowers, or the flight of birds" (*JMN* 7:442).

While this baroque style was both admired and imitated by Waldo, its exuberance often precludes clarity. Mary's method is far different from that prescribed by the classical curriculum at Harvard, where her grandfathers, father, brothers, cousins, and nephews received their educations. Nephew William thought that Carlyle's description of the fantastic style of Richter could also be applied to that of his aunt, and the boys traded jokes about the latest "ludicrous profoundness" of "she-Isaiah . . . alive to the comedy of her pretensions & costume [who] quotes as wildly as she talks" (*L* 1:242), as Waldo described a recent communication from his aunt in 1828. Letters begin in medias res and stop abruptly; spelling, punctuation, and grammar are careless; they are maddeningly allusive; their language ranges from the wonderfully poetic and highly rhetorical to the grandiose and trite. Nevertheless, in the best letters, the form is rich and fluid: it circles and weaves together topics appropriated from reading, conversation, and the lives and letters of correspondents, making the writing of Mary Emerson more difficult than if she were logical and linear.[15]

Reading these letters can prove a daunting experience. Mary recognized that she wrote obsessively on "one subject . . . the joy of reason & sensibility," or religion; and she conceded that her "homilies" might be as tedious as a "thrice-told tale" (MH: 670). Filled with questions and exclamations, her letters are also elusive: they require "much commentary," as Waldo recognized (*JMN* 16:15). Still, especially with that commentary (provided in this edition through both extensive annotation and introductory material), it is possible to appreciate her uniquely provocative voice; to discover the "she-Isaiah," the "weird-woman of her religion"; to see the "lightnings of [her] ladyship's satire" and hear her "hortatory eloquence," as her nephews described her and her writing in 1832 and 1828 (MT/MH).

The letter was Mary Emerson's art form, which she used to counsel, provoke, engage, inspire, and always challenge her audience. In her earliest letter, she calls herself an "epistler of *common size*," and numerous statements about the method, value, and purpose of letters indicate this was not a form she practiced casually. She strove to make each letter, as she did with each meeting with an interesting person, a "conversation" rather than a mere "narration" of facts (MH: 220[76]). Most often, her letters are feminized sermons on texts appropriated from her culture, especially as that culture was mediated by her correspondents.

A good example of how she uses texts from her correspondents' lives is a letter, written in February 1826 at Elm Vale, to nephew Charles Emerson, then a sophomore at Harvard. Mary's topics derive from Charles's letters to her over the past half year: society's advancement toward perfectibility; the Grecian oracles, the topic for the upcoming dissertation competition at Harvard; Charles's New Year's greeting; and his reference to Mary as a "weird woman." In each case, though the text is borrowed, Mary uses it to express her own ideas. Without apparent argument, she questions the idea of societal perfection by substituting the "higher order" toward which God is moving, the millennium; and she offers the present state of the law ("cumbered" by the "rubbish of barbarous ages") as a counterexample to his claim. A fantastically mixed metaphor perfectly embodies her own sense of the incomprehensible complexities of the legal system: law is "so loaded with [rubbish] and with artificial (and I fear fraudulent) apparatus that it takes years of the flower of life to pass thro' their dadalian volumns and . . . often the rights of an individual are lost in their involutions." From this she moves to her larger view: fifty years hence, perhaps, the law may be "regenerated" (with the help of her nephews, she hints) by a return to "those few grand principles" sufficient to all legal practice.

Other topics from Charles's letter receive similar treatment: though she wants to read his essay on the Grecian oracles, she immediately uses the subject for her own miniessay, an imagined re-creation of the human journey after the flood. Charles's New Year's greeting opens the door for her view of time, which she expresses in a cryptically poetic passage built on an image of the self as the pointer (or "gnomon") on a sundial, which marks time by its own shadow; but the time toward which she points is incomprehensible to her. Charles's epithet "weird woman" prompts her to define herself: "I who live so as to try never to offend by one singular word—whose whole time is devoted to one & the same object, pray you spare my age & vocation."

In each case, Mary relocates herself at the center of Charles's text, makes his tenor serve as vehicle for her object: to regenerate the world through perception of a few grand principles. To some extent, this is a variation on the Puritan moralizing habit. But her use of this technique in many letters goes beyond such an inheritance; her transformation of the events and ideas of her correspondents' lives is a way of insinuating herself into their texts. Whereas Beatrice Didier has called the letter the "place of conflict"[16] between woman's desire to write and society's silencing of her, the "society" of letter writing opens Mary's mind by giving her a place to speak. Her method is organic; her thoughts grow naturally out of the texts she takes from her correspondents. She creates a feminized version of orthodox realities: a universe designed and controlled by an all-powerful God; the authority of Scripture and the testimony of revelation; human depravity and the need for redemption by Christ, but one in which the God-given gift of inquiry is the guiding spark, and feelings (or "affections") are the enabling power.

It is impossible to appreciate these letters without some idea of the religious view of reality Mary Emerson took for granted. For Waldo her writing was "the best example I have known of the power of the religion of the Puritans in full energy. . . . The central theme of these endless diaries, is, her relation to the Divine Being" (*JMN* 16:15-16). She practiced what she preached to seventeen-year-old Ann Brewer in 1811: "Make religion the great business of your life. Accept with humble zeal every possible method of improving yourself. [Contemplate] *Death, Judgment* and *Eternity*" (MWA).

"Religion" was central to her life, and she held steadfastly to some of the outward forms of an earlier Puritanism (such as her solemn observance of fast days and her refusal to travel on Sunday). However, she was less "Puritan" than the word connotes to many people, less Calvinistic than the legends about her suggest.[17] Jonathan Edwards's statement in his preface to *Freedom of the Will* adequately describes her basic position: "Of all kinds of knowledge that we can ever obtain, the knowledge of God, and the knowledge of ourselves, are the most important. As religion is the great business, for which we are created, and on which our happiness depends; and as religion consists in an intercourse between ourselves and our Maker; and so has its foundation in God's nature and ours, and in the relation that God and we stand in to each other; therefore a true knowledge of both must be needful in order to true religion."[18] Like Edwards, she stressed "connection" and "relation," not separation and sin. She saw life as a "web" of "eternity," the "long woven scheme of man's creation and redemption." The practice of religion was the discovery of the "golden links w'h bind [the individual] to the great end of existence" (MH: 704). She urged Waldo to study the "relations that bind the universe and God" (MH: 863), desired to know the "intimate relations . . . of the other world with our souls," and constantly saw correspondences, analogies, and emblems in nature, a harmony between works and word. Reason connected her with Being; nature connected with spirit, cause with effect.

Mary Emerson's theological position was actually quite complex. Writing to Elizabeth Hoar in 1846, she said, "I who never know nor talk of sects can be fed with crumbs every where. tho' I rarely enter a Chh." Her "religion" combined orthodoxy with the more rational and evangelical tendencies alive in her day. Just as Waldo, in his 1837 Phi Beta Kappa address, insisted on the excitement of being born in an age of revolution, when old meets new, Mary Emerson rejoiced that she lived in an era of intense theological dispute: "In the wanderings of your imajanation, dear Charles," she asked in 1829 (in a letter Waldo probably reread only a few months before composing "The American Scholar" in 1837), "can you find a world where it is likely there are such differences in theology?" Rather than despairing, she found her time a "period of wonderfull revolutions," as new and old views clamored to be heard: Calvinistic, Trinitarian, liberal, old and new Unitarian, orthodox, Universalist, materialist, Deist, humanitarian, Arian, Socinian, pantheist, transcendentalist. She claimed to follow the "religion of Paul," calling herself a "bible theist," an "old Unitarian," and "orthodox." In fact, she advocated a middle position between "coarse damnatory Calvinism," many of whose doctrines she found "horrible" and "exclusive," and the timid, easy faith of the liberals or "new Unitarians," as she called them. Her theology was broad enough to encompass both God's sovereignty and human freedom, both God's benevolence and man's sin and redemption—and the nexus was the human mind.

In many respects, her theology closely resembled the post-Awakening, liberal, Arminian position that began to develop in about 1734. As Conrad Wright shows, in this period New England liberals rewrote Christian theology to conform to the basic principles of the Age of Reason, shifting the emphasis from the inscrutable sovereignty of God and innate human depravity to the benevolence of God and humans' free agency in working out their own salvation. The new doctrinal position that emerged combined Arminianism, supernatural rationalism, and anti-Trinitarianism.[19] Her grandfather, father, and brother played important roles in the early stages of the shift from orthodox to liberal religion, after the Awakening's revivalism and the theology of Edwards and his heirs had done their work and the Revolution had radically changed the social and political landscape. Her maturity coincided with intellectual movements of great influence: the "Unitarian controversy" that began with the appointment of Henry Ware, Sr., to the Hollis professorship at Harvard in 1805, when Harvard Unitarians clashed with the Andover orthodox and when William Ellery Channing emerged as the leader of Unitarianism; Americans' discovery of German metaphysics in the 1820s and 1830s; and the transcendentalist challenge that grew out of this ferment.

For the "bible theist," Scripture provides the only secure proof of the truths arrived at by human reason and experience. Mary Emerson's theology rested on a very traditional bedrock. She stated it simply in an 1825 letter to Waldo: "Man has deeply fallen. An Enymy *hath sown tares*. A friend is plucking them up—is renovating the fallen & guilty." She proceeded to reiterate this scheme, paraphrasing the words of Saint Paul, for which another baroque artist (George Frideric Handel) created a memorable setting: "*As by means of Adam* sin *entered and death so by means of a divine man death & sin are destroyed!*" (1 Cor. 15:21).

This account, written for twenty-one-year-old Waldo when he was considering studying for the ministry, restates her earliest epistolary expression of her religious ideas, written thirty years earlier to her future sister-in-law Ruth Haskins, when Mary herself was twenty-one. Much like Anne Bradstreet in "Contemplations," the writer finds her subject in the appearance of nature on one exquisite October day, which led her with "wonder and inquiry" to meditate on the fall in Eden, on the sad loss of happiness of this first pair, but without imputing to them a legacy of original sin. "How aggravating and painfull to see them falling by that very capacity, freedom of will," that could raise them, she exclaimed. At the same time, she stressed the whole scheme of redemption and man's reinstatement to divine favor. She goes on to emphasize the essentially Arminian belief in human potential: she speaks emotionally of the "power of man" to rise above his fallen state, through "persevering dilligence and activity to regain what is lost . . . and secure the offer of life and glory."

Most of the homilies or sermons in these letters, however, explore nonbiblical texts drawn from Mary Emerson's wide reading in theology, philosophy, and literature, and they reveal her Enlightenment interests in "evidences," natural and supernatural, external and internal, and her joy in the harmony between Scripture and the voice within, history, nature, and philosophy. "Without evidence [faith] has no charms," she insisted, and she believed the inquiring human spirit was designed to lead the mind to God. In the "earthly Eden of xianity . . . the intellect gathers most effectually the fruit from the tree of knowledge," she asserted; ten years later, she called reason the "godlike spark . . . ordained to thread it's way to the first Cause—to find it's origin—to build it's faith by it's own sternest laws." Her thought was never static: each encounter with a new idea led to a new synthesis. By 1832 she had arrived, through her explorations of German thought, at a more "transcendental" expression of the paradox of the will: she speaks of the only true philosophy—the religion of Paul—as the "divine personal agency as of your own consciousness—God within the heart but not the heart."

However, these appeals to the intellect never obscured Mary Emerson's emphasis on the primacy of the "affections," often experienced in rapturous encounters with nature. The theme of her earliest letters is the "feelings of the human heart"; later she called these nonrational experiences "miracles," and miracles, she asserted, are "the foundation of our faith." In 1830 she worried about Charles's "lack of enthusiasm" and "sacred fire," and she reminded him that "one great ice berg is a shallow theology" (MH: 681). Reason meant not "cool thoughts," but emotional experiences, found in the mystical, idealistic, and Platonic side of Puritanism as well as the intuitionist moral sense described by the English philosopher and theologian Richard Price and the Scots philosoper Thomas Reid. The unassailable sense of Being, the "it is," as Samuel Clarke expressed it,[20] was the spark that set the mind in motion; consciousness, feelings, the connection between God and the self, created "moral epochs" or the *"feeling infinite,"* which was evidence of immortality. She repeatedly stresses the joy of religion, the excitement of the "ardent enlarged mind" as it pursues "the glorious prize of immortal glory," and the importance of nature as a source of "symbols of character human & divine."

Despite her enthusiasm and her open-minded quest for religious knowledge, Mary Emerson never repudiated her ancestors' sense of the mysterious, the inexplicable, the inscrutable nature of God, of the "divine agency," and of what she frequently calls "the enigma of human nature." As was the case with Melville and

Hawthorne, these dark questions fascinated her and drove her inquiries. She trusted in an infinite design, but one image for that design was a "measureless dial" with dread and veiled "numbers." She faced head-on the complex issues of sin and atonement ignored by the liberals, while she avoided the extreme doctrines of innate depravity and election. In her Christology, which was essentially Arian, Jesus is the eternally created Son of God and necessary mediator in the redemption of humankind. His death and sacrifice are an "astonishing apparatus" miraculously constructed to reveal God's will and attributes, as do Scripture and the book of nature. Like Edwards, she arrived at a paradoxical synthesis of the problem of free will and divine providence: "necessity . . . in its' perfect accordance with . . . liberty."

Her letters are full of wonderful expressions of this remarkable "scheme" devised by God, of the "divine econymy" that unites chance and Providence, the "liberty of the creature & the agency of Creator": she describes "liberty . . . girdled . . . within the infinite Orb of Being" (MH: 679) and claims that "Destiny allows of much freedom." The "true metaphysicks," she insists, is the "glorious secret" that God is in all; this is the "ground fact" that makes us free agents.

The continuing presence of this harsh, stern, demanding thread in her religious framework has led to Mary Emerson's being classified as a latter-day Puritan. She believed the liberal school had failed to deal with questions of necessity, "the nature of man & of the origin & nature of evil," the origin and meaning of Christianity. In their emphasis on God's benevolence and man's potential, the liberals had lost sight of eternity. Even the Scriptures, she admitted, "are misterioss there," for they cast both "light & darkness" on these matters—but, she adds in a significant image, "Perhaps it is this feeling [of "misteriossness"] which leads us on with unwearied curiosty to search it's meaning, as we should follow some supernal vision that was always the same yet never the same." This was the gleam she followed in her letters and conversation.

Comparing God to a human father in his 1828 sermon "Likeness to God," William Ellery Channing asked, "And what is it to be a father? It is to communicate one's own nature, to give life to kindred beings; and the highest function of a father is to educate the mind of the child, and to impart to it what is noblest and happiest in his own mind." It is hard to imagine Mary Emerson reading this sermon without thinking of the father she had never really known, the education she had missed, and the pilgrim life she had led. In connection with the subject of war, she wrote, in 1832, "Of the widows & orphans—Oh I could give facts of the long drawn years of imprisoned minds & hearts w'h uneducated orphans endure. But it is among the means of discipline and no worse than other warfare with poverty and ill & ignorance." Perhaps it was her marginal position in society, as a woman and "orphan," cut off from her inheritance, that made her cling at times to a stern view of God's sovereignty and human weakness, of God's inscrutability and incomprehensible plan—to a gap between God and human that prevented her, finally, from accepting the transcendentalists' belief in the God within. Within this spiritual reality, her own suffering made sense.

At the end of his lecture-essay "Mary Moody Emerson," Waldo commented sardonically that, despite the appeal of his aunt's "arcana," "it is easy to believe that Cassandra domesticated in a lady's house would have proved a troublesome boarder" (CW 10:432). She has indeed proven difficult to domesticate. But, like Mary herself, these letters are perhaps most welcome in small doses—which is, after all, how her regular correspondents experienced them. Usually arriving fortnightly or monthly, a letter was written on a 9¾-by-15-inch sheet of old-fashioned, heavy ivory or thin, pale-blue paper bought by the quire and folded to give four full sides, the last typically reserved for the address. The folded letter was sealed with a wax wafer—often red, or black flecked with green, if she could get it—stamped with the thimble that had pressed against more letters than needles (JMN 3:98).

In black ink now faded to brown, she filled at least three sides of each folded sheet with an elegant, slightly spindly, not entirely ladylike hand: right-sloping, angular, her handwriting was characterized by bold downstrokes and many loops (which make distinguishing both capital letters and lowercase vowels particularly difficult). She frequently used the space on the address side for afterthoughts or continuations (in the style of Richardson, as she explained). Typically she caught up on family matters first (marriages, illnesses, deaths, moves, distinctions), asked questions and made requests, and continued a dialogue, at the same time that she was writing her sermon on a text from her correspondent's life and letters. Each letter contains a world of ideas, as passed through her personal lens of family, religion, and the revolutionary period in which she lived.

It should not be surprising that this "auction of the mind" (I borrow Emily Dickinson's metaphor for publication) of Mary Moody Emerson has been so long in coming. From her handwriting to the volume of her output, from the complexity to the tediousness of many of her missives, these letters present a challenge to general reader and editor alike. However, this edition, through its judicious selection of letters to significant correspondents on representative topics, makes it possible to see her and her world anew. I hope it will enable a new generation of readers and scholars to see beyond the anecdotes and around the eccentricities, to see into the mind and heart of a remarkable woman writer who obviously had something to say to her contemporaries and who can continue to speak to ours.

Depositories and Collections

MH—Houghton Library, Harvard University, Cambridge, Mass.: MH: 000 = RWEMA, bMS Am 1280.226; MH: 220(00) or 225(00) = bMS Am 1280.220 or bMS Am 1280.225

MH-AH—Andover-Harvard Theological Library, Harvard University, Cambridge, Mass.

MT/EW—Joel Myerson Transcription, Collection of Dr. Ethel Emerson Wortis (Privately Owned)

MT/MH—Joel Myerson Transcription, RWEMA

MWA—American Antiquarian Society, Worcester, Mass.

RWEMA—Ralph Waldo Emerson Memorial Association Collection, Houghton Library, Harvard University, Cambridge, Mass.

Primary and Secondary Sources

CS—Ralph Waldo Emerson. *The Complete Sermons of Ralph Waldo Emerson*. 3 vols. to date. Ed. Albert J. von Frank, Teresa Toulouse, Andrew Delbanco. and Ronald J. Bosco. Columbia: University of Mo. Press, 1989- .

CW—Ralph Waldo Emerson. *The Complete Works of Ralph Waldo Emerson*. Ed. Joseph Slater et al. 5 vols. to date. Cambridge: Harvard University Press, 1971-.

DAB—*Dictionary of American Biography*

JMN—Ralph Waldo Emerson. *The Journals and Miscellaneous Notebooks of Ralph Waldo Emerson*. Ed. William H. Gilman et al. 16 vols. Cambridge: Harvard University Press, 1960-82.

L—Ralph Waldo Emerson. *The Letters of Ralph Waldo Emerson*. Ed. Ralph L. Rusk. Vols. 1-6. New York: Columbia University Press, 1939. Ed. Eleanor Tilton. Vols. 7-8. New York: Columbia University Press, 1990-91.

MWW-M—Elizabeth Amelia Dwight. *Memorials of Mary Wilder White*. Ed. Mary Wilder Tileston. Boston: Everett Press, 1903.

RevSR—James B. Thayer. *Reverend Samuel Ripley of Waltham*. Cambridge: John Wilson, 1897.

SAR—*Studies in the American Renaissance*. Ed. Joel Myerson. Boston: Twayne, 1977-82; Charlottesville: University Press of Va., 1983-.

W—Ralph Waldo Emerson. *The Complete Works of Ralph Waldo Emerson*. Ed. Edward Waldo Emerson and James Elliot Cabot. 12 vols. Boston: Houghton Mifflin, 1903-4.

Notes

[1] Ursula K. Le Guin, "The Fisherwoman's Daughter," *Dancing at the Edge of the World: Thoughts on Words, Women, Places* (New York: Harper and Row, 1989), 213.

[2] Francis H. Allen, ed., *Men of Concord and Some Others as Portrayed in the Journal of Henry David Thoreau*, with illustrations by N. C. Wyeth (Boston: Houghton Mifflin, 1936), pl. 4. The painting is in the Concord Free Public Library.

[3] Abbreviations of depositories are used to identify locations of manuscripts cited in the Introductions and notes. Citations of letters by MME not printed in this edition that are in the RWEMA Collection (MH) will be further identified by one of two notations: "MH: 000" designates a letter in bMS Am 1280.226(000); "MH: 220(00) or 225(00)" refer to bMS Am 1280.220(00) or 1280.225(00). Non-MME manuscripts will be cited by depository designation only. My use of Joel Myerson's transcriptions of letters by the Emerson brothers is indicated by "MT/MH" (where the manuscript is in the RWEMA Collection) or "MT/EW" (where the manuscript is in the Ethel Wortis Collection).

[4] To date, the most significant work on MME is by Phyllis Cole. In "The Advantage of Loneliness: Mary Moody Emerson's Almanacks, 1802-1855," in *Emerson: Prospect and Retrospect*, ed. Joel Porter (Cambridge: Harvard University Press, 1982), 1-32, Cole describes the spiritual diary (she discovered MME's manuscript in the uncataloged RWEMA Collection) and begins to explore it as a major woman's text. In "From the Edwardses to the Emersons," *CEA Critic* 49 (Winter 1946-Summer 1987): 70-78, Cole reflects further on MME's place within the larger generational history of the Emersons, especially the family-centered "opposing culture" of women (71), the basis for her forthcoming book on MME. A useful genealogical chart of the Emersons is on p. 78.

[5] RWE, "Mary Moody Emerson" (*W* 10:399-433), a portrait that James Elliot Cabot believed was "somewhat softened by [Emerson's] veneration" (*A Memoir of Ralph Waldo Emerson* [Boston: Houghton Mifflin, 1887], 1:30).

[6] The lesser-known sources include several by Franklin B. Sanborn, who prints portions of six letters in "A Concord NoteBook," *The Critic* 48 (Feb., Apr. 1906): 154-60, 338-50; Sanborn reprints this material in *Recollections of Seventy Years*, 2 vols. (Boston: R. G.

Badger, 1909); *Sixty Years of Concord, 1855-1905,* ed. Kenneth W. Cameron (Hartford, Conn.: Transcendental Books, 1975); and *The Personality of Emerson* (Boston: Charles Goodspeed, 1903). *RevSR* includes excerpts from three letters by MME (as well as many letters from SR to MME); manuscripts for these letters seem to be among the now-lost Ames family papers, privately owned, transcribed by Joan Goodwin in 1954. *MWW-M* prints portions of four letters by MME (all but one located in MH-AH).

Along with a few additional anecdotes in Edward W. Emerson's *Emerson in Concord* (Boston: Houghton Mifflin, 1889), RWE's and Sanborn's accounts have served as the major texts for most subsequent writing about MME, which skews the material in several ways (as the following titles suggest): R. F. Dibble, "She Lived to Give Pain," *Century Magazine* 112 (July 1926): 326-32; Van Wyck Brooks, "The Cassandra of New England," *Scribner's Magazine* 81 (Feb. 1927): 125-29; and Rosalie Feltenstein, "Mary Moody Emerson: The Gadfly of Concord," *American Quarterly* 5 (Fall 1953): 231-46. An earlier Sanborn piece is "Thoreau's *Autumn* and Mary Moody Emerson," dated 13 Sept. [1892], in *Transcendental Writers and Heroes,* ed. Kenneth Walter Cameron (Hartford, Conn.: Transcendental Books, 1978), 97-98. Remarkably few scholars have made use of George Tolman's more liberal and varied selection of texts (from both her letters and her "Almanack") in his *Mary Moody Emerson* (privately printed, by Edward Waldo Forbes, in 1929), read at the Concord Antiquarian Society in 1902. MME has always figured in some way in RWE's biography, with perhaps the most interesting earlier comments appearing in O. W. Firkins, *Ralph Waldo Emerson* (Boston: Houghton Mifflin, 1915), esp. 4-8, and Phillips Russell, *Emerson: The Wisest American* (New York: Brentano's, 1929), 19-30. Ralph L. Rusk's edition of the letters and his *Life of Ralph Waldo Emerson* print extracts from previously unpublished manuscripts; and Tilton's two volumes of additional letters continue the tradition. Publication of *JMN* provided additional materials for exploring connections between RWE and MME, including many (but not all) of the letters between them that RWE copied there. Scholars who have used this material include John McAleer, *Ralph Waldo Emerson: Days of Encounter* (Boston: Little, Brown, 1984); David R. Williams, "The Wilderness Rapture of Mary Moody Emerson: One Calvinist Link to Transcendentalism," *SAR 1986:* 1-16; Lawrence Rosenwald, *Emerson and the Art of the Diary* (New York: Oxford University Press, 1988); and Alan D. Hodder, *Emerson's Rhetoric of Revelation* (University Park: Pa. State University Press, 1989). While Williams has used the "MME Notebooks" (MH) into which RWE and his son Edward copied many extracts from MME's manuscripts, none of these studies draws on the manuscripts themselves.

The "intrepid" scholars are Phyllis Cole (see above, n. 4), and Evelyn Barish, whose *Emerson: The Roots of Prophecy* (Princeton: Princeton University Press, 1989) is the first major study since Rusk's *Life* to make extensive use of these materials. See also Barbara Packer, "Origin and Authority: Emerson and the Higher Criticism," in *Reconstructing American Literary History,* ed. Sacvan Bercovitch (Cambridge: Harvard University Press, 1986), 67-92.

[7] Jean Baker Miller, *Toward a New Psychology of Women,* 2d ed. (Boston: Beacon Press, 1986), xii, xvi; Cole, "Edwardses to Emersons," 71.

[8] Most of these stories are preserved in sources cited in nn. 5, 6, above, and *JMN;* see also the articles on MME in *DAB* and *Notable American Women, 1607-1950: A Biographical Dictionary,* ed. Edward T. James, Janet Wilson James, and Paul S. Boyer, 3 vols. (Cambridge: Harvard University Press, 1971), 1:580-81; HDT, *Journals* (Boston: Houghton Mifflin, 1906; Princeton: Princeton University Press, 1981-); Susan Loring, "Reminiscences of Concord," *The Concord Saunterer* 17, no. 3 (Dec. 1984): 12-17; [F. B. Sanborn], untitled obituary notice, *Boston Commonwealth,* 8 May 1863; and EPP's tribute to MME, in Thomas Hovey Gage, Jr., *Notes on the History of Waterford, Maine* (Worcester, Mass., 1913), 54-57. For EH's comments, see *MWW-M,* 109-17, probably the source for Sanborn's use of the same material. HDT's comment is in a letter to H. G. O. Blake, 9 Dec. 1855 (*The Correspondence of Henry D. Thoreau,* ed. Walter Harding and Carl Bode [New York: New York University Press, 1958], 401-2). In this biographical overview I have drawn freely on printed and manuscript sources concerning MME; much family information comes from *IpsE*.

[9] MME called her early years in Malden a "slavery of poverty and ignorance and long orphanship" ("Almanack," Phyllis Cole transcription).

[10] "Reverend Samuel Ripley," *Christian Examiner* 44 (Mar. 1848): 178.

[11] Somewhat different versions of this story are told by EH in *MWW-M,* 114, and RWE, "Mary Moody Emerson."

[12] Whereas Tolman says MME "attended the district school" in Malden (4), Barish, *Emerson,* assumes she had "little or no schooling" (39). MME is silent on the subject.

[13] See Introduction to part 1, n. 6. Phyllis Cole first recognized MME's authorship of the "Constance" letters ("Nature Within and Without," New World Colloquium, Concord, Mass., 6 Jan. 1988, 5-8). Three other publications (all printed anonymously) are an obituary notice of LG, *Christian Witness* (Boston), 13 May 1842; a fictional piece, "Meeting of Two Friends after Long Separation by Death" ("from a fragment of 1830"),

Portland Register, 27 June 1846, rpt. in *Christian Register* (Boston), 22 Aug. 1846; and an article, "The Sabbath," *Middlesex Freeman* (Concord), 14 Nov. 1851. " 'The Woman': A Reminiscence," *Christian Register,* 24 Jan. 1852, signed "An Octogenarian," may have been written by MME, but heavily revised by someone else.

[14] Most of MME's surviving correspondence is addressed to her family and to ASG and EH, both of whom she came to consider her nieces. However, references in her letters make it clear that she corresponded extensively with Sarah Hurd; MWW; Ann Bromfield Tracy; niece Louisa Farnham Dewey and her husband Orville; TTS; her sisters Hannah Farnham, PER, and REH; and their children, numerous Emerson cousins, and others. Very few of these letters survive. Other references point to additional letters addressed to her major correspondents.

[15] Compare, for example, Edmund Wilson's puzzled response to Harriet Beecher Stowe's style (*Patriotic Gore* [New York: Oxford University Press, 1962], 34-35) to RWE's description of MME's writing: both point to a need to consider these features in the context of a "feminist poetics": to look at what Elaine Showalter calls the "social dimensions and determinants of language use, the shaping of linguistic behavior by cultural ideals" ("Feminist Criticism in the Wilderness," in *The New Feminist Criticism,* ed. Showalter [New York: Pantheon, 1985], 259-60).

[16] In *Le Journal intime* (Paris: Presses Universitaires de France, 1976), 11, Beatrice Didier calls the letter "le lieu d'un conflict."

[17] See, for example, the entry for Sarah Alden Bradford Ripley in *Notable American Women:* "When Mary tried to force her own grim Calvinism on [Sarah], she refused to accept a creed that might close her mind 'against the light of truth' " (164). Three recent examples of the persistence of this label of Calvinist are McAleer, *Ralph Waldo Emerson,* 34; Lawrence Buell, *New England Literary Culture* (Cambridge: Cambridge University Press, 1986), 168; and David M. Robinson, "Historical Introduction," *CS* 1:3. On the other hand, David R. Williams recognizes the difficulty of codifying her position, and he distinguishes between the "literal and legal side of Calvinism" and MME's more "imaginative and lively" version ("Wilderness Rapture," 4). Eleanor Tilton concludes that MME was "just what she claimed to be: an old-fashioned Unitarian. She cannot be called a Calvinist" (*L* 7:3). Although I would argue that MME was moving beyond old-fashioned Unitarianism, Tilton's term is usefully free of connotations of rigidity, narrowness, and dogmatism. MME communicates an open and joyful vision of a meaningful universe of connections presided over by a designing God, who is first discovered in "*those keen vibrations of soul* which . . . immortalizes moments and which give to life all the zest of enjoyment."

[18] Jonathan Edwards, *Freedom of the Will,* ed. Paul Ramsey, vol. 1 of *The Works of Jonathan Edwards,* ed. Perry Miller, Sydney E. Ahlstrom, John E. Smith, et al., 7 vols. to date (New Haven: Yale University Press, 1957-), 133.

[19] Conrad Wright, *The Beginnings of Unitarianism in America* (Boston: Beacon Press, 1955), 3-5, 252; see also Ahlstrom, 391-402.

[20] Samuel Clarke, *A Demonstration of the Being and Attributes of God: Works, 1738* (New York: Garland Publishing, 1978), 2:527.

FURTHER READING

Barish, Evelyn. "Aunt" and "The Angel of Midnight." In *Emerson: The Roots of Prophecy,* pp. 36-53 and 132-44. Princeton: Princeton University Press, 1989.

    Examines the intellectual interactions of Mary Moody Emerson and Ralph Waldo Emerson, with specific regard to issues of spirituality.

Brooks, Van Wyck. "The Cassandra of New England." *Scribner's Magazine* 81 (February 1927): 125-9.

    Describes the unconventional behavior and interests of Emerson, including her persistently Calvinist criticisms of nineteenth-century society.

Cole, Phyllis. "From the Edwardses to the Emersons." *CEA Critic* 49, Nos. 2-4 (Winter 1986-Summer 1987): 70-8.

    Discusses the religious and intellectual influence of Mary Moody Emerson on Ralph Waldo Emerson, and emphasizes the role of autonomy and individualism in the former's brand of Calvinism.

Dibble, R. F. "She Lived to Give Pain: Aunt Mary Emerson's Eye Went Through You Like a Needle." *The Century Magazine* 112, No. 3 (July 1926): 326-32.

    Describes in an anecdotal manner the social position and personality of Mary Moody Emerson.

Eisler, Benita. " 'Up to the Mind's Elbows': The Instructive Friendship of Emerson's Aunts." *American Voice* 3 (Summer 1986): 96-107.

    Claims that Emerson's gender prevented her from fulfilling her intellectual potential beyond the outlets of theological discussion and correspondence, which led to an influential relationship with Ralph Waldo Emerson and earned her the label of an "eccentric."

Feltenstein, Rosalie. "Mary Moody Emerson: The Gadfly of Concord." *American Quarterly* 5, No. 3 (Fall 1953): 231-46.

A short biography of Emerson and account of her original ideas.

Sanborn, F. B. "The Women of Concord." *The Critic* 48, No. 2 (February 1906): 154-60.
Provides anecdotal information about the influential women, including Emerson, who contributed to the intellectual life and reputation of Concord, Massachusetts.

———. "Thoreau's *Autumn* and Mary Moody Emerson." In *Transcendental Writers and Heroes: Papers Chiefly on Emerson, Thoreau, Literary Friends and Contemporaries with Regional and Critical Backgrounds*, edited by Kenneth Walter Cameron, pp. 97-8. Hartford: Transcendental Books, 1978.
An account—written by Sanborn on September 13, 1892—of the relationship between Henry David Thoreau and Emerson.

Madame Bovary

Gustave Flaubert

The following entry covers criticism of Flaubert's novel *Madame Bovary* from the late 1970s to the present. For additional information on Flaubert's career and works, see *NCLC*, Volumes 2, 10, 19, and 62.

INTRODUCTION

Madame Bovary, first published in 1857, is considered Flaubert's masterpiece and one of the most influential French novels of the nineteenth century. Through painstaking attention to detail and constant revision, Flaubert created a highly accurate rendering of his characters' motivations and personalities, achieving an exquisite prose style that has served as a model for numerous writers. A meticulous craftsman, Flaubert attempted to create a narrative "as rhythmical as verse and as precise as the language of science." The novel has significantly influenced literary criticism; since its publication, *Madame Bovary* has been one of the most frequently discussed books in the history of world literature. Many scholars have concurred with Paul de Man's assertion that "contemporary criticism of fiction owes more to this novel than to any other nineteenth-century work."

Biographical Information

In 1849, Flaubert completed the first version of his novel *La tentation de Saint Antoine* (1874; *The Temptation of Saint Antony*). Flaubert's friends Maxime Du Camp and Louis Bouilhet declared the work a failure and persuaded him to abandon historical subjects in favor of a novel that would be contemporary in content and realistic in intent. Flaubert subsequently began *Madame Bovary*. Although he had contempt for his bourgeois subject, he nevertheless strove to achieve stylistic perfection in the novel by working slowly and carefully for more than five years, often producing only one page in several days. Various sources have been cited as possible inspirations for the novel's plot, among them an anecdote related by Maxime Du Camp, and the autobiography of Flaubert's friend Louise Pradier, wife of the painter James Pradier. Other critics have concluded that Flaubert's imagination was in fact the primary source for the novel, pointing to the author's famous declaration: "Madame Bovary, c'est moi." *Madame Bovary*—Flaubert's first published novel, despite having previously completed several other manuscripts—initially appeared in installments in *La Revue de Paris* from October 1 through December 15, 1856. Although critics recognized the novel as

a work of immense significance, the French government was of a different opinion: Flaubert, his printer, and his publisher were all tried for blasphemy and offense against public morals. All were eventually acquitted, however, and *Madame Bovary* acquired an elevated notoriety as a result of the publicity generated by the trial. Despite the novel's success, biographers have noted that Flaubert came to resent the fame of *Madame Bovary*, which greatly overshadowed his subsequent works.

Plot and Major Characters

Madame Bovary is often described as a satire on romantic beliefs and the ineffectual lives of the provincial bourgeoisie of nineteenth-century France. The novel relates the story of Emma Bovary, a bored, frustrated housewife whose dreams of romantic love—primarily inspired by popular novels of her time—are unfulfilled through her marriage to a simple country doctor, Charles Bovary. She attempts to realize her fantasies through love affairs with a local landowner and a law clerk and, later, through extravagant purchases. Unable to pay her debts and unwilling to tolerate or to conform to bourgeois values, she ultimately commits suicide by poisoning herself. Charles is comfortable with his bourgeois simplicity, in contrast with his wife's rage and frustration at the limitations of her life. Throughout the story, Charles becomes increasingly happy and content with his married life, as Emma secretly grows to hate him. Although affectionate and loyal, Charles is portrayed as an obtuse character, oblivious to the sources of his wife's unhappiness and completely naive concerning her affairs. Even the revelation of financial ruin and his wife's infidelity does not alter his adulation for Emma. Her suicide sends him into a devastating episode of grief and seems to contribute to his death at the novel's conclusion. The character Homais, the village pharmacist and champion of scientific progress and traditional patriarchal values, has been viewed by some critics as the novel's most prominent symbol of bourgeois conventionality. While depicted as the focus of satire due to his frequent use of platitudes, Homais also proves to be the most successful figure at the culmination of the plot. Geoffrey Wall has remarked: "Homais becomes ever more powerful in the final chapters, now that . . . the wifeless Charles is fading away with grief. He is enthroned as 'the happiest of fathers, the most fortunate of men'. His public apotheosis comes in the book's closing sentence, as he is awarded the Legion of Honour."

Major Themes

Social and historical themes are among the most frequently discussed motifs of *Madame Bovary*. Read as a social commentary, the novel depicts Flaubert's view of the conventionality and banality of the French middle class during the nineteenth century. Rosemary Lloyd has stated: "From the opening pages, with their depiction of the way in which both children and teachers impose on individuals patterns of behaviour they are obliged to copy slavishly, to the concluding lines, which record Homais's reward for conforming to the image of the successful man, *Madame Bovary* reveals the mechanisms of middle-class society, the way in which it creates a form of fatality." The portrayal of gender roles has also received attention in recent years. Several critics have emphasized the novel's depiction of a society in which women received a relatively useless, "ornamental" education, with Emma Bovary's largely superfluous social position being viewed as one of the sources of her malaise and unhappiness. Tony Williams has commented: "The fictional world of *Madame Bovary* is marked by the over-differentiation of the sexes which characterizes patriarchal society." Other important themes in the novel include the blurred relationship between fantasy and reality and the duplicitous nature of language and meaning. Emma's fruitless search for the heightened passion that she has read about in novels illustrates a dichotomy between language and real-life experience. Many critics have therefore interpreted the novel as a skeptical commentary on the escapist Romantic literature of the era, emphasizing Flaubert's demystification of Romantic and sentimental stereotypes. Others, however, have offered a more ambiguous reading of Flaubert's commentary on the Romantic imagination. A product of the Romantic temperament in conflict with practical, conventional bourgeois society, Emma Bovary can be interpreted as a victim both of her banal circumstances and of her own impressionability.

Critical Reception

Much recent criticism of *Madame Bovary* has evidenced a feminist or historicist perspective. Several critics have taken a feminist interest in Emma's position in a patriarchal society, interpreting her existential malaise and obsession with fantasy as a product of her limited role in bourgeois society. Tony Tanner, for example, has argued that "[Emma's] sickness must be connected to the vagueness of her position in society: after being a daughter (and thus entirely defined by the father . . .), she exists on the threshold in a sort of pronominal limbo." Also examining the novel's portrayal of gender roles, Janet Todd has perceived a conflict between Emma Bovary's conventional feminine role and increasingly powerful "masculine" urges which ultimately undermine her social position and contribute to her suicide. Reading *Madame Bovary* through a historical perspective, Rosemary Lloyd has argued that "the novel draws largely on three main currents of thought: the sentimentalism prevalent in the eighteenth century, which leads into the Romanticism of the 1820s to 1840s; the analytical explorations of love that develop, in part, from other eighteenth-century writers; and the pragmatism of bourgeois thought, which had grown increasingly dominant since the 1830 revolution." Another major focus of critical interest has been the problematic relationship, suggested by Flaubert's narrative techniques, between language, meaning, and reality. "The division between language and experience is a major concern of the novel," Nathaniel Wing has remarked. Exploring the juxtaposition of imagination and reality, Lawrence Thornton has emphasized Emma Bovary's subjective responses to "two equally counterfeit versions of reality": the "marvelous," derived from romantic stories, and the conventional cultural codes of behavior that are defined by her middle-class society.

CRITICISM

Lawrence Thornton (essay date 1978)

SOURCE: "The Fairest of Them All: Modes of Vision in *Madame Bovary*," in *PMLA: Publications of the*

Modern Language Association, Vol. 93, No. 5, October, 1978, pp. 982-91.

[*In the following essay, Thornton examines the sources of Emma Bovary's fantasies in a conflation of fairy tales and romantic literature. He notes that "Flaubert presents Emma's fantasy life through a series of tableaux in which her imagination is associated with images of mirrors."*]

> She had a magic looking-glass and when she stood before it and looked at herself she used to say: "Mirror, mirror, on the wall, who is fairest of us all?" Then the glass replied: "Queen, thou'rt fairest of them all."
>
> "Snow White"

I

On her first evening in Yonville, Emma Bovary becomes involved in a discussion of esthetics with the local litterateur, Léon Dupuis. "[Q]uelle meilleure chose," he argues, "que d'être le soir au coin du feu avec un livre, pendant que le vent bat les carreaux, que la lampe brûle?"

—N'est-ce pas? dit-elle, en fixant sur lui ses grands yeux noirs tout ouverts.

—On ne songe à rien, continuait-il, les heures passent. On se promène immobile dans des pays que l'on croit voir, et votre pensée, s'enlaçant à la fiction, se joue dans les détails ou poursuit le contour des aventures. Elle se mêle aux personnages; il semble que c'est vous qui palpitez sous leurs costumes.

—C'est vrai! c'est vrai! disait-elle.¹

Léon's banalities radiate insights for Emma. Here, at last, is someone who responds as she does to the vicarious pleasures of books. But Emma is a more passionate and engaged reader than the clerk who tests her knowledge of *idées reçues*. For her, books encapsulate life itself; people, emotions, even objects are significant only to the degree that they validate the discoveries of her reading, and much of her time is spent re-creating her experience to make it conform with the demands of her imagination.

To render this process, Flaubert presents Emma's fantasy life through a series of tableaux in which her imagination is associated with images of mirrors. This imagery always signals a movement toward subjectivity in *Madame Bovary,* and there is a close relationship here with Tzvetan Todorov's perception about the world of the fantastic, where, he argues, "every appearance of a supernatural element is accompanied by the parallel introduction of an element belonging to the realm of sight. It is, in particular, eyeglasses and mirrors that permit penetration into the marvelous universe." These symbols of "indirect, distorted, subverted vision" mediate between reality and the supernatural, reifying the "marvelous universe" for character and reader alike.² However, while Todorov's construct offers an illuminating context for Flaubert's imagery, we need to be aware that the motif of the mirror provides only one element in the structure of a marvelous tale (an element whose function is transitional and therefore generally limited in thematic significance), whereas in *Madame Bovary* it eventually symbolizes Emma's whole subjective life. This is a large claim to make, especially since the initial connection I wish to point out among Todorov's "marvelous universe," Emma's subjectivity, and the mirror motif begins with an examination of the character of the Queen in "Snow White." But the incongruity of this association is superficial, giving way to likeness between novel and fairy tale in both theme and setting.

When the Queen asks her question of the magic mirror, the reader witnesses an act of schizophrenia taking place simultaneously with the unfolding of the dialectic between fantasy and reality. From a psychological perspective, it is not the mirror but her own selfish desires that subvert the Queen's vision and permit her to penetrate the "marvelous universe." While the voice in the mirror originates in the supernatural, what the Queen sees reflected in the mirror is her own subjective conception of herself, which is manifested by projecting an ideal version of herself onto her own image. In other words, the Queen gains access to the subjective equivalent of Todorov's supernatural world by an act of mind so powerful that she can see what she wants to see. Every visual and psychological element in this scene is repeated in the ninth chapter of Part II of *Madame Bovary,* where Emma contemplates her own image after having been seduced by Rodolphe. The tableau of the Queen before her mirror covers Emma like a transparency, and these fused images symbolize Emma's life from the moment she enters the convent until her death. Given this congruence, the "mœurs de Province" Flaubert chose to anatomize involve elements one would scarcely attribute, at least at first glance, to the kingdom of the bourgeoisie: magic mirrors, fantastic visions, high adventure in the most ephemeral reaches of the romantic's imagination.

At the same time, more is at stake here than allusions to the world of fairy tales and the marvelous, for these elements lead directly to what I take to be Flaubert's most devastating irony. Just as there is a dialectic in Emma's consciousness, so is there in the structure of the novel itself. The external events of *Madame Bovary* deal with nuances of boredom exemplified in the lives of those who inhabit the monochromatic countrysides' of Tostes and Yonville. Opposed to the banalities of everyday life in these dusty villages is all that Emma sees, and in the congeries of images cast on her imagination we encounter a beautifully contrived paradox: that which is most vital in the novel is most ephemeral, existing only in the distorted world of Emma's visual imagination. More complex than Todorov's, this world resonates with the syllables of Flaubert's *idées reçues,* Aristotle's *endoxon* ("current opinion"),[3] Barthes's codes. For each time Emma sees (or hears) something in the depths of her own subjectivity, "one might say that off-stage voices can [also] be heard"—Barthes's cultural codes "whose origin is 'lost' in the vast perspective of the *already-written.* . . ."[4] As I hope the following discussion of modes of vision will show, Emma's universe consists of two equally counterfeit versions of reality: the marvelous, whose elements are derived from her reading, and the endoxal, whose terms are derived from her culture and repeated in the symbols and themes of her reading.

Flaubert discloses Emma's subjectivity in three visual modes, which I call descriptive, hallucinatory, and autoscopic. The descriptive mode provided Erich Auerbach with the materials for his analysis of Flaubertian realism in *Mimesis;* he begins by citing the following domestic scene:[5]

> Mais c'était surtout aux heures des repas qu'elle n'en pouvait plus, dans cette petite salle au rez-dechaussée, avec le poêle qui fumait, la parte qui criait, les murs qui suintaient, les pavés humides; toute l'amertume de l'existence lui semblait servie sur son assiette, et, à la fumée du bouilli, il montrait du fond de son âme comme d'autres bouffées d'affadissement. Charles était long à manger; elle grignotait quelques noisettes, ou bien, appuyée du coude, s'amusait, avec la pointe de son couteau, de faire des raies sur la toile cirée.

Auerbach shows how Emma's subjective responses to Charles are indicated by a series of essentially descriptive images, and since his argument is familiar enough not to require lengthy rehearsal, it should be sufficient to reiterate the main points of his conclusion.

The picture above is not presented for itself; it is subordinated to Emma's despair, which has impressed itself more and more heavily on her soul since her marriage. The drabness of the scene "appears to her, and through her to the reader also, as something that is connected with [Charles] . . . yet she is . . . herself part of the picture, she is situated within it" (Auerbach, p. 427). And Auerbach isolates the major characteristic of the descriptive mode when he tells us that Emma "does not simply see, but is herself seen as one seeing, and is thus judged, simply through a plain description of her subjective life, out of her own feelings" (pp. 427-28). In this sense, visual phenomena can become symptoms of subjective states of being.

The scene at the Banneville groves illustrates how this mode functions, even more clearly than Auerbach's example. After asking herself why she married, Emma begins to think of her companions at the convent, imagining them in the theaters and ballrooms of Paris. The contrast is unbearable: "Mais elle, sa vie était froide comme un grenier dont la lucarne est au nord, et l'ennui, araignée silencieuse, filait sa toile dans l'ombre, à tous les coins de son cœur." With her emotional condition thus established, Flaubert goes on to describe the countryside:

> Il arrivait parfois des rafales de vent, brises de la mer qui, roulant d'un bond sur tout le plateau du pays de Caux, apportaient, jusqu'au loin dans les champs, une fraîcheur salée. Les joncs sifflaient à ras de terre et les feuilles des hêtres bruissaient en un frisson rapide, tandis que les cimes, se balançant toujours, continuaient leur grand murmure. Emma serrait son châle contre ses épaules et se levait.
>
> (pp. 42-43)

The movement of the rushes and branches, the swaying of the crowns of the beech trees, the mournful sound of the wind and the onomatopoetic effect produced by the rhymes of "toujours," "leur," and "murmure" present a composite description (with sound effects) of Emma's internal condition, a description, in fact, of the ennui that "filait sa toile" in her soul. Here, as in the Auerbach example, her subjective responses are reported by an omniscient narrator.

In the hallucinatory mode, images of the external world decode subjective images present in the reservoir of Emma's memory, and she frequently perceives images of both sorts simultaneously. It has been suggested that this simultaneity may be related to the hallucinations Flaubert suffered from as a young man,[6] and in a letter to Taine, Flaubert records their effects in a way that illuminates a good deal about the function of Emma's memory:

> Puis, tout à coup, comme la foudre, envahissement car l'hallucination proprement dite n'est pas autre chose,—pour moi, du moins. C'est une maladie de la mémoire, un relâchement de ce qu'elle recele. On sent les images s'échapper de vous comme des flots de sang. Il vous semble que tout ce qu'on a dans la tête éclate à la fois comme les mille pièces d'un feu d'artifice, et on n'a pas le temps de regarder ces images internes qui défilent avec furie.—En d'autres circonstances, ça commence par une seule image qui grandit, se développe et finit par couvrir la réalité objective, comme par exemple une étincelle qui voltige et devient un grand feu flambant. Dans ce dernier cas, on peut très bien penser à autre chose, *en même temps;* et cela se confond presque avec ce qu'on appelle les papillons noirs, c'est-à-dire ces rondelles de satin que certaines personnes voient flotter dans l'air, quand le ciel est grisâtre et qu'elles ont la vue fatiguée.[7]

Or, more simply:

> Au contraire, dans l'hallucination pure et simple on peut très bien voir une image fausse d'un œil, et les objets vrais de l'autre.
>
> (*Correspondance*, II, 96)

This multiplication of images and the ensuing dysfunction of memory occur during Emma's final retreat from Rodolphe's chateau, when she gazes dumbly at the surrounding countryside and sees images "qui défilent avec furie":

> Tout ce qu'il y avait dans sa tête de réminiscences, d'idées, s'échappait à la fois, d'un seul bond, comme le mille pièces d'un feu d'artifice. Elle vit son père, le cabinet de Lheureux, leur chambre là-bas, un autre paysage. . . .
>
> La nuit tombait, des corneilles volaient.
>
> Il lui sembla tout à coup que des globules couleur de feu éclataient dans l'air comme des balles fulminantes en s'aplatissant, et tournaient, tournaient, pour aller se fondre dans la neige, entre les branches des arbres. Au milieu de chacun d'eux, la figure de Rodolphe apparaissait. Ils se multiplièrent, et ils se rapprochaient, la pénétraient; tout disparut. Elle reconnut les lumières des maisons, qui rayonnaient de loin dans le brouillard. (pp. 290-91)

In this highly sensitized condition, Emma cannot distinguish the present from the past, reality from hallucination. Fragmented images impinge on her mind's eye for a millisecond before merging in the vortex where everything "tournaient, tournaient" and she is engulfed by the multiple faces of Rodolphe.

Less dramatic situations affect her vision in the same way, as in the following scene from the ball at Vaubyessard:

> L'air du bal était lourd; les lampes pâlissaient. On refluait dans la salle de billard. Un domestique monta sur une chaise et cassa deux vitres; au bruit des éclats de verre, Mme Bovary tourna la tête et aperçut dans le jardin, contre les barreaux, des faces de paysans qui regardaient. Alors le souvenir des Bertaux lui arriva. Elle revit la ferme, la mare bourbeuse, son père en blouse sous les pommiers, et elle se revit elle-même, comme autrefois, écrémant avec son doigt les terrines de lait dans la laiterie.
>
> (pp. 48-49)

Immersed in the present splendor of the chateau, she sees herself as she used to be, the intensity of the recovered experience so great that it has tactile as well as visual qualities. Here the omniscient narrator has vanished, and it is Emma herself who links external and internal, past and present. But there is more here than simultaneity. This scene, like the previous one, is epiphanic: there is a "showing forth" of the quintessential Emma Bovary as she exists in two places at once, her visual imagination the node of intersecting planes of time. Not only does the encroachment of the past into the present exemplify the power of her imagination, it also epitomizes the tragedy of a life in which it will become increasingly difficult to distinguish the real from the marvelous, phenomena from dreams, the world of actuality and logical possibility from the world of fantasy and endoxal codes. Emma's problem, as opposed to Flaubert's, is not a "maladie de la mémorie," but a sickness of consciousness in which the ego has been cut loose from its moorings in a stable psyche and allowed to contemplate itself in the "marvelous universe" of its own reflections: the domain of the autoscopic mode of vision, where mirrors abound under the sign of Narcissus.

III

At the convent Emma is exposed to the virus of romantic literature, whose virulence results from the melding of the marvelous plots of fairy tales with identifiable but unspecified glandular longings. Following an exhaustive catalog of images and codes running through Emma's reading, Flaubert adds that "l'abat-jour du quinquet, accroché dans la muraille au-dessus de la tête d'Emma, éclairait tous ces tableaux du monde, qui passaient devant elle les uns après les autres, dans le silence du dortoir et au bruit lointain de quelque fiacre attardé qui roulait encore sur les boulevards" (p. 36). These "tableaux du monde," moving in parataxis through her mind to the rhythm of the "fiacre attardé" (whose "bruit lointain" underscores Emma's sense of mimesis), adumbrate a crucial structure in her imagination. For the only images that ever achieve autonomy are of young women, and in the process of differentiating them from their surroundings, and from the young men who are sometimes present, Emma reveals the cause of her perpetual dissatisfaction with her lovers.

Consider the details of the "tableaux" etched on her memory. Dreaming over Scott's novels, "elle aurait voulu vivre dans quelque vieux manoir, comme ces châtelaines au long corsage qui, sous le trèfle des ogives, passaient leurs jours, le coude sur la pierre et le menton dans la main, à regarder venir du fond de la campagne un cavalier à plume blanche qui galope sur un cheval noir" (p. 35). Here the focus of her attention is disclosed in the perspective of the "tableaux." Compared to the detailed description of the composite châtelaine occupying the foreground of the scene, the knight is only an impressionistic blur in the middle distance, a catalyst, as it were, for *rêverie*. But this fantasy is only the first in a series that includes a "culte de Marie Stuart et des vénérations enthousiastes à l'endroit des femmes illustres ou infortunées." Emma is equally fascinated by "ladies anglaises à boucles blondes qui, sous leur chapeau de paille rond, vous regardent avec leurs grands yeux clairs" (p. 36), as well as by others "rêvant sur des sofas près d'un billet décacheté, contemplaient la lune, par la fenêtre entr'ouverte, à demi drapée d'un rideau noir." The catalog of heroines is completed by "naïves, une larme sur la joue, becquetaient une tourterelle à travers les barreaux d'une cage gothique, ou, souriant, la tête sur l'épaule, effeuillaient une marguerite de leurs doigts pointus, retroussés comme des souliers à la poulaine."

The convent tableaux prefigure Emma's increasingly dangerous fantasies, which begin to turn up shortly after the ball at Vaubyessard. As the weeks following her experience there fade away, "ce fut donc une occupation pour Emma que le souvenir de ce bal" (p. 53). At the center of these memories is an image of the Viscount who "revenait toujours dans ses lectures. Entre lui et les personnages inventés, elle établissait des rapprochements. Mais le cercle dont il était le centre peu à peu s'élargit autour de lui, et cette auréole qu'il avait, s'écartant de sa figure, s'étala plus au loin, pour illuminer d'autres rêves" (p. 54). This light, once shed on the "tableaux du monde," now illuminates Paris as it emerges from her imagination like Mallarmé's flower absent from the bouquets of this world:

> Paris, plus vaste que l'Océan, miroitait donc aux yeux d'Emma dans une atmosphère vermeille. La vie nombreuse qui s'agitait en ce tumulte y était cependant divisée par parties, classée en tableaux distincts, Emma n'en apercevait que deux ou trois, qui lui cachaient tous les autres et représentaient à eux seuls l'humanité complète. Le monde des ambassadeurs marchait sur des parquets luisants, dans des salons lambrissés de miroirs, autour de tables ovales couvertes d'un tapis de velours à crépines d'or. Il y avait là des robes à queue, de grands mystères, des angoisses dissimulées sous des sourires. Venait ensuite la société des duchesses: on y était pâle; on se levait à quatre heures; les femmes, pauvres anges! portaient du point d'Angleterre au bas de leur jupon, et les hommes, capacités méconnues sous des dehors futiles, crevaient leurs chevaux par partie de plaisir, allaient passer à Bade la saison d'été, et, vers la quarantaine enfin, épousaient des héritières. (pp. 54-55)

A street map; a magazine; novels by Sue, Balzac, and Sand; memories of her convent reading and of the waltz at Vaubyessard; a green cigar case—this is a reasonably accurate inventory of the data that nurtured the Parisian *rêverie*. In the paragraph preceding that fantasia the Viscount is momentarily the brightest star in Emma's constellation, but his image soon fades; the aureole emanating from him is first diffused and then reconstituted in the dream of Paris that emerges slowly in her imagination. The subject of the *rêverie* is not the Viscount, but rather the aureole he bears, which irradiates details of the larger dream of Paris. And it is important to see that in both examples the Viscount cannot maintain his position at the center of Emma's imaginative circle. Although the fantasy begins with her memory of him, he is absorbed into the mirrored images of the Parisian drawing rooms and the *women who move among them*. Compared to these "pauvres anges" with "robes à queue, de grands mystères, des angoisses dissimulées sous des sourires," pale faces and delicate petticoats, the men Emma imagines remain undifferentiated abstractions. Clearly, the Viscount has become another of the disappearing men, reduced to a charge of light shed on bright images of women.

Vaubyessard "avait fait un trou dans sa vie" (p. 52) by juxtaposing the dreariness of village life with the ambience of chateaux; at the same time, it provided Emma with an experience whereby she could synthesize the disparate images that had crowded her imagination since adolescence, when solitary heroines in stylized attitudes of melancholy longing became her emblem of love. Moreover, it is in the nature of her fascination with these heroines that their significance to her own personality and to the mirror motif becomes apparent. As a girl, Emma perceived an embryonic ideal of herself in these women, which she realizes in her maturity, and, I have tried to show, it is always the avatar of herself that survives in Emma's fantasies. Men function exclusively as catalysts in the process of her self-discovery, vehicles for her journeys toward herself. Consequently, her narcissism goes beyond the self-love normally associated with the word to infatuation with women in general and particularly with women as erotic objects. Emma's attraction to herself thus participates in a larger attraction to her own sex.[8] And it can be argued, I think, that the dialectic formed by the phenomena of the disappearing men and the photographically envisioned women at least partially explains Emma's dissatisfaction with Charles, Rodolphe, and Léon. This aspect of Emma's character is examined below in detail, following a discussion of her response to herself after she has been seduced by Rodolphe. At this point, it should be sufficient to say that narcissism ultimately displaces infidelity as the source of her most intense erotic experience.

IV

The Parisian fantasy marks the end of the first stage of Emma's voyage into the "marvelous universe." Afterward, she is conscious of nothing for days on end but the gap in her life, and during the last weeks she spends in Tostes, ennui settles over her soul as if it were dust raised by carts passing in the street below her window, where she sits for hours waiting for something to happen. Occasionally it does:

Dans l'après-midi, quelquefois, une tête d'homme apparaissait derrière les vitres de la salle, tête hâlée, à favoris noirs, et qui souriait lentement, d'un large sourire doux à dents blanches. Une valse aussitôt commençait, et, sur l'orgue, dans un petit salon, des danseurs hauts comme le doigt, femmes en turban rose, Tyroliens en jaquette, singes en habit noir, messieurs en culotte courte, tournaient, tournaient entre les fauteuils, les canapés, les consoles, se répétant dans les morceaux de miroir que raccordait à leurs angles un filet de papier doré. . . . [L]a musique de la boîte s'échappait en bourdonnant à travers un rideau de taffetas rose, sous une griffe de cuivre en arabesque. C'étaient des airs que l'on jouait ailleurs, sur les théâtres, que l'on chantait dans les salons, que l'on dansait le soir sous des lustres éclairés, échos du monde qui arrivaient jusqu'à Emma. Des sarabandes à n'en plus finir se déroulaient dans sa tête, et, comme une bayadère sur les fleurs d'un tapis, sa pensée bondissait avec les notes, se balançait de rêve en rêve, de tristesse en tristesse. Quand l'homme avait reçu l'aumône dans sa casquette, il rabattait une vieille couverture de laine bleue, passait son orgue sur son dos et s'éloignait s'un pas lourd. Elle le regardait partir. (p. 61)

Adumbrating the transformational qualities of her mirrors, Emma's window gives onto a scene that illustrates how the marvelous and endoxal worlds are fused in her imagination. Set against a mirrored background, the figures in the organ-grinder's "petit salon" are symbolic of that congeries of *idées reçues* apprehended in Emma's society magazines and childhood books. Moreover, these miniatures move in time to music played in imaginary theaters and drawing rooms, and the melodies she hears become "échos du monde," audible equivalents of the pictures already examined. The configuration of an ironic pattern emerges here, for the images of the "petit salon" parody the content of the Parisian *rêverie* just as that scene parodied the "tableaux du monde" of the convent, and hereafter Flaubert's ironic rendering of Emma's consciousness depends increasingly on the repetition of such images.

Up to this point in the novel, Emma has passively looked on at the imaginary actions unfolding in her mind. In the next phase of her development, soon after she realizes that she is in love with Léon, she projects herself into this world:

Mais plus Emma s'apercevait de son amour, plus elle le refoulait, afin qu'il ne parût pas, et pour le diminuer. Elle aurait voulu que Léon s'en doutât; et elle imaginait des hasards, des catastrophes qui l'eussent facilité. Ce qui la retenait, sans doute, c'était la paresse ou l'épouvante, et la pudeur aussi. Elle songeait qu'elle l'avait repoussé trop loin, qu'il n'était plus temps, que tout était perdu. Puis l'orgueil, la joie de se dire: «Je suis vertueuse», et de se regarder dans la glace en prenant des poses résignées, la consolait un peu du sacrifice qu'elle croyait faire.

(p. 101)

The images and music of the world apprehended in the "petit salon" are replaced by her own image and voice as she stands before her mirror. But though she experiences the "joie de se dire: «Je suis vertueuse»," she is only repeating the statement of some sloe-eyed heroine of her reading. And it is that remembered utterance, in turn, which triggers the mime of "poses résignées" practiced before the mirror. The source of the phrase and gesture is less important than the remarkable change taking place, for in the mirror, that symbol of distorted vision, Emma sees herself in a "tableau du monde." Little wonder that she should feel consoled by what she sees; it is as if she had entered that green world of her youthful reading. As if. The identification with a phantom figure in her reading flickers out quickly, never having quite freed itself from conscious analogy. Not until the advent of Rodolphe will Emma become one of the women she has so longingly gazed at in her imagination.

The fastidious comportment that limited her relationship with Léon to exchanges of cactus plants and definitions from the **Dictionnaire des Idées Reçues** is undermined by Rodolphe at the agricultural fair, finally collapsing before his strange smile and comic-opera clenched teeth. Freeing herself from Charles on the night of her seduction, Emma rushes upstairs to her bedroom:

D'abord, ce fut comme un étourdissement; elle voyait les arbres, les chemins, les fossés, Rodolphe, et elle sentait encore l'étreinte de ses bras, tandis que le feuillage frémissait et que les joncs sifflaient.

Mais, en s'apercevant dans la glace, elle s'étonna de son visage. Jamais elle n'avait eu les yeux si grands, si noirs, ni d'une telle profondeur. Quelque chose de subtil épandu sur sa personne la transfigurait.

Elle se répétait: «J'ai un amant! un amant!» se délectant à cette idée comme à celle d'une autre puberté qui lui serait survenue. Elle allait donc posséder enfin ces joies de l'amour, cette fièvre du bonheur dont elle avait désespéré. Elle entrait dans quelque chose de merveilleux où tout serait passion, extase, délire; une immensité bleuâtre l'entourant les sommets du sentiment étincelaient sous sa pensée, l'existence ordinaire n'apparaissait qu'au loin, tout en bas, dans l'ombre, entre les intervalles de ces hauteurs.

Alors elle se rappela les héroïnes des livres qu'elle avait lus, et la légion lyrique de ces femmes adultères se mit à chanter dans sa mémoire avec des voix de sœurs qui la charmaient. Elle devenait elle-même comme une partie véritable de ces imaginations et réalisait la longue rêverie de sa jeunesse, en se considérant dans ce type d'amoureuse qu'elle avait tant envié. (pp. 151-52)

Personae metamorphose with lightning rapidity in these four brief paragraphs, where a by-now-familiar process is once again at work. Emma sees Rodolphe, feels the pressure of his arms, hears the rustling of the leaves. And then self-absorption reveals the real source of her ecstasy. "Mais," Flaubert writes, "Mais en s'apercevant dans la glace": the simple conjunction signals an act of mind that soon relegates Rodolphe to a linguistic category. From an image he is changed into a word: "amant." As Emma confronts her transfigured image in the mirror, Rodolphe becomes another of the disappearing men, his essence subsumed by Emma's vision of herself. He is more important as a concept than as a person, and "amant," that linguistic talisman of her imagination, easily leads Emma to the endoxal world zoned by its synonyms—"passion, extase, délire." Rising into the fantastic blue space that these words create (an apotheosis is taking place here), the reality of her illusions is confirmed by a choir of "héroines des livres qu'elle avait lus"; and accompanied by "la légion lyrique de ces femmes adultères," Emma moves into the marvelous world of the mirror: "Elle devenait elle-même comme une partie véritable de ces imaginations et réalisait la longue rêverie de sa jeunesse, en se considérant dans ce type d'amoureuse qu'elle avait tant envié." Like Rodolphe, Emma has been changed into a verbal substance, a character in a novel, the fairest of them all.

While Emma's fulfillment is achieved through linguistic manipulation (first, her culture's, whereby emotions are debased to serve the definitions of Romantic Love; second, her own, whereby the eviscerated words are made to correspond to her imaginative life), it is also language that leads to her destruction. Todorov's comments about the function of words in the genre of the fantastic explain precisely what takes place here and in virtually every other scene given over to Emma's dreams of love: "the fantastic has what . . . appears to be a tautological function: it permits the description of a fantastic universe, one that has no reality outside language: *the description and what is described are not of a different nature*" (p. 92; italics mine). The language of the fantastic, I submit, is only a dialect of Romanticism—Emma's mother tongue—and her fate stems from believing that the words she reads, speaks, or thinks describe palpable realities, whereas in fact they are signifiers with no referable matrix for the signified. Such language becomes literally destructive because it sets up an irresolvable opposition between reality and fantasy.[9]

Thus, Emma's narcissism, in which the language of the fantastic is deeply implicated, exacerbates an already difficult situation. Scrambled and fragmentarily articulated as it may be, thought almost always precedes feeling for Emma, and this sequence is central to an examination of her narcissism because she has ideas both about the kinds of emotions appropriate to a given situation (a set of beliefs that amounts to a complicated taxonomy) and about herself experiencing those emotions. Whenever she is in her lover's arms, Emma is most fully aware of herself and what she feels in circumstances recapitulating the data of her reading, but this goes considerably beyond the extrapolation of a personality from the texts of Romantic Love: her erotic life is equally borrowed, equally linked to imagination. If we look back over the course of her involvement with Rodolphe and Léon, it is easy enough to see that the passionate sensations she experiences during her visits to La Huchette or the Hôtel-de-Boulogne are relatively mild compared to her erotic fantasies about what takes place. This is true, not because Flaubert was prohibited from frank sexual description, but rather because Emma simply feels *more* when she imagines erotic sensations. The emphasis Flaubert placed on the autoscopic nature of Emma's sexuality—a sustained and often devastatingly ironic emphasis—can be illustrated by juxtaposing three scenes that enclose the central mirror epiphany.

After settling into Yonville, Emma confronts Léon's coded sensitivities, against which she is defenseless:

Elle était amoureuse de Léon, et elle recherchait la solitude, afin de pouvoir plus à l'aise se délecter en son image. La vue de sa personne troublait la volupté de cette méditation. Emma palpitait au bruit de ses pas: puis, en sa présence, l'émotion tombait, et il ne lui restait ensuite qu'un immense étonnement qui se finissait en tristesse. (p. 100)

Three years later, when she is having an affair with him, she feels compelled to write letters. Although the task seems wearisome at first, something strange begins to happen as she joins word to word:

Mais, en écrivant, elle percevait un autre homme, un fantôme fait de ses plus ardents souvenirs, de ses lectures les plus belles, de ses convoitises les plus fortes; et il devenait à la fin si véritable, et accessible, qu'elle en palpitait émerveillée, sans pouvoir néanmoins le nettement imaginer, tant il se perdait comme un dieu, sous l'abondance de ses attributs. Il habitait la contrée bleuâtre ou les échelles de soie se balancent à des balcons, sous le souffle des fleurs, dans la clarté de la lune. Elle le sentait près d'elle, il allait venir et l'enlèverait tout entière dans un baiser. Ensuite elle retombait à plat, brisée; car ces élans d'amour vague la fatiguaient plus que de grandes débauches. (p. 270)

In addition to presenting variations of the disappearing-man motif, both examples bring forward into

Emma's erotic life the central predilection of her adolescent fantasies. However, more is revealed here than the continuation of an imagery pattern, for two sentences condense the essence of her sexuality:

> La vue de sa personne troublait la volupté de cette méditation.
>
> Ensuite elle retombait à plat, brisée; car ces élans d'amour vague la fatiguaient plus que des grandes débauches.

Given the ultraromantic nature of her character, how can "élans d'amour vague" be more satisfying than the actual pleasures of the boudoir? The answer is there in the pendant noun of the first sentence, "méditation," for narcissism is a *contemplative* affliction that cannot be actualized; the self can only be experienced imaginatively. If, like Emma, one has not been able to make the shift from ego- to object-libido, one's fullest erotic sensations must take place in fantasies, because that is where the inward-turning libido has no competition. The homoerotic aspect of Emma's narcissism becomes clear when we realize that her erotic fantasies are always linked to a female avatar born of her reading.

This process is confirmed at the opera, where she gives herself up to the melodies, costumes, scenery, actors, and "toutes ces imaginations qui s'agitaient dans l'harmonie comme dans l'atmosphère d'un autre monde" (p. 208). These "imaginations" once furnished the images of the "tableaux de monde" of the convent; now they are transformed into a *tableau vivant* on the rickety stage of Rouen's opera house, where Emma begins to see herself in Lucie, who "se plaignait d'amour . . . demandait des ailes." Primed by the words of the libretto, Emma is overwhelmed by Lagardy's appearance and "se penchait pour le voir, égratignant avec ses ongles le velours de sa loge." Unrivaled in the suspension of disbelief, Emma is drawn to Lagardy "par l'illusion du personnage" as she slips once again into the world of Romantic Love:

> Ils se seraient connus, ils se seraient aimés! Avec lui, par tous les royaumes de l'Europe, elle aurait voyagé de capitale en capitale, partageant ses fatigues et son orgueil. . . . Chaque soir, au fond d'une loge, derrière la grille à treillis d'or, elle eût recueilli, béante, les expansions de cette âme qui n'aurait chanté que pour elle seule; de la scène, tout en jouant, il l'aurait regardée. Mais une folie la saisit: il la regardait, c'est sûr! (pp. 210-11)

Emma has created a demanding role for herself as Lucie of Yonville, and after the curtain "elle retomba dans son fauteuil avec des palpitations qui la suffoquaient." These palpitations are the result of experienced sensuality, of passionate emotion; the problem, of course, is that Emma has all along been communing with herself in the image of another woman.

This brings us full circle to Todorov's perception that the fantastic "has no reality outside language," and I think the same can be said about Emma's erotic life. With Rodolphe and Léon she acts out her ideal of herself, but the pleasures available are of herself involved in the pleasures of her reading. In this sense, she reminds one of Roland Barthes, who takes pleasure in a "reported pleasure" by making himself the text's voyeur.[10] But Emma is really a step ahead of Barthes. In page after page of *Madame Bovary,* we see her emotionally engaged in a special kind of voyeurism. Since her imagination has developed in such a way that the women in her texts all become versions of herself, Emma is her own voyeur: the perfect narcissist, meditating on successions of . . . words.

V

Regardless of her efforts, that world of words and mirrors cannot survive in the world of unpaid bills assumed to buy time and the furnishings of dreams. Eroded by a series of collisions with reality, the marvelous, whose perfect expression occurred when Emma realized the "longue rêverie de sa jeunesse," deliquesces during her last visit to Rodolphe's chateau.

Although she takes arsenic to avoid any further confrontations with reality, habits persist even on the deathbed, where Emma gazes at herself one last time:

> En effet, elle regarda tout autour d'elle, lentement, comme quelqu'un qui se réveille d'un songe, puis, d'une voix distincte, elle demanda son miroir, et elle resta penchée dessus quelque temps; jusqu'au moment où de grosses larmes lui découlèrent des yeux. Alors elle se renversa la tête en poussant un soupir et retomba sur l'oreiller. (pp. 301-02)

Suddenly Flaubert's scathing irony is vividly before us in the synecdoche of the dream metaphor. Awakening into life, Emma requests the mirror that gave form to her dream of life only to discover that the magic is gone. Like the Queen's in "Snow White," Emma's mirror now tells the truth, and what she sees at last is herself—not Rodolphe's mistress, not Léon's, not Lagardy's imaginary lover. The avatar of the "amoureuse qu'elle avait tant envié" has vanished, and the face looking back at her is no longer the fairest of them all: it is now her memento mori.

The significance of the mirror motif and the destructive power brought into play by autoscopic vision are reinforced by the projected ending of an early draft of *Madame Bovary*. Wearing the Croix de la Légion d'Honneur, Homais was to have walked up and down in a room full of mirrors, admiring himself. The ensuing crisis, and the probable reason for Flaubert's canceling this ending, bears importantly on Emma's final vision. Here is the text:

> Le jour qu'il (l') reçue n'y voulut pas croire. Mr. X deputé lui avait envoyé un bout de ruban—le met se regarde dans la glace éblouissement.—....
>
> Doute de lui—regarde les bocaux—doute de son existence (délire, effets fantastiques, la croix répétée dans les glaces, pluie foudre de ruban rouge)—"ne suis-je qu'un personnage de roman, le fruit d'une imagination en délire, l'invention d'un petit paltoquot que j'ai vu naître/et qui m'a inventé pour faire croire que je j'existe pas/—Oh cela n'est pas possible, voilà les fœtus, (voilà mes enfants, voilà, voilà)
>
> Puis se résumant, il finit par le grand mot du rationalisme moderne, Cogito, ergo sum.[11]

Christopher Prendergast, rightly calling Homais "the supreme incarnation of the endoxal," takes this scene as an illustration of the existential "néant" (p. 212). While it is easy enough to see how such an ending would have appealed to the pessimist in Flaubert, to have concluded **Madame Bovary** with Homais's crisis and his relatively easy resolution of that crisis would have deflected, even muted, the carefully wrought irony inhering in the mirror motif. It would also have repeated, with much less force, the insight Emma achieves on her deathbed. While her initial response is to the ravaged features reflected in her mirror, the dream metaphor suggests a discovery that goes beyond Homais's brief moment of doubt. Awakening to reality during the last moments of her life, she discovers the nature of the dream she has lived, "le fruit d'une imagination en délire," and the horror of that realization cannot be avoided by uttering a Cartesian dictum whose terms have been responsible for her own misapprehension of the world. Emma is all too aware of the gap between who she is and what she has thought.

That awareness begins with her contemplation of herself in the mirror, and it is completed when she hears the beggar's voice beyond her window as he stridently sings of love and seduction:

> —L'aveugle! s'écria-t-elle.
>
> Et Emma se mit á rire, d'un rire atroce, frénétique, désespéré, croyant voir la face hideuse du misérable, qui se dressait dans les ténèbres éternelles comme un épouvantement. (p. 302)

At the peak of her imaginative powers, what Emma perceived in her mind's eye and in her mirrors were "tableaux du monde" that graphed a culture's myths. As her life flickers out, these pictures are replaced by her own death mask and the image of the beggar's "face hideuse" looming out of the eternal darkness. Emma is demystified, and while the world of the mirror paradoxically brought her to the threshold of reality, death spares her the agony of living with her newly acquired knowledge.

Notes

[1] Gustave Flaubert, *Madame Bovary* (Paris: Garnier, 1961), p. 78: hereafter cited in the text by page number only.

[2] Tzvetan Todorov, *The Fantastic: A Structural Approach to a Literary Genre,* trans. Richard Howard (Cleveland: Press of Case Western Reserve Univ., 1973), p. 121.

[3] I am endebted to Christopher Prendergast's fine study of *idées reçues* in "Flaubert: Writing and Negativity," *Novel,* 8 (1975), 197-213. Prendergast offers an elaborate definition of *endoxon* as it applies to *Madame Bovary*: "The consensus of received opinion which a given society assumes and offers as Reality ... is what Aristotle called *endoxon* ('current opinion') and, following Aristotle, we may perhaps call the discourse which repeats and reinforces consensus knowledge the endoxal discourse, the language of common-sense, the language of the stereotype, whose function is to cover a world historically produced with the mantle of the universal and the permanent and of which the classic forms are the maxim, the proverb, the platitude, the *idée reçue*" (p. 207).

[4] Roland Barthes, *S/Z: An Essay,* trans. Richard Miller (New York: Hill and Wang, 1974), p. 21.

[5] Erich Auerbach, *Mimesis: The Representation of Reality in Western Literature,* trans. Willard Trask (New York: Doubleday, 1953), p. 426.

[6] John C. Lapp explores this congruence in "Art and Hallucination in Flaubert," *French Studies,* 10 (1956), 322-44.

[7] Gustave Flaubert, *Correspondance. Supplément,* ed. R. Dumesnil, J. Pommier, and C. Digeon (Paris, Conard, 1954), II, 94-95.

[8] Robert Rogers, in *A Psychoanalytic Study of the Double in Literature* (Detroit: Wayne State Univ. Press, 1970), makes a similar observation about Narcissus' self-love (p. 20). He also defines narcissism in a way I have found useful: "Narcissism is a kind of love, but it is misleading to translate the concept into what is known commonly as 'self-love.' Self-love in the everyday sense of 'egotism' is a metaphorical expression. In narcissism the self-love is literal. The only difference between this kind of love and the erotic love of another person is in the object. Narcissism

paradoxically involves a relationship, a relationship of self to self in which one's self is regarded as though it were another person" (p. 18). In addition, *Romanticism and Consciousness*, ed. Harold Bloom (New York: Norton, 1970), contains several outstanding essays that touch on the relationship between narcissism and Romanticism. Bloom's "The Internalization of Quest-Romance" (pp. 3-24) is especially good on the Freudian view of this subject. See also J. H. Van den Berg's "The Subject and His Landscape" (pp. 57-65) and Paul de Man's "Intentional Structure of the Romantic Image" (pp. 65-77).

[9] This is true not only for Emma and her prototype. Don Quixote, but also for Conrad's Lord Jim, Ford's Edward Ashburnham, Fitzgerald's Jay Gatsby. Each character's death is closely linked to this aspect of the language of Romanticism. For more on this connection, see my "Ford Madox Ford and *The Great Gatsby*" in *Fitzgerald/Hemingway Annual 1975*, ed. Matthew J. Bruccoli (Englewood, N.J.: Microcard Editions Books, 1975), pp. 57-74, and "Escaping the Impasse: Criticism and the Mitosis of *The Good Soldier*," *Modern Fiction Studies*, 21 (Summer 1975), 237-41.

[10] Roland Barthes, *The Pleasure of the Text*, trans. Richard Miller (New York: Hill and Wang, 1975), p. 17. Here is the relevant *prose:* "How can we take pleasure in a *reported* pleasure (boredom of all narratives of dreams, of parties)? How can we read criticism? Only one way: since I am here a second-degree reader, I must shift my position: instead of agreeing to be the confidant of this critical pleasure—a sure way to miss it—I can make myself its voyeur: I observe clandestinely the pleasure of others, I enter perversion: the commentary then becomes in my eyes a text, a fiction, a fissured envelope. The writer's perversity (his pleasure in writing is *without function*), the doubled, the trebled, the infinite perversity of the critic and of his reader."

[11] Jean Pommier and Gabrielle Leleu, Madame Bovary, *nouvelle version* (Paris: Corti, 1949), p. 129. Quoted in Prendergast.

Tony Tanner (essay date 1979)

SOURCE: "Flaubert's *Madame Bovary*," in *Adultery in the Novel: Contract and Transgression*, The Johns Hopkins University Press, 1979, pp. 233-367.

[*In the following excerpt, Tanner links Emma Bovary's vague but persistent mental unease and unhappiness with her male-defined and largely superfluous role in society. He then examines "why Emma's story should start with Charles Bovary's somewhat inauspicious entry into a schoolroom" and connects this scene with the larger theme of language and meaning in the novel.*]

Emma Bovary and Abbey Bournisien.

The Fog in Emma Bovary's Head

"Ah yes!" returned Félicité. "You're like old Guérin's daughter, the fisherman at Le Pollet, that I knew at Dieppe before I came to you. She was that wretched, you'd think to see her standing in the doorway there was a funeral pall hung up over the door. It seems she'd got a soft of fog in her head, the doctors couldn't do a thing with her, and no more could the *curé*. When she got it real bad she'd go off by herself long the beach, and the coastguard often used to find her there on his rounds. Stretched flat out on the shingle she'd be, crying her eyes out. . . . They say it went when she got married, though."

"But with me," replied Emma, "it didn't come on till I was married."[1]

(p. 122)

—Ah! oui, reprenait Félicité, vous êtes justement comme la Guérine, la fille au père Guérin, le pêcheur du Pollet, que j'ai connue á Dieppe, avant de venir chez vous. Elle était si triste, si triste, qu'à la voir debout sur le seuil de sa maison, elle vous faisait l'effet d'un drap d'enterrement tendu devant la porte. Son mal, à ce qu'il paraît, était une manière de brouillard qu'elle avait dans la tête, et les médecins n'y pouvaient rien, ni le curé non plus. Quand ça la prenait trop fort, elle s'en allait toute seule sur le bord de la mer, si bien que le lieutenant de la douane, en faisant sa tournée, souvent la trouvait étendue à plat ventre et pleurant sur les galets. Puis, après son mariage, ça lui a passé, dit-on.

—Mais, moi, reprenait Emma, c'est après le mariage que ça m'est venu.

(P. 154)

The "sort of fog" in the head of Guérin's daughter is imprecise, indefinable, unamenable to the diagnoses and the remedies of the constituted secular and sacred authorities who can supposedly analyze and aid the maladies of body and spirit. It is not something indistinct that can be brought into focus with superior modes of definition—it is *indistinctness* itself as a presence in the head. The effects of this malady of oppressive interior indistinctness are notable. Standing in the doorway, she gives the impression of having been transformed into a funeral pall, into cloth ("drap") that wraps up the dead body, so this fog can cause an apparent loss of substance, a deformation or translation of flesh into material. As a response to these attacks, she would make her way alone to the edge of the sea, fall prostrate, and weep. This instinctive withdrawal from society to the point where the land dissolves into the sea, accompanied by the abandonment of the upright or vertical posture of the body and the internal dissolving intimated by weeping, is an act of obvious archetypal significance, a symbolic gesture of thalassic regression, and of devolutionary collapse, that indicates that life within the city, governed by the rules of the fathers (note that this girl is not named, she is "la fille au père Guérin"), has become insupportable, unlivable. Then the indistinctness in the head prompts the body toward the undifferentiation of the sea, as though it offered the only possible "cure": the name of the father contains the pun *guérir,* to "cure"—and this touches on the whole problem of sickness and cure, which recurs in many contexts and is central to the book. Who is to decide what is to be classified as sickness, and who is to dictate what shall constitute a cure? In this little vignette it is quite clear. For when the unnamed girl seeks some kind of cure for her unnamable illness in a solitary movement toward the sea, she is found by *le lieutenant de la douane*—coastguard, or literally lieutenant of customs—who is making his rounds ("faisant sa tournée"). It is almost as if it is his presence on the beach that prevented her total abandonment to the sea, and the fact that the guardian of the customs (to rephrase his title only slightly) is always "making his rounds" suggests that it is precisely this motion, his constant "circulation" as it were, that both prevents the girl's self-annihilatory escape (he is effectively *between* her and the sea) and helps to facilitate her restoration to society where the "cure" is completed by her "marriage." Thus, in brief, her life is determined and defined by three males—her father, the lieutenant, and the husband. Between being daughter and wife she (simply "elle") suffers from the fog of interior indistinctness. Her sickness must be connected to the vagueness of her position in society: after being a daughter (and thus entirely defined by the father—she was "la Guérine"), she exists on the threshold ("sur le seuil") in a sort of pronominal limbo. And indeed what will she become when she crosses the threshold of her father's house? All the problems of liminality, both those connected with crossing thresholds in the stages of the individual chronological life and those involving literal and lateral movement from edifice to edifice within the governing architecture of society, are adumbrated in the girl's sad hovering on the threshold of her father's house, at which point ontologically she seems more like cloth than flesh. She is there, but what is she? Hence the fog in the head. And the flight to the beach. And the repudiation of human identity that is implicit in that most primitive of gestures, the negation of the upright position by an act of self-prostration. But the customs man finds her and . . . after her marriage the fog went away. She has been renamed, redefined, absorbed back into society. For if there is one thing that the guardians of society—including "le pére," "les médecins," "le curé," and "le lieutenant de la douane"—seek either to check or to dispel, it is that nameless fog of indistinctness that threatens the whole edifice of consciousness of the individual and by implication the architecture of society itself. For one of the governing impulses in any society is, and must be, a terror of indistinctness. At its most extreme this can manifest itself as suppression of all deviation and diversity. But even in societies that may tolerate a very high degree of variety, something of that dread must still be there. "La Guérine" is thus cured by marriage. Her life story, as compressed in this one apparently casual paragraph, recapitulates a comparatively orthodox process of socialization and initiation, and her temporary sickness is the understandable result of the temporary nonidentity of adolescence. The fog in the head then can be seen as a by-product of that ontological lacuna in her life when she can no longer identify herself with her father but has not yet been initiated into a new identity as a wife. It is indeed a critical period of great sadness and may even produce suicidal moods. But, as we may say, she was rescued by "custom." This is indeed a conventional pattern of life in bourgeois or petit-bourgeois terms.

But what, then, of Emma, for whom marriage was not the cure but, much more worryingly, apparently part of the cause of that "manière de brouillard qu'elle avait dans la tête"? In trying to sense the connections between marriage and the fog in the head in the life of Emma Bovary I think we can begin to discover what Flaubert was doing in what is, after all, the most important and far-reaching novel of adultery in Western literature. Rather than trying to approach the problem of Emma Bovary directly, I want first to consider select aspects of the various men who in one way of another make up the male context within which she must articulate her life, or have it shaped and defined for her. . . .

Charles Bovary Goes to School, Drops His Cap, and Tries to Say His Name

Why Emma's story should start with Charles Bovary's somewhat inauspicious entry into a schoolroom is a matter that prompts some careful consideration. We should note, first of all, that the title of the book, **Madame Bovary,** does not refer unequivocally to Emma, since there are three Madame Bovarys[2] in the book and two of them, Charles's mother and his first wife, are encountered in the first chapter. Emma is, initially, Emma Rouault, and one of the matters the first chapter concentrates on is the origin, or more accurately the transmission, of a name. Whatever else he is, Charles is the bearer of the name of Bovary; it is not the least of the burdens that he has to carry. (The name itself, of course, suggests bovine qualities, indeed it could be said to contain both something of the bullock and the cow since *bouveau* is "bullock" and *bouverie* is "cowshed." The name can also be almost heard as Beau-voir-y, a latent cunning irony given the marked absence of both beautiful views and perceptive vision in the book—and it can hardly be a textual coincidence that the Bovarys stay at a hotel in "la place Beauvoisine" (French—p. 290) on their visit to Rouen to go to the theatre—an excursion that proves to be the final undoing of Emma. It is not an idle exercise to point out the presence of such latent puns and homonyms, as I hope to show in a later section.) But the first thing he is described as carrying is a large desk ("un grand pupitre" [p. 21]), and it is to his initial appearance in the book, which is also his initial (and initiatory) appearance in the school, that I want to turn.

The first word of the novel is *nous,* a nonspecific "we" that is dropped after the first chapter. It would be possible to make endless speculations about the implications of this, but whatever else we (as readers) understand by the *we* we read, the first scene reveals that *we* comprises the staring, mocking, speaking, aggressive communality into which "le nouveau" is introduced. Charles is of course not named in the opening paragraph but is "a new boy dressed in 'civies'" (p. 15) "un *nouveau* habillé en bourgeois" [p. 21]). The word *nouveau* is italicized every time it occurs in the opening paragraphs, and while it of course implies "the new boy," it also has more unrestricted connotations meaning simply—the new. It is an adjective used as a noun, suggesting that this new presence is as yet only a quality and not an entity. That is to say that we (not "they," since we as readers, in possession of the language, are also implicated) are watching the introduction into the schoolroom of some unnamed "newness," a presence, an object, a phenomenon, that can be classified by its clothes, but as yet has no social identity. The schoolroom will do very well for a paradigm of society, since it is there that we study ("Nous étions à l'étude" [p. 21]) the texts and discourses that will constitute us (no matter how imperfectly) in later life. The Headmaster ("le Proviseur") who leads this *nouveau* into the classroom incorporates the male authority that sanctions the imposition of the particular forms of study and work ("l'étude" and "travail") of society. So, that entering "newness" is already encumbered with a desk, the epitomous object of the socializing and enculturating process. It is the first of many ambiguous containers and containing objects that we will encounter in the book. Carrying one's own desk is the ultimate secular inversion of Christ carrying his own cross. What we are watching is the painful insertion of "*le nouveau*" into "nous"; or, to put it another way, the incorporation or absorption of "*le nouveau*" by the "nous." This involves the placing of "*le nouveau*" in the "ranks," or rows and lines, by which a school operates (the master has to direct him toward the others, toward us—"le maître d'études fut obligé de l'avertir, pour qu'il si mît avec nous dans les rangs" [p. 22]). It is a difficult and harsh moment of transition, and as I shall suggest, it would seem to be intimately involved with the general trauma of entering language itself and the more specific trauma of nomination, which that process necessarily involves.

But before considering that part of the process, we must consider that famous cap that is given to us in such legible detail before we hear the name of the bearer of the cap. In a book in which we will everywhere encounter the primacy of clothes and garments of all kinds—particularly hats and shoes—over the wearers, it is entirely appropriate that we should be given a detailed account of how *le nouveau* was "habillé" before we learn how he has been named. But the cap has a special priority over any other garment in the book in the length and detail of its description, and this in itself is an exhortation to consider it very carefully. Certain features of the cap are very well known—for instance, that it contains elements of a fur hat, a lancer's cap, a bowler hat, an otterskin cap, and a night cap; this in itself suggests a deterioration in social roles, from the military and the hunting hat, down through the business hat, ending in the night cap, and there is no doubt that such degenerative hints are intended. But I want to look at the cap once again in its entirety. And the first thing that becomes apparent is that it is impossible to visualize this cap. It is *lisible* but not *visible*. It is as if, from the start, Flaubert is demonstrating that there can be written verbal constructs that the other senses cannot translate: language can create impossible objects that can be read and deciphered, but not seen and experienced. This potentially dangerous and disproportionate power of language over the senses is, in fact, a key part of Emma's dilemma. The cap itself is an assemblage of decontextualized quotations; a combination, or rather a weird tressage, of anomalous and incongruous fragments from other areas of experience; a cluster of signs taken from other fields of reference. The transposition of elements from the wild-animal kingdom and from the military ethos and business ethos to a schoolboy's cap is one obvious example of this, as though nature and history were dwindling into a random assortment of sartorial echoes. But there is even more going on in that "composite" cap ("une de ces coiffures d'ordre composite" [p. 22]), as begins to emerge when you try to figure out—literally—what is being described in the second long sentence dedicated to it. It requires quoting in full. "An oval splayed out with whale-bone, it started off with three pompons; these were followed by lozenges of velvet and rabbit's fur alternately, separated by a red band, and after that came a kind of bag ending in a polygon of cardboard with intricate braiding on it; and from this there hung down like a tassel, at the end of a long, too slender cord, a little sheaf of gold threads" (p. 16). ("Ovoïde et renflée de baleines, elle commençait par trois boudins circulairs; puis s'alternaient, séparés par une bande rouge, des losanges de velours et de poils de lapin; venait ensuite une façon de sac que se terminait par un polygone cartonné, couvert d'une broderie en soutache compliquée, et d'où pendait, au bout d'un long cordon trop mince, un petit croisillon de fil d'or, en manière de gland" [p. 22].) Brought together here in a very strange way—the cap is a nexus of incongruities!—are words of shape (oval, circular, lozenge, polygon, etc.) with words connected with construction (*renflée* implies "swollen" or "stretched out": *boudins* is a particularly difficult word in this context, since it can mean "torus," "flange," "spiral," as well as "pudding"; *croisillon* refers to a "crosspiece" or "brace," etc.). These fairly firm, even rigid words of shape and construction are mixed in with words referring to all kinds of soft material (velvet, cardboard, even gold, which is a very soft metal), just as we have the firm bones of the largest animal in nature (*baleines*—"whale bone") conjoined in the same artefact with the soft fur of one of the reputedly most timid, the rabbit ("de poils de lapin"). The cap is a mélange of processed nature and produced material, of architecture and embroidery, and the most disparate shapes, qualities, and material converge in it. And there is one more aspect to the cap that is hard to define and isolate, since it shimmers evasively somewhere within the unfolding of this whole mélangerie, but it seems to me undeniably to be there. I can perhaps approach it indirectly by pointing out that the word *sac* is also used for the amniotic sac; the word *cordon* is also used for the umbilical cord; and the word *gland*, while undoubtedly meaning "tassel," as the standard translations indicate, is also used in anatomy to refer to the glans and is even now used colloquially to refer to the testicles (hardly surprising, since it also means acorn). What the cap seems to contain among all the other things mentioned is a fragmented recapitulation of the period in the womb and the birth process. These fragments, or echoes, are mixed in with the fragmentary references to animals existing at a much earlier evolutionary stage than man (whales, otters) and an animal renowned for its timidity and fecundity alike (the rabbit); with references to earlier professions and roles; and references to various shapes, containers, materials. Thus the cap is a tissue of ontogenetic, philogenetic, and epigenetic hints. It is exactly a composite object "ou l'on retrouve les éléments," not where you can *find* the elements or basic constituents, but where you can find them *again*—displaced from their original context, which range widely through time and space, and reappearing in vestigial bits in a particular garment, an irrational collation of shapes, textures and materials, a "casquette" that seems to carry within it barely distinguishable memories of immemorial realms and times but that now serves to contain the head of a schoolboy. The putting on of the cap thus represents a kind of second "birth" into a confusion of signs. If we accept that traditional initiation tends to fall into the three stages of baptism, chrism, and communion (confirmation), we can recognize that in this grotesque parody of initiation into the prevailing culture, the cap plays the chrismal role—when it is placed on the head, *le nouveau* is annointed with incoherence.

We have then these *two* objects at the start of the book: *Le nouveau*, unnamed, silent, frightened, volitionless, a piece of manipulable flesh—not yet defined, identified, human; and *le casquette*, a manufactured object that is an assemblage of displacements, not only from nature into clothing, but from thing to sign. Indeed it is only because everything has been transformed to the status of sign that the cap can be "written" at all. In the cap the whalebone has lost its whaleness, just as the hint of lancer's cap brings with it no martial echoes. Everything meets and merges at the level of *costume*. Whatever else the cap means, it bespeaks the homogenization of initially utterly disparate elements, and this is possible because these elements have been treated as disposable and displaceable signs. All cultures necessarily employ this process in some way or another, even if only by turning animals into food and skins into clothing, etc. The point about this cap, with the absurd miscellaneousness and unvisualizable overabundance of its signs, is that it operates here as the representative object of the kind of bourgeois culture Flaubert was writing about. This is the object that is put over the head of *le nouveau*; it sums up the enculturation process by which *le nouveau* is initiated into and prepared for the established society. Such an object, and all that it implies, instead of making for a clarification and enrichment of consciousness, works to produce its confusion and obfuscation. How it does this is one of the issues that the book explores.

The fact that "nous," the boys already established within the school, like to throw their caps under their seats and against the wall—to leave their hands freer—may indicate some initial disinclination to rest easy under the allotted headgear of their society. *Le nouveau* is certainly uncertain in his relationship with his cap, and his hold on it is of the most tenuous, as is made clear when the master tells them all to stand up and "he" stands up, letting his cap fall to the ground. ("Il se leva; sa casquette tomba" [p. 22].) When he tries to pick it up, his neighbor knocks it to the floor again with a blow of the elbow ("un coup de coude" [p. 22]—I will return to these words later on) and "he" is still fumbling for it when the master makes his pedantic joke—"Débarrassez-vous de votre casque" ("Disburden yourself of your helmet" in the Penguin translation, p. 16). Inasmuch as how and whether a person in that society can disburden him or herself of the helmet or hood that society has clamped over him or her becomes a basic concern of the book, the "joke" sends prophetic echoes through the following text. But at this point it serves as a prelude to the ordeal of nomination, or the traumatic entry into language, that *le nouveau* now has to undergo. Significantly, he does not know what to do with his cap—hold it, put it on his head, or put it on the ground. He leaves it lying on his knees, as yet having established no relationship with it. As long as *le nouveau* remains *le nouveau*, he will never comprehend what to do with the cap. For the essence of the cap is precisely to eliminate the *nouveauté* of *le nouveau* and turn it into part of the existing "nous." He will know what to do with his cap once he has entered the given circuit of discourse, which is why he first has to say his name in front of all the others, in front of "us." And in the ensuing description Flaubert compresses the painful stages by which *le nouveau* enters into *la condition linguistique*. It must be quoted in full.

"Stand up and tell me your name."

The boy stammered out some unintelligible noise.

"Again!"

The same halting syllables, smothered by hoots from the class.

"Louder! Louder!"

This time the new boy plucked up his courage, opened his mouth to an enormous width, brought out at the top of his voice, as if he were hailing someone, the word *Charbovari*.

(Pp. 116-17)

—Levez-vous, reprit le professeur, et dites moi votre nom.

Le *nouveau* articula, d'une voix bredouillante, un nom inintelligible.

—Répétez!

Le même bredouillement de syllabes se fit entendre, couvert par les huées de la classe.

—Plus haut! cria le maître, plus haut!

Le *nouveau*, prenant alors une résolution extrême, ouvrit une bouche démesurée et lança à pleins poumons, comme pour appeler quelqu'un, ce mot: *Charbovari*.

(p. 23)

The master's summons, a summons to verticality, to speech, to self-nomination, is a précis of the imperatives and exhortations by which the child, or *le nouveau*, is initiated into its social-linguistic identity.[3] And the three attempts to comply that *le nouveau* makes also offer a foreshortened paradigmatic enactment of the difficulties involved in this entry into language. At first he "articulates" in a mumbling voice an unintelligible name—"nom inintelligible." The choice of words is particularly interesting for *articuler* means "clear utterance," and what is uttered is indeed a "nom." But it is unintelligible to the listeners because of the mumbling voice, "voix bredouillante." It is as though *le nouveau* can talk perfectly clearly to himself but has not mastered the ability to participate in audible discourse. The voice dissolves into a mumble or stammer. This kind of failure or disintegration of speech implied in words like *bredouiller* and *balbutier* ("Stammer") occurs frequently throughout the book, and among other things we may detect in it some trace of the traumatic period spent on the threshold of speech (in it yet not in it, mastered by it yet not master of it) such as is here being described. It is a graphic reminder of how precarious our position is in language. The second attempt to obey the master's imperative results in a significant shift in the description even though it would seem to be a repetition of the same noise. This time there is no "voix" but a "bredouillement de syllabes" that makes itself heard. The initiative seems to have passed from *le nouveau* (who in the first attempt was said to articulate) to a kind of inchoate speech-noise, or rather to something between the two. That is to say, it is not a voice saying a name, nor is it a totally nonsematic cry or jabber, but rather a kind of trembling of syllables ("syllabes"), a painful midway point between the private lalling of a young child and the full speech act, a point at which—following the implications of this description—the would-be speaker is not the controlling agent but rather the locus or venue where sounds and syllables foregather preparatory to transforming that venue into a public voice. At this point *le nouveau* is indeed more spoken, or rather half-spoken, than speaking. The pain involved in this period of transition is dramatized by the response of the listeners ("nous"), for those pathetic mumbling syllables trying to make themselves heard are covered or smothered by the hoots of the class ("couvert par les huées de la classe"). *Huées* ("hooting," "jeering," "booing," etc.), is a nonsemantic noise, but this time indicative, not of the helpless state of the infant (which means literally "without speech"), but of the aggression of "la classe"—or, we may say, society in its mob form, the mocking destructive roar of the deindividualized and thus dehumanized group. The fact that society both imposes the imperative to enter into language (the orders of the master) and can also, as it were, turn on language and negate it, nihilating individual articulation in a smothering communal noise, is a paradox that Flaubert puts before us at the very beginning of his book. We may refer then to the latent double humiliation in language—the painful ordeal of having to speak, and the continual risk of having your speech mockingly denied and erased by the surrounding others ("nous," "la classe," etc.).

The third attempt to obey the master ("Louder! Louder!") results in an almost orgasmic effort on the part of *le nouveau,* and the result this time is not a "*nom* intelligible" nor a "bredouillement de *syllabes*" but a *"mot"*. It is, to be sure, a rather strange word, and I will come to that. But here again let us note just how Flaubert describes this climactic moment when *le nouveau* finally speaks an audible word. First of all it takes extreme determination, as though the whole being had to concentrate and come together to focus on this one act. Then the description of the opening of a mouth "démesurée" seems to anticipate many of the problems encountered later in the book. For while the word means simply "huge," it does also mean "beyond measure" or "unmeasured." A mouth beyond measure is a very suggestive paradox. Physically it is an impossibility; however big the mouth, it could still be "measured." But when the mouth is seen as the part of the body particularly involved with speech, then the word becomes very suggestive. Here we should note this: although the open mouth is a constant motif in the book (Charles dies with his mouth open) and is of course intimately connected with the whole problem of the satisfying of appetites and the vast amount of simple eating in the course of the narrative, it is in connection with the effort involved in *speaking* (i.e., not eating) that the mouth becomes an organ "beyond measure"—the unmeasurable dimension of the mouth is not primarily its hunger but its participation in language. That this unmeasurability might readily affect all the other appetites is of course a crucial aspect of the whole book. In a society where the dominant people live by *measure* of all kinds (number, law, finance—boxing, bottling, labeling—the world epitomized by Homais and his shop), the problems of "une bouche démesurée" may become acute, even unbearable. This will not be the case with *le nouveau,* but rather with the girl who takes on his name. Two other aspects of the description should be noted. First of all, there is something sexual about it: the full lungs (and Flaubert makes us vividly aware of differences in breathing, or what Dickens calls "the office of respiration," and its effects, throughout), then the release and the "throwing," or hurling, of the word, do suggest (through displacement or isomorphism, or something of both) that the final discharge of the whole being in a thrown word is in some way connected to the release in orgasm. The other point concerns the simile that Flaubert inserts—"comme pour appeler quelqu'un" (as if calling someone). Needless to say, there are no idle similes in this book, but this one brings more into the text than one might think at first glance. For in speaking, one is inevitably involved in "calling" someone. Here the multiple meanings involved in *appeler* are crucial, since it can refer both to calling out (hailing) and to naming and giving a term to. Once we are in language, we are forever "calling someone," calling for someone to help us, to love us, to answer us, and forever naming and labeling. It is as though in learning to speak, we first become fully aware of our own severance and state of separateness, so Flaubert carefully makes the first utterance of the word (in terms of this book) coeval with the need or compulsion to "call someone." And indeed in many ways they are one and the same act, since in speech there is always involved some element of a desire for connection, a reaching out, an attempt to join. And since the words we speak come from those around us, we are necessarily calling them in using their words. Once you move beyond unintelligibility and syllabic indeterminacy and gain the word, you are doomed forever to be calling someone. No one learns this lesson more thoroughly and painfully than Emma Bovary.

Notes

[1] Unless otherwise indicated, French and English quotations from Flaubert's novel within this chapter are from Gustave Flaubert, *Madame Bovary* (Paris: Gallimard, 1972), and Flaubert, *Madame Bovary,* trans. Alan Russell (Harmondsworth, Middlesex: Penguin, 1950).

[2] The phenomenon of "trebling" or "triplication," is deeply rooted in narrative and has been identified by Vladimir Propp in his classic work, *The Morphology of the Folk Tale* (ed. Louis A. Wagner, trans. Lawrence Salt, 2d ed., rev. [Austin and London: University of Texas Press, 1968], p. 74). It is a recurrent phenomenon in the book. There are three Madame Bovarys, there are three primary men (i.e., sexual partners) in Emma's life (as there are three men in the life of "la Guérine"): when Rodolphe starts his seduction of Emma at the Agricultural Show, he draws up three, not two, stools; she is buried in three coffins; at her funeral there are three choristers, three batons, and her father

sees three black hens and promises three chasubles to the church; and the book itself is in three parts. The phenomenon of triplication is, in this novel, related to the phenomenon of duplication, as I will suggest in another context.

[3] It could be said that in this scene Charles Bovary is being forcibly recruited into the dominant ideology of his class. Cf. Louis Althusser: "I shall then suggest that ideology 'acts' or 'functions' in such a way that it 'recruits' subjects among the individuals (it recruits them all), or 'transforms' the individuals into subjects (it transforms them all) by that very precise operation which I have called *interpellation* or hailing, and which can be imagined along the lines of the most commonplace everyday police (or other) hailing: 'Hey, you there!'" For that parenthetic "other" in this case read "school-teacher." See Althusser's whole essay on "Ideology and Ideological State Apparatuses" in *Lenin and Philosophy and Other Essays* (trans. Ben Brewster [New York: Monthly Review Press, 1972]).

Diana Festa-McCormick (essay date 1980)

SOURCE: "Emma Bovary's Masculinization: Convention of Clothes and Morality of Conventions," in *Gender and Literary Voice*, edited by Janet Todd, Holmes & Meier Publishers, Inc., 1980, pp. 223-35.

[*In the following essay, Festa-McCormick examines how the motif of clothing illustrates Emma Bovary's conflicted experience of her feminine gender role. She notes that "the encroachment of masculinity on [Emma's] personality stands as a betrayal of her social role, progressively mirrored in the masculinization of her attire."*]

Emma Bovary has long been a favorite character for critics of fiction, analyzed from all angles, praised and vilified in turn, held as a type or treated as an individual, as a free spirit or a product of circumstances, the essence of femininity or the portrait of a man within a woman. We shall study here the problematic aspect of her womanhood in order to show how the encroachment of masculinity on her personality stands as a betrayal of her social role, progressively mirrored in the masculinization of her attire. The corruption of the teachings she has received assumes visible and recognizable manifestations: in the very process of betraying her assigned functions as a spouse and mother, she allows maculinity to intrude upon her appearance. This essay will deal not so much with Emma's feminity "per se," as with her obedience to, or discord with, her role as a woman illustrated through her clothing.

When she is first introduced at the Bertaux's farm, Emma presents a domestic image, quite in keeping with accepted notions of a nubile young woman tending her father's home. "A young woman wearing a dress of blue merino adorned with three flounces welcomed Monsieur Bovary at the front door, and showed him into the kitchen where a huge fire was blazing."[1] Critics have pointed out that the first part of the novel is a projection of Charles's visual perception.[2] Emma's introduction, therefore, is to be considered as a mirror of her future husband's eye. It is of interest then to notice that Charles's initial impression is dictated not by the girl's striking beauty but by what she is wearing—not by her unusually large eyes, raven hair or tumescent lower lip, but by the color of her dress and its three ruffles.

Beyond Emma's portrait of delicate femininity and coquettishness thus presented, stands a background of domestic warmth: a kitchen with a blazing fire. The stage is clearly set to convey an image in keeping with general expectations where the presence of a maiden is concerned. Emma appears like the embodiment of filial duties, foreshadowing, one is tempted to assume, those of spouse and mother in days to come. The dress is a symbol of the femininity she has perhaps culled in dreams and shaped within the demands of her society. That femininity is both her function and her prerogative, the immaterial evidence of harmony between a chosen path and assigned roles.

The remaining part of the paragraph introducing Emma at the Bertaux establishes the social condition to which she belongs—one that affords her a measure of distinction in a world rooted in work and in pride of possession. "Breakfast for the farm-hands stood bubbling in little pots of different sizes. Wet clothes hung drying within the great chimney-place. The shovel, the tongs, and the nozzle of the bellows, all of gigantic proportions, shone like polished steel, and along the walls were ranged a rich variety of kitchen utensils" (15).[3] Emma is the mistress in that well-to-do-farm house: order reigns over the scene, and the shining utensils point to the striking cleanliness of the place. The impression received is that Emma herself has prepared the meal for the farm hands, or at least has been responsible for it, as well as for the spotless decor. That this impression is somewhat called into question when, needing to make bandages for her father's broken leg. "She took a long time, however, to find her needle case" is of little consequence. Her individual weaknesses have hardly any bearing upon her image as a woman and her own private understanding of it—for she has not yet betrayed the premises upon which it stands.

More important is a detail added to Emma's clothing, as if haphazardly, and noticed only a little later: "A pair of shell-rimmed glasses was stuck, masculine fashion between the buttons of her bodice" (17). The deliberate use of the adjective "masculine" here plays a false note in the otherwise well orchestrated feminine details, and points to the latent potential for violation of the feminine quintessence in Emma. The glasses are a warning through which we may later recognize a pattern of deterioration reflected in Emma's raiment and general attire.

The picture of a girl acting in accord with the postulates of her condition is developed in the pages that follow. Emma's "blushing furiously" when her back brushes inadvertently against Charles's arm, is consonant with the "tiny clogs" she wears, or the high heels the spell-bound suitor admires (18). Charles's jealous wife may well resent the fact that Emma looks "like a countess in a silken gown" (19), but it would be preposterous for her to see anything offensive—or masculine—in it.

If Emma's clothing can be used as a code for her adherence to prescribed behavior, it follows that the height of her feminine apparel should coincide with the crowning of her womanhood on her wedding day. "Emma's dress was too long and it touched a little on the ground; now and then she stopped to raise it, and then delicately, with her gloved fingers, she picked off the wild grasses and thistles, while Charles, empty handed, waited for her to finish" (29). The dress falling to the ground seems designed to hide her small shoes, thus removing from view what from the onset was presented as a source of sensuous appeal. White and pure, the bride's overly long gown emphasizes the steps that have led, from provocative postures and the frivolity of ruffles and high heels, to the solemn moment of a woman swearing life-long allegiance to a man. That man, significantly "empty handed" when Emma's arm is removed from his, holds his rightful place by her side.

A period of moderate well-being follows, in which clothing and gestures illustrate at least the simulation of fulfillment. The quiet intimacy of the couple, with their evening meals across from each other, or the walks along the dusky road, finds confirmation in the gentle shadow of Emma's "scalloped night-cap," as she sleeps under her husband's mesmerized gaze. The young bride's fluttering activities in reshaping the order of her new home are corroborated in the soft roundness of her straw hat hanging by the window; as Charles leaves for work in the morning, she steals to the window "wrapped in a dressing gown that fell loosely about her," still evocative of her bridal dress (34-35). The first signs of restlessness in the face of continued monotony assume for Emma the shape of clothing in deep hues and alluring contours. She dreams of faraway places reached by post-chaise with blue silk curtains, next to a husband—alas, so little resembling the Charles at her side—"dressed in black, long-skirted velvet coat, soft leather boots, a pointed hat, and ruffles at his wrist" (41-43). This effeminate, or at least dandyfied, image of a nonexistent husband, could be seen to point, by contrast, to Emma's embryonic "masculinization." The "long skirted coat" she envisions, anticipates the Vicomte's tight waistcoast at La Vaubyessard, the graceful figures floating by on the dance floor, and Emma's first languorous dizziness, during the waltz, in the arms of a man.[4]

The pattern that began with precious little feet sheathed in high-heel clogs and a frilled skirt with light ruffles, and that had led to the exaggerated discreetness of Emma's wedding gown, is repeated during the intervening months, but in distorted fashion. As she begins to muse about a more glamorous existence than the one she lives, Emma decks herself in "wine red slippers" that show beneath an open dressing gown revealing a pleated bodice adorned "with three gold buttons" (62)—somewhat more obvious and eye-catching than the image at the Bertaux. When Emma's courtesanlike apparel finds no support in outer reality and the actual presence of an adoring cavalier, it is discarded, and the dreamy mood is replaced by despondency. The listless young woman now wears "gray cotton stockings" and is loth to dress (68), implicitly renouncing her natural role in the home along with the more feminine and gauzy wraps of the past. Then, coinciding with her first meeting of Léon when she arrives at the inn in Yonville, the dainty movement of lifting her skirt with two fingers reappears. But the gesture now brings the dress "up to the ankles" and reveals a "foot shod in a little black boot," gingerly extended toward the flames in the fireplace. That same evening, the first slight suggestion of a perhaps discordant element in her travelling costume becomes evident: "She was wearing a small tie of blue silk which held straight, as a stiff ruff, a collar of pleated batiste" (86). Emma is on the look out, half consciously, for the kind of love that would confirm vague expectations, not totally in keeping with connubial fidelity. This mood of anticipation contains the potential for deviation from her womanly role, suggestively the potential for presence of the masculine tie around her neck.

Alison Fairlie, in her sensitive study of the novel, observes that "between the origins and the fulfilment of passion may come the stage of resistance," and that "the mere discovery of love may in itself be so satisfying that there is a momentary pause with no urge to go further."[5] Just as "one dreams before contemplating," in Bachelard's words, the contemplation itself is a stage that needs full maturation before it can be translated into action.[6] Emma has gone from the dream—which, albeit with a different demeanor, still contained the image of her husband—to the contemplation, which envisages the delicate features of Léon. The first stage was heralded by the presence of red slippers and a provocative negligé, still traditionally feminine if devoid of delicacy; the second is ushered in by a small tie, inconspicuous if vaguely masculine, and blue colored—a masculine symbol that remains obstinately delicate in shade and texture. If this is the first time that Emma's musing about love assumes the distinctive features of a man other than her husband, she is not yet tempted to transgress accepted bonds. This resistance against the "urge to go further" becomes a kind of triumph against the little blue tie she wore on the first encounter, and it is mirrored in the soft folds of her dress in subsequent images: "A dark hue fell on her back from her hair pulled up, becoming gradually paler as it fell in the shadow. Her garment then cascaded over from both sides of the chair, in billows full of pleats and spreading down to the ground" (101). Where bright and suggestive colors had dominated the period of Emma's lustful dreams, somber shades seem to hind her body during the assuaging contemplation of sentiment; where seductive booties had been proffered to the glow of embers, ample folds of material now reach to the ground in sign of demure chastity.

All contemplation of love that is not sublimated, however, leads to musings that unavoidably assume the urgency for fulfilment. When such an exigency is frustrated, chastity is no longer an elevating virtue, but a source of resentment. After Emma has pondered with wonderment on the inebriating flutters of her heart, the love she discerns soon exacts the price of desire. "But she was full of greed, rage, and hatred. The straight folds of her dress concealed a distressed heart, her chaste lips did not tell of the tempest within" (110). The storm of desire that now rages in her has erased all softness in her dress and replaced it with vertical and abrupt lines. Léon then leaves, and the earlier pattern that had gone from vague expectations to despondency after La Vaubyessard is repeated, but in reverse order. The thwarting of inner longings brings a period of misery—which is followed by a phase of self-indulgence and the renewal of feminine elegance, in brooding solitude, behind closed shutters, in the languid poses of an Odalisque (128).

Madame Bovary, Richard Blackmur has poetically written, "is a novel which is the shape of a life which is the shape of a woman which is the shape of a desire."[7] It is not the purpose of this essay to measure the energetic femininity that emerges from Blackmur's portrait of Emma, against the virility that ransoms her away from the banality of a woman's universe, in Baudelaire's appraisal. The aim here is to examine Emma's masculinity in the very manifestations of her desires against accepted modes. Emma's eventual flaunting of a freedom which in reality she does not possess, and which is not sanctioned by the morals of her society, can easily be seen as the exasperation of a woman not resigned to boredom at the side of an eminently boring man. But her transgression against the age-old pattern of submissiveness can only be seen as virile; that virility assumes the shape of masculinity in the particulars of her clothing.

In an author such as Flaubert, who left in his composition so little room for spontaneous inspiration, and who carefully pondered over all details with more deliberation than the wariest of generals before a battle, it would be rash to venture that the progressive intrusion of masculine details in Emma's dress is fortuitous. The steps that lead from her chance meeting with Rodolphe in her own kitchen, to her swooning surrender in the fields, are indeed signaled by a movement which, along with the disorder to the senses, points to a crescendo in distance between her and the marks of her femininity. As Emma bends by the kitchen table, she presents to Rodolphe's appreciative gaze a picture of delectable femininity: "her dress (it was a summer dress, with four flounces, yellow colored, long waisted, full skirted), her dress spread around her and over the tiles of the room" (132). The word "dress" repeated three times in the space of these very few lines, and reiterated after the parenthesis with an emphasis that can only point to its intrinsic value, in the face of no grammatical justification—marks the critical point in Emma's role as a woman. She is, and somewhat vaguely senses it, at the threshold. She can still cling, figuratively, to the light flounces and billowing folds that have constituted her realm—or she can step over, into the domain of the forbidden, and affirm her independence from customary principles.

Emma, we know, rushes forward with an impetus that only the long tarrying and period of dejection after Léon's departure explain. Symptomatically, on her way to the agricultural fair, leaning on Rodolphe's arm, the soft roundness of the straw hat hanging by the window latch during the initial days of her marriage, is replaced by an "oval bonnet" (139). Interestingly, a study of the variants shows that a previous version of the text read: "the large oval of her bonnet."[8] One may presume that the adjective "large" was subsequently eliminated so as to stress the "ovality" of the hat—and thus prevent all association of the new shape with the previous "roundness" and wide flaps.[9] The ensuing picture, with Emma's cavalcade in the woods, reinforces this assumption. On that day so predictably ushering her surrender into Rodolphe's arms, Emma's dress stands literally in the way: "But her dress, too long, hampered her, although she held it up by the train" (163). The image of her holding the dress reappears for the third time—so removed in context, however, from that of the wedding day with the candor of her expectations. The dress is now black, and beneath it there show, as on her arrival in Yonville, little black boots. More to the point, Emma is wearing "a man's hat" (164). Masculinity is the equivalent, with Emma, of a daring out of place, of an empty challenge against the postulates of her condition. She can only be the loser in that challenge, for her condition is indeed that of a woman, whose identity is inexorably bound to recognized canons. Each jolt against the invisible wheel of her destiny leaves a cleft in her integrity as a woman.

Circularly, her blemished integrity assumes the shape of masculinity.

Love spelled with a capital L, in the name of which many transgressions have been justified, will not be allowed by Flaubert to assume here redeeming qualities. Love itself is placed within the context of Emma's condition, which is that of a married woman. No romantic eulogizing on her part, no amount of sentiment or passionate endeavor to change the decrees of her lot, can detract from that initial premise. As she violates it, she begins to lose the core upon which rests the collective aspect of her social personality. Modesty—or "pudeur," that untranslatable French word—is the first casualty in the marring of her femininity. Rodolphe, well versed in the games of love, "judged all modesty importunate. He treated it without regard. He made of it something malleable and corrupt" (196). At the mercy of her discovered sensuality, Emma basks in the debasement of all the stipulations that had held her world together. "Her demeanor changed. Her looks became bolder, her talk more unrestrained; she even had the indecorousness of walking with Rodolphe, a cigarette at her lips, *as if to flout public opinion*" (197). Without any need to indulge in considerations of the symbolic value of a cigarette in the hands of this pre-Freudian heroine, one may nevertheless recall that smoking was strictly relegated to men's use at that time. The public opinion she flouts (and the cursive in the text emphasizes the importance of the statement) is the very foundation for her identity as a woman. The cigarette itself, however, explicit as it might seem in denouncing Emma's process of masculinization—and hence of perversion—pales in import when measured against the slow metamorphosis in her clothing: "finally, those who still doubted did not doubt any longer when they saw her, one day, alighting from the *Hirondelle*, her waist held tight in a vest, like a man" (197). It is the presence of the close-fitting, man-like garment that removes all doubt and reveals to the shocked bourgeois of Yonville the degree of Emma's abasement. There is no mention of blue color to relieve the masculine aspect of the vest, no description of vast folds in the dress to mitigate its presence by contrast. The very absence of a description of her dress, in fact, underlies the impact of that vest, which points both to Emma's physical and to her moral decline as a woman.

If Emma's downfall is defined by her social reality, it does not necessarily touch upon all aspects of her psychology as an individual. She continues, in fact, to "dream" as a woman. She envisions a Paradise of joy next to her lover, in far-away lands where flowers and maidens in red bodices would salute them. The dream fades when Rodolphe disappears.

When consciousness returns after months of anguish, Emma's first action, in keeping with the thesis of a woman's identity tied to social concepts, is to mend the broken links in her femininity. She could not do this, at this point, simply by reestablishing softness in her dressing; she instinctively turns to social work, in order to restore her social image, and sews "clothing for the poor" (120). Her mother-in-law is not happy with her "knitting little tops for orphans, instead of mending her own dusters" (221). She does not understand that only through improving her public image can Emma come closer to the morality she has lost. Gradually, as the Yonville world begins to accept the decorous image she now presents, Emma can, little by little, remove the milling crowd of well wishers and become once again mistress in her own home. Eventually, she puts on "a dress of blue silk with four flounces" (226), buys a hat (of unspecified shape), gloves, a bouquet of flowers for her outing to the opera in Rouen.

There is, however, no road back, no possibility of reconquering a mystical purity. The blue gown with the flounces underlies at this point the irony, rather than the sincerity, in Emma's efforts—as vacuous as the letter of disengagement she intended to give to Léon on the following day, instead of meeting him. That blue dress and those flounces stand also for the intermission before events continue along the by now predictable road. The only deep resentment Emma nourishes, in reality, is against her marriage. Her aspiration, at least unconsciously, remains tied to the fulfillment of a dream of love that takes no notice of Charles. No amount of lace or silk can undo her longing for the renewal, not the obliteration, of past felicities in Rodolphe's arms. She thinks of marriage as "defilement" ("les souillures du marriage"), while she merely avows "disillusion" in her adulterous relation (p. 230). The frenzy with which she heads toward a new venture reveals in fact that, camouflaged under domestic mien, the corruption of moral standards had been burrowing within her, before bursting anew in visible manifestation.

The three stages that revealed Emma's betrayal of her marital commitment through changes in her clothing—very "feminine" when first meeting Rodolphe, followed by the presence of an "oval" hat and finally by a "man's hat"—are repeated more deliberately during the second time around. The vest, earlier found so shocking and revealing of her corruption by the Yonville society, represented an unambiguous substitution for a more acceptable and feminine bodice. But Emma has since gone a long way in the process of masculinization. She has learned, as all experienced lovers must—and as indeed Rodolphe had done—to be more circumspect in her exhibition of licentiousness. Thus, outwardly, she caters now to a display of femininity: ribbons and lace abound, wide skirts, veils and shawls. Away from the scrutinizing eyes of her society, however, the three phases mentioned take on a more brutal manifestation of masculinity than ever before. They go from the gradual removal of her womanly garments to the outright wearing of a man's costume.

Along the road, Emma now walks discreetly, brushing the walls, her eyes cast down. She usually wears black, and if the dress makes her look taller and more imposing perhaps than women are wont to be, it has nevertheless "folds widening like a fan" (262). But in the hotel room where she steals every Thursday to meet Léon, details of nudity are suddenly revealed that were never mentioned before. "She would even say 'my slippers,' a gift from Léon, a whim she had had. They were slippers of pink satin, trimmed with swandown. When she sat on his lap, her leg, too short then, hung in the air; and the cute shoe, which had no back, held only by the toes of her naked foot" (270). The nakedness of that foot brings to fore what had until now been only suggested eroticism, through high heels or soft leather boots. Booties, we now understand, were alluring for the imagination, but acting as a kind of screen, and hence still feminine in the traditional concept. The precariously balanced satin slippers on the other hand—reminiscent of the "red wine" pair worn earlier, when Emma was half-consciously trying out provocative poses for still nonexistent lovers—suggest their own eventual dropping, and hence the act of undressing and removing a vestige of femininity.

What has been implied with the little slippers about to fall from Emma's bare feet is later amplified and restated in unambiguous terms. Emma's gradual appropriation of men's prerogatives—and Léon has meekly become "her mistress rather than she his" (283)—is mirrored in her attitudes to clothing. The dress, which at her initial outing with Rodolphe was "in the way," is now unceremoniously discarded. "She pulled off her clothes brutally, tearing at the thin lace of the stays in the corset, which hissed around her things like a slithering snake. She went tiptoeing on her naked feet to see once more if the door was locked, and then with a single gesture she let her clothes drop to the floor;—and, pale, without talking, solemn, she threw herself down on his chest, with a prolonged shudder" (228). The violence of Emma's undressing and flinging her clothes to the ground is followed by the taking possession of her lover, and of falling on his supine and receptive body. Clearly, the roles have been reversed and, in the intimacy of the hotel room, Emma has shed all semblance of her past femininity. There is hardly an inkling left of the demure attitudes of the early stages of her loves and dreams, not a bit of that "pudeur" so indispensable to her role as a woman. There is also not a shred of silk or lace, not a dress, not even a slipper.

The last stage in Emma's process of masculinization assumes the unmistakable shape of a complete male costume. The dreams she had nourished before her marriage are hardly even a memory by now. Long gone too are the illusions of her first love with Rodolphe. This final phase no longer holds any respect even for the outward rituals of what had constituted her world. Emma has embraced a moral depravity that recognizes no law outside of her immediate urges. She toys briefly with the temptation of assuring herself of Léon's loyalty, but haughtily dismisses it. "Eh! never mind!" she concludes, "let him betray me, what do I care! does it matter?" (289)—thoughts which would have been inconceivable earlier. Benjamin Bart points out that Emma is defeated not by love but by materialism.[10] Her materialism, in fact, is as such a part of her inherited culture (witness the shining utensils in her kitchen at the Bertaux farm) as love and marriage are: all have been corrupted, reduced to grasping and crushing, where caring and holding had been prescribed. The schism that now exists not only between Emma and the world in which she lives, but within herself, finds manifestations in her outward appearance. Moving parallel to her decline, as she reaches the lowest ebb, clothes become once again the denouncing factor.

Emma, who is now oppressed by an "incessant" sense of fatigue (297)—incapable, one may conclude, of sustaining any longer the weight of a femininity she does not in truth honor—assumes the guise of a man. "The day of Mid-Lent, she did not go back to Yonville; she went in the evening to the masked ball. She put on velvet trousers and red socks, a knotted wig and a lantern on her ear" (297). The ostensible masquerade is but a visible evidence of the final shattering of a public image. No longer a gesture of daring, the male costume stands in reality for an act of surrender, confirming Emma's defeat in the dominion of the woman. Symptomatically, the wearing of the velvet pants coincides with a night of orgy and the forsaking of home and family. An ominous air weighs upon the near empty house in Yonville, where the child Berthe, who plays such a diminutive role in the novel, now cries for the absent mother, sensing, perhaps, her irremediable loss. The "red socks" contain all the defiance previously denied by the "gray socks," worn in muted resignation against the plays of destiny. The wig might help confer on Emma the male elegance she had so longed for in a lover; but why "the lantern on her ear"? Maybe all inner light, dulled by now, refuted, could have as substitute only a derisive imitation and the artificial glow of a paper lantern. Emma is in effect "no more," degradation having conquered her.

In death alone will Emma resume the candor of that day long ago, when her womanhood was crowned. Away at last from all temptation that impugned her image as a woman, she is finally restored to that very image: a fey beauty in the filmy white of her gown, laid upon the velvet softness of the casket. Guided by the visionary force of his love, Charles vindicates the very femininity that was at the core of Emma's tragedy: "I want her to be buried in her wedding dress, with white shoes, a wreath. Her hair is to be arranged on her shoulders" (334).

Notes

[1] All quotations from *Madame Bovary* are taken from the same edition (Paris: Garnier Frères, 1971) and only the page number will be given in parentheses. All translations are mine.

[2] See in this connection Jean Rousset's "*Madame Bovary* ou le livre sur rien," *Forme et Signification* (Paris: Librairie José Corti, 1962), pp. 109-133.

[3] See Pierre Danger's book, *Sensations et Objets dans le Roman de Flaubert* (Paris: Librairie Armand Colin, 1973), particularly Chapter V, "Le vocabulaire des objets," p. 160.

[4] Victor Brombert points out that the waltz was "considered immoral by the Imperial Prosecutor," *The Novels of Flaubert* (Princeton: Princeton University Press, 1966), p. 46. The dance itself then is an initial transgression for Emma, and an opening into a forbidden world of sensations.

[5] Alison Fairlie, *Flaubert: Madame Bovary* (London: Edward Arnold Publishers, 1962), p. 47.

[6] Gaston Bachelard, *L'Eau et les Rêves* (Paris: Librairie José Corti, 1942), p. 6.

[7] Richard Blackmur, "Beauty out of Place: Flaubert's *Madame Bovary*," in *Eleven Essays in the European Novel* (New York: Harcourt, Brace & World, 1964), p. 48.

[8] *Madame Bovary. Nouvelle Version précédée des Scénarios inédits,* edited by Jean Pommier and Gabrielle Leleu (Paris: Librairie José Corti, 1949), p. 342.

[9] That hats play a considerable role in foreshadowing personalities is indicated from the beginning: young Charles's carefully detailed, multi-shaped, multicolored cap presumably stands for incongruity or absence of reason in his character.

[10] Benjamin Bart, *Flaubert* (Syracuse University Press, 1967), p. 319: "Her materialism, not her sensuality, causes her death, although she does not understand it."

Dominick LaCapra (essay date 1982)

SOURCE: "Aspects of the Novel," in Madame Bovary On Trial, Cornell University Press, 1982, pp. 169-208.

[*In the following excerpt, LaCapra argues that "Madame Bovary is not simply a 'tragedy of dreams' that places responsibility for Emma's 'fate' on her reading of romantic novels." He focuses instead on "how modifications in narrative perspective provide a nonlinear subplot" which he relates to the novel's theme of temporality.*]

> Do not speak to me about modern times, with respect to the grandiose. There is not enough there to satisfy the imagination of a feuilletonist of the lowest order.
>
> Flaubert, June 7, 1844

> It's equally fatal for the mind to have a system and to have none. It will simply have to decide to combine the two.
>
> Friedrich Schlegel, *Athenaeum Fragments* (1798)

Approaching more general aspects of the novel, I shall enlarge the focus on narrative perspective to include other dimensions of Flaubert's novelistic practice, for his "dual style" affected other standard components of the novel: themes, plot, characterization, and setting or context. While my treatment of these issues may in certain respects be anticipated given the preceding discussion, it is nonetheless useful to render more explicit the manner in which **Madame Bovary** recast the traditional novel.

In the analysis of cliché, irony, and stupidity [presented in *Madame Bovary on Trial*], I intimated that **Madame Bovary** lends itself to thematic unification up to a point but also provokes a questioning of the very thematic lines or leads it holds out to the reader. The trial centered its readings upon the themes of the family and religion. Associated with them was the theme of the novel itself in influencing behavior in "real" life. The prosecution and the defense were in agreement on the ability of fiction to trigger "mimetic" effects in ordinary life, for good or ill. They both assumed that readers would read **Madame Bovary** as Emma herself read novels, and, in attributing great importance to this theme, they joined literary critics who present Emma's own quixotic attempt to live what she reads as the unifying explanation which the novel seems to furnish in accounting for her life.

It might, however, be argued that within the novel itself the explanation of Emma's "fate" through the reading of novels has only a limited validity. It is in no sense a total or univocal explanation of her life. That Emma attempts to lead her life as if she were living a novel and that her actual reading of "romantic" novels as a girl helped to shape her conception of life are blatantly apparent postulations of the novel itself. But they are mediated, qualified, and dislocated by other considerations in a complex of relations that is not entirely coherent. There is, for example, a tension between Emma's more transcendent aspirations toward an absolute and her earth-bound, indeed vulgar, de-

Drawing of Emma Bovary.

sires: both are in some sense "romantic," but they cohabit uneasily. Nor is there any simple coincidence between Emma's romantic excesses and her financial imprudence. Love and money are two forms of impropriety in her life, and they combine to help undermine the status of the bourgeois family. But they do so from different directions that intersect only at certain points (gifts for her lovers or expenditures for the planned escape with Rodolphe). What they share is an extremely transgressive relation to conventional norms of bourgeois respectability, but the mode of transgression is not unitary: there is little romance in Emma's financial problems. A similar relation holds between erotic dreams and conventional religious inclinations in Emma, for they merge in mawkish amalgams that attest to the implausibility of their combination. Indeed Emma, in paradoxical contrast to her idealizing romanticization of secular love, takes too literally the image of a celestial lover and the belief that material practices are the path to true religious faith.

In all these senses, **Madame Bovary** is not simply a "tragedy of dreams" that places responsibility for Emma's "fate" on her reading of romantic novels which create "mimetic" desire in her. One telling defect of this interpretation is that it does not inquire into the way in which it is both invited and critically situated by the novel itself. The fact that Emma's mother-in-law offers the reading of romantic novels as the cause of Emma's "problems" is enough to give one pause and to cast a shadow of doubt upon the explanation. The shadow is lengthened by the additional fact that Charles and Rodolphe are the bearers of the belated Greek message that "fate" determined the course of events. Indeed a general problem in offering any given interpretation of a Flaubert novel is to see whether and how that interpretation is already put forth and positioned in the novel itself, for example, which of the characters one sounds like in offering it. One may then find that the trojan horse in which one takes refuge has a rather uncomfortable fit.

On a related level of composition, symbols and images also raise problems in providing agencies of unification or coherent organization that tend to break down or become questionable. We have already mentioned [in previous chapters of this work] Charles's hat—a symbol that manifestly seems to stand for him yet is both too full and too empty for adequate interpretation. The image of the window serves as another remarkable instance of the possibilities and limits of unified thematic interpretation. Jean Rousset begins his famous discussion of **Madame Bovary** as the "book about nothing" (in which the art of narrative transition is nonetheless crucial) only to have his analysis veer in the direction of making the novel a book about windows.[1] This Alice-in-Wonderland metamorphosis from a formalistic reading of the novel as the realization of pure art to a thematic and image-centered reading may be emblematic of the duality of the novel itself in exploring the interplay of opposites without being reducible to them. The window in **Madame Bovary** does partially lend itself to thematic analysis as an image inducing phenomenological reverie that is more subtle and extensive than Emma's own. The closed window is often related to claustration and self-enclosure, while the open window is the scene of dreams in the provinces—dreams that provide at least imaginary communication with an outside world. Yet there are instances in the novel that block the comprehensive coverage of this interpretation. For in the use of the window with its quivering hook as the father's signal to announce Emma's acceptance of the proposal of marriage to the inarticulate Charles, as well as in the "absurdist" gesticulations of Emma and Binet as perceived by the two old busy-bodies, it is the open window that functions as a barrier to communication and a bar to dreams.

All this is not to say that thematic organization is beside the point. But the text puts into practice a complex interplay between thematic determinacy and indeterminacy, proffering certain consistent lines of interpretation to the reader while simultaneously indicating their shortcomings or possible dead-ends. Jonathan Culler has written extensively about the uses of uncertainty in Flaubert.[2] It is important to recognize that it is a question of *uses* of uncertainty and not simply a provision of "a *theory* of the indeterminacy of experience."[3] The reader may of course attempt to formulate this theory. The novel furnishes certain elements for it and tests the limits of their validity, thereby raising the question of the tenability of such theories in its world and, by implication, in other possible worlds. Here one sees again how **Madame Bovary** is a novel situated on the threshold between traditional novels and experimental texts. The latter will often leave the furnishing of conventional interpretations or expectations up to the reader rather than inscribe them within the text itself. **The Sentimental Education** and **Bouvard and Pécuchet** move further in this direction. But **Madame Bovary** is positioned between tradition and its often disorienting critique, and for this reason is accessible to large numbers of readers (or misreaders) and even seems to invite misreading or at least reading on only a relatively "naive" level. This active use of "deviations" that are unremarkable enough to pass unnoticed, yet insistent enough to disconcert once they are noticed or even subconsciously sensed, may also be observed on the levels of plot and characterization.

When one attempts to provide a linear plot summary of **Madame Bovary**, one invariably begins to echo either the prosecution or the defense at the trial. Rather than repeat the story of adultery in the provinces, I shall try to indicate how modifications in narrative perspective provide a nonlinear subplot—one in which the use of language engages the problem of sense-making and its limits. And I shall relate this story to the role of temporality in the novel.

Chronology in the ordinary sense is not very well defined in **Madame Bovary** (in contrast to a novel such as **The Sentimental Education** where the implausible length of Rosanette's pregnancy or the gap between 1851 and 1867 are marked by their contrast to the precise dating of other events). For the world represented in **Madame Bovary** is that of everyday life in the provinces where *plus ça change, plus c'est la même chose*. The events of the novel can be roughly dated as taking place in the late 1830s and the 1840s, and drawing to a close somewhere around 1848. (Why 1848 is not mentioned may be formulated as a problem, and one may suggest that Emma's suicide takes its place.) But dating is possible on the basis of inferences from a few passing allusions, for example, Homais' reference to floods in Lyon and the government's reaction to insurrection in Poland. The novel is definitely not a chronicle of its time in any topical or circumstantially detailed way. It rather brings out the nature of life in a provincial context that is characterized by what recent social historians call *la longue durée*.

But the proverbial cliché about change and sameness does not fully account for the treatment of time in the novel. On an other than chronological level, the novel treats at least three forms of temporality that are woven together in a fourth dimension of time—that of nonlinear narrative itself. These three temporalities are those of the project, of hollow or deadly repetitiveness, and of reverie.

The time of the project is closest to that of linear plot in the ordinary neo-Aristotelian sense. Plot is itself the comprehensive structure modelled on the project and including specific projects as subplots. Here one's attention is drawn mostly to the story of Emma. Indeed she is distinctive in the novel in that she is the one character who does have some semblance of dynamic projects or goals. (Her closest counterpart in this respect is, paradoxically, Homais who has a sustained will to succeed.) Emma at least wants to escape the constraints of her tedious milieu and will go to any lengths to get what she wants. She creates her men in her image and uses them as crosses on which to nail her dreams. She is in the "active" position, clearly with Léon who is described as her mistress, also with Charles who behaves after their wedding night as the virgin of the day before, and even with Rodolphe who, superficially in control, is a stock figure given substance by Emma's imagination and overwhelmed by her demands.

Emma's projects transcend her environment only in the most evanescent of fashions—just as she is a tragic heroine only in the most equivocal of senses. Indeed another fault in the interpretation of her fate as a "tragedy of dreams" is that tragedy requires substantial oppositions while her dreams and imaginings are as friable as her realities. Her world in general is too messy and low-life for "tragic seriousness" but too pathetic and, in one attenuated sense (that of a displaced metaphysical quest for the absolute), elevated for full absurdity. She is in the zone between the tragic (including Erich Auerbach's modern realistic sense) and the absurd, for her tragic potential is dubious, and the absurdist possibilities in her position have yet to emerge clearly.

Thus Emma has projects—at least projects of escape—but they flare up only to collapse into the repetitive pattern that permeates the world from which she would escape. She moves in a vicious cycle of boredom and hysteria: a situation she cannot stand, a man she cannot tolerate (or who can no longer tolerate her), provoke dreams of another scene, another man. But these dreams deflate after a time only to rise again—repetition as death in life, repetition also as the path frayed to suicide. Emma is of course in love with her own idea of a lover and in this sense in love with herself. The other is never on the level of her projections, imaginings, and dreams. The dreams are emptied of content or compromised in sordid reality, and they retain some semblance of force only on a metaphysical level where desire cannot but meet with frustration in the mundane round of daily life.

This time of empty, deadly repetition is the dominant mode of existence represented in the novel. Things in it may follow one another, but sequence does not add up to progress or even to a promise of renewal. Cliché is the sociolinguistic definition of this social reality, and all life seems consumed by it. Here, for example, is what is written of the days of Emma's life:

> So now they would keep following one another, always the same, immovable and bringing nothing new. Other lives, however flat, had at least the chance of some event. One adventure sometimes brought with it infinite consequences and the scene changed. But nothing happened to her; God had willed it so! The future was a dark corridor, with its door at the end shut tight. [45]

The one escape from hollow repetition into a seemingly atemporal realm is provided by extremely fleeting moments of reverie. And Emma is the mistress of reverie. With Charles and the narrator, she is the one "person" allowed these transient experiences of time out of time, especially at her window where she stands framed by her desires of escape. The narrator is closest to Emma at these moments. Yet the longest passage of "pantheistic" reverie is reserved for a narratorial description of nature which displaces the reader's attention from the first sexual encounter between Rodolphe and Emma and is itself rudely interrupted by the depiction of Rodolphe after the event. Dreamlike moments of relief, besides being immediately dislocated, are frustratingly brief: they are not developed with the flow of metaphor that might give them more duration and a greater chance to alleviate daily routine. Indeed Flaubert's practice in revision might anachronistically be termed decidedly anti-Proustian, for he pared down the more protracted figures of oblivion or metaphoric embrace until they no longer even seemed to provide havens of bliss in the lives of his characters or the movement of events. That he was capable of writing those passages is revealed in the Leleu-Pommier edition of variants. That he was aware of their allure is evident in his letters.

> It is a delicious thing to write, whether well or badly—to be no longer yourself but to circulate in the entire creation of which one speaks. Today, for example, man and woman together, lover and mistress at the same time, I rode on horseback in a forest, on an autumn afternoon, and I was the horses, the leaves, the wind, the words they spoke to one another, and the red sun that made them half-shut their eyes drenched with love. Is this pride or pity? Is it a silly overflow of exaggerated self-satisfaction? Or a vague and noble religious sentiment? But when I turn over these experiences of bliss, after having undergone them, I am tempted to offer a prayer of thanks to the good Lord, if only I knew he could hear me. Let him be praised for not having me be born a cotton merchant, a vaudevillian, a wit, etc.!

> Let me sing to Apollo as in the first days, and breathe deeply the cold air of Parnassus; let us strike our guitars and our cymbals, and whirl like dervishes in the eternal clash [*brouhaha*] of Forms and Ideas. [December 23, 1853]

But that the indulgence of these flights would be at best a minor part of Flaubert's novelistic practice is a matter of record. His whirling dervishes would take other forms. In ***Madame Bovary,*** reverie is and remains fleeting—a hinted iridescence in the collapse of projects and the course of empty repetitiveness. Indeed the world represented in the novel seems to be one of almost unrelieved frustration of hope, punctuated by ineffectual reverie (and by the equally evanescent appearance of characters one is tempted to describe as "positive": the adolescent Justin, the old servant Catherine Leroux, and the good doctor Larivière). Insofar as the reader inserts himself into this world through identification, it is plausible to argue that demoralization is the result.

Yet Flaubert's narrative practice does not simply conform to the three modalities of temporality represented in the novel. It binds and unbinds them, as the narrator weaves in and out of the story told. For the time of narration is itself punctuated by the variations of proximity and distance and the inflexions of irony and empathy that we have already discussed at length. And, on this level, the issue of temporality is related to the imbrication of reinforcing, critical, and transformative tendencies in the interaction between what is "represented" in the novel and its mode of "representation" or narration. But here, perhaps more clearly than elsewhere, one has in the foreground the problem of the possibilities and limits of language in coming to terms with things. Insofar as the mode of narration sensitizes the reader to this problem, it does not demoralize him. It confronts him with a range of issues which its own periodicity in the use of language may help to resolve or at least to pose in more articulate ways.

It may be observed that, in discussing plot and temporality, I have also been discussing characterization. This is unavoidable given the mutually implicated parallelism of the two. On a linear level, the story begins with Charles, moves to Emma, and ends with Charles. On a nonlinear level, it involves characters in the temporal movements I have just evoked. Rather than trace this process in detail, I shall attempt to take the discussion of characterization in somewhat different directions.

The relation of narrator to characters at times goes beyond the boundaries of empathy and irony to less sublimated forms of love and hate, and nowhere is this ambivalence more pronounced than in relation to Emma. The narrator-character relationship is even further complicated by the relation of the author to the narrator. "Madame Bovary, c'est moi" is one of

Flaubert's most quoted pronouncements. Yet the enigma lies in the nature of the "moi." For Flaubert also said repeatedly that the novel was so difficult for him to write because he put nothing of himself in it and because the characters were so antipathetic to him.

The one thing that is clear in this oscillation between identification and denial is the intensity of Flaubert's investment in the novel. The readiest way to resolve the ambivalence of that investment would be in terms of the dialectic between romantic illusion and novelistic truth.[4] Emma is a deluded romantic infected by mimetic desire that is caused by her participatory reading of novels. She tries to lead her own life as if it were a romantic novel. Flaubert, recognizing that this illusion has no future, lucidly reveals its true status and writes fiction ironically and critically serving the interest of a higher truth. That the relationship between "Flaubert" and his "creation" cannot be so simple is bound up with the suspicion that the mutual implication of author, narrator, and characters is more intricate and even bewildering than this scenario allows. Let us raise a few questions that will resurface in the course of our discussion. Does "Flaubert" face problems comparable to those of Emma (as well as of other characters), and can we be altogether sure about whose response is most justifiable or "authentic"? Can we be entirely reassured that "Flaubert" masters the hysteresis unleashed by this "hysterical" woman who fascinates him to the point of identification and denial? These questions may in certain respects be taken as variations of a question raised by the prosecutor at the trial (who is in a position to condemn Emma?), but the point of our inquiry is rather different, for it may generate residual doubts about directions taken by our own analysis. I shall not pretend to eliminate these doubts, but I shall attempt to situate them to the extent that I find it possible.

Emma was the central figure in the novel for both the prosecution and the defense at the trial. She is also the character in whom metaphysical desire for an absolute—desire which ennobles and sets one apart—is endangered, even hopelessly contaminated, by banal and pathetic attempts at evasion that are symptomatic of the milieu they would transcend. She has velleities of purity and a thirst for something better: she makes demands on her environment. Yet she is a narcissistic creature of her romantic dreams and longings with little or no concern for the needs or the existence of others. She oscillates between boredom and hysteria, recognizes only what comes in cliché, and unites the "pleasure principle" with a deadly pattern of repetition. "Incapable . . . of understanding what she did not experience or of believing anything that did not take on a conventional form," Emma "rejected as useless whatever did not contribute to the immediate satisfaction of her heart's desire—being of a temperament more sentimental than artistic, looking for emotions, not landscapes" (31, 26).

The narrator who can analyze her ironically and critically is also fascinated with her—as are the other men who come into contact with her. When narratorial fascination reaches the limit of identification, it approaches the emulation of Emma that marks Charles at the end of the novel. The sense that the narrator in relating to Emma is also relating to himself—and beyond his fictive role to the authorial or biographical Flaubert—makes his ambivalence all the more difficult to pin down. Emma is manifestly, as the prosecutor at the trial (who himself courted becoming "involved" with her) observed, the most forceful creature in the book—more forceful perhaps than the author-narrator who gives birth to her. Men cannot handle her; she cannot handle herself. And "Flaubert" threatens to be overwhelmed by her less sophisticated, less sublimated, and in certain respects more powerful desires and demands. She insistently wants something out of life and is willing to take major risks to get it. If one can speak of her "problem," it is in no sense a simple problem, and it is perplexingly bound up with the "problems" of her world.

Indeed the figure of Emma represents a crucial breakdown in the circuits of sexual, socioeconomic, and linguistic exchange and reproduction. Given the interference of these circuits with one another, she also signals a more general short-circuiting in society and culture at large.

Sexually, Emma's position is not fixed: it is far from stable in any regard. She is a woman who refuses to play the traditional woman's role. And, despite her own weaknesses, she is the most active and "masculine" figure in the novel, dominating not only other characters but threatening to dominate the author-narrator as well. For Baudelaire, Flaubert poured his own masculine blood into Emma's veins, while for Sartre, in a kind of reverse transfusion, Emma is Flaubert feminized. This chiasmic criss-crossing of perspectives—each turn of which is equally plausible or equally exorbitant—indicates that Emma's masculinity is not a question of ordinary role reversal and that her relation to Flaubert is implicated in a tangled web of involvements. Indeed Baudelaire saw Emma's hysteria in terms that broached the problem of androgeny:

> The Academy of Medicine has not as yet been able to explain the mysterious condition of hysteria. In woman, it acts like a stifling ball rising in the body (I mention only the main symptom), while in nervous men it can be the cause of many forms of impotence as well as of a limitless ability at excess. Why could this physiological mystery not serve as the central subject, the true core, of a literary work?[5]

The image of a ball rising in the body might suggest that of a cat that chokes "hysterically" on a fur ball caused by licking the self, and it metaphorically links hysteria and narcissism. The relation between impotence—for example, that felt by the epigone—and excess points to the interplay between lack and limitlessness that preoccupied Flaubert in the world he represented and in his own narrative practice.

Emma herself is in character neither for the traditional man nor for the traditional woman, for her desires both exceed and fall short of the expectations of both. She does at times affect masculine dress and behavior, but she does not simply want to be a man in the traditional sense. Nor does she want to have this kind of man, assuming that he exists in her world. The man of whom she dreams transcends ordinary incarnations of "manhood" to the point of becoming vaguely utopian.

Nor will Emma assume the role of traditional housewife. Her activity in the family departs from the conventional code in an extravagant way. She performs her duties with obsessive finesse, or she abandons them with peremptory negligence. In both cases, she really seems to be elsewhere. She does wish that her child were a boy, and she loses interest in the poor creature who has the misfortune to be born a girl. "George" might have had the chances denied to Emma and provided her with a vicarious sense of fulfillment—at least as long as "George" remained as imaginary as Emma's other longed-for men. The girl child is an absence in the novel, almost a literal figure of castration. Emma takes leave of the role of *"mère de famille"* before the standard Oedipal triangle has a chance to get started, for the child is a blank in her life. In this sense, even her pregnancy was hysterical, and its product, which is not an object of imaginary investments or narcissistic identification, loses all interest for her.

Equally significant for the rupture of the generational cycle is the fact that Emma's mother is dead as the story opens, and she does not seem to play a significant part in Emma's life. Far from identifying with her mother, Emma escapes motherhood and behaves in a way that establishes an association between the position of her mother and that of her child: both are absences. Indeed the first explicit reference to Emma's mother in the novel comes from the mouth of her father, and it is an analogy between the woman and Charles's first wife. The analogy is situationally ironic, for it is intended to console Charles after the passing of the unlamented Héloïse—herself a widow he had married under false pretenses. The second and last reference to Emma's mother recalls that Emma cried much the first few days when her mother died, and she sent her father a letter "full of sad reflections on life" and requesting that she be buried in her mother's grave (27). This reference is followed by her father's anticlimactic reaction (the "old man" thinks she is ill and comes to see her) and by Emma's own self-satisfaction in attaining "at a first attempt the rare ideal of delicate lives, never attained by mediocre hearts"—an ideal immediately linked to "Lamartine, . . . harps on lakes, . . . all the songs of dying swans, . . . the falling of the leaves, the pure virgins ascending to heaven, and the voice of the Eternal discoursing down the valleys" (28). Thus Emma reduces and assimilates her mother's death to her ordinary romantic musings.

Economically as well as socially, Emma has no productive or reproductive function. She is a pure consumer in a world where commodities tend to be reduced to counters in a largely imaginary game. And her pattern of consumption, which is more heedless and imprudent than wasteful, creates financial difficulties that adulterate the purity of "romantic" fate—the one thing she would like to attain, perhaps even in its more elevated tragic form. In fact, her financial mismanagement is itself paradoxically traditional rather than modern: she behaves like a displaced *grande dame* in her desire to give gifts, unconcerned with mere money matters, and like a good *bourgeoise* in her will to possess fully what she has bought. Yet her lack of prudence is capitalized upon by those, such as Lheureux, who are more in tune with existing economic demands in their own small scale and petty fashion. Emma is less a victim of Capitalism than someone whose desires cannot be accommodated within its limits—and perhaps within any limits, even largely technical or formal ones. But the system she chooses to disdain returns to her with a vengeance, bringing her both to the verge of prostitution and to the absurdly virtuous and highly conventional affirmation that she cannot be bought. Emma is a scandal both to the traditional bourgeois family and to its modern economic setting.

Linguistically, Emma herself disrupts the code of realistic representation. Her primary use of language is incantatory. Her magical clichés and rhythmic repetitions create their object—one that can never be attained in the world of mundane realities. Indeed an "other" attains reality for her only when it may be perceived as the incarnation of a memory recast through the imagination. A perverse Platonist, she is also a small-town Proustian *avant la lettre*. Rodolphe registers as a lover only after the event of seduction when Emma may intone him into imaginary existence through an appeal to an evanescent but transcendent archetype.

> She repeated: 'I have a lover! a lover!' delighting at the idea as if a second puberty had come to her. So at last she was to know those joys of love, that fever of happiness of which she had despaired! She was entering upon a marvelous world where all would be passion, ecstasy, delirium. She felt herself surrounded by an endless rapture. A blue space surrounded her and ordinary existence appeared only intermittently between these heights, dark and far away beneath her.

> Then she recalled the heroines of books that she had read, and the lyric legion of their adulterous women began to sing in her memory with the voice of sisters that charmed her. [117]

Cliché and stereotype are as much the vehicles of Emma's dreams as they are the powers that help to create them. The one thing they are not is a simple representation of a preexistent reality. Emma herself is both utterly conventional and insistently unconventional—so much so that it becomes difficult to distinguish between what is and is not "ordinary" in her behavior. Her disaffection for her child is the conventional response of a "narcissistic" woman who would have her progeny be what she is not but would like to be. But her reaction goes beyond the limits of convention in its hyperbole. And her various "men" always have something dubious about them: Rodolphe is a hackneyed, hollow phallus that crudely signifies the imaginary; Léon is her mistress; and Charles as fool and saint is both less and more than the average man. . . .

Notes

[1] *Forme et signification* (Paris: Librairie José Corti, 1962), 109-33. Included in Paul de Man, ed., *Madame Bovary* (New York: Norton, 1965), 439-57.

[2] Jonathan Culler, *Flaubert: The Uses of Uncertainty* (Ithaca: Cornell University Press, 1974).

[3] The idea that Flaubert provides such a theory is put forth by Gerald Graff, *Literature against Itself* (Chicago: University of Chicago Press, 1979), 160.

[4] For this analysis, as well as for a discussion of "mimetic desire," see René Girard, *Mensonge romantique et vérité romanesque* (Paris: Grasset, 1961).

[5] "*Madame Bovary*, by Gustave Flaubert" in Paul de Man, ed., *Madame Bovary*, 341. . . .

Dennis Porter (essay date 1984)

SOURCE: "*Madame Bovary* and the Question of Pleasure," in *Flaubert and Postmodernism*, edited by Naomi Schor and Henry F. Majewski, University of Nebraska Press, 1984, pp. 116-38.

[*In the following essay, Porter categorizes* Madame Bovary *according to the three main types of reading pleasure identified by Roland Barthes in* The Pleasure of the Text. *Following a Barthian analysis of* Madame Bovary, *Porter considers the work in relation to its "central theme of the duplicity of language."*]

One of the more interesting developments in narrative theory over the past decade or so has been a renewed interest in pleasure. Subsequent to the structuralist enterprise there have grown up a reader-centered, a psychoanalytic, a new textual, and a feminist criticism which in their different ways have been attentive among other things to the experience of the reader reading a literary text and to the subject positions the reader is required to assume. For those interested in that experience and those positions, the guiding critical questions have been, neither "What does the work tell us, and how well is it made?" (New Criticism) nor "What is the model narrative structure of which this particular work is an example?" (structuralism), but "What does this work do to us as we read it, and how does it do what it does?" (reader response) and, to paraphrase Roland Barthes, "How is this text to be unmade, exploded, disseminated?" (poststructuralism).[1] As the result of such inquiry, we have come to appreciate more fully that reading literary works is not like breathing. It is, on the contrary, a complex learned activity with a corporeal and psychic as well as a social dimension, and one that we choose to engage in under certain conditions for a variety of reasons, paramount among which is the pursuit of pleasure. Through an interest in the way a reader is both constituted by and processes a text, we have been led back to ask the question why it is we enjoy reading literary works at all.

Probably the most suggestive account of the varieties of pleasure to be derived from reading, if not the most comprehensive and systematic, remains Barthes's *The Pleasure of the Text*.[2] And I would like in what follows to consider how Barthes's work can help in rethinking the question of pleasure as it relates to a more traditional form of narrative than he once championed. *The Pleasure of the Text* is, of course, in itself a characteristically allusive piece of writing that raises almost as many questions as it suggests answers. But it is a work that conveniently gathers together much that has been thought about literature in France over the past decade or so and reformulates it with a provocative incisiveness. It has, in fact, something of the character of a manifesto of the postmodernist sensibility that draws on Lacanian psychoanalysis, deconstructionism, and French feminist theory. Consequently, I have chosen to put Barthes's thought to the challenge of *Madame Bovary,* a novel that for many readers still has a canonical stature as the most fully developed example of classic French realism. The exchange is suggestive not only for the challenge Barthes's book throws down to reread a monument but also for the questions that Flaubert's novel in its turn raises about postmodernist narrative theory.

As far as *The Pleasure of the Text* is concerned, it will be remembered that Barthes distinguishes there between two major categories of texts, the *texte de plaisir* and the *texte de jouissance,* and makes a passing reference to a third category, the *texte de désir,* that he mentions only to dismiss. Further, a hierarchy of literary value based on these three categories is established whose two extremes are more easily defined than the middle term. The despised *texte de désir* takes the form of a popular work of erotica or a detective story that represents not so much a scene of sex or violence as its imminence—"its expectation, its preparation, its rise" (p. 92). At the other extreme a *texte de jouissance* is one which "leaves you in a state of loss, which disturbs . . . which causes the reader's historical, cultural and psychological foundations to wobble . . . provokes a crisis in his relation to language" (p. 25). As for the middle category, the *texte de plaisir,* the range of sensations encompassed by the word *plaisir* itself suggests the ambiguity of the concept. *Plaisir* is the general term which includes the particular experience of *jouissance* but which also needs to be distinguished from it. In Barthes's scheme, the former generalized concept of *plaisir* refers to an "excess of the text" and includes such notions as "euphoria, satisfaction, comfort, the sensation of fullness into which culture freely enters." It does not include "shock, agitation, loss" (p. 34), which are exclusive to *jouissance*. On the one hand, there is, in Stephen Heath's phrase, "a pleasure (*plaisir*) linked to cultural enjoyment and identity, to the cultural enjoyment of identity, to a homogenizing movement of the ego; on the other, a radically violent pleasure (*jouissance*) which shatters—dissipates, loses—that cultural identity, that ego."[3]

Isolated from Barthes's work, such categories appear to have a peculiarly abstract quality of a kind that one associates with pre-Freudian psychologizing in spite of the obvious Lacanian derivation. They also suffer from the imprecision inherent in definitions founded on the effects of a text on a reader—what is experienced as "euphoria" by one reader may be felt as "shock" by another. Yet in practice Barthes's categories are useful because they go further than any other contemporary critical text in introducing the idea of a range of qualitatively different pleasurable emotions that may be excited in a reader by a work of literature.

From Barthes's point of view, the highest level that a traditional work of prose fiction such as **Madame Bovary** might attain is that of a *texte de plaisir*. However, the effort to rethink the responses that Flaubert's novel excites in the light of Barthes's theory shows how at least two of the categories are present at the same time and that there are occasional intimations of the third.[4]

In the first place, then, **Madame Bovary** is a *texte de désir*. That is to say, like popular romantic fiction, it has an erotic theme and engages the reader in the progress of not one but three love affairs—named respectively Charles, Léon and Rodolphe—the second of which is suspended in medias res in order to be resumed in a spirit of intenser expectation after the third has run its predictable course. As in that popular romance which takes the crooked path to coupling or in the detective story that goes the long way round to an unveiling and the reconstruction of an original scene of suffering, Flaubert's novel alternately promises and postpones gratification. **Madame Bovary** offers an example of the familiar tension-building device of trebling, but it is complicated here by an overlapping—the affair with Léon begins and ends after the affair with Rodolphe—and in each case the author lingers over scenes of anticipation, preparation, and arousal. The titillation of deferment is particularly marked in the affair with Léon, but in each case there is an important element of the suspense that is inherent in narrative structures at all levels and that may be exploited more or less thoroughly. Before they are anything else, the novels of James and Proust are also novels of desire whose complex sentences are paradigms of halting progression toward an anticipated end. And in **Madame Bovary** many of the celebrated early episodes that involve Emma are designed to arouse desire in a reader through the lingering evocation of female sensuality. But after Emma's wedding there is no representation of the night of love. Moreover, the climactic moments in the subsequent affairs with Rodolphe and Léon are also deliberately elided—the first, in the woods, evokes the sharpness of sensations after the act; and the second, in the closed cab, is represented from outside as grotesque pantomime.

The only scenes which follow Emma through preparation to a kind of consummation are those evoking her suicide and death. In this case, suspense as an unresolved narrative sequence that alternates in the reader fear of the worst and hope for the best sustains reader concentration down to Emma's final paroxysm. Thus Emma is represented in the labor neither of love nor of childbirth but in that of death. Flaubert exploits for his own purposes a strange morality that imposed a taboo on the representation of sex, yet finds no indecency in dying. But more of that later.

At the same time that it is a *texte de désir,* **Madame Bovary** is also a *texte de plaisir*. That this is the case it confirmed early on through scenes that are not simply designed to stimulate desire; they are more than brief stopping places on the journey to fulfillment. The story of Emma is, in fact, chiefly told through the device of matching scenes of expectation with others that represent apparent plentitude and final disillusionment. Those equivalences which in the poetic function of language Jakobson found projected from the axis of selection onto the axis of combination are constituted here by *scenes à faire* in paired relationships. As a result, the linearity of basic narrative is overlaid in Flaubert's novel by a complex patterning that on the level of the action is cyclical in nature. As she moves from anticipation to fulfillment to disillusionment, Emma is made to repeat herself before the alerted eyes of the reader. Moreover, Flaubert's novel is rich in such equivalences at all levels from that of episode, scene, paragraph, and sentence down to word and phoneme. Consequently, the work's texture is thickened to a point where its linear sequences come close to being overwhelmed by complex cross-references. It frequently happens that the reader ceases to be impelled by the dynamism of the end-oriented forces of desire and is invited to enjoy the play of the text; in Jakobson's terminology, the reader is distracted from the referential function by the pull of the poetic function of language.

It will be remembered that in Barthes's view one sign that we are in the presence of a *texte de plaisir* is the apparent excess of signifier over signified. And the realist subject matter of Flaubert's novel is not enough to prevent a characteristic indulgence in such excess on a number of fronts. The classic example, in fact, sits astride the entrance to the text and presents its challenge to each fresh critical probe of the work's significance. I refer, of course, to the description of Charles's hat that can, if one is so inclined, be reduced to narrative sense, recuperated by reference to plot and character, but whose verbal extravagance on the printed page always remains uncomfortably in excess both of any signified in the text and of any referent in the world.[5]

The description of Charles's hat is a verbal *pièce montée,* which is introduced as "one of those hats of a composite kind."[6] In other words, the hat that is produced at this early point in the novel faces the reader with the category of the monstrous. A *monster* according to the *Concise Oxford* is: "1. [A] Misshapen animal or plant. 2. [An] Imaginary animal compounded of incongruous elements." And Charles's hat is just such an imaginary beast. In brief, Flaubert's apparently realist novel begins, not with an "effet de réel," not with the ordinary, but with the extraordinary. Flaubert imagines a hat that is five different hats in one. In its composition, he knowingly confuses a variety of shapes and orders; it is familiar and exotic, organic and inorganic, formless and geometric. The description combines references to three animals—a rabbit, an otter, and a whale—to food, fur, gold, and an acorn. In other words, largely as the result of the juxtaposition of disparate elements, a verbal context is established such that beyond the derived meanings of *baleine* ("whalebone stiffners"), *boudin* ("roll") and *gland* ("tassel") their concrete sense reasserts itself. The effect is particularly marked in the sentence beginning "Ovoïde et renflée de baleines, elle commençait par trois boudins circulaires" ("Oval and reinforced with whalebone, it began with three circular rolls")—a line of print that manages to combine references to eggs, whales, and blood-sausages. At the same time, because of its exposed position at the opening of the sentence, the peculiar sonority of *ovoïde* ("oval") forces itself briefly on the reader's attention. Two full-sounded back vowels echo each other across the labio-dental fricative, and the second [o] is followed by a glide into the high thin front vowel, which is terminated by the voiced dental stop consonant, [d]. Further, that prominent *ovo* anticipates the *ova* of the mumbled "Charbovari" a few lines later. And it is the spelling of the name which provides a further clue to the ways in which **Madame Bovary** occasionally promises to transcend *plaisir* in the direction of *jouissance.*

Charbovari is a Joycean neologism that contains an ox and a cart and a discordant noise—"un charivari." After a composite hat, a composite word; the monster here is metalingual. The linguistic sign is suddenly made to lose its self-evident discreteness, and the code itself is put into question. Moreover, one might urge against Culler that at the center of the hat paragraph itself Flaubert seems to invite the kind of symbolic interpretation that the object's eclecticism apparently mocks. The passage is a signifier that claims as its signified "la laideur muette" ("the mute ugliness"). By virtue of the following simile, however—"comme le visage d'un imbécile" ("of an idiot's face")—Flaubert makes such interpretation specular. The hat is like the human type of which it is the image. Like a pun or a misspelling, words whose referents seem limited to other words are, I assume, capable of provoking the sudden sense of loss which can follow the collapse of an order. Depending on one's point of view, therefore, speech may appear as beyond culture and thrillingly carnivalesque or shockingly irresponsible. At such moments, one is reminded that **Madame Bovary** is the product of the same mind that conceived the outrageous figure of the Garçon, bred different monsters in the **Tentation de saint Antoine,** and typically reinvented an adjective in his youthful correspondence to express the world's outrageousness, "Hénaurme" ("He-normous"). That splendid orthography is in itself an example of the way in which the extravagance of a signifier may lead to one of those vertiginous moments when the word subverts the word. If Flaubert brings classical realist representation to a new level of fullness in **Madame Bovary** in the celebrated pictorial tableaux, he also subverts such representation by rematerializing his medium.

Similar if less spectacular effects are to be found throughout the novel, including the apparently straightforward episode which describes the operation Charles performs on Hippolyte's clubfoot (part 2, chapter 11). On the level of the signified, the extravagance here is in *bêtise* made visible in its actions upon others; it is in particular an example of the macabre which begins with the verbal construction of another monstrous object, namely the strangely material box destined to contain the deformed foot: "a kind of box that weighed about eight pounds and in which there was no shortage of iron, wood, metal, leather, screws, and nuts" (p.

633). At the same time, the episode turns out to be a characteristically disturbing and comic example of linguistic self-reflexiveness in which categories are collapsed and cultural identities are blurred. In short, the register of the reader's pleasure alternates between *plaisir* and *jouissance*.

As so often in **Madame Bovary,** long sections of this chapter are constituted of pastiche in one form or another. The narrator's voice is not absent, as was once thought, but it tends to disappear because it is only one voice among many others, a tissue of voices. That hierarchy of discourses which characterizes classic realist narration and which is dominated by the privileged discourse of the narrator is temporarily subverted. The technique used is that of quotation, both direct and indirect, handled in a less obvious way than in the *comices agricoles* section.

In the form of a foregrounded intertextual exchange that is related to the novel's central theme of the duplicity of language ("La parole est un laminoir"), the chapter begins with Homais *reading* about the operation and, assisted by Emma, *talking* Charles into performing it, with Charles *reading* up on the relevant medical *literature* and with Homais *talking* Hippolyte into undergoing the operation: "While he Charles was studying equinus, varus and valgus, that is to say, strephocatopody, strephendodopy and strephexopody (or, more precisely, the different malformations of the foot, downwards, inwards or outwards) with strephypopody and strephanopody (or, in other words, torsion below and straightening above), Mr. Homais used all kinds of arguments in exhorting the boy to undergo the operation" (p. 633). The passage is characteristic above all because it reveals a word-merchant's delight in words as material objects independent of any referent. Thus the page is briefly overwhelmed by the alien wordhoard of the medical lexicon. The echoing Greek syllables in particular amount, in the context of French, to a formidable obstacle for the tongue and are also experienced as a comic cacophony by the ear. Moreover, there is interlinguistic irony in the fact that Flaubert takes the opportunity to turn the tables and make Greek for once seem "barbarous." Such prose in any case may be said to provoke a crisis in the reader's relation to language insofar as it objectifies speech in its material strangeness. It effects a shift out of the geometrical space of theatrical representation or narrative tableaux into nonrepresentative music, Barthean stereophony.

Further, in the rest of the chapter the circulation of words continues, either in the form of dialogues in direct and indirect speech or in the form of musings in *discours indirect libre* or in the form of reproductions of the written word. Flaubert quotes a nineteenth-century druggist, an incompetent medical man, an unhappy housewife, a parish priest, a chorus of village characters, a medical textbook, and a newspaper article. Yet the voice of his hidden narrator is finally made to emerge from the network of borrowed words in order to confront the reader with the reality of a gangrenous leg: "A livid tumefaction spread over the leg with here and there phlyctena whence oozed a black liquid" (p. 635). The task of the words here is different. It derives from the familiar Flaubertian intention of making his reader feel the material impact of what is evoked or, in other words, to disguise the fact that this reality, too, is only verbal. Moreover, in order to achieve such an effect, Flaubert steps outside the circle of quotations and reverts to realist reportage, employing a privileged narrative discourse that presents itself as the discourse of knowledge. Such sentences are an expression of his continuing trust in the power of words to communicate with the force of experience. Thus, in spite of the fact that so much in this chapter is put into inverted commas, by no means everything is self-reproducing speech. **Madame Bovary** is not simply an echo chamber in which all combinations of words have the appearance of having come from somewhere else. The conception of the novel itself as a ***Dictionary of Received Ideas*** will have to wait for ***Bouvard et Pécuchet***, but Flaubert's first major work sometimes points in that direction.

On such occasions as those just referred to, then, and there are many others, **Madame Bovary** hints at the form a sustained *texte de jouissance* might take. From time to time it invites what Barthes has called reading "à la dérive" ("adrift"): "Drifting occurs whenever *I do not respect the whole,* whenever apparently borne away here and there at the whim of the illusions, seductions, and intimidations of language, like a cork on a wave, I remain still, pivoting upon that intractable *jouissance* which binds me to the text (to the world)" (*The Pleasure of the Text,* pp. 32-33).

As far as Flaubert is concerned, the paradox, of course, is in the fact that the great craftsman of fiction, the inventor of the novel as grand poetic design, should have created a work that seems to encourage irresponsible readings, readings which do not "respect the whole," but which dismantle what was so carefully laid together. Yet such insidious encouragements are only intermittent and are perhaps perceptible chiefly to those who share something of our postmodernist sensibility. For the most part Flaubert submits the fragmenting potential of his text to the traditional discipline of end-oriented narrative. Consequently, excess as a characteristic of a *texte de plaisir* mostly takes quieter forms in **Madame Bovary** than those mentioned above and is carefully delimited as an episodic unit within an advancing action. A famous passage suggests how:

> Elle le reconduisait toujours jusqu'à la première marche du perron. Lorsqu'on n'avait pas encore

amené son cheval, elle restait là. On s'était dit adieu, on ne parlait plus; le grand air l'entourait, levant pêle-mêle les petits cheveux follets de sa nuque, ou secouant sur sa hanche les cordons de son tablier, qui se tortillaient comme des banderoles. Une fois, par un temps de dégel, l'écorce des arbres suintait dans la cour, la neige sur les couvertures des bâtiments se fondait. Elle était sur le seuil; elle alla chercher son ombrelle; elle l'ouvrit. L'ombrelle, de soie gorge-de-pigeon, que traversait le soleil, éclairait de reflets mobiles la peau blanche de sa figure. Elle souriait là-dessous à la chaleur tiède; et on entendait les gouttes d'eau, une à une, tomber sur la moire tendue. [P. 580]

[She always accompanied him outside as far as the first step of the stairs. When his horse had not been brought up, she waited there. They had said goodbye; no further words were spoken. The open air surrounded her, carelessly lifting the soft little curls at the nape of her neck or raising on her hips her apron strings which twisted in the wind like streamers. Once during a thaw, when the bark of the trees in the courtyard was oozing and the snow of the roofs of the buildings was melting, she stood on the threshold. She went to fetch her sunshade. She opened it. The silk sunshade was pigeon-breast in color, and the sunlight passed through it to illuminate the white skin of her face with shifting hues. She smiled as she stood there at the gentle warmth, and drops of water could be heard, falling one by one on the taut silk.]

At first glance the passage appears to be a tableau of the kind associated with classical realism, namely, a word painting that in its transparency offers itself as an equivalent for a slice of already given reality. It turns out, however, that the passage is an example of the way in which representation may achieve the status of a "text," of a "writable" potential within a "readable" work. Such potential is experienced first of all by a reader as a consciousness of thickened verbal texture, of the materiality of the medium.

On a first reading the passage gives the impression of a *plein-air* Impressionist canvas. That is to say, it imitates a scene from life that appears to be flooded with light and air. Yet, as we all know, if one comes too close to an Impressionist canvas, the represented scene suddenly disintegrates into a chaos of brush strokes. One step too many leads the observer out of the illusion of a dappled world and into the presence of paint. And a comparable attention to the verbal medium of Flaubert's scene may give rise to a similar effect. The passage is perceived to exist simultaneously on a referential and a material level. A form of play occurs that is dependent on the double nature of the linguistic sign. And it becomes clear at such moments that if Flaubert was, in fact, the first novelist to write as a poet, the first to pay systematic attention to the acoustic substance of words, it is because he was the novelist of the "gueuloir." He put his prose to the test of declamation. In formalist terms, he worked the verbal texture of his fiction so hard his linguistic signs became palpable; by trying out his words in the mouth he foregrounded in his text those sound values that are the units of word-units, thus disclosing phonemic equivalences which communication usually dissimulates.[7] On the one hand, therefore, the passage evokes erotic expectation on the representational level. On the other hand, it is a tissue of patterned sounds that generates a concurrent pleasure in the reader, not because of some supposed imitative harmony, of a posited natural connection between sound and sense, but because as we read—and to read Flaubert properly is to read him as he wrote, aloud—we are obliged to play the instrument constituted by our organs of speech. Flaubert's text is a score to be played in the mouth.

Like any *texte de plaisir*, like the *Sarrasine* that Barthes analyzes in *S/Z*, the passage speaks to the reader on a number of levels in the same way as the novel which contains it. From the beginning it displays the referential and sequential qualities of realist narrative, but by the third sentence the complex interrelatedness of the concepts and sounds is clear. Word music begins to subvert word painting.[8] Repetition in the form of assonance, alliteration, rhyme, words, and syntactic structures insists on a recognition that impedes the forward momentum of the narrative. The two consciously unremarkable opening sentences suggest a potential for union in the play of the gender-specific personal pronouns and the personal adjective—"Elle le reconduisait" ("She always accompanied him"), "son cheval, elle restait là" ("his horse, she waited there")—a union that takes a grammatical form with the opening "On" ("They") of the third sentence. But it is the second half of that third sentence which reveals how in a *texte de plaisir* pleasure is located as much, if not more, in the play of the signifiers as in the signifieds, in the decomposition and recomposition of acoustical images in unaccustomed proximity as in the concepts they speak.

". . . le grand air l'entourait, levant pêle-mêle les petits cheveux follets de sa nuque, ou secouant sur sa hanche les cordons de son tablier, qui se tortillaient comme des banderoles" ("The open air surrounded her, carelessly lifting the soft little curls at the nape of her neck or raising on her hips her apron strings which twisted in the wind like streamers.") As is often the case in Flaubert, the semicolon preceding this passage signals the fixing of the attention; it is a sign of the intention to linger and savor sensation through and across words. On this occasion, the author makes use of the capacity of language to isolate a part in the absence of a whole—in painting before cubism a breast was never detached from its body. And Flaubert isolates a part in order to focus with fetishistic relish not so much on a woman as on the nape of a neck and a hip. In such a context the linguistic signs constituted by *nuque* ("nape") and *hanche* ("hip") are calculated to excite desire on the conceptual level. But before considering the peculiar power of this passage as erotic scene, I would like to look briefly at its phonetic complexity, paying attention not only to audition but also the production of speech.

The opening clause—"le grand air l'entourait" ("the open air surrounded her")—breaks down into two sequences of three syllables, both of which begin with an [l] and end with an open [ε], either followed or preceded by the liquid [r]. All the phonemes used occur at least once in each sequence with the exception of the [g]—the voiced dental consonant [d] recurs in the unvoiced form [t]. Liquid consonants, open [ε]s and the nasal [ã]s dominate. And the same sounds are repeated in the following phrase, "levant pêle-mêle les petits cheveux follets de sa nuque" ("carelessly lifting the soft little curls at the nape of her neck"), the [l] no less than five times, the open [ε] three, the [ã] once. Moreover, in this phrase the open [ε]s and the [l]s combine in "pêle-mêle" to form a back-to-back rhyme which is introduced by two bilabial consonants, so that a closing of the mouth is followed by an opening of the mouth and a final rise of the tongue behind the teeth. The phrase, "les petits cheveux follets de sa nuque," with the play of the [l]s, is most marked for its series of fricatives . . . and the surprise of the velar positive [k], a new sound. Fricatives dominate in the next phrase, no less than four in the following four words. Also, the word "hanche" which ends the series repeats the open nasal sound before sliding into the palatal [sound]. In the final dozen words of the sentence, the sound texture is chiefly dominated by the phoneme [k] that originally appeared in "nuque," [and] by the voiced and unvoiced dentals, [d] and [t]. . . .

From the point of view of phonetic analysis, the most striking feature of the last three sentences is the frequent repetition of the two phonemes [εl], either alone or combined with the nasal . . . "ombrelle" ("sunshade")—"Elle était sur le seuil; elle alla chercher son ombrelle; elle l'ouvrit." ("She stood on the threshold. She went to fetch her sunshade. She opened it.") The combination of the two phonemes [ε] and [l] involves, of course, an opening of the mouth followed by a darting forward of the tongue against the teeth. In the word "ombrelle" the production of the two phonemes together is preceded by the full sound of the rounded nasal vowel, a shift forward in the mouth to the bilabial stop consonant [b] and a swift movement back again to the resonant velar [r]. In short, the production of the five phonemes of the word "ombrelle" involves considerable motor activity on the part of the organs of speech, so much so that as a result of repetition the sound values achieve a substantiality we can almost taste. It is at such moments that one is forced to recognize that speaking is, like eating, an oral activity capable of engendering a similar range of pleasures.

That Flaubert is the novelist of the "gueuloir" is confirmed finally by the second half of the final sentence—"et on entendait les gouttes d'eau, une à une, tomber sur la moire tendue" ("and drops of water could be heard, falling one by one upon the taut silk"). Within the space of little more than a dozen short words, Flaubert uses six of the eleven regular vowels of French and two of four nasals, most of them more than once, and one, [y], no less than four times. The effect is the same as that of playing musical notes in sequence at different points on the scale on an instrument whose range of sonorities is unusually wide. If one isolates the phrases beginning "gouttes d'eau, une à une," for example, and concentrates on the vowels, one notes a slide down the rounded back vowels from [u] to [o], followed by a shift forward of the point of articulation to the rounded middle vowel [y]. Further, in this play of similarity and difference, the postponed infinitive "tomber" finds an echo first in the opening nasal phoneme of "moire" and then in the resonant last word of the paragraph "tendue." Moreover, both "tomber" and "tendue" are two-syllable words, and both begin with the unvoiced dental [t] followed by two relatively similar nasal sounds, which in their turn are followed by two consonants pronounced well forward in the mouth, [b] and [d]. And they end with two fairly closely related front vowels, [e] and [y].

If I have concentrated so pedantically on the sounds of what is after all a familiar passage, it is because Flaubert's prose here illustrates so well how the different elements in a text that trigger pleasure begin with motor activity in the mouth. And in this respect the technical terminology of phonetics is suggestive to the extent that it locates speech precisely in the bodily organs—lips, teeth, tongue, and palate—which produce it, and supplies a word for the manner of its production—fricative, resonant, sibilant.

Not only qualities of sound but also most of the other forms of pleasure that I have so far discussed find an analogue in this passage. In the first place, it has the power of a *texte de désir* insofar as it is a tableau that generates sexual suspense by representing, not an erotic scene, but its preparation; it is on its most obvious representational level a scene of early courtship. At the same time it is a *texte de plaisir* to the extent that it is suggestively polysemic and, in effect, manages to represent figuratively what it merely looks forward to literally, namely, physical union. The fact that it is only the wind which touches a bare neck or a hip does not prevent the gesture from being read as delicate foreplay. And from that point on the passage moves successively through images of unfreezing and flowing to the offering of an "ombrelle"—a word that both through the shape of its referent and through the combination of two syllables evoking respectively the concept of shadow and of the female gender may be said to suggest the traditional essence of femininity. From "ombrelle" it moves on to refer to a face expressing pleasure—"sourire" ("smile")—humid warmth and the insistence of drops on a taut membrane—"moire tendue." The erotic charge concentrated in that final "tendue," in any case, is unmistakable. And it is an erotic charge that depends for its power on all the verbal factors isolated above, including, finally, the word's emphatic position at the end of a developing narrative sequence.

In brief, the passage is a paradigm of narrative at the level of a *texte de plaisir*. It moves in a linear fashion from an initial neutral situation to a point of climax via a series of sentences whose syntactic variety is calculated to produce an alternating rhythm of advance and delay. At the same time, like a dream, it embodies effects of displacement and condensation that are, nevertheless, controlled by considerations of secondary revision in the interest of narratability. As a result, it suggests a latent significance that it does not declare; like certain gauzy Victorian portraits of women, it manages both to profess innocence and to invite the spectator's erotic absorption. Insofar as it is a portrait of a woman, it also serves to remind us how in literature as in film women have been traditionally produced by and for the male gaze, within a regime of pleasure, in other words, whose characteristic perversions are voyeurism and fetishism. The effect of such production, as Laura Mulvey has noted in connection with film, is to freeze the flow of the action.[9] Where women are concerned, classic realist representation in both the literary and the film media has typically combined spectacle with narrative.

The passage achieves the polysemic suggestiveness of a *texte de plaisir*, then, but it stops short of *jouissance*. If *jouissance* is a symptom recognizable by the loss of self and the collapse of meaning and is produced by the play of detached signifiers, it is not a symptom excited by Flaubert's prose here. His linguistic signs retain for the most part their dual status. They achieve through juxtaposition a new substantiality that one is obliged to stop and taste in the mouth, but they are at the same time under traditional syntactic control, and their location in an unfolding realist narrative limits signification.

In a remarkable passage at the end of *The Pleasure of the Text*, Barthes refers to "a writing aloud" ("une écriture à haute voix") whose goal is not communication. Instead, it promotes "desiring incidents, it is language hung with skin, a text in which one can hear the grain of a throat, the patina of consonants, the sensuousness of vowels, a whole stereophony from deep in the flesh" (pp. 104-5). It is a passage whose choice of words makes particularly clear how a mouth supplied with appropriate combinations of words is a formidable organ of pleasure-taking. It is also clear that such a noncommunicational goal for the written language is only possible in the form of a nonreferential writing that subverts the traditional order of words by employing such devices as the dislocation of syntax, the absence of punctuation, multiple punning, or calculated misspellings. Under such conditions it is possible to offer the pleasures of sound pigment in place of sense; the written word is made simply material. But this is not the case with the Flaubert passage quoted above. More systematically than any other novelist before him, Flaubert obliges his reader to refer his printed words back to their production by the organs of speech. Yet context is not dissolved in pure auto-referential play. Instead, the reader's attention is solicited now by the scene represented, now by the acoustical material of the linguistic signs. The passage has the status of a Monet canvas, not of a Jackson Pollock; to read it carefully is to be absorbed in a game of now you see it, now you don't.

It could hardly be otherwise, since without such a play of the text between the referential and poetic functions of speech in the sole interest of the latter, the story of Emma would disappear. In short, the price of *jouissance* is the end of narrative. But it is a price that Barthes, along with other postmodernists, including particularly certain French feminists, has seemed willing to pay. In common with moralists from at least the seventeenth century, Barthes recognizes that novel reading is an erotic activity. However, what he advocates in the theory of *jouissance* is eroticism with a difference, eroticism that is not end-oriented. The fundamental distinction affirmed in "Diderot, Brecht, Eisenstein" between mathematics and acoustics, on the one hand, and geometry and theater, on the other, is finally one between the voice and the look, between stereophony and representation. And it is precisely this distinction which has been taken up by French feminists who, extrapolating from Freud and Lacan, affirm the qualities of (feminine) voice over the phallocentric representation of the (male) gaze.[10]

In any case, whereas narrative has traditionally been constructed according to principles similar to those which Freud viewed as characterizing normal adult sexuality, a *texte de jouissance* repudiates such principles. It stands in relation to a *texte de plaisir* as in Freud's theory the sexual perversions do to the genital aim of the mature sexual norm. In the second of the *Three Essays on the Theory of Sexuality* Freud contrasts infantile sexual life in which "its individual component instincts are upon the whole disconnected and independent of one another in their search for pleasure" with that of the normal adult "in which the component instincts . . . form a firm organization directed towards a sexual aim attached to some extraneous sexual object."[11] And Freud goes on to speak of "organization" and "subordination to the reproductive function." As the key terms "organization" and "subordination" make clear, it is a view of sexuality that is both directional and hierarchical in its structure and is, therefore, subject to the same strictures that Barthes applies to the sentence and a fortiori to the form of narrative which is the sentence writ large, namely the novel.

In effect, the theory of textuality as elaborated by Barthes in collaboration with a certain French avantgarde amounts to what was once known as a polymorphous perversity of the written word and has more recently been seen as a feminine form of sexuality, an *écriture féminine*. In a *texte de jouissance* the reading aim is diverted from taking pleasure in the parts of a text in the anticipation of an end to a total absorption in those parts—"like a cork on a wave." The goal of writing has become "a definitive discontinuity" (*The Pleasure of the Text,* p. 79). The new criteria of literary value are founded on such concepts as semantic undecidability, sonic reversibility, and a text's energy in transgressing all taboos, including particularly those which hold that narrative should be both linear and representational. The reader is invited to join in the play of the self-dismantling text in the same way that in the activity of critical deconstruction the text itself is made to collaborate in dethroning its authorial subject and in exposing the failures of authorial intentionality. The ideal of the text is a writing in which nothing is privileged. And a similar purpose is served through the critical subversion of the hierarchies in a canonical text. There is *jouissance* in a world without categories and identities where everything reverberates with utopian possibility. The utopian character—in the sense of desired but unrealizable—of an unlimited textuality is conceded by Barthes himself: "How could art, in a society that has not yet found peace, cease to be metaphysical? that is, significant, readable, representational? fetishist? When are we to have music, the Text?"[12]

If among nineteenth-century novels **Madame Bovary** seems particularly receptive to analysis along Barthean lines, therefore, it is in part because Flaubert's novel embodies attitudes that are sympathetic to the postmodernist and post-Freudian sensibility. And this is the case not only in the ways suggested above but also in relation to the work's central themes. **Madame Bovary** knowingly thematizes the question of the relationship between erotic pleasure and the reading process, both in the novel's content, or in its account of Emma's experience in the world, and in the novel's structure, to the extent that it exploits the mechanisms of popular romance in order in the end to entrap its reader.

First, then, the theme of eroticism and reading is represented directly in a heroine whose experience of life is shown to be less satisfactory than her early novel reading had prepared her for. But this is not simply because men in reality prove to be inferior to the heroic lovers of literature. It is rather because in Emma's case the sharpness of sensations stimulated by the reading activity itself is never quite matched, let alone sustained, in the world. Neither the content of reading-inspired fantasies nor the intensity of feeling aroused by the activity of reading literary romances has, in fact, been suggested with greater precision than in the sixth chapter of **Madame Bovary**. The sight and touch of "keepsakes" and novels as objects stimulate an anticipatory physiological reaction in Flaubert's adolescent heroine: "Delicately handling their beautiful satin bindings, Emma fixed her dazzled eyes on the names of unknown authors whose signature lay there. . . . She trembled as she lifted with her breath the silk paper of the engravings which rose half-folded back and then fell again gently on to the page." Emma's most important discovery will perhaps be that, though they have much in common, making love turns out in the end to be less exciting than reading or writing it.[13] Although she is not let into the secret, it is clear that the only alternative to suicide—the author's alternative—was aestheticism.

Second, the theme of the relationship between erotic experience and reading is embodied in the structure of **Madame Bovary**. If as was noted earlier, Flaubert consciously employs the mechanisms of a *texte de désir*, however, he only does so in order to frustrate his reader at the denouement. The promise of fulfillment seems implied by a great many scenes in **Madame Bovary;** the early representations of Emma particularly excite expectations in the reader—"the rise"—that the text does not satisfy. In the end, however, apart from the clubfoot operation, the only scene which represents directly down to its denouement a physical action carried out by a body on a body is that of Emma's suicide. Instead of a consummating act of generation, Flaubert inflicts on his reader a scene of self-destruction. As the text makes clear, Emma's suicide is the gesture of a *révolté* in which the means of death is particularly significant. The cramming of arsenic directly from her hand into the mouth is not only a defiantly self-destructive act, it is also a regressive one. It has in itself the force of an anti-Freudian, radical feminist gesture. By that I mean that there is a return to an oral form of gratification which under the circumstances is the essence of perversity,[14] in Freud's sense, since it is a return that occurs after the disappointing experience of three male lovers, of sexuality under the regime of the phallus. In other words, the mode as well as the choice of Emma's death constitute a bitter comment on male sexuality. Autoerotic gestures are associated with Emma from the beginning—witness the early incident when she pricks her finger and sucks it and the subsequent reference to the movements of her tongue licking the bottom of a glass. Moreover, such moments knowingly appeal to that voyeuristic reader pleasure which consists in observing someone else taking their pleasure. Nevertheless, the climax of all the rich foreplay of Flaubert's novel is an autoerotic *Liebestod* that can please nobody. No wonder Lamartine was so upset. The reader gets something significantly stronger than he bargained for. If Flaubert seems for long stretches of his novel to be appealing to the reader of a *texte de désir,* the denouement reveals that such an appeal is only simulated. Flaubert punishes the reader of Madame Bovary as *texte de désir* at the same time that he rewards anyone who is responsive to his work as a *texte de plaisir.*

In short, if in the end Flaubert's first and apparently most traditional novel continues to interest us so much, I suggest it is because a consciousness of the Barthean registers as well as of male desire and female sexuality is embodied in his fiction on a number of levels. **Madame Bovary** is exemplary because it implicitly acknowledges the existence of the three kinds of reading pleasure that Barthes isolates. It consciously combines the characteristics of a *texte de désir* and a *texte de plaisir* and occasionally confronts its reader with the thrilling vertigo of a *texte de jouissance.* Unlike the latter, however, it always locates its auto-referential digressive elements within a strongly articulated progressive structure. It displays to an unusual degree the features of "organization" and "subordination" that characterize linear narrative, but it does so at least in part because of the powerful centrifugal pull of its parts down to the level of its phonemes. The lesson of **Madame Bovary,** in fact, is that unlike a run-of-the-mill traditional novel or a *nouveau nouveau roman,* it manages to maintain a balance of tension such that the reader's interest is invariably divided between local excitements and the expectation of yet greater rewards. The risk run by a *texte de jouissance,* on the other hand, is similar to that described by Freud in the section of his third essay on the theory of sexuality entitled "Dangers of Fore-pleasure." There is, in Freud's view, "danger" "if at any point in the preparatory sexual processes the fore-pleasure turns out to be too great and the element of tension too small. The motive for proceeding further with the sexual process then disappears, the whole path is cut short, and the preparatory act in question takes the place of the normal sexual aim" (p. 77).

If **Madame Bovary** continues to exercise a hold over its readers, I would suggest that it is because, in spite of the richness of its preliminaries, "the whole path is not cut short." It still leads its reader on through promise and postponement toward an end. The verbal distractions of Flaubert's text are multiple and operate on the registers of both *plaisir* and *jouissance.* Above all, perhaps, the story of Emma is accompanied throughout by a sonorous subliminal buzz, by a stereophony which is registered by the reader as a reading in the body. At such moments the reader enjoys the play of language released briefly from the tyranny of sense and representation. Yet it is this (male) reader's experience that he is not unhappy in being returned to them. Although **Madame Bovary** submits its reader throughout to the various regimes of pleasure, it comes down in the end on the side of the currently despised phallocentric closure.[15] In spite of Barthes, therefore, Flaubert's novel persuades me that the most pleasurable fictional mode my own male difference can learn to love is one which navigates between the shores of *désir, plaisir,* and *jouissance* without stopping off at any single one. In the back and forth movement between such loss and reappearance is the *Fort / Da* of narrative itself.

Notes

[1] Roland Barthes, *Image-Music-Text: Essays Selected and Translated by Stephen Heath* (Fontana: London, 1977), p. 127.

[2] Roland Barthes, *Le Plaisir du Texte* (Paris: Éditions du Seuil, 1973). With the exception of the Barthes quotations from *Image-Music-Text,* translations from the French throughout are my own.

[3] Barthes, *Image-Music-Text,* p. 9.

[4] Barthes himself is, of course, aware of the provocative originality of Flaubert's writing. He refers in passing to the fact that "a generalized asyndeton takes hold of the whole enunciation so that this very readable discourse is beneath it all one of the craziest one can imagine" ibid., (p. 18).

[5] See Jonathan Culler's nice account of how Flaubert's description resists the traditional interpreting process, in *Flaubert: The Uses of Uncertainty* (Ithaca, N.Y.: Cornell University Press, 1974), pp. 91-94.

[6] It hardly seems necessary to repeat once more in print what is by now one of the most celebrated artifacts in literature. Yet critical good manners perhaps require it. "C'était une de ces coiffures d'ordre composite, où l'on retrouve les éléments du bonnet à poil, du chapska, du chapeau rond, de la casquette de loutre et du bonnet de coton, une de ces pauvres choses, enfin, dont la laideur muette a des profondeurs d'expression comme le visage d'un imbécile. Ovoïde et renflée de baleines, elle commençait par trois boudins circulaires; puis s'alternaient, séparés par une bande rouge, des losanges de velours et de poil de lapin; venait ensuite une façon de sac qui se terminait par un polygone cartonné, couvert d'une broderie en soutache compliquée, et d'où pendait, au bout d'un long cordon trop mince, un petit croisillon de fils d'or en manière de gland. Elle était neuve; la visière brillait." In *Oeuvres complètes,* 2 vols. (Paris: Seuil, 1964), 1:575. ("It was one of those headgears of the composite kind in which one can find elements of a fur hat, a shako, a billycock hat, a sealskin cap and a cotton bonnet. It was, in short, one of those poor things whose mute ugliness

has the expressive depths of an idiot's face. Oval and reinforced with whalebone, it began with three rolls. There followed in order, separated by a red band, lozenges in velvet and rabbit skin; then came a sort of bag which culminated in a cardboard polygon covered with ornate braid and to which in turn was appended by means of a long, excessively thin cord a tassel of plaited gold. It was new; its peak gleamed.") Subsequent page references in the text are to volume 1 of this edition.

[7] The spelling of French shares with English the advantage of often disguising congruences of sound behind graphic difference. From the point of view of the poetic function of speech, therefore, there is pleasure in the surprise of an identity heard but not seen. Spelling reform would be a disaster for poetry.

[8] In a typically suggestive essay, Barthes notes aphoristically on Western theater: "Thus is founded—against music (against the text)—*representation*" ("Diderot, Brecht, Eisenstein," in *Image-Music-Text*, p. 69).

[9] "The presence of woman is an indispensable element of spectacle in normal narrative film, yet her visual presence tends to work against the development of a story line, to freeze the flow of action in moments of erotic contemplation. The alien presence then has to be integrated into cohesion with the narrative." "Visual Pleasure and Narrative Cinema," *Screen* 16, no. 3 (Autumn 1975): 11.

[10] "All the feminine texts that I have read are very close to the Voice, are very close to the flesh of the language, much more than in masculine texts" (Hélène Cixous). "Investment in the look is not privileged in women as in men. More than the other senses, the eye objectifies and masters. It sets at a distance, maintains the distance. In our culture, the predominance of the look over smell, taste, touch, hearing has brought impoverishment of bodily relations" (Luce Irigaray). Quoted by Stephen Heath, "Difference," *Screen* 19, no. 3 (Autumn 1978): 83-84.

[11] Sigmund Freud, *Three Essays on the Theory of Sexuality*, trans. James Strachey (New York: Basic Books, 1962), pp. 63, 65.

[12] Barthes, "Diderot, Brecht, Eisenstein," p. 77.

[13] When toward the end of her affair with Léon, Emma feels obliged to conform to her received idea of the role of a mistress by writing letters to her lover, she manages once again to relocate the ideal lover of her fantasy. Once the letter is finished, however, "she collapsed, broken, since these outbursts of vague love tired her more than grand orgies" (p. 672).

[14] One is also reminded of Freud's formulation that "poison is nourishment that makes us ill." *The New Introductory Lectures on Psychoanalysis,* trans. James Strachey (New York: Norton, 1965), p. 122.

[15] Commenting on the relationships between male desire and feminine sexuality, Jane Gallop has noted that they both function in the same dimension of metonymy: "The difference is that desire is metonymical impatience, anticipation pressing ever forward along the line of discourse so as to close signification, whereas feminine sexuality is a '*jouissance* enveloped in its own contiguity.' Such *jouissance* would be sparks of pleasure ignited by *contact* at any point, any moment along the line, not waiting for a closure, but enjoying the touching." *The Daughter's Seduction: Feminism and Psychoanalysis* (Ithaca, N.Y.: Cornell University Press, 1982), pp. 30-31.

Michal Peled Ginsburg (essay date 1986)

SOURCE: "*Madame Bovary*," in *Flaubert Writing: A Study in Narrative Strategies*, Stanford University Press, 1986, pp. 82-107.

[*In the following excerpt, Ginsburg examines how an analysis of Flaubert's early works contributes to an understanding of* Madame Bovary. *"Instead of beginning a new mode of narration, as most critics claim it does,"* Ginsburg argues, "Madame Bovary *marks a return—with important modifications—. . . to the early works.*"]

In the first version of the **Tentation,** the narrator and his surrogate Antoine disappeared—"died"—and gave their places to a spectacle that faced them as an independent reality. The citational character of the work, its rhetorical order, the conventional, cliché nature of the visions, the emphasis on the problem of incarnation—all contributed to making Antoine a passive and empty figure. In the person of Antoine, the self does not express its original, individual desires through language, but instead is seen as predetermined and passively manipulated by a world of discourse that is exterior and anterior to it. In contrast to the **Mémoires** or **Novembre,** where the narration repeatedly reached a narcissistic impasse and had to stop and start afresh (using each time a new mode of narration), the text of the first **Tentation** flows without interruption and without end: the difficulty in generating the text has been overcome. But this textual richness is accompanied by a psychological poverty; the superabundance of the text is counterbalanced by the emptiness of the self whose story the text is supposed to recount.

How does this analysis of the early works contribute to our understanding of **Madame Bovary**? Of all the works of Flaubert, **Madame Bovary** is the one that has always invited analysis in terms of the entire oeuvre. The first of his works to be published and to enjoy

Title page for Madame Bovary *(1857)*.

recognition, it has always been acclaimed as the first "mature" work, with maturity understood as a break with his previous, so-called romantic view of life and art. Possibly the reason for this view of maturity is to be found within *Madame Bovary* itself, where characters (Charles or Léon, for example) outgrow romantic, "poetic" dreams and accept prosaic (novelistic, bourgeois) reality. Charles and Léon can thus be seen as deliberate, though ironic, self-portraits. But the parallel evolution of characters and author suggests another possibility: if, as I assume is agreed, characters in a novel "grow" according to narrative constraints, then the process of "embourgeoisement" is in fact determined by narative rather than socio-cultural pressure. Can we not then interpret the development of Flaubert's work—that is to say, the passage from the first *Tentation* to *Madame Bovary*—in the same terms? On this interpretation *Madame Bovary* and Flaubert's realism in general could be seen as growing out of the unsolved problems of the earlier works. In what follows I shall examine *Madame Bovary* from this particular point of view—as an attempt to remedy the central flaw of the first *Tentation*. I will claim that where the first version of the *Tentation*, following the first *Education sentimentale*, tried to circumvent the narcissistic impasse, *Madame Bovary* attempts to generate a narration by accepting and radicalizing the narcissistic predicament in order to save a self, even if it is an imaginary one. Instead of beginning a new mode of narration, as most critics claim it does, *Madame Bovary* marks a return—with important modifications, to be sure—to the early works.

Madame Bovary can be interpreted as an elaboration of those scenes in Flaubert's early works in which the narrator, having eliminated the all-too-menacing mirror image, tries to create a story around a specter that replaces it. Like that specter, Emma is an imaginary character: a character whose life, desire and even body are created and shaped by others. Never allowed to gain life and independence, she remains a character deprived of the capacity to fully become a narrator.

The imaginary nature of Emma's existence can be understood in different but complementary ways. Most obviously, her existence is "doubly bookish."[1] Not only is she a fictive character in a book, but as a character—as a desiring subject—she has been created by literature: "And Emma tried to find out what one meant exactly in life by the words *bliss, passion, ecstasy,* that had seemed to her so beautiful in books" (586; *24;* Flaubert's emphasis); "Then she recalled the heroines of the books that she had read. . . . She became herself, as it were, an actual part of these imaginings" (629; *117*). The theme of the dangers of reading, the corrupting influence of literature (a cliché theme, of course),[2] is the most obvious expression of Emma's imaginary existence.

That a character's desire should be determined by a previous text is not in itself something new in Flaubert. We saw this happen in both the early works and the first version of the *Tentation*. But in the early works the non-originality of desire was recognized and felt as a menace (by the narrator-hero of the *Mémoires* or *Novembre,* by the hero-artist Jules of the first *Education*), and in the *Tentation* it was exploited (by the narrator and his various surrogates) as a way of generating a text. What characterizes *Madame Bovary* and distinguishes it from those works is that Emma—unlike the narrator—is not aware of the borrowed nature of her desire. Her inability to see repetition, to recognize clichés as clichés—her blindness to the fact that her desire is the desire of the other—manifest her narcissism.

On the level of plot Emma's imaginary existence is conveyed by the fact that she is always seen and chosen—created as an object of desire—by others. As most critics have observed, in the first encounter between Emma and the various men who shape her life, we are not given Emma's point of view. Instead of a description of Charles, Léon, or Rodolphe as seen by Emma, we have a description of Emma as seen by the desiring eyes of Charles, Léon, or Rodolphe.[3] We are not told what Emma's feelings, impressions, or desires are when she first meets these men. We are told of her feelings toward Charles only after the consummation of their marriage: "Before marriage she thought herself in love. . . . The uneasiness of her new position, or perhaps the disturbance caused by the presence of this man, had sufficed to make her believe that she at last felt that wondrous passion" (586, 587; *24, 28*); her love for Léon is described only when she realizes he loves her: "Looking from her bed at the bright fire that was burning, she still saw, as she had down there, Léon standing up. . . . She thought him charming; she could not tear herself away from him. . . . Is he not in love? she asked herself; but with whom? . . . with me!" (608-9; *73*); we get a glimpse of her feelings toward Rodolphe only at the end of the *Comices,* when, on hearing Rodolphe's words, "something gave way in her. . . . The sweetness of this sensation revived her past desires, and like grains of sand under a gust of wind, they swirled around in the subtle breath of the perfume that diffused over her soul" (624; *106*). This fact of narrative technique should not be taken lightly; it means that in terms of the novel, Emma does not exist as a desiring subject before she is made such, first by literature, then by the men who choose her. [Ginsburg notes: "It is rather obvious, and important, that the literature Emma reads is written by men: among the authors mentioned or alluded to in the chapter dealing with her readings, we do not find Madame de Staël or Georges Sand, for example. The heroines of the novels Emma reads are the images of perfect femininity as conceived by men, in response to *their* desire. When Emma dreams of becoming like one of those heroines, she desires to become the ideal object of a man's desire."] Rather than being an autonomous subject whose desire originates within herself and whose consciousness of herself is independent of other people, Emma exists only as an object of desire created by the others (men and literature). This "inessentiality" is emphasized by her never being the "first one" for any of the men around her: she is Charles' second wife, one of many mistresses for Rodolphe, and Léon's only after he has lost his virginity to some working girl in Paris. She is not even the first victim of Lheureux (who shapes her life financially rather than erotically). Being second means filling in the place left by someone else, fitting into a preexisting slot. Just as the theme of reading shows that the self is produced by the order of language that precedes it and determines it, so the plot inscribes Emma in a circle of exchange where she is not an autonomous subject but an object of substitution.

Emma is, then, in spite of her hyperactivity, as passive as the Saint Antoine of the first version. His temptations, orchestrated by a medieval Devil, were the "clichés" of the old morality plays; her dreams, like his, are stereotypical and banal, and her "temptations" are always controlled by others. Why is it, then, that we feel that Emma is so different from Saint Antoine of the first version, that whereas he is an empty figure, a pretext for the unfolding of images, she is a real woman? The reason is that unlike Antoine, whose attention always moves from one image or temptation to the next without lingering too long on any of them, Emma "succumbs to temptation" and fixes her attention on successive single images.

In the first **Tentation** constant movement from one image to another, from one "possible life" to another, generated a text, but at the same time prevented it from being the story of a self. A self can come into being as a self (can have a story) only by arresting its attention on one image, fixing its flow at one "possible life." To have an identity, it must be narcissistic, must enter into an exclusive, specular relation with the image that its desire has created or that has created its desire. Emma, like Félicité of "Un Coeur simple" later on, repeatedly tries to anchor her shifting existence in a single image, be it Charles, Léon, Rodolphe, God, or Lagardy. But because the relation that constitutes her as a desiring self is specular and exclusive, its end means her death. Just as the narrator in the **Mémoires** or **Novembre** was shaped by the narcissistic cycle and therefore periodically reached an impasse, then had to stop and start afresh, so too in **Madame Bovary** Emma's life is punctuated by points of rupture, "little deaths," followed each time by a new departure.

But, again, Emma's particularity is her refusal to recognize the repetition in her life. A product of the desire of the other, a fragment in a chain of substitutions that constitutes her as a desiring subject, ironically she experiences each successive desire as something totally new, as something that has not happened before and cannot happen again—hence, as an "original" desire. On the one hand, every new lover is a totally new beginning, and it is as if nothing has existed before; on the other hand, all her lovers tend to collapse into a single image of a lover: "Then something gave way in her. . . . It seemed to her that she was again turning in the waltz under the light of the lustres on the arm of the Viscount, and that Léon was not far away, that he was coming . . . and yet all the time she was conscious of Rodolphe's head by her side" (624; *105-6*). What Emma experiences each time as newness and originality is precisely what never stops repeating itself; it is the "virginity" of the prostitute in *Novembre*—the inability ever to possess what she is possessed by. [Ginsburg observes: "The difference between Emma, who sees every relation as "first," as new and original, and Charles, Rodolphe, Léon, and

Lheureux, for whom she is never the first, establishes a binary opposition Emma / men. Charles, however, resembles not only the three other men, but also Emma herself: though he has been married, he is still "virgin" ("It was he who might rather have been taken for the virgin of the evening before"; 584; *21*), and his relation to Emma is, like her relation to the other men, so exclusive that her death means his own death. Thus, Charles' position is essentially double and ambiguous. I discuss this topic in greater detail in the next part of the chapter."] But unlike Marie of *Novembre,* Emma cannot recognize this repetition: she is "not in the least conscious of her prostitution" (678; *225*). Thus, though Emma's story is similar to Marie's (both tell of the impossibility of satisfying desire) and also to Helen's in the *Tentation* (both tell of a growing sensuality, of a gradual "incarnation"[4]), Emma remains only half aware of her "story" and, unlike the other two, cannot narrate it herself.

Every character in Flaubert is potentially a narrator. But Emma's imaginary existence (her narcissism) prevents her from fully realizing this potential. In the same way that the narrators (of the *Mémoires, Novembre,* the *Tentation*) create characters by doubling, by externalizing a part of themselves, magically evoking the other, so does Emma:

> But while writing to him, it was another man she saw, a phantom fashioned out of her most ardent memories, of her favorite books, her strongest desires, and at last he became so real, so tangible, that her heart beat wildly in awe and admiration, though unable to see him distinctly, for, like God, he was hidden beneath the abundance of his attributes. He dwelt in that azure land where silken ladders swung from balconies in the moonlight, beneath a flower-scented breeze. She felt him near her; he was coming and would ravish her entire being in a kiss. (672; *211*)

Emma creates by doubling herself, by projecting images, spectacles. But she can never go very far in giving these images life and specificity. Even in this passage, which marks the greatest concretization she ever achieves ("he became so real, so tangible"), the image of the lover, the idealized other ("another man"), remains vague and abstract. The description ("he dwelt in that azure land . . .") reminds us of the description of Helen before she became "real" ("I was the moonlight, I penetrated the foliage, I rolled over the flowers, I illuminated with my face the azure ether of summer nights"; 394), before she became specified in time and place, with a body, with a history. The images Emma conjures up do not "come to life" because she cannot let them become concrete, specific, that is, different from and independent of her. Emma dreams not too much but too little— too little not in terms of the practical welfare of a provincial woman but in terms of the possibility of creating fiction, of coming into being as a narrator.

Emma does not understand why her dreams never come true ("Why was her life so unsatisfactory," she asks herself; 670; *206*). She tends to blame her unhappiness on "fate" ("If fate had willed it"; 651; *163*), her bad luck, her particular situation in time and space—her reality. But we already know that in Flaubert "reality" is whatever has been externalized and differentiated enough to become totally different from the self that gave rise to it. That Emma's dreams do not come to life is therefore the fault not of her reality but of her dreaming. Her dreams could come to life if she let them take on some life. But Emma always arrests her dreams before they become concrete and specific, independent of and different from her, real. Emma's dreams, in other words, do not have plots; the images she projects remain so amorphous, so lacking life and concreteness, that they cannot act at all and so, of course, can neither fulfill her desires nor provide her with a story to narrate. This becomes clear when we compare Emma's dreams with one of the dreams of the narrator-hero in *Novembre.*

In *Novembre* the "I" narcissistically doubles itself for the sake of erotic satisfaction: "I called to Love! My lips trembled and went out as if I had scented the breath of some other mouth" (258; *61*). But the hero does not stop here. The "double" becomes more and more real, concrete, alive, independent, so that when the hero goes back to the city, he "sees" women who "seemed to smile on me, to invite me to silken loves; ladies in wraps bent from their balconies to see me, saying: 'Love us! Love us!'" (258-59; *62-63*). Finally, this generalized femininity becomes even more concrete and particularized when it is incarnated in the figure of Marie: "There was Woman everywhere. . . . When I came to the street at last, after I walked for a century, I thought I should choke. . . . I went forward, forward. . . . Finally I entered a room. . . . A woman was seated. . . . She was wearing a white dress" (259; *63-65*). The dream comes true (and the price, as we have seen, will have to be paid).

But Emma's dreams never become stories: "With Walter Scott, later on, she fell in love with historical events, dreamed of guard-rooms, old oak chests and minstrels. She would have liked to live in some old manor-house, like those long-waisted chatelaines who, in the shade of pointed arches, spent their days leaning on the stone, chin in hand, watching a white-plumed knight galloping on his black horse from the distant field" (586-87; *26*). This dream, like every other "vision" in Flaubert, is "en abîme": Emma sees herself as a lady of the manor who sees a knight coming toward her. But what is curious about this dream (and characteristic of all Emma's dreams) is its complete immobility; it is a frozen tableau, wholly lacking in action. Emma sees herself, but not, basically, as different from herself. Though the lady lives in an "old manor-house" and wears gowns with "long-waisted" bodices, she shares Emma's predicament and "activity," and spends her day dreaming, looking, expecting someone to come to her, waiting for her dream lover to become real. This in itself is not entirely surprising or new; after all, Saint Antoine, lying passive next to his hut, saw himself lying in a boat. But the similarity in the positions of the two Antoines was complemented by the difference—the activity—of the next relay, where the Saint was seen walking in Alexandria, killing and destroying, conversing with the Emperor. In Emma's dream the lack of action and mobility, the lack of difference, characterizes all relays. The dream lover is seen coming toward the lady but never actually reaching her—he is frozen on his black horse, and no matter how fast he gallops, he never arrives; he never comes true.

In her narcissism, then, Emma can neither see herself as different from herself nor give life to something that is independent of and different from herself. When she looks at keepsakes, what she sees are not different "possible lives," but different settings ("behind the balustrade of a balcony," "in carriages, gliding through parks," etc.; 587; 27) for an activity that is always the same: dreaming, looking, desiring. In her dream of a honeymoon with a dream lover, the only activity she can imagine is that of going toward another place ("to fly to those lands with sonorous names"; 588; 28); and after one arrives (but where?) the only activity possible remains that of desiring: "One looks at the stars, making plans for the future" (ibid.). Even when, just before she is to go away with Rodolphe, this dream of a perfect honeymoon seems about to come true, the situation is no different: she dreams about going away, and when, in the dream, they do arrive, nothing actually happens: "They would row in gondolas, swing in hammocks, and their existence would be easy and free as their wide silk gowns, warm and star-spangled as the nights they would contemplate. However, in the immensity of this future that she conjured up, nothing specific stood out; the days, all magnificent, resembled each other like waves; and the vision swayed in the horizon, infinite, harmonized, azure, and bathed in sunshine" (641; 141-42). [Ginsburg contends: "As we can see in this passage, the complete narcissism of Emma's dreams is also conveyed by the "intradiegetic" similes used here, on which Jacques Neef has commented in his "La Figuration réaliste." To a certain extent, in this novel Flaubert shares Emma's need to limit the narration to a reiteration of the same, to suppress developments that are different and differentiated. This is seen most clearly in his reworking of the drafts, where all deviations, all metaphors that were not "intradiegetic," all beginnings of other *récits* (especially through metaphors), have been ruthlessly eliminated. Flaubert, however, does not just repeat Emma's activity. The relation between implied author, narrator, and character is developed in the next part of this chapter."] Emma can conceive of herself only as what she is: desiring, expecting, going toward something. If she never actually arrives, if her dreams and expectations never come true, it is because she always stops too short: "At the end of some indefinite distance there was always a confused spot, into which her dream died" (594; 41).

Emma's dream about Paris is a particularly striking example of her incapability of generating difference. The dream is divided into distinct pictures, each of which is slightly more animated than the previous one, so that we engage in the typical Flaubertian movement toward materialization and concretization. The world of the ambassadors is simply the world of reflections, with its "polished floors" and "drawing rooms lined with mirrors" (594; 42). The only activity is that of "moving" (going elsewhere?). It is a totally specular world in which nothing can happen to ruffle its surface and break the reflection (hence, it is also a world of mystery and dissimulation). In the world of the duchesses, the women's activity is limited to being pale and wearing English point on their petticoats, and though the men are slightly more active, their activity is marked by futility (they "don't get anywhere"): "The men, their talents hidden under a frivolous appearance, rode horses to death at pleasure, spent the summer season at Baden, and finally, on reaching their forties, married heiresses" (ibid.). The world of the "writers and actresses" is clearly more alive (one eats there!) though again its activity is rather close to home: "They were . . . full of ambitious ideals and fantastic frenzies" (ibid.). What comes next? We might expect something more active still, something that will finally become fully alive (will develop into a story, into a plot); but no: "As for the rest of the world, it was lost, with no particular place, and as if nonexistent" (ibid.). This is what always happens to Emma's dreams: they always expire—die into "a confused spot"—when they arrive at a place where an activity other than looking, going elsewhere, dreaming, contemplating, desiring (that is, other than repetition without difference) would allow them to reveal difference and independence, become real. This place where the dream has to expire, that "rest of the world" she cannot bear to make precise, is "all her immediate surroundings" (ibid.). The locus of difference is, paradoxically, not "elsewhere," not far away, but right next to her, within arm's reach. That which surrounds her is what is different from her, independent of her, not subject to her control (hence, antagonistic, hostile); this is "real"—"real" being whatever escapes the control of narcissistic projection.

The reality that is totally independent of Emma is crystallized in the figure of Homais. Though Homais probably speaks more than any other character in the novel, we are very seldom presented with his inner thoughts and feelings, either through direct discourse or through narrative description. This is because Homais, as an incarnation of "reality," cannot be represented as an individual: he does not have an interiority; he is totally empty, desexualized; he is the incarnation of the ***Dictionnaire des idées reçues***.⁵

As a representation of reality, Homais is totally excluded by Emma. He is the only important character in the novel who does not play a role in her drama, who is entirely superfluous to the main line of the story: her love relations and her gradual entanglement in monetary difficulties. Even at the very end of the novel, when Emma tries to borrow money from Guillaumin and goes so far as attempting to seduce Binet, the possibility of establishing some relation with the pharmacist never occurs to her. Though they live as neighbors and meet very often, they appear to be totally unaware of each other. We never see Homais looking at Emma; we never see her through his eyes (as we do through the eyes of Charles, Léon, and Rodolphe). Occasionally, we hear his "opinion" of her: "You are prettier than ever. You'll make *quite an impression* [*vous allez* faire flores] in Rouen" (649; *159;* Flaubert's emphasis), or "She is a real lady! She would not be out of place in a sous-préfecture!" (610; *76*), but these opinions are always impersonal pronouncements rather than revelations of his private thoughts. About Emma's view of Homais we know even less: we never see him through her eyes; we never hear her opinion of him or her feelings toward him. We do know what Emma and Léon think of Madame Homais (610; *75*)—because she exists as an object that can conceivably be desired (Léon thinks of this possibility, though negatively; 606; *68*). Homais, however, simply does not exist as a subject or as an object of desire.

The independence and autonomy that Homais enjoys, as an incarnation of reality, explain his menacing power—"he was becoming dangerous" (690; *251*)—and justify his role as the impersonal agent of Emma's death. Even though he is not involved directly and actively in Emma's destruction (as is Lheureux), the poison that kills her has to come from his pharmacy.

It is this menacing quality of reality that explains Emma's refusal to think about or accept what is close to her, though this is the only way to make her dreams come true. And indeed, Homais, as an incarnation of reality, is not only external to Emma's existence and a threat; he is also represented as the place where Emma's desires are fulfilled. Whereas she is frustrated in her desire for a son, he is the father of two; whereas she falls further and further into debt, he is economically successful. He is famous, his name is known to all; he achieves the reputation that Emma would like to have, and that she tries to achieve, vicariously and without success, through Charles: "Why at least, was not her husband one of those silently determined men who work at their books all night, and at last . . . at sixty . . . wear a string of medals on their ill-fitting black coat? She would have wished this name of Bovary, which was hers, to be illustrious, to see it displayed at the booksellers', repeated in the newspapers, known to all France" (595; *44*).

Homais fulfills these desires: "He busied himself with great questions: the social problem, the moral plight of the poorer classes, pisciculture, rubber, railways, &c. . . . He by no means gave up his store. On the contrary, he kept well abreast of new discoveries" (690-91; *251-52*); "The crowds . . . threatened at times to smash the window of the pharmacy . . . so great was Homais' reputation in the neighboring villages" (617; *90-91*); "He has just been given the cross of the Legion of Honor" (692; *255*).

Emma's failure and frustration are the result of her narcissism, of her imaginary existence, which does not allow any real difference. The only difference Emma can permit is that of scenery, of setting, so that although she retains her sameness and holds the projected image in specular subordination to herself, she can still create the illusion of difference. Her preoccupation with the smallest details of clothes and scenery, furniture or accessories, points to her desire to create an illusion of difference where actually only sameness and repetition exist. What characterizes her both as a "dreamer" (a potential, though abortive, narrator) and as a character is her belief that a change in decor is sufficient to create a difference in experience.⁶

Notes

[1] Bonnefis, p. 157.

[2] Culler sees the centrality of this cliché theme as the novel's greatest flaw. "If there is anything that justifies our finding the novel limited and tendentious," he says, "it is the seriousness with which Emma's corruption is attributed to novels and romances" (*Flaubert*, p. 146). As my analysis demonstrates, however, the centrality of this cliché theme is necessary for articulating the relation between character and narrator in the novel. Although the implied author does not perfectly coincide with the character of Emma, he is like her in being a divided subject, inhabited by the language of the other.

[3] See, for example, Gothot-Mersch, "Le Point de vue dans *Madame Bovary*," p. 257. See also Rousset, "*Madame Bovary*," p. 114.

[4] This gradual incarnation can be seen both in Emma herself and in the specular images, her lovers: Charles is almost nonexistent as a character, the Viscount is just a shadow (a name), and Léon I is a quotation from Lamartine, but Rodolphe and Léon II have concrete material and psychological reality. Both of them have more life of their own, more of an independent existence outside the relation with Emma. A character's independence is correlated with its materiality and

incarnation. Similarly, Emma herself moves toward greater and greater sensuality and incarnation, which, as in the case of Helen, is indicated by a descent on the social ladder: "On the day of Mid-Lent she did not return to Yonville; that evening she went to a masked ball . . . and in the morning she found herself on the steps of the theater together with five or six other masked dancers, dressed as stevedores or sailors. . . . There were a clerk, two medical students, and a shop assistant: what company for her! As to the women, Emma soon perceived from the tone of their voices that most of them probably came from the lowest class" (672-73; *212*).

[5] Gothot-Mersch, "Le point de vue dans *Madame Bovary*," p. 257. See also Sartre, "Notes sur *Madame Bovary*," p. 42.

[6] This belief of Emma's is demystified by the narrator. As Bal has shown, the description of the "splendid city" about which Emma dreams when she wants to run away with Rodolphe has strong similarities to the descriptions of Rouen, the chateau of the Vaubyessard, and Yonville. For a detailed analysis of those description, see Bal, pp. 89-111. . . .

Nathaniel Wing (essay date 1986)

SOURCE: "Emma's Stories: Narrative, Repetition and Desire in *Madame Bovary*," in *The Limits of Narrative: Essays on Baudelaire, Flaubert, Rimbaud and Mallarmé*, Cambridge University Press, 1986, pp. 41-77.

[*In the following excerpt, Wing argues that "the division between language and experience is a major concern of* [Madame Bovary]." *He focuses on the problematic nature of the novel's narrative voice and structure, noting ways in which its "authority," or believability, is undermined.*]

> —Eh bien! reprit Homais, il faudrait en faire une analyse. Car il savait qu'il faut, dans tous les empoisonnements, faire une analyse . . . (295)
>
> *Qu'on n'accuse personne.* (294)[1]

Flaubert's use of narrative in ***Madame Bovary*** demystifies in many ways the desires which motivate Emma's stories, her fantasies, dreams and her extended fictions of escape and romantic love. Emma's narratives, her protonarratives (fantasies and dreams), her letters to her lovers, the account of her financial ruin told to Lheureux, Binet, Rodolphe and others in the last desperate moments of her life, can be read as repeated and unsuccessful attempts to give order to desires which are destabilizing in their effects and ultimately unattainable. Emma's narratives of desire presuppose closure, bringing on, paradoxically, the death

Monsieur Bovary.

of desire, which cannot live on images of fulfillment, but only on displacements and deferrals.

The division between language and experience is a major concern of the novel. Emma's stories oppose the events which constitute her world, yet lack the force to transform that world. One can attribute Emma's difficulties throughout the novel, then, not just to her foolishness and to the mediocrity of her milieu (although Flaubert clearly treats ironically the shop-worn topos of provincial adultery) but to the more general problems of desire and its realization, and of language and illusion.

Throughout the novel desire, narrative and writing in general produce corrosive effects. These are figured most directly and powerfully, perhaps, during Emma's agony, with the likening of the taste of poison to the taste of ink, and later in the same sequence when the narrator describes a certain black fluid oozing from Emma's mouth. Only a very limited reading, however, would link Emma's desires and her narratives unequivocally to an ultimately mortal alienation of the desiring subject and to writing as death. However demystifying its narrative, the novel *is* a story about desire, with "characters," organized with extraordinary control at certain points of the text by a narrator whose production of fiction must necessarily be interpreted not only as a denial but also a repetition of Emma's relations to narrative and . . . to desire. Once again, what are the possible meanings of that famous statement which Flaubert may or may not have made "Madame Bovary. C'est moi"?

While this chapter focuses on the context and the order of Emma's narratives, it will also re-examine the general problematic of writing in the novel, in the hope that the subject of Emma's narratives will implicate the performance of narrative in the novel itself and, ultimately, the performance of the critical text as well. If Emma is a figure for the writer at a certain point in the history of the novel, this figure does not function exclusively as an uncomplex emblem of the deluded Romantic in an already post-Romantic moment.[2] It may be suspected that the demystification of Emma's narratives does not in fact validate without reserve the control of an enlightened narrator whose understanding transcends the dilemmas of Romantic subjectivity and Romantic literary stereotypes. In many ways, of course, that control is exercised with remarkable force, yet an omniscient narrator is caught in an intricate web of repetition and difference which includes and radically exceeds the logic of identification between narrator and protagonist; includes and exceeds a simple demystification which would deny altogether the links between protagonist and narrator.

An omniscient narrator in **Madame Bovary** is only one among several figures through which narrative is articulated. One of the most fascinating aspects of the novel is the dispersal and fragmentation of authority for narrative. As Barthes has noted, it is impossible to establish with certainty in any comprehensive sense "who speaks" as narrator in this text or from what "point of view."[3] Point of view in **Madame Bovary** can be characterized only by its instability and indeterminacy. It alternates between an omniscient narrator, who knows the motivations of all the protagonists and the truths of the world in which they are placed; a limited point of view, circumscribed by the thoughts and feelings of a particular protagonist; and the even more limited scope of certain minor figures in the text, spectators who have no immediate connection with the major protagonists. The frequent use of free indirect discourse, with its blurring of distinctions between reported speech and narrative, is another complex amalgam of narrative authority.[4] The resulting indeterminacy of point of view, as Culler has demonstrated, is one of the major features of the novel.[5] Those passages which organize narrative according to one or another point of view are countered by others which function in a very different way. The "impersonality" of Flaubert's text, then, is not a distanced objectivity, but a mix of modes of presentation which prevent the reader from identifying a consistent pattern or, to use Rousset's term, modulation. Objectivity is not the absence of narrative authority but a dispersal of that authority which makes it ultimately resistant to recuperative interpretation.

This chapter will question how authority for narrative, both the story of the novel, and Emma's stories framed by the main narrative, is assumed and at the same time problematized. An examination of the composition of Emma's narratives elucidates the ways in which those narratives ironically construct the subject as radically different from what she would be. My assumption is that both narrative form, as well as the stereotypes of narrative content, are necessary to the assertion of desire and intimately related to its failures. The dissolution of the protagonist will be interpreted through perceptible shifts in her relations both to the fictions of desire, the narrative *énoncé,* and to narrative form, both *énoncé* and *énonciation,* as means of ordering and appropriating objects of desire. Finally I will ask how the account and the interpretation of Emma's narratives implicate at once narrators and the reader, as producers of stories: the narratives of desire and the allegories of interpretation.

In a broad sense, **Madame Bovary** gives considerable attention to questions of reading and writing; it narrativizes the interpretation of narrative. The effects of narrative are never merely limited to an explicit content, a subject's relation to the objects of desire, but always open up the more troublesome problematic of how narratives attempt to organize and control desire, how they interpret and construct "reality" and the desiring subject.[6] The power of narrative ordering as a means to fulfil desire and attain knowledge is a ubiquitous motif in this novel. That power fails consistently, as I have suggested, for the effects of fiction-making are quite different from those projected by the desiring subject.

The very control which encourages metanarrative commentary is itself problematized, as in the opening pages of the second part of the novel, when a statement, rare for its explicitness, speaks of the aporia of fictions. The comment serves as a sweeping demystification, yet it doesn't simply write off narrative, for it is set in a transition between the first and second parts of the novel and serves as a preface to a major section of the story. Following a realistic description of the countryside and the village of Yonville, just prior to Charles's and Emma's arrival at their new home, the narrator states simply:

> Depuis les événements que l'on va raconter, rien, en effet, n'a changé à Yonville. La drapeau tricolore

de fer blanc tourne toujours au haut du clocher de l'église; la boutique du marchand de nouveautés agite encore au vent ses deux banderoles d'indienne; les foetus du pharmacien, comme des paquets d'amadou blanc, se pourrissent de plus en plus dans leur alcool bourbeux, et, au-dessus de la grande porte de l'auberge, le vieux lion d'or, déteint par les pluies, montre toujours aux passants sa frisure de caniche.

(68)

There is a curious complex of meanings here, the sort which will interest me throughout this study. First, a narrator announces in a traditional manner that a new story sequence is about to be related. In an equally traditional fashion, the statement is proleptic; it alludes to the conclusion of the story, known to an omniscient narrator who will relate it to the reader. A moment "beyond narrative" is also posited here, when the main story will have been told and events will return to a meaningless repetition of the same (*toujours, encore*). Narrative, according to this passage, seems to be invested with a significance which is superior to "reality." The world of Yonville after the story, "outside" of narrative, is set against narrative as an endless and seemingly meaningless repetition, which is figured by random motion, the weather vane turning in place, the pennants flapping in the wind, and by the degeneration of the bottled foetuses.

One can also interpret the first sentence of the passage in a very different way, however, as signifying something like: "Events occur, nothing changes." The narrative signified would then be undercut as ultimately insignificant. Thus read, this passage denies the closure of the story about to be told even before it is narrated, as it sets these events against an insignificant post-narrative "reality." While establishing demarcations between story and non-story, the comment problematizes the meaningful difference produced by narrative. I have said that the passage serves as a preface to a section of the novel, and at the same time suggests much about the inconsequentiality of the story; things are further complicated, however, because this is not the *beginning* of the story, but the opening of the second of three major sequences. Whatever is being said about stories in general must be applied retrospectively to the first part of the novel. The commentary which seems to set itself outside of the main narrative is already framed by the earlier narrative, which can be read as a *commentary* on the metanarrative statement. What is at issue here is less the knowing control over the story by an omniscient narrator who demystifies the fiction from a privileged position, than the impossibility of narrating and at the same time placing oneself outside of the rhetorical operations of fiction. The passage thus becomes engaged in a crisis of narrative whose terms it reiterates in an inevitable play of repetition.[7]

I have already hinted at some of my conclusions about the operations of desire, narrative and interpretation, which can be ordered tentatively in terms of the two statements quoted at the beginning of this chapter. Both quotations are taken from the last pages of the novel. The first is uttered by Homais, panicked when he discovers that Emma has taken poison: "Eh bien! reprit Homais, il faudrait en faire l'analyse. Car il savait qu'il faut, dans tous les empoisonnements, faire une analyse; . . ." (295). In this moment of crisis, the pharmacist unhesitatingly turns toward his science to determine what action must be taken to save Emma from herself. Rapidly moving events prevent Homais from performing his diagnosis, but the critic faced with unsettling problems of interpretation is not subject to such constraints. If we are to analyze the reasons for Emma's destruction in terms of the workings of narrative and accept the guidance of an ironically illusive and sophisticated narrator, we must also accept the tutelage of the pharmacist, that other patron of the analytic process. The imperative to analyze and to achieve interpretive validity allies us unwittingly, yet unfailingly, with Homais.

The other statement informing my reading is a fragment of Emma's suicide letter, which Charles has torn open as Emma lies convulsed on her bed: "*Qu'on n'accuse personne . . .*" (294). At the very moment when it becomes a most urgent concern, we are told in a curiously ambiguous fashion that interpretation is to be suspended. In what ways does Emma's statement serve as an antidote to Homais's disastrously inadequate imperative to undertake analysis? What, in fact, are we being asked not to evaluate? the immediate responsibility for Emma's death? her adultery? or perhaps in a more sweeping sense, those wider issues I have raised—the destructive effects of Emma's relations to fiction? This imperative regarding interpretation, however, is literally suspended, broken by deletion marks in the text. I will return later to the interpretive space opened up by those marks, but let us note for the moment that Homais's and Emma's statements, taken together, point to radically different and incompatible positions concerning the finality of fiction and the necessity for interpretation.[8] The first aims at masterly control and is killing in its effects; the second invites the suspension of judgment and is powerfully productive of interpretation. Inevitably, the reader is engaged by these two imperatives, simultaneously; interpretation circulates between Homais's inept, but nonetheless murderous authority, and Emma's call for the suspension of interpretation.

Learning narrative: a story of one's own

The first part of the novel establishes certain constants in Emma's relation to her desires and the law of the father, which will be repeated throughout the text, and through reiteration, modified. From the outset, Emma's desires are articulated within another's story: paradoxically "her" story is explicitly spoken or already composed by another. In its simplest form, she is the silent and passive object of the story of another's desire, the alienated object of masculine appropriation.

Some of the major preoccupations of the text concerning language and desire, that language is always inadequate to desire, that the language of desire is never unique, but always a common and alienating discourse, are figured early in the novel by the account of Charles's stammering attempts to ask for Emma's hand. This passage marks Emma's entry into the discourse of desire. It is paralleled, as we shall see, by an extensive sequence at the end of the novel which explicitly links the economy of romantic desire with the economy of bourgeois capitalism, when Emma tells the story of her ruin to the men who directly or indirectly contributed to its design. In Part One of the novel Emma undergoes what might be called an apprenticeship to narrative, in which she acquires an individual "voice" for her desires and elaborates them in narrative fictions. Although this section ends with the classic impasse of feminine desire, the "silence" of hysteria, Emma emerges in Part One from the position of a passive voiceless object of desire, to an active fiction making "subject." She theorizes about love, passion and happiness, and composes stories of fulfilled desire. There is an earlier pre-narrative moment, however, which informs all of Emma's subsequent relations to narratives and to desire. Charles attempts to tell Emma's father of his wish to marry her:

> Maître Rouault, murmura-t-il, je voudrais bien vous dire quelque chose.
>
> Ils s'arrêtèrent. Charles se taisait.
>
> —*Mais contez-moi votre histoire!* Est-ce que je ne sais pas tout! dit le père Rouault, en riant doucement. (23, italics added)

The formulation of desire here, early in the text, is associated significantly with the ability to compose a story. Charles, of course, has difficulty with stories throughout the novel, and that is part of the reason why his demand is relayed to Emma by her father. There are further implications of this episode, however, which are worth exploring. Throughout the novel Charles will remain deprived of the status of acting subject in the stories of desire. In terms of Emma's stories, he is the silent institutionalized opponent. There is more at issue, however, than Charles's silence and his ultimate exclusion from the stories of desire. Here the figure of the prospective husband and that of the father are conflated in a manner which *Emma* never fully overcomes, in spite of the transformations of Charles's role later in the narrative from subject to opponent. The story of feminine desire remains linked consistently with the figure of the father, for the voice of the father always reverberates in the voice of the lover. The "position" Emma occupies here, as determined by the possessive adjective *votre,* and by her role as the object of a story in which the male formulates desire through the voice of the father, or functions as his symbolic equivalent, remains constant throughout the novel. Even as Emma becomes the teller of stories, she can exercise that role only in imitation of this initial model, within the structure of masculine desire.[9] The chapter ends with a paragraph in which the first sentence confirms the displacement of Emma as a subject of her desire: "*Emma eût, au contraire, désiré se marier à minuit, aux flambeaux,* mais le père Rouault ne comprit rien à cette idée." (24, italics added). The sentence derives as much meaning from its syntax as from its semantic content; the adversitive *au contraire,* which interrupts the verbal structure interrupts the language of Emma's desire, which in asserting itself against the father (lover) becomes disintegrated, deferred.

Shortly after her marriage, at the end of chapter 5, Emma's disappointments take the form of speculation about the full meaning of the words of love; they remain in a pre-narrative mode:

> Avant qu'elle se mariât, elle avait cru avoir de l'amour; mais le bonheur qui aurait dû résulter de cet amour n'étant pas venu, il fallait qu'elle se fut trompée, songeait-elle. Et Emma cherchait à savoir ce que l'on entendait au juste dans la vie par les mots de *félicité,* de *passion* et *d'ivresse,* qui lui avaient paru si beaux dans les livres. (32)

From the outset, Emma's experience of desire is linked to the elusive meanings of words; access to pleasure and knowledge will "take place" in language. Language is doubly deficient, however; on the one hand it is always the discourse of the other ("ce que *l'on* entendait par les mots . . .") never the unique property of the desiring subject. On the other hand, the words mark a radical flaw in the system. Scandalously, they require but utterly lack reference. This dilemma, as critics have shown, is a key element of *bovarysm,* a desire/writing which maniacally seeks the *mot juste* without the ultimate guarantee of a reality which would validate the relations of signification. In a general sense, the object of desire in Flaubert's novels retreats under the proliferation of the signs which are necessary to its representation.[10] These words also have a particular relation to narrative: they mark a pre-narrative moment for Emma, in which the signifiers of desire are presented as pure nomination, not yet engaged in a verbal sequence. This moment is in many ways similar to the intransitive position which Anna O., in Breuer's famous analysis, assumes in her reveries, at one stage in her treatment. During her "absences," Anna murmurs the impersonal "tormenting, tormenting." Anna has lost the position of grammatical subject; she repeats an impersonal form with no immediate link to the first person, standing outside any narrative ordering of a fantasm.[11] Emma, too, at this point in the story has not yet appropriated a discursive form which will be charged with giving meaning to the signifiers of desire. The experience of desire here is the interpretation of the already spoken or written, which the subject cannot know until she assumes a relation to narrative.[12]

The retrospective account of Emma's emotional formation, in chapter 6 of the first part of the novel, is the story of her first seduction, the seduction by romantic fiction. The terms which refer to Emma's readings have significant erotic implications not simply in their themes, but in reference to the act of reading itself. The narratives of desire are invested with erotic intensity not only because of their content, but also because they are read in secret. Of reading keepsakes it is said: "Il les fallait cacher, c'était une affaire . . ." (35). Erotic transgression thus becomes linked from the outset with concealment and an intimate relation is established between narratives of desire and secrecy.

Emma not only fantasizes by imitating the stereotypes of romantic fiction throughout the novel, but her imaginings imitate the second-rate copy. Her representation of romantic fiction will be associated not only with erotic intensity, but also with the dissolution of energy. The texts which establish the models of desire are themselves set in a structure of destructive repetition. Emma reads the classics of romantic fiction, yet she reads with even greater pleasure the second-rate reproductions of romantic stereotypes; keepsakes and popular novels. By interiorizing the stereotype it becomes a fantasm, which Emma assumes as her personal history. The text does not repress the knowledge of the repetition, which implicates an omniscient narrator as well as the protagonist; it becomes one of the major motifs of the novel. In demystifying Emma's blindness to her engagement in these repetitions, the narrator assumes a largely sadistic role, which we may suspect is the effect of a powerful nostalgia for the lost power of now obsolete stories of desire, still painfully contemporary.

The relation of desire to language here is similar to that discussed above in the context of Emma's wish to know the meanings of the words of bliss, but there are significant differences. Attention shifts from the static paradigm (metaphor) to the mobile syntagmatic order of narrative (metonymy). Desire, when associated with the nouns which serve as its signifier, can only remain virtual, a possibility forever suspended. When it is articulated as the narrative of fulfilled pleasure, however, desire is linked inevitably with the alienating repetitions of the stereotype. The private strategy of concealment only renders more apparent this alienation within romantic narratives.

Other constants of Emma's relation to desire and narrative are also established in this chapter. Desire is experienced as an imperative to appropriate objects for personal profit. Emma's personal narratives will later provide the means for that appropriation, but here the motif of the pleasures of reading and the motif of appropriation are simply contiguous, not yet joined explicitly as they will be later in the novel. Certain links between the personally pleasurable and bourgeois economy, however, are already formed in this chapter:

> Il fallait qu'elle pût retirer des choses une sorte de *profit personnel;* et elle rejetait comme *inutile* tout ce qui ne contribuait pas à *la consommation immédiate* de son coeur, étant de tempérament plus sentimental qu'artiste . . . (34, italics added)

Pleasure is set in a system of exchange which conflates the emotional and the commercial, in which the subject seeks to consume the object of desire. Flaubert's correspondence repeatedly underscores implications in this passage that Emma is a perverted emblem of the artist and that her experiences of desire are characteristic of bourgeois sensibility. Desiring, for Emma, is a form of imitation whose object is the recuperation of sense, without difference or loss.

In terms of the novel's narrative order, this chapter is analeptic to the main narrative, its events situated in the protagonist's childhood.[13] Clearly, chapter 6 provides information about attributes of Emma's "character" which will remain remarkably static throughout the novel. Emma will attain maturity as a "subject," however, only when she actively orders the elements of Romantic narratives according to an economic and sentimental schema already set by these earliest reported experiences of literature.

In the remaining chapters of Part One, Emma's desires are confined to a narcissistic silence. She now spins out her narratives as voiceless fantasies. In the opening lines of chapter 7, Emma composes hypothetical stories of travel to far-away places:

> il eût fallu, sans doute, s'en aller vers ces pays à noms sonores où les lendemains de mariage ont de plus suaves paresses! Dans des chaises de poste, sous des stores de soie bleue, on monte au pas des routes escarpées, écoutant la chanson du postillon, qui se répète dans la montagne avec les clochettes des chèvres et le bruit sourd de la cascade. (38)

Moments of daydreaming such as this, as Genette notes in an excellent study of description and narrative in Flaubert, are doubly silent.[14] The protagonists have ceased to speak to each other; Emma turns toward the world of her dreams. The narrative of the novel is also silent here, immobile, interrupted by a fantasy narrative which suspends the sequence of events in the main story. Emma's narratives, although they intrude upon the sequence of the main story, never acquire the power to take over from that story the initiative for ordering events.

Following this passage, the text focuses specifically on the illocutionary context of communication: Emma's needs are formulated less in terms which characterize a specific object of desire than in terms of a discursive situation.[15] She lacks that *other*, necessary to the circuit of communication:

> Peut-être aurait-elle souhaité faire à quelqu'un la confidence de toutes ces choses. Mais comment dire un insaisissable malaise, qui change d'aspect comme les nuées, qui tourbillonne comme le vent? Les mots lui manquaient donc, l'occasion, la hardiesse. (38)

This passage opens up questions considerably more complex than the problem posed for Emma by the absence of an interlocutor. On the one hand the role of the other can never fulfill the function which Emma desires, for the other is to be always elsewhere and different from what the subject wishes. The images and the stories of desire, furthermore, are to be located beyond a particular and immediately accessible reality, a particular time and space contemporary to the subject, yet they can be constructed only with the aid of what they attempt to reject: reality . . . *another* reality. As for the formation of images and stories of pure desire, a further paradox makes itself felt. From the outset, there is a fundamental problem: these things, objects of desire, are lacking, and the elements which might constitute objects are heterogeneous, disparate, incapable of acquiring a stable configuration. Language cannot fix them, nor can they be generated by "reality" to be retrieved by language.[16]

Emma's attempts to arouse passion in herself pursue an illusive, provisional and ultimately inadequate solution. She develops theories about desire, narrative explanations of the empty signifiers. She repeats passionate verse in the manner of a sentimental catechism:

> d'après des théories qu'elle croyait bonnes, elle voulut se donner de l'amour. Au clair de lune, dans le jardin, elle récitait tout ce qu'elle savait par coeur de rimes passionnées . . . (41)

Theory, for Emma, is auto-erotic, a solitary gesture directed toward narcissistic fulfillment. Knowing pleasure is repeating *by heart* the language of another's passion.

The major "event" of Part One, the trip to the chateau de Vaubeyssard, the dinner and the ball, appears to provide the occasion or access to the passion about which Emma had mused earlier. She remains excluded, however, from the language of potential partners in communication. What she wishes for most fervently is a passionate interlocutor, yet, in the conversations which take place in this sequence, she occupies an unmistakably marginal position; the language of the people at the chateau is incomprehensible, foreign to her. Emma is excluded because she is ignorant of the meanings of the speaker's words who "causait Italie":

> A trois pas d'Emma, un cavalier en habit bleu causait Italie avec une jeune femme pâle, . . . Ils vantaient la grosseur des piliers de Saint-Pierre, Tivoli, le Vésuve, Castellamare et les Cassines, les roses de Gênes, le Colisée au clair de lune. Emma écoutait de son autre oreille une conversation pleine de mots qu'elle ne comprenait pas. (48)

Her alienation is also figured by the space in which she is caught, a space between two centers of desire. Although the swirling movements of her dance with the Vicomte transform the swirling, formless malaise (*qui tourbillone comme le vent . . .*) into intense pleasure, Emma is excluded from the verbal articulations of desire which she seeks to know. Two passages specifically underscore the link between silence and the enforced solitude of Emma's desire. In the first, Emma composes a brief narrative about a cigar case of green silk, which Charles finds by the road on their return to Tostes. Emma supposes that its owner is the Vicomte; her fantasy narrative transforms the case into a fetishized object:

> A qui appartenait-il? . . . Au vicomte. C'était peut-être un cadeau de sa maîtresse. On avait brodé cela sur quelque métier de palissandre, meuble mignon que l'on cachait à tous les yeux, qui avait occupé bien des heures et où s'étaient penchées les boucles molles de la travailleuse pensive. Un souffle d'amour avait passé parmi les mailles du canevas; chaque coup d'aiguille avait fixé là une espérance ou un souvenir, et tous ces fils de soie entrelacés n'étaient que le continuité de la même passion silencieuse. (53)

A cigar case here, is not "just" a cigar case. Once again, Emma's silent narrative is both erotic and the reproduction of the fabric of another text; she composes her story upon the already woven surface of a fetishized object. Paradoxically, however, in seeking a sense which would attain the continuity of "authentic" passion, meanings become a play of surface effects, incapable of evoking the desired presence. The fiction of desire, quite literally, is a fabrication which affirms distance, not presence; "Elle était à Tostes. Lui, il était à Paris, maintenant; là-bas!" (53). The desired moment of absolute presence (*maintenant*) is deferred, and metaphorized as spatial disjunction (*là-bas*).

Emma's taste for stories is not easily satisfied, however, and the inadequacies of this narrative produce more fiction, generated by a word which, in its very emptiness, can accommodate all meaning:

> Comment était ce Paris? Quel nom démesuré! Elle se le répétait à demi-voix, pour se faire plaisir; il sonnait à ses oreilles comme un bourdon de cathédrale; il flamboyait à ses yeux jusque sur l'étiquette de ses pots de pommade.
>
> . . . . .
>
> Paris, plus vaste qu'un océan. (53-4)

This passage maintains a certain structural symmetry with the end of chapter 5, in which Emma had speculated on the meaning of the words *félicité, passion* and *ivresse,* yet there are meaningful differences between the two contexts which are due to the increasing importance of narrative to Emma's desire. The passages are similar in that each is an act of denomination, the terms in each case being devoid of semantic substance. The word Paris here must be referential, but is meaningful only as a figure. *Paris* is as empty a signifier as the words of passion, yet a fantasmatic geography has replaced the atopical terms of bliss, and Emma's imaginings move closer to narrative. The term *Paris* justifies the fantasmatic representation of desire, for it has historical, topographical reference, but it only functions effectively as a signifier which can accommodate the projections of desire when it becomes detached from that reference.

The act of naming is followed by another debauchery of reading, similar to that in the retrospective chapter 6. In the later episode, Emma subscribes to "feminine" reviews and studies descriptions of Parisian decors in E. Sue, Balzac and Georges Sand; "y cherchant des assouvissements imaginaires pour ses convoitises personnelles" (54). The same desire to consume the text and the same relation between desire and writing of both the first (Balzac, etc.) and the second order (*le journal de femmes*) are asserted as before. Emma takes the realist project literally; if the word is able to represent adequately the essence of things, then that essence is available to appropriation as language. Emma wants writing without difference, a desire figured here by her turning away from the symbolic mode of romantic narratives toward realist description and, beyond that, toward the iconic figure of a map of Paris. She buys a map and traces imaginary walks through the city:

> Elle s'acheta un plan de Paris, et du bout de son doigt, sur la carte, elle faisait des courses dans la capitale. Elle remontait des boulevards, s'arrêtait à chaque angle entre les lignes des rues, devant des carrés blancs qui figurent des maisons. (54)

Like Félicité, in **"Un Coeur simple,"** who asks to be shown the house of her nephew on a map of Cuba, Emma's interpretation of the map seeks the real, where there is only the surface of an iconic figure. Her misreading in this passage allegorizes the separation between figures of desire and referents. Emma's finger on this fetishized surface of the map attempts an impossible coincidence between her imaginings and the abstract surface on which desire has been projected.

It is at this time that Emma begins to wear an open house coat, buys paper and a blotter and dreams of *Charles* becoming a famous writer:

> Elle s'était acheté un buvard, une papeterie, un porte-plume et des enveloppes, quoiqu'elle n'eût persone à qui écrire. (56)

Emma fills the space of lack not by writing herself, but by displacing the feminine subject in favor of a masculine proper name, which is to assume phallocentric mastery and circulate within a bourgeois economy:

> Elle aurait voulu que *ce nom de Bovary, qui était le sien,* fût illustre, le voir étalé chez les libraries, répété dans les journaux, connu par toute la France
> (58, italics added)

At the very moment when Emma might begin to write, her enclosure by the bourgeois family permits access to writing through the name of the husband, which can circulate only in accordance with the laws of commerce. Emma has effaced feminine difference in favor of the workings of the *non(m) propre*.[17]

Emma has come full circle; having gained access to narrative as the medium of desire she now refuses the role of the writing subject and in her fantasies seeks to give over that role to a man. The "solution" takes the form of denial and displacement; it produces a re-emergence of desire in the symptoms of a "nervous disorder": "Elle devenait difficile, capricieuse . . ." "Elle pâlissait et avait des battements de coeur" (62, 63). This sequence, then, repeats regressively the order of Emma's initiation to narrative; from symptom, to fantasm, to the nominal terms (*félicité,* etc.) to narrative . . . the silenced narratives of desire have been reconverted into the symptoms of hysteria. At the end of Part One of the novel, Emma can give voice to her desire only through the "silent" metaphor by which she is strangled: "Elle eut des étouffements aux premières chaleurs . . ." (59). . . .

Notes

[1] All references to *Madame Bovary* are to the Garnier edition (Paris: Garnier, 1961). References to Flaubert's other writings are to the *Oeuvres complètes* (Paris: Seuil, "L'Intégrale," 1964).

[2] Of the many studies which treat the problematic of language and writing in Flaubert, and in particular in

Madame Bovary, I have found the following to be most valuable: Charles Bernheimer, *Flaubert and Kafka: Studies in Psychopoetic Structure* (New Haven and London: Yale University Press, 1982); Leo Bersani, *A Future for Astyanax* (Boston-Toronto: Little, Brown, 1976), 89-105; Victor Brombert, *The Novels of Flaubert* (Princeton: Princeton University Press, 1966); Dominick La Capra, *Madame Bovary on Trial* (Ithaca and London: Cornell University Press, 1982); Jonathan Culler, *Flaubert: The Uses of Uncertainty* (Ithaca, NY: Cornell University Press, 1974); Alain de Lattre, *La Bêtise d'Emma Bovary* (Paris: Corti, 1980); Françoise Gaillard, "L'En-signement du réel," in *La Production du sens chez Flaubert,* ed. C. Gothot-Mersch, Colloque de Cérisy (Paris: Union générale d'éditions, 10/18, 1975), 197-220; "La Représentation comme mis en scène du voyeurisme," *RSH* vol. 154, no. 2 (1874), 267-82; Jean Rousset, *Forme et signification* (Paris: Corti, 1962), 109-33; Jean-Paul Sartre, *L' Idiot de la famille,* II (Paris: Gallimard, 1971), 1611-20; III (Paris: Gallimard, 1972), 178-201; Naomi Schor, "Pour une thématique restreinte: Ecriture, parole et différence dans *Madame Bovary,*" *Litt.* 22 (1975), 30-46; R. J. Sherrington, *Three Novels by Flaubert* (Oxford: Clarendon Press, 1970); Tony Tanner, *Adultery in the Novel* (Baltimore and London: The Johns Hopkins Press, 1979), 233-367; Albert Thibaudet, *Gustave Flaubert* (Paris: Gallimard, 1935); Anthony Thorlby, *Gustave Flaubert and the Art of Realism* (London: Bowes and Bowes, 1956). Most of these analyses, in so far as they offer any extended study of Emma's stories, treat them as framed by the narrative of an authoritative narrator. Although that perspective must be taken into account, this chapter will focus more directly on Emma's stories and will trace their effects on a general interpretation of narrative in the novel. Reversing the conventional perspective produces unanticipated effects which lead to a re-examination of framing, desire and the impulses of power in narrative.

[3] Roland Barthes, *S/Z* (Paris: Seuil, 1970), 146: "Flaubert . . . , en maniant une ironie frappée d'incertitude, opère un malaise salutaire de l'écriture: il n'arrête pas le jeu des codes (ou l'arrête mal), en sorte que (c'est là sans doute la *preuve* de l'écriture) *on ne sait jamais s'il est responsable de ce qu'il écrit* (s'il y a un sujet *derrière* son langage); car l'être de l'écriture (le sens du travail qui la constitue) est d'empêcher de jamais répondre à cette question: *Qui parle?*"

[4] For a discussion of the combination of impersonal narration and *erlebte Rede,* or free, indirect discourse in *Madame Bovary* see Hans Robert Jauss, "Literary History as a Challenge to Literary Theory," *New Literary History,* II, No. 1 (1970), 7-38.

[5] Culler, 109-22.

[6] The troublesome word "reality" will assert itself frequently in my text. I will define my uses of the term here to avoid the repeated intrusion of cumbersome definitions in the course of my discussion. On the one hand, the term will refer to what the fiction designates as real, what is generally understood as an *effet de réel*. See Roland Barthes, "L'Effet de réel," *Communications,* 11 (1968), 84-9. In other instances the meaning of the term will be closer to what Lacan has called *le Réel,* which, precisely, cannot be named and resists symbolization. The *Real* can only be approximated by narrative in asymptotic fashion, as Frederic Jameson has noted: "Imaginary and Symbolic in Lacan: Marxism, Psychoanalytic Criticism and the Problem of the Subject," *Yale French Studies,* 55/56 (1977), 338-95, esp. 383-95. Very often in reading *Madame Bovary* it is not possible to assert with any confidence which of these two senses is appropriate and much of the force of the novel is generated by this indeterminacy.

[7] Gaillard, "L'En-signement du réel": "on ne peut triompher de l'écriture qu'en s'absorbant en elle: par un mouvement vertigineux de répétition en abîme, il faut être le livre en recopiant le livre que l'on recopie dans le livre," 201.

[8] Naomi Schor's very suggestive article, "Pour une Thématique restreinte," discusses the similarities between Homais and Emma, both of whom aspire to be writers. It should also be noted that, as interpreters, Emma and Homais are set in opposition to each other at the end of the novel. On the legal implications of a stable narrative signified see La Capra, *Madame Bovary on Trial* and the final chapter of this book.

[9] Luce Irigaray, in *Speculum de l'autre femme* (Paris: Minuit, 1974), 9-162, discusses the displacement of a feminine libidinal economy and the imposition of masculine mimetic models of desire in the Freudian theory of sexual difference. In Freud's analysis of the early relation between the daughter and her mother, the young girl's role is determined by that of the male child; the daughter is said to understand her sexual difference as a lack, a defect, an absence of the phallus. The terms in which Irigaray discusses this suppression of feminine difference and its assimilation by the story of masculine desire are strikingly pertinent to this crucial passage in *Madame Bovary:* "Laissée au *vide,* au *manque* de toute représentation, re-presentation, et en toute rigueur aussi mimésis, de son désir (d')origine. Lequel en passera, dès lors, par le désir-discours-loi du désir de l'homme: tu seras ma femmemère, ma femme si tu veux, tu peux, être (comme) ma mère = tu seras pour moi la possibilité de répéter-représenter-reproduire-m'approprier le (mon) rapport à l'origine . . . Mais disons qu'*au commencement s'arrêterait son historie,* [l'histoire de la fillette] pour se laisser prescrire par celle d'un autre: celle de l'homme père," 47.

[10] See de Lattre's discussion of the "paradox of the image," *La Bêtise* . . . , 20.

[11] Laurent Jenny, "Il n'y a pas de récit cathartique," *Poétique,* 41 (février, 1980), 1-21. "Cette douleur impossible, c'est celle, pour un sujet, de ne pouvoir se conjuguer au noyau verbal de son fantasme, dans la syntaxe d'une narration," 7.

[12] Paradoxically, Emma seeks a fully expressive, unmediated language of desire by imitating, as if they were "her own," the stories of others' passion. In the most fundamental way, the possibility of appropriating meaning for the self is determined as a process of censorship imposed by discourse. The language of "self-expression" imposes what Pierre Bourdieu has called *euphémisation:* "toute expression est un ajustement entre un *intérêt expressif* et une *censure* constituée par la structure du champ dans lequel s'offre cette expression, et cet ajustement est le produit d'un travail d'euphémisation pouvant aller jusqu'au silence, limite du discours censuré." "La Censure," in *Questions de sociologie* (Paris: Minuit, 1980), 138.

[13] Gérard Genette, *Figures* III (Paris: Seuil, 1972), 90.

[14] Genette, "Silences de Flaubert," *Figures* (Paris: Seuil, 1966), 223-43.

[15] On illocutionary speech acts, see Mary Louise Pratt, *Toward a Speech Act Theory of Literary Discourse* (Bloomington, London: Indiana University Press, 1977), 80-1.

[16] de Lattre, *La Bêtise* . . . , 20-1.

[17] C. Clément, H. Cixous, *La Jeune née* (Paris: Union générale d'éditions, 10/18, 1975), 144-7: Irigaray, *Speculum,* 165-82. . . .

Tony Williams (essay date 1992)

SOURCE: "Gender Stereotypes in *Madame Bovary*," in *Forum for Modern Language Studies,* Vol. XXVIII, No. 2, April, 1992, pp. 130-9.

[*In the following essay, Williams discusses Flaubert's belief in the influence of cultural conditioning as a determinant of gender roles, pointing to motifs in* Madame Bovary *that illustrate the restricted and highly artificial role of women in a patriarchal society.*]

Madame Bovary was put on trial when it was first published largely on account of its intense critical interrogation of the assumptions that collectively make up the common-sense outlook on life in nineteenth-century France. The subversive force of the novel is directed most obviously against that cornerstone of

Emma Bovary and Rudolphe encounter each other at the agricultural fair.

bourgeois society, marriage.[1] This subversion of the conventional view of marriage is, however, connected with a more fundamental attack upon another received idea, what, in a different context, has been described as the "ideological image, repeated and naturalised a thousand times in the fiction of the period, of the very reality of 'woman' as the passive, inert creature of the domestic world of the nineteenth-century family".[2] Although the objection against Flaubert's novel was not formulated in these terms, it is against the conventional view of woman as essentially passive and inert that the novel offended most deeply. At an earlier point in the writing of the novel, Emma appears dressed in a waistcoat and Charles's mother is shocked by "ce bouleversement des sexes et de toutes les convenances".[3] It is the implications of this and other examples of overturning of conventional gender distinctions which this article will explore.

In many respects it is surprising that Flaubert should have mounted one of the most ferocious and sustained attacks upon conventional gender distinctions. In his letters he often sounds like a typical nineteenth-century misogynist, slipping into what sounds like mindless denigration of the opposite sex.[4] The negative views expressed in the letters are, however, directed not so much against something innate in women as against a pattern of behaviour which has been induced by social conditioning. Flaubert has a strong awareness that women are not born but made: "La femme est un produit de l'homme. *Dieu a créé la femelle et l'homme a fait la femme;* elle est le résultat de la civilisation, une œuvre factice."[5] Flaubert's view coincides with that of his contemporary, Stuart Mill, who in *The Subjection of Women* asserted that "what is now called the nature of woman is an eminently artificial thing—the result of forced repression in some directions, unnatural stimulation in others". Flaubert clearly recognises that what are commonly regarded as the principal characteristics of the opposite sex are in fact the result of a process of cultural conditioning. Central to this process of cultural conditioning is the conventional education to which girls are submitted:

> On apprend aux femmes à mentir d'une façon infâme. L'apprentissage dure toute leur vie. [. . .] Le puritanisme, la bégueulerie, le système du *renfermé,* de l'*étroit,* dénature et perd dans sa fleur les plus charmantes créations du bon Dieu. [. . .] J'ai peur du corset moral, voilà tout. Les premières impressions ne s'effacent pas, tu le sais.[6]

Like Stendhal, Flaubert believes that the cultural conditioning of women entails the radical loss of half of humanity which becomes alienated from an original femaleness.[7] Flaubert's strategic distinction between "la femelle" and "la femme" is close to the now familiar distinction between sex and gender. Although sex and gender have frequently been confused in the past, "the threadbare tactic of justifying social and temperamental differences by biological ones" is now largely discredited. As Angela Carter insists, although sexual differentiation of a biological nature is an unarguable fact, "separate from it, and only partially derived from it, are the behavioural modes of masculine and feminine, which are culturally defined variables translated in the language of common usage to the status of universals".[8] Flaubert, arguably, shows a similar awareness of the relativity of gender stereotypes.

The fictional world of **Madame Bovary** is marked by the over-differentiation of the sexes which characterises patriarchal society. Despite his considerable limitations, Charles receives an education as a health officer which equips him for a useful role in society whilst Emma, despite her greater intelligence and ability, receives an education in the Rouen convent-school which provides her with skills which have little practical relevance to her subsequent life. The marriage between Charles and Emma is arranged initially between Charles and Emma's father; Charles is legally the head of the household and special powers of attorney have to be granted to Emma in order to allow her to settle his financial affairs after the death of his father. Adultery, like marriage, is organised more according to the man's convenience and this is perhaps one of the reasons why, in Flaubert's memorable comment, Emma "retrouvait dans l'adultère toutes les platitudes du mariage" (p. 296).[9] Rodolphe's early display of chivalry gives way to brutality—"Il la traita sans façon" (p. 196)—and it soon becomes clear, as Tony Tanner puts it, that adultery has no manners.[10] This rigid division according to sex is underpinned by gender stereotypes which command wide assent. Emma has an exalted conception of the opposite sex: "Un homme, au contraire, ne devait-il pas tout connaître, exceller en des activités multiples, vous initier aux énergies de la passion, aux raffinements de la vie, à tous les mystères?" (p. 42). Her view of women is correspondingly low; she complains to Rodolphe that women are deprived of the right to roam the world and to Léon that they live useless lives. When she is angry with Léon she thinks of him as being "plus mou qu'une femme" (p. 288). Significantly Emma wishes to have a boy child:

> Un homme, au moins est libre; il peut parcourir les passions et les pays, traverser les obstacles, mordre aux bonheurs les plus lointains. Mais une femme est empêchée continuellement. Inerte et flexible à la fois, elle a contre elle les mollesses de la chair avec les dépendances de la loi. Sa volonté, comme le voile de son chapeau retenu par un cordon, palpite à tous les vents. (p. 91)

This naive view of the differences between the sexes gave rise in an early version to the following significant comment:

> Chaque sexe [. . .] par ignorance de l'autre, lui suppose des qualités qu'il n'a pas, comme les siècles supposent aux siècles précédents des énergies que la distance seule leur donne. (*Nouvelle version,* p. 265)

Given the exalted notion of what it is to be man, it is hardly surprising that Emma repeatedly wishes she *were* a man: "Que n'était-elle un homme! Comme elle aurait fait siffler au vent la mèche de sa cravache! Comme elle aurait couru dans le monde!" (*Nouvelle version,* p. 226). Likewise Charles also experiences envy of the opposite sex: "Que n'était-il pas la mère, lui! comme il aurait du plaisir à se relever la nuit et à allaiter la petite fille, en lui parlant doucement!" (*Nouvelle version,* p. 269). In this kind of instance, gender stereotypes provide the focus for a kind of existential dissatisfaction. Neither Charles nor Emma is entirely happy with the masculine or feminine role accorded to their sex.

Gender distinctions may be completely fallacious, but they die hard. If Emma is unable to shake off an idealised image of the opposite sex, which has the unfortunate effect of making the actual men she knows seem totally defective, it is largely on account of the cultural conditioning which has taken place in the convent-school. *Madame Bovary* is attentive to the construction of gender stereotypes in the sentimental novel. The world of the sentimental novel and the keepsake projects an image of man as strong and active and of the woman as weak and passive. Whilst the gentlemen are strikingly mobile, riding horses to death or galloping out of the distant countryside on a black charger, the ladies are shown lolling in carriages or reclining on sofas (p. 39). It is the "literature of patriarchy" which leads Emma to believe that fulfilment can be found only through a man.[11] Despite all the evidence to the contrary, she thinks marriage to Charles will allow her to possess "cette passion merveilleuse qui jusqu'alors s'était tenue comme un grand oiseau au plumage rose planant dans la splendeur des ciels poétiques", only to find that the quietness of married life is far removed from "le bonheur qu'elle avait rêvé" (p. 41). Subsequently she continues to believe that she needs simply to "placer sa vie sur quelque cœur solide" in order to be happy, only to discover that neither of her lovers is able to sustain his devotion. Emma's behaviour is highly contradictory: she strives with an energy and forcefulness unrivalled by any of the male characters to put herself in a position of complete dependence upon a man who she hopes will sweep her off her feet. The masculine counterpart of this process of self-mutilation involves Charles being conditioned into believing that a man should be strong: as a medical student in Rouen, he finds work in the hospital difficult to stomach but "se raidit de son mieux dans l'idée qu'il était un homme, et qu'il fallait faire bonne mine et qu'il faut qu'un homme soit énergique" (*Nouvelle version,* p. 143). Flaubert shows, particularly in earlier drafts, how both Emma and Charles try to live up to highly questionable gender stereotypes and are led into patterns of behaviour which run counter to their natural inclinations.

The validity of the conventional view of the sexes is on occasion challenged directly in narratorial comments. Rodolphe, we are told, has avoided Emma "par suite de cette lâcheté naturelle qui caractérise le sexe fort" (p. 316). Flaubert prefers, however, to allow the behaviour of his characters to speak for itself. If one takes a global view, Emma, in particular, shows more audacity, resolution and courage than all the male characters, though the goals to which these qualities are directed may seem misplaced. She is also a good deal more self-centred, strong-willed, forceful and domineering than both Charles and Léon. In contrast, Charles is more "feminine"—he is placid, undemanding, submissive, the passive partner in the marriage. Whilst Emma dreams of escaping to some exotic never-never land, Charles directs all his desire and energy to the domestic sphere.

Flaubert's presentation of the development of Emma Bovary points to a malleability as she draws upon a repertoire of both "masculine" and "feminine" roles. Emma's so-called "masculine" qualities are not immediately apparent; they gradually emerge in the course of the novel, leading to a slow dismantling of the conventional view of woman. Emma seeks to get the upper hand in all of her relationships with men. Once she has made the rather belated discovery that Charles does not conform to the image of the perfect man she has derived from her reading of the sentimental novel, Emma takes the initiative, reading him romantic poems by moonlight in the hope that he might be elevated to a higher plane. Charles cannot be prodded into the kind of artificial response she requires and Emma treats him in an increasingly scornful and imperious manner. Compared to other literary husbands, Charles is strikingly decent and devoted, but, for Emma, he becomes "l'obstacle à toute félicité, la cause de toute misère, et comme l'ardillon pointu de cette courroie complexe qui la bouclait de tous côtés" (p. 111). In the course of the novel, he is divested of all the trappings of patriarchal power as Emma adds to the sexual supremacy gained on the first night of their marriage emotional, intellectual and financial control. In contrast, Rodolphe conforms to the traditional image of the strong male and Emma is sexually subjugated by him: "Ce n'était pas de l'attachement, c'était comme une séduction permanente. Il la subjugait. Elle en avait presque peur" (p. 175). Even with Rodolphe, however, Emma gains a kind of supremacy, forcing him to act out the charade of the romantic lover and showering him with humiliating gifts: "Cependant ces cadeaux l'humiliaient. Il en refusa plusieurs; elle insista, et Rodolphe finit par obéir, la trouvant tyrannique et trop envahissante" (p. 195). There is something profoundly contradictory about Emma's behaviour as, with an authority Rodolphe finds difficult to resist, she urges him to play the part of the masterful lover and carry her away. His final failure to do this points both to the falsity of the image of the romantic lover and the limits of the woman's power in adultery. It is with Léon, in the third part of the novel, that Emma achieves a kind of apotheosis. Léon, we are told, "devenait sa maîtresse plutôt qu'elle n'était la sienne" (p. 283). Emma uses him in the same way as Rodolphe has used her—as a convenience. Léon is powerless to resist Emma's total domination: "Il en voulait à Emma de cette victoire permanente. Il s'efforçait même à ne pas la chérir; puis, au craquement de ses bottines, il se sentait lâche, comme les ivrognes à la vue des liqueurs fortes" (pp. 288-9). Once again, however, the limits of Emma's control are exposed; Léon does not extricate her from her financial crisis, just as Rodolphe has resisted running away with her. At the end of the novel, Emma experiences a generalised anger against the opposite sex. After Guillaumin has attempted to take advantage of her position, "Elle aurait voulu battre les hommes, leur cracher au visage, les broyer tous" (p.

310). She cannot bear the thought of Charles pardoning her ("Cette idée de la supériorité de Bovary sur elle l'exaspérait", p. 311) and when Rodolphe refuses to lend her money, she flings his cufflinks against the wall (p. 318). The heroism she has failed to elicit from men finally wells up in Emma herself: 'Puis, dans un transport d'héroïsme qui la rendait presque joyeuse, elle descendit la côte en courant [. . .] et arriva devant la boutique du pharmacien" (p. 320). There is, however, one final symbolic confrontation to come. As Emma is about to die she hears the Blind Man's coarsely sexist ditty and responds with despairing laughter: "Et Emma se mit à rire, d'un rire atroce, frénétique, désespéré, croyant voir la face hideuse du misérable qui se dressait dans les ténèbres éternelles comme un épouvantement" (pp. 332-3). One crucial feature of this horrific figure, as of "Dieu le Père tout éclatant de majesté" of her earlier, contrasting, "vision splendide" (p. 219), is its sex: whether she is to be saved or damned, Emma's cultural conditioning puts her at the mercy of an embodiment of ultimate power and authority who is male.

Gender distinctions are explored in a more oblique and suggestive way through the novel's extraordinarily rich web of symbolic suggestion. A number of motifs can be related to the position of the woman in society. The motif of bending, for instance, according to Tanner's reading, suggests not simply the sexual dominance of the male but more generally the inevitable female submission to the matrix of the male world around her: "She must and can only 'bend' under it to the shapes, postures, and positions that it offers, imposes, or dictates."[12] This interpretation is supported by the implications of the words of the Blind Man's song.[13] Emma's bending, however, has an energetic quality which belies the notion of submission. When Charles's whip slips behind some wheat-sacks, Emma bends over to retrieve it:

> Et il se mit à fureter sur le lit, derrière les portes, sous les chaises; elle [the whip] était tombée à terre, entre les sacs et la muraille. Mademoiselle Emma l'aperçut; elle se pencha sur les sacs de blé. Charles, par galanterie, se précipita et, comme il allongeait son bras dans le même mouvement, il sentit sa poitrine effleurer le dos de la jeune fille, courbée sous lui. Elle se redressa toute rouge et le regarda par-dessus l'épaule, en lui tendant son nerf de bœuf. (p. 17)

A similar incident can be found in George Eliot's *Middlemarch*, where it serves to confirm rather than undermine traditional gender distinctions. At one point Rosamond is portrayed going towards her whip, which lies at a distance:

> Lydgate was quick in anticipating her. He reached the whip before she did, and turned to present it to her. She bowed and looked at him: he of course was looking at her, and their eyes met with that peculiar meeting which is never arrived at by effort, but seems like a sudden divine clearance of haze. I think that Lydgate turned a little paler than usual, but Rosamond blushed deeply and felt a certain astonishment.[14]

There is no bending in Rosamond's case but there is no implied symbolic exchange of power either since the whip in question is her own and Lydgate gets to it first. The power relations between the sexes remain undisturbed, whereas in **Madame Bovary** Emma counteracts the notion of submission implicit in her bending by reaching the whip first and handing it over to Charles. In another highly charged episode, Emma is shown bending over to remove the bowl of blood which has caused Justin to faint:

> Madame Bovary prit la cuvette. Pour la mettre sous la table, dans le mouvement qu'elle fit en s'inclinant, sa robe (c'était une robe d'été à quatre volants, de couleur jaune, longue de taille, large de jupe), sa robe s'évasa autour d'elle sur les carreaux de la salle;—et, comme Emma, baissée, chancelait un peu en écartant les bras, le gonflement de l'étoffe se crevait de place en place, selon les inflexions de son corsage. (p. 132)

Once again Emma is handling something with strong masculine associations and this, combined with the energetic connotations of the description of her dress, partially offsets the humiliating implications of her action.

A second motif which defines the domestic imperative governing the woman's role is sewing. Emma either sews incompetently or endows sewing with an autoerotic quality. The one time her heart is in her work is when she is undoing the lining of a dress, just as in adultery she has unravelled the very fabric of married life (p. 258). Appropriately, it is Charles who performs the classically restorative function of sewing properly, sewing up his daughter's dolls when they split open (p. 350). A third motif which points to the essential nature of the woman's lot is constriction. On numerous occasions Emma is depicted within an enclosed space, and she perceives her existence in terms of cold rooms, narrow houses, belts that hem her in. Her natural inclination, however, is to try to break out of narrow confines in order to soar in the vast open spaces of the romantic dream. In contrast, Charles takes fright at open spaces and longs for enclosed domesticity. Once again, therefore, what emerges from a traditional motif associated with the woman's position is a powerful resistance on Emma's part, suggesting that she is not at ease within the conventional role accorded to her.

Further suggestions are made through the close descriptions of Emma's physical appearance. Her frequently bulky garments can point to something burdensome in her condition as a woman—whether married or adulterous—but her dress can also have an expansive grace which evokes a triumphant femininity.[15] Throughout the novel, however, Flaubert describes various items and appendages which have strong masculine associations in order to measure, as it were, an increasing quotient of "masculinity". The tortoiseshell eyeglasses, attached, in masculine fashion, to two buttonholes of her bodice, and introduced in the first description of Emma (p. 17), represent a key component, a deliberately dissonant note in an otherwise traditionally orchestrated feminine appearance. Subsequently, she will wear a blue silk tie on arriving in Yonville, and a man's hat and riding costume for the ride with Rodolphe; and she will step out of the coach "la taille serrée dans un gilet, à la façon d'un homme" (p. 197) and dress in masculine attire for the masked ball (p. 297). These masculine elements have been regarded negatively. Diana Festa-McCormick, for instance, claims that "no longer a gesture of daring, the male costume stands in reality for an act of surrender, confirming Emma's defeat in the dominion of the woman";[16] but this is to subscribe to a highly questionable view of woman's role. Emma is also made to manipulate a wide range of patently phallic substitutes. Emma not only retrieves Charles's whip, she also makes Rodolphe a present of a handsome riding-whip. Emma may be shown "regrettant de n'être pas un homme pour sauter sur un poignard" (*Nouvelle version*, p. 586), but she can "look daggers" at Charles.[17] The main male characters all have knives which they use in symbolically appropriate fashion, but Emma too has a knife which she uses disconsolately to make lines on the waxed table cloth: "[elle] s'amusait, avec la pointe de son couteau, à faire des raies sur la toile cirée" (p. 67). A particularly ambiguous appendage is the sunshade, whose fragility is often associated with femininity. On the occasion when for the first time her thoughts about her marriage become clear, Emma is shown poking the ground with its tip: "Puis ses idées peu à peu se fixaient, et, assise sur le gazon, qu'elle fouillait à petits coups avec le bout de son ombrelle, Emma se répétait: 'Pourquoi, mon Dieu! me suis-je mariée?'" (p. 46). She also usurps what at the time was a specifically male prerogative, smoking in public "*comme pour narguer le monde*" (p. 197), as well as playfully putting Rodolphe's big pipe into her mouth (p. 169).

The significance of Emma's adoption of masculine modes of dress and manipulation of phallic substitutes requires careful consideration. The first point to be made is that they do not displace feminine modes, and that Emma continues to exhibit many of the traditional features of femininity against which Flaubert railed in his correspondence—role-playing, sentimentality, lack of frankness, the pursuit of an impossible ideal. It is clearly inappropriate, therefore, to speak of Emma's masculinisation since masculine modes do not take the place of feminine modes. She also possesses what Baudelaire referred to as a "charmant corps féminin",[18] a delicately realised physical presence. One interpretation might be that the adoption of masculine modes is yet another example of role-playing, which is no more privileged than her adoption of feminine modes the rest of the time. There does, however, seem to be more at stake than such a view implies. The broader context in which some of the developments discussed take place is one of symbolic exchange.[19] Male characters undergo a symbolic emasculation—Emma's father breaks his leg, Hippolyte has his amputated. A large number of objects associated with the power and influence of men are broken, or given to men by Emma. Flaubert has created a fictional world where the masculinity of men is, symbolically, in retreat and males in various ways shown to be defective. In this context, Emma's assumption of masculine modes suggests a takeover or exchange and has as its counterpart Charles's assumption of feminine modes. What Flaubert has engineered in the elaboration of a number of symbolic patterns is a full-scale realignment of the sexes in relation to gender stereotypes. René Girard has stressed the way in which, as Flaubert develops, there is a tendency for oppositions to be subverted and polarities to collapse with the end result that what are traditionally viewed as contraries are shown to share a good deal, if not to be identical.[20] This seems to be what happens to the opposition between the sexes. By endowing Emma with marked masculine traits and Charles with feminine traits, Flaubert problematises, or perhaps even collapses, the conventional opposition between male and female. In order to subvert such an opposition, however, Flaubert relies on well-defined gender stereotypes. A hard-and-fast distinction between the sexes is nullified by the way in which Emma displays "masculine" traits and Charles "feminine" traits.

Flaubert's creation of a heroine with masculine traits has often been viewed as a failure to create a completely convincing character. From Baudelaire to Sartre, critics have argued that a man's blood—Flaubert's own—flows through Emma's veins. Such comments are based, however, on precisely those categories that the novel queries and make us aware just how radical Flaubert's critique of traditional gender stereotypes was.[21] It would, however, be wrong to think of Flaubert as a champion of the androgynous ideal which attracted many nineteenth-century writers. This is largely because so-called feminine and masculine traits are not brought into a state of harmony. Indeed it could be argued that Emma is destroyed by her failure to resolve the contradiction between her "masculine" and "feminine" tendencies.[22] Although Flaubert subverts the rigid opposition between male and female which characterises patriarchal society; although, in his private life, Flaubert declared that he wanted Louise Colet to become an "hermaphrodite sublime"; and although in his own person he detected "les deux sexes",[23]

Madame Bovary suggests that a free, non-problematic choice of gender roles—the androgynous ideal—is a long way off. Emma's adoption of masculine modes does not, after all, do her much good and it is profoundly ironic that her most forceful act is to commit suicide. Nor is Charles's gravitation to the feminine pole a recipe for survival. Like Emma, he too comes to an untimely end, dying pathetically of a broken heart. It is partly a question of the kind of society in which cross-gender behaviour takes place but, whilst he clearly rejects the conventional view of sexual difference, Flaubert does not offer the reader any new, heady, gender cocktail.

Notes

[1] Louis Bouilhet's comment on Flaubert's use of the generalising definite article (*du* mariage) in the famous sentence "Emma retrouvait dans l'adultère toutes les platitudes du mariage" is significant: "tu attaques la société par une de ses bases" (Quoted in C. Gothot-Mersch's edition of the novel, (Paris: 1971), p. 463). D. LaCapra has argued that Flaubert's novel was put on trial because "the ideological image of the modern family as the holy family is called into question" (*"Madame Bovary" on Trial*, (Cornell: 1982), p. 9).

[2] C. Prendergast, *Balzac: Fiction and Melodrama*, (London: 1977), p. 139.

[3] *Madame Bovary: Nouvelle version*, ed. J. Pommier and G. Leleu, (Paris: 1949), p. 424. All references to earlier versions of the novel will be to this edition.

[4] Flaubert's complex and contradictory attitude to women has been discussed most fully by L. Czyba in *Mythes et idéologie de la femme dans les romans de Flaubert*, (Lyon: 1983).

[5] *Correspondance*, ed. J. Bruneau, (Paris: 1980), ii, 284.

[6] *Correspondance*, ed. J. Bruneau, (Paris: 1973), i, 711.

[6] Flaubert does not, however, acknowledge the difficulty of determining the characteristics of this original female nature. Cf. John Stuart Mill: "I deny that anyone knows, or can know, the nature of the two sexes, as long as they have only been seen in their present relations to one another" (quoted in M. Midgley and J. Hughes, *Women's Choices: Philosophical Problems facing Feminism*, (London: 1983), p. 207).

[8] *The Sadeian Woman*, (London: 1979), p. 6.

[9] Pages references are to the Gothot-Mersch edition (Paris: 1971).

[10] *Adultery in the Novel*, (Princeton: 1979), p. 367.

[11] See R. W. Greene, "Clichés, moral censure and heroism in Flaubert's *Madame Bovary*", *Symposium*, 32 (1978), pp. 289-302.

[12] *Adultery in the Novel*, p. 354.

[13] The words of the Blind Man's song, relayed fully at the moment of Emma's death (p. 332) are: "Pour amasser diligemment / Les épis que la faux moissonne, / Ma Nanette va s'inclinant / Vers le sillon qui nous les donne." The complex relationship between Emma's bending and that of Nanette is discussed in my "Quotation in *Madame Bovary*", *Romance Studies*, 12 (1988), pp. 29-43.

[14] *Middlemarch*, Part I, xii, (Harmondsworth: 1965), p. 145. I am grateful to my colleague, David Roe of Leeds University, for drawing my attention to the similarity between the two passages.

[15] See, in addition to the passage on p. 132 already quoted, the description on p. 101: "Son vêtement, ensuite, retombait des deux côtés sur le siège, en bouffant, plein de plis, et s'étalait jusqu'à terre."

[16] "Emma Bovary's masculinisation. Convention of clothes and morality of conventions", in *Gender and Literary Voice*, ed. J. Todd, (New York, 1980) (*Women and Literature*. I, 1980), p. 234.

[17] See p. 190: "elle fixait sur Charles la pointe ardente de ses prunelles, comme deux flèches de feu prêtes à partir."

[18] See *"Madame Bovary"* in *L'Art romantique*, (Paris: 1968), p. 224: "Comme la Pallas armée, sortie du cerveau de Zeus, ce bizarre androgyne a gardé toutes les séductions d'une âme virile dans un charmant corps féminin."

[19] See M. Picard's excellent article, to which this discussion is indebted, "La prodigalité d'Emma", *Littérature*, 10 (1973), pp. 77-97.

[20] "A mesure que mûrit le génie romanesque flaubertien, les oppositions se font toujours plus creuses; l'identité des contraires s'affirme avec toujours plus de force", *Mensonge romantique et vérité romanesque*, (Paris: 1961), p. 157.

[21] R. Lloyd rightly points out in her recent study that "a gendered reading might begin to unravel many of the male-centred misinterpretations that have grown up around the novel ever since Baudelaire depicted as masculine all Emma's positive and active attributes", *Madame Bovary*, (London: 1990), p. 172.

[22] J. F. Hamilton has argued that "the apparent contradictions in Emma's character and behaviour" reflect

"the salutary urge to unite the female and male aspects of her being"; see "*Madame Bovary* and the Myth of Androgyny", *University of South Florida Language Quarterly,* 19 (1981), p. 19. Two more recent considerations of the problematic relationship between masculine and feminine elements in Emma's behaviour are N. Schor's "For a restricted thematics. Writing, speech and difference in *Madame Bovary*", in *Breaking the Chain. Women, Theory and French Realist Fiction,* (Columbia: 1985) and D. Kelly's "Gender and Representation" in *Fictional Genders. Role and Representation in Nineteenth-Century French Narrative,* (Nebraska: 1989). Both of these critics emphasise Flaubert's exploration of significant differences between male and female attitudes to language, a topic which this article has not examined.

[23] See "J'ai toujours essayé de faire de toi un hermaphrodite sublime" (*Correspondance,* ii, 548) and "C'est que j'ai les deux sexes, peut-être" (*Correspondance,* (Paris: 1929), v, 268).

Anne Green (essay date 1995)

SOURCE: "Time and History in *Madame Bovary,*" in *French Studies: A Quarterly Review,* Vol. XLIX, No. 3, July, 1995, pp. 283-91.

[*In the following essay, Green explores "the way in which [Flaubert's] value-laden approach to [the concept of] time informs* Madame Bovary.*"*]

—Nous ne sommes jamais au Présent qui seul est important dans la vie.[1]

—Le Présent est tout ce qu'il y a de moins important, car il est très court, insaisissable. Le vrai, c'est le Passé, et l'Avenir.[2]

These mutually contradictory comments from Flaubert's *Correspondance* are evidence of his long-standing preoccupation with the way in which we perceive time. His letters show him to be particularly sensitive to the personal and subjective nature of time, which he variously sees as destructive or consoling, as a force for change or an indicator of stasis, or as evidence of a particular state of mind.[3] But the comments I have quoted also hint at the moral overtones which Flaubert attributes to the subject: for him, the stances which can be adopted towards past, present or future are clearly open to moral judgment, although his judgment on them may change over the years. The purpose of this article is to explore the way in which this value-laden approach to time informs *Madame Bovary.*

The novel carries an extraordinary number of references to time. There are 105 references to *le temps* (in the temporal sense) and 14 to *l'* or *les heure(s),* making them two of the most frequently recurring nouns in the book.[4] Alongside these, the large number of references to past, present and future and the clusters of clocks, watches and other timepieces make it clear that something of significance is happening in the text. But critics who have tried to analyse *Madame Bovary's* timescale on a realistic level have encountered problems. There are very few specific dates in the novel, and those that do exist can be misleading. For example, the date of Emma and Rodolphe's planned elopement, 'le 4 septembre, un lundi' has been used by Jacques Seebacher as a *point de repère* for an elaborate calculation of the timing of other events in the novel, culminating in his claim that Emma poisons herself on 23 March 1846, the day of Flaubert's sister Caroline's death.[5] But as Claudine Gothot-Mersch has meticulously shown, that kind of detective work is doomed to failure because the novel does not follow a coherent chronology. Dates and other numbers undergo changes in the different manuscript versions of the novel (the elopement date figures variously as 4, 12, and 23 September) and seem often to have been chosen for their sound and lack of associations rather than for any more specific purpose. Any attempt to impose a strict and realistic time-scale on the novel will reveal all kinds of logical inconsistencies, including characters who age at different rates.[6] Flaubert was clearly interested less in paying scrupulous attention to consistent chronology in his plots, than in creating a coherent impression; he sets crucial events against an appropriate seasonal background rather than calculating them by the calendar. His deep concern with the significance of time takes a quite different focus—it is not on the level of events that we shall find it, but in the narrative itself.

Much has been written about the opening 'Nous' of *Madame Bovary,* but one of the most important qualities of that striking use of the first-person is the way in which it effectively anchors the story to the present. This is confirmed a little later when, after a few pages describing Charles's childhood, we read: 'Il serait *maintenant* impossible à aucun de nous de se rien rappeler de lui' (p. 8)[7]—a curious sentence which again establishes the link with the present, with 'us', but which at the same time emphasizes the past, vanished, forgotten nature of the story—a paradox to which I shall return later.

The 'nous' makes its final appearance here, and the narrative plunges back into the past, not resurfacing in the present again until the beginning of Part II with the description of the little town of Yonville, static in time ('Yonville l'Abbaye est demeuré stationnaire'), and described from the perspective of the present: 'Depuis les événements que l'on va raconter, rien [. . .] n'a changé à Yonville' (p. 68). The present is evoked for the third time at the end of the novel, where the fortunes of Justin, Berthe and

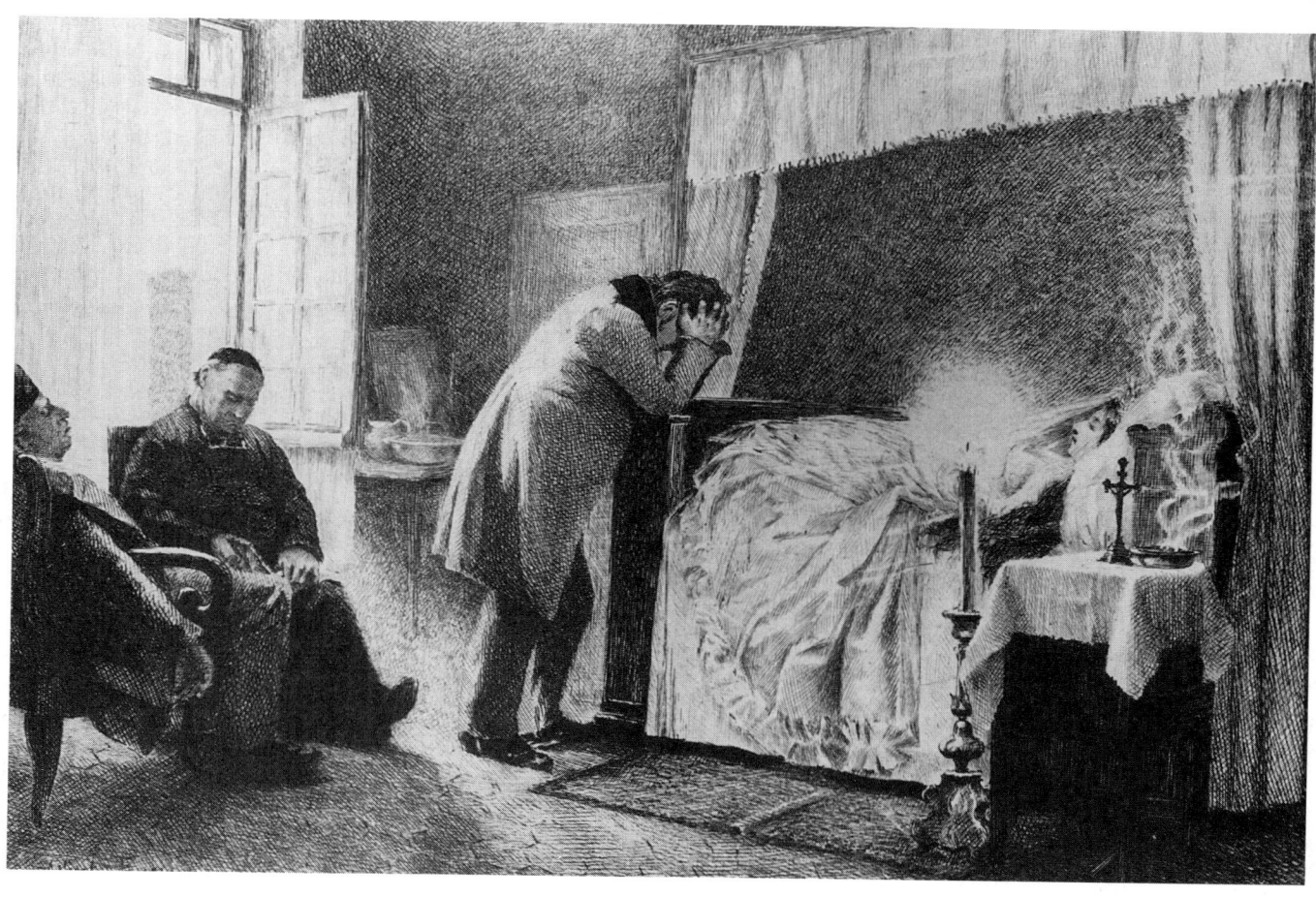

The death of Emma Bovary.

Homais are recorded in the present tense. The narrative, then, is set in a past which has three explicit links to the present at the beginning, middle and end of the novel. But the past narrative never quite flows up to the present: there remains a curious gap between the events of the narrative and these three 'presents', a gap that is emphasized by the comment that it would now be impossible for us to remember anything, and by the suggestion of a lapse of time between the events of the story ('les événements que l'on va raconter') and Yonville 'now'.

Within the past and fragmented narrative,[8] Flaubert presents us with different concepts of time. One of the most striking is ordered time—time as it is measured and counted. Time is often measured very precisely in this novel: Charles, waiting for a sign from Emma's father to let him know whether she has agreed to marry him, counts nineteen minutes by his watch (p. 23). But the apparent precision of the nineteen minutes is undermined by the fact that he does not start measuring his wait until about half an hour has already elapsed. The precise calculation made by Hivert as he waits for Emma to catch the coach to Rouen is similarly pointless: he gives up and drives off after exactly fifty-three minutes. Why fifty-three?

Flaubert's manner of describing the many clocks and watches that figure in the novel leaves us in no doubt that this kind of measurement of time is both artificial and suspect. The timepieces are highly ornate, over-decorated, visually elaborate; their function of telling the time has been eclipsed by their function as social symbols. The simple slate sundial in the garden at Tostes is soon 'improved' by Emma who surrounds it with garden seats and plans a fountain with ornamental fish (p. 30); the Bovarys' living-room at Tostes is dominated by 'une pendule à tête d'Hippocrate' (p. 30); 'les pendules Pompadour' feature in Emma's dreams of the vicomte (p. 53); in Rouen, she notices ladies wearing clusters of charms hanging from their watches, and so buys charms for her own watch (p. 57); all the *notables* at the agricultural fair have watches decorated with an oval cornelian seal dangling from a long ribbon (p. 131); the wig-maker has a cuckoo-clock (p. 222); in Emma and Léon's room in Rouen the clock is decorated with a simpering bronze Cupid clutching a gilded garland (p. 247); and when Emma makes her final visit to Rodolphe to plead for money and is told that he cannot afford to lend her any, her fury at the hypocrisy of his reply is roused by the sight of his Boule clock with its tortoiseshell inlay, and the expensive decorations, the *breloques,* that hang from his watch-chain (p. 289). This is bourgeois time, decorative and artificial, time as display, time as money.[9] The function of these elaborate clocks and watches is not to tell the time—they never do—but instead to reflect the bourgeoisie's own image back at themselves: Hippocrates for the doctor, Cupid for the lovers, Boule and 'breloques' for the wealthy, and Pompadour as the emblem of Emma's dreams of passion and social advancement intertwined.[10]

The ultimate absurdity of this concept of time is found in Binet, obsessive in his habits, who always arrives for dinner on the stroke of six—'son pareil n'existe pas sur la terre pour l'exactitude' (p. 70). But later in the novel Binet has moved his mealtime forward by an hour, eating every night at precisely five o'clock but often grumbling that the clock is slow (p. 240). Not only is any rationale behind his obsessive time-keeping thrown into question when he arbitrarily switches from six to five, but the clock's role in the rigorous apportionment of time is also challenged: Binet's complaint that 'la *vieille patraque retardait*' highlights the inadequacy of clock-time as a means of imposing order on life.

Set against this, at the end of the novel, is a different and simpler approach to time—the pre-industrial time of la Mère Rollet, the wet-nurse. She has no clock or watch in her little cottage, and when Emma asks her the time she gets up from her spinning-wheel, goes outside, holds her fingers up to the light, and unhurriedly returns to tell Emma that it will soon be three o'clock (p. 285). La Mère Rollet has a natural, unforced experience of time which contrasts sharply with the narcissistic, 'bourgeois' time already described.

Also set against 'bourgeois' time, and making a nonsense of those attempts to measure time meticulously, is what one might call subjective time—time as it is felt, rather than time as it is measured.[11] So, for example, when Charles returns to Les Bertaux for the first time since his first wife's death, 'Il retrouva tout comme la veille, comme il y avait cinq mois, c'est-à-dire' (p. 20)—five months have flashed by as if overnight. Elsewhere time has stretched rather than contracted. Waiting in la Mère Rollet's clockless cottage, Emma cannot tell 'si elle était là depuis un siècle ou une minute' (p. 286); and her memories of the ball at la Vaubyessard demonstrate a similar disorientation: 'Comme le bal déjà lui semblait loin! Qui donc écartait, à tant de distance, le matin d'avant-hier et le soir d'aujourd'hui? Son voyage à la Vaubyessard avait fait un trou dans sa vie, à la manière de ces grandes crevasses qu'un orage, en une seule nuit, creuse quelquefois dans les montagnes' (p. 53). Emma's sense of time is quite out of step with clock-time; it is repeatedly projected backwards, as she reminisces about her past or has dreams of living in the Middle Ages. At times she can imagine no future: 'L'avenir était un corridor tout noir, et qui avait au fond sa porte bien fermée' (p. 59). The everyday events of the village go on around her at a regular pace, slow and repeated like the bell that tolls throughout the novel, but Emma's inner time is erratic—either frenetic, flashing past without trace, or deathly slow.[12] Unlike Emma, whose dreams send her back into an imaginary past or into nostalgic reminiscence, Homais tends to look towards the future. Virtually his first words in the novel are, 'Il faut marcher avec son siècle!' (p. 70). On the outing to the linen factory, it is he who holds forth about 'l'importance future de cet établissement' (p. 94), foreseeing the progress of industrialization, and it is he who has the vision of the future as a time when the blind will see, the deaf will hear, and the lame will walk—a prophecy which is of course ironically undermined by the ubiquitous blind beggar, and by the failure of the operation on Hippolyte's club foot. Indeed, Homais's vicious and sustained attack on the blind beggar at the end of the novel is an expression of his frustration at this living challenge to his perception of the future as progress: for Homais, the beggar is a throwback to 'ces temps monstrueux du moyen-âge, où il était permis aux vagabonds d'étaler par nos places publiques la lèpre et les scrofules qu'ils avaient rapportées de la croisade' (p. 319).

But Homais's and Emma's subjective and self-serving temporal projections are set against a very different concept of time represented by the beggar himself: time as natural, cyclical, eternal. His bawdy song tells metaphorically of a cycle of death and rebirth—ripe grain cut down by the scythe, Nanette stooping down to the furrowed earth from which new grain will spring. The cyclical continuum of 'natural' time runs through the novel in counterpoint to the linear and anguished personal senses of time which the main characters experience. For, of course, the story of Emma and Charles is embedded in the broader timescale of a repeated cycle of births, marriages and deaths. Seen from that perspective, Emma takes her place in a series of Madame Bovarys, and the title itself highlights the contrast between the self-absorption of Emma's viewpoint and the broad, inevitable continuum within which her life is set. Our awareness of a natural continuity is heightened by repeated references to the sound of the river which flows on in the background of many of the most dramatic episodes, and which continues its 'gros murmure [. . .] dans les ténèbres' (p. 306) after Emma's death.

Yet we are not allowed to find any consolation in this continuity. The symbolic river may always run on into the darkness, but much else is threatened. The long, placid description of Yonville in the first chapter of Part II suggests that this village which has stood since the Middle Ages is now approaching its end. 'Il n'y a plus [. . .] rien à voir dans Yonville' (p. 68). The road stops dead, and the one path leads only to the cemetery. Nothing has changed since the events of the story took place, we are told, and Homais's collection of preserved foetuses still rot in their murky liquid (p. 68). That striking image seems to hint that the natural cycle of birth and death has collapsed in on itself and become corrupted and stagnant, just as the repeated cycle of Madame Bovarys finishes with the death of Charles's mother on the last page. Berthe can never be a Madame Bovary: the line has died out.

This counterpoint between continuity and collapse, between progress and stagnation, shows Flaubert exploring ideas about time whose implications stretch beyond the lives of his characters. Perhaps the most important of these concerns historical time—the all-pervasive presence of the historical past. References to the history of France, to past monarchs and vanished régimes, abound. But these references are always fleeting and partial, suggesting a history fragmented and debased. When Emma and her father are served a meal at the inn, it comes on plates depicting scenes from the life of Louise de La Vallière, mistress of Louis XIV, but the writing round the plate-rims offering reductive explanations of the pictures has been partly obliterated by the constant scraping of cutlery (p. 33). Flaubert's description of Emma's fascination with the past emphasizes the superficial, disconnected nature of her historical perception which reduces the history of France to a few *idées reçues,* and reinforces the emblematic value of these scratched dinner-plates as an image of the reduction and virtual obliteration of history:

> Elle eut dans ce temps-là le culte de Marie Stuart et des vénérations enthousiastes à l'endroit des femmes illustres ou infortunées. Jeanne d'Arc, Héloïse, Agnès Sorel, la belle Ferronnière et Clémence Isaure, pour elle, se détachaient comme des comètes sur l'immensité ténébreuse de l'histoire, où saillissaient encore çà et là, mais plus perdus dans l'ombre et sans aucun rapport entre eux, saint Louis avec son chêne, Bayard mourant, quelques férocités de Louis XI, un peu de Saint-Barthélemy, le panache du Béarnais, et toujours le souvenir des assiettes peintes où Louis XIV était vanté.[13] (p. 35)

This is one of the tragedies of **Madame Bovary**. History itself has become fragmented and erased; it vanishes into the 'immensité ténébreuse' of the past, leaving only isolated, incoherent details which are quickly reduced to platitudes. The history of France from the earliest times is evoked in this novel, but in a debased and splintered form. The names Homais gives his four children are emblematic of that process—Athalie, so called to evoke the French classical period; Irma, the romantic period; Napoléon, the Empire; and Franklin, the American republic.[14] The disconnected, sentimental jumble of historical figures and events which crowd in on Emma during her craze for '[les] choses historiques' at the convent (p. 35) has its counterpart in the flurry of disparate and inappropriate historical allusions dotted throughout the text, ranging from the Empire and the Revolution to Diane de Poitiers (p. 225), Richard the Lion Heart (p. 226), Cincinnatus, Diocletian and the Emperors of China, and fading away into prehistory when men wore animal skins and lived on acorns (pp. 138-39). Elsewhere, history is reduced to a mere mouthful[15]—the turban-shaped bread rolls which Homais buys for his wife evoke the time of the Crusades, for the rolls are said to be the 'dernier échantillon des nourritures gothiques, qui remonte peut-être au siècle des croisades, et dont les robustes Normands s'emplissaient autrefois, croyant voir sur la table [. . .] des têtes de Sarrasins à dévorer' (p. 277). In this example, any remaining shred of an historical allusion is further obscured by the determinedly industrial connotations of the rolls' name: *cheminots.* By the end of the novel Homais is distorting history for his own ends, evoking the Crusades and the Middle Ages in his campaign against the blind beggar, sycophantically comparing the king to Henri IV, and raising the spectre of the massacre of St Bartholemew's Day in protest against a small grant paid to the Church; 'Homais sapait; il devenait dangereux' (pp. 319-22). Flaubert thus makes it clear that when history is fragmented and reduced, and when all sense of chronology and historical perspective is ignored, the historical past dissolves into a jumble of elements, as incongruous as the juxtaposed images of one of Emma's keepsake pictures. Such a debased awareness of the past can contribute nothing to an understanding of the present or the future; furthermore, it is dangerous.

The most striking example of that danger is central to the novel—literally central, for the middle section of the middle chapter of the middle part contains M. Lieuvain's extraordinarily complacent speech in which he praises the government and 'notre souverain, [. . .] ce roi bien-aimé' in the most fulsome terms before declaring that civil unrest is now a thing of the past:

> 'Le temps n'est plus, messieurs, où la discorde civile ensanglantait nos places publiques, où le propriétaire, le négociant, l'ouvrier lui-même, en s'endormant le soir d'un sommeil paisible, tremblaient de se voir réveillés tout à coup au bruit des tocsins incendiaires [. . .] la religion, plus affermie, sourit à tous les cœurs: nos ports sont pleins, la confiance renaît, et enfin la France respire! . . .' (p. 133)

It is here that the gap between the novel's narrative time and the present time postulated at the beginning by the narrator is finally made clear. Emma's death is set in the last years of the July Monarchy,[16] the novel first appeared in 1856, and so that temporal gap between the events of the novel and the 'maintenant' of the narrator is implicitly filled by the revolution of 1848 and its immediate aftermath.[17] The conspicuous absence of explicit references to those events—an absence underlined by the fact that the significant dates of 'mardi 22 février 1848' and 'jeudi 4 décembre 1851' which appear in the early drafts have been omitted from the final version[18]—subtly emphasizes their importance. The reader's awareness of the impending revolution and its consequences inevitably colours a reading of **Madame Bovary,** undermining Lieuvain's confident assertions about France's political stability just as knowledge of the subsequent destruction of Carthage colours the events of **Salammbô** and makes a mockery of those Carthaginians who, at the end of that work, feel that 'partout on sentait l'ordre rétabli, une existence nouvelle qui recommençait, un vaste bonheur épandu'. We read these novels from the ironic perspective of historical hindsight, for the gap between the events of both novels and our awareness of subsequent, devastating events highlights the danger of ignoring lessons from the past. In his first **Education sentimentale** Flaubert had written of the way in which the same ideas and the same crises periodically return in a chain of cause and effect so evident that it seems to have been planned in advance; he likens the whole historical process to a constantly developing organism which appears to work to a regular pattern.[19] But for the characters of **Madame Bovary** there is no awareness of any such causal links between past, present and future.

Flaubert told the Goncourt brothers: 'J'aime l'histoire, follement. [. . .] Le sens historique . . . est peut-être ce que le XIXe siècle a de meilleur.'[20] But as I have shown, the characters of **Madame Bovary**—even those most ready to evoke the great names of the past—are singularly lacking in 'sens historique'. Flaubert seems to suggest that we shall never be able to learn from the past or understand the present if, like them, we live in that superficial, narcissistic, 'bourgeois' time which I have described. If we do, we shall drift helplessly on like Emma, unable to salvage any sense from the past: 'aux fulgurations de l'heure présente', we are told, 'sa vie passée, si nette jusqu'alors, s'évanouissait tout entière, et elle doutait presque de l'avoir vécue' (p. 49). She is as unable to understand her own history as she is incapable of understanding the history of France. Past and future, dreams and memories merge and blur ('le passé, l'avenir, les réminiscences et les rêves, tout se trouvait confondu') (p. 219), and she has no firm points of reference.[21] Emma can never learn, because she has no proper sense of time or history.[22]

After the Commune, Flaubert wrote of his contemporaries: 'Si l'on eût été plus éclairé, s'il y avait eu à Paris plus de gens connaissant l'histoire, nous n'aurions subi ni Gambetta, ni la Prusse, ni la Commune.'[23] His value-laden presentation of time in **Madame Bovary** portrays a similarly flawed awareness of the past, and seems to hint that the revolution of 1848 and its violent aftermath might possibly have been avoided if only there had been 'plus de gens connaissant l'histoire'.

Notes

[1] *Correspondance,* ed. by J. Bruneau, Pléiade (Paris, Gallimard, 1973-), II (1980), 413. (24 August 1853, to Louis Bouilhet). Unless otherwise indicated, all references to Flaubert's correspondence are to this edition.

[2] *Correspondance* (Paris, Conard, 1926-33), VII (1930), 363 (4 December 1876, to Caroline).

[3] E.g. 'je me méfie du temps [. . .] qui pourrit tout, comme la pluie qui ronge les marbres les plus durs et les sentiments les plus solides' (*Corr.* I, 402, November 1846, to Gertrude Collier); 'Le temps, les choses sont plus forts que nous.' (*Corr.* I, 268, 31 May 1846, to A. Le Poittevin); 'Il semble, à certains moments, que l'univers s'est immobilisé, que tout est devenu statue et que nous seuls, vivons' (*Corr.* II, 412, 24 August 1853, to L. Bouilhet); 'Ce qui prouve peut-être qu'on vieillit, c'est que le temps, à mesure qu'il y en a derrière vous, vous semble moins long' (*Corr.* II. 424, 2 September 1853, to L. Colet), etc.

[4] Charles Carlut, Pierre H. Dubé, and J. Raymond Dugan, *A Concordance to Flaubert's 'Madame Bovary',* 2 vols (Garland, New York-London, 1978).

[5] Jacques Seebacher, 'Chiffres, dates, écritures, inscriptions dans *Madame Bovary*', in *La Production du sens chez Flaubert,* colloque de Cerisy (10/18, Paris, 1975), pp. 286-96. In fact Caroline died on 22 March, not 23 March.

[6] See C. Gothot-Mersch, 'Aspects de la temporalité dans les romans de Flaubert', in *Flaubert, la dimension du texte,* ed. by P. M. Wetherill (Manchester University Press, 1982), pp. 6-55. She points out that 'Si le père Bovary meurt à 58 ans, à une époque où Charles approache de la trentaine, le fils devait avoir 16 ans quand son pére, ruiné, s'est retiré à la campagne; or il semble bien qu'il n'était pas encore né' (p. 38).

[7] Page numbers refer to *Madame Bovary,* ed. by E. Maynial (Paris, Garnier, 1961).

[8] See Rosemary Lloyd, *Madame Bovary* (London, Unwin Hyman, 1990), pp. 130ff. for a discussion of the novel's temporal fluctuations and nesting techniques, which Lloyd sees as 'one of the means Flaubert uses to create an image of fragmented time, an image that intensifies the suggestion that existence is purposeless and directionless' (p. 131).

[9] Note that Emma tries to give Lheureux her watch in lieu of payment (p. 184).

[10] Cf. the *Dictionnaire des Idées reçues* entry: 'TROUBADOUR.—Beau sujet de pendule'.

[11] Cf. *Corr.* I, 384 (10 October 1846, to L. Colet): 'Chacun de nous a dans le cœur un calendrier particulier d'après lequel il mesure le temps. Il y a des minutes qui sont des années, des jours qui marquent comme des siècles.'

[12] See especially Part I, chapter 9.

[13] This fragmentation and diminution of history in Emma's mind has another visual parallel in the description of the series of paintings of the ancestors of the marquis d'Andervilliers. The first two portraits are clear and have complete captions, but the remainder of the series is lost in the shadows. Here and there a patch of reflected light picks out a fragment—a pale forehead, the buckle of a garter on a rounded calf, a powdered wig—but these are isolated and disparate details which do not coalesce into a meaningful whole; they cannot be made sense of (p. 45).

[14] Cf. the lack of temporal coherence in the funerary monument which Homais plans for Emma. First of all he suggests a broken pillar, then a pyramid, then a round Vestal temple, then a mock ruin, each to be accompanied by a weeping willow—moving randomly between ancient Egypt, classical Greece and Rome, and the romantic period (p. 320).

[15] Cf. the 'puddings à la Trafalgar' served at La Vaubyessard (p. 49).

[16] Roger Bismut and Jacques Seebacher place Emma's suicide in 1846, but Claudine Gothot-Mersch shows that 'la date de 1846 n'est pas sûre, puisqu'elle se fonde sur un 1843 douteux'. Art cit., pp. 44-46.

[17] 1848 is also subliminally present in *Un cœur simple*. Flaubert's notes for the story include a page of calculations comparing the ages of Mme Aubain, her children and Félicité at different stages of their lives; all the calculations converge in 1848, when Mme Aubain, Paul and Félicité are 71, 45, and 60 respectively. See *Plans, notes et scénarios de 'Un cœur simple'*, ed. by F. Fleury (Rouen. Lecerf, 1977), p. 26 (fol. 387r).

[18] MS gg 223, 17606, fol. 139r; 17610, fol. 52r; 17610, fol. 60r. See Gothot-Mersch, art. cit., p. 46.

[19] See Flaubert, *Œuvres complètes*, ed. by B. Masson, 2 vols (Paris, Editions du Seuil, 1964), I. 356.

[20] *Corr.* III, 95 (3 July 1860, to E. and J. de Goncourt).

[21] Contrast with Flaubert's own method in Chapter 6 of *Bouvard et Pécuchet*, where Flaubert refers to precise historical dates and well-known events, and gives coherence to his fiction by linking his characters to the 'moments reçus' of the unfolding Second Republic. See Jean-Luc Seylaz, 'Bouvard et Pécuchet ou l'Histoire au présent', in *Etudes de Lettres,* revue de la Faculté des Lettres, Université de Lausanne (1989.2), pp. 63-78.

[22] Ironically, Emma and Charles are themselves subject to this process of vanishing into the past. After his wife's death we read that 'Bovary, tout en pensant à Emma continuellement, l'oubliait; et il se désespérait à sentir cette image lui échapper de la mémoire au milieu des efforts qu'il faisait pour la retenir' (p. 320), while of Charles himself we are told that 'il serait maintenant impossible à aucun de nous de se rien rappeler de lui' (p. 8).

[23] *Corr.* (Conard edition), VI (1930), 228 (29 April 1871, to G. Sand,).

FURTHER READING

Ahearn, Edward J. "Using Marx to Read Flaubert: The Case of *Madame Bovary*." In *L'Hénaurme Siècle: A Miscellany of Essays on Nineteenth-Century French Literature*, edited by Will L. McLendon, pp. 73-91. Heidelbert: Carl Winter Universitätsverlag, 1984.

    Argues that "the relevance of Marx for the study of Flaubert" is "*formally* as well as historically pertinent."

Cascardi, Anthony J. "The Female Quixote: Aesthetics and Seduction." In *The Bounds of Reason: Cervantes, Dostoevsky, Flaubert*, pp. 159-82. New York: Columbia University Press, 1986.

    Considers the depiction of irony and sentimentality in *Madame Bovary* and Cervantes's *Don Quixote.*

Church, Margaret. "A Triad of Images: Nature as Structure in *Madame Bovary*." In *Structure and Theme: Don Quixote to James Joyce*, pp. 61-80. Columbus: Ohio State University Press, 1983.

    Examines "the means by which Flaubert fashions coherence within and among the three parts of [*Madame Bovary*], building slowly triadic structures within the larger triad of the book itself."

Collas, Ion K. *Madame Bovary: A Psychoanalytic Reading.* Geneve: Librairie Droz, 1985, 138 p.

    Scrutinizes the text of *Madame Bovary* "in an effort to discover the deeper cause of the sufferings of its heroine, the mysterious Emma Bovary, whose melancholy moods and tragic death have never been satisfactorily explained."

Culler, Jonathan. "The Uses of *Madame Bovary*." *Diacritics: A Review of Contemporary Criticism* 11 (Fall 1981): 74-81.

> Discusses how the "celebration of *Madame Bovary* as the novel of novels is closely connected with the celebration of Emma as a model of human nature" and the "use of *Madame Bovary* as a model of the post-modern."

Goodwin, Sarah Webster. "Emma Bovary's Dance of Death." *Novel* 19, No. 3 (Spring 1986): 197-215.

> Argues that Emma Bovary's "death-wish" is shaped in the text of *Madame Bovary* by "the popular motif of the dance of death, transformed and embedded by Flaubert in the novel's structures."

Greene, Robert W. "Clichés, Moral Censure, and Heroism in Flaubert's *Madame Bovary*." *Symposium* XXXII, No. 4 (Winter 1978): 289-302.

> Discusses Flaubert's satirical use of clichés in *Madame Bovary*.

Haig, Stirling. "*Madame Bovary*." In *Flaubert and the Gift of Speech: Dialogue and Discourse in Four 'Modern' Novels*, pp. 53-105. Cambridge: Cambridge University Press, 1986.

> Examines how Flaubert's use of dialogue in *Madame Bovary* "dramatizes narratorial irony" and also "allows him to reduce authorial presence, thus achieving the ideal of [authorial] objectivity."

——. "The *Madame Bovary* Blues." In *The Madame Bovary Blues: The Pursuit of Illusion in Nineteenth-Century French Fiction*, pp. 79-93. Baton Rouge: Louisiana State University Press, 1987.

> Argues that "while we are certainly witnessing the deflation of a [Romantic] myth in [*Madame Bovary*] . . . that deflation in no sense invalidates the myth's urgency or even destroys it."

Hamilton, James F. "*Madame Bovary* and the Myth of Androgyny." *The USF Language Quarterly* XIX, Nos. 3-4 (Spring-Summer 1981): 19-22.

> Maintains that the "apparent contradictions in [Emma Bovary's] character and conduct . . . reflect the salutary urge to unite the female and male aspects of her being."

Heath, Stephen. *Gustave Flaubert: Madame Bovary.* Cambridge: Cambridge University Press, 1992, 157 p.

> Examines Flaubert's authorial "identification" with *Madame Bovary*, focusing on the composition process and themes of personal relevance to Flaubert.

Johnsen, William A. "*Madame Bovary*: Romanticism, Modernism, and Bourgeois Style." *Modern Language Notes* 94, No. 4 (May 1979): 843-50.

> Argues that "Flaubert's attempt to go beyond the derivative romanticism of others [in *Madame Bovary*] only exposes, once again, his kinship to the bourgeois."

Kelly, Dorothy. "Gender and Representation: Flaubert's Androgynous Representations." In *Fictional Genders: Role and Representation in Nineteenth-Century French Narrative*, pp. 119-68. Lincoln: University of Nebraska Press, 1989.

> Argues that the "androgynous mix-up of feminine birthing metaphors and masculine phallo-pens [in *Madame Bovary*] must lead us away from purely historical and thematic questions to look at gender in relation to the real literary problem of this text: the problem of meaning."

Lloyd, Rosemary. "The Intellectual and Social Background." In *Madame Bovary,* pp. 21-45. London: Unwin Hyman, 1990.

> Focuses on *Madame Bovary*'s "evocation of contemporary convictions and codes of behaviour," arguing that the characters are confined by "a net of beliefs and expectations instilled in them by all the means society has at its disposal for making its citizens conform."

Pascal, Roy. "The French Masters." In *The Dual Voice: Free Indirect Speech and Its Functioning in the Nineteenth-Century European Novel*, pp. 98-122. Manchester: Manchester University Press, 1977.

> Offers "a bare and schematic indication of Flaubert's use of free indirect speech, limit[ed] . . . to a few issues that are of the most general significance."

Peterson, Carla L. "The Heroine as Reader in the Nineteenth-Century Novel: Emma Bovary and Maggie Tulliver." *Comparative Literature Studies* XVII, No. 2 (June 1980): 168-83.

> Discusses Emma Bovary in the context of the social position of women in England and France during the nineteenth century.

Reynaud, Patricia. "Economics as Lure in *Madame Bovary*." In *Money: Lure, Lore, and Literature*, edited by John Louis DiGaetani, pp. 163-74.

> Links the erosion of economic value with the decline of linguistic meaning and examines how this concept functions in the text of *Madame Bovary*.

Schor, Naomi. "For a Restricted Thematics: Writing, Speech, and Difference in *Madame Bovary*." In *Breaking the Chain: Women, Theory, and French Realist Fiction*, pp. 3-28. New York: Columbia University Press, 1985.

> Argues for a thematic approach to critical interpretation of *Madame Bovary*.

Wall, Geoffrey, trans. Introduction to *Madame Bovary: Provincial Lives,* by Gustave Flaubert, pp. vii-xxv. London: Penguin Books, 1992.

> Focuses on the biographical context for Flaubert's composition of *Madame Bovary* and provides an overview of the novel's plot.

Additional coverage of Flaubert's life and career can be found in the following sources published by Gale Research: *Nineteenth-Century Literature Criticism,* Vols. 2, 10, 19, and 62; *DISCovering Authors; Short Story Criticism,* Vol. 11; *World Literature Criticism, 1500 to the Present;* and *Dictionary of Literary Biography,* Vol. 119.

"Goblin Market"

Christina Georgina Rossetti

Poem by Christina Georgina Rossetti (1830-1894), composed in 1859 and published in 1862 in *Goblin Market and Other Poems*. For more information on Rossetti's life and her other works, see *Nineteenth-Century Literature Criticism*, Volumes 1 and 50.

INTRODUCTION

"Goblin Market," an early work considered to be one of Rossetti's masterpieces, was intended simply as a fairy story. Despite Rossetti's assertions that she meant nothing profound by the tale, its rich, complex, and suggestive language has caused the poem to be practically ignored as children's literature and instead regarded variously as an erotic exploration of sexual fantasy, a commentary on capitalism and Victorian market economy, a feminist glorification of "sisterhood," and a Christian allegory about temptation and redemption, among other readings. Additionally, in attempts to decode what is often described as the poem's subversive text, critics have looked to Rossetti's life for interpretive keys. The biographical aspects which have been examined by critics as means toward achieving a greater understanding of the poem include Rossetti's love affairs, her work with the Oxford Movement's "women's mission to women" in which she helped "rehabilitate" prostitutes, and her association with her brother, Dante Gabriel Rossetti, and the Pre-Raphaelite brotherhood. Since the language of "Goblin Market" suggests a variety of meanings, critics rarely agree on what the poem is about. Although scholars have failed to concur about something as elemental to the poem as its themes, "Goblin Market" is generally viewed as one of Rossetti's greatest works.

Biographical Information

Although Rossetti was a frequent contributor to her brother Dante's Pre-Raphaelite journal *The Germ*, she achieved immediate and significant recognition as a skilled poet with the 1862 publication of *Goblin Market and Other Poems*. The publication of the volume was hailed as the first literary success of the Pre-Raphaelites, earned critical and popular acclaim, and paved the way for the publication of Rossetti's next volume of poetry, *The Prince's Progress and Other Poems* (1866). Rossetti went on to publish religious poetry, devotional prose, and nursery rhymes for children. Due to the early success of "Goblin Market," Rossetti rarely fell out of favor with critics or her reading public and remains a focal point of critical study of nineteenth-century literary figures.

Plot and Major Characters

The story narrated in "Goblin Market" is often described as simple. Two sisters, Laura and Lizzie, who apparently live together without parents, are taunted by goblin merchant men to buy luscious and tantalizing fruits. Lizzie is able to resist their coaxing and runs home, but Laura succumbs. She pays for the wares with a lock of her hair and gorges herself on the exotic fare, but her desire increases rather than being satisfied. She returns home and informs Lizzie that she will venture back into the glen and seek the goblins again. But Laura can no longer hear the call of the goblins and grows increasingly apathetic. She refuses to eat and begins to age prematurely. Fearing for her sister's life, Lizzie decides to seek out the goblins in order to purchase an "antidote" for her sister. When the goblins learn that Lizzie does not intend to eat the fruit herself, they throw her money back at her and verbally and physically abuse her, pinching and kicking, tearing at her clothing, and smearing the juice and pulp of their fruit on her. Lizzie refuses to open her mouth and returns home with the penny in her purse. She invites her sister to suck the juices from her body, which Laura does. The juice of the goblin fruit now tastes bitter to Laura, and she writhes in pain from having consumed it. But the antidote works. Laura returns to her former self, and the epilogue of the poem describes Laura and Lizzie as wives and mothers. Laura now tells the story to their children, reminding them that "there is no friend like a sister."

Major Themes

Critics look to the language and structure of "Goblin Market" to identify the poem's themes. The argument for the poem's erotic and sexual nature is supported by the language of the poem. The nature of the goblins' fruit is extensively detailed and described as luscious and succulent. Laura consumes the fruit ravenously ("She sucked until her lips were sore" [l. 136]) and physically pays for it with a lock of her hair. Once Lizzie decides to seek the goblin men, their taunts carry heavy sexual overtones as well. First they "Squeezed and caressed her" (l. 349) and then invite her to "Bob at our cherries / Bite at our peaches" (ll. 354-55), and to "Pluck them and suck them" (l. 361). When she refuses to eat, they "Held her hands and squeezed their fruits / Against her mouth to make her eat" (ll. 406-07). Finally, when Lizzie returns home, battered and bruised, she invites her sister's embrace: "Come and kiss me. / Never mind my bruises, / Hug me, kiss me, suck my juices / . . . Eat me, drink me, love me; / Laura, make much of me" (ll. 466-68; 471-72). This erotic language has been used to support readings of the poem as a sexual fantasy and an examination of the sexuality and cruelty of children. Some critics focus primarily on Lizzie's suffering and subsequent offering of herself to her sister, reading this not as a sexual advance but as a sacrifice similar to Christ's redemption of humanity's sins or as exemplifying the power of sisterhood in a secular or feminist sense.

The language of the poem is also filled with terms of commerce, economics, and exchange. The goblins sell exotic fruits to Laura, who pays for them with a lock of her hair. Lizzie attempts to pay for the fruit with money, which is refused. Such elements of the poem have been examined as statements about capitalism and the Victorian economy, as an exploration of the role of women within the economy and society, and, more specifically, as a discussion of the place of female literature within the economy. Some critics take this one step further and maintain that the poem represents Rossetti's own aesthetic theory. The theme of renunciation in the poem, demonstrated primarily through Lizzie's actions, is sometimes used to prove that Rossetti believed in the necessity of renouncing pleasure or art's gratification in order for poetry to have purpose or significance. On a more religious level, renunciation of pleasure is read as a means of achieving spiritual redemption.

The basic structure of the poem lends itself to a reading of "Goblin Market" as a Christian allegory of temptation, fall, and redemption, and some critics have contended that this is the main purpose of the tale. In this reading, Laura represents the biblical Eve who yields to temptation, and Lizzie is the Christ figure who sacrifices herself to save her sister. Yet other scholars have maintained that the sexual language of the poem compromises its reading as a moral tale. Additionally, some aspects of the poem fail to coincide with the allegory. For example, as several critics have noted, Laura's desire itself is never criticized by either the poem's narrator or by Lizzie, and Lizzie's act is not one of overcoming temptation or desire, for she never longs for goblin fruit herself. This, some critics argue, undercuts Lizzie's standing as a Christ figure.

Critical Reception

Twentieth-century criticism of "Goblin Market" is remarkably similar to its contemporary commentary. In an early review (1863), Caroline Norton wrote that the poem "is one of the works which are said to 'defy criticism.' Is it a fable—or a mere fairy story—or an allegory against the pleasures of sinful love—or what is it?" These comments reflect modern criticism, as "Goblin Market" still perplexes and inspires scholars. Perhaps the most common means of investigating the poem is based in biography. Most modern analyses of "Goblin Market" refer in some way to aspects of Rossetti's life. Some critics, such as Lona Mosk Packer (1958), suggest ways in which Rossetti's romantic relationships influenced the poem. Packer describes Rossetti's "intimate friendship" with William Bell Scott, and Scott's subsequent, perhaps romantic, friendship with another woman. By Packer's account, Rossetti's sister Maria may have informed Christina of Scott's new interest and "saved" her sister from misplaced desire in much the same way that Lizzie saves Laura.

Another biographical angle from which the poem is approached is that of Rossetti's work as a "sister" within the Anglican Sisterhoods of the Oxford Movement during the 1850s and 1860s. The work of the sisterhoods involved the reform of prostitutes and the reintroduction of reformed women into mainstream society. Critics such as Mary Wilson Carpenter (1991) argue that interaction with these women accounts for both the feminism and homoeroticism of "Goblin Market." Other critics suggest that the poem was meant as a means of cautioning these women about returning to their former ways. Additionally, critics such as Janet Galligani Casey (1991) suggest a more secular interpretation of "sisterhood." Casey points to the work of Florence Nightingale, and Rossetti's interest in this work, arguing that Nightingale popularized the notion of "sisters" as nurses. Casey goes on to suggest that, having been familiar with this concept and the fact that Nightingale attempted to elevate the role of nurturer (a traditionally female role) to that of the nurtured (a traditionally male role), Rossetti perhaps intended to emphasize that Lizzie heals or nurtures Laura and that the idea of "sisterhood" is really genderless.

One other way in which critics have used Rossetti's life as a key to interpreting the poem centers on Rossetti's involvement with the Pre-Raphaelite brotherhood, in which Rossetti's brother Dante played a prominent role. The Pre-Raphaelite movement was primarily Christian in emphasis and was a reaction against both Victorian materialism and artistic neoclassicism. At the time of its publication, "Goblin Market" was considered to be the first major literary achievement of the movement. Dorothy Mermin (1983) described "Goblin Market" as a "vision of a Pre-Raphaelite world from a woman's point of view." Furthermore, Mermin supports a biographical reading of the poem in which Rossetti imagines a Pre-Raphaelite sisterhood which she did not feel existed in reality.

Finally, some critics have sought to synthesize various biographical aspects in interpreting "Goblin Market." Sean C. Grass (1996) attempts to account for the "commingling" of the influences of Rossetti's love affairs, her work in the sisterhoods of the Oxford Movement, and her association with the Pre-Raphaelites, through her writing of "Goblin Market." Grass emphasizes the importance of letting the poem point to the most "fruitful" ways of approaching it and identifies the use of lists within the poem as the "interpretive key." In his analysis, Grass finds that Rossetti experienced a conflict between her love of nature's variety and her belief that reveling in nature would cloud moral judgement; this conflict, concludes Grass, is the focus of "Goblin Market."

CRITICISM

Caroline Norton (essay date 1863)

SOURCE: " 'The Angel in the House' and 'The Goblin Market'," in *Macmillan's Magazine*, Vol. VIII, No. 47, September, 1863, pp. 398-404.

[*In the following excerpt, Norton offers a favorable assessment of "Goblin Market," maintaining that the work is Rossetti's best and that its linking of fantastic imagery to everyday life allows "Goblin Market" to "vie with Coleridge's 'Ancient Mariner'."*]

The **"Goblin Market,"** by Miss Christina Rossetti, is one of the works which are said to "defy criticism." Is it a fable—or a mere fairy story—or an allegory against the pleasures of sinful love—or what is it? Let us not too rigorously inquire, but accept it in all its quaint and pleasant mystery, and quick and musical rhythm—a ballad which children will con with delight, and which riper minds may ponder over, as we do with poems written in a foreign language which we only half understand.

One thing is certain; we ought not to buy fruit from goblin men. We ought not; and we will not. The cost of doing so, is too passionately portrayed in Miss Rossetti's verses to permit us to err in such a sort. The cunning, and selfish overreaching of the goblins is too faithfully rendered in Mr. D. G. Rossetti's picture—"Buy from us with a golden curl"—to allow us to be taken in. Decidedly not all the list of delicious fruits with which the volume opens shall make us waver in our resolution. We agree with Lizzie, the conscientious sister—

> 'We must not look at goblin men,
> We must not buy their fruits:
> Who knows upon what soil they fed
> Their hungry thirsty roots?'
> 'Come buy,' call the goblins
> Hobbling down the glen.
> 'Oh,' cried Lizzie, 'Laura, Laura,
> You should not peep at goblin men.'
> Lizzie covered up her eyes,
> Covered close lest they should look;
> Laura reared her glossy head,
> And whispered like the restless brook:
> 'Look, Lizzie, look, Lizzie,
> Down the glen tramp little men.
> One hauls a basket,
> One bears a plate,
> One lugs a golden dish
> Of many pounds weight.
> How fair the vine must grow
> Whose grapes are so luscious;
> How warm the wind must blow
> Through those fruit bushes.'
> 'No.' said Lizzie: 'No, no, no;
> Their offers should not charm us,
> Their evil gifts would harm us.'

We regret Laura's fall in spite of such sweet warning:—

> But sweet-tooth Laura spoke in haste:
> 'Good folk, I have no coin;
> To take were to purloin:
> I have no copper in my purse,
> I have no silver either,
> And all my gold is on the furze
> That shakes in windy weather
> Above the rusty heather.'
> 'You have much gold upon your head,'
> They answered all together:
> 'Buy from us with a golden curl.'

> She clipped a precious golden lock,
> She dropped a tear more rare than pearl,
> Then sucked their fruit globes fair or red:
> Sweeter than honey from the rock,
> Stronger than man-rejoicing wine,
> Clearer than water flowed that juice;
> She never tasted such before,
> How should it cloy with length of use?
> She sucked and sucked and sucked the more
> Fruits which that unknown orchard bore;
> She sucked until her lips were sore;
> Then flung the emptied rinds away,
> But gathered up one kernel-stone,
> And knew not was it night or day
> As she turned home alone.
>
> Lizzie met her at the gate
> Full of wise upbraidings:
> 'Dear, you should not stay so late,
> Twilight is not good for maidens;
> Should not loiter in the glen
> In the haunts of goblin men.
> Do you not remember Jeanie,
> How she met them in the moonlight,
> Took their gifts both choice and many,
> Ate their fruits and wore their flowers
> Plucked from bowers
> Where summer ripens at all hours?
> But ever in the moonlight
> She pined and pined away;
> Sought them by night and day,
> Found them no more but dwindled and grew grey;
> Then fell with the first snow,
> While to this day no grass will grow
> Where she lies low:
> I planted daisies there a year ago
> That never blow.
> You should not loiter so.'

We tremble as we read the contrast, suddenly resulting, between the two golden-haired sisters:—

> Early in the morning
> When the first cock crowed his warning,
> Neat like bees, as sweet and busy,
> Laura rose with Lizzie:
> Fetched in honey, milked the cows,
> Aired and set to rights the house,
> Kneaded cakes of whitest wheat,
> Cakes for dainty months to eat,
> Next churned butter, whipped up cream,
> Fed their poultry, sat and sewed;
> Talked as modest maidens should:
> Lizzie with an open heart,
> Laura in an absent dream,
> One content, one sick in part;
> One warbling for the mere bright day's delight,
> One longing for the night.

We shudder over the weird change in poor Laura:—

> Day after day, night after night,
> Laura kept watch in vain
> In sullen silence of exceeding pain.
> She never caught again the goblin cry:
> 'Come buy, come buy;'—
> She never spied the goblin men
> Hawking their fruits along the glen:
> But when the noon waxed bright
> Her hair grew thin and grey;
> She dwindled, as the fair full moon doth turn
> To swift decay and burn
> Her fire away.
>
> She no more swept the house,
> Tended the fowls or cows,
> Fetched honey, kneaded cakes of wheat,
> Brought water from the brook:
> But sat down listless in the chimney-nook
> And would not eat.

Till at last, as with Effie and Jeanie Deans, the one sister risks all to save the other; and Lizzie, putting a silver penny in her purse, sets out to buy from the goblin-men!—

> Laughed every goblin
> When they spied her peeping:
> Came towards her hobbling,
> Flying, running, leaping,
> Puffing and blowing,
> Chuckling, clapping, crowing,
> Clucking and gobbling,
> Mopping and mowing,
> Full of airs and graces,
> Pulling wry faces,
> Demure grimaces,
> Cat-like and rat-like,
> Ratel- and wombat-like,
> Snail-paced in a hurry,
> Parrot-voiced and whistler,
> Helter skelter, hurry skurry,
> Chattering like magpies,
> Fluttering like pigeons,
> Gliding like fishes,—
> Hugged her and kissed her,
> Squeezed and caressed her:
> Stretched up their dishes,
> Panniers, and plates:
> 'Look at our apples
> Russet and dun,
> Bob at our cherries,
> Bite at our peaches,
> Citrons and dates,
> Grapes for the asking,
> Pears red with basking
> Ont in the sun,
> Plums on their twigs;

> Pluck them and suck them,
> Pomegranates, figs.'

Here is a picture of the spite which goblin-men show, when you will not eat with them of their strange fruits:—

> They trod and hustled her,
> Elbowed and jostled her,
> Clawed with their nails,
> Barking, mewing, hissing, mocking,
> Tore her gown and soiled her stocking,
> Twitched her hair out by the roots,
> Stamped upon her tender feet,
> Held her hands and squeezed their fruits
> Against her mouth to make her eat.

We are relieved to find that Lizzie nevertheless escapes in safety:—

> At last the evil people,
> Worn out by her resistance,
> Flung back her penny, kicked their fruit
> Along whichever road they took,
> Not leaving root or stone or shoot;
> Some writhed into the ground,
> Some dived into the brook
> With ring and ripple,
> Some scudded on the gale without a sound,
> Some vanished in the distance.
>
> She cried 'Laura,' up the garden,
> 'Did you miss me?
> Come and kiss me.
> Never mind my bruises,
> Hug me, kiss me, suck my juices
> Squeezed from goblin fruits for you,
> Goblin pulp and goblin dew.
> Eat me, drink me, love me;
> Laura, make much of me:
> For your sake I have braved the glen
> And had to do with goblin merchant men.

Laura's penitence is as mysterious as her sin; but we are beyond measure soothed and comforted when we learn this:—

> But when the first birds chirped about their eaves,
> And early reapers plodded to the place
> Of golden sheaves,
> And dew-wet grass
> Bowed in the morning winds so brisk to pass,
> And new buds with new day
> Opened of cup-like lilies on the stream,
> Laura awoke as from a dream,
> Laughed in the innocent old way,
> Hugged Lizzie but not twice or thrice;
> Her gleaming locks showed not one thread of grey,
> Her breath was sweet as May,
> And light danced in her eyes.

Very beautiful are the simple lines which follow:—

> Days, weeks, months, years,
> Afterwards, when both were wives
> With children of their own;
> *Their mother-hearts beset with fears,*
> *Their lives bound up in tender lives;*
> Laura would call the little ones
> And tell them of her early prime,
> Those pleasant days long gone
> Of not-returning time:
> Would talk about the haunted glen,
> The wicked, quaint fruit-merchant men,
> Their fruits like honey to the throat
> But poison in the blood.

There are other poems in the volume full of serious power and purpose, and full also of poetry and passion. The sonnet, entitled **"Rest,"** is one of the finest of these; and the brief, but full of meaning, **"Up-hill,"** the gentle page, **"Consider the Lilies of the Field,"** and the less openly intelligible but beautiful **"From House to Home,"** prove the versatility, as well as the originality of genius, which has fallen to the share of this young writer. Many verses of Miss Rossetti, scattered through other works, make many readers familiar with her writings; but incomparably the best of her compositions is the **"Goblin Market,"** which may vie with Coleridge's "Ancient Mariner," in its degree, for the vivid and wonderful power by which things unreal and mystic are made to blend and link themselves with the everyday images and events of common life.

J. Ashcroft Noble (essay date 1895)

SOURCE: "The Burden of Christina Rossetti," in *Impressions and Memories*, J. M. Dent and Co., 1895, pp. 55-64.

[*In the following excerpt, Noble praises "Goblin Market" as a "spiritual drama" about the redemptive power of love.*]

For those who love letters so well that even its mere chronology has for them no barren aridity, there are certain years to which are assigned specially honourable places in the chambers of memory; and 1862 has a double claim to such honour, for it witnessed the publication of the "Last Poems" of Elizabeth Barrett Browning, and of the first really representative work of Christina Rossetti. When the latter poet was but sixteen, a little collection of her girlish verse had been proudly though privately printed by her maternal grandfather, Mr Polidori, and in 1850 her pen-name, "Ellen Alleyn," had appeared as the signature of seven youthful poems published in

The Germ; but the slim volume containing **"Goblin Market"** and its lyrical companions was the first revelation to the world of the matured powers of the new singer, and to those who had ears to hear, the little book came as a welcome assurance that, though one rich penetrating strain was silenced, a woman's voice not less strong and tender, and with a new, strange quality of charm, was still to be heard in the Victorian choir.

It is probable, however, that few of Miss Rossetti's earliest readers and critics fully recognised the importance of the new contribution to English poetry. Its grace, sweetness, purity, and tenderness could not well be missed, and there was a certain obviously natural quaintness which gave to many of the poems a haunting, exotic charm; but at this early day, there seems to have been but scant discernment of that simple directness of imaginative vision and that power of rendering by one set of symbols truths of the material and of the spiritual worlds, which gave to these first poems, not less truly than to the poems which have succeeded them, their power of subtle fascination. For it must be noted in passing that Miss Rossetti is not one of the many poets whose works represent successive stages of an intellectual or artistic development, and can therefore only be studied with full appreciation in the order of their production. Of course, it was impossible that thirty years of the life of any earnest worker should come and go and leave no result of gain behind them; but in Miss Rossetti's case it was simply the inevitable gain of facility and finish, for in all essential qualities of vision and the rendering of it her earliest work is as characteristically opulent as any of the work that succeeded it.

Of various elusive impressions left upon the reader's emotional consciousness by Miss Rossetti's poems, the one which finally achieves supremacy both of distinctness and permanence can only be described with apparent paradox as an impression of familiar remoteness. Wordsworth, in his most frequently quoted line, has spoken of the imaginative vision to which all objects appear in "the light that never was on sea or land," and the true magical quality of this light is best discerned, not when it flames on Shelley's mountain peaks, or pierces with lurid illumination the recesses of Milton's Pandemonium, but when, as in this more human poet's pages, it falls on homely figures and homely scenes, and confers upon them a strange and beautiful transfiguration like that which is wrought by moonlight or by dream. It shines even in such comparatively unimportant poems as **"Maiden Song," "Maggie, a Lady,"** and **"Noble Sisters,"** which have much of the form and all the spirit of the old ballads—that spirit which charms and soothes us, because where it reigns the weary complexities and sophistications of our confused thought and business can find no place, and the primitive simplicities of action and emotion live their own glad unconscious life.

> Long ago and long ago,
> And long ago still,
> There dwelt three merry maidens,
> Upon a distant hill.
> One was tall Meggan,
> And one was dainty May,
> But one was fair Margaret,
> More fair than I can say—
> Long ago and long ago.

The song itself, as well as the maidens, seems to come to us from an immemorial long ago. How sweet, fresh, and unstrained are its notes, but today how few can sing them! Many are the strivers after that simplicity which in an artificial age serves as well as anything else to gratify the lust for change; but the true simplicity comes not by seeking; it is a grace of instinct that is given, not won, and in our century it has been given to but two singers—to William Blake and Christina Rossetti.

But it is elsewhere than in these simple ballad verses that the strange light gleams with spiritual, rather than merely natural, magic. In the larger body of Miss Rossetti's poetry the familiar things of sense win their special quality of fascination from an atmosphere of spiritual suggestion by which they are surrounded and permeated. In thus making us conscious of two worlds at once, Miss Rossetti does not use the mechanical method of the allegorist, who chooses a set of arbitrary symbols, and labels each with its special spiritual significance; for she is a true mystic, to whom each simple thing of nature or each homely human relation tells its own secret of meaning, and tomorrow's meaning may not be that of today, because the object is not a figure in a cipher, but a true symbol with infinite variety of revelation. The poem, [**"Goblin Market"**] . . . for example, which gave its name to her first volume, may be read and enjoyed merely as a charming fairy-fantasy, and as such it is delightful and satisfying; but behind the simple story of the two children and the goblin fruit-sellers is a little spiritual drama of love's vicarious redemption, in which the child redeemer goes into the wilderness to be tempted of the devil, that by her painful conquest she may succour and save the sister who has been vanquished and all but slain. The luscious juices of the goblin fruit, sweet and deadly when sucked by selfish greed, become bitter and medicinal when spilt in unselfish conflict; and the girl who knows that she has won love's victory can call exultantly—

> Did you miss me?
> Come and kiss me,
> Never mind my bruises,
> Hug me, kiss me, suck my juices
> Squeezed from goblin fruits for you,
> Goblin pulp and goblin dew.
> Eat me, drink me, love me;

Laura, make much of me;
For your sake I have braved the glen
And had to do with goblin merchant men.

Marian Shalkhauser (essay date 1956)

SOURCE: "The Feminine Christ," in *The Victorian Newsletter,* No. 10, Autumn, 1956, pp. 19-20.

[*In the following essay, Shalkhauser examines "Goblin Market" as a "Christian fairy tale" in which Lizzie represents Christ and Laura signifies sinful humanity.*]

Christina Rossetti's **"Goblin Market"** is a unique Christian fairy tale in which a feminine cast of characters is substituted for the masculine cast of the Biblical sin-redemption sequence. Lizzie, the pure sister, is the symbol of Christ; Laura represents Adam-Eve and consequently all of sinful mankind.

The basic symbolic pattern begins immediately: "Morning and evening / Maids heard the goblins cry." Throughout their lives sin beckons to God's creatures. Notice that only maidens are mentioned as hearing the cry of sin, and that they are innocent until corrupted by the animalistic masculine goblins. The cry of these goblins is that of the fruit-hawker, as was Satan's in the Garden of Eden, and their fruit comes from the un-Anglican South. The cry itself is encased within lines indicative of early mortality, for it is "evening by evening" that the sisters hear it. Lizzie warns Laura, "We must not look at goblin men, / We must not buy their fruits." Goblins are creatures of the Devil, symbols of Satan himself, who carry with them all the temptations of the world, as did Satan when he tempted Adam, and later, Christ. How ironic it is then when Laura tries to envision the fair lands from which these goblin fruits come, for of course sin is of Hell. Lizzie intimates as much when she admonishes Laura: "No, no, no; / Their offers should not charm us, / Their evil gifts would harm us." Christ closed his ears to the charms of Satan's offers; Lizzie "thrust a dimpled finger / In each ear, shut eyes and ran." But Laura, and Adam, stayed to listen.

Satan appears typically in the form of depraved animals—cat, rat, snail, wombat—whose eeriness is enhanced by Christina's endowing them with the voices of paradisal doves. The shock of this contrast between repulsive appearance and heavenly sound produces in the reader a chaos of inverted values such as that produced by hearing from a serpent's mouth the voice of an angel. Laura has the innocent beauty of Adam before the Fall; she is like a swan, a lily, a moonlit poplar branch, a vessel. Satanic goblins offer her the lures of the world: a crown, wealth, a golden plate of fruit, which Laura says is "too huge for me to hold," and which the goblins later tell Lizzie "no man can carry," for no man can bear alone the burden of sin. Laura, with a golden curl and a tear "more rare than pearl," sells her soul to taste of the fruit, as had Adam and Eve. Immediately her sense of the difference between right and wrong is obscured, for when she turns to go home, she knows not "was it night or day," but she clutches in her hand a seed of the fruit, a seed of sin to which she clings.

Lizzie meets her as God had once met Adam, upbraiding her for listening to Satan, but, like mankind, Laura cannot return to innocence without help. Man persists in feasting greedily upon the pleasures of this world. Laura says, "I ate and ate my fill, / Yet my mouth waters still: / Tomorrow night I will / Buy more." Tasks are tedious to Laura next day, for she longs after the sombre, dark, guilt-infested night. At last night comes, and the sisters go back to the sin-haunted glen. Laura is "most like a leaping flame," the unhealthy and destructive fire of guilt. Lizzie begs her to come home, as Christ through His prophets had pleaded with mankind to return to God, "For clouds may gather / Though this is summer weather, / Put out the lights and drench us through"—though this is the summer of life, clouds of evil, brought by the night of sin, may darken the path of mankind—and "then if we lost our way what should we do?"

Laura will not hear Lizzie; she is listening for sin, and when she does not hear its cry, "her tree of life drooped from the root," and the fire of guilt gnaws at her soul until it produces a sterile desert within her: "She dreamed of melons, as a traveller sees / False waves in desert drouth / With shade of leaf-crowned trees, / And burns the thirstier in the sandful breeze." Mankind declines, and Christ sees that He must offer Himself as sacrifice to redeem His brothers. Lizzie goes to the glen, the valley of the shadow, and for the first time in her life begins "to listen and look" when sin appears. The Devil rejoices prematurely in his victory: "Laughed every goblin / When they spied her peeping." As the multitude lauded Christ when He entered Jerusalem, so the goblins fawn on Lizzie, assuring her, "Our feast is but beginning. / Night yet is early. . . ." But when she refuses to taste of sin, they become hostile and Lizzie assumes the stance of Christ buffeted by the mob, upright amidst her tormentors. To the mockery of the Devil, Christ answered never a word, and Lizzie likewise "uttered not a word." And at last evil is routed, as it must be when it challenges complete innocence.

Laura benefits by the sacrifice when she is reborn in tears that drop "like rain / After long and sultry drouth." She "rent all her robe" and "beat her breast" in her agony of repentance; she "loathed the feast" of sin. The fire of purification overcomes the "lesser flame" of guilt in her soul, and Christina Rossetti cannot forebear to point out the wages of sin and its folly: "She gorged on bitterness without a name: / Ah fool, to choose such part / Of soul-consuming care!" Laura faints from the stress of her struggle—"Is it death or is it life?" For the Christian the answer is patent: "Life out of death." Laura dies into life when she renounces her sin, is baptized by tears into salvation, and accepts her sister's sacrifice. All night Lizzie watches over her while Laura gathers strength, and when day comes Laura wakens and laughs "in the innocent old way." Thus does Christ comfort mankind through his darkest hours, bringing him at last to everlasting innocence. Years later, Laura tells her children, the successive generations of mankind, that a sister is one "to cheer one on the tedious way, / To fetch one if one goes astray, / To lift one if one totters down, / To strengthen whilst one stands." Is not this the ideal relationship between mankind and Christ?

Though there are surely many other elements, particularly that of folklore, which contribute to the composition of the entire poem, **"Goblin Market"** sets forth Christina Rossetti's beliefs in original sin and in the sacrificial nature of Christ's death through her creation of a Christian fairy tale in which a feminine Christ redeems a feminine mankind from a masculine Satan.

Lona Mosk Packer (essay date 1958)

SOURCE: "Symbol and Reality in Christina Rossetti's *Goblin Market*," in *PMLA*, Vol. LXXIII, No. 4, Part I, September, 1958, pp. 375-85.

[*In the following essay, Packer argues that the symbolism—which is often vague—in "Goblin Market" reflects the realities of Rossetti's life, just as the symbols in her other works correspond with her life, and that the poem should not be read simply as a "Pre-Raphaelite masterpiece."*]

I

In common with other such enduring works of art as *The Faery Queen, Gulliver's Travels,* and *Alice in Wonderland,* Christina Rossetti's **"Goblin Market"** has many levels of meaning. At the narrative level it offers a charming and delicate fairy tale to delight a child—if a somewhat precocious one. At the symbolic and allegorical level, it conveys certain Christian ethical assumptions. At the psychological level, it suggests emotional experience universally valid.

Unlike Christina's other long autobiographical poems, notably **"Convent Threshold," "From House to Home,"** and **"Prince's Progress,"** this poem, acknowledged her masterpiece, has no hero.[1] No fiery intellectual such as we find in **"Convent Threshold,"** no poet-lover similar to the one who first shares and then shatters the speaker's earthly paradise in **"From House to Home,"** no tardy and loitering Prince failing to make hymeneal progress graces this work. It can hardly be said to have a heroine, for the sisters, Laura and Lizzie, between them share the narrative interest. Golden-haired, ivory-skinned, "like two blossoms on one stem," they seem but different aspects of the same maiden. They may in fact be regarded as Christina Rossetti's version of sacred and profane love. For once in her poetry, she presents love in large, abstract, general terms. But although the individual contours are lacking, no poem of Christina's is more clearly based upon personal experience.

Despite the fact that William Michael Rossetti, Christina's brother and editor, remembered that he had often heard her say she did not mean anything profound by this fairy tale and it was not to be taken as a moral apologue, he himself admitted finding "the incidents . . . suggestive," and in his comments about the poem encouraged an interpretation at a deeper level than that of a fairy tale fantasy (*Works,* p. 459, n.). Although modern critics have been inclined to drop the whole matter of meaning and to regard the poem as a Pre-Raphaelite masterpiece which combines a realistic use of detail with the vague symbolism and religiosity of a **"Blessed Damozel,"** in interpreting the poem it would seem more fruitful to pay attention to William Rossetti's various hints and admissions, particularly since Christina herself, for reasons of her own, apparently wished to discourage explication. Indeed these very reasons are what give the poem its organizing principle.

Once **"Goblin Market"** is read as the complex, rich, and meaningful work it actually, is, the prevalent critical view that the poem has the bright, clear, obvious pigmentation and the lightly woven surface texture of a Pre-Raphaelite painting will no longer be tenable. An analysis of the poem in the light of the emotional facts in Christina's life will reveal that the symbolism, vague and suggestive as it may appear, actually has the same underlying contact with reality that her other poems display. Ford Madox Ford once remarked that although love among the Pre-Raphaelites was a romantic and glamorous affair of generalizations, Christina alone regarded it concretely and individually.[2]

II

The story is simple. Two lovely sisters are tempted by the little goblin merchants who haunt the glens and woods and toward evening allure unwary maidens with fruit, rich, glowing, delicious to the taste. Lizzie resists; Laura succumbs to temptation. Once the victim has tasted the fruit, she is tormented by a wild craving for a second taste, but this the goblin merchants never grant. Fearing for Laura's life, Lizzie braves the seductions of the goblins, exposing herself to their tempting wares, so that she may secure the "fiery antidote" to save her sister's life. The antidote is the fruit itself. The goblins taunt, tease, maul, and torment Lizzie, but she stands firm amidst the turmoil. At length she triumphs, and with the rich juices smeared over her face, she runs home to let Laura kiss and suck them off her cheeks and chin. A second taste gratifies Laura's longing. She is saved, and the poem concludes with the well-known tribute to a sister.

Temptation, both in its human and its theological sense, is the thematic core of **"Goblin Market."** Even more than in Christina's **"Convent Threshold,"** which Alice Meynell described as "a song of penitence for love that yet praises love more fervently than would a chorus hymeneal," **"Goblin Market"** celebrates by condemning sensuous passion. Seldom in nineteenth-century poetry, even in the verse of Christina's brother Dante Gabriel Rossetti and of Swinburne, has the lure of the senses been so convincingly portrayed. Indirection is Christina's method, and its subtlety and delicacy can be appreciated only when **"Goblin Market"** is compared to poems as frankly and openly sensuous as Rossetti's **"Eden Bower"** and **"Troy Town,"** or Swinburne's "Dolores." The symbolism in which Christina veils her own tribute to Eros is all the more persuasive in that it is rooted in both the legendry of pagan German romanticism and the morality of the Christian tradition.

To Mackenzie Bell, Christina's first biographer, William Rossetti admitted that the main subject of the poem was the problem of temptation. Despite Christina's denial of some "profound or ulterior meaning . . ." he said, "one can discern that it implies at any rate this much—that to succumb to a temptation makes one a victim to that same temptation . . ."[3]

The problem itself was one which throughout her literary life attracted Christina. In **"Three Enemies,"** a poem of 1851, she treated the subject according to the traditional conception of Christian orthodoxy, dramatizing her theme much as Herbert did in "The Quip." The World, the Flesh, and the Devil are portrayed as the conventional three-pronged fork of temptation. Other poems exploring the same subject are **"Two Pursuits"** (1849), **"The World"** (1854), **"Amor Mundi"** (1865), and **"Sister Louise de la Misericorde"** (B. 1882).

Frequent allusions to the problem crop up in her prose works as well as in her verse. In *Annus Domini* (London, 1874), p. 103, she acknowledges as major temptations the seduction of the flesh and the allurements of the world, but for the devil she substitutes angry rebellion, a form of temptation to which, as she admitted upon more than one occasion, she herself was peculiarly susceptible.[4] In *Time Flies* (London, 1885), p. 184, she portrays temptation figuratively as Satan's sieve. In theological language which nevertheless suggests an accepted insight of modern psychology, she writes: "For he can never . . . destroy us, unless we first make a covenant with death . . . Meanwhile he is doing us an actual service by bringing to the surface what already lurks within. However tormenting and humiliating declared leprosy may be, it is less desperate than suppressed leprosy." From these and other statements, it can be seen that Christina wrote about sensual temptation not as one academically interested in a theological question, but as one who had herself crossed Dante's flaming path of arrowy fire, the last barrier to *Paradiso*.

Temptation in **"Goblin Market"** is symbolized by the fruit, the great traditional symbol of sin and temptation in the Bible. Clearly the fruit sold by the goblin merchants, those "bloom-down-cheeked peaches," the "rare pears," and "bright fire-like barberries," the iced melons, and the sun-ripened citrons from the South, of which the taste brings decay and death, are the forbidden fruit of Scripture. They belong to the order of fruit which tempted Eve, and which in Revelation (xviii.14) appears as "the fruit that thy soul lusteth after." In Christina's poem Laura even asks Lizzie if she has tasted "For my sake the fruit forbidden?"

Fruit also appears as the symbolic inducement to sin in St. Augustine's *Confessions*. In this work, one of Christina's early favorites, the plucking of the forbidden fruit is dramatized and symbolized in the famous pear tree incident. As a young lad, Augustine with his comrades steals the ripe pears from the farmer's tree. For Augustine, this irresponsible act of a mischievous boy represents the first free choice of the evil will.

Although in **"Goblin Market"** the powerful lure of love is primarily represented by the traditional symbol of fruit, it is also symbolized by the goblin men of Teutonic fairy lore, the elves, dwarfs, and little men that B. Ifor Evans thought Christina found ready-made in Keightley's collection of fairy tales and in William Allingham's poem "The Fairies."[5] But one hardly needs to go back either to Keightley or to Allingham for the little merchant men. In 1840, when Christina was ten years old, Dr. Adolf Heimann, a family friend, offered to teach the four Rossetti children German in exchange for Italian lessons from the elder Rossetti, at that time professor of Italian at King's College, London. With her brothers, Dante Gabriel and William, and her sister Maria, Christina studied German with Dr. Heimann for three years. Her first simple reading assignment in that language was *Sagen und Mährchen,* the popular collection of folk and fairy lore in which the customary Teutonic dwarf makes a frequent appearance.[6]

What distinguishes Christina's little men from the conventional figure of the dwarf is their partial resemblance to animals:

One had a cat's face,
One whisked a tail,

One tramped at a rat's pace,
One crawled like a snail,
One like a wombat prowled obtuse and furry,
One like a ratel tumbled hurry skurry.

In "**From House to Home,**" which Christina wrote only six months before "**Goblin Market,**" such small animals form part of the speaker's earthly paradise:

> My trees were full of songs and flowers and
>   fruit;
> Their branches spread a city to the air
> And mice lodged in their root.
>
> My heath lay farther off, where lizards lived
> In strange metallic mail, just spied and gone;
> Like darted lightnings here and there perceived
> But nowhere dwelt upon.
>
> Frogs and fat toads were there to hop or plod
> And propagate in peace, an uncouth crew,
> Where velvet-headed rushes rustling nod
> And spill the morning dew.
>
> All caterpillars throve beneath my rule,
> With snails and slugs in corners out of sight;
> I never marred the curious sudden stool
> That perfects in a night.
>
> Safe in his excavated gallery
> The burrowing mole groped on from year to
>   year;
> No harmless hedgehog curled because of me
> His prickly back for fear.

This innocent Eden strikes one as a child's rather than an adult's conception of the earthly paradise, and in fact probably originated in Christina's childhood memories of Holmer Green, her grandfather's country cottage in Buckinghamshire where until she was nine she was accustomed to spend her summers. Its grounds, she said, were her "familiar haunt" and "inexhaustible delight." To Edmund Gosse she confided once, "If any one thing schooled me in the direction of poetry, it was perhaps the delightful idle liberty to prowl all alone about my grandfather's cottage-grounds some thirty miles from London . . ."[7] To the end of her life she remembered and described the effect that Holmer Green had had upon her "youthful imagination."

As a child, then, she could have found the originals both of the fruit and the animal-faced goblins in her grandfather's cottage grounds. Undoubtedly she first saw in the orchards surrounding Holmer Green those "sun-red apples," nectarines, peaches, and ripe plums, which she initially idealized in an early poem ("**The Dead City,**" 1847), and later glorified in "**Goblin Market.**" From William's reminiscences of the common childhood shared by the four Rossettis as well as from Christina's own random recollections in *Time Flies,* we can be sure that she had ample opportunity to observe directly the frogs, toads, snails, mice, cats, rabbits, squirrels, and pigeons that invariably make up her earthly paradise.[8] Such animal images grafted upon the imaginary German dwarfs and elves of *Sagen und Mährchen* could have resulted in the poetic conception of the goblin merchants.

The question then arises, if she was so partial to these small animals dear to her childhood, why in "**Goblin Market**" did she portray them in such sinister guise, as the agents of evil and the vendors of temptation?

For the purposes of the poem itself, no contradiction exists. The joys of the earthly paradise must be renounced, if one is to achieve spiritual redemption. The lusciousness of the forbidden fruit and the charm of the little animal-faced goblins are but different aspects of nature, the core of which is sexual passion. "Nature worshipped under divers aspects," Christina wrote in *Letter and Spirit* (London, 1883), "exacts under each aspect her victims; or rather, man's consciousness of guilt invests her with a punitive energy backed by a will to punish greater than he can bear" (p. 74).

But if she recognized and acknowledged the dangerous potentialities inherent in sexual love, she did not puritanically condemn it as such. At the conclusion of "**Goblin Market**" both sisters, Laura as well as Lizzie, are portrayed as happily married women with children of their own, to whom they relate the old tale. By such a traditionally "happy ending," Christina seems to be implying that neither the fruit nor the animals are in themselves harmful, although in the poem one is the object and the other the agent of temptation; it is only "man's consciousness of guilt"—that is, the Christian concept of guilt incurred through sin embedded in the evil will—which charges them with a dangerous and punitive malignity. In short, man is his own destroyer.

Christina was explicit on this point, that is, man's capacity for self-destruction, in *The Face of the Deep* (London, 1892). In this, the last of her devotional prose works, she wrote:

> There is a mystery of evil which I suppose no man during his tenure of mortal life will ever fathom. But there is a second mystery of evil. . . . I pursuing my own evil from point to point find that it leads me not outward amid a host of foes laid against me, but inward within myself: it is not mine enemy that doeth me this dishonour, neither is it mine adversary that magnifieth himself against me: it is I, it is not another, not primarily any other; it is I who undo, defile, deface myself. True, I am summoned to wrestle on my own scale against principalities, powers, rulers of the darkness of this world, spiritual wickedness in high places; but none of these can crush me unless I simultaneously undermine my own

citadel. . . . Nothing outside myself can destroy me by main force and in my own despite. (pp. 489-490)

How well this philosophy is illustrated in **"Goblin Market"** appears in Christina's conception of the two sisters. Both are equally tempted. One resists. The other succumbs. Laura is destroyed by her own weakness, not by goblin fruit. Even the taste of goblin fruit which the little men force upon Lizzie's lips does not corrupt her whose strength is formidable enough to put the goblins themselves to rout.

III

The poem opens with the sisters exposed at dusk to the cries of the goblins. Hearing them, Lizzie "veiled her blushes." The two sisters crouch close together "with tingling cheeks and finger tips." Obviously these girls understand the call; their antennae feel love in the air. So certain is it what the goblins mean that

> Lizzie covered up her eyes,
> Covered close lest they should look.

Laura, however, takes a covetous peep at the goblin men and their "evil gifts." In the *Purgatorio* of the *Commedia,* it may be recalled, Virgil advises Dante to keep guard "with the curb tight over the eyes" when coming to the great fire.

Ready and eager for love, Laura stretches out her gleaming neck, looks and listens. She attracts her own temptation. And then as the goblin merchants, sniffing a victim, turn and troop "backwards up the mossy glen," Laura assists in her own undoing. She does this primarily by means of her imagination. Elsewhere Christina said that "the seduction of imaginative emotion" was frequently an inducement to sin (***Letter and Spirit,*** p. 101). And again: "How shall a heart preserve its purity if once the rein be given to imagination; if vivid pictures be conjured up, and stormy or melting emotions indulged?" (*Face of the Deep,* p. 339).

Perceiving that Laura, through the instrumentality of her imagination, is ready for love, one of the little men "began to weave a crown." In Christina's system of symbolism the crown and the feast represent love's fulfillment. "Only they had lost a crown," she wrote in describing the separation of lovers in the lyric **"One Day."** And in **"Three Stages"** the invitation to love is rejected in the words

> I cannot crown my head
> With royal purple blossoms for the feast,

a combination of the two symbols. Poems in which the feast symbol similarly appears are **"At Home," "Shadow of Dorothea," "From House to Home," "A Peal of Bells," "Friends," "I Commend You," "Laughing Life Cries at the Feast,"** and others.

As might be expected, the feast symbol runs throughout **"Goblin Market."** After Laura's fall, Lizzie is invited by the goblins to "sit down and feast with us," obviously an invitation to erotic pleasure. Later she is told by them that "our feast is but beginning." After Lizzie has risked her own peace of mind to bring Laura the antidote, its first effect is to make Laura "loathe the feast." Furthermore, the sensuous joys of love, for which Laura pays with the products of her own body, a curl and a tear, are described as a lustful feasting on the fruit:

> Then sucked their fruit globes fair or red.
> Sweeter than honey from the rock,
> Stronger than man-rejoicing wine,
> Clearer than water flowed that juice;
> She never tasted such before,
> How should it cloy with length of use?
> She sucked and sucked and sucked the more
> Fruits which that unknown orchard bore;
> She sucked until her lips were sore;
> Then flung the emptied rinds away.[9]

But satiety does not come with repletion. After the feasting, Laura complains to Lizzie that "I ate and ate my fill, / Yet my mouth waters still," a common lover's complaint.

Retribution follows swiftly as Laura begins to suffer and starve from the lack of the exhilarating food upon which she has fed so sweetly. "Like a leaping flame," she goes again with Lizzie to the goblin-haunted glen, alert for the sound of the "sugar-baited words." In lines which recall Christina's **"Listening"** of October 1854, Laura is shown "Listening ever, but not catching the customary cry."[10]

That there may be no doubt about what the symbolic fruit is intended to represent, Christina describes its effect upon another girl victim:

> She thought of Jeannie in her grave,
> Who should have been a bride;
> But who for joys brides hope to have
> Fell sick and died.

In this stanza, again the distinction we have already observed is drawn between the two sorts of love, that which is domestic and legitimate, and the other, which is outlawed.

Elsewhere in the poem love itself is stigmatized as the carrier of death. In a piece of 1847 Christina had already characterized love as "a poison-cup," and in a lyric of 1853 as

A poisoned fount to take from,
But oh how sweet the stream!

And so we are not surprised to find in **"Goblin Market"** the little merchant men's wares described similarly:

Their fruits like honey to the throat
But poison in the blood.

Now we begin to understand why, for Laura, the fulfillment of love is followed by the passionate and rebellious anguish of love frustrated. Denied sight and sound of the goblins, perishing for another taste of their deadly fruit, Laura pines and sickens. Like the heroines of **"From House to Home"** and **"Convent Threshold,"** who likewise suffer from the deprivation of love, Laura

Then sat up in a passionate yearning,
And gnashed her teeth for baulked desire, and wept
As if her heart would break.

In **"From House to Home"** (19 Nov. 1858) "baulked desire" is also the cause of weeping and the gnashing of teeth:

O love, I knew that I should meet my love,
Should find my love no more.

'My love no more,' I muttered, stunned with pain:
I shed no tear, I wrung no passionate hand,
Till something whispered: 'You shall meet again,
Meet in a distant land.'

Then with a cry like famine I arose,
I lit my candle, searched from room to room,
Searched up and down; a war of winds that froze
Swept through the blank of gloom.

I searched day after day, night after night;
Scant change there came to me of night or day:
'No more,' I wailed, 'No more:' and trimmed my light,
And gnashed, but did not pray.

And in **"Convent Threshold"** (9 July 1858) the novice who has sent away her lover spends the kind of wakeful, feverish nights familar to Laura:

For all night long I dreamed of you:
I woke and prayed against my will,
Then slept to dream of you again,
At length I rose and knelt and prayed.
I cannot write the words I said,

My words were slow, my tears were few;
But through the dark my silence spoke
Like thunder. When this morning broke,
My face was pinched, my hair was grey,
And frozen blood was on the sill
Where stifling in my struggle I lay.

IV

"No woman," observed C. M. Bowra in discussing another poem of Christina's, "could write with this terrible directness if she did not to some degree know the experience which she describes."[11] Indeed, it is difficult to believe that an emotive effect so powerful as that evoked in these poems could be the result of the imaginative fantasy of an untried woman who has put together her ideas about love from observation and books.

And yet a Christina Rossetti experienced in the passion of love, and understanding the bereaved torment of one who has been deprived of love, is totally unlike the conventional portrait which has come down to us. This legendary figure of the saintly recluse is the subject of Ellen A. Proctor's *A Brief Memoir of Christina Rossetti* (London, 1895). Miss Proctor's Christina "never realised evil." Living a sheltered and retired life like that of a nun, commented Miss Proctor, Christina was guarded carefully from all contact with evil.

Christina herself granted that "some innocent souls there are who from cradle to grave remain as it were veiled and cloistered from knowledge of evil," but clearly she did not consider herself one of their number. Like Milton in the *Areopagitica* she could not praise such a fugitive and cloistered virtue: "For most persons contact with evil and consequently knowledge of evil being unavoidable . . . they must achieve a more difficult sanctity, touching pitch yet continuing clean, enduring evil communications yet without corruption . . ." (***The Face of the Deep***, p. 399). How difficult she knew this to be is evident from another statement in the same work: "Evil knowledge acquired in one wilful moment of curiosity may harass and haunt us to the end of our time" (p. 19). One recognizes here an apt description of Laura's predicament.

It is Lizzie who must achieve the "more difficult sanctity," who must gain a knowledge of evil and still remain pure. And so she must sally out to seek her adversary on that field "which is not without dust and heat." Fearing for Laura's life, she goes back to the glen at dusk in order to obtain the "fiery antidote." She dares the elfin men; she seduces the seducers. But she finds out what her creator undoubtedly knew from actual experience, that nature balked and frustrated takes a terrible revenge. The goblins scratch and grunt and snarl at Lizzie. They lash her with their tails, they claw and hustle her, they

Twitched out her hair by the roots,
Stamped upon her tender feet,
Held her hands and squeezed their fruits
Against her mouth to make her eat.

But Lizzie, by now no longer a youngling in the contemplation of evil, wears out the little evil people by her resistance. Disregarding her aches and bruises, the love-juices smeared triumphantly over her face, lodging in her dimples and streaking her neck, Lizzie runs home rejoicing to give the antidote to Laura:

Hug me, kiss me, suck my juices
Squeezed from goblin fruits for you,
Goblin pulp and goblin dew.
Eat me, drink me, love me.

she cries exultantly.

When Laura tastes again love's justices, this time vicariously from the face of Lizzie, her human redeemer, she reacts violently to the antidote:

Her lips began to scorch,
That juice was wormwood to her tongue.

Like the woman in the dream vision of **"From House to Home"** who, deprived of love, was likewise forced to drain the bitter and loathsome cup, Laura "gorges on bitterness without a name."

A passage from *The Face of the Deep* throws additional light upon Laura's condition: "the knowledge of foulness welcomed, entertained, gloated over, breeds in us foulness like itself; it acts like blood poison which, infused from without, turns the man himself, or the woman herself, to a death-struck mass of corruption" (pp. 97-98). The reference to blood poison provides the clue. If we recall that Christina had already compared the effect of the honey-tasting goblin fruit to "poison in the blood," and that elsewhere she used the figures of the poisoned fount and the poison-cup to describe love, we will have no difficulty in identifying the corrupting and deathbringing "foulness." The source of Laura's malady now becomes increasingly comprehensible.

Laura's extreme torment of repentance brought on by the antidote which, paradoxically, is no more than love itself, at last reaches the pitch of the unendurable and results in her loss of consciousness, the swoon of the speaker in **"From House to Home."** Lizzie, a human angel, watches by Laura's bedside during her perilous crisis of soul, just as superhuman agents watch by the swooner of **"From House to Home."**

At this point one of Christina Rossetti's leading concepts begins to emerge: the paradox of love as both destroyer and redeemer. Nowhere is this concept dramatized with more striking originality and imaginative power than in **"Goblin Market;"** but what distinguishes this long narrative poem from the many short lyrics expressing the same idea is that here human rather than divine love is the agent of redemption. Despite its bizarre features, Lizzie's is nonetheless a sacrifice. Her love brings Laura back from spiritual death; and in her traffic with the goblins she hazards the kind of human suffering that results from an insatiable craving of the unsatisfied appetite, Laura's own affliction.

The conception of love as both destructive and redemptive is not an original one, nor was it original with Christina. But like Dante, from whom she probably derived it, she uses fire symbolism to reinforce it. In the *Commedia* fire imagery expresses both carnal and divine love. When Dante and Virgil arrive at the seventh circle of Purgatory, they see those spirits who, having indulged their lusts on earth, must thereafter plunge into and burn in the great fire. But the higher Dante mounts in paradise, the more clearly he perceives that divine love is also fire. In **"Goblin Market"** fire symbolism performs the same function, that of emphasizing through imagery the concept of the paradoxical nature of love. As we have seen, Laura is "most like a leaping flame" in her wild longing for love. And when it is denied her,

She dwindled, as the fair full moon doth turn
To swift decay and burn
Her fire away.

And Lizzie, white and golden, standing firmly in the midst of the goblins' cruel attack, is figuratively

Like a beacon left alone
In a hoary roaring sea
Sending up a golden fire.

V

It would be a mistake to identify Christina herself with either Laura or Lizzie. And yet one senses that she uses both her heroines to express her own attitude toward the moral question she raises in the poem. If at times the reader is inclined to read into Lizzie Christina's own integrity and firmness of character, he should remember that Lizzie has been identified with Maria Rossetti, Christina's older sister. She even dedicated the poem to her sister M. F. R., and she concluded it with the significant tribute,

'For there is no friend like a sister
In calm or stormy weather;
To cheer one on the tedious way,
To fetch one if one goes astray,
To lift one if one totters down,
To strengthen whilst one stands.'

William did not doubt that Christina had some good reason for her dedication, "but what it was I know not." Yet when Mackenzie Bell questioned him closely on this point, William was more explicit: "I don't remember that there was at that time any personal circumstances of a marked kind," he said, "but I certainly think (with you) that the lines at the close, 'There is nothing like a sister,' etc., indicate *something:* apparently C. considered herself to be chargeable with some sort of spiritual backsliding, against which Maria's influence had been exerted beneficially." As usual when writing of his family, William hints and suggests that he knows more than he is revealing.[12]

Violet Hunt, a writer who professed to know a great deal about the personal affairs of the Rossettis, wrote in her *Wife of Rossetti* (London, 1932) that there was a "well-kept secret" in Christina's life, and that this secret, which Miss Hunt asserted Christina could not stay away from in her verse, was one that concerned the poet's emotional life:

> Maria did not, like Lizzie to save Laura, hold converse and traffic with goblin men on the hillside and eat their delicious deadly fruits. But for a week of nights the kind, sonsy creature crouched on the mat by the house door and saved her sister from the horrors of an elopement with a man who belonged to another. (p. xiii)

This man Miss Hunt identified as James Collinson, the Pre-Raphaelite painter to whom Christina became engaged when she was eighteen and whom she refused to marry two years later. "For Collinson, when she threw him over . . ." continued Miss Hunt, "consoled himself"; but apparently inadequately, for according to this writer, some nine years later he returned, a married man, to ask Christina to elope with him. Despite the fact that this absurd story has gained credence with some writers, one need not consider it seriously, so wildly does it veer away from probability.[13]

And yet I believe that Miss Hunt had a clue to the central situation, mistaken as she was about the circumstantial details. Elsewhere I have set forth my view that Christina was at no time in love with Collinson; and that was why in 1850 she broke her engagement to him.[14] I have also produced evidence to the effect that in 1859, when she wrote **"Goblin Market,"** she could not have been enamored of Charles Bagot Cayley, the second man she is supposed to have loved. Cayley was the scholarly recluse who began to court her between 1862 and 1864, who proposed in September 1866, but whom she refused to marry, conceivably for the same reason she had rejected Collinson some sixteen years earlier.

But I have suggested above that Christina was not inexperienced in the passion of love. Assuming, then, that her love poetry was not written in an emotional vacuum, as the frenzied and erotic fantasies of a love-starved spinster, but that it was rooted in emotional reality directly experienced, the conclusion emerges that she loved someone other than Collinson or Cayley.

I have identified this man as William Bell Scott, painter and poet, intimate friend of Christina's brothers, a man, said William Rossetti, whom she "viewed with great predilection" ("Memoir," **Works,** p. lviii). She met Scott in 1847, when she was seventeen, presumably loved him all her life, and addressed a poem to him in 1882 when she was in her fifties. That Scott was married gives some support to Miss Hunt's theory; but that he ever asked Christina to elope with him is extremely unlikely.

At this point we might return to William's statement to Mackenzie Bell which raises the question: Were there actually any "personal circumstances of a marked kind" in 1858-59 that might have inspired or at least influenced the genesis of **"Goblin Market?"** If so, what were they? And what part did Maria Rossetti play in what William has called Christina's "hushed life-drama"?

In order to answer these questions, at least in part, we will first need to learn a little about Scott, his personality and his emotional commitments; and second, to understand Christina's relationship with him prior to the writing of **"Goblin Market."**

VI

Not only was Scott married, although he is said never to have consummated his marriage with Letitia Norquoy, but he was also in the habit of forming intimate friendships with women. Two of these relationships were known to Scott's contemporaries and acknowledged by him in his autobiography.[15] Both are important for their effect upon Christina's life and poetry.

The first, Scott's friendship with Lady Pauline Trevelyan of Wallington Hall, the friend of Ruskin and Swinburne, began in the autumn of 1854 and continued until her death in 1866. About 1857, however, Scott appears to have cooled off somewhat, and from then on we hear less of Lady Trevelyan in his autobiography. The second woman in Scott's life was Alice Boyd of Penkill Castle, Ayrshire, Scotland, whom he met in 1859 and with whom he formed a permanent alliance similar to the union of Mary Ann Evans and George Henry Lewes.[16]

Scott's interest in Christina apparently reached its peak in June 1858, just after his friendship with Lady Trevelyan had become less ardent. At their first meeting in the winter of 1847-48, Christina and Scott made a memorable impression upon one another. Scott's description of Christina as a young girl has been frequently quoted. Calling upon Dante Gabriel who was not at home, Scott introduced himself to the elder Rossetti and Christina, who was standing by the window in front of a high narrow reading-desk, writing poetry. She was "a slight girl with a serious regular profile, dark against the pallid wintry light without." For Scott she was by far "the most interesting of the two inmates." He particularly admired the "formal and graceful curtsey" she made upon his entrance (*Notes*, I, 247-248).

Scott evidently produced an equally favorable effect upon her. Both William Rossetti and Holman Hunt agree Scott was a handsome and interesting-looking man. William reports that upon first meeting him the Rossettis, "female as well as male took very warmly indeed to Mr. Scott," and found him "not only attractive, but even fascinating." For the phrase, "female as well as male," William's daughter, Helen Rossetti Angeli, substitutes the less discreet phrase, "From Gabriele the elder to Christina." All reports agree that Christina was the only female Rossetti present at Scott's introduction to the family.[17] She, then, and not her mother or older sister, found Scott attractive and fascinating.

One cannot say how soon this initial attraction developed into a more intimate friendship. Probably it remained dormant during Christina's engagement to Collinson in 1848-50, started up again in 1851, reached a preliminary crisis of feeling in the summer of 1854 (when Christina wrote **"Dream-Love"** and **"Three Stages"**), and declined in intensity upon Scott's meeting with Lady Trevelyan in November 1854.

But by 1857 Scott was seeing much less of Pauline Trevelyan, and apparently in the autumn of that year his interest in Christina revived, a supposition suggested by her lyric, **"Birthday,"** of 18 November 1857. In this familiar anthology piece, which even William regards as emotional autobiography, she celebrates with "exuberant joy" the advent of love as the dawn of a new life:

> Because the birthday of my life
> Is come, my love is come to me.

The date of the lyric precludes the possibility of associating it with either Collinson or Cayley. The former lay buried some seven years back in the past, and the latter was not to show an interest in Christina for some five years in the future. But Scott appears prominently in the chronicle of Christina's life during this midperiod between wooers.

It was in June 1858, some seven months after the writing of **"Birthday,"** that Christina visited Scott and his wife at Newcastle-on-Tyne, where he held the position of Head Master at the Government School of Design. She left his home on 15 June. On the train speeding her away from Newcastle and Scott, she wrote the poem **"Parting After Parting,"** entitled "Goodbye" in manuscript. Although to part, she wrote, brought "Sore loss and gnawing pain," to meet was

> worth living for;
> Worth dying for, to meet;
> To meet, worth parting for,
> Bitter forgot in sweet:
> To meet, worth parting before,
> Never to part more.

To this lyric Christina joined a second written 11 June 1864, the year Scott moved permanently from Newcastle to London (*Notes*, II, 70). She called it **"Meeting."**[18]

Shortly after Christina left him in June 1858, Scott went to Oxford (*Notes*, II, 41, n.). No record exists of his presence in London at this time, but it is not improbable that he went there before or after his stay at Oxford. It was his custom to visit London during the summer. Perhaps, like Christina, he too was unable to bear the "sore loss and gnawing pain" of separation, and followed her to London, hoping to renew the happy association they had enjoyed during her visit to Newcastle. If so, he was doomed to disappointment. For by 9 July, the date of **"Convent Threshold,"** presumably she had reached the decision to send him away, a decision she was to implement and to regret all the days of her life.

It did not take Scott long to find consolation elsewhere. Ten months after Christina's stay at his home, he "had a visit from a lady some few years over thirty," whose name he had not heard before. "She wanted to find a new interest in life," he wrote, "and thought to find it in art. She was somehow or other possessed, to me, of the most interesting face and voice I had ever heard or seen. I devoted myself to answering this desire of hers," he continued naïvely, "and from day to day the interest on either side increased" (*Notes*, II, 56-57).

Alice Boyd, the lady in question, proved to be a formidable rival. Descendant of an ancient and aristocratic Scottish family, she was, according to Dante Gabriel, "a rarely precious woman," and according to Christina herself, "the prettiest handsome woman I ever met."[19] Himself an egoist, Scott particularly prized Alice's unselfishness and nobility of character. Eager to please, he wrote, she "enjoyed others' happiness and others' ideas exactly as if they were her own" (*Notes*, II, 293). Moreover, she did not have a jealous disposition.

From what we know of him, we cannot doubt that Scott gave her cause for jealousy. "Common prudence," he protested, "is always howling against turning from one study to another, from one love to another, from one form of art to another" (*Notes* II, 220). In putting his theory into practice, not only did Scott turn from one study to another, and from one form of art, poetry, to another, painting, but he also turned with ease from one love to another, sometimes maintaining relations with two or more women simultaneously. "It may be," he wrote, "that few can do this without losing their way, coming to grief; it requires tact to hold half a dozen lines without allowing them to tangle, or to ride six horses as they do in the circus."

His own skill at this kind of management was masterly. He introduced the women in his life to each other, and sometimes they became warm friends. Several times Scott lived harmoniously in Penkill Castle with Mrs. Scott, Alice Boyd, and Christina.[20] He conducted his emotional affairs with a bold and truly regal disregard of conventional attitudes and mores.

VII

How soon Christina found out about what Scott discreetly called his "friendship at first sight" is uncertain. We know that he first met Alice Boyd on 18 March 1859, and that Christina finished **"Goblin Market"** on 27 April of that year. Allowing some time for Scott's new attachment to have become known to her, and additional time for her to have reacted to it, to have assimilated and absorbed the unwelcome experience emotionally before expressing it artistically, we may conclude that forty days would not be too long a lapse of time between the two events. Dante Gabriel and William must have found out about Scott's new friend almost immediately, for Scott lived on terms of fraternal intimacy with the Rossetti brothers, and he was a man more inclined to boast of his love affairs than to keep them a secret. If he told Gabriel and William about Alice within the fortnight, the Rossetti sisters could have learned about her shortly thereafter. Possibly Maria was the first to be informed, and it might have been through her agency that Christina was told. At any rate, not much longer than a month intervened between what may be called "a personal circumstance of a marked kind," and the writing of **"Goblin Market."**[21]

Unlike the two major poems preceding **"Goblin Market"** (they are **"Convent Threshold"** of July and **"From House to Home"** of November) in which the central idea is the renunciation of love, **"Goblin Market,"** we have noted, has as its theme not renunciation but temptation. Laura, far from the thought of renouncing love, tastes the poisoned honey, longs for a second taste and is denied it. Hence, one might conclude that it is one thing to renounce love voluntarily, but quite another thing to be arbitrarily deprived of it.

That Scott could have "turned from one love to another" with such apparent ease must have been a serious shock to Christina. His behavior would have shown her the unstable nature of his earlier attachment to her, would have revealed the depth of the abyss into which she had almost plunged, the peril of the temptation from which, like Laura, she had been saved.

Was it Maria who had saved her? If so, when? And in what manner? Although these questions cannot be conclusively answered, we ought to take William's word for it that Christina's tribute to her sister at the conclusion of **"Goblin Market"** "indicated *something*." Perhaps, as I have already suggested, it was Maria who informed Christina about Scott's new love. If so, the strait-laced Maria would not have been the one to have omitted pointing out the moral lesson to be derived. She may even have been responsible for breaking up Christina's friendship with Scott after the Newcastle visit. Possibly in June of 1858, after Christina's return from Scott's home, Maria might have wrestled with her to prevent that "spiritual backsliding" Christina might have both desired and feared.[22]

That Maria's intervention was probably of an active and positive nature is suggested not only by **"Goblin Market"** but by two poems written the following year which have as their theme the interference of one sister in the love affair of another. But instead of regarding the interfering sister as a human redeemer, the saved sister in the two ballads of 1860, **"Sister Maude"** and **"The Noble Sisters,"** resents the other's busybody meddling. In fact, the tone of **"Sister Maude"** is noticeably vindictive:

> Who told my mother of my shame,
> Who told my father of my dear?
> O who but Maude, my sister Maude,
> Who lurked to spy and peer.

"The Noble Sisters" is almost a travesty upon the **"Goblin Market"** situation. One sister sends away all the messengers of her sister's lover, the falcon, the ruddy hound, the pretty page. Finally she turns the lover himself from the door, thereby bringing down upon herself the angry denunciation of the saved one:

> 'Fie, sister, fie, a wicked lie,
> A lie, a wicked lie!
> I have none other love but him,
> Nor will have till I die.
> And you have turned him from our door,
> And stabbed him with a lie:
> I will go seek him thro' the world
> In sorrow till I die.'

These two poems together with several others were originally included in Christina's 1862 *Goblin Market* volume, but were omitted from subsequent editions. According to William, at a later date she considered the "moral tone" of all four pieces open to reproach, and hence excluded them. But even by Victorian standards this judgment is hardly applicable to the two sister poems we have been examining. Could Christina have had a different reason for not wishing them to appear in the *Goblin Market* collection? Could she have feared that they might be construed as showing an attitude of resentment, even temporary resentment, against a sister she loved dearly and had long ago forgiven for any well-meant meddling?

If we read **"Goblin Market"** in the context of the other poems of the period, both those preceding and those following it, we are obliged to conclude that **"Goblin Market"** is not the artistic mutation in the body of Christina's work that critics have occasionally implied, but that it has both chronological significance and emotional relevance in the order of her creative productions. We may additionally conclude that the emotional intensity the poem achieves is not altogether a feat of imaginative virtuosity, but is the result of deeply felt experience directly known and poetically assimilated. It is solidly rooted in the reality of Christina's own knowledge of the passions.

Skilled in what Henry James has called "the art of covering one's tracks," Christina strove to conceal rather than to reveal her intention through the use of symbolism. William Rossetti has told us that hers "was a life which did not consist of incidents: in few things external; in all its deeper currents, internal." It is only by attempting to sound these subterranean currents that we are able to gauge the depth, pressure, and density of meaning in **"Goblin Market."** In referring to a different poem, Christina said that it gave "a subtle hint by symbol" of its meaning. Not, she added, that she "expected the general public to catch these refined clues; but there they are for minds such as mine" (*Rossetti Papers*, p. 81).[23]

Notes

[1] References in my text to "Goblin Market" and other of Christina Rossetti's poems are from *The Poetical Works*, ed. William Michael Rossetti (London, 1904)—hereafter cited as *Works*. The parenthetical date "(B. 1882)" means 'before 1882,' William Rossetti's method of dating Christina's poems before her *Pageant* volume of 1881 was published.

[2] *Memories and Impressions* (New York, 1911), pp. 69 ff.

[3] Mackenzie Bell, *Christina Rossetti: A Biographical and Critical Study* (London, 1898), p. 207.

[4] See "Symbols" (1849) and "An Old World Thicket" (B. 1882). To William Sharp Christina admitted that she was "the ill-tempered one in the family" (William Sharp, "Some Reminiscences of Christina Rossetti," *Atlantic Monthly*, LXXV [June 1895], 740). And to William Rossetti's wife Lucy she wrote in 1883, "It is such a triumph for ME to attain to philosophic calm, that, even if that subdued temper is applied by me without common sense, 'color che sanno' may still congratulate me on some sort of improvement! Ask William, who knew me in my early story days: he could a tale unfold—" (*Family Letters of Christina Rossetti*, ed. W. M. Rossetti, New York, 1908, p. 138—hereafter cited as *Family Letters*).

[5] "The Sources of Christina Rossetti's 'Goblin Market,'" *MLR*, XXVIII, ii (April 1933), 157-158.

[6] *Dante Gabriel Rossetti's Family Letters with a Memoir*, ed. W. M. Rossetti (London, 1895), I, 87—hereafter cited as *DGRFL*.

[7] Gosse, *Critical Kitkats* (New York, 1896), p. 140.

[8] W. M. Rossetti, *Some Reminiscences* (New York, 1906), I, 5; *DGRFL*, I, 79; Christina Rossetti, *Time Flies* (London, 1885), pp. 45, 128, 137, et passim. The wombat was a much later addition to the earthly paradise. It was in 1858 that Christina and William discovered this exotic little creature at the Zoological Gardens, and in 1862 that Christina made the pencil drawing of it that William used to illustrate her *Family Letters* (opposite p. 45). "In or about 1858," William writes in *Some Reminiscences*, "we two were in the Zoological Gardens, and our steps led us towards a certain enclosure hitherto unknown to us, and little scrutinized by most visitors. Christina, who had as good an eye for a 'beast' as Dante Gabriel, caught sight of 'phascolomys ursinus' a second before myself, and exclaimed, 'O look at that delightful object!'" (I, 285-286). Shortly afterwards, Dante Gabriel was shown the delightful object which later occupied a conspicuous position in his celebrated Tudor House menagerie.

[9] Cf. "At Home" (*Works*, p. 339). In this lyric Christina similarly used the feast symbolism to express sensuous joy:

> Feasting beneath green orange boughs;
> From hand to hand they pushed the wine,
> They sucked the pulp of plum and peach . . .

[10] Cf.:

> She listened like a cushat dove
> That listens to its mate alone:
> She listened like a cushat dove
> That loves but only one.

[11] *The Romantic Imagination* (Cambridge, Mass., 1949), p. 263. The poem referred to is "Twice."

[12] Bell, p. 231. In William's preface to his edition of Gabriel's family letters, he commented upon the fact

that he was accused of concealing relevant information about his brother. His answer to this charge is significant in indicating the position he took, not only as Gabriel's but also as Christina's editor and biographer. He said, "... I have told what I choose to tell and left untold what I do not choose to tell: if you want more, be pleased to consult some other informant" (I, xli). In his preface to his own *Some Reminiscences,* he likewise admitted frankly that "it does not follow that I know nothing beyond which I write. In some cases I do know a good deal more; but to cast a slur here or violate a confidence there would make me contemptible to myself" (I, xi). Janet Troxell in *Three Rossettis* (Cambridge, Mass., 1937) produced what she considered incontrovertible "evidence that William was suppressing something about Christina" (p. 202).

[13] Marya Zaturenska (*Christina Rossetti,* New York, 1949, pp. 59-60) and Margaret Sawtell (*Christina Rossetti,* London, 1955, pp. 54-55) are the writers in question. For a refutation of Violet Hunt's allegation see Helen Rossetti Angeli, *Dante Gabriel Rossetti* (London, 1949), pp. 6, n., and 272.

[14] See my unpub. diss. (Univ. of Calif., L. A., 1957), "Beauty for Ashes: A Biographical Study of Christina Rossetti's Poetry." Unless otherwise stated, the following material in my text is derived from this source.

[15] *Autobiographical Notes,* ed. W. Minto, 2 vols. (London, 1892)—hereafter cited as *Notes.* My information about Scott is drawn from this work.

[16] In Scott's youth he and Lewes were intimate friends (*Notes,* I, 129-134).

[17] *DGRFL,* I, 114-115; *Some Remin.,* I, 131; Holman W. Hunt, *Pre-Raphaelitism and the Pre-Raphaelite Brotherhood* (London, 1905), I, 230; Helen Rossetti Angeli, *Dante Gabriel Rossetti,* p. 151. Ford Madox Brown once remarked that women in general and his own wife in particular were "enchanted" by Scott (W. M. Rossetti, *Ruskin: Rossetti: Pre-raphaelitism,* London, 1900, p. 39).

[18] My information about this poem (*Works,* p. 200) is derived from William's enlightening comment about it in his notes (*Works,* p. 473, n.).

[19] *DGRFL,* I, 266; *Anna Gilchrist,* ed. Herbert H. Gilchrist (London, 1887), p. 161.

[20] In the summers of 1866 and 1869, although Mrs. Scott may not have been present upon the latter occasion (*The Rossetti Papers,* ed. W. M. Rossetti, New York, 1903, pp. 203, 396; *Gilchrist,* pp. 160-161, 175; *Three Rossettis,* pp. 155-156; *DGRFL,* II, 201; *Dante Gabriel Rossetti: Letters to Miss Alice Boyd,* ed. John Purves, *Fortnightly Rev.,* CXXIX [May 1928], 583).

[21] We cannot suppose that the actual writing of "Goblin Market" was a lengthy process, for upon more than one occasion William has assured us that his sister's "habits of composition were eminently of the spontaneous kind," that she seldom meditated or deliberated before writing a poem, but on the contrary, after "something impelled her feeling or 'came into her head'," she wrote rapidly, easily, and without hesitation, almost as though "her hand obeyed dictation" (*Works,* pp. lxviii-lxix; *New Poems,* ed. W. M. Rossetti, London, 1896, pp. xii-xiii). And of all her long poems, "Goblin Market" strikes the reader as the one the most likely to have been produced in the mood of direct inspiration. I take it that she wrote the poem out as a whole first, and later made whatever revisions and alterations she deemed necessary. It would not have been impossible for a poet with her working habits to have turned out the approximately 550 lines within a week or so.

[22] Much has been written about Maria's harmful influence over Christina. Posterity's conception of Maria as a narrow-minded, gloomy fanatic partially originated in Christina's own portrait of her sister in *Time Flies.* Maria, she wrote, "shrank from entering the Mummy Room at the British Museum under a vivid realisation of how the general resurrection might occur even as one stood among those solemn corpses turned into a sight for sightseers" (p. 128). This vivid portrait was reinforced by Sir Edmund Gosse's view that "the influence of Maria Francesca on her sister seemed to be like that of Newton upon Cowper, a species of police surveillance exercised by a hard, convinced mind over a softer and more fanciful one" (*Critical Kitkats,* p. 160). R. D. Waller was the first critic to detect and to expose the fallacy of such a conception of Maria. He emphasized the love existing between the two sisters and quoted Gabriel's opinion that Maria was "the healthiest in mind and cheeriest of us all, with William coming next, and Christina and I nowhere" (*The Rossetti Family, 1824-54,* Univ. Manchester, No. CCXVII, Eng. Ser. No. 21 [Manchester, 1932], pp. 179-180). This observation is borne out by the fact that in the depths of her last fatal illness in 1876 Maria could still write a bright little letter to Christina playfully calling her "the crowned Queen of Dears" (*Family Letters,* p. 56). On her deathbed Maria unsentimentally scoffed at what she called the "hood and hatband" style of mourning (*Time Flies,* p. 213). Cheerful and loving though she may have been, Maria, who joined an Anglican sisterhood in 1874, was undoubtedly strait-laced and Puritanical in her attitude toward sex, and would have considered it her unquestioned duty to rescue Christina from an affair with Scott.

[23] The reference is to Christina's "Prince's Progress" of 1865.

Ellen Moers (essay date 1976)

SOURCE: "Female Gothic," in *Literary Women*, Doubleday and Company, Inc., 1976, pp. 90-110.

[*In the excerpt that follows, Moers regards "Goblin Market" as Rossetti's contribution to Gothic fiction, or the "literature of the monster," and maintains that the poem serves as an examination of the cruelty and sexuality of children rather than as a Christian allegory.*]

Thinking about *Wuthering Heights* as part of a literary women's tradition may open up a new approach to a faded classic of Victorian poetry by a woman who was in fact, as Emily Brontë certainly was not, gentle, pious, and conservative: Christina Rossetti's **"Goblin Market."** In 1859, twelve years after the Brontë novel, Rossetti wrote her own contribution to the literature of the monster in the form of a narrative poem. Published in 1862, **"Goblin Market"** quickly became one of the most familiar and best-loved Victorian poems, and was given to little children to read in the days when children had stronger stomachs than they do today. Perhaps the last generation to grow up with **"Goblin Market"** was that of Willa Cather, who published her first book of short stories a decade after Rossetti's death, called it *The Troll Garden,* and gave it an epigraph from **"Goblin Market:"**

> We must not look at Goblin men,
> We must not buy their fruits;
> Who knows upon what soil they fed
> Their hungry thirsty roots?

The roots of Christina Rossetti's goblins are themselves mysterious. In its modest way, her fable was as original a creation as *Frankenstein;* that is, as a maker of monsters Rossetti swerved as sharply from her sources in literary and folk materials as did Mary Shelley. There seems little doubt that particularly female experiences, in both cases, contributed to the disturbing eccentricity of the tale.

Two little girls, two sisters Laura and Lizzie, seem to be living alone together as **"Goblin Market"** opens, and running their own household without parents. Their relationship is one of spiritual and physical affection:

> Golden head by golden head,
> Like two pigeons in one nest
> Folded in each other's wings,
> They lay down in their curtained bed . . .
> Cheek to cheek and breast to breast
> Locked together in one nest.

Into their neighborhood come goblin men known to all the maids round about as dangerous tempters: they sell fruit which intoxicates and then destroys. One feast upon the goblin fruit and girls turn prematurely gray, sicken, fade, and die young. In verses that seem unquestionably to associate goblin fruit with forbidden sexual experience, Rossetti cites the case of one goblin victim,

> Jeanie in her grave,
> Who should have been a bride;
> But who for joys brides hope to have
> Fell sick and died. . . .

The goblins themselves are monstrosities of a special kind that Emily Brontë, too, worked with in *Wuthering Heights.* Like Heathcliff, who is set off from the norm by animal metaphors ("a fierce, pitiless, wolfish man," or a tiger, a serpent, a mad dog that howls "like a savage beast" or prowls like "an evil beast [between the sheep] and the fold"), Rossetti's goblins are animal people:

> One had a cat's face,
> One whisked a tail,
> One tramped at a rat's pace,
> One crawled like a snail,
> One like a wombat prowled obtuse and furry,
> One like a ratel tumbled hurry scurry.

The sinister music here, one of the numerous auditory variations played by Rossetti's apparently simple verse, establishes that these goblins are not lovable little hobbits, but true monsters.

What are monsters? Creatures who scare because they look different, wrong, non-human. Distortion of scale was the first visual effect employed by Gothic novelists in creating monsters, particularly gigantism: well before Frankenstein's outsize monster, Walpole had filled the *Castle of Otranto* with specters of giant stature. But the classically Victorian device to create monsters was the crossing of species, animal with human. I am thinking of the sneezing pigs, smiling cats, preaching caterpillars, and gourmandizing walruses of Lewis Carroll's *Wonderland;* of Kingsley's *Water Babies,* and Jean Ingelow's Pre-Raphaelite fairy tales; of Melville's *Moby-Dick* and H. G. Wells's *Island of Dr. Moreau*—all fantasies in the Gothic or other modes, with monsters that are animaloid humans.

But there is something more to Christina Rossetti's goblins that suggests to me a specifically feminine Victorian fantasy: that is, that they are brothers. They are not, in so many words, brothers to the sisters Laura and Lizzie in the poem, but a separate breed:

> Leering at each other,
> Brother with queer brother;

> Signalling each other,
> Brother with sly brother.

The brothers stand opposed to the sisters as tempters of clearly double intention: to intoxicate them with forbidden fruit, and also to harass, torture, and destroy them. One of the sisters, Laura, succumbs to the goblin song. She buys their fruit with a lock of her golden hair:

> Then sucked their fruit globes fair or red. . . .
> She never tasted such before. . . .
> She sucked and sucked and sucked the more
> Fruits which that unknown orchard bore;
> She sucked until her lips were sore.

"Suck" is the central verb of **"Goblin Market;"** sucking with mixed lust and pain is, among the poem's Pre-Raphaelite profusion of colors and tastes, the particular sensation carried to an extreme that must be called perverse. I am suggesting not that **"Goblin Market"** belongs to the history of pornography as a Victorian celebration of oral sex, but that Christina Rossetti wrote a poem, as Emily Brontë wrote a novel, about the erotic life of children.

Gorged on goblin fruit, Laura craves with all the symptoms of addiction for another feast, but craves in vain, for the goblins' sinister magic makes their victims incapable of hearing the fruit-selling cry a second time. However, the other sister, Lizzie, who through strength of character has resisted the temptation to eat the goblins' fruit, can still hear their cry. Lizzie sets out to buy of the goblins in order to save her fallen sister, who, "dwindling, / Seemed knocking at Death's door."

Lizzie's venture in redemption opens up the question of the spiritual implications of **"Goblin Market,"** for it is, of course, as a Christian poet that Christina Rossetti is best known. In the view of C. M. Bowra and others, she is one of the finest religious poets in the language, and, until recognition came to Gerard Manley Hopkins (who read her with admiration), she was widely accepted as the greatest religious poet of the nineteenth century. Most of her poems (there are about a thousand) are Christian poems of remarkable fervor and orthodoxy, but not all of them—not, in my opinion, **"Goblin Market,"** which, if it were in conception a Christian work, would surely be resolved by an act of piety. Rossetti would have Lizzie save her sister through some ceremony of exorcism, a prayer, at least an act symbolizing her own essential purity. What Rossetti does give us at the end is something quite different, for it is in a spirit of heroism rather than of sainthood that Lizzie engages fully with the goblin experience:

She goes to trade with the goblins:

> At twilight, halted by the brook:
> And for the first time in her life
> Began to listen and look.

The goblins rush to greet her:

> Hugged her and kissed her:
> Squeezed and caressed her.

They force their fruit upon her, urging her to "Pluck them and suck them." But when Lizzie makes clear her intention to buy and carry off the fruits to save her sister, without tasting them herself, the goblins become enraged and attack her:

> Grunting and snarling. . . .
> Their tones waxed loud,
> Their looks were evil.
> Lashing their tails
> They trod and hustled her,
> Elbowed and jostled her,
> Clawed with their nails,
> Barking, mewing, hissing, mocking,
> Tore her gown and soiled her stocking,
> Twitched her hair out by the roots,
> Stamped upon her tender feet,
> Held her hands and squeezed their fruits
> Against her mouth to make her eat.

But Lizzie keeps her mouth clenched tightly shut. Though the goblin attack turns even nastier and crueler, she resists, survives, and runs home to Laura to offer herself physically—it is the most eloquent, most erotic moment in the poem—to her sister. For Lizzie bears away not only cuts and bruises from her battle with the goblin brothers; she is also smeared with the juices of their fruit. "Laura," she cries,

> "Did you miss me?
> Come and kiss me.
> Never mind my bruises,
> Hug me, kiss me, suck my juices
> Squeezed from goblin fruits for you,
> Goblin pulp and goblin dew.
> Eat me, drink me, love me;
> Laura, make much of me;
> For your sake I have braved the glen
> And had to do with goblin merchant men."

Laura responds: "She kissed and kissed her with a hungry mouth." The effect is at first disastrous (loathing, bitterness, feverish fires in the blood) but at last Laura's cure is complete and permanent. Rossetti concludes with a sober *envoi:* "Days, weeks, months, years / Afterwards . . ." Both sisters, she says, grow to a maturity which includes marriage and motherhood. In reality Christina Rossetti remained a spinster, and her sister Maria, to whom **"Goblin Market"** was dedicated, became an Anglican nun.

That some kind of biographical fact or event lies behind **"Goblin Market"** has been a matter of general agreement among Rossetti scholars, starting with William Michael Rossetti, who edited his sister's poems. I find the usual biographical speculations ingenious but not wholly satisfying; I can also go only part way with the standard reading of "Goblin Market" as a poem about the divided self, for it makes too little of the two sisters theme that Rossetti handled with particular intensity. Not only in "Goblin Market" but in many other poems Christina Rossetti presents symbolic oppositions by means of a pair of sisters; sometimes, as in "Noble Sisters" or "Sister Maude," they are rivals in love or hostile to each other's passion.

> Who told my mother of my shame,
>   Who told my father of my dear?
> Oh who but Maude, my sister Maude,
>   Who lurked to spy and peer.

Rossetti brings a special, hissing vigor to the sisters-in-opposition theme which, not surprisingly, is pervasive in women's literature, at least from *Sense and Sensibility* to *Middlemarch*. Its most neurotic variation can be found in Harriet Martineau's *Deerbrook;* its most dramatically symbolic presentation in *Lélia,* where George Sand opposes a sister courtesan to her intellectually frigid heroine.

Laura and Lizzie, in "Goblin Market," may very possibly symbolize profane versus sacred love, or weak sensuality versus strong reason. But to say that as criticism is no more illuminating than to say (as has been said) that Heathcliff is the Id, and Catherine the Ego. A purely symbolic interpretation of *Wuthering Heights* and "Goblin Market" makes them out to be a sort of Tennysonian "Two Voices," or something different from what they are in fact: perverse and also realistic works in the Victorian Gothic mode. It was a mode to which I suspect both Emily Brontë and Christina Rossetti had access through fantasies derived from the night side of the Victorian nursery—a world where childish cruelty and childish sexuality come to the fore.

In one important respect their formation was similar: both women grew up in a family of four siblings male and female, bound together in a closed circle by affection and by imaginative genius, as well as by remoteness from the social norm. Several Victorian women writers—the Brontë sister and Christina Rossetti among them—derived a valuable professional leavening from starting out as infant poets, dramatists, or tellers of tales with an audience of enthusiastic and collaborating siblings. That not only much of the technical expertise but also some of the material of their adult work derived from the nursery circle should not surprise us. Quentin Bell's recent biography of Virginia Stephen, a girl in another family of talented, like-minded sisters and brothers, allows us at least to speculate openly on the sexual drama of the Victorian nursery. (Though Mr. Bell does not, for me at least, settle the question of the factual component in Virginia Woolf's memories of fraternal incest, to the reality of a sister's incest fantasy he brings important evidence, if evidence be needed.)

Every reader of Dickens knows the importance of a sister to a brother struggling to resolve the extreme Victorian separation between the purity and the desirability of womanhood. But to Victorian women the sister-brother relationship seems to have had a different and perhaps even greater significance—especially to those women, so commonplace in the intellectual middle class, who in a sexual sense never lived to full maturity. The rough-and-tumble sexuality of the nursery loomed large for sisters: it was the *only* heterosexual world that Victorian literary spinsters were ever freely and physically to explore. Thus the brothers of their childhood retained in their fantasy life a prominent place somewhat different in kind from that of the father figures who dominated them all.

Little sisters were briefly and tantalizingly the equals of little brothers, sharers of infant pains and pleasures that boys quickly grew out of, but that girls—as Maggie Tulliver bitterly tells us—clung to despairingly at an inappropriate age. Women authors of Gothic fantasies appear to testify that the physical teasing they received from their brothers—the pinching, mauling, and scratching we dismiss as the most unimportant of children's games—took on outsize proportions and powerful erotic overtones in their adult imaginations. (Again, the poverty of their physical experience may have caused these disproportions, for it was not only sexual play but *any* kind of physical play for middle-class women that fell under the Victorian ban.) . . .

Sandra M. Gilbert and Susan Gubar (essay date 1979)

SOURCE: "The Aesthetics of Renunciation," in *The Madwoman in the Attic: The Woman Writer and the Nineteenth-Century Literary Imagination,* Yale University Press, 1979, pp. 539-80.

[*In the following excerpt, Gilbert and Gubar argue that "Goblin Market" demonstrates Rossetti's opinion of the necessity for female renunciation of the "risks and gratifications of art."*]

Like [Rossetti's] *Maude,* "Goblin Market" (1859) depicts multiple heroines, each representing alternative possibilities of selfhood for women. Where *Maude*'s options were divided rather bewilderingly among Agnes, Mary, Magdalen, and Maude herself, however, "Goblin Market" offers just the twinlike sisters Lizzie and Laura (together with Laura's shadowy precursor Jeanie) who live in a sort of surrealistic fairytale cottage by the side of a "restless brook" and not far from a sinister glen. Every morning and evening, so the story goes, scuttling, furry, animal-like goblins ("One had a cat's face, / One whisked a tail, / One tramped at a rat's pace, / One crawled like a snail") emerge from the glen to peddle magically delicious fruits that "Men sell not . . . in any town"—"Bloom-down-cheeked peaches, / Swart-headed mulberries, / Wild free-born cranberries," and so forth.[62] Of course the two girls know that "We must not look at goblin men, / We must not buy their fruits: / Who knows upon what soil they fed / Their hungry thirsty roots?" But of course, nevertheless, one of the two—Laura—does purchase the goblin fruit, significantly with "a lock of her golden hair," and sucks and sucks upon the sweet food "until her lips [are] sore."

The rest of the poem deals with the dreadful consequences of Laura's act, and with her ultimate redemption. To begin with, as soon as she has eaten the goblin fruit, the disobedient girl no longer hears the cry of the tiny "brisk fruit-merchant men," though her more dutiful sister does continue to hear their "sugar-baited words." Then, as time goes by, Laura sickens, dwindles, and ages unnaturally: her hair grows "thin and grey," she weeps, dreams of melons, and does none of the housework she had shared with Lizzie in the old fruitless days when they were both "neat like bees, as sweet and busy." Finally, Lizzie resolves to save her sister by purchasing some fruit from the goblin peddlers, who still do appear to her. When she does this, however, they insist that she herself eat their wares on the spot, and when she refuses, standing motionless and silent like "a lily in a flood" or "a beacon left alone / In a hoary roaring sea," they assault her with the fruit, smearing her all over with its pulp. The result is that when she goes home to her sick sister she is able to offer herself to the girl as almost a sacramental meal: "Eat me, drink me, love me . . . make much of me." But when Laura kisses her sister hungrily, she finds that the juice is "wormwood to her tongue, / She loathed the feast; / Writhing as one possessed she leaped and sung." Finally she falls into a swoon. When she wakens, she is her old, girlish self again: "Her gleaming locks showed not one thread of gray, / Her breath was sweet as May." In after years, when she and her sister, now happy wives and mothers, are warning their own daughters about the fruit-merchant men, she tells them the tale of "how her sister stood / In deadly peril to do her good. . . . 'For there is no friend like a sister, / In calm or stormy weather; / To cheer one on the tedious way, / To fetch one if one goes astray, / To lift one if one totters down, / To strengthen whilst one stands.'"

Obviously the conscious or semi-conscious allegorical intention of this narrative poem is sexual/religious. Wicked men offer Laura forbidden fruits, a garden of sensual delights, in exchange for the golden treasure that, like any young girl, she keeps in her "purse," or for permission to "rape" a lock of her hair. Once she has lost her virginity, however, she is literally valueless and therefore not worth even further seduction. Her exaggerated fall has, in fact, intensified the processes of time which, for all humanity, began with Eve's eating of the forbidden fruit, when our primordial parents entered the realm of generation. Thus Laura goes into a conventional Victorian decline, then further shrinks and grays, metamorphosing into a witchlike old woman. But at this point, just as Christ intervened to save mankind by offering his body and blood as bread and wine for general spiritual consumption, so Laura's "good" sister Lizzie, like a female Saviour, negotiates with the goblins (as Christ did with Satan) and offers herself to be eaten and drunk in a womanly holy communion. And just as Christ redeemed mankind from Original Sin, restoring at least the possibility of heaven to Eve's erring descendents, so Lizzie rehabilitates Laura, changing her back from a lost witch to a virginal bride and ultimately leading her into a heaven of innocent domesticity.

Beyond such didacticism, however, **"Goblin Market"** seems to have a tantalizing number of other levels of meaning—meanings about and for women in particular—so that it has recently begun to be something of a textual crux for feminist critics. To such readers, certainly, the indomitable Lizzie, standing like a lily, a rock, a beacon, a "fruit-crowned orange tree" or "a royal virgin town / Topped with gilded dome and spire," may well seem almost a Victorian Amazon, a nineteenth-century reminder that "sisterhood is powerful." Certainly, too, from one feminist perspective **"Goblin Market,"** with its evil and mercantile little men and its innocent, high-minded women, suggests that men *hurt* while women redeem. Significantly, indeed, there are no men in the poem other than the unpleasant goblins; even when Laura and Lizzie become "wives and mothers" their husbands never appear, and they evidently have no sons. Rossetti does, then, seem to be dreamily positing an effectively matrilineal and matriarchal world, perhaps even, considering the strikingly sexual redemption scene between the sisters, a covertly (if ambivalently) lesbian world.

At the same time, however, what are we to think when the redeemed Eden into which Lizzie leads Laura turns out to be a heaven of domesticity? Awakening from her consumptive trance, Laura laughs "in the innocent old way," but in fact, like Blake's Thel withdrawing from the pit of Experience, she has retreated to a psychic stage prior even to the one she was in when the poem began. Living in a virginal female world and rejecting any notions of sexuality, of self-assertion, of personal pleasure (for men are beasts, as the animal-like goblins proved), she devotes herself now entirely to guarding the "tender lives" of her daughters from dangers no doubt equivalent to the one with which the fruit-merchants threatened her. For her, however, the world no longer contains such dangers, and a note of nostalgia steals into Rossetti's verse as she describes

Laura's reminiscences of "Those pleasant days long gone / Of not-returning time," the days of the "haunted glen" and the "wicked quaint fruit-merchant men." Like Lizzie, Laura has become a true Victorian angel-in-the-house—selfless and smiling—so naturally (we intuitively feel the logic of this) the "haunted glen" and the "quaint" goblins have disappeared.

But why is it natural that the glen with its merchants should vanish when Laura becomes angelically selfless? Do the goblins incarnate anything besides beastly and exploitative male sexuality? Does their fruit signify something more than fleshly delight? Answers to these questions may be embedded in the very Miltonic imagery Rossetti exploits. In *Paradise Lost,* we should remember, the Satanic serpent persuades Eve to eat the apple not because it is delicious but because it has brought about a "Strange alteration" in him, adding both "Reason" and "Speech" to his "inward Powers." But, he argues, if he, a mere animal, has been so transformed by this "Sacred, Wise, and Wisdom-giving Plant," the fruit will surely make Eve, a human being, "as Gods," presumably in speech as in other powers.[63] Rossetti's goblin men, more enigmatic than Milton's snake, make no such promises to Laura, but **"Goblin Market"**'s fruit-eating scene parallels the *Paradise Lost* scene in so many other ways that there may well be a submerged parallel here too.

Certainly Eve, devouring the garden's "intellectual food," acts just like her descendent Laura. "Intent now wholly on her taste," she regards "naught else," for "such delight till then . . . In Fruit she never tasted . . . Greedily she ingorg'd without restraint," until at last she is "hight'n'd as with Wine, jocund and boon."[64] But though she is pleasuring herself physically, Eve's true goal is intellectual divinity, equality with or superiority to Adam (and God), pure self-assertion. Her first resolve, when she is finally "Satiate," is to worship the Tree daily, "Not without Song." Given this Miltonic context, it seems quite possible that Laura too—sucking on the goblin fruit, asserting and indulging her own desires "without restraint"—is enacting an affirmation of intellectual (or poetic) as well as sexual selfhood. There is a sense, after all, in which she is metaphorically eating *words* and enjoying the taste of *power,* just as Eve before her did. "A Word made Flesh is seldom / And tremblingly partook / Nor then perhaps reported," wrote Emily Dickinson. She might have been commenting on **"Goblin Market"**'s central symbolism, for she added, as if to illuminate the dynamics of Laura's Satanically unholy Communion,

> But have I not mistook
> Each one of us has tasted
> With ecstasies of stealth
> The very food debated
> To our specific strength—
>
> [J. 1651]

Both the taste and the "Philology" of power are steeped in guilt, she seems to be saying. And as we have seen, for women like Eve and Laura (and Rossetti herself), they can only be partaken "with ecstasies of stealth."

Such connections between female pleasure and female power, between assertive female sexuality and assertive female speech, have been traditional ones. Both the story of Eve and Dickinson's poem make such links plain, as do the kinds of attacks that were leveled against iconoclastic feminists like Mary Wollstonecraft—the accusation, for instance, that *The Rights of Woman* was "a scripture archly fram'd for propagating whores."[65] (Richard Polwhele, one of Wollstonecraft's most virulent critics, even associated "bliss botanic" with the "imperious mien" and "proud defiance" of Wollstonecraft's "unsex'd" female followers.)[66] We should remember, too, that Barrett Browning was praised for her blameless sexual life, since "the lives of women of genius have so frequently been sullied by sin . . . that their intellectual gifts are [usually] a curse rather than a blessing." In this last remark, indeed, the relationship between sexuality and female genius becomes virtually causal: female genius triggers uncontrollable sexual desires, and perhaps, conversely, uncontrollable sexual desires even cause the disease of female genius.

That genius and sexuality *are* diseases in women, diseases akin to madness, is implied in **"Goblin Market"** both by Laura's illness and by the monitory story of Jeanie, "who should have been a bride; / But who for joys brides hope to have / Fell sick and died / In her gay prime." For though Rossetti's allusion to bridal joys does seem to reinforce our first notion that the forbidden goblin fruit simply signifies forbidden sexuality, an earlier reference to Jeanie renders the fruit symbolism in her case just as ambiguous as it is in Laura's. Jeanie, Lizzie reminds Laura, met the goblin men "in the moonlight, / Took their gifts both choice and many, / Ate their fruits and wore their flowers / Plucked from bowers / Where summer ripens at all hours." In other words, wandering in the moonlight and trafficking with these strange creatures from the glen, Jeanie became a witch or madwoman, yielding herself entirely to an "unnatural" or at least unfeminine life of dream and inspiration. Her punishment, therefore, was that decline which was essentially an outer sign of her inner disease.[67]

That the goblins' fruits and flowers are unnatural and out-of-season, however, associates them further with works of art—the fruits of the mind—as well as with sinful sexuality. More, that they do not reproduce themselves in the ordinary sense and even seem to hinder the reproduction of ordinary vegetation reinforces our sense of their curious and guilty artificiality. Jeanie and Laura are both cursed with physical barrenness, unlike most Victorian fallen women, who almost always (like Eliot's Hetty Sorel or Barrett Browning's

Marian Erle) bear bastard children to denote their shame. But not even daisies will grow on Jeanie's grave, and the kernelstone Laura has saved refuses to produce a new plant. Sickening and pining, both Jeanie and Laura are thus detached not only from their own healthful, child-oriented female sexuality, but also from their socially ordained roles as "modest maidens." The day after her visit to the goblin men Laura still helps Lizzie milk, sweep, sew, knead, and churn, but while Lizzie is content, Laura is already "Sick in part," pining for the fruits of the haunted glen, and eventually, like Jeanie, she refuses to participate in the tasks of domesticity.

Finally, while the haunted glen itself is on one level a female sexual symbol, it becomes increasingly clear that on another, equally significant level it represents a chasm in the mind, analogous to that enchanted romantic chasm Coleridge wrote of in "Kubla Khan," to the symbolic Red Deeps George Eliot described in *The Mill on the Floss,* or to the mental chasms Dickinson defined in numerous poems. When we realize this we can more thoroughly understand the disease—the strange weeping, the dreamy lassitude, the sexual barrenness, and witchlike physical deformity—that afflicts both Laura and Jeanie. The goblin men were not, after all, real human-sized, sexually charismatic men. Indeed, at every point Rossetti distinguishes them from the *real* men who never do appear in the poem. Instead, they are—were all along—the desirous little creatures so many women writers have recorded encountering in the haunted glens of their own minds, hurrying scurrying furry ratlike *its* or *ids,* inescapable *incubi.* "Cunning" as animal-like Bertha Rochester, "bad" as that "rat" or "bad cat" the nine-year-old Jane Eyre, they remind us too of the "it" goblin-dark Heathcliff was to Catherine Earnshaw, and the "it" Dickinson sometimes saw herself becoming, the "sweet wolf" she said "we all have inside us." Out of an enchanted but earthly chasm in the self, a mossy cave of the unconscious, these it-like inner selves, "mopping and mowing" with masculine assertiveness, arise to offer Jeanie, Laura, Lizzie, and Rossetti herself the unnatural but honey-sweet fruit of art, fruit that is analogous to (or identical with) the luscious fruit of self-gratifying sensual pleasure.

As *Maude* predicted, however, either Rossetti or one of the surrogate selves into whom she projected her literary anxieties would have to reject the goblin fruit of art. With its attendant invitation to such solipsistic luxuries as vanity and self-assertion, such fruit has "hungry thirsty roots" that have fed on suspicious soil indeed. **"From House to Home,"** one of Rossetti's other major poems of renunciation, was written in the same year as **"Goblin Market,"** and it makes the point more directly. She had inhabited, the poet-speaker confides, "a pleasure-place within my soul; / An earthly paradise supremely fair."[68] But her inner Eden "lured me from the goal." Merely "a tissue of hugged lies," this paradise is complete with a castle of "white transparent glass," woods full of "songs and flowers and fruit," and a muse-like male spirit who has eyes "like flames of fire . . . Fulfilling my desire." Rossetti's "pleasure-place" is thus quite clearly a paradise of self-gratifying art, a paradise in which the lures of **"Goblin Market"**'s masculine fruit-merchants are anticipated by the seductions of the male muse, and the sensual delights of the goblin fruit are embodied in an artfully arranged microcosmos of happy natural creatures. Precisely because this inner Eden *is* a "pleasure-place," however, it soon becomes a realm of banishment in which the poet-speaker, punitively abandoned by her muse, is condemned to freeze, starve, and age, like Laura and Jeanie. For again like Laura and Jeanie, Rossetti must learn to suffer and renounce the self-gratifications of art and sensuality.

As a representative female poet-speaker, moreover, Rossetti believes she must learn to sing selflessly, despite pain, rather than selfishly, in celebration of pleasure. A key passage in **"From House to Home"** describes an extraordinary, masochistic vision which strikingly illuminates the moral aesthetic on which **"Goblin Market"** is also based.

> I saw a vision of a woman, where
>   Night and new morning strive for
>   domination;
> Incomparably pale, and almost fair,
>   And sad beyond expression.
>
>   . . . . .
>
> I stood upon the outer barren ground
>   She stood on inner ground that budded
>   flowers;
> While circling in their never-slackening round
>   Danced by the mystic hours.
>
> But every flower was lifted on a thorn,
>   And every thorn shot upright from its sands
> To gall her feet; hoarse laughter pealed in scorn
>   With cruel clapping hands.
>
> She bled and wept, yet did not shrink; her
>   strength
>   Was strung up until daybreak of delight:
> She measured measureless sorrow toward its
>   length,
>   And breadth, and depth, and height.
>
> Then marked I how a chain sustained her
>   form,
>   A chain of living links not made nor riven:
> It stretched sheer up through lightning, wind,
>   and storm,
>   And anchored fast in heaven.

One cried: "How long? Yet founded on the
    Rock
She shall do battle, suffer, and attain."—
One answered: "Faith quakes in the tempest
    shock:
Strengthen her soul again."

I saw a cup sent down and come to her
    Brimful of loathing and of bitterness:
She drank with livid lips that seemed to stir
    The depth, not make it less.

But as she drank I spied a hand distil
    New wine and virgin honey; making it
First bitter-sweet, then sweet indeed, until
    She tasted only sweet.

Her lips and cheeks waxed rosy-fresh and
    young;
Drinking she sang: "My soul shall nothing
    want";
And drank anew: while soft a song was sung,
    A mystical slow chant.

What the female poet-speaker must discover, this passage suggests, is that for the woman poet only renunciation, even anguish, can be a suitable source of song. Bruised and tortured, the Christ-like poet of Rossetti's vision drinks the bitterness of self-abnegation, and *then* sings. For the pure sweetness of the early "pleasure-place," Rossetti implies, is merely a "tissue of lies." The woman artist can be strengthened "to live" only through doses of paradoxically bittersweet pain.

Like the sweet "pleasaunce" of **"From House to Home,"** the fruit of **"Goblin Market"** has fed on the desirous substrata of the psyche, the childishly self-gratifying fantasies of the imagination. Superegoistic Lizzie, therefore, is the agent of necessity and necessity's "white and golden" virtue, repression. When Laura returns from eating the forbidden fruit, Lizzie meets her "at the gate / Full of wise upbraidings: 'Dear, you should not stay so late, / Twilight is not good for maidens; / Should not loiter in the glen / In the haunts of goblin men.' " Although, as we noted earlier, the goblin men are not "real" men, they are of course integrally associated with masculinity's prerogatives of self-assertion, so that what Lizzie is telling Laura (and what Rossetti is telling herself) is that the risks and gratifications of art are "not good for maidens," a moral Laura must literally assimilate here just as the poet-speaker had to learn it in **"From House to Home."** Young ladies like Laura, Maude, and Christina Rossetti should not loiter in the glen of imagination, which is the haunt of goblin men like Keats and Tennyson—or like Dante Gabriel Rossetti and his compatriots of the Pre-Raphaelite Brotherhood.

Later, becoming a eucharistic Messiah, a female version of the patriarchal (rather than Satanic) Word made flesh, Lizzie insists that Laura must devour her—must, that is, ingest her bitter repressive wisdom, the wisdom, of necessity's virtue, in order to be redeemed. And indeed, when Laura does feast on Lizzie, the goblin juice on her repressive sister's skin is "wormwood to the tongue." As in **"From House to Home,"** the aesthetic of pleasure has been transformed by censorious morality into an aesthetic of pain. And, again, just as in **"From House to Home"** the female hero bleeds, weeps, and *sings* because she suffers, so in **"Goblin Market"** Laura does at last begin to leap and sing "like a caged thing freed" at the moment in which she learns the lesson of renunciation. At this moment, in other words, she reaches what Rossetti considers the height of a woman poet's art, and here, therefore, she is truly Rossetti's surrogate. Later, she will lapse into childlike domesticity, forgoing all feasts, but here, for a brief interval of ecstatic agony, she "stems the light / Straight toward the sun" and gorges "on bitterness without a name," a masochistic version of what Dickinson called "the banquet of abstemiousness." Then, having assimilated her repressive but sisterly superego, she dies utterly to her old poetic / sexual life of self-assertion.

Once again a comparison with Keats seems appropriate, for just as he was continually obsessed with the same poetic apprenticeship that concerned Rossetti in *Maude,* he too wrote a resonantly symbolic poem about the relationship of poetry and starvation to an encounter with interior otherness incarnated in a magical being of the opposite sex. Like Rossetti's goblin men, Keats's "belle dame" fed his vulnerable knight mysterious but luscious food—"roots of relish sweet, / And honey-wild, and manna dew—" and, cementing the connection between food and speech, she told him "in language strange . . . 'I love thee true.' " Like Rossetti's Laura (and like the speaker of **"From House to Home"**), Keats's knight was also inexplicably deserted by the muselike lady whom he had met in the meads and wooed in an eerie "elfin grot" analogous to the goblin's haunted glen, once she had had her will of him. Like Laura, too, he pined, starved, and sickened on the cold hillside of reality where his *anima* and his author abandoned him. Yet in Keats's case, unlike Rossetti's, we cannot help feeling that the poet's abandonment is only temporary, no matter what the knight's fate might be. Where her betrayal by goblin men (and the distinction between a beautiful queen and rat-faced goblin men is relevant here too) persuades Laura/Rossetti that her original desire to eat the forbidden fruit of art was a vain and criminal impulse, the knight's abandonment simply enhances our sense of his tragic grandeur.

Art, Keats says, is ultimately worth any risk, even the risk of alienation or desolation. The ecstasy of the beautiful lady's "kisses sweet" and "language strange" is more than worth the starvation and agony to come. Indeed, the ecstasy of the kisses, deceptive though they are, itself constitutes the only redemption possible for both Keats and his knight. Certainly any redemption of the kind Lizzie offers Laura, though it might return the knight to the fat land where "the squirrel's granary is full," would destroy what is truly valuable to him—his memory of the elfin grot, the fairy's song, the "honey wild"—just as Laura's memory of the haunted glen and the "fruits like honey to the throat" is ultimately destroyed by her ritual consumption of repressive domesticity. And that **"Goblin Market"** is not just an observation of the lives of other women but an accurate account of the aesthetics Rossetti worked out for herself helps finally to explain why, although Keats can imagine asserting himself from beyond the grave, Rossetti, banqueting on bitterness, must bury herself alive in a coffin of renunciation. . . .

Notes

. . .[62] "Goblin Market," *The Poetical Works of Christina G. Rossetti*, 1:3-22.

[63] *Paradise Lost*, 9. 599-600, and 679.

[64] Ibid., 9. 790-800.

[65] See Ralph Wardle, *Mary Wollstonecraft*, p. 322.

[66] Richard Polwhele, *The Unsex'd Females: A Poem* (New York: Garland, 1974; first published 1798), pp. 6-9. Polwhele complained in a footnote that "Botany has lately become a fashionable amusement with the ladies. But how the study of the sexual system of plants can accord with female modesty, I am not able to comprehend." And in his diatribe against Wollstonecraft he wrote that "I shudder at the new unpictur'd scene, / Where unsex'd woman vaunts the imperious mien; / Where girls . . . With bliss botanic as their bosoms heave, / Still pluck forbidden fruit, with mother Eve, / For puberty in sighing florets pant, / Or point the prostitution of a plant; / Dissect its organ of unhallow'd lust, / And fondly gaze the titillating dust." He felt, in other words, that botanizing literally accompanied sexual and political self-assertion, as a sign of female depravity.

[67] The dynamics of Jeanie's (and Laura's) disease are further illuminated by Rossetti's sonnet "The World." Here the speaker describes "The World" as a woman who is beautiful by day, offering "Ripe fruits, sweet flowers, and full satiety," but who becomes "a very monster void of love and prayer" by night. Thus "By day she stands a lie: by night she stands, / In all the naked horror of the truth, / With pushing horns and clawed and clutching hands." Clearly Rossetti has converted the traditional allegorical threesome of "the world, the flesh, and the devil" into a single terrifying figure who incarnates, among other things, her deep anxieties about female ambition, inspiration, and self-assertion. (See *Poetical Works*, 1: 96.)

[68] "From House to Home," Ibid., pp. 103-12. . . .

Cora Kaplan (essay date 1979)

SOURCE: "The Indefinite Disclosed: Christina Rossetti and Emily Dickinson," in *Women Writing and Writing about Women*, edited by Mary Jacobus, Croom Helm, London, 1979, pp. 61-79.

[*In the excerpt below, Kaplan surveys feminist readings of "Goblin Market" and argues that the poem explores female sexual fantasy.*]

> To fill a Gap
> Insert the Thing that caused it—
> Block it up
> With Other—and 'twill yawn the more—
> You cannot solder an Abyss
> With Air.
> (Emily Dickinson, *c.* 1862)[1]

This curious, compacted lyric is one of a group of poems that form a distinct category in the work of two Victorian women poets, Emily Dickinson and Christina Rossetti. Such lyrics speak directly to and about the psyche, expressing and querying feelings that are deliberately abstracted from any reference to, or analysis of, the social causes of psychological states. They attempt to escape immediate or specific social determination, a project that cannot be finally realised since all representation as such must exist within a cultural discourse. Most of Dickinson's verse, and the larger part of Rossetti's, exclude the social in this way; but in this particular subgenre their poetry also employs atypical forms of imagery. Instead of straightforward metaphorical constructions, comparisons of like to unlike (as in the metaphysical mode for which Dickinson is famous, or the more traditional late Romantic style preferred by Rossetti), these lyrics are marked by their use of synecdoche, where the part stands for the whole, and metonymy, where the images are narratively or associatively related rather than expressly compared.[2] Images and their meanings are left dangling, as in 'To fill a Gap' where 'Gap', 'Other', 'Abyss' and 'Air' are not meant as metaphors for each other but as substitutes. 'Gaps' are caused by absence and loss and can only be described through an articulation which opens rather than blocks the 'Abyss'.

Such strategies were not vulnerable to the type of textual explication used by Victorian critics, which depended on a text susceptible to paraphrase. Similarly, their richness of reference makes them texts puzzling to modern critics intent on extracting a single or definitive interpretation; dream-form, too, either directly stated or implied, becomes an important means of presenting distorted or unclear images with impunity. While these modes are idiosyncratic to Dickinson and

Rossetti, conveying powerful ideas and feelings past internal and external censors, they are by no means the monopoly of women writers. But they deserve the special attention of feminist critics because they seem to 'fill a Gap' in our understanding of women's subjectivity—their sense of themselves—and because their very openness renders the poems at once problematic and vulnerable to particular kinds of misreading. It is too easy to bind them into biographical interpretations of the poets' lives or build them into additional 'literary' evidence to buttress interpretations of women's experience drawn from their prose fiction. Worst of all, because these lyrics are so clearly 'about' the psychological, they can be used to substantiate specific psychoanalytic theories of femininity. The use of psychoanalysis in literary criticism as a way of exploring the conjunction between specific historical ideologies and individual literary works has become popular in recent years, partly in response to the attempt to integrate Marxism and psychoanalytic theory. Feminists have supported and added substantially to such integration, and my reservations about interpretation are intended, not to denounce this enterprise as such, but to serve as a critique of its least useful tendencies.

Why should such common uses of the lyric of feeling, particularly when its meaning is difficult or obscure, be inappropriate? These texts speak to and about psychic phenomena in ways that are unique in women's writing of the period. However formal their presentation, they are, by virtue of their fragmentary and opaque language, torn away from a chain of meaning which would secure them to larger interpretations. Their sybilline quality means that they can be inserted into almost any theory about women as social subjects and about high culture as an expression of women's suppressed and distorted subjectivity. Most of the poems that follow, would, for example support either a phallocentric theory of women's psychological development as espoused by Freud and some of his modern followers, or a concentric theory, lately in vogue in feminist psychoanalysis and already popularised in feminist literary criticism as the concept of 'inner space'.[3] Phallocentric theories see language and gender-socialisation organised around the phallus as a privileged signifier of 'difference'; concentric theory sees the vagina as an equally powerful force in the organisation of women's social, psychic and sexual being, also expressed through their use of language. These theories are still in the early stages of development, and although I am myself tentatively aligned with neo-Freudians such as Lacan, I cannot see the lyrics which I am examining as decisive witness for either side. Their real strength, in relation to the casual reader and the critical theorist alike, is that they are shapes, like ink-blots, from which to decipher related images in our own experience and intellectual orientation. These poems interrogate states for which the poets themselves had no ready explanations; in turn they interrogate our own theory and politics. The symbolic strategies which they employ ensure that this is their main effect, making them stand apart from other lyrics by the same poets which are more precisely metaphorical and more immediately didactic, as well as standing in opposition to narrative, the dominant genre of women's prose writing.

In focusing on the work of two poets who were exact contemporaries (both born in 1830) certain ironic anomalies are apparent. Emily Dickinson's verse, unpublished in her lifetime, has been much more fully worked over by modern critics than Christina Rossetti's, which enjoyed considerable popularity until the turn of the century. Rossetti belongs to the pre-Raphaelite school; her poetry has an obvious niche in English literature, but the twentieth century has virtually ignored her, and for this reason I shall devote more of my attention to her. On the other hand, Dickinson's thousands of short lyrics, as edited by Thomas H. Johnson, have proved a scholar's gift to scholars, a virgin œuvre on which to make their mark. Yet even though Dickinson's poetry has been tackled from almost every critical position, she, like Christina Rossetti, figures much less prominently in the new feminist literary criticism than women novelists of the same period.

One can only suggest some reasons why their work has been slighted by feminists. A large portion of both poets' writing is devotional, it is true; but so is much well-thought-of poetry. More important, perhaps, is the reflexive nature of the verse, its concentration on the inner life, its virtual exclusion of the contemporary or social. Emily Dickinson's approach is analytic, intellectual even; she read more widely than her urban British contemporary. Her lyrics most typically seek to analyse emotions through analogy; that is the way in which she uses the metaphysical. Rossetti's poems offer a sensuous appreciation of emotion. A conscious preoccupation with the constricting demands of femininity does not often surface in the poetry of either. Even in life their protests against the constraints of gender were muted at the social level, where they presented exaggerated examples of retiring women. Unlike contemporary women novelists, many of whom were also perfect Victorian gentlewomen, they hardly ever make combative social relations with lovers or family the subject of their poetry. Instead, their verse is preoccupied with a melancholy inner struggle for peace of mind. This introspective, almost morbid preoccupation marked not only their verse but also that of many lesser women poets of the century—so much so that in the mid-1890s the young Alice Thompson, who would become the poet and feminist Alice Meynell, wrote bitterly of her 'rhyming faculty' that 'whatever I write will be melancholy and self-conscious, as are all women's poems.'[4]

Dickinson's and Rossetti's lyrics are so meagre in description of their cultural surroundings that they do not date, except in certain turns of speech, and therefore withhold the crucial historical distance that places the nineteenth-century novel in a convenient conceptual past; the modern reader cannot see them through the wrong end of the binoculars, from a progressive present in which a better world for women is implicit. Such poetry accentuates the way in which the female psyche has a recalcitrant tendency to remain recognisable in its supposedly 'weaker' aspects, despite a variety of ostensible improvements in women's social and political status. This emphasis may suggest the difficulty which they present for a new feminist criticism. The women's movement today—Marxist, bourgeois or radical feminist—tends to endorse women's struggle through social and political action and to resist as weakening those psychoanalytic interpretations of femininity which seem to confirm or eternalise women's passive and masochistic behaviour. Both Rossetti and Dickinson represented very fully the internal struggles of women of their day as well as ours, without the comforting assurance that their spiritual malaise would be cured by egalitarian marriage, revision of the laws of inheritance, education, employment, a more equitable division of labour, the loosening of sexual prohibitions, or the curtailment of parental authority.

Since the most intractable problem facing feminists today is the relationship between the psychological components of femininity, female socialisation, and the social and political elements of women's subordination, it is not surprising that the writing of Dickinson and Rossetti should provide much thought but small comfort. Their poetry—particularly at its most arcane and difficult points—does, however, help us to understand the relationship between the imaginative act and the dominant ideology. Despite considerable prejudice against women writers in the nineteenth century, imaginative writing was, of all forms of public discourse, the one in which women were most able to participate and, in England, become prominent. Perhaps it was thought to be the least dangerous to bourgeois hegemony and hence to patriarchal power. This being so (and it is, of course, open to debate), we might come at their poetry in a new way, understanding that even when its overt intention is revolutionary it is only rarely a force which ruptures or alters existing social and political forms. In their most radical sallies it may be said that Rossetti and Dickinson conformed to the judgement of an approving contemporary critic who compared Christina Rossetti favourably with Elizabeth Barrett Browning because Rossetti accepted 'the burden of womanhood'. Where their strategies of subversion are subtle, even subliminal, the effect may still be to confirm traditional arrangements by substituting fantasy for anger. Both a clearer definition of the place of literary discourse in women's oppression and the place of literature in resistance to it is needed. Such an approach would begin by accepting the contradiction posed by women's writing as simultaneously a historical record of their oppression and a definitive mark of their defiance, hence making the conservative implications of the work of these two major poets less embarrassing for feminist criticism.

Christina Rossetti

Two recent feminist readings of Christina Rossetti's **"Goblin Market"** (1862) may help to distinguish between useful and misleading analyses of such poetry. **"Goblin Market"** has for some years had an underground reputation as a forgotten feminist classic. Christina Rossetti adamantly resisted attempts to press an interpretation on the poem, insisting that it was what its surface suggests—a fairy story. It unquestionably belongs to the genre of 'faery' which had a long tradition in English and underwent a late-nineteenth-century revival. A narrative (like many of Rossetti's longer poems), it is the story of two sisters, Laura and Lizzie, who live alone together. Wilful Laura looks at and listens to the fairy men, then buys and sucks the goblins' magical fruit which produces a violent addiction. The goblins sell only once to each buyer and Lizzie, older and more careful, watches her sister waste away in 'baulked desire'. Finally she takes a silver penny and seeks out the goblins who literally assault her with their wares, but cannot make her open her lips to eat the fruit herself. The sexual analogy is quite explicit:

> Like a royal virgin town
> Topped with gilded dome and spire
> Close beleaguered by a fleet
> Mad to tug her standard down.[5]

Finally they toss back her penny and, covered in juice, 'In a smart, ache, tingle', Lizzie rushes back to Laura crying 'Hug me, kiss me, suck my juices'.[6] Laura obeys and recovers; Lizzie does not suffer, and the two sisters live to marry and tell their tale to their own children, both as cautionary and as heroic, with the moral that 'there is no friend like a sister.'[7]

My first example, Maureen Duffy's interpretation in *The Erotic World of Faery,* is full of suggestive insights culled from psychoanalytic theory; but it is never clear how the text is being defined in relation to her analysis. It is not just that the text is left unspecified as a product of Christina Rossetti's conscious intention or as unconscious displacement—the problem of conscious or unconscious production of images is never even taken up. Sometimes it seems as if Duffy views the poem as a loose but evocative series of representations in which each reader can find a metaphor to suit his or her fantasy; at other points the poem is seen to be grounded in Victorian sexual taboos; at still others the text is used as a 'timeless' example of the way in which the unconscious displaces and condenses sexual meanings. We might start by asking what conscious sexual under- and overtones Rossetti meant the poem to carry. To the extent that it is allegorical, the goblins' fruit and the serpent's apple are constant, implied metaphors. The lines already quoted about the 'virgin town' make clear Rossetti's basic analogy between goblins-with-fruit and sexual temptation. But the last thing **"Goblin Market"** intends is a recapitulation of Eve's fall. The analogy is there to set up a different, contradictory set of relations to the story of Adam and Eve. While the snake's apple produces sensations of shame in the Edenic couple, the goblins' fruit gives Laura knowledge of desire but not shame. This, and the fact that Laura and Lizzie are sisters instead of mates, constitutes the deliberate contrast which Rossetti establishes between her fairy tale and the Edenic myth.

Duffy's basic assumption is that the poem concerns fantasy sex, desire and masturbation. But read as an allegory (bad thoughts equal bad fairies, forbidden fruit is the female body itself), the narrative breaks down; the point about the goblins is that they represent—whether consciously, unconsciously, or as a result of ambiguity—both real tempters of the other sex (i.e. males) and paranoid projections of temptation. Duffy sees Laura devouring the fruit as 'a powerful masturbatory fantasy of feeding at the breast', quoting Rossetti in support: 'She sucked until her lips were sore.'[8] But even this simple image is too condensed to be reduced to a single connotation; childish greed and undifferentiated sensual pleasure may be indicated, but a contradiction remains: children can get sore lips from eating too much tart fruit, but babies don't get sore lips from breast-feeding. *Mothers* do, however, get sore nipples from being sucked, and if we are to pursue the masturbatory implications of Duffy's reading then presumably sore lips must be transposed from mouth to vagina. But what is important about the passage is not the physical site or source of sensual excitement, but the moral overtone: you can hurt from too much pleasure, oral or genital. As with Duffy's suggestion that the goblins' invitation to Lizzie to 'Bob at our cherries / Bite at our peaches' is a temptation closer to fellatio (surely the sexual practice least likely to have been known to the author), we are confronted by the poem's ability to induce fantasy, its power to stir further erotic association in the reader.

Duffy's attempt to historicise the poem produces further difficulties. Quoting William Acton's *The Functions and Disorders of the Reproductive Organs* (1857), she suggests that the symptoms of Laura's decline are those which Acton ascribes to the habitual masturbator. Although Acton's text conveniently precedes the poem's writing by a few years, it is highly unlikely that Christina Rossetti, who refused to dip into a racy novel, would have read it. True, Acton simply repeats and gives spurious scientific valorisation to current beliefs about masturbation, but his symptoms are punitive projection rather than medical reality. If one wanted to look for a 'real' medical analogy for Laura's decline, and one moreover that Christina Rossetti might have witnessed, one could point to drug addiction, of course, but possibly to anorexia, now commonly thought to be associated with pubescent crises at the onset of adult female sexuality. This explanation is equally hypothetical; its only advantage is that it is less specific and coincides both with the mysterious ailments of adolescence and with the traditional malaise following fairy curses on either sex. But pursuit of Laura's disease distracts from what is really important: its place in the moral narrative. Laura is ill with 'baulked desire', not guilt; Lizzie goes out determined to cure, not absolve, her, by getting her sister more of what she wants. Most important for the structure of the poem, Laura's illness is an excuse for the next 'erotic' episode in the poem, Lizzie's assault by the goblins.

Finally, Duffy sees in Laura and Lizzie 'the sisters who appear repeatedly in paintings and drawings from Millais to Sargent. This double female image is an interesting component of the period's eroticism akin to the heterosexual desire to see blue films about lesbians.'[9] The sisterly relationship in the poem has definite and unsuppressed sensuous elements, but are we really to believe that Christina Rossetti produced a representation of female eroticism pandering to male taste? Blue films about lesbians are made for and by men, as distinct from representations by lesbians about lesbian relationships made by and for women. Both may satisfy the erotic fantasies of either sex in different ways, but it is hardly useful to talk about a 'period's eroticism' as if it were a unified phenomenon. In addition, the 'erotic' encounter between Laura and Lizzie is far more daring than any scene, however suggestive, portrayed in the high art of the period. It is protected from censure through its enclosure in fairy tale and through the pain and anguish of the cure (Lizzie's embrace) which now tastes of bitterest wormwood. The poem operates its own internal censorship by making joint motifs of pleasure and punishment strongest at the most significant erotic moments. What such historicising in relation to Victorian sexual attitude and high art may locate is the site of contradiction within a poem which struggles to represent female sexual fantasy while being constrained nevertheless by the guilt inherent in even the most displaced expression of such fantasy.

Ellen Moers, in *Literary Women,* provides a much tauter commentary on the poem. More careful in her use of psychoanalytic interpretations, she contributes to our understanding of the punitive elements in **"Goblin Market"** by examining the mixed elements of sensuality, sadism and violence in the sisters' confrontation with the goblins. Moers places the poem within her discussion of female Gothic, a genre in which violence to women in supernatural settings is a leading trope. However, Moers' argument for the prominence of hand-to-hand sadism, pinching and plaguing is based on her assessment of the limited heterosexual experience open to single women writers in the nineteenth century. Their sexual experience and subsequent sexual fantasy are linked to the night side of the Victorian nursery, where siblings, cousins and friends were allowed a pre-pubescent freedom denied to young men and women:

> Women authors of Gothic fantasies appear to testify that the physical teasing they received from their brothers—the pinching, mauling, and scratching we dismiss as the most unimportant of children's games—took on outsize proportions and powerful erotic overtones in their adult imaginations . . . (it was not only sexual play but *any* kind of physical play for middle-class women that fell under the Victorian ban).[10]

Moers extends her argument by pointing to the prominence of the nursery-tussle motif in the writing of many other Victorian women. Her clear and cautious use of the relation between socialisation, fantasy and literature is a model for feminist criticism. She does not attempt to prove anything about Christina Rossetti's individual experience; rather, she generalises illuminatingly about the social components of women's sexual imagination. She is, if anything, a little too eager to clean up the poem by locating its more disturbing elements in a harmless practice which demonstrates the poverty rather than the richness of women's sexual fantasy.

While "Goblin Market" cannot be decoded as an elaborate adult sexual scenario, it undoubtedly remains an exploration of women's sexual fantasy which includes suggestions of masochism, homoeroticism, rape or incest. The images are incomplete and blurred for several possible reasons. Most obviously the blurring can be seen as a form of both conscious and unconscious censorship; it is also (perhaps primarily) the result of sexual ignorance. Christina Rossetti was sexually uninitiated, and while we may not have to fix her imagination at the level of a ten-year-old, we may legitimately see transformed fantasies as indistinct, referring characteristically to sensations rather than particular practices. Blurring occurs typically in fantasy anyway, where images condense and overlay each other, while condensed images often contract pleasure and punishment into a single act. The most interesting element of the poem remains this obscure level of internal reference combined with its very precise form. The narrative shape of the poem signals the primacy of erotic fantasy. The two sisters are given to the reader without social context. The absence of all social detail except their apparently orphaned state fits in well with the conventional frame of the fairy or folk tale as well as that of sexual fantasy, where too much specificity can impede the erotic message. The encounters with the goblins, and Laura's and Lizzie's embrace at the end of the poem, are presented within a surprisingly threadbare narrative scheme; the poet's words and attention are lavished instead on the 'erotic' incidents.

This rich concentration on the sensuous moment is typical of erotic fantasy; but the fairy story or folk tale similarly often contains irrelevant narrative elements which have little direct bearing on the dramatic crises. Thus the closing of the poem, like its opening, is compatible with both. Rather than leaving the girls locked in the annealing embrace, Rossetti projects them forwards into marriage and motherhood. This social ending—traditional in many narrative forms—is odd here only because the poem does not begin with a typical fairy story introduction. Instead it dives right into the heart of the matter: 'Morning and evening / Maids heard the goblins' cry . . . ' My analysis of the poem does not attempt to refute Duffy and Moers by going one better. Rather, it attempts to locate the poem within Christina Rossetti's work, and to identify particular strategies, conscious or unconscious, for conveying the pleasurable but forbidden past the Victorian censor. More important, I have tried to suggest the difficulty of disentangling the text as a historical structure of meaning and the text as read by the critic at any point after its production. Most simply, I suppose, "Goblin Market" can be seen as a comical-tragical view of the erotic from the women's position with conscious and unconscious elements inextricably mingled. A brief funny-sad lyric of *c.* 1861 by Emily Dickinson reads like a marginal gloss on Rossetti's poem:

> Over the fence—
> Strawberries—grow—
> Over the fence—
> I could climb—if I tried, I know—
> Berries are nice!
>
> But—if I stained my Apron—
> God would certainly scold!
> Oh, dear—I guess if He were a Boy—
> He'd—climb—if He could![11]

Like a number of Victorian poets, Christina Rossetti used dream-form as a favourite device when she wanted to exempt her poems from the demands of clarity. Poetry did not have to be very difficult to be thought obscure—witness contemporary verdicts on Robert Browning. Fancy, faery, dream-form and the absurd, as in Edward Lear's verse, were acceptable ways round the expectation that each metaphor be complete in itself, not too far-fetched, and related to the one that followed. For Tennyson, too, dream-form was a means of introducing irrational, private states of being into a canon built round a literature concerned with socially conventional ideas and feelings. Such alien psychic levels find their representation elsewhere in Victorian writing not only through the convention of the dream (both Alice's adventures are dreams), but through methods of displacement such as setting poem or novel in the past or in another country where things can be ordered differently. English writers themselves (the Brownings are perhaps the most celebrated example) went abroad in order to be released from the claustrophobic mores of their class and culture. The other scenes—Wonderland, the world of Tennyson's *The Princess*, **"Goblin Market,"** Arthur's Court—are all in part used to suspend social rules; the dream-state, as one of these other worlds, permits the expression of feelings and the enactment of dramas taboo in genteel households. . . .

Notes

[1] Thomas H. Johnson (ed.), *The Complete Poems of Emily Dickinson* (London, 1975), p. 266. All references are to this edition.

[2] My use of these distinctions is largely drawn from Roman Jakobson, *Studies on Child Language and Aphasia* (The Hague, 1971), pp. 44-5 and *passim*.

[3] The leading modern theoretician of phallocentric theory is the French psychoanalyst, Jacques Lacan. See *Écrits*, trans. Alan Sheridan (London, 1977). For concentric theory see Karen Horney, *Feminine Psychology* (London, 1967). More recent discussion of 'phallocentric' versus 'concentric' include Luce Irigaray, 'Women's Exile', *Ideology and Consciousness*, vol. i (1977), pp. 62-76; Parveen Adams, 'Representation and Sexuality', *m/f*, vol. i (1978), pp. 66-82; and Michèle Montrelay, 'Inquiry into Femininity', *m/f*, vol. i (1978), pp. 83-101.

[4] See *Salt and Bitter and Good: Three Centuries of English and American Women Poets* (New York and London, 1975), p. 181.

[5] William Michael Rossetti (ed.), *The Poetical Works of Christina Rossetti with Memoir and Notes etc.* (London, 1904), p. 6. All references are to this edition.

[6] Ibid., p. 7.

[7] Ibid., p. 8.

[8] Maureen Duffy, *The Erotic World of Faery* (London, 1972), p. 290.

[9] Ibid., pp. 288-9.

[10] Ellen Moers, *Literary Women* (New York, 1976), p. 105.

[11] Johnson, *Complete Poems of Emily Dickinson*, p. 115. . . .

Dorothy Mermin (essay date 1983)

SOURCE: "Heroic Sisterhood in *Goblin Market*," in *Victorian Poetry*, Vol. 21, No. 2, Summer, 1983, pp. 107-18.

[*In the following essay, Mermin argues that "Goblin Market" explores the feminine fantasies of "freedom, heroism, and self-sufficiency," celebrates "sisterly and maternal love," and suggests the possibility of a Pre-Raphaelite sisterhood.*]

"Goblin Market" is usually read as an allegory of the poet's self-division that shows, in Lionel Stevenson's representative summary, the conflict between "the two sides of Christina's own character, the sensuous and the ascetic," and demonstrates "the evil of self-indulgence, the fraudulence of sensuous beauty, and the supreme duty of renunciation."[1] Readings of his sort even when they are not reductively biographical (as Stevenson's is not) do not allow for the openness and multiplicity of meanings that we acknowledge in such predecessor poems as Coleridge's *The Ancient Mariner* or Keats's "La Belle Dame Sans Merci." They usually assume that the poem welled up spontaneously and artlessly from Rossetti's unconscious and press towards exclusively psycho-sexual interpretations. By turning the two sisters into parts of one person, they minimize or distort the central action in which one sister saves the other; they shy away from the powerful image of Lizzie as Christ saying, "'Eat me, drink me, love me'" (l. 471);[2] they ignore the energy, triumph, and joy of the poem; and they give insufficient weight to the ending. Recent readings have suggested other dimensions to the poem: that it is about art as well as sex, and that it represents the development of female autonomy in a largely female world.[3] An inclusive reading will demonstrate what is evident from the sensuousness, luxuriance, cheerfulness, and energy of the poem and from the serenity of the ending: that it is not a poem of bitter repression but rather a fantasy of feminine freedom, heroism, and self-sufficiency and a celebration of sisterly and maternal love. It is a dream or a vision of the Pre-Raphaelite world from a woman's point of view.

The goblins represent the temptations of sexual desire, but of a highly imaginative kind.[4] Jeanie "for joys brides hope to have / Fell sick and died" (ll. 314-315). This sexuality is without marriage or issue: no grass grows on Jeanie's grave and the kernel Laura brings back does not sprout. As in much of Rossetti's poetry and that of others in the Pre-Raphaelite circle, desire here has no end or final object. The goblins are like odd, furry, cuddly little animals of the sort Rossetti loved, sometimes childlike and charming, purveyors of desire but not its object. The fruits are not the real object either, since they feed the appetite instead of satisfying it; once tasted, they have served their purpose and cannot be found again. They are unreal even in the fairy-tale world of the poem—"Men sell not such in any town" (ll. 101, 556)—seeming to come from a paradise "'Where summer ripens at all hours'" (l. 152) but where no one ever goes. They represent desire for a paradise of the imagination that does not exist and therefore can be only desired, never obtained. The conflation of erotic and imaginative significance in a story about non-human objects of desire which exist outside of time recalls La Belle Dame Sans Merci, whose victims eat strange fruit in fairyland and then loiter, turn pale, starve, and waste away, and also Tennyson's "Tithonus" and (proleptically) "The Holy Grail." In Tennyson's poem the Grail quest begins with a nun who starves herself to a shadow after her love has been thwarted; the quest leads Percivale through a world of shadows and into a monastery and gives (as in **"Goblin Market"**) a framework of explicitly Christian meaning to a deeply ambiguous story. In all these poems the sexualized imaginative world is infinitely attractive but sterile and destructive, and those who commit themselves to longing for it waste away in gloom and frustration, cut off from natural human life.

Rossetti's knowledge of the lives and art of the Pre-Raphaelites, especially her brother Gabriel's, as well as the idea of Keats that was current at mid-century would have enforced the association between imaginary worlds, sexuality, and art. In her story **"The Lost Titian"** (1856) she describes a party at Titian's studio that resembles both a glorified version of Gabriel's house and the goblins' feast:

> The studio was elegant with clusters of flowers, sumptuous with crimson, gold-bordered hangings, and luxurious with cushions and perfumes. From the walls peeped pictured fruit and fruit-like faces.... On the table were silver dishes, filled with leaves and choice fruits; wonderful vessels of Venetian glass, containing rare wines and iced waters; and footless goblets, which allowed the guest no choice but to drain his bumper.[5]

The fruit both attracts and frightens Laura by suggesting a combination of sensuous richness, moral irresponsibility, and sinister eroticism that is frequent in Pre-Raphaelite art. "'Who knows upon what soil they fed / Their hungry thirsty roots?'" (ll. 44-45), she warns; but then: "'How fair the vine must grow. . . . How warm the wind must blow / Thro' those fruit bushes'" (ll. 60-63). The fruit seems to her to offer access to a paradise of art; she herself, moreover, is described in terms that suggest that she belongs in a Pre-Raphaelite picture. She "stretched her gleaming neck" like a swan, a lily, "a moonlit poplar branch" (ll. 81-84)—or like the long-necked women in Gabriel's paintings—and finally like a "vessel" (l. 85) about to break free, an association of woman and drifting boat that recalls a favorite Pre-Raphaelite subject, the Lady of Shalott. The other extended description of Laura refers to the most notable attribute of Pre-Raphaelite women, long loosened hair (ll. 500-506).

Laura sounds, in fact, like Lizzie Siddal, with her long neck and fabulously luxuriant red-gold hair[6]—Laura's hair "streamed" like a "torch" (l. 500) even though it had turned "thin and gray" (l. 277). Elizabeth Siddal, Dante Gabriel Rossetti's model and eventually his wife, was a painter and a poet too; she was reclusive, thin, and unhealthy, and took large quantities of laudanum, dying of an overdose shortly before **"Goblin Market"** was published. The goblins, "Brother with queer brother" (l. 94), suggest the Pre-Raphaelite brotherhood with their queer lives and also, perhaps, childhood memories and fantasies of Rossetti's own two brothers; as Ellen Moers points out, the goblins seem to reflect "fantasies derived from the night side of the Victorian nursery."[7] They call Lizzie "proud, / Cross-grained, uncivil" (ll. 394-395)—terms that Rossetti could well have imagined applied to herself by the Brotherhood, among whom she was often both sharp-tongued and reserved.[8] She was cool to Lizzie Siddal; nor did she get on well later with her other sister-in-law, Lucy (a name fortuitously apposite in sound to **"Goblin Market"**), the daughter of Ford Madox Brown, whom William Rossetti married in 1874. On the simplest biographical level, the poem seems to describe possible lives for women among the Pre-Raphaelites and to imagine a sisterly feeling among them that did not, so far as Christina Rossetti was concerned, actually exist.

In narrative terms the story is a transformation of a traditional fairy tale.[9] The sisters live alone in a cosy little house. Asleep, they are compared to blossoms, snow, "wands of ivory / Tipped with gold for awful kings" (ll. 188-191). Their sleep is protected as if by enchantment: "Wind sang to them lullaby, / Lumbering owls forebore to fly, / Not a bat flapped" (ll. 193-195). A verbal ambiguity makes them seem imprisoned: "Cheek to cheek and breast to breast / Locked together in one nest" (ll. 197-198) like sleeping princesses waiting for princes (or "awful kings") to rescue them. But this is a fairy tale that Rossetti usually tells with a difference. Her princes are dilatory and lovers seldom come to those who wait. (They are more likely to come to women who are doing something: making music in **"Maiden-Song,"** getting married in **"Love from the North."**) Once Laura yields to desire she becomes that central figure in Rossetti's poems and stories, the woman "Grown old before [her] time" ("Song: Oh roses for the flush of youth," l. 4), doomed to pine away like the princess in **"The Prince's Progress"** who dies before her lover gets there. Laura is cured, however, by discovering that what she pined for is not really desirable. Rossetti tells the same story again in **"Commonplace"** (1870), in which Lucy (again, a name fit for **"Goblin Market"**) learns that the man she loved has married someone else. Immediately she ages, fades, and withdraws from her family and the world. Then she meets him again, sees that he's not worth pining for, regains her health, looks, and cheerfulness, and marries a nicer man. Similarly, the goblins show their evil nature when Lizzie resists them and the juice she brings back tastes bitter. Knowing the bitterness is the "fiery antidote" (l. 559) to Laura's yearning. She is cured not because her fairy prince comes but because she ceases to want him.

Since the goblin fruit has explicitly sexual connotations, however, and since in the moral logic of poetry desire and deed blur together, Laura is in effect a "fallen woman"—an object that fascinated Victorians from the Pre-Raphaelities up the social and moral scale to Gladstone. Several of Rossetti's poems deal with women who have been seduced and abandoned. Like **"Goblin Market,"** these poems are remarkably uncensorious, particularly in contrast to the sentimental cruelty of works like Dante Gabriel Rossetti's painting "Found" or his poem "Jenny," to which the name "Jeanie" in **"Goblin Market"** may allude. Rossetti treats such women sympathetically, reserving her scorn for the men. Thus in **"The Iniquity of the Fathers Upon the Children"** the speaker forgives the mother who does not dare to acknowledge her and blames her unknown father, and in **"Cousin Kate"** and **"Light Love"** illegitimate children cause their mothers more pride than shame. The speaker in "Jenny" compares the prostitute to "a rose shut in a book / In which pure women may not look" and contrasts her with his virtuous cousin:

> Of the same lump (as it is said)
> For honour and dishonour made,
> Two sister vessels. Here is one.
>
> It makes a goblin of the sun.[10]

"Sister," "vessels," and "goblin" all suggest **"Goblin Market."** For Christina Rossetti, however, sin does not necessarily cancel sisterhood, and she thought like Barrett Browning that women should know and write about such things. In the 1860's she spent a considerable amount of time at a "Home for Fallen Women,"[11] a form of social welfare work that allowed respectable middle-class women to read in the "book" that Gabriel's "Jenny" says "pure women" may not look into. So Lizzie, emboldened by love for her sister, "for the first time in her life / Began to listen and look" (ll. 327-328); and what she sees does not, in the end, hurt her. Laura's heated imagination inhabits the erotic world of Pre-Raphaelite art, while Lizzie's imagination leads her towards—if not actually into—a realistic, socially responsible moral world like Barrett Browning's. Rossetti's defense of **"The Iniquity of the Fathers"** against Gabriel's disapproval can serve as a reply to "Jenny" and an explanation of **"Goblin Market:"**

> Whilst I endorse your opinion of the unavoidable and indeed much-to-be-desired unreality of women's work on many social matters, I yet incline to include within female range such an attempt as this: where the certainly possible circumstances are merely indicated as it were in skeleton.... Moreover the sketch only gives the girl's own deductions, feelings... and whilst it may truly be urged that unless white could be black and Heaven Hell my experience (thank God) precludes me from hers, I yet don't see why "the Poet mind" should be less able to construct her from its own inner consciousness than a hundred other unknown quantities.[12]

Lizzie's rescue of Laura, the main action of the poem, has several aspects. As in *The Ancient Mariner* redemption comes—thirst is sated—through imaginative identification analogous to the poet's own. Primarily, however, it is an heroic exploit. Lizzie stands firm under attack like a large, substantial object, mixing male and female qualities: a lily, a rock, a beacon, an orange-tree, a beleaguered town (ll. 409-421). It is a triumph of cleverness and daring: she would not open her mouth, she made no bargain, she "laughed in heart" (l. 433) while the goblins attacked her. She outwits them like a folktale heroine, getting their treasure without paying their price; the "bounce" of her unspent penny in her purse is "music to her ear" (l. 454), an image as much simply economic as sexual. She runs home in the sheer physical pleasure of strength and freedom, impelled not by fear (l. 460) but by joy and filled again with "inward laughter" (l. 463). As her laughter indicates, her story has to do not with temptation resisted—neither the goblins nor their fruit attract her, and what she is resisting is attempted rape—but with danger braved and overcome, an heroic deed accomplished.

She brings the "fiery antidote" (l. 559) and she *is* the antidote. She brings proof that the goblin fruit is bitter, and she offers as an alternative both a gift of love and an example of a better way of life. She brings back "'the fruit forbidden'" (l. 479) without tasting it herself—that is, she shows that it is possible in erotic and artistic matters, if not in Genesis, to know good and evil and not succumb to evil. "'Eat me, drink me, love me'" (l. 471): like Christ, she saves both by her self-sacrifice and by her example. "The next Christ will perhaps be a female Christ," Florence Nightingale wrote in *Cassandra;* "at last there shall arise a woman, who will resume, in his own soul, all the sufferings of her race, and that woman will be the Saviour of her race."[13] The speaker in Rossetti's **"From House to Home,"** written shortly before **"Goblin Market,"** is saved from despair after losing her paradise of love by a vision of a woman suffering torment like the crucifixion. In simpler terms, the moral is a good Victorian one, familiar from many novels: moral and emotional salvation comes from a loving response to selfless love.

"'Hug me, kiss me, suck my juices'," cries Lizzie (l. 468), and Laura "kissed and kissed her with a hungry mouth" (l. 492). The eroticism troubles many readers; we are more nervous about manifestations of affection between women than Victorians were, and we find it hard to allow a nineteenth-century religious poet the conflation of spiritual and erotic intensity that we accept without question in Crashaw or Donne.[14] Calmer traditional images of eating and drinking are used to exemplify the relation of Christ to mankind in several of the devotional poems published with **"Goblin Market"** (**"The Love of Christ Which Passeth Knowledge,"** ll. 9-12; **"A Bruised Reed Shall He Not Break,"** l.4; **"A Better Resurrection,"** ll. 17-24; **"Advent,"** ll. 31-32). Embodying this symbolic relationship in two women evokes strange overtones. But there is nothing erotic in Lizzie's jubilant shouts of triumph, heroic boasting even: "'Laura, make much of me: / For your sake I have braved the glen'" (ll. 472-473). Laura's reaction is excessive, but the excess here as in her gluttonous sucking at the fruit is part of the evil as well as its cure. She falls into a highly stylized, rather Biblical frenzy that is like a ritual of exorcism:

> Writhing as one possessed she leaped and sung,
> Rent all her robe, and wrung
> Her hands in lamentable haste,
> And beat her breast.
>
> (ll. 496-499)

Then, "Pleasure past and anguish past" (l. 522)—the mixture of pleasure and pain, poison and delight characteristic of Pre-Raphaelite formulations of alluring, evil love—she falls senseless, almost dies, and is reborn at dawn into the natural cycle of life: chirping birds, reapers, dewy grass and buds, and moderate behavior. She "Hugged Lizzie but not twice or thrice" (l. 539).

The full meaning of the story, however, is seen in its consequences. "Afterwards, when both were wives" (l. 544), Laura would tell their children about the goblins and how her sister "stood / In deadly peril to do her good" (ll. 557-558), and then,

> joining hands to little hands
> Would bid them cling together,
> "For there is no friend like a sister."
>
> (ll. 560-562)

The story thus completed is clear and simple in its essential structure: two girls live alone; they encounter goblin men; they have children. Except for the word "wives," which legitimizes the children, there is no mention of any men but the goblins, who are explicitly male. The children are apparently all girls and are exhorted to keep the female circle closed and complete. This is a world in which men serve only the purpose of impregnation. Once both sisters have gone to the goblins and acquired the juices of their fruits, they have no further need of them.

Many of Rossetti's poems and stories suggest that the fantasy of such a world might well attract her. *Sing-Song*, for instance, is filled with a yearning for children that is so intense as to be painful:

> Motherless baby and babyless mother,
> Bring them together to love one another.
>
> My baby has a mottled fist,
>   My baby has a neck in creases;
>   My baby kisses and is kissed.[15]

In **"Commonplace"** childlessness is regarded as a terrible sorrow, and the death of children, a recurrent motif in her writings, is the worst of calamities (see **"Eve," "Vanna's Twins,"** and much of *Sing-Song*). Relationships between mothers and babies and between women, usually sisters, are central to her poems and stories, whereas men are generally peripheral or absent; often the relationship is the darker side of the sisterly coin, competitiveness and envy, but even then it is a source of dramatic excitement and energy. Marriage is seldom depicted as wholly desirable. **"A Triad"** gives the most negative view, telling of three women:

> One shamed herself in love; one temperately
>   Grew gross in soulless love, a sluggish
>   wife;
> One famished died for love.
>
> (ll. 9-11)

In **"Maude Clare"** the speaker denounces her lover, who is marrying another woman; he quakes inarticulately with shame, but Nell (the name, perhaps significantly, of the virtuous cousin in Gabriel's "Jenny") answers her:

> "Yea, tho' you're taller by the head,
>   More wise, and much more fair;
> I'll love him till he loves me best."
>
> (ll. 45-47)

Maude Clare is strong, proud, and bold, while a good wife is humble, unambitious, uncensorious, and loving, like Nell: virtues that most of Rossetti's speakers find almost impossible to attain and hard even to praise, although admitting that in fact they lead to happiness. The speaker in "The Lowest Room" who reads Homer and is restless with her "'aimless life'" (l. 81) ends up unmarried, bitterly envious of her sister's cosy family—which a woman who is not content with a woman's lot cannot, evidently, hope for. But such discontent is a strong and persistent undercurrent in Rossetti's poems, and a good deal of poetic and moral energy goes into resisting it. She was encouraged to resist it, too: her brother Gabriel saw in **"The Lowest Room"** a "taint" of "falsetto muscularity" which he attributed to the influence of Barrett Browning and thought "utterly foreign" to his sister's "primary impulses."[16]

As in "Goblin Market," however, Rossetti sometimes imagines other alternatives than soft domesticity, resentful loneliness, and "falsetto muscularity." In *Maude* (written in 1850) the only mode of life the heroine admires is that of a friend who joins an Anglican sisterhood and is seen just once more "walking with some poor children," "thoughtful, but very calm and happy";[17] like Laura and Lizzie, she has both sisterhood and children. Rossetti was much attracted to sisterhoods; her work with fallen women made her an "Associate" of one, and in 1873 her older sister Maria became an Anglican nun, as she had long wanted to do—and thereby (as Lona Mosk Packer points out, p. 304) left the seclusion and limited sphere of home and entered a wider and busier world. The Anglican sisterhoods, like the central fantasy of "Goblin Market," satisfied the need that haunts *Maude* and such poems as "The Lowest Room," "A Royal Princess," and "Maggie a Lady": the need for a sphere of significant activity, combined with emotional fulfillment, within the limits of women's traditional roles. In 1854 Rossetti wanted to join Florence Nightingale in her Crimean venture—that apotheosis of a traditionally feminine activity into strenuous, serious, public deeds—but was rejected as too young. She thought that motherhood, too, could confer heroic strength and even masculine status: "I do think if anything ever does sweep away the barrier of sex, and make the female not a giantess or a heroine but at once and full grown a hero and giant, it is that mighty maternal love which makes little birds and little beasts as well as little women matches for very big adversaries."[18] Unwed mothers, furthermore, are among the strongest figures in her poetry ("Cousin Kate," "Light Love"), and female strength often goes with rejecting a man, as in "Maude Clare" and "No, Thank You, John" (in which Gabriel found the objectionable Barrett Browning "taint" recurring).[19] Virgin saints also offered a model of female independence. In *Time Flies*, Rossetti tells of St. Etheldreda, who remained virgin through two marriages and "after twelve years of successful contest, ended strife by separating from her enamoured husband." "Thus she fought the battle of life," Rossetti comments, carrying out the martial image, "thus she triumphed." Having escaped from husbands, Etheldreda founded and ruled "a monastery for men and women."[20] She is evidently one of Rossetti's favorite saints.

A world of female potency and exclusively female happiness appears in Rossetti's works only covertly, as fantasy, and in clearly unrealistic modes: ballads, fairy tales, and legends of saints. Her lyrics generally keep to conventional lyric themes, and when women in her narrative poems lose or leave their lovers, religion is usually their only solace. She accepted these limitations, writing with some wryness to her brother Gabriel in 1870:

> It is impossible to go on singing out-loud to one's one-stringed lyre. It is not in me, and therefore it will never come out of me, to turn to politics or philanthropy with Mrs. Browning: such many-sidedness I leave to a greater than I, and, having said my say, may well sit silent. . . . Here is a great discovery, "Women are not Men," and you must not expect me to possess a tithe of your capacities, though I humbly—or proudly—lay claim to family-likeness.[21]

Religious belief both curbed her ambition and offered escape from the restrictions imposed by her sex. Her didactic and devotional works assert women's inferiority with relentless stringency and with an undertone of rebellion and pain that she finds hard to subdue; but part of the comfort she finds in religion is the promise that in the soul's relation to Christ gender, finally, does not matter. She says in *Seek and Find*: "if our proud waves will after all . . . not be allayed (for stayed they must be) by the limit of God's ordinance concerning our sex, one final consolation yet remains to careful and troubled hearts: in Christ there is neither male nor female, for we are all one."[22]

The optimistic plot of "Goblin Market" reappears, however, in *Speaking Likenesses* (1874), an unpretentious little book of three fairy tales told in one narrative frame by a very prim aunt to her nieces. In the first story a little girl finds herself at a fantastic party with terrible children who torment her as the goblins do Lizzie and whose marvellously tempting food she does not eat; from this she learns to put up with the normally unpleasant children at her birthday party. In the second a little girl goes into the woods and tries unsuccessfully, with the help of friendly but ineffectual animals, to boil a kettle for tea; she learns that she cannot manage to live alone. In the third story a little girl walking through the woods on a generous errand refuses to join the terrible children's party, to feed or eat with a monstrous boy whose face has only a huge mouth, or to fall asleep with a band of gypsies. The way is cold and difficult and the recipients of her generosity are ungrateful, but she completes her errands. Apparently as a reward, she finds a pigeon, a kitten, and a puppy which she brings back to her cosy house and loving grandmother. As in "Goblin Market," resistance to male figures which attract some sympathy and yet repel and refusal to eat their food or join their dreams are parts of a painful and strenuous quest that frees the heroine both from a disagreeable social world of males and females together (as in the first story) and from helplessness (as in the second), and leaves two women self-sufficient and happy with baby creatures to care for. The frame is conventional, repressive, and moralistic, but the unstated theme is not.

Much of Rossetti's poetry presents frustrated, unhappy women yearning for love. **"Goblin Market,"** in contrast, shows women testing the allurements of male sexuality and exploring the imaginative world that male eroticism has created. By entering but finally rejecting that world, they discover that a woman can be strong, bold, and clever, Christ-like in active self-sacrifice as well as in silent endurance, and that sisters and daughters can live happy lives together. For Rossetti this may have been as unrealizable a dream as the variously uninhabitable realms of art imagined by Keats and his Victorian followers; but it was a dream that sought to integrate passion and art into life and not, as critics often say, merely to reject or repress them. Sexuality is not repressed in the poem—it is quite evidently and undisguisedly there—but its proper function is shown to be the generation of children and literary works. Laura turns the encounter with the goblins into a tale told and retold as a ritual to bind the children together, and the moral she draws from it is not that girls should avoid goblins—the sisters seem to remember them, in fact, with some pleasure—but that "'there is no friend like a sister'" (l. 562). Similarly, the imaginative experience of the goblin world appears to generate the poem that includes and goes beyond it. Rossetti's sense of poetical possibilities was restricted by Pre-Raphaelite assumptions about the subjects, moods, and tones appropriate to art, but in **"Goblin Market"** she shows that the erotic and imaginative intensity cultivated by the Brotherhood need not be self-enclosing, all-engrossing, or male. The energy, freedom, and easy control of the fluent irregular meter (which seems to have shocked Ruskin with its apparent waywardness)[23] reflect Rossetti's triumphant appropriation of Pre-Raphaelite materials for her own purposes. She uses a literary form, furthermore, that purports to be nothing more serious than a tale told by a woman to amuse and instruct children; the form, like the content, seems to betray an assumption that women can only be grown-up, independent, productive, and active in a life without men.

Notes

[1] *The Pre-Raphaelite Poets* (Univ. of North Carolina Press, 1972), p. 105. Winston Weathers gives the fullest explication of the sisters as two halves of one self in "Christina Rossetti: The Sisterhood of Self," *VP*, 3 (1965), 81-89.

[2] Citations from the poems unless otherwise specified are from *The Complete Poems of Christina Rossetti: A Variorum Edition*, ed. R. W. Crump (Louisiana State Univ. Press, 1979), I.

[3] A. A. DeVitis sees the sisters as two halves of an artist in "*Goblin Market*: Fairy Tale and Reality," *JPC*, I (1967), 418-426. The poem is read as showing, in part, growth into adulthood and the development of female autonomy by Martine Watson Brownley in "Love and Sensuality in Christina Rossetti's 'Goblin Market'," *ELWIU*, 6 (1979), 179-186; Ellen Golub in "Untying Goblin Apron Strings: A Psychoanalytic Reading of 'Goblin Market'," *L&P*, 25 (1975), 158-165; and Miriam Sagan in "Christina Rossetti's 'Goblin Market' and Feminist Literary Criticism," *PRR*, 3 (1980), 66-76. Sandra M. Gilbert and Susan Gubar find hints of "an effectively matrilineal and matriarchal world" as well as "bitter repressive wisdom" in *The Madwoman in the Attic: The Woman Writer and the Nineteenth-Century Literary Imagination* (Yale Univ. Press, 1979), pp. 567, 573. William T. Going shows that the poem draws significantly on the life of the Pre-Raphaelite Brotherhood in "'Goblin Market' and the Pre-Raphaelite Brotherhood," *PRR*, 3 (1979), I-II, and Jerome J. McGann analyzes it as an enactment of the sisters' discovery that they need not be emotionally dependent on goblin men in "Christina Rossetti's Poems: A New Edition and a Revaluation," *VS*, 23 (1980), 237-254.

[4] Weathers says that the goblins tempt to "a kind of imaginative, fanciful, visionary—even hallucinatory—state of mind" (p. 82), and Lona Mosk Packer sees it as (in Rossetti's own words) "'the seduction of imaginative emotion'" (*Christina Rossetti* [Univ. of California Press, 1963], p. 145). Gilbert and Gubar suggest that the fruits are works of art (pp. 568-570).

[5] *Commonplace, and Other Short Stories* (London, 1870), p. 149.

[6] In her edition of "Goblin Market" (New York, 1975), Germaine Greer notes the likeness and makes it more impressive by calling Laura and Lizzie by each other's names (p. xxxi and passim). Violet Hunt associates Lizzie with Maria Rossetti and Laura with Christina herself. The story she tells is highly implausible (that Maria kept Christina from eloping by crouching for several nights on the door mat), but some general allusion to Maria, to whom the poem is dedicated, seems likely. See Violet Hunt, *The Wife of Rossetti: Her Life and Death* (New York, 1932), p. xiii.

[7] *Literary Women* (Garden City, N. Y., 1976), p. 105.

[8] Violet Hunt's characterization of her suggests that such opinions were held by some Pre-Raphaelites; see *The Wife of Rossetti*, pp. xii-xiii, 45, 58.

[9] Thomas Burnett Swann points out that they are like fairy-tale princesses in *Wonder and Whimsy: The Fantastic World of Christina Rossetti* (Francestown, New Hampshire, 1960), pp. 103, 105. Readings of the fairy-tale element in terms of repressed eroticism are given by Stephen Prickett in *Victorian Fantasy* (Indiana Univ. Press, 1979), pp. 103-106, and Maureen Duffy in *The Erotic World of Faery* (London, 1972), pp. 288-291.

[10] "Jenny," *The Works of Dante Gabriel Rossetti*, ed. William M. Rossetti (London, 1911).

[11] Packer notes the connection between "Goblin Market" and this welfare work, p. 154.

[12] *Three Rossettis: Unpublished Letters to and from Dante Gabriel, Christina, William*, ed. Janet Camp Troxell (Harvard Univ. Press, 1937), p. 143.

[13] *Cassandra*, ed. Myra Stark (Old West bury, 1979), pp. 53, 50. *Cassandra* was written in 1852.

[14] Greer finds the poem "deeply perverse" (p. xxxvi). Brownley says, "Her sexual fall requires a sexual redemption" (p. 183). Cora Kaplan finds the poem "an exploration of women's sexual fantasy which includes suggestions of masochism, homoeroticism, rape or incest" ("The Indefinite Disclosed: Christina Rossetti and Emily Dickinson," in *Women Writing and Writing About Women*, ed. Mary Jacobus [London, 1979], p. 69). None of these critics thinks that Rossetti knew what she was doing when she wrote passages like this.

[15] *Sing-Song, Speaking Likenesses, Goblin Market*, ed. R. Loring Taylor (New York, 1976), pp. 125, 23.

[16] *Letters of Dante Gabriel Rossetti*, ed. Oswald Doughty and John Robert Wahl (Oxford, 1967), III, 1380.

[17] *Maude: Prose & Verse* (Chicago, 1897), p. 83.

[18] Mackenzie Bell, *Christina Rossetti: A Biographical and Critical Study* (Boston, 1898), p. 124.

[19] *Letters*, III, 1380.

[20] *Time Flies: A Reading Diary* (Boston, 1886), p. 244. As a child Rossetti would have read the legend in Hone's *Every-Day Book*.

[21] *The Family Letters of Christina Georgina Rossetti*, ed. William Michael Rossetti (London, 1908), p. 31.

[22] *Seek and Find: A Double Series of Short Studies of the Benedicite* (New York, [1897]), p. 32.

[23] See William Michael Rossetti, ed., *Ruskin: Rossetti: Pre-Raphaelitism: Papers 1854 to 1862* (London, 1899), pp. 258-259.

Jeanie Watson (essay date 1984)

SOURCE: "'Men Sell Not Such in Any Town': Christina Rossetti's Goblin Fruit of Fairy Tale," in *Children's Literature*, Vol. 12, Yale University Press, 1984, pp. 61-77.

[*In the following essay, Watson maintains that while the Christian allegorical framework of "Goblin Market" is the means by which the story is made "acceptable," the fairy tale subtext of the poem subverts the Christian moral of renunciation and extolls the virtues of imagination and knowledge.*]

Although **"Goblin Market"** has long enjoyed a reputation as one of the finest of children's poems[1] and has repeatedly been labeled a fairy tale, in line with Christina Rossetti's own insistence on this point, there has been no serious, extensive consideration of **"Goblin Market"** as a children's poem drawing upon the themes and forms of traditional children's literature. This is true because, in large part, readers from the beginning to the present have had difficulty concentrating on anything other than the framework of Christian allegory—a more "adult" genre—which is so apparent in the poem. This overriding critical attention to the allegorical moral, while it has produced a number of instructive and illuminating readings, has been less than entirely satisfactory. It is the contention of this essay that only by viewing **"Goblin Market"** as a tale for children, a tale which is structurally based on the interweaving of the predominant nineteenth-century strands of children's literature—the fairy tale and the moral tale—can the poem's true moral, for children and adults, be understood. Further, it is the interplay between moral tale and fairy tale that allows **"Goblin Market's"** thematic statement to be utterly subversive and yet ultimately moral.

I

In 1898, Mackenzie Bell, Christina Rossetti's early biographer, quotes Christina's surviving brother as having written: "I have more than once heard C[hristina] aver that the poem has not any profound or ulterior meaning—it is just a fairy story: yet one can discern that it implies at any rate this much—that to succumb to a temptation makes one a victim to that same continuous temptation; that the remedy does not always lie with oneself; and that a stronger and more righteous will may prove of avail to restore one's lost estate."[2] The ambivalent reaction to the dual elements of fairy tale and allegory are neatly summarized by Bell's commentary on a contemporary critic:

> James Ashcroft Noble, in a penetrating essay called "The Burden of Christina Rossetti," . . . says that "'Goblin Market' may be read and enjoyed merely as a charming fairy-fantasy, and as such it is delightful and satisfying; but behind the simple story of two children and the goblin fruit-sellers is a little spiritual drama of love's vicarious redemption, in which the child redeemer goes into the wilderness to be tempted of the devil, that by her painful conquest she may succour and save the sister who has been vanquished and all but slain. The luscious juices of the goblin fruit, bitter and deadly when

sucked by selfish greed, become bitter and medicinal when spilt in unselfish conflict." This is admirably and eloquently put, but it may be questioned whether the critic has not perhaps somewhat overstated the case for didacticism in the poem. [pp. 206-07]

With only a few dissenting voices,[3] the moral of **"Goblin Market"** has, then, from the beginning been seen primarily within the framework of the Christian allegory of temptation, fall, and redemption. The goblin fruits become the forbidden fruit of Genesis and Revelation, the fruit of illicit sensuality. Knowing she should not, Laura trafficks with the goblin men, buys their fruit with a golden curl and a single tear. Having once eaten of the fruit, she is no longer a maiden and can no longer hear the goblins' cry, "Come buy, come buy" (1.4).[4] She is saved from death only by the redemptive act of her sister Lizzie. Laura's commentary at the end that "there is no friend like a sister" becomes a tribute to Lizzie's saving love.

The moral is very clearly stated and seems to fit the allegorical redemption:

> For there is no friend like a sister
> In calm or stormy weather;
> To cheer one on the tedious way,
> To fetch one if one goes astray,
> To lift one if one totters down,
> To strengthen whilst one stands.
>
> [ll. 562-67]

It *should* be a neat and satisfactory ending, but it is not. Indeed, far from being satisfactory, the allegorical moral makes many readers very uncomfortable, although they cannot readily explain their lack of ease. Eleanor Walter Thomas, a Rossetti biographer, writes about an early critic who sounds frustrated, almost angry: "The critic, F. A. Rudd, wrote paragraph after paragraph in solemn condemnation of the fantastic **'Goblin Market'** as immoral: he could find not a syllable in the poem to show that yielding to evil as incarnate in the goblins was at all wrong in itself. What is the moral? he weightily inquires. 'Not resist the devil and he will flee from you, but cheat the devil and he won't catch you. Now all these sayings and silences are gravely wrong and false to a writer's true functions.'"[5] Similarly, other readers simply do not believe that the poem says what the allegory says it says. They argue that rather than condemning physical passion, the story of Laura and Lizzie celebrates that passion: "Temptation, in both its human and theological sense, is the thematic core of **'Goblin Market'**. . . . **'Goblin Market'** celebrates by condemning sensuous passion."[6] In the same vein, Ellen Golub says: "Rossetti seems to condemn such [sexual] passion, but in her condemnation she offers much description of it. Eros being very much present, it is the seduction of girls by goblins which engages reader attention."[7]

Those who are able to accept the moral at face value either have the courage of an appalling lack of sensibility (for example, "The most charming scene of all is that of the sisters, grown to woman's estate, telling their own children of their terrific adventure" [Meigs, p. 291]), or they read the lines as an accommodation to the prevailing status of women, and women writers in particular, in Victorian times, the very necessity of that accommodation calling forth a proud and defiant independence. Jerome J. McGann argues that the goblins represent the Victorian marketplace, "institutionalized patterns of social destructiveness operating in nineteenth-century England" that promise women fulfillment of their desires through love and marriage, promises which are illusionary and by which women are betrayed.[8] But, continues McGann, "the poem is unusual in Christina Rossetti's canon in that it has developed a convincing positive symbol for an alternative, uncorrupted mode of social relations—the love of sisters" (p. 250). Gilbert and Gubar also see Rossetti as making a virtue of necessity: "Christina Rossetti and, to a lesser extent, Elizabeth Barrett Browning build their art on a willing acceptance of passionate or demure destitution. They . . . are the nineteenth-century women singers of renunciation as necessity's highest and noblest virtue."[9] Gilbert and Gubar discuss the important connection which **"Goblin Market"** sets up between "the unnatural but honey-sweet fruit of art" and the "luscious fruit of self-gratifying sensual pleasure" (p. 570), and they rightly assert that "the fruit of **'Goblin Market'** has fed on the desirous substrata of the psyche, the childishly self-gratifying fantasies of the imagination." But, they conclude, since "young ladies like Laura, Maude, and Christina Rossetti should not loiter in the glen of imagination, which is the haunt of goblin men like Keats and Tennyson," they must learn "the lesson of renunciation" and feed on "bitter repressive wisdom, the wisdom of necessity's virtue, in order to be redeemed" (p. 573).

As insightful as many of these readings of **"Goblin Market"** are, they still do not banish our discomfort over the ending of the poem. That this is so is because, finally, Christina Rossetti does not want us to be comfortable. It may well be that Victorian institutions necessitate a positive sisterly alliance in a male-less world. And it may be that women's sexuality and creative impulses are systematically and severely repressed. But Rossetti does not believe that it should be so. To be redeemed in this kind of world is to be damned. **"Goblin Market"** is an extremely subversive poem which, while acknowledging the "wisdom of necessity's virtue," refuses to accept it, insisting instead on the right to dearly bought goblin fruit. This stance is made possible through Rossetti's choice of form for the poem: the interplay of fairy tale and moral tale. This interplay subverts the accepted moral into the immoral and makes imaginative knowledge the only righteousness acceptable.

II

Mary F. Thwaite, in her history of children's books, *From Primer to Pleasure in Reading,* lauds **"Goblin Market"** by saying: "With Christina Rossetti . . . the children's muse found the crystal springs of true poetry. There had been nothing of the quality of her lyrics for the young since *Songs of Innocence.* Finest of all is her fairy poem 'Goblin Market'. . . . Both the theme and the style are fascinating, expressed with a lilt and pace new in children's verse" (p. 135). Although the poem may appear to be something new, its form is firmly rooted in two traditional genres of children's literature. **"Goblin Market"** is, as Christina Rossetti repeatedly insisted, a fairy tale. But the poem is also a moral tale. Both genres have had a long history in children's literature, and both were popular in Rossetti's time. That she was familiar with the whole range of moral tales and fairy tales is clear from her own and others' accounts of her youthful reading.[10] However, the forms are essentially antithetical, one being used for didactic purposes to teach children proper spiritual and social conduct, the other being secular or amoral, or even immoral, in its lesson.

Moral tales of the mid-nineteenth century, some of which emphasized a virtuous life founded on right conduct and some of which were unabashedly religious in their didacticism, had their source in the emblem books, Christian allegories, and stories of saints and martyrs of earlier centuries. The subsequent evolution of the moral tale occurred in response to social and philosophical changes, stimulated by the theories of John Locke, who held that books for children should be pleasant and entertaining to read. Morality and right conduct were seen as more important than knowledge, and reason as preferable to imagination. "Fairies and fairy lore, 'goblins and spirits'; with other superstitions, he [Locke] regarded as belonging to the useless trumpery. Imagination and enthusiasm were to be avoided— as were unintelligible ideas about God, the Supreme Being whom children should be taught to love and reverence. The sober light of reason and common-sense was to illumine the child's life" (Thwaite, p. 34).[11]

The strictures against fairy tales, which had caused them to be available for many years primarily only in chapbooks, had, by the end of the eighteenth century, been eased by the tales being transformed—albeit through truncation and softening—into models for moral instruction. The fairy tale, thus bowdlerized, became domesticated and acceptable. "The moralizing of fairy tales (when they were admitted by the creators of juvenile literature at this period) was recognized as a cunning method of utilizing for good the youthful predilection for the fabulous" (Thwaite, p. 72). Still, reputable English editions of the Perrault tales were published in the last half of the eighteenth century, and *German Popular Stories,* or *Grimm's Fairy Tales,* was published in English in two volumes (1823-26). Therefore, by mid-nineteenth century, legitimate fairy tales were readily available.

In **"Goblin Market,"** Christina Rossetti combines the social and religious forms of the nineteenth-century moral tale, making the religious allegory seem to serve the social function of warning against any illicit desire or action outside the boundaries accepted by society. At the same time, the context for this moral tale is the goblin fairy tale, precisely the imaginative, out-of-bounds kind of story that had aroused so much suspicion.[12] Rossetti uses these two popular, but embattled, forms for her own purposes, simultaneously diffusing and intensifying the true moral of her poem by making it a poem for children.

The musical lilt and fast-paced narrative of **"Goblin Market,"** the short, easily read lines and the concrete, sensory imagery of color, taste, sound, and texture all argue for the poem's special appeal to children, as do also the fantastic goblin creatures and the fairy "haunted glen" (l. 552). But it is not only on the level of the Victorian child as audience that **"Goblin Market"** is a tale for children. within the poem itself, the story of Laura and Lizzie's encounter with the goblins is the story told the children, time after enraptured time, by the maiden turned mother. The tale that Laura lived becomes the tale her children—and we—hear. There is a shift in critical perspective when we listen as a child to the poem. What seduces us into wanting to hear the story again and again is not the moral tale warning but the same thing that enthralls the children and seduced Laura: the goblin fruit of a fairy tale. The overt text of the moral tale makes the story "acceptable"; the subtext of the fairy tale presents Rossetti's moral. And we believe the fairy tale.

III

"Goblin Market"'s Laura and Lizzie live in the safe and orderly daytime world of the moral tale in which one event follows another in predictable, simple fashion:

> Early in the morning
> When the first cock crowed his warning,
> Neat like bees, as sweet and busy,
> Laura rose with Lizzie:
> Fetched in honey, milked the cows,
> Aired and set to rights the house,
> Kneaded cakes of whitest wheat,
> Cakes for dainty mouths to eat,
> Next churned butter, whipped up cream,
> Fed their poultry, sat and sewed;
> Talked as modest maidens should:
> [ll. 199-209]

In this domestic scene, work, common sense, and right conduct prevail, and the moral tale assures us that this, indeed, is the way things ought to be. The maidens' orderly lives are lived within boundaries, a life of milk and honey, cakes and cream, wholesome food of innocence and righteousness. They are, in fact, as Rossetti makes clear through her verbal allusions, following the moral percept of Isaac Watts's well-known poem "Against Idleness and Mischief," published in 1715 as one of his *Divine Songs for Children:*

> How doth the little busy bee
> Improve each shining hour,
> And gather honey all the day
> From every opening flower![13]

The admonition to be as neat as the bee is followed by the warning that Satan will find mischief for idle hands. Presumably, as long as one is industrious, one is safe. However, Laura has always been busy as a bee, and still she has eaten goblin fruit. In addition, it is after her eating of the fruit that the passage comparing the sisters to bees occurs. It is not until Laura realizes that she cannot have more goblin fruit that

> She no more swept the house,
> Tended the fowls or cows,
> Fetched honey, kneaded cakes of wheat,
> Brought water from the brook:
> But sat down listless in the chimney-nook
> And would not eat.
>
> [ll. 293-98]

If Laura cannot have the goblin fruit, she will not eat the cake and honey either.

There is other evidence as well that the overt didacticism of the moral tale is at variance the actual message of the poem, that the fairy tale, in other words, is subverting the moral tale. By not doing her chores, Laura leaves herself open to the punishment warned against in country superstition for those who do not keep their houses clean and tidy—to be pinched by the fairies. Although a visit by the goblins is precisely what Laura desires, they do not come to her. It is, instead, Lizzie who is pinched "black as ink," having offered the goblins the payment of a "silver penny" (ll. 427, 324)—the traditional reward left in the shoe of the neat housekeeper. The moral tale sequence of cause and effect and the usual admonitory system of punishments do not seem to hold in the expected way. We are in the out-of-bounds world of fairy tale rather than the orderly world of the moral tale.

Wariness of **"Goblin Market"**'s moral tale message increases when we recall another instance from the earlier moral tale tradition of the bee's being used for moral instruction. In 1686, John Bunyan published *A Book for Boys and Girls; or Country Rhimes for Children.* This book, known in the mid-nineteenth-century as *Divine Emblems; Or Temporal Things Spiritualized,* has as one of its figures the bee:

> Upon the Bee
> The Bee goes out and Honey home doth bring;
> And some who seek that Honey find a sting.
> Now wouldst thou have the Honey and be free
> From stinging; in the first place kill the Bee.
>
> Comparison
> This Bee an Emblem truly is of sin
> Whose sweet unto a many death hath been.
> Now wouldst have Sweet from sin, and yet not dye,
> Do thou it in the first place mortifie.[14]

In his poem on the busy bee, Watts had domesticated the bee, turning it into an example of industry and order. Rossetti, through the force of her fairy tale, undercuts this meaning and goes back to Bunyan's earlier identification of the bee with sin. Bunyan advises those who wish the honey without the sting to first kill the bee. The fruits of the goblin men are "like honey to the throat / But poison in the blood" (ll. 554-55). The words are spoken by Laura at the end of **"Goblin Market,"** and like the speaker in Bunyan's poem, she has wished to divide the honey from the sting. The moral of Rossetti's poem is that one who would have the sweet "and yet not dye" must "in the first place mortifie" the neat and busy little bee of the moral tale. Goblin gifts often bring a curse with them;[15] in this case, the curse is the painful death of the view which the moral tale embodies.

In **"Goblin Market,"** the bounded and orderly world of cottage and domesticity is juxtaposed to the "haunted glen" of "wicked quaint fruit-merchant men" (ll. 552 53). Traditionally, goblins were "evil and malicious spirits, usually small and grotesque in appearance,"[16] who were known "to tempt mortals to their undoing" (Thwaite, p. 135). The temptation in **"Goblin Market"** is to leave the world of moral tale and enter the world of fairy tale. Katherine Briggs notes in *The Faeries in English Tradition and Literature* that "the plot of ['**Goblin Market**'] is a variant of three main fairy themes: the danger of peeping at the fairies, the TABOO against eating FAIRY FOOD, and the rescue from Fairyland" (p. 193). Christina Rossetti's original title for the poem was *A Peep at the Fairies,* indicating perhaps that the poem is her own dangerous peep at the fairies, despite the injunctions against such a look.

True fairy tales often bear little resemblance to light, delightful fantasies; in fact, they are stories of abandonment, betrayal, violence, and irrationality. To enter the world of fairy tales is to enter a world different from the world of order and reason and common sense which we inhabit in our daytime lives; there are ordering principles in fairy tales, but they operate the boundaries of ordinary life. As Bettelheim argues, "The 'truth' of fairy stories is the truth of our imagination, not that of moral causality."[17] Fairy tales are "spiritual explorations" and hence "the most life-like," revealing "human life as seen, or felt, or divined from the inside."[18] The world of fairy tale is a world of knowledge, knowledge not accessible within the limits of the real world. The real world limits us to the known; it is safe, rational, capable of empirical proof. The fairy tale world is the "long, long ago" world of infinite possibility, existent now only in and through the imagination. Entering into the realm of possibility is dangerous—for possibility includes both vision and nightmare—but necessary for wholeness. The risk of imagination is most assuredly a temptation, the risk of chaos for the possibility of knowledge which is truth, truth which is beauty.

The temptation of fairy tale is immediate and urgent in **"Goblin Market"**. Maidens are urged to eat the luscious fruits of the natural world, which are also, paradoxically and magically, the fruits of imaginative creativity. The fairy tale world is inhabited by creatures of the imagination, born out of the human psyche. Here, natural and supernatural meet. Here, there is a suspension of disbelief. Here is the place where the oxymoronic exists. In the fairy tale world, one risks going beyond the boundaries of empirical rationality to experience more fundamental and intuitive truths. The fairy tale world is tempting because it promises knowledge and because we sense the underlying truth of that knowledge. "Subjected to the rational teachings of others, the child only buries his 'true knowledge' deeper in his soul and it remains untouched by rationality" (Bettelheim, p. 46). It is this "true knowledge" that **"Goblin Market"** tempts us to, away from the rational teachings which limit and restrict the imagination. The cry of the goblin men is almost hypnotic in its rich catalogue of fruits so numerous as to be virtually unending. The kinds and quantities and combinations of taste and color are unlimited, appealing to the senses and to the possibilities of imagination. The fruits are all ripe to the bursting point and "All ripe together / In summer weather" (ll. 15-16); they are "full and fine," ready to "fill" the mouth (ll. 21, 28), very like "Joy's grape" of Keats's *Ode to Melancholy*:

> Joy, whose hand is ever at his lips
> Bidding adieu; and aching Pleasure nigh,
> Turning to Poison while the bee-mouth sips:
> [ll. 22-24][19]

Intensity of experience, whether sensual or imaginative, requires the reconciliation of opposites, Melancholy and Delight. Joy that dwells with Beauty is achieved only through the sacramental bursting of the grape. "Honey to the throat" and "Poison in the blood" are necessary accompaniments.

The "mossy glen" (l. 87) where maidens may hear the cry of goblin men is a haunted, fairy place with "brookside rushes" (l. 33), fertile and rich and erotic in its connotations. It is a place as much feminine as masculine. In addition, as Gilbert and Gubar point out, the glen "represents a chasm in the mind, analogous to that enchanted romantic chasm" (p. 570) of Coleridge's *Kubla Khan*, a "holy and enchanted" place, "haunted / By woman wailing for her demon lover!"[20] Coleridge's chasm is itself the fertile ground of the androgynous creative imagination. The goblin men, who presumably also eat the fruit they sell, are similar to Coleridge's poet of whom one should beware and around whom one should weave a circle thrice since "he on honeydew hath fed, / And drunk the milk of Paradise" (ll. 53-54). So Lizzie says, "We must not look at goblin men" (l. 42). The goblin men may be seen as androgynous creatures, unlike the men—or the women—of the town. Rossetti's liking for animals, especially unusual or bizarre ones,[21] should keep us from assuming that she intends us to see the appearance of the goblin men in a negative way. Rather, their form combines the parts of the masculine-rational-mind and feminine-animal passion-emotion traditional dichotomy. It is they who are the possessors of the sensuous fruits of the imagination, but they also desire that maidens buy the fruit. "We must not buy their fruits," says Laura. "Who knows upon what soil they fed / Their hungry thirsty roots?" (ll. 43-45). Since the fruit shapes are full and round, erotically masculine and feminine, the soil would seem to be the androgynous ground of creative imagination.

A number of critics have noted in passing the resemblance between Christina Rossetti's poetry and that of Coleridge.[22] *The Rime of the Ancient Mariner*, in both its similarities and dissimilarities, seems a particularly instructive gloss for **"Goblin Market"** since the same concerns are at issue in both poems. To begin with, the *Rime* and **"Goblin Market"** are both, broadly speaking, fairy tales. Both are journey stories, quests for the fruits of knowledge. The Mariner leaves the safe harbor of the rational and the known to enter, through an act of "irrationality," the world of fairy tale, that is, the world of the supernatural. Out-of-bounds and separated from the support provided by the dependable order of the natural world, community with his fellows, and a domesticated religious structure, he suffers the nightmare time of life-in-death. Finally, through an intuitive act of imagination and love, he perceives the beauty of the water snakes and the spell breaks. If one participates fully in the imaginative world, then that world is perceived in its wholeness and perceived as beautiful. Lack of participation shifts the perception so that the beautiful becomes ugly and destructive. In his spiritual alienation, the Mariner is repulsed by the crawling, slimy water snakes. Reconciled with, and by, the wholeness of love, he says, "No tongue / Their beauty might declare" (ll. 282-83). At last, he is spirited back to the safety of the land where he is compelled to tell his story to those who are receptive to its meaning.

Laura leaves the cottage and goes to the haunted glen. Despite all the warnings, she moves outside the limits of safety to buy with the coin of her body and the anguish of experience the fruits which cannot be had in any other way: "(Men sell not such in any town)" (l. 101). The goblin men invite maidens to "sit down and feast with us, / Be welcome guest with us" (ll. 380-81), and as long as the maidens do feast, the merchants' voices coo like doves and sound "kind and full of loves" (l. 79). It is only when Lizzie tries to give them back the silver fairy penny, in accordance with the moral tale, that the goblins revenge themselves on her. The punishing "rape" in which the goblin men try to force Lizzie to eat the fruit is a nightmare vision not unlike the "viper's thoughts" of the "dark dream" (ll. 94-95) summoned by the imaginative storm of Coleridge's *Dejection: An Ode.*

Laura, like the Mariner, becomes a storyteller, and the overt moral at the end of **"Goblin Market"** is strikingly similar to the moral at the end of the *Rime*:

> He prayeth best, who loveth best
> All things both great and small;
> For the dear God who loveth us,
> He made and loveth all.
>
> [ll. 614-17]

Both morals, childishly sing-songey in cadence and almost simple-minded in tone, sound disconcertingly inadequate to the reader as summary statements for the turmoil that has preceded them. In both cases, we as readers are supposed to understand more than the speaker. What the Mariner says is true, but truer than he can explain. What Laura says is true, but not true enough; her vision is insufficient and, therefore, true to the moral tale but not to the fairy tale. The Mariner is changed by his experience. His tale is a "ghastly" one, and his glittering eye holds the listener. Because his moral is true to the fairy tale, the listener, the Wedding-Guest, is also changed:

> He went like one that hath been stunned,
> And is of sense forlorn:
> A sadder and a wiser man,
> He rose the morrow morn.
>
> [ll. 622-25]

Laura and Lizzie repudiate the fruits of knowledge. They are neither sadder nor wiser the following morning. For a terrifying experience of grace, they substitute a formulaic religiosity. We believe the Mariner's moral, but we do not believe in the efficacy of Laura's. What we *do* believe in **"Goblin Market"** is the truth of the fairy tale. Laura and Lizzie are saved to their damnation, and we and Christina Rossetti know it, even if they do not. The whole poem then becomes a moral poem of a different kind, one in which the immoral moral triumphs.

To see with the eye of imagination is to be outside the safe confines of conventional life; it calls for perception and participation in whole vision. The institutions and cultural attitudes of Victorian society make goblin fruit forbidden to maidens—and almost kindly so: one taste of the fruit cuts them off from expected female domesticity, and yet they are not allowed full and continued feasting. "Must your light like mine be hidden / Your young life like mine be wasted," Laura asks Lizzie. The light of imagination must be hidden, and thus life is wasted. Girls like Jeanie, who eat the goblins' fruit and wear the crown of flowers, pine away in "noonlight" (l. 153), lost equally to the glen and to the town. Lizzie's intervention keeps Laura from Jeanie's fate, but the "salvation" scene is strangely ambiguous. Laura, admonished by Lizzie to "Hug me, kiss me, suck my juices" (l. 468), "Kissed and kissed and kissed her." And again, "She kissed and kissed her with a hungry mouth" (ll. 486, 492) in an orgy of hunger for goblin fruit. But at the same time that she writhes "as one possessed," leaping and singing in a frenzy of Dionysian ecstasy,[23] she "loathed the feast" and "gorged on bitterness without a name" (ll. 495-96, 510). Does the bitterness come from having eaten the fruit or from having to be saved from her desire for its taste? Similarly, who is speaking the lines, "Ah fool, to choose such part / Of soul-consuming care!" (ll. 511-12)— Laura or the narrator? And where, exactly, is the foolishness? There is a tone of longing even at the point of rejection. Laura has desired that which is forbidden her, though it should be hers by right. Perhaps what we hear in her voice is frustrated anger.

What is clear to the reader at the end of the poem is that the progression from innocence to experience and back to original innocence is no progression at all; it is at best, sad—we are the ones sadder and wiser—and at worst, immoral. Had Keats's Madeline in *The Eve of St. Agnes*[24] remained

> Blissfully havened both from joy and pain;
>
> . . . . .
>
> Blinded alike from sunshine and from rain,
> As though a rose should shut, and be a bud again,
>
> [ll. 240, 242-43]

she would have been lost. For a rose to become a bud again is no more natural than to regain one's innocence; therefore, Laura's salvation becomes ironic:

> Sense failed in the mortal strife:
> Like the watch-tower of a town
> Which an earthquake shatters down,
> Like a lightning-stricken mast,
> Like a wind up-rooted tree
> Spun about,

> Like a foam-topped waterspout
> Cast down headlong in the sea,
> She fell at last;
> Pleasure past and anguish past,
> Is it death or is it life?
>
> [ll. 513-23]

The Mariner falls "down in a swound" (392); when his "living life returned" (l. 394), he prays, "O let me be awake, my God! / Or let me sleep alway" (ll. 470-71). He awakes to speak of the unity of life. Laura, her sense having failed, chooses "Life out of death" and falls at last, past the possibilities of both pleasure and anguish, "Blinded alike from sunshine and from rain." She has become a bud again.

Fairy tales have traditionally been able to triumph over the morals attached to them. The moral tags may or may not fit the story; they may be cynical or comforting; they may disappear altogether.[25] But, as Christina Rossetti knows, the power of the story remains, impervious to attack, reaching out like Laura's own yearning after goblin fruit:

> Like a rush-imbedded swan,
> Like a lily from the beck,
> Like a moonlit poplar branch,
> Like a vessel at the launch
> When its last restraint is gone
>
> [ll. 82-86]

The power of the fairy tale remains as long as the story is told, passed down from generation to generation, whatever the intent of the teller. Thus,

> Laura would call the little ones
> And tell them of her early prime,
> Those pleasant days long gone
> Of not-returning time:
> Would talk about the haunted glen,
> The wicked quaint fruit-merchant men,
> Their fruits like honey to the throat
> But poison in the blood
> (Men sell not such in any town).
>
> [ll. 548-56]

The children listen—as do we—fascinated and intrigued by the story of the goblin men and their fruit. And Christina Rossetti, by letting her female character tell a fairy tale which delights and entertains as the children join "hands to little hands" (l. 560) to form a magic circle, affirms the truth of imagination and knowledge over conventional moral conduct. Maidens have the right to buy the fruit of Goblin Market.

Notes

[1] The following is typical commentary found in histories of children's literature: "In the midst of what was, for the most part, merely pleasant verse for children, Christina Rossetti (1830-1894) provided them with one real, one can even say, one great poem in 'Goblin Market' (1862)," in Cornelia Meigs, et al., *A Critical History of Children's Literature* (New York: The Macmillan Co., 1953), p. 290. See also Mary F. Thwaite, *From Primer to Pleasure in Reading* (Boston: Horn Book, 1963), p. 135.

[2] Mackenzie Bell, *Christina Rossetti: A Biographical and Critical Study* (1898; rpt. New York: Haskell House Publishers, 1971), p. 206.

[3] Delores Rosenblum, in "Christina Rossetti: The Inward Pose," in Sandra M. Gilbert and Susan Gubar, eds., *Shakespeare's Sisters: Feminist Essays on Women Poets* (Bloomington: Indiana University Press, 1979), says, "The poem really has less to do with temptation than with the consequences of indulgence" (p. 95).

[4] Christina Rossetti, *The Complete Poems,* ed. R. W. Crump, 3 vols. (Baton Rouge: Louisiana State University Press, 1979), 1:11-26. References to 'Goblin Market' will be taken from this edition.

[5] Eleanor Walter Thomas, *Christina Georgina Rossetti* (New York: Columbia University Press, 1931), p. 60.

[6] Lona Mosk Packer, *Christina Rossetti* (Berkeley: The University of California Press, 1963), p. 142.

[7] Ellen Golub, "Untying Goblin Apron Strings: A Psychoanalytic Reading of 'Goblin Market,'" *Literature and Psychology,* 25 (1975), 158.

[8] Jerome J. McGann, "Christina Rossetti's Poems: A New Edition and a Revaluation," *Victorian Studies,* 23 (1979-80), 237-54.

[9] Sandra M. Gilbert and Susan Gubar, *The Madwoman in the Attic: The Woman Writer and the Nineteenth-Century Literary Imagination* (New Haven: Yale University Press, 1979), p. 564.

[10] Packer, pp. 13-14, discusses Rossetti's early reading, as does B. Ifor Evans, "The Sources of Christina Rossetti's 'Goblin Market,'" *Modern Language Review,* 28 (1933), 156-65. See also Thomas, pp. 151-52.

[11] For a full treatment of John Locke's influence on children's literature, see Samuel F. Pickering, Jr., *John Locke and Children's Books in Eighteenth-Century England* (Knoxville: The University of Tennessee Press, 1981).

[12] For accounts of this controversy see F. J. Harvey Darton, *Children's Books in England: Five Centuries of Social Life* (1939; rpt. Cambridge: Cambridge University Press, 1970), pp. 218 ff.; Paul Hazard, *Books,*

Children and Men (Boston: The Horn Book, 1944); Michael Rotzin, "The Fairy Tale in England, 1800-1870," *Journal of Popular Culture*, 4 (Summer 1970), 130-54; Anita Moss, "Varieties of Literary Fairy Tale," *Children's Literature Association Quarterly*, 7, No. 4 (Summer 1982), 15-17.

[13] Patricia Demers and Gordon Moyles, eds., *From Instruction to Delight: An Anthology of Children's Literature* (Toronto: Oxford University Press, 1982), p. 68.

[14] *John Bunyan: The Poems*, ed. Graham Midgley (Oxford: Clarenden Press, 1980), which is vol. 6 of *The Miscellaneous Works of Paul Bunyan*, gen. ed. Roger Sharrock.

[15] Katherine Briggs, *The Fairies in English Tradition and Literature* (Chicago: University of Chicago Press, 1967), p. 59.

[16] Katherine Briggs, *An Encyclopedia of Fairies* (New York: Pantheon Books, 1976), p. 194.

[17] Bruno Bettelheim, *The Uses of Enchantment* (New York: Alfred A. Knopf, 1976), p. 117.

[18] Quoted by Bettelheim, p. 24, from G. K. Chesterton, *Orthodoxy* (London: John Lane, 1909) and from C. S. Lewis, *The Allegory of Love* (Oxford: Oxford University Press, 1936).

[19] John Keats, *The Poems*, ed. Jack Stillinger (Cambridge: The Belknap Press, Harvard University, 1978). Quotations from Keats's poetry will be taken from this edition.

[20] Samuel Taylor Coleridge, *Complete Poetical Works*, ed., E. H. Coleridge, 2 vols. (Oxford, 1912). Quotations from Coleridge's poetry will be taken from this edition.

[21] See, for example, Packer, who observes: "We have seen that in 'From House to Home,' written only six months before 'Goblin Market,' such small animals form part of the speaker's earthly paradise" (p. 143).

[22] See, for example, Zaturenska, p. 79; Packer, pp. 129, 132, 135, 198. D. M. Stuart, in *Christina Rossetti* (London: Macmillan and Co., 1930), says explicitly: "One of the earliest admirers of 'Goblin Market' was Mrs. Caroline Norton, who compared it to 'The Ancient Mariner.' It has, indeed, certain vague affinities with more than one of Coleridge's dream poems" (p. 54).

[23] Carolyn G. Heilbrun's quotation from critic Thomas Rosenmeyer's discussion of *The Bacchae* of Euripides is interestingly appropriate: "Dionysus appears to be neither woman nor man; or, better, he represents himself as woman-in-man, or man-in-woman, the unlimited personality. . . . To follow him or to comprehend him we must ourselves give up our precariously controlled, socially desirable limitations," in *Toward a Recognition of Androgyny* (New York: Colophon Books, 1974), p. xi.

[24] "It was in Hone's three-volume popular miscellany (1825) that Christina at nine discovered Keats. . . . She, and not Gabriel or Holman Hunt, was the first 'Pre-Raphaelite' to appreciate Keats. The poem which caught her fancy . . . was *The Eve of St. Agnes*" (Packer, p. 14). Barbara Foss, in "Christina Rossetti and St. Agnes' Eve," *Victorian Poetry*, 14 (1976), 33-46, discusses Rossetti's awareness of the passive role of Victorian woman and the frustration of always having to wait in inactivity. Rossetti's lines in *From the Antique*:

> It's a weary life, it is, she said:—
> Doubly blank in a woman's lot:
> I wish and I wish I were a man:
> Or, better than any being, were not:
>
> [ll. 1-4]

echo Tennyson's "Mariana" in the weariness and wish for death that often accompanies the unimaginative passivity of "a woman's lot." It is little wonder that the goblin fruits are so tempting and being forbidden to feast on them so frustrating.

[25] For example, in Perrault's *Little Red Riding Hood*, the girl learns that "young lasses . . . do very wrong to listen to strangers" (Charles Perrault, *Perrault's Complete Fairy Tales*, trans. A. E. Johnson et al. [New York: Dodd, Mead & Company, 1961], p. 77). What Red Cap learns in the Grimms' tale is to obey her mother. The moral at the end of *Puss in Boots* adjuring young people to value "industry, knowledge, and a clever mind" (Perrault, p. 25) is totally at variance with the success through deception taught by the tale itself. *Moralités* have now all but disappeared in the hands of today's publishers of fairy tales.

Steven Conner (essay date 1984)

SOURCE: "'Speaking Likenesses': Language and Repetition in Christina Rossetti's *Goblin Market*," in *Victorian Poetry*, Vol. 22, No. 4, Winter, 1984, pp. 439-48.

[*In the following essay, Conner explores the relationships between "Goblin Market" and Rossetti's other works, maintaining that the use of repetition in Rossetti's devotional poetry establishes a sense of "confirmed redemption," while in her nursery rhymes this repetition formula creates a sense of "irresolution." Similarly, Conner suggests, this "irresolution" is the result of the use of repetition in "Goblin Market."*]

"Goblin Market" remains one of the most persistently puzzling poems of the nineteenth century; familiarity has seemed to increase rather than to diminish our uncertainty about its form, style, meaning, and even content. The poem has been treated too much, however, as sui generis, without reference to the rest of Christina Rossetti's work and especially to her other writing for children.[1] The aim of this brief essay is to make the links between her other work and **"Goblin Market"** a little clearer and thus to throw light on some of the peculiarities of this poem, as well as to suggest ways in which Christina Rossetti's poetry as a whole shares with **"Goblin Market"** the capacity to unsettle.

First, it is important to note the power which nursery rhyme had over Christina Rossetti; indeed the title of the volume of nursery rhymes which she published hints at the kinds of attraction which the form had for her, particularly its tendency to organize meaning and expression in terms of pair and antithesis. Critics have noted this predominance of pairings and opposites in Christina Rossetti's own poetry: the pairing relationship of sisterhood, for instance,[2] or the pairing and counterposing of different conditions of existence, the earthly and the transcendental, or indeed the dualistic sense displayed in many of the very titles of the poems, such as **"Life and Death," "He and She," "One Foot in Sea and One on Shore,"** and **"From Sunset to Star-Rise,"**[3] This pattern is restated in the dialogic form of many of her lyrics and similarly in many of the nursery rhymes in *Sing-Song* which are poised in the hesitant space between question and answer:

> Why did baby die,
> Making Father sigh,
> Mother cry?
>
> Flowers that bloom to die
> Make no reply
> Of "Why?"
> But bow and die.[4]

But more than this, Christina Rossetti found in nursery rhyme that same attention to the density of language which is a feature of many of her lyrics. Released from reference to the real world, or even to a strongly experienced world of feeling, her verse often enacts in the shifting of its appositions a drama which is to be apprehended at the level of the signifier:

> Ah changed and cold, how changed and very cold,
> With stiffened smiling lips and cold calm eyes!
> Changed, yet the same.
>   (**"Dead Before Death,"** pp. 313-314)

> There's blood between us, love, my love,
> There's father's blood, there's brother's blood;
> And blood's a bar I cannot pass.
>   (**"The Convent Threshold,"** p. 340)

This shifting is displayed in the poem **"Cobwebs,"** where the actual subject of the poem recedes into invisibility under the pressure of the continuous negatives: "no moons or seasons wax or wane, / . . . / No budtime, no leaf-falling, there for aye" (p. 317). The subject slips away behind the elaborate dance of denials. One of the attractions of nursery rhyme shown in *Sing-Song* is the opportunity to indulge the expressivity of a language emptied of content. This point is obviously of great importance for the understanding of a poem such as **"Goblin Market,"** where the apparent garrulousness of the verse is an enactment quite as much as a representation of sexual/linguistic energy. This is not to imply, however, that this kind of poetic language is sprawling or incoherent; we know that Christina Rossetti devoted considerable time to the writing of these nursery rhymes (and their translation into Italian). What follows, in fact, is the conception of language as a game—an essentially closed, self-sustaining activity. Included under the heading of "Poems for Children, and Minor Verse" in William Rossetti's edition of his sister's poetry is a series of poems which testify to Christina Rossetti's interest in language games. There are riddles (**"Two Enigmas," "Two Charades,"** p. 422), alphabets, counting rhymes, sonnets written to bouts-rimés, and playful conceits:

> A pin has a head, but has no hair;
> A clock has a face, but no mouth there;
> Needles have eyes, but they cannot see;
> A fly has a trunk without lock or key.
>   (p. 432)

or mnemonics:

> O Lady Moon, your horns point toward the east;
>   Shine, be increased:
> O Lady Moon, your horns point toward the west;
>   Wane, be at rest.
>   (p. 442)

The important point about a mnemonic is that it locates within language, within its chimings and assonances, the ordering of experience. The signifier becomes self-motivating, turning the fortuitous into the systematic.

Nevertheless, although Christina Rossetti indulged herself in her poetry in game playing, she is remarkably dogmatic in her devotional works about such frivolity in language. The end of the entry for February 3 in her *Time Flies: A Reading Diary* (London, 1885) reads, "Can a pun profit? Seldom, I fear. Puns and

Chalk drawing of Christina Rossetti by her brother Dante Gabriel Rossetti, 1877.

such like are a frivolous crew likely to misbehave unless kept within strict bounds. 'Foolish talking' and 'jesting' writes St. Paul, 'are not convenient.' Can the majority of puns be classed as *wise* talking?" (p. 26). It is clear that Christina Rossetti was both appalled and fascinated by the profitless and frivolous nature of unrestricted language. (We should note, for example, her enjoyment of the slight bending of the sense of "convenient.")

We might expect certain conflicts in any mingling of the highly subjective form of the lyric with the nursery rhyme and its impersonality. In her devotional writing, Christina Rossetti shows a fiercely tenacious individualism: "In rising out of my grave I must carry on that very life which was mine before I died, of which death itself could not altogether snap the thread. Who I was I am, who I am I am, who I am I must be for ever and ever. . . . I may loathe myself, or be amazed at myself, but I cannot *unself myself* for ever and ever."[5] But in her poetry, this omnipresence of the self is manifested not in the gathering of threads of experience back to an originating subject but rather in their casting outwards upon the world, the generation of the subject by things outside itself, and, in particular, by language. The speaking personality extends itself along the filaments of the signifier. This decentering of the subject is often achieved in Christina Rossetti's poetry by the contortions of syntax, and the inversion, or disturbance, of subject-object categories which these effect. In a sonnet such as "I have done I know not what,—what have I done?" (p. 261), the subject is spread syntactically across the roles of interrogator, confessor, and supplicant. "**An Old-World Thicket,**" a poem dramatizing the emptiness of being, opens with the same giving over of personality, knowledge, and experience to the play of grammatical and semantic alternatives: "Awake or sleeping, (for I know not which) / I was or was not mazed within a wood" (p. 64).

Another way in which the language of the self is highlighted over and above the preverbal experience of the self is by the use of repetition, a common syntactic device. The repetitive or appositional mode of thought is very common in Christina Rossetti; one of her favorite verse-forms was the roundel, imitated from Swinburne. Repetition exists too as translation, or repetition with variation, as in "**A Birthday**" (p. 335) with its creative transformation of objects into symbols, the singing bird, the apple-tree and the seashell assuming on repetition the status of emblems. Here repetition means a move away from a universe of casual things to a universe of sanctified signs. Similarly, in the poem "**Twice**" (p. 366), repetition of the act of offering the heart to God and not to the feckless lover means a kind of redemption. The doubling or echoing of a poetic moment has the effect of blurring the particularity of that moment; in a transformation analogous to the diffusion of personality which we have mentioned, the punctual, momentary nature of the individual experience is translated, made part of a pattern. This doubling impulse is found in Christina Rossetti's devotional writings too. *Time Flies* is a calendar of Christian thoughts which seeks to fuse the individual's experience of day-to-day reality with the larger signifying system of the Church seasons, while *Letter and Spirit* is a double commentary on the *Benedicite*, illustrating the repetitive relationship between the Old and New Testaments.

Sometimes, though, the repetition formula in the nursery rhymes produces a sense of openness and irresolution rather than confirmed redemption. This is also true of her lyric poetry:

> A boat that sails upon the sea,
>   Sails far and far and far away:
> Who sail in her sing songs of glee,
>   Or watch and pray.
>
> A boat that drifts upon the sea,
>   Silent and void to sun and air:
> Who sailed in her have ended glee
>   And watch and prayer.
>   ("**The Way of the World,**" p. 415)

Sometimes, again, this parallelism can be put to ironic use, to generate a false sense of closure, and to produce a certain superfluity of meaning, a sense of hesitation or inconclusiveness. The remarkable poem **"A Life's Parallels"** is very like one of Christina Rossetti's nursery rhymes in its simplicity, in the ascendancy of its form over its apparent content. And yet the implied reconciliation which the poem produces is an illusion. The deliberate mistaking of "ever" and "never" for antonyms produces a surplus of meaning, which, increased by the asymmetrical indefiniteness of the participles, leaves a deep sense of doubt and shifting uncertainty:

> Never on this side of the grave again,
>   On this side of the river,
> On this side of the garner of the grain,
>   Never.
>
> Ever while time flows on and on and on,
>   That narrow noiseless river,
> Ever while corn bows heavy-headed, wan,
>   Ever.
>
> Never despairing, often fainting, rueing,
>   But looking back, ah never!
> Faint yet pursuing, faint yet still pursuing
>   Ever.
>
> (p. 405)

The same inconclusiveness is developed in other Rossetti lyrics, especially **"Sleeping at last"** which similarly suspends its active verbs (p. 417).

Of course, the most urgent exploration of the idea of the ritualizing reenactment of experience through alternation and repetition is found in **"Goblin Market."** The point must be made initially that the poem was not intended originally for children, although a letter from Alexander Macmillan to Dante Gabriel Rossetti in 1861 reveals that the artlessness of the diction produced an uncertainty as to its intended audience: "I took the liberty of reading the **"Goblin Market"** aloud to a number of people belonging to a small working-man's society here. They seemed at first to wonder whether I was making fun of them; by degrees they got as still as death, and when I finished there was a tremendous burst of applause."[6]

The poem is fundamentally a fairy tale, but a highly self-conscious fairy tale, too. There are intrusions into, disturbances of the economy of the fairy-tale structure. Alice Meynell remarked of it that "the story, for all its freshness and freedom, has not the reasonableness we have the right to expect even from a fairy-tale—or especially from a fairy-tale. The moral is hardly intelligible—we miss any perceptible reason why the goblin fruits should be deadly at one time and restorative at another."[7] Actually, dual utility, the fact that objects can be put to different uses and have different, often contradictory effects, is a common motif in fairy tale, although the comparison which one might equally draw in the case of **"Goblin Market"** is the double use of symbols in Christian eschatology. As we have seen, though, this kind of syncretism through repetition is not always guaranteed in Christina Rossetti's poetry.

True, the picturesquencess and facility of rhyme and rhythm in **"Goblin Market,"** along with the categorical moral, do seem initially to mark the poem out as children's fare:

> One had a cat's face,
> One whisked a tail,
> One tramped at a rat's pace,
> One crawled like a snail,
> One like a wombat prowled obtuse and furry,
> One like a ratel tumbled hurry-skurry.
>
> (p. 2)

But it is precisely the infelicity of the relationship between the gamesome accretiveness of the story with the "reasonableness" of its subject, between the experience and the "moral" affixed to it, which constitutes the pivotal ambivalence of the poem. The remarkable undisguised sensuousness of **"Goblin Market"** is luxuriated in by the language itself, as it were, generated out of the richness and variety of its own linguistic textures. The temptation to sin which the goblins represent is as much to indulge oneself in language, in a kind of verbal promiscuity, as in sexual or sensual abandon. (At one point, Laura is said to be unable to hear the "iterated jingle / Of sugar-baited words," which seems to make the identification explicit.) And when Lizzie endures the assault of the goblin men, she must keep her lips shut tight together, lest they should cram in a mouthful of fruit. But to keep one's lips together is a refusal not only of food but of language: "Lizzie uttered not a word; / Would not open lip from lip" (p. 7). The goblin men, on the other hand, are characterized by the furious variegation of their discourse as much as of their shapes:

> The whisk-tailed merchant bade her taste
> In tones as smooth as honey,
> The cat-faced purr'd,
> The rat-paced spoke a word
> Of welcome, and the snail-paced even was
>   heard;
> One parrot-voiced and jolly
> Cried "Pretty Goblin" still for "Pretty Polly";
> One whistled like a bird.
>
> (p. 2)

The incantatory language of the poem offers participation in this variety and energy, and the special status of the children's poem as something spoken aloud reinforces this. But the density of this verbal superflux must be overcome before the two sisters can make their entry into adult married life.

One way which this is attained is by the peculiarity of the rhyme pattern of the piece. The eccentricity of the meter we have already noticed: masculine and feminine line endings agitate and jostle with each other, and the length of the line varies from the curtness of "Spun about" to the cantering briskness of:

> "We must not look at goblin men,
> We must not buy their fruits:
> Who knows upon what soil they fed
> Their hungry thirsty roots?"
>
> (p. 1)

It even modulates briefly into blank verse. But this volatile prankishness is kept in check, as it were, by the rhyme structure. While there is no consistent pattern of rhyme as such, the rhymes are relatively few and recurrent, and on at least one occasion the recurrence of a particular rhyme seems to serve a definite purpose. In the first half of the poem, Laura laments that she can no longer hear the "iterated jingle" of the goblins. This rhyme reappears briefly over 200 lines later, after Lizzie has successfully withstood the buffetings of the goblin men:

> In a smart, ache, tingle,
> Lizzie went her way;
> Knew not was it night or day;
> Sprang up the bank, tore thro' the furze,
> Threaded copse and dingle,
> And heard her penny jingle
> Bouncing in her purse,—
> Its bounce was music to her ear.
>
> (p. 7)

Iteration is clearly seen as in itself threatening, though by this point in the poem we see that the threat and temptation of the "iterated jingle" have been transformed, through the repetitions of the poem itself, into exulation and triumph. In fact, iteration is the predominating mode of the poem with the circulation of recurring rhyme elements now expressing congruence, now difference. Repetition paradoxically keeps awareness alive of otherness and alteration, so that, by the time we reach the end of the poem, "sisterhood" seems to stand for more than just chumminess: it seems to stand for the life beyond the limitations of the individual personality, the life, in language, of otherness.

Christina Rossetti's imagery also enacts a conflict between fixity and restlessness: images designed to convey stability habitually dissolve into images of instability. The question which attaches itself habitually to the goblins' fruit, for instance, is the question of its origin. "How fair the vine must grow / Whose grapes are so luscious," thinks Laura (p. 1). She talks about the "unknown orchard" whence come the fruits and conjectures, "Odorous indeed must be the mead / Whereon they grow, and pure the wave they drink." Christina Rossetti seems to regard it as an important feature of these fruits that they are not nourished in conventional soil: the kernelstone which Laura picks up will not grow. And their phantom insubstantiality seems to be a factor in the agonizing thirst and longing which they induce. But set over against this idea of rootlessness, of unnatural self-reproduction, is a series of images of nourishment in flowing water. The two sisters go to draw water from a well:

> Lizzie most placid in her look,
> Laura most like a leaping flame.
> They drew the gurgling water from its deep.
> Lizzie plucked purple and rich golden flags
>
> (p. 4)

The significance of the flag flower is elucidated partially in Christina Rossetti's devotional work, *Called to Be Saints*:

> Let us take for our subject the Yellow Flag or Iris, which frequents river banks, marsh lands and pools; not disdaining to unfurl even from ditches its golden standard adorned with rare gradations of texture and pencillings of colour. That which it craves is water: and thence whether presented to it in sweet running shallows or in cups of stagnant ponds, it sucks uncontaminated nourishment, thriving on food convenient for it; swaying and stooping amid shifting winds and ripples, yet steadied by its great creeping root as by an anchor.[8]

She finishes her portrait of the flag with an allusion to Job 8. 11, "Can the flag grow without water?" This symbol of the nourishing flow of water as emblematic of redemptive faith in Christ is found elsewhere in her poetry, notably in **"A Birthday"**: in the first stanza the poet says her heart is like "a singing bird / Whose nest is in a watered shoot" (p. 335).

The long passage just quoted suggests a further quality of the flag, namely that it can derive benefit from all environments; but the language of the passage induces the awareness of other less comfortable possibilities: the craving, for instance, of the flag, and the term "uncontaminated nourishment" which seems to conjure up the possibility of its opposite and brings to mind Lizzie's caution about the soil upon which the fruits have been fed. We should note, too, the reappearance of that word "convenient," to connote propriety and fitness of relation—a propriety which seems progressively to be undone in **"Goblin Market."**

The image of fire is called upon extensively in the poem, too. Laura's desire is expressed as "a leaping flame." But this flame, recoiling back upon itself for want of a proper object, dwindles to the self-consuming condition of an ember:

> She dwindled, as the fair full moon doth turn
> To swift decay and burn
> Her fire away.
>
> (p. 5)

Her thirst is called a "burning" (p. 5). Lizzie, as she stands triumphantly dumb amidst the goblins, is also compared to a flame:

> Like a beacon left alone
> In a hoary roaring sea,
> Sending up a golden fire.
>
> (p. 6)

But, significantly, she is compared to a flame set in water; and the image attempts to reconcile the opposed ideas of static, self-consuming desire and a nourishing, redeeming fire. The juice of the goblin fruits which Laura licks from her sister's lips scorches her. It is called "the fiery antidote":

> Swift fire spread through her veins, knocked at her heart,
> Met the fire smouldering there
> And overbore its lesser flame.
>
> (p. 8)

Laura's agony at tasting the goblin fruit is described as well in a succession of images suggestive of speed, power, and urgency:

> Her locks streamed like the torch
> Borne by a racer at full speed,
> Or like the mane of horses in their flight,
> Or like an eagle when she stems the light
> Straight toward the sun,
> Or like a caged thing freed,
> Or like a flying flag when armies run.
>
> (p. 8)

The flag image of the final line is perhaps suggested by the flag-flower. For the passage which this parallels (quoted earlier) showing Lizzie, steadfast amid the tumult of the goblins' temptation, ends, "Close beleaguered by a fleet / Mad to tug her standard down" (p. 6). Interestingly enough, even the rhymes "town"/"down" are maintained. Also, Lizzie has been compared to "a lily in a flood" (p. 6), which is not without significance, bearing in mind the symbolic pattern of flowers nourished by water which the poem generates. A curious thing is that these relationships arise not entirely out of symbolic correspondences but also out of inconvenient puns and verbal associations. Perhaps an indication of the attentiveness of Christina Rossetti's imagination to the signifier is the appearance of the word "flagging," in another sense, as Lizzie tries to revive Laura:

> That night long Lizzie watched by her,
> Counted her pulse's flagging stir,
> Felt for her breath.
>
> (p. 8)

The word may have suggested itself as an involuntary echo of the earlier line "Like a flying flag when armies run." The word is the same, but the meaning is modified; where earlier the flag had been streaming in the wind, now Laura's pulse flags because of the absence of breath which, incidentally, is restored by Lizzie cooling her face "With tears and fanning leaves" (p. 8).

The effect of this method of internal suggestion and assonance—made peculiarly effective by the adoption of the form of the children's poem—is to enact the ceremonial ritualism of the poem at the most basic level. The poem institutes an energetic but self-validating sign-system, the incremental accumulation of terms acquiring internally a kind of parodied sacramental value. But repeatedly, as we have seen, images designed to quell difference end up reactivating it.

There is a worrying violence about Lizzie's refusal to eat, which has a kind of prurience about it, so that abstinence becomes a kind of masochistic indulgence in erotic assault. The account of the conversion of eating into sacramental Feast is incomplete, as signifier drifts away from signified. It is precisely this kind of expressive energy which cannot be fixed or sedated by Laura's retrospective moral:

> Days, weeks, months, years
> Afterwards, when both were wives
> With children of their own;
> Their mother-hearts beset with fears,
> Their lives bound up in tender lives;
> Laura would call the little ones
> And tell them of her early prime,
> Those pleasant days long gone
> Of not-returning time.
>
> (p. 8)

An analogy suggesting itself immediately is the end of *Alice's Adventures in Wonderland*. In both worlds the dispelling of the mood of climactic anxiety is followed by a vignette of the child-heroine grown into a woman with children of her own recounting her own story to them. (Interestingly, Carroll introduces Alice's sister again at this point and imagines her thoughts mingling dreamily with Alice's adventure, as she looks forward to Alice telling the story.)

But the sentimentality of Carroll's ending is, if not deliberate, then certainly functional. Like his melancholy epilogue "All in a golden afternoon," it works by suggesting its own inadequacy as paraphrase. We feel that the *Alice* text is misrepresented by the posterity ascribed to it, just as Laura's account of the "pleasant days" of her youth shockingly misremembers the events of the poem we have just read.[9] So, in both stories, the bland conclusion provokes a return to the unruly discourse of the goblins which forms so large a part of the poem. And, significantly, the poem ends, as it begins, with quotation—so that, in a sense, as readers we hover undecidedly between them; repetition in the form of this kind of paraphrase reveals itself as a series of theoretically endless substitutions.[10]

It is important not to underestimate the need which **"Goblin Market"** supplies for a sanative repression of ugly and frightening experience, but its achievement lies in the fact that we are able to join both in the poetic forgetting of the experience and in retaining a living awareness of it, something which connects with its indeterminacy of genre: in its peculiar status as adult fairy tale, **"Goblin Market"** set up an oddly dual reading. The poem addresses its adult audience, as it were, over the shoulder of its child audience, and is then able to compact innocence and awareness, the happy ending with the disturbing inconclusiveness of language as process. Like the best of Victorian children's writing, it requires adult and child to construct and deconstruct themselves as readers.

Notes

[1] Aside from the difficult case of *Goblin Market*, Christina Rossetti wrote three works specifically for children: *Sing-Song: A Nursery-Rhyme Book* (London, 1872), *Speaking Likenesses* (London, 1874), and *Maude: A Story for Girls* (London, 1897).

[2] See Winston Weathers, "Christina Rossetti: The Sisterhood of Self," *VP*, 3 (1965), 81-89.

[3] See, for instance, Theo Dombrowski, "Dualism in the Poetry of Christina Rossetti," *VP*, 14 (1976), 70-76; Friedrich Dubslaff, *Die Sprachform der Lyrik Christina Rossettis* (Halle, 1933), p. 75 ff.

[4] *The Poetical Works of Christina Georgina Rossetti*, ed. W. M. Rossetti (London, 1904), pp. 428-429. Subsequent references to Rossetti's poetry will be cited by page number to this text.

[5] *The Face of the Deep* (London, 1892), p. 42.

[6] *The Rossetti-Macmillan Letters*, ed. Lona Mosk Packer (Univ. of California Press, 1963), p. 7.

[7] "Christina Rossetti," *Prose and Poetry* (1947; rpt. Freeport, N.Y., 1970), p. 147.

[8] *Called to Be Saints* (London, 1881), pp. 333-334.

[9] Lewis Carroll and Christina Rossetti enjoyed a cordial relationship for over thirty years and frequently exchanged their books. There are obvious affinities of life and temperament between the two writers. Of more particular interest, I think, is the mutual influence exerted between them. Carroll records reading "Goblin Market" with admiration on May 12, 1862—a matter of days before the expedition upon which he says that *Alice in Wonderland* was first extemporized. If some elements from "Goblin Market" strayed into *Alice*, then Christina Rossetti repaid the compliment some years later with *Speaking Likenesses* (1874), her sinister imitation of Carroll's work (*The Diaries of Lewis Carroll*, ed. Roger Lancelyn Green [London, 1953], pp. 203-204).

[10] As Winston Weathers points out, this final hymn of praise to sister-love is strikingly inverted in "Sister Maude" and "The Noble Sisters" (p. 348), two poems which Christina Rossetti wrote shortly after completing "Goblin Market," and which deal with the betrayal of sister by sister.

Elizabeth K. Helsinger (essay date 1991)

SOURCE: "Consumer Power and the Utopia of Desire: Christina Rossetti's 'Goblin Market'," in *ELH*, Vol. 58, No. 4, Winter, 1991, pp. 903-33.

[*In the essay below, Helsinger reviews "Goblin Market" as a "fantasy of consumer power, where the empowered consumer is a woman," concluding that such power is gained by women through the "withholding of desire" and that the poem describes a utopian withdrawal from the economics of sex and marriage.*]

The language of Christina Rossetti's best-known poem, **"Goblin Market,"** is remarkably mercantile. "Come buy, come buy," the iterated cry of the "merchant men" that punctuates the poem, has few parallels in English poetry in the nineteenth century. While buying and selling, markets and merchants and their customers, are a staple of nursery rhymes—"To market, to market, jiggety jig"—most literary Victorian poetry, like the little pig, resolutely stays home from commercial encounters. **"Goblin Market"** not only adopts the forms of the nursery rhyme but also carries the mercantile preoccupations of Mother Goose into a volume of serious poetry.[1] Much of the criticism of **"Goblin Market"** treats its story of buying and selling, like its rhymes and goblins, as the figurative dress for a narrative of spiritual temptation, fall, and redemption.[2] But what happens if instead we read the figure as the subject: buying and selling, or more specifically, the relation of women to those markets of the nursery tales?

Rossetti's merchants are goblin men; their customers are maidens. When Lizzie and Laura step from home into the male marketplace of Rossetti's poem, they cross a fictive but strongly invested boundary separating not only serious poetry from nursery rhymes but also moral from economic space, private from public, "natural" creativity from the alienated labor of capitalist production, and—underwriting and sustaining these distinctions—female from male.[3] Victorian culture acknowledges only one figure who transgresses this boundary—the prostitute. The threat she inevitably poses to the security of these distinctions is contained when she is cast out from the company of moral women. Rossetti's poem is haunted by that shadowy figure. As in so many Victorian narratives of the fallen woman, Laura purchases pleasure only to discover that her own body is ultimately consumed. But Laura is not a prostitute; she is never excluded from the company of moral women by Lizzie or by her author. Rossetti avoids what might be thought the bolder move: she does not take the prostitute as a defining instance of all women's relation to buying and selling, thus negating the fiction of separate spheres. The poem stops short of identifying Laura with the prostitute, for reasons to which I shall return, but its fiction that Laura buys fruit (however magical), not sex, may make the same point more effectively. Rossetti's poem makes visible the contradictory assumptions that render women's relation to the most ordinary forms of consumption, in both the Victorian marketplace and texts about that marketplace, unique and peculiarly risky—both to themselves and to the fragile fictions that legitimize some activities as properly economic while refusing to recognize others. In **"Goblin Market"** and a related group of Rossetti's poems, the domestic desires of women are examined as dramas of competitive buying and selling in which women are always at risk as objects to be purchased, yet also implicated as agents of consumption. Rossetti's poems do not acknowledge the fiction of separate spheres; the mercantile language of **"Goblin Market"** is one sign of her persistent inclination to consider tales of female love and desire as caught up in the operations of a contemporary economics that extends to sex and marriage. A Victorian ideology of separate spheres returns (but with quite a different figuration) only as the utopian fiction that concludes **"Goblin Market."**

"Goblin Market," then, is a transgressive poem that denies (or at least defers) a series of linked distinctions constructed on the fiction of moral woman's difference from economic man, a fiction that much Victorian writing and thinking posited as normal and natural. The story of Lizzie and Laura represents a specifically female experience of Victorian political economy—one which is often occluded or erased from imaginative and analytic accounts of that economy's operations in the service of maintaining gendered distinctions. Rossetti's economics of sex and marriage is primarily an economics of consumption. A very brief look at some other texts on consumption may suggest how conceptions of gender difference have paradoxically erased women's different experience of consumption, even in the most critical accounts of capitalist relations.

At first glance women are far from absent from such accounts. A surprising number of texts, from the eighteenth through the twentieth centuries, specify that the consumer is female or feminized. For example, both novels in England and rococo art in France were condemned in the eighteenth century for encouraging a love of luxury and idleness by associating them with women.[4] Yet the real targets of these critiques of consumption were all those, from the working classes to the aristocracy, who did not share bourgeois values of hard work and careful saving. The taste for luxury and idleness attributed to women stood for similar tastes in the socially useless aristocrat or the lazy domestic servant. By attributing such dangerous consumption to women's appetites and influence, these criticisms acknowledged a power they intended to contain. Both then and later, the association of luxurious tastes with women outran the facts—women need not be the primary or exclusive buyers, authors, or patrons of novels or rococo art in order to activate denunciations of a consumption with which they were identified.[5]

The grounds for the strong associations between women and consumption probably lie in the fact that in eighteenth and nineteenth-century monied society women were themselves a sign of luxury, indicating in their persons the power of their fathers, husbands, or lovers to consume. Where this power was feared, female consumption was criticized; where it was applauded, women were expected to buy and display the ornaments of a luxury and leisure that they also represented. In the rococo world of eighteenth-century France but also, much later, in the bourgeois world of mid-Victorian England, women displayed the conspicuous consumption that conferred social status on men. Their role as luxury objects of consumption, in other words, influenced their characterization as agents of consumption, enabling them to stand for—and sometimes, deflect criticism from—those whose consuming passions they represented. The speaker of Dante Gabriel Rossetti's "Jenny" only half grasps the evasions that shape his meditations on the prostitute who *is* the pleasure men consume while (he imagines) she herself shares—and can therefore embody—that morally suspect but consuming passion.[6]

Marx carefully points out the contradiction between the bourgeois asceticism expressed in critiques of consumption and capitalism's own dependence on consumers. But his argument, in the "Economic and Philosophic Manuscripts" of 1844, employs the same associations between consumption and the feminine, this time to portray both capitalists and the consumers they dupe as emasculated or feminized. The capitalist is an "industrial eunuch" who puts himself at the service of the consumer's most depraved fancies, plays the pimp between him and his need, excites in him morbid appetites, lies in wait for each of his weaknesses—all so that he can then demand the cash for this service of love. The capitalist-pimp seeks to compensate with money for his lack of (masculine) power by preying on the "weaknesses," the longings for "potency," of the consumer-other.[7] Like Christina Rossetti a few years later, Marx uses the buying and selling of sexual pleasure to stand for all markets. But in his version of the exchange of money for sex there is no place for women as either buyers or sellers. Like money, women represent a power properly belonging to masculinity and are the objects, not the agents, of the exchange.

Returning to the same subject a century later, Max Horkheimer and Theodor Adorno bring their condemnation of mass culture to a climax by repeating Marx's charge: the consumer under late capitalism is a man wrongly placed in the feminine position, deprived of economic subjecthood and hence of the dignity of the father, like a boy perpetually subjected to the symbolic castration of an initiation rite:

> The possibility of becoming a subject in the economy, an entrepreneur or a proprietor, has been completely liquidated. Right down to the humblest shop, the independent enterprise, on the management and inheritance of which the bourgeois family and the position of its head had rested, became hopelessly dependent. Everybody became an employee; and in this civilization of employees the dignity of the father (questionable anyhow) vanishes. . . . The attitude into which everybody is forced in order to give repeated proof of his moral suitability for this society reminds one of the boys who, during tribal initiation, go round in a circle with a stereotyped smile on their faces while the priest strikes them. Life in the late capitalist era is a constant initiation rite. . . . The eunuch-like voice of the crooner on the radio, the heiress's smooth suitor, who falls into the swimming pool in his dinner jacket, are models for those who must become whatever the system wants.[8]

Where the female consumer of eighteenth-century critiques of capitalism represented a threatening male power, from above or below, that critics were eager to contain, the feminized consumer of these Marxist accounts represents a male subject shamefully deprived of power. But some things do not change: not only can the feminine never represent a legitimate possessor of power, it can never represent itself. None of these accounts considers how or why the sexes may be differently related to consumption. Indeed, in most of them, women disappear. One could continue this history and argue, as Tania Modleski has recently, that when postmodernist writers like Jean Baudrillard or the novelist Manuel Puig appear to place a higher value on consumption (as against political activism, for example) and thereby to imply that such consumption is feminist, they are only reinscribing a time-honored association between consumption and the feminine. The suppression of real gender differences in the power relations of the marketplace, Modleski concludes, can offer very little to a feminist politics.[9]

Against this history of texts in which women appear only to figure male power or powerlessness, Christina Rossetti's fable of female consumption stands out as an exception. Like many other Victorian writers, Rossetti is deeply suspicious of a world of unrestricted buying and selling associated primarily with men; unlike her contemporaries, however, she assumes that women are already implicated as both agents and objects in an economics of consumption—but differently from men.[10] In the utopian conclusion of her poem, the female protagonists undo the erasure with which a male market, like male texts on the market, threatens their existence. The poem becomes a fantasy of consumer power, where the empowered consumer is a woman.

Yet Lizzie and Laura triumph over the market only to withdraw from it. At the point when women seem most empowered, the poem reaches the limits of its ability to conceive their relations to the market. Rossetti's women must consume and be consumed, or declare an impossible independence of all economic relations. An analysis that looked more closely at women's relations to production (as Rossetti, for reasons I will suggest below, hesitates to do) might argue that women in the marketplace are also producers of the product with which they are identified—that femininity and female sexuality, like books, are cultural artifacts in the construction of which women participate, "the masquerade of femininity."[11] In this analysis the prostitute who produces herself for sale would figure not only all women's risky relation to consumption but also a (hidden) relation to production. The prostitute so understood threatens any distinction between public, male, spheres of labor shaped by market relations and private, female spheres where work remains unpaid and thus "natural." It is not surprising that the prostitute should be a figure of scandal—nor that women who wrote for a market, like Rossetti, should especially fear an association with prostitutes, whose trangressive appearance in the market place was not so different from their own.[12] **"Goblin Market"** acknowledges no relation to production for Lizzie and Laura except one that is naturalized by its apparent independence from all markets—like butter-making (represented without reference to sale or exchange) or mothering. I will return to the question of the poem's ideological limits, but I want first to recover its critical potential as an account of Victorian women's relation to consumption.

I

Though the poems of a reclusive Victorian woman may seem an unlikely place to look for such an account, two aspects of Rossetti's biography may suggest why she has a particular interest in the gendering of market relations. First, as a number of critics have noted, she was a lay "Sister" at a home for fallen women in the late 1850s and 60s.[13] Charitable institutions like St. Mary Magdalene's Penitentiary, Highgate, run by the Diocese of London, were intended to redeem through spiritual reformation women who had strayed into a moral abyss. But they were also a means of keeping women off the market until they had something to sell other than their bodies—until they could return as domestic servants or needlewomen, not as prostitutes. Rossetti joined the "self-devoted ladies" whose influence and instruction was to bring about a moral and economic reformation.[14] Though she did not, as an Associate, live at St. Mary's, she evidently stayed there for occasional periods of several days or weeks over a decade, until ill health curtailed her activities in 1870. Her duties while in residence probably included reading aloud to the penitents while they worked at sewing. Her association may not have permitted much detailed knowledge of the lives of these women (they were enjoined to silence about their past, partly to protect the Sisters and partly, one suspects, as part of the process of remaking their identities). It did, however, keep vividly before Rossetti's eyes the consequences of a market in which women participated at great risk.

Rossetti also had complicated relations with another market where gender seemed to make a difference. Her interest in art sales and literary publication was elicited by both her own and her brothers' productions. Rossetti's attitudes suggest a combination of ambivalence and ironic awareness of her status as woman with respect to the aesthetic market. On the one hand, she allowed her writing to be produced, if not authored, almost entirely through the mediation of the male members of her family, particularly Dante Gabriel. Between 1847 and 1850, she wrote and published a number of poems, but her only volume was privately printed by her grandfather, and six of eight published poems appeared in *The Germ*, the Pre-Raphaelite journal organized by her brothers, under a pseudonym chosen for her by Dante Gabriel. He was active again in 1852-54 in soliciting (mostly unsuccessfully) publication on her behalf, and it was he who finally arranged in 1861 with Macmillan for her first published volume, whose title poem—**"Goblin Market"**—he had named.[15] He also designed the book's cover and that of the second edition, in 1865, which appeared with his frontispiece and title page designs—as did her second volume, *The Prince's Progress,* in 1866. With respect to that project she wrote him, "I foresee you will charitably do the business-details."[16] Dante Gabriel not only arranged terms, invented titles and pseudonyms, and designed covers and title pages, he also suggested revisions and made selections and arrangements of the poems themselves. Rossetti sent her manuscript to Macmillan by way of Dante Gabriel for his final advice, and he had Macmillan send separate proof sets to him and to her. But though Christina was apparently willing to concede her brother most of the responsibility for the participation of her work in the public literary market, she could on occasion firmly resist his revisions and intervene when he tried to alter her arrangement with Macmillan in a way she did not approve. "So please wash your hands of the vexatious business; I will settle it now myself with him," she wrote her brother in 1865.[17] In fact, by 1861 she was corresponding directly with Macmillan, despite her willingness to employ Dante Gabriel as a go-between—or at least, to let him believe that he handled her business matters for her.

This combination of apparent reluctance to enter the literary market except under her brother's auspices with a retention of some degree of control over the marketing of her product may have more than one explanation. Certainly Rossetti was not indifferent to the value of her writing as property which might be sold for money; she never resists her brother's efforts to publish her poems and joins gleefully in speculations about earning money from literary production. But her eagerness for publication and its profits is tempered in part by her own scruples against close dealing, reinforced by a not unrealistic estimate of the small commercial value of her work, and in part by a sense that writing is sullied by commercial exchange (a sense she shared with her brother, as well as with many other Victorian artists). Dante Gabriel, for example, drew a sharp distinction between the paintings by which he made his living and the poems which remained until 1870 largely unpublished. The former he often spoke of derogatorily as a prostitution of his talents; the latter, he wrote to a friend in 1860, he had a special regard for as "depend[ing] mainly on their having no trade associations, and being still a thing of one's own."[18] Christina catches her brother's tone when she distinguishes between the poems she published in *Macmillan's Magazine,* for which she was directly paid in return for the copyright—her "potboilers"—and those she saved for her volumes, in which she would have a share in any profits, but did not exchange her property rights for direct cash payments.[19]

But this not uncommon ambivalence toward the commercial market for art is exaggerated by her awareness, often expressed obliquely and ironically, that women's products are undervalued, while they incur particular risks in a public market as agents of exchanges. In a letter to her brother William in 1853, she imagines a comic scenario in which she will reverse a decline in the family fortunes through the publication of her short story "Nick." In the letter, the story is accepted because it is accompanied by her portrait, which appears to be the reason why the "man of business," who is also "a susceptible individual of great discernment," "risks the loss of his situation by immediately forwarding me a cheque for £20."[20] Christina leaves it quite ambiguous whether this is a portrait *of* her (Dante Gabriel had painted her more than once) or *by* her, since she had been trying her hand at portraits that year. If read as a portrait of her, the fantasy suggests it is not her literary talents but her brother's artistic ones (and the lure of a female face) that will sell her work. If she is the artist, her estimate of her talents is more assertively made—though there may still be some ironic note taken of her greater commercial success as a face than as an author or artist. The letter would seem to put all these meanings deliberately into play.

Rossetti had plenty of opportunities to observe that the commercial value of women's faces might be at odds with their ability to get what they wanted in a world structured by an exchange economy. Just a few months before this letter, itself a fantasy partly generated by her failure to sell anything for publication, Dante Gabriel succeeded in selling his painting, *Ecce Ancilla Domina!* (1850), an annunciation for which Christina had been the model for the Virgin (as she had been for the first painting he sold, *The Girlhood of Mary Virgin* [1849]). Perhaps more disturbing, Rossetti was also witness to the fate of her brother's favorite model, Elizabeth Siddal, who by 1853 was herself writing poems and painting pictures (with no commercial success), suffering chronic ill health, and waiting—as she would until 1860—for Rossetti to redeem his promise to marry her. Christina's poem **"In an Artist's Studio"** (dated December, 1856) is usually understood to represent her brother's tortuous relations with Lizzie. "One face looks out from all his canvases," it begins, "We found her hidden just behind those screens." The painted face is lovely: "Fair as the moon and joyful as the light"—not, like the real woman, "wan with waiting, not with sorrow dim." The dim, silent, hidden woman has been drained of all vitality by what the poem depicts as the artist's act of consumption: "He feeds upon her face by day and night." The woman who perhaps aspired to be an agent of exchange, to negotiate money or love or marriage for the use of her face—even, like Lizzie (and Christina), to author her own exchangeable objects of beauty—has been herself reduced to that object, and consumed.

This memento mori (in 1862, Lizzie was in fact to die), like the silenced, fallen women she observed at St. Mary's, underlines the hazards of exchange economies for women and points to the conclusion Rossetti entertains in her 1853 letter to William—women can more easily sell themselves than what they can produce—and to its consequence: if they enter the marketplace, they risk being literally consumed. Rossetti's preoccupation with consumption (to the virtual exclusion of any consideration of women as producers) is evidently strongly shaped by market relations that she perceives as substituting women's bodies for women's productions. Well before Lizzie's death, Rossetti had begun to explore women's precarious relation to production and consumption in a group of poems that considerably extend these speculations on what she could observe in her brother's studio or at St. Mary's, Highgate. Though I shall focus on **"Goblin Market"** (dated April, 1859), I would like to look first at several lesser-known poems written between October 1856 (the year St. Mary's opened) and the mid-1860s.

II

The poems I shall be considering allude to but revise two different traditions of poetry about sex and marriage current in the mid-nineteenth century. They can be viewed as responses to the prose idylls made popular in the 1820s and 30s by Mary Russell Mitford and mined as material for poetry by Tennyson, several of whose "English Idyls" from the 1830s and 40s draw on stories by Mitford. These were sketches of rural English life, short narratives of domestic romance intended for a middle-class reading audience.[21] Both Mitford's tales and Tennyson's poems depict courtships leading to marriage, not seductions and betrayals. Their women are successful at what many Victorians saw as an exchange situation parallel to that of the market in sex: female love and beauty exchanged for the security of a home and family offered by men. Mitford's tales usually end with the achievement of such security, though not always marriage, for the woman, while Tennyson's adaptations of her stories conclude with marriage or, failing that, happy return to a patriarchal family. Mitford's stories reveal a great deal of anxiety about economic security, a subject generally displaced or suppressed in Tennyson's versions, but both portray sentiment as the key to domestic content. For example, in Mitford's "The Queen of the Meadow," a gentleman farmer falls in love with Katy, the miller's daughter.[22] Though Katy fears that her lover has abandoned her for her beautiful, educated cousin from the city, it turns out that lover and cousin are simply conspiring to bring about his marriage to Katy. In Tennyson's version of this story, "The Miller's Daughter," class barriers themselves play the role dramatized by the "cousin": the neighboring squire falls in love and marries despite the social distance that divides them. The poem is a retrospective account of this idyllic, cross-class rural romance by the husband, after years of "wedded bliss."[23]

Rossetti's poems, however, view the marriage of the rural idyll from the perspective of women who fail to achieve emotional or economic security. Seduced and abandoned women contemplate their married rivals as successful competitors in a market they have belatedly learned to recognize. In what might be read as her version of the Mitford-Tennyson story, **"Cousin Kate"** (dated November, 1859, a few months after **"Goblin Market"**), a "cottage maiden" laments her abandonment by "a great lord" who has seduced her and then left her for her cousin, who "grew more fair than I." Kate gets the wedding ring, the gold, and the land; the speaker is left with a child and very little else. In Rossetti's version of the story, to succeed in this market is to consume, while to fail is to be consumed (the speaker loses her beauty).

Where the sentimental middle-class rural romance excludes the exchange of sexual beauty for money from its account of how marriages are achieved, ballad stories and their remnants in nursery song readily adopt the language of the market. In its franker treatment of money and sex (there are no illegitimate children in Mitford or Tennyson), **"Cousin Kate,"** like Rossetti's other rural idylls, has much in common with ballad narratives of seduction.[24] But the pragmatic acceptance of economic and gender inequalities that often underlies the ballad stories is missing from Rossetti's. In the popular song "Where are you going to, my pretty maid?" (published in a number of versions in the eighteenth and nineteenth centuries), for example, the dialogue between milkmaid and gentleman reveals no illusions on either side: seduction is a possibility, but not marriage.

> What if I do lay you down on the ground,
>   With your white face and your yellow hair?
>
> I will rise up again, sweet Sir, she said,
>   For strawberry leaves make maidens fair.
>
> What if I do bring you with child
>   With your white face and your yellow hair?
>
> I will bear it, sweet Sir, she said,
>   For strawberry leaves make maidens fair.[25]

Another popular version of the ballad makes the economic and class terms of the transaction equally explicit:

> What is your father, my pretty maid?
> My father's a farmer, sir, she said.
>
> What is your fortune, my pretty maid?
> My face is my fortune, sir, she said.
>
> Then I can't marry you, my pretty maid.
> Nobody asked you, sir, she said.[26]

The song implies that the attempted seduction is legitimate because the girl accepts the bargain she's offered (pleasure, but no prospect of marriage)—though her confidence that nature will always renew the face that is her fortune may be quite unrealistic.

Rossetti's cottage maiden is, by contrast, quite innocent of the need to bargain with her beauty:

> I was a cottage maiden
>   Hardened by sun and air,
> Contented with my cottage mates,
>   Not mindful I was fair.
> Why did a great lord find me out,
>   And praise my flaxen hair?
>
> (1-8)

Unlike Cousin Kate, she does not know that her beauty is a commodity, to be guarded until it can be exchanged advantageously. The speaker of **"An Apple-Gathering,"** who plucked her apple blossoms to wear for her lover only to find herself without lover or fruit at apple-gathering time, is similarly unable to estimate values or obey the economic law (save now to buy later) of courtship:

> Ah Willie, Willie, was my love less worth
>   Than apples with their green leaves piled above?
> I counted rosiest apples on the earth
>   Of far less worth than love.
>
> (17-20)

Rossetti's naive speakers begin with the expectations of the heroines of Mitford's and Tennyson's idylls, and learn—too late—to perceive courtship as an economic transaction, a matter of "value" and "worth." But although the poems may seem to endorse the more realistic views of Cousin Kate and "plump Gertrude" (who wins Willie), the questions of the naive speakers linger: "Was my love less worth?" Or as the speaker asks Cousin Kate: "Now which of us has tenderer heart? / You had the stronger wing" (31-32).

In fact the poems use each woman's position to criticize the other: the speakers for their sentimental naivete (and for their misplaced resentments of their rivals, a point to which I shall return), Kate and Gertrude for their too-ready acceptance of gender relations as competitive bargaining, sex for money (or beauty and pleasure for marriage and children). The implied criticism of Kate and Gertrude, made strong and plump and complacent by their success, is not simply or perhaps not even primarily moral. The poems attempt to unravel the economic logic by which Kate's and Gertrude's actions are justified by showing, not that it is morally repugnant, but that it is faulty. Bargaining for the security of marriage, women become the objects as well as the agents of exchange.

Rossetti's point may be clearer if we contrast her stories with a classic ballad narrative. Both versions of "Where are you going, my pretty maid?" quoted above appear in collections of nursery songs and are probably fragments. In the longer ballad to which they are related, "The Knight and Shepherd's Daughter," the seduced maiden runs to the king, protests that she's been robbed of her maidenhead, and is promised the body of her seducer—as a corpse, if he is married, as a husband, if he is not. Rejecting offers of money, she holds out for a fair exchange, his body for hers, and manages—thanks to the king—to turn the tables on her seducer and redeem her loss with marriage:

> "O I'le have none of your gold," she said,
> "Nor I'le have none of your fee;
> But I must have your fair body
> The king hath given me."[27]

Most other popular ballads of seduction, like "The Knight and Shepherd's Daughter," conclude by mitigating what first looks like a very unequal transaction by allowing a persistent woman (provided she is neither wanton nor a child murderer) the recompense of revenge or marriage.[28] Such conclusions disguise but do not deny the facts of class and gender inequality that structure the exchange of sex and marriage. The shepherdess who wins the king's support turns out to be herself a king's daughter. While this revelation explains her apparent power, the ballad's final lines reinscribe her within the patriarchal hierarchy of the family. The Knight comes out quite well in the exchange, after all: "He had both purse and person too, / And all at his command."

In Rossetti's several versions of the rural seduction story (**"Light Love"** as well as **"Cousin Kate"** and **"An Apple-Gathering"**) woman's disadvantage in these transactions is exposed but not overcome. Even the apparent successes of Kate or Gertrude are necessarily called into question. Kate and Gertrude seem to illustrate how women can participate in such bargaining and win—even without the hidden capital held by the pseudo-shepherdess—by recognizing and obeying economic laws. They prudently withhold their bodies and their beauty until they can exchange them for the security of marriage. But the poems suggest there are at least three things wrong with such advice, quite apart from any moral objections to an economic model for love relationships. Management of commodified sex and beauty depends upon an economy of scarcity that the poems belie. There is always another maid in the cottage for the great lord; the apple orchard is full of maidens (Lilian and Lilias as well as Gertrude). Moreover, as Rossetti's imagery of blossoms and fruit and seasonal change constantly stresses, beauty is a highly perishable commodity (a fact the maid of "Where are you going" has overlooked). The speaker of **"Cousin Kate"** finds the great lord "changed me like a glove" when Kate "grew more fair than I." The male speaker in the dialogue poem **"Light Love"** taunts the mistress he is abandoning with her powerlessness in a world where new beauties are abundantly available:

> For nigh at hand there blooms a bride,
>   My bride before the morn;
> Ripe-blooming she, as thou forlorn.
>   (43-45)

Though it may appear that brides are safe from abandonment, the mistress's reply reminds us that all women who bargain for marriage risk being reduced from consumer to consumed. Trading with their beauty, they become wholly identified with it, and hence subject to the inevitable natural process of decay. Wives can also be abandoned when their beauty withers:

> Change new again for new;
> Pluck up, enjoy—yea, trample too.
>
> Alas for her, poor faded rose,
>   Alas for her, like me,
> Cast down and trampled in the snows.
>   (59-63)

The lover's reply suggests that permanent success in the market depends not on prudent bargains for beauty but on some prior security: "Like thee? nay, not like thee: / She leans, but from a guarded tree" (64-65). The speaker of **"An Apple-Gathering"** associates the cheerful confidence of Lilian and Lilias with the fact that "their mother's home was near" (12). Milly Brandon, who loves her cousin but has lost him to a cottage maiden, "has no mother," while her successful rival Nelly "dwells at home beneath her mother's eyes" (**"Brandons Both,"** 25, 22). Without protection, Rossetti's stories imply, women cannot participate on equal terms in courtships structured by economic laws of exchange. Unlike the pseudo-shepherdess, they have no independent power as consumers; at best they can manipulate male consumption to avoid becoming consumed themselves. Those who are "guarded"—for Rossetti, significantly, by a mother's watchfulness, not a father's wealth or authority—have a far better chance of succeeding at even this limited venture. Rossetti's poems show her under no illusions that the markets of sex and marriage can be either avoided or made safe for women.[29]

By pairing abandoned with safely coupled women, Rossetti calls into question both the account of cross-class courtship presented in the sentimental rural tale and that of cross-class seduction found in the ballads. She also draws attention to the way participation in these economic and sexual exchanges affects relations between women. In nearly every one of Rossetti's tales the woman who has failed to find and hold a mate talks about, and often directly addresses, a woman successful in love and marriage (**"Cousin Kate," "An Apple-Gathering," "Maude Clare," "The Lowest Room," "Brandons Both"**). In a related group of poems (**"Noble Sisters," "Sister Maude"**), one sister blocks the marriage or elopement of another, in the name of family honor. In all of these poems, sisters, cousins, and female friends are the objects of jealousy and barely suppressed resentments that complicate our attitudes toward the otherwise sympathetically presented speakers. Indeed, one might argue that Rossetti's critical focus on the problem of male and class supremacy is at least partially displaced in her poems by that of female competition for a limited supply of male love. Or as Rossetti herself might see it, a second economy of exchange and competition is generated by the first. The lingering questions of **"An Apple-Gathering"** and **"Cousin Kate"**—"was my love less worth?" "which of us has the tenderer heart?"—may move us as the pathos of a wronged speaker, but they are also presented as ungenerous attempts to devalue a rival.

"Maude Clare," Rossetti's reworking of a well-known ballad ("Lord Thomas and Lady Ellinor" in the English version, "Lord Thomas and Fair Annet" in the Scottish) makes this point quite clearly.[30] In the original ballad, Lord Thomas loves Fair Ellinor/Annet but takes the advice of his mother (father, brother) and marries a "nut-browne bride" who has the lands and gold his love does not. Ellinor/Annet, resplendently dressed, confronts the two at the wedding; Lord Thomas places a rose in her lap, and his bride stabs her. The wronged heroine has class on her side, however, and romance, an aristocratic possession, has its revenge on nut-brown brides and their money when Lord Thomas draws his sword and kills first his bride and then himself. Rossetti wrote three progressively more concise versions of the ballad, each focusing on the confrontation at the wedding between Lord Thomas, Maude Clare ("like a queen") and Nell ("like a village maid").[31] As in the ballad, Maude Clare, especially in the first version, is clearly the suffering wronged woman whose love and romantic, aristocratic beauty have been valued less than the lands and gold of the rural middle-class heroine of domesticity (bride and bridegroom are imagistically linked to mated pigeons). But where the bride of the ballad taunts and then stabs Ellinor/Annet, in all three versions of Rossetti's poem Maude Clare taunts both Lord Thomas and Nell. (In the first version she explicitly tells Nell he's married her for her gold.) Nell's reply is neither a verbal nor a physical stab but a spirited defense against Maude Clare's accusations. In this poem, Nell has the last words:

> "And what you leave," said Nell, "I'll take,
>   And what you spurn, I'll wear;
> For he's my lord for better and worse,
>   And him I love, Maude Clare.
>
> Yea, tho' you're taller by the head,
>   More wise, and much more fair;
> I'll love him till he loves me best,
>   Me best of all, Maude Clare."
>
> (41-48)

The traditional ballad turns the gendered marketplace of marriage into a reaffirmation of aristocratic values; Rossetti, however, lets Lord Thomas keep his middle-class bride. The tale's transformation seems to replicate a literary history in which aristocratic romance gives way to the middle-class rural idyll, where the squire does marry the miller's daughter. But in the poem's final version, Rossetti eliminates Maude Clare's scornful reference to the bride's material assets. Though she thus uncharacteristically suppresses the economic bargain which underlies the marriage—as Tennyson and Mitford do in "The Miller's Daughter" and "The Queen of the Meadow"—the omission helps refocus the poem away from the differences of class and toward the ties of gender, toward what the two women have in common. **"Cousin Kate"** or **"An Apple-Gathering"** suggest that the rural idyll misrepresents courtship as an affair of sentiment only, and thus fails to depict women's dangerously disadvantaged situation where they must use themselves as currency to purchase security. **"Maude Clare"** also emphasizes the insidious effects on female relationships of women's powerlessness in the competitive marriage market. Neither Maude Clare nor Nell is allowed moral authority in Rossetti's version of their confrontation, even though Nell has profited from Lord Thomas's faithlessness, and Maude Clare may be a compromised woman (she has exchanged love tokens and waded barefoot in the beck with Lord Thomas). Rossetti refuses to place exclusive value on either purity or wronged beauty. Rather, both women are implicated in the morally dubious enterprise of devaluing each other, the more subtle but equally destructive consequence of their participation in a market of sex and marriage. Though Rossetti's poems implicitly criticize a male-dominated economy in which women are consumed, they can also be read as an account of competition between women as would-be consumers of men. Both these dangers, as Rossetti sees them, are circumvented in her utopian fable of female consumer power. **"Goblin Market"** is fantasy not because its men are goblins and its consumer goods magical ("Men sell not such in any town" [101]), but because, for once, sisterhood intervenes so that women can successfully buy in markets run by merchant men.

III

Like **"Cousin Kate," "An Apple-Gathering,"** or **"Maude Clare,"** Rossetti's **"Goblin Market"** responds to a literary representation as well as to its author's own observations of sexual and economic exchange. In Dante Gabriel Rossetti's dramatic monologue, to which Christina's poem alludes, a young student addresses a sleeping prostitute, meditating on the dissimilar fates of two initially like women, the prostitute Jenny and his cousin Nell.[32] The poem's epigraph identifies the eponymous Jenny as a character borrowed from Shakespeare ("Vengeance of Jenny's case! Fie on her! Never name her, child!"). Despite Mrs. Quickly's admonition, Dante Gabriel's speaker ponders over both Jenny and her "case" for all of one long night. The heroines of Christina Rossetti's poem cannot forget her either:

> She thought of Jeanie in her grave,
> Who should have been a bride;
> But who for joys brides hope to have
> Fell sick and died.
>
> (312-15)

Jenny lives out her fate as whore as she circulates through these authors' texts. She is the shadow figure of the prostitute that haunts **"Goblin Market"** and its initially innocent female consumers, Laura and Lizzie. We should not be surprised to find her unexamined presence in another contemporary discussion of consumption, Marx's 1844 manuscript "On Money."

Marx too has Shakespeare in mind, and in two passages apostrophizing money in *Timon of Athens* he finds concisely expressed the double nature of money as "Thou common whore of mankind" and "Thou *visible God!*" Money is a "visible God" because it is, in Marx's words, "the alienated *ability of mankind,*" the "*truly creative* power" that can transform "essential powers which are really impotent, which exist only in the imagination of the individual—into *real powers* and *faculties*"; god also because it is an *un*creative power that can change real human abilities into "tormenting chimeras." Money is a common whore because it circulates between men, and because it has no intrinsic value—it is a means to an end, not an end in itself. In fact the whore, like the god, is a power whose source is ultimately man; money as whore is a bearer of power or meaning alienated from man that he must constantly struggle to repossess. In Marx's text gender difference appears only to disappear; god, whores, and money alike reduce to one, and that one is man. Yet Marx cannot leave the fascinating scene of prostitution. "Money's properties are my properties and essential powers—the properties and powers of its possessor.... I am ugly, but I can buy for myself the most *beautiful* of women. Therefore I am not *ugly.*" Woman as woman has constantly to be reduced to "the properties and powers of its possessor," to be appropriated as money in the text and yet still to be purchased with money in the world again and again.[33] Marx's text points to money as an objectified human power which in turn threatens him and must be constantly reclaimed as his own. But it also suggests unwittingly that for women the dangers of the marketplace are rather different. What women have to fear is not (or not just) the alienated power of money, but the efforts of men to reappropriate that power by buying women. Male consumption, in other words, takes place through feminized figures. The female consumer, no less than the prostitute, risks being reduced from the agent who consumes to an object to be consumed in a chain of substitutions by which an alienated power is reappropriated by more powerful consumers, usually men. Money is a whore is a woman. Male texts on the marketplace, like Marx's own, repeat this process of substitution, appropriating the power of an alienating representation, money, by refiguring it: money is a woman who can be possessed. **"Goblin Market"** sets out to undo this double consumption or erasure of woman, textual and sexual or economic.

Dante Gabriel Rossetti's poem acts out the scenario suggested by Marx's words; it is the text which Christina Rossetti's poem most directly rewrites. As an allusion to Shakespeare's Jenny, the woman in Dante Gabriel's poem is already doubly in circulation, as whore and as a literary property. The poet, however, must exercise countless strategies to deprive her once again of difference. He makes her unconscious throughout the poem; then he articulates her thoughts for her; finally he constantly figures her as money, itself of course both the bearer of and the power for the satisfaction of his own desires.[34] Thus at one point the speaker himself notes that

> Jenny, looking long at you,
> The woman almost fades from view.
> A cipher of man's changeless sum
> Of lust, past, present, and to come,
> Is left.
>
> (276-80)

But even a thoroughly silenced Jenny is not simply the figure of man's lust, another number in a "changeless sum," and so as the poem ends the speaker must both buy her and replace her with his money yet again:

> I lay among your golden hair
> Perhaps the subject of your dreams,
> These golden coins . . .
>
> . . . . .
>
> I think I see you when you wake,
> And rub your eyes for me, and shake
> My gold, in rising, from your hair,
> A Danaë for a moment there.
>
> (340-42, 376-79)

As Zeus descending in a shower of gold, the speaker achieves in imagination the sexual climax that pointedly has not occurred in Jenny's room that night. But he also attempts another kind of victory over Jenny; laying the coins in Jenny's golden hair, he signifies that Jenny is for him the gold he claims she dreams of. Money is a whore, and a whore is money.

When the heroine of Christina Rossetti's **"Goblin Market"** is "mindful of Jeanie" (364), she is thinking not just of Jenny's sexual fall but of her failure to take her place in the market as a consumer. Laura and Lizzie, the poem's sister protagonists, live in a state of pastoral maidenhood like that enjoyed by Lilian and Lilias in **"An Apple-Gathering,"** or by the speaker and her cottage mates, before the great lord came along, in

"**Cousin Kate**." They sleep at night "Golden head by golden head, / Like two pigeons in one nest" (184-85), united in an image of domestic, even conjugal unity (as the image implied in "**Maude Clare**") that is guarded by nature: the moon, the stars, the wind, and some solicitous owls. At cock crow, "neat like bees, as sweet and busy" (201) they

> Fetched in honey, milked the cows,
> Aired and set to rights the house,
> Kneaded cakes of whitest wheat,
> Cakes for dainty mouths to eat,
> Next churned butter, whipped up cream,
> Fed their poultry, sat and sewed;
> Talked as modest maidens should.
> (203-9)

But "goblin men" have set up their market even in this place of pastoral childhood and "natural" domestic production. (Christina Rossetti is never under any illusions about the chances of innocence remaining so in the countryside more than in the city.) The luscious fruits these merchants sell are reputed to be harmful to maidens, and Lizzie, mindful of Jeanie's case, refuses to look or listen to the goblin men with their cries of "Come buy, come buy!" But "curious Laura" takes her chances, succumbing to the peculiar dangers that beset women in the marketplace. At the goblin men's suggestion, Laura pays for her purchase with a golden curl of her hair, and in so doing she becomes both the buyer and the bought, the agent and the object of exchange. She uses her body as money—and money, of course, is a whore.

Rossetti's account of Laura's fall is markedly different from the usual (male) Victorian version, however. Unlike Dante Gabriel's Jenny, Laura suffers no instant loss of purity. She is not transformed from maiden to fallen woman.[35] Her mind does not become an open sewer ("Jenny" [164-66]). She goes home to the domestic nest and sleeps the sleep of innocence, rises and cheerfully performs her pastoral chores. But having placed her body in circulation, she cannot reenter the market as consumer or as object of exchange. She can no longer see or hear the goblin men to buy their fruit, but must suffer the debilitating effects of her unsatisfied desires. She begins to pine and wither away. Like Jeanie, it appears that she will die a maiden, without tasting "joys brides hope to have." The fairy tale form of the poem suggests that this may be a fable of the passage from childhood to adulthood, where participation in the marketplace of sex and marriage is the task whose successful accomplishment marks the transition. Laura, however, has failed; she will not grow up. Attempting to exercise the power of the consumer, she has been consumed.

Her sister Lizzie succeeds where Laura has failed. But her success (and her "redemption" of Laura, as her act is usually read) is not, I think, simply a function of her greater moral strength to resist temptation. Lizzie goes to market doubly armed. Unlike Laura, Lizzie has money in her pocket, and she knows how to use it. She has learned from the examples of Jeanie and Laura enough to know that she must not "pay too dear." She does not offer herself as money. With a penny in her purse, "for the first time in her life" she begins "to listen and to look." The goblin men are not to be put off easily. They don't want her to participate in the market on her terms. They insist that she not only buy the fruit that her sister wants, but eat it herself. Lizzie emerges unscathed with her purchase not only because she has money but also because she does not bring her desire—the intellectual or sexual hunger signified by Laura's curiosity—to market with her. She buys for her sister, not herself. The goblin men cannot force her to eat what she has purchased. Lizzie is allowed to triumph all around: the disgusted goblin men throw her back her penny, and its jingle in her purse is "music to her ear" as she runs home, covered with the juices of the fruit that will prove a bitter but successful antidote to the poisonous desire that is destroying Laura.

Lizzie is the heroine of this poem because she gets what she wants without giving in to the pressure that a male marketplace, like male texts about the marketplace, exerts on women—to become that which is exchanged, to become money. She retains the power of the consumer, but to do so she must limit the meaning of consumption. For Lizzie, consuming is understood in its strictest (and etymologically originating) sense as buying (Latin *consumere,* from the root verb *emere,* to buy). She refuses the ordinary metaphorical extensions of the word: to take wholly, to use, burn, or devour. A linguistic purist, Lizzie resists male pressures to make economic acts express desire. She will not say "I want," even if resistance means she cannot speak at all:

> The goblins cuffed and caught her,
>
> . . . . .
>
> Lizzie uttered not a word;
> Would not open lip from lip
> Lest they should cram a mouthful in.
> (424, 430-32)

The danger she avoids is of course exemplified by Jeanie's fate. For Jeanie and Laura, purchase becomes inseparable from desire. Laura's consumption—her purchase of the luscious fruits from the goblin men—is rendered primarily as a scene of pleasure in eating.

> She clipped a precious golden lock,
> She dropped a tear more rare than pearl,
> Then sucked their fruit globes fair or red:
> Sweeter than honey from the rock,

> Stronger than man-rejoicing wine,
> Clearer than water flowed that juice;
> She never tasted such before,
> How should it cloy with length of use?
> She sucked and sucked and sucked the more...
>
> (126-34)

To consume in this extended sense, however, is to expose oneself to the same uses—not only to risk becoming the object rather than the subject of exchange, but also to risk becoming the devoured rather than the devourer. So both Jeanie and Laura waste away, self-consumed by their own desire, the desire that is fed by participation in the marketplace:

> But when the noon waxed bright
> Her hair grew thin and grey;
> She dwindled, as the fair full moon doth turn
> To swift decay and burn
> Her fire away.
>
> (276-80)

Lizzie arrests the horrifying, or "soul-consuming" (512), progress of desire by reestablishing a necessary separation between acts of economic exchange and the expression of desire. She buys but does not consume; Laura is then allowed to consume what she has not bought but been given. The second scene of Laura's eating is fully as passionate as the first, as many readers have noticed, sometimes with embarrassment:

> She clung about her sister
> Kissed and kissed and kissed her:
>
> . . . . .
>
> She kissed and kissed her with a hungry mouth.
>
> (485-86, 492)

But this is the first scene played in reverse: as the kiss replaces her voracious sucking, so the luscious juice becomes "wormwood to her tongue" (494); "She gorged on bitterness without a name" (510). Wasted Laura is purged and restored to health. The desire to consume which made her long to buy again became a smouldering fire consuming her, but in this scene it is overcome by a stronger fire:

> Swift fire spread thro' her veins, knocked at
>   her heart,
> Met the fire smouldering there
> And overbore its lesser flame.
>
> (507-9)

What is this stronger fire? As the poem would have it, love between women. Love, that is, as mutual care and support, surviving and defeating the competitive ethos of the market. The play of desire has been reprivatized, divorced from the play of money, and hence no longer, according to the logic of the poem, an issue of consuming or being consumed.

The poem has its happy fairy tale ending. Lizzie and Laura, having learned to operate successfully in the marketplace of sex and marriage, both grow up. Their reciprocal aid—Lizzie learns from Laura and uses what she learns to help her—enables them to get all the rewards of participating in both the money and the sexual economies, without succumbing fatally to their dangers. Unlike the Jennys of the world, they live to know "the joys brides hope to have," though significantly, the joys of marriage are in this poem the joys of motherhood. This conflation of terms is significant because heterosexual desire is banished from the poem. Lizzie can get her money back because she does not want to enjoy the fruits of merchant men. To achieve power as a consumer, she leaves desire at home, not, for Rossetti, a place of heterosexual desire.

In **"Goblin Market"** home is a place for love between women. The startling passion with which Laura receives from Lizzie the antidote to goblin fruit suggests that such love may be sexual, though consumption, in the literal as well as the economic sense, is to be interdicted after this moment (the luscious juice turns to wormwood in Laura's mouth). The narrative seems to assure us that this scene of sexual passion is the first and last in the sisters' lives, serving to guarantee their passage into marriage and maternity. But Rossetti may be insisting on a different conception of desire altogether: desire not expressed in special acts of passionate, literal consumption, but in the daily sensuous relationships of nurturance that mark the pastoral childhood of the sisters ("Golden head by golden head, / Like two pigeons in one nest / Folded in each other's wings") and their adult experience of maternity ("Their lives bound up in tender lives"). This world of sisters and mothers without fathers (conspicuously absent in the poem) is utopian—as is the "distant place" of the Christian afterlife (the "home" of **"From House to Home"**) to which woman's desire is displaced in much of Rossetti's poetry, when that desire is not, as in her other fairy tale **"The Prince's Progress,"** perpetually deferred.[36] Whether displaced to another world or located in a wholly feminized domestic space, women's desire is withdrawn from sexual and money economies dominated by merchant men.

"Goblin Market" is a tale of women's survival in a world where "the market offers itself to women and girls as a stage for the production of themselves as public beings, [but] on particularly unfavorable terms."[37] However qualified its happy ending may turn out to be, on closer examination, it depicts with considerable acuteness the terms on which girls succeed or fail to reach adulthood. To become adults they must enter a marketplace in which they are always at risk. As the texts of Shakespeare, Marx, and Dante Gabriel Rossetti all suggest, women in the marketplace have not only to reclaim the power of money as their own, but also to resist the tendency of men to exercise their mastery of money through women. The key to this resistance is the separation of economic acts from consuming desires. What makes it possible is the mutual support of women for women. Christina Rossetti reads Jenny's silence as death: reduced to money, the maiden dies. Her death also marks the suppression of gender in the marketplace. The story of survival offered in **"Goblin Market"**—consumer power achieved by withholding female desire—culminates in the production of its heroines as "public beings" who can publish female difference. Laura lives not only to marry and have children, but to tell her story:

> Days, weeks, months, years
> Afterwards, when both were wives
> With children of their own;
>
> . . . . .
>
> Laura would call the little ones
> And tell them of her early prime,
>
> . . . . .
>
> Would talk about the haunted glen,
> The wicked, quaint fruit-merchant men,
>
> . . . . .
>
> Would tell them how her sister stood
> In deadly peril to do her good,
>
> . . . . .
>
> Would bid them cling together,
> "For there is no friend like a sister . . ."
> (543-45, 548-49, 552-53, 557-58, 561-62)

The access to adulthood is also an access to speech—for Laura, to speech within the family, the extent of her sphere, but for her author, Christina Rossetti, to the published speech of literature. Like Lizzie and Laura, Rossetti avoided Jenny's fate in the market of sex and marriage. She did not allow her body to circulate as the currency of exchange between men. The story of **"Goblin Market"** is in this respect its author's story as well. Nor did she engage in the competitive consumption with other women that was, for Rossetti, the equal or greater danger posed by a heterosexual exchange economy. The poem was dedicated to Christina's sister Maria, who was later to become a Sister in an Anglican religious order, and thus, like Christina through the lay Sisterhood at St. Mary Magdalene's, to affirm the mutual ties of women to women, both inside and outside the family, as a refuge from the double threat of an exchange economy.[38]

Laura's concluding celebration of a sister's act, telling the tale to others, mimics her author's efforts to save sisters from the consuming passions of the marketplace.

As my reading of **"Goblin Market"** should make clear, Rossetti herself is finally less interested in exposing the fictions of separate spheres through the transgressive figure of the female consumer (and her shadow sister, the prostitute), than in rescuing the possibility of a utopian place for women outside the marketplace. The fantasy of consumer power and the retreat to a utopia of desire is, however, powerfully attractive to feminist readers. I want to urge that we resist this attraction in order to retain the critical power of the poem. The resistance might begin with a critique like this.

"Goblin Market"'s conclusion may be altogether too self-congratulating—for feminist critics as much as for Christina Rossetti. The triumphant jingle of Lizzie's coin, like the reiteration of Jeanie's name, jars on the ears, suggesting as it does that Lizzie, her author, and her author's critics embrace the laws of exchange and use that whore, money, as long as we do not become it. The apparent displacement of desire from the marketplace to no-place or *utopia* perhaps conceals a greater investment in a political economy, both sexual and literary, than this interpretation of the poem's ending admits. Rossetti's heroines, one might argue, are never really outside the economies from which they appear to triumphantly withdraw, because they are always participants in production that presumes exchange. The butter, milk, and honey of their pastoral childhood, the babies of their adult lives, and, in a different sense, even the femininity or female sexuality that they bring to the goblin market, all belie the possibility of women's work or a woman's sphere untouched by the political economy of the dominant, "male" world. Rossetti herself was, of course, an economic agent, whose books, as well as her face, were for sale—however mediated and disguised her relations with the literary market. The shadowy figure of the prostitute, so named because she shows herself in the public market rather than staying home (*prostituere,* to place before, expose publicly, offer for sale), may after all be an inescapable meaning of the feminine as it is constructed in a market economy.

The withdrawal from the marketplace that **"Goblin Market"** recommends, even were it possible, would have the unwanted consequence of silencing women as totally as Jenny is silenced: Lizzie, refusing to open her lips to consume the goblins' fruit, cannot utter a word. But neither Rossetti nor her heroines mean to swallow their words permanently. Perhaps the fantasy of withdrawal from exchange relations played out in **"Goblin Market"** conceals the desire, not to give and nurture, but to hoard—goods, words, sex, children, and even money (Lizzie's jingling coin). This hoarding becomes itself a kind of power, but only in the context of the exchange relations that women might—a teasing possibility—choose at moments to reenter. Consumer power is then dependent on the power to produce, and ultimately, of course, on the intertwined systems of production and exchange that Rossetti would keep separate for women. Although Rossetti's fable imagines that women who successfully exercise consumer power can then leave the marketplace for the privacy of sisterhood or marriage and motherhood, that withdrawal hardly describes her own activity as author, and it does not describe ours. We would be deluding ourselves if we confused the utopia constructed by Rossetti's strategy for survival, the withholding of desire (which, on closer inspection, turns out to be the reinvestment of desire in hoarding what we have produced) with any real retreat from the public marketplace. Not only is Jenny's case always potentially ours. We also remain invested in the political economies of production and exchange that make utopian desire both necessary—and utopian.

Notes

My special thanks to Lauren Berlant, an acute critic of many versions of this essay.

[1] Though Rossetti later insisted "Goblin Market" was only a nursery tale, she published it as the title poem in a volume of serious verse (1862). Among the 550 rhymes collected by Iona and Peter Opie in *The Oxford Dictionary of Nursery Rhymes* (Oxford: Clarendon, 1951)—taken from late 18th and 19th century published collections—almost a fifth concern buying and selling. One continuing favorite in Mother Goose collections goes: "To market, to market, to buy a fat pig, / Home again, home again, jiggety-jig; / To market, to market, to buy a fat hog, / Home again, home again, jiggety-jog." Browning describes the purchase of the Old Yellow Book at a street market in Florence in detail in the first book of *The Ring and the Book*. That poem, like Dante Gabriel Rossetti's "Jenny" (see discussion below), is also concerned with the figurative prostitution of the artist for money and its relation to women's participation in such exchanges. Other poems by Browning and Rossetti explore related themes; see Browning's "Andrea del Sarto" and "Fra Filippo Lippi," for example, and (more obliquely), the introductory poem "The Sonnet," to Rossetti's *House of Life* (where the poem is a coin). Elsewhere in Victorian literary poetry, however, markets, whether of sex or other commodities, are rare.

[2] Thus Jerome McGann, opening his discussion of the poem, can state: "Everyone agrees that the poem contains the story of temptation, fall, and redemption, and some go so far as to say that the work is fundamentally a Christian allegory" ("Christina Rossetti's Poems: A New Edition and a Revaluation," *Victorian Studies* 23 [Winter 1980]: 247). A variant of this common reading interprets the temptation in terms of Rossetti's internal spiritual history or psychodrama; thus Dorothy Mermin begins her discussion: "*Goblin Market* is usually read as an allegory of the poet's self-division that shows, in Lionel Stevenson's representative summary, the conflict between 'the two sides of Christina's own character, the sensuous and the ascetic,' and demonstrates 'the evil of self-indulgence, the fraudulence of sensuous beauty, and the supreme duty of renunciation'" ("Heroic Sisterhood in *Goblin Market*," *Victorian Poetry* 21 [Summer 1983]: 107; the Stevenson quotation is from his *The Pre-Raphaelite Poets* [Chapel Hill: Univ. of North Carolina Press, 1972], 105). Many critics also recognize that the spiritual narrative has a social referent in the Victorian fallen woman, perhaps specifically those Christina encountered in her association with the Diocesan Penitentiary, St. Mary Magdalene's, Highgate, a home for fallen women. A recent example that argues that the poem may have been actually read aloud at the home is D. M. R. Bentley's "The Meretricious and the Meritorious in *Goblin Market*: A Conjecture and an Analysis," in *The Achievement of Christina Rossetti,* ed. David A. Kent (Ithaca: Cornell Univ. Press, 1987), 57-81.

[3] Market relations in nursery rhymes are not especially gendered: neither the little piggy who went to market ("This little piggy went to market / This little piggy stayed home . . .") nor the fat pig who was sold there ("To market, to market, to buy a fat pig") is assigned a gender. Little old women feature as often as merchant men among the sellers in nursery lore (as they surely did at village markets). The ideology of separate spheres apparently is not reflected in Mother Goose—whose origins, after all, are neither Victorian nor middle class. On the historicity of the distinction between public and private, see Jurgen Habermas, *The Structural Transformation of the Public Sphere: An Inquiry into a Category of Bourgeois Society* (Cambridge: MIT Press, 1989). The critical literature on the gendering of public and private spheres in Victorian discourses is extensive; for an excellent recent discussion, see Mary Poovey, *Uneven Developments: The Ideological Work of Gender in Mid-Victorian England* (Chicago: Univ. of Chicago Press, 1988).

[4] For English attacks on novel reading as a feminine vice, see Terry Lovell, *Consuming Fiction* (London: Verso, 1987), especially 8-11; also John Tinnon Taylor, *Early Opposition to the English Novel* (New York: King's Crown Press, 1943). For the attacks on women as the patrons and consumers of rococo art in France, see Erica Rand, "Boucher, David, and the French Revolution: Politics and Gender in Eighteenth-Century French History Painting" (Ph.D. diss., University of Chicago, 1988), especially chapters 2 and 3.

[5] See Lovell (note 4), 9 and 36-44; and Rand (note 4). Lovell points out not only that the novel was far from an exclusively feminine province, but that perceptions of women readers as "leisured" or "idle" have also been strongly challenged by recent scholarship. For a similarly debunking account of women's relation to rococo art, see, besides Rand, Danielle Rice, "Women and the Visual Arts," in *French Women and the Age of Enlightenment,* ed. Samia I. Spencer (Bloomington: Indiana Univ. Press, 1985), 242-55.

[6] For analyses of how women's desires are employed in contemporary advertising and popular culture, see Judith Williamson, *Decoding Advertisements: Ideology and Meaning in Advertising* (London: Marion Boyars, 1978) and *Consuming Passions: The Dynamics of Popular Culture* (London: Marion Boyars, 1986); and Rosalind Coward, *Female Desires: How They Are Sought, Bought and Packaged* (New York: Grove Press, 1985).

[7] Karl Marx, "Economic and Philosophic Manuscripts," in *The Marx-Engels Reader,* ed. Robert C. Tucker, rev. ed. (New York: W. W. Norton, 1978), 93-94.

[8] Max Horkheimer and Theodor W. Adorno, "The Culture Industry: Enlightenment as Mass Deception," in *Dialectic of Enlightenment,* trans. John Cumming (New York: Continuum, 1987), 153.

[9] Tania Modleski, "Femininity as Mas[s]querade: A Feminist Approach to Mass Culture," in *High Theory/Low Culture: Analysing Popular Television and Film,* ed. Colin MacCabe (New York: St. Martin's Press, 1986), 37-52.

[10] Catherine Gallagher has pointed out the way Henry Mayhew rejects a whole political economy embodied in the figure of the Victorian costermonger; one might argue that "Goblin Market" starts from a similar point, but Mayhew's costermongers (female as well as male) have become Rossetti's goblin *men.* See Gallagher, "The Body Versus the Social Body in the Works of Thomas Malthus and Henry Mayhew," *Representations* 14 (Spring 1986), especially 98-106.

[11] This is the argument made by Joan Riviere in "Womanliness as a Masquerade," *Formations of Fantasy,* ed. Victor Burgin, James Donald, and Cora Kaplan (London: Methuen, 1986).

[12] Mary Poovey and Catherine Gallagher have written illuminatingly on the place of authorship within a Victorian ideology of separate spheres; Gallagher discusses the association between production for a market economy and prostitution as a special danger for women authors. See Mary Poovey, *Uneven Developments* (note 3), especially chap. 4; and Catherine Gallagher, "George Eliot and *Daniel Deronda*: The Prostitute and the Jewish Question," *Sex, Politics and Science in the Nineteenth-Century Novel,* ed. Ruth Bernard Yeazell (Baltimore: Johns Hopkins Univ. Press, 1986), 39-62.

[13] William Michael Rossetti is the source for this information; see Mackenzie Bell, *Christina Rossetti: A Biographical and Critical Study* (Boston: Roberts, 1898), 60; *The Poetical Works of Christina Georgina Rossetti,* ed. William Michael Rossetti (London: Macmillan, 1904), 485; and *The Family Letters of Christina Georgina Rossetti,* ed. William Michael Rossetti (1908; reprint, New York: Haskell House, 1969), 26. The most recent discussions of Rossetti's association with St. Mary's are D. M. R. Bentley's (note 3) and Diane D'Amico, "Christina Rossetti and Highgate Penitentiary: Working Among Fallen Women" (Paper delivered at the Victorians Institute Conference, Univ. of North Carolina at Chapel Hill, 17 October 1987). I have drawn especially on the latter.

[14] The phrase is quoted by D'Amico from Thomas Carter, *A Memoir of John Armstrong* (London: John Henry and James Parker, 1859), 199. Armstrong and Carter were both central figures in the movement to establish penitentiaries for fallen women. On the reforming role of the penitentiary, see John B. Bender, *Imagining the Penitentiary* (Chicago: Univ. of Chicago Press, 1987) and Michel Foucault, *Discipline and Punish: The Birth of the Prison,* trans. Alan Sheridan (London: Allen Lane, 1977).

[15] Christina had originally called it "A Peep at the Goblins"; Dante Gabriel, she later recorded, "substituted the greatly improved title as it now stands." See her note in an 1893 copy of the volume (Iowa State Department of History and Archives, Des Moines), which concludes, "And here I like to acknowledge the general indebtedness of my first and second volumes to his suggestive wit and revising hand." (Note quoted by Rebecca Crump in the textual notes to her edition, *The Complete Poems of Christina Rossetti,* 3 vols. [Baton Rouge: Louisiana State Univ. Press, 1979, 1986], 1:234.) Unless otherwise noted, all quotations from Christina Rossetti's poems will be taken from this edition; line numbers will be given in the text.

[16] Letter to Dante Gabriel Rossetti, 3 March 1865, *The Rossetti-Macmillan Letters,* ed. Lona Mosk Packer (Berkeley: Univ. of California Press, 1963), 44 note 1. The Macmillan correspondence provides much of the information I have drawn on in this paragraph. For pre-1860 publication, see also William Michael Rossetti, ed., *Family Letters of Dante Gabriel Rossetti,* 2 vols. (London: Ellis & Elvey, 1895), and *The Family Letters of Christina Georgina Rossetti* (note 13).

[17] Letter to Dante Gabriel, April-May 1865, *The Rossetti-Macmillan Letters* (note 16), 51.

[18] Letter to William Allingham, September-October 1860, in *Letters of Dante Gabriel Rossetti,* ed. Oswald Doughty and John Robert Wahl, 2 vols. (Oxford: Clarendon Press, 1965), 1:377.

[19] For the reference to her "pot-boilers," see *The Rossetti-Macmillan Letters* (note 16), 46n1. For Christina's decided wish to retain copyright for her published volumes, see especially her letter to Alexander Macmillan, 20 April 1881 (*The Rossetti-Macmillan Letters,* 133-34). One could argue that Christina's insistence on retaining copyright to her volumes came as much from shrewd business sense as from distaste for selling poems. No doubt both motives were at work.

[20] Quoted by Antony H. Harrison, "Eighteen Early Letters by Christina Rossetti," in *The Achievement of Christina Rossetti* (note 2), 198.

[21] See A. Dwight Culler's discussion of prose and poetic idylls in the early nineteenth century, in *The Poetry of Tennyson* (New Haven: Yale Univ. Press, 1977), 114-16.

[22] Collected in Volume 3 of Mary Russell Mitford's *Our Village* (1828); cited here from *Our Village,* 2 vols. (1828; reprint, London: Bell & Daldy, 1865), 2:70-84.

[23] First published in *Poems, Chiefly Lyrical* (1830). That it was influenced by Mitford's story is generally acknowledged. See *The Poems of Tennyson,* 2nd ed., ed. Christopher Ricks, 3 vols. (Berkeley: Univ. of California Press, 1987), 1:406-17.

[24] Her choice of form suggests as much. Most of her rural poems use ballad stanza or more complex combinations of alternately rhymed tetrameter and trimeter lines, together with frequent repetitions, a good deal of dialogue or direct speech, and concise, minimal narration. All the Rossettis seem to have been very interested in ballads, from the 1840s. Dante Gabriel, who avidly read Bishop Percy's *Reliques,* experimented with ballad stories and ballad forms throughout his poetic career. Christina did so too.

[25] Opie, *Oxford Companion* (note 1), 282.

[26] Opie, 282.

[27] Quoted from Francis James Child, ed., *The English and Scottish Popular Ballads,* 5 vols. (1882-98; reprint, New York: Dover, 1965), 2:460. This, the English version of the ballad, was published in Bishop Percy's *Reliques of Ancient English Poetry,* 3 vols. (London: J. Dodsley, 1765), 3:75. Closely related Scottish versions appeared in several late eighteenth and nineteenth-century publications (see Child, 2:457-59). As Child notes, the ballad has many parallels with tales in Gower and Chaucer ("The Wife of Bath's Tale"). The ballad version seems to have been popular in Elizabeth I's time; a stanza was quoted in Fletcher's comedy, *The Pilgrim.*

[28] See, for example, "Fair Annie" and "Child Waters" (in Child (note 27), 2:63, 83). "Mary Hamilton" gets nothing, but she is both wanton and a child murderer (Child, 3:379).

[29] Rossetti's conviction that women are always at a disadvantage in dealing with men seems to be one consequence she drew from the Biblical injunction (that woman is the helpmeet to man) that she accepted. In her prose work, *The Face of the Deep* (London: Society for Promoting Christian Knowledge, 1892), she concluded: "Society may be personified as a human figure whose right hand is man, whose left woman; in one sense equal, in another sense unequal. The right hand is labourer, acquirer, achiever: the left hand helps, but has little independence, and is more apt at carrying than at executing. The right hand runs the risks, fights the battles; the left hand abides in comparative quiet and safety; except (a material exception) that in the *mutual* relationship of the twain it is in some ways far more liable to undergo than to inflict hurt, to be cut (for instance) than to cut" (410; quoted by Diane D'Amico, "Eve, Mary, and Mary Magdalene: Christina Rossetti's Feminine Triptych," in *The Achievement of Christina Rossetti* [note 2], 181).

[30] Both versions were published in Percy's *Reliques* (note 27). Christina Rossetti appears to have followed the English version (which has the explicit comparison of the scorned woman to a queen, as does her poem); this would also have been available in several other late eighteenth and nineteenth-century published collections. See Child (note 27), 2:179-99. To my knowledge, no one has noted that "Maude Clare" is based on an existing popular ballad.

[31] Antony H. Harrison discusses the differences between the three versions in his *Christina Rossetti in Context* (Chapel Hill: Univ. of North Carolina Press, 1988), 4-8. See Crump (note 15), 244-47 for the manuscript and first published versions.

[32] First published in Rossetti's *Poems* of 1870, but begun more than twenty years earlier. Rossetti worked on it in the late 1850s, when Christina was composing her poem.

[33] Karl Marx, "The Power of Money in Bourgeois Society," from "Economic and Philosophic Manuscripts of 1844," in *The Marx-Engels Reader* (note 7), 102-5.

[34] Of the many recent critical essays on Rossetti's "Jenny," only one to my knowledge discusses the mutual figuring of woman as money and money as woman in the text. See Daniel A. Harris's suggestive piece, "D. G. Rossetti's 'Jenny': Sex, Money, and the

Interior Monologue," *Victorian Poetry* 22 (Summer 1984), 197-215. Harris, however, reads the poem as a much more radical statement than I do.

[35] This assertion of the initial innocence of female desire is maintained by Rossetti in her interpretations of the fall of Eve. As Diane D'Amico has pointed out, not only is Eve presented sympathetically in Rossetti's poetry; her commentary on the scriptural event in *Letter and Spirit* (London: Society for Promoting Christian Knowledge, 1883) insists: "It is in no degree at variance with the Sacred Record to picture to ourselves Eve, that first and typical woman, as indulging quite innocently sundry refined tastes and aspirations, a castle-building spirit (if so it may be called), a feminine boldness and directness of aim combined with a no less feminine guessiness as to means. Her very virtues may have opened the door to temptation" (17-18). Eve's desire is "prideful, not lustful," as D'Amico puts it. Sexual desire is her punishment, not her sin: "Eve, the representative woman, received as part of her sentence 'desire': the assigned object of her desire being such that satisfaction must depend not on herself but on one stronger than she, who might grant or deny," Rossetti wrote in another of her prose works, *The Face of the Deep* (1892). See D'Amico's "Eve, Mary, and Mary Magdalene," which quotes these passages, especially 175-80. The sequence of sexually innocent desire, disobedience, and punishment through desire is exactly followed in Laura's story.

[36] Dorothy Mermin, in a particularly sensible essay, argues that "Goblin Market" is a utopian fantasy of "female potency and exclusively female happiness"—disputing Gilbert and Gubar's influential reading of it as conveying "bitter repressive wisdom." See Mermin, "Heroic Sisterhood in *Goblin Market*" (note 2), 116; and Sandra M. Gilbert and Susan Gubar, *The Madwoman in the Attic: The Woman Writer and the Nineteenth-Century Literary Imagination* (New Haven: Yale Univ. Press, 1979), 573. "From House to Home" (composed November, 1858) is a good example of a poem about the need to relocate desire to "a distant place," not in this world but the next.

[37] Erica Carter, "Alice in the Consumer Wonderland: West German case studies in gender and consumer culture," in *Gender and Generation*, ed. Angela McRobbie and Mica Nava (Basingstoke: Macmillan, 1984), 198.

[38] For the dedication, deleted in the published version, see Crump (note 15), 1:234.

Janet Galligani Casey (essay date 1991)

SOURCE: "The Potential of Sisterhood: Christina Rossetti's *Goblin Market*," in *Victorian Poetry*, Vol. 29, No. 1, Spring, 1991, pp. 63-78.

[*In the following essay, Casey studies the meaning of "sisterhood" in "Goblin Market," arguing that the term implies a variety of meanings and "potentially includes the experience of both sexes." Additionally, Casey examines the Victorian conception of the nature of sisterhood as popularized by the work of Florence Nightingale and suggests how Rossetti's own work as a "sister" may have influenced her writing of "Goblin Market."*]

"For there is no friend like a sister."[1]

Critics of Christina Rossetti's **"Goblin Market"** have long noted the prominence of "sisterhood" in this poem. In particular, feminist readings of the poem center on the sisterhood theme in an attempt to argue that Rossetti has created a world which deliberately excludes men. For these critics, the term "sisterhood" marks a reaffirmation of the potentialities of women for independence and productivity.[2] However, **"Goblin Market"** is also recognized as a work which successfully sustains several levels of meaning simultaneously; its rich "suggestive[ness]," first commented upon by William Michael Rossetti,[3] prompts numerous and varied interpretations. In reducing the concept of "sisterhood" to a single unwavering level of meaning, feminist critics, among others, are disregarding this resonance that is the hallmark of the poem. "Sisterhood" in **"Goblin Market"** is not an exclusionary term: rather, it implies several meanings in the same way that it potentially includes the experience of both sexes.

"Goblin Market" exploits two Biblical stories (those of Christ and Eve) which have important implications concerning the traditional roles of men and women. In the Judeo-Christian tradition, the male is the Redeemer; Church hierarchy, male suffrage, and other patriarchal practices carried this religious tradition of male power into the cultural realm. With the role of "savior" reserved exclusively for males, females are relegated to the supporting role (Mary/Martha) or the role of the person in need of salvation (Eve). As Mary or Martha, the female fulfills the secondary function of nurturing the male, the Christ figure. As Eve, the female is the archetypal "fallen woman" who, contrasted to savior, the embodiment of spiritual love, is traditionally associated with carnal love. Both female roles, of course, are inferior to the role of the male.[4]

Our perception of nineteenth-century sexual politics is in accordance with this dichotomy. We tend to view the Victorian female as an egoless, domestic "angel" in the service of the male, who possesses all social and political power; diametrically opposed to this "ideal" of womanhood is the "fallen" woman, whose sins are of a sexual nature. Yet our stereotypical view of Victorian sexual roles has recently been called into question,[5] and a careful sampling of women's writing throughout the Victorian age demonstrates how reductive our mythology of Victorian sexuality can be. Specifically, many of the books on female conduct written by nineteenth-century women prove that these writers did not always perceive themselves as impotent. Their works consistently question the traditional sexual dichotomy by revealing a belief in the power—especially the moral power—of women.

In fact, the concept of a "female Christ"—of woman as moral regenerator—was not uncommon among Victorian female writers, especially insofar as they perceived their maternal role as endowing them with the power to teach—and hence morally guide—the race. A good example is Mrs. Ellis' *The Women of England: Their Social Duties, and Domestic Habits* (1839), in which women are referred to as "supporters of their country's moral worth" (p. 35). Significantly, Mrs. Ellis also emphasizes the importance of female suffering, which creates a "sisterly" bond: "But women do know what their sex was formed to suffer; and for this very reason, there is sometimes a bond existing between sisters, the most endearing, the most pure and disinterested, of any description of affection which this world affords" (p. 224). Although the author is referring here to biological sisterhood, her tendency to address her readers as "my sisters" (e.g., p. 216) suggests that she views "sisterhood" as a sexual identification as much as a biological kinship. More importantly, her assertions concerning "sisters" as "unpretending" sufferers and vehicles of "moral power" suggest that women are metaphorically akin to Christ. In a similar vein, the female author of *Woman's Mission* (1840) claims for women "no less an office than that of instruments (under God) for the regeneration of the world,—restorers of God's image in the human soul."[6]

Such a stance was not as unusual as we may think: other female writers of the period expressed similar views regarding woman's superior capacity for provoking society's moral rebirth. In fact, later in the century, the argument of the female's moral power was used by some women to oppose the suffrage movement: they asserted that women did not need the vote because they already held supreme sway over the male children, whom they could inculcate with their own moral and social ideals.[7] In a basic sense this position is connected to that of Florence Nightingale, who played an integral role in establishing the popular nineteenth-century notion of "sisterhood": as we shall see, her explicit reference to a "female Christ" reflects her belief that the traditional female role of nurturer may take on heroic proportions. All of these women wholeheartedly embraced the role of nurturer without considering themselves consequently barred from the role of redemptor; in fact, they perceived the two roles as inextricably entwined.

Christina Rossetti's writings demonstrate her accordance with such views: like other female Victorian writers, she sees a connection between the "male" and "female" roles that are traditionally mutually exclusive. In a letter to Augusta Webster, an eminent writer and advocate of women's suffrage, Rossetti asserts that maternal love makes a woman "not a giantess or a heroine but at once and full grown a hero and giant."[8] Even more significant is Rossetti's statement in *Seek and Find* of woman's likeness to Christ:

> In many ways the feminine lot copies very closely the voluntarily assumed position of our Lord and Pattern. Woman must obey: and Christ "learned obedience." . . . She by natural constitution is adapted not to serve herself, but to be subordinate: and He came not to be ministered unto but to minister. . . . And well may she glory, inasmuch as one of the tenderest of divine promises takes (so to say) the feminine form: "As one whom his mother comforteth, so will I comfort you" (Is. lxvi.13).[9]

While this is assuredly not a feminist statement, it does assert that women, in their nurturing roles, are indeed Christ-like: they too have access to the redemptive power traditionally assigned to men.

Christina Rossetti's use of the term "sisterhood" in **"Goblin Market"** reveals the same underlying concept: that both "male" and "female" roles are in fact available to everyone. Through the central figures, Lizzie and Laura, Rossetti demonstrates that the female—and ultimately, all people—may potentially act as redeemer and redeemed, as nurturer and nurtured, as lover and beloved. At the end of **"Goblin Market"** Rossetti posits not a world without men, but a world in which all people are allowed to play all parts, to embrace a wholeness that is only possible with the dissolution of the traditional male/female dichotomy. This poem, in part, defines "sisterhood" as the interdependence, rather than isolation, of antinomies, and demonstrates this interdependence both within each of the girls and between them.

At the same time that she advocates this fundamental dynamism between polarities, however, Rossetti also argues on a simpler—and for many of her nineteenth-century readers, a more recognizable—plane that the most traditional female role, that of nurturer, is equal to the traditional roles of men. She plays on the late nineteenth-century definition of "sisterhood" as a religious order of nurses, suggesting that nurturing, rather than being a secondary function, embodies a heroism of its own. In this Rossetti was heavily influenced by Florence Nightingale, whose brave service in the Crimea made her an atypical Victorian female and whose outspoken views on the role of women, especially in her essay *Cassandra*, have clear affinities with **"Goblin Market."**

Consequently, the meaning of the word "sisterhood" in this poem is anything but simple. On the contrary, these competing issues of the dissolution of the male/female dichotomy and of the dignity of the female role of nurturer seem to echo and re-echo throughout the work until the word "sisterhood" achieves a new richness of meaning through these reverberations. To understand fully this intertwining of meanings, it is necessary to investigate each of them individually.

According to Hélène Cixous' conception of patriarchal binary thought,[10] the "weaker" side of all polarities (day/night, sun/moon, etc.) is traditionally associated with women: thus erotic love is conventionally the realm of females (the Eve figures, and also the bearers of children) while the "higher," spiritual love is associated with men (the Christ figures). In **"Goblin Market,"** however, Christina Rossetti has created a world in which women embody both the "strong," male side of life as well as the "weak," female side. Furthermore, Rossetti achieves this end by subverting the Biblical stories of Eve and Christ, which have deep roots in religious and cultural conceptions and which have helped to shape and define both the scope and relative importance of the roles which men and women may play in a patriarchal society. This poem undercuts the traditional patriarchal binary concept that the redeemer is somehow "better" than the redeemed and the spiritual superior to the erotic. Instead, **"Goblin Market"** celebrates a dynamism—a "sisterhood"—between polarities, and allows Laura and Lizzie to represent this interdependence in both narrative and metaphoric terms.

The narrative impetus for the poem is provided by the encounter between Lizzie and Laura and the "goblin men." Most critics have quickly identified these goblins with eroticism: their fruits, an obvious reference to the Eve story, are described in sensual terms (e.g., "Plump, unpecked cherries," "Bloom-down-cheeked peaches," "Pomegranates full and fine" [ll. 5-31]); the goblins have seductive voices, sounding "kind and full of loves" (l. 79) and with "tones as smooth as honey" (l. 108); when Laura eats their fruits there is a marked repetition of the word "sucked" (ll. 128-137). Laura has to pay for the goblins' fruit with part of her body, Lizzie is physically molested by the goblins, and the fate of Jeannie, "Who should have been a bride; / But who for joys brides hope to have / Fell sick and died" (ll. 313-315), is also apparently related to the goblins' carnal nature.[11] These lascivious creatures most certainly represent the lure of erotic love.

Some critics, including Jerome McGann, Dorothy Mermin, and Sandra Gilbert and Susan Gubar,[12] further argue that the goblins represent men. Note, however, the goblins' explicit assertion that "No man can carry" their fruits (l. 376), and a twice repeated parenthetical refrain that "Men sell not such in any town" (ll. 101 and 556). Clearly, "goblin men" are not human men. In order to provide erotic temptation for the women and consequently to make a statement about carnal versus spiritual love, the goblins had to be, in some sense, "male": for a Victorian audience, such a temptation could only be presented in heterosexual (or pseudo-heterosexual) terms. Nevertheless, to suggest that the lustful nature of the goblins and their craftiness in preying on young women represents the nature of human males as Rossetti sees them is, I think, to grossly misread the poem. Both Lizzie and Laura seem contentedly married at the end of the work: this would certainly be inappropriate if the fearful goblin men were intended to represent all members of the male sex.

Lizzie's and Laura's reactions to these goblins indicate immediately the differences in their personalities. At the goblins' cry, "Laura bowed her head to hear / Lizzie veiled her blushes" (ll. 34-35); Lizzie "thrust a dimpled finger / In each ear, shut eyes and ran: / Curious Laura chose to linger" (ll. 67-69). We later learn more about Lizzie's prudence: she worries about the possibility of the girls "los[ing their] way" and urges Laura to "get home before the night grows dark" (ll. 248-252); unlike Laura, she approaches the goblins "Mindful of Jeannie" (l. 364). From the beginning it is clear that Laura is the more daring of the two while Lizzie is the more cautious.

Yet, while there are marked differences between them, the girls are meant to be identified with one another. They lead virtually identical daily lives, sharing all of their domestic activities:

> Laura rose with Lizzie:
> Fetched in honey, milked the cows,
> Aired and set to rights the house
>
> . . . . .
>
> Next churned butter, whipped up cream,
> Fed their poultry, sat and sewed;
> Talked as modest maidens should.
> (ll. 202-209)

And, though the sisters' subsequent actions are quite different, Rossetti pointedly uses the same phrase (in separate sections of the poem) to describe first Laura's, then Lizzie's, initial confused reaction to the goblins: both "knew not was it night or day" (ll. 139, 449). An important passage further emphasizes their closeness:

> Golden head by golden head,
> Like two pigeons in one nest
> Folded in each other's wings,
> They lay down in their curtained bed:
> Like two blossoms on one stem,
> Like two flakes of new-fall'n snow

> . . . . .
> Cheek to cheek and breast to breast
> Locked together in one nest.
>
> (ll. 184-198)

Several critics cite this passage in asserting that the two girls represent two halves of one personality, which becomes "divided" after Laura's "fall" and must reintegrate.[13] The girls' personalities, however, were already markedly different prior to Laura's eating of the goblin fruit; to view them as two parts of one whole also presents difficulties regarding the ending of the poem, in which both girls are married, leading separate—albeit similar—lives. I believe that it is more correct to view them as two distinct individuals who are equally incomplete. Each lacks the trait that is dominant in the other: Laura is wanting in Lizzie's prudence, while Lizzie has none of Laura's daring. There is even a subtle suggestion that the timid Lizzie recognizes her need to acquire some of Laura's courage:

> Tender Lizzie could not bear
> To watch her sister's cankerous care
> Yet not to share.
>
> (ll. 299-301)

Thus, although Laura and Lizzie are quite different, they are equal in two very important ways. First, their personalities are equally deficient. Secondly, and more significantly, as Jerome McGann insightfully points out (p. 253), neither sister is morally superior to the other. Although Laura alone succumbs to the temptations of the goblin fruit, neither Lizzie nor the narrator offers a negative judgment of her. Moreover, the passage in which the closeness of the girls is emphasized ("two pigeons in one nest," etc.) occurs immediately after Laura's "fall," further stressing the equality of the sisters: they remain entwined even after Laura succumbs to the goblins' eroticism.

This pointed restraint from moral judgment is integral to the climax of the poem, when Lizzie secures the antidote to cure Laura and thus becomes the bearer of the "spiritual" love that saves her. At first glance, their roles seem obvious: Lizzie is the redeemer and Laura the redeemed. Just as Laura is the fallen Eve figure, Lizzie becomes a Christ figure, scourged by the goblins and ultimately presenting herself to Laura as a kind of Eucharist: "Eat me, drink me, love me" (l. 471). Similarly, while it is clear that Laura has yielded to the eroticism offered by the goblins, Lizzie embodies a more spiritual, sisterly love that is equally illuminated by the Christian typology. At first she "longed to buy fruit" to save Laura, but "feared to pay too dear" (ll. 310-311). Nevertheless, she finally saves Laura out of Christ-like selflessness:

> Till Laura dwindling
> Seemed knocking at Death's door:
> Then Lizzie weighed no more
> Better and worse.
>
> (ll. 320-323)

In a very subtle manner, however, Rossetti allows Lizzie to play the part of the redeemed as well as that of the redeemer. As we have already seen, Lizzie lacks the courage of action that is Laura's. Laura's fall sets in motion the chain of events which forces Lizzie to gain that courage.[14] When she first decides to confront the goblins for Laura's sake, Lizzie "for the first time in her life / Began to listen and look" (ll. 327-328); she stands resolutely before the goblins, who become "worn out by her resistance" (l. 438); "nor was she pricked by fear" (l. 460) when she finally triumphs over them. When she faces Laura with the antidote, Lizzie is giddy with "inward laughter" (l. 463) and proud of her new-found courage: "For your sake I have braved the glen / And had to do with goblin merchant men" (ll. 473-474). Furthermore, Lizzie's experience forces her to confront her fears about the eroticism that the goblins represent. In procuring the antidote, she submits to a metaphorical rape:

> Lashing their tails
> They trod and hustled her,
> Elbowed and jostled her,
> Clawed with their nails,
> Barking, mewing, hissing, mocking,
> Tore her gown and soiled her stocking.
>
> (ll. 398-403)

When the goblins finally free her, she is "In a smart, ache, tingle" (l. 447). However, this molestation has allowed her to confront and defeat her own fear of sensuality. When she returns to Laura with the antidote, it is Lizzie who initiates the erotic scene which is the climax of the poem:

> Come and kiss me.
> Never mind my bruises,
> Hug me, kiss me, suck my juices
> Squeezed from goblin fruits for you.
>
> (ll. 466-469)

In these lines Lizzie combines both her spiritual love for Laura and her new appreciation of the physical aspects of love: in the proper context, erotic love can indeed be a positive thing. What Lizzie (and consequently, Laura) learns is that sexual love for its own sake leads only to empty desire, but that it acquires a healing and fulfilling element when it has a spiritual dimension.[15]

Laura's fall, therefore, is a fortunate one, for through it she indirectly becomes the redeemer of Lizzie. Prudent Lizzie has now learned that caution must sometimes give way to bold action and that physical love is both beautiful and integral to the human experience. In turn, Laura discovers that daring should be tempered with prudence and that erotic love is empty without emotional commitment: she has been a "fool" to choose only "part / Of soul-consuming care!" (ll. 511-512). Significantly, Laura, the sister who originally succumbed to erotic temptation, is also the one who, at the end of the poem, encourages the children to sing the song of sisterhood. At this moment, the sisters have come full circle: they have both acted as redeemer and redeemed, and they both recognize the value of the erotic and the spiritual sides of love. Realizing that strength is derived from the interaction, rather than isolation, of opposite states, Laura and Lizzie have achieved true "sisterhood."

With this in mind, the closure of "Goblin Market" appears less problematic than some critics have found it. The theme of interdependence, which prior to this point has only been hinted at, finally surfaces. "Is it death or is it life?" the narrator asks as Laura suffers with the antidote. The answer is both: "Life out of death" (ll. 523-524). The placement of these two lines, which mark the ending and beginning of consecutive verse paragraphs, gives them added emphasis. At the climax of the poem, Rossetti has taken the most basic polarity—life versus death—and shown us the interdependent nature of these two states. Suffering and metaphorical death are integral to Laura's redemption and rebirth.

Likewise, both sisters are now depicted as evincing spiritual and erotic love, and the interplay between the two types is positive: their children represent the generative aspects of physical love, and the song they sing reveals the value placed on spiritual love. The final lines of the poem stress this theme of interdependence as well as the concept of equity, the idea that neither side of a polarity is superior:

> For there is no friend like a sister
> In calm or stormy weather;
> To cheer one on the tedious way,
> To fetch one if one goes astray,
> To lift one if one totters down,
> To strengthen whilst one stands.
>
> (ll. 562-567)

The final line—"To strengthen whilst one stands"—echoes the careful avoidance in the poem of passing judgment on either sister: the cheerful and the dispirited, the standing and the fallen, the redeemer and the redeemed remain equal. The equivocal use of the pronoun "one" subtly extends this conviction to the relationship between women and men: we all are both redeemer and redeemed, and we may find ourselves, at different times, playing one part or the other or both. "Sisterhood," at least in part, refers to this state of interdependence, this sense that the strong and the weak are equally necessary and may be fully embodied in both women and men.

Moreover, Rossetti implies that our language practices do not reflect this shared potential. Her emphasis on "sisterhood" as a kind of universal emotional kinship seems to mark a deliberate subversion of the traditional use of "brotherhood"—that term which ostensibly refers to any spiritually kindred state, but which is nevertheless based on an exclusive, patriarchal language. To be a "sister," as to be a "brother," is to share with another person an emotional relationship—a psychic affinity—not necessarily dependent on an actual blood relationship. By substituting "sisterhood" for the term "brotherhood," Rossetti calls attention to those language practices that assign masculine terminology to conditions which do not have a sexual dimension or bias and which rightfully should include women as well as men ("humanity," "mankind," "brotherhood"). Rossetti, however, does not want to replace "brotherhood" with "sisterhood," but to show that both terms are equally valid—or, perhaps, equally invalid. Significantly, she refrains from identifying Laura's and Lizzie's children by their sex: they are referred to only as "children" and "little ones" (ll. 545, 548). Rossetti is careful not to suggest that a "sisterhood" must consist only of females.

"Sisterhood" in this poem also carries other connotations which were no doubt much more obvious to Rossetti's nineteenth-century readers. To be a "sister" is also to play the part of Mary and Martha, to fill the role of nurturer: Lizzie nourishes Laura in both a physical and emotional sense, assuming this traditional maternal role. In the Victorian period this concept was institutionalized in the various orders of religious sisters. By the time Rossetti was writing **"Goblin Market"** the popularity of organized sisterhoods—groups of trained single women dedicated to nursing, teaching, and ministering to the unfortunate—had become a controversial national issue.

The widespread establishment of these groups had begun in the 1840s, when Anglican sisterhoods were advocated by Oxford Movement leaders John Henry Newman and E. B. Pusey; such organizations were considered to accomplish the dual purpose of providing useful occupation for the nation's single women and assisting the increasing numbers of the poor. Many of these sisterhoods were located in London, and they were widely criticized because they actively recruited women from families of good standing. It was believed that they enticed young ladies from their "natural" positions in the home and encouraged a lifestyle that would eventually lead to the dissolution of the family in England. Predictably, the establishment of special sisterhoods to minister specifically to fallen women stirred even greater concern. Yet, as Martha Vicinus points out, there was a certain fascination with, and admiration for, the women who chose to become sisters, particularly those who ministered to prostitutes:

> Only the very highest type of religious woman could succor the ill or penitent, according to the new mythology rapidly gaining ground at midcentury.... The cool cleanliness of the devoted sisters would wipe away the physical illness and its moral implications. Not surprisingly, then, should sisters—the cleanest and purest of women—seek out as their special responsibility the reform of prostitutes—the vilest and most impure of women.... In a society fascinated with sexuality as a symbol of man's fallen nature, the picture of highly controlled and pure women caring for prostitutes had a peculiar appeal and reassurance.[16]

Hence the sisters simultaneously posed a threat to society and provided a model that could be appropriated on both Christian and feminist terms. This dual nature naturally sparked an emotional and often angry controversy which can be traced through the numerous pamphlets on the subject which appeared throughout the 1850s and 1860s. The controversy raged on religious, social, and political grounds as the pamphleteers debated such points as the education of women in these societies, the advantages and disadvantages of the communal lifestyle required by many of the sisterhoods, the possible "contamination" of the women by their association with the poor and fallen, and the issue of celibacy.

In the years immediately preceding **"Goblin Market"** the popularity of these sisterhoods had been greatly spurred by the reputation of Florence Nightingale, who became a national heroine due to her work in the Crimea. Nightingale's "sisters" were, of course, nurses, and Nightingale's continuous fight to establish professional standards for these women—which would consequently lend them dignity and respect—kept the sisterhood issue in the public eye. As a national figure, Nightingale was tremendously popular, so much so that her brief illness in 1855 as the result of Crimean fever elicited national sympathy and prompted the creation of the Nightingale Fund, designated for the establishment of a training school for nurses. Although there were certainly critics who regarded her attempted legitimization of the nursing profession as a silly fad, she was nevertheless revered by the populace, particularly the soldiers. The respect accorded to "The Lady with the Lamp" was an important catalyst for the increasing growth of sisterhoods.[17]

Largely due to Nightingale's renown, the concept of "sister" became increasingly secularized in that its meaning was associated less with organized religion than with the profession of nursing and the general attitude of ministering to the unfortunate. Nurses—with or without religious affiliation—were known as "sisters," as Nightingale's writings of the period (notably *Notes on Hospitals* [1859]) attest. As early as 1855, Anna Jameson, a noted art critic and feminist, gave a lecture entitled "Sisters of Charity" in which she extolled Nightingale's virtues at length and began by defining the term "sister" not only "as the designation of a particular order of religious women, belonging to a particular church, but also in a far more comprehensive sense, as indicating the vocation of a large number of women in every country, class, and creed."[18] Hence the term "sisterhood" had taken on a wide range of implications and had come to represent a larger endeavor: through the concept of sisterhood, women acquired a sense of themselves as an identifiable group with its own aims, talents, and capacities for social power.

Rossetti was certainly not ignorant of the sisterhood phenomenon. As Lona Mosk Packer has pointed out,[19] this poem was originally dedicated to Maria Francesca Rossetti, Christina Rossetti's sister, who later joined the Anglican Sisterhood of All Saints (Bell, p. 54). Moreover, Christina herself spent considerable time during the 1860s working at the St. Mary Magdalene Home for Fallen Women at Highgate Hill.[20] Even more significant is Rossetti's interest in the activities of Florence Nightingale. William Michael Rossetti reports that in 1854 "Christina wished to join her Aunt Eliza Polidori in going out as a nurse to Scutari, in connection with the Crimean War, under the scheme planned out by Miss Nightingale; but she was pronounced to be below the stipulated age."[21] In the same year, Maria made inquiries concerning Nightingale's "sanatorium," in the hope that Lizzie Siddal, the future wife of Dante Gabriel Rossetti, might be treated there.[22] Thus, for the Rossetti family, particularly Christina, Nightingale constituted a significant presence.

Rossetti's interest in Florence Nightingale and the sisterhood movement largely accounts for the diverse ramifications of "sisterhood" in **"Goblin Market."** The association of "sister" with the profession of nursing, the redemption of fallen women, and female communal life relates clearly to the tale of Lizzie and Laura and is important to a full conception of the poem. These associations certainly provided reverberations of meaning for a nineteenth-century audience that are largely lost on readers today. Moreover, Rossetti's exploitation of the various concepts of "sisterhood" places her within that group of contemporary women writers who were grappling with similar issues: the unique relationships among women, their capacity for social awareness and activism, and their ability to take on the role of moral redeemer.

One of these other writers was Florence Nightingale herself. In particular, *Cassandra,* her essay protesting the subordinate status of Victorian women, has remarkable affinities with **"Goblin Market."** Although Rossetti could not have read this essay before writing her poem (it was not published until after Nightingale's death in 1910), much of *Cassandra* was written contemporaneously with **"Goblin Market;"** moreover, Nightingale was well known for her outspokenness concerning both the nursing profession and women in general, so that at least some of the thoughts expressed in *Cassandra* may have been known to the public long before its publication.[23] In any event, the marked similarities between the two works suggest that these women were not writing in ideological isolation, but that both were working within a larger current of female thought that was sweeping the age. The connections between *Cassandra* and **"Goblin Market"** demonstrate that Rossetti shared with Nightingale similar ideas concerning the restrictions placed on women in Victorian society, and that both women viewed "sisterhood"—both the nurturing avocation and the nursing profession—as a pursuit endowed with inherent dignity.

One insistent question serves as the primary focus of *Cassandra:* "Why have women passion, intellect, moral activity—these three—and a place in society where no one of the three can be exercised?" (p. 25). Nightingale feels that it is the woman's prescribed domestic role that stunts her intellectual and emotional growth, and that a fantasy world for women would therefore include few family ties. This, she asserts, is one reason for the Victorian female's love of fiction: "The heroine has *generally* no family ties . . . or, if she has, these do not interfere with her entire independence" (p. 28). **"Goblin Market"** seems to suit such criteria: perhaps Rossetti, too, was positing a world in which women are largely freed from the ties of family to explore themselves and each other. Of course, the solidly domestic ending of **"Goblin Market"** would seem to negate such a view; yet in one sense the domestic ending may simply signify a return from fantasy to an "imaginary reality"—a domestic reality, to be sure, but an "improved" domesticity in which the woman's role as nurturer achieves dignity and respect.

Rossetti's (and also Nightingale's) love for this fostering role would necessitate her continued advocacy of such roles for women. Note the tender care with which Lizzie nurses Laura:

> That night long Lizzie watched by her,
> Counted her pulse's flagging stir,
> Felt for her breath,
> Held water to her lips, and cooled her face
> With tears and fanning leaves.
> (ll. 525-529)

However, it is the manner in which these nurturing roles are perceived by society as a whole that determines their ability to provide women with psychic fulfillment: this is the focus of Rossetti's concern. At the end of **"Goblin Market,"** Rossetti depicts Lizzie and Laura in blissful motherhood, indicating that she does not believe that the traditional role of "sisterhood," of nurturing, should be abandoned by women. Rather, she extols it in its fullest, most complete, form, a form which insists that it is not inferior to the roles of the nurtured—that is, of men.

Rossetti and Nightingale also agree on the centrality of suffering. In *Cassandra,* Nightingale rails against the "indifferentism" of Victorian women, arguing that "out of nothing comes nothing. But out of suffering may come the cure" (p. 29). Rossetti shares this attitude in **"Goblin Market,"** for she subjects not just Laura, but also Lizzie, to suffering in order to arrive at new self-awareness. Like Nightingale, Rossetti feels that it is suffering for the sake of others (and not sex) that makes one Christ-like. Rossetti apparently agrees with Nightingale that "it is a privilege for you [women] to suffer for your race—a privilege not reserved to the Redeemer, and the martyrs alone" (p. 30). Nightingale, however, goes a step further, saying explicitly what Rossetti touches on in this poem only metaphorically:

> At last there shall arise a woman, who will resume, in her own soul, all the sufferings of her race, and that woman will be the Saviour of her race. (p. 50)

> The next Christ will perhaps be a female Christ. (p. 53)

This concept of a female Christ figures prominently in both *Cassandra* and **"Goblin Market,"** for both Nightingale and Rossetti believe that women, like men, may be redeemers. For both of these writers, women have been unfairly relegated to the roles of Mary/Martha and Eve, when the role of Christ is within their grasp as well. To nurture, to love, and even to redeem—these, imply both Nightingale and Rossetti, are indeed the proper spheres of women as well as men.

The potential meaning of "sisterhood" in **"Goblin Market"** is therefore expanded by considering its peculiar nineteenth-century implications—namely, the controversy surrounding organized sisterhoods and the attempt by women such as Florence Nightingale to endow these groups with dignity. Rossetti's personal involvement with sisterhoods and her admiration for the work of Nightingale suggest that her exploitation of the concept of "sisterhood" in **"Goblin Market"** was not coincidental; for both Rossetti and her readers, that term evoked a complex set of ideas concerning woman's attempt to expand her social role, and her pursuit of a special kind of heroism both through and beyond her traditional sphere.

However, like Nightingale, Rossetti also suggests that this traditional sphere—the nurturing role—should ideally be shared by all of society and should be weighed equally with the traditional roles of men. Thus "sisterhood" in this poem transcends the obvious meaning of the relationship between Lizzie and Laura and, I believe, even transcends those definitions of the word which hinge on "femaleness." "Sisterhood" in **"Goblin Market"** is, ultimately, a kinship which is purged of its sexual bias in that it allows each sex to openly embrace both the "stronger" and the "weaker" sides of life in the knowledge that both aspects are necessary for completeness.

Hence **"Goblin Market"** is not, as some critics have suggested, a feminist manifesto in which women assume the roles of men. Rather, it is the positing of a world in which the interdependence or dynamism of contrasting states is a positive thing, and in which women are permitted to take part in the achievement of that wholeness. Like other female writers of the nineteenth century, Rossetti believed in the potentially redemptive power of women. In this poem she subverts Christian allegory in order to allow women to participate equally in the positive roles of Christian mythology: they are not limited to being Eve figures, can achieve new dignity as Mary/Martha figures, and may even go so far as to become Christ figures. Furthermore, the traditional moral judgments regarding these roles have been removed, so that Lizzie and Laura learn that they are all equally important, that it is no more degrading to play the part of Eve or Mary/Martha than it is to play the part of Christ. The assumption that the redeemer is above the redeemed, the nurtured better than the nurturer, and the spiritual superior to the erotic has been undermined, leaving the sisters to play the parts of both the fallen and the savior, the nursing and the nursed, and to fuse the joys of both erotic and spiritual love. "Sisterhood" in all of its non-sexual ramifications is, for Lizzie and Laura as well as for Christina Rossetti, the primary goal.

Notes

[1] Quotations from *Goblin Market* are taken from *The Complete Poems of Christina Rossetti,* ed. R. W. Crump (Baton Rouge, 1979), vol. 1.

[2] See, for example, Dorothy Mermin's "Heroic Sisterhood in 'Goblin Market,'" *VP* 21 (1983): 107-118. In a similar vein, Jerome J. McGann argues that "all men [have] been banished from this world so that the iniquity of the fathers might not be passed on to the children" ("Christina Rossetti's Poems: A New Edition and a Revaluation," *VS* 23 [1980]: 237-254). For a good overview of feminist approaches up to 1980 see Miriam Sagan's "Christina Rossetti's 'Goblin Market' and Feminist Literary Criticism" (*Pre-Raphaelite Review* 3, no. 2 [1980]: 66-76).

[3] *The Poetical Works of Christina Georgina Rossetti,* ed. William Michael Rossetti (London, 1904), p. 459.

[4] One woman who seems to encompass both of these roles, at least in popular tradition, is Mary Magdalene, who is "saved" from her Eve-like sinfulness only to become Christ's nurturer at the foot of the Cross. By contrast, Christ's male followers (e.g., Saul/Paul) forsake sin in order to take part in the redemption of the masses by becoming teachers. What is even more interesting about the Mary Magdalene tradition, however, is that it lacks Biblical authority. There is no evidence that Mary Magdalene was a reformed adultress: early in Church history her identity was confused by Church Fathers with that of two other women in the Bible (Mary of Bethany and an unnamed adultress), and the tradition of Mary Magdalene as both Eve figure and nurturer of Christ has been maintained to this day. For an introduction to this issue see *The New Catholic Encyclopedia* (New York, 1967), vol. 9.

[5] See especially Nina Auerbach, *Woman and the Demon: The Life of a Victorian Myth* (Cambridge, Massachusetts, 1982).

[6] *Woman's Mission* (Boston, 1840), p. 11. The author of this work is designated only as "an English lady, residing near London."

[7] For a presentation of this stance by a Victorian female novelist who was widely read and admired by her contemporaries, see Marie Corelli, "Man's War Against Women," *Harper's Bazaar* 41 (May-June 1907): 425-428, 550-553.

[8] Quoted in Mackenzie Bell, *Christina Rossetti: A Biographical and Critical Study* (London, 1898), pp. 111-112.

[9] Christina Rossetti, *Seek and Find: Double Series of Short Stories of the Benedicite* (London, 1879), pp. 30-31.

[10] For a succinct summary of Cixous' theories, see Toril Moi, *Sexual/Textual Politics: Feminist Literary Theory* (London, 1985), pp. 102-126.

[11] The traditional alignment of females with the "lower," erotic form of love did not wholly suit the Victorian sensibility: although woman was indeed perceived as inferior, she was also viewed as having no sexual appetite. By emphasizing the generative aspect of erotic love, however, the Victorians maintained the tradition of the female's inferior nature without referring to sex. Jeannie's fate, then, can be interpreted in two ways: her hoped-for "joys" may be purely sensual, or they may refer to the birth of children. Either way, these "joys" certainly represent some aspect of erotic love.

[12] McGann's and Mermin's articles have been previously cited. See also Gilbert and Gubar's reading of "Goblin Market" in *The Madwoman in the Attic* (New Haven, 1979).

[13] See especially Winston Weathers, "Christina Rossetti: The Sisterhood of Self," *VP* 3 (1965): 81-89. Similar arguments are asserted by Alan P. Barr in "Sensuality Survived: Christina Rossetti's 'Goblin Market,'" *EM* 28-29 (1979-80): 267-282, and by A. A. DeVitis in "'Goblin Market': Fairy Tale and Reality," *JPC* 1 (1967): 418-426.

[14] I am indebted to Martine Watson Brownley ("Love and Sensuality in Christina Rossetti's 'Goblin Market,'" *Essays in Literature* 6 [1979]: 179-186) for her insight regarding Lizzie's need to confront the goblins. Jerome McGann also considers the "dialectical relationship" of the two girls, noting that they both gain something through the redemptive process.

[15] Some may object to this reading by pointing out that Christina Rossetti never idealized erotic love. This is true; in fact, her devotional poetry often emphasizes the superiority of the spiritual over the carnal. For example, the title and content of the poem "Doeth Well . . . Doeth Better" clearly suggest the teachings of St. Paul, who says that spiritual devotion is "better" than earthly love (1 Corinthians 7.38). However, St. Paul also insists that marriage, though inferior to celibate devotion to God, can be a sacred thing as well. In "Goblin Market," Rossetti seems to follow a similar line of thought: the spiritual element of the love between the sisters somehow validates their erotic act, in contrast to the empty eroticism which Laura experiences through the goblins.

[16] Martha Vicinus, *Independent Women: Work and Community for Single Women 1850-1920* (Chicago, 1985), pp. 77-78. This is one of several excellent studies of the sisterhood phenomenon; see also A. M. Allchin, *The Silent Rebellion: Anglican Religious Communities 1845-1900* (London, 1958) and the relevant chapter of Michael Hill's *The Religious Order* (London, 1973).

[17] For more information concerning Nightingale's work throughout this period and her popular reception in England, see Sir Edward Cook, *The Life of Florence Nightingale* (London, 1913), vol. 2.

[18] Delivered February 14, 1855, and first published in 1857 in *"Sisters of Charity" and "The Communion of Labor" by Mrs. Jameson* (rpt. Westport, Connecticut, 1976).

[19] Lona Mosk Packer, "Symbol and Reality in Christina Rossetti's 'Goblin Market,'" *PMLA* 73 (1958): 375-385.

[20] In light of Christina Rossetti's interests in this area, D.M.R. Bentley hypothesizes that "Goblin Market" was intended to be read aloud to an audience of fallen women ("The Meretricious and the Meritorious in 'Goblin Market': A Conjecture and an Analysis" in *The Achievement of Christina Rossetti*, ed. David A. Kent [Ithaca, New York, 1987], pp. 57-81). Rossetti's sonnet "From Sunset to Star Rise" has also been associated with her charity work; for a recent view of the historical context of this poem, see Diane D'Amico, "Christina Rossetti's 'From Sunset to Star Rise': A New Reading," *VP* 27 (1989): 95-100.

[21] See William Michael Rossetti's Introduction to *The Poetical Works of Christina Georgina Rossetti*, p. lvi. A brief account of Eliza Polidori's adventures in Crimea is included in *Dante Gabriel Rossetti: His Family Letters*, ed. William Michael Rossetti (London, 1895), p. 32.

[22] Georgina Battiscombe, *Christina Rossetti: A Divided Life* (New York, 1981), p. 82.

[23] See Myra Stark's introduction to Nightingale's *Cassandra* (Westbury, New York, 1979). All page references regarding *Cassandra* refer to this text.

Mary Wilson Carpenter (essay date 1991)

SOURCE: "'Eat me, drink me, love me': The Consumable Female Body in Christina Rossetti's *Goblin Market*," in *Victorian Poetry*, Vol. 29, No. 4, Winter, 1991, pp. 415-34.

[*In the following essay, Carpenter suggests that "Goblin Market" presents a radical view of women's bodies and appetites that was influenced by Rossetti's participation in the Oxford Movement's "women's mission to women," in which she worked with prostitutes and homeless women.*]

When Alice falls down the rabbit-hole she behaves, as Nancy Armstrong has pointed out, like a typical shopper—picking out and then putting back a jar of orange marmalade from the shelves of the rabbit-hole.[1] Later, she discovers that objects in Wonderland tend to come inscribed with such unsubtle advertising ploys as "eat me" or "drink me." Noting that all Alice's troubles seem to "begin and end with her mouth," Armstrong relates Alice's dilemma to "a new moment in the history of desire," a moment when the burgeoning "consumer culture" based on British imperialism changed the nature of middle-class English femininity (p. 17). *Alice in Wonderland* (1865) demonstrates the logic that links the colonial venture to the appetite of a little girl through the image of a "double-bodied woman"—a conflation of non-European women with European prostitutes and madwomen, all three of which were thought to exhibit the same features of face and genitals and, more crucially, to display the disfiguring results of unrestrained "appetite."[2] Victorian consumer culture both produced objects of desire and dictated that little Alices must learn to control their desires, in imagined contrast to women of the "dark continents" and prostitutes on the dark streets of their own cities.

So runs Armstrong's persuasive reading of a Victorian "children's" classic known to as many adults as children. Christina Rossetti's poem, **"Goblin Market,"** first published in 1862, suggests its location in the same intersection of imperialist culture and consumer capitalism that Armstrong elucidates for *Alice in Wonderland*.[3] Opening with the sensuous advertisement of exotic fruits hawked by goblin men to innocent young women, Rossetti's poem presents an explicitly articulated image of a marketplace in which female "appetite" is at stake. But whereas in Carroll's narrative, according to Armstrong's reading of it, *"all possibility for pleasure splits off from appetite and attaches itself to self-control,"* in Rossetti's poem female appetite is simply re-directed toward another female figure, where it is provoked, encouraged, and satiated in the undeniably homoerotic text of the poem (p. 20; Armstrong's emphasis). Lizzie urges Laura to "Hug me, kiss me, suck my juices" as well as to "Eat me, drink me, love me" (ll. 468, 471). While Laura is said to loathe this "feast" proffered on her sister's body, it makes her leap and sing "like a caged thing freed" (l. 505). The result of Laura's totally unrestrained, orgiastic consumption of the "juices" on her sister's body is her restoration to life and health and, I will argue, to desire. The female body in the poem is subject to "consumption" as a commodity—as Laura's near-fatal experience demonstrates—but it is also "consumable" as a regenerative and self-propagating "fruit," as Lizzie's example shows us.

If *Alice in Wonderland* is structured on the "problem" of female desire in the imperialist marketplace, then Christina Rossetti's **"Goblin Market"** presents a startlingly different assessment of female sexual appetite. Yet the drive to evoke and regulate female appetite is not unique to the Rev. Charles Dodgson's children's story or even to children's literature conceived by Victorian clergymen. Charles Bernheimer argues that for nineteenth-century French male artists and novelists, the image of the prostitute stimulated representational strategies to control and dispel the fantasmatic threat of female "sexual ferment."[4] These artists associated the female body with "animality, disease, castration, excrement, and decay" (p. 2). Bernheimer acknowledges that in writing his book he "had to confront powerful expressions of disgust for female sexuality" (p. 4). As the nineteenth century progressed, the fear of "contamination" by the prostitute's unrestricted sexuality was given medical justification in France by "theories of degenerate heredity and syphilitic infection" (p. 2). Similarly, as Judith R. Walkowitz shows, the passage of the Contagious Diseases Acts in England in the 1860s suggests that prostitution was increasingly perceived there also as a dangerously contaminating form of sexual activity, one "whose boundaries had to be controlled and defined by the state."[5]

Even closer to Christina Rossetti's artistic context was her brother Dante Gabriel Rossetti's poem about a prostitute, "Jenny," which articulates a typical construction of female sexuality as diseased and contagious appetite:

> For is there hue or shape defin'd
> In Jenny's desecrated mind,
> Where all contagious currents meet,
> A Lethe of the middle street?[6]

If, as Armstrong argues, the 1860s represent a new moment in the history of desire in which consumer culture changed the nature of middle-class English femininity, both producing the desire for objects and structuring femininity in relation to that desire, then what accounts for the radically different representation of female appetite in **"Goblin Market"**? How was it possible for Christina Rossetti, devout Victorian practitioner of what Jerome McGann has called a "severe Christianity," to produce a poem in which fear of the contagion of the female body is radically disavowed?[7] And is it nonetheless possible to locate a "deviant counterpart"—the "double-bodied" figure of the prostitute-cum-African or -Asian woman—as a structuring figure repressed from **"Goblin Market"**?

D. M. R. Bentley has recently speculated that Christina Rossetti may have written **"Goblin Market"** with the intention of reading it not to children but to the inmates—"fallen women" or prostitutes—of the St. Mary Magdalene Home, Highgate, where she is known to have volunteered during the 1860s.[8] However much this possibility may alter our perception of the poem, Rossetti's intentions are not my concern here. Rather, I would propose that the foundation of Anglican Sisterhoods associated directly with the two churches which Rossetti is known to have attended, and the work of those Sisterhoods with homeless, destitute, and fallen women, gave the poet access to a uniquely feminocentric view of women's sexuality and simultaneously opened her eyes to its problematic position in Victorian culture. In particular, her immediate experience with the interaction between prostitutes and women's religious communities may have constructed Rossetti's representation of a "marketplace" in which "appetite" puts a woman at risk, but where her salvation is to be found not in controlling her appetite but in turning to another woman.

Like the other "fruits of empire," women's bodies were vended in the streets surrounding the churches, and zealous churchwomen like Christina Rossetti went out to "buy" them back. But these shoppers were themselves commodified by the market in which they bargained, their own bodies and appetites implicated in the exploitative sexual economy they sought to resist and evade. In this scene of "compulsory heterosexuality," **"Goblin Market"** suggests that female erotic pleasure cannot be imagined without pain, yet the poem not only affirms the female body and its appetites but constructs "sisterhood" as a saving female homoerotic bond.[9]

While **"Goblin Market"** pushes the normative realm of heterosexual marriage to the margins of its narrative—invoking husbands only by implication in the final lines of the poem—that normative realm with its inscription of gender, class, and racial hierarchies is nevertheless exhibited in the poem which followed **"Goblin Market"** in its 1862 edition (Crump, I, p. 26).[10] In that little-discussed poem, **"In the Round Tower at Jhansi,"** I find a final comment on what **"Goblin Market"** is, and is not, about.

Sisterhoods and the Female Gaze

The extraordinary homoerotic energies of **"Goblin Market"** seem particularly unaccountable in relation to the familiar assessment of Christina Rossetti as a devout Anglo-Catholic spinster who lived out her entire life with her mother, sister, and elderly aunts. William Rossetti described her as a "devotee," instancing her "perpetual church-going and communions, her prayers and fasts, her submission to clerical direction, her oblations, her practice of confession"—a catalog that suggests a religious practice stripped of much social interaction and certainly of all pleasure.[11] Yet the histories of Christ Church, Albany Street, and All Saints' Margaret Street, and of the Sisterhoods founded at these two churches produce a very different reading of the Oxford Movement that constructed both Rossetti's religious practice and her poetic texts. Far from McGann's conception of a "severe Christianity," the "Church" as represented in these histories appears to have been a hotbed of social reforms and sexual tensions generated by those reforms. The work of the newly formed Anglican Sisterhoods proved to be inseparable from the "work" of "fallen women," producing an unprecedented mingling of "pure" and "tainted" women. Moreover, as Martha Vicinus has noted, the Anglican Sisterhoods empowered women, validating their work and values.[12] The feminism and intense homoeroticism of **"Goblin Market"** are fully accountable when read intertextually with this unconventional "social text" of the Victorian Anglican church.

In speaking of the homoeroticism of the poem as "accountable," I am assuming, as Mary Poovey states, that "the representation of biological sexuality, the definition of sexual difference, and the social organization of sexual relations are social, not natural, phenomena."[13] Rather than reading **"Goblin Market"** as "expressing" by virtue of the poet's creative genius an "inner" and unaccountable desire—a reading which might be called a humanist Freudian interpretation—I look for the "origins" of Rossetti's representation of female sexual desire in the complex interactions between the social institutions and texts of her culture. Thus, I will argue that the characteristics of the historical institution of "sisterhood" unique to Christina Rossetti's churches constituted a social and discursive matrix which enabled the production of a radical subjectivity in **"Goblin Market:"** that is, a female speaker or subject of discourse which does not take up the conventional phallocentric position, in which the female body is the object of a male gaze.[14] In a text exemplary of the Oxford Movement's "women's mission to women," as I will show, the female body is represented as the object of a female gaze, and in **"Goblin Market"** we find a similarly radical female subjectivity.

What I will be arguing here is that the writer, though determined by the ideological structuring of her society, may also be emancipated in some degree by exposure to unconventional or disruptive ideological discourses. Such "uneven developments," as Poovey says, result from the different positioning of individuals within the social formation, and from the different articulation of the ideological formulation by different institutions, discourses, and practices (p. 3). While Marxist or materialist readings may position the writer as the "simple" subject of the dominant ideology, subjectivities are constituted at the intersection of multiple and competing discourses.[15] This multiplicity accounts for such "uneven developments" as a powerfully feminist and homoerotic text written by a devout Victorian lady poet.

Previous attempts to link **"Goblin Market"** with Rossetti's associations with "sisters" and "fallen women" have focused on her involvement with the institution at Highgate, despite William Rossetti's recollection that this work did not begin until 1860, while the manuscript of **"Goblin Market"** is dated April 27, 1859. So little is known about the 1850s in Christina Rossetti's life that they have been described as the "grey years."[16] Scholars have relied largely on William's reminiscences, but these are often vague and spotty and may also be inaccurate, as demonstrated in his comments to Mackenzie Bell about Christina's church-related work:

> She was (I rather think) an outer Sister—but in no sort of way professed—of the Convent which Maria afterwards joined—Also at one time (1860-'70) she used pretty often to go to an Institution at Highgate for redeeming 'Fallen Women'—It seems to me that at one time they wanted to make her a sort of superintendent there, but she declined—In her own neighbourhood, Albany Street, she did a deal of district visiting and the like.[17]

William's use of the term "Convent," which suggests an enclosed community of women, to refer to the All Saints' Sisterhood which Maria joined in 1873 shows how unacquainted he must have been with the Sisterhood and its activities, for it was primarily a nursing order which occupied an ever increasing number of buildings adjacent to All Saints' Church and administered various institutions both in London and outside it. The headnote, "House of Charity," which Christina penciled in on her poem, **"From Sunset to Star Rise,"** and which William thought referred to the Highgate institution, may have referred to the All Saints' Home run by these Sisters, since the Rev. W. Upton Richards described it as an institution entirely dependent on voluntary gifts and commended to the "Christian charity of all."[18]

William's statement that Christina did district visiting in "her own neighbourhood, Albany Street" may also be misleading, as this implies that she did this kind of work only after March, 1854, when the Rossetti family moved to 45 Upper Albany Street. Since the Rossetti women began attending Christ Church in 1843, it seems probable that Christina participated in its social work and reform efforts well before 1854 (Battiscombe, p. 30). Built in 1837 at the instigation of William Dodsworth, a fiery young preacher who was then the incumbent at the Margaret Street Chapel (whose remaining parishioners went on to build All Saints' Church), Christ Church was characterized by "zeal" for social reform from its beginnings.[19] According to Canon Burrows, who became the incumbent in 1851, Christ Church became "the leading church in the [Oxford] movement," and the scene of sermons by such well-known preachers as Archdeacon Manning, Dr. Pusey, and Dr. Hook (Burrows, p. 14). Doubtless much more important to Christina Rossetti and her sister Maria was the fact that the first Anglican Sisterhood since the Reformation was founded there.

Pusey seems to have been the guiding force for the formation of this Sisterhood, which some thought might "save" certain Anglican members from converting to Roman Catholicism while others despaired that it would only further encourage such "Romanising."[20] Pusey's desires for the Sisterhood, however, appear to have been intimately linked with his grief for his own daughter, who died tragically on the very day of the meeting which decided to establish such a community (Cameron, p. 31). Pusey thought that for a Bishop to have anything to do with the Sisterhood, which should consist simply of a few young women living together, would be to violate "the sacredness of domestic charity and devotion" (Cameron, p. 32). His close and even tender relationship with the Sisters began on March 26, 1845, when the first two aspirants arrived. As Pusey later wrote to Keble, "We (i.e. Dodsworth and myself) had a little service with them on Wednesday; they were in floods of tears, but in joy" (Cameron, p. 33).

If Pusey imagined a sanctified domestic enclave of perpetual daughters, others—particularly the women who either entered or founded such Sisterhoods—seem to have had quite a different vision. Far from seeking out an ecclesiastical version of the patriarchal families most of them were leaving, they saw themselves as embarking on a new and independent existence in which they would undertake useful, important work. The Park Village Sisters are reported to have immediately begun to visit the "low Irish people" and the brothels in their district (Williams and Campbell, p. 23).[21] Before founding the All Saints' Sisterhood, Harriet Brownlow Byron took a nursing course.[22] She then began the work of this Sisterhood by taking homeless women and orphan girls right into the house where the Sisters lived, the All Saints' Home. By 1862 this "Home" occupied four buildings on Margaret Street, and the Sisters' various enterprises eventually occupied every building on Margaret Street as far as Great Titchfield Street. By 1866 they were conducting an asylum for aged women, an industrial school for girls, an orphanage, a home for incurables, two convalescent homes, and the nursing service for the entire University College Hospital, in addition to teaching in the district night-school and nursing the sick poor in their own homes.[23]

Unlike the more successful All Saints' Sisterhood, the Park Village Sisterhood encountered many difficulties, finding itself at the center of fierce religious controversy in Christ Church.[24] Throughout the years of 1849 and 1850 Dodsworth—increasingly convinced that he should convert to Catholicism—was preaching sermons at Christ Church of such a nature that Pusey said "he wished he could induce the sisters to read their Bibles during his sermons or shut their ears."[25] One of the Sisters was actually kidnapped by a "Miss White" and taken to a Roman Catholic convent. She was eventually released, only to be assailed and accused of "apostasy" the following Sunday as she tried to enter the door of Christ Church (Williams and Campbell, pp. 81-82). Christina Rossetti could hardly have escaped involvement in the parish turmoil. She was at this time engaged to James Collinson, who had converted from the Roman Catholic to the Anglican Church to further his courtship of Christina. During the early months of 1850, Collinson decided that he must rejoin the Catholic Church, and upon hearing this, Christina decided to end their engagement. The Rev. Mr. Dodsworth "romanized" on the last day of 1850.[26]

Despite such disruptions, both Christ Church and the Sisterhood moved ahead vigorously with new plans for ministering to the poor. A second church was to be built at the south end of the parish near "the notoriously evil York Square," where brothels flourished because of the nearby Cumberland Barracks (Coombs, pp. 9-12). On July 15, 1849, the laying of the foundation stone for "St. Mary Magdalene" was planned, with the congregation to make a procession from

Christ Church to the site.[27] John Keble, who preached the sermon, hinted that troublemakers might be encountered and begged the congregation to "go reverently . . . as we pass through the streets of Babylon." The "long tramping procession" accordingly wound its way silently through the "sordid district" (Coombs, p. 13). A little over a year later, in September, 1850, Pusey laid the foundation stone for the "House of Religion," which was to be occupied by the Sisters of Park Village but was also intended to accommodate fourteen homeless women, forty orphan girls, and fourteen "ladies" (Coombs, p. 15). This building was very near the site for the new St. Mary Magdalene Church (and therefore near the brothels). On All Saints' Day (November 1) in 1850, Pusey also laid the foundation stone for what would become the extravagantly beautiful All Saints' Church, built on the site of the old Margaret Street Chapel.

Christina Rossetti, her sister Maria, her mother Frances, and her aunts could all have been a part of that unprecedented outdoor procession through the neighboring "red light" district to the site chosen for the new church.[28] That Christina and one of her aunts were very much caught up in the new fervor for women's work with the needy is known from the fact that they were among some "ladies of the [Christ Church] congregation" who joined the Park Village Sisters and others in volunteering to go with Florence Nightingale to the Crimea in December, 1854.[29] Nightingale rejected Christina on the grounds that she was too young, but her aunt was accepted.

Neither the Park Village nor the All Saints' Sisters had a mandate for working with "fallen women," but their work with "homeless women" and "orphan girls" would in fact have been inseparable from work with "fallen women."[30] Other Anglican Sisterhoods which were newly forming at this time, however, displayed a predominant interest in work with prostitutes. The first Sister at St. Mary's, Wantage, felt called to penitentiary work and founded a penitentiary there in 1850, despite the distress of the Vicar, who had wanted this Sisterhood to be dedicated to educational work. The Clewer Sisterhood was formed because three women moved into a "House of Mercy" in 1851, simultaneously undertaking the religious life and the work of the "penitentiary."[31] This "House of Mercy" had been founded two years earlier by a Mrs. Tennant, a laywoman living in the village of Clewer who offered to take the "abandoned women" of the parish into her own home. She was said to have an unparalleled ability to control the "most undisciplined and impassioned natures" of these women and to attach them to herself "in a marvellous manner" (Cameron, pp. 58-59).

Such enthusiasm for work with prostitutes and willingness to share living-quarters with them was not confined to religious sisterhoods. Josephine Butler, who led the Ladies' National Association in its campaign against the Contagious Diseases Acts, began her career by taking women from the work-houses, jails, and streets of Liverpool into her own home, where she devotedly nursed them herself. Walkowitz reports that by 1878 the LNA leadership had actually grown wary of the "rescue impulse," recognizing by then that there were "a 'hundred women' who would engage in rescue work for the 'one' who would bravely enter the political arena to combat the acts" (Walkowitz, p. 133).

The St. Mary Magdalene Home at which Christina Rossetti worked in the 1860s may have been staffed by lay "sisters" who committed themselves to the work but took no permanent religious vows. According to its Annual Reports, St. Mary's "sisters" were to be divided into two groups, "approved sisters" and "sisters under probation," either of whom were to be free to resign at any time.[32] Christina Rossetti's work at St. Mary's in the 1860s appears to have been only a continuation of her involvement with the "rescue work" which had appealed to the desires of British women in general, and Anglican Sisterhoods in particular, including the two Sisterhoods associated with the churches attended by the Rossetti women. **"Goblin Market,"** written sometime during the late 1850s, is inscribed by the turbulent history of "women's mission to women" in the Oxford Movement during this period. In this ecclesiastical "female world of love and ritual," how was the female body and its "appetite" represented?[33]

I would like to begin by noting that ecclesiastical discourse constituted saving "sisters" and "fallen women" together, as if part of a unitary entity. In a preface to two sermons on penitentiary work, W. J. Butler, Vicar of Wantage, wrote that, "so soon as the evil [prostitution] was fairly faced . . . nothing could quell it so much as purity and tender love, that these would foster habits of prayer and industry and faith in virtue and goodness, . . . the lack of which had occasioned so fearful a moral wreck."[34] The Sisters' "purity and tender love" are defined by the "moral wreck" so in need of them.

Like the discourses of nineteenth-century male artists, the discourses of the Oxford Movement also reveal a fear of "contamination." But while the male artists' imagery suggests a fear of physical and moral pollution from the prostitute's body, male clerics appear to have feared that the sisters would be contaminated by the attractions of the "fallen women" and their way of life. In a sermon preached at St. Mary's Home, Wantage, in 1861, Samuel Wilberforce, the Bishop of Oxford, displays this anxiety by taking as his opening subject the prevailing notion that those who work to reform the corrupted are themselves liable to be corrupted. He also labors to disprove the idea that institutions such as St. Mary's tended to "discredit homely virtue and to throw a gloss over vice" (*On Penitentiary Work*, p. 5).

In a second sermon preached on the same occasion, Henry Parry Liddon indicates that the "decay" of prostitution begins with a woman's "act of rebellion," and that this first act of rebellion is generally followed by a second and a third, such that "you find yourself in the presence of a new and formidable force—the force of habit" (p. 19). This habit of rebellion, he suggests, must be met by "a counter-habit of purity" (p. 20).

These sermons thus articulate a fear that, far from experiencing "disgust for female sexuality" or "sexual repulsion," the sisters who worked with fallen women might themselves be "corrupted" by these living examples of active female sexuality and "rebellion." In an 1867 sermon to the Parochial Mission-Women Association, Canon Burrows' text fairly resonates with the fear that rescue work might encourage the development of an unwomanly sense of authority, and that after going into the streets, mission women might not return exactly as they had been before. Noting uneasily at the outset that he was not often called upon to "address a body so largely composed of women" and that there were many "Managers and Superintendents here today," he takes as his theme the imperative of maintaining a proper sense of humility amidst the heady excitement of this mission work:

> "Many of you, Mission Women, must be tempted to think . . . when you find yourselves associated with rank and talent, the clergy co-operating, congregations applauding, and all men speaking well of you, that surely success is certain; but you come together to-day to the House of God, to humble yourselves."[35]

Commenting that "yours is woman's work, and a true woman's best work is modest, retiring, humble, self-sacrificing," Burrows reminds his feminine audience of "the special deference to authority" involved in their "constitution" and urges his hearers to be always willing to "take the lowest place" and to be "persistent" in humility (pp. 7, 9, 11). He mentions that these mission women not only have no house or institution, no official dress, but that they almost always work singly. They go out on the streets and bring women in to the Mission room, the School, the Church. They must never forget, he concludes, that they should be "the servant of all" (p. 11).

Although always organized hierarchically and on the assumption that class differences were part of God's plan and not to be interfered with, the Oxford Movement actually fostered associations between middle-class church women and working-class women on the belief that the former could help prevent the latter from "falling." In 1856 Upton Richards founded an organization called the All Saints Confraternity for Girls and Young Women.[36] According to the 1866 Manual, the association was intended for the "mutual help and encouragement of Girls and Young Women wishing to lead a Christian life amidst the difficulties and temptations of the world." The Objects of the Confraternity further specified that the organization was to help "carefully brought up" and pious girls retain their beliefs and good behavior after they were sent out into the world to earn a living.[37]

These objectives obviously suggest another possibility for an intended audience for **"Goblin Market,"** which certainly can be read as a cautionary tale for girls and young women wishing to lead a Christian life amidst the temptations of the "world," for which read the streets of London. Again, however, my interest is not to speculate on an "intended" audience but rather to examine certain texts produced by or for the Confraternity which I believe are paradigmatic of female relations in the Oxford Movement, and to read in them a construction of the female gaze that I think is highly pertinent to the reading of **"Goblin Market."** In this construction of the female gaze we may find a "look" exchanged between women that constitutes an unorthodox (feminine) subjectivity.

Class difference and hierarchy clearly structured the Confraternity, like all of the Sisterhood enterprises. In 1866 its membership consisted of sixty "members" and twenty "Lady-Associates," headed by a "Superior-General" or the Rev. Upton Richards, and a "Sister-Superior," who was one of the All Saints Sisters.[38] But these rigid demarcations of class and authority do not appear in the Confraternity hymns to the Virgin Mother, or to the Virgin's mother, St. Anne. In a hymn to St. Anne I find a particularly significant revision of Jacques Lacan's construction of the "mirror stage" as the moment when the infant first perceives itself as a coherent image. In Lacan's theorization of this moment, the infant is constituted by its perception of this mirrored image, an image which the mother who holds the infant only "guarantees." In short, the infant, not the mother, is the subject here.[39]

If we take the Confraternity hymn to St. Anne as textual exemplar, we read in it instead an egalitarian exchange of gazes between the Virgin's mother and the future Virgin Mother:

> Blest among women shall thy daughter be!
>   Yes, highly favoured above every other;
> The little one reposing on thy knee,
>   (Believe, and fear not) shall be GOD's own Mother.
> The clear, grave eyes that now look up to thine,
>   In the calm faith that sheds its radiance o'er her,
> Thus shall they gaze upon the form divine
>   Of God's bright Angel, as he stands before her.
>
> (*Manual*, pp. 65-66)

There are several important points here. For one, it is the gaze of the infant daughter which is represented as guaranteeing the mother's subjectivity. The Virgin's mother looks down on the "little one reposing" on her knee, and in the infant's mirroring gaze sees the promise of a future divine motherhood. Rather than beginning (and ending) with the infant and ignoring the mother as anything but "guarantee," it starts (though it does not end) with the mother.

Another interesting difference is the hymn's explicit construction of the gaze between two feminine subjects. The hymn virtually excludes males from this female exchange, and what is male appears only as prophetic image that grants permission to the mother's gaze: the female child can be taken as "object" because she is validated by the divine form of the angel who will announce that she is a virgin mother. The hymn thus authorizes the female gaze to take a feminine object as its focus.

The infant daughter here, however, obviously functions as subject herself: her look "up" to the mother's look is already a gaze upon a future "form divine" that is in turn a guarantee of her subjectivity. As such, I think the exchange can be said to undo the hierarchy of mother and daughter as it does of infant and "mirror." How shall we describe the relationship constructed by such an exchange of looks between female subjects? As "sisterhood"—a "sisterhood" which represses hierarchical differences and permits the female gaze to feast on the female form.

"Goblin Market" and Feminine Guessiness

Criticism of **"Goblin Market"** can be divided into two camps in the reading of Lizzie and Laura: one camp assumes that Laura represents the "fallen woman" and Lizzie the "pure woman," or that Laura is a type of Eve and Lizzie a type of Mary; the other camp asserts that the poem does not construct either sister as morally superior and that Lizzie is as much "redeemed" by her confrontation with the goblins as Laura is by ingesting Lizzie's "antidote."[40]

I take my stance very much in this second camp, for it seems to me the poem quite deliberately denies any suggestion of categorical differences between the two women. That is, the text excludes any suggestion of sexual, racial, class, or any other kind of hierarchical difference between the two women—or girls, since the difference between sexual maturity and childish innocence also seems to be blurred. We cannot find in the text of this poem or in the illustration Dante Gabriel designed for it of the two "golden heads" any suggestion of Armstrong's "double-bodied woman." On the contrary, even after Laura has eaten of the goblin fruits—an act many readers regard as synonymous with a "fall"—the poem constructs them in what Jerome McGann appropriately calls "unspeakably beautiful litanies" of identical innocence (p. 253):

> Like two blossoms on one stem,
> Like two flakes of new-fall'n snow,
> Like two wands of ivory.
>
> (ll. 188-198)

I would like to suggest that the poem excludes difference between the two girls or women in order to focus on women's common plight as commodities in the linked capitalist and sexual economies. By erasing categorical differences between Laura and Lizzie, the poem can construct those various characterological differences among women which make them vulnerable to the market, on the one hand, but which the poem, on the other hand, argues "sisters" can also capitalize upon in order to rescue each other from exploitation.

Christina Rossetti's own reflective interpretation of Eve and her "fall" in an 1882 work of biblical commentary, *Letter and Spirit,* is relevant here:

> It is in no degree at variance with the Sacred Record to picture to ourselves Eve, that first and typical woman, as indulging quite innocently sundry refined tastes and aspirations, a castle-building spirit (if so it may be called), a feminine boldness and directness of aim combined with a no less feminine guessiness as to means. Her very virtues may have opened the door to temptation.[41]

So it appears with Laura in **"Goblin Market"**—her very virtues open the door to temptation. She combines a "feminine boldness and directness of aim" with "sundry refined tastes and aspirations." She exhibits a "castle-building spirit," if so we may read the heroic similes which describe her as stretching her "gleaming neck" and being like a "moonlit poplar branch," or a "vessel at the launch / When its last restraint is gone" (ll. 81-86).

But she also exhibits a "feminine guessiness as to means." Untutored in the deceptive strategies employed in the goblin market, she gets herself in for more than she bargained for. Although her desire to indulge "refined tastes" for the exotic and delicious fruits hawked by the goblin men is nowhere condemned in the poem, Laura finds that in consuming those fruits a part of herself has also been "consumed." What has been stolen from her in this shady transaction is her "desire" itself, a desire which far exceeds that for real fruits, however exotic.

Yet we should not fail to notice how infinitely more potent as locus of desire these "fruits" are than that pathetically domesticated jar of marmalade that is supposed to tempt Alice. The very words for these fruits are quite literally mouth-filling and sensuously delectable, but they are also packed with metaphorical and associational meanings. Both a woman and the product of her womb may be called a "fruit," but with what different valances! And "fruits" can refer to the profits of any kind of enterprise—economic, spiritual, or sexual.

The poem, moreover, specifically links the fruits to "the fruits of empire": these are not just common, home-grown English apples and cherries, but also a rich variety of gourmet fruits imported from foreign climes—pomegranates, dates, figs, lemons and oranges, "citrons from the South." These are luxury fruits that appeal to "sundry refined tastes" such as have been cultivated by Britain's colonial empire. That Rossetti associated the availability of such luxuries with the capitalistic exploitation of the poor is clearly indicated in her 1892 commentary on the Book of Revelation, *The Face of the Deep,* where she identifies her country with the apocalyptic Babylon and assails it with prophetic wrath: " 'Alas England full of luxuries and thronged by stinted poor, whose merchants are princes and whose dealings crooked, whose packed storehouses stand amid bare homes, whose gorgeous array has rags for neighbours!' "[42]

Amidst this market with its packed storehouses and gorgeous array, Laura, who has not a single "copper" in her purse, is taken in by the crooked dealings of the goblin men. When they tell her she does not need any money because they will be happy with a "golden curl," she hands over this emblem of her virginity with only a single tear. Her "feminine guessiness as to means"—her naiveté about the marketplace—has condemned her to a loss far greater than she knows.

So far it would almost be permissible to read the poem as a sort of feminist guide to shopping: watch out for those so-called bargains, sister, especially the ones offered by the funny little men—you'll be taken for a lot more than you know. But to read it as such a sororal cautionary tale is to neglect what the poem has to say about the importance of looking. While one can get into trouble by satisfying the desire to look and listen, the trouble is precisely the loss of that desire. Christina Rossetti herself wanted to name the poem, "A Peep at the Goblins," but when her brother Dante Gabriel suggested **"Goblin Market,"** Christina accepted this as a "greatly improved title."[43] Yet while the poem is certainly about the "traffic in women," it also seems to be about the desire to "peep." Even more interestingly, the poem does not appear to condemn this voyeuristic desire in itself but rather to represent its risks in the goblin market.

Thus, Laura at first warns Lizzie, "We must not look at goblin men," as well as "We must not buy their fruits." But apparently sensing her sister's weakening control, Lizzie responds, "Laura, Laura, / You should not peep at goblin men" (ll. 42, 43, 48, 49). Lizzie sticks her fingers in her ears and shuts her eyes, but Laura lingers and looks, "Wondering at each merchant man."[44]

When she returns after having made her unwittingly disastrous bargain, and "sucked and sucked and sucked" the goblin fruit until her lips were sore, Lizzie meets her "at the gate / Full of wise upbraidings" (ll. 141-142). " 'Dear, you should not stay so late, / Twilight is not good for maidens," she reminds her sister primly, and now already too late tells her the sad tale of Jeanie who "lies low" because she loitered so (ll. 143-163). But when Laura first suffers agonies because of the frustration of her "baulked desire," and then, like her "kernel-stone," begins to dry up, dwindle, and face the prospect of a "sandful" sterility (how painful that "sandful" is!), Lizzie is jarred out of her maidenly correctness by her sister's "cankerous care." After taking the prudent precaution of supplying herself with a silver penny, Lizzie ventures out, "And for the first time in her life / Began to listen and look" (ll. 327-328).

The narrative thus clearly affirms woman's listening and looking—Lizzie needs to listen and look, the line suggests, or she will remain merely a happy little bird in her closed domestic cage. The decision to confront the goblins of the twilight, to open her eyes and unstop her ears, is as crucial to Lizzie as the recovery of desire will be to Laura. So long as Lizzie remains safely behind her garden gate, she will never know desire or taste its fulfillment and she will be no better off—though her case will be different—than her sister, whose desire has been stolen from her. The sisters represent women's double plight in the Victorian sexual economy: either risk becoming a commodity yourself, or risk never tasting desire, never letting yourself "peep."

The poem demonstrates for us how listening may be as seductive as looking: the goblins laugh when they spy Lizzie "peeping," and they slither towards her in a fascinating cacophony of sounds that fills the ear just as the earlier listing of fruits fills the mouth. These sounds are full of sinister, sexual, spell-binding implications—snake-like, we might say.

But looking and listening are not enough to accomplish the poem's desire for Lizzie here. She must also suffer, putting up at first with name-calling, then with what we would call sexual harassment and physical abuse. The goblins push her and jostle her, rip her dress, tear out her hair, and step on her feet. Finally, they try to force their "fruits" into her mouth. Under this treatment, Lizzie is transformed into a heroic and unviolated figure. The list of similes here interestingly refers both to colonial and sexual economies: she's like a "fruit-crowned orange tree" beset by wasps and bees, or like "a royal virgin town" beleaguered by a fleet "Mad to tug her standard down." Laughing in her heart, Lizzie gleefully lets the goblins "syrup" her face with their juices, but she keeps her mouth shut. The goblins are unable to penetrate her. When she leaves the glen, the penny jingling in her purse is testimony that she got what she wanted for a smaller price than she thought she might have to pay. The price was only "a smart, ache, tingle"—not so bad, under the circumstances.

Ecstatically, she offers Laura the "juices" of her sexual knowledge, spread over the surface of her bruised body:

> She cried "Laura," up the garden,
> "Did you miss me?
> Come and kiss me.
> Never mind my bruises,
> Hug me, kiss me, suck my juices
> Squeezed from goblin fruits for you,
> Goblin pulp and goblin dew.
> Eat me, drink me, love me;
> Laura, make much of me:
> For your sake I have braved the glen
> And had to do with goblin merchant men."
> (ll. 464-474)

Laura clings about her sister, "kissed and kissed and kissed her," and is transformed in her turn. Though the juice is "wormwood" to her tongue, and she "loathes" the feast, she appears to experience a masochistic orgy—writhing like one possessed, leaping and singing, and beating her breast. In simile, she streams upward like an eagle toward the sun, like a caged thing freed, like a flying flag when armies run. And then she falls—falls like a mast struck by lightning, like a tree uprooted by the wind, like a waterspout that falls into the sea. She falls, "pleasure past and anguish past," into a deep sleep, from which she awakens as innocent as ever, and quite healthy.

Lizzie appears to have restored her sister by recirculating the erotic energies first set into motion by the goblin market. Inviting her sister to feast on her instead of on the goblin fruits produces a saving satisfaction. But all such exchanges involve the paying of some price, and here the price is pain—a pain which seems always to originate from the "goblin merchant men." However, the pain does not seem to be part of a sadistic-masochistic pairing. Rather, the pain which accompanies the women's erotic pleasure appears to be the inevitable effect of that dimly glimpsed other world that frames and constructs the sisters' relationship to each other. Nevertheless, within their own sphere, sisters can do a lot for each other. Or, as Laura teaches the little ones to sing, "there is no friend like a sister."

In the end, however, we must acknowledge that the poem accomplishes this transformative sisterhood by pushing the heterosexual world to its margins—husbands are not completely excluded, they are implied in the last paragraph—and by wiping out all reference to class or racial differences as if they did not exist. That they did exist, and that they determine the vision in **"Goblin Market"** of non-hierarchical sisterhood, is demonstrated by the poem which has been placed immediately after **"Goblin Market"** in the 1862 volume. This poem, **"In the Round Tower at Jhansi, June 8, 1857,"** carries in its title the specific reference to time and place, and to empire and colony, that has been excluded from **"Goblin Market."**

The title of the poem refers to an incident in what was called the "Indian Mutiny" but was actually part of the Indian rebellion against the British Empire, an incident in which a young white officer reportedly shot first his wife and then himself in order to protect her from the threat of rape by "The swarming howling wretches below." These "wretches below" are, presumably, the Indian troops. In this poem, then, we find the traces of the imperialist discourse missing from the preceding poem: the purity of the (English) female body here is constituted by its absolute difference from "The swarming howling wretches below." Lizzie's consumable body is, after all, offered to an equally blond sister—those "wretches below" on the London streets have not been invited to the saving feast.

I have suggested that **"Goblin Market"** constructs a radically different view of the female body and its appetites, and that the poet's access to the social and discursive matrix of the Oxford Movement's "women's mission to women" accounts for this radical discourse. Read in this context, the poem articulates women's common vulnerability to sexual and economic exploitation while affirming the bodies and appetites that are implicated in that exploitation. But **"In the Round Tower at Jhansi"** demonstrates that **"Goblin Market"** achieves this seemingly radical vision of women's bodies through its deliberate exclusion of racial and class differences. Like that first and typical woman, Christina Rossetti's work is still limited by a "feminine guessiness as to means."

Notes

[1] Nancy Armstrong, "The Occidental Alice," *Differences* 2 (Summer 1990):3-40.

[2] Armstrong, p. 9. On the "double-bodied image," see also Sander Gilman, "Black Bodies, White Bodies: Toward an Iconography of Female Sexuality in Late Nineteenth-Century Art, Medicine, and Literature," in Henry Louis Gates, Jr., ed. *"Race," Writing, and Difference* (Chicago, 1985), pp. 223-261.

[3] All references to "Goblin Market" are to *The Complete Poems of Christina Rossetti*, ed. R. W. Crump (Baton Rouge, 1979), vol. 1, pp. 11-26. Perhaps the

"eat me" and "drink me" labels in *Wonderland* are already a more restrained and heterosexually-oriented version of Lizzie's "eat me, drink me, love me," for "Lewis Carroll" (Rev. Charles Dodgson) not only knew Rossetti well but was extremely enamored of little girls and very likely to have been intrigued by "Goblin Market". See *The Annotated Alice,* ed. Martin Gardner (Harmondsworth, England, 1960), pp. 11-13, and U. C. Knoepflmacher's "Avenging Alice: Christina Rossetti and Lewis Carroll," *NCL* 41 (1986): 302, 311.

[4] Charles Bernheimer, *Figures of Ill Repute: Representing Prostitution in Nineteenth-Century France* (Cambridge, Massachusetts, 1989), p. 2.

[5] Judith R. Walkowitz, *Prostitution and Victorian Society: Women, Class and the State* (Cambridge, 1980), p. 3.

[6] *The Poetical Works of Dante Gabriel Rossetti,* ed. William M. Rossetti (London, 1911), p. 39. D.M.R. Bentley points out that Dante Gabriel turned "intensively to the fallen-woman theme between 1853 and 1858," and that William Rossetti stated that "Jenny" was finished toward 1858, though revised in 1869 ("The Meretricious and the Meritorious in *Goblin Market*: A Conjecture and an Analysis," in David A. Kent, ed., *The Achievement of Christina Rossetti* [Ithaca, 1987], p. 60). *Goblin Market,* dated April 27, 1859, would appear to have been written in roughly the same period as "Jenny."

[7] Jerome J. McGann, "Christina Rossetti's Poems: A New Edition and a Revaluation," *VS* 23 (1980): 254.

[8] "The Meretricious and the Meritorious in *Goblin Market,*" p. 58.

[9] See Adrienne Rich's foundational analysis of the strategies universally employed by cultures to make heterosexuality compulsory by discouraging and even punishing homosexuality, thus coercing women into "choosing" heterosexuality. Rich theorizes that all women remain more attached to their mothers than men do, and that all women are therefore part of a "lesbian continuum." See "Compulsory Heterosexuality and Lesbian Existence" in Ann Snitow, Christine Stansell, and Sharon Thompson, eds., *Powers of Desire: The Politics of Sexuality* (New York, 1983), pp. 177-205.

[10] As Dorothy Mermin comments, "This is a world in which men serve only the purpose of impregnation" ("Heroic Sisterhood in *Goblin Market,*" *VP* 21 [1983]: 114.

[11] *The Poetical Works of Christina Georgina Rossetti,* with memoir and notes by William Michael Rossetti (London, 1924), p. lv.

[12] Martha Vicinus, *Independent Women: Work and Community for Single Women,* 1850-1920 (Chicago, 1985), p. 83.

[13] Mary Poovey, *Uneven Developments: The Ideological Work of Gender in Mid-Victorian England* (Chicago, 1988), p. 2.

[14] Laura Mulvey, referring to Jacque Lacan's theory, explains how "the unconscious of patriarchal society" structures Western narrative so that woman is the object of the male gaze ("Visual Pleasure and Narrative Cinema," reprinted in Constance Penley, ed., *Feminism and Film Theory* [New York, 1988], pp. 57-68).

[15] Terrence Holt's otherwise insightful reading of sexual and economic exchange in "Goblin Market," for example, is limited by its reading of the language of the poem exclusively in relation to a dominant phallocentrism. Not surprisingly, Holt ignores the female homoeroticism of the poem. See " 'Men sell not such in any town': Exchange in *Goblin Market,*" *VP* 28 (1990): 51-67.

[16] Georgina Battiscombe, *Christina Rossetti: A Divided Life* (New York, 1981), p. 76.

[17] Mackenzie Bell, *Christina Rossetti: A Biographical and Critical Study* (Boston, 1898), p. 60. Interestingly, William's letter goes on to document the interaction between Christina's church-related social work and the consumer culture of her day. One thing which occupied Christina "to an extent one would hardly credit," William writes, "was the making-up of scrapbooks for Hospital patients or children—This may possibly have begun before she removed to Torrington Sq[uare]: was certainly in very active exercise for several years ensuing—say up to 1885. When I called to see her and my mother it was 9 chances out of 10 that I found her thus occupied—I daresay she may have made up at least 50 biggish scrapbooks of this kind—taking some pains in adapting borderings to the pages etc. etc." These scrapbooks, no longer extant but presumably compiled from popular magazines and newspapers, suggest the poet's interest in popular culture.

[18] *Poetical Works,* p. 485. Diane D'Amico, in "Christina Rossetti's 'From Sunset to Star Rise': A New Reading," (*VP* 27 [1989]: 95-100) has also pointed out that William was probably mistaken in this surmise, not only because "House of Charity" is never used in the records for this institution, but because an Anglican institution for the "fallen" was much more usually referred to as a "House of Mercy." Concluding that Christina's note, "House of Charity," probably refers to some other institution—perhaps the House of Charity in Soho—D'Amico suggests that the poet probably worked in more than one charitable institution.

19 Canon Burrows described its foundation as "a time of fervour and revival of church principles." By January, 1839, only a year and a half after its founding, for example, the congregation had set up schools in which no fewer than 871 district children were enrolled. See Henry W. Burrows, *The Half-Century of Christ Church, Albany Street, St. Pancras* (London, 1887), pp. 12-14.

20 Allan T. Cameron, *The Religious Communities of the Church of England* (London, 1918), pp. 28-34.

21 Thomas Jay Williams and Allan Walter Campbell, *The Park Village Sisterhood* (London, 1965), p. 23.

22 Pitkin Guide, *All Saints Margaret Street* (London, 1990), p. 18.

23 *All Saints' Church, Margaret Street*. Reprinted from *The Orchestra* (London, [1866]).

24 The Park Village Sisterhood merged with the Devonport Sisterhood in 1856. See Chapter 12 in Williams and Campbell, *The Park Village Sisterhood*, pp. 112-117.

25 Joyce Coombs, *One Aim: Edward Stuart, 1820-1877* (London, 1975), p. 11.

26 Battiscombe, pp. 55-57. Burrows, p. 22.

27 So far as I have been able to determine, there was no connection between this church and the St. Mary Magdalene institution at Highgate.

28 Christina visited Collinson's family (James Collinson himself was not there) at Pleasley Hill during August 1849, but there is no evidence that she was not in London during July 1849. See *The Family-Letters of Christina Georgina Rossetti*, ed. William Michael Rossetti (London, 1908), pp. 5-8; also Lona Mosk Packer, *Christina Rossetti* (Berkeley, 1963), p. 35.

29 Janet Galligani Casey, in "The Potential of Sisterhood: Christina Rossetti's *Goblin Market*," VP 29 (1991): 63-78, also gives an account of Rossetti's interest in Nightingale and the "sisterhood movement," but argues that "sisterhood" in the poem "potentially includes the experience of both sexes" (p. 63).

30 Walkowitz notes that women who moved into prostitution were most often girls in their late teens, living outside the family, in fact often half or full orphan, and frequently having previously been casual maids of all work. See *Prostitution and Victorian Society*, p. 19.

31 Cameron, pp. 43, 59. Interestingly, these two Sisterhoods which took work with prostitutes as their primary focus grew to be two of the largest Anglican communities (Vicinus, *Independent Women*, p. 72).

32 First organized under a council formed by the Bishop of London in 1854, this "penitentiary" at Highgate was known originally as "Park House" but called "St. Mary Magdalene's" in order to give it a "distinctive name." See Deed to the London Diocesan Penitentiary, St. Mary Magdalene, London Guildhall Library, MS. 18532 and the Annual Reports of the London Diocesan Penitentiary, St. Mary Magdalene's, London Guildhall Library, MS. 18535. The institution is not listed among those institutions supervised by the All Saints' Sisterhood, nor is it mentioned in accounts of the Park Village Sisters. Cameron notes that "The House of Mercy," North Hill, Highgate, was taken over by the Clewer Sisters in 1901 (p. 65).

33 Carroll Smith-Rosenberg, "The Female World of Love and Ritual" in *Disorderly Conduct: Visions of Gender in Victorian America* (New York, 1985), pp. 53-76.

34 *On Penitentiary Work . . . Two Sermons Preached At the Opening of the Chapel of St. Mary's Home, Wantage, July* 30, 1861, *by Samuel [Wilberforce], Lord Bishop of Oxford, and Henry Parry Liddon, M. A., with a Short Preface on Sisterhoods, by W. J. Butler, M. A., Vicar of Wantage* (Oxford and London, 1861), pp. iv-v.

35 *Parochial Mission-Women Association. A Sermon Preached at St. James's, Westminster, on June 20th, 1867, by the Rev. H. W. Burrows, B.D., Perpetual Curate of Christ Church, St. Pancras* (Oxford and London, 1867), pp. 4-5.

36 Although there is no evidence that Christina Rossetti was a member of this particular organization, a Young Women's Friendly Society was organized at Christ Church for the benefit of servant girls. Tea, Bible lessons, and other "religious recreations" were offered on Sunday afternoons (*Half-Century of Christ Church*, p. 34). Maria Rossetti not only worked with this society but wrote a series of letters (dated 1860-61) to the young women in it, published as *Letters to My Bible Class on Thirty-Nine Sundays* (London, n.d. [1872]).

37 *The Manual of the Confraternity of All Saints, for Girls and Young Women*, in connection with the All Saints' Home, 82, Margaret Street, Cavendish Square, 2nd ed. (London, 1866), p. 1.

38 In a notice to the public, the Superior of the All Saints' Home stated that "women of a superior class are received to be trained for Nursing the Sick Poor in Hospitals; and for Private Nursing in the Families of the rich" ("Nurses for the Sick, in Private Families," All Saints' Home, 82, Margaret Street, Cavendish Square [1862]). Vicinus comments on the "upper-class character" of the All Saints' and Clewer Sisterhoods and notes that both were known as "fashionable" (*Independent Women*, pp. 55-56).

[39] Jacques Lacan, "The mirror stage as formative of the function of the I as revealed in psychoanalytic experience," in *Écrits: A Selection*, trans. Alan Sheridan (New York, 1977), pp. 1-7. As Jane Gallop notes, "In Lacanian models she [the mother] is the prohibited object of desire; in object-relations she is the mirror where the infant can find his or her subjectivity. In either case her only role is to complement the infant's subjectivity; in neither story is she ever a subject" ("Reading the Mother Tongue: Psychoanalytic Feminist Criticism," *CritI* 13 [1987]: p. 324).

[40] Helena Michie, for example, speaks of Laura and Lizzie as representing a culturally constructed difference between sisters, in which one sister is the "fallen" and the other the "unfallen," one the "sexual" and the other the "pure woman," in "'There is No Friend Like a Sister': Sisterhood as Sexual Difference," *ELH* 56 (1989): p. 404. Jerome McGann typifies the other reading which argues that without Laura's "precipitous act the women would have remained forever in a condition of childlike innocence" and that "Lizzie's timidity is by no means condemned, but its limitations are very clear," in "Christina Rossetti's Poems," p. 250).

[41] Christina Rossetti, *Letter and Spirit* (London, [1882]), p. 17.

[42] *The Face of the Deep: A Devotional Commentary* (London, 1892), p. 422.

[43] *Poetical Works*, p. 459; Crump, 1:234.

[44] We should not overlook the fact that "merchant man" also refers to a cargocarrying ship.

David B. Drake (essay date 1992)

SOURCE: "Rossetti's *Goblin Market*," in *The Explicator*, Vol. 51, No. 1, Fall, 1992, pp. 22-24.

[*In the following essay, Drake discusses "Goblin Market" as a modified epyllion—a small epic—in which Lizzie plays the role of the epic heroine.*]

Christina Rossetti's **"Goblin Market"** exhibits several of the characteristics and conventions of epic poetry and should be studied as a somewhat modified version of the epyllion—a poem that emulates the classical epic in subject matter and technique, but is decidedly shorter (typically depicting just a single heroic episode) and narrower in scope—modified because the epyllion is ideally composed using dactylic hexameter, and **"Goblin Market"** is, of course, written in free verse.

A substantial number of critics have noted that Rossetti's heroine, Lizzie, resembles a transfigured Christ who redeems her peccant sister by sacrificing herself to the malevolent goblins.[1] Feminist critics, meanwhile, have designated Lizzie a pioneering member of their own movement who is earnestly determined to protect the sanctity of sisterhood against any form of patriarchal corruption (i.e. the goblin men).[2] Inherent in both these persuasive exegeses is the understanding that Lizzie is an individual of historic, or even cosmic, consequence. Moreover, one need not examine her victorious encounter with the goblins (lines 363-446) too scrupulously to recognize that Lizzie's actions are not only valorous, but utterly herculean in magnitude (keep in mind that she is but a child and is greatly outnumbered). In short, Lizzie, while ostensibly not an imposing personage, is truly an epic heroine.

Thematically, **"Goblin Market"** incorporates a pair of archetypal motifs that frequently appear in epic poetry. To begin with, Lizzie's journey into the glen to combat the demonic, preternatural goblins—the poem's epic machinery—is analogous to a descent into the underworld. And accordingly, her subsequent reemergence from this underworld clearly signifies a resurrection, not so much for herself, but more precisely for the moribund Laura (again, Lizzie the Christlike healer), as well as for all maidens, since Lizzie (the seminal feminist) has emphatically demonstrated that they indeed possess more resourcefulness and tenaciousness than the goblins, and consequently need no longer be the victims of their misogynistic tyranny.

Besides featuring an epic heroine who engages in quintessentially epical exploits, Rossetti's poem also features some of the unifying stylistic devices commonly employed by epic poets, such as the refrain (exemplified here by the goblins' exhortation, "Come buy, come buy") and anaphoristic repetition. In fact, the anaphora in **"Goblin Market"** repeatedly involves the clustering of similes, with each cluster devoted to describing a lone primary object and thus functioning much like an aggregate epic simile. In other words, when making a comparison, Rossetti does not offer merely one secondary vehicle developed well beyond its patent correspondence with a primary object (as occurs in the epic simile), but rather a consecutive string of secondary vehicles, of similes. Granted, none of these secondary vehicles is intricately developed; still the immediate effect is exactly the same as in the epic simile: the primary object is deemphasized. Perhaps this is best explained through illustration:

> Laura stretched her gleaming neck
> Like a rush-imbedded swan,
> Like a lily from the beck,
> Like a moonlit poplar branch,
> Like a vessel at the launch
> When its last restraint is gone.
>
> (81-86)

These simile clusters appear throughout the poem, most notably to depict a somnolent embrace between Laura and Lizzie (184-91), a steadfast Lizzie as she prepares to face the goblins (408-21), and Laura's frenzied reaction after ingesting the vivifying fruit juice that her sister has so courageously procured for her (510-20).

"Goblin Market" additionally includes two epic catalogues, albeit these martial catalogues, like those found in Pope's mock-heroic "Rape of the Lock," are metaphoric. The first comes at the start of the poem (5-29), listing the goblins' poisonous produce, their armaments, while another, itemizing the goblins or warriors themselves, occurs approximately between lines 55 and 76.

In his essay "Simple Surfaces: Christina Rossetti's Work for Children," Roderick McGillis briefly mentions that Laura's miraculous reanimation near the close of **"Goblin Market"** recalls the passage in Homer's *Odyssey* when "Odysseus' sailors return to human form after Odysseus has overpowered Circe" (211). They, like Laura, actually seem to have been favorably transformed by virtue of surviving their mystical ordeal. Unfortunately, however, McGillis neglects to develop this evocative thesis further and comment explicitly upon the striking number of parallels between **"Goblin Market"** and epic poetry in general. Because Rossetti's poem manifests not simply one or two, but a number of epic attributes, it seems thoroughly unlikely that their presence is entirely coincidental. And seeing that a poem need not be written in dactylic hexameter to be considered an epyllion (e.g. Arnold's "Sohrab and Rustum"; Tennyson's "Idylls of the King"), it is only appropriate that **"Goblin Market"** be likewise regarded as an epyllion or small epic.

Notes

[1] See, for instance, James Ashcroft Noble, "The Burden of Christina Rossetti," *Impressions and Memories,* 8 vols. (London, 1895) 55-64; Marian Shaulkhauser, "The Feminine Christ," *Victorian Newsletter* 10 (1956): 19-20; D.M.R. Bentley, "The Meretricious and the Meritorious," *The Achievement of Christina Rossetti,* ed. David A. Kent (Ithaca: Cornell UP, 1987) 57-81; Antony H. Harrison, *Christina Rossetti in Context* (Chapel Hill: U of North Carolina P, 1988) 115.

[2] See Miriam Sagan, "Christina Rossetti's 'Goblin Market' and Feminist Literary Criticism," *Pre-Raphaelite Review* 3 (1980): 66-76; Dorothy Mermin, "Heroic Sisterhood in 'Goblin Market,'" *Victorian Poetry* 21 (1983): 107-18; Jeanie Watson, "'Eat Me, Drink Me, Love Me,': The Dilemma of Sisterly Self-Sacrifice," *Journal of Pre-Raphaelite Studies* 7.1 (1986): 50-62.

Works Cited

McGillis, Roderick. "Simple Surfaces: Christina Rossetti's Work for Children." *The Achievement of Christina Rossetti.* Ed. David A. Kent. Ithaca: Cornell UP, 1987. 208-30.

Rossetti, Christina. *The Complete Poems of Christina Rossetti.* Ed. R. W. Crump. Vol. 1. Baton Rouge: Louisiana State UP, 1979. 3 vols. 1979-90.

Sean C. Grass (essay date 1996)

SOURCE: "Nature's Perilous Variety in Rossetti's 'Goblin Market'," in *Nineteenth-Century Literature,* Vol. 51, No. 3, December, 1996, pp. 356-76.

[*In the essay that follows, Grass examines the influence of various aspects of Rossetti's life on her writing of "Goblin Market." He identifies Rossetti's extensive use of lists as the "interpretive key" in determining which biographical events correspond to the events in "Goblin Market."*]

The critical interpretations of Christina Rossetti's **"Goblin Market"** that have been advanced during the last two decades are nearly as multifarious as the goblin fruits so lavishly depicted in her verse. A cursory glance at the introduction to virtually any critical essay on **"Goblin Market"** provides a healthy catalog of the disparate readings of the poem: as commentary on the capitalist marketplace; as tale of sexual, sometimes homoerotic yearning; as feminist glorification of sisterhood; and perhaps most often as Christian allegory of temptation and redemption, "inescapably a Genesis story."[1] Many early criticisms of Rossetti's poetry focus on the location of biographical events that correspond to the situations described in her verse, apparently in an attempt to show Rossetti's poetry as grappling with the symbolic meanings in events of her quiet, retiring life.[2] But this body of criticism as a whole tends to be too narrowly focused on Rossetti's poetry as a product of a singular aspect of her life—either her ill-fated love affairs, her association with Tractarianism and the Oxford Movement, or her affiliation with Dante Gabriel Rossetti and the Pre-Raphaelite Brotherhood. However, seeing her poetry as influenced by only one or another of these forces provides an inadequate and myopic view of her verse as a whole and of **"Goblin Market"** in particular. Instead, we should at least attempt to account for the commingling of these influences as they manifest themselves in her verse if we are to arrive at any comprehensive understanding of the several layers of meaning in **"Goblin Market"**—the poem that continues to be the enigmatic core of Rossetti's work—and if we are to defy the inquiry of any narrowly ideological approach.

In attempting to arrive at such an understanding we necessarily must let the poem itself determine the avenues of inquiry that are most fruitful, and in **"Goblin Market"** Rossetti's use of lists may provide an interpretive key. Nearly fifteen years have passed since Miriam Sagan observed that "the major trope of the poem is the *list*" (p. 71), but little has been done to explore the ramifications of this accurate assessment. More often than not the goblin fruits and goblin characteristics have been relegated to strictly symbolic or allegorical significance by critics, or they have been vaguely referred to only insofar as they overwhelm the senses or render the goblins and their fruits in ambiguous terms.[3] Katherine Mayberry has by and large discarded the possibility of any literal significance in the lists, attributing "the proliferation of words, rhythms, metaphors, and similes" to "the poet's breathless inebriation with the process of writing" (p. 90). To assume that these meticulously structured lists are strictly symbolic or that they are only illustrative of Rossetti's poetic self-indulgence, however, is to underrate the breadth and clarity of her poetic vision.

The lists in **"Goblin Market"** construct a vision of a bounteous and abundant nature that is seductive in its infinite variety—not a surprising vision considering Rossetti's love of the natural world around her. In fact, the use of lists in **"Goblin Market"** in such diverse ways—in cataloging the goblin fruits, in describing the physiognomies and behaviors of the goblins themselves, and in developing the imagery associated with Laura and Lizzie—suggests that variety and multiplicity in the natural world, especially when juxtaposed against the harmony and unity of the sisters, are more central to Rossetti's themes of temptation and moral discernment than has previously been thought. Such variety is threatening for Rossetti, for not only does it have the potential to lead one to dissatisfaction with a simple and retiring life, but it can also cause a spiritual crisis as the desire to celebrate the variety of nature clashes with the necessity of viewing nature morally.

That Christina Rossetti loved the natural world—especially all sorts of animals—has been thoroughly documented by her biographers and by literary critics. She and her siblings were frequent visitors to the Regent's Park Zoological Gardens throughout her adolescence and early womanhood, and one such trip is recounted by her in a letter to her brother William dated 18 August 1858, only one year before **"Goblin Market"** was written. "We have revisited the Z. Gardens," she writes; "Lizards are in strong force, tortoises active, alligators looking up. The weasel-headed armadillo as usual evaded us. . . . The blind wombat and neighbouring porcupine broke forth into short-lived hostilities, but apparently without permanent results."[4] In this passage we see not only the interest (and good humor) with which she surveyed the animals during her visits, but also, in the "weasel-headed armadillo," we glimpse perhaps the beginnings of her goblin men with their humanoid forms and animal components. William also indicates that "she knew . . . Ratel at the Zoological Gardens," and that "it was C[hristina] and I who jointly discovered the Wombat in the Zoological Gardens."[5] Packer in her biography has discussed Christina's experiences of 1854 when, in a time of depression, "she walked in the Botanical Gardens of Regent's Park" to relieve her melancholy (p. 98).[6] This interest in and love of nature in its infinite varieties is reflected in many of Rossetti's poems, including works like **"From House to Home," "Another Spring,"** and **"A Birthday."**

The artistic sensibilities of Dante Gabriel and of the Pre-Raphaelite Brotherhood surely served to nurture and perhaps even to heighten the love of nature Christina already felt. The painters of the Pre-Raphaelite Brotherhood had "the overt aim of . . . a 'return to nature,' " much as the Romantics before them, although in a very stylized way.[7] Such a return meant precision and saturation of detail in depicting nature to produce an aesthetically pleasing effect. Pre-Raphaelite poetry tended to exhibit many of these same characteristics, with meticulous attention being paid to minute natural phenomena, and with poets attempting to use meter and melody playfully to delight the senses.[8] **"Goblin Market,"** with its lavish attention to the cataloging of natural phenomena and with its highly irregular but melodic rhythms, would seem to be an archetypical example of both of these characteristics. And, if anything, the Pre-Raphaelite influences shaping Christina's verse would certainly have heightened her desire to represent faithfully and at length the variety she found and so doted upon in the natural world, both as she observed it at the Zoological Gardens and as she experienced it as a girl during her visits to the English countryside.[9] Thus Christina's own predisposition to celebrate nature received certain encouragement from at least one of the forces helping to shape her poetic sensibility.

Christina's desire to revel in and glorify the splendor of the natural world in her verse was mitigated, however, by her religious apprehension that nature must be scrutinized for its moral and sacred meanings—a belief characteristic of the writings of Tractarians John Keble and John Newman. Christina, along with her mother and sister Maria, probably came under the influence of the Oxford Movement as early as 1840, and in fact both sisters cultivated longstanding relationships with the Anglican Sisterhood of All Saints.[10] As the Oxford Movement influenced Christina's spirituality, so Tractarianism and the writings of Keble and Newman informed her sense of symbolism and interpretation with regard to the natural world.[11] Tractarian thought included a central tenet of intense sacramentalism in which things visible in the natural world were thought to symbolize things invisible and divine, and Tractarians saw in nature "the signs of the Creator."[12] Since the incarnation of Christ, the beauty of the physical world was shaped by his continuing presence here on earth. The job of the Christian was to look for the signs of Christ on earth and to understand the natural world in terms of his continuing presence and incarnation in order to achieve ultimate Christian salvation.[13] Moreover, the very composition of poetry was based, according to Newman, "on correct moral perception . . . where there is no sound principle in exercise there will be no poetry."[14] In order for Christina to produce excellent poetry, she therefore needed to attempt to resolve the underlying tension between her desire to celebrate the sheer variety of nature and the spiritual and moral need to make sense of that variety. The collision between her own affinity for nature and her religiously imposed moral doctrine produced Rossetti the poet: a poet who worried that reveling in nature could confuse moral judgment, thereby imperiling salvation. Understanding Rossetti in these various contexts shows us that she was deeply concerned with her own love of nature's variety and its depiction in her Pre-Raphaelite verse.

This concern takes center stage in Rossetti's poetic world, from the very outset of **"Goblin Market,"** in the form of lists. The first fourteen lines of the poem list for us no fewer than sixteen types of goblin fruit:

> Morning and evening
> Maids heard the goblins cry:
> "Come buy our orchard fruits,
> Come buy, come buy:
> Apples and quinces,
> Lemons and oranges,
> Plump unpecked cherries,
> Melons and raspberries,
> Bloom-down-cheeked peaches,
> Swart-headed mulberries,
> Wild free-born cranberries,
> Crab-apples, dewberries,
> Pine-apples, blackberries,
> Apricots, strawberries;—[15]

Then, after a five-line respite, Rossetti goes on to catalog another thirteen of the goblin fruits for us. The effect upon the senses is overwhelming, as many critics have pointed out, but such an observation is only particularly relevant within the context of Rossetti's Tractarianism. While the common view has been to see these fruits as together symbolic of the "fruit forbidden" (l. 479) of Eve's fall in Eden, thus rendering the poem wholly allegorical, the case is not quite so simple. In other poems Rossetti utilized individual types of fruit as symbolic of sin and temptation (such as in **"An Apple Gathering"**), but here the forbidden fruit is not of any single type. The Edenic fruit of the Tree of Knowledge, unique as it is, serves as the means of Eve's fall from innocence and grace, and Rossetti could certainly have made use of the single tempting fruit here had the poem been intended as simple Genesis allegory. Instead, Rossetti makes use of twenty-nine different fruits, all meticulously listed, some with accompanying details. This vision of the multifarious goblin fruits does overwhelm, but more important, this overwhelming of the senses can confuse moral discernment, the spiritual problem Rossetti battled herself.

The way to combat this sensory overload, in Laura and Lizzie's initial view, is twofold: the sisters must remain united, and they also must close their senses entirely to the avalanche of sensory input the situation attempts to force upon them:

> Crouching close together
> In the cooling weather,
> With clasping arms and cautioning lips,
> With tingling cheeks and finger tips.
> (ll. 36-39)

As they crouch, Laura iterates what must be their credo for action if they are to resist the jumbling of their moral judgment:

> "We must not look at goblin men,
> We must not buy their fruits:
> Who knows upon what soil they fed
> Their hungry thirsty roots?"
> (ll. 42-45)

The maintenance of unity of both mind and purpose is a means of coping with the multiplicity and abundance of the scene. Unfortunately for Laura and Lizzie both, however, Laura is breaking their unity even as she acknowledges its necessity, for she is "pricking up her golden head" (l. 41) to look. Very early in the poem, then, the variety of nature with its potential to overwhelm and mislead is pitted against the unity and resolve of the sisters.

Just as the multiplicity of the forbidden fruit in Rossetti's poetic world is at odds with the uniqueness of the Edenic fruit, the variety of the tempters in the forms of the goblin men provide us with no unique Satan. The goblin men not only look very different in their animal aspects:

> One had a cat's face,
> One whisked a tail,
> One tramped at a rat's pace,
> One crawled like a snail,
> One like a wombat prowled obtuse and furry,
> One like a ratel tumbled hurry skurry,
> (ll. 71-76; see fig. 1)

but they also are engaged in differentiated activities:

> One hauls a basket,
> One bears a plate,

>   One lugs a golden dish
>   Of many pounds weight.
>
>   (ll. 56-59)

The repetition of the word "one" reinforces that for Laura no two of the goblin men look alike. The particular wonder of each is unique, and we are told that although Lizzie "thrust a dimpled finger / In each ear, shut eyes and ran" (ll. 67-68), Laura chooses to remain, "wondering at *each* merchant man [emphasis added]" (l. 70). Once again the variety and multiplicity of the experience are what confuse Laura's intellectual and moral instincts, causing her to react improperly. The result is a complete fragmentation of the harmony of the sisters, for now they are separated—a situation that we feel inevitably leads to Laura's fall.

The goblin men, strictly speaking, are more manifestations of the supernatural than of the natural world, and their origins in the books of Rossetti's childhood have been convincingly traced.[16] But the goblins are no more entirely supernatural than they are entirely humanoid, like the traditional goblins of mythology. Rossetti has provided us with a rather curious admixture of mythology and her own experiences at the Zoological Gardens, as we can see from her references to animals like the wombat and the ratel. The goblins' supernatural aura, though, is not what draws Laura to them; rather, the focus of the poem is on the aspects of the goblins that are most closely connected with the natural world—namely, their fruits and their animal characteristics. Moreover, these animal characteristics are precisely what differentiate the goblins from one another. Despite their partially supernatural origins, the goblins are unmistakably part of Rossetti's concern with the variety of nature as she depicts it in this poem; and insofar as they are, they interfere with Laura's moral judgment almost immediately. Even though Laura has taken time to examine each particular goblin man and found each unique, to her ear they sound entirely harmonious:

>   She heard a voice like voice of doves
>   Cooing all together:
>   They sounded kind and full of loves
>   In the pleasant weather.
>
>   (ll. 77-80)

Later in the poem Laura's perception of the goblins' apparent harmony will be contrasted sharply with Lizzie's own uncorrupted and morally discerning recognition of their discordant voices. Also, as Mary Arseneau has perceptively pointed out (p. 86), Laura's comparison of the goblin voices with the cooing of doves is a clear indicator that Laura's discernment has been muddled, for the dove is the traditional Christian symbol of the Holy Spirit, while the goblins themselves are dangerous and perhaps even evil.

Laura's inability to locate any moral meaning in all of this natural variety results in the complete loss of her ability to make morally proper decisions, as we learn from yet another list that Rossetti has assembled for us:

>   Laura stretched her gleaming neck
>   Like a rush-imbedded swan,
>   Like a lily from the beck,
>   Like a moonlit poplar branch,
>   Like a vessel at the launch
>   When its last restraint is gone.
>
>   (ll. 81-86)

In this list of images Laura is compared with and thereby closely associated with both the animal and vegetable natural worlds; she is finally a vessel, then, something associated with humanity, but only insofar as she has lost all restraint. She has been entirely assimilated into a nature that is devoid of moral meaning and that exists outside the possibility of exercising judgment and restraint to mitigate the desire for self-indulgence. The first three images, picturesque and attractive though they are, provide an interpretation of Laura that, for Rossetti, would have been terrifying.

Later in the poem, when we come upon a similar list of images associated with Lizzie's stand against the goblins, we are first reminded of Laura's fall. In fact, the first simile used to describe Lizzie is "like a lily in a flood" (l. 409), intentionally bringing to mind the lily with which Laura was compared during her encounter with the goblins. The imagery used for Lizzie is subtly, but decidedly, of a different sort. The narrative voice says:

>   White and golden Lizzie stood,
>   Like a lily in a flood,—
>   Like a rock of blue-veined stone
>   Lashed by tides obstreperously,—
>   Like a beacon left alone
>   In a hoary roaring sea,
>   Sending up a golden fire,—
>   Like a fruit-crowned orange-tree
>   White with blossoms honey-sweet
>   Sore beset by wasp and bee,—
>   Like a royal virgin town
>   Topped with gilded dome and spire
>   Close beleaguered by a fleet
>   Mad to tug her standard down.
>
>   (ll. 408-21)

Unlike Laura, Lizzie is part of both the beauty and variety of the natural world—as reflected by her comparison to a lily and a blossom-laden orange tree—and the world of human, Christian understanding. The color blue and her comparison to a virgin certainly indicate a reference to the Virgin Mary, and, despite the beauty of the natural world, Lizzie realizes her precarious position "sore beset by wasp and bee" and under assault by "a hoary roaring sea." Indeed, her depiction as a beacon "sending up a golden fire" is accurate, for she is a moral example, shedding a Christian light through the chaos of nature so that others—especially Laura—may find the moral grounding and direction they require.

Without Lizzie to guide her, however, Laura during her encounter with the goblins remains morally ungrounded, cast adrift without a guiding principle for conduct. Laura is oblivious to the threat the goblins pose, even though the narrative voice depicts them in steadily more ominous terms, "leering at" (l. 93) and "signalling" (l. 95) each other. As if they are acting on cue, the various activities of the goblins begin afresh, and they all speak to Laura to encourage her to eat:

> The whisk-tailed merchant bade her taste
> In tones as smooth as honey,
> The cat-faced purr'd,
> The rat-paced spoke a word
> Of welcome, and the snail-paced even was heard;
> One parrot-voiced and jolly
> Cried "Pretty Goblin" still for "Pretty Polly;"—
> One whistled like a bird.
> (ll. 107-14)

The goblins no longer sound like cooing doves, but Laura is too far adrift at this point to realize her danger and speaks "in haste" (l. 115) to seal her moral collapse by purchasing the goblin fruits with "a precious golden lock" (l. 126; see fig. 2).

The result of Laura's self-immersion in the bounteous variety offered by the goblin men is her engagement in a frenzied, gluttonous feast during which she is unable even to differentiate which fruits she is eating. Perhaps more important is the fact that Laura does not *care* to distinguish between the different fruits, indicating her complete abandonment of even the pretense of moral awareness. Not until she returns home and is subjected to Lizzie's "wise upbraidings" (l. 142) does Laura try to reconstruct exactly what her experience with the goblins has consisted of. Laura's description of her adventure, as she tells us of it in her own voice, sounds frighteningly like the opening speech of the goblins themselves:

> "I'll bring you plums tomorrow
> Fresh on their mother twigs,
> Cherries worth getting;
> You cannot think what figs
> My teeth have met in,
> What melons icy-cold
> Piled on a dish of gold
> Too huge for me to hold,
> What peaches with a velvet nap,
> Pellucid grapes without one seed."
> (ll. 170-79)

Like the goblins, Laura is intoxicated by the sheer excess of her indulgence in the variety of the fruits. No single kind of fruit appealed to her more than any other, and she has no particular fruit in mind for her return visit—she desires them all again. Even free from direct contact with the goblins, Laura is consumed by the remembrance of her experience in all its forms.

The experience of eating the goblin fruit and the results of that experience mark the poem's most significant departure from the Genesis story, for Laura does not immediately suffer any consequences for her transgression. Unlike Adam and Eve, Laura is not overburdened with either a feeling of guilt, a fear of "the potentially mortal consequences of disobedience," or a knowledge that she has done evil (Sturrock, p. 99).[17] On the contrary, she is in a state of exhilaration when she reaches home, and even that night in bed the sisters present what D. M. R. Bentley calls "a stability that opposes itself to the anarchic . . . nature of the goblins" (p. 71). At least for this one night the sisters regain and retain the harmony that could have shielded Laura had they maintained it at the start of the poem. According to the narrative voice:

> Golden head by golden head,
> Like two pigeons in one nest
> Folded in each other's wings,
> They lay down in their curtained bed:
> Like two blossoms on one stem,
> Like two flakes of new-fall'n snow,
> Like two wands of ivory
> Tipped with gold for awful kings.
>
> . . . . .
>
> Cheek to cheek and breast to breast
> Locked together in one nest.
> (ll. 184-91, 197-98)

This picture of serenity differs from the lists describing the goblins and from the lists of images describing the sisters individually, for here neither solitariness nor true variety exists. While snowflakes and blossoms are not identical natural phenomena, their freshness and purity suggest that these sisters remain even now unmarred by ugliness or defect. The absence of variety, at least as it is presented here, is the happiest and least threatening of all possible states and exists even after Laura's physical consumption of the goblin fruit.

If Laura's subsequent decline is not linked to the actual eating of the fruit, as in the Genesis story, to what can we attribute it? It is not surprising that the key providing an answer for this question lies in another of Rossetti's lists. Although Laura and Lizzie pass a peaceful and harmonious night, the following day brings the advent of another loss of harmony between the sisters.

Laura rose with Lizzie:
Fetched in honey, milked the cows,
Aired and set to rights the house,
Kneaded cakes of whitest wheat,
Cakes for dainty mouths to eat,
Next churned butter, whipped up cream,
Fed their poultry, sat and sewed;
Talked as modest maidens should:
Lizzie with an open heart,
Laura in an absent dream,
One content, one sick in part.

(ll. 202-12)

The list here, unlike the lists of goblin fruits, suggests a tedium of routine inherent in domestic pastoral life—a life, incidentally, that seems to have been satisfying enough for Laura before but now is a wearisome burden for her. The dizzying effect of her self-indulgence in the variety of nature has been so pleasurable that Laura now finds a return to her previous routines impossibly constraining.

Such a dilemma is particularly interesting in light of what we know of Rossetti's own life. Her various biographers have indicated that Rossetti led a quiet, retiring life, devoting much of her time as a young woman to caring for her invalid father and later working closely with the nuns at Highgate Hall. According to Lionel Stevenson, 'by the time [Rossetti] was eighteen she had given up going to the theater, in spite of her love of drama and music, because she believed that actors and other stage folk were prone to too much self-indulgence" (p. 80). And according to Katherine Mayberry, "from 1854 until 1866 [the period during which **"Goblin Market"** was written], Christina Rossetti led a comparatively quiet life, dividing her time between her three central interests: her art, her religion, and her family" (p. 8). The theme of distaste for a life of excitement and society runs through much of her poetry, most noticeably in **"Repining,"** in which she depicts a girl who "begs to return to her quiet isolation" (Stevenson, p. 84). We should not be surprised, then, to see Rossetti struggling with the same sort of conflict—between a life of self-indulgent excitement and one of ascetic simplicity—within the verse of **"Goblin Market."** From what we know of Rossetti's love of nature, perhaps her greatest temptation to leave her quiet life was the wonder of the natural world around her. We see this same inner tension in Laura, after her experience with the goblins.

The mounting tension in Laura and her increasing spiritual desolation as she pines away are reflected by a corresponding change in her appearance. Her hair, which was golden less than one hundred lines before, "when the noon waxed bright / . . . grew thin and gray" (ll. 276-77). Her behavior changes also, for she is no longer able to keep herself in bed with Lizzie during the night. The peaceful and harmonious scene of the two of them asleep side by side is interrupted, for after Lizzie falls asleep Laura rises and spends the night "in a passionate yearning" (l. 266), weeping and gnashing her teeth "for baulked desire" (l. 267) of a repeat of her previous exhilarating experience. Finally, we are told that Laura does not even attempt to participate any longer in the simple chores of her domestic country life.

In order to redeem her rapidly failing sister, Lizzie must find a way to reestablish that harmony and unity so splintered by Laura's goblin experience:

Tender Lizzie could not bear
To watch her sister's cankerous care
Yet not to share.

(ll. 299-301)

The only course of action that Lizzie can conceive of taking that will provide both her and her sister with a commonality of experience is to encounter the fruit-merchant men herself, and to do so she must overcome her own fears "and for the first time in her life / Beg[i]n to listen and look" (ll. 327-28). But Lizzie's visit to the haunted glen is fundamentally different from her sister's because of their different motivations in dealing with the goblins. Whereas Laura's determination to experience the goblin fruits was based first on her fascination with their infinite variety and second on her own inability to refrain from self-indulgence, Lizzie's visit to the goblins is driven by Christian values. First, and most important, Lizzie is moved to take this course of action by a pure, unconditional love for her degenerating sister. Moreover, Lizzie's aim is not simply to experience nature but to meet it and wrest from it the secret of her sister's salvation—and, by association, her own. Thus Laura's failure in Tractarian terms to scrutinize nature for signs of a greater purpose than mere self-indulgence is redeemed by Lizzie's fundamentally Tractarian approach to the problem of redemption and salvation. In approaching the overwhelming natural world that seduced her sister, Lizzie begins on much firmer moral ground.

The difference between Lizzie's experience and Laura's becomes apparent as the scene of Lizzie's encounter unfolds. For thirty-four lines (ll. 329-62) the bewildering description of the goblins goes on—the longest and most dizzying such catalog in the poem. Everything about them is described in rapid succession and with meticulous differentiation: means of locomotion, demeanors, features, sounds, activities, and finally their fruits. The cumulative images overwhelm the imaginative eye as the poetic language of the catalog rises to a cacophonic crescendo. Yet in spite of this most furious of the poem's assaults upon the senses, Lizzie remains morally upright and physically composed, never indicating that she is for a moment tempted to experience nature for a reason other than her professed purpose. When Lizzie speaks of her desire to buy goblin fruits she does not do so hastily, as Laura has done; rather, Lizzie is "mindful of Jeanie" (l. 364) in her reserved approach to the array of fruits.

Further, the goblins seem much more threatening to Lizzie's perceptions than they seemed to Laura's. None of the goblins speak in honey-sweet tones or purr as they approach; instead, they make harsher, less melodic sounds as they come,

> Puffing and blowing,
> Chuckling, clapping, crowing,
> Clucking and gobbling.
>
> (ll. 333-35)

Rossetti's use of harsher sounds in this passage, compared with those describing the goblins' seduction of Laura, emphasizes the goblins' more grating approach to Lizzie. The goblins have become representative of the uglier, less seductive side of the natural world, though they are still the same goblins that accosted Laura. But because of her morally discerning eyes and ears, Lizzie interprets the goblins not as benevolently cooing like doves but as "chattering like magpies" (l. 345)—birds with decidedly less attractive reputations and lacking Christian resonance.

As Lizzie's resistance to the temptations of the goblins mounts, their frenzied and disharmonious activities intensify. The variety of the goblins and their actions has become, at this point of the poem, a threatening and dangerous repulsion rather than an exciting attraction. The lists in these lines detail a multitude of malevolent and violent activities, rendering this portion of the poem, at least superficially, as a symbolic, if not a literal, rape of Lizzie at the goblins' hands. Despite the violence and struggle of the scene, though, the rape is a failed one. Lizzie has encountered the ambiguous variety of the goblins and their fruits, but through her moral stability she has come to a realization that Laura failed to reach. Lizzie has discovered that the seductive beauty of nature's variety is neither good nor evil in itself but instead has the ability to produce either good or evil results, depending upon the viewer's response. The goblin experience and her initial taste of the fruits produced for Laura an evil result, primarily because her approach to that experience was self-indulgent and, if not immoral, at least amoral. But when the same experience is encountered with a discerning moral eye and a pure heart, as Lizzie has approached it, the result can be spiritual rejuvenation and moral salvation.

Many critics have pointed to Lizzie's return to Laura as a barely veiled moment of sexuality and homoeroticism, primarily because of Lizzie's words to Laura:

> "Did you miss me?
> Come and kiss me.
> Never mind my bruises,
> Hug me, kiss me, suck my juices
> Squeezed from goblin fruits for you,
> Goblin pulp and goblin dew.
> Eat me, drink me, love me;
> Laura, make much of me."
>
> (ll. 465-72)

While the language of this passage is both erotic and suggestive, Rossetti's intense sacramentalism and devout Christianity render rather hollow any strictly sexual or homoerotic interpretation. As we have seen, much of the poem is concerned with the temptation offered by the variety of the natural world, a temptation to which Laura succumbed earlier. The more likely interpretation of this scene is a Christian one in which Lizzie becomes a representative of Christ, offering communion and Christian salvation. This salvation also renders **"Goblin Market"** as an unlikely (although much improved from a Christian perspective) variation of the Genesis story, for only in the New Testament do we finally reach the possibility of Christian salvation. Lizzie has finally and ultimately turned the variety of the goblin fruits into a physical mode of salvation for her ailing sister, for Lizzie is morally astute enough to understand what can be taken away from nature to provide meaning for her sister's experiences.

After tasting the juices of the goblin fruits again, in the form of communion from her sister, Laura undergoes a spiritual transformation that is described in imagery highly suggestive of a rending of the soul, followed by a resurrection from a state indistinguishable from death. Once again, as occurred with her decline into spiritual desolation, Laura's recovery is dramatized by a corresponding change in physical appearance and behavior. After she regains consciousness, we are told:

> Laura awoke as from a dream,
> Laughed in the innocent old way,
> Hugged Lizzie but not twice or thrice;
> Her gleaming locks showed not one thread of grey,
> Her breath was sweet as May
> And light danced in her eyes.
>
> (ll. 537-42)

For Rossetti a return to spiritual wholeness and a state of Christian grace seems necessarily to require a harmony and unity among the sisters. Throughout **"Goblin Market,"** in fact, such a state of harmony and unity has always provided the surest means of happiness and the starkest contrast to the ambiguity and variety of the mysterious goblin men who threaten to upset both domestic tranquility and the moral judgment that provides for Christian salvation.

In this context the concluding lines of Rossetti's poem seem to offer a more than satisfactory resolution to the experiences of Laura and Lizzie:

> "For there is no friend like a sister
> In calm or stormy weather;
> To cheer one on the tedious way,
> To fetch one if one goes astray,
> To lift one if one totters down,
> To strengthen whilst one stands."
>
> (ll. 562-67)

By arriving at this conclusion herself in her own storytelling, Laura makes clear that she has learned the lesson exemplified by Lizzie. But more significant, the message contained in Laura's final speech is not merely an affirmation of biological sisterhood; rather, having a sister can be the means of achieving a human harmony that allows one to stand, fortified rather than forlorn, upright amid the bewildering array of human experience from which one may be unable, alone, to make moral sense. In **"Goblin Market"** the bewilderment comes specifically from nature, and it is in unearthing the secrets of Christian salvation in nature that a sister can light the way as a spiritual beacon.[18] Understanding this crucial conflict that lies at the center of **"Goblin Market"** requires a reconsideration of Rossetti's use of the list to present in quite real and literal terms the fear she felt of the seductive and multifarious natural world.

Notes

[1] June Sturrock, "Protective Pastoral: Innocence and Female Experience in William Blake's *Songs* and Christina Rossetti's *Goblin Market*," *Colby Quarterly*, 30 (1994), 99. See also Terrence Holt, "'Men sell not such in any town': Exchange in *Goblin Market*," *Victorian Poetry*, 28 (1990), 51-67. In *The Madwoman in the Attic: The Woman Writer and the Nineteenth-Century Literary Imagination* (New Haven: Yale Univ. Press, 1979), Sandra M. Gilbert and Susan Gubar explore the poem as a story of sexual temptation and renunciation (see pp. 564-75). Two examples of articles that treat "Goblin Market" as a glorification of sisterhood are Dorothy Mermin, "Heroic Sisterhood in *Goblin Market*," *Victorian Poetry*, 21 (1983), 107-18; and Miriam Saga, "Christina Rossetti's 'Goblin Market' and Feminist Literary Criticism," *Pre-Raphaelite Review*, 3, no. 2 (1980), 66-76.

[2] In her biography *Christina Rossetti* (Berkeley and Los Angeles: Univ. of California Press, 1963) Lona Mosk Packer attempts to portray the poem as a description of Rossetti's sexual yearnings for William Bell Scott (see p. 120).

[3] In *Christina Rossetti and the Poetry of Discovery* (Baton Rouge: Louisiana State Univ. Press, 1989) Katherine J. Mayberry writes that the fruits "by [their] sheer variety and number" "threaten to overpower Lizzie completely," and she goes on to claim that "the multiple implications of the goblin experience" are reflected by the multiplicity of the fruits (p. 98). Sagan claims only that the multiple fruits seem to intensify the images and overwhelm the senses (p. 71).

[4] *The Family Letters of Christina Georgina Rossetti*, ed. William Michael Rossetti (London: Brown, Langham, and Co., 1908), pp. 25-26.

[5] Mackenzie Bell, *Christina Rossetti: A Biographical and Critical Study*, 4th ed. (1898; rpt. New York: Haskell House, 1971), p. 209.

[6] Making use of such visits to the Zoological Gardens was not an uncommon practice in attempting to relieve particularly emotional or psychological ailments in Rossetti's time. In Samuel Butler's *The Way of All Flesh* (Garden City, N.Y.: Doubleday, 1960), "one of the most eminent doctors in London" suggests that such walks are medicinal when he says, "I have found the Zoological Gardens of service to many of my patients" (pp. 379-80).

[7] John Heath-Stubbs, "Pre-Raphaelitism and the Aesthetic Withdrawal," in *Pre-Raphaelitism: A Collection of Critical Essays*, ed. James Sambrook (Chicago: Univ. of Chicago Press, 1974), p. 169.

[8] See Lionel Stevenson, *The Pre-Raphaelite Poets* (Chapel Hill: Univ. of North Carolina Press, 1972), p. 6.

[9] Biographers have noted several vacations in which Christina would have had opportunity to explore the English countryside, such as at Holmer Green (Packer, p. 144) and at Frome Selwood, where she lived with her parents for an eleven-month stint (see Bell, p. 24).

[10] See Georgina Battiscombe, *Christina Rossetti: A Divided Life* (London: Constable, 1981), p. 154. Christina was an Associate of this same Order and worked at its House of Charity from 1860 to 1870 (Battiscombe, p. 94), which explains her support of Maria's decision to become a nun with the Anglican Sisterhood of All Saints in 1873 (p. 154). In fact, D.M.R. Bentley explores, intriguingly though not wholly convincingly, the hypothesis that "Goblin Market" was in fact written to be read aloud to the fallen women of Highgate Hill, with whom Christina was associated through her involvement with the Anglican Sisterhood (see "The Meretricious and the Meritorious in *Goblin Market*: A Conjecture and an Analysis," in *The Achievement of Christina Rossetti*, ed. David A. Kent [Ithaca: Cornell Univ. Press, 1987], p. 58).

[11] See Mary Arseneau, "Incarnation and Interpretation: Christina Rossetti, the Oxford Movement, and *Goblin Market*," *Victorian Poetry*, 31 (1993), 80. Rossetti in fact "took the trouble to illustrate her own copy of

[Keble's] *The Christian Year* with naive little marginal drawings" despite her lack of true affinity for Keble's verse (Battiscombe, p. 180).

[12] G. B. Tennyson, *Victorian Devotional Poetry: The Tractarian Mode* (Cambridge, Mass.: Harvard Univ. Press, 1981), p. 21. Tennyson presents perhaps the most thorough treatment of the influences of Tractarianism upon Victorian poetry and includes a discussion of Rossetti's work (and Hopkins's) in his "Postscript: Christina Rossetti and Gerard Manley Hopkins" (pp. 197-211).

[13] See Arseneau, p. 81.

[14] Quoted in Tennyson, p. 39.

[15] "Goblin Market," in *The Complete Poems of Christina Rossetti: A Variorum Edition*, ed. R. W. Crump, 3 vols. (Baton Rouge: Louisiana State Univ. Press, 1979-1995), I, 11, ll. 1-14. Further references to "Goblin Market" are from this edition and are cited parenthetically by line number in the text.

[16] B. Ifor Evans traces the origins of the goblins back to such sources as Thomas Keightley's *The Fairy Mythology* (1828), and he makes convincing arguments for the sources of many other aspects of the poem, including the merchant cries, the lavish scenery, and the animal features of the goblin men (see "The Sources of Christina Rossetti's 'Goblin Market,'" *Modern Language Review*, 28 [1933], 156-65).

[17] Sturrock argues that "Goblin Market" is "inescapably a Genesis story: it involves arbitrary taboo, forbidden fruit, and the potentially mortal consequences of disobedience," but in her argument she does not explicitly connect Laura's suffering to her disobedience, per se. It seems to me that Laura's suffering is more accurately a result of her desire to repeat her experience than of her original transgression. The goblin fruit is not intrinsically harmful, nor is an omnipotent arbiter of the "taboo" involved in meting out punishment, as in the Genesis story. Sturrock's description of the poem as "inescapably a Genesis story," then, remains unconvincing.

[18] Bentley, too, argues that the culmination of the poem lies in the "right-thinking Laura who draws upon her own past experiences, as well as Lizzie's, to emphasize the importance of community and mutuality" (p. 79).

FURTHER READING

Arseneau, Mary. "Incarnation and Interpretation: Christina Rossetti, the Oxford Movement, and *Goblin Market*." *Victorian Poetry* 31, No. 1 (Spring 1993): 79-93.

Advances a religious interpretation of "Goblin Market" not as Christian allegory but in light of the "intense incarnationalism and sacramentalism of the Oxford Movement" in which Rossetti participated.

Bentley, D. M. R. "The Meretricious and the Meritorious in *Goblin Market*: A Conjecture and an Analysis." In *The Achievement of Christina Rossetti*, edited by David A. Kent, pp. 57-81. Ithaca, N.Y.: Cornell University Press, 1987.

Argues that not only is "Goblin Market" a reflection of Rossetti's work with "fallen women" but was intended as a "cautionary tale" to be read aloud by Rossetti to an audience of such women.

Campbell, Elizabeth. "Of Mothers and Merchants: Female Economics in Christina Rossetti's 'Goblin Market'." *Victorian Studies* 33, No. 3 (Spring 1990): 393-410.

Maintains that "Goblin Market" represents Rossetti's critique of capitalist society and that the poem affirms the "vital socioeconomic function" of women in the Victorian economy.

Crump, R. W. An Introduction to *The Complete Poems of Christina Rossetti*, edited by R. W. Crump, pp. 3-7. Baton Rouge: Louisiana State University Press, 1979.

Traces the printing history of two volumes of Rossetti's poetry—*Goblin Market and Other Poems* and *The Prince's Progress*—and maintains that an understanding of this history will aid in the "determination" of Rossetti's poems.

Evans, B. Ifor. "The Sources of Christina Rossetti's 'Goblin Market'." *Modern Language Review* 28, No. 2 (1933): 156-65.

Discusses the works which may have influenced Rossetti's writing of "Goblin Market," including *The Fairy Mythology* (1828) by Thomas Keightley.

Golub, Ellen. "Untying Goblin Apron Strings: A Psychoanalytic Reading of 'Goblin Market'." *Literature and Psychology* XXV, No. 4 (1975): 158-65.

Examines the issues suggested by the poem itself rather than by Rossetti's life, including the flight from a love relationship and the attraction to and threat of the gratification of desires.

Holt, Terrence. "'Men sell not such in any town': Exchange in *Goblin Market*." *Victorian Poetry* 28, No. 1 (Spring 1990): 51-67.

Analyzes the terms of commerce and exchange in "Goblin Market" and argues that the poem focuses as much on power relations as it does on gender relations. The critic further maintains that, contrary to his reading of Sandra Gilbert's and Susan Gubar's conclusions, "Goblin Market" does not reject women's literature.

Mayberry, Katherine J. "'Goblin Market': A Reconciling Poetic." In *Christina Rossetti and the Poetry of Discovery*, pp. 84-108. Baton Rouge: Louisiana State University Press, 1989.

> Examines "Goblin Market" as Rossetti's statement of her aesthetic theory, which partially reflected Tractarian poetic theory and which asserted that poetry was justified provided that it "expressed moral truth."

McGann, Jerome J. "Christina Rossetti's Poems: A New Edition and a Revaluation." *Victorian Studies* 23, No. 2 (Winter 1980): 237-54.

> In the section of the essay devoted to "Goblin Market," McGann asserts that the poem serves as a "serious critique of its age and the age's cultural institutions."

Morrill, David F. " 'Twilight is not good for maidens': Uncle Polidori and the Psychodynamics of Vampirism in 'Goblin Market'." *Victorian Poetry* 23, No. 1 (Spring 1990): 1-16.

> Suggests that John Polidori's novel *The Vampyre* may have inspired portions of "Goblin Market" by providing Rossetti with "certain details of the vampire myth."

Rosenblum, Dolores. " 'Goblin Market': Dearth and Sufficiency." In *Christina Rossetti: The Poetry of Endurance*, pp. 63-108. Carbondale, Ill.: Southern Illinois University Press, 1986.

> Offers a "psychological-phenomenological" discussion of "Goblin Market" in order to analyze the poem's structure and key motifs. The second part of the chapter examines other Rossetti poems which may be viewed as commentary on "Goblin Market."

Sturrock, June. "Protective Pastoral: Innocence and Female Experience in William Blake's *Songs* and Christina Rossetti's 'Goblin Market'." *Colby Quarterly* 30, No. 2 (June 1994): 98-108.

> Maintains that Blake's *Songs of Innocence and Experience* and Rossetti's "Goblin Market" examine the "protective implications of pastoral in connection with the early stages of maturation" and that only these two works explore the female connection to the protective pastoral.

Thompson, Deborah Ann. "Anorexia as a Lived Trope: Christina Rossetti's 'Goblin Market'." *Mosaic* 24, Nos. 3-4 (Summer-Fall 1991): 89-106.

> Agrees that both food and the female body are metaphors in "Goblin Market" but maintains that the two are already metaphors outside the poem and examines what food signifies in the poem.

Weathers, Winston. "Christina Rossetti: The Sisterhood of Self." *Victorian Poetry* III, No. 2 (Spring 1965): 81-9.

> Argues that in "Goblin Market" the two sisters, Lizzie and Laura, are "aspects of one self" and that the poem traces the movement of the self through innocence to "sickness and fragmentation" and finally to balance.

Additional coverage of Rossetti's life and career is contained in the following sources published by Gale Research: *Nineteenth-Century Literature Criticism,* **Vols. 2 and 50;** *DISCovering Authors; Poetry Criticism,* **Vol. 7;** *World Literature Criticism, 1500 to the Present;* **and** *Dictionary of Literary Biography,* **Vols. 35 and 163.**

Nineteenth-Century Literature Criticism

Cumulative Indexes
Volumes 1-66

How to Use This Index

The main references

> Calvino, Italo
> 1923-1985.....CLC 5, 8, 11, 22, 33, 39, 73; SSC 3

list all author entries in the following Gale Literary Criticism series:

BLC = Black Literature Criticism
CLC = Contemporary Literary Criticism
CLR = Children's Literature Review
CMLC = Classical and Medieval Literature Criticism
DA = DISCovering Authors
DAB = DISCovering Authors: British
DAC = DISCovering Authors: Canadian
DAM = DISCovering Authors Modules
    DRAM: Dramatists module
    MST: Most-studied authors module
    MULT: Multicultural authors module
    NOV: Novelists module
    POET: Poets module
    POP: Popular/genre writers module

DC = Drama Criticism
HLC = Hispanic Literature Criticism
LC = Literature Criticism from 1400 to 1800
NCLC = Nineteenth-Century Literature Criticism
PC = Poetry Criticism
SSC = Short Story Criticism
TCLC = Twentieth-Century Literary Criticism
WLC = World Literature Criticism, 1500 to the Present

The cross-references

> See also CANR 23; CA 85-88;
> obituary CA 116

list all author entries in the following Gale biographical and literary sources:

AAYA = Authors & Artists for Young Adults
AITN = Authors in the News
BEST = Bestsellers
BW = Black Writers
CA = Contemporary Authors
CAAS = Contemporary Authors Autobiography Series
CABS = Contemporary Authors Bibliographical Series
CANR = Contemporary Authors New Revision Series
CAP = Contemporary Authors Permanent Series
CDALB = Concise Dictionary of American Literary Biography
CDBLB = Concise Dictionary of British Literary Biography
DLB = Dictionary of Literary Biography
DLBD = Dictionary of Literary Biography Documentary Series
DLBY = Dictionary of Literary Biography Yearbook
HW = Hispanic Writers
JRDA = Junior DISCovering Authors
MAICYA = Major Authors and Illustrators for Children and Young Adults
MTCW = Major 20th-Century Writers
NNAL = Native North American Literature
SAAS = Something about the Author Autobiography Series
SATA = Something about the Author
YABC = Yesterday's Authors of Books for Children

Literary Criticism Series
Cumulative Author Index

Abasiyanik, Sait Faik 1906-1954
　See Sait Faik
　See also CA 123
Abbey, Edward 1927-1989 .... **CLC 36, 59**
　See also CA 45-48; 128; CANR 2, 41
Abbott, Lee K(ittredge) 1947- .... **CLC 48**
　See also CA 124; CANR 51; DLB 130
Abe, Kobo 1924-1993**CLC 8, 22, 53, 81; DAM NOV**
　See also CA 65-68; 140; CANR 24, 60; DLB 182; MTCW
Abelard, Peter c. 1079-c. 1142 ...... **CMLC 11**
　See also DLB 115
Abell, Kjeld 1901-1961 .... **CLC 15**
　See also CA 111
Abish, Walter 1931- .... **CLC 22**
　See also CA 101; CANR 37; DLB 130
Abrahams, Peter (Henry) 1919- .... **CLC 4**
　See also BW 1; CA 57-60; CANR 26; DLB 117; MTCW
Abrams, M(eyer) H(oward) 1912- ... **CLC 24**
　See also CA 57-60; CANR 13, 33; DLB 67
Abse, Dannie 1923-.. **CLC 7, 29; DAB; DAM POET**
　See also CA 53-56; CAAS 1; CANR 4, 46; DLB 27
Achebe, (Albert) Chinua(lumogu) 1930-**C L C 1, 3, 5, 7, 11, 26, 51, 75; BLC; DA; DAB; DAC; DAM MST, MULT, NOV; WLC**
　See also AAYA 15; BW 2; CA 1-4R; CANR 6, 26, 47; CLR 20; DLB 117; MAICYA; MTCW; SATA 40; SATA-Brief 38
Acker, Kathy 1948- .... **CLC 45**
　See also CA 117; 122; CANR 55
Ackroyd, Peter 1949- .... **CLC 34, 52**
　See also CA 123; 127; CANR 51; DLB 155; INT 127
Acorn, Milton 1923- .... **CLC 15; DAC**
　See also CA 103; DLB 53; INT 103
Adamov, Arthur 1908-1970**CLC 4, 25; DAM DRAM**
　See also CA 17-18; 25-28R; CAP 2; MTCW
Adams, Alice (Boyd) 1926-**CLC 6, 13, 46; SSC 24**
　See also CA 81-84; CANR 26, 53; DLBY 86; INT CANR-26; MTCW
Adams, Andy 1859-1935 .... **TCLC 56**
　See also YABC 1
Adams, Douglas (Noel) 1952- .... **CLC 27, 60; DAM POP**
　See also AAYA 4; BEST 89:3; CA 106; CANR 34; DLBY 83; JRDA
Adams, Francis 1862-1893 .... **NCLC 33**
Adams, Henry (Brooks) 1838-1918 **TCLC 4, 52; DA; DAB; DAC; DAM MST**
　See also CA 104; 133; DLB 12, 47
Adams, Richard (George) 1920-**CLC 4, 5, 18; DAM NOV**
　See also AAYA 16; AITN 1, 2; CA 49-52; CANR 3, 35; CLR 20; JRDA; MAICYA; MTCW; SATA 7, 69
Adamson, Joy(-Friederike Victoria) 1910-1980
CLC 17
　See also CA 69-72; 93-96; CANR 22; MTCW; SATA 11; SATA-Obit 22
Adcock, Fleur 1934- .... **CLC 41**
　See also CA 25-28R; CAAS 23; CANR 11, 34; DLB 40
Addams, Charles (Samuel) 1912-1988**CLC 30**
　See also CA 61-64; 126; CANR 12
Addams, Jane 1860-1935 .... **TCLC 76**
Addison, Joseph 1672-1719 .... **LC 18**
　See also CDBLB 1660-1789; DLB 101
Adler, Alfred (F.) 1870-1937 .... **TCLC 61**
　See also CA 119; 159
Adler, C(arole) S(chwerdtfeger) 1932- . **C L C 35**
　See also AAYA 4; CA 89-92; CANR 19, 40; JRDA; MAICYA; SAAS 15; SATA 26, 63
Adler, Renata 1938- .... **CLC 8, 31**
　See also CA 49-52; CANR 5, 22, 52; MTCW
Ady, Endre 1877-1919 .... **TCLC 11**
　See also CA 107
A.E. 1867-1935 .... **TCLC 3, 10**
　See also Russell, George William
Aeschylus 525B.C.-456B.C. . **CMLC 11; DA; DAB; DAC; DAM DRAM, MST; DC 8; WLCS**
　See also DLB 176
Africa, Ben
　See Bosman, Herman Charles
Afton, Effie
　See Harper, Frances Ellen Watkins
Agapida, Fray Antonio
　See Irving, Washington
Agee, James (Rufus) 1909-1955 **TCLC 1, 19; DAM NOV**
　See also AITN 1; CA 108; 148; CDALB 1941-1968; DLB 2, 26, 152
Aghill, Gordon
　See Silverberg, Robert
Agnon, S(hmuel) Y(osef Halevi) 1888-1970
CLC 4, 8, 14; SSC 29
　See also CA 17-18; 25-28R; CANR 60; CAP 2; MTCW
Agrippa von Nettesheim, Henry Cornelius 1486-1535 .... **LC 27**
Aherne, Owen
　See Cassill, R(onald) V(erlin)
Ai 1947- .... **CLC 4, 14, 69**
　See also CA 85-88; CAAS 13; DLB 120
Aickman, Robert (Fordyce) 1914-1981 . **C L C 57**
　See also CA 5-8R; CANR 3
Aiken, Conrad (Potter) 1889-1973**CLC 1, 3, 5, 10, 52; DAM NOV, POET; SSC 9**
　See also CA 5-8R; 45-48; CANR 4, 60; CDALB 1929-1941; DLB 9, 45, 102; MTCW; SATA 3, 30
Aiken, Joan (Delano) 1924- .... **CLC 35**
　See also AAYA 1; CA 9-12R; CANR 4, 23, 34; CLR 1, 19; DLB 161; JRDA; MAICYA; MTCW; SAAS 1; SATA 2, 30, 73
Ainsworth, William Harrison 1805-1882
NCLC 13
　See also DLB 21; SATA 24
Aitmatov, Chingiz (Torekulovich) 1928-**C L C 71**
　See also CA 103; CANR 38; MTCW; SATA 56
Akers, Floyd
　See Baum, L(yman) Frank
Akhmadulina, Bella Akhatovna 1937-..**C L C 53; DAM POET**
　See also CA 65-68
Akhmatova, Anna 1888-1966**CLC 11, 25, 64; DAM POET; PC 2**
　See also CA 19-20; 25-28R; CANR 35; CAP 1; MTCW
Aksakov, Sergei Timofeyvich 1791-1859
NCLC 2
Aksenov, Vassily
　See Aksyonov, Vassily (Pavlovich)
Aksyonov, Vassily (Pavlovich) 1932-**CLC 22, 37, 101**
　See also CA 53-56; CANR 12, 48
Akutagawa, Ryunosuke 1892-1927 **TCLC 16**
　See also CA 117; 154
Alain 1868-1951 .... **TCLC 41**
Alain-Fournier .... **TCLC 6**
　See also Fournier, Henri Alban
　See also DLB 65
Alarcon, Pedro Antonio de 1833-1891**NCLC 1**
Alas (y Urena), Leopoldo (Enrique Garcia) 1852-1901 .... **TCLC 29**
　See also CA 113; 131; HW
Albee, Edward (Franklin III) 1928-**CLC 1, 2, 3, 5, 9, 11, 13, 25, 53, 86; DA; DAB; DAC; DAM DRAM, MST; WLC**
　See also AITN 1; CA 5-8R; CABS 3; CANR 8, 54; CDALB 1941-1968; DLB 7; INT CANR-8; MTCW
Alberti, Rafael 1902- .... **CLC 7**
　See also CA 85-88; DLB 108
Albert the Great 1200(?)-1280 ...... **CMLC 16**
　See also DLB 115
Alcala-Galiano, Juan Valera y
　See Valera y Alcala-Galiano, Juan
Alcott, Amos Bronson 1799-1888 .... **NCLC 1**
　See also DLB 1
Alcott, Louisa May 1832-1888 . **NCLC 6, 58; DA; DAB; DAC; DAM MST, NOV; SSC 27; WLC**
　See also AAYA 20; CDALB 1865-1917; CLR 1, 38; DLB 1, 42, 79; DLBD 14; JRDA; MAICYA; YABC 1
Aldanov, M. A.
　See Aldanov, Mark (Alexandrovich)
Aldanov, Mark (Alexandrovich) 1886(?)-1957
TCLC 23
　See also CA 118
Aldington, Richard 1892-1962 .... **CLC 49**
　See also CA 85-88; CANR 45; DLB 20, 36, 100, 149
Aldiss, Brian W(ilson) 1925- . **CLC 5, 14, 40; DAM NOV**

See also CA 5-8R; CAAS 2; CANR 5, 28; DLB 14; MTCW; SATA 34

Alegria, Claribel 1924- **CLC 75; DAM MULT**
See also CA 131; CAAS 15; DLB 145; HW

Alegria, Fernando 1918- .... **CLC 57**
See also CA 9-12R; CANR 5, 32; HW

Aleichem, Sholom .... **TCLC 1, 35**
See also Rabinovitch, Sholem

Aleixandre, Vicente 1898-1984 ... **CLC 9, 36; DAM POET; PC 15**
See also CA 85-88; 114; CANR 26; DLB 108; HW; MTCW

Alepoudelis, Odysseus
See Elytis, Odysseus

Aleshkovsky, Joseph 1929-
See Aleshkovsky, Yuz
See also CA 121; 128

Aleshkovsky, Yuz .... **CLC 44**
See also Aleshkovsky, Joseph

Alexander, Lloyd (Chudley) 1924- .. **CLC 35**
See also AAYA 1; CA 1-4R; CANR 1, 24, 38, 55; CLR 1, 5; DLB 52; JRDA; MAICYA; MTCW; SAAS 19; SATA 3, 49, 81

Alexie, Sherman (Joseph, Jr.) 1966- **CLC 96; DAM MULT**
See also CA 138; DLB 175; NNAL

Alfau, Felipe 1902- .... **CLC 66**
See also CA 137

Alger, Horatio, Jr. 1832-1899 .... **NCLC 8**
See also DLB 42; SATA 16

Algren, Nelson 1909-1981 .... **CLC 4, 10, 33**
See also CA 13-16R; 103; CANR 20, 61; CDALB 1941-1968; DLB 9; DLBY 81, 82; MTCW

Ali, Ahmed 1910- .... **CLC 69**
See also CA 25-28R; CANR 15, 34

Alighieri, Dante 1265-1321 ...... **CMLC 3, 18; WLCS**

Allan, John B.
See Westlake, Donald E(dwin)

Allan, Sydney
See Hartmann, Sadakichi

Allan, Sydney
See Hartmann, Sadakichi

Allen, Edward 1948- .... **CLC 59**

Allen, Paula Gunn 1939- .... **CLC 84; DAM MULT**
See also CA 112; 143; DLB 175; NNAL

Allen, Roland
See Ayckbourn, Alan

Allen, Sarah A.
See Hopkins, Pauline Elizabeth

Allen, Sidney H.
See Hartmann, Sadakichi

Allen, Woody 1935- **CLC 16, 52; DAM POP**
See also AAYA 10; CA 33-36R; CANR 27, 38; DLB 44; MTCW

Allende, Isabel 1942- . **CLC 39, 57, 97; DAM MULT, NOV; HLC; WLCS**
See also AAYA 18; CA 125; 130; CANR 51; DLB 145; HW; INT 130; MTCW

Alleyn, Ellen
See Rossetti, Christina (Georgina)

Allingham, Margery (Louise) 1904-1966 **CLC 19**
See also CA 5-8R; 25-28R; CANR 4, 58; DLB 77; MTCW

Allingham, William 1824-1889 ...... **NCLC 25**
See also DLB 35

Allison, Dorothy E. 1949- .... **CLC 78**
See also CA 140

Allston, Washington 1779-1843 .... **NCLC 2**
See also DLB 1

Almedingen, E. M. .... **CLC 12**
See also Almedingen, Martha Edith von
See also SATA 3

Almedingen, Martha Edith von 1898-1971
See Almedingen, E. M.
See also CA 1-4R; CANR 1

Almqvist, Carl Jonas Love 1793-1866 **NCLC 42**

Alonso, Damaso 1898-1990 .... **CLC 14**
See also CA 110; 131; 130; DLB 108; HW

Alov
See Gogol, Nikolai (Vasilyevich)

Alta 1942- .... **CLC 19**
See also CA 57-60

Alter, Robert B(ernard) 1935- .... **CLC 34**
See also CA 49-52; CANR 1, 47

Alther, Lisa 1944- .... **CLC 7, 41**
See also CA 65-68; CANR 12, 30, 51; MTCW

Altman, Robert 1925- .... **CLC 16**
See also CA 73-76; CANR 43

Alvarez, A(lfred) 1929- .... **CLC 5, 13**
See also CA 1-4R; CANR 1, 33; DLB 14, 40

Alvarez, Alejandro Rodriguez 1903-1965
See Casona, Alejandro
See also CA 131; 93-96; HW

Alvarez, Julia 1950- .... **CLC 93**
See also CA 147

Alvaro, Corrado 1896-1956 .... **TCLC 60**

Amado, Jorge 1912- **CLC 13, 40; DAM MULT, NOV; HLC**
See also CA 77-80; CANR 35; DLB 113; MTCW

Ambler, Eric 1909- .... **CLC 4, 6, 9**
See also CA 9-12R; CANR 7, 38; DLB 77; MTCW

Amichai, Yehuda 1924- .... **CLC 9, 22, 57**
See also CA 85-88; CANR 46, 60; MTCW

Amichai, Yehudah
See Amichai, Yehuda

Amiel, Henri Frederic 1821-1881 .... **NCLC 4**

Amis, Kingsley (William) 1922-1995 **CLC 1, 2, 3, 5, 8, 13, 40, 44; DA; DAB; DAC; DAM MST, NOV**
See also AITN 2; CA 9-12R; 150; CANR 8, 28, 54; CDBLB 1945-1960; DLB 15, 27, 100, 139; DLBY 96; INT CANR-8; MTCW

Amis, Martin (Louis) 1949- **CLC 4, 9, 38, 62, 101**
See also BEST 90:3; CA 65-68; CANR 8, 27, 54; DLB 14; INT CANR-27

Ammons, A(rchie) R(andolph) 1926- **CLC 2, 3, 5, 8, 9, 25, 57; DAM POET; PC 16**
See also AITN 1; CA 9-12R; CANR 6, 36, 51; DLB 5, 165; MTCW

Amo, Tauraatua i
See Adams, Henry (Brooks)

Anand, Mulk Raj 1905- ... **CLC 23, 93; DAM NOV**
See also CA 65-68; CANR 32; MTCW

Anatol
See Schnitzler, Arthur

Anaximander c. 610B.C.-c. 546B.C. **CMLC 22**

Anaya, Rudolfo A(lfonso) 1937- ...... **CLC 23; DAM MULT, NOV; HLC**
See also AAYA 20; CA 45-48; CAAS 4; CANR 1, 32, 51; DLB 82; HW 1; MTCW

Andersen, Hans Christian 1805-1875 **NCLC 7; DA; DAB; DAC; DAM MST, POP; SSC 6; WLC**
See also CLR 6; MAICYA; YABC 1

Anderson, C. Farley
See Mencken, H(enry) L(ouis); Nathan, George Jean

Anderson, Jessica (Margaret) Queale 1916- **CLC 37**
See also CA 9-12R; CANR 4, 62

Anderson, Jon (Victor) 1940- .. **CLC 9; DAM POET**
See also CA 25-28R; CANR 20

Anderson, Lindsay (Gordon) 1923-1994 **CLC 20**
See also CA 125; 128; 146

Anderson, Maxwell 1888-1959 **TCLC 2; DAM DRAM**
See also CA 105; 152; DLB 7

Anderson, Poul (William) 1926- ...... **CLC 15**
See also AAYA 5; CA 1-4R; CAAS 2; CANR 2, 15, 34; DLB 8; INT CANR-15; MTCW; SATA 90; SATA-Brief 39

Anderson, Robert (Woodruff) 1917- **CLC 23; DAM DRAM**
See also AITN 1; CA 21-24R; CANR 32; DLB 7

Anderson, Sherwood 1876-1941 **TCLC 1, 10, 24; DA; DAB; DAC; DAM MST, NOV; SSC 1; WLC**
See also CA 104; 121; CANR 61; CDALB 1917-1929; DLB 4, 9, 86; DLBD 1; MTCW

Andier, Pierre
See Desnos, Robert

Andouard
See Giraudoux, (Hippolyte) Jean

Andrade, Carlos Drummond de .... **CLC 18**
See also Drummond de Andrade, Carlos

Andrade, Mario de 1893-1945 .... **TCLC 43**

Andreae, Johann V(alentin) 1586-1654 **LC 32**

Andreas-Salome, Lou 1861-1937 ... **TCLC 56**
See also DLB 66

Andress, Lesley
See Sanders, Lawrence

Andrewes, Lancelot 1555-1626 .... **LC 5**
See also DLB 151, 172

Andrews, Cicily Fairfield
See West, Rebecca

Andrews, Elton V.
See Pohl, Frederik

Andreyev, Leonid (Nikolaevich) 1871-1919 **TCLC 3**
See also CA 104

Andric, Ivo 1892-1975 .... **CLC 8**
See also CA 81-84; 57-60; CANR 43, 60; DLB 147; MTCW

Androvar
See Prado (Calvo), Pedro

Angelique, Pierre
See Bataille, Georges

Angell, Roger 1920- .... **CLC 26**
See also CA 57-60; CANR 13, 44; DLB 171

Angelou, Maya 1928- **CLC 12, 35, 64, 77; BLC; DA; DAB; DAC; DAM MST, MULT, POET, POP; WLCS**
See also AAYA 7, 20; BW 2; CA 65-68; CANR 19, 42; DLB 38; MTCW; SATA 49

Annensky, Innokenty (Fyodorovich) 1856-1909 **TCLC 14**
See also CA 110; 155

Annunzio, Gabriele d'
See D'Annunzio, Gabriele

Anodos
See Coleridge, Mary E(lizabeth)

Anon, Charles Robert
See Pessoa, Fernando (Antonio Nogueira)

Anouilh, Jean (Marie Lucien Pierre) 1910-1987 **CLC 1, 3, 8, 13, 40, 50; DAM DRAM; DC 8**
See also CA 17-20R; 123; CANR 32; MTCW

Anthony, Florence
See Ai

Anthony, John
See Ciardi, John (Anthony)

Anthony, Peter
See Shaffer, Anthony (Joshua); Shaffer, Peter (Levin)

Anthony, Piers 1934- ...... **CLC 35; DAM POP**
See also AAYA 11; CA 21-24R; CANR 28, 56; DLB 8; MTCW; SAAS 22; SATA 84

Antoine, Marc

See Proust, (Valentin-Louis-George-Eugene-) Marcel
Antoninus, Brother
See Everson, William (Oliver)
Antonioni, Michelangelo 1912- .... **CLC 20**
See also CA 73-76; CANR 45
Antschel, Paul 1920-1970
See Celan, Paul
See also CA 85-88; CANR 33, 61; MTCW
Anwar, Chairil 1922-1949 .... **TCLC 22**
See also CA 121
Apollinaire, Guillaume 1880-1918 **TCLC 3, 8, 51; DAM POET; PC 7**
See also Kostrowitzki, Wilhelm Apollinaris de
See also CA 152
Appelfeld, Aharon 1932- .... **CLC 23, 47**
See also CA 112; 133
Apple, Max (Isaac) 1941- .... **CLC 9, 33**
See also CA 81-84; CANR 19, 54; DLB 130
Appleman, Philip (Dean) 1926- .... **CLC 51**
See also CA 13-16R; CAAS 18; CANR 6, 29, 56
Appleton, Lawrence
See Lovecraft, H(oward) P(hillips)
Apteryx
See Eliot, T(homas) S(tearns)
Apuleius, (Lucius Madaurensis) 125(?)-175(?) **CMLC 1**
Aquin, Hubert 1929-1977 .... **CLC 15**
See also CA 105; DLB 53
Aragon, Louis 1897-1982 .. **CLC 3, 22; DAM NOV, POET**
See also CA 69-72; 108; CANR 28; DLB 72; MTCW
Arany, Janos 1817-1882 .... **NCLC 34**
Arbuthnot, John 1667-1735 .... **LC 1**
See also DLB 101
Archer, Herbert Winslow
See Mencken, H(enry) L(ouis)
Archer, Jeffrey (Howard) 1940- ..... **CLC 28; DAM POP**
See also AAYA 16; BEST 89:3; CA 77-80; CANR 22, 52; INT CANR-22
Archer, Jules 1915- .... **CLC 12**
See also CA 9-12R; CANR 6; SAAS 5; SATA 4, 85
Archer, Lee
See Ellison, Harlan (Jay)
Arden, John 1930- **CLC 6, 13, 15; DAM DRAM**
See also CA 13-16R; CAAS 4; CANR 31; DLB 13; MTCW
Arenas, Reinaldo 1943-1990 . **CLC 41; DAM MULT; HLC**
See also CA 124; 128; 133; DLB 145; HW
Arendt, Hannah 1906-1975 .... **CLC 66, 98**
See also CA 17-20R; 61-64; CANR 26, 60; MTCW
Aretino, Pietro 1492-1556 .... **LC 12**
Arghezi, Tudor .... **CLC 80**
See also Theodorescu, Ion N.
Arguedas, Jose Maria 1911-1969 **CLC 10, 18**
See also CA 89-92; DLB 113; HW
Argueta, Manlio 1936- .... **CLC 31**
See also CA 131; DLB 145; HW
Ariosto, Ludovico 1474-1533 .... **LC 6**
Aristides
See Epstein, Joseph
Aristophanes 450B.C.-385B.C. **CMLC 4; DA; DAB; DAC; DAM DRAM, MST; DC 2; WLCS**
See also DLB 176
Arlt, Roberto (Godofredo Christophersen) 1900-1942 **TCLC 29; DAM MULT; HLC**
See also CA 123; 131; HW
Armah, Ayi Kwei 1939- .... **CLC 5, 33; BLC; DAM MULT, POET**
See also BW 1; CA 61-64; CANR 21; DLB 117; MTCW

Armatrading, Joan 1950- .... **CLC 17**
See also CA 114
Arnette, Robert
See Silverberg, Robert
Arnim, Achim von (Ludwig Joachim von Arnim) 1781-1831 ...... **NCLC 5; SSC 29**
See also DLB 90
Arnim, Bettina von 1785-1859 .... **NCLC 38**
See also DLB 90
Arnold, Matthew 1822-1888 **NCLC 6, 29; DA; DAB; DAC; DAM MST, POET; PC 5; WLC**
See also CDBLB 1832-1890; DLB 32, 57
Arnold, Thomas 1795-1842 .... **NCLC 18**
See also DLB 55
Arnow, Harriette (Louisa) Simpson 1908-1986 **CLC 2, 7, 18**
See also CA 9-12R; 118; CANR 14; DLB 6; MTCW; SATA 42; SATA-Obit 47
Arp, Hans
See Arp, Jean
Arp, Jean 1887-1966 .... **CLC 5**
See also CA 81-84; 25-28R; CANR 42
Arrabal
See Arrabal, Fernando
Arrabal, Fernando 1932- .... **CLC 2, 9, 18, 58**
See also CA 9-12R; CANR 15
Arrick, Fran .... **CLC 30**
See also Gaberman, Judie Angell
Artaud, Antonin (Marie Joseph) 1896-1948 **TCLC 3, 36; DAM DRAM**
See also CA 104; 149
Arthur, Ruth M(abel) 1905-1979 ...... **CLC 12**
See also CA 9-12R; 85-88; CANR 4; SATA 7, 26
Artsybashev, Mikhail (Petrovich) 1878-1927 **TCLC 31**
Arundel, Honor (Morfydd) 1919-1973 **CLC 17**
See also CA 21-22; 41-44R; CAP 2; CLR 35; SATA 4; SATA-Obit 24
Arzner, Dorothy 1897-1979 .... **CLC 98**
Asch, Sholem 1880-1957 .... **TCLC 3**
See also CA 105
Ash, Shalom
See Asch, Sholem
Ashbery, John (Lawrence) 1927- **CLC 2, 3, 4, 6, 9, 13, 15, 25, 41, 77; DAM POET**
See also CA 5-8R; CANR 9, 37; DLB 5, 165; DLBY 81; INT CANR-9; MTCW
Ashdown, Clifford
See Freeman, R(ichard) Austin
Ashe, Gordon
See Creasey, John
Ashton-Warner, Sylvia (Constance) 1908-1984 **CLC 19**
See also CA 69-72; 112; CANR 29; MTCW
Asimov, Isaac 1920-1992 **CLC 1, 3, 9, 19, 26, 76, 92; DAM POP**
See also AAYA 13; BEST 90:2; CA 1-4R; 137; CANR 2, 19, 36, 60; CLR 12; DLB 8; DLBY 92; INT CANR-19; JRDA; MAICYA; MTCW; SATA 1, 26, 74
Assis, Joaquim Maria Machado de
See Machado de Assis, Joaquim Maria
Astley, Thea (Beatrice May) 1925- ... **CLC 41**
See also CA 65-68; CANR 11, 43
Aston, James
See White, T(erence) H(anbury)
Asturias, Miguel Angel 1899-1974 **CLC 3, 8, 13; DAM MULT, NOV; HLC**
See also CA 25-28; 49-52; CANR 32; CAP 2; DLB 113; HW; MTCW
Atares, Carlos Saura
See Saura (Atares), Carlos
Atheling, William
See Pound, Ezra (Weston Loomis)

Atheling, William, Jr.
See Blish, James (Benjamin)
Atherton, Gertrude (Franklin Horn) 1857-1948 **TCLC 2**
See also CA 104; 155; DLB 9, 78
Atherton, Lucius
See Masters, Edgar Lee
Atkins, Jack
See Harris, Mark
Atkinson, Kate .... **CLC 99**
Attaway, William (Alexander) 1911-1986 **CLC 92; BLC; DAM MULT**
See also BW 2; CA 143; DLB 76
Atticus
See Fleming, Ian (Lancaster)
Atwood, Margaret (Eleanor) 1939- **CLC 2, 3, 4, 8, 13, 15, 25, 44, 84; DA; DAB; DAC; DAM MST, NOV, POET; PC 8; SSC 2; WLC**
See also AAYA 12; BEST 89:2; CA 49-52; CANR 3, 24, 33, 59; DLB 53; INT CANR-24; MTCW; SATA 50
Aubigny, Pierre d'
See Mencken, H(enry) L(ouis)
Aubin, Penelope 1685-1731(?) .... **LC 9**
See also DLB 39
Auchincloss, Louis (Stanton) 1917- **CLC 4, 6, 9, 18, 45; DAM NOV; SSC 22**
See also CA 1-4R; CANR 6, 29, 55; DLB 2; DLBY 80; INT CANR-29; MTCW
Auden, W(ystan) H(ugh) 1907-1973 **CLC 1, 2, 3, 4, 6, 9, 11, 14, 43; DA; DAB; DAC; DAM DRAM, MST, POET; PC 1; WLC**
See also AAYA 18; CA 9-12R; 45-48; CANR 5, 61; CDBLB 1914-1945; DLB 10, 20; MTCW
Audiberti, Jacques 1900-1965 **CLC 38; DAM DRAM**
See also CA 25-28R
Audubon, John James 1785-1851 .. **NCLC 47**
Auel, Jean M(arie) 1936- **CLC 31; DAM POP**
See also AAYA 7; BEST 90:4; CA 103; CANR 21; INT CANR-21; SATA 91
Auerbach, Erich 1892-1957 .... **TCLC 43**
See also CA 118; 155
Augier, Emile 1820-1889 .... **NCLC 31**
August, John
See De Voto, Bernard (Augustine)
Augustine, St. 354-430 .... **CMLC 6; DAB**
Aurelius
See Bourne, Randolph S(illiman)
Aurobindo, Sri 1872-1950 .... **TCLC 63**
Austen, Jane 1775-1817 **NCLC 1, 13, 19, 33, 51; DA; DAB; DAC; DAM MST, NOV; WLC**
See also AAYA 19; CDBLB 1789-1832; DLB 116
Auster, Paul 1947- .... **CLC 47**
See also CA 69-72; CANR 23, 52
Austin, Frank
See Faust, Frederick (Schiller)
Austin, Mary (Hunter) 1868-1934 . **TCLC 25**
See also CA 109; DLB 9, 78
Autran Dourado, Waldomiro
See Dourado, (Waldomiro Freitas) Autran
Averroes 1126-1198 .... **CMLC 7**
See also DLB 115
Avicenna 980-1037 .... **CMLC 16**
See also DLB 115
Avison, Margaret 1918- **CLC 2, 4, 97; DAC; DAM POET**
See also CA 17-20R; DLB 53; MTCW
Axton, David
See Koontz, Dean R(ay)
Ayckbourn, Alan 1939- **CLC 5, 8, 18, 33, 74; DAB; DAM DRAM**
See also CA 21-24R; CANR 31, 59; DLB 13;

MTCW
Aydy, Catherine
See Tennant, Emma (Christina)
Ayme, Marcel (Andre) 1902-1967 ... **CLC 11**
See also CA 89-92; CLR 25; DLB 72; SATA 91
Ayrton, Michael 1921-1975 .... **CLC 7**
See also CA 5-8R; 61-64; CANR 9, 21
Azorin .... **CLC 11**
See also Martinez Ruiz, Jose
Azuela, Mariano 1873-1952 . **TCLC 3; DAM MULT; HLC**
See also CA 104; 131; HW; MTCW
Baastad, Babbis Friis
See Friis-Baastad, Babbis Ellinor
Bab
See Gilbert, W(illiam) S(chwenck)
Babbis, Eleanor
See Friis-Baastad, Babbis Ellinor
Babel, Isaac
See Babel, Isaak (Emmanuilovich)
Babel, Isaak (Emmanuilovich) 1894-1941(?) **TCLC 2, 13; SSC 16**
See also CA 104; 155
Babits, Mihaly 1883-1941 .... **TCLC 14**
See also CA 114
Babur 1483-1530 .... **LC 18**
Bacchelli, Riccardo 1891-1985 .... **CLC 19**
See also CA 29-32R; 117
Bach, Richard (David) 1936- **CLC 14; DAM NOV, POP**
See also AITN 1; BEST 89:2; CA 9-12R; CANR 18; MTCW; SATA 13
Bachman, Richard
See King, Stephen (Edwin)
Bachmann, Ingeborg 1926-1973 ...... **CLC 69**
See also CA 93-96; 45-48; DLB 85
Bacon, Francis 1561-1626 .... **LC 18, 32**
See also CDBLB Before 1660; DLB 151
Bacon, Roger 1214(?)-1292 .... **CMLC 14**
See also DLB 115
Bacovia, George .... **TCLC 24**
See also Vasiliu, Gheorghe
Badanes, Jerome 1937- .... **CLC 59**
Bagehot, Walter 1826-1877 .... **NCLC 10**
See also DLB 55
Bagnold, Enid 1889-1981 ...... **CLC 25; DAM DRAM**
See also CA 5-8R; 103; CANR 5, 40; DLB 13, 160; MAICYA; SATA 1, 25
Bagritsky, Eduard 1895-1934 .... **TCLC 60**
Bagrjana, Elisaveta
See Belcheva, Elisaveta
Bagryana, Elisaveta .... **CLC 10**
See also Belcheva, Elisaveta
See also DLB 147
Bailey, Paul 1937- .... **CLC 45**
See also CA 21-24R; CANR 16, 62; DLB 14
Baillie, Joanna 1762-1851 .... **NCLC 2**
See also DLB 93
Bainbridge, Beryl (Margaret) 1933- **CLC 4, 5, 8, 10, 14, 18, 22, 62; DAM NOV**
See also CA 21-24R; CANR 24, 55; DLB 14; MTCW
Baker, Elliott 1922- .... **CLC 8**
See also CA 45-48; CANR 2
Baker, Jean H. .... **TCLC 3, 10**
See also Russell, George William
Baker, Nicholson 1957- . **CLC 61; DAM POP**
See also CA 135
Baker, Ray Stannard 1870-1946 .... **TCLC 47**
See also CA 118
Baker, Russell (Wayne) 1925- .... **CLC 31**
See also BEST 89:4; CA 57-60; CANR 11, 41, 59; MTCW
Bakhtin, M.
See Bakhtin, Mikhail Mikhailovich

Bakhtin, M. M.
See Bakhtin, Mikhail Mikhailovich
Bakhtin, Mikhail
See Bakhtin, Mikhail Mikhailovich
Bakhtin, Mikhail Mikhailovich 1895-1975 **CLC 83**
See also CA 128; 113
Bakshi, Ralph 1938(?)- .... **CLC 26**
See also CA 112; 138
Bakunin, Mikhail (Alexandrovich) 1814-1876 **NCLC 25, 58**
Baldwin, James (Arthur) 1924-1987 **CLC 1, 2, 3, 4, 5, 8, 13, 15, 17, 42, 50, 67, 90; BLC; DA; DAB; DAC; DAM MST, MULT, NOV, POP; DC 1; SSC 10; WLC**
See also AAYA 4; BW 1; CA 1-4R; 124; CABS 1; CANR 3, 24; CDALB 1941-1968; DLB 2, 7, 33; DLBY 87; MTCW; SATA 9; SATA-Obit 54
Ballard, J(ames) G(raham) 1930- **CLC 3, 6, 14, 36; DAM NOV, POP; SSC 1**
See also AAYA 3; CA 5-8R; CANR 15, 39; DLB 14; MTCW; SATA 93
Balmont, Konstantin (Dmitriyevich) 1867-1943 **TCLC 11**
See also CA 109; 155
Balzac, Honore de 1799-1850 **NCLC 5, 35, 53; DA; DAB; DAC; DAM MST, NOV; SSC 5; WLC**
See also DLB 119
Bambara, Toni Cade 1939-1995 **CLC 19, 88; BLC; DA; DAC; DAM MST, MULT; WLCS**
See also AAYA 5; BW 2; CA 29-32R; 150; CANR 24, 49; DLB 38; MTCW
Bamdad, A.
See Shamlu, Ahmad
Banat, D. R.
See Bradbury, Ray (Douglas)
Bancroft, Laura
See Baum, L(yman) Frank
Banim, John 1798-1842 .... **NCLC 13**
See also DLB 116, 158, 159
Banim, Michael 1796-1874 .... **NCLC 13**
See also DLB 158, 159
Banjo, The
See Paterson, A(ndrew) B(arton)
Banks, Iain
See Banks, Iain M(enzies)
Banks, Iain M(enzies) 1954- .... **CLC 34**
See also CA 123; 128; CANR 61; INT 128
Banks, Lynne Reid .... **CLC 23**
See also Reid Banks, Lynne
See also AAYA 6
Banks, Russell 1940- .... **CLC 37, 72**
See also CA 65-68; CAAS 15; CANR 19, 52; DLB 130
Banville, John 1945- .... **CLC 46**
See also CA 117; 128; DLB 14; INT 128
Banville, Theodore (Faullain) de 1832-1891 **NCLC 9**
Baraka, Amiri 1934- **CLC 1, 2, 3, 5, 10, 14, 33; BLC; DA; DAC; DAM MST, MULT, POET, POP; DC 6; PC 4; WLCS**
See also Jones, LeRoi
See also BW 2; CA 21-24R; CABS 3; CANR 27, 38, 61; CDALB 1941-1968; DLB 5, 7, 16, 38; DLBD 8; MTCW
Barbauld, Anna Laetitia 1743-1825 **NCLC 50**
See also DLB 107, 109, 142, 158
Barbellion, W. N. P. .... **TCLC 24**
See also Cummings, Bruce F(rederick)
Barbera, Jack (Vincent) 1945- .... **CLC 44**
See also CA 110; CANR 45
Barbey d'Aurevilly, Jules Amedee 1808-1889 **NCLC 1; SSC 17**
See also DLB 119

Barbusse, Henri 1873-1935 .... **TCLC 5**
See also CA 105; 154; DLB 65
Barclay, Bill
See Moorcock, Michael (John)
Barclay, William Ewert
See Moorcock, Michael (John)
Barea, Arturo 1897-1957 .... **TCLC 14**
See also CA 111
Barfoot, Joan 1946- .... **CLC 18**
See also CA 105
Baring, Maurice 1874-1945 .... **TCLC 8**
See also CA 105; DLB 34
Barker, Clive 1952- .... **CLC 52; DAM POP**
See also AAYA 10; BEST 90:3; CA 121; 129; INT 129; MTCW
Barker, George Granville 1913-1991 **CLC 8, 48; DAM POET**
See also CA 9-12R; 135; CANR 7, 38; DLB 20; MTCW
Barker, Harley Granville
See Granville-Barker, Harley
See also DLB 10
Barker, Howard 1946- .... **CLC 37**
See also CA 102; DLB 13
Barker, Pat(ricia) 1943- .... **CLC 32, 94**
See also CA 117; 122; CANR 50; INT 122
Barlow, Joel 1754-1812 .... **NCLC 23**
See also DLB 37
Barnard, Mary (Ethel) 1909- .... **CLC 48**
See also CA 21-22; CAP 2
Barnes, Djuna 1892-1982 **CLC 3, 4, 8, 11, 29; SSC 3**
See also CA 9-12R; 107; CANR 16, 55; DLB 4, 9, 45; MTCW
Barnes, Julian(Patrick) 1946- **CLC 42; DAB**
See also CA 102; CANR 19, 54; DLBY 93
Barnes, Peter 1931- .... **CLC 5, 56**
See also CA 65-68; CAAS 12; CANR 33, 34; DLB 13; MTCW
Baroja (y Nessi), Pio 1872-1956 **TCLC 8; HLC**
See also CA 104
Baron, David
See Pinter, Harold
Baron Corvo
See Rolfe, Frederick (William Serafino Austin Lewis Mary)
Barondess, Sue K(aufman) 1926-1977 **CLC 8**
See also Kaufman, Sue
See also CA 1-4R; 69-72; CANR 1
Baron de Teive
See Pessoa, Fernando (Antonio Nogueira)
Barres, Maurice 1862-1923 .... **TCLC 47**
See also DLB 123
Barreto, Afonso Henrique de Lima
See Lima Barreto, Afonso Henrique de
Barrett, (Roger) Syd 1946- .... **CLC 35**
Barrett, William (Christopher) 1913-1992 **CLC 27**
See also CA 13-16R; 139; CANR 11; INT CANR-11
Barrie, J(ames) M(atthew) 1860-1937 **TCLC 2; DAB; DAM DRAM**
See also CA 104; 136; CDBLB 1890-1914; CLR 16; DLB 10, 141, 156; MAICYA; YABC 1
Barrington, Michael
See Moorcock, Michael (John)
Barrol, Grady
See Bograd, Larry
Barry, Mike
See Malzberg, Barry N(athaniel)
Barry, Philip 1896-1949 .... **TCLC 11**
See also CA 109; DLB 7
Bart, Andre Schwarz
See Schwarz-Bart, Andre
Barth, John (Simmons) 1930- **CLC 1, 2, 3, 5, 7, 9, 10, 14, 27, 51, 89; DAM NOV; SSC 10**

See also AITN 1, 2; CA 1-4R; CABS 1; CANR 5, 23, 49; DLB 2; MTCW

Barthelme, Donald 1931-1989 CLC **1, 2, 3, 5, 6, 8, 13, 23, 46, 59; DAM NOV; SSC 2**
See also CA 21-24R; 129; CANR 20, 58; DLB 2; DLBY 80, 89; MTCW; SATA 7; SATA-Obit 62

Barthelme, Frederick 1943- .... CLC **36**
See also CA 114; 122; DLBY 85; INT 122

Barthes, Roland (Gerard) 1915-1980 CLC **24, 83**
See also CA 130; 97-100; MTCW

Barzun, Jacques (Martin) 1907- ...... CLC **51**
See also CA 61-64; CANR 22

Bashevis, Isaac
See Singer, Isaac Bashevis

Bashkirtseff, Marie 1859-1884 .... NCLC **27**

Basho
See Matsuo Basho

Bass, Kingsley B., Jr.
See Bullins, Ed

Bass, Rick 1958- .... CLC **79**
See also CA 126; CANR 53

Bassani, Giorgio 1916- .... CLC **9**
See also CA 65-68; CANR 33; DLB 128, 177; MTCW

Bastos, Augusto (Antonio) Roa
See Roa Bastos, Augusto (Antonio)

Bataille, Georges 1897-1962 .... CLC **29**
See also CA 101; 89-92

Bates, H(erbert) E(rnest) 1905-1974 CLC **46; DAB; DAM POP; SSC 10**
See also CA 93-96; 45-48; CANR 34; DLB 162; MTCW

Bauchart
See Camus, Albert

Baudelaire, Charles 1821-1867 NCLC **6, 29, 55; DA; DAB; DAC; DAM MST, POET; PC 1; SSC 18; WLC**

Baudrillard, Jean 1929- .... CLC **60**

Baum, L(yman) Frank 1856-1919 ... TCLC **7**
See also CA 108; 133; CLR 15; DLB 22; JRDA; MAICYA; MTCW; SATA 18

Baum, Louis F.
See Baum, L(yman) Frank

Baumbach, Jonathan 1933- .... CLC **6, 23**
See also CA 13-16R; CAAS 5; CANR 12; DLBY 80; INT CANR-12; MTCW

Bausch, Richard (Carl) 1945- .... CLC **51**
See also CA 101; CAAS 14; CANR 43, 61; DLB 130

Baxter, Charles 1947- CLC **45, 78; DAM POP**
See also CA 57-60; CANR 40; DLB 130

Baxter, George Owen
See Faust, Frederick (Schiller)

Baxter, James K(eir) 1926-1972 ...... CLC **14**
See also CA 77-80

Baxter, John
See Hunt, E(verette) Howard, (Jr.)

Bayer, Sylvia
See Glassco, John

Baynton, Barbara 1857-1929 .... TCLC **57**

Beagle, Peter S(oyer) 1939- .... CLC **7, 104**
See also CA 9-12R; CANR 4, 51; DLBY 80; INT CANR-4; SATA 60

Bean, Normal
See Burroughs, Edgar Rice

Beard, Charles A(ustin) 1874-1948 TCLC **15**
See also CA 115; DLB 17; SATA 18

Beardsley, Aubrey 1872-1898 .... NCLC **6**

Beattie, Ann 1947- CLC **8, 13, 18, 40, 63; DAM NOV, POP; SSC 11**
See also BEST 90:2; CA 81-84; CANR 53; DLBY 82; MTCW

Beattie, James 1735-1803 .... NCLC **25**
See also DLB 109

Beauchamp, Kathleen Mansfield 1888-1923
See Mansfield, Katherine
See also CA 104; 134; DA; DAC; DAM MST

Beaumarchais, Pierre-Augustin Caron de 1732-1799 .... DC **4**
See also DAM DRAM

Beaumont, Francis 1584(?)-1616 LC **33; DC 6**
See also CDBLB Before 1660; DLB 58, 121

Beauvoir, Simone (Lucie Ernestine Marie Bertrand) de 1908-1986 CLC **1, 2, 4, 8, 14, 31, 44, 50, 71; DA; DAB; DAC; DAM MST, NOV; WLC**
See also CA 9-12R; 118; CANR 28, 61; DLB 72; DLBY 86; MTCW

Becker, Carl (Lotus) 1873-1945 ..... TCLC **63**
See also CA 157; DLB 17

Becker, Jurek 1937-1997 .... CLC **7, 19**
See also CA 85-88; 157; CANR 60; DLB 75

Becker, Walter 1950- .... CLC **26**

Beckett, Samuel (Barclay) 1906-1989 CLC **1, 2, 3, 4, 6, 9, 10, 11, 14, 18, 29, 57, 59, 83; DA; DAB; DAC; DAM DRAM, MST, NOV; SSC 16; WLC**
See also CA 5-8R; 130; CANR 33, 61; CDBLB 1945-1960; DLB 13, 15; DLBY 90; MTCW

Beckford, William 1760-1844 .... NCLC **16**
See also DLB 39

Beckman, Gunnel 1910- .... CLC **26**
See also CA 33-36R; CANR 15; CLR 25; MAICYA; SAAS 9; SATA 6

Becque, Henri 1837-1899 .... NCLC **3**

Beddoes, Thomas Lovell 1803-1849 NCLC **3**
See also DLB 96

Bede c. 673-735 .... CMLC **20**
See also DLB 146

Bedford, Donald F.
See Fearing, Kenneth (Flexner)

Beecher, Catharine Esther 1800-1878 N C L C **30**
See also DLB 1

Beecher, John 1904-1980 .... CLC **6**
See also AITN 1; CA 5-8R; 105; CANR 8

Beer, Johann 1655-1700 .... LC **5**
See also DLB 168

Beer, Patricia 1924- .... CLC **58**
See also CA 61-64; CANR 13, 46; DLB 40

Beerbohm, Max
See Beerbohm, (Henry) Max(imilian)

Beerbohm, (Henry) Max(imilian) 1872-1956 TCLC **1, 24**
See also CA 104; 154; DLB 34, 100

Beer-Hofmann, Richard 1866-1945 TCLC **60**
See also CA 160; DLB 81

Begiebing, Robert J(ohn) 1946- .... CLC **70**
See also CA 122; CANR 40

Behan, Brendan 1923-1964 CLC **1, 8, 11, 15, 79; DAM DRAM**
See also CA 73-76; CANR 33; CDBLB 1945-1960; DLB 13

Behn, Aphra 1640(?)-1689 LC **1, 30; DA; DAB; DAC; DAM DRAM, MST, NOV, POET; DC 4; PC 13; WLC**
See also DLB 39, 80, 131

Behrman, S(amuel) N(athaniel) 1893-1973 CLC **40**
See also CA 13-16; 45-48; CAP 1; DLB 7, 44

Belasco, David 1853-1931 .... TCLC **3**
See also CA 104; DLB 7

Belcheva, Elisaveta 1893- .... CLC **10**
See also Bagryana, Elisaveta

Beldone, Phil "Cheech"
See Ellison, Harlan (Jay)

Beleno
See Azuela, Mariano

Belinski, Vissarion Grigoryevich 1811-1848 NCLC **5**

Belitt, Ben 1911- .... CLC **22**
See also CA 13-16R; CAAS 4; CANR 7; DLB 5

Bell, Gertrude 1868-1926 .... TCLC **67**
See also DLB 174

Bell, James Madison 1826-1902 ... TCLC **43; BLC; DAM MULT**
See also BW 1; CA 122; 124; DLB 50

Bell, Madison Smartt 1957- ...... CLC **41, 102**
See also CA 111; CANR 28, 54

Bell, Marvin (Hartley) 1937- CLC **8, 31; DAM POET**
See also CA 21-24R; CAAS 14; CANR 59; DLB 5; MTCW

Bell, W. L. D.
See Mencken, H(enry) L(ouis)

Bellamy, Atwood C.
See Mencken, H(enry) L(ouis)

Bellamy, Edward 1850-1898 .... NCLC **4**
See also DLB 12

Bellin, Edward J.
See Kuttner, Henry

Belloc, (Joseph) Hilaire (Pierre Sebastien Rene Swanton) 1870-1953 TCLC **7, 18; DAM POET**
See also CA 106; 152; DLB 19, 100, 141, 174; YABC 1

Belloc, Joseph Peter Rene Hilaire
See Belloc, (Joseph) Hilaire (Pierre Sebastien Rene Swanton)

Belloc, Joseph Pierre Hilaire
See Belloc, (Joseph) Hilaire (Pierre Sebastien Rene Swanton)

Belloc, M. A.
See Lowndes, Marie Adelaide (Belloc)

Bellow, Saul 1915- CLC **1, 2, 3, 6, 8, 10, 13, 15, 25, 33, 34, 63, 79; DA; DAB; DAC; DAM MST, NOV, POP; SSC 14; WLC**
See also AITN 2; BEST 89:3; CA 5-8R; CABS 1; CANR 29, 53; CDALB 1941-1968; DLB 2, 28; DLBD 3; DLBY 82; MTCW

Belser, Reimond Karel Maria de 1929-
See Ruyslinck, Ward
See also CA 152

Bely, Andrey .... TCLC **7; PC 11**
See also Bugayev, Boris Nikolayevich

Benary, Margot
See Benary-Isbert, Margot

Benary-Isbert, Margot 1889-1979 .... CLC **12**
See also CA 5-8R; 89-92; CANR 4; CLR 12; MAICYA; SATA 2; SATA-Obit 21

Benavente (y Martinez), Jacinto 1866-1954 TCLC **3; DAM DRAM, MULT**
See also CA 106; 131; HW; MTCW

Benchley, Peter (Bradford) 1940- . CLC **4, 8; DAM NOV, POP**
See also AAYA 14; AITN 2; CA 17-20R; CANR 12, 35; MTCW; SATA 3, 89

Benchley, Robert (Charles) 1889-1945 T C L C **1, 55**
See also CA 105; 153; DLB 11

Benda, Julien 1867-1956 .... TCLC **60**
See also CA 120; 154

Benedict, Ruth (Fulton) 1887-1948 TCLC **60**
See also CA 158

Benedikt, Michael 1935- .... CLC **4, 14**
See also CA 13-16R; CANR 7; DLB 5

Benet, Juan 1927- .... CLC **28**
See also CA 143

Benet, Stephen Vincent 1898-1943 . TCLC **7; DAM POET; SSC 10**
See also CA 104; 152; DLB 4, 48, 102; YABC 1

Benet, William Rose 1886-1950 ... TCLC **28; DAM POET**
See also CA 118; 152; DLB 45

Benford, Gregory (Albert) 1941- ...... CLC **52**
See also CA 69-72; CAAS 27; CANR 12, 24, 49; DLBY 82

Bengtsson, Frans (Gunnar) 1894-1954 TCLC 48
Benjamin, David
    See Slavitt, David R(ytman)
Benjamin, Lois
    See Gould, Lois
Benjamin, Walter 1892-1940 .... TCLC 39
Benn, Gottfried 1886-1956 .... TCLC 3
    See also CA 106; 153; DLB 56
Bennett, Alan 1934- CLC 45, 77; DAB; DAM MST
    See also CA 103; CANR 35, 55; MTCW
Bennett, (Enoch) Arnold 1867-1931 TCLC 5, 20
    See also CA 106; 155; CDBLB 1890-1914; DLB 10, 34, 98, 135
Bennett, Elizabeth
    See Mitchell, Margaret (Munnerlyn)
Bennett, George Harold 1930-
    See Bennett, Hal
    See also BW 1; CA 97-100
Bennett, Hal .... CLC 5
    See also Bennett, George Harold
    See also DLB 33
Bennett, Jay 1912- .... CLC 35
    See also AAYA 10; CA 69-72; CANR 11, 42; JRDA; SAAS 4; SATA 41, 87; SATA-Brief 27
Bennett, Louise (Simone) 1919- CLC 28; BLC; DAM MULT
    See also BW 2; CA 151; DLB 117
Benson, E(dward) F(rederic) 1867-1940 TCLC 27
    See also CA 114; 157; DLB 135, 153
Benson, Jackson J. 1930- .... CLC 34
    See also CA 25-28R; DLB 111
Benson, Sally 1900-1972 .... CLC 17
    See also CA 19-20; 37-40R; CAP 1; SATA 1, 35; SATA-Obit 27
Benson, Stella 1892-1933 .... TCLC 17
    See also CA 117; 155; DLB 36, 162
Bentham, Jeremy 1748-1832 .... NCLC 38
    See also DLB 107, 158
Bentley, E(dmund) C(lerihew) 1875-1956 TCLC 12
    See also CA 108; DLB 70
Bentley, Eric (Russell) 1916- .... CLC 24
    See also CA 5-8R; CANR 6; INT CANR-6
Beranger, Pierre Jean de 1780-1857 NCLC 34
Berdyaev, Nicolas
    See Berdyaev, Nikolai (Aleksandrovich)
Berdyaev, Nikolai (Aleksandrovich) 1874-1948 TCLC 67
    See also CA 120; 157
Berdyayev, Nikolai (Aleksandrovich)
    See Berdyaev, Nikolai (Aleksandrovich)
Berendt, John (Lawrence) 1939- ..... CLC 86
    See also CA 146
Berger, Colonel
    See Malraux, (Georges-)Andre
Berger, John (Peter) 1926- .... CLC 2, 19
    See also CA 81-84; CANR 51; DLB 14
Berger, Melvin H. 1927- .... CLC 12
    See also CA 5-8R; CANR 4; CLR 32; SAAS 2; SATA 5, 88
Berger, Thomas (Louis) 1924- CLC 3, 5, 8, 11, 18, 38; DAM NOV
    See also CA 1-4R; CANR 5, 28, 51; DLB 2; DLBY 80; INT CANR-28; MTCW
Bergman, (Ernst) Ingmar 1918- CLC 16, 72
    See also CA 81-84; CANR 33
Bergson, Henri 1859-1941 .... TCLC 32
Bergstein, Eleanor 1938- .... CLC 4
    See also CA 53-56; CANR 5
Berkoff, Steven 1937- .... CLC 56
    See also CA 104
Bermant, Chaim (Icyk) 1929- .... CLC 40

See also CA 57-60; CANR 6, 31, 57
Bern, Victoria
    See Fisher, M(ary) F(rances) K(ennedy)
Bernanos, (Paul Louis) Georges 1888-1948 TCLC 3
    See also CA 104; 130; DLB 72
Bernard, April 1956- .... CLC 59
    See also CA 131
Berne, Victoria
    See Fisher, M(ary) F(rances) K(ennedy)
Bernhard, Thomas 1931-1989 CLC 3, 32, 61
    See also CA 85-88; 127; CANR 32, 57; DLB 85, 124; MTCW
Bernhardt, Sarah (Henriette Rosine) 1844-1923 TCLC 75
    See also CA 157
Berriault, Gina 1926- .... CLC 54
    See also CA 116; 129; DLB 130
Berrigan, Daniel 1921- .... CLC 4
    See also CA 33-36R; CAAS 1; CANR 11, 43; DLB 5
Berrigan, Edmund Joseph Michael, Jr. 1934-1983
    See Berrigan, Ted
    See also CA 61-64; 110; CANR 14
Berrigan, Ted .... CLC 37
    See also Berrigan, Edmund Joseph Michael, Jr.
    See also DLB 5, 169
Berry, Charles Edward Anderson 1931-
    See Berry, Chuck
    See also CA 115
Berry, Chuck .... CLC 17
    See also Berry, Charles Edward Anderson
Berry, Jonas
    See Ashbery, John (Lawrence)
Berry, Wendell (Erdman) 1934- CLC 4, 6, 8, 27, 46; DAM POET
    See also AITN 1; CA 73-76; CANR 50; DLB 5, 6
Berryman, John 1914-1972 CLC 1, 2, 3, 4, 6, 8, 10, 13, 25, 62; DAM POET
    See also CA 13-16; 33-36R; CABS 2; CANR 35; CAP 1; CDALB 1941-1968; DLB 48; MTCW
Bertolucci, Bernardo 1940- .... CLC 16
    See also CA 106
Berton, Pierre (Francis De Marigny) 1920- CLC 104
    See also CA 1-4R; CANR 2, 56; DLB 68
Bertrand, Aloysius 1807-1841 .... NCLC 31
Bertran de Born c. 1140-1215 .... CMLC 5
Besant, Annie (Wood) 1847-1933 .... TCLC 9
    See also CA 105
Bessie, Alvah 1904-1985 .... CLC 23
    See also CA 5-8R; 116; CANR 2; DLB 26
Bethlen, T. D.
    See Silverberg, Robert
Beti, Mongo ...... CLC 27; BLC; DAM MULT
    See also Biyidi, Alexandre
Betjeman, John 1906-1984 CLC 2, 6, 10, 34, 43; DAB; DAM MST, POET
    See also CA 9-12R; 112; CANR 33, 56; CDBLB 1945-1960; DLB 20; DLBY 84; MTCW
Bettelheim, Bruno 1903-1990 .... CLC 79
    See also CA 81-84; 131; CANR 23, 61; MTCW
Betti, Ugo 1892-1953 .... TCLC 5
    See also CA 104; 155
Betts, Doris (Waugh) 1932- ...... CLC 3, 6, 28
    See also CA 13-16R; CANR 9; DLBY 82; INT CANR-9
Bevan, Alistair
    See Roberts, Keith (John Kingston)
Bialik, Chaim Nachman 1873-1934 TCLC 25
Bickerstaff, Isaac
    See Swift, Jonathan
Bidart, Frank 1939- .... CLC 33

See also CA 140
Bienek, Horst 1930- .... CLC 7, 11
    See also CA 73-76; DLB 75
Bierce, Ambrose (Gwinett) 1842-1914(?) TCLC 1, 7, 44; DA; DAC; DAM MST; SSC 9; WLC
    See also CA 104; 139; CDALB 1865-1917; DLB 11, 12, 23, 71, 74
Biggers, Earl Derr 1884-1933 .... TCLC 65
    See also CA 108; 153
Billings, Josh
    See Shaw, Henry Wheeler
Billington, (Lady) Rachel (Mary) 1942- CLC 43
    See also AITN 2; CA 33-36R; CANR 44
Binyon, T(imothy) J(ohn) 1936- ...... CLC 34
    See also CA 111; CANR 28
Bioy Casares, Adolfo 1914- CLC 4, 8, 13, 88; DAM MULT; HLC; SSC 17
    See also CA 29-32R; CANR 19, 43; DLB 113; HW; MTCW
Bird, Cordwainer
    See Ellison, Harlan (Jay)
Bird, Robert Montgomery 1806-1854 NCLC 1
Birney, (Alfred) Earle 1904- CLC 1, 4, 6, 11; DAC; DAM MST, POET
    See also CA 1-4R; CANR 5, 20; DLB 88; MTCW
Bishop, Elizabeth 1911-1979 CLC 1, 4, 9, 13, 15, 32; DA; DAC; DAM MST, POET; PC 3
    See also CA 5-8R; 89-92; CABS 2; CANR 26, 61; CDALB 1968-1988; DLB 5, 169; MTCW; SATA-Obit 24
Bishop, John 1935- .... CLC 10
    See also CA 105
Bissett, Bill 1939- .... CLC 18; PC 14
    See also CA 69-72; CAAS 19; CANR 15; DLB 53; MTCW
Bitov, Andrei (Georgievich) 1937- .. CLC 57
    See also CA 142
Biyidi, Alexandre 1932-
    See Beti, Mongo
    See also BW 1; CA 114; 124; MTCW
Bjarme, Brynjolf
    See Ibsen, Henrik (Johan)
Bjornson, Bjornstjerne (Martinius) 1832-1910 TCLC 7, 37
    See also CA 104
Black, Robert
    See Holdstock, Robert P.
Blackburn, Paul 1926-1971 .... CLC 9, 43
    See also CA 81-84; 33-36R; CANR 34; DLB 16; DLBY 81
Black Elk 1863-1950 TCLC 33; DAM MULT
    See also CA 144; NNAL
Black Hobart
    See Sanders, (James) Ed(ward)
Blacklin, Malcolm
    See Chambers, Aidan
Blackmore, R(ichard) D(oddridge) 1825-1900 TCLC 27
    See also CA 120; DLB 18
Blackmur, R(ichard) P(almer) 1904-1965 CLC 2, 24
    See also CA 11-12; 25-28R; CAP 1; DLB 63
Black Tarantula
    See Acker, Kathy
Blackwood, Algernon (Henry) 1869-1951 TCLC 5
    See also CA 105; 150; DLB 153, 156, 178
Blackwood, Caroline 1931-1996 CLC 6, 9, 100
    See also CA 85-88; 151; CANR 32, 61; DLB 14; MTCW
Blade, Alexander
    See Hamilton, Edmond; Silverberg, Robert
Blaga, Lucian 1895-1961 .... CLC 75

Blair, Eric (Arthur) 1903-1950
See Orwell, George
See also CA 104; 132; DA; DAB; DAC; DAM MST, NOV; MTCW; SATA 29
Blais, Marie-Claire 1939-**CLC 2, 4, 6, 13, 22; DAC; DAM MST**
See also CA 21-24R; CAAS 4; CANR 38; DLB 53; MTCW
Blaise, Clark 1940- .... **CLC 29**
See also AITN 2; CA 53-56; CAAS 3; CANR 5; DLB 53
Blake, Fairley
See De Voto, Bernard (Augustine)
Blake, Nicholas
See Day Lewis, C(ecil)
See also DLB 77
Blake, William 1757-1827 **NCLC 13, 37, 57; DA; DAB; DAC; DAM MST, POET; PC 12; WLC**
See also CDBLB 1789-1832; DLB 93, 163; MAICYA; SATA 30
Blasco Ibanez, Vicente 1867-1928 **TCLC 12; DAM NOV**
See also CA 110; 131; HW; MTCW
Blatty, William Peter 1928-**CLC 2; DAM POP**
See also CA 5-8R; CANR 9
Bleeck, Oliver
See Thomas, Ross (Elmore)
Blessing, Lee 1949- .... **CLC 54**
Blish, James (Benjamin) 1921-1975 **CLC 14**
See also CA 1-4R; 57-60; CANR 3; DLB 8; MTCW; SATA 66
Bliss, Reginald
See Wells, H(erbert) G(eorge)
Blixen, Karen (Christentze Dinesen) 1885-1962
See Dinesen, Isak
See also CA 25-28; CANR 22, 50; CAP 2; MTCW; SATA 44
Bloch, Robert (Albert) 1917-1994 ... **CLC 33**
See also CA 5-8R; 146; CAAS 20; CANR 5; DLB 44; INT CANR-5; SATA 12; SATA-Obit 82
Blok, Alexander (Alexandrovich) 1880-1921 **TCLC 5**
See also CA 104
Blom, Jan
See Breytenbach, Breyten
Bloom, Harold 1930- .... **CLC 24, 103**
See also CA 13-16R; CANR 39; DLB 67
Bloomfield, Aurelius
See Bourne, Randolph S(illiman)
Blount, Roy (Alton), Jr. 1941- .... **CLC 38**
See also CA 53-56; CANR 10, 28, 61; INT CANR-28; MTCW
Bloy, Leon 1846-1917 .... **TCLC 22**
See also CA 121; DLB 123
Blume, Judy (Sussman) 1938-... **CLC 12, 30; DAM NOV, POP**
See also AAYA 3; CA 29-32R; CANR 13, 37; CLR 2, 15; DLB 52; JRDA; MAICYA; MTCW; SATA 2, 31, 79
Blunden, Edmund (Charles) 1896-1974 **CLC 2, 56**
See also CA 17-18; 45-48; CANR 54; CAP 2; DLB 20, 100, 155; MTCW
Bly, Robert (Elwood) 1926-**CLC 1, 2, 5, 10, 15, 38; DAM POET**
See also CA 5-8R; CANR 41; DLB 5; MTCW
Boas, Franz 1858-1942 .... **TCLC 56**
See also CA 115
Bobette
See Simenon, Georges (Jacques Christian)
Boccaccio, Giovanni 1313-1375 .. **CMLC 13; SSC 10**
Bochco, Steven 1943- .... **CLC 35**
See also AAYA 11; CA 124; 138
Bodenheim, Maxwell 1892-1954 .... **TCLC 44**

See also CA 110; DLB 9, 45
Bodker, Cecil 1927- .... **CLC 21**
See also CA 73-76; CANR 13, 44; CLR 23; MAICYA; SATA 14
Boell, Heinrich (Theodor) 1917-1985 **CLC 2, 3, 6, 9, 11, 15, 27, 32, 72; DA; DAB; DAC; DAM MST, NOV; SSC 23; WLC**
See also CA 21-24R; 116; CANR 24; DLB 69; DLBY 85; MTCW
Boerne, Alfred
See Doeblin, Alfred
Boethius 480(?)-524(?) .... **CMLC 15**
See also DLB 115
Bogan, Louise 1897-1970 . **CLC 4, 39, 46, 93; DAM POET; PC 12**
See also CA 73-76; 25-28R; CANR 33; DLB 45, 169; MTCW
Bogarde, Dirk ....**CLC 19**
See also Van Den Bogarde, Derek Jules Gaspard Ulric Niven
See also DLB 14
Bogosian, Eric 1953- .... **CLC 45**
See also CA 138
Bograd, Larry 1953- .... **CLC 35**
See also CA 93-96; CANR 57; SAAS 21; SATA 33, 89
Boiardo, Matteo Maria 1441-1494 .... **LC 6**
Boileau-Despreaux, Nicolas 1636-1711 **LC 3**
Bojer, Johan 1872-1959 .... **TCLC 64**
Boland, Eavan (Aisling) 1944- .. **CLC 40, 67; DAM POET**
See also CA 143; CANR 61; DLB 40
Bolt, Lee
See Faust, Frederick (Schiller)
Bolt, Robert (Oxton) 1924-1995 ..... **CLC 14; DAM DRAM**
See also CA 17-20R; 147; CANR 35; DLB 13; MTCW
Bombet, Louis-Alexandre-Cesar
See Stendhal
Bomkauf
See Kaufman, Bob (Garnell)
Bonaventura .... **NCLC 35**
See also DLB 90
Bond, Edward 1934- **CLC 4, 6, 13, 23; DAM DRAM**
See also CA 25-28R; CANR 38; DLB 13; MTCW
Bonham, Frank 1914-1989 .... **CLC 12**
See also AAYA 1; CA 9-12R; CANR 4, 36; JRDA; MAICYA; SAAS 3; SATA 1, 49; SATA-Obit 62
Bonnefoy, Yves 1923- .. **CLC 9, 15, 58; DAM MST, POET**
See also CA 85-88; CANR 33; MTCW
Bontemps, Arna(ud Wendell) 1902-1973**CLC 1, 18; BLC; DAM MULT, NOV, POET**
See also BW 1; CA 1-4R; 41-44R; CANR 4, 35; CLR 6; DLB 48, 51; JRDA; MAICYA; MTCW; SATA 2, 44; SATA-Obit 24
Booth, Martin 1944- ....**CLC 13**
See also CA 93-96; CAAS 2
Booth, Philip 1925- .... **CLC 23**
See also CA 5-8R; CANR 5; DLBY 82
Booth, Wayne C(layson) 1921- .... **CLC 24**
See also CA 1-4R; CAAS 5; CANR 3, 43; DLB 67
Borchert, Wolfgang 1921-1947 .... **TCLC 5**
See also CA 104; DLB 69, 124
Borel, Petrus 1809-1859 .... **NCLC 41**
Borges, Jorge Luis 1899-1986**CLC 1, 2, 3, 4, 6, 8, 9, 10, 13, 19, 44, 48, 83; DA; DAB; DAC; DAM MST, MULT; HLC; SSC 4; WLC**
See also AAYA 19; CA 21-24R; CANR 19, 33; DLB 113; DLBY 86; HW; MTCW
Borowski, Tadeusz 1922-1951 .... **TCLC 9**
See also CA 106; 154

Borrow, George (Henry) 1803-1881 **NCLC 9**
See also DLB 21, 55, 166
Bosman, Herman Charles 1905-1951 **TCLC 49**
See also Malan, Herman
See also CA 160
Bosschere, Jean de 1878(?)-1953 ... **TCLC 19**
See also CA 115
Boswell, James 1740-1795 . **LC 4; DA; DAB; DAC; DAM MST; WLC**
See also CDBLB 1660-1789; DLB 104, 142
Bottoms, David 1949- .... **CLC 53**
See also CA 105; CANR 22; DLB 120; DLBY 83
Boucicault, Dion 1820-1890 .... **NCLC 41**
Boucolon, Maryse 1937(?)-
See Conde, Maryse
See also CA 110; CANR 30, 53
Bourget, Paul (Charles Joseph) 1852-1935 **TCLC 12**
See also CA 107; DLB 123
Bourjaily, Vance (Nye) 1922- .... **CLC 8, 62**
See also CA 1-4R; CAAS 1; CANR 2; DLB 2, 143
Bourne, Randolph S(illiman) 1886-1918 **TCLC 16**
See also CA 117; 155; DLB 63
Bova, Ben(jamin William) 1932- ...... **CLC 45**
See also AAYA 16; CA 5-8R; CAAS 18; CANR 11, 56; CLR 3; DLBY 81; INT CANR-11; MAICYA; MTCW; SATA 6, 68
Bowen, Elizabeth (Dorothea Cole) 1899-1973 **CLC 1, 3, 6, 11, 15, 22; DAM NOV; SSC 3, 28**
See also CA 17-18; 41-44R; CANR 35; CAP 2; CDBLB 1945-1960; DLB 15, 162; MTCW
Bowering, George 1935- .... **CLC 15, 47**
See also CA 21-24R; CAAS 16; CANR 10; DLB 53
Bowering, Marilyn R(uthe) 1949- .... **CLC 32**
See also CA 101; CANR 49
Bowers, Edgar 1924- .... **CLC 9**
See also CA 5-8R; CANR 24; DLB 5
Bowie, David .... **CLC 17**
See also Jones, David Robert
Bowles, Jane (Sydney) 1917-1973 **CLC 3, 68**
See also CA 19-20; 41-44R; CAP 2
Bowles, Paul (Frederick) 1910-**CLC 1, 2, 19, 53; SSC 3**
See also CA 1-4R; CAAS 1; CANR 1, 19, 50; DLB 5, 6; MTCW
Box, Edgar
See Vidal, Gore
Boyd, Nancy
See Millay, Edna St. Vincent
Boyd, William 1952- .... **CLC 28, 53, 70**
See also CA 114; 120; CANR 51
Boyle, Kay 1902-1992**CLC 1, 5, 19, 58; SSC 5**
See also CA 13-16R; 140; CAAS 1; CANR 29, 61; DLB 4, 9, 48, 86; DLBY 93; MTCW
Boyle, Mark
See Kienzle, William X(avier)
Boyle, Patrick 1905-1982 .... **CLC 19**
See also CA 127
Boyle, T. C. 1948-
See Boyle, T(homas) Coraghessan
Boyle, T(homas) Coraghessan 1948-**CLC 36, 55, 90; DAM POP; SSC 16**
See also BEST 90:4; CA 120; CANR 44; DLBY 86
Boz
See Dickens, Charles (John Huffam)
Brackenridge, Hugh Henry 1748-1816**NCLC 7**
See also DLB 11, 37
Bradbury, Edward P.

Bradbury
See Moorcock, Michael (John)
Bradbury, Malcolm (Stanley) 1932- CLC 32, 61; DAM NOV
See also CA 1-4R; CANR 1, 33; DLB 14; MTCW
Bradbury, Ray (Douglas) 1920-CLC 1, 3, 10, 15, 42, 98; DA; DAB; DAC; DAM MST, NOV, POP; SSC 29; WLC
See also AAYA 15; AITN 1, 2; CA 1-4R; CANR 2, 30; CDALB 1968-1988; DLB 2, 8; MTCW; SATA 11, 64
Bradford, Gamaliel 1863-1932 ...... TCLC 36
See also CA 160; DLB 17
Bradley, David (Henry, Jr.) 1950-.. CLC 23; BLC; DAM MULT
See also BW 1; CA 104; CANR 26; DLB 33
Bradley, John Ed(mund, Jr.) 1958- CLC 55
See also CA 139
Bradley, Marion Zimmer 1930- ..... CLC 30; DAM POP
See also AAYA 9; CA 57-60; CAAS 10; CANR 7, 31, 51; DLB 8; MTCW; SATA 90
Bradstreet, Anne 1612(?)-1672 LC 4, 30; DA; DAC; DAM MST, POET; PC 10
See also CDALB 1640-1865; DLB 24
Brady, Joan 1939- .... CLC 86
See also CA 141
Bragg, Melvyn 1939- .... CLC 10
See also BEST 89:3; CA 57-60; CANR 10, 48; DLB 14
Braine, John (Gerard) 1922-1986 CLC 1, 3, 41
See also CA 1-4R; 120; CANR 1, 33; CDBLB 1945-1960; DLB 15; DLBY 86; MTCW
Bramah, Ernest 1868-1942 .... TCLC 72
See also CA 156; DLB 70
Brammer, William 1930(?)-1978 ..... CLC 31
See also CA 77-80
Brancati, Vitaliano 1907-1954 .... TCLC 12
See also CA 109
Brancato, Robin F(idler) 1936- .... CLC 35
See also AAYA 9; CA 69-72; CANR 11, 45; CLR 32; JRDA; SAAS 9; SATA 23
Brand, Max
See Faust, Frederick (Schiller)
Brand, Millen 1906-1980 .... CLC 7
See also CA 21-24R; 97-100
Branden, Barbara .... CLC 44
See also CA 148
Brandes, Georg (Morris Cohen) 1842-1927 TCLC 10
See also CA 105
Brandys, Kazimierz 1916- .... CLC 62
Branley, Franklyn M(ansfield) 1915-CLC 21
See also CA 33-36R; CANR 14, 39; CLR 13; MAICYA; SAAS 16; SATA 4, 68
Brathwaite, Edward Kamau 1930- CLC 11; DAM POET
See also BW 2; CA 25-28R; CANR 11, 26, 47; DLB 125
Brautigan, Richard (Gary) 1935-1984 CLC 1, 3, 5, 9, 12, 34, 42; DAM NOV
See also CA 53-56; 113; CANR 34; DLB 2, 5; DLBY 80, 84; MTCW; SATA 56
Brave Bird, Mary 1953-
See Crow Dog, Mary (Ellen)
See also NNAL
Braverman, Kate 1950- .... CLC 67
See also CA 89-92
Brecht, (Eugen) Bertolt (Friedrich) 1898-1956 TCLC 1, 6, 13, 35; DA; DAB; DAC; DAM DRAM, MST; DC 3; WLC
See also CA 104; 133; CANR 62; DLB 56, 124; MTCW
Brecht, Eugen Berthold Friedrich
See Brecht, (Eugen) Bertolt (Friedrich)
Bremer, Fredrika 1801-1865 .... NCLC 11
Brennan, Christopher John 1870-1932 TCLC 17
See also CA 117
Brennan, Maeve 1917- .... CLC 5
See also CA 81-84
Brentano, Clemens (Maria) 1778-1842 NCLC 1
See also DLB 90
Brent of Bin Bin
See Franklin, (Stella Maraia Sarah) Miles
Brenton, Howard 1942- .... CLC 31
See also CA 69-72; CANR 33; DLB 13; MTCW
Breslin, James 1930-
See Breslin, Jimmy
See also CA 73-76; CANR 31; DAM NOV; MTCW
Breslin, Jimmy .... CLC 4, 43
See Breslin, James
See also AITN 1
Bresson, Robert 1901- .... CLC 16
See also CA 110; CANR 49
Breton, Andre 1896-1966 CLC 2, 9, 15, 54; PC 15
See also CA 19-20; 25-28R; CANR 40, 60; CAP 2; DLB 65; MTCW
Breytenbach, Breyten 1939(?)- . CLC 23, 37; DAM POET
See also CA 113; 129; CANR 61
Bridgers, Sue Ellen 1942- .... CLC 26
See also AAYA 8; CA 65-68; CANR 11, 36; CLR 18; DLB 52; JRDA; MAICYA; SAAS 1; SATA 22, 90
Bridges, Robert (Seymour) 1844-1930 TCLC 1; DAM POET
See also CA 104; 152; CDBLB 1890-1914; DLB 19, 98
Bridie, James .... TCLC 3
See also Mavor, Osborne Henry
See also DLB 10
Brin, David 1950- .... CLC 34
See also AAYA 21; CA 102; CANR 24; INT CANR-24; SATA 65
Brink, Andre (Philippus) 1935- . CLC 18, 36
See also CA 104; CANR 39, 62; INT 103; MTCW
Brinsmead, H(esba) F(ay) 1922- .... CLC 21
See also CA 21-24R; CANR 10; CLR 47; MAICYA; SAAS 5; SATA 18, 78
Brittain, Vera (Mary) 1893(?)-1970 . CLC 23
See also CA 13-16; 25-28R; CANR 58; CAP 1; MTCW
Broch, Hermann 1886-1951 .... TCLC 20
See also CA 117; DLB 85, 124
Brock, Rose
See Hansen, Joseph
Brodkey, Harold (Roy) 1930-1996 ... CLC 56
See also CA 111; 151; DLB 130
Brodsky, Iosif Alexandrovich 1940-1996
See Brodsky, Joseph
See also AITN 1; CA 41-44R; 151; CANR 37; DAM POET; MTCW
Brodsky, Joseph 1940-1996 CLC 4, 6, 13, 36, 100; PC 9
See also Brodsky, Iosif Alexandrovich
Brodsky, Michael (Mark) 1948- .... CLC 19
See also CA 102; CANR 18, 41, 58
Bromell, Henry 1947- .... CLC 5
See also CA 53-56; CANR 9
Bromfield, Louis (Brucker) 1896-1956 TCLC 11
See also CA 107; 155; DLB 4, 9, 86
Broner, E(sther) M(asserman) 1930-CLC 19
See also CA 17-20R; CANR 8, 25; DLB 28
Bronk, William 1918- .... CLC 10
See also CA 89-92; CANR 23; DLB 165
Bronstein, Lev Davidovich
See Trotsky, Leon
Bronte, Anne 1820-1849 .... NCLC 4
See also DLB 21
Bronte, Charlotte 1816-1855 NCLC 3, 8, 33, 58; DA; DAB; DAC; DAM MST, NOV; WLC
See also AAYA 17; CDBLB 1832-1890; DLB 21, 159
Bronte, Emily (Jane) 1818-1848 NCLC 16, 35; DA; DAB; DAC; DAM MST, NOV, POET; PC 8; WLC
See also AAYA 17; CDBLB 1832-1890; DLB 21, 32
Brooke, Frances 1724-1789 .... LC 6
See also DLB 39, 99
Brooke, Henry 1703(?)-1783 .... LC 1
See also DLB 39
Brooke, Rupert (Chawner) 1887-1915 TCLC 2, 7; DA; DAB; DAC; DAM MST, POET; WLC
See also CA 104; 132; CANR 61; CDBLB 1914-1945; DLB 19; MTCW
Brooke-Haven, P.
See Wodehouse, P(elham) G(renville)
Brooke-Rose, Christine 1926(?)- ...... CLC 40
See also CA 13-16R; CANR 58; DLB 14
Brookner, Anita 1928-CLC 32, 34, 51; DAB; DAM POP
See also CA 114; 120; CANR 37, 56; DLBY 87; MTCW
Brooks, Cleanth 1906-1994 .... CLC 24, 86
See also CA 17-20R; 145; CANR 33, 35; DLB 63; DLBY 94; INT CANR-35; MTCW
Brooks, George
See Baum, L(yman) Frank
Brooks, Gwendolyn 1917- CLC 1, 2, 4, 5, 15, 49; BLC; DA; DAC; DAM MST, MULT, POET; PC 7; WLC
See also AAYA 20; AITN 1; BW 2; CA 1-4R; CANR 1, 27, 52; CDALB 1941-1968; CLR 27; DLB 5, 76, 165; MTCW; SATA 6
Brooks, Mel .... CLC 12
See also Kaminsky, Melvin
See also AAYA 13; DLB 26
Brooks, Peter 1938- .... CLC 34
See also CA 45-48; CANR 1
Brooks, Van Wyck 1886-1963 .... CLC 29
See also CA 1-4R; CANR 6; DLB 45, 63, 103
Brophy, Brigid (Antonia) 1929-1995 CLC 6, 11, 29, 105
See also CA 5-8R; 149; CAAS 4; CANR 25, 53; DLB 14; MTCW
Brosman, Catharine Savage 1934- ..... CLC 9
See also CA 61-64; CANR 21, 46
Brother Antoninus
See Everson, William (Oliver)
Broughton, T(homas) Alan 1936- .... CLC 19
See also CA 45-48; CANR 2, 23, 48
Broumas, Olga 1949- .... CLC 10, 73
See also CA 85-88; CANR 20
Brown, Alan 1951- .... CLC 99
Brown, Charles Brockden 1771-1810 NCLC 22
See also CDALB 1640-1865; DLB 37, 59, 73
Brown, Christy 1932-1981 .... CLC 63
See also CA 105; 104; DLB 14
Brown, Claude 1937- .. CLC 30; BLC; DAM MULT
See also AAYA 7; BW 1; CA 73-76
Brown, Dee (Alexander) 1908-.. CLC 18, 47; DAM POP
See also CA 13-16R; CAAS 6; CANR 11, 45, 60; DLBY 80; MTCW; SATA 5
Brown, George
See Wertmueller, Lina
Brown, George Douglas 1869-1902 TCLC 28
Brown, George Mackay 1921-1996 CLC 5, 48, 100
See also CA 21-24R; 151; CAAS 6; CANR 12,

37, 62; DLB 14, 27, 139; MTCW; SATA 35
Brown, (William) Larry 1951- .... **CLC 73**
See also CA 130; 134; INT 133
Brown, Moses
See Barrett, William (Christopher)
Brown, Rita Mae 1944-**CLC 18, 43, 79; DAM NOV, POP**
See also CA 45-48; CANR 2, 11, 35, 62; INT CANR-11; MTCW
Brown, Roderick (Langmere) Haig-
See Haig-Brown, Roderick (Langmere)
Brown, Rosellen 1939- .... **CLC 32**
See also CA 77-80; CAAS 10; CANR 14, 44
Brown, Sterling Allen 1901-1989 **CLC 1, 23, 59; BLC; DAM MULT, POET**
See also BW 1; CA 85-88; 127; CANR 26; DLB 48, 51, 63; MTCW
Brown, Will
See Ainsworth, William Harrison
Brown, William Wells 1813-1884 .. **NCLC 2; BLC; DAM MULT; DC 1**
See also DLB 3, 50
Browne, (Clyde) Jackson 1948(?)- ... **CLC 21**
See also CA 120
Browning, Elizabeth Barrett 1806-1861
NCLC 1, 16, 61, 66; DA; DAB; DAC; DAM MST, POET; PC 6; WLC
See also CDBLB 1832-1890; DLB 32
Browning, Robert 1812-1889 **NCLC 19; DA; DAB; DAC; DAM MST, POET; PC 2; WLCS**
See also CDBLB 1832-1890; DLB 32, 163; YABC 1
Browning, Tod 1882-1962 .... **CLC 16**
See also CA 141; 117
Brownson, Orestes (Augustus) 1803-1876
NCLC 50
Bruccoli, Matthew J(oseph) 1931- ... **CLC 34**
See also CA 9-12R; CANR 7; DLB 103
Bruce, Lenny .... **CLC 21**
See also Schneider, Leonard Alfred
Bruin, John
See Brutus, Dennis
Brulard, Henri
See Stendhal
Brulls, Christian
See Simenon, Georges (Jacques Christian)
Brunner, John (Kilian Houston) 1934-1995
CLC 8, 10; DAM POP
See also CA 1-4R; 149; CAAS 8; CANR 2, 37; MTCW
Bruno, Giordano 1548-1600 .... **LC 27**
Brutus, Dennis 1924- ... **CLC 43; BLC; DAM MULT, POET**
See also BW 2; CA 49-52; CAAS 14; CANR 2, 27, 42; DLB 117
Bryan, C(ourtlandt) D(ixon) B(arnes) 1936-
CLC 29
See also CA 73-76; CANR 13; INT CANR-13
Bryan, Michael
See Moore, Brian
Bryant, William Cullen 1794-1878. **NCLC 6, 46; DA; DAB; DAC; DAM MST, POET; PC 20**
See also CDALB 1640-1865; DLB 3, 43, 59
Bryusov, Valery Yakovlevich 1873-1924
TCLC 10
See also CA 107; 155
Buchan, John 1875-1940 .... **TCLC 41; DAB; DAM POP**
See also CA 108; 145; DLB 34, 70, 156; YABC 2
Buchanan, George 1506-1582 .... **LC 4**
Buchheim, Lothar-Guenther 1918- .... **CLC 6**
See also CA 85-88
Buchner, (Karl) Georg 1813-1837. **NCLC 26**
Buchwald, Art(hur) 1925- .... **CLC 33**
See also AITN 1; CA 5-8R; CANR 21; MTCW; SATA 10
Buck, Pearl S(ydenstricker) 1892-1973**CLC 7, 11, 18; DA; DAB; DAC; DAM MST, NOV**
See also AITN 1; CA 1-4R; 41-44R; CANR 1, 34; DLB 9, 102; MTCW; SATA 1, 25
Buckler, Ernest 1908-1984 ... **CLC 13; DAC; DAM MST**
See also CA 11-12; 114; CAP 1; DLB 68; SATA 47
Buckley, Vincent (Thomas) 1925-1988**CLC 57**
See also CA 101
Buckley, William F(rank), Jr. 1925- . **CLC 7, 18, 37; DAM POP**
See also AITN 1; CA 1-4R; CANR 1, 24, 53; DLB 137; DLBY 80; INT CANR-24; MTCW
Buechner, (Carl) Frederick 1926-**CLC 2, 4, 6, 9; DAM NOV**
See also CA 13-16R; CANR 11, 39; DLBY 80; INT CANR-11; MTCW
Buell, John (Edward) 1927- .... **CLC 10**
See also CA 1-4R; DLB 53
Buero Vallejo, Antonio 1916- .... **CLC 15, 46**
See also CA 106; CANR 24, 49; HW; MTCW
Bufalino, Gesualdo 1920(?)- .... **CLC 74**
Bugayev, Boris Nikolayevich 1880-1934
See Bely, Andrey
See also CA 104
Bukowski, Charles 1920-1994**CLC 2, 5, 9, 41, 82; DAM NOV, POET; PC 18**
See also CA 17-20R; 144; CANR 40, 62; DLB 5, 130, 169; MTCW
Bulgakov, Mikhail (Afanas'evich) 1891-1940
TCLC 2, 16; DAM DRAM, NOV; SSC 18
See also CA 105; 152
Bulgya, Alexander Alexandrovich 1901-1956
TCLC 53
See also Fadeyev, Alexander
See also CA 117
Bullins, Ed 1935- ... **CLC 1, 5, 7; BLC; DAM DRAM, MULT; DC 6**
See also BW 2; CA 49-52; CAAS 16; CANR 24, 46; DLB 7, 38; MTCW
Bulwer-Lytton, Edward (George Earle Lytton) 1803-1873 .... **NCLC 1, 45**
See also DLB 21
Bunin, Ivan Alexeyevich 1870-1953**TCLC 6; SSC 5**
See also CA 104
Bunting, Basil 1900-1985 ..... **CLC 10, 39, 47; DAM POET**
See also CA 53-56; 115; CANR 7; DLB 20
Bunuel, Luis 1900-1983 ... **CLC 16, 80; DAM MULT; HLC**
See also CA 101; 110; CANR 32; HW
Bunyan, John 1628-1688 ... **LC 4; DA; DAB; DAC; DAM MST; WLC**
See also CDBLB 1660-1789; DLB 39
Burckhardt, Jacob (Christoph) 1818-1897
NCLC 49
Burford, Eleanor
See Hibbert, Eleanor Alice Burford
Burgess, AnthonyCLC 1, 2, 4, 5, 8, 10, 13, 15, 22, 40, 62, 81, 94; DAB
See also Wilson, John (Anthony) Burgess
See also AITN 1; CDBLB 1960 to Present; DLB 14
Burke, Edmund 1729(?)-1797 **LC 7, 36; DA; DAB; DAC; DAM MST; WLC**
See also DLB 104
Burke, Kenneth (Duva) 1897-1993**CLC 2, 24**
See also CA 5-8R; 143; CANR 39; DLB 45, 63; MTCW
Burke, Leda
See Garnett, David
Burke, Ralph
See Silverberg, Robert
Burke, Thomas 1886-1945 .... **TCLC 63**
See also CA 113; 155
Burney, Fanny 1752-1840 .... **NCLC 12, 54**
See also DLB 39
Burns, Robert 1759-1796 .... **PC 6**
See also CDBLB 1789-1832; DA; DAB; DAC; DAM MST, POET; DLB 109; WLC
Burns, Tex
See L'Amour, Louis (Dearborn)
Burnshaw, Stanley 1906- .... **CLC 3, 13, 44**
See also CA 9-12R; DLB 48
Burr, Anne 1937- .... **CLC 6**
See also CA 25-28R
Burroughs, Edgar Rice 1875-1950 . **TCLC 2, 32; DAM NOV**
See also AAYA 11; CA 104; 132; DLB 8; MTCW; SATA 41
Burroughs, William S(eward) 1914-1997**CLC 1, 2, 5, 15, 22, 42, 75; DA; DAB; DAC; DAM MST, NOV, POP; WLC**
See also AITN 2; CA 9-12R; 160; CANR 20, 52; DLB 2, 8, 16, 152; DLBY 81; MTCW
Burton, Richard F. 1821-1890 .... **NCLC 42**
See also DLB 55, 184
Busch, Frederick 1941- ..... **CLC 7, 10, 18, 47**
See also CA 33-36R; CAAS 1; CANR 45; DLB 6
Bush, Ronald 1946- .... **CLC 34**
See also CA 136
Bustos, F(rancisco)
See Borges, Jorge Luis
Bustos Domecq, H(onorio)
See Bioy Casares, Adolfo; Borges, Jorge Luis
Butler, Octavia E(stelle) 1947-**CLC 38; DAM MULT, POP**
See also AAYA 18; BW 2; CA 73-76; CANR 12, 24, 38; DLB 33; MTCW; SATA 84
Butler, Robert Olen (Jr.) 1945-**CLC 81; DAM POP**
See also CA 112; DLB 173; INT 112
Butler, Samuel 1612-1680 .... **LC 16**
See also DLB 101, 126
Butler, Samuel 1835-1902 **TCLC 1, 33; DA; DAB; DAC; DAM MST, NOV; WLC**
See also CA 143; CDBLB 1890-1914; DLB 18, 57, 174
Butler, Walter C.
See Faust, Frederick (Schiller)
Butor, Michel (Marie Francois) 1926-**CLC 1, 3, 8, 11, 15**
See also CA 9-12R; CANR 33; DLB 83; MTCW
Buzo, Alexander (John) 1944- .... **CLC 61**
See also CA 97-100; CANR 17, 39
Buzzati, Dino 1906-1972 .... **CLC 36**
See also CA 160; 33-36R; DLB 177
Byars, Betsy (Cromer) 1928- .... **CLC 35**
See also AAYA 19; CA 33-36R; CANR 18, 36, 57; CLR 1, 16; DLB 52; INT CANR-18; JRDA; MAICYA; MTCW; SAAS 1; SATA 4, 46, 80
Byatt, A(ntonia) S(usan Drabble) 1936-**CLC 19, 65; DAM NOV, POP**
See also CA 13-16R; CANR 13, 33, 50; DLB 14; MTCW
Byrne, David 1952- .... **CLC 26**
See also CA 127
Byrne, John Keyes 1926-
See Leonard, Hugh
See also CA 102; INT 102
Byron, George Gordon (Noel) 1788-1824
NCLC 2, 12; DA; DAB; DAC; DAM MST, POET; PC 16; WLC
See also CDBLB 1789-1832; DLB 96, 110
Byron, Robert 1905-1941 .... **TCLC 67**
See also CA 160

C. 3. 3.
See Wilde, Oscar (Fingal O'Flahertie Wills)
Caballero, Fernan 1796-1877 .... **NCLC 10**
Cabell, Branch
See Cabell, James Branch
Cabell, James Branch 1879-1958 .... **TCLC 6**
See also CA 105; 152; DLB 9, 78
Cable, George Washington 1844-1925 **TCLC 4; SSC 4**
See also CA 104; 155; DLB 12, 74; DLBD 13
Cabral de Melo Neto, Joao 1920- ... **CLC 76; DAM MULT**
See also CA 151
Cabrera Infante, G(uillermo) 1929- . **CLC 5, 25, 45; DAM MULT; HLC**
See also CA 85-88; CANR 29; DLB 113; HW; MTCW
Cade, Toni
See Bambara, Toni Cade
Cadmus and Harmonia
See Buchan, John
Caedmon fl. 658-680 .... **CMLC 7**
See also DLB 146
Caeiro, Alberto
See Pessoa, Fernando (Antonio Nogueira)
Cage, John (Milton, Jr.) 1912- .... **CLC 41**
See also CA 13-16R; CANR 9; INT CANR-9
Cahan, Abraham 1860-1951 .... **TCLC 71**
See also CA 108; 154; DLB 9, 25, 28
Cain, G.
See Cabrera Infante, G(uillermo)
Cain, Guillermo
See Cabrera Infante, G(uillermo)
Cain, James M(allahan) 1892-1977 **CLC 3, 11, 28**
See also AITN 1; CA 17-20R; 73-76; CANR 8, 34, 61; MTCW
Caine, Mark
See Raphael, Frederic (Michael)
Calasso, Roberto 1941- .... **CLC 81**
See also CA 143
Calderon de la Barca, Pedro 1600-1681 . **LC 23; DC 3**
Caldwell, Erskine (Preston) 1903-1987 **CLC 1, 8, 14, 50, 60; DAM NOV; SSC 19**
See also AITN 1; CA 1-4R; 121; CAAS 1; CANR 2, 33; DLB 9, 86; MTCW
Caldwell, (Janet Miriam) Taylor (Holland) 1900-1985 **CLC 2, 28, 39; DAM NOV, POP**
See also CA 5-8R; 116; CANR 5
Calhoun, John Caldwell 1782-1850 **NCLC 15**
See also DLB 3
Calisher, Hortense 1911- **CLC 2, 4, 8, 38; DAM NOV; SSC 15**
See also CA 1-4R; CANR 1, 22; DLB 2; INT CANR-22; MTCW
Callaghan, Morley Edward 1903-1990 **CLC 3, 14, 41, 65; DAC; DAM MST**
See also CA 9-12R; 132; CANR 33; DLB 68; MTCW
Callimachus c. 305B.C.-c. 240B.C. **CMLC 18**
See also DLB 176
Calvin, John 1509-1564 .... **LC 37**
Calvino, Italo 1923-1985 **CLC 5, 8, 11, 22, 33, 39, 73; DAM NOV; SSC 3**
See also CA 85-88; 116; CANR 23, 61; MTCW
Cameron, Carey 1952- .... **CLC 59**
See also CA 135
Cameron, Peter 1959- .... **CLC 44**
See also CA 125; CANR 50
Campana, Dino 1885-1932 .... **TCLC 20**
See also CA 117; DLB 114
Campanella, Tommaso 1568-1639 ..... **LC 32**
Campbell, John W(ood, Jr.) 1910-1971 **CLC 32**
See also CA 21-22; 29-32R; CANR 34; CAP 2; DLB 8; MTCW

Campbell, Joseph 1904-1987 .... **CLC 69**
See also AAYA 3; BEST 89:2; CA 1-4R; 124; CANR 3, 28, 61; MTCW
Campbell, Maria 1940- .... **CLC 85; DAC**
See also CA 102; CANR 54; NNAL
Campbell, (John) Ramsey 1946-**CLC 42; SSC 19**
See also CA 57-60; CANR 7; INT CANR-7
Campbell, (Ignatius) Roy (Dunnachie) 1901-1957 .... **TCLC 5**
See also CA 104; 155; DLB 20
Campbell, Thomas 1777-1844 .... **NCLC 19**
See also DLB 93; 144
Campbell, Wilfred .... **TCLC 9**
See also Campbell, William
Campbell, William 1858(?)-1918
See Campbell, Wilfred
See also CA 106; DLB 92
Campion, Jane .... **CLC 95**
See also CA 138
Campos, Alvaro de
See Pessoa, Fernando (Antonio Nogueira)
Camus, Albert 1913-1960**CLC 1, 2, 4, 9, 11, 14, 32, 63, 69; DA; DAB; DAC; DAM DRAM, MST, NOV; DC 2; SSC 9; WLC**
See also CA 89-92; DLB 72; MTCW
Canby, Vincent 1924- .... **CLC 13**
See also CA 81-84
Cancale
See Desnos, Robert
Canetti, Elias 1905-1994**CLC 3, 14, 25, 75, 86**
See also CA 21-24R; 146; CANR 23, 61; DLB 85, 124; MTCW
Canin, Ethan 1960- .... **CLC 55**
See also CA 131; 135
Cannon, Curt
See Hunter, Evan
Cape, Judith
See Page, P(atricia) K(athleen)
Capek, Karel 1890-1938 ... **TCLC 6, 37; DA; DAB; DAC; DAM DRAM, MST, NOV; DC 1; WLC**
See also CA 104; 140
Capote, Truman 1924-1984**CLC 1, 3, 8, 13, 19, 34, 38, 58; DA; DAB; DAC; DAM MST, NOV, POP; SSC 2; WLC**
See also CA 5-8R; 113; CANR 18, 62; CDALB 1941-1968; DLB 2; DLBY 80, 84; MTCW; SATA 91
Capra, Frank 1897-1991 .... **CLC 16**
See also CA 61-64; 135
Caputo, Philip 1941- .... **CLC 32**
See also CA 73-76; CANR 40
Caragiale, Ion Luca 1852-1912 ...... **TCLC 76**
See also CA 157
Card, Orson Scott 1951-**CLC 44, 47, 50; DAM POP**
See also AAYA 11; CA 102; CANR 27, 47; INT CANR-27; MTCW; SATA 83
Cardenal, Ernesto 1925- .... **CLC 31; DAM MULT, POET; HLC**
See also CA 49-52; CANR 2, 32; HW; MTCW
Cardozo, Benjamin N(athan) 1870-1938 **TCLC 65**
See also CA 117
Carducci, Giosue 1835-1907 .... **TCLC 32**
Carew, Thomas 1595(?)-1640 .... **LC 13**
See also DLB 126
Carey, Ernestine Gilbreth 1908- ...... **CLC 17**
See also CA 5-8R; SATA 2
Carey, Peter 1943- .... **CLC 40, 55, 96**
See also CA 123; 127; CANR 53; INT 127; MTCW; SATA 94
Carleton, William 1794-1869 .... **NCLC 3**
See also DLB 159
Carlisle, Henry (Coffin) 1926- .... **CLC 33**
See also CA 13-16R; CANR 15

Carlsen, Chris
See Holdstock, Robert P.
Carlson, Ron(ald F.) 1947- .... **CLC 54**
See also CA 105; CANR 27
Carlyle, Thomas 1795-1881 . **NCLC 22; DA; DAB; DAC; DAM MST**
See also CDBLB 1789-1832; DLB 55; 144
Carman, (William) Bliss 1861-1929**TCLC 7; DAC**
See also CA 104; 152; DLB 92
Carnegie, Dale 1888-1955 .... **TCLC 53**
Carossa, Hans 1878-1956 .... **TCLC 48**
See also DLB 66
Carpenter, Don(ald Richard) 1931-1995**CLC 41**
See also CA 45-48; 149; CANR 1
Carpentier (y Valmont), Alejo 1904-1980 **CLC 8, 11, 38; DAM MULT; HLC**
See also CA 65-68; 97-100; CANR 11; DLB 113; HW
Carr, Caleb 1955(?)- .... **CLC 86**
See also CA 147
Carr, Emily 1871-1945 .... **TCLC 32**
See also CA 159; DLB 68
Carr, John Dickson 1906-1977 .... **CLC 3**
See also Fairbairn, Roger
See also CA 49-52; 69-72; CANR 3, 33, 60; MTCW
Carr, Philippa
See Hibbert, Eleanor Alice Burford
Carr, Virginia Spencer 1929- .... **CLC 34**
See also CA 61-64; DLB 111
Carrere, Emmanuel 1957- .... **CLC 89**
Carrier, Roch 1937-**CLC 13, 78; DAC; DAM MST**
See also CA 130; CANR 61; DLB 53
Carroll, James P. 1943(?)- .... **CLC 38**
See also CA 81-84
Carroll, Jim 1951- .... **CLC 35**
See also AAYA 17; CA 45-48; CANR 42
Carroll, Lewis .... **NCLC 2, 53; PC 18; WLC**
See also Dodgson, Charles Lutwidge
See also CDBLB 1832-1890; CLR 2, 18; DLB 18, 163, 178; JRDA
Carroll, Paul Vincent 1900-1968 ..... **CLC 10**
See also CA 9-12R; 25-28R; DLB 10
Carruth, Hayden 1921- **CLC 4, 7, 10, 18, 84; PC 10**
See also CA 9-12R; CANR 4, 38, 59; DLB 5, 165; INT CANR-4; MTCW; SATA 47
Carson, Rachel Louise 1907-1964 .. **CLC 71; DAM POP**
See also CA 77-80; CANR 35; MTCW; SATA 23
Carter, Angela (Olive) 1940-1992 **CLC 5, 41, 76; SSC 13**
See also CA 53-56; 136; CANR 12, 36, 61; DLB 14; MTCW; SATA 66; SATA-Obit 70
Carter, Nick
See Smith, Martin Cruz
Carver, Raymond 1938-1988**CLC 22, 36, 53, 55; DAM NOV; SSC 8**
See also CA 33-36R; 126; CANR 17, 34, 61; DLB 130; DLBY 84, 88; MTCW
Cary, Elizabeth, Lady Falkland 1585-1639 **LC 30**
Cary, (Arthur) Joyce (Lunel) 1888-1957 **TCLC 1, 29**
See also CA 104; CDBLB 1914-1945; DLB 15, 100
Casanova de Seingalt, Giovanni Jacopo 1725-1798 .... **LC 13**
Casares, Adolfo Bioy
See Bioy Casares, Adolfo
Casely-Hayford, J(oseph) E(phraim) 1866-1930 **TCLC 24; BLC; DAM MULT**
See also BW 2; CA 123; 152

Casey, John (Dudley) 1939- .... **CLC 59**
See also BEST 90:2; CA 69-72; CANR 23
Casey, Michael 1947- .... **CLC 2**
See also CA 65-68; DLB 5
Casey, Patrick
See Thurman, Wallace (Henry)
Casey, Warren (Peter) 1935-1988 ... **CLC 12**
See also CA 101; 127; INT 101
Casona, Alejandro .... **CLC 49**
See also Alvarez, Alejandro Rodriguez
Cassavetes, John 1929-1989 .... **CLC 20**
See also CA 85-88; 127
Cassian, Nina 1924- .... **PC 17**
Cassill, R(onald) V(erlin) 1919- ... **CLC 4, 23**
See also CA 9-12R; CAAS 1; CANR 7, 45; DLB 6
Cassirer, Ernst 1874-1945 .... **TCLC 61**
See also CA 157
Cassity, (Allen) Turner 1929- ...... **CLC 6, 42**
See also CA 17-20R; CAAS 8; CANR 11; DLB 105
Castaneda, Carlos 1931(?)- .... **CLC 12**
See also CA 25-28R; CANR 32; HW; MTCW
Castedo, Elena 1937- .... **CLC 65**
See also CA 132
Castedo-Ellerman, Elena
See Castedo, Elena
Castellanos, Rosario 1925-1974 **CLC 66; DAM MULT; HLC**
See also CA 131; 53-56; CANR 58; DLB 113; HW
Castelvetro, Lodovico 1505-1571 .... **LC 12**
Castiglione, Baldassare 1478-1529 ..... **LC 12**
Castle, Robert
See Hamilton, Edmond
Castro, Guillen de 1569-1631 .... **LC 19**
Castro, Rosalia de 1837-1885 **NCLC 3; DAM MULT**
Cather, Willa
See Cather, Willa Sibert
Cather, Willa Sibert 1873-1947 **TCLC 1, 11, 31; DA; DAB; DAC; DAM MST, NOV; SSC 2; WLC**
See also CA 104; 128; CDALB 1865-1917; DLB 9, 54, 78; DLBD 1; MTCW; SATA 30
Cato, Marcus Porcius 234B.C.-149B.C. **CMLC 21**
Catton, (Charles) Bruce 1899-1978 . **CLC 35**
See also AITN 1; CA 5-8R; 81-84; CANR 7; DLB 17; SATA 2; SATA-Obit 24
Catullus c. 84B.C.-c. 54B.C. .... **CMLC 18**
Cauldwell, Frank
See King, Francis (Henry)
Caunitz, William J. 1933-1996 .... **CLC 34**
See also BEST 89:3; CA 125; 130; 152; INT 130
Causley, Charles (Stanley) 1917- .... **CLC 7**
See also CA 9-12R; CANR 5, 35; CLR 30; DLB 27; MTCW; SATA 3, 66
Caute, David 1936- .... **CLC 29; DAM NOV**
See also CA 1-4R; CAAS 4; CANR 1, 33; DLB 14
Cavafy, C(onstantine) P(eter) 1863-1933 **TCLC 2, 7; DAM POET**
See also Kavafis, Konstantinos Petrou
See also CA 148
Cavallo, Evelyn
See Spark, Muriel (Sarah)
Cavanna, Betty .... **CLC 12**
See also Harrison, Elizabeth Cavanna
See also JRDA; MAICYA; SAAS 4; SATA 1, 30
Cavendish, Margaret Lucas 1623-1673 **LC 30**
See also DLB 131
Caxton, William 1421(?)-1491(?) .... **LC 17**
See also DLB 170
Cayrol, Jean 1911- .... **CLC 11**
See also CA 89-92; DLB 83
Cela, Camilo Jose 1916- **CLC 4, 13, 59; DAM MULT; HLC**
See also BEST 90:2; CA 21-24R; CAAS 10; CANR 21, 32; DLBY 89; HW; MTCW
Celan, Paul .... **CLC 10, 19, 53, 82; PC 10**
See also Antschel, Paul
See also DLB 69
Celine, Louis-Ferdinand **CLC 1, 3, 4, 7, 9, 15, 47**
See also Destouches, Louis-Ferdinand
See also DLB 72
Cellini, Benvenuto 1500-1571 .... **LC 7**
Cendrars, Blaise .... **CLC 18**
See also Sauser-Hall, Frederic
Cernuda (y Bidon), Luis 1902-1963 **CLC 54; DAM POET**
See also CA 131; 89-92; DLB 134; HW
Cervantes (Saavedra), Miguel de 1547-1616 **LC 6, 23; DA; DAB; DAC; DAM MST, NOV; SSC 12; WLC**
Cesaire, Aime (Fernand) 1913- . **CLC 19, 32; BLC; DAM MULT, POET**
See also BW 2; CA 65-68; CANR 24, 43; MTCW
Chabon, Michael 1963- .... **CLC 55**
See also CA 139; CANR 57
Chabrol, Claude 1930- .... **CLC 16**
See also CA 110
Challans, Mary 1905-1983
See Renault, Mary
See also CA 81-84; 111; SATA 23; SATA-Obit 36
Challis, George
See Faust, Frederick (Schiller)
Chambers, Aidan 1934- .... **CLC 35**
See also CA 25-28R; CANR 12, 31, 58; JRDA; MAICYA; SAAS 12; SATA 1, 69
Chambers, James 1948-
See Cliff, Jimmy
See also CA 124
Chambers, Jessie
See Lawrence, D(avid) H(erbert Richards)
Chambers, Robert W. 1865-1933 .. **TCLC 41**
Chandler, Raymond (Thornton) 1888-1959 **TCLC 1, 7; SSC 23**
See also CA 104; 129; CANR 60; CDALB 1929-1941; DLBD 6; MTCW
Chang, Eileen 1920- .... **SSC 28**
Chang, Jung 1952- .... **CLC 71**
See also CA 142
Channing, William Ellery 1780-1842 **NCLC 17**
See also DLB 1, 59
Chaplin, Charles Spencer 1889-1977 **CLC 16**
See also Chaplin, Charlie
See also CA 81-84; 73-76
Chaplin, Charlie
See Chaplin, Charles Spencer
See also DLB 44
Chapman, George 1559(?)-1634 **LC 22; DAM DRAM**
See also DLB 62, 121
Chapman, Graham 1941-1989 .... **CLC 21**
See also Monty Python
See also CA 116; 129; CANR 35
Chapman, John Jay 1862-1933 .... **TCLC 7**
See also CA 104
Chapman, Lee
See Bradley, Marion Zimmer
Chapman, Walker
See Silverberg, Robert
Chappell, Fred (Davis) 1936- ...... **CLC 40, 78**
See also CA 5-8R; CAAS 4; CANR 8, 33; DLB 6, 105
Char, Rene(-Emile) 1907-1988 **CLC 9, 11, 14, 55; DAM POET**
See also CA 13-16R; 124; CANR 32; MTCW
Charby, Jay
See Ellison, Harlan (Jay)
Chardin, Pierre Teilhard de
See Teilhard de Chardin, (Marie Joseph) Pierre
Charles I 1600-1649 .... **LC 13**
Charriere, Isabelle de 1740-1805 .. **NCLC 66**
Charyn, Jerome 1937- .... **CLC 5, 8, 18**
See also CA 5-8R; CAAS 1; CANR 7, 61; DLBY 83; MTCW
Chase, Mary (Coyle) 1907-1981 .... **DC 1**
See also CA 77-80; 105; SATA 17; SATA-Obit 29
Chase, Mary Ellen 1887-1973 .... **CLC 2**
See also CA 13-16; 41-44R; CAP 1; SATA 10
Chase, Nicholas
See Hyde, Anthony
Chateaubriand, Francois Rene de 1768-1848 **NCLC 3**
See also DLB 119
Chatterje, Sarat Chandra 1876-1936(?)
See Chatterji, Saratchandra
See also CA 109
Chatterji, Bankim Chandra 1838-1894 **NCLC 19**
Chatterji, Saratchandra .... **TCLC 13**
See also Chatterje, Sarat Chandra
Chatterton, Thomas 1752-1770 . **LC 3; DAM POET**
See also DLB 109
Chatwin, (Charles) Bruce 1940-1989 **CLC 28, 57, 59; DAM POP**
See also AAYA 4; BEST 90:1; CA 85-88; 127
Chaucer, Daniel
See Ford, Ford Madox
Chaucer, Geoffrey 1340(?)-1400 **LC 17; DA; DAB; DAC; DAM MST, POET; PC 19; WLCS**
See also CDBLB Before 1660; DLB 146
Chaviaras, Strates 1935-
See Haviaras, Stratis
See also CA 105
Chayefsky, Paddy .... **CLC 23**
See also Chayefsky, Sidney
See also DLB 7, 44; DLBY 81
Chayefsky, Sidney 1923-1981
See Chayefsky, Paddy
See also CA 9-12R; 104; CANR 18; DAM DRAM
Chedid, Andree 1920- .... **CLC 47**
See also CA 145
Cheever, John 1912-1982 **CLC 3, 7, 8, 11, 15, 25, 64; DA; DAB; DAC; DAM MST, NOV, POP; SSC 1; WLC**
See also CA 5-8R; 106; CABS 1; CANR 5, 27; CDALB 1941-1968; DLB 2, 102; DLBY 80, 82; INT CANR-5; MTCW
Cheever, Susan 1943- .... **CLC 18, 48**
See also CA 103; CANR 27, 51; DLBY 82; INT CANR-27
Chekhonte, Antosha
See Chekhov, Anton (Pavlovich)
Chekhov, Anton (Pavlovich) 1860-1904 **TCLC 3, 10, 31, 55; DA; DAB; DAC; DAM DRAM, MST; SSC 2, 28; WLC**
See also CA 104; 124; SATA 90
Chernyshevsky, Nikolay Gavrilovich 1828-1889 .... **NCLC 1**
Cherry, Carolyn Janice 1942-
See Cherryh, C. J.
See also CA 65-68; CANR 10
Cherryh, C. J. .... **CLC 35**
See also Cherry, Carolyn Janice
See also DLBY 80; SATA 93
Chesnutt, Charles W(addell) 1858-1932 **TCLC 5, 39; BLC; DAM MULT; SSC 7**
See also BW 1; CA 106; 125; DLB 12, 50, 78;

MTCW
Chester, Alfred 1929(?)-1971 .... **CLC 49**
See also CA 33-36R; DLB 130
Chesterton, G(ilbert) K(eith) 1874-1936
TCLC 1, 6, 64; DAM NOV, POET; SSC 1
See also CA 104; 132; CDBLB 1914-1945;
DLB 10, 19, 34, 70, 98, 149, 178; MTCW;
SATA 27
Chiang Pin-chin 1904-1986
See Ding Ling
See also CA 118
Ch'ien Chung-shu 1910- .... **CLC 22**
See also CA 130; MTCW
Child, L. Maria
See Child, Lydia Maria
Child, Lydia Maria 1802-1880 .... **NCLC 6**
See also DLB 1, 74; SATA 67
Child, Mrs.
See Child, Lydia Maria
Child, Philip 1898-1978 .... **CLC 19, 68**
See also CA 13-14; CAP 1; SATA 47
Childers, (Robert) Erskine 1870-1922 **TCLC 65**
See also CA 113; 153; DLB 70
Childress, Alice 1920-1994 **CLC 12, 15, 86, 96;**
BLC; DAM DRAM, MULT, NOV; DC 4
See also AAYA 8; BW 2; CA 45-48; 146;
CANR 3, 27, 50; CLR 14; DLB 7, 38; JRDA;
MAICYA; MTCW; SATA 7, 48, 81
Chin, Frank (Chew, Jr.) 1940- .... **DC 7**
See also CA 33-36R; DAM MULT
Chislett, (Margaret) Anne 1943- ..... **CLC 34**
See also CA 151
Chitty, Thomas Willes 1926- .... **CLC 11**
See Hinde, Thomas
See also CA 5-8R
Chivers, Thomas Holley 1809-1858 **NCLC 49**
See also DLB 3
Chomette, Rene Lucien 1898-1981
See Clair, Rene
See also CA 103
Chopin, Kate TCLC 5, 14; DA; DAB; SSC 8;
WLCS
See Chopin, Katherine
See also CDALB 1865-1917; DLB 12, 78
Chopin, Katherine 1851-1904
See Chopin, Kate
See also CA 104; 122; DAC; DAM MST, NOV
Chretien de Troyes c. 12th cent. - . **CMLC 10**
Christie
See Ichikawa, Kon
Christie, Agatha (Mary Clarissa) 1890-1976
CLC 1, 6, 8, 12, 39, 48; DAB; DAC; DAM NOV
See also AAYA 9; AITN 1, 2; CA 17-20R; 61-64; CANR 10, 37; CDBLB 1914-1945; DLB 13, 77; MTCW; SATA 36
Christie, (Ann) Philippa
See Pearce, Philippa
See also CA 5-8R; CANR 4
Christine de Pizan 1365(?)-1431(?) ...... **LC 9**
Chubb, Elmer
See Masters, Edgar Lee
Chulkov, Mikhail Dmitrievich 1743-1792 **LC 2**
See also DLB 150
Churchill, Caryl 1938- ..... **CLC 31, 55; DC 5**
See also CA 102; CANR 22, 46; DLB 13; MTCW
Churchill, Charles 1731-1764 .... **LC 3**
See also DLB 109
Chute, Carolyn 1947- .... **CLC 39**
See also CA 123
Ciardi, John (Anthony) 1916-1986. **CLC 10, 40, 44; DAM POET**
See also CA 5-8R; 118; CAAS 2; CANR 5, 33; CLR 19; DLB 5; DLBY 86; INT CANR-5;

MAICYA; MTCW; SATA 1, 65; SATA-Obit 46
Cicero, Marcus Tullius 106B.C.-43B.C.
CMLC 3
Cimino, Michael 1943- .... **CLC 16**
See also CA 105
Cioran, E(mil) M. 1911-1995 .... **CLC 64**
See also CA 25-28R; 149
Cisneros, Sandra 1954-**CLC 69; DAM MULT; HLC**
See also AAYA 9; CA 131; DLB 122, 152; HW
Cixous, Helene 1937- .... **CLC 92**
See also CA 126; CANR 55; DLB 83; MTCW
Clair, Rene .... **CLC 20**
See also Chomette, Rene Lucien
Clampitt, Amy 1920-1994 .... **CLC 32; PC 19**
See also CA 110; 146; CANR 29; DLB 105
Clancy, Thomas L., Jr. 1947-
See Clancy, Tom
See also CA 125; 131; CANR 62; INT 131; MTCW
Clancy, Tom .... **CLC 45; DAM NOV, POP**
See also Clancy, Thomas L., Jr.
See also AAYA 9; BEST 89:1, 90:1
Clare, John 1793-1864 **NCLC 9; DAB; DAM POET**
See also DLB 55, 96
Clarin
See Alas (y Urena), Leopoldo (Enrique Garcia)
Clark, Al C.
See Goines, Donald
Clark, (Robert) Brian 1932- .... **CLC 29**
See also CA 41-44R
Clark, Curt
See Westlake, Donald E(dwin)
Clark, Eleanor 1913-1996 .... **CLC 5, 19**
See also CA 9-12R; 151; CANR 41; DLB 6
Clark, J. P.
See Clark, John Pepper
See also DLB 117
Clark, John Pepper 1935- ..... **CLC 38; BLC; DAM DRAM, MULT; DC 5**
See also Clark, J. P.
See also BW 1; CA 65-68; CANR 16
Clark, M. R.
See Clark, Mavis Thorpe
Clark, Mavis Thorpe 1909- .... **CLC 12**
See also CA 57-60; CANR 8, 37; CLR 30; MAICYA; SAAS 5; SATA 8, 74
Clark, Walter Van Tilburg 1909-1971**CLC 28**
See also CA 9-12R; 33-36R; DLB 9; SATA 8
Clarke, Arthur C(harles) 1917-**CLC 1, 4, 13, 18, 35; DAM POP; SSC 3**
See also AAYA 4; CA 1-4R; CANR 2, 28, 55; JRDA; MAICYA; MTCW; SATA 13, 70
Clarke, Austin 1896-1974 .... **CLC 6, 9; DAM POET**
See also CA 29-32; 49-52; CAP 2; DLB 10, 20
Clarke, Austin C(hesterfield) 1934-**CLC 8, 53; BLC; DAC; DAM MULT**
See also BW 1; CA 25-28R; CAAS 16; CANR 14, 32; DLB 53, 125
Clarke, Gillian 1937- .... **CLC 61**
See also CA 106; DLB 40
Clarke, Marcus (Andrew Hislop) 1846-1881
NCLC 19
Clarke, Shirley 1925- .... **CLC 16**
Clash, The
See Headon, (Nicky) Topper; Jones, Mick; Simonon, Paul; Strummer, Joe
Claudel, Paul (Louis Charles Marie) 1868-1955
TCLC 2, 10
See also CA 104
Clavell, James (duMaresq) 1925-1994**CLC 6, 25, 87; DAM NOV, POP**
See also CA 25-28R; 146; CANR 26, 48; MTCW

Cleaver, (Leroy) Eldridge 1935- ..... **CLC 30; BLC; DAM MULT**
See also BW 1; CA 21-24R; CANR 16
Cleese, John (Marwood) 1939- .... **CLC 21**
See also Monty Python
See also CA 112; 116; CANR 35; MTCW
Cleishbotham, Jebediah
See Scott, Walter
Cleland, John 1710-1789 .... **LC 2**
See also DLB 39
Clemens, Samuel Langhorne 1835-1910
See Twain, Mark
See also CA 104; 135; CDALB 1865-1917; DA; DAB; DAC; DAM MST, NOV; DLB 11, 12, 23, 64, 74; JRDA; MAICYA; YABC 2
Cleophil
See Congreve, William
Clerihew, E.
See Bentley, E(dmund) C(lerihew)
Clerk, N. W.
See Lewis, C(live) S(taples)
Cliff, Jimmy .... **CLC 21**
See also Chambers, James
Clifton, (Thelma) Lucille 1936- **CLC 19, 66; BLC; DAM MULT, POET; PC 17**
See also BW 2; CA 49-52; CANR 2, 24, 42; CLR 5; DLB 5, 41; MAICYA; MTCW; SATA 20, 69
Clinton, Dirk
See Silverberg, Robert
Clough, Arthur Hugh 1819-1861 ... **NCLC 27**
See also DLB 32
Clutha, Janet Paterson Frame 1924-
See Frame, Janet
See also CA 1-4R; CANR 2, 36; MTCW
Clyne, Terence
See Blatty, William Peter
Cobalt, Martin
See Mayne, William (James Carter)
Cobbett, William 1763-1835 .... **NCLC 49**
See also DLB 43, 107, 158
Coburn, D(onald) L(ee) 1938- .... **CLC 10**
See also CA 89-92
Cocteau, Jean (Maurice Eugene Clement)
1889-1963**CLC 1, 8, 15, 16, 43; DA; DAB; DAC; DAM DRAM, MST, NOV; WLC**
See also CA 25-28; CANR 40; CAP 2; DLB 65; MTCW
Codrescu, Andrei 1946-**CLC 46; DAM POET**
See also CA 33-36R; CAAS 19; CANR 13, 34, 53
Coe, Max
See Bourne, Randolph S(illiman)
Coe, Tucker
See Westlake, Donald E(dwin)
Coetzee, J(ohn) M(ichael) 1940- **CLC 23, 33, 66; DAM NOV**
See also CA 77-80; CANR 41, 54; MTCW
Coffey, Brian
See Koontz, Dean R(ay)
Cohan, George M(ichael) 1878-1942**TCLC 60**
See also CA 157
Cohen, Arthur A(llen) 1928-1986 **CLC 7, 31**
See also CA 1-4R; 120; CANR 1, 17, 42; DLB 28
Cohen, Leonard (Norman) 1934- **CLC 3, 38; DAC; DAM MST**
See also CA 21-24R; CANR 14; DLB 53; MTCW
Cohen, Matt 1942- .... **CLC 19; DAC**
See also CA 61-64; CAAS 18; CANR 40; DLB 53
Cohen-Solal, Annie 19(?)- .... **CLC 50**
Colegate, Isabel 1931- .... **CLC 36**
See also CA 17-20R; CANR 8, 22; DLB 14; INT CANR-22; MTCW
Coleman, Emmett

See Reed, Ishmael
Coleridge, M. E.
See Coleridge, Mary E(lizabeth)
Coleridge, Mary E(lizabeth) 1861-1907 TCLC 73
See also CA 116; DLB 19, 98
Coleridge, Samuel Taylor 1772-1834 NCLC 9, 54; DA; DAB; DAC; DAM MST, POET; PC 11; WLC
See also CDBLB 1789-1832; DLB 93, 107
Coleridge, Sara 1802-1852 .... NCLC 31
Coles, Don 1928- .... CLC 46
See also CA 115; CANR 38
Colette, (Sidonie-Gabrielle) 1873-1954 TCLC 1, 5, 16; DAM NOV; SSC 10
See also CA 104; 131; DLB 65; MTCW
Collett, (Jacobine) Camilla (Wergeland) 1813-1895 .... NCLC 22
Collier, Christopher 1930- .... CLC 30
See also AAYA 13; CA 33-36R; CANR 13, 33; JRDA; MAICYA; SATA 16, 70
Collier, James L(incoln) 1928- CLC 30; DAM POP
See also AAYA 13; CA 9-12R; CANR 4, 33, 60; CLR 3; JRDA; MAICYA; SAAS 21; SATA 8, 70
Collier, Jeremy 1650-1726 .... LC 6
Collier, John 1901-1980 .... SSC 19
See also CA 65-68; 97-100; CANR 10; DLB 77
Collingwood, R(obin) G(eorge) 1889(?)-1943 TCLC 67
See also CA 117; 155
Collins, Hunt
See Hunter, Evan
Collins, Linda 1931- .... CLC 44
See also CA 125
Collins, (William) Wilkie 1824-1889 NCLC 1, 18
See also CDBLB 1832-1890; DLB 18, 70, 159
Collins, William 1721-1759 . LC 4, 40; DAM POET
See also DLB 109
Collodi, Carlo 1826-1890 .... NCLC 54
See also Lorenzini, Carlo
See also CLR 5
Colman, George
See Glassco, John
Colt, Winchester Remington
See Hubbard, L(afayette) Ron(ald)
Colter, Cyrus 1910- .... CLC 58
See also BW 1; CA 65-68; CANR 10; DLB 33
Colton, James
See Hansen, Joseph
Colum, Padraic 1881-1972 .... CLC 28
See also CA 73-76; 33-36R; CANR 35; CLR 36; MAICYA; MTCW; SATA 15
Colvin, James
See Moorcock, Michael (John)
Colwin, Laurie (E.) 1944-1992 CLC 5, 13, 23, 84
See also CA 89-92; 139; CANR 20, 46; DLBY 80; MTCW
Comfort, Alex(ander) 1920- .... CLC 7; DAM POP
See also CA 1-4R; CANR 1, 45
Comfort, Montgomery
See Campbell, (John) Ramsey
Compton-Burnett, I(vy) 1884(?)-1969 CLC 1, 3, 10, 15, 34; DAM NOV
See also CA 1-4R; 25-28R; CANR 4; DLB 36; MTCW
Comstock, Anthony 1844-1915 ...... TCLC 13
See also CA 110
Comte, Auguste 1798-1857 .... NCLC 54
Conan Doyle, Arthur
See Doyle, Arthur Conan

Conde, Maryse 1937- .... CLC 52, 92; DAM MULT
See also Boucolon, Maryse
See also BW 2
Condillac, Etienne Bonnot de 1714-1780 . LC 26
Condon, Richard (Thomas) 1915-1996 CLC 4, 6, 8, 10, 45, 100; DAM NOV
See also BEST 90:3; CA 1-4R; 151; CAAS 1; CANR 2, 23; INT CANR-23; MTCW
Confucius 551B.C.-479B.C. . CMLC 19; DA; DAB; DAC; DAM MST; WLCS
Congreve, William 1670-1729 LC 5, 21; DA; DAB; DAC; DAM DRAM, MST, POET; DC 2; WLC
See also CDBLB 1660-1789; DLB 39, 84
Connell, Evan S(helby), Jr. 1924- CLC 4, 6, 45; DAM NOV
See also AAYA 7; CA 1-4R; CAAS 2; CANR 2, 39; DLB 2; DLBY 81; MTCW
Connelly, Marc(us Cook) 1890-1980 .. CLC 7
See also CA 85-88; 102; CANR 30; DLB 7; DLBY 80; SATA-Obit 25
Connor, Ralph .... TCLC 31
See also Gordon, Charles William
See also DLB 92
Conrad, Joseph 1857-1924 TCLC 1, 6, 13, 25, 43, 57; DA; DAB; DAC; DAM MST, NOV; SSC 9; WLC
See also CA 104; 131; CANR 60; CDBLB 1890-1914; DLB 10, 34, 98, 156; MTCW; SATA 27
Conrad, Robert Arnold
See Hart, Moss
Conroy, Donald Pat(rick) 1945- CLC 30, 74; DAM NOV, POP
See also AAYA 8; AITN 1; CA 85-88; CANR 24, 53; DLB 6; MTCW
Constant (de Rebecque), (Henri) Benjamin 1767-1830 .... NCLC 6
See also DLB 119
Conybeare, Charles Augustus
See Eliot, T(homas) S(tearns)
Cook, Michael 1933- .... CLC 58
See also CA 93-96; DLB 53
Cook, Robin 1940- .... CLC 14; DAM POP
See also BEST 90:2; CA 108; 111; CANR 41; INT 111
Cook, Roy
See Silverberg, Robert
Cooke, Elizabeth 1948- .... CLC 55
See also CA 129
Cooke, John Esten 1830-1886 .... NCLC 5
See also DLB 3
Cooke, John Estes
See Baum, L(yman) Frank
Cooke, M. E.
See Creasey, John
Cooke, Margaret
See Creasey, John
Cook-Lynn, Elizabeth 1930- . CLC 93; DAM MULT
See also CA 133; DLB 175; NNAL
Cooney, Ray .... CLC 62
Cooper, Douglas 1960- .... CLC 86
Cooper, Henry St. John
See Creasey, John
Cooper, J(oan) California ...... CLC 56; DAM MULT
See also AAYA 12; BW 1; CA 125; CANR 55
Cooper, James Fenimore 1789-1851 NCLC 1, 27, 54
See also AAYA 22; CDALB 1640-1865; DLB 3; SATA 19
Coover, Robert (Lowell) 1932- CLC 3, 7, 15, 32, 46, 87; DAM NOV; SSC 15
See also CA 45-48; CANR 3, 37, 58; DLB 2;

DLBY 81; MTCW
Copeland, Stewart (Armstrong) 1952-CLC 26
Coppard, A(lfred) E(dgar) 1878-1957 TCLC 5; SSC 21
See also CA 114; DLB 162; YABC 1
Coppee, Francois 1842-1908 .... TCLC 25
Coppola, Francis Ford 1939- .... CLC 16
See also CA 77-80; CANR 40; DLB 44
Corbiere, Tristan 1845-1875 .... NCLC 43
Corcoran, Barbara 1911- .... CLC 17
See also AAYA 14; CA 21-24R; CAAS 2; CANR 11, 28, 48; DLB 52; JRDA; SAAS 20; SATA 3, 77
Cordelier, Maurice
See Giraudoux, (Hippolyte) Jean
Corelli, Marie 1855-1924 .... TCLC 51
See also Mackay, Mary
See also DLB 34, 156
Corman, Cid .... CLC 9
See also Corman, Sidney
See also CAAS 2; DLB 5
Corman, Sidney 1924-
See Corman, Cid
See also CA 85-88; CANR 44; DAM POET
Cormier, Robert (Edmund) 1925-CLC 12, 30; DA; DAB; DAC; DAM MST, NOV
See also AAYA 3, 19; CA 1-4R; CANR 5, 23; CDALB 1968-1988; CLR 12; DLB 52; INT CANR-23; JRDA; MAICYA; MTCW; SATA 10, 45, 83
Corn, Alfred (DeWitt III) 1943- .... CLC 33
See also CA 104; CAAS 25; CANR 44; DLB 120; DLBY 80
Corneille, Pierre 1606-1684 .... LC 28; DAB; DAM MST
Cornwell, David (John Moore) 1931-CLC 9, 15; DAM POP
See also le Carre, John
See also CA 5-8R; CANR 13, 33, 59; MTCW
Corso, (Nunzio) Gregory 1930- ... CLC 1, 11
See also CA 5-8R; CANR 41; DLB 5, 16; MTCW
Cortazar, Julio 1914-1984 CLC 2, 3, 5, 10, 13, 15, 33, 34, 92; DAM MULT, NOV; HLC; SSC 7
See also CA 21-24R; CANR 12, 32; DLB 113; HW; MTCW
CORTES, HERNAN 1484-1547 .... LC 31
Corwin, Cecil
See Kornbluth, C(yril) M.
Cosic, Dobrica 1921- .... CLC 14
See also CA 122; 138; DLB 181
Costain, Thomas B(ertram) 1885-1965 . CLC 30
See also CA 5-8R; 25-28R; DLB 9
Costantini, Humberto 1924(?)-1987 . CLC 49
See also CA 131; 122; HW
Costello, Elvis 1955- .... CLC 21
Cotes, Cecil V.
See Duncan, Sara Jeannette
Cotter, Joseph Seamon Sr. 1861-1949 TCLC 28; BLC; DAM MULT
See also BW 1; CA 124; DLB 50
Couch, Arthur Thomas Quiller
See Quiller-Couch, Arthur Thomas
Coulton, James
See Hansen, Joseph
Couperus, Louis (Marie Anne) 1863-1923 TCLC 15
See also CA 115
Coupland, Douglas 1961-CLC 85; DAC; DAM POP
See also CA 142; CANR 57
Court, Wesli
See Turco, Lewis (Putnam)
Courtenay, Bryce 1933- .... CLC 59
See also CA 138

Courtney, Robert
See Ellison, Harlan (Jay)

Cousteau, Jacques-Yves 1910-1997. **CLC 30**
See also CA 65-68; 159; CANR 15; MTCW; SATA 38

Cowan, Peter (Walkinshaw) 1914- .... **SSC 28**
See also CA 21-24R; CANR 9, 25, 50

Coward, Noel (Peirce) 1899-1973 **CLC 1, 9, 29, 51; DAM DRAM**
See also AITN 1; CA 17-18; 41-44R; CANR 35; CAP 2; CDBLB 1914-1945; DLB 10; MTCW

Cowley, Malcolm 1898-1989 .... **CLC 39**
See also CA 5-8R; 128; CANR 3, 55; DLB 4, 48; DLBY 81, 89; MTCW

Cowper, William 1731-1800. **NCLC 8; DAM POET**
See also DLB 104, 109

Cox, William Trevor 1928- ... **CLC 9, 14, 71; DAM NOV**
See also Trevor, William
See also CA 9-12R; CANR 4, 37, 55; DLB 14; INT CANR-37; MTCW

Coyne, P. J.
See Masters, Hilary

Cozzens, James Gould 1903-1978. **CLC 1, 4, 11, 92**
See also CA 9-12R; 81-84; CANR 19; CDALB 1941-1968; DLB 9; DLBD 2; DLBY 84; MTCW

Crabbe, George 1754-1832 .... **NCLC 26**
See also DLB 93

Craddock, Charles Egbert
See Murfree, Mary Noailles

Craig, A. A.
See Anderson, Poul (William)

Craik, Dinah Maria (Mulock) 1826-1887 **NCLC 38**
See also DLB 35, 163; MAICYA; SATA 34

Cram, Ralph Adams 1863-1942 ..... **TCLC 45**
See also CA 160

Crane, (Harold) Hart 1899-1932 **TCLC 2, 5; DA; DAB; DAC; DAM MST, POET; PC 3; WLC**
See also CA 104; 127; CDALB 1917-1929; DLB 4, 48; MTCW

Crane, R(onald) S(almon) 1886-1967 **CLC 27**
See also CA 85-88; DLB 63

Crane, Stephen (Townley) 1871-1900 **TCLC 11, 17, 32; DA; DAB; DAC; DAM MST, NOV, POET; SSC 7; WLC**
See also AAYA 21; CA 109; 140; CDALB 1865-1917; DLB 12, 54, 78; YABC 2

Crase, Douglas 1944- .... **CLC 58**
See also CA 106

Crashaw, Richard 1612(?)-1649 .... **LC 24**
See also DLB 126

Craven, Margaret 1901-1980. **CLC 17; DAC**
See also CA 103

Crawford, F(rancis) Marion 1854-1909 **TCLC 10**
See also CA 107; DLB 71

Crawford, Isabella Valancy 1850-1887 **NCLC 12**
See also DLB 92

Crayon, Geoffrey
See Irving, Washington

Creasey, John 1908-1973 .... **CLC 11**
See also CA 5-8R; 41-44R; CANR 8, 59; DLB 77; MTCW

Crebillon, Claude Prosper Jolyot de (fils) 1707-1777 .... **LC 28**

Credo
See Creasey, John

Credo, Alvaro J. de
See Prado (Calvo), Pedro

Creeley, Robert (White) 1926- **CLC 1, 2, 4, 8, 11, 15, 36, 78; DAM POET**
See also CA 1-4R; CAAS 10; CANR 23, 43; DLB 5, 16, 169); MTCW

Crews, Harry (Eugene) 1935- **CLC 6, 23, 49**
See also AITN 1; CA 25-28R; CANR 20, 57; DLB 6, 143; MTCW

Crichton, (John) Michael 1942- **CLC 2, 6, 54, 90; DAM NOV, POP**
See also AAYA 10; AITN 2; CA 25-28R; CANR 13, 40, 54; DLBY 81; INT CANR-13; JRDA; MTCW; SATA 9, 88

Crispin, Edmund .... **CLC 22**
See also Montgomery, (Robert) Bruce
See also DLB 87

Cristofer, Michael 1945(?)- ... **CLC 28; DAM DRAM**
See also CA 110; 152; DLB 7

Croce, Benedetto 1866-1952 .... **TCLC 37**
See also CA 120; 155

Crockett, David 1786-1836 .... **NCLC 8**
See also DLB 3, 11

Crockett, Davy
See Crockett, David

Crofts, Freeman Wills 1879-1957 .. **TCLC 55**
See also CA 115; DLB 77

Croker, John Wilson 1780-1857 .... **NCLC 10**
See also DLB 110

Crommelynck, Fernand 1885-1970 .. **CLC 75**
See also CA 89-92

Cronin, A(rchibald) J(oseph) 1896-1981 **CLC 32**
See also CA 1-4R; 102; CANR 5; SATA 47; SATA-Obit 25

Cross, Amanda
See Heilbrun, Carolyn G(old)

Crothers, Rachel 1878(?)-1958 ...... **TCLC 19**
See also CA 113; DLB 7

Croves, Hal
See Traven, B.

Crow Dog, Mary (Ellen) (?)- .... **CLC 93**
See also Brave Bird, Mary
See also CA 154

Crowfield, Christopher
See Stowe, Harriet (Elizabeth) Beecher

Crowley, Aleister .... **TCLC 7**
See also Crowley, Edward Alexander

Crowley, Edward Alexander 1875-1947
See Crowley, Aleister
See also CA 104

Crowley, John 1942- .... **CLC 57**
See also CA 61-64; CANR 43; DLBY 82; SATA 65

Crud
See Crumb, R(obert)

Crumarums
See Crumb, R(obert)

Crumb, R(obert) 1943- .... **CLC 17**
See also CA 106

Crumbum
See Crumb, R(obert)

Crumski
See Crumb, R(obert)

Crum the Bum
See Crumb, R(obert)

Crunk
See Crumb, R(obert)

Crustt
See Crumb, R(obert)

Cryer, Gretchen (Kiger) 1935- .... **CLC 21**
See also CA 114; 123

Csath, Geza 1887-1919 .... **TCLC 13**
See also CA 111

Cudlip, David 1933- .... **CLC 34**

Cullen, Countee 1903-1946 **TCLC 4, 37; BLC; DA; DAC; DAM MST, MULT, POET; PC 20; WLCS**
See also BW 1; CA 108; 124; CDALB 1917-1929; DLB 4, 48, 51; MTCW; SATA 18

Cum, R.
See Crumb, R(obert)

Cummings, Bruce F(rederick) 1889-1919
See Barbellion, W. N. P.
See also CA 123

Cummings, E(dward) E(stlin) 1894-1962 **CLC 1, 3, 8, 12, 15, 68; DA; DAB; DAC; DAM MST, POET; PC 5; WLC 2**
See also CA 73-76; CANR 31; CDALB 1929-1941; DLB 4, 48; MTCW

Cunha, Euclides (Rodrigues Pimenta) da 1866-1909 .... **TCLC 24**
See also CA 123

Cunningham, E. V.
See Fast, Howard (Melvin)

Cunningham, J(ames) V(incent) 1911-1985 **CLC 3, 31**
See also CA 1-4R; 115; CANR 1; DLB 5

Cunningham, Julia (Woolfolk) 1916- **CLC 12**
See also CA 9-12R; CANR 4, 19, 36; JRDA; MAICYA; SAAS 2; SATA 1, 26

Cunningham, Michael 1952- .... **CLC 34**
See also CA 136

Cunninghame Graham, R(obert) B(ontine) 1852-1936 .... **TCLC 19**
See also Graham, R(obert) B(ontine) Cunninghame
See also CA 119; DLB 98

Currie, Ellen 19(?)- .... **CLC 44**

Curtin, Philip
See Lowndes, Marie Adelaide (Belloc)

Curtis, Price
See Ellison, Harlan (Jay)

Cutrate, Joe
See Spiegelman, Art

Cynewulf c. 770-c. 840 .... **CMLC 23**

Czaczkes, Shmuel Yosef
See Agnon, S(hmuel) Y(osef Halevi)

Dabrowska, Maria (Szumska) 1889-1965 **CLC 15**
See also CA 106

Dabydeen, David 1955- .... **CLC 34**
See also BW 1; CA 125; CANR 56

Dacey, Philip 1939- .... **CLC 51**
See also CA 37-40R; CAAS 17; CANR 14, 32; DLB 105

Dagerman, Stig (Halvard) 1923-1954 **TCLC 17**
See also CA 117; 155

Dahl, Roald 1916-1990 **CLC 1, 6, 18, 79; DAB; DAC; DAM MST, NOV, POP**
See also AAYA 15; CA 1-4R; 133; CANR 6, 32, 37, 62; CLR 1, 7, 41; DLB 139; JRDA; MAICYA; MTCW; SATA 1, 26, 73; SATA-Obit 65

Dahlberg, Edward 1900-1977 .. **CLC 1, 7, 14**
See also CA 9-12R; 69-72; CANR 31, 62; DLB 48; MTCW

Daitch, Susan 1954- .... **CLC 103**
See also CA 161

Dale, Colin .... **TCLC 18**
See also Lawrence, T(homas) E(dward)

Dale, George E.
See Asimov, Isaac

Daly, Elizabeth 1878-1967 .... **CLC 52**
See also CA 23-24; 25-28R; CANR 60; CAP 2

Daly, Maureen 1921- .... **CLC 17**
See also AAYA 5; CANR 37; JRDA; MAICYA; SAAS 1; SATA 2

Damas, Leon-Gontran 1912-1978 ... **CLC 84**
See also BW 1; CA 125; 73-76

Dana, Richard Henry Sr. 1787-1879 **NCLC 53**

Daniel, Samuel 1562(?)-1619 .... **LC 24**
See also DLB 62

Daniels, Brett
See Adler, Renata

Dannay, Frederic 1905-1982 . **CLC 11; DAM POP**
See also Queen, Ellery
See also CA 1-4R; 107; CANR 1, 39; DLB 137; MTCW

D'Annunzio, Gabriele 1863-1938 **TCLC 6, 40**
See also CA 104; 155

Danois, N. le
See Gourmont, Remy (-Marie-Charles) de

d'Antibes, Germain
See Simenon, Georges (Jacques Christian)

Danticat, Edwidge 1969- .... **CLC 94**
See also CA 152

Danvers, Dennis 1947- .... **CLC 70**

Danziger, Paula 1944- .... **CLC 21**
See also AAYA 4; CA 112; 115; CANR 37; CLR 20; JRDA; MAICYA; SATA 36, 63; SATA-Brief 30

Da Ponte, Lorenzo 1749-1838 .... **NCLC 50**

Dario, Ruben 1867-1916 .... **TCLC 4; DAM MULT; HLC; PC 15**
See also CA 131; HW; MTCW

Darley, George 1795-1846 .... **NCLC 2**
See also DLB 96

Darwin, Charles 1809-1882 .... **NCLC 57**
See also DLB 57, 166

Daryush, Elizabeth 1887-1977 ..... **CLC 6, 19**
See also CA 49-52; CANR 3; DLB 20

Dashwood, Edmee Elizabeth Monica de la Pasture 1890-1943
See Delafield, E. M.
See also CA 119; 154

Daudet, (Louis Marie) Alphonse 1840-1897 **NCLC 1**
See also DLB 123

Daumal, Rene 1908-1944 .... **TCLC 14**
See also CA 114

Davenport, Guy (Mattison, Jr.) 1927- **CLC 6, 14, 38; SSC 16**
See also CA 33-36R; CANR 23; DLB 130

Davidson, Avram 1923-
See Queen, Ellery
See also CA 101; CANR 26; DLB 8

Davidson, Donald (Grady) 1893-1968 **CLC 2, 13, 19**
See also CA 5-8R; 25-28R; CANR 4; DLB 45

Davidson, Hugh
See Hamilton, Edmond

Davidson, John 1857-1909 .... **TCLC 24**
See also CA 118; DLB 19

Davidson, Sara 1943- .... **CLC 9**
See also CA 81-84; CANR 44

Davie, Donald (Alfred) 1922-1995 **CLC 5, 8, 10, 31**
See also CA 1-4R; 149; CAAS 3; CANR 1, 44; DLB 27; MTCW

Davies, Ray(mond Douglas) 1944- .. **CLC 21**
See also CA 116; 146

Davies, Rhys 1903-1978 .... **CLC 23**
See also CA 9-12R; 81-84; CANR 4; DLB 139

Davies, (William) Robertson 1913-1995 **C L C 2, 7, 13, 25, 42, 75, 91; DA; DAB; DAC; DAM MST, NOV, POP; WLC**
See also BEST 89:2; CA 33-36R; 150; CANR 17, 42; DLB 68; INT CANR-17; MTCW

Davies, W(illiam) H(enry) 1871-1940 **TCLC 5**
See also CA 104; DLB 19, 174

Davies, Walter C.
See Kornbluth, C(yril) M.

Davis, Angela (Yvonne) 1944- **CLC 77; DAM MULT**
See also BW 2; CA 57-60; CANR 10

Davis, B. Lynch
See Bioy Casares, Adolfo; Borges, Jorge Luis

Davis, Gordon
See Hunt, E(verette) Howard, (Jr.)

Davis, Harold Lenoir 1896-1960 ..... **CLC 49**
See also CA 89-92; DLB 9

Davis, Rebecca (Blaine) Harding 1831-1910 **TCLC 6**
See also CA 104; DLB 74

Davis, Richard Harding 1864-1916 **TCLC 24**
See also CA 114; DLB 12, 23, 78, 79; DLBD 13

Davison, Frank Dalby 1893-1970 ..... **CLC 15**
See also CA 116

Davison, Lawrence H.
See Lawrence, D(avid) H(erbert Richards)

Davison, Peter (Hubert) 1928- .... **CLC 28**
See also CA 9-12R; CAAS 4; CANR 3, 43; DLB 5

Davys, Mary 1674-1732 .... **LC 1**
See also DLB 39

Dawson, Fielding 1930- .... **CLC 6**
See also CA 85-88; DLB 130

Dawson, Peter
See Faust, Frederick (Schiller)

Day, Clarence (Shepard, Jr.) 1874-1935 **TCLC 25**
See also CA 108; DLB 11

Day, Thomas 1748-1789 .... **LC 1**
See also DLB 39; YABC 1

Day Lewis, C(ecil) 1904-1972 .. **CLC 1, 6, 10; DAM POET; PC 11**
See also Blake, Nicholas
See also CA 13-16; 33-36R; CANR 34; CAP 1; DLB 15, 20; MTCW

Dazai, Osamu .... **TCLC 11**
See also Tsushima, Shuji
See also DLB 182

de Andrade, Carlos Drummond
See Drummond de Andrade, Carlos

Deane, Norman
See Creasey, John

de Beauvoir, Simone (Lucie Ernestine Marie Bertrand)
See Beauvoir, Simone (Lucie Ernestine Marie Bertrand) de

de Beer, P.
See Bosman, Herman Charles

de Brissac, Malcolm
See Dickinson, Peter (Malcolm)

de Chardin, Pierre Teilhard
See Teilhard de Chardin, (Marie Joseph) Pierre

Dee, John 1527-1608 .... **LC 20**

Deer, Sandra 1940- .... **CLC 45**

De Ferrari, Gabriella 1941- .... **CLC 65**
See also CA 146

Defoe, Daniel 1660(?)-1731 **LC 1; DA; DAB; DAC; DAM MST, NOV; WLC**
See also CDBLB 1660-1789; DLB 39, 95, 101; JRDA; MAICYA; SATA 22

de Gourmont, Remy(-Marie-Charles)
See Gourmont, Remy (-Marie-Charles) de

de Hartog, Jan 1914- .... **CLC 19**
See also CA 1-4R; CANR 1

de Hostos, E. M.
See Hostos (y Bonilla), Eugenio Maria de

de Hostos, Eugenio M.
See Hostos (y Bonilla), Eugenio Maria de

Deighton, Len .... **CLC 4, 7, 22, 46**
See also Deighton, Leonard Cyril
See also AAYA 6; BEST 89:2; CDBLB 1960 to Present; DLB 87

Deighton, Leonard Cyril 1929-
See Deighton, Len
See also CA 9-12R; CANR 19, 33; DAM NOV, POP; MTCW

Dekker, Thomas 1572(?)-1632 . **LC 22; DAM DRAM**
See also CDBLB Before 1660; DLB 62, 172

Delafield, E. M. 1890-1943 .... **TCLC 61**
See also Dashwood, Edmee Elizabeth Monica de la Pasture

See also DLB 34

de la Mare, Walter (John) 1873-1956 **TCLC 4, 53; DAB; DAC; DAM MST, POET; SSC 14; WLC**
See also CDBLB 1914-1945; CLR 23; DLB 162; SATA 16

Delaney, Franey
See O'Hara, John (Henry)

Delaney, Shelagh 1939- **CLC 29; DAM DRAM**
See also CA 17-20R; CANR 30; CDBLB 1960 to Present; DLB 13; MTCW

Delany, Mary (Granville Pendarves) 1700-1788 **LC 12**

Delany, Samuel R(ay, Jr.) 1942- . **CLC 8, 14, 38; BLC; DAM MULT**
See also BW 2; CA 81-84; CANR 27, 43; DLB 8, 33; MTCW

De La Ramee, (Marie) Louise 1839-1908
See Ouida
See also SATA 20

de la Roche, Mazo 1879-1961 .... **CLC 14**
See also CA 85-88; CANR 30; DLB 68; SATA 64

De La Salle, Innocent
See Hartmann, Sadakichi

Delbanco, Nicholas (Franklin) 1942- **CLC 6, 13**
See also CA 17-20R; CAAS 2; CANR 29, 55; DLB 6

del Castillo, Michel 1933- .... **CLC 38**
See also CA 109

Deledda, Grazia (Cosima) 1875(?)-1936 **TCLC 23**
See also CA 123

Delibes, Miguel .... **CLC 8, 18**
See also Delibes Setien, Miguel

Delibes Setien, Miguel 1920-
See Delibes, Miguel
See also CA 45-48; CANR 1, 32; HW; MTCW

DeLillo, Don 1936- **CLC 8, 10, 13, 27, 39, 54, 76; DAM NOV, POP**
See also BEST 89:1; CA 81-84; CANR 21; DLB 6, 173; MTCW

de Lisser, H. G.
See De Lisser, H(erbert) G(eorge)
See also DLB 117

De Lisser, H(erbert) G(eorge) 1878-1944 **TCLC 12**
See also de Lisser, H. G.
See also BW 2; CA 109; 152

Deloria, Vine (Victor), Jr. 1933- ...... **CLC 21; DAM MULT**
See also CA 53-56; CANR 5, 20, 48; DLB 175; MTCW; NNAL; SATA 21

Del Vecchio, John M(ichael) 1947- ... **CLC 29**
See also CA 110; DLBD 9

de Man, Paul (Adolph Michel) 1919-1983 **CLC 55**
See also CA 128; 111; CANR 61; DLB 67; MTCW

De Marinis, Rick 1934- .... **CLC 54**
See also CA 57-60; CAAS 24; CANR 9, 25, 50

Dembry, R. Emmet
See Murfree, Mary Noailles

Demby, William 1922- **CLC 53; BLC; DAM MULT**
See also BW 1; CA 81-84; DLB 33

de Menton, Francisco
See Chin, Frank (Chew, Jr.)

Demijohn, Thom
See Disch, Thomas M(ichael)

de Montherlant, Henry (Milon)
See Montherlant, Henry (Milon) de

Demosthenes 384B.C.-322B.C. .... **CMLC 13**
See also DLB 176

de Natale, Francine
See Malzberg, Barry N(athaniel)

Denby, Edwin (Orr) 1903-1983 .... **CLC 48**
See also CA 138; 110

Denis, Julio
See Cortazar, Julio

Denmark, Harrison
See Zelazny, Roger (Joseph)

Dennis, John 1658-1734 .... **LC 11**
See also DLB 101

Dennis, Nigel (Forbes) 1912-1989 .... **CLC 8**
See also CA 25-28R; 129; DLB 13, 15; MTCW

Dent, Lester 1904(?)-1959 .... **TCLC 72**
See also CA 112; 161

De Palma, Brian (Russell) 1940- ...... **CLC 20**
See also CA 109

De Quincey, Thomas 1785-1859 ...... **NCLC 4**
See also CDBLB 1789-1832; DLB 110; 144

Deren, Eleanora 1908(?)-1961
See Deren, Maya
See also CA 111

Deren, Maya 1917-1961 .... **CLC 16, 102**
See also Deren, Eleanora

Derleth, August (William) 1909-1971 **CLC 31**
See also CA 1-4R; 29-32R; CANR 4; DLB 9; SATA 5

Der Nister 1884-1950 .... **TCLC 56**

de Routisie, Albert
See Aragon, Louis

Derrida, Jacques 1930- .... **CLC 24, 87**
See also CA 124; 127

Derry Down Derry
See Lear, Edward

Dersonnes, Jacques
See Simenon, Georges (Jacques Christian)

Desai, Anita 1937- **CLC 19, 37, 97; DAB; DAM NOV**
See also CA 81-84; CANR 33, 53; MTCW; SATA 63

de Saint-Luc, Jean
See Glassco, John

de Saint Roman, Arnaud
See Aragon, Louis

Descartes, Rene 1596-1650 .... **LC 20, 35**

De Sica, Vittorio 1901(?)-1974 .... **CLC 20**
See also CA 117

Desnos, Robert 1900-1945 .... **TCLC 22**
See also CA 121; 151

Destouches, Louis-Ferdinand 1894-1961 **CLC 9, 15**
See Celine, Louis-Ferdinand
See also CA 85-88; CANR 28; MTCW

de Tolignac, Gaston
See Griffith, D(avid Lewelyn) W(ark)

Deutsch, Babette 1895-1982 .... **CLC 18**
See also CA 1-4R; 108; CANR 4; DLB 45; SATA 1; SATA-Obit 33

Devenant, William 1606-1649 .... **LC 13**

Devkota, Laxmiprasad 1909-1959 . **TCLC 23**
See also CA 123

De Voto, Bernard (Augustine) 1897-1955 **TCLC 29**
See also CA 113; 160; DLB 9

De Vries, Peter 1910-1993 **CLC 1, 2, 3, 7, 10, 28, 46; DAM NOV**
See also CA 17-20R; 142; CANR 41; DLB 6; DLBY 82; MTCW

Dexter, John
See Bradley, Marion Zimmer

Dexter, Martin
See Faust, Frederick (Schiller)

Dexter, Pete 1943- .. **CLC 34, 55; DAM POP**
See also BEST 89:2; CA 127; 131; INT 131; MTCW

Diamano, Silmang
See Senghor, Leopold Sedar

Diamond, Neil 1941- .... **CLC 30**
See also CA 108

Diaz del Castillo, Bernal 1496-1584 ... **LC 31**

di Bassetto, Corno
See Shaw, George Bernard

Dick, Philip K(indred) 1928-1982 **CLC 10, 30, 72; DAM NOV, POP**
See also CA 49-52; 106; CANR 2, 16; DLB 8; MTCW

Dickens, Charles (John Huffam) 1812-1870 **NCLC 3, 8, 18, 26, 37, 50; DA; DAB; DAC; DAM MST, NOV; SSC 17; WLC**
See also CDBLB 1832-1890; DLB 21, 55, 70, 159, 166; JRDA; MAICYA; SATA 15

Dickey, James (Lafayette) 1923-1997 **CLC 1, 2, 4, 7, 10, 15, 47; DAM NOV, POET, POP**
See also AITN 1, 2; CA 9-12R; 156; CABS 2; CANR 10, 48, 61; CDALB 1968-1988; DLB 5; DLBD 7; DLBY 82, 93, 96; INT CANR-10; MTCW

Dickey, William 1928-1994 .... **CLC 3, 28**
See also CA 9-12R; 145; CANR 24; DLB 5

Dickinson, Charles 1951- .... **CLC 49**
See also CA 128

Dickinson, Emily (Elizabeth) 1830-1886 **NCLC 21; DA; DAB; DAC; DAM MST, POET; PC 1; WLC**
See also AAYA 22; CDALB 1865-1917; DLB 1; SATA 29

Dickinson, Peter (Malcolm) 1927- **CLC 12, 35**
See also AAYA 9; CA 41-44R; CANR 31, 58; CLR 29; DLB 87, 161; JRDA; MAICYA; SATA 5, 62, 95

Dickson, Carr
See Carr, John Dickson

Dickson, Carter
See Carr, John Dickson

Diderot, Denis 1713-1784 .... **LC 26**

Didion, Joan 1934- **CLC 1, 3, 8, 14, 32; DAM NOV**
See also AITN 1; CA 5-8R; CANR 14, 52; CDALB 1968-1988; DLB 2, 173; DLBY 81, 86; MTCW

Dietrich, Robert
See Hunt, E(verette) Howard, (Jr.)

Dillard, Annie 1945- . **CLC 9, 60; DAM NOV**
See also AAYA 6; CA 49-52; CANR 3, 43, 62; DLBY 80; MTCW; SATA 10

Dillard, R(ichard) H(enry) W(ilde) 1937- **CLC 5**
See also CA 21-24R; CAAS 7; CANR 10; DLB 5

Dillon, Eilis 1920-1994 .... **CLC 17**
See also CA 9-12R; 147; CAAS 3; CANR 4, 38; CLR 26; MAICYA; SATA 2, 74; SATA-Obit 83

Dimont, Penelope
See Mortimer, Penelope (Ruth)

Dinesen, Isak .... **CLC 10, 29, 95; SSC 7**
See also Blixen, Karen (Christentze Dinesen)

Ding Ling .... **CLC 68**
See also Chiang Pin-chin

Disch, Thomas M(ichael) 1940- ... **CLC 7, 36**
See also AAYA 17; CA 21-24R; CAAS 4; CANR 17, 36, 54; CLR 18; DLB 8; MAICYA; MTCW; SAAS 15; SATA 92

Disch, Tom
See Disch, Thomas M(ichael)

d'Isly, Georges
See Simenon, Georges (Jacques Christian)

Disraeli, Benjamin 1804-1881 .... **NCLC 2, 39**
See also DLB 21, 55

Ditcum, Steve
See Crumb, R(obert)

Dixon, Paige
See Corcoran, Barbara

Dixon, Stephen 1936- .... **CLC 52; SSC 16**
See also CA 89-92; CANR 17, 40, 54; DLB 130

Doak, Annie
See Dillard, Annie

Dobell, Sydney Thompson 1824-1874 **NCLC 43**
See also DLB 32

Doblin, Alfred .... **TCLC 13**
See also Doeblin, Alfred

Dobrolyubov, Nikolai Alexandrovich 1836-1861 .... **NCLC 5**

Dobyns, Stephen 1941- .... **CLC 37**
See also CA 45-48; CANR 2, 18

Doctorow, E(dgar) L(aurence) 1931- **CLC 6, 11, 15, 18, 37, 44, 65; DAM NOV, POP**
See also AAYA 22; AITN 2; BEST 89:3; CA 45-48; CANR 2, 33, 51; CDALB 1968-1988; DLB 2, 28, 173; DLBY 80; MTCW

Dodgson, Charles Lutwidge 1832-1898
See Carroll, Lewis
See also CLR 2; DA; DAB; DAC; DAM MST, NOV, POET; MAICYA; YABC 2

Dodson, Owen (Vincent) 1914-1983 **CLC 79; BLC; DAM MULT**
See also BW 1; CA 65-68; 110; CANR 24; DLB 76

Doeblin, Alfred 1878-1957 .... **TCLC 13**
See also Doblin, Alfred
See also CA 110; 141; DLB 66

Doerr, Harriet 1910- .... **CLC 34**
See also CA 117; 122; CANR 47; INT 122

Domecq, H(onorio) Bustos
See Bioy Casares, Adolfo; Borges, Jorge Luis

Domini, Rey
See Lorde, Audre (Geraldine)

Dominique
See Proust, (Valentin-Louis-George-Eugene-) Marcel

Don, A
See Stephen, Leslie

Donaldson, Stephen R. 1947- **CLC 46; DAM POP**
See also CA 89-92; CANR 13, 55; INT CANR-13

Donleavy, J(ames) P(atrick) 1926- **CLC 1, 4, 6, 10, 45**
See also AITN 2; CA 9-12R; CANR 24, 49, 62; DLB 6, 173; INT CANR-24; MTCW

Donne, John 1572-1631 **LC 10, 24; DA; DAB; DAC; DAM MST, POET; PC 1**
See also CDBLB Before 1660; DLB 121, 151

Donnell, David 1939(?)- .... **CLC 34**

Donoghue, P. S.
See Hunt, E(verette) Howard, (Jr.)

Donoso (Yanez), Jose 1924-1996 **CLC 4, 8, 11, 32, 99; DAM MULT; HLC**
See also CA 81-84; 155; CANR 32; DLB 113; HW; MTCW

Donovan, John 1928-1992 .... **CLC 35**
See also AAYA 20; CA 97-100; 137; CLR 3; MAICYA; SATA 72; SATA-Brief 29

Don Roberto
See Cunninghame Graham, R(obert) B(ontine)

Doolittle, Hilda 1886-1961 **CLC 3, 8, 14, 31, 34, 73; DA; DAC; DAM MST, POET; PC 5; WLC**
See also H. D.
See also CA 97-100; CANR 35; DLB 4, 45; MTCW

Dorfman, Ariel 1942- ...... **CLC 48, 77; DAM MULT; HLC**
See also CA 124; 130; HW; INT 130

Dorn, Edward (Merton) 1929- ... **CLC 10, 18**
See also CA 93-96; CANR 42; DLB 5; INT 93-96

Dorsan, Luc
See Simenon, Georges (Jacques Christian)

Dorsange, Jean
See Simenon, Georges (Jacques Christian)

Dos Passos, John (Roderigo) 1896-1970 **C L C**

1, 4, 8, 11, 15, 25, 34, 82; DA; DAB; DAC; DAM MST, NOV; WLC
See also CA 1-4R; 29-32R; CANR 3; CDALB 1929-1941; DLB 4, 9; DLBD 1, 15; DLBY 96; MTCW

Dossage, Jean
See Simenon, Georges (Jacques Christian)

Dostoevsky, Fedor Mikhailovich 1821-1881 NCLC 2, 7, 21, 33, 43; DA; DAB; DAC; DAM MST, NOV; SSC 2; WLC

Doughty, Charles M(ontagu) 1843-1926 .... TCLC 27
See also CA 115; DLB 19, 57, 174

Douglas, Ellen .... CLC 73
See also Haxton, Josephine Ayres; Williamson, Ellen Douglas

Douglas, Gavin 1475(?)-1522 .... LC 20

Douglas, Keith (Castellain) 1920-1944 TCLC 40
See also CA 160; DLB 27

Douglas, Leonard
See Bradbury, Ray (Douglas)

Douglas, Michael
See Crichton, (John) Michael

Douglas, Norman 1868-1952 .... TCLC 68

Douglass, Frederick 1817(?)-1895 NCLC 7, 55; BLC; DA; DAC; DAM MST, MULT; WLC
See also CDALB 1640-1865; DLB 1, 43, 50, 79; SATA 29

Dourado, (Waldomiro Freitas) Autran 1926- .... CLC 23, 60
See also CA 25-28R; CANR 34

Dourado, Waldomiro Autran
See Dourado, (Waldomiro Freitas) Autran

Dove, Rita (Frances) 1952- CLC 50, 81; DAM MULT, POET; PC 6
See also BW 2; CA 109; CAAS 19; CANR 27, 42; DLB 120

Dowell, Coleman 1925-1985 .... CLC 60
See also CA 25-28R; 117; CANR 10; DLB 130

Dowson, Ernest (Christopher) 1867-1900 TCLC 4
See also CA 105; 150; DLB 19, 135

Doyle, A. Conan
See Doyle, Arthur Conan

Doyle, Arthur Conan 1859-1930 TCLC 7; DA; DAB; DAC; DAM MST, NOV; SSC 12; WLC
See also AAYA 14; CA 104; 122; CDBLB 1890-1914; DLB 18, 70, 156, 178; MTCW; SATA 24

Doyle, Conan
See Doyle, Arthur Conan

Doyle, John
See Graves, Robert (von Ranke)

Doyle, Roddy 1958(?)- .... CLC 81
See also AAYA 14; CA 143

Doyle, Sir A. Conan
See Doyle, Arthur Conan

Doyle, Sir Arthur Conan
See Doyle, Arthur Conan

Dr. A
See Asimov, Isaac; Silverstein, Alvin

Drabble, Margaret 1939- CLC 2, 3, 5, 8, 10, 22, 53; DAB; DAC; DAM MST, NOV, POP
See also CA 13-16R; CANR 18, 35; CDBLB 1960 to Present; DLB 14, 155; MTCW; SATA 48

Drapier, M. B.
See Swift, Jonathan

Drayham, James
See Mencken, H(enry) L(ouis)

Drayton, Michael 1563-1631 .... LC 8

Dreadstone, Carl
See Campbell, (John) Ramsey

Dreiser, Theodore (Herman Albert) 1871-1945 TCLC 10, 18, 35; DA; DAC; DAM MST, NOV; WLC
See also CA 106; 132; CDALB 1865-1917; DLB 9, 12, 102, 137; DLBD 1; MTCW

Drexler, Rosalyn 1926- .... CLC 2, 6
See also CA 81-84

Dreyer, Carl Theodor 1889-1968 ..... CLC 16
See also CA 116

Drieu la Rochelle, Pierre(-Eugene) 1893-1945 TCLC 21
See also CA 117; DLB 72

Drinkwater, John 1882-1937 .... TCLC 57
See also CA 109; 149; DLB 10, 19, 149

Drop Shot
See Cable, George Washington

Droste-Hulshoff, Annette Freiin von 1797-1848 NCLC 3
See also DLB 133

Drummond, Walter
See Silverberg, Robert

Drummond, William Henry 1854-1907 TCLC 25
See also CA 160; DLB 92

Drummond de Andrade, Carlos 1902-1987 CLC 18
See also Andrade, Carlos Drummond de
See also CA 132; 123

Drury, Allen (Stuart) 1918- .... CLC 37
See also CA 57-60; CANR 18, 52; INT CANR-18

Dryden, John 1631-1700 LC 3, 21; DA; DAB; DAC; DAM DRAM, MST, POET; DC 3; WLC
See also CDBLB 1660-1789; DLB 80, 101, 131

Duberman, Martin 1930- .... CLC 8
See also CA 1-4R; CANR 2

Dubie, Norman (Evans) 1945- .... CLC 36
See also CA 69-72; CANR 12; DLB 120

Du Bois, W(illiam) E(dward) B(urghardt) 1868-1963 CLC 1, 2, 13, 64, 96; BLC; DA; DAC; DAM MST, MULT, NOV; WLC
See also BW 1; CA 85-88; CANR 34; CDALB 1865-1917; DLB 47, 50, 91; MTCW; SATA 42

Dubus, Andre 1936- CLC 13, 36, 97; SSC 15
See also CA 21-24R; CANR 17; DLB 130; INT CANR-17

Duca Minimo
See D'Annunzio, Gabriele

Ducharme, Rejean 1941- .... CLC 74
See also DLB 60

Duclos, Charles Pinot 1704-1772 .... LC 1

Dudek, Louis 1918- .... CLC 11, 19
See also CA 45-48; CAAS 14; CANR 1; DLB 88

Duerrenmatt, Friedrich 1921-1990 CLC 1, 4, 8, 11, 15, 43, 102; DAM DRAM
See also CA 17-20R; CANR 33; DLB 69, 124; MTCW

Duffy, Bruce (?)- .... CLC 50

Duffy, Maureen 1933- .... CLC 37
See also CA 25-28R; CANR 33; DLB 14; MTCW

Dugan, Alan 1923- .... CLC 2, 6
See also CA 81-84; DLB 5

du Gard, Roger Martin
See Martin du Gard, Roger

Duhamel, Georges 1884-1966 .... CLC 8
See also CA 81-84; 25-28R; CANR 35; DLB 65; MTCW

Dujardin, Edouard (Emile Louis) 1861-1949 TCLC 13
See also CA 109; DLB 123

Dulles, John Foster 1888-1959 .... TCLC 72
See also CA 115; 149

Dumas, Alexandre (Davy de la Pailleterie) 1802-1870.. NCLC 11; DA; DAB; DAC; DAM MST, NOV; WLC
See also DLB 119; SATA 18

Dumas, Alexandre 1824-1895 NCLC 9; DC 1
See also AAYA 22

Dumas, Claudine
See Malzberg, Barry N(athaniel)

Dumas, Henry L. 1934-1968 .... CLC 6, 62
See also BW 1; CA 85-88; DLB 41

du Maurier, Daphne 1907-1989 CLC 6, 11, 59; DAB; DAC; DAM MST, POP; SSC 18
See also CA 5-8R; 128; CANR 6, 55; MTCW; SATA 27; SATA-Obit 60

Dunbar, Paul Laurence 1872-1906 TCLC 2, 12; BLC; DA; DAC; DAM MST, MULT, POET; PC 5; SSC 8; WLC
See also BW 1; CA 104; 124; CDALB 1865-1917; DLB 50, 54, 78; SATA 34

Dunbar, William 1460(?)-1530(?) .... LC 20
See also DLB 132, 146

Duncan, Dora Angela
See Duncan, Isadora

Duncan, Isadora 1877(?)-1927 .... TCLC 68
See also CA 118; 149

Duncan, Lois 1934- .... CLC 26
See also AAYA 4; CA 1-4R; CANR 2, 23, 36; CLR 29; JRDA; MAICYA; SAAS 2; SATA 1, 36, 75

Duncan, Robert (Edward) 1919-1988 CLC 1, 2, 4, 7, 15, 41, 55; DAM POET; PC 2
See also CA 9-12R; 124; CANR 28, 62; DLB 5, 16; MTCW

Duncan, Sara Jeannette 1861-1922 TCLC 60
See also CA 157; DLB 92

Dunlap, William 1766-1839 .... NCLC 2
See also DLB 30, 37, 59

Dunn, Douglas (Eaglesham) 1942- CLC 6, 40
See also CA 45-48; CANR 2, 33; DLB 40; MTCW

Dunn, Katherine (Karen) 1945- .... CLC 71
See also CA 33-36R

Dunn, Stephen 1939- .... CLC 36
See also CA 33-36R; CANR 12, 48, 53; DLB 105

Dunne, Finley Peter 1867-1936 ...... TCLC 28
See also CA 108; DLB 11, 23

Dunne, John Gregory 1932- .... CLC 28
See also CA 25-28R; CANR 14, 50; DLBY 80

Dunsany, Edward John Moreton Drax Plunkett 1878-1957
See Dunsany, Lord
See also CA 104; 148; DLB 10

Dunsany, Lord .... TCLC 2, 59
See also Dunsany, Edward John Moreton Drax Plunkett
See also DLB 77, 153, 156

du Perry, Jean
See Simenon, Georges (Jacques Christian)

Durang, Christopher (Ferdinand) 1949- CLC 27, 38
See also CA 105; CANR 50

Duras, Marguerite 1914-1996 CLC 3, 6, 11, 20, 34, 40, 68, 100
See also CA 25-28R; 151; CANR 50; DLB 83; MTCW

Durban, (Rosa) Pam 1947- .... CLC 39
See also CA 123

Durcan, Paul 1944- CLC 43, 70; DAM POET
See also CA 134

Durkheim, Emile 1858-1917 .... TCLC 55

Durrell, Lawrence (George) 1912-1990 CLC 1, 4, 6, 8, 13, 27, 41; DAM NOV
See also CA 9-12R; 132; CANR 40; CDBLB 1945-1960; DLB 15, 27; DLBY 90; MTCW

Durrenmatt, Friedrich
See Duerrenmatt, Friedrich

Dutt, Toru 1856-1877 .... NCLC 29

Dwight, Timothy 1752-1817 .... NCLC 13

See also DLB 37
Dworkin, Andrea 1946- .... **CLC 43**
　See also CA 77-80; CAAS 21; CANR 16, 39; INT CANR-16; MTCW
Dwyer, Deanna
　See Koontz, Dean R(ay)
Dwyer, K. R.
　See Koontz, Dean R(ay)
Dye, Richard
　See De Voto, Bernard (Augustine)
Dylan, Bob 1941- ...... **CLC 3, 4, 6, 12, 77**
　See also CA 41-44R; DLB 16
Eagleton, Terence (Francis) 1943-
　See Eagleton, Terry
　See also CA 57-60; CANR 7, 23; MTCW
Eagleton, Terry .... **CLC 63**
　See also Eagleton, Terence (Francis)
Early, Jack
　See Scoppettone, Sandra
East, Michael
　See West, Morris L(anglo)
Eastaway, Edward
　See Thomas, (Philip) Edward
Eastlake, William (Derry) 1917-1997 **CLC 8**
　See also CA 5-8R; 158; CAAS 1; CANR 5; DLB 6; INT CANR-5
Eastman, Charles A(lexander) 1858-1939
　TCLC 55; DAM MULT
　See also DLB 175; NNAL; YABC 1
Eberhart, Richard (Ghormley) 1904- **CLC 3, 11, 19, 56; DAM POET**
　See also CA 1-4R; CANR 2; CDALB 1941-1968; DLB 48; MTCW
Eberstadt, Fernanda 1960- .... **CLC 39**
　See also CA 136
Echegaray (y Eizaguirre), Jose (Maria Waldo) 1832-1916 .... **TCLC 4**
　See also CA 104; CANR 32; HW; MTCW
Echeverria, (Jose) Esteban (Antonino) 1805-1851 .... **NCLC 18**
Echo
　See Proust, (Valentin-Louis-George-Eugene-) Marcel
Eckert, Allan W. 1931- .... **CLC 17**
　See also AAYA 18; CA 13-16R; CANR 14, 45; INT CANR-14; SAAS 21; SATA 29, 91; SATA-Brief 27
Eckhart, Meister 1260(?)-1328(?) ... **CMLC 9**
　See also DLB 115
Eckmar, F. R.
　See de Hartog, Jan
Eco, Umberto 1932- **CLC 28, 60; DAM NOV, POP**
　See also BEST 90:1; CA 77-80; CANR 12, 33, 55; MTCW
Eddison, E(ric) R(ucker) 1882-1945 **TCLC 15**
　See also CA 109; 156
Eddy, Mary (Morse) Baker 1821-1910 **TCLC 71**
　See also CA 113
Edel, (Joseph) Leon 1907-1997 .. **CLC 29, 34**
　See also CA 1-4R; 161; CANR 1, 22; DLB 103; INT CANR-22
Eden, Emily 1797-1869 .... **NCLC 10**
Edgar, David 1948- .. **CLC 42; DAM DRAM**
　See also CA 57-60; CANR 12, 61; DLB 13; MTCW
Edgerton, Clyde (Carlyle) 1944- ..... **CLC 39**
　See also AAYA 17; CA 118; 134; INT 134
Edgeworth, Maria 1768-1849 .... **NCLC 1, 51**
　See also DLB 116, 159, 163; SATA 21
Edmonds, Paul
　See Kuttner, Henry
Edmonds, Walter D(umaux) 1903- .. **CLC 35**
　See also CA 5-8R; CANR 2; DLB 9; MAICYA; SAAS 4; SATA 1, 27
Edmondson, Wallace

See Ellison, Harlan (Jay)
Edson, Russell .... **CLC 13**
　See also CA 33-36R
Edwards, Bronwen Elizabeth
　See Rose, Wendy
Edwards, G(erald) B(asil) 1899-1976 **CLC 25**
　See also CA 110
Edwards, Gus 1939- .... **CLC 43**
　See also CA 108; INT 108
Edwards, Jonathan 1703-1758 ..... **LC 7; DA; DAC; DAM MST**
　See also DLB 24
Efron, Marina Ivanovna Tsvetaeva
　See Tsvetaeva (Efron), Marina (Ivanovna)
Ehle, John (Marsden, Jr.) 1925- .... **CLC 27**
　See also CA 9-12R
Ehrenbourg, Ilya (Grigoryevich)
　See Ehrenburg, Ilya (Grigoryevich)
Ehrenburg, Ilya (Grigoryevich) 1891-1967
　CLC 18, 34, 62
　See also CA 102; 25-28R
Ehrenburg, Ilyo (Grigoryevich)
　See Ehrenburg, Ilya (Grigoryevich)
Eich, Guenter 1907-1972 .... **CLC 15**
　See also CA 111; 93-96; DLB 69, 124
Eichendorff, Joseph Freiherr von 1788-1857 **NCLC 8**
　See also DLB 90
Eigner, Larry .... **CLC 9**
　See also Eigner, Laurence (Joel)
　See also CAAS 23; DLB 5
Eigner, Laurence (Joel) 1927-1996
　See Eigner, Larry
　See also CA 9-12R; 151; CANR 6
Einstein, Albert 1879-1955 .... **TCLC 65**
　See also CA 121; 133; MTCW
Eiseley, Loren Corey 1907-1977 .... **CLC 7**
　See also AAYA 5; CA 1-4R; 73-76; CANR 6
Eisenstadt, Jill 1963- .... **CLC 50**
　See also CA 140
Eisenstein, Sergei (Mikhailovich) 1898-1948
　TCLC 57
　See also CA 114; 149
Eisner, Simon
　See Kornbluth, C(yril) M.
Ekeloef, (Bengt) Gunnar 1907-1968 **CLC 27; DAM POET**
　See also CA 123; 25-28R
Ekelof, (Bengt) Gunnar
　See Ekeloef, (Bengt) Gunnar
Ekelund, Vilhelm 1880-1949 .... **TCLC 75**
Ekwensi, C. O. D.
　See Ekwensi, Cyprian (Odiatu Duaka)
Ekwensi, Cyprian (Odiatu Duaka) 1921- **CLC 4; BLC; DAM MULT**
　See also BW 2; CA 29-32R; CANR 18, 42; DLB 117; MTCW; SATA 66
Elaine .... **TCLC 18**
　See also Leverson, Ada
El Crummo
　See Crumb, R(obert)
Elder, Lonne III 1931-1996 .... **DC 8**
　See also BLC; BW 1; CA 81-84; 152; CANR 25; DAM MULT; DLB 7, 38, 44
Elia
　See Lamb, Charles
Eliade, Mircea 1907-1986 .... **CLC 19**
　See also CA 65-68; 119; CANR 30, 62; MTCW
Eliot, A. D.
　See Jewett, (Theodora) Sarah Orne
Eliot, Alice
　See Jewett, (Theodora) Sarah Orne
Eliot, Dan
　See Silverberg, Robert
Eliot, George 1819-1880 **NCLC 4, 13, 23, 41, 49; DA; DAB; DAC; DAM MST, NOV; PC 20; WLC**

See also CDBLB 1832-1890; DLB 21, 35, 55
Eliot, John 1604-1690 .... **LC 5**
　See also DLB 24
Eliot, T(homas) S(tearns) 1888-1965 **CLC 1, 2, 3, 6, 9, 10, 13, 15, 24, 34, 41, 55, 57; DA; DAB; DAC; DAM DRAM, MST, POET; PC 5; WLC 2**
　See also CA 5-8R; 25-28R; CANR 41; CDALB 1929-1941; DLB 7, 10, 45, 63; DLBY 88; MTCW
Elizabeth 1866-1941 .... **TCLC 41**
Elkin, Stanley L(awrence) 1930-1995 **CLC 4, 6, 9, 14, 27, 51, 91; DAM NOV, POP; SSC 12**
　See also CA 9-12R; 148; CANR 8, 46; DLB 2, 28; DLBY 80; INT CANR-8; MTCW
Elledge, Scott .... **CLC 34**
Elliot, Don
　See Silverberg, Robert
Elliott, Don
　See Silverberg, Robert
Elliott, George P(aul) 1918-1980 .... **CLC 2**
　See also CA 1-4R; 97-100; CANR 2
Elliott, Janice 1931- .... **CLC 47**
　See also CA 13-16R; CANR 8, 29; DLB 14
Elliott, Sumner Locke 1917-1991 .... **CLC 38**
　See also CA 5-8R; 134; CANR 2, 21
Elliott, William
　See Bradbury, Ray (Douglas)
Ellis, A. E. .... **CLC 7**
Ellis, Alice Thomas .... **CLC 40**
　See also Haycraft, Anna
Ellis, Bret Easton 1964- .. **CLC 39, 71; DAM POP**
　See also AAYA 2; CA 118; 123; CANR 51; INT 123
Ellis, (Henry) Havelock 1859-1939 **TCLC 14**
　See also CA 109
Ellis, Landon
　See Ellison, Harlan (Jay)
Ellis, Trey 1962- .... **CLC 55**
　See also CA 146
Ellison, Harlan (Jay) 1934- ... **CLC 1, 13, 42; DAM POP; SSC 14**
　See also CA 5-8R; CANR 5, 46; DLB 8; INT CANR-5; MTCW
Ellison, Ralph (Waldo) 1914-1994 **CLC 1, 3, 11, 54, 86; BLC; DA; DAB; DAC; DAM MST, MULT, NOV; SSC 26; WLC**
　See also AAYA 19; BW 1; CA 9-12R; 145; CANR 24, 53; CDALB 1941-1968; DLB 2, 76; DLBY 94; MTCW
Ellmann, Lucy (Elizabeth) 1956- ...... **CLC 61**
　See also CA 128
Ellmann, Richard (David) 1918-1987 **CLC 50**
　See also BEST 89:2; CA 1-4R; 122; CANR 2, 28, 61; DLB 103; DLBY 87; MTCW
Elman, Richard 1934- .... **CLC 19**
　See also CA 17-20R; CAAS 3; CANR 47
Elron
　See Hubbard, L(afayette) Ron(ald)
Eluard, Paul .... **TCLC 7, 41**
　See also Grindel, Eugene
Elyot, Sir Thomas 1490(?)-1546 .... **LC 11**
Elytis, Odysseus 1911-1996 **CLC 15, 49, 100; DAM POET**
　See also CA 102; 151; MTCW
Emecheta, (Florence Onye) Buchi 1944- **CLC 14, 48; BLC; DAM MULT**
　See also BW 2; CA 81-84; CANR 27; DLB 117; MTCW; SATA 66
Emerson, Mary Moody 1774-1863 **NCLC 66**
Emerson, Ralph Waldo 1803-1882 . **NCLC 1, 38; DA; DAB; DAC; DAM MST, POET; PC 18; WLC**
　See also CDALB 1640-1865; DLB 1, 59, 73
Eminescu, Mihail 1850-1889 .... **NCLC 33**

Empson, William 1906-1984 CLC 3, 8, 19, 33, 34
See also CA 17-20R; 112; CANR 31, 61; DLB 20; MTCW

Enchi Fumiko (Ueda) 1905-1986 ..... CLC 31
See also CA 129; 121

Ende, Michael (Andreas Helmuth) 1929-1995 CLC 31
See also CA 118; 124; 149; CANR 36; CLR 14; DLB 75; MAICYA; SATA 61; SATA-Brief 42; SATA-Obit 86

Endo, Shusaku 1923-1996 CLC 7, 14, 19, 54, 99; DAM NOV
See also CA 29-32R; 153; CANR 21, 54; DLB 182; MTCW

Engel, Marian 1933-1985 .... CLC 36
See also CA 25-28R; CANR 12; DLB 53; INT CANR-12

Engelhardt, Frederick
See Hubbard, L(afayette) Ron(ald)

Enright, D(ennis) J(oseph) 1920- CLC 4, 8, 31
See also CA 1-4R; CANR 1, 42; DLB 27; SATA 25

Enzensberger, Hans Magnus 1929- . CLC 43
See also CA 116; 119

Ephron, Nora 1941- .... CLC 17, 31
See also AITN 2; CA 65-68; CANR 12, 39

Epicurus 341B.C.-270B.C. .... CMLC 21
See also DLB 176

Epsilon
See Betjeman, John

Epstein, Daniel Mark 1948- .... CLC 7
See also CA 49-52; CANR 2, 53

Epstein, Jacob 1956- .... CLC 19
See also CA 114

Epstein, Joseph 1937- .... CLC 39
See also CA 112; 119; CANR 50

Epstein, Leslie 1938- .... CLC 27
See also CA 73-76; CAAS 12; CANR 23

Equiano, Olaudah 1745(?)-1797 LC 16; BLC; DAM MULT
See also DLB 37, 50

ER.. TCLC 33
See also CA 160; DLB 85

Erasmus, Desiderius 1469(?)-1536 ..... LC 16

Erdman, Paul E(mil) 1932- .... CLC 25
See also AITN 1; CA 61-64; CANR 13, 43

Erdrich, Louise 1954- ..... CLC 39, 54; DAM MULT, NOV, POP
See also AAYA 10; BEST 89:1; CA 114; CANR 41, 62; DLB 152, 175; MTCW; NNAL; SATA 94

Erenburg, Ilya (Grigoryevich)
See Ehrenburg, Ilya (Grigoryevich)

Erickson, Stephen Michael 1950-
See Erickson, Steve
See also CA 129

Erickson, Steve 1950- .... CLC 64
See also Erickson, Stephen Michael
See also CANR 60

Ericson, Walter
See Fast, Howard (Melvin)

Eriksson, Buntel
See Bergman, (Ernst) Ingmar

Ernaux, Annie 1940- .... CLC 88
See also CA 147

Eschenbach, Wolfram von
See Wolfram von Eschenbach

Eseki, Bruno
See Mphahlele, Ezekiel

Esenin, Sergei (Alexandrovich) 1895-1925 TCLC 4
See also CA 104

Eshleman, Clayton 1935- .... CLC 7
See also CA 33-36R; CAAS 6; DLB 5

Espriella, Don Manuel Alvarez
See Southey, Robert

Espriu, Salvador 1913-1985 .... CLC 9
See also CA 154; 115; DLB 134

Espronceda, Jose de 1808-1842 ..... NCLC 39

Esse, James
See Stephens, James

Esterbrook, Tom
See Hubbard, L(afayette) Ron(ald)

Estleman, Loren D. 1952- ...... CLC 48; DAM NOV, POP
See also CA 85-88; CANR 27; INT CANR-27; MTCW

Eugenides, Jeffrey 1960(?)- .... CLC 81
See also CA 144

Euripides c. 485B.C.-406B.C.CMLC 23; DA; DAB; DAC; DAM DRAM, MST; DC 4; WLCS
See also DLB 176

Evan, Evin
See Faust, Frederick (Schiller)

Evans, Evan
See Faust, Frederick (Schiller)

Evans, Marian
See Eliot, George

Evans, Mary Ann
See Eliot, George

Evarts, Esther
See Benson, Sally

Everett, Percival L. 1956- .... CLC 57
See also BW 2; CA 129

Everson, R(onald) G(ilmour) 1903- . CLC 27
See also CA 17-20R; DLB 88

Everson, William (Oliver) 1912-1994 CLC 1, 5, 14
See also CA 9-12R; 145; CANR 20; DLB 5, 16; MTCW

Evtushenko, Evgenii Aleksandrovich
See Yevtushenko, Yevgeny (Alexandrovich)

Ewart, Gavin (Buchanan) 1916-1995 CLC 13, 46
See also CA 89-92; 150; CANR 17, 46; DLB 40; MTCW

Ewers, Hanns Heinz 1871-1943 ..... TCLC 12
See also CA 109; 149

Ewing, Frederick R.
See Sturgeon, Theodore (Hamilton)

Exley, Frederick (Earl) 1929-1992 CLC 6, 11
See also AITN 2; CA 81-84; 138; DLB 143; DLBY 81

Eynhardt, Guillermo
See Quiroga, Horacio (Sylvestre)

Ezekiel, Nissim 1924- .... CLC 61
See also CA 61-64

Ezekiel, Tish O'Dowd 1943- .... CLC 34
See also CA 129

Fadeyev, A.
See Bulgya, Alexander Alexandrovich

Fadeyev, Alexander .... TCLC 53
See also Bulgya, Alexander Alexandrovich

Fagen, Donald 1948- .... CLC 26

Fainzilberg, Ilya Arnoldovich 1897-1937
See Ilf, Ilya
See also CA 120

Fair, Ronald L. 1932- .... CLC 18
See also BW 1; CA 69-72; CANR 25; DLB 33

Fairbairn, Roger
See Carr, John Dickson

Fairbairns, Zoe (Ann) 1948- .... CLC 32
See also CA 103; CANR 21

Falco, Gian
See Papini, Giovanni

Falconer, James
See Kirkup, James

Falconer, Kenneth
See Kornbluth, C(yril) M.

Falkland, Samuel
See Heijermans, Herman

Fallaci, Oriana 1930- .... CLC 11
See also CA 77-80; CANR 15, 58; MTCW

Faludy, George 1913- .... CLC 42
See also CA 21-24R

Faludy, Gyoergy
See Faludy, George

Fanon, Frantz 1925-1961 CLC 74; BLC; DAM MULT
See also BW 1; CA 116; 89-92

Fanshawe, Ann 1625-1680 .... LC 11

Fante, John (Thomas) 1911-1983 ..... CLC 60
See also CA 69-72; 109; CANR 23; DLB 130; DLBY 83

Farah, Nuruddin 1945- CLC 53; BLC; DAM MULT
See also BW 2; CA 106; DLB 125

Fargue, Leon-Paul 1876(?)-1947 ... TCLC 11
See also CA 109

Farigoule, Louis
See Romains, Jules

Farina, Richard 1936(?)-1966 .... CLC 9
See also CA 81-84; 25-28R

Farley, Walter (Lorimer) 1915-1989 CLC 17
See also CA 17-20R; CANR 8, 29; DLB 22; JRDA; MAICYA; SATA 2, 43

Farmer, Philip Jose 1918- .... CLC 1, 19
See also CA 1-4R; CANR 4, 35; DLB 8; MTCW; SATA 93

Farquhar, George 1677-1707 ... LC 21; DAM DRAM
See also DLB 84

Farrell, J(ames) G(ordon) 1935-1979 CLC 6
See also CA 73-76; 89-92; CANR 36; DLB 14; MTCW

Farrell, James T(homas) 1904-1979 CLC 1, 4, 8, 11, 66; SSC 28
See also CA 5-8R; 89-92; CANR 9, 61; DLB 4, 9, 86; DLBD 2; MTCW

Farren, Richard J.
See Betjeman, John

Farren, Richard M.
See Betjeman, John

Fassbinder, Rainer Werner 1946-1982 . CLC 20
See also CA 93-96; 106; CANR 31

Fast, Howard (Melvin) 1914- CLC 23; DAM NOV
See also AAYA 16; CA 1-4R; CAAS 18; CANR 1, 33, 54; DLB 9; INT CANR-33; SATA 7

Faulcon, Robert
See Holdstock, Robert P.

Faulkner, William (Cuthbert) 1897-1962 CLC 1, 3, 6, 8, 9, 11, 14, 18, 28, 52, 68; DA; DAB; DAC; DAM MST, NOV; SSC 1; WLC
See also AAYA 7; CA 81-84; CANR 33; CDALB 1929-1941; DLB 9, 11, 44, 102; DLBD 2; DLBY 86; MTCW

Fauset, Jessie Redmon 1884(?)-1961 CLC 19, 54; BLC; DAM MULT
See also BW 1; CA 109; DLB 51

Faust, Frederick (Schiller) 1892-1944(?) TCLC 49; DAM POP
See also CA 108; 152

Faust, Irvin 1924- .... CLC 8
See also CA 33-36R; CANR 28; DLB 2, 28; DLBY 80

Fawkes, Guy
See Benchley, Robert (Charles)

Fearing, Kenneth (Flexner) 1902-1961 . CLC 51
See also CA 93-96; CANR 59; DLB 9

Fecamps, Elise
See Creasey, John

Federman, Raymond 1928- .... CLC 6, 47
See also CA 17-20R; CAAS 8; CANR 10, 43; DLBY 80

Federspiel, J(uerg) F. 1931- .... CLC 42
See also CA 146

Feiffer, Jules (Ralph) 1929- ..... **CLC 2, 8, 64; DAM DRAM**
See also AAYA 3; CA 17-20R; CANR 30, 59; DLB 7, 44; INT CANR-30; MTCW; SATA 8, 61

Feige, Hermann Albert Otto Maximilian
See Traven, B.

Feinberg, David B. 1956-1994 .... **CLC 59**
See also CA 135; 147

Feinstein, Elaine 1930- .... **CLC 36**
See also CA 69-72; CAAS 1; CANR 31; DLB 14, 40; MTCW

Feldman, Irving (Mordecai) 1928- ..... **CLC 7**
See also CA 1-4R; CANR 1; DLB 169

Felix-Tchicaya, Gerald
See Tchicaya, Gerald Felix

Fellini, Federico 1920-1993 .... **CLC 16, 85**
See also CA 65-68; 143; CANR 33

Felsen, Henry Gregor 1916- .... **CLC 17**
See also CA 1-4R; CANR 1; SAAS 2; SATA 1

Fenton, James Martin 1949- .... **CLC 32**
See also CA 102; DLB 40

Ferber, Edna 1887-1968 .... **CLC 18, 93**
See also AITN 1; CA 5-8R; 25-28R; DLB 9, 28, 86; MTCW; SATA 7

Ferguson, Helen
See Kavan, Anna

Ferguson, Samuel 1810-1886 .... **NCLC 33**
See also DLB 32

Fergusson, Robert 1750-1774 .... **LC 29**
See also DLB 109

Ferling, Lawrence
See Ferlinghetti, Lawrence (Monsanto)

Ferlinghetti, Lawrence (Monsanto) 1919(?)- **CLC 2, 6, 10, 27; DAM POET; PC 1**
See also CA 5-8R; CANR 3, 41; CDALB 1941-1968; DLB 5, 16; MTCW

Fernandez, Vicente Garcia Huidobro
See Huidobro Fernandez, Vicente Garcia

Ferrer, Gabriel (Francisco Victor) Miro
See Miro (Ferrer), Gabriel (Francisco Victor)

Ferrier, Susan (Edmonstone) 1782-1854 **NCLC 8**
See also DLB 116

Ferrigno, Robert 1948(?)- .... **CLC 65**
See also CA 140

Ferron, Jacques 1921-1985 .... **CLC 94; DAC**
See also CA 117; 129; DLB 60

Feuchtwanger, Lion 1884-1958 .... **TCLC 3**
See also CA 104; DLB 66

Feuillet, Octave 1821-1890 .... **NCLC 45**

Feydeau, Georges (Leon Jules Marie) 1862-1921 .... **TCLC 22; DAM DRAM**
See also CA 113; 152

Fichte, Johann Gottlieb 1762-1814 **NCLC 62**
See also DLB 90

Ficino, Marsilio 1433-1499 .... **LC 12**

Fiedeler, Hans
See Doeblin, Alfred

Fiedler, Leslie A(aron) 1917- . **CLC 4, 13, 24**
See also CA 9-12R; CANR 7; DLB 28, 67; MTCW

Field, Andrew 1938- .... **CLC 44**
See also CA 97-100; CANR 25

Field, Eugene 1850-1895 .... **NCLC 3**
See also DLB 23, 42, 140; DLBD 13; MAICYA; SATA 16

Field, Gans T.
See Wellman, Manly Wade

Field, Michael .... **TCLC 43**

Field, Peter
See Hobson, Laura Z(ametkin)

Fielding, Henry 1707-1754 **LC 1; DA; DAB; DAC; DAM DRAM, MST, NOV; WLC**
See also CDBLB 1660-1789; DLB 39, 84, 101

Fielding, Sarah 1710-1768 .... **LC 1**
See also DLB 39

Fierstein, Harvey (Forbes) 1954- .... **CLC 33; DAM DRAM, POP**
See also CA 123; 129

Figes, Eva 1932- .... **CLC 31**
See also CA 53-56; CANR 4, 44; DLB 14

Finch, Robert (Duer Claydon) 1900- **CLC 18**
See also CA 57-60; CANR 9, 24, 49; DLB 88

Findley, Timothy 1930- **CLC 27, 102; DAC; DAM MST**
See also CA 25-28R; CANR 12, 42; DLB 53

Fink, William
See Mencken, H(enry) L(ouis)

Firbank, Louis 1942-
See Reed, Lou
See also CA 117

Firbank, (Arthur Annesley) Ronald 1886-1926 **TCLC 1**
See also CA 104; DLB 36

Fisher, M(ary) F(rances) K(ennedy) 1908-1992 **CLC 76, 87**
See also CA 77-80; 138; CANR 44

Fisher, Roy 1930- .... **CLC 25**
See also CA 81-84; CAAS 10; CANR 16; DLB 40

Fisher, Rudolph 1897-1934 **TCLC 11; BLC; DAM MULT; SSC 25**
See also BW 1; CA 107; 124; DLB 51, 102

Fisher, Vardis (Alvero) 1895-1968 ..... **CLC 7**
See also CA 5-8R; 25-28R; DLB 9

Fiske, Tarleton
See Bloch, Robert (Albert)

Fitch, Clarke
See Sinclair, Upton (Beall)

Fitch, John IV
See Cormier, Robert (Edmund)

Fitzgerald, Captain Hugh
See Baum, L(yman) Frank

FitzGerald, Edward 1809-1883 .... **NCLC 9**
See also DLB 32

Fitzgerald, F(rancis) Scott (Key) 1896-1940 **TCLC 1, 6, 14, 28, 55; DA; DAB; DAC; DAM MST, NOV; SSC 6; WLC**
See also AITN 1; CA 110; 123; CDALB 1917-1929; DLB 4, 9, 86; DLBD 1, 15, 16; DLBY 81, 96; MTCW

Fitzgerald, Penelope 1916- ... **CLC 19, 51, 61**
See also CA 85-88; CAAS 10; CANR 56; DLB 14

Fitzgerald, Robert (Stuart) 1910-1985 **CLC 39**
See also CA 1-4R; 114; CANR 1; DLBY 80

FitzGerald, Robert D(avid) 1902-1987 **CLC 19**
See also CA 17-20R

Fitzgerald, Zelda (Sayre) 1900-1948 **TCLC 52**
See also CA 117; 126; DLBY 84

Flanagan, Thomas (James Bonner) 1923- **CLC 25, 52**
See also CA 108; CANR 55; DLBY 80; INT 108; MTCW

Flaubert, Gustave 1821-1880 **NCLC 2, 10, 19, 62, 66; DA; DAB; DAC; DAM MST, NOV; SSC 11; WLC**
See also DLB 119

Flecker, Herman Elroy
See Flecker, (Herman) James Elroy

Flecker, (Herman) James Elroy 1884-1915 **TCLC 43**
See also CA 109; 150; DLB 10, 19

Fleming, Ian (Lancaster) 1908-1964 . **CLC 3, 30; DAM POP**
See also CA 5-8R; CANR 59; CDBLB 1945-1960; DLB 87; MTCW; SATA 9

Fleming, Thomas (James) 1927- .... **CLC 37**
See also CA 5-8R; CANR 10; INT CANR-10; SATA 8

Fletcher, John 1579-1625 .... **LC 33; DC 6**
See also CDBLB Before 1660; DLB 58

Fletcher, John Gould 1886-1950 ... **TCLC 35**

See also CA 107; DLB 4, 45

Fleur, Paul
See Pohl, Frederik

Flooglebuckle, Al
See Spiegelman, Art

Flying Officer X
See Bates, H(erbert) E(rnest)

Fo, Dario 1926- .... **CLC 32; DAM DRAM**
See also CA 116; 128; MTCW

Fogarty, Jonathan Titulescu Esq.
See Farrell, James T(homas)

Folke, Will
See Bloch, Robert (Albert)

Follett, Ken(neth Martin) 1949- ..... **CLC 18; DAM NOV, POP**
See also AAYA 6; BEST 89:4; CA 81-84; CANR 13, 33, 54; DLB 87; DLBY 81; INT CANR-33; MTCW

Fontane, Theodor 1819-1898 .... **NCLC 26**
See also DLB 129

Foote, Horton 1916- **CLC 51, 91; DAM DRAM**
See also CA 73-76; CANR 34, 51; DLB 26; INT CANR-34

Foote, Shelby 1916- **CLC 75; DAM NOV, POP**
See also CA 5-8R; CANR 3, 45; DLB 2, 17

Forbes, Esther 1891-1967 .... **CLC 12**
See also AAYA 17; CA 13-14; 25-28R; CAP 1; CLR 27; DLB 22; JRDA; MAICYA; SATA 2

Forche, Carolyn (Louise) 1950- **CLC 25, 83, 86; DAM POET; PC 10**
See also CA 109; 117; CANR 50; DLB 5; INT 117

Ford, Elbur
See Hibbert, Eleanor Alice Burford

Ford, Ford Madox 1873-1939 **TCLC 1, 15, 39, 57; DAM NOV**
See also CA 104; 132; CDBLB 1914-1945; DLB 162; MTCW

Ford, Henry 1863-1947 .... **TCLC 73**
See also CA 115; 148

Ford, John 1586-(?) .... **DC 8**
See also CDBLB Before 1660; DAM DRAM; DLB 58

Ford, John 1895-1973 .... **CLC 16**
See also CA 45-48

Ford, Richard .... **CLC 99**

Ford, Richard 1944- .... **CLC 46**
See also CA 69-72; CANR 11, 47

Ford, Webster
See Masters, Edgar Lee

Foreman, Richard 1937- .... **CLC 50**
See also CA 65-68; CANR 32

Forester, C(ecil) S(cott) 1899-1966 .. **CLC 35**
See also CA 73-76; 25-28R; SATA 13

Forez
See Mauriac, Francois (Charles)

Forman, James Douglas 1932- .... **CLC 21**
See also AAYA 17; CA 9-12R; CANR 4, 19, 42; JRDA; MAICYA; SATA 8, 70

Fornes, Maria Irene 1930- .... **CLC 39, 61**
See also CA 25-28R; CANR 28; DLB 7; HW; INT CANR-28; MTCW

Forrest, Leon 1937- .... **CLC 4**
See also BW 2; CA 89-92; CAAS 7; CANR 25, 52; DLB 33

Forster, E(dward) M(organ) 1879-1970 **C L C 1, 2, 3, 4, 9, 10, 13, 15, 22, 45, 77; DA; DAB; DAC; DAM MST, NOV; SSC 27; WLC**
See also AAYA 2; CA 13-14; 25-28R; CANR 45; CAP 1; CDBLB 1914-1945; DLB 34, 98, 162, 178; DLBD 10; MTCW; SATA 57

Forster, John 1812-1876 .... **NCLC 11**
See also DLB 144, 184

Forsyth, Frederick 1938- **CLC 2, 5, 36; DAM NOV, POP**
See also BEST 89:4; CA 85-88; CANR 38, 62;

Forten, Charlotte L. .... TCLC 16; BLC
See also Grimke, Charlotte L(ottie) Forten
See also DLB 50
Foscolo, Ugo 1778-1827 .... NCLC 8
Fosse, Bob .... CLC 20
See also Fosse, Robert Louis
Fosse, Robert Louis 1927-1987
See Fosse, Bob
See also CA 110; 123
Foster, Stephen Collins 1826-1864 NCLC 26
Foucault, Michel 1926-1984 . CLC 31, 34, 69
See also CA 105; 113; CANR 34; MTCW
Fouque, Friedrich (Heinrich Karl) de la Motte 1777-1843 .... NCLC 2
See also DLB 90
Fourier, Charles 1772-1837 .... NCLC 51
Fournier, Henri Alban 1886-1914
See Alain-Fournier
See also CA 104
Fournier, Pierre 1916- .... CLC 11
See also Gascar, Pierre
See also CA 89-92; CANR 16, 40
Fowles, John 1926-CLC 1, 2, 3, 4, 6, 9, 10, 15, 33, 87; DAB; DAC; DAM MST
See also CA 5-8R; CANR 25; CDBLB 1960 to Present; DLB 14, 139; MTCW; SATA 22
Fox, Paula 1923- .... CLC 2, 8
See also AAYA 3; CA 73-76; CANR 20, 36, 62; CLR 1, 44; DLB 52; JRDA; MAICYA; MTCW; SATA 17, 60
Fox, William Price (Jr.) 1926- .... CLC 22
See also CA 17-20R; CAAS 19; CANR 11; DLB 2; DLBY 81
Foxe, John 1516(?)-1587 .... LC 14
Frame, Janet 1924-CLC 2, 3, 6, 22, 66, 96; SSC 29
See also Clutha, Janet Paterson Frame
France, Anatole .... TCLC 9
See also Thibault, Jacques Anatole Francois
See also DLB 123
Francis, Claude 19(?)- .... CLC 50
Francis, Dick 1920-CLC 2, 22, 42, 102; DAM POP
See also AAYA 5, 21; BEST 89:3; CA 5-8R; CANR 9, 42; CDBLB 1960 to Present; DLB 87; INT CANR-9; MTCW
Francis, Robert (Churchill) 1901-1987 . C L C 15
See also CA 1-4R; 123; CANR 1
Frank, Anne(lies Marie) 1929-1945TCLC 17; DA; DAB; DAC; DAM MST; WLC
See also AAYA 12; CA 113; 133; MTCW; SATA 87; SATA-Brief 42
Frank, Elizabeth 1945- .... CLC 39
See also CA 121; 126; INT 126
Frankl, Viktor E(mil) 1905-1997 ..... CLC 93
See also CA 65-68; 161
Franklin, Benjamin
See Hasek, Jaroslav (Matej Frantisek)
Franklin, Benjamin 1706-1790 .. LC 25; DA; DAB; DAC; DAM MST; WLCS
See also CDALB 1640-1865; DLB 24, 43, 73
Franklin, (Stella Maraia Sarah) Miles 1879-1954 .... TCLC 7
See also CA 104
Fraser, (Lady) Antonia (Pakenham) 1932- CLC 32
See also CA 85-88; CANR 44; MTCW; SATA-Brief 32
Fraser, George MacDonald 1925- ...... CLC 7
See also CA 45-48; CANR 2, 48
Fraser, Sylvia 1935- .... CLC 64
See also CA 45-48; CANR 1, 16, 60
Frayn, Michael 1933-CLC 3, 7, 31, 47; DAM DRAM, NOV
See also CA 5-8R; CANR 30; DLB 13, 14; MTCW

Fraze, Candida (Merrill) 1945- .... CLC 50
See also CA 126
Frazer, J(ames) G(eorge) 1854-1941TCLC 32
See also CA 118
Frazer, Robert Caine
See Creasey, John
Frazer, Sir James George
See Frazer, J(ames) G(eorge)
Frazier, Ian 1951- .... CLC 46
See also CA 130; CANR 54
Frederic, Harold 1856-1898 .... NCLC 10
See also DLB 12, 23; DLBD 13
Frederick, John
See Faust, Frederick (Schiller)
Frederick the Great 1712-1786 .... LC 14
Fredro, Aleksander 1793-1876 .... NCLC 8
Freeling, Nicolas 1927- .... CLC 38
See also CA 49-52; CAAS 12; CANR 1, 17, 50; DLB 87
Freeman, Douglas Southall 1886-1953T C L C 11
See also CA 109; DLB 17
Freeman, Judith 1946- .... CLC 55
See also CA 148
Freeman, Mary Eleanor Wilkins 1852-1930 TCLC 9; SSC 1
See also CA 106; DLB 12, 78
Freeman, R(ichard) Austin 1862-1943T C L C 21
See also CA 113; DLB 70
French, Albert 1943- .... CLC 86
French, Marilyn 1929-CLC 10, 18, 60; DAM DRAM, NOV, POP
See also CA 69-72; CANR 3, 31; INT CANR-31; MTCW
French, Paul
See Asimov, Isaac
Freneau, Philip Morin 1752-1832 ... NCLC 1
See also DLB 37, 43
Freud, Sigmund 1856-1939 .... TCLC 52
See also CA 115; 133; MTCW
Friedan, Betty (Naomi) 1921- .... CLC 74
See also CA 65-68; CANR 18, 45; MTCW
Friedlander, Saul 1932- .... CLC 90
See also CA 117; 130
Friedman, B(ernard) H(arper) 1926-.CLC 7
See also CA 1-4R; CANR 3, 48
Friedman, Bruce Jay 1930- .... CLC 3, 5, 56
See also CA 9-12R; CANR 25, 52; DLB 2, 28; INT CANR-25
Friel, Brian 1929- .... CLC 5, 42, 59; DC 8
See also CA 21-24R; CANR 33; DLB 13; MTCW
Friis-Baastad, Babbis Ellinor 1921-1970C L C 12
See also CA 17-20R; 134; SATA 7
Frisch, Max (Rudolf) 1911-1991CLC 3, 9, 14, 18, 32, 44; DAM DRAM, NOV
See also CA 85-88; 134; CANR 32; DLB 69, 124; MTCW
Fromentin, Eugene (Samuel Auguste) 1820-1876 .... NCLC 10
See also DLB 123
Frost, Frederick
See Faust, Frederick (Schiller)
Frost, Robert (Lee) 1874-1963CLC 1, 3, 4, 9, 10, 13, 15, 26, 34, 44; DA; DAB; DAC; DAM MST, POET; PC 1; WLC
See also AAYA 21; CA 89-92; CANR 33; CDALB 1917-1929; DLB 54; DLBD 7; MTCW; SATA 14
Froude, James Anthony 1818-1894NCLC 43
See also DLB 18, 57, 144
Froy, Herald
See Waterhouse, Keith (Spencer)
Fry, Christopher 1907- CLC 2, 10, 14; DAM DRAM
See also CA 17-20R; CAAS 23; CANR 9, 30; DLB 13; MTCW; SATA 66
Frye, (Herman) Northrop 1912-1991CLC 24, 70
See also CA 5-8R; 133; CANR 8, 37; DLB 67, 68; MTCW
Fuchs, Daniel 1909-1993 .... CLC 8, 22
See also CA 81-84; 142; CAAS 5; CANR 40; DLB 9, 26, 28; DLBY 93
Fuchs, Daniel 1934- .... CLC 34
See also CA 37-40R; CANR 14, 48
Fuentes, Carlos 1928-CLC 3, 8, 10, 13, 22, 41, 60; DA; DAB; DAC; DAM MST, MULT, NOV; HLC; SSC 24; WLC
See also AAYA 4; AITN 2; CA 69-72; CANR 10, 32; DLB 113; HW; MTCW
Fuentes, Gregorio Lopez y
See Lopez y Fuentes, Gregorio
Fugard, (Harold) Athol 1932-CLC 5, 9, 14, 25, 40, 80; DAM DRAM; DC 3
See also AAYA 17; CA 85-88; CANR 32, 54; MTCW
Fugard, Sheila 1932- .... CLC 48
See also CA 125
Fuller, Charles (H., Jr.) 1939-CLC 25; BLC; DAM DRAM, MULT; DC 1
See also BW 2; CA 108; 112; DLB 38; INT 112; MTCW
Fuller, John (Leopold) 1937- .... CLC 62
See also CA 21-24R; CANR 9, 44; DLB 40
Fuller, Margaret .... NCLC 5, 50
See also Ossoli, Sarah Margaret (Fuller marchesa d')
Fuller, Roy (Broadbent) 1912-1991CLC 4, 28
See also CA 5-8R; 135; CAAS 10; CANR 53; DLB 15, 20; SATA 87
Fulton, Alice 1952- .... CLC 52
See also CA 116; CANR 57
Furphy, Joseph 1843-1912 .... TCLC 25
Fussell, Paul 1924- .... CLC 74
See also BEST 90:1; CA 17-20R; CANR 8, 21, 35; INT CANR-21; MTCW
Futabatei, Shimei 1864-1909 .... TCLC 44
See also DLB 180
Futrelle, Jacques 1875-1912 .... TCLC 19
See also CA 113; 155
Gaboriau, Emile 1835-1873 .... NCLC 14
Gadda, Carlo Emilio 1893-1973 .... CLC 11
See also CA 89-92; DLB 177
Gaddis, William 1922- CLC 1, 3, 6, 8, 10, 19, 43, 86
See also CA 17-20R; CANR 21, 48; DLB 2; MTCW
Gage, Walter
See Inge, William (Motter)
Gaines, Ernest J(ames) 1933- CLC 3, 11, 18, 86; BLC; DAM MULT
See also AAYA 18; AITN 1; BW 2; CA 9-12R; CANR 6, 24, 42; CDALB 1968-1988; DLB 2, 33, 152; DLBY 80; MTCW; SATA 86
Gaitskill, Mary 1954- .... CLC 69
See also CA 128; CANR 61
Galdos, Benito Perez
See Perez Galdos, Benito
Gale, Zona 1874-1938TCLC 7; DAM DRAM
See also CA 105; 153; DLB 9, 78
Galeano, Eduardo (Hughes) 1940- ... CLC 72
See also CA 29-32R; CANR 13, 32; HW
Galiano, Juan Valera y Alcala
See Valera y Alcala-Galiano, Juan
Gallagher, Tess 1943- ..... CLC 18, 63; DAM POET; PC 9
See also CA 106; DLB 120
Gallant, Mavis 1922-... CLC 7, 18, 38; DAC; DAM MST; SSC 5
See also CA 69-72; CANR 29; DLB 53; MTCW

Gallant, Roy A(rthur) 1924- .... **CLC 17**
  See also CA 5-8R; CANR 4, 29, 54; CLR 30; MAICYA; SATA 4, 68
Gallico, Paul (William) 1897-1976 ..... **CLC 2**
  See also AITN 1; CA 5-8R; 69-72; CANR 23; DLB 9, 171; MAICYA; SATA 13
Gallo, Max Louis 1932- .... **CLC 95**
  See also CA 85-88
Gallois, Lucien
  See Desnos, Robert
Gallup, Ralph
  See Whitemore, Hugh (John)
Galsworthy, John 1867-1933 **TCLC 1, 45; DA; DAB; DAC; DAM DRAM, MST, NOV; SSC 22; WLC 2**
  See also CA 104; 141; CDBLB 1890-1914; DLB 10, 34, 98, 162; DLBD 16
Galt, John 1779-1839 .... **NCLC 1**
  See also DLB 99, 116, 159
Galvin, James 1951- .... **CLC 38**
  See also CA 108; CANR 26
Gamboa, Federico 1864-1939 .... **TCLC 36**
Gandhi, M. K.
  See Gandhi, Mohandas Karamchand
Gandhi, Mahatma
  See Gandhi, Mohandas Karamchand
Gandhi, Mohandas Karamchand 1869-1948 **TCLC 59; DAM MULT**
  See also CA 121; 132; MTCW
Gann, Ernest Kellogg 1910-1991 ..... **CLC 23**
  See also AITN 1; CA 1-4R; 136; CANR 1
Garcia, Cristina 1958- .... **CLC 76**
  See also CA 141
Garcia Lorca, Federico 1898-1936 **TCLC 1, 7, 49; DA; DAB; DAC; DAM DRAM, MST, MULT, POET; DC 2; HLC; PC 3; WLC**
  See also CA 104; 131; DLB 108; HW; MTCW
Garcia Marquez, Gabriel (Jose) 1928- **CLC 2, 3, 8, 10, 15, 27, 47, 55, 68; DA; DAB; DAC; DAM MST, MULT, NOV, POP; HLC; SSC 8; WLC**
  See also AAYA 3; BEST 89:1, 90:4; CA 33-36R; CANR 10, 28, 50; DLB 113; HW; MTCW
Gard, Janice
  See Latham, Jean Lee
Gard, Roger Martin du
  See Martin du Gard, Roger
Gardam, Jane 1928- .... **CLC 43**
  See also CA 49-52; CANR 2, 18, 33, 54; CLR 12; DLB 14, 161; MAICYA; MTCW; SAAS 9; SATA 39, 76; SATA-Brief 28
Gardner, Herb(ert) 1934- .... **CLC 44**
  See also CA 149
Gardner, John (Champlin), Jr. 1933-1982 **CLC 2, 3, 5, 7, 8, 10, 18, 28, 34; DAM NOV, POP; SSC 7**
  See also AITN 1; CA 65-68; 107; CANR 33; DLB 2; DLBY 82; MTCW; SATA 40; SATA-Obit 31
Gardner, John (Edmund) 1926- ..... **CLC 30; DAM POP**
  See also CA 103; CANR 15; MTCW
Gardner, Miriam
  See Bradley, Marion Zimmer
Gardner, Noel
  See Kuttner, Henry
Gardons, S. S.
  See Snodgrass, W(illiam) D(e Witt)
Garfield, Leon 1921-1996 .... **CLC 12**
  See also AAYA 8; CA 17-20R; 152; CANR 38, 41; CLR 21; DLB 161; JRDA; MAICYA; SATA 1, 32, 76; SATA-Obit 90
Garland, (Hannibal) Hamlin 1860-1940 **TCLC 3; SSC 18**
  See also CA 104; DLB 12, 71, 78
Garneau, (Hector de) Saint-Denys 1912-1943 **TCLC 13**
  See also CA 111; DLB 88
Garner, Alan 1934- **CLC 17; DAB; DAM POP**
  See also AAYA 18; CA 73-76; CANR 15; CLR 20; DLB 161; MAICYA; MTCW; SATA 18, 69
Garner, Hugh 1913-1979 .... **CLC 13**
  See also CA 69-72; CANR 31; DLB 68
Garnett, David 1892-1981 .... **CLC 3**
  See also CA 5-8R; 103; CANR 17; DLB 34
Garos, Stephanie
  See Katz, Steve
Garrett, George (Palmer) 1929- **CLC 3, 11, 51**
  See also CA 1-4R; CAAS 5; CANR 1, 42; DLB 2, 5, 130, 152; DLBY 83
Garrick, David 1717-1779 .... **LC 15; DAM DRAM**
  See also DLB 84
Garrigue, Jean 1914-1972 .... **CLC 2, 8**
  See also CA 5-8R; 37-40R; CANR 20
Garrison, Frederick
  See Sinclair, Upton (Beall)
Garth, Will
  See Hamilton, Edmond; Kuttner, Henry
Garvey, Marcus (Moziah, Jr.) 1887-1940 **TCLC 41; BLC; DAM MULT**
  See also BW 1; CA 120; 124
Gary, Romain .... **CLC 25**
  See also Kacew, Romain
  See also DLB 83
Gascar, Pierre .... **CLC 11**
  See also Fournier, Pierre
Gascoyne, David (Emery) 1916- .... **CLC 45**
  See also CA 65-68; CANR 10, 28, 54; DLB 20; MTCW
Gaskell, Elizabeth Cleghorn 1810-1865 **NCLC 5; DAB; DAM MST; SSC 25**
  See also CDBLB 1832-1890; DLB 21, 144, 159
Gass, William H(oward) 1924- **CLC 1, 2, 8, 11, 15, 39; SSC 12**
  See also CA 17-20R; CANR 30; DLB 2; MTCW
Gasset, Jose Ortega y
  See Ortega y Gasset, Jose
Gates, Henry Louis, Jr. 1950- **CLC 65; DAM MULT**
  See also BW 2; CA 109; CANR 25, 53; DLB 67
Gautier, Theophile 1811-1872 . **NCLC 1, 59; DAM POET; PC 18; SSC 20**
  See also DLB 119
Gawsworth, John
  See Bates, H(erbert) E(rnest)
Gay, Oliver
  See Gogarty, Oliver St. John
Gaye, Marvin (Penze) 1939-1984 ..... **CLC 26**
  See also CA 112
Gebler, Carlo (Ernest) 1954- .... **CLC 39**
  See also CA 119; 133
Gee, Maggie (Mary) 1948- .... **CLC 57**
  See also CA 130
Gee, Maurice (Gough) 1931- .... **CLC 29**
  See also CA 97-100; SATA 46
Gelbart, Larry (Simon) 1923- .... **CLC 21, 61**
  See also CA 73-76; CANR 45
Gelber, Jack 1932- .... **CLC 1, 6, 14, 79**
  See also CA 1-4R; CANR 2; DLB 7
Gellhorn, Martha (Ellis) 1908- ... **CLC 14, 60**
  See also CA 77-80; CANR 44; DLBY 82
Genet, Jean 1910-1986 **CLC 1, 2, 5, 10, 14, 44, 46; DAM DRAM**
  See also CA 13-16R; CANR 18; DLB 72; DLBY 86; MTCW
Gent, Peter 1942- .... **CLC 29**
  See also AITN 1; CA 89-92; DLBY 82
Gentlewoman in New England, A
  See Bradstreet, Anne
Gentlewoman in Those Parts, A
  See Bradstreet, Anne
George, Jean Craighead 1919- .... **CLC 35**
  See also AAYA 8; CA 5-8R; CANR 25; CLR 1; DLB 52; JRDA; MAICYA; SATA 2, 68
George, Stefan (Anton) 1868-1933 **TCLC 2, 14**
  See also CA 104
Georges, Georges Martin
  See Simenon, Georges (Jacques Christian)
Gerhardi, William Alexander
  See Gerhardie, William Alexander
Gerhardie, William Alexander 1895-1977 **CLC 5**
  See also CA 25-28R; 73-76; CANR 18; DLB 36
Gerstler, Amy 1956- .... **CLC 70**
  See also CA 146
Gertler, T. .... **CLC 34**
  See also CA 116; 121; INT 121
Ghalib .... **NCLC 39**
  See also Ghalib, Hsadullah Khan
Ghalib, Hsadullah Khan 1797-1869
  See Ghalib
  See also DAM POET
Ghelderode, Michel de 1898-1962 **CLC 6, 11; DAM DRAM**
  See also CA 85-88; CANR 40
Ghiselin, Brewster 1903- .... **CLC 23**
  See also CA 13-16R; CAAS 10; CANR 13
Ghose, Zulfikar 1935- .... **CLC 42**
  See also CA 65-68
Ghosh, Amitav 1956- .... **CLC 44**
  See also CA 147
Giacosa, Giuseppe 1847-1906 .... **TCLC 7**
  See also CA 104
Gibb, Lee
  See Waterhouse, Keith (Spencer)
Gibbon, Lewis Grassic .... **TCLC 4**
  See also Mitchell, James Leslie
Gibbons, Kaye 1960- **CLC 50, 88; DAM POP**
  See also CA 151
Gibran, Kahlil 1883-1931 . **TCLC 1, 9; DAM POET, POP; PC 9**
  See also CA 104; 150
Gibran, Khalil
  See Gibran, Kahlil
Gibson, William 1914- .. **CLC 23; DA; DAB; DAC; DAM DRAM, MST**
  See also CA 9-12R; CANR 9, 42; DLB 7; SATA 66
Gibson, William (Ford) 1948- ... **CLC 39, 63; DAM POP**
  See also AAYA 12; CA 126; 133; CANR 52
Gide, Andre (Paul Guillaume) 1869-1951 **TCLC 5, 12, 36; DA; DAB; DAC; DAM MST, NOV; SSC 13; WLC**
  See also CA 104; 124; DLB 65; MTCW
Gifford, Barry (Colby) 1946- .... **CLC 34**
  See also CA 65-68; CANR 9, 30, 40
Gilbert, Frank
  See De Voto, Bernard (Augustine)
Gilbert, W(illiam) S(chwenck) 1836-1911 **TCLC 3; DAM DRAM, POET**
  See also CA 104; SATA 36
Gilbreth, Frank B., Jr. 1911- .... **CLC 17**
  See also CA 9-12R; SATA 2
Gilchrist, Ellen 1935- **CLC 34, 48; DAM POP; SSC 14**
  See also CA 113; 116; CANR 41, 61; DLB 130; MTCW
Giles, Molly 1942- .... **CLC 39**
  See also CA 126
Gill, Patrick
  See Creasey, John
Gilliam, Terry (Vance) 1940- .... **CLC 21**
  See also Monty Python
  See also AAYA 19; CA 108; 113; CANR 35;

INT 113
Gillian, Jerry
See Gilliam, Terry (Vance)
Gilliatt, Penelope (Ann Douglass) 1932-1993 CLC 2, 10, 13, 53
See also AITN 2; CA 13-16R; 141; CANR 49; DLB 14
Gilman, Charlotte (Anna) Perkins (Stetson) 1860-1935 .... TCLC 9, 37; SSC 13
See also CA 106; 150
Gilmour, David 1949- .... CLC 35
See also CA 138, 147
Gilpin, William 1724-1804 .... NCLC 30
Gilray, J. D.
See Mencken, H(enry) L(ouis)
Gilroy, Frank D(aniel) 1925- .... CLC 2
See also CA 81-84; CANR 32; DLB 7
Gilstrap, John 1957(?)- .... CLC 99
See also CA 160
Ginsberg, Allen 1926-1997 CLC 1, 2, 3, 4, 6, 13, 36, 69; DA; DAB; DAC; DAM MST, POET; PC 4; WLC 3
See also AITN 1; CA 1-4R; 157; CANR 2, 41; CDALB 1941-1968; DLB 5, 16, 169; MTCW
Ginzburg, Natalia 1916-1991 CLC 5, 11, 54, 70
See also CA 85-88; 135; CANR 33; DLB 177; MTCW
Giono, Jean 1895-1970 .... CLC 4, 11
See also CA 45-48; 29-32R; CANR 2, 35; DLB 72; MTCW
Giovanni, Nikki 1943- CLC 2, 4, 19, 64; BLC; DA; DAB; DAC; DAM MST, MULT, POET; PC 19; WLCS
See also AAYA 22; AITN 1; BW 2; CA 29-32R; CAAS 6; CANR 18, 41, 60; CLR 6; DLB 5, 41; INT CANR-18; MAICYA; MTCW; SATA 24
Giovene, Andrea 1904- .... CLC 7
See also CA 85-88
Gippius, Zinaida (Nikolayevna) 1869-1945
See Hippius, Zinaida
See also CA 106
Giraudoux, (Hippolyte) Jean 1882-1944 TCLC 2, 7; DAM DRAM
See also CA 104; DLB 65
Gironella, Jose Maria 1917- .... CLC 11
See also CA 101
Gissing, George (Robert) 1857-1903 TCLC 3, 24, 47
See also CA 105; DLB 18, 135, 184
Giurlani, Aldo
See Palazzeschi, Aldo
Gladkov, Fyodor (Vasilyevich) 1883-1958 TCLC 27
Glanville, Brian (Lester) 1931- .... CLC 6
See also CA 5-8R; CAAS 9; CANR 3; DLB 15, 139; SATA 42
Glasgow, Ellen (Anderson Gholson) 1873(?)-1945 .... TCLC 2, 7
See also CA 104; DLB 9, 12
Glaspell, Susan 1882(?)-1948 .... TCLC 55
See also CA 110; 154; DLB 7, 9, 78; YABC 2
Glassco, John 1909-1981 .... CLC 9
See also CA 13-16R; 102; CANR 15; DLB 68
Glasscock, Amnesia
See Steinbeck, John (Ernst)
Glasser, Ronald J. 1940(?)- .... CLC 37
Glassman, Joyce
See Johnson, Joyce
Glendinning, Victoria 1937- .... CLC 50
See also CA 120; 127; CANR 59; DLB 155
Glissant, Edouard 1928- . CLC 10, 68; DAM MULT
See also CA 153
Gloag, Julian 1930- .... CLC 40
See also AITN 1; CA 65-68; CANR 10

Glowacki, Aleksander
See Prus, Boleslaw
Gluck, Louise (Elisabeth) 1943-CLC 7, 22, 44, 81; DAM POET; PC 16
See also CA 33-36R; CANR 40; DLB 5
Glyn, Elinor 1864-1943 .... TCLC 72
See also DLB 153
Gobineau, Joseph Arthur (Comte) de 1816-1882 .... NCLC 17
See also DLB 123
Godard, Jean-Luc 1930- .... CLC 20
See also CA 93-96
Godden, (Margaret) Rumer 1907- ... CLC 53
See also AAYA 6; CA 5-8R; CANR 4, 27, 36, 55; CLR 20; DLB 161; MAICYA; SAAS 12; SATA 3, 36
Godoy Alcayaga, Lucila 1889-1957
See Mistral, Gabriela
See also BW 2; CA 104; 131; DAM MULT; HW; MTCW
Godwin, Gail (Kathleen) 1937- CLC 5, 8, 22, 31, 69; DAM POP
See also CA 29-32R; CANR 15, 43; DLB 6; INT CANR-15; MTCW
Godwin, William 1756-1836 .... NCLC 14
See also CDBLB 1789-1832; DLB 39, 104, 142, 158, 163
Goebbels, Josef
See Goebbels, (Paul) Joseph
Goebbels, (Paul) Joseph 1897-1945 TCLC 68
See also CA 115; 148
Goebbels, Joseph Paul
See Goebbels, (Paul) Joseph
Goethe, Johann Wolfgang von 1749-1832 NCLC 4, 22, 34; DA; DAB; DAC; DAM DRAM, MST, POET; PC 5; WLC 3
See also DLB 94
Gogarty, Oliver St. John 1878-1957 TCLC 15
See also CA 109; 150; DLB 15, 19
Gogol, Nikolai (Vasilyevich) 1809-1852 NCLC 5, 15, 31; DA; DAB; DAC; DAM DRAM, MST; DC 1; SSC 4, 29; WLC
Goines, Donald 1937(?)-1974 CLC 80; BLC; DAM MULT, POP
See also AITN 1; BW 1; CA 124; 114; DLB 33
Gold, Herbert 1924- .... CLC 4, 7, 14, 42
See also CA 9-12R; CANR 17, 45; DLB 2; DLBY 81
Goldbarth, Albert 1948- .... CLC 5, 38
See also CA 53-56; CANR 6, 40; DLB 120
Goldberg, Anatol 1910-1982 .... CLC 34
See also CA 131; 117
Goldemberg, Isaac 1945- .... CLC 52
See also CA 69-72; CAAS 12; CANR 11, 32; HW
Golding, William (Gerald) 1911-1993 CLC 1, 2, 3, 8, 10, 17, 27, 58, 81; DA; DAB; DAC; DAM MST, NOV; WLC
See also AAYA 5; CA 5-8R; 141; CANR 13, 33, 54; CDBLB 1945-1960; DLB 15, 100; MTCW
Goldman, Emma 1869-1940 .... TCLC 13
See also CA 110; 150
Goldman, Francisco 1955- .... CLC 76
Goldman, William (W.) 1931- ..... CLC 1, 48
See also CA 9-12R; CANR 29; DLB 44
Goldmann, Lucien 1913-1970 .... CLC 24
See also CA 25-28; CAP 2
Goldoni, Carlo 1707-1793 LC 4; DAM DRAM
Goldsberry, Steven 1949- .... CLC 34
See also CA 131
Goldsmith, Oliver 1728-1774 LC 2; DA; DAB; DAC; DAM DRAM, MST, NOV, POET; DC 8; WLC
See also CDBLB 1660-1789; DLB 39, 89, 104, 109, 142; SATA 26
Goldsmith, Peter

See Priestley, J(ohn) B(oynton)
Gombrowicz, Witold 1904-1969 CLC 4, 7, 11, 49; DAM DRAM
See also CA 19-20; 25-28R; CAP 2
Gomez de la Serna, Ramon 1888-1963 CLC 9
See also CA 153; 116; HW
Goncharov, Ivan Alexandrovich 1812-1891 NCLC 1, 63
Goncourt, Edmond (Louis Antoine Huot) de 1822-1896 .... NCLC 7
See also DLB 123
Goncourt, Jules (Alfred Huot) de 1830-1870 NCLC 7
See also DLB 123
Gontier, Fernande 19(?)- .... CLC 50
Gonzalez Martinez, Enrique 1871-1952 TCLC 72
See also HW
Goodman, Paul 1911-1972 ..... CLC 1, 2, 4, 7
See also CA 19-20; 37-40R; CANR 34; CAP 2; DLB 130; MTCW
Gordimer, Nadine 1923- CLC 3, 5, 7, 10, 18, 33, 51, 70; DA; DAB; DAC; DAM MST, NOV; SSC 17; WLCS
See also CA 5-8R; CANR 3, 28, 56; INT CANR-28; MTCW
Gordon, Adam Lindsay 1833-1870 NCLC 21
Gordon, Caroline 1895-1981 . CLC 6, 13, 29, 83; SSC 15
See also CA 11-12; 103; CANR 36; CAP 1; DLB 4, 9, 102; DLBY 81; MTCW
Gordon, Charles William 1860-1937
See Connor, Ralph
See also CA 109
Gordon, Mary (Catherine) 1949- CLC 13, 22
See also CA 102; CANR 44; DLB 6; DLBY 81; INT 102; MTCW
Gordon, N. J.
See Bosman, Herman Charles
Gordon, Sol 1923- .... CLC 26
See also CA 53-56; CANR 4; SATA 11
Gordone, Charles 1925-1995 CLC 1, 4; DAM DRAM; DC 8
See also BW 1; CA 93-96; 150; CANR 55; DLB 7; INT 93-96; MTCW
Gore, Catherine 1800-1861 .... NCLC 65
See also DLB 116
Gorenko, Anna Andreevna
See Akhmatova, Anna
Gorky, Maxim TCLC 8; DAB; SSC 28; WLC
See also Peshkov, Alexei Maximovich
Goryan, Sirak
See Saroyan, William
Gosse, Edmund (William) 1849-1928 T C L C 28
See also CA 117; DLB 57, 144, 184
Gotlieb, Phyllis Fay (Bloom) 1926- .. CLC 18
See also CA 13-16R; CANR 7; DLB 88
Gottesman, S. D.
See Kornbluth, C(yril) M.; Pohl, Frederik
Gottfried von Strassburg fl. c. 1210- . C M L C 10
See also DLB 138
Gould, Lois .... CLC 4, 10
See also CA 77-80; CANR 29; MTCW
Gourmont, Remy (-Marie-Charles) de 1858-1915 .... TCLC 17
See also CA 109; 150
Govier, Katherine 1948- .... CLC 51
See also CA 101; CANR 18, 40
Goyen, (Charles) William 1915-1983 CLC 5, 8, 14, 40
See also AITN 2; CA 5-8R; 110; CANR 6; DLB 2; DLBY 83; INT CANR-6
Goytisolo, Juan 1931- . CLC 5, 10, 23; DAM MULT; HLC
See also CA 85-88; CANR 32, 61; HW; MTCW

Gozzano, Guido 1883-1916 .... **PC 10**
  See also CA 154; DLB 114
Gozzi, (Conte) Carlo 1720-1806 .... **NCLC 23**
Grabbe, Christian Dietrich 1801-1836 **N C L C 2**
  See also DLB 133
Grace, Patricia 1937- .... **CLC 56**
Gracian y Morales, Baltasar 1601-1658 **LC 15**
Gracq, Julien .... **CLC 11, 48**
  See also Poirier, Louis
  See also DLB 83
Grade, Chaim 1910-1982 .... **CLC 10**
  See also CA 93-96; 107
Graduate of Oxford, A
  See Ruskin, John
Grafton, Garth
  See Duncan, Sara Jeannette
Graham, John
  See Phillips, David Graham
Graham, Jorie 1951- .... **CLC 48**
  See also CA 111; DLB 120
Graham, R(obert) B(ontine) Cunninghame
  See Cunninghame Graham, R(obert) B(ontine)
  See also DLB 98, 135, 174
Graham, Robert
  See Haldeman, Joe (William)
Graham, Tom
  See Lewis, (Harry) Sinclair
Graham, W(illiam) S(ydney) 1918-1986 **C L C 29**
  See also CA 73-76; 118; DLB 20
Graham, Winston (Mawdsley) 1910- **CLC 23**
  See also CA 49-52; CANR 2, 22, 45; DLB 77
Grahame, Kenneth 1859-1932 **TCLC 64; DAB**
  See also CA 108; 136; CLR 5; DLB 34, 141, 178; MAICYA; YABC 1
Grant, Skeeter
  See Spiegelman, Art
Granville-Barker, Harley 1877-1946 **TCLC 2; DAM DRAM**
  See also Barker, Harley Granville
  See also CA 104
Grass, Guenter (Wilhelm) 1927- **CLC 1, 2, 4, 6, 11, 15, 22, 32, 49, 88; DA; DAB; DAC; DAM MST, NOV; WLC**
  See also CA 13-16R; CANR 20; DLB 75, 124; MTCW
Gratton, Thomas
  See Hulme, T(homas) E(rnest)
Grau, Shirley Ann 1929- .. **CLC 4, 9; SSC 15**
  See also CA 89-92; CANR 22; DLB 2; INT CANR-22; MTCW
Gravel, Fern
  See Hall, James Norman
Graver, Elizabeth 1964- .... **CLC 70**
  See also CA 135
Graves, Richard Perceval 1945- ...... **CLC 44**
  See also CA 65-68; CANR 9, 26, 51
Graves, Robert (von Ranke) 1895-1985 **C L C 1, 2, 6, 11, 39, 44, 45; DAB; DAC; DAM MST, POET; PC 6**
  See also CA 5-8R; 117; CANR 5, 36; CDBLB 1914-1945; DLB 20, 100; DLBY 85; MTCW; SATA 45
Graves, Valerie
  See Bradley, Marion Zimmer
Gray, Alasdair (James) 1934- .... **CLC 41**
  See also CA 126; CANR 47; INT 126; MTCW
Gray, Amlin 1946- .... **CLC 29**
  See also CA 138
Gray, Francine du Plessix 1930- ..... **CLC 22; DAM NOV**
  See also BEST 90:3; CA 61-64; CAAS 2; CANR 11, 33; INT CANR-11; MTCW
Gray, John (Henry) 1866-1934 ...... **TCLC 19**
  See also CA 119
Gray, Simon (James Holliday) 1936- **CLC 9, 14, 36**
  See also AITN 1; CA 21-24R; CAAS 3; CANR 32; DLB 13; MTCW
Gray, Spalding 1941- **CLC 49; DAM POP; DC 7**
  See also CA 128
Gray, Thomas 1716-1771 **LC 4, 40; DA; DAB; DAC; DAM MST; PC 2; WLC**
  See also CDBLB 1660-1789; DLB 109
Grayson, David
  See Baker, Ray Stannard
Grayson, Richard (A.) 1951- .... **CLC 38**
  See also CA 85-88; CANR 14, 31, 57
Greeley, Andrew M(oran) 1928- .... **CLC 28; DAM POP**
  See also CA 5-8R; CAAS 7; CANR 7, 43; MTCW
Green, Anna Katharine 1846-1935 **TCLC 63**
  See also CA 112; 159
Green, Brian
  See Card, Orson Scott
Green, Hannah
  See Greenberg, Joanne (Goldenberg)
Green, Hannah 1927(?)-1996 .... **CLC 3**
  See also CA 73-76; CANR 59
Green, Henry 1905-1973 .... **CLC 2, 13, 97**
  See also Yorke, Henry Vincent
  See also DLB 15
Green, Julian (Hartridge) 1900-
  See Green, Julien
  See also CA 21-24R; CANR 33; DLB 4, 72; MTCW
Green, Julien .... **CLC 3, 11, 77**
  See also Green, Julian (Hartridge)
Green, Paul (Eliot) 1894-1981 **CLC 25; DAM DRAM**
  See also AITN 1; CA 5-8R; 103; CANR 3; DLB 7, 9; DLBY 81
Greenberg, Ivan 1908-1973
  See Rahv, Philip
  See also CA 85-88
Greenberg, Joanne (Goldenberg) 1932- **C L C 7, 30**
  See also AAYA 12; CA 5-8R; CANR 14, 32; SATA 25
Greenberg, Richard 1959(?)- .... **CLC 57**
  See also CA 138
Greene, Bette 1934- .... **CLC 30**
  See also AAYA 7; CA 53-56; CANR 4; CLR 2; JRDA; MAICYA; SAAS 16; SATA 8
Greene, Gael .... **CLC 8**
  See also CA 13-16R; CANR 10
Greene, Graham (Henry) 1904-1991 **CLC 1, 3, 6, 9, 14, 18, 27, 37, 70, 72; DA; DAB; DAC; DAM MST, NOV; SSC 29; WLC**
  See also AITN 2; CA 13-16R; 133; CANR 35, 61; CDBLB 1945-1960; DLB 13, 15, 77, 100, 162; DLBY 91; MTCW; SATA 20
Greer, Richard
  See Silverberg, Robert
Gregor, Arthur 1923- .... **CLC 9**
  See also CA 25-28R; CAAS 10; CANR 11; SATA 36
Gregor, Lee
  See Pohl, Frederik
Gregory, Isabella Augusta (Persse) 1852-1932 **TCLC 1**
  See also CA 104; DLB 10
Gregory, J. Dennis
  See Williams, John A(lfred)
Grendon, Stephen
  See Derleth, August (William)
Grenville, Kate 1950- .... **CLC 61**
  See also CA 118; CANR 53
Grenville, Pelham
  See Wodehouse, P(elham) G(renville)
Greve, Felix Paul (Berthold Friedrich) 1879-1948
  See Grove, Frederick Philip
  See also CA 104; 141; DAC; DAM MST
Grey, Zane 1872-1939 .. **TCLC 6; DAM POP**
  See also CA 104; 132; DLB 9; MTCW
Grieg, (Johan) Nordahl (Brun) 1902-1943 **TCLC 10**
  See also CA 107
Grieve, C(hristopher) M(urray) 1892-1978 **CLC 11, 19; DAM POET**
  See also MacDiarmid, Hugh; Pteleon
  See also CA 5-8R; 85-88; CANR 33; MTCW
Griffin, Gerald 1803-1840 .... **NCLC 7**
  See also DLB 159
Griffin, John Howard 1920-1980 .... **CLC 68**
  See also AITN 1; CA 1-4R; 101; CANR 2
Griffin, Peter 1942- .... **CLC 39**
  See also CA 136
Griffith, D(avid Lewelyn) W(ark) 1875(?)-1948 **TCLC 68**
  See also CA 119; 150
Griffith, Lawrence
  See Griffith, D(avid Lewelyn) W(ark)
Griffiths, Trevor 1935- .... **CLC 13, 52**
  See also CA 97-100; CANR 45; DLB 13
Grigson, Geoffrey (Edward Harvey) 1905-1985 **CLC 7, 39**
  See also CA 25-28R; 118; CANR 20, 33; DLB 27; MTCW
Grillparzer, Franz 1791-1872 .... **NCLC 1**
  See also DLB 133
Grimble, Reverend Charles James
  See Eliot, T(homas) S(tearns)
Grimke, Charlotte L(ottie) Forten 1837(?)-1914
  See Forten, Charlotte L.
  See also BW 1; CA 117; 124; DAM MULT, POET
Grimm, Jacob Ludwig Karl 1785-1863 **NCLC 3**
  See also DLB 90; MAICYA; SATA 22
Grimm, Wilhelm Karl 1786-1859 ... **NCLC 3**
  See also DLB 90; MAICYA; SATA 22
Grimmelshausen, Johann Jakob Christoffel von 1621-1676 .... **LC 6**
  See also DLB 168
Grindel, Eugene 1895-1952
  See Eluard, Paul
  See also CA 104
Grisham, John 1955- ...... **CLC 84; DAM POP**
  See also AAYA 14; CA 138; CANR 47
Grossman, David 1954- .... **CLC 67**
  See also CA 138
Grossman, Vasily (Semenovich) 1905-1964 **CLC 41**
  See also CA 124; 130; MTCW
Grove, Frederick Philip .... **TCLC 4**
  See also Greve, Felix Paul (Berthold Friedrich)
  See also DLB 92
Grubb
  See Crumb, R(obert)
Grumbach, Doris (Isaac) 1918- **CLC 13, 22, 64**
  See also CA 5-8R; CAAS 2; CANR 9, 42; INT CANR-9
Grundtvig, Nicolai Frederik Severin 1783-1872 **NCLC 1**
Grunge
  See Crumb, R(obert)
Grunwald, Lisa 1959- .... **CLC 44**
  See also CA 120
Guare, John 1938- . **CLC 8, 14, 29, 67; DAM DRAM**
  See also CA 73-76; CANR 21; DLB 7; MTCW
Gudjonsson, Halldor Kiljan 1902-
  See Laxness, Halldor
  See also CA 103
Guenter, Erich
  See Eich, Guenter

Guest, Barbara 1920- .... CLC 34
  See also CA 25-28R; CANR 11, 44; DLB 5
Guest, Judith (Ann) 1936- . CLC 8, 30; DAM NOV, POP
  See also AAYA 7; CA 77-80; CANR 15; INT CANR-15; MTCW
Guevara, Che .... CLC 87; HLC
  See also Guevara (Serna), Ernesto
Guevara (Serna), Ernesto 1928-1967
  See Guevara, Che
  See also CA 127; 111; CANR 56; DAM MULT; HW
Guild, Nicholas M. 1944- .... CLC 33
  See also CA 93-96
Guillemin, Jacques
  See Sartre, Jean-Paul
Guillen, Jorge 1893-1984 .... CLC 11; DAM MULT, POET
  See also CA 89-92; 112; DLB 108; HW
Guillen, Nicolas (Cristobal) 1902-1989 . C L C 48, 79; BLC; DAM MST, MULT, POET; HLC
  See also BW 2; CA 116; 125; 129; HW
Guillevic, (Eugene) 1907- .... CLC 33
  See also CA 93-96
Guillois
  See Desnos, Robert
Guillois, Valentin
  See Desnos, Robert
Guiney, Louise Imogen 1861-1920 TCLC 41
  See also CA 160; DLB 54
Guiraldes, Ricardo (Guillermo) 1886-1927 TCLC 39
  See also CA 131; HW; MTCW
Gumilev, Nikolai Stephanovich 1886-1921 TCLC 60
Gunesekera, Romesh 1954- .... CLC 91
  See also CA 159
Gunn, Bill .... CLC 5
  See also Gunn, William Harrison
  See also DLB 38
Gunn, Thom(son William) 1929- CLC 3, 6, 18, 32, 81; DAM POET
  See also CA 17-20R; CANR 9, 33; CDBLB 1960 to Present; DLB 27; INT CANR-33; MTCW
Gunn, William Harrison 1934(?)-1989
  See Gunn, Bill
  See also AITN 1; BW 1; CA 13-16R; 128; CANR 12, 25
Gunnars, Kristjana 1948- .... CLC 69
  See also CA 113; DLB 60
Gurdjieff, G(eorgei) I(vanovich) 1877(?)-1949 TCLC 71
  See also CA 157
Gurganus, Allan 1947- .. CLC 70; DAM POP
  See also BEST 90:1; CA 135
Gurney, A(lbert) R(amsdell), Jr. 1930- CLC 32, 50, 54; DAM DRAM
  See also CA 77-80; CANR 32
Gurney, Ivor (Bertie) 1890-1937 ... TCLC 33
Gurney, Peter
  See Gurney, A(lbert) R(amsdell), Jr.
Guro, Elena 1877-1913 .... TCLC 56
Gustafson, James M(oody) 1925- .. CLC 100
  See also CA 25-28R; CANR 37
Gustafson, Ralph (Barker) 1909- .... CLC 36
  See also CA 21-24R; CANR 8, 45; DLB 88
Gut, Gom
  See Simenon, Georges (Jacques Christian)
Guterson, David 1956- .... CLC 91
  See also CA 132
Guthrie, A(lfred) B(ertram), Jr. 1901-1991 CLC 23
  See also CA 57-60; 134; CANR 24; DLB 6; SATA 62; SATA-Obit 67
Guthrie, Isobel
  See Grieve, C(hristopher) M(urray)
Guthrie, Woodrow Wilson 1912-1967
  See Guthrie, Woody
  See also CA 113; 93-96
Guthrie, Woody .... CLC 35
  See also Guthrie, Woodrow Wilson
Guy, Rosa (Cuthbert) 1928- .... CLC 26
  See also AAYA 4; BW 2; CA 17-20R; CANR 14, 34; CLR 13; DLB 33; JRDA; MAICYA; SATA 14, 62
Gwendolyn
  See Bennett, (Enoch) Arnold
H. D. .... CLC 3, 8, 14, 31, 34, 73; PC 5
  See also Doolittle, Hilda
H. de V.
  See Buchan, John
Haavikko, Paavo Juhani 1931- .. CLC 18, 34
  See also CA 106
Habbema, Koos
  See Heijermans, Herman
Habermas, Juergen 1929- .... CLC 104
  See also CA 109
Habermas, Jurgen
  See Habermas, Juergen
Hacker, Marilyn 1942- CLC 5, 9, 23, 72, 91; DAM POET
  See also CA 77-80; DLB 120
Haggard, H(enry) Rider 1856-1925 TCLC 11
  See also CA 108; 148; DLB 70, 156, 174, 178; SATA 16
Hagiosy, L.
  See Larbaud, Valery (Nicolas)
Hagiwara Sakutaro 1886-1942 TCLC 60; PC 18
Haig, Fenil
  See Ford, Ford Madox
Haig-Brown, Roderick (Langmere) 1908-1976 CLC 21
  See also CA 5-8R; 69-72; CANR 4, 38; CLR 31; DLB 88; MAICYA; SATA 12
Hailey, Arthur 1920- CLC 5; DAM NOV, POP
  See also AITN 2; BEST 90:3; CA 1-4R; CANR 2, 36; DLB 88; DLBY 82; MTCW
Hailey, Elizabeth Forsythe 1938- ..... CLC 40
  See also CA 93-96; CAAS 1; CANR 15, 48; INT CANR-15
Haines, John (Meade) 1924- .... CLC 58
  See also CA 17-20R; CANR 13, 34; DLB 5
Hakluyt, Richard 1552-1616 .... LC 31
Haldeman, Joe (William) 1943- .... CLC 61
  See also CA 53-56; CAAS 25; CANR 6; DLB 8; INT CANR-6
Haley, Alex(ander Murray Palmer) 1921-1992 CLC 8, 12, 76; BLC; DA; DAB; DAC; DAM MST, MULT, POP
  See also BW 2; CA 77-80; 136; CANR 61; DLB 38; MTCW
Haliburton, Thomas Chandler 1796-1865 NCLC 15
  See also DLB 11, 99
Hall, Donald (Andrew, Jr.) 1928- CLC 1, 13, 37, 59; DAM POET
  See also CA 5-8R; CAAS 7; CANR 2, 44; DLB 5; SATA 23
Hall, Frederic Sauser
  See Sauser-Hall, Frederic
Hall, James
  See Kuttner, Henry
Hall, James Norman 1887-1951 ..... TCLC 23
  See also CA 123; SATA 21
Hall, (Marguerite) Radclyffe 1886-1943 TCLC 12
  See also CA 110; 150
Hall, Rodney 1935- .... CLC 51
  See also CA 109
Halleck, Fitz-Greene 1790-1867 .... NCLC 47
  See also DLB 3
Halliday, Michael
  See Creasey, John
Halpern, Daniel 1945- .... CLC 14
  See also CA 33-36R
Hamburger, Michael (Peter Leopold) 1924- CLC 5, 14
  See also CA 5-8R; CAAS 4; CANR 2, 47; DLB 27
Hamill, Pete 1935- .... CLC 10
  See also CA 25-28R; CANR 18
Hamilton, Alexander 1755(?)-1804 NCLC 49
  See also DLB 37
Hamilton, Clive
  See Lewis, C(live) S(taples)
Hamilton, Edmond 1904-1977 .... CLC 1
  See also CA 1-4R; CANR 3; DLB 8
Hamilton, Eugene (Jacob) Lee
  See Lee-Hamilton, Eugene (Jacob)
Hamilton, Franklin
  See Silverberg, Robert
Hamilton, Gail
  See Corcoran, Barbara
Hamilton, Mollie
  See Kaye, M(ary) M(argaret)
Hamilton, (Anthony Walter) Patrick 1904-1962 CLC 51
  See also CA 113; DLB 10
Hamilton, Virginia 1936- ...... CLC 26; DAM MULT
  See also AAYA 2, 21; BW 2; CA 25-28R; CANR 20, 37; CLR 1, 11, 40; DLB 33, 52; INT CANR-20; JRDA; MAICYA; MTCW; SATA 4, 56, 79
Hammett, (Samuel) Dashiell 1894-1961 C L C 3, 5, 10, 19, 47; SSC 17
  See also AITN 1; CA 81-84; CANR 42; CDALB 1929-1941; DLBD 6; DLBY 96; MTCW
Hammon, Jupiter 1711(?)-1800(?). NCLC 5; BLC; DAM MULT, POET; PC 16
  See also DLB 31, 50
Hammond, Keith
  See Kuttner, Henry
Hamner, Earl (Henry), Jr. 1923- .... CLC 12
  See also AITN 2; CA 73-76; DLB 6
Hampton, Christopher (James) 1946- CLC 4
  See also CA 25-28R; DLB 13; MTCW
Hamsun, Knut .... TCLC 2, 14, 49
  See also Pedersen, Knut
Handke, Peter 1942- CLC 5, 8, 10, 15, 38; DAM DRAM, NOV
  See also CA 77-80; CANR 33; DLB 85, 124; MTCW
Hanley, James 1901-1985 ..... CLC 3, 5, 8, 13
  See also CA 73-76; 117; CANR 36; MTCW
Hannah, Barry 1942- .... CLC 23, 38, 90
  See also CA 108; 110; CANR 43; DLB 6; INT 110; MTCW
Hannon, Ezra
  See Hunter, Evan
Hansberry, Lorraine (Vivian) 1930-1965 CLC 17, 62; BLC; DA; DAB; DAC; DAM DRAM, MST, MULT; DC 2
  See also BW 1; CA 109; 25-28R; CABS 3; CANR 58; CDALB 1941-1968; DLB 7, 38; MTCW
Hansen, Joseph 1923- .... CLC 38
  See also CA 29-32R; CAAS 17; CANR 16, 44; INT CANR-16
Hansen, Martin A. 1909-1955 .... TCLC 32
Hanson, Kenneth O(stlin) 1922- .... CLC 13
  See also CA 53-56; CANR 7
Hardwick, Elizabeth 1916- .... CLC 13; DAM NOV
  See also CA 5-8R; CANR 3, 32; DLB 6; MTCW
Hardy, Thomas 1840-1928 TCLC 4, 10, 18, 32, 48, 53, 72; DA; DAB; DAC; DAM MST,

NOV, POET; PC 8; SSC 2; WLC
   See also CA 104; 123; CDBLB 1890-1914; DLB 18, 19, 135; MTCW
Hare, David 1947- .... **CLC 29, 58**
   See also CA 97-100; CANR 39; DLB 13; MTCW
Harewood, John
   See Van Druten, John (William)
Harford, Henry
   See Hudson, W(illiam) H(enry)
Hargrave, Leonie
   See Disch, Thomas M(ichael)
Harjo, Joy 1951- .... **CLC 83; DAM MULT**
   See also CA 114; CANR 35; DLB 120, 175; NNAL
Harlan, Louis R(udolph) 1922- .... **CLC 34**
   See also CA 21-24R; CANR 25, 55
Harling, Robert 1951(?)- .... **CLC 53**
   See also CA 147
Harmon, William (Ruth) 1938- .... **CLC 38**
   See also CA 33-36R; CANR 14, 32, 35; SATA 65
Harper, F. E. W.
   See Harper, Frances Ellen Watkins
Harper, Frances E. W.
   See Harper, Frances Ellen Watkins
Harper, Frances E. Watkins
   See Harper, Frances Ellen Watkins
Harper, Frances Ellen
   See Harper, Frances Ellen Watkins
Harper, Frances Ellen Watkins 1825-1911
      TCLC 14; BLC; DAM MULT, POET
   See also BW 1; CA 111; 125; DLB 50
Harper, Michael S(teven) 1938- .. **CLC 7, 22**
   See also BW 1; CA 33-36R; CANR 24; DLB 41
Harper, Mrs. F. E. W.
   See Harper, Frances Ellen Watkins
Harris, Christie (Lucy) Irwin 1907- **CLC 12**
   See also CA 5-8R; CANR 6; CLR 47; DLB 88; JRDA; MAICYA; SAAS 10; SATA 6, 74
Harris, Frank 1856-1931 .... **TCLC 24**
   See also CA 109; 150; DLB 156
Harris, George Washington 1814-1869**NCLC 23**
   See also DLB 3, 11
Harris, Joel Chandler 1848-1908 ... **TCLC 2; SSC 19**
   See also CA 104; 137; DLB 11, 23, 42, 78, 91; MAICYA; YABC 1
Harris, John (Wyndham Parkes Lucas) Beynon 1903-1969
   See Wyndham, John
   See also CA 102; 89-92
Harris, MacDonald .... **CLC 9**
   See also Heiney, Donald (William)
Harris, Mark 1922- .... **CLC 19**
   See also CA 5-8R; CAAS 3; CANR 2, 55; DLB 2; DLBY 80
Harris, (Theodore) Wilson 1921- .... **CLC 25**
   See also BW 2; CA 65-68; CAAS 16; CANR 11, 27; DLB 117; MTCW
Harrison, Elizabeth Cavanna 1909-
   See Cavanna, Betty
   See also CA 9-12R; CANR 6, 27
Harrison, Harry (Max) 1925- .... **CLC 42**
   See also CA 1-4R; CANR 5, 21; DLB 8; SATA 4
Harrison, James (Thomas) 1937- **CLC 6, 14, 33, 66; SSC 19**
   See also CA 13-16R; CANR 8, 51; DLBY 82; INT CANR-8
Harrison, Jim
   See Harrison, James (Thomas)
Harrison, Kathryn 1961- .... **CLC 70**
   See also CA 144
Harrison, Tony 1937- .... **CLC 43**

   See also CA 65-68; CANR 44; DLB 40; MTCW
Harriss, Will(ard Irvin) 1922- .... **CLC 34**
   See also CA 111
Harson, Sley
   See Ellison, Harlan (Jay)
Hart, Ellis
   See Ellison, Harlan (Jay)
Hart, Josephine 1942(?)-**CLC 70; DAM POP**
   See also CA 138
Hart, Moss 1904-1961**CLC 66; DAM DRAM**
   See also CA 109; 89-92; DLB 7
Harte, (Francis) Bret(t) 1836(?)-1902**TCLC 1, 25; DA; DAC; DAM MST; SSC 8; WLC**
   See also CA 104; 140; CDALB 1865-1917; DLB 12, 64, 74, 79; SATA 26
Hartley, L(eslie) P(oles) 1895-1972**CLC 2, 22**
   See also CA 45-48; 37-40R; CANR 33; DLB 15, 139; MTCW
Hartman, Geoffrey H. 1929- ....**CLC 27**
   See also CA 117; 125; DLB 67
Hartmann, Sadakichi 1867-1944 ... **TCLC 73**
   See also CA 157; DLB 54
Hartmann von Aue c. 1160-c. 1205**CMLC 15**
   See also DLB 138
Hartmann von Aue 1170-1210 ...... **CMLC 15**
Haruf, Kent 1943- ....**CLC 34**
   See also CA 149
Harwood, Ronald 1934- .... **CLC 32; DAM DRAM, MST**
   See also CA 1-4R; CANR 4, 55; DLB 13
Hasek, Jaroslav (Matej Frantisek) 1883-1923
      TCLC 4
   See also CA 104; 129; MTCW
Hass, Robert 1941- ... **CLC 18, 39, 99; PC 16**
   See also CA 111; CANR 30, 50; DLB 105; SATA 94
Hastings, Hudson
   See Kuttner, Henry
Hastings, Selina ....**CLC 44**
Hathorne, John 1641-1717 .... **LC 38**
Hatteras, Amelia
   See Mencken, H(enry) L(ouis)
Hatteras, Owen .... **TCLC 18**
   See also Mencken, H(enry) L(ouis); Nathan, George Jean
Hauptmann, Gerhart (Johann Robert) 1862-1946 .... **TCLC 4; DAM DRAM**
   See also CA 104; 153; DLB 66, 118
Havel, Vaclav 1936- .. **CLC 25, 58, 65; DAM DRAM; DC 6**
   See also CA 104; CANR 36; MTCW
Haviaras, Stratis ....**CLC 33**
   See also Chaviaras, Strates
Hawes, Stephen 1475(?)-1523(?) .... **LC 17**
Hawkes, John (Clendennin Burne, Jr.) 1925-
      CLC 1, 2, 3, 4, 7, 9, 14, 15, 27, 49
   See also CA 1-4R; CANR 2, 47; DLB 2, 7; DLBY 80; MTCW
Hawking, S. W.
   See Hawking, Stephen W(illiam)
Hawking, Stephen W(illiam) 1942- **CLC 63, 105**
   See also AAYA 13; BEST 89:1; CA 126; 129; CANR 48
Hawthorne, Julian 1846-1934 .... **TCLC 25**
Hawthorne, Nathaniel 1804-1864 **NCLC 39; DA; DAB; DAC; DAM MST, NOV; SSC 29; WLC**
   See also AAYA 18; CDALB 1640-1865; DLB 1, 74; YABC 2
Haxton, Josephine Ayres 1921-
   See Douglas, Ellen
   See also CA 115; CANR 41
Hayaseca y Eizaguirre, Jorge
   See Echegaray (y Eizaguirre), Jose (Maria Waldo)
Hayashi Fumiko 1904-1951 .... **TCLC 27**

   See also CA 161; DLB 180
Haycraft, Anna
   See Ellis, Alice Thomas
   See also CA 122
Hayden, Robert E(arl) 1913-1980 **CLC 5, 9, 14, 37; BLC; DA; DAC; DAM MST, MULT, POET; PC 6**
   See also BW 1; CA 69-72; 97-100; CABS 2; CANR 24; CDALB 1941-1968; DLB 5, 76; MTCW; SATA 19; SATA-Obit 26
Hayford, J(oseph) E(phraim) Casely
   See Casely-Hayford, J(oseph) E(phraim)
Hayman, Ronald 1932- .... **CLC 44**
   See also CA 25-28R; CANR 18, 50; DLB 155
Haywood, Eliza (Fowler) 1693(?)-1756 **LC 1**
Hazlitt, William 1778-1830 ....**NCLC 29**
   See also DLB 110, 158
Hazzard, Shirley 1931- .... **CLC 18**
   See also CA 9-12R; CANR 4; DLBY 82; MTCW
Head, Bessie 1937-1986 .. **CLC 25, 67; BLC; DAM MULT**
   See also BW 2; CA 29-32R; 119; CANR 25; DLB 117; MTCW
Headon, (Nicky) Topper 1956(?)- .... **CLC 30**
Heaney, Seamus (Justin) 1939- **CLC 5, 7, 14, 25, 37, 74, 91; DAB; DAM POET; PC 18; WLCS**
   See also CA 85-88; CANR 25, 48; CDBLB 1960 to Present; DLB 40; DLBY 95; MTCW
Hearn, (Patricio) Lafcadio (Tessima Carlos) 1850-1904 .... **TCLC 9**
   See also CA 105; DLB 12, 78
Hearne, Vicki 1946- .... **CLC 56**
   See also CA 139
Hearon, Shelby 1931- .... **CLC 63**
   See also AITN 2; CA 25-28R; CANR 18, 48
Heat-Moon, William Least .... **CLC 29**
   See also Trogdon, William (Lewis)
   See also AAYA 9
Hebbel, Friedrich 1813-1863**NCLC 43; DAM DRAM**
   See also DLB 129
Hebert, Anne 1916-**CLC 4, 13, 29; DAC; DAM MST, POET**
   See also CA 85-88; DLB 68; MTCW
Hecht, Anthony (Evan) 1923- **CLC 8, 13, 19; DAM POET**
   See also CA 9-12R; CANR 6; DLB 5, 169
Hecht, Ben 1894-1964 .... **CLC 8**
   See also CA 85-88; DLB 7, 9, 25, 26, 28, 86
Hedayat, Sadeq 1903-1951 .... **TCLC 21**
   See also CA 120
Hegel, Georg Wilhelm Friedrich 1770-1831
      NCLC 46
   See also DLB 90
Heidegger, Martin 1889-1976 .... **CLC 24**
   See also CA 81-84; 65-68; CANR 34; MTCW
Heidenstam, (Carl Gustaf) Verner von 1859-1940 .... **TCLC 5**
   See also CA 104
Heifner, Jack 1946- .... **CLC 11**
   See also CA 105; CANR 47
Heijermans, Herman 1864-1924 .... **TCLC 24**
   See also CA 123
Heilbrun, Carolyn G(old) 1926- ...... **CLC 25**
   See also CA 45-48; CANR 1, 28, 58
Heine, Heinrich 1797-1856 ....**NCLC 4, 54**
   See also DLB 90
Heinemann, Larry (Curtiss) 1944- .. **CLC 50**
   See also CA 110; CAAS 21; CANR 31; DLBD 9; INT CANR-31
Heiney, Donald (William) 1921-1993
   See Harris, MacDonald
   See also CA 1-4R; 142; CANR 3, 58
Heinlein, Robert A(nson) 1907-1988**CLC 1, 3, 8, 14, 26, 55; DAM POP**

See also AAYA 17; CA 1-4R; 125; CANR 1, 20, 53; DLB 8; JRDA; MAICYA; MTCW; SATA 9, 69; SATA-Obit 56

Helforth, John
See Doolittle, Hilda

Hellenhofferu, Vojtech Kapristian z
See Hasek, Jaroslav (Matej Frantisek)

Heller, Joseph 1923-CLC **1, 3, 5, 8, 11, 36, 63; DA; DAB; DAC; DAM MST, NOV, POP; WLC**
See also AITN 1; CA 5-8R; CABS 1; CANR 8, 42; DLB 2, 28; DLBY 80; INT CANR-8; MTCW

Hellman, Lillian (Florence) 1906-1984CLC **2, 4, 8, 14, 18, 34, 44, 52; DAM DRAM; DC 1**
See also AITN 1, 2; CA 13-16R; 112; CANR 33; DLB 7; DLBY 84; MTCW

Helprin, Mark 1947-CLC **7, 10, 22, 32; DAM NOV, POP**
See also CA 81-84; CANR 47; DLBY 85; MTCW

Helvetius, Claude-Adrien 1715-1771 . **LC 26**

Helyar, Jane Penelope Josephine 1933-
See Poole, Josephine
See also CA 21-24R; CANR 10, 26; SATA 82

Hemans, Felicia 1793-1835 .... **NCLC 29**
See also DLB 96

Hemingway, Ernest (Miller) 1899-1961 **C L C 1, 3, 6, 8, 10, 13, 19, 30, 34, 39, 41, 44, 50, 61, 80; DA; DAB; DAC; DAM MST, NOV; SSC 25; WLC**
See also AAYA 19; CA 77-80; CANR 34; CDALB 1917-1929; DLB 4, 9, 102; DLBD 1, 15, 16; DLBY 81, 87, 96; MTCW

Hempel, Amy 1951- .... **CLC 39**
See also CA 118; 137

Henderson, F. C.
See Mencken, H(enry) L(ouis)

Henderson, Sylvia
See Ashton-Warner, Sylvia (Constance)

Henderson, Zenna (Chlarson) 1917-1983S S C **29**
See also CA 1-4R; 133; CANR 1; DLB 8; SATA 5

Henley, Beth .... **CLC 23; DC 6**
See also Henley, Elizabeth Becker
See also CABS 3; DLBY 86

Henley, Elizabeth Becker 1952-
See Henley, Beth
See also CA 107; CANR 32; DAM DRAM, MST; MTCW

Henley, William Ernest 1849-1903 .. **TCLC 8**
See also CA 105; DLB 19

Hennissart, Martha
See Lathen, Emma
See also CA 85-88

Henry, O. .... **TCLC 1, 19; SSC 5; WLC**
See also Porter, William Sydney

Henry, Patrick 1736-1799 .... **LC 25**

Henryson, Robert 1430(?)-1506(?) ..... **LC 20**
See also DLB 146

Henry VIII 1491-1547 .... **LC 10**

Henschke, Alfred
See Klabund

Hentoff, Nat(han Irving) 1925- .... **CLC 26**
See also AAYA 4; CA 1-4R; CAAS 6; CANR 5, 25; CLR 1; INT CANR-25; JRDA; MAICYA; SATA 42, 69; SATA-Brief 27

Heppenstall, (John) Rayner 1911-1981 **C L C 10**
See also CA 1-4R; 103; CANR 29

Heraclitus c. 540B.C.-c. 450B.C. .... **CMLC 22**
See also DLB 176

Herbert, Frank (Patrick) 1920-1986CLC **12, 23, 35, 44, 85; DAM POP**
See also AAYA 21; CA 53-56; 118; CANR 5, 43; DLB 8; INT CANR-5; MTCW; SATA 9, 37; SATA-Obit 47

Herbert, George 1593-1633 ..... **LC 24; DAB; DAM POET; PC 4**
See also CDBLB Before 1660; DLB 126

Herbert, Zbigniew 1924- ...**CLC 9, 43; DAM POET**
See also CA 89-92; CANR 36; MTCW

Herbst, Josephine (Frey) 1897-1969 **CLC 34**
See also CA 5-8R; 25-28R; DLB 9

Hergesheimer, Joseph 1880-1954 .. **TCLC 11**
See also CA 109; DLB 102, 9

Herlihy, James Leo 1927-1993 .... **CLC 6**
See also CA 1-4R; 143; CANR 2

Hermogenes fl. c. 175- .... **CMLC 6**

Hernandez, Jose 1834-1886 .... **NCLC 17**

Herodotus c. 484B.C.-429B.C. .... **CMLC 17**
See also DLB 176

Herrick, Robert 1591-1674LC **13; DA; DAB; DAC; DAM MST, POP; PC 9**
See also DLB 126

Herring, Guilles
See Somerville, Edith

Herriot, James 1916-1995CLC **12; DAM POP**
See also Wight, James Alfred
See also AAYA 1; CA 148; CANR 40; SATA 86

Herrmann, Dorothy 1941- .... **CLC 44**
See also CA 107

Herrmann, Taffy
See Herrmann, Dorothy

Hersey, John (Richard) 1914-1993CLC **1, 2, 7, 9, 40, 81, 97; DAM POP**
See also CA 17-20R; 140; CANR 33; DLB 6; MTCW; SATA 25; SATA-Obit 76

Herzen, Aleksandr Ivanovich 1812-1870 **NCLC 10, 61**

Herzl, Theodor 1860-1904 .... **TCLC 36**

Herzog, Werner 1942- .... **CLC 16**
See also CA 89-92

Hesiod c. 8th cent. B.C.- .... **CMLC 5**
See also DLB 176

Hesse, Hermann 1877-1962CLC **1, 2, 3, 6, 11, 17, 25, 69; DA; DAB; DAC; DAM MST, NOV; SSC 9; WLC**
See also CA 17-18; CAP 2; DLB 66; MTCW; SATA 50

Hewes, Cady
See De Voto, Bernard (Augustine)

Heyen, William 1940- .... **CLC 13, 18**
See also CA 33-36R; CAAS 9; DLB 5

Heyerdahl, Thor 1914- .... **CLC 26**
See also CA 5-8R; CANR 5, 22; MTCW; SATA 2, 52

Heym, Georg (Theodor Franz Arthur) 1887-1912 .... **TCLC 9**
See also CA 106

Heym, Stefan 1913- .... **CLC 41**
See also CA 9-12R; CANR 4; DLB 69

Heyse, Paul (Johann Ludwig von) 1830-1914 **TCLC 8**
See also CA 104; DLB 129

Heyward, (Edwin) DuBose 1885-1940 **T C L C 59**
See also CA 108; 157; DLB 7, 9, 45; SATA 21

Hibbert, Eleanor Alice Burford 1906-1993 **CLC 7; DAM POP**
See also BEST 90:4; CA 17-20R; 140; CANR 9, 28, 59; SATA 2; SATA-Obit 74

Hichens, Robert S. 1864-1950 .... **TCLC 64**
See also DLB 153

Higgins, George V(incent) 1939-CLC **4, 7, 10, 18**
See also CA 77-80; CAAS 5; CANR 17, 51; DLB 2; DLBY 81; INT CANR-17; MTCW

Higginson, Thomas Wentworth 1823-1911 **TCLC 36**
See also DLB 1, 64

Highet, Helen
See MacInnes, Helen (Clark)

Highsmith, (Mary) Patricia 1921-1995CLC **2, 4, 14, 42, 102; DAM NOV, POP**
See also CA 1-4R; 147; CANR 1, 20, 48, 62; MTCW

Highwater, Jamake (Mamake) 1942(?)- **C L C 12**
See also AAYA 7; CA 65-68; CAAS 7; CANR 10, 34; CLR 17; DLB 52; DLBY 85; JRDA; MAICYA; SATA 32, 69; SATA-Brief 30

Highway, Tomson 1951-CLC **92; DAC; DAM MULT**
See also CA 151; NNAL

Higuchi, Ichiyo 1872-1896 .... **NCLC 49**

Hijuelos, Oscar 1951-CLC **65; DAM MULT, POP; HLC**
See also BEST 90:1; CA 123; CANR 50; DLB 145; HW

Hikmet, Nazim 1902(?)-1963 .... **CLC 40**
See also CA 141; 93-96

Hildegard von Bingen 1098-1179 . **CMLC 20**
See also DLB 148

Hildesheimer, Wolfgang 1916-1991 . **CLC 49**
See also CA 101; 135; DLB 69, 124

Hill, Geoffrey (William) 1932- CLC **5, 8, 18, 45; DAM POET**
See also CA 81-84; CANR 21; CDBLB 1960 to Present; DLB 40; MTCW

Hill, George Roy 1921- .... **CLC 26**
See also CA 110; 122

Hill, John
See Koontz, Dean R(ay)

Hill, Susan (Elizabeth) 1942- . **CLC 4; DAB; DAM MST, NOV**
See also CA 33-36R; CANR 29; DLB 14, 139; MTCW

Hillerman, Tony 1925- .. **CLC 62; DAM POP**
See also AAYA 6; BEST 89:1; CA 29-32R; CANR 21, 42; SATA 6

Hillesum, Etty 1914-1943 .... **TCLC 49**
See also CA 137

Hilliard, Noel (Harvey) 1929- .... **CLC 15**
See also CA 9-12R; CANR 7

Hillis, Rick 1956- .... **CLC 66**
See also CA 134

Hilton, James 1900-1954 .... **TCLC 21**
See also CA 108; DLB 34, 77; SATA 34

Himes, Chester (Bomar) 1909-1984CLC **2, 4, 7, 18, 58; BLC; DAM MULT**
See also BW 2; CA 25-28R; 114; CANR 22; DLB 2, 76, 143; MTCW

Hinde, Thomas .... **CLC 6, 11**
See also Chitty, Thomas Willes

Hindin, Nathan
See Bloch, Robert (Albert)

Hine, (William) Daryl 1936- .... **CLC 15**
See also CA 1-4R; CAAS 15; CANR 1, 20; DLB 60

Hinkson, Katharine Tynan
See Tynan, Katharine

Hinton, S(usan) E(loise) 1950- CLC **30; DA; DAC; DAM MST, NOV**
See also AAYA 2; CA 81-84; CANR 32, 62; CLR 3, 23; JRDA; MAICYA; MTCW; SATA 19, 58

Hippius, Zinaida .... **TCLC 9**
See also Gippius, Zinaida (Nikolayevna)

Hiraoka, Kimitake 1925-1970
See Mishima, Yukio
See also CA 97-100; 29-32R; DAM DRAM; MTCW

Hirsch, E(ric) D(onald), Jr. 1928- ..... **CLC 79**
See also CA 25-28R; CANR 27, 51; DLB 67; INT CANR-27; MTCW

Hirsch, Edward 1950- .... **CLC 31, 50**
See also CA 104; CANR 20, 42; DLB 120

Hitchcock, Alfred (Joseph) 1899-1980 **CLC 16**
See also AAYA 22; CA 159; 97-100; SATA 27; SATA-Obit 24

Hitler, Adolf 1889-1945 .... **TCLC 53**
See also CA 117; 147

Hoagland, Edward 1932- .... **CLC 28**
See also CA 1-4R; CANR 2, 31, 57; DLB 6; SATA 51

Hoban, Russell (Conwell) 1925- .. **CLC 7, 25; DAM NOV**
See also CA 5-8R; CANR 23, 37; CLR 3; DLB 52; MAICYA; MTCW; SATA 1, 40, 78

Hobbes, Thomas 1588-1679 .... **LC 36**
See also DLB 151

Hobbs, Perry
See Blackmur, R(ichard) P(almer)

Hobson, Laura Z(ametkin) 1900-1986 **CLC 7, 25**
See also CA 17-20R; 118; CANR 55; DLB 28; SATA 52

Hochhuth, Rolf 1931- .. **CLC 4, 11, 18; DAM DRAM**
See also CA 5-8R; CANR 33; DLB 124; MTCW

Hochman, Sandra 1936- .... **CLC 3, 8**
See also CA 5-8R; DLB 5

Hochwaelder, Fritz 1911-1986 **CLC 36; DAM DRAM**
See also CA 29-32R; 120; CANR 42; MTCW

Hochwalder, Fritz
See Hochwaelder, Fritz

Hocking, Mary (Eunice) 1921- .... **CLC 13**
See also CA 101; CANR 18, 40

Hodgins, Jack 1938- .... **CLC 23**
See also CA 93-96; DLB 60

Hodgson, William Hope 1877(?)-1918 **TCLC 13**
See also CA 111; DLB 70, 153, 156, 178

Hoeg, Peter 1957- .... **CLC 95**
See also CA 151

Hoffman, Alice 1952- ... **CLC 51; DAM NOV**
See also CA 77-80; CANR 34; MTCW

Hoffman, Daniel (Gerard) 1923- **CLC 6, 13, 23**
See also CA 1-4R; CANR 4; DLB 5

Hoffman, Stanley 1944- .... **CLC 5**
See also CA 77-80

Hoffman, William M(oses) 1939- ..... **CLC 40**
See also CA 57-60; CANR 11

Hoffmann, E(rnst) T(heodor) A(madeus) 1776-1822 .... **NCLC 2; SSC 13**
See also DLB 90; SATA 27

Hofmann, Gert 1931- .... **CLC 54**
See also CA 128

Hofmannsthal, Hugo von 1874-1929 .. **TCLC 11; DAM DRAM; DC 4**
See also CA 106; 153; DLB 81, 118

Hogan, Linda 1947- ... **CLC 73; DAM MULT**
See also CA 120; CANR 45; DLB 175; NNAL

Hogarth, Charles
See Creasey, John

Hogarth, Emmett
See Polonsky, Abraham (Lincoln)

Hogg, James 1770-1835 .... **NCLC 4**
See also DLB 93, 116, 159

Holbach, Paul Henri Thiry Baron 1723-1789 **LC 14**

Holberg, Ludvig 1684-1754 .... **LC 6**

Holden, Ursula 1921- .... **CLC 18**
See also CA 101; CAAS 8; CANR 22

Holderlin, (Johann Christian) Friedrich 1770-1843 .... **NCLC 16; PC 4**

Holdstock, Robert
See Holdstock, Robert P.

Holdstock, Robert P. 1948- .... **CLC 39**
See also CA 131

Holland, Isabelle 1920- .... **CLC 21**
See also AAYA 11; CA 21-24R; CANR 10, 25, 47; JRDA; MAICYA; SATA 8, 70

Holland, Marcus
See Caldwell, (Janet Miriam) Taylor (Holland)

Hollander, John 1929- .... **CLC 2, 5, 8, 14**
See also CA 1-4R; CANR 1, 52; DLB 5; SATA 13

Hollander, Paul
See Silverberg, Robert

Holleran, Andrew 1943(?)- .... **CLC 38**
See also CA 144

Hollinghurst, Alan 1954- .... **CLC 55, 91**
See also CA 114

Hollis, Jim
See Summers, Hollis (Spurgeon, Jr.)

Holly, Buddy 1936-1959 .... **TCLC 65**

Holmes, Gordon
See Shiel, M(atthew) P(hipps)

Holmes, John
See Souster, (Holmes) Raymond

Holmes, John Clellon 1926-1988 ...... **CLC 56**
See also CA 9-12R; 125; CANR 4; DLB 16

Holmes, Oliver Wendell 1809-1894 **NCLC 14**
See also CDALB 1640-1865; DLB 1; SATA 34

Holmes, Raymond
See Souster, (Holmes) Raymond

Holt, Victoria
See Hibbert, Eleanor Alice Burford

Holub, Miroslav 1923- .... **CLC 4**
See also CA 21-24R; CANR 10

Homer c. 8th cent. B.C.- ... **CMLC 1, 16; DA; DAB; DAC; DAM MST, POET; WLCS**
See also DLB 176

Honig, Edwin 1919- .... **CLC 33**
See also CA 5-8R; CAAS 8; CANR 4, 45; DLB 5

Hood, Hugh (John Blagdon) 1928- **CLC 15, 28**
See also CA 49-52; CAAS 17; CANR 1, 33; DLB 53

Hood, Thomas 1799-1845 .... **NCLC 16**
See also DLB 96

Hooker, (Peter) Jeremy 1941- .... **CLC 43**
See also CA 77-80; CANR 22; DLB 40

hooks, bell .... **CLC 94**
See also Watkins, Gloria

Hope, A(lec) D(erwent) 1907- .... **CLC 3, 51**
See also CA 21-24R; CANR 33; MTCW

Hope, Brian
See Creasey, John

Hope, Christopher (David Tully) 1944- **CLC 52**
See also CA 106; CANR 47; SATA 62

Hopkins, Gerard Manley 1844-1889 .. **NCLC 17; DA; DAB; DAC; DAM MST, POET; PC 15; WLC**
See also CDBLB 1890-1914; DLB 35, 57

Hopkins, John (Richard) 1931- .... **CLC 4**
See also CA 85-88

Hopkins, Pauline Elizabeth 1859-1930 **TCLC 28; BLC; DAM MULT**
See also BW 2; CA 141; DLB 50

Hopkinson, Francis 1737-1791 .... **LC 25**
See also DLB 31

Hopley-Woolrich, Cornell George 1903-1968
See Woolrich, Cornell
See also CA 13-14; CANR 58; CAP 1

Horatio
See Proust, (Valentin-Louis-George-Eugene-) Marcel

Horgan, Paul (George Vincent O'Shaughnessy) 1903-1995 .... **CLC 9, 53; DAM NOV**
See also CA 13-16R; 147; CANR 9, 35; DLB 102; DLBY 85; INT CANR-9; MTCW; SATA 13; SATA-Obit 84

Horn, Peter
See Kuttner, Henry

Hornem, Horace Esq.
See Byron, George Gordon (Noel)

Horney, Karen (Clementine Theodore Danielsen) 1885-1952 .... **TCLC 71**
See also CA 114

Hornung, E(rnest) W(illiam) 1866-1921 **TCLC 59**
See also CA 108; 160; DLB 70

Horovitz, Israel (Arthur) 1939- **CLC 56; DAM DRAM**
See also CA 33-36R; CANR 46, 59; DLB 7

Horvath, Odon von
See Horvath, Oedoen von
See also DLB 85, 124

Horvath, Oedoen von 1901-1938 ... **TCLC 45**
See also Horvath, Odon von
See also CA 118

Horwitz, Julius 1920-1986 .... **CLC 14**
See also CA 9-12R; 119; CANR 12

Hospital, Janette Turner 1942- .... **CLC 42**
See also CA 108; CANR 48

Hostos, E. M. de
See Hostos (y Bonilla), Eugenio Maria de

Hostos, Eugenio M. de
See Hostos (y Bonilla), Eugenio Maria de

Hostos, Eugenio Maria
See Hostos (y Bonilla), Eugenio Maria de

Hostos (y Bonilla), Eugenio Maria de 1839-1903 .... **TCLC 24**
See also CA 123; 131; HW

Houdini
See Lovecraft, H(oward) P(hillips)

Hougan, Carolyn 1943- .... **CLC 34**
See also CA 139

Household, Geoffrey (Edward West) 1900-1988 **CLC 11**
See also CA 77-80; 126; CANR 58; DLB 87; SATA 14; SATA-Obit 59

Housman, A(lfred) E(dward) 1859-1936 **TCLC 1, 10; DA; DAB; DAC; DAM MST, POET; PC 2; WLCS**
See also CA 104; 125; DLB 19; MTCW

Housman, Laurence 1865-1959 .... **TCLC 7**
See also CA 106; 155; DLB 10; SATA 25

Howard, Elizabeth Jane 1923- ..... **CLC 7, 29**
See also CA 5-8R; CANR 8, 62

Howard, Maureen 1930- .... **CLC 5, 14, 46**
See also CA 53-56; CANR 31; DLBY 83; INT CANR-31; MTCW

Howard, Richard 1929- .... **CLC 7, 10, 47**
See also AITN 1; CA 85-88; CANR 25; DLB 5; INT CANR-25

Howard, Robert E(rvin) 1906-1936 **TCLC 8**
See also CA 105; 157

Howard, Warren F.
See Pohl, Frederik

Howe, Fanny 1940- .... **CLC 47**
See also CA 117; CAAS 27; SATA-Brief 52

Howe, Irving 1920-1993 .... **CLC 85**
See also CA 9-12R; 141; CANR 21, 50; DLB 67; MTCW

Howe, Julia Ward 1819-1910 .... **TCLC 21**
See also CA 117; DLB 1

Howe, Susan 1937- .... **CLC 72**
See also CA 160; DLB 120

Howe, Tina 1937- .... **CLC 48**
See also CA 109

Howell, James 1594(?)-1666 .... **LC 13**
See also DLB 151

Howells, W. D.
See Howells, William Dean

Howells, William D.
See Howells, William Dean

Howells, William Dean 1837-1920 . **TCLC 7, 17, 41**
See also CA 104; 134; CDALB 1865-1917; DLB 12, 64, 74, 79

Howes, Barbara 1914-1996 .... **CLC 15**

See also CA 9-12R; 151; CAAS 3; CANR 53; SATA 5
Hrabal, Bohumil 1914-1997 .... **CLC 13, 67**
See also CA 106; 156; CAAS 12; CANR 57
Hsun, Lu
See Lu Hsun
Hubbard, L(afayette) Ron(ald) 1911-1986 **CLC 43; DAM POP**
See also CA 77-80; 118; CANR 52
Huch, Ricarda (Octavia) 1864-1947 **TCLC 13**
See also CA 111; DLB 66
Huddle, David 1942- .... **CLC 49**
See also CA 57-60; CAAS 20; DLB 130
Hudson, Jeffrey
See Crichton, (John) Michael
Hudson, W(illiam) H(enry) 1841-1922 **TCLC 29**
See also CA 115; DLB 98, 153, 174; SATA 35
Hueffer, Ford Madox
See Ford, Ford Madox
Hughart, Barry 1934- .... **CLC 39**
See also CA 137
Hughes, Colin
See Creasey, John
Hughes, David (John) 1930- .... **CLC 48**
See also CA 116; 129; DLB 14
Hughes, Edward James
See Hughes, Ted
See also DAM MST, POET
Hughes, (James) Langston 1902-1967 **CLC 1, 5, 10, 15, 35, 44; BLC; DA; DAB; DAC; DAM DRAM, MST, MULT, POET; DC 3; PC 1; SSC 6; WLC**
See also AAYA 12; BW 1; CA 1-4R; 25-28R; CANR 1, 34; CDALB 1929-1941; CLR 17; DLB 4, 7, 48, 51, 86; JRDA; MAICYA; MTCW; SATA 4, 33
Hughes, Richard (Arthur Warren) 1900-1976 **CLC 1, 11; DAM NOV**
See also CA 5-8R; 65-68; CANR 4; DLB 15, 161; MTCW; SATA 8; SATA-Obit 25
Hughes, Ted 1930- **CLC 2, 4, 9, 14, 37; DAB; DAC; PC 7**
See also Hughes, Edward James
See also CA 1-4R; CANR 1, 33; CLR 3; DLB 40, 161; MAICYA; MTCW; SATA 49; SATA-Brief 27
Hugo, Richard F(ranklin) 1923-1982 **CLC 6, 18, 32; DAM POET**
See also CA 49-52; 108; CANR 3; DLB 5
Hugo, Victor (Marie) 1802-1885 **NCLC 3, 10, 21; DA; DAB; DAC; DAM DRAM, MST, NOV, POET; PC 17; WLC**
See also DLB 119; SATA 47
Huidobro, Vicente
See Huidobro Fernandez, Vicente Garcia
Huidobro Fernandez, Vicente Garcia 1893-1948 .... **TCLC 31**
See also CA 131; HW
Hulme, Keri 1947- .... **CLC 39**
See also CA 125; INT 125
Hulme, T(homas) E(rnest) 1883-1917 **TCLC 21**
See also CA 117; DLB 19
Hume, David 1711-1776 .... **LC 7**
See also DLB 104
Humphrey, William 1924-1997 .... **CLC 45**
See also CA 77-80; 160; DLB 6
Humphreys, Emyr Owen 1919- .... **CLC 47**
See also CA 5-8R; CANR 3, 24; DLB 15
Humphreys, Josephine 1945- ..... **CLC 34, 57**
See also CA 121; 127; INT 127
Huneker, James Gibbons 1857-1921 **TCLC 65**
See also DLB 71
Hungerford, Pixie
See Brinsmead, H(esba) F(ay)
Hunt, E(verette) Howard, (Jr.) 1918- **CLC 3**
See also AITN 1; CA 45-48; CANR 2, 47
Hunt, Kyle
See Creasey, John
Hunt, (James Henry) Leigh 1784-1859 **NCLC 1; DAM POET**
Hunt, Marsha 1946- .... **CLC 70**
See also BW 2; CA 143
Hunt, Violet 1866-1942 .... **TCLC 53**
See also DLB 162
Hunter, E. Waldo
See Sturgeon, Theodore (Hamilton)
Hunter, Evan 1926- **CLC 11, 31; DAM POP**
See also CA 5-8R; CANR 5, 38, 62; DLBY 82; INT CANR-5; MTCW; SATA 25
Hunter, Kristin (Eggleston) 1931- .... **CLC 35**
See also AITN 1; BW 1; CA 13-16R; CANR 13; CLR 3; DLB 33; INT CANR-13; MAICYA; SAAS 10; SATA 12
Hunter, Mollie 1922- .... **CLC 21**
See also McIlwraith, Maureen Mollie Hunter
See also AAYA 13; CANR 37; CLR 25; DLB 161; JRDA; MAICYA; SAAS 7; SATA 54
Hunter, Robert (?)-1734 .... **LC 7**
Hurston, Zora Neale 1903-1960 **CLC 7, 30, 61; BLC; DA; DAC; DAM MST, MULT, NOV; SSC 4; WLCS**
See also AAYA 15; BW 1; CA 85-88; CANR 61; DLB 51, 86; MTCW
Huston, John (Marcellus) 1906-1987 **CLC 20**
See also CA 73-76; 123; CANR 34; DLB 26
Hustvedt, Siri 1955- .... **CLC 76**
See also CA 137
Hutten, Ulrich von 1488-1523 .... **LC 16**
See also DLB 179
Huxley, Aldous (Leonard) 1894-1963 **CLC 1, 3, 4, 5, 8, 11, 18, 35, 79; DA; DAB; DAC; DAM MST, NOV; WLC**
See also AAYA 11; CA 85-88; CANR 44; CDBLB 1914-1945; DLB 36, 100, 162; MTCW; SATA 63
Huysmans, Charles Marie Georges 1848-1907
See Huysmans, Joris-Karl
See also CA 104
Huysmans, Joris-Karl .... **TCLC 7, 69**
See also Huysmans, Charles Marie Georges
See also DLB 123
Hwang, David Henry 1957- ... **CLC 55; DAM DRAM; DC 4**
See also CA 127; 132; INT 132
Hyde, Anthony 1946- .... **CLC 42**
See also CA 136
Hyde, Margaret O(ldroyd) 1917- ..... **CLC 21**
See also CA 1-4R; CANR 1, 36; CLR 23; JRDA; MAICYA; SAAS 8; SATA 1, 42, 76
Hynes, James 1956(?)- .... **CLC 65**
Ian, Janis 1951- .... **CLC 21**
See also CA 105
Ibanez, Vicente Blasco
See Blasco Ibanez, Vicente
Ibarguengoitia, Jorge 1928-1983 ...... **CLC 37**
See also CA 124; 113; HW
Ibsen, Henrik (Johan) 1828-1906 **TCLC 2, 8, 16, 37, 52; DA; DAB; DAC; DAM DRAM, MST; DC 2; WLC**
See also CA 104; 141
Ibuse Masuji 1898-1993 .... **CLC 22**
See also CA 127; 141; DLB 180
Ichikawa, Kon 1915- .... **CLC 20**
See also CA 121
Idle, Eric 1943- .... **CLC 21**
See also Monty Python
See also CA 116; CANR 35
Ignatow, David 1914- .... **CLC 4, 7, 14, 40**
See also CA 9-12R; CAAS 3; CANR 31, 57; DLB 5
Ihimaera, Witi 1944- .... **CLC 46**
See also CA 77-80
Ilf, Ilya .... **TCLC 21**
See also Fainzilberg, Ilya Arnoldovich
Illyes, Gyula 1902-1983 .... **PC 16**
See also CA 114; 109
Immermann, Karl (Lebrecht) 1796-1840 **NCLC 4, 49**
See also DLB 133
Inchbald, Elizabeth 1753-1821 ...... **NCLC 62**
See also DLB 39, 89
Inclan, Ramon (Maria) del Valle
See Valle-Inclan, Ramon (Maria) del
Infante, G(uillermo) Cabrera
See Cabrera Infante, G(uillermo)
Ingalls, Rachel (Holmes) 1940- .... **CLC 42**
See also CA 123; 127
Ingamells, Rex 1913-1955 .... **TCLC 35**
Inge, William (Motter) 1913-1973 **CLC 1, 8, 19; DAM DRAM**
See also CA 9-12R; CDALB 1941-1968; DLB 7; MTCW
Ingelow, Jean 1820-1897 .... **NCLC 39**
See also DLB 35, 163; SATA 33
Ingram, Willis J.
See Harris, Mark
Innaurato, Albert (F.) 1948(?)- .. **CLC 21, 60**
See also CA 115; 122; INT 122
Innes, Michael
See Stewart, J(ohn) I(nnes) M(ackintosh)
Ionesco, Eugene 1909-1994 **CLC 1, 4, 6, 9, 11, 15, 41, 86; DA; DAB; DAC; DAM DRAM, MST; WLC**
See also CA 9-12R; 144; CANR 55; MTCW; SATA 7; SATA-Obit 79
Iqbal, Muhammad 1873-1938 .... **TCLC 28**
Ireland, Patrick
See O'Doherty, Brian
Iron, Ralph
See Schreiner, Olive (Emilie Albertina)
Irving, John (Winslow) 1942- **CLC 13, 23, 38; DAM NOV, POP**
See also AAYA 8; BEST 89:3; CA 25-28R; CANR 28; DLB 6; DLBY 82; MTCW
Irving, Washington 1783-1859 **NCLC 2, 19; DA; DAB; DAM MST; SSC 2; WLC**
See also CDALB 1640-1865; DLB 3, 11, 30, 59, 73, 74; YABC 2
Irwin, P. K.
See Page, P(atricia) K(athleen)
Isaacs, Susan 1943- .... **CLC 32; DAM POP**
See also BEST 89:1; CA 89-92; CANR 20, 41; INT CANR-20; MTCW
Isherwood, Christopher (William Bradshaw) 1904-1986 .... **CLC 1, 9, 11, 14, 44; DAM DRAM, NOV**
See also CA 13-16R; 117; CANR 35; DLB 15; DLBY 86; MTCW
Ishiguro, Kazuo 1954- **CLC 27, 56, 59; DAM NOV**
See also BEST 90:2; CA 120; CANR 49; MTCW
Ishikawa, Hakuhin
See Ishikawa, Takuboku
Ishikawa, Takuboku 1886(?)-1912 **TCLC 15; DAM POET; PC 10**
See also CA 113; 153
Iskander, Fazil 1929- .... **CLC 47**
See also CA 102
Isler, Alan (David) 1934- .... **CLC 91**
See also CA 156
Ivan IV 1530-1584 .... **LC 17**
Ivanov, Vyacheslav Ivanovich 1866-1949 **TCLC 33**
See also CA 122
Ivask, Ivar Vidrik 1927-1992 .... **CLC 14**
See also CA 37-40R; 139; CANR 24
Ives, Morgan
See Bradley, Marion Zimmer

J. R. S.
See Gogarty, Oliver St. John
Jabran, Kahlil
See Gibran, Kahlil
Jabran, Khalil
See Gibran, Kahlil
Jackson, Daniel
See Wingrove, David (John)
Jackson, Jesse 1908-1983 .... **CLC 12**
See also BW 1; CA 25-28R; 109; CANR 27; CLR 28; MAICYA; SATA 2, 29; SATA-Obit 48
Jackson, Laura (Riding) 1901-1991
See Riding, Laura
See also CA 65-68; 135; CANR 28; DLB 48
Jackson, Sam
See Trumbo, Dalton
Jackson, Sara
See Wingrove, David (John)
Jackson, Shirley 1919-1965 . **CLC 11, 60, 87; DA; DAC; DAM MST; SSC 9; WLC**
See also AAYA 9; CA 1-4R; 25-28R; CANR 4, 52; CDALB 1941-1968; DLB 6; SATA 2
Jacob, (Cyprien-)Max 1876-1944 .... **TCLC 6**
See also CA 104
Jacobs, Jim 1942- .... **CLC 12**
See also CA 97-100; INT 97-100
Jacobs, W(illiam) W(ymark) 1863-1943
TCLC 22
See also CA 121; DLB 135
Jacobsen, Jens Peter 1847-1885 ..... **NCLC 34**
Jacobsen, Josephine 1908- .... **CLC 48, 102**
See also CA 33-36R; CAAS 18; CANR 23, 48
Jacobson, Dan 1929- .... **CLC 4, 14**
See also CA 1-4R; CANR 2, 25; DLB 14; MTCW
Jacqueline
See Carpentier (y Valmont), Alejo
Jagger, Mick 1944- .... **CLC 17**
Jakes, John (William) 1932- . **CLC 29; DAM NOV, POP**
See also BEST 89:4; CA 57-60; CANR 10, 43; DLBY 83; INT CANR-10; MTCW; SATA 62
James, Andrew
See Kirkup, James
James, C(yril) L(ionel) R(obert) 1901-1989
CLC 33
See also BW 2; CA 117; 125; 128; CANR 62; DLB 125; MTCW
James, Daniel (Lewis) 1911-1988
See Santiago, Danny
See also CA 125
James, Dynely
See Mayne, William (James Carter)
James, Henry Sr. 1811-1882 .... **NCLC 53**
James, Henry 1843-1916 **TCLC 2, 11, 24, 40, 47, 64; DA; DAB; DAC; DAM MST, NOV; SSC 8; WLC**
See also CA 104; 132; CDALB 1865-1917; DLB 12, 71, 74; DLBD 13; MTCW
James, M. R.
See James, Montague (Rhodes)
See also DLB 156
James, Montague (Rhodes) 1862-1936 **T C L C 6; SSC 16**
See also CA 104
James, P. D. .... **CLC 18, 46**
See also White, Phyllis Dorothy James
See also BEST 90:2; CDBLB 1960 to Present; DLB 87
James, Philip
See Moorcock, Michael (John)
James, William 1842-1910 .... **TCLC 15, 32**
See also CA 109
James I 1394-1437 .... **LC 20**
Jameson, Anna 1794-1860 .... **NCLC 43**
See also DLB 99, 166
Jami, Nur al-Din 'Abd al-Rahman 1414-1492
LC 9
Jammes, Francis 1868-1938 .... **TCLC 75**
Jandl, Ernst 1925- .... **CLC 34**
Janowitz, Tama 1957- ... **CLC 43; DAM POP**
See also CA 106; CANR 52
Japrisot, Sebastien 1931- .... **CLC 90**
Jarrell, Randall 1914-1965 **CLC 1, 2, 6, 9, 13, 49; DAM POET**
See also CA 5-8R; 25-28R; CABS 2; CANR 6, 34; CDALB 1941-1968; CLR 6; DLB 48, 52; MAICYA; MTCW; SATA 7
Jarry, Alfred 1873-1907 . **TCLC 2, 14; DAM DRAM; SSC 20**
See also CA 104; 153
Jarvis, E. K.
See Bloch, Robert (Albert); Ellison, Harlan (Jay); Silverberg, Robert
Jeake, Samuel, Jr.
See Aiken, Conrad (Potter)
Jean Paul 1763-1825 .... **NCLC 7**
Jefferies, (John) Richard 1848-1887**NCLC 47**
See also DLB 98, 141; SATA 16
Jeffers, (John) Robinson 1887-1962**CLC 2, 3, 11, 15, 54; DA; DAC; DAM MST, POET; PC 17; WLC**
See also CA 85-88; CANR 35; CDALB 1917-1929; DLB 45; MTCW
Jefferson, Janet
See Mencken, H(enry) L(ouis)
Jefferson, Thomas 1743-1826 .... **NCLC 11**
See also CDALB 1640-1865; DLB 31
Jeffrey, Francis 1773-1850 .... **NCLC 33**
See also DLB 107
Jelakowitch, Ivan
See Heijermans, Herman
Jellicoe, (Patricia) Ann 1927- .... **CLC 27**
See also CA 85-88; DLB 13
Jen, Gish .... **CLC 70**
See also Jen, Lillian
Jen, Lillian 1956(?)-
See Jen, Gish
See also CA 135
Jenkins, (John) Robin 1912- .... **CLC 52**
See also CA 1-4R; CANR 1; DLB 14
Jennings, Elizabeth (Joan) 1926-. **CLC 5, 14**
See also CA 61-64; CAAS 5; CANR 8, 39; DLB 27; MTCW; SATA 66
Jennings, Waylon 1937- .... **CLC 21**
Jensen, Johannes V. 1873-1950 ..... **TCLC 41**
Jensen, Laura (Linnea) 1948- .... **CLC 37**
See also CA 103
Jerome, Jerome K(lapka) 1859-1927**TCLC 23**
See also CA 119; DLB 10, 34, 135
Jerrold, Douglas William 1803-1857**NCLC 2**
See also DLB 158, 159
Jewett, (Theodora) Sarah Orne 1849-1909
TCLC 1, 22; SSC 6
See also CA 108; 127; DLB 12, 74; SATA 15
Jewsbury, Geraldine (Endsor) 1812-1880
NCLC 22
See also DLB 21
Jhabvala, Ruth Prawer 1927-**CLC 4, 8, 29, 94; DAB; DAM NOV**
See also CA 1-4R; CANR 2, 29, 51; DLB 139; INT CANR-29; MTCW
Jibran, Kahlil
See Gibran, Kahlil
Jibran, Khalil
See Gibran, Kahlil
Jiles, Paulette 1943- .... **CLC 13, 58**
See also CA 101
Jimenez (Manteclon), Juan Ramon 1881-1958
TCLC 4; DAM MULT, POET; HLC; PC 7
See also CA 104; 131; DLB 134; HW; MTCW

Jimenez, Ramon
See Jimenez (Mantecon), Juan Ramon
Jimenez Mantecon, Juan
See Jimenez (Mantecon), Juan Ramon
Joel, Billy .... **CLC 26**
See also Joel, William Martin
Joel, William Martin 1949-
See Joel, Billy
See also CA 108
John of the Cross, St. 1542-1591 .... **LC 18**
Johnson, B(ryan) S(tanley William) 1933-1973
CLC 6, 9
See also CA 9-12R; 53-56; CANR 9; DLB 14, 40
Johnson, Benj. F. of Boo
See Riley, James Whitcomb
Johnson, Benjamin F. of Boo
See Riley, James Whitcomb
Johnson, Charles (Richard) 1948-**CLC 7, 51, 65; BLC; DAM MULT**
See also BW 2; CA 116; CAAS 18; CANR 42; DLB 33
Johnson, Denis 1949- .... **CLC 52**
See also CA 117; 121; DLB 120
Johnson, Diane 1934- .... **CLC 5, 13, 48**
See also CA 41-44R; CANR 17, 40, 62; DLBY 80; INT CANR-17; MTCW
Johnson, Eyvind (Olof Verner) 1900-1976
CLC 14
See also CA 73-76; 69-72; CANR 34
Johnson, J. R.
See James, C(yril) L(ionel) R(obert)
Johnson, James Weldon 1871-1938 **TCLC 3, 19; BLC; DAM MULT, POET**
See also BW 1; CA 104; 125; CDALB 1917-1929; CLR 32; DLB 51; MTCW; SATA 31
Johnson, Joyce 1935- .... **CLC 58**
See also CA 125; 129
Johnson, Lionel (Pigot) 1867-1902 **TCLC 19**
See also CA 117; DLB 19
Johnson, Mel
See Malzberg, Barry N(athaniel)
Johnson, Pamela Hansford 1912-1981**CLC 1, 7, 27**
See also CA 1-4R; 104; CANR 2, 28; DLB 15; MTCW
Johnson, Robert 1911(?)-1938 .... **TCLC 69**
Johnson, Samuel 1709-1784**LC 15; DA; DAB; DAC; DAM MST; WLC**
See also CDBLB 1660-1789; DLB 39, 95, 104, 142
Johnson, Uwe 1934-1984 .. **CLC 5, 10, 15, 40**
See also CA 1-4R; 112; CANR 1, 39; DLB 75; MTCW
Johnston, George (Benson) 1913- ..... **CLC 51**
See also CA 1-4R; CANR 5, 20; DLB 88
Johnston, Jennifer 1930- .... **CLC 7**
See also CA 85-88; DLB 14
Jolley, (Monica) Elizabeth 1923-**CLC 46; SSC 19**
See also CA 127; CAAS 13; CANR 59
Jones, Arthur Llewellyn 1863-1947
See Machen, Arthur
See also CA 104
Jones, D(ouglas) G(ordon) 1929- ...... **CLC 10**
See also CA 29-32R; CANR 13; DLB 53
Jones, David (Michael) 1895-1974**CLC 2, 4, 7, 13, 42**
See also CA 9-12R; 53-56; CANR 28; CDBLB 1945-1960; DLB 20, 100; MTCW
Jones, David Robert 1947-
See Bowie, David
See also CA 103
Jones, Diana Wynne 1934- .... **CLC 26**
See also AAYA 12; CA 49-52; CANR 4, 26, 56; CLR 23; DLB 161; JRDA; MAICYA; SAAS 7; SATA 9, 70

Jones, Edward P. 1950- .... CLC 76
See also BW 2; CA 142

Jones, Gayl 1949- ...... CLC 6, 9; BLC; DAM MULT
See also BW 2; CA 77-80; CANR 27; DLB 33; MTCW

Jones, James 1921-1977 ...... CLC 1, 3, 10, 39
See also AITN 1, 2; CA 1-4R; 69-72; CANR 6; DLB 2, 143; MTCW

Jones, John J.
See Lovecraft, H(oward) P(hillips)

Jones, LeRoi .... CLC 1, 2, 3, 5, 10, 14
See also Baraka, Amiri

Jones, Louis B. .... CLC 65
See also CA 141

Jones, Madison (Percy, Jr.) 1925- ...... CLC 4
See also CA 13-16R; CAAS 11; CANR 7, 54; DLB 152

Jones, Mervyn 1922- .... CLC 10, 52
See also CA 45-48; CAAS 5; CANR 1; MTCW

Jones, Mick 1956(?)- .... CLC 30

Jones, Nettie (Pearl) 1941- .... CLC 34
See also BW 2; CA 137; CAAS 20

Jones, Preston 1936-1979 .... CLC 10
See also CA 73-76; 89-92; DLB 7

Jones, Robert F(rancis) 1934- .... CLC 7
See also CA 49-52; CANR 2, 61

Jones, Rod 1953-................ CLC 50
See also CA 128

Jones, Terence Graham Parry 1942-CLC 21
See also Jones, Terry; Monty Python
See also CA 112; 116; CANR 35; INT 116

Jones, Terry
See Jones, Terence Graham Parry
See also SATA 67; SATA-Brief 51

Jones, Thom 1945(?)- .... CLC 81
See also CA 157

Jong, Erica 1942- CLC 4, 6, 8, 18, 83; DAM NOV, POP
See also AITN 1; BEST 90:2; CA 73-76; CANR 26, 52; DLB 2, 5, 28, 152; INT CANR-26; MTCW

Jonson, Ben(jamin) 1572(?)-1637 .. LC 6, 33; DA; DAB; DAC; DAM DRAM, MST, POET; DC 4; PC 17; WLC
See also CDBLB Before 1660; DLB 62, 121

Jordan, June 1936- ...... CLC 5, 11, 23; DAM MULT, POET
See also AAYA 2; BW 2; CA 33-36R; CANR 25; CLR 10; DLB 38; MAICYA; MTCW; SATA 4

Jordan, Pat(rick M.) 1941- .... CLC 37
See also CA 33-36R

Jorgensen, Ivar
See Ellison, Harlan (Jay)

Jorgenson, Ivar
See Silverberg, Robert

Josephus, Flavius c. 37-100 .... CMLC 13

Josipovici, Gabriel 1940- .... CLC 6, 43
See also CA 37-40R; CAAS 8; CANR 47; DLB 14

Joubert, Joseph 1754-1824 .... NCLC 9

Jouve, Pierre Jean 1887-1976 .... CLC 47
See also CA 65-68

Joyce, James (Augustine Aloysius) 1882-1941 TCLC 3, 8, 16, 35, 52; DA; DAB; DAC; DAM MST, NOV, POET; SSC 26; WLC
See also CA 104; 126; CDBLB 1914-1945; DLB 10, 19, 36, 162; MTCW

Jozsef, Attila 1905-1937 .... TCLC 22
See also CA 116

Juana Ines de la Cruz 1651(?)-1695 ..... LC 5

Judd, Cyril
See Kornbluth, C(yril) M.; Pohl, Frederik

Julian of Norwich 1342(?)-1416(?) .... LC 6
See also DLB 146

Juniper, Alex
See Hospital, Janette Turner

Junius
See Luxemburg, Rosa

Just, Ward (Swift) 1935- .... CLC 4, 27
See also CA 25-28R; CANR 32; INT CANR-32

Justice, Donald (Rodney) 1925- .. CLC 6, 19, 102; DAM POET
See also CA 5-8R; CANR 26, 54; DLBY 83; INT CANR-26

Juvenal c. 55-c. 127 .... CMLC 8

Juvenis
See Bourne, Randolph S(illiman)

Kacew, Romain 1914-1980
See Gary, Romain
See also CA 108; 102

Kadare, Ismail 1936-.......................... CLC 52
See also CA 161

Kadohata, Cynthia ....CLC 59
See also CA 140

Kafka, Franz 1883-1924TCLC 2, 6, 13, 29, 47, 53; DA; DAB; DAC; DAM MST, NOV; SSC 29; WLC
See also CA 105; 126; DLB 81; MTCW

Kahanovitsch, Pinkhes
See Der Nister

Kahn, Roger 1927- .... CLC 30
See also CA 25-28R; CANR 44; DLB 171; SATA 37

Kain, Saul
See Sassoon, Siegfried (Lorraine)

Kaiser, Georg 1878-1945 .... TCLC 9
See also CA 106; DLB 124

Kaletski, Alexander 1946-.................CLC 39
See also CA 118; 143

Kalidasa fl. c. 400-............................. CMLC 9

Kallman, Chester (Simon) 1921-1975 CLC 2
See also CA 45-48; 53-56; CANR 3

Kaminsky, Melvin 1926-
See Brooks, Mel
See also CA 65-68; CANR 16

Kaminsky, Stuart M(elvin) 1934- ..... CLC 59
See also CA 73-76; CANR 29, 53

Kane, Francis
See Robbins, Harold

Kane, Paul
See Simon, Paul (Frederick)

Kane, Wilson
See Bloch, Robert (Albert)

Kanin, Garson 1912-.......................... CLC 22
See also AITN 1; CA 5-8R; CANR 7; DLB 7

Kaniuk, Yoram 1930- .... CLC 19
See also CA 134

Kant, Immanuel 1724-1804 .... NCLC 27
See also DLB 94

Kantor, MacKinlay 1904-1977 .... CLC 7
See also CA 61-64; 73-76; CANR 60; DLB 9, 102

Kaplan, David Michael 1946- .... CLC 50

Kaplan, James 1951-.......................... CLC 59
See also CA 135

Karageorge, Michael
See Anderson, Poul (William)

Karamzin, Nikolai Mikhailovich 1766-1826 NCLC 3
See also DLB 150

Karapanou, Margarita 1946-............CLC 13
See also CA 101

Karinthy, Frigyes 1887-1938 .... TCLC 47

Karl, Frederick R(obert) 1927- ....CLC 34
See also CA 5-8R; CANR 3, 44

Kastel, Warren
See Silverberg, Robert

Kataev, Evgeny Petrovich 1903-1942
See Petrov, Evgeny
See also CA 120

Kataphusin
See Ruskin, John

Katz, Steve 1935- ....CLC 47
See also CA 25-28R; CAAS 14; CANR 12; DLBY 83

Kauffman, Janet 1945- ....CLC 42
See also CA 117; CANR 43; DLBY 86

Kaufman, Bob (Garnell) 1925-1986 .CLC 49
See also BW 1; CA 41-44R; 118; CANR 22; DLB 16, 41

Kaufman, George S. 1889-1961CLC 38; DAM DRAM
See also CA 108; 93-96; DLB 7; INT 108

Kaufman, Sue .... CLC 3, 8
See also Barondess, Sue K(aufman)

Kavafis, Konstantinos Petrou 1863-1933
See Cavafy, C(onstantine) P(eter)
See also CA 104

Kavan, Anna 1901-1968 .... CLC 5, 13, 82
See also CA 5-8R; CANR 6, 57; MTCW

Kavanagh, Dan
See Barnes, Julian (Patrick)

Kavanagh, Patrick (Joseph) 1904-1967 C L C 22
See also CA 123; 25-28R; DLB 15, 20; MTCW

Kawabata, Yasunari 1899-1972 CLC 2, 5, 9, 18; DAM MULT; SSC 17
See also CA 93-96; 33-36R; DLB 180

Kaye, M(ary) M(argaret) 1909- ....CLC 28
See also CA 89-92; CANR 24, 60; MTCW; SATA 62

Kaye, Mollie
See Kaye, M(ary) M(argaret)

Kaye-Smith, Sheila 1887-1956 .... TCLC 20
See also CA 118; DLB 36

Kaymor, Patrice Maguilene
See Senghor, Leopold Sedar

Kazan, Elia 1909- .... CLC 6, 16, 63
See also CA 21-24R; CANR 32

Kazantzakis, Nikos 1883(?)-1957 TCLC 2, 5, 33
See also CA 105; 132; MTCW

Kazin, Alfred 1915- .... CLC 34, 38
See also CA 1-4R; CAAS 7; CANR 1, 45; DLB 67

Keane, Mary Nesta (Skrine) 1904-1996
See Keane, Molly
See also CA 108; 114; 151

Keane, Molly ....CLC 31
See also Keane, Mary Nesta (Skrine)
See also INT 114

Keates, Jonathan 19(?)- .... CLC 34

Keaton, Buster 1895-1966 ....CLC 20

Keats, John 1795-1821 . NCLC 8; DA; DAB; DAC; DAM MST, POET; PC 1; WLC
See also CDBLB 1789-1832; DLB 96, 110

Keene, Donald 1922-........................... CLC 34
See also CA 1-4R; CANR 5

Keillor, Garrison .... CLC 40
See also Keillor, Gary (Edward)
See also AAYA 2; BEST 89:3; DLBY 87; SATA 58

Keillor, Gary (Edward) 1942-
See Keillor, Garrison
See also CA 111; 117; CANR 36, 59; DAM POP; MTCW

Keith, Michael
See Hubbard, L(afayette) Ron(ald)

Keller, Gottfried 1819-1890NCLC 2; SSC 26
See also DLB 129

Kellerman, Jonathan 1949- ...CLC 44; DAM POP
See also BEST 90:1; CA 106; CANR 29, 51; INT CANR-29

Kelley, William Melvin 1937- .... CLC 22
See also BW 1; CA 77-80; CANR 27; DLB 33

Kellogg, Marjorie 1922- .... CLC 2
See also CA 81-84

Kellow, Kathleen
See Hibbert, Eleanor Alice Burford
Kelly, M(ilton) T(erry) 1947- .... **CLC 55**
See also CA 97-100; CAAS 22; CANR 19, 43
Kelman, James 1946- .... **CLC 58, 86**
See also CA 148
Kemal, Yashar 1923- .... **CLC 14, 29**
See also CA 89-92; CANR 44
Kemble, Fanny 1809-1893 .... **NCLC 18**
See also DLB 32
Kemelman, Harry 1908-1996............. **CLC 2**
See also AITN 1; CA 9-12R; 155; CANR 6; DLB 28
Kempe, Margery 1373(?)-1440(?) .... **LC 6**
See also DLB 146
Kempis, Thomas a 1380-1471 .... **LC 11**
Kendall, Henry 1839-1882 .... **NCLC 12**
Keneally, Thomas (Michael) 1935- **CLC 5, 8, 10, 14, 19, 27, 43; DAM NOV**
See also CA 85-88; CANR 10, 50; MTCW
Kennedy, Adrienne (Lita) 1931- ...... **CLC 66; BLC; DAM MULT; DC 5**
See also BW 2; CA 103; CAAS 20; CABS 3; CANR 26, 53; DLB 38
Kennedy, John Pendleton 1795-1870 **NCLC 2**
See also DLB 3
Kennedy, Joseph Charles 1929-
See Kennedy, X. J.
See also CA 1-4R; CANR 4, 30, 40; SATA 14, 86
Kennedy, William 1928- .. **CLC 6, 28, 34, 53; DAM NOV**
See also AAYA 1; CA 85-88; CANR 14, 31; DLB 143; DLBY 85; INT CANR-31; MTCW; SATA 57
Kennedy, X. J. .... **CLC 8, 42**
See Kennedy, Joseph Charles
See also CAAS 9; CLR 27; DLB 5; SAAS 22
Kenny, Maurice (Francis) 1929- ..... **CLC 87; DAM MULT**
See also CA 144; CAAS 22; DLB 175; NNAL
Kent, Kelvin
See Kuttner, Henry
Kenton, Maxwell
See Southern, Terry
Kenyon, Robert O.
See Kuttner, Henry
Kerouac, Jack .... **CLC 1, 2, 3, 5, 14, 29, 61**
See also Kerouac, Jean-Louis Lebris de
See also CDALB 1941-1968; DLB 2, 16; DLBD 3; DLBY 95
Kerouac, Jean-Louis Lebris de 1922-1969
See Kerouac, Jack
See also AITN 1; CA 5-8R; 25-28R; CANR 26, 54; DA; DAB; DAC; DAM MST, NOV, POET, POP; MTCW; WLC
Kerr, Jean 1923- .... **CLC 22**
See also CA 5-8R; CANR 7; INT CANR-7
Kerr, M. E. .... **CLC 12, 35**
See also Meaker, Marijane (Agnes)
See also AAYA 2; CLR 29; SAAS 1
Kerr, Robert .... **CLC 55**
Kerrigan, (Thomas) Anthony 1918- **CLC 4, 6**
See also CA 49-52; CAAS 11; CANR 4
Kerry, Lois
See Duncan, Lois
Kesey, Ken (Elton) 1935- **CLC 1, 3, 6, 11, 46, 64; DA; DAB; DAC; DAM MST, NOV, POP; WLC**
See also CA 1-4R; CANR 22, 38; CDALB 1968-1988; DLB 2, 16; MTCW; SATA 66
Kesselring, Joseph (Otto) 1902-1967 **CLC 45; DAM DRAM, MST**
See also CA 150
Kessler, Jascha (Frederick) 1929- ...... **CLC 4**
See also CA 17-20R; CANR 8, 48
Kettelkamp, Larry (Dale) 1933- .... **CLC 12**
See also CA 29-32R; CANR 16; SAAS 3; SATA 2
Key, Ellen 1849-1926 .... **TCLC 65**
Keyber, Conny
See Fielding, Henry
Keyes, Daniel 1927- **CLC 80; DA; DAC; DAM MST, NOV**
See also CA 17-20R; CANR 10, 26, 54; SATA 37
Keynes, John Maynard 1883-1946 **TCLC 64**
See also CA 114; DLBD 10
Khanshendel, Chiron
See Rose, Wendy
Khayyam, Omar 1048-1131 **CMLC 11; DAM POET; PC 8**
Kherdian, David 1931- .... **CLC 6, 9**
See also CA 21-24R; CAAS 2; CANR 39; CLR 24; JRDA; MAICYA; SATA 16, 74
Khlebnikov, Velimir .... **TCLC 20**
See also Khlebnikov, Viktor Vladimirovich
Khlebnikov, Viktor Vladimirovich 1885-1922
See Khlebnikov, Velimir
See also CA 117
Khodasevich, Vladislav (Felitsianovich) 1886-1939 .... **TCLC 15**
See also CA 115
Kielland, Alexander Lange 1849-1906 **TCLC 5**
See also CA 104
Kiely, Benedict 1919- .... **CLC 23, 43**
See also CA 1-4R; CANR 2; DLB 15
Kienzle, William X(avier) 1928- ..... **CLC 25; DAM POP**
See also CA 93-96; CAAS 1; CANR 9, 31, 59; INT CANR-31; MTCW
Kierkegaard, Soren 1813-1855 .... **NCLC 34**
Killens, John Oliver 1916-1987 .... **CLC 10**
See also BW 2; CA 77-80; 123; CAAS 2; CANR 26; DLB 33
Killigrew, Anne 1660-1685 .... **LC 4**
See also DLB 131
Kim
See Simenon, Georges (Jacques Christian)
Kincaid, Jamaica 1949- .. **CLC 43, 68; BLC; DAM MULT, NOV**
See also AAYA 13; BW 2; CA 125; CANR 47, 59
King, Francis (Henry) 1923- **CLC 8, 53; DAM NOV**
See also CA 1-4R; CANR 1, 33; DLB 15, 139; MTCW
King, Martin Luther, Jr. 1929-1968 **CLC 83; BLC; DA; DAB; DAC; DAM MST, MULT; WLCS**
See also BW 2; CA 25-28; CANR 27, 44; CAP 2; MTCW; SATA 14
King, Stephen (Edwin) 1947- **CLC 12, 26, 37, 61; DAM NOV, POP; SSC 17**
See also AAYA 1, 17; BEST 90:1; CA 61-64; CANR 1, 30, 52; DLB 143; DLBY 80; JRDA; MTCW; SATA 9, 55
King, Steve
See King, Stephen (Edwin)
King, Thomas 1943- .... **CLC 89; DAC; DAM MULT**
See also CA 144; DLB 175; NNAL
Kingman, Lee .... **CLC 17**
See also Natti, (Mary) Lee
See also SAAS 3; SATA 1, 67
Kingsley, Charles 1819-1875 .... **NCLC 35**
See also DLB 21, 32, 163; YABC 2
Kingsley, Sidney 1906-1995 .... **CLC 44**
See also CA 85-88; 147; DLB 7
Kingsolver, Barbara 1955- **CLC 55, 81; DAM POP**
See also AAYA 15; CA 129; 134; CANR 60; INT 134

Kingston, Maxine (Ting Ting) Hong 1940- **CLC 12, 19, 58; DAM MULT, NOV; WLCS**
See also AAYA 8; CA 69-72; CANR 13, 38; DLB 173; DLBY 80; INT CANR-13; MTCW; SATA 53
Kinnell, Galway 1927- **CLC 1, 2, 3, 5, 13, 29**
See also CA 9-12R; CANR 10, 34; DLB 5; DLBY 87; INT CANR-34; MTCW
Kinsella, Thomas 1928- .... **CLC 4, 19**
See also CA 17-20R; CANR 15; DLB 27; MTCW
Kinsella, W(illiam) P(atrick) 1935- **CLC 27, 43; DAC; DAM NOV, POP**
See also AAYA 7; CA 97-100; CAAS 7; CANR 21, 35; INT CANR-21; MTCW
Kipling, (Joseph) Rudyard 1865-1936 **TCLC 8, 17; DA; DAB; DAC; DAM MST, POET; PC 3; SSC 5; WLC**
See also CA 105; 120; CANR 33; CDBLB 1890-1914; CLR 39; DLB 19, 34, 141, 156; MAICYA; MTCW; YABC 2
Kirkup, James 1918- .... **CLC 1**
See also CA 1-4R; CAAS 4; CANR 2; DLB 27; SATA 12
Kirkwood, James 1930(?)-1989 .... **CLC 9**
See also AITN 2; CA 1-4R; 128; CANR 6, 40
Kirshner, Sidney
See Kingsley, Sidney
Kis, Danilo 1935-1989 .... **CLC 57**
See also CA 109; 118; 129; CANR 61; DLB 181; MTCW
Kivi, Aleksis 1834-1872 .... **NCLC 30**
Kizer, Carolyn (Ashley) 1925- **CLC 15, 39, 80; DAM POET**
See also CA 65-68; CAAS 5; CANR 24; DLB 5, 169
Klabund 1890-1928 .... **TCLC 44**
See also DLB 66
Klappert, Peter 1942- .... **CLC 57**
See also CA 33-36R; DLB 5
Klein, A(braham) M(oses) 1909-1972 **CLC 19; DAB; DAC; DAM MST**
See also CA 101; 37-40R; DLB 68
Klein, Norma 1938-1989 .... **CLC 30**
See also AAYA 2; CA 41-44R; 128; CANR 15, 37; CLR 2, 19; INT CANR-15; JRDA; MAICYA; SAAS 1; SATA 7, 57
Klein, T(heodore) E(ibon) D(onald) 1947- **CLC 34**
See also CA 119; CANR 44
Kleist, Heinrich von 1777-1811 **NCLC 2, 37; DAM DRAM; SSC 22**
See also DLB 90
Klima, Ivan 1931- .... **CLC 56; DAM NOV**
See also CA 25-28R; CANR 17, 50
Klimentov, Andrei Platonovich 1899-1951
See Platonov, Andrei
See also CA 108
Klinger, Friedrich Maximilian von 1752-1831 **NCLC 1**
See also DLB 94
Klingsor the Magician
See Hartmann, Sadakichi
Klopstock, Friedrich Gottlieb 1724-1803 **NCLC 11**
See also DLB 97
Knapp, Caroline 1959- .... **CLC 99**
See also CA 154
Knebel, Fletcher 1911-1993 .... **CLC 14**
See also AITN 1; CA 1-4R; 140; CAAS 3; CANR 1, 36; SATA 36; SATA-Obit 75
Knickerbocker, Diedrich
See Irving, Washington
Knight, Etheridge 1931-1991 **CLC 40; BLC; DAM POET; PC 14**
See also BW 1; CA 21-24R; 133; CANR 23;

DLB 41
Knight, Sarah Kemble 1666-1727 .... **LC 7**
See also DLB 24
Knister, Raymond 1899-1932 .... **TCLC 56**
See also DLB 68
Knowles, John 1926- .. **CLC 1, 4, 10, 26; DA; DAC; DAM MST, NOV**
See also AAYA 10; CA 17-20R; CANR 40; CDALB 1968-1988; DLB 6; MTCW; SATA 8, 89
Knox, Calvin M.
See Silverberg, Robert
Knox, John c. 1505-1572 .... **LC 37**
See also DLB 132
Knye, Cassandra
See Disch, Thomas M(ichael)
Koch, C(hristopher) J(ohn) 1932- ... **CLC 42**
See also CA 127
Koch, Christopher
See Koch, C(hristopher) J(ohn)
Koch, Kenneth 1925- .... **CLC 5, 8, 44; DAM POET**
See also CA 1-4R; CANR 6, 36, 57; DLB 5; INT CANR-36; SATA 65
Kochanowski, Jan 1530-1584 .... **LC 10**
Kock, Charles Paul de 1794-1871 .. **NCLC 16**
Koda Shigeyuki 1867-1947
See Rohan, Koda
See also CA 121
Koestler, Arthur 1905-1983 **CLC 1, 3, 6, 8, 15, 33**
See also CA 1-4R; 109; CANR 1, 33; CDBLB 1945-1960; DLBY 83; MTCW
Kogawa, Joy Nozomi 1935- .. **CLC 78; DAC; DAM MST, MULT**
See also CA 101; CANR 19, 62
Kohout, Pavel 1928- .... **CLC 13**
See also CA 45-48; CANR 3
Koizumi, Yakumo
See Hearn, (Patricio) Lafcadio (Tessima Carlos)
Kolmar, Gertrud 1894-1943 .... **TCLC 40**
Komunyakaa, Yusef 1947- .... **CLC 86, 94**
See also CA 147; DLB 120
Konrad, George
See Konrad, Gyoergy
Konrad, Gyoergy 1933- .... **CLC 4, 10, 73**
See also CA 85-88
Konwicki, Tadeusz 1926- .... **CLC 8, 28, 54**
See also CA 101; CAAS 9; CANR 39, 59; MTCW
Koontz, Dean R(ay) 1945- ..... **CLC 78; DAM NOV, POP**
See also AAYA 9; BEST 89:3, 90:2; CA 108; CANR 19, 36, 52; MTCW; SATA 92
Kopit, Arthur (Lee) 1937-**CLC 1, 18, 33; DAM DRAM**
See also AITN 1; CA 81-84; CABS 3; DLB 7; MTCW
Kops, Bernard 1926- .... **CLC 4**
See also CA 5-8R; DLB 13
Kornbluth, C(yril) M. 1923-1958 .... **TCLC 8**
See also CA 105; 160; DLB 8
Korolenko, V. G.
See Korolenko, Vladimir Galaktionovich
Korolenko, Vladimir
See Korolenko, Vladimir Galaktionovich
Korolenko, Vladimir G.
See Korolenko, Vladimir Galaktionovich
Korolenko, Vladimir Galaktionovich 1853-1921 .... **TCLC 22**
See also CA 121
Korzybski, Alfred (Habdank Skarbek) 1879-1950 .... **TCLC 61**
See also CA 123; 160
Kosinski, Jerzy (Nikodem) 1933-1991**CLC 1, 2, 3, 6, 10, 15, 53, 70; DAM NOV**
See also CA 17-20R; 134; CANR 9, 46; DLB 2; DLBY 82; MTCW
Kostelanetz, Richard (Cory) 1940-... **CLC 28**
See also CA 13-16R; CAAS 8; CANR 38
Kostrowitzki, Wilhelm Apollinaris de 1880-1918
See Apollinaire, Guillaume
See also CA 104
Kotlowitz, Robert 1924- .... **CLC 4**
See also CA 33-36R; CANR 36
Kotzebue, August (Friedrich Ferdinand) von 1761-1819 .... **NCLC 25**
See also DLB 94
Kotzwinkle, William 1938-..... **CLC 5, 14, 35**
See also CA 45-48; CANR 3, 44; CLR 6; DLB 173; MAICYA; SATA 24, 70
Kowna, Stancy
See Szymborska, Wislawa
Kozol, Jonathan 1936- ....**CLC 17**
See also CA 61-64; CANR 16, 45
Kozoll, Michael 1940(?)- ....**CLC 35**
Kramer, Kathryn 19(?)- ....**CLC 34**
Kramer, Larry 1935-**CLC 42; DAM POP; DC 8**
See also CA 124; 126; CANR 60
Krasicki, Ignacy 1735-1801 .... **NCLC 8**
Krasinski, Zygmunt 1812-1859 .... **NCLC 4**
Kraus, Karl 1874-1936 .... **TCLC 5**
See also CA 104; DLB 118
Kreve (Mickevicius), Vincas 1882-1954**TCLC 27**
Kristeva, Julia 1941- .... **CLC 77**
See also CA 154
Kristofferson, Kris 1936- .... **CLC 26**
See also CA 104
Krizanc, John 1956- .... **CLC 57**
Krleza, Miroslav 1893-1981 .... **CLC 8**
See also CA 97-100; 105; CANR 50; DLB 147
Kroetsch, Robert 1927-**CLC 5, 23, 57; DAC; DAM POET**
See also CA 17-20R; CANR 8, 38; DLB 53; MTCW
Kroetz, Franz
See Kroetz, Franz Xaver
Kroetz, Franz Xaver 1946- ....**CLC 41**
See also CA 130
Kroker, Arthur (W.) 1945- .... **CLC 77**
See also CA 161
Kropotkin, Peter (Alekseevich) 1842-1921 **TCLC 36**
See also CA 119
Krotkov, Yuri 1917- .... **CLC 19**
See also CA 102
Krumb
See Crumb, R(obert)
Krumgold, Joseph (Quincy) 1908-1980 **CLC 12**
See also CA 9-12R; 101; CANR 7; MAICYA; SATA 1, 48; SATA-Obit 23
Krumwitz
See Crumb, R(obert)
Krutch, Joseph Wood 1893-1970 ..... **CLC 24**
See also CA 1-4R; 25-28R; CANR 4; DLB 63
Krutzch, Gus
See Eliot, T(homas) S(tearns)
Krylov, Ivan Andreevich 1768(?)-1844**NCLC 1**
See also DLB 150
Kubin, Alfred (Leopold Isidor) 1877-1959 **TCLC 23**
See also CA 112; 149; DLB 81
Kubrick, Stanley 1928- ....**CLC 16**
See also CA 81-84; CANR 33; DLB 26
Kumin, Maxine (Winokur) 1925- **CLC 5, 13, 28; DAM POET; PC 15**
See also AITN 2; CA 1-4R; CAAS 8; CANR 1, 21; DLB 5; MTCW; SATA 12
Kundera, Milan 1929-.. **CLC 4, 9, 19, 32, 68; DAM NOV; SSC 24**
See also AAYA 2; CA 85-88; CANR 19, 52; MTCW
Kunene, Mazisi (Raymond) 1930- .... **CLC 85**
See also BW 1; CA 125; DLB 117
Kunitz, Stanley (Jasspon) 1905-**CLC 6, 11, 14; PC 19**
See also CA 41-44R; CANR 26, 57; DLB 48; INT CANR-26; MTCW
Kunze, Reiner 1933- ....**CLC 10**
See also CA 93-96; DLB 75
Kuprin, Aleksandr Ivanovich 1870-1938 **TCLC 5**
See also CA 104
Kureishi, Hanif 1954(?)- .... **CLC 64**
See also CA 139
Kurosawa, Akira 1910-**CLC 16; DAM MULT**
See also AAYA 11; CA 101; CANR 46
Kushner, Tony 1957(?)-**CLC 81; DAM DRAM**
See also CA 144
Kuttner, Henry 1915-1958 .... **TCLC 10**
See also Vance, Jack
See also CA 107; 157; DLB 8
Kuzma, Greg 1944- .... **CLC 7**
See also CA 33-36R
Kuzmin, Mikhail 1872(?)-1936 .... **TCLC 40**
Kyd, Thomas 1558-1594**LC 22; DAM DRAM; DC 3**
See also DLB 62
Kyprianos, Iossif
See Samarakis, Antonis
La Bruyere, Jean de 1645-1696 .... **LC 17**
Lacan, Jacques (Marie Emile) 1901-1981 **CLC 75**
See also CA 121; 104
Laclos, Pierre Ambroise Francois Choderlos de 1741-1803 .... **NCLC 4**
La Colere, Francois
See Aragon, Louis
Lacolere, Francois
See Aragon, Louis
La Deshabilleuse
See Simenon, Georges (Jacques Christian)
Lady Gregory
See Gregory, Isabella Augusta (Persse)
Lady of Quality, A
See Bagnold, Enid
La Fayette, Marie (Madelaine Pioche de la Vergne Comtes 1634-1693 .... **LC 2**
Lafayette, Rene
See Hubbard, L(afayette) Ron(ald)
Laforgue, Jules 1860-1887**NCLC 5, 53; PC 14; SSC 20**
Lagerkvist, Paer (Fabian) 1891-1974 **CLC 7, 10, 13, 54; DAM DRAM, NOV**
See also Lagerkvist, Par
See also CA 85-88; 49-52; MTCW
Lagerkvist, Par .... **SSC 12**
See also Lagerkvist, Paer (Fabian)
Lagerloef, Selma (Ottiliana Lovisa) 1858-1940 **TCLC 4, 36**
See also Lagerlof, Selma (Ottiliana Lovisa)
See also CA 108; SATA 15
Lagerlof, Selma (Ottiliana Lovisa)
See Lagerloef, Selma (Ottiliana Lovisa)
See also CLR 7; SATA 15
La Guma, (Justin) Alex(ander) 1925-1985 **CLC 19; DAM NOV**
See also BW 1; CA 49-52; 118; CANR 25; DLB 117; MTCW
Laidlaw, A. K.
See Grieve, C(hristopher) M(urray)
Lainez, Manuel Mujica
See Mujica Lainez, Manuel
See also HW
Laing, R(onald) D(avid) 1927-1989 .. **CLC 95**
See also CA 107; 129; CANR 34; MTCW

Lamartine, Alphonse (Marie Louis Prat) de 1790-1869 **NCLC 11; DAM POET; PC 16**

Lamb, Charles 1775-1834 .... **NCLC 10; DA; DAB; DAC; DAM MST; WLC**
See also CDBLB 1789-1832; DLB 93, 107, 163; SATA 17

Lamb, Lady Caroline 1785-1828 ... **NCLC 38**
See also DLB 116

Lamming, George (William) 1927- **CLC 2, 4, 66; BLC; DAM MULT**
See also BW 2; CA 85-88; CANR 26; DLB 125; MTCW

L'Amour, Louis (Dearborn) 1908-1988 **CLC 25, 55; DAM NOV, POP**
See also AAYA 16; AITN 2; BEST 89:2; CA 1-4R; 125; CANR 3, 25, 40; DLBY 80; MTCW

Lampedusa, Giuseppe (Tomasi) di 1896-1957 **TCLC 13**
See also Tomasi di Lampedusa, Giuseppe
See also DLB 177

Lampman, Archibald 1861-1899 ... **NCLC 25**
See also DLB 92

Lancaster, Bruce 1896-1963 .... **CLC 36**
See also CA 9-10; CAP 1; SATA 9

Lanchester, John .... **CLC 99**

Landau, Mark Alexandrovich
See Aldanov, Mark (Alexandrovich)

Landau-Aldanov, Mark Alexandrovich
See Aldanov, Mark (Alexandrovich)

Landis, Jerry
See Simon, Paul (Frederick)

Landis, John 1950- .... **CLC 26**
See also CA 112; 122

Landolfi, Tommaso 1908-1979 .. **CLC 11, 49**
See also CA 127; 117; DLB 177

Landon, Letitia Elizabeth 1802-1838 . **NCLC 15**
See also DLB 96

Landor, Walter Savage 1775-1864 **NCLC 14**
See also DLB 93, 107

Landwirth, Heinz 1927-
See Lind, Jakov
See also CA 9-12R; CANR 7

Lane, Patrick 1939- .... **CLC 25; DAM POET**
See also CA 97-100; CANR 54; DLB 53; INT 97-100

Lang, Andrew 1844-1912 .... **TCLC 16**
See also CA 114; 137; DLB 98, 141, 184; MAICYA; SATA 16

Lang, Fritz 1890-1976 .... **CLC 20, 103**
See also CA 77-80; 69-72; CANR 30

Lange, John
See Crichton, (John) Michael

Langer, Elinor 1939- .... **CLC 34**
See also CA 121

Langland, William 1330(?)-1400(?)... **LC 19; DA; DAB; DAC; DAM MST, POET**
See also DLB 146

Langstaff, Launcelot
See Irving, Washington

Lanier, Sidney 1842-1881 ..... **NCLC 6; DAM POET**
See also DLB 64; DLBD 13; MAICYA; SATA 18

Lanyer, Aemilia 1569-1645 .... **LC 10, 30**
See also DLB 121

Lao Tzu .... **CMLC 7**

Lapine, James (Elliot) 1949- .... **CLC 39**
See also CA 123; 130; CANR 54; INT 130

Larbaud, Valery (Nicolas) 1881-1957 **TCLC 9**
See also CA 106; 152

Lardner, Ring
See Lardner, Ring(gold) W(ilmer)

Lardner, Ring W., Jr.
See Lardner, Ring(gold) W(ilmer)

Lardner, Ring(gold) W(ilmer) 1885-1933 **TCLC 2, 14**
See also CA 104; 131; CDALB 1917-1929; DLB 11, 25, 86; DLBD 16; MTCW

Laredo, Betty
See Codrescu, Andrei

Larkin, Maia
See Wojciechowska, Maia (Teresa)

Larkin, Philip (Arthur) 1922-1985 **CLC 3, 5, 8, 9, 13, 18, 33, 39, 64; DAB; DAM MST, POET**
See also CA 5-8R; 117; CANR 24, 62; CDBLB 1960 to Present; DLB 27; MTCW

Larra (y Sanchez de Castro), Mariano Jose de 1809-1837 .... **NCLC 17**

Larsen, Eric 1941- .... **CLC 55**
See also CA 132

Larsen, Nella 1891-1964 **CLC 37; BLC; DAM MULT**
See also BW 1; CA 125; DLB 51

Larson, Charles R(aymond) 1938- ... **CLC 31**
See also CA 53-56; CANR 4

Larson, Jonathan 1961(?)-1996 .... **CLC 99**

Las Casas, Bartolome de 1474-1566 .. **LC 31**

Lasch, Christopher 1932-1994 .... **CLC 102**
See also CA 73-76; 144; CANR 25; MTCW

Lasker-Schueler, Else 1869-1945 .. **TCLC 57**
See also DLB 66, 124

Latham, Jean Lee 1902- .... **CLC 12**
See also AITN 1; CA 5-8R; CANR 7; MAICYA; SATA 2, 68

Latham, Mavis
See Clark, Mavis Thorpe

Lathen, Emma .... **CLC 2**
See also Hennissart, Martha; Latsis, Mary J(ane)

Lathrop, Francis
See Leiber, Fritz (Reuter, Jr.)

Latsis, Mary J(ane)
See Lathen, Emma
See also CA 85-88

Lattimore, Richmond (Alexander) 1906-1984 **CLC 3**
See also CA 1-4R; 112; CANR 1

Laughlin, James 1914- .... **CLC 49**
See also CA 21-24R; CAAS 22; CANR 9, 47; DLB 48; DLBY 96

Laurence, (Jean) Margaret (Wemyss) 1926-1987 .. **CLC 3, 6, 13, 50, 62; DAC; DAM MST; SSC 7**
See also CA 5-8R; 121; CANR 33; DLB 53; MTCW; SATA-Obit 50

Laurent, Antoine 1952- .... **CLC 50**

Lauscher, Hermann
See Hesse, Hermann

Lautreamont, Comte de 1846-1870 **NCLC 12; SSC 14**

Laverty, Donald
See Blish, James (Benjamin)

Lavin, Mary 1912-1996 **CLC 4, 18, 99; SSC 4**
See also CA 9-12R; 151; CANR 33; DLB 15; MTCW

Lavond, Paul Dennis
See Kornbluth, C(yril) M.; Pohl, Frederik

Lawler, Raymond Evenor 1922- .... **CLC 58**
See also CA 103

Lawrence, D(avid) H(erbert Richards) 1885-1930 **TCLC 2, 9, 16, 33, 48, 61; DA; DAB; DAC; DAM MST, NOV, POET; SSC 4, 19; WLC**
See also CA 104; 121; CDBLB 1914-1945; DLB 10, 19, 36, 98, 162; MTCW

Lawrence, T(homas) E(dward) 1888-1935 **TCLC 18**
See also Dale, Colin
See also CA 115

Lawrence of Arabia
See Lawrence, T(homas) E(dward)

Lawson, Henry (Archibald Hertzberg) 1867-1922 .... **TCLC 27; SSC 18**
See also CA 120

Lawton, Dennis
See Faust, Frederick (Schiller)

Laxness, Halldor .... **CLC 25**
See also Gudjonsson, Halldor Kiljan

Layamon fl. c. 1200- .... **CMLC 10**
See also DLB 146

Laye, Camara 1928-1980 . **CLC 4, 38; BLC; DAM MULT**
See also BW 1; CA 85-88; 97-100; CANR 25; MTCW

Layton, Irving (Peter) 1912- **CLC 2, 15; DAC; DAM MST, POET**
See also CA 1-4R; CANR 2, 33, 43; DLB 88; MTCW

Lazarus, Emma 1849-1887 .... **NCLC 8**

Lazarus, Felix
See Cable, George Washington

Lazarus, Henry
See Slavitt, David R(ytman)

Lea, Joan
See Neufeld, John (Arthur)

Leacock, Stephen (Butler) 1869-1944 **TCLC 2; DAC; DAM MST**
See also CA 104; 141; DLB 92

Lear, Edward 1812-1888 .... **NCLC 3**
See also CLR 1; DLB 32, 163, 166; MAICYA; SATA 18

Lear, Norman (Milton) 1922- .... **CLC 12**
See also CA 73-76

Leavis, F(rank) R(aymond) 1895-1978 . **CLC 24**
See also CA 21-24R; 77-80; CANR 44; MTCW

Leavitt, David 1961- ...... **CLC 34; DAM POP**
See also CA 116; 122; CANR 50, 62; DLB 130; INT 122

Leblanc, Maurice (Marie Emile) 1864-1941 **TCLC 49**
See also CA 110

Lebowitz, Fran(ces Ann) 1951(?)- **CLC 11, 36**
See also CA 81-84; CANR 14, 60; INT CANR-14; MTCW

Lebrecht, Peter
See Tieck, (Johann) Ludwig

le Carre, John .... **CLC 3, 5, 9, 15, 28**
See also Cornwell, David (John Moore)
See also BEST 89:4; CDBLB 1960 to Present; DLB 87

Le Clezio, J(ean) M(arie) G(ustave) 1940- **CLC 31**
See also CA 116; 128; DLB 83

Leconte de Lisle, Charles-Marie-Rene 1818-1894 .... **NCLC 29**

Le Coq, Monsieur
See Simenon, Georges (Jacques Christian)

Leduc, Violette 1907-1972 .... **CLC 22**
See also CA 13-14; 33-36R; CAP 1

Ledwidge, Francis 1887(?)-1917 .... **TCLC 23**
See also CA 123; DLB 20

Lee, Andrea 1953- .... **CLC 36; BLC; DAM MULT**
See also BW 1; CA 125

Lee, Andrew
See Auchincloss, Louis (Stanton)

Lee, Chang-rae 1965- .... **CLC 91**
See also CA 148

Lee, Don L. .... **CLC 2**
See also Madhubuti, Haki R.

Lee, George W(ashington) 1894-1976 **CLC 52; BLC; DAM MULT**
See also BW 1; CA 125; DLB 51

Lee, (Nelle) Harper 1926- .. **CLC 12, 60; DA; DAB; DAC; DAM MST, NOV; WLC**
See also AAYA 13; CA 13-16R; CANR 51; CDALB 1941-1968; DLB 6; MTCW; SATA 11

Lee, Helen Elaine 1959(?)- .... **CLC 86**
See also CA 148

Lee, Julian
See Latham, Jean Lee

Lee, Larry
See Lee, Lawrence

Lee, Laurie 1914-1997 **CLC 90; DAB; DAM POP**
See also CA 77-80; 158; CANR 33; DLB 27; MTCW

Lee, Lawrence 1941-1990 .... **CLC 34**
See also CA 131; CANR 43

Lee, Manfred B(ennington) 1905-1971 . **CLC 11**
See also Queen, Ellery
See also CA 1-4R; 29-32R; CANR 2; DLB 137

Lee, Shelton Jackson 1957(?)-**CLC 105; DAM MULT**
See also Lee, Spike
See also BW 2; CA 125; CANR 42

Lee, Spike
See Lee, Shelton Jackson
See also AAYA 4

Lee, Stan 1922- .... **CLC 17**
See also AAYA 5; CA 108; 111; INT 111

Lee, Tanith 1947- .... **CLC 46**
See also AAYA 15; CA 37-40R; CANR 53; SATA 8, 88

Lee, Vernon .... **TCLC 5**
See also Paget, Violet
See also DLB 57, 153, 156, 174, 178

Lee, William
See Burroughs, William S(eward)

Lee, Willy
See Burroughs, William S(eward)

Lee-Hamilton, Eugene (Jacob) 1845-1907 **TCLC 22**
See also CA 117

Leet, Judith 1935- .... **CLC 11**

Le Fanu, Joseph Sheridan 1814-1873**NCLC 9, 58; DAM POP; SSC 14**
See also DLB 21, 70, 159, 178

Leffland, Ella 1931- .... **CLC 19**
See also CA 29-32R; CANR 35; DLBY 84; INT CANR-35; SATA 65

Leger, Alexis
See Leger, (Marie-Rene Auguste) Alexis Saint-Leger

Leger, (Marie-Rene Auguste) Alexis Saint-Leger 1887-1975 **CLC 11; DAM POET**
See also Perse, St.-John
See also CA 13-16R; 61-64; CANR 43; MTCW

Leger, Saintleger
See Leger, (Marie-Rene Auguste) Alexis Saint-Leger

Le Guin, Ursula K(roeber) 1929- **CLC 8, 13, 22, 45, 71; DAB; DAC; DAM MST, POP; SSC 12**
See also AAYA 9; AITN 1; CA 21-24R; CANR 9, 32, 52; CDALB 1968-1988; CLR 3, 28; DLB 8, 52; INT CANR-32; JRDA; MAICYA; MTCW; SATA 4, 52

Lehmann, Rosamond (Nina) 1901-1990**CLC 5**
See also CA 77-80; 131; CANR 8; DLB 15

Leiber, Fritz (Reuter, Jr.) 1910-1992**CLC 25**
See also CA 45-48; 139; CANR 2, 40; DLB 8; MTCW; SATA 45; SATA-Obit 73

Leibniz, Gottfried Wilhelm von 1646-1716**LC 35**
See also DLB 168

Leimbach, Martha 1963-
See Leimbach, Marti
See also CA 130

Leimbach, Marti .... **CLC 65**
See also Leimbach, Martha

Leino, Eino .... **TCLC 24**
See also Loennbohm, Armas Eino Leopold

Leiris, Michel (Julien) 1901-1990 ..... **CLC 61**
See also CA 119; 128; 132

Leithauser, Brad 1953- .... **CLC 27**
See also CA 107; CANR 27; DLB 120

Lelchuk, Alan 1938- .... **CLC 5**
See also CA 45-48; CAAS 20; CANR 1

Lem, Stanislaw 1921- .... **CLC 8, 15, 40**
See also CA 105; CAAS 1; CANR 32; MTCW

Lemann, Nancy 1956- .... **CLC 39**
See also CA 118; 136

Lemonnier, (Antoine Louis) Camille 1844-1913 **TCLC 22**
See also CA 121

Lenau, Nikolaus 1802-1850 .... **NCLC 16**

L'Engle, Madeleine (Camp Franklin) 1918- **CLC 12; DAM POP**
See also AAYA 1; AITN 2; CA 1-4R; CANR 3, 21, 39; CLR 1, 14; DLB 52; JRDA; MAICYA; MTCW; SAAS 15; SATA 1, 27, 75

Lengyel, Jozsef 1896-1975 .... **CLC 7**
See also CA 85-88; 57-60

Lenin 1870-1924
See Lenin, V. I.
See also CA 121

Lenin, V. I. .... **TCLC 67**
See also Lenin

Lennon, John (Ono) 1940-1980 . **CLC 12, 35**
See also CA 102

Lennox, Charlotte Ramsay 1729(?)-1804 **NCLC 23**
See also DLB 39

Lentricchia, Frank (Jr.) 1940- .... **CLC 34**
See also CA 25-28R; CANR 19

Lenz, Siegfried 1926- .... **CLC 27**
See also CA 89-92; DLB 75

Leonard, Elmore (John, Jr.) 1925- **CLC 28, 34, 71; DAM POP**
See also AAYA 22; AITN 1; BEST 89:1, 90:4; CA 81-84; CANR 12, 28, 53; DLB 173; INT CANR-28; MTCW

Leonard, Hugh .... **CLC 19**
See also Byrne, John Keyes
See also DLB 13

Leonov, Leonid (Maximovich) 1899-1994 **CLC 92; DAM NOV**
See also CA 129; MTCW

Leopardi, (Conte) Giacomo 1798-1837**NCLC 22**

Le Reveler
See Artaud, Antonin (Marie Joseph)

Lerman, Eleanor 1952- .... **CLC 9**
See also CA 85-88

Lerman, Rhoda 1936- .... **CLC 56**
See also CA 49-52

Lermontov, Mikhail Yuryevich 1814-1841 **NCLC 47; PC 18**

Leroux, Gaston 1868-1927 .... **TCLC 25**
See also CA 108; 136; SATA 65

Lesage, Alain-Rene 1668-1747 .... **LC 28**

Leskov, Nikolai (Semyonovich) 1831-1895 **NCLC 25**

Lessing, Doris (May) 1919-**CLC 1, 2, 3, 6, 10, 15, 22, 40, 94; DA; DAB; DAC; DAM MST, NOV; SSC 6; WLCS**
See also CA 9-12R; CAAS 14; CANR 33, 54; CDBLB 1960 to Present; DLB 15, 139; DLBY 85; MTCW

Lessing, Gotthold Ephraim 1729-1781 **LC 8**
See also DLB 97

Lester, Richard 1932- .... **CLC 20**

Lever, Charles (James) 1806-1872 **NCLC 23**
See also DLB 21

Leverson, Ada 1865(?)-1936(?) ...... **TCLC 18**
See also Elaine
See also CA 117; DLB 153

Levertov, Denise 1923-**CLC 1, 2, 3, 5, 8, 15, 28, 66; DAM POET; PC 11**
See also CA 1-4R; CAAS 19; CANR 3, 29, 50; DLB 5, 165; INT CANR-29; MTCW

Levi, Jonathan .... **CLC 76**

Levi, Peter (Chad Tigar) 1931-......... **CLC 41**
See also CA 5-8R; CANR 34; DLB 40

Levi, Primo 1919-1987 . **CLC 37, 50; SSC 12**
See also CA 13-16R; 122; CANR 12, 33, 61; DLB 177; MTCW

Levin, Ira 1929- .... **CLC 3, 6; DAM POP**
See also CA 21-24R; CANR 17, 44; MTCW; SATA 66

Levin, Meyer 1905-1981 . **CLC 7; DAM POP**
See also AITN 1; CA 9-12R; 104; CANR 15; DLB 9, 28; DLBY 81; SATA 21; SATA-Obit 27

Levine, Norman 1924- .... **CLC 54**
See also CA 73-76; CAAS 23; CANR 14; DLB 88

Levine, Philip 1928- .. **CLC 2, 4, 5, 9, 14, 33; DAM POET**
See also CA 9-12R; CANR 9, 37, 52; DLB 5

Levinson, Deirdre 1931- .... **CLC 49**
See also CA 73-76

Levi-Strauss, Claude 1908- .... **CLC 38**
See also CA 1-4R; CANR 6, 32, 57; MTCW

Levitin, Sonia (Wolff) 1934-................. **CLC 17**
See also AAYA 13; CA 29-32R; CANR 14, 32; JRDA; MAICYA; SAAS 2; SATA 4, 68

Levon, O. U.
See Kesey, Ken (Elton)

Levy, Amy 1861-1889 .... **NCLC 59**
See also DLB 156

Lewes, George Henry 1817-1878 ... **NCLC 25**
See also DLB 55, 144

Lewis, Alun 1915-1944 .... **TCLC 3**
See also CA 104; DLB 20, 162

Lewis, C. Day
See Day Lewis, C(ecil)

Lewis, C(live) S(taples) 1898-1963**CLC 1, 3, 6, 14, 27; DA; DAB; DAC; DAM MST, NOV, POP; WLC**
See also AAYA 3; CA 81-84; CANR 33; CDBLB 1945-1960; CLR 3, 27; DLB 15, 100, 160; JRDA; MAICYA; MTCW; SATA 13

Lewis, Janet 1899- .... **CLC 41**
See also Winters, Janet Lewis
See also CA 9-12R; CANR 29; CAP 1; DLBY 87

Lewis, Matthew Gregory 1775-1818**NCLC 11, 62**
See also DLB 39, 158, 178

Lewis, (Harry) Sinclair 1885-1951 . **TCLC 4, 13, 23, 39; DA; DAB; DAC; DAM MST, NOV; WLC**
See also CA 104; 133; CDALB 1917-1929; DLB 9, 102; DLBD 1; MTCW

Lewis, (Percy) Wyndham 1882(?)-1957**TCLC 2, 9**
See also CA 104; 157; DLB 15

Lewisohn, Ludwig 1883-1955 .... **TCLC 19**
See also CA 107; DLB 4, 9, 28, 102

Lewton, Val 1904-1951 .... **TCLC 76**

Leyner, Mark 1956- .... **CLC 92**
See also CA 110; CANR 28, 53

Lezama Lima, Jose 1910-1976**CLC 4, 10, 101; DAM MULT**
See also CA 77-80; DLB 113; HW

L'Heureux, John (Clarke) 1934- ...... **CLC 52**
See also CA 13-16R; CANR 23, 45

Liddell, C. H.
See Kuttner, Henry

Lie, Jonas (Lauritz Idemil) 1833-1908(?) **TCLC 5**
See also CA 115

Lieber, Joel 1937-1971 .... **CLC 6**

See also CA 73-76; 29-32R
Lieber, Stanley Martin
See Lee, Stan
Lieberman, Laurence (James) 1935- **CLC 4, 36**
See also CA 17-20R; CANR 8, 36
Lieksman, Anders
See Haavikko, Paavo Juhani
Li Fei-kan 1904-
See Pa Chin
See also CA 105
Lifton, Robert Jay 1926- .... **CLC 67**
See also CA 17-20R; CANR 27; INT CANR-27; SATA 66
Lightfoot, Gordon 1938- .... **CLC 26**
See also CA 109
Lightman, Alan P. 1948- .... **CLC 81**
See also CA 141
Ligotti, Thomas (Robert) 1953- **CLC 44; SSC 16**
See also CA 123; CANR 49
Li Ho 791-817 .... **PC 13**
Liliencron, (Friedrich Adolf Axel) Detlev von 1844-1909 .... **TCLC 18**
See also CA 117
Lilly, William 1602-1681 .... **LC 27**
Lima, Jose Lezama
See Lezama Lima, Jose
Lima Barreto, Afonso Henrique de 1881-1922 **TCLC 23**
See also CA 117
Limonov, Edward 1944- .... **CLC 67**
See also CA 137
Lin, Frank
See Atherton, Gertrude (Franklin Horn)
Lincoln, Abraham 1809-1865 .... **NCLC 18**
Lind, Jakov .... **CLC 1, 2, 4, 27, 82**
See also Landwirth, Heinz
See also CAAS 4
Lindbergh, Anne (Spencer) Morrow 1906- **CLC 82; DAM NOV**
See also CA 17-20R; CANR 16; MTCW; SATA 33
Lindsay, David 1878-1945 .... **TCLC 15**
See also CA 113
Lindsay, (Nicholas) Vachel 1879-1931 **T C L C 17; DA; DAC; DAM MST, POET; WLC**
See also CA 114; 135; CDALB 1865-1917; DLB 54; SATA 40
Linke-Poot
See Doeblin, Alfred
Linney, Romulus 1930- .... **CLC 51**
See also CA 1-4R; CANR 40, 44
Linton, Eliza Lynn 1822-1898 .... **NCLC 41**
See also DLB 18
Li Po 701-763 .... **CMLC 2**
Lipsius, Justus 1547-1606 .... **LC 16**
Lipsyte, Robert (Michael) 1938- **CLC 21; DA; DAC; DAM MST, NOV**
See also AAYA 7; CA 17-20R; CANR 8, 57; CLR 23; JRDA; MAICYA; SATA 5, 68
Lish, Gordon (Jay) 1934- ... **CLC 45; SSC 18**
See also CA 113; 117; DLB 130; INT 117
Lispector, Clarice 1925-1977 .... **CLC 43**
See also CA 139; 116; DLB 113
Littell, Robert 1935(?)- .... **CLC 42**
See also CA 109; 112
Little, Malcolm 1925-1965
See Malcolm X
See also BW 1; CA 125; 111; DA; DAB; DAC; DAM MST, MULT; MTCW
Littlewit, Humphrey Gent.
See Lovecraft, H(oward) P(hillips)
Litwos
See Sienkiewicz, Henryk (Adam Alexander Pius)
Liu E 1857-1909 .... **TCLC 15**

See also CA 115
Lively, Penelope (Margaret) 1933- . **CLC 32, 50; DAM NOV**
See also CA 41-44R; CANR 29; CLR 7; DLB 14, 161; JRDA; MAICYA; MTCW; SATA 7, 60
Livesay, Dorothy (Kathleen) 1909- **CLC 4, 15, 79; DAC; DAM MST, POET**
See also AITN 2; CA 25-28R; CAAS 8; CANR 36; DLB 68; MTCW
Livy c. 59B.C.-c. 17 .... **CMLC 11**
Lizardi, Jose Joaquin Fernandez de 1776-1827 **NCLC 30**
Llewellyn, Richard
See Llewellyn Lloyd, Richard Dafydd Vivian
See also DLB 15
Llewellyn Lloyd, Richard Dafydd Vivian 1906-1983 .... **CLC 7, 80**
See also Llewellyn, Richard
See also CA 53-56; 111; CANR 7; SATA 11; SATA-Obit 37
Llosa, (Jorge) Mario (Pedro) Vargas
See Vargas Llosa, (Jorge) Mario (Pedro)
Lloyd Webber, Andrew 1948-
See Webber, Andrew Lloyd
See also AAYA 1; CA 116; 149; DAM DRAM; SATA 56
Llull, Ramon c. 1235-c. 1316 .... **CMLC 12**
Locke, Alain (Le Roy) 1886-1954 .. **TCLC 43**
See also BW 1; CA 106; 124; DLB 51
Locke, John 1632-1704 .... **LC 7, 35**
See also DLB 101
Locke-Elliott, Sumner
See Elliott, Sumner Locke
Lockhart, John Gibson 1794-1854 .. **NCLC 6**
See also DLB 110, 116, 144
Lodge, David (John) 1935- .... **CLC 36; DAM POP**
See also BEST 90:1; CA 17-20R; CANR 19, 53; DLB 14; INT CANR-19; MTCW
Loennbohm, Armas Eino Leopold 1878-1926
See Leino, Eino
See also CA 123
Loewinsohn, Ron(ald William) 1937- **CLC 52**
See also CA 25-28R
Logan, Jake
See Smith, Martin Cruz
Logan, John (Burton) 1923-1987 .... **CLC 5**
See also CA 77-80; 124; CANR 45; DLB 5
Lo Kuan-chung 1330(?)-1400(?) .... **LC 12**
Lombard, Nap
See Johnson, Pamela Hansford
London, Jack . **TCLC 9, 15, 39; SSC 4; WLC**
See also London, John Griffith
See also AAYA 13; AITN 2; CDALB 1865-1917; DLB 8, 12, 78; SATA 18
London, John Griffith 1876-1916
See London, Jack
See also CA 110; 119; DA; DAB; DAC; DAM MST, NOV; JRDA; MAICYA; MTCW
Long, Emmett
See Leonard, Elmore (John, Jr.)
Longbaugh, Harry
See Goldman, William (W.)
Longfellow, Henry Wadsworth 1807-1882 **NCLC 2, 45; DA; DAB; DAC; DAM MST, POET; WLCS**
See also CDALB 1640-1865; DLB 1, 59; SATA 19
Longley, Michael 1939- .... **CLC 29**
See also CA 102; DLB 40
Longus fl. c. 2nd cent. - .... **CMLC 7**
Longway, A. Hugh
See Lang, Andrew
Lonnrot, Elias 1802-1884 .... **NCLC 53**
Lopate, Phillip 1943- .... **CLC 29**
See also CA 97-100; DLBY 80; INT 97-100

Lopez Portillo (y Pacheco), Jose 1920- . **C L C 46**
See also CA 129; HW
Lopez y Fuentes, Gregorio 1897(?)-1966 **CLC 32**
See also CA 131; HW
Lorca, Federico Garcia
See Garcia Lorca, Federico
Lord, Bette Bao 1938- .... **CLC 23**
See also BEST 90:3; CA 107; CANR 41; INT 107; SATA 58
Lord Auch
See Bataille, Georges
Lord Byron
See Byron, George Gordon (Noel)
Lorde, Audre (Geraldine) 1934-1992 **CLC 18, 71; BLC; DAM MULT, POET; PC 12**
See also BW 1; CA 25-28R; 142; CANR 16, 26, 46; DLB 41; MTCW
Lord Houghton
See Milnes, Richard Monckton
Lord Jeffrey
See Jeffrey, Francis
Lorenzini, Carlo 1826-1890
See Collodi, Carlo
See also MAICYA; SATA 29
Lorenzo, Heberto Padilla
See Padilla (Lorenzo), Heberto
Loris
See Hofmannsthal, Hugo von
Loti, Pierre .... **TCLC 11**
See also Viaud, (Louis Marie) Julien
See also DLB 123
Louie, David Wong 1954- .... **CLC 70**
See also CA 139
Louis, Father M.
See Merton, Thomas
Lovecraft, H(oward) P(hillips) 1890-1937 **TCLC 4, 22; DAM POP; SSC 3**
See also AAYA 14; CA 104; 133; MTCW
Lovelace, Earl 1935- .... **CLC 51**
See also BW 2; CA 77-80; CANR 41; DLB 125; MTCW
Lovelace, Richard 1618-1657 .... **LC 24**
See also DLB 131
Lowell, Amy 1874-1925 .... **TCLC 1, 8; DAM POET; PC 13**
See also CA 104; 151; DLB 54, 140
Lowell, James Russell 1819-1891 .... **NCLC 2**
See also CDALB 1640-1865; DLB 1, 11, 64, 79
Lowell, Robert (Traill Spence, Jr.) 1917-1977 **CLC 1, 2, 3, 4, 5, 8, 9, 11, 15, 37; DA; DAB; DAC; DAM MST, NOV; PC 3; WLC**
See also CA 9-12R; 73-76; CABS 2; CANR 26, 60; DLB 5, 169; MTCW
Lowndes, Marie Adelaide (Belloc) 1868-1947 **TCLC 12**
See also CA 107; DLB 70
Lowry, (Clarence) Malcolm 1909-1957 **TCLC 6, 40**
See also CA 105; 131; CANR 62; CDBLB 1945-1960; DLB 15; MTCW
Lowry, Mina Gertrude 1882-1966
See Loy, Mina
See also CA 113
Loxsmith, John
See Brunner, John (Kilian Houston)
Loy, Mina .... **CLC 28; DAM POET; PC 16**
See also Lowry, Mina Gertrude
See also DLB 4, 54
Loyson-Bridet
See Schwob, (Mayer Andre) Marcel
Lucas, Craig 1951- .... **CLC 64**
See also CA 137
Lucas, E(dward) V(errall) 1868-1938 **T C L C 73**

See also DLB 98, 149, 153; SATA 20
Lucas, George 1944- .... **CLC 16**
See also AAYA 1; CA 77-80; CANR 30; SATA 56
Lucas, Hans
See Godard, Jean-Luc
Lucas, Victoria
See Plath, Sylvia
Ludlam, Charles 1943-1987 .... **CLC 46, 50**
See also CA 85-88; 122
Ludlum, Robert 1927- .... **CLC 22, 43; DAM NOV, POP**
See also AAYA 10; BEST 89:1, 90:3; CA 33-36R; CANR 25, 41; DLBY 82; MTCW
Ludwig, Ken .... **CLC 60**
Ludwig, Otto 1813-1865 .... **NCLC 4**
See also DLB 129
Lugones, Leopoldo 1874-1938 .... **TCLC 15**
See also CA 116; 131; HW
Lu Hsun 1881-1936 .... **TCLC 3; SSC 20**
See also Shu-Jen, Chou
Lukacs, George .... **CLC 24**
See also Lukacs, Gyorgy (Szegeny von)
Lukacs, Gyorgy (Szegeny von) 1885-1971
See Lukacs, George
See also CA 101; 29-32R; CANR 62
Luke, Peter (Ambrose Cyprian) 1919-1995
CLC 38
See also CA 81-84; 147; DLB 13
Lunar, Dennis
See Mungo, Raymond
Lurie, Alison 1926- .... **CLC 4, 5, 18, 39**
See also CA 1-4R; CANR 2, 17, 50; DLB 2; MTCW; SATA 46
Lustig, Arnost 1926- .... **CLC 56**
See also AAYA 3; CA 69-72; CANR 47; SATA 56
Luther, Martin 1483-1546 .... **LC 9, 37**
See also DLB 179
Luxemburg, Rosa 1870(?)-1919 ..... **TCLC 63**
See also CA 118
Luzi, Mario 1914- .... **CLC 13**
See also CA 61-64; CANR 9; DLB 128
Lyly, John 1554(?)-1606 .... **DC 7**
See also DAM DRAM; DLB 62, 167
L'Ymagier
See Gourmont, Remy (-Marie-Charles) de
Lynch, B. Suarez
See Bioy Casares, Adolfo; Borges, Jorge Luis
Lynch, David (K.) 1946- .... **CLC 66**
See also CA 124; 129
Lynch, James
See Andreyev, Leonid (Nikolaevich)
Lynch Davis, B.
See Bioy Casares, Adolfo; Borges, Jorge Luis
Lyndsay, Sir David 1490-1555 .... **LC 20**
Lynn, Kenneth S(chuyler) 1923- ..... **CLC 50**
See also CA 1-4R; CANR 3, 27
Lynx
See West, Rebecca
Lyons, Marcus
See Blish, James (Benjamin)
Lyre, Pinchbeck
See Sassoon, Siegfried (Lorraine)
Lytle, Andrew (Nelson) 1902-1995 .. **CLC 22**
See also CA 9-12R; 150; DLB 6; DLBY 95
Lyttelton, George 1709-1773 .... **LC 10**
Maas, Peter 1929- .... **CLC 29**
See also CA 93-96; INT 93-96
Macaulay, Rose 1881-1958 .... **TCLC 7, 44**
See also CA 104; DLB 36
Macaulay, Thomas Babington 1800-1859
NCLC 42
See also CDBLB 1832-1890; DLB 32, 55
MacBeth, George (Mann) 1932-1992 **CLC 2, 5, 9**
See also CA 25-28R; 136; CANR 61; DLB 40; MTCW; SATA 4; SATA-Obit 70
MacCaig, Norman (Alexander) 1910-**CLC 36; DAB; DAM POET**
See also CA 9-12R; CANR 3, 34; DLB 27
MacCarthy, (Sir Charles Otto) Desmond 1877-1952 .... **TCLC 36**
MacDiarmid, Hugh CLC 2, 4, 11, 19, 63; PC 9
See also Grieve, C(hristopher) M(urray)
See also CDBLB 1945-1960; DLB 20
MacDonald, Anson
See Heinlein, Robert A(nson)
Macdonald, Cynthia 1928- .... **CLC 13, 19**
See also CA 49-52; CANR 4, 44; DLB 105
MacDonald, George 1824-1905 .... **TCLC 9**
See also CA 106; 137; DLB 18, 163, 178; MAICYA; SATA 33
Macdonald, John
See Millar, Kenneth
MacDonald, John D(ann) 1916-1986 **CLC 3, 27, 44; DAM NOV, POP**
See also CA 1-4R; 121; CANR 1, 19, 60; DLB 8; DLBY 86; MTCW
Macdonald, John Ross
See Millar, Kenneth
Macdonald, Ross .... **CLC 1, 2, 3, 14, 34, 41**
See also Millar, Kenneth
See also DLBD 6
MacDougal, John
See Blish, James (Benjamin)
MacEwen, Gwendolyn (Margaret) 1941-1987
CLC 13, 55
See also CA 9-12R; 124; CANR 7, 22; DLB 53; SATA 50; SATA-Obit 55
Macha, Karel Hynek 1810-1846 .... **NCLC 46**
Machado (y Ruiz), Antonio 1875-1939 **TCLC 3**
See also CA 104; DLB 108
Machado de Assis, Joaquim Maria 1839-1908
TCLC 10; BLC; SSC 24
See also CA 107; 153
Machen, Arthur .... **TCLC 4; SSC 20**
See also Jones, Arthur Llewellyn
See also DLB 36, 156, 178
Machiavelli, Niccolo 1469-1527**LC 8, 36; DAB; DAC; DAM MST; WLCS**
MacInnes, Colin 1914-1976 .... **CLC 4, 23**
See also CA 69-72; 65-68; CANR 21; DLB 14; MTCW
MacInnes, Helen (Clark) 1907-1985**CLC 27, 39; DAM POP**
See also CA 1-4R; 117; CANR 1, 28, 58; DLB 87; MTCW; SATA 22; SATA-Obit 44
Mackay, Mary 1855-1924
See Corelli, Marie
See also CA 118
Mackenzie, Compton (Edward Montague) 1883-1972 .... **CLC 18**
See also CA 21-22; 37-40R; CAP 2; DLB 34, 100
Mackenzie, Henry 1745-1831 .... **NCLC 41**
See also DLB 39
Mackintosh, Elizabeth 1896(?)-1952
See Tey, Josephine
See also CA 110
MacLaren, James
See Grieve, C(hristopher) M(urray)
Mac Laverty, Bernard 1942- .... **CLC 31**
See also CA 116; 118; CANR 43; INT 118
MacLean, Alistair (Stuart) 1922(?)-1987**CLC 3, 13, 50, 63; DAM POP**
See also CA 57-60; 121; CANR 28, 61; MTCW; SATA 23; SATA-Obit 50
Maclean, Norman (Fitzroy) 1902-1990 . **CLC 78; DAM POP; SSC 13**
See also CA 102; 132; CANR 49
MacLeish, Archibald 1892-1982**CLC 3, 8, 14, 68; DAM POET**
See also CA 9-12R; 106; CANR 33; DLB 4, 7, 45; DLBY 82; MTCW
MacLennan, (John) Hugh 1907-1990 **CLC 2, 14, 92; DAC; DAM MST**
See also CA 5-8R; 142; CANR 33; DLB 68; MTCW
MacLeod, Alistair 1936-**CLC 56; DAC; DAM MST**
See also CA 123; DLB 60
Macleod, Fiona
See Sharp, William
MacNeice, (Frederick) Louis 1907-1963**CLC 1, 4, 10, 53; DAB; DAM POET**
See also CA 85-88; CANR 61; DLB 10, 20; MTCW
MacNeill, Dand
See Fraser, George MacDonald
Macpherson, James 1736-1796 .... **LC 29**
See also DLB 109
Macpherson, (Jean) Jay 1931- .... **CLC 14**
See also CA 5-8R; DLB 53
MacShane, Frank 1927- .... **CLC 39**
See also CA 9-12R; CANR 3, 33; DLB 111
Macumber, Mari
See Sandoz, Mari(e Susette)
Madach, Imre 1823-1864 .... **NCLC 19**
Madden, (Jerry) David 1933- .... **CLC 5, 15**
See also CA 1-4R; CAAS 3; CANR 4, 45; DLB 6; MTCW
Maddern, Al(an)
See Ellison, Harlan (Jay)
Madhubuti, Haki R. 1942- **CLC 6, 73; BLC; DAM MULT, POET; PC 5**
See also Lee, Don L.
See also BW 2; CA 73-76; CANR 24, 51; DLB 5, 41; DLBD 8
Maepenn, Hugh
See Kuttner, Henry
Maepenn, K. H.
See Kuttner, Henry
Maeterlinck, Maurice 1862-1949 ... **TCLC 3; DAM DRAM**
See also CA 104; 136; SATA 66
Maginn, William 1794-1842 .... **NCLC 8**
See also DLB 110, 159
Mahapatra, Jayanta 1928- .... **CLC 33; DAM MULT**
See also CA 73-76; CAAS 9; CANR 15, 33
Mahfouz, Naguib (Abdel Aziz Al-Sabilgi) 1911(?)-
See Mahfuz, Najib
See also BEST 89:2; CA 128; CANR 55; DAM NOV; MTCW
Mahfuz, Najib .... **CLC 52, 55**
See also Mahfouz, Naguib (Abdel Aziz Al-Sabilgi)
See also DLBY 88
Mahon, Derek 1941- .... **CLC 27**
See also CA 113; 128; DLB 40
Mailer, Norman 1923-**CLC 1, 2, 3, 4, 5, 8, 11, 14, 28, 39, 74; DA; DAB; DAC; DAM MST, NOV, POP**
See also AITN 2; CA 9-12R; CABS 1; CANR 28; CDALB 1968-1988; DLB 2, 16, 28; DLBD 3; DLBY 80, 83; MTCW
Maillet, Antonine 1929- .... **CLC 54; DAC**
See also CA 115; 120; CANR 46; DLB 60; INT 120
Mais, Roger 1905-1955 .... **TCLC 8**
See also BW 1; CA 105; 124; DLB 125; MTCW
Maistre, Joseph de 1753-1821 .... **NCLC 37**
Maitland, Frederic 1850-1906 .... **TCLC 65**
Maitland, Sara (Louise) 1950- .... **CLC 49**
See also CA 69-72; CANR 13, 59
Major, Clarence 1936- **CLC 3, 19, 48; BLC; DAM MULT**
See also BW 2; CA 21-24R; CAAS 6; CANR

13, 25, 53; DLB 33
Major, Kevin (Gerald) 1949- . **CLC 26; DAC**
　See also AAYA 16; CA 97-100; CANR 21, 38; CLR 11; DLB 60; INT CANR-21; JRDA; MAICYA; SATA 32, 82
Maki, James
　See Ozu, Yasujiro
Malabaila, Damiano
　See Levi, Primo
Malamud, Bernard 1914-1986 **CLC 1, 2, 3, 5, 8, 9, 11, 18, 27, 44, 78, 85; DA; DAB; DAC; DAM MST, NOV, POP; SSC 15; WLC**
　See also AAYA 16; CA 5-8R; 118; CABS 1; CANR 28, 62; CDALB 1941-1968; DLB 2, 28, 152; DLBY 80, 86; MTCW
Malan, Herman
　See Bosman, Herman Charles; Bosman, Herman Charles
Malaparte, Curzio 1898-1957 .... **TCLC 52**
Malcolm, Dan
　See Silverberg, Robert
Malcolm X .... **CLC 82; BLC; WLCS**
　See also Little, Malcolm
Malherbe, Francois de 1555-1628 .... **LC 5**
Mallarme, Stephane 1842-1898 **NCLC 4, 41; DAM POET; PC 4**
Mallet-Joris, Francoise 1930- .... **CLC 11**
　See also CA 65-68; CANR 17; DLB 83
Malley, Ern
　See McAuley, James Phillip
Mallowan, Agatha Christie
　See Christie, Agatha (Mary Clarissa)
Maloff, Saul 1922- .... **CLC 5**
　See also CA 33-36R
Malone, Louis
　See MacNeice, (Frederick) Louis
Malone, Michael (Christopher) 1942- **CLC 43**
　See also CA 77-80; CANR 14, 32, 57
Malory, (Sir) Thomas 1410(?)-1471(?) **LC 11; DA; DAB; DAC; DAM MST; WLCS**
　See also CDBLB Before 1660; DLB 146; SATA 59; SATA-Brief 33
Malouf, (George Joseph) David 1934- **CLC 28, 86**
　See also CA 124; CANR 50
Malraux, (Georges-)Andre 1901-1976 **CLC 1, 4, 9, 13, 15, 57; DAM NOV**
　See also CA 21-22; 69-72; CANR 34, 58; CAP 2; DLB 72; MTCW
Malzberg, Barry N(athaniel) 1939- .... **CLC 7**
　See also CA 61-64; CAAS 4; CANR 16; DLB 8
Mamet, David (Alan) 1947- **CLC 9, 15, 34, 46, 91; DAM DRAM; DC 4**
　See also AAYA 3; CA 81-84; CABS 3; CANR 15, 41; DLB 7; MTCW
Mamoulian, Rouben (Zachary) 1897-1987 **CLC 16**
　See also CA 25-28R; 124
Mandelstam, Osip (Emilievich) 1891(?)-1938(?) **TCLC 2, 6; PC 14**
　See also CA 104; 150
Mander, (Mary) Jane 1877-1949 ... **TCLC 31**
Mandeville, John fl. 1350- .... **CMLC 19**
　See also DLB 146
Mandiargues, Andre Pieyre de .... **CLC 41**
　See also Pieyre de Mandiargues, Andre
　See also DLB 83
Mandrake, Ethel Belle
　See Thurman, Wallace (Henry)
Mangan, James Clarence 1803-1849 **NCLC 27**
Maniere, J.-E.
　See Giraudoux, (Hippolyte) Jean
Manley, (Mary) Delariviere 1672(?)-1724 **LC 1**
　See also DLB 39, 80
Mann, Abel
　See Creasey, John
Mann, Emily 1952- .... **DC 7**
　See also CA 130; CANR 55
Mann, (Luiz) Heinrich 1871-1950 ... **TCLC 9**
　See also CA 106; DLB 66
Mann, (Paul) Thomas 1875-1955 **TCLC 2, 8, 14, 21, 35, 44, 60; DA; DAB; DAC; DAM MST, NOV; SSC 5; WLC**
　See also CA 104; 128; DLB 66; MTCW
Mannheim, Karl 1893-1947 .... **TCLC 65**
Manning, David
　See Faust, Frederick (Schiller)
Manning, Frederic 1887(?)-1935 ... **TCLC 25**
　See also CA 124
Manning, Olivia 1915-1980 .... **CLC 5, 19**
　See also CA 5-8R; 101; CANR 29; MTCW
Mano, D. Keith 1942- .... **CLC 2, 10**
　See also CA 25-28R; CAAS 6; CANR 26, 57; DLB 6
Mansfield, Katherine TCLC 2, 8, 39; DAB; SSC 9, 23; WLC
　See also Beauchamp, Kathleen Mansfield
　See also DLB 162
Manso, Peter 1940- .... **CLC 39**
　See also CA 29-32R; CANR 44
Mantecon, Juan Jimenez
　See Jimenez (Mantecon), Juan Ramon
Manton, Peter
　See Creasey, John
Man Without a Spleen, A
　See Chekhov, Anton (Pavlovich)
Manzoni, Alessandro 1785-1873 .... **NCLC 29**
Mapu, Abraham (ben Jekutiel) 1808-1867 **NCLC 18**
Mara, Sally
　See Queneau, Raymond
Marat, Jean Paul 1743-1793 .... **LC 10**
Marcel, Gabriel Honore 1889-1973 . **CLC 15**
　See also CA 102; 45-48; MTCW
Marchbanks, Samuel
　See Davies, (William) Robertson
Marchi, Giacomo
　See Bassani, Giorgio
Margulies, Donald .... **CLC 76**
Marie de France c. 12th cent. - .... **CMLC 8**
Marie de l'Incarnation 1599-1672 ...... **LC 10**
Marier, Captain Victor
　See Griffith, D(avid Lewelyn) W(ark)
Mariner, Scott
　See Pohl, Frederik
Marinetti, Filippo Tommaso 1876-1944 **TCLC 10**
　See also CA 107; DLB 114
Marivaux, Pierre Carlet de Chamblain de 1688-1763 .... **LC 4; DC 7**
Markandaya, Kamala .... **CLC 8, 38**
　See also Taylor, Kamala (Purnaiya)
Markfield, Wallace 1926- .... **CLC 8**
　See also CA 69-72; CAAS 3; DLB 2, 28
Markham, Edwin 1852-1940 .... **TCLC 47**
　See also CA 160; DLB 54
Markham, Robert
　See Amis, Kingsley (William)
Marks, J
　See Highwater, Jamake (Mamake)
Marks-Highwater, J
　See Highwater, Jamake (Mamake)
Markson, David M(errill) 1927- .... **CLC 67**
　See also CA 49-52; CANR 1
Marley, Bob .... **CLC 17**
　See also Marley, Robert Nesta
Marley, Robert Nesta 1945-1981
　See Marley, Bob
　See also CA 107; 103
Marlowe, Christopher 1564-1593 **LC 22; DA; DAB; DAC; DAM DRAM, MST; DC 1; WLC**
　See also CDBLB Before 1660; DLB 62
Marlowe, Stephen 1928-
　See Queen, Ellery
　See also CA 13-16R; CANR 6, 55
Marmontel, Jean-Francois 1723-1799 . **LC 2**
Marquand, John P(hillips) 1893-1960 **CLC 2, 10**
　See also CA 85-88; DLB 9, 102
Marques, Rene 1919-1979 ..... **CLC 96; DAM MULT; HLC**
　See also CA 97-100; 85-88; DLB 113; HW
Marquez, Gabriel (Jose) Garcia
　See Garcia Marquez, Gabriel (Jose)
Marquis, Don(ald Robert Perry) 1878-1937 **TCLC 7**
　See also CA 104; DLB 11, 25
Marric, J. J.
　See Creasey, John
Marrow, Bernard
　See Moore, Brian
Marryat, Frederick 1792-1848 .... **NCLC 3**
　See also DLB 21, 163
Marsden, James
　See Creasey, John
Marsh, (Edith) Ngaio 1899-1982 **CLC 7, 53; DAM POP**
　See also CA 9-12R; CANR 6, 58; DLB 77; MTCW
Marshall, Garry 1934- .... **CLC 17**
　See also AAYA 3; CA 111; SATA 60
Marshall, Paule 1929- **CLC 27, 72; BLC; DAM MULT; SSC 3**
　See also BW 2; CA 77-80; CANR 25; DLB 157; MTCW
Marsten, Richard
　See Hunter, Evan
Marston, John 1576-1634 **LC 33; DAM DRAM**
　See also DLB 58, 172
Martha, Henry
　See Harris, Mark
Marti, Jose 1853-1895 .... **NCLC 63; DAM MULT; HLC**
Martial c. 40-c. 104 .... **PC 10**
Martin, Ken
　See Hubbard, L(afayette) Ron(ald)
Martin, Richard
　See Creasey, John
Martin, Steve 1945- .... **CLC 30**
　See also CA 97-100; CANR 30; MTCW
Martin, Valerie 1948- .... **CLC 89**
　See also BEST 90:2; CA 85-88; CANR 49
Martin, Violet Florence 1862-1915 **TCLC 51**
Martin, Webber
　See Silverberg, Robert
Martindale, Patrick Victor
　See White, Patrick (Victor Martindale)
Martin du Gard, Roger 1881-1958 **TCLC 24**
　See also CA 118; DLB 65
Martineau, Harriet 1802-1876 .... **NCLC 26**
　See also DLB 21, 55, 159, 163, 166; YABC 2
Martines, Julia
　See O'Faolain, Julia
Martinez, Enrique Gonzalez
　See Gonzalez Martinez, Enrique
Martinez, Jacinto Benavente y
　See Benavente (y Martinez), Jacinto
Martinez Ruiz, Jose 1873-1967
　See Azorin; Ruiz, Jose Martinez
　See also CA 93-96; HW
Martinez Sierra, Gregorio 1881-1947 **TCLC 6**
　See also CA 115
Martinez Sierra, Maria (de la O'LeJarraga) 1874-1974 .... **TCLC 6**
　See also CA 115
Martinsen, Martin
　See Follett, Ken(neth Martin)
Martinson, Harry (Edmund) 1904-1978 **CLC**

14
See also CA 77-80; CANR 34
Marut, Ret
See Traven, B.
Marut, Robert
See Traven, B.
Marvell, Andrew 1621-1678 LC 4; DA; DAB; DAC; DAM MST, POET; PC 10; WLC
See also CDBLB 1660-1789; DLB 131
Marx, Karl (Heinrich) 1818-1883 . NCLC 17
See also DLB 129
Masaoka Shiki .... TCLC 18
See also Masaoka Tsunenori
Masaoka Tsunenori 1867-1902
See Masaoka Shiki
See also CA 117
Masefield, John (Edward) 1878-1967 CLC 11, 47; DAM POET
See also CA 19-20; 25-28R; CANR 33; CAP 2; CDBLB 1890-1914; DLB 10, 19, 153, 160; MTCW; SATA 19
Maso, Carole 19(?)- .... CLC 44
Mason, Bobbie Ann 1940- CLC 28, 43, 82; SSC 4
See also AAYA 5; CA 53-56; CANR 11, 31, 58; DLB 173; DLBY 87; INT CANR-31; MTCW
Mason, Ernst
See Pohl, Frederik
Mason, Lee W.
See Malzberg, Barry N(athaniel)
Mason, Nick 1945- .... CLC 35
Mason, Tally
See Derleth, August (William)
Mass, William
See Gibson, William
Masters, Edgar Lee 1868-1950 TCLC 2, 25; DA; DAC; DAM MST, POET; PC 1; WLCS
See also CA 104; 133; CDALB 1865-1917; DLB 54; MTCW
Masters, Hilary 1928- .... CLC 48
See also CA 25-28R; CANR 13, 47
Mastrosimone, William 19(?)- .... CLC 36
Mathe, Albert
See Camus, Albert
Mather, Cotton 1663-1728 .... LC 38
See also CDALB 1640-1865; DLB 24, 30, 140
Mather, Increase 1639-1723 .... LC 38
See also DLB 24
Matheson, Richard Burton 1926- ..... CLC 37
See also CA 97-100; DLB 8, 44; INT 97-100
Mathews, Harry 1930- .... CLC 6, 52
See also CA 21-24R; CAAS 6; CANR 18, 40
Mathews, John Joseph 1894-1979 .. CLC 84; DAM MULT
See also CA 19-20; 142; CANR 45; CAP 2; DLB 175; NNAL
Mathias, Roland (Glyn) 1915- .... CLC 45
See also CA 97-100; CANR 19, 41; DLB 27
Matsuo Basho 1644-1694 .... PC 3
See also DAM POET
Mattheson, Rodney
See Creasey, John
Matthews, Greg 1949- .... CLC 45
See also CA 135
Matthews, William 1942- .... CLC 40
See also CA 29-32R; CAAS 18; CANR 12, 57; DLB 5
Matthias, John (Edward) 1941- .... CLC 9
See also CA 33-36R; CANR 56
Matthiessen, Peter 1927- CLC 5, 7, 11, 32, 64; DAM NOV
See also AAYA 6; BEST 90:4; CA 9-12R; CANR 21, 50; DLB 6, 173; MTCW; SATA 27
Maturin, Charles Robert 1780(?)-1824 NCLC 6
See also DLB 178
Matute (Ausejo), Ana Maria 1925- .. CLC 11
See also CA 89-92; MTCW
Maugham, W. S.
See Maugham, W(illiam) Somerset
Maugham, W(illiam) Somerset 1874-1965 CLC 1, 11, 15, 67, 93; DA; DAB; DAC; DAM DRAM, MST, NOV; SSC 8; WLC
See also CA 5-8R; 25-28R; CANR 40; CDBLB 1914-1945; DLB 10, 36, 77, 100, 162; MTCW; SATA 54
Maugham, William Somerset
See Maugham, W(illiam) Somerset
Maupassant, (Henri Rene Albert) Guy de 1850-1893 NCLC 1, 42; DA; DAB; DAC; DAM MST; SSC 1; WLC
See also DLB 123
Maupin, Armistead 1944- CLC 95; DAM POP
See also CA 125; 130; CANR 58; INT 130
Maurhut, Richard
See Traven, B.
Mauriac, Claude 1914-1996 .... CLC 9
See also CA 89-92; 152; DLB 83
Mauriac, Francois (Charles) 1885-1970 C L C 4, 9, 56; SSC 24
See also CA 25-28; CAP 2; DLB 65; MTCW
Mavor, Osborne Henry 1888-1951
See Bridie, James
See also CA 104
Maxwell, William (Keepers, Jr.) 1908- . C L C 19
See also CA 93-96; CANR 54; DLBY 80; INT 93-96
May, Elaine 1932- .... CLC 16
See also CA 124; 142; DLB 44
Mayakovski, Vladimir (Vladimirovich) 1893-1930 .... TCLC 4, 18
See also CA 104; 158
Mayhew, Henry 1812-1887 .... NCLC 31
See also DLB 18, 55
Mayle, Peter 1939(?)- .... CLC 89
See also CA 139
Maynard, Joyce 1953- .... CLC 23
See also CA 111; 129
Mayne, William (James Carter) 1928- CLC 12
See also AAYA 20; CA 9-12R; CANR 37; CLR 25; JRDA; MAICYA; SAAS 11; SATA 6, 68
Mayo, Jim
See L'Amour, Louis (Dearborn)
Maysles, Albert 1926- .... CLC 16
See also CA 29-32R
Maysles, David 1932- .... CLC 16
Mazer, Norma Fox 1931- .... CLC 26
See also AAYA 5; CA 69-72; CANR 12, 32; CLR 23; JRDA; MAICYA; SAAS 1; SATA 24, 67
Mazzini, Guiseppe 1805-1872 .... NCLC 34
McAuley, James Phillip 1917-1976 .. CLC 45
See also CA 97-100
McBain, Ed
See Hunter, Evan
McBrien, William Augustine 1930- .. CLC 44
See also CA 107
McCaffrey, Anne (Inez) 1926- CLC 17; DAM NOV, POP
See also AAYA 6; AITN 2; BEST 89:2; CA 25-28R; CANR 15, 35, 55; DLB 8; JRDA; MAICYA; MTCW; SAAS 11; SATA 8, 70
McCall, Nathan 1955(?)- .... CLC 86
See also CA 146
McCann, Arthur
See Campbell, John W(ood, Jr.)
McCann, Edson
See Pohl, Frederik
McCarthy, Charles, Jr. 1933-
See McCarthy, Cormac
See also CANR 42; DAM POP
McCarthy, Cormac 1933- CLC 4, 57, 59, 101
See also McCarthy, Charles, Jr.
See also DLB 6, 143
McCarthy, Mary (Therese) 1912-1989 CLC 1, 3, 5, 14, 24, 39, 59; SSC 24
See also CA 5-8R; 129; CANR 16, 50; DLB 2; DLBY 81; INT CANR-16; MTCW
McCartney, (James) Paul 1942- CLC 12, 35
See also CA 146
McCauley, Stephen (D.) 1955- .... CLC 50
See also CA 141
McClure, Michael (Thomas) 1932- CLC 6, 10
See also CA 21-24R; CANR 17, 46; DLB 16
McCorkle, Jill (Collins) 1958- .... CLC 51
See also CA 121; DLBY 87
McCourt, James 1941- .... CLC 5
See also CA 57-60
McCoy, Horace (Stanley) 1897-1955 TCLC 28
See also CA 108; 155; DLB 9
McCrae, John 1872-1918 .... TCLC 12
See also CA 109; DLB 92
McCreigh, James
See Pohl, Frederik
McCullers, (Lula) Carson (Smith) 1917-1967 CLC 1, 4, 10, 12, 48, 100; DA; DAB; DAC; DAM MST, NOV; SSC 9, 24; WLC
See also AAYA 21; CA 5-8R; 25-28R; CABS 1, 3; CANR 18; CDALB 1941-1968; DLB 2, 7, 173; MTCW; SATA 27
McCulloch, John Tyler
See Burroughs, Edgar Rice
McCullough, Colleen 1938(?)- CLC 27; DAM NOV, POP
See also CA 81-84; CANR 17, 46; MTCW
McDermott, Alice 1953- .... CLC 90
See also CA 109; CANR 40
McElroy, Joseph 1930- .... CLC 5, 47
See also CA 17-20R
McEwan, Ian (Russell) 1948- .... CLC 13, 66; DAM NOV
See also BEST 90:4; CA 61-64; CANR 14, 41; DLB 14; MTCW
McFadden, David 1940- .... CLC 48
See also CA 104; DLB 60; INT 104
McFarland, Dennis 1950- .... CLC 65
McGahern, John 1934- CLC 5, 9, 48; SSC 17
See also CA 17-20R; CANR 29; DLB 14; MTCW
McGinley, Patrick (Anthony) 1937- . CLC 41
See also CA 120; 127; CANR 56; INT 127
McGinley, Phyllis 1905-1978 .... CLC 14
See also CA 9-12R; 77-80; CANR 19; DLB 11, 48; SATA 2, 44; SATA-Obit 24
McGinniss, Joe 1942- .... CLC 32
See also AITN 2; BEST 89:2; CA 25-28R; CANR 26; INT CANR-26
McGivern, Maureen Daly
See Daly, Maureen
McGrath, Patrick 1950- .... CLC 55
See also CA 136
McGrath, Thomas (Matthew) 1916-1990 CLC 28, 59; DAM POET
See also CA 9-12R; 132; CANR 6, 33; MTCW; SATA 41; SATA-Obit 66
McGuane, Thomas (Francis III) 1939- CLC 3, 7, 18, 45
See also AITN 2; CA 49-52; CANR 5, 24, 49; DLB 2; DLBY 80; INT CANR-24; MTCW
McGuckian, Medbh 1950- ...... CLC 48; DAM POET
See also CA 143; DLB 40
McHale, Tom 1942(?)-1982 .... CLC 3, 5
See also AITN 1; CA 77-80; 106
McIlvanney, William 1936- .... CLC 42
See also CA 25-28R; CANR 61; DLB 14

McIlwraith, Maureen Mollie Hunter
See Hunter, Mollie
See also SATA 2

McInerney, Jay 1955- ... **CLC 34; DAM POP**
See also AAYA 18; CA 116; 123; CANR 45; INT 123

McIntyre, Vonda N(eel) 1948- .... **CLC 18**
See also CA 81-84; CANR 17, 34; MTCW

McKay, Claude **TCLC 7, 41; BLC; DAB; PC 2**
See also McKay, Festus Claudius
See also DLB 4, 45, 51, 117

McKay, Festus Claudius 1889-1948
See McKay, Claude
See also BW 1; CA 104; 124; DA; DAC; DAM MST, MULT, NOV, POET; MTCW; WLC

McKuen, Rod 1933- .... **CLC 1, 3**
See also AITN 1; CA 41-44R; CANR 40

McLoughlin, R. B.
See Mencken, H(enry) L(ouis)

McLuhan, (Herbert) Marshall 1911-1980 **CLC 37, 83**
See also CA 9-12R; 102; CANR 12, 34, 61; DLB 88; INT CANR-12; MTCW

McMillan, Terry (L.) 1951-**CLC 50, 61; DAM MULT, NOV, POP**
See also AAYA 21; BW 2; CA 140; CANR 60

McMurtry, Larry (Jeff) 1936-**CLC 2, 3, 7, 11, 27, 44; DAM NOV, POP**
See also AAYA 15; AITN 2; BEST 89:2; CA 5-8R; CANR 19, 43; CDALB 1968-1988; DLB 2, 143; DLBY 80, 87; MTCW

McNally, T. M. 1961- .... **CLC 82**

McNally, Terrence 1939- ... **CLC 4, 7, 41, 91; DAM DRAM**
See also CA 45-48; CANR 2, 56; DLB 7

McNamer, Deirdre 1950- .... **CLC 70**

McNeile, Herman Cyril 1888-1937
See Sapper
See also DLB 77

McNickle, (William) D'Arcy 1904-1977 **CLC 89; DAM MULT**
See also CA 9-12R; 85-88; CANR 5, 45; DLB 175; NNAL; SATA-Obit 22

McPhee, John (Angus) 1931- .... **CLC 36**
See also BEST 90:1; CA 65-68; CANR 20, 46; MTCW

McPherson, James Alan 1943- ... **CLC 19, 77**
See also BW 1; CA 25-28R; CAAS 17; CANR 24; DLB 38; MTCW

McPherson, William (Alexander) 1933-**CLC 34**
See also CA 69-72; CANR 28; INT CANR-28

Mead, Margaret 1901-1978 .... **CLC 37**
See also AITN 1; CA 1-4R; 81-84; CANR 4; MTCW; SATA-Obit 20

Meaker, Marijane (Agnes) 1927-
See Kerr, M. E.
See also CA 107; CANR 37; INT 107; JRDA; MAICYA; MTCW; SATA 20, 61

Medoff, Mark (Howard) 1940- ... **CLC 6, 23; DAM DRAM**
See also AITN 1; CA 53-56; CANR 5; DLB 7; INT CANR-5

Medvedev, P. N.
See Bakhtin, Mikhail Mikhailovich

Meged, Aharon
See Megged, Aharon

Meged, Aron
See Megged, Aharon

Megged, Aharon 1920-......................... **CLC 9**
See also CA 49-52; CAAS 13; CANR 1

Mehta, Ved (Parkash) 1934- .... **CLC 37**
See also CA 1-4R; CANR 2, 23; MTCW

Melanter
See Blackmore, R(ichard) D(oddridge)

Melikow, Loris
See Hofmannsthal, Hugo von

Melmoth, Sebastian
See Wilde, Oscar (Fingal O'Flahertie Wills)

Meltzer, Milton 1915- .... **CLC 26**
See also AAYA 8; CA 13-16R; CANR 38; CLR 13; DLB 61; JRDA; MAICYA; SAAS 1; SATA 1, 50, 80

Melville, Herman 1819-1891**NCLC 3, 12, 29, 45, 49; DA; DAB; DAC; DAM MST, NOV; SSC 1, 17; WLC**
See also CDALB 1640-1865; DLB 3, 74; SATA 59

Menander c. 342B.C.-c. 292B.C. ... **CMLC 9; DAM DRAM; DC 3**
See also DLB 176

Mencken, H(enry) L(ouis) 1880-1956 **TCLC 13**
See also CA 105; 125; CDALB 1917-1929; DLB 11, 29, 63, 137; MTCW

Mendelsohn, Jane 1965(?)-................. **CLC 99**
See also CA 154

Mercer, David 1928-1980 .... **CLC 5; DAM DRAM**
See also CA 9-12R; 102; CANR 23; DLB 13; MTCW

Merchant, Paul
See Ellison, Harlan (Jay)

Meredith, George 1828-1909 . **TCLC 17, 43; DAM POET**
See also CA 117; 153; CDBLB 1832-1890; DLB 18, 35, 57, 159

Meredith, William (Morris) 1919-**CLC 4, 13, 22, 55; DAM POET**
See also CA 9-12R; CAAS 14; CANR 6, 40; DLB 5

Merezhkovsky, Dmitry Sergeyevich 1865-1941 **TCLC 29**

Merimee, Prosper 1803-1870**NCLC 6, 65; SSC 7**
See also DLB 119

Merkin, Daphne 1954- .... **CLC 44**
See also CA 123

Merlin, Arthur
See Blish, James (Benjamin)

Merrill, James (Ingram) 1926-1995**CLC 2, 3, 6, 8, 13, 18, 34, 91; DAM POET**
See also CA 13-16R; 147; CANR 10, 49; DLB 5, 165; DLBY 85; INT CANR-10; MTCW

Merriman, Alex
See Silverberg, Robert

Merritt, E. B.
See Waddington, Miriam

Merton, Thomas 1915-1968**CLC 1, 3, 11, 34, 83; PC 10**
See also CA 5-8R; 25-28R; CANR 22, 53; DLB 48; DLBY 81; MTCW

Merwin, W(illiam) S(tanley) 1927- **CLC 1, 2, 3, 5, 8, 13, 18, 45, 88; DAM POET**
See also CA 13-16R; CANR 15, 51; DLB 5, 169; INT CANR-15; MTCW

Metcalf, John 1938-............................. **CLC 37**
See also CA 113; DLB 60

Metcalf, Suzanne
See Baum, L(yman) Frank

Mew, Charlotte (Mary) 1870-1928 .. **TCLC 8**
See also CA 105; DLB 19, 135

Mewshaw, Michael 1943- .... **CLC 9**
See also CA 53-56; CANR 7, 47; DLBY 80

Meyer, June
See Jordan, June

Meyer, Lynn
See Slavitt, David R(ytman)

Meyer-Meyrink, Gustav 1868-1932
See Meyrink, Gustav
See also CA 117

Meyers, Jeffrey 1939- .... **CLC 39**
See also CA 73-76; CANR 54; DLB 111

Meynell, Alice (Christina Gertrude Thompson) 1847-1922.................... **TCLC 6**
See also CA 104; DLB 19, 98

Meyrink, Gustav .... **TCLC 21**
See also Meyer-Meyrink, Gustav
See also DLB 81

Michaels, Leonard 1933- **CLC 6, 25; SSC 16**
See also CA 61-64; CANR 21, 62; DLB 130; MTCW

Michaux, Henri 1899-1984 .... **CLC 8, 19**
See also CA 85-88; 114

Micheaux, Oscar 1884-1951 .... **TCLC 76**
See also DLB 50

Michelangelo 1475-1564 .... **LC 12**

Michelet, Jules 1798-1874 .... **NCLC 31**

Michener, James A(lbert) 1907(?)-1997 **CLC 1, 5, 11, 29, 60; DAM NOV, POP**
See also AITN 1; BEST 90:1; CA 5-8R; 161; CANR 21, 45; DLB 6; MTCW

Mickiewicz, Adam 1798-1855 .... **NCLC 3**

Middleton, Christopher 1926- .... **CLC 13**
See also CA 13-16R; CANR 29, 54; DLB 40

Middleton, Richard (Barham) 1882-1911 **TCLC 56**
See also DLB 156

Middleton, Stanley 1919-.............. **CLC 7, 38**
See also CA 25-28R; CAAS 23; CANR 21, 46; DLB 14

Middleton, Thomas 1580-1627 **LC 33; DAM DRAM, MST; DC 5**
See also DLB 58

Migueis, Jose Rodrigues 1901- .... **CLC 10**

Mikszath, Kalman 1847-1910 .... **TCLC 31**

Miles, Jack .... **CLC 100**

Miles, Josephine (Louise) 1911-1985**CLC 1, 2, 14, 34, 39; DAM POET**
See also CA 1-4R; 116; CANR 2, 55; DLB 48

Militant
See Sandburg, Carl (August)

Mill, John Stuart 1806-1873 ... **NCLC 11, 58**
See also CDBLB 1832-1890; DLB 55

Millar, Kenneth 1915-1983 ...**CLC 14; DAM POP**
See also Macdonald, Ross
See also CA 9-12R; 110; CANR 16; DLB 2; DLBD 6; DLBY 83; MTCW

Millay, E. Vincent
See Millay, Edna St. Vincent

Millay, Edna St. Vincent 1892-1950**TCLC 4, 49; DA; DAB; DAC; DAM MST, POET; PC 6; WLCS**
See also CA 104; 130; CDALB 1917-1929; DLB 45; MTCW

Miller, Arthur 1915-**CLC 1, 2, 6, 10, 15, 26, 47, 78; DA; DAB; DAC; DAM DRAM, MST; DC 1; WLC**
See also AAYA 15; AITN 1; CA 1-4R; CABS 3; CANR 2, 30, 54; CDALB 1941-1968; DLB 7; MTCW

Miller, Henry (Valentine) 1891-1980**CLC 1, 2, 4, 9, 14, 43, 84; DA; DAB; DAC; DAM MST, NOV; WLC**
See also CA 9-12R; 97-100; CANR 33; CDALB 1929-1941; DLB 4, 9; DLBY 80; MTCW

Miller, Jason 1939(?)-........................... **CLC 2**
See also AITN 1; CA 73-76; DLB 7

Miller, Sue 1943- .... **CLC 44; DAM POP**
See also BEST 90:3; CA 139; CANR 59; DLB 143

Miller, Walter M(ichael, Jr.) 1923-**CLC 4, 30**
See also CA 85-88; DLB 8

Millett, Kate 1934- .... **CLC 67**
See also AITN 1; CA 73-76; CANR 32, 53; MTCW

Millhauser, Steven 1943- .... **CLC 21, 54**
See also CA 110; 111; DLB 2; INT 111

Millin, Sarah Gertrude 1889-1968 .. **CLC 49**
See also CA 102; 93-96

Milne, A(lan) A(lexander) 1882-1956 TCLC 6; DAB; DAC; DAM MST
See also CA 104; 133; CLR 1, 26; DLB 10, 77, 100, 160; MAICYA; MTCW; YABC 1

Milner, Ron(ald) 1938- CLC 56; BLC; DAM MULT
See also AITN 1; BW 1; CA 73-76; CANR 24; DLB 38; MTCW

Milnes, Richard Monckton 1809-1885 NCLC 61
See also DLB 32, 184

Milosz, Czeslaw 1911- CLC 5, 11, 22, 31, 56, 82; DAM MST, POET; PC 8; WLCS
See also CA 81-84; CANR 23, 51; MTCW

Milton, John 1608-1674 ..... LC 9; DA; DAB; DAC; DAM MST, POET; PC 19; WLC
See also CDBLB 1660-1789; DLB 131, 151

Min, Anchee 1957- .... CLC 86
See also CA 146

Minehaha, Cornelius
See Wedekind, (Benjamin) Frank(lin)

Miner, Valerie 1947- .... CLC 40
See also CA 97-100; CANR 59

Minimo, Duca
See D'Annunzio, Gabriele

Minot, Susan 1956- .... CLC 44
See also CA 134

Minus, Ed 1938- .... CLC 39

Miranda, Javier
See Bioy Casares, Adolfo

Mirbeau, Octave 1848-1917 .... TCLC 55
See also DLB 123

Miro (Ferrer), Gabriel (Francisco Victor) 1879-1930 .... TCLC 5
See also CA 104

Mishima, Yukio 1925-1970 CLC 2, 4, 6, 9, 27; DC 1; SSC 4
See also Hiraoka, Kimitake
See also DLB 182

Mistral, Frederic 1830-1914 .... TCLC 51
See also CA 122

Mistral, Gabriela .... TCLC 2; HLC
See also Godoy Alcayaga, Lucila

Mistry, Rohinton 1952- .... CLC 71; DAC
See also CA 141

Mitchell, Clyde
See Ellison, Harlan (Jay); Silverberg, Robert

Mitchell, James Leslie 1901-1935
See Gibbon, Lewis Grassic
See also CA 104; DLB 15

Mitchell, Joni 1943- .... CLC 12
See also CA 112

Mitchell, Joseph (Quincy) 1908-1996 CLC 98
See also CA 77-80; 152; DLBY 96

Mitchell, Margaret (Munnerlyn) 1900-1949 TCLC 11; DAM NOV, POP
See also CA 109; 125; CANR 55; DLB 9; MTCW

Mitchell, Peggy
See Mitchell, Margaret (Munnerlyn)

Mitchell, S(ilas) Weir 1829-1914 ... TCLC 36

Mitchell, W(illiam) O(rmond) 1914- CLC 25; DAC; DAM MST
See also CA 77-80; CANR 15, 43; DLB 88

Mitford, Mary Russell 1787-1855 .... NCLC 4
See also DLB 110, 116

Mitford, Nancy 1904-1973 .... CLC 44
See also CA 9-12R

Miyamoto, Yuriko 1899-1951 .... TCLC 37
See also DLB 180

Miyazawa Kenji 1896-1933 .... TCLC 76
See also CA 157

Mizoguchi, Kenji 1898-1956 .... TCLC 72

Mo, Timothy (Peter) 1950(?)- .... CLC 46
See also CA 117; MTCW

Modarressi, Taghi (M.) 1931- .... CLC 44
See also CA 121; 134; INT 134

Modiano, Patrick (Jean) 1945- .... CLC 18
See also CA 85-88; CANR 17, 40; DLB 83

Moerck, Paal
See Roelvaag, O(le) E(dvart)

Mofolo, Thomas (Mokopu) 1875(?)-1948 TCLC 22; BLC; DAM MULT
See also CA 121; 153

Mohr, Nicholasa 1935- CLC 12; DAM MULT; HLC
See also AAYA 8; CA 49-52; CANR 1, 32; CLR 22; DLB 145; HW; JRDA; SAAS 8; SATA 8

Mojtabai, A(nn) G(race) 1938- CLC 5, 9, 15, 29
See also CA 85-88

Moliere 1622-1673 . LC 28; DA; DAB; DAC; DAM DRAM, MST; WLC

Molin, Charles
See Mayne, William (James Carter)

Molnar, Ferenc 1878-1952 . TCLC 20; DAM DRAM
See also CA 109; 153

Momaday, N(avarre) Scott 1934- CLC 2, 19, 85, 95; DA; DAB; DAC; DAM MST, MULT, NOV, POP; WLCS
See also AAYA 11; CA 25-28R; CANR 14, 34; DLB 143, 175; INT CANR-14; MTCW; NNAL; SATA 48; SATA-Brief 30

Monette, Paul 1945-1995 .... CLC 82
See also CA 139; 147

Monroe, Harriet 1860-1936 .... TCLC 12
See also CA 109; DLB 54, 91

Monroe, Lyle
See Heinlein, Robert A(nson)

Montagu, Elizabeth 1917- .... NCLC 7
See also CA 9-12R

Montagu, Mary (Pierrepont) Wortley 1689-1762 .... LC 9; PC 16
See also DLB 95, 101

Montagu, W. H.
See Coleridge, Samuel Taylor

Montague, John (Patrick) 1929- CLC 13, 46
See also CA 9-12R; CANR 9; DLB 40; MTCW

Montaigne, Michel (Eyquem) de 1533-1592 LC 8; DA; DAB; DAC; DAM MST; WLC

Montale, Eugenio 1896-1981 CLC 7, 9, 18; PC 13
See also CA 17-20R; 104; CANR 30; DLB 114; MTCW

Montesquieu, Charles-Louis de Secondat 1689-1755 .... LC 7

Montgomery, (Robert) Bruce 1921-1978
See Crispin, Edmund
See also CA 104

Montgomery, L(ucy) M(aud) 1874-1942 TCLC 51; DAC; DAM MST
See also AAYA 12; CA 108; 137; CLR 8; DLB 92; DLBD 14; JRDA; MAICYA; YABC 1

Montgomery, Marion H., Jr. 1925- .... CLC 7
See also AITN 1; CA 1-4R; CANR 3, 48; DLB 6

Montgomery, Max
See Davenport, Guy (Mattison, Jr.)

Montherlant, Henry (Milon) de 1896-1972 CLC 8, 19; DAM DRAM
See also CA 85-88; 37-40R; DLB 72; MTCW

Monty Python
See Chapman, Graham; Cleese, John (Marwood); Gilliam, Terry (Vance); Idle, Eric; Jones, Terence Graham Parry; Palin, Michael (Edward)
See also AAYA 7

Moodie, Susanna (Strickland) 1803-1885 NCLC 14
See also DLB 99

Mooney, Edward 1951-
See Mooney, Ted

See also CA 130

Mooney, Ted .... CLC 25
See also Mooney, Edward

Moorcock, Michael (John) 1939- CLC 5, 27, 58
See also CA 45-48; CAAS 5; CANR 2, 17, 38; DLB 14; MTCW; SATA 93

Moore, Brian 1921- CLC 1, 3, 5, 7, 8, 19, 32, 90; DAB; DAC; DAM MST
See also CA 1-4R; CANR 1, 25, 42; MTCW

Moore, Edward
See Muir, Edwin

Moore, George Augustus 1852-1933 TCLC 7; SSC 19
See also CA 104; DLB 10, 18, 57, 135

Moore, Lorrie .... CLC 39, 45, 68
See also Moore, Marie Lorena

Moore, Marianne (Craig) 1887-1972 CLC 1, 2, 4, 8, 10, 13, 19, 47; DA; DAB; DAC; DAM MST, POET; PC 4; WLCS
See also CA 1-4R; 33-36R; CANR 3, 61; CDALB 1929-1941; DLB 45; DLBD 7; MTCW; SATA 20

Moore, Marie Lorena 1957-
See Moore, Lorrie
See also CA 116; CANR 39

Moore, Thomas 1779-1852 .... NCLC 6
See also DLB 96, 144

Morand, Paul 1888-1976 .... CLC 41; SSC 22
See also CA 69-72; DLB 65

Morante, Elsa 1918-1985 .... CLC 8, 47
See also CA 85-88; 117; CANR 35; DLB 177; MTCW

Moravia, Alberto 1907-1990 CLC 2, 7, 11, 27, 46; SSC 26
See also Pincherle, Alberto
See also DLB 177

More, Hannah 1745-1833 .... NCLC 27
See also DLB 107, 109, 116, 158

More, Henry 1614-1687 .... LC 9
See also DLB 126

More, Sir Thomas 1478-1535 .... LC 10, 32

Moreas, Jean .... TCLC 18
See also Papadiamantopoulos, Johannes

Morgan, Berry 1919- .... CLC 6
See also CA 49-52; DLB 6

Morgan, Claire
See Highsmith, (Mary) Patricia

Morgan, Edwin (George) 1920- .... CLC 31
See also CA 5-8R; CANR 3, 43; DLB 27

Morgan, (George) Frederick 1922- .. CLC 23
See also CA 17-20R; CANR 21

Morgan, Harriet
See Mencken, H(enry) L(ouis)

Morgan, Jane
See Cooper, James Fenimore

Morgan, Janet 1945- .... CLC 39
See also CA 65-68

Morgan, Lady 1776(?)-1859 .... NCLC 29
See also DLB 116, 158

Morgan, Robin 1941- .... CLC 2
See also CA 69-72; CANR 29; MTCW; SATA 80

Morgan, Scott
See Kuttner, Henry

Morgan, Seth 1949(?)-1990 .... CLC 65
See also CA 132

Morgenstern, Christian 1871-1914 . TCLC 8
See also CA 105

Morgenstern, S.
See Goldman, William (W.)

Moricz, Zsigmond 1879-1942 .... TCLC 33

Morike, Eduard (Friedrich) 1804-1875 NCLC 10
See also DLB 133

Mori Ogai .... TCLC 14
See also Mori Rintaro

Mori Rintaro 1862-1922

See Mori Ogai
See also CA 110
Moritz, Karl Philipp 1756-1793 .... **LC 2**
See also DLB 94
Morland, Peter Henry
See Faust, Frederick (Schiller)
Morren, Theophil
See Hofmannsthal, Hugo von
Morris, Bill 1952- .... **CLC 76**
Morris, Julian
See West, Morris L(anglo)
Morris, Steveland Judkins 1950(?)-
See Wonder, Stevie
See also CA 111
Morris, William 1834-1896 .... **NCLC 4**
See also CDBLB 1832-1890; DLB 18, 35, 57, 156, 178, 184
Morris, Wright 1910- ...... **CLC 1, 3, 7, 18, 37**
See also CA 9-12R; CANR 21; DLB 2; DLBY 81; MTCW
Morrison, Arthur 1863-1945 .... **TCLC 72**
See also CA 120; 157; DLB 70, 135
Morrison, Chloe Anthony Wofford
See Morrison, Toni
Morrison, James Douglas 1943-1971
See Morrison, Jim
See also CA 73-76; CANR 40
Morrison, Jim .... **CLC 17**
See also Morrison, James Douglas
Morrison, Toni 1931-**CLC 4, 10, 22, 55, 81, 87;**
BLC; DA; DAB; DAC; DAM MST,
MULT, NOV, POP
See also AAYA 1, 22; BW 2; CA 29-32R; CANR 27, 42; CDALB 1968-1988; DLB 6, 33, 143; DLBY 81; MTCW; SATA 57
Morrison, Van 1945- .... **CLC 21**
See also CA 116
Morrissy, Mary 1958- .... **CLC 99**
Mortimer, John (Clifford) 1923-**CLC 28, 43;**
DAM DRAM, POP
See also CA 13-16R; CANR 21; CDBLB 1960 to Present; DLB 13; INT CANR-21; MTCW
Mortimer, Penelope (Ruth) 1918- ...... **CLC 5**
See also CA 57-60; CANR 45
Morton, Anthony
See Creasey, John
Mosca, Gaetano 1858-1941 .... **TCLC 75**
Mosher, Howard Frank 1943- .... **CLC 62**
See also CA 139
Mosley, Nicholas 1923- .... **CLC 43, 70**
See also CA 69-72; CANR 41, 60; DLB 14
Mosley, Walter 1952-**CLC 97; DAM MULT,**
POP
See also AAYA 17; BW 2; CA 142; CANR 57
Moss, Howard 1922-1987 **CLC 7, 14, 45, 50;**
DAM POET
See also CA 1-4R; 123; CANR 1, 44; DLB 5
Mossgiel, Rab
See Burns, Robert
Motion, Andrew (Peter) 1952- .... **CLC 47**
See also CA 146; DLB 40
Motley, Willard (Francis) 1909-1965**CLC 18**
See also BW 1; CA 117; 106; DLB 76, 143
Motoori, Norinaga 1730-1801 .... **NCLC 45**
Mott, Michael (Charles Alston) 1930-**CLC 15, 34**
See also CA 5-8R; CAAS 7; CANR 7, 29
Mountain Wolf Woman 1884-1960 . **CLC 92**
See also CA 144; NNAL
Moure, Erin 1955- .... **CLC 88**
See also CA 113; DLB 60
Mowat, Farley (McGill) 1921-**CLC 26; DAC;**
DAM MST
See also AAYA 1; CA 1-4R; CANR 4, 24, 42; CLR 20; DLB 68; INT CANAR-24; JRDA; MAICYA; MTCW; SATA 3, 55
Moyers, Bill 1934- .... **CLC 74**

See also AITN 2; CA 61-64; CANR 31, 52
Mphahlele, Es'kia
See Mphahlele, Ezekiel
See also DLB 125
Mphahlele, Ezekiel 1919-**CLC 25; BLC; DAM**
MULT
See also Mphahlele, Es'kia
See also BW 2; CA 81-84; CANR 26
Mqhayi, S(amuel) E(dward) K(rune Loliwe)
1875-1945**TCLC 25; BLC; DAM MULT**
See also CA 153
Mrozek, Slawomir 1930- .... **CLC 3, 13**
See also CA 13-16R; CAAS 10; CANR 29; MTCW
Mrs. Belloc-Lowndes
See Lowndes, Marie Adelaide (Belloc)
Mtwa, Percy (?)- ....**CLC 47**
Mueller, Lisel 1924- .... **CLC 13, 51**
See also CA 93-96; DLB 105
Muir, Edwin 1887-1959 .... **TCLC 2**
See also CA 104; DLB 20, 100
Muir, John 1838-1914 .... **TCLC 28**
Mujica Lainez, Manuel 1910-1984 ... **CLC 31**
See also Lainez, Manuel Mujica
See also CA 81-84; 112; CANR 32; HW
Mukherjee, Bharati 1940-**CLC 53; DAM NOV**
See also BEST 89:2; CA 107; CANR 45; DLB 60; MTCW
Muldoon, Paul 1951-**CLC 32, 72; DAM POET**
See also CA 113; 129; CANR 52; DLB 40; INT 129
Mulisch, Harry 1927- .... **CLC 42**
See also CA 9-12R; CANR 6, 26, 56
Mull, Martin 1943- .... **CLC 17**
See also CA 105
Mulock, Dinah Maria
See Craik, Dinah Maria (Mulock)
Munford, Robert 1737(?)-1783 .... **LC 5**
See also DLB 31
Mungo, Raymond 1946- .... **CLC 72**
See also CA 49-52; CANR 2
Munro, Alice 1931-.... **CLC 6, 10, 19, 50, 95;**
DAC; DAM MST, NOV; SSC 3; WLCS
See also AITN 2; CA 33-36R; CANR 33, 53; DLB 53; MTCW; SATA 29
Munro, H(ector) H(ugh) 1870-1916
See Saki
See also CA 104; 130; CDBLB 1890-1914; DA; DAB; DAC; DAM MST, NOV; DLB 34, 162; MTCW; WLC
Murasaki, Lady .... **CMLC 1**
Murdoch, (Jean) Iris 1919-**CLC 1, 2, 3, 4, 6, 8, 11, 15, 22, 31, 51; DAB; DAC; DAM MST, NOV**
See also CA 13-16R; CANR 8, 43; CDBLB 1960 to Present; DLB 14; INT CANR-8; MTCW
Murfree, Mary Noailles 1850-1922 ... **SSC 22**
See also CA 122; DLB 12, 74
Murnau, Friedrich Wilhelm
See Plumpe, Friedrich Wilhelm
Murphy, Richard 1927- .... **CLC 41**
See also CA 29-32R; DLB 40
Murphy, Sylvia 1937- .... **CLC 34**
See also CA 121
Murphy, Thomas (Bernard) 1935- ... **CLC 51**
See also CA 101
Murray, Albert L. 1916- .... **CLC 73**
See also BW 2; CA 49-52; CANR 26, 52; DLB 38
Murray, Judith Sargent 1751-1820**NCLC 63**
See also DLB 37
Murray, Les(lie) A(llan) 1938-**CLC 40; DAM POET**
See also CA 21-24R; CANR 11, 27, 56
Murry, J. Middleton
See Murry, John Middleton

Murry, John Middleton 1889-1957 **TCLC 16**
See also CA 118; DLB 149
Musgrave, Susan 1951- .... **CLC 13, 54**
See also CA 69-72; CANR 45
Musil, Robert (Edler von) 1880-1942 **T C L C 12, 68; SSC 18**
See also CA 109; CANR 55; DLB 81, 124
Muske, Carol 1945- .... **CLC 90**
See also Muske-Dukes, Carol (Anne)
Muske-Dukes, Carol (Anne) 1945-
See Muske, Carol
See also CA 65-68; CANR 32
Musset, (Louis Charles) Alfred de 1810-1857 **NCLC 7**
My Brother's Brother
See Chekhov, Anton (Pavlovich)
Myers, L(eopold) H(amilton) 1881-1944 **TCLC 59**
See also CA 157; DLB 15
Myers, Walter Dean 1937- ....**CLC 35; BLC;**
DAM MULT, NOV
See also AAYA 4; BW 2; CA 33-36R; CANR 20, 42; CLR 4, 16, 35; DLB 33; INT CANR-20; JRDA; MAICYA; SAAS 2; SATA 41, 71; SATA-Brief 27
Myers, Walter M.
See Myers, Walter Dean
Myles, Symon
See Follett, Ken(neth Martin)
Nabokov, Vladimir (Vladimirovich) 1899-1977
CLC 1, 2, 3, 6, 8, 11, 15, 23, 44, 46, 64;
DA; DAB; DAC; DAM MST, NOV; SSC 11; WLC
See also CA 5-8R; 69-72; CANR 20; CDALB 1941-1968; DLB 2; DLBD 3; DLBY 80, 91; MTCW
Nagai Kafu 1879-1959 .... **TCLC 51**
See also Nagai Sokichi
See also DLB 180
Nagai Sokichi 1879-1959
See Nagai Kafu
See also CA 117
Nagy, Laszlo 1925-1978 .... **CLC 7**
See also CA 129; 112
Naipaul, Shiva(dhar Srinivasa) 1945-1985
CLC 32, 39; DAM NOV
See also CA 110; 112; 116; CANR 33; DLB 157; DLBY 85; MTCW
Naipaul, V(idiadhar) S(urajprasad) 1932-
CLC 4, 7, 9, 13, 18, 37, 105; DAB; DAC;
DAM MST, NOV
See also CA 1-4R; CANR 1, 33, 51; CDBLB 1960 to Present; DLB 125; DLBY 85; MTCW
Nakos, Lilika 1899(?)- .... **CLC 29**
Narayan, R(asipuram) K(rishnaswami) 1906-
CLC 7, 28, 47; DAM NOV; SSC 25
See also CA 81-84; CANR 33, 61; MTCW; SATA 62
Nash, (Frediric) Ogden 1902-1971 . **CLC 23;**
DAM POET
See also CA 13-14; 29-32R; CANR 34, 61; CAP 1; DLB 11; MAICYA; MTCW; SATA 2, 46
Nathan, Daniel
See Dannay, Frederic
Nathan, George Jean 1882-1958 .... **TCLC 18**
See also Hatteras, Owen
See also CA 114; DLB 137
Natsume, Kinnosuke 1867-1916
See Natsume, Soseki
See also CA 104
Natsume, Soseki 1867-1916 .... **TCLC 2, 10**
See also Natsume, Kinnosuke
See also DLB 180
Natti, (Mary) Lee 1919-
See Kingman, Lee

See also CA 5-8R; CANR 2
Naylor, Gloria 1950- **CLC 28, 52; BLC; DA; DAC; DAM MST, MULT, NOV, POP; WLCS**
See also AAYA 6; BW 2; CA 107; CANR 27, 51; DLB 173; MTCW
Neihardt, John Gneisenau 1881-1973 **CLC 32**
See also CA 13-14; CAP 1; DLB 9, 54
Nekrasov, Nikolai Alekseevich 1821-1878 **NCLC 11**
Nelligan, Emile 1879-1941 .... **TCLC 14**
See also CA 114; DLB 92
Nelson, Willie 1933- .... **CLC 17**
See also CA 107
Nemerov, Howard (Stanley) 1920-1991 **C L C 2, 6, 9, 36; DAM POET**
See also CA 1-4R; 134; CABS 2; CANR 1, 27, 53; DLB 5, 6; DLBY 83; INT CANR-27; MTCW
Neruda, Pablo 1904-1973 **CLC 1, 2, 5, 7, 9, 28, 62; DA; DAB; DAC; DAM MST, MULT, POET; HLC; PC 4; WLC**
See also CA 19-20; 45-48; CAP 2; HW; MTCW
Nerval, Gerard de 1808-1855 **NCLC 1; PC 13; SSC 18**
Nervo, (Jose) Amado (Ruiz de) 1870-1919 **TCLC 11**
See also CA 109; 131; HW
Nessi, Pio Baroja y
See Baroja (y Nessi), Pio
Nestroy, Johann 1801-1862 .... **NCLC 42**
See also DLB 133
Netterville, Luke
See O'Grady, Standish (James)
Neufeld, John (Arthur) 1938- .... **CLC 17**
See also AAYA 11; CA 25-28R; CANR 11, 37, 56; MAICYA; SAAS 3; SATA 6, 81
Neville, Emily Cheney 1919- .... **CLC 12**
See also CA 5-8R; CANR 3, 37; JRDA; MAICYA; SAAS 2; SATA 1
Newbound, Bernard Slade 1930-
See Slade, Bernard
See also CA 81-84; CANR 49; DAM DRAM
Newby, P(ercy) H(oward) 1918-1997 **CLC 2, 13; DAM NOV**
See also CA 5-8R; 161; CANR 32; DLB 15; MTCW
Newlove, Donald 1928- .... **CLC 6**
See also CA 29-32R; CANR 25
Newlove, John (Herbert) 1938- .... **CLC 14**
See also CA 21-24R; CANR 9, 25
Newman, Charles 1938- .... **CLC 2, 8**
See also CA 21-24R
Newman, Edwin (Harold) 1919- .... **CLC 14**
See also AITN 1; CA 69-72; CANR 5
Newman, John Henry 1801-1890 ... **NCLC 38**
See also DLB 18, 32, 55
Newton, Suzanne 1936- .... **CLC 35**
See also CA 41-44R; CANR 14; JRDA; SATA 5, 77
Nexo, Martin Andersen 1869-1954 **TCLC 43**
Nezval, Vitezslav 1900-1958 .... **TCLC 44**
See also CA 123
Ng, Fae Myenne 1957(?)- .... **CLC 81**
See also CA 146
Ngema, Mbongeni 1955- .... **CLC 57**
See also BW 2; CA 143
Ngugi, James T(hiong'o) .... **CLC 3, 7, 13**
See also Ngugi wa Thiong'o
Ngugi wa Thiong'o 1938- **CLC 36; BLC; DAM MULT, NOV**
See also Ngugi, James T(hiong'o)
See also BW 2; CA 81-84; CANR 27, 58; DLB 125; MTCW
Nichol, B(arrie) P(hillip) 1944-1988 **CLC 18**
See also CA 53-56; DLB 53; SATA 66
Nichols, John (Treadwell) 1940- ...... **CLC 38**

See also CA 9-12R; CAAS 2; CANR 6; DLBY 82
Nichols, Leigh
See Koontz, Dean R(ay)
Nichols, Peter (Richard) 1927- **CLC 5, 36, 65**
See also CA 104; CANR 33; DLB 13; MTCW
Nicolas, F. R. E.
See Freeling, Nicolas
Niedecker, Lorine 1903-1970 .... **CLC 10, 42; DAM POET**
See also CA 25-28; CAP 2; DLB 48
Nietzsche, Friedrich (Wilhelm) 1844-1900 **TCLC 10, 18, 55**
See also CA 107; 121; DLB 129
Nievo, Ippolito 1831-1861 .... **NCLC 22**
Nightingale, Anne Redmon 1943-
See Redmon, Anne
See also CA 103
Nik. T. O.
See Annensky, Innokenty (Fyodorovich)
Nin, Anais 1903-1977 **CLC 1, 4, 8, 11, 14, 60; DAM NOV, POP; SSC 10**
See also AITN 2; CA 13-16R; 69-72; CANR 22, 53; DLB 2, 4, 152; MTCW
Nishiwaki, Junzaburo 1894-1982 .... **PC 15**
See also CA 107
Nissenson, Hugh 1933- .... **CLC 4, 9**
See also CA 17-20R; CANR 27; DLB 28
Niven, Larry .... **CLC 8**
See also Niven, Laurence Van Cott
See also DLB 8
Niven, Laurence Van Cott 1938-
See Niven, Larry
See also CA 21-24R; CAAS 12; CANR 14, 44; DAM POP; MTCW; SATA 95
Nixon, Agnes Eckhardt 1927- .... **CLC 21**
See also CA 110
Nizan, Paul 1905-1940 .... **TCLC 40**
See also CA 161; DLB 72
Nkosi, Lewis 1936- ...... **CLC 45; BLC; DAM MULT**
See also BW 1; CA 65-68; CANR 27; DLB 157
Nodier, (Jean) Charles (Emmanuel) 1780-1844 **NCLC 19**
See also DLB 119
Nolan, Christopher 1965- .... **CLC 58**
See also CA 111
Noon, Jeff 1957- .... **CLC 91**
See also CA 148
Norden, Charles
See Durrell, Lawrence (George)
Nordhoff, Charles (Bernard) 1887-1947 **TCLC 23**
See also CA 108; DLB 9; SATA 23
Norfolk, Lawrence 1963- .... **CLC 76**
See also CA 144
Norman, Marsha 1947- **CLC 28; DAM DRAM; DC 8**
See also CA 105; CABS 3; CANR 41; DLBY 84
Norris, Frank 1870-1902 .... **SSC 28**
See also Norris, (Benjamin) Frank(lin, Jr.)
See also CDALB 1865-1917; DLB 12, 71
Norris, (Benjamin) Frank(lin, Jr.) 1870-1902 **TCLC 24**
See also Norris, Frank
See also CA 110; 160
Norris, Leslie 1921- .... **CLC 14**
See also CA 11-12; CANR 14; CAP 1; DLB 27
North, Andrew
See Norton, Andre
North, Anthony
See Koontz, Dean R(ay)
North, Captain George
See Stevenson, Robert Louis (Balfour)
North, Milou
See Erdrich, Louise

Northrup, B. A.
See Hubbard, L(afayette) Ron(ald)
North Staffs
See Hulme, T(homas) E(rnest)
Norton, Alice Mary
See Norton, Andre
See also MAICYA; SATA 1, 43
Norton, Andre 1912- .... **CLC 12**
See also Norton, Alice Mary
See also AAYA 14; CA 1-4R; CANR 2, 31; DLB 8, 52; JRDA; MTCW; SATA 91
Norton, Caroline 1808-1877 .... **NCLC 47**
See also DLB 21, 159
Norway, Nevil Shute 1899-1960
See Shute, Nevil
See also CA 102; 93-96
Norwid, Cyprian Kamil 1821-1883 **NCLC 17**
Nosille, Nabrah
See Ellison, Harlan (Jay)
Nossack, Hans Erich 1901-1978 .... **CLC 6**
See also CA 93-96; 85-88; DLB 69
Nostradamus 1503-1566 .... **LC 27**
Nosu, Chuji
See Ozu, Yasujiro
Notenburg, Eleanora (Genrikhovna) von
See Guro, Elena
Nova, Craig 1945- .... **CLC 7, 31**
See also CA 45-48; CANR 2, 53
Novak, Joseph
See Kosinski, Jerzy (Nikodem)
Novalis 1772-1801 .... **NCLC 13**
See also DLB 90
Novis, Emile
See Weil, Simone (Adolphine)
Nowlan, Alden (Albert) 1933-1983 . **CLC 15; DAC; DAM MST**
See also CA 9-12R; CANR 5; DLB 53
Noyes, Alfred 1880-1958 .... **TCLC 7**
See also CA 104; DLB 20
Nunn, Kem .... **CLC 34**
See also CA 159
Nye, Robert 1939- ... **CLC 13, 42; DAM NOV**
See also CA 33-36R; CANR 29; DLB 14; MTCW; SATA 6
Nyro, Laura 1947- .... **CLC 17**
Oates, Joyce Carol 1938- **CLC 1, 2, 3, 6, 9, 11, 15, 19, 33, 52; DA; DAB; DAC; DAM MST, NOV, POP; SSC 6; WLC**
See also AAYA 15; AITN 1; BEST 89:2; CA 5-8R; CANR 25, 45; CDALB 1968-1988; DLB 2, 5, 130; DLBY 81; INT CANR-25; MTCW
O'Brien, Darcy 1939- .... **CLC 11**
See also CA 21-24R; CANR 8, 59
O'Brien, E. G.
See Clarke, Arthur C(harles)
O'Brien, Edna 1936- **CLC 3, 5, 8, 13, 36, 65; DAM NOV; SSC 10**
See also CA 1-4R; CANR 6, 41; CDBLB 1960 to Present; DLB 14; MTCW
O'Brien, Fitz-James 1828-1862 ..... **NCLC 21**
See also DLB 74
O'Brien, Flann .... **CLC 1, 4, 5, 7, 10, 47**
See also O Nuallain, Brian
O'Brien, Richard 1942- .... **CLC 17**
See also CA 124
O'Brien, (William) Tim(othy) 1946- . **CLC 7, 19, 40, 103; DAM POP**
See also AAYA 16; CA 85-88; CANR 40, 58; DLB 152; DLBD 9; DLBY 80
Obstfelder, Sigbjoern 1866-1900 ... **TCLC 23**
See also CA 123
O'Casey, Sean 1880-1964 **CLC 1, 5, 9, 11, 15, 88; DAB; DAC; DAM DRAM, MST; WLCS**
See also CA 89-92; CANR 62; CDBLB 1914-1945; DLB 10; MTCW

O'Cathasaigh, Sean
See O'Casey, Sean
Ochs, Phil 1940-1976 .... CLC 17
See also CA 65-68
O'Connor, Edwin (Greene) 1918-1968 . C L C 14
See also CA 93-96; 25-28R
O'Connor, (Mary) Flannery 1925-1964 C L C 1, 2, 3, 6, 10, 13, 15, 21, 66, 104; DA; DAB; DAC; DAM MST, NOV; SSC 1, 23; WLC
See also AAYA 7; CA 1-4R; CANR 3, 41; CDALB 1941-1968; DLB 2, 152; DLBD 12; DLBY 80; MTCW
O'Connor, Frank .... CLC 23; SSC 5
See also O'Donovan, Michael John
See also DLB 162
O'Dell, Scott 1898-1989 .... CLC 30
See also AAYA 3; CA 61-64; 129; CANR 12, 30; CLR 1, 16; DLB 52; JRDA; MAICYA; SATA 12, 60
Odets, Clifford 1906-1963 CLC 2, 28, 98; DAM DRAM; DC 6
See also CA 85-88; CANR 62; DLB 7, 26; MTCW
O'Doherty, Brian 1934- .... CLC 76
See also CA 105
O'Donnell, K. M.
See Malzberg, Barry N(athaniel)
O'Donnell, Lawrence
See Kuttner, Henry
O'Donovan, Michael John 1903-1966 CLC 14
See also O'Connor, Frank
See also CA 93-96
Oe, Kenzaburo 1935- CLC 10, 36, 86; DAM NOV; SSC 20
See also CA 97-100; CANR 36, 50; DLB 182; DLBY 94; MTCW
O'Faolain, Julia 1932- .... CLC 6, 19, 47
See also CA 81-84; CAAS 2; CANR 12, 61; DLB 14; MTCW
O'Faolain, Sean 1900-1991 CLC 1, 7, 14, 32, 70; SSC 13
See also CA 61-64; 134; CANR 12; DLB 15, 162; MTCW
O'Flaherty, Liam 1896-1984 CLC 5, 34; SSC 6
See also CA 101; 113; CANR 35; DLB 36, 162; DLBY 84; MTCW
Ogilvy, Gavin
See Barrie, J(ames) M(atthew)
O'Grady, Standish (James) 1846-1928 T C L C 5
See also CA 104; 157
O'Grady, Timothy 1951- .... CLC 59
See also CA 138
O'Hara, Frank 1926-1966 . CLC 2, 5, 13, 78; DAM POET
See also CA 9-12R; 25-28R; CANR 33; DLB 5, 16; MTCW
O'Hara, John (Henry) 1905-1970 CLC 1, 2, 3, 6, 11, 42; DAM NOV; SSC 15
See also CA 5-8R; 25-28R; CANR 31, 60; CDALB 1929-1941; DLB 9, 86; DLBD 2; MTCW
O Hehir, Diana 1922- .... CLC 41
See also CA 93-96
Okigbo, Christopher (Ifenayichukwu) 1932-1967 ... CLC 25, 84; BLC; DAM MULT, POET; PC 7
See also BW 1; CA 77-80; DLB 125; MTCW
Okri, Ben 1959- .... CLC 87
See also BW 2; CA 130; 138; DLB 157; INT 138
Olds, Sharon 1942- .... CLC 32, 39, 85; DAM POET
See also CA 101; CANR 18, 41; DLB 120
Oldstyle, Jonathan
See Irving, Washington

Olesha, Yuri (Karlovich) 1899-1960 .. CLC 8
See also CA 85-88
Oliphant, Laurence 1829(?)-1888 .. NCLC 47
See also DLB 18, 166
Oliphant, Margaret (Oliphant Wilson) 1828-1897 .... NCLC 11, 61; SSC 25
See also DLB 18, 159
Oliver, Mary 1935- .... CLC 19, 34, 98
See also CA 21-24R; CANR 9, 43; DLB 5
Olivier, Laurence (Kerr) 1907-1989 CLC 20
See also CA 111; 150; 129
Olsen, Tillie 1913- CLC 4, 13; DA; DAB; DAC; DAM MST; SSC 11
See also CA 1-4R; CANR 1, 43; DLB 28; DLBY 80; MTCW
Olson, Charles (John) 1910-1970 CLC 1, 2, 5, 6, 9, 11, 29; DAM POET; PC 19
See also CA 13-16; 25-28R; CABS 2; CANR 35, 61; CAP 1; DLB 5, 16; MTCW
Olson, Toby 1937- .... CLC 28
See also CA 65-68; CANR 9, 31
Olyesha, Yuri
See Olesha, Yuri (Karlovich)
Ondaatje, (Philip) Michael 1943-CLC 14, 29, 51, 76; DAB; DAC; DAM MST
See also CA 77-80; CANR 42; DLB 60
Oneal, Elizabeth 1934-
See Oneal, Zibby
See also CA 106; CANR 28; MAICYA; SATA 30, 82
Oneal, Zibby .... CLC 30
See also Oneal, Elizabeth
See also AAYA 5; CLR 13; JRDA
O'Neill, Eugene (Gladstone) 1888-1953 TCLC 1, 6, 27, 49; DA; DAB; DAC; DAM DRAM, MST; WLC
See also AITN 1; CA 110; 132; CDALB 1929-1941; DLB 7; MTCW
Onetti, Juan Carlos 1909-1994 ... CLC 7, 10; DAM MULT, NOV; SSC 23
See also CA 85-88; 145; CANR 32; DLB 113; HW; MTCW
O Nuallain, Brian 1911-1966
See O'Brien, Flann
See also CA 21-22; 25-28R; CAP 2
Opie, Amelia 1769-1853 .... NCLC 65
See also DLB 116, 159
Oppen, George 1908-1984 ...... CLC 7, 13, 34
See also CA 13-16R; 113; CANR 8; DLB 5, 165
Oppenheim, E(dward) Phillips 1866-1946 TCLC 45
See also CA 111; DLB 70
Origen c. 185-c. 254 .... CMLC 19
Orlovitz, Gil 1918-1973 .... CLC 22
See also CA 77-80; 45-48; DLB 2, 5
Orris
See Ingelow, Jean
Ortega y Gasset, Jose 1883-1955 .... TCLC 9; DAM MULT; HLC
See also CA 106; 130; HW; MTCW
Ortese, Anna Maria 1914- .... CLC 89
See also DLB 177
Ortiz, Simon J(oseph) 1941-.. CLC 45; DAM MULT, POET; PC 17
See also CA 134; DLB 120, 175; NNAL
Orton, Joe .... CLC 4, 13, 43; DC 3
See also Orton, John Kingsley
See also CDBLB 1960 to Present; DLB 13
Orton, John Kingsley 1933-1967
See Orton, Joe
See also CA 85-88; CANR 35; DAM DRAM; MTCW
Orwell, George TCLC 2, 6, 15, 31, 51; DAB; WLC
See also Blair, Eric (Arthur)
See also CDBLB 1945-1960; DLB 15, 98

Osborne, David
See Silverberg, Robert
Osborne, George
See Silverberg, Robert
Osborne, John (James) 1929-1994 CLC 1, 2, 5, 11, 45; DA; DAB; DAC; DAM DRAM, MST; WLC
See also CA 13-16R; 147; CANR 21, 56; CDBLB 1945-1960; DLB 13; MTCW
Osborne, Lawrence 1958- .... CLC 50
Oshima, Nagisa 1932- .... CLC 20
See also CA 116; 121
Oskison, John Milton 1874-1947 . TCLC 35; DAM MULT
See also CA 144; DLB 175; NNAL
Ossoli, Sarah Margaret (Fuller marchesa d') 1810-1850
See Fuller, Margaret
See also SATA 25
Ostrovsky, Alexander 1823-1886 NCLC 30, 57
Otero, Blas de 1916-1979 .... CLC 11
See also CA 89-92; DLB 134
Otto, Whitney 1955- .... CLC 70
See also CA 140
Ouida .... TCLC 43
See also De La Ramee, (Marie) Louise
See also DLB 18, 156
Ousmane, Sembene 1923- .... CLC 66; BLC
See also BW 1; CA 117; 125; MTCW
Ovid 43B.C.-18(?)CMLC 7; DAM POET; PC 2
Owen, Hugh
See Faust, Frederick (Schiller)
Owen, Wilfred (Edward Salter) 1893-1918 TCLC 5, 27; DA; DAB; DAC; DAM MST, POET; PC 19; WLC
See also CA 104; 141; CDBLB 1914-1945; DLB 20
Owens, Rochelle 1936- .... CLC 8
See also CA 17-20R; CAAS 2; CANR 39
Oz, Amos 1939-CLC 5, 8, 11, 27, 33, 54; DAM NOV
See also CA 53-56; CANR 27, 47; MTCW
Ozick, Cynthia 1928-CLC 3, 7, 28, 62; DAM NOV, POP; SSC 15
See also BEST 90:1; CA 17-20R; CANR 23, 58; DLB 28, 152; DLBY 82; INT CANR-23; MTCW
Ozu, Yasujiro 1903-1963 .... CLC 16
See also CA 112
Pacheco, C.
See Pessoa, Fernando (Antonio Nogueira)
Pa Chin .... CLC 18
See also Li Fei-kan
Pack, Robert 1929- .... CLC 13
See also CA 1-4R; CANR 3, 44; DLB 5
Padgett, Lewis
See Kuttner, Henry
Padilla (Lorenzo), Heberto 1932- .... CLC 38
See also AITN 1; CA 123; 131; HW
Page, Jimmy 1944- .... CLC 12
Page, Louise 1955- .... CLC 40
See also CA 140
Page, P(atricia) K(athleen) 1916- CLC 7, 18; DAC; DAM MST; PC 12
See also CA 53-56; CANR 4, 22; DLB 68; MTCW
Page, Thomas Nelson 1853-1922 .... SSC 23
See also CA 118; DLB 12, 78; DLBD 13
Pagels, Elaine Hiesey 1943- .... CLC 104
See also CA 45-48; CANR 2, 24, 51
Paget, Violet 1856-1935
See Lee, Vernon
See also CA 104
Paget-Lowe, Henry
See Lovecraft, H(oward) P(hillips)
Paglia, Camille (Anna) 1947- .... CLC 68

See also CA 140
Paige, Richard
See Koontz, Dean R(ay)
Paine, Thomas 1737-1809 .... **NCLC 62**
See also CDALB 1640-1865; DLB 31, 43, 73, 158
Pakenham, Antonia
See Fraser, (Lady) Antonia (Pakenham)
Palamas, Kostes 1859-1943 .... **TCLC 5**
See also CA 105
Palazzeschi, Aldo 1885-1974 .... **CLC 11**
See also CA 89-92; 53-56; DLB 114
Paley, Grace 1922-**CLC 4, 6, 37; DAM POP; SSC 8**
See also CA 25-28R; CANR 13, 46; DLB 28; INT CANR-13; MTCW
Palin, Michael (Edward) 1943- .... **CLC 21**
See also Monty Python
See also CA 107; CANR 35; SATA 67
Palliser, Charles 1947- .... **CLC 65**
See also CA 136
Palma, Ricardo 1833-1919 .... **TCLC 29**
Pancake, Breece Dexter 1952-1979
See Pancake, Breece D'J
See also CA 123; 109
Pancake, Breece D'J .... **CLC 29**
See also Pancake, Breece Dexter
See also DLB 130
Panko, Rudy
See Gogol, Nikolai (Vasilyevich)
Papadiamantis, Alexandros 1851-1911**TCLC 29**
Papadiamantopoulos, Johannes 1856-1910
See Moreas, Jean
See also CA 117
Papini, Giovanni 1881-1956 .... **TCLC 22**
See also CA 121
Paracelsus 1493-1541 .... **LC 14**
See also DLB 179
Parasol, Peter
See Stevens, Wallace
Pareto, Vilfredo 1848-1923 .... **TCLC 69**
Parfenie, Maria
See Codrescu, Andrei
Parini, Jay (Lee) 1948- .... **CLC 54**
See also CA 97-100; CAAS 16; CANR 32
Park, Jordan
See Kornbluth, C(yril) M.; Pohl, Frederik
Park, Robert E(zra) 1864-1944 ...... **TCLC 73**
See also CA 122
Parker, Bert
See Ellison, Harlan (Jay)
Parker, Dorothy (Rothschild) 1893-1967**CLC 15, 68; DAM POET; SSC 2**
See also CA 19-20; 25-28R; CAP 2; DLB 11, 45, 86; MTCW
Parker, Robert B(rown) 1932-**CLC 27; DAM NOV, POP**
See also BEST 89:4; CA 49-52; CANR 1, 26, 52; INT CANR-26; MTCW
Parkin, Frank 1940- .... **CLC 43**
See also CA 147
Parkman, Francis, Jr. 1823-1893 ..**NCLC 12**
See also DLB 1, 30
Parks, Gordon (Alexander Buchanan) 1912-**CLC 1, 16; BLC; DAM MULT**
See also AITN 2; BW 2; CA 41-44R; CANR 26; DLB 33; SATA 8
Parmenides c. 515B.C.-c. 450B.C. **CMLC 22**
See also DLB 176
Parnell, Thomas 1679-1718 .... **LC 3**
See also DLB 94
Parra, Nicanor 1914- ...... **CLC 2, 102; DAM MULT; HLC**
See also CA 85-88; CANR 32; HW; MTCW
Parrish, Mary Frances
See Fisher, M(ary) F(rances) K(ennedy)

Parson
See Coleridge, Samuel Taylor
Parson Lot
See Kingsley, Charles
Partridge, Anthony
See Oppenheim, E(dward) Phillips
Pascal, Blaise 1623-1662 .... **LC 35**
Pascoli, Giovanni 1855-1912 .... **TCLC 45**
Pasolini, Pier Paolo 1922-1975**CLC 20, 37; PC 17**
See also CA 93-96; 61-64; DLB 128, 177; MTCW
Pasquini
See Silone, Ignazio
Pastan, Linda (Olenik) 1932- **CLC 27; DAM POET**
See also CA 61-64; CANR 18, 40, 61; DLB 5
Pasternak, Boris (Leonidovich) 1890-1960 **CLC 7, 10, 18, 63; DA; DAB; DAC; DAM MST, NOV, POET; PC 6; WLC**
See also CA 127; 116; MTCW
Patchen, Kenneth 1911-1972 ... **CLC 1, 2, 18; DAM POET**
See also CA 1-4R; 33-36R; CANR 3, 35; DLB 16, 48; MTCW
Pater, Walter (Horatio) 1839-1894 . **NCLC 7**
See also CDBLB 1832-1890; DLB 57, 156
Paterson, A(ndrew) B(arton) 1864-1941 **TCLC 32**
See also CA 155
Paterson, Katherine (Womeldorf) 1932-**CLC 12, 30**
See also AAYA 1; CA 21-24R; CANR 28, 59; CLR 7; DLB 52; JRDA; MAICYA; MTCW; SATA 13, 53, 92
Patmore, Coventry Kersey Dighton 1823-1896 **NCLC 9**
See also DLB 35, 98
Paton, Alan (Stewart) 1903-1988 **CLC 4, 10, 25, 55; DA; DAB; DAC; DAM MST, NOV; WLC**
See also CA 13-16; 125; CANR 22; CAP 1; MTCW; SATA 11; SATA-Obit 56
Paton Walsh, Gillian 1937-
See Walsh, Jill Paton
See also CANR 38; JRDA; MAICYA; SAAS 3; SATA 4, 72
Paulding, James Kirke 1778-1860 ... **NCLC 2**
See also DLB 3, 59, 74
Paulin, Thomas Neilson 1949-
See Paulin, Tom
See also CA 123; 128
Paulin, Tom .... **CLC 37**
See also Paulin, Thomas Neilson
See also DLB 40
Paustovsky, Konstantin (Georgievich) 1892-1968 .... **CLC 40**
See also CA 93-96; 25-28R
Pavese, Cesare 1908-1950 ... **TCLC 3; PC 13; SSC 19**
See also CA 104; DLB 128, 177
Pavic, Milorad 1929- .... **CLC 60**
See also CA 136; DLB 181
Payne, Alan
See Jakes, John (William)
Paz, Gil
See Lugones, Leopoldo
Paz, Octavio 1914-**CLC 3, 4, 6, 10, 19, 51, 65; DA; DAB; DAC; DAM MST, MULT, POET; HLC; PC 1; WLC**
See also CA 73-76; CANR 32; DLBY 90; HW; MTCW
p'Bitek, Okot 1931-1982**CLC 96; BLC; DAM MULT**
See also BW 2; CA 124; 107; DLB 125; MTCW
Peacock, Molly 1947- .... **CLC 60**
See also CA 103; CAAS 21; CANR 52; DLB 120
Peacock, Thomas Love 1785-1866 **NCLC 22**
See also DLB 96, 116
Peake, Mervyn 1911-1968 .... **CLC 7, 54**
See also CA 5-8R; 25-28R; CANR 3; DLB 15, 160; MTCW; SATA 23
Pearce, Philippa .... **CLC 21**
See also Christie, (Ann) Philippa
See also CLR 9; DLB 161; MAICYA; SATA 1, 67
Pearl, Eric
See Elman, Richard
Pearson, T(homas) R(eid) 1956- .... **CLC 39**
See also CA 120; 130; INT 130
Peck, Dale 1967- .... **CLC 81**
See also CA 146
Peck, John 1941- .... **CLC 3**
See also CA 49-52; CANR 3
Peck, Richard (Wayne) 1934- .... **CLC 21**
See also AAYA 1; CA 85-88; CANR 19, 38; CLR 15; INT CANR-19; JRDA; MAICYA; SAAS 2; SATA 18, 55
Peck, Robert Newton 1928- ...... **CLC 17; DA; DAC; DAM MST**
See also AAYA 3; CA 81-84; CANR 31; CLR 45; JRDA; MAICYA; SAAS 1; SATA 21, 62
Peckinpah, (David) Sam(uel) 1925-1984**CLC 20**
See also CA 109; 114
Pedersen, Knut 1859-1952
See Hamsun, Knut
See also CA 104; 119; MTCW
Peeslake, Gaffer
See Durrell, Lawrence (George)
Peguy, Charles Pierre 1873-1914 .. **TCLC 10**
See also CA 107
Pena, Ramon del Valle y
See Valle-Inclan, Ramon (Maria) del
Pendennis, Arthur Esquir
See Thackeray, William Makepeace
Penn, William 1644-1718 .... **LC 25**
See also DLB 24
PEPECE
See Prado (Calvo), Pedro
Pepys, Samuel 1633-1703 **LC 11; DA; DAB; DAC; DAM MST; WLC**
See also CDBLB 1660-1789; DLB 101
Percy, Walker 1916-1990**CLC 2, 3, 6, 8, 14, 18, 47, 65; DAM NOV, POP**
See also CA 1-4R; 131; CANR 1, 23; DLB 2; DLBY 80, 90; MTCW
Perec, Georges 1936-1982 .... **CLC 56**
See also CA 141; DLB 83
Pereda (y Sanchez de Porrua), Jose Maria de 1833-1906 .... **TCLC 16**
See also CA 117
Pereda y Porrua, Jose Maria de
See Pereda (y Sanchez de Porrua), Jose Maria de
Peregoy, George Weems
See Mencken, H(enry) L(ouis)
Perelman, S(idney) J(oseph) 1904-1979 **CLC 3, 5, 9, 15, 23, 44, 49; DAM DRAM**
See also AITN 1, 2; CA 73-76; 89-92; CANR 18; DLB 11, 44; MTCW
Peret, Benjamin 1899-1959 .... **TCLC 20**
See also CA 117
Peretz, Isaac Loeb 1851(?)-1915 .. **TCLC 16; SSC 26**
See also CA 109
Peretz, Yitzkhok Leibush
See Peretz, Isaac Loeb
Perez Galdos, Benito 1843-1920 .... **TCLC 27**
See also CA 125; 153; HW
Perrault, Charles 1628-1703 .... **LC 2**
See also MAICYA; SATA 25

Perry, Brighton
See Sherwood, Robert E(mmet)
Perse, St.-John .... **CLC 4, 11, 46**
See also Leger, (Marie-Rene Auguste) Alexis Saint-Leger
Perutz, Leo 1882-1957 .... **TCLC 60**
See also DLB 81
Peseenz, Tulio F.
See Lopez y Fuentes, Gregorio
Pesetsky, Bette 1932- .... **CLC 28**
See also CA 133; DLB 130
Peshkov, Alexei Maximovich 1868-1936
See Gorky, Maxim
See also CA 105; 141; DA; DAC; DAM DRAM, MST, NOV
Pessoa, Fernando (Antonio Nogueira) 1888-1935 .... **TCLC 27; HLC; PC 20**
See also CA 125
Peterkin, Julia Mood 1880-1961 ...... **CLC 31**
See also CA 102; DLB 9
Peters, Joan K(aren) 1945- .... **CLC 39**
See also CA 158
Peters, Robert L(ouis) 1924- .... **CLC 7**
See also CA 13-16R; CAAS 8; DLB 105
Petofi, Sandor 1823-1849 .... **NCLC 21**
Petrakis, Harry Mark 1923- .... **CLC 3**
See also CA 9-12R; CANR 4, 30
Petrarch 1304-1374 **CMLC 20; DAM POET; PC 8**
Petrov, Evgeny .... **TCLC 21**
See also Kataev, Evgeny Petrovich
Petry, Ann (Lane) 1908-1997 ... **CLC 1, 7, 18**
See also BW 1; CA 5-8R; 157; CAAS 6; CANR 4, 46; CLR 12; DLB 76; JRDA; MAICYA; MTCW; SATA 5; SATA-Obit 94
Petursson, Halligrimur 1614-1674 .... **LC 8**
Phaedrus 18(?)B.C.-55(?) .... **CMLC 24**
Philips, Katherine 1632-1664 .... **LC 30**
See also DLB 131
Philipson, Morris H. 1926- .... **CLC 53**
See also CA 1-4R; CANR 4
Phillips, Caryl 1958- . **CLC 96; DAM MULT**
See also BW 2; CA 141; DLB 157
Phillips, David Graham 1867-1911 **TCLC 44**
See also CA 108; DLB 9, 12
Phillips, Jack
See Sandburg, Carl (August)
Phillips, Jayne Anne 1952- **CLC 15, 33; SSC 16**
See also CA 101; CANR 24, 50; DLBY 80; INT CANR-24; MTCW
Phillips, Richard
See Dick, Philip K(indred)
Phillips, Robert (Schaeffer) 1938- ... **CLC 28**
See also CA 17-20R; CAAS 13; CANR 8; DLB 105
Phillips, Ward
See Lovecraft, H(oward) P(hillips)
Piccolo, Lucio 1901-1969 .... **CLC 13**
See also CA 97-100; DLB 114
Pickthall, Marjorie L(owry) C(hristie) 1883-1922 .... **TCLC 21**
See also CA 107; DLB 92
Pico della Mirandola, Giovanni 1463-1494 **LC 15**
Piercy, Marge 1936- **CLC 3, 6, 14, 18, 27, 62**
See also CA 21-24R; CAAS 1; CANR 13, 43; DLB 120; MTCW
Piers, Robert
See Anthony, Piers
Pieyre de Mandiargues, Andre 1909-1991
See Mandiargues, Andre Pieyre de
See also CA 103; 136; CANR 22
Pilnyak, Boris .... **TCLC 23**
See also Vogau, Boris Andreyevich
Pincherle, Alberto 1907-1990 .... **CLC 11, 18; DAM NOV**
See also Moravia, Alberto

See also CA 25-28R; 132; CANR 33; MTCW
Pinckney, Darryl 1953- .... **CLC 76**
See also BW 2; CA 143
Pindar 518B.C.-446B.C. ..... **CMLC 12; PC 19**
See also DLB 176
Pineda, Cecile 1942- .... **CLC 39**
See also CA 118
Pinero, Arthur Wing 1855-1934 .. **TCLC 32; DAM DRAM**
See also CA 110; 153; DLB 10
Pinero, Miguel (Antonio Gomez) 1946-1988 **CLC 4, 55**
See also CA 61-64; 125; CANR 29; HW
Pinget, Robert 1919-1997 .... **CLC 7, 13, 37**
See also CA 85-88; 160; DLB 83
Pink Floyd
See Barrett, (Roger) Syd; Gilmour, David; Mason, Nick; Waters, Roger; Wright, Rick
Pinkney, Edward 1802-1828 .... **NCLC 31**
Pinkwater, Daniel Manus 1941- .... **CLC 35**
See also Pinkwater, Manus
See also AAYA 1; CA 29-32R; CANR 12, 38; CLR 4; JRDA; MAICYA; SAAS 3; SATA 46, 76
Pinkwater, Manus
See Pinkwater, Daniel Manus
See also SATA 8
Pinsky, Robert 1940- **CLC 9, 19, 38, 94; DAM POET**
See also CA 29-32R; CAAS 4; CANR 58; DLBY 82
Pinta, Harold
See Pinter, Harold
Pinter, Harold 1930- **CLC 1, 3, 6, 9, 11, 15, 27, 58, 73; DA; DAB; DAC; DAM DRAM, MST; WLC**
See also CA 5-8R; CANR 33; CDBLB 1960 to Present; DLB 13; MTCW
Piozzi, Hester Lynch (Thrale) 1741-1821 **NCLC 57**
See also DLB 104, 142
Pirandello, Luigi 1867-1936 **TCLC 4, 29; DA; DAB; DAC; DAM DRAM, MST; DC 5; SSC 22; WLC**
See also CA 104; 153
Pirsig, Robert M(aynard) 1928- **CLC 4, 6, 73; DAM POP**
See also CA 53-56; CANR 42; MTCW; SATA 39
Pisarev, Dmitry Ivanovich 1840-1868 **NCLC 25**
Pix, Mary (Griffith) 1666-1709 .... **LC 8**
See also DLB 80
Pixerecourt, Guilbert de 1773-1844 **NCLC 39**
Plaatje, Sol(omon) T(shekisho) 1876-1932 **TCLC 73**
See also BW 2; CA 141
Plaidy, Jean
See Hibbert, Eleanor Alice Burford
Planche, James Robinson 1796-1880 **NCLC 42**
Plant, Robert 1948- .... **CLC 12**
Plante, David (Robert) 1940- **CLC 7, 23, 38; DAM NOV**
See also CA 37-40R; CANR 12, 36, 58; DLBY 83; INT CANR-12; MTCW
Plath, Sylvia 1932-1963 **CLC 1, 2, 3, 5, 9, 11, 14, 17, 50, 51, 62; DA; DAB; DAC; DAM MST, POET; PC 1; WLC**
See also AAYA 13; CA 19-20; CANR 34; CAP 2; CDALB 1941-1968; DLB 5, 6, 152; MTCW
Plato 428(?)B.C.-348(?)B.C. .. **CMLC 8; DA; DAB; DAC; DAM MST; WLCS**
See also DLB 176
Platonov, Andrei .... **TCLC 14**
See also Klimentov, Andrei Platonovich
Platt, Kin 1911- .... **CLC 26**

See also AAYA 11; CA 17-20R; CANR 11; JRDA; SAAS 17; SATA 21, 86
Plautus c. 251B.C.-184B.C. .... **DC 6**
Plick et Plock
See Simenon, Georges (Jacques Christian)
Plimpton, George (Ames) 1927- .... **CLC 36**
See also AITN 1; CA 21-24R; CANR 32; MTCW; SATA 10
Pliny the Elder c. 23-79 .... **CMLC 23**
Plomer, William Charles Franklin 1903-1973 **CLC 4, 8**
See also CA 21-22; CANR 34; CAP 2; DLB 20, 162; MTCW; SATA 24
Plowman, Piers
See Kavanagh, Patrick (Joseph)
Plum, J.
See Wodehouse, P(elham) G(renville)
Plumly, Stanley (Ross) 1939- .... **CLC 33**
See also CA 108; 110; DLB 5; INT 110
Plumpe, Friedrich Wilhelm 1888-1931 **TCLC 53**
See also CA 112
Po Chu-i 772-846 .... **CMLC 24**
Poe, Edgar Allan 1809-1849 **NCLC 1, 16, 55; DA; DAB; DAC; DAM MST, POET; PC 1; SSC 1, 22; WLC**
See also AAYA 14; CDALB 1640-1865; DLB 3, 59, 73, 74; SATA 23
Poet of Titchfield Street, The
See Pound, Ezra (Weston Loomis)
Pohl, Frederik 1919- .... **CLC 18; SSC 25**
See also CA 61-64; CAAS 1; CANR 11, 37; DLB 8; INT CANR-11; MTCW; SATA 24
Poirier, Louis 1910-
See Gracq, Julien
See also CA 122; 126
Poitier, Sidney 1927- .... **CLC 26**
See also BW 1; CA 117
Polanski, Roman 1933- .... **CLC 16**
See also CA 77-80
Poliakoff, Stephen 1952- .... **CLC 38**
See also CA 106; DLB 13
Police, The
See Copeland, Stewart (Armstrong); Summers, Andrew James; Sumner, Gordon Matthew
Polidori, John William 1795-1821 . **NCLC 51**
See also DLB 116
Pollitt, Katha 1949- .... **CLC 28**
See also CA 120; 122; MTCW
Pollock, (Mary) Sharon 1936- **CLC 50; DAC; DAM DRAM, MST**
See also CA 141; DLB 60
Polo, Marco 1254-1324 .... **CMLC 15**
Polonsky, Abraham (Lincoln) 1910- **CLC 92**
See also CA 104; DLB 26; INT 104
Polybius c. 200B.C.-c. 118B.C. .... **CMLC 17**
See also DLB 176
Pomerance, Bernard 1940- ... **CLC 13; DAM DRAM**
See also CA 101; CANR 49
Ponge, Francis (Jean Gaston Alfred) 1899-1988 **CLC 6, 18; DAM POET**
See also CA 85-88; 126; CANR 40
Pontoppidan, Henrik 1857-1943 .... **TCLC 29**
Poole, Josephine .... **CLC 17**
See also Helyar, Jane Penelope Josephine
See also SAAS 2; SATA 5
Popa, Vasko 1922-1991 .... **CLC 19**
See also CA 112; 148; DLB 181
Pope, Alexander 1688-1744 **LC 3; DA; DAB; DAC; DAM MST, POET; WLC**
See also CDBLB 1660-1789; DLB 95, 101
Porter, Connie (Rose) 1959(?)- .... **CLC 70**
See also BW 2; CA 142; SATA 81
Porter, Gene(va Grace) Stratton 1863(?)-1924 **TCLC 21**
See also CA 112

Porter, Katherine Anne 1890-1980 CLC 1, 3, 7, 10, 13, 15, 27, 101; DA; DAB; DAC; DAM MST, NOV; SSC 4
See also AITN 2; CA 1-4R; 101; CANR 1; DLB 4, 9, 102; DLBD 12; DLBY 80; MTCW; SATA 39; SATA-Obit 23
Porter, Peter (Neville Frederick) 1929- C L C 5, 13, 33
See also CA 85-88; DLB 40
Porter, William Sydney 1862-1910
See Henry, O.
See also CA 104; 131; CDALB 1865-1917; DA; DAB; DAC; DAM MST; DLB 12, 78, 79; MTCW; YABC 2
Portillo (y Pacheco), Jose Lopez
See Lopez Portillo (y Pacheco), Jose
Post, Melville Davisson 1869-1930 TCLC 39
See also CA 110
Potok, Chaim 1929- . CLC 2, 7, 14, 26; DAM NOV
See also AAYA 15; AITN 1, 2; CA 17-20R; CANR 19, 35; DLB 28, 152; INT CANR-19; MTCW; SATA 33
Potter, (Helen) Beatrix 1866-1943
See Webb, (Martha) Beatrice (Potter)
See also MAICYA
Potter, Dennis (Christopher George) 1935-1994 CLC 58, 86
See also CA 107; 145; CANR 33, 61; MTCW
Pound, Ezra (Weston Loomis) 1885-1972 CLC 1, 2, 3, 4, 5, 7, 10, 13, 18, 34, 48, 50; DA; DAB; DAC; DAM MST, POET; PC 4; WLC
See also CA 5-8R; 37-40R; CANR 40; CDALB 1917-1929; DLB 4, 45, 63; DLBD 15; MTCW
Povod, Reinaldo 1959-1994 .... CLC 44
See also CA 136; 146
Powell, Adam Clayton, Jr. 1908-1972 CLC 89; BLC; DAM MULT
See also BW 1; CA 102; 33-36R
Powell, Anthony (Dymoke) 1905-CLC 1, 3, 7, 9, 10, 31
See also CA 1-4R; CANR 1, 32, 62; CDBLB 1945-1960; DLB 15; MTCW
Powell, Dawn 1897-1965 .... CLC 66
See also CA 5-8R
Powell, Padgett 1952- .... CLC 34
See also CA 126
Power, Susan 1961- .... CLC 91
Powers, J(ames) F(arl) 1917-CLC 1, 4, 8, 57; SSC 4
See also CA 1-4R; CANR 2, 61; DLB 130; MTCW
Powers, John J(ames) 1945-
See Powers, John R.
See also CA 69-72
Powers, John R. .... CLC 66
See also Powers, John J(ames)
Powers, Richard (S.) 1957- .... CLC 93
See also CA 148
Pownall, David 1938- .... CLC 10
See also CA 89-92; CAAS 18; CANR 49; DLB 14
Powys, John Cowper 1872-1963 CLC 7, 9, 15, 46
See also CA 85-88; DLB 15; MTCW
Powys, T(heodore) F(rancis) 1875-1953 TCLC 9
See also CA 106; DLB 36, 162
Prado (Calvo), Pedro 1886-1952 ... TCLC 75
See also CA 131; HW
Prager, Emily 1952- .... CLC 56
Pratt, E(dwin) J(ohn) 1883(?)-1964 CLC 19; DAC; DAM POET
See also CA 141; 93-96; DLB 92
Premchand .... TCLC 21

See also Srivastava, Dhanpat Rai
Preussler, Otfried 1923- .... CLC 17
See also CA 77-80; SATA 24
Prevert, Jacques (Henri Marie) 1900-1977 CLC 15
See also CA 77-80; 69-72; CANR 29, 61; MTCW; SATA-Obit 30
Prevost, Abbe (Antoine Francois) 1697-1763 LC 1
Price, (Edward) Reynolds 1933-CLC 3, 6, 13, 43, 50, 63; DAM NOV; SSC 22
See also CA 1-4R; CANR 1, 37, 57; DLB 2; INT CANR-37
Price, Richard 1949- .... CLC 6, 12
See also CA 49-52; CANR 3; DLBY 81
Prichard, Katharine Susannah 1883-1969 CLC 46
See also CA 11-12; CANR 33; CAP 1; MTCW; SATA 66
Priestley, J(ohn) B(oynton) 1894-1984 CLC 2, 5, 9, 34; DAM DRAM, NOV
See also CA 9-12R; 113; CANR 33; CDBLB 1914-1945; DLB 10, 34, 77, 100, 139; DLBY 84; MTCW
Prince 1958(?)- .... CLC 35
Prince, F(rank) T(empleton) 1912- .. CLC 22
See also CA 101; CANR 43; DLB 20
Prince Kropotkin
See Kropotkin, Peter (Aleksieevich)
Prior, Matthew 1664-1721 .... LC 4
See also DLB 95
Prishvin, Mikhail 1873-1954 .... TCLC 75
Pritchard, William H(arrison) 1932-CLC 34
See also CA 65-68; CANR 23; DLB 111
Pritchett, V(ictor) S(awdon) 1900-1997 C L C 5, 13, 15, 41; DAM NOV; SSC 14
See also CA 61-64; 157; CANR 31; DLB 15, 139; MTCW
Private 19022
See Manning, Frederic
Probst, Mark 1925- .... CLC 59
See also CA 130
Prokosch, Frederic 1908-1989 ..... CLC 4, 48
See also CA 73-76; 128; DLB 48
Prophet, The
See Dreiser, Theodore (Herman Albert)
Prose, Francine 1947- .... CLC 45
See also CA 109; 112; CANR 46
Proudhon
See Cunha, Euclides (Rodrigues Pimenta) da
Proulx, E. Annie 1935- .... CLC 81
Proust, (Valentin-Louis-George-Eugene-) Marcel 1871-1922 TCLC 7, 13, 33; DA; DAB; DAC; DAM MST, NOV; WLC
See also CA 104; 120; DLB 65; MTCW
Prowler, Harley
See Masters, Edgar Lee
Prus, Boleslaw 1845-1912 .... TCLC 48
Pryor, Richard (Franklin Lenox Thomas) 1940- .... CLC 26
See also CA 122
Przybyszewski, Stanislaw 1868-1927 TCLC 36
See also CA 160; DLB 66
Pteleon
See Grieve, C(hristopher) M(urray)
See also DAM POET
Puckett, Lute
See Masters, Edgar Lee
Puig, Manuel 1932-1990 CLC 3, 5, 10, 28, 65; DAM MULT; HLC
See also CA 45-48; CANR 2, 32; DLB 113; HW; MTCW
Pulitzer, Joseph 1847-1911 .... TCLC 76
See also CA 114; DLB 23
Purdy, Al(fred Wellington) 1918-. CLC 3, 6, 14, 50; DAC; DAM MST, POET
See also CA 81-84; CAAS 17; CANR 42; DLB 88
Purdy, James (Amos) 1923-CLC 2, 4, 10, 28, 52
See also CA 33-36R; CAAS 1; CANR 19, 51; DLB 2; INT CANR-19; MTCW
Pure, Simon
See Swinnerton, Frank Arthur
Pushkin, Alexander (Sergeyevich) 1799-1837 NCLC 3, 27; DA; DAB; DAC; DAM DRAM, MST, POET; PC 10; SSC 27; WLC
See also SATA 61
P'u Sung-ling 1640-1715 .... LC 3
Putnam, Arthur Lee
See Alger, Horatio, Jr.
Puzo, Mario 1920-CLC 1, 2, 6, 36; DAM NOV, POP
See also CA 65-68; CANR 4, 42; DLB 6; MTCW
Pygge, Edward
See Barnes, Julian (Patrick)
Pyle, Ernest Taylor 1900-1945
See Pyle, Ernie
See also CA 115; 160
Pyle, Ernie 1900-1945 .... TCLC 75
See also Pyle, Ernest Taylor
See also DLB 29
Pym, Barbara (Mary Crampton) 1913-1980 CLC 13, 19, 37
See also CA 13-14; 97-100; CANR 13, 34; CAP 1; DLB 14; DLBY 87; MTCW
Pynchon, Thomas (Ruggles, Jr.) 1937-CLC 2, 3, 6, 9, 11, 18, 33, 62, 72; DA; DAB; DAC; DAM MST, NOV, POP; SSC 14; WLC
See also BEST 90:2; CA 17-20R; CANR 22, 46; DLB 2, 173; MTCW
Pythagoras c. 570B.C.-c. 500B.C. . CMLC 22
See also DLB 176
Qian Zhongshu
See Ch'ien Chung-shu
Qroll
See Dagerman, Stig (Halvard)
Quarrington, Paul (Lewis) 1953- ...... CLC 65
See also CA 129; CANR 62
Quasimodo, Salvatore 1901-1968 ..... CLC 10
See also CA 13-16; 25-28R; CAP 1; DLB 114; MTCW
Quay, Stephen 1947- .... CLC 95
Quay, The Brothers
See Quay, Stephen; Quay, Timothy
Quay, Timothy 1947- .... CLC 95
Queen, Ellery .... CLC 3, 11
See also Dannay, Frederic; Davidson, Avram; Lee, Manfred B(ennington); Marlowe, Stephen; Sturgeon, Theodore (Hamilton); Vance, John Holbrook
Queen, Ellery, Jr.
See Dannay, Frederic; Lee, Manfred B(ennington)
Queneau, Raymond 1903-1976 CLC 2, 5, 10, 42
See also CA 77-80; 69-72; CANR 32; DLB 72; MTCW
Quevedo, Francisco de 1580-1645 ...... LC 23
Quiller-Couch, Arthur Thomas 1863-1944 TCLC 53
See also CA 118; DLB 135, 153
Quin, Ann (Marie) 1936-1973 .... CLC 6
See also CA 9-12R; 45-48; DLB 14
Quinn, Martin
See Smith, Martin Cruz
Quinn, Peter 1947- .... CLC 91
Quinn, Simon
See Smith, Martin Cruz
Quiroga, Horacio (Sylvestre) 1878-1937 TCLC 20; DAM MULT; HLC
See also CA 117; 131; HW; MTCW

Quoirez, Francoise 1935- .... CLC 9
See also Sagan, Francoise
See also CA 49-52; CANR 6, 39; MTCW
Raabe, Wilhelm 1831-1910 .... TCLC 45
See also DLB 129
Rabe, David (William) 1940- .. CLC 4, 8, 33; DAM DRAM
See also CA 85-88; CABS 3; CANR 59; DLB 7
Rabelais, Francois 1483-1553 LC 5; DA; DAB; DAC; DAM MST; WLC
Rabinovitch, Sholem 1859-1916
See Aleichem, Sholom
See also CA 104
Rachilde 1860-1953 .... TCLC 67
See also DLB 123
Racine, Jean 1639-1699 . LC 28; DAB; DAM MST
Radcliffe, Ann (Ward) 1764-1823 NCLC 6, 55
See also DLB 39, 178
Radiguet, Raymond 1903-1923 ...... TCLC 29
See also DLB 65
Radnoti, Miklos 1909-1944 .... TCLC 16
See also CA 118
Rado, James 1939- .... CLC 17
See also CA 105
Radvanyi, Netty 1900-1983
See Seghers, Anna
See also CA 85-88; 110
Rae, Ben
See Griffiths, Trevor
Raeburn, John (Hay) 1941- .... CLC 34
See also CA 57-60
Ragni, Gerome 1942-1991 .... CLC 17
See also CA 105; 134
Rahv, Philip 1908-1973 .... CLC 24
See Greenberg, Ivan
See also DLB 137
Raine, Craig 1944- .... CLC 32, 103
See also CA 108; CANR 29, 51; DLB 40
Raine, Kathleen (Jessie) 1908- ..... CLC 7, 45
See also CA 85-88; CANR 46; DLB 20; MTCW
Rainis, Janis 1865-1929 .... TCLC 29
Rakosi, Carl .... CLC 47
See also Rawley, Callman
See also CAAS 5
Raleigh, Richard
See Lovecraft, H(oward) P(hillips)
Raleigh, Sir Walter 1554(?)-1618 . LC 31, 39
See also CDBLB Before 1660; DLB 172
Rallentando, H. P.
See Sayers, Dorothy L(eigh)
Ramal, Walter
See de la Mare, Walter (John)
Ramon, Juan
See Jimenez (Mantecon), Juan Ramon
Ramos, Graciliano 1892-1953 .... TCLC 32
Rampersad, Arnold 1941- .... CLC 44
See also BW 2; CA 127; 133; DLB 111; INT 133
Rampling, Anne
See Rice, Anne
Ramsay, Allan 1684(?)-1758 .... LC 29
See also DLB 95
Ramuz, Charles-Ferdinand 1878-1947 TCLC 33
Rand, Ayn 1905-1982 CLC 3, 30, 44, 79; DA; DAC; DAM MST, NOV, POP; WLC
See also AAYA 10; CA 13-16R; 105; CANR 27; MTCW
Randall, Dudley (Felker) 1914- CLC 1; BLC; DAM MULT
See also BW 1; CA 25-28R; CANR 23; DLB 41
Randall, Robert
See Silverberg, Robert
Ranger, Ken
See Creasey, John
Ransom, John Crowe 1888-1974 CLC 2, 4, 5, 11, 24; DAM POET
See also CA 5-8R; 49-52; CANR 6, 34; DLB 45, 63; MTCW
Rao, Raja 1909- ...... CLC 25, 56; DAM NOV
See also CA 73-76; CANR 51; MTCW
Raphael, Frederic (Michael) 1931- CLC 2, 14
See also CA 1-4R; CANR 1; DLB 14
Ratcliffe, James P.
See Mencken, H(enry) L(ouis)
Rathbone, Julian 1935- .... CLC 41
See also CA 101; CANR 34
Rattigan, Terence (Mervyn) 1911-1977 C L C 7; DAM DRAM
See also CA 85-88; 73-76; CDBLB 1945-1960; DLB 13; MTCW
Ratushinskaya, Irina 1954- .... CLC 54
See also CA 129
Raven, Simon (Arthur Noel) 1927-...CLC 14
See also CA 81-84
Rawley, Callman 1903-
See Rakosi, Carl
See also CA 21-24R; CANR 12, 32
Rawlings, Marjorie Kinnan 1896-1953 TCLC 4
See also AAYA 20; CA 104; 137; DLB 9, 22, 102; JRDA; MAICYA; YABC 1
Ray, Satyajit 1921-1992 .. CLC 16, 76; DAM MULT
See also CA 114; 137
Read, Herbert Edward 1893-1968 ..... CLC 4
See also CA 85-88; 25-28R; DLB 20, 149
Read, Piers Paul 1941- .... CLC 4, 10, 25
See also CA 21-24R; CANR 38; DLB 14; SATA 21
Reade, Charles 1814-1884 .... NCLC 2
See also DLB 21
Reade, Hamish
See Gray, Simon (James Holliday)
Reading, Peter 1946- .... CLC 47
See also CA 103; CANR 46; DLB 40
Reaney, James 1926- ... CLC 13; DAC; DAM MST
See also CA 41-44R; CAAS 15; CANR 42; DLB 68; SATA 43
Rebreanu, Liviu 1885-1944 .... TCLC 28
Rechy, John (Francisco) 1934- CLC 1, 7, 14, 18; DAM MULT; HLC
See also CA 5-8R; CAAS 4; CANR 6, 32; DLB 122; DLBY 82; HW; INT CANR-6
Redcam, Tom 1870-1933 .... TCLC 25
Reddin, Keith .... CLC 67
Redgrove, Peter (William) 1932- . CLC 6, 41
See also CA 1-4R; CANR 3, 39; DLB 40
Redmon, Anne .... CLC 22
See also Nightingale, Anne Redmon
See also DLBY 86
Reed, Eliot
See Ambler, Eric
Reed, Ishmael 1938- CLC 2, 3, 5, 6, 13, 32, 60; BLC; DAM MULT
See also BW 2; CA 21-24R; CANR 25, 48; DLB 2, 5, 33, 169; DLBD 8; MTCW
Reed, John (Silas) 1887-1920 .... TCLC 9
See also CA 106
Reed, Lou .... CLC 21
See also Firbank, Louis
Reeve, Clara 1729-1807 .... NCLC 19
See also DLB 39
Reich, Wilhelm 1897-1957 .... TCLC 57
Reid, Christopher (John) 1949- .... CLC 33
See also CA 140; DLB 40
Reid, Desmond
See Moorcock, Michael (John)
Reid Banks, Lynne 1929-
See Banks, Lynne Reid
See also CA 1-4R; CANR 6, 22, 38; CLR 24; JRDA; MAICYA; SATA 22, 75
Reilly, William K.
See Creasey, John
Reiner, Max
See Caldwell, (Janet Miriam) Taylor (Holland)
Reis, Ricardo
See Pessoa, Fernando (Antonio Nogueira)
Remarque, Erich Maria 1898-1970 CLC 21; DA; DAB; DAC; DAM MST, NOV
See also CA 77-80; 29-32R; DLB 56; MTCW
Remizov, A.
See Remizov, Aleksei (Mikhailovich)
Remizov, A. M.
See Remizov, Aleksei (Mikhailovich)
Remizov, Aleksei (Mikhailovich) 1877-1957 TCLC 27
See also CA 125; 133
Renan, Joseph Ernest 1823-1892 ... NCLC 26
Renard, Jules 1864-1910 .... TCLC 17
See also CA 117
Renault, Mary .... CLC 3, 11, 17
See also Challans, Mary
See also DLBY 83
Rendell, Ruth (Barbara) 1930- . CLC 28, 48; DAM POP
See also Vine, Barbara
See also CA 109; CANR 32, 52; DLB 87; INT CANR-32; MTCW
Renoir, Jean 1894-1979 .... CLC 20
See also CA 129; 85-88
Resnais, Alain 1922- .... CLC 16
Reverdy, Pierre 1889-1960 .... CLC 53
See also CA 97-100; 89-92
Rexroth, Kenneth 1905-1982 CLC 1, 2, 6, 11, 22, 49; DAM POET; PC 20
See also CA 5-8R; 107; CANR 14, 34; CDALB 1941-1968; DLB 16, 48, 165; DLBY 82; INT CANR-14; MTCW
Reyes, Alfonso 1889-1959 .... TCLC 33
See also CA 131; HW
Reyes y Basoalto, Ricardo Eliecer Neftali
See Neruda, Pablo
Reymont, Wladyslaw (Stanislaw) 1868(?)-1925 TCLC 5
See also CA 104
Reynolds, Jonathan 1942- .... CLC 6, 38
See also CA 65-68; CANR 28
Reynolds, Joshua 1723-1792 .... LC 15
See also DLB 104
Reynolds, Michael Shane 1937- .... CLC 44
See also CA 65-68; CANR 9
Reznikoff, Charles 1894-1976 .... CLC 9
See also CA 33-36; 61-64; CAP 2; DLB 28, 45
Rezzori (d'Arezzo), Gregor von 1914- CLC 25
See also CA 122; 136
Rhine, Richard
See Silverstein, Alvin
Rhodes, Eugene Manlove 1869-1934 TCLC 53
R'hoone
See Balzac, Honore de
Rhys, Jean 1890(?)-1979 CLC 2, 4, 6, 14, 19, 51; DAM NOV; SSC 21
See also CA 25-28R; 85-88; CANR 35, 62; CDBLB 1945-1960; DLB 36, 117, 162; MTCW
Ribeiro, Darcy 1922-1997 .... CLC 34
See also CA 33-36R; 156
Ribeiro, Joao Ubaldo (Osorio Pimentel) 1941- CLC 10, 67
See also CA 81-84
Ribman, Ronald (Burt) 1932- .... CLC 7
See also CA 21-24R; CANR 46
Ricci, Nino 1959- .... CLC 70
See also CA 137
Rice, Anne 1941- .... CLC 41; DAM POP
See also AAYA 9; BEST 89:2; CA 65-68;

CANR 12, 36, 53
Rice, Elmer (Leopold) 1892-1967 **CLC 7, 49; DAM DRAM**
See also CA 21-22; 25-28R; CAP 2; DLB 4, 7; MTCW
Rice, Tim(othy Miles Bindon) 1944- **CLC 21**
See also CA 103; CANR 46
Rich, Adrienne (Cecile) 1929-**CLC 3, 6, 7, 11, 18, 36, 73, 76; DAM POET; PC 5**
See also CA 9-12R; CANR 20, 53; DLB 5, 67; MTCW
Rich, Barbara
See Graves, Robert (von Ranke)
Rich, Robert
See Trumbo, Dalton
Richard, Keith .... **CLC 17**
See also Richards, Keith
Richards, David Adams 1950- **CLC 59; DAC**
See also CA 93-96; CANR 60; DLB 53
Richards, I(vor) A(rmstrong) 1893-1979 **CLC 14, 24**
See also CA 41-44R; 89-92; CANR 34; DLB 27
Richards, Keith 1943-
See Richard, Keith
See also CA 107
Richardson, Anne
See Roiphe, Anne (Richardson)
Richardson, Dorothy Miller 1873-1957 **TCLC 3**
See also CA 104; DLB 36
Richardson, Ethel Florence (Lindesay) 1870-1946
See Richardson, Henry Handel
See also CA 105
Richardson, Henry Handel .... **TCLC 4**
See also Richardson, Ethel Florence (Lindesay)
Richardson, John 1796-1852 **NCLC 55; DAC**
See also DLB 99
Richardson, Samuel 1689-1761 ... **LC 1; DA; DAB; DAC; DAM MST, NOV; WLC**
See also CDBLB 1660-1789; DLB 39
Richler, Mordecai 1931-**CLC 3, 5, 9, 13, 18, 46, 70; DAC; DAM MST, NOV**
See also AITN 1; CA 65-68; CANR 31, 62; CLR 17; DLB 53; MAICYA; MTCW; SATA 44; SATA-Brief 27
Richter, Conrad (Michael) 1890-1968 **CLC 30**
See also AAYA 21; CA 5-8R; 25-28R; CANR 23; DLB 9; MTCW; SATA 3
Ricostranza, Tom
See Ellis, Trey
Riddell, J. H. 1832-1906 .... **TCLC 40**
Riding, Laura.................................. **CLC 3, 7**
See also Jackson, Laura (Riding)
Riefenstahl, Berta Helene Amalia 1902-
See Riefenstahl, Leni
See also CA 108
Riefenstahl, Leni .... **CLC 16**
See also Riefenstahl, Berta Helene Amalia
Riffe, Ernest
See Bergman, (Ernst) Ingmar
Riggs, (Rolla) Lynn 1899-1954 .... **TCLC 56; DAM MULT**
See also CA 144; DLB 175; NNAL
Riley, James Whitcomb 1849-1916 **TCLC 51; DAM POET**
See also CA 118; 137; MAICYA; SATA 17
Riley, Tex
See Creasey, John
Rilke, Rainer Maria 1875-1926 **TCLC 1, 6, 19; DAM POET; PC 2**
See also CA 104; 132; CANR 62; DLB 81; MTCW
Rimbaud, (Jean Nicolas) Arthur 1854-1891 **NCLC 4, 35; DA; DAB; DAC; DAM MST, POET; PC 3; WLC**

Rinehart, Mary Roberts 1876-1958 **TCLC 52**
See also CA 108
Ringmaster, The
See Mencken, H(enry) L(ouis)
Ringwood, Gwen(dolyn Margaret) Pharis 1910-1984 .... **CLC 48**
See also CA 148; 112; DLB 88
Rio, Michel 19(?)- .... **CLC 43**
Ritsos, Giannes
See Ritsos, Yannis
Ritsos, Yannis 1909-1990 .... **CLC 6, 13, 31**
See also CA 77-80; 133; CANR 39, 61; MTCW
Ritter, Erika 1948(?)- .... **CLC 52**
Rivera, Jose Eustasio 1889-1928 ... **TCLC 35**
See also HW
Rivers, Conrad Kent 1933-1968 .... **CLC 1**
See also BW 1; CA 85-88; DLB 41
Rivers, Elfrida
See Bradley, Marion Zimmer
Riverside, John
See Heinlein, Robert A(nson)
Rizal, Jose 1861-1896 .... **NCLC 27**
Roa Bastos, Augusto (Antonio) 1917-**CLC 45; DAM MULT; HLC**
See also CA 131; DLB 113; HW
Robbe-Grillet, Alain 1922-**CLC 1, 2, 4, 6, 8, 10, 14, 43**
See also CA 9-12R; CANR 33; DLB 83; MTCW
Robbins, Harold 1916-... **CLC 5; DAM NOV**
See also CA 73-76; CANR 26, 54; MTCW
Robbins, Thomas Eugene 1936-
See Robbins, Tom
See also CA 81-84; CANR 29, 59; DAM NOV, POP; MTCW
Robbins, Tom .... **CLC 9, 32, 64**
See also Robbins, Thomas Eugene
See also BEST 90:3; DLBY 80
Robbins, Trina 1938- .... **CLC 21**
See also CA 128
Roberts, Charles G(eorge) D(ouglas) 1860-1943 **TCLC 8**
See also CA 105; CLR 33; DLB 92; SATA 88; SATA-Brief 29
Roberts, Elizabeth Madox 1886-1941 **TCLC 68**
See also CA 111; DLB 9, 54, 102; SATA 33; SATA-Brief 27
Roberts, Kate 1891-1985 .... **CLC 15**
See also CA 107; 116
Roberts, Keith (John Kingston) 1935-**CLC 14**
See also CA 25-28R; CANR 46
Roberts, Kenneth (Lewis) 1885-1957 **TCLC 23**
See also CA 109; DLB 9
Roberts, Michele (B.) 1949- .... **CLC 48**
See also CA 115; CANR 58
Robertson, Ellis
See Ellison, Harlan (Jay); Silverberg, Robert
Robertson, Thomas William 1829-1871 **NCLC 35; DAM DRAM**
Robeson, Kenneth
See Dent, Lester
Robinson, Edwin Arlington 1869-1935 **TCLC 5; DA; DAC; DAM MST, POET; PC 1**
See also CA 104; 133; CDALB 1865-1917; DLB 54; MTCW
Robinson, Henry Crabb 1775-1867 **NCLC 15**
See also DLB 107
Robinson, Jill 1936- .... **CLC 10**
See also CA 102; INT 102
Robinson, Kim Stanley 1952-........... **CLC 34**
See also CA 126
Robinson, Lloyd
See Silverberg, Robert
Robinson, Marilynne 1944- .... **CLC 25**
See also CA 116
Robinson, Smokey .... **CLC 21**

See also Robinson, William, Jr.
Robinson, William, Jr. 1940-
See Robinson, Smokey
See also CA 116
Robison, Mary 1949-.................. **CLC 42, 98**
See also CA 113; 116; DLB 130; INT 116
Rod, Edouard 1857-1910 .... **TCLC 52**
Roddenberry, Eugene Wesley 1921-1991
See Roddenberry, Gene
See also CA 110; 135; CANR 37; SATA 45; SATA-Obit 69
Roddenberry, Gene .... **CLC 17**
See also Roddenberry, Eugene Wesley
See also AAYA 5; SATA-Obit 69
Rodgers, Mary 1931- .... **CLC 12**
See also CA 49-52; CANR 8, 55; CLR 20; INT CANR-8; JRDA; MAICYA; SATA 8
Rodgers, W(illiam) R(obert) 1909-1969 **CLC 7**
See also CA 85-88; DLB 20
Rodman, Eric
See Silverberg, Robert
Rodman, Howard 1920(?)-1985 .... **CLC 65**
See also CA 118
Rodman, Maia
See Wojciechowska, Maia (Teresa)
Rodriguez, Claudio 1934-.................. **CLC 10**
See also DLB 134
Roelvaag, O(le) E(dvart) 1876-1931 **TCLC 17**
See also CA 117; DLB 9
Roethke, Theodore (Huebner) 1908-1963 **CLC 1, 3, 8, 11, 19, 46, 101; DAM POET; PC 15**
See also CA 81-84; CABS 2; CDALB 1941-1968; DLB 5; MTCW
Rogers, Thomas Hunton 1927- .... **CLC 57**
See also CA 89-92; INT 89-92
Rogers, Will(iam Penn Adair) 1879-1935 **TCLC 8, 71; DAM MULT**
See also CA 105; 144; DLB 11; NNAL
Rogin, Gilbert 1929-........................... **CLC 18**
See also CA 65-68; CANR 15
Rohan, Koda .... **TCLC 22**
See also Koda Shigeyuki
Rohlfs, Anna Katharine Green
See Green, Anna Katharine
Rohmer, Eric .... **CLC 16**
See also Scherer, Jean-Marie Maurice
Rohmer, Sax .... **TCLC 28**
See also Ward, Arthur Henry Sarsfield
See also DLB 70
Roiphe, Anne (Richardson) 1935- . **CLC 3, 9**
See also CA 89-92; CANR 45; DLBY 80; INT 89-92
Rojas, Fernando de 1465-1541 .... **LC 23**
Rolfe, Frederick (William Serafino Austin Lewis Mary) 1860-1913 .... **TCLC 12**
See also CA 107; DLB 34, 156
Rolland, Romain 1866-1944 .... **TCLC 23**
See also CA 118; DLB 65
Rolle, Richard c. 1300-c. 1349 ...... **CMLC 21**
See also DLB 146
Rolvaag, O(le) E(dvart)
See Roelvaag, O(le) E(dvart)
Romain Arnaud, Saint
See Aragon, Louis
Romains, Jules 1885-1972 .... **CLC 7**
See also CA 85-88; CANR 34; DLB 65; MTCW
Romero, Jose Ruben 1890-1952 .... **TCLC 14**
See also CA 114; 131; HW
Ronsard, Pierre de 1524-1585 ...**LC 6; PC 11**
Rooke, Leon 1934-.. **CLC 25, 34; DAM POP**
See also CA 25-28R; CANR 23, 53
Roosevelt, Theodore 1858-1919 ..... **TCLC 69**
See also CA 115; DLB 47
Roper, William 1498-1578 .... **LC 10**
Roquelaure, A. N.
See Rice, Anne

Rosa, Joao Guimaraes 1908-1967 ... **CLC 23**
See also CA 89-92; DLB 113
Rose, Wendy 1948-**CLC 85; DAM MULT; PC 13**
See also CA 53-56; CANR 5, 51; DLB 175; NNAL; SATA 12
Rosen, R. D.
See Rosen, Richard (Dean)
Rosen, Richard (Dean) 1949- ... **CLC 39**
See also CA 77-80; CANR 62; INT CANR-30
Rosenberg, Isaac 1890-1918 ... **TCLC 12**
See also CA 107; DLB 20
Rosenblatt, Joe ... **CLC 15**
See also Rosenblatt, Joseph
Rosenblatt, Joseph 1933-
See Rosenblatt, Joe
See also CA 89-92; INT 89-92
Rosenfeld, Samuel 1896-1963
See Tzara, Tristan
See also CA 89-92
Rosenstock, Sami
See Tzara, Tristan
Rosenstock, Samuel
See Tzara, Tristan
Rosenthal, M(acha) L(ouis) 1917-1996 . **C L C 28**
See also CA 1-4R; 152; CAAS 6; CANR 4, 51; DLB 5; SATA 59
Ross, Barnaby
See Dannay, Frederic
Ross, Bernard L.
See Follett, Ken(neth Martin)
Ross, J. H.
See Lawrence, T(homas) E(dward)
Ross, Martin
See Martin, Violet Florence
See also DLB 135
Ross, (James) Sinclair 1908- **CLC 13; DAC; DAM MST; SSC 24**
See also CA 73-76; DLB 88
Rossetti, Christina (Georgina) 1830-1894
NCLC 2, 50, 66; DA; DAB; DAC; DAM MST, POET; PC 7; WLC
See also DLB 35, 163; MAICYA; SATA 20
Rossetti, Dante Gabriel 1828-1882 **NCLC 4; DA; DAB; DAC; DAM MST, POET; WLC**
See also CDBLB 1832-1890; DLB 35
Rossner, Judith (Perelman) 1935-**CLC 6, 9, 29**
See also AITN 2; BEST 90:3; CA 17-20R; CANR 18, 51; DLB 6; INT CANR-18; MTCW
Rostand, Edmond (Eugene Alexis) 1868-1918
TCLC 6, 37; DA; DAB; DAC; DAM DRAM, MST
See also CA 104; 126; MTCW
Roth, Henry 1906-1995 ... **CLC 2, 6, 11, 104**
See also CA 11-12; 149; CANR 38; CAP 1; DLB 28; MTCW
Roth, Philip (Milton) 1933-**CLC 1, 2, 3, 4, 6, 9, 15, 22, 31, 47, 66, 86; DA; DAB; DAC; DAM MST, NOV, POP; SSC 26; WLC**
See also BEST 90:3; CA 1-4R; CANR 1, 22, 36, 55; CDALB 1968-1988; DLB 2, 28, 173; DLBY 82; MTCW
Rothenberg, Jerome 1931- ... **CLC 6, 57**
See also CA 45-48; CANR 1; DLB 5
Roumain, Jacques (Jean Baptiste) 1907-1944
TCLC 19; BLC; DAM MULT
See also BW 1; CA 117; 125
Rourke, Constance (Mayfield) 1885-1941
TCLC 12
See also CA 107; YABC 1
Rousseau, Jean-Baptiste 1671-1741 ... **LC 9**
Rousseau, Jean-Jacques 1712-1778**LC 14, 36; DA; DAB; DAC; DAM MST; WLC**
Roussel, Raymond 1877-1933 ... **TCLC 20**
See also CA 117

Rovit, Earl (Herbert) 1927-... **CLC 7**
See also CA 5-8R; CANR 12
Rowe, Nicholas 1674-1718 ... **LC 8**
See also DLB 84
Rowley, Ames Dorrance
See Lovecraft, H(oward) P(hillips)
Rowson, Susanna Haswell 1762(?)-1824
NCLC 5
See also DLB 37
Roy, Gabrielle 1909-1983 **CLC 10, 14; DAB; DAC; DAM MST**
See also CA 53-56; 110; CANR 5, 61; DLB 68; MTCW
Rozewicz, Tadeusz 1921- ...**CLC 9, 23; DAM POET**
See also CA 108; CANR 36; MTCW
Ruark, Gibbons 1941- ... **CLC 3**
See also CA 33-36R; CAAS 23; CANR 14, 31, 57; DLB 120
Rubens, Bernice (Ruth) 1923- ... **CLC 19, 31**
See also CA 25-28R; CANR 33; DLB 14; MTCW
Rubin, Harold
See Robbins, Harold
Rudkin, (James) David 1936- ... **CLC 14**
See also CA 89-92; DLB 13
Rudnik, Raphael 1933- ... **CLC 7**
See also CA 29-32R
Ruffian, M.
See Hasek, Jaroslav (Matej Frantisek)
Ruiz, Jose Martinez ... **CLC 11**
See also Martinez Ruiz, Jose
Rukeyser, Muriel 1913-1980**CLC 6, 10, 15, 27; DAM POET; PC 12**
See also CA 5-8R; 93-96; CANR 26, 60; DLB 48; MTCW; SATA-Obit 22
Rule, Jane (Vance) 1931- ... **CLC 27**
See also CA 25-28R; CAAS 18; CANR 12; DLB 60
Rulfo, Juan 1918-1986 ... **CLC 8, 80; DAM MULT; HLC; SSC 25**
See also CA 85-88; 118; CANR 26; DLB 113; HW; MTCW
Rumi, Jalal al-Din 1297-1373 ... **CMLC 20**
Runeberg, Johan 1804-1877 ... **NCLC 41**
Runyon, (Alfred) Damon 1884(?)-1946**T C L C 10**
See also CA 107; DLB 11, 86, 171
Rush, Norman 1933- ... **CLC 44**
See also CA 121; 126; INT 126
Rushdie, (Ahmed) Salman 1947-**CLC 23, 31, 55, 100; DAB; DAC; DAM MST, NOV, POP; WLCS**
See also BEST 89:3; CA 108; 111; CANR 33, 56; INT 111; MTCW
Rushforth, Peter (Scott) 1945- ... **CLC 19**
See also CA 101
Ruskin, John 1819-1900 ... **TCLC 63**
See also CA 114; 129; CDBLB 1832-1890; DLB 55, 163; SATA 24
Russ, Joanna 1937- ... **CLC 15**
See also CA 25-28R; CANR 11, 31; DLB 8; MTCW
Russell, George William 1867-1935
See Baker, Jean H.
See also CA 104; 153; CDBLB 1890-1914; DAM POET
Russell, (Henry) Ken(neth Alfred) 1927-**C L C 16**
See also CA 105
Russell, Willy 1947-............**CLC 60**
Rutherford, Mark ... **TCLC 25**
See also White, William Hale
See also DLB 18
Ruyslinck, Ward 1929- ... **CLC 14**
See also Belser, Reimond Karel Maria de
Ryan, Cornelius (John) 1920-1974 ... **CLC 7**

See also CA 69-72; 53-56; CANR 38
Ryan, Michael 1946- ... **CLC 65**
See also CA 49-52; DLBY 82
Ryan, Tim
See Dent, Lester
Rybakov, Anatoli (Naumovich) 1911-**CLC 23, 53**
See also CA 126; 135; SATA 79
Ryder, Jonathan
See Ludlum, Robert
Ryga, George 1932-1987**CLC 14; DAC; DAM MST**
See also CA 101; 124; CANR 43; DLB 60
S. H.
See Hartmann, Sadakichi
S. S.
See Sassoon, Siegfried (Lorraine)
Saba, Umberto 1883-1957 ... **TCLC 33**
See also CA 144; DLB 114
Sabatini, Rafael 1875-1950 ... **TCLC 47**
Sabato, Ernesto (R.) 1911-**CLC 10, 23; DAM MULT; HLC**
See also CA 97-100; CANR 32; DLB 145; HW; MTCW
Sacastru, Martin
See Bioy Casares, Adolfo
Sacher-Masoch, Leopold von 1836(?)-1895
NCLC 31
Sachs, Marilyn (Stickle) 1927- ... **CLC 35**
See also AAYA 2; CA 17-20R; CANR 13, 47; CLR 2; JRDA; MAICYA; SAAS 2; SATA 3, 68
Sachs, Nelly 1891-1970 ... **CLC 14, 98**
See also CA 17-18; 25-28R; CAP 2
Sackler, Howard (Oliver) 1929-1982 **CLC 14**
See also CA 61-64; 108; CANR 30; DLB 7
Sacks, Oliver (Wolf) 1933- ... **CLC 67**
See also CA 53-56; CANR 28, 50; INT CANR-28; MTCW
Sadakichi
See Hartmann, Sadakichi
Sade, Donatien Alphonse Francois Comte 1740-1814 ... **NCLC 47**
Sadoff, Ira 1945- ... **CLC 9**
See also CA 53-56; CANR 5, 21; DLB 120
Saetone
See Camus, Albert
Safire, William 1929- ... **CLC 10**
See also CA 17-20R; CANR 31, 54
Sagan, Carl (Edward) 1934-1996 ... **CLC 30**
See also AAYA 2; CA 25-28R; 155; CANR 11, 36; MTCW; SATA 58; SATA-Obit 94
Sagan, Francoise ... **CLC 3, 6, 9, 17, 36**
See also Quoirez, Francoise
See also DLB 83
Sahgal, Nayantara (Pandit) 1927- ... **CLC 41**
See also CA 9-12R; CANR 11
Saint, H(arry) F. 1941- ... **CLC 50**
See also CA 127
St. Aubin de Teran, Lisa 1953-
See Teran, Lisa St. Aubin de
See also CA 118; 126; INT 126
Saint Birgitta of Sweden c. 1303-1373**C M L C 24**
Sainte-Beuve, Charles Augustin 1804-1869
NCLC 5
Saint-Exupery, Antoine (Jean Baptiste Marie Roger) de 1900-1944**TCLC 2, 56; DAM NOV; WLC**
See also CA 108; 132; CLR 10; DLB 72; MAICYA; MTCW; SATA 20
St. John, David
See Hunt, E(verette) Howard, (Jr.)
Saint-John Perse
See Leger, (Marie-Rene Auguste) Alexis Saint-Leger
Saintsbury, George (Edward Bateman) 1845-

1933 .... **TCLC 31**
  See also CA 160; DLB 57, 149
Sait Faik .... **TCLC 23**
  See also Abasiyanik, Sait Faik
Saki .... **TCLC 3; SSC 12**
  See also Munro, H(ector) H(ugh)
Sala, George Augustus .... **NCLC 46**
Salama, Hannu 1936- .... **CLC 18**
Salamanca, J(ack) R(ichard) 1922-**CLC 4, 15**
  See also CA 25-28R
Sale, J. Kirkpatrick
  See Sale, Kirkpatrick
Sale, Kirkpatrick 1937- .... **CLC 68**
  See also CA 13-16R; CANR 10
Salinas, Luis Omar 1937- ...... **CLC 90; DAM MULT; HLC**
  See also CA 131; DLB 82; HW
Salinas (y Serrano), Pedro 1891(?)-1951
  TCLC 17
  See also CA 117; DLB 134
Salinger, J(erome) D(avid) 1919-**CLC 1, 3, 8, 12, 55, 56; DA; DAB; DAC; DAM MST, NOV, POP; SSC 2, 28; WLC**
  See also AAYA 2; CA 5-8R; CANR 39; CDALB 1941-1968; CLR 18; DLB 2, 102, 173; MAICYA; MTCW; SATA 67
Salisbury, John
  See Caute, David
Salter, James 1925- .... **CLC 7, 52, 59**
  See also CA 73-76; DLB 130
Saltus, Edgar (Everton) 1855-1921 . **TCLC 8**
  See also CA 105
Saltykov, Mikhail Evgrafovich 1826-1889
  NCLC 16
Samarakis, Antonis 1919- .... **CLC 5**
  See also CA 25-28R; CAAS 16; CANR 36
Sanchez, Florencio 1875-1910 .... **TCLC 37**
  See also CA 153; HW
Sanchez, Luis Rafael 1936- .... **CLC 23**
  See also CA 128; DLB 145; HW
Sanchez, Sonia 1934- ..... **CLC 5; BLC; DAM MULT; PC 9**
  See also BW 2; CA 33-36R; CANR 24, 49; CLR 18; DLB 41; DLBD 8; MAICYA; MTCW; SATA 22
Sand, George 1804-1876**NCLC 2, 42, 57; DA; DAB; DAC; DAM MST, NOV; WLC**
  See also DLB 119
Sandburg, Carl (August) 1878-1967**CLC 1, 4, 10, 15, 35; DA; DAB; DAC; DAM MST, POET; PC 2; WLC**
  See also CA 5-8R; 25-28R; CANR 35; CDALB 1865-1917; DLB 17, 54; MAICYA; MTCW; SATA 8
Sandburg, Charles
  See Sandburg, Carl (August)
Sandburg, Charles A.
  See Sandburg, Carl (August)
Sanders, (James) Ed(ward) 1939- ... **CLC 53**
  See also CA 13-16R; CAAS 21; CANR 13, 44; DLB 16
Sanders, Lawrence 1920-**CLC 41; DAM POP**
  See also BEST 89:4; CA 81-84; CANR 33, 62; MTCW
Sanders, Noah
  See Blount, Roy (Alton), Jr.
Sanders, Winston P.
  See Anderson, Poul (William)
Sandoz, Mari(e Susette) 1896-1966 . **CLC 28**
  See also CA 1-4R; 25-28R; CANR 17; DLB 9; MTCW; SATA 5
Saner, Reg(inald Anthony) 1931- .... **CLC 9**
  See also CA 65-68
Sannazaro, Jacopo 1456(?)-1530 .... **LC 8**
Sansom, William 1912-1976 **CLC 2, 6; DAM NOV; SSC 21**
  See also CA 5-8R; 65-68; CANR 42; DLB 139; MTCW
Santayana, George 1863-1952 .... **TCLC 40**
  See also CA 115; DLB 54, 71; DLBD 13
Santiago, Danny .... **CLC 33**
  See also James, Daniel (Lewis)
  See also DLB 122
Santmyer, Helen Hoover 1895-1986 **CLC 33**
  See also CA 1-4R; 118; CANR 15, 33; DLBY 84; MTCW
Santoka, Taneda 1882-1940 .... **TCLC 72**
Santos, Bienvenido N(uqui) 1911-1996 . **CLC 22; DAM MULT**
  See also CA 101; 151; CANR 19, 46
Sapper .... **TCLC 44**
  See also McNeile, Herman Cyril
Sapphire 1950- .... **CLC 99**
Sappho fl. 6th cent. B.C.- ..... **CMLC 3; DAM POET; PC 5**
  See also DLB 176
Sarduy, Severo 1937-1993 .... **CLC 6, 97**
  See also CA 89-92; 142; CANR 58; DLB 113; HW
Sargeson, Frank 1903-1982 .... **CLC 31**
  See also CA 25-28R; 106; CANR 38
Sarmiento, Felix Ruben Garcia
  See Dario, Ruben
Saroyan, William 1908-1981**CLC 1, 8, 10, 29, 34, 56; DA; DAB; DAC; DAM DRAM, MST, NOV; SSC 21; WLC**
  See also CA 5-8R; 103; CANR 30; DLB 7, 9, 86; DLBY 81; MTCW; SATA 23; SATA-Obit 24
Sarraute, Nathalie 1900-**CLC 1, 2, 4, 8, 10, 31, 80**
  See also CA 9-12R; CANR 23; DLB 83; MTCW
Sarton, (Eleanor) May 1912-1995**CLC 4, 14, 49, 91; DAM POET**
  See also CA 1-4R; 149; CANR 1, 34, 55; DLB 48; DLBY 81; INT CANR-34; MTCW; SATA 36; SATA-Obit 86
Sartre, Jean-Paul 1905-1980**CLC 1, 4, 7, 9, 13, 18, 24, 44, 50, 52; DA; DAB; DAC; DAM DRAM, MST, NOV; DC 3; WLC**
  See also CA 9-12R; 97-100; CANR 21; DLB 72; MTCW
Sassoon, Siegfried (Lorraine) 1886-1967**CLC 36; DAB; DAM MST, NOV, POET; PC 12**
  See also CA 104; 25-28R; CANR 36; DLB 20; MTCW
Satterfield, Charles
  See Pohl, Frederik
Saul, John (W. III) 1942-**CLC 46; DAM NOV, POP**
  See also AAYA 10; BEST 90:4; CA 81-84; CANR 16, 40
Saunders, Caleb
  See Heinlein, Robert A(nson)
Saura (Atares), Carlos 1932- .... **CLC 20**
  See also CA 114; 131; HW
Sauser-Hall, Frederic 1887-1961 ...... **CLC 18**
  See also Cendrars, Blaise
  See also CA 102; 93-96; CANR 36, 62; MTCW
Saussure, Ferdinand de 1857-1913 **TCLC 49**
Savage, Catharine
  See Brosman, Catharine Savage
Savage, Thomas 1915- .... **CLC 40**
  See also CA 126; 132; CAAS 15; INT 132
Savan, Glenn 19(?)- .... **CLC 50**
Sayers, Dorothy L(eigh) 1893-1957 **TCLC 2, 15; DAM POP**
  See also CA 104; 119; CANR 60; CDBLB 1914-1945; DLB 10, 36, 77, 100; MTCW
Sayers, Valerie 1952- .... **CLC 50**
  See also CA 134; CANR 61
Sayles, John (Thomas) 1950- . **CLC 7, 10, 14**
  See also CA 57-60; CANR 41; DLB 44
Scammell, Michael 1935-................... **CLC 34**
  See also CA 156
Scannell, Vernon 1922- .... **CLC 49**
  See also CA 5-8R; CANR 8, 24, 57; DLB 27; SATA 59
Scarlett, Susan
  See Streatfeild, (Mary) Noel
Schaeffer, Susan Fromberg 1941-**CLC 6, 11, 22**
  See also CA 49-52; CANR 18; DLB 28; MTCW; SATA 22
Schary, Jill
  See Robinson, Jill
Schell, Jonathan 1943- .... **CLC 35**
  See also CA 73-76; CANR 12
Schelling, Friedrich Wilhelm Joseph von 1775-1854 .... **NCLC 30**
  See also DLB 90
Schendel, Arthur van 1874-1946 ... **TCLC 56**
Scherer, Jean-Marie Maurice 1920-
  See Rohmer, Eric
  See also CA 110
Schevill, James (Erwin) 1920- .... **CLC 7**
  See also CA 5-8R; CAAS 12
Schiller, Friedrich 1759-1805**NCLC 39; DAM DRAM**
  See also DLB 94
Schisgal, Murray (Joseph) 1926- .... **CLC 6**
  See also CA 21-24R; CANR 48
Schlee, Ann 1934- .... **CLC 35**
  See also CA 101; CANR 29; SATA 44; SATA-Brief 36
Schlegel, August Wilhelm von 1767-1845
  NCLC 15
  See also DLB 94
Schlegel, Friedrich 1772-1829 .... **NCLC 45**
  See also DLB 90
Schlegel, Johann Elias (von) 1719(?)-1749**L C 5**
Schlesinger, Arthur M(eier), Jr. 1917-**CLC 84**
  See also AITN 1; CA 1-4R; CANR 1, 28, 58; DLB 17; INT CANR-28; MTCW; SATA 61
Schmidt, Arno (Otto) 1914-1979 .... **CLC 56**
  See also CA 128; 109; DLB 69
Schmitz, Aron Hector 1861-1928
  See Svevo, Italo
  See also CA 104; 122; MTCW
Schnackenberg, Gjertrud 1953- .... **CLC 40**
  See also CA 116; DLB 120
Schneider, Leonard Alfred 1925-1966
  See Bruce, Lenny
  See also CA 89-92
Schnitzler, Arthur 1862-1931**TCLC 4; SSC 15**
  See also CA 104; DLB 81, 118
Schoenberg, Arnold 1874-1951 ...... **TCLC 75**
  See also CA 109
Schonberg, Arnold
  See Schoenberg, Arnold
Schopenhauer, Arthur 1788-1860 . **NCLC 51**
  See also DLB 90
Schor, Sandra (M.) 1932(?)-1990 ...... **CLC 65**
  See also CA 132
Schorer, Mark 1908-1977 .... **CLC 9**
  See also CA 5-8R; 73-76; CANR 7; DLB 103
Schrader, Paul (Joseph) 1946- .... **CLC 26**
  See also CA 37-40R; CANR 41; DLB 44
Schreiner, Olive (Emilie Albertina) 1855-1920
  TCLC 9
  See also CA 105; DLB 18, 156
Schulberg, Budd (Wilson) 1914-.. **CLC 7, 48**
  See also CA 25-28R; CANR 19; DLB 6, 26, 28; DLBY 81
Schulz, Bruno 1892-1942**TCLC 5, 51; SSC 13**
  See also CA 115; 123
Schulz, Charles M(onroe) 1922- .... **CLC 12**
  See also CA 9-12R; CANR 6; INT CANR-6; SATA 10

Schumacher, E(rnst) F(riedrich) 1911-1977
CLC 80
See also CA 81-84; 73-76; CANR 34

Schuyler, James Marcus 1923-1991. CLC 5, 23; DAM POET
See also CA 101; 134; DLB 5, 169; INT 101

Schwartz, Delmore (David) 1913-1966 CLC 2, 4, 10, 45, 87; PC 8
See also CA 17-18; 25-28R; CANR 35; CAP 2; DLB 28, 48; MTCW

Schwartz, Ernst
See Ozu, Yasujiro

Schwartz, John Burnham 1965- ...... CLC 59
See also CA 132

Schwartz, Lynne Sharon 1939- .... CLC 31
See also CA 103; CANR 44

Schwartz, Muriel A.
See Eliot, T(homas) S(tearns)

Schwarz-Bart, Andre 1928- .... CLC 2, 4
See also CA 89-92

Schwarz-Bart, Simone 1938- .... CLC 7
See also BW 2; CA 97-100

Schwob, (Mayer Andre) Marcel 1867-1905
TCLC 20
See also CA 117; DLB 123

Sciascia, Leonardo 1921-1989. CLC 8, 9, 41
See also CA 85-88; 130; CANR 35; DLB 177; MTCW

Scoppettone, Sandra 1936- .... CLC 26
See also AAYA 11; CA 5-8R; CANR 41; SATA 9, 92

Scorsese, Martin 1942- .... CLC 20, 89
See also CA 110; 114; CANR 46

Scotland, Jay
See Jakes, John (William)

Scott, Duncan Campbell 1862-1947 TCLC 6; DAC
See also CA 104; 153; DLB 92

Scott, Evelyn 1893-1963 .... CLC 43
See also CA 104; 112; DLB 9, 48

Scott, F(rancis) R(eginald) 1899-1985 CLC 22
See also CA 101; 114; DLB 88; INT 101

Scott, Frank
See Scott, F(rancis) R(eginald)

Scott, Joanna 1960- .... CLC 50
See also CA 126; CANR 53

Scott, Paul (Mark) 1920-1978 ...... CLC 9, 60
See also CA 81-84; 77-80; CANR 33; DLB 14; MTCW

Scott, Walter 1771-1832 NCLC 15; DA; DAB; DAC; DAM MST, NOV, POET; PC 13; WLC
See also AAYA 22; CDBLB 1789-1832; DLB 93, 107, 116, 144, 159; YABC 2

Scribe, (Augustin) Eugene 1791-1861 NCLC 16; DAM DRAM; DC 5

Scrum, R.
See Crumb, R(obert)

Scudery, Madeleine de 1607-1701 .... LC 2

Scum
See Crumb, R(obert)

Scumbag, Little Bobby
See Crumb, R(obert)

Seabrook, John
See Hubbard, L(afayette) Ron(ald)

Sealy, I. Allan 1951- .... CLC 55

Search, Alexander
See Pessoa, Fernando (Antonio Nogueira)

Sebastian, Lee
See Silverberg, Robert

Sebastian Owl
See Thompson, Hunter S(tockton)

Sebestyen, Ouida 1924- .... CLC 30
See also AAYA 8; CA 107; CANR 40; CLR 17; JRDA; MAICYA; SAAS 10; SATA 39

Secundus, H. Scriblerus
See Fielding, Henry

Sedges, John
See Buck, Pearl S(ydenstricker)

Sedgwick, Catharine Maria 1789-1867 NCLC 19
See also DLB 1, 74

Seelye, John 1931- .... CLC 7

Seferiades, Giorgos Stylianou 1900-1971
See Seferis, George
See also CA 5-8R; 33-36R; CANR 5, 36; MTCW

Seferis, George .... CLC 5, 11
See also Seferiades, Giorgos Stylianou

Segal, Erich (Wolf) 1937- .. CLC 3, 10; DAM POP
See also BEST 89:1; CA 25-28R; CANR 20, 36; DLBY 86; INT CANR-20; MTCW

Seger, Bob 1945- .... CLC 35

Seghers, Anna .... CLC 7
See also Radvanyi, Netty
See also DLB 69

Seidel, Frederick (Lewis) 1936- .... CLC 18
See also CA 13-16R; CANR 8; DLBY 84

Seifert, Jaroslav 1901-1986 .. CLC 34, 44, 93
See also CA 127; MTCW

Sei Shonagon c. 966-1017(?) .... CMLC 6

Selby, Hubert, Jr. 1928- CLC 1, 2, 4, 8; SSC 20
See also CA 13-16R; CANR 33; DLB 2

Selzer, Richard 1928- .... CLC 74
See also CA 65-68; CANR 14

Sembene, Ousmane
See Ousmane, Sembene

Senancour, Etienne Pivert de 1770-1846
NCLC 16
See also DLB 119

Sender, Ramon (Jose) 1902-1982 ..... CLC 8; DAM MULT; HLC
See also CA 5-8R; 105; CANR 8; HW; MTCW

Seneca, Lucius Annaeus 4B.C.-65 CMLC 6; DAM DRAM; DC 5

Senghor, Leopold Sedar 1906- CLC 54; BLC; DAM MULT, POET
See also BW 2; CA 116; 125; CANR 47; MTCW

Serling, (Edward) Rod(man) 1924-1975 CLC 30
See also AAYA 14; AITN 1; CA 65-68; 57-60; DLB 26

Serna, Ramon Gomez de la
See Gomez de la Serna, Ramon

Serpieres
See Guillevic, (Eugene)

Service, Robert
See Service, Robert W(illiam)
See also DAB; DLB 92

Service, Robert W(illiam) 1874(?)-1958 TCLC 15; DA; DAC; DAM MST, POET; WLC
See also Service, Robert
See also CA 115; 140; SATA 20

Seth, Vikram 1952- CLC 43, 90; DAM MULT
See also CA 121; 127; CANR 50; DLB 120; INT 127

Seton, Cynthia Propper 1926-1982 .. CLC 27
See also CA 5-8R; 108; CANR 7

Seton, Ernest (Evan) Thompson 1860-1946
TCLC 31
See also CA 109; DLB 92; DLBD 13; JRDA; SATA 18

Seton-Thompson, Ernest
See Seton, Ernest (Evan) Thompson

Settle, Mary Lee 1918- .... CLC 19, 61
See also CA 89-92; CAAS 1; CANR 44; DLB 6; INT 89-92

Seuphor, Michel
See Arp, Jean

Sevigne, Marie (de Rabutin-Chantal) Marquise de 1626-1696 .... LC 11

Sewall, Samuel 1652-1730 .... LC 38

See also DLB 24

Sexton, Anne (Harvey) 1928-1974 CLC 2, 4, 6, 8, 10, 15, 53; DA; DAB; DAC; DAM MST, POET; PC 2; WLC
See also CA 1-4R; 53-56; CABS 2; CANR 3, 36; CDALB 1941-1968; DLB 5, 169; MTCW; SATA 10

Shaara, Michael (Joseph, Jr.) 1929-1988 CLC 15; DAM POP
See also AITN 1; CA 102; 125; CANR 52; DLBY 83

Shackleton, C. C.
See Aldiss, Brian W(ilson)

Shacochis, Bob .... CLC 39
See also Shacochis, Robert G.

Shacochis, Robert G. 1951-
See Shacochis, Bob
See also CA 119; 124; INT 124

Shaffer, Anthony (Joshua) 1926- .... CLC 19; DAM DRAM
See also CA 110; 116; DLB 13

Shaffer, Peter (Levin) 1926- CLC 5, 14, 18, 37, 60; DAB; DAM DRAM, MST; DC 7
See also CA 25-28R; CANR 25, 47; CDBLB 1960 to Present; DLB 13; MTCW

Shakey, Bernard
See Young, Neil

Shalamov, Varlam (Tikhonovich) 1907(?)-1982
CLC 18
See also CA 129; 105

Shamlu, Ahmad 1925- .... CLC 10

Shammas, Anton 1951- .... CLC 55

Shange, Ntozake 1948- ..... CLC 8, 25, 38, 74; BLC; DAM DRAM, MULT; DC 3
See also AAYA 9; BW 2; CA 85-88; CABS 3; CANR 27, 48; DLB 38; MTCW

Shanley, John Patrick 1950- .... CLC 75
See also CA 128; 133

Shapcott, Thomas W(illiam) 1935- . CLC 38
See also CA 69-72; CANR 49

Shapiro, Jane .... CLC 76

Shapiro, Karl (Jay) 1913- ... CLC 4, 8, 15, 53
See also CA 1-4R; CAAS 6; CANR 1, 36; DLB 48; MTCW

Sharp, William 1855-1905 .... TCLC 39
See also CA 160; DLB 156

Sharpe, Thomas Ridley 1928-
See Sharpe, Tom
See also CA 114; 122; INT 122

Sharpe, Tom .... CLC 36
See also Sharpe, Thomas Ridley
See also DLB 14

Shaw, Bernard .... TCLC 45
See also Shaw, George Bernard
See also BW 1

Shaw, G. Bernard
See Shaw, George Bernard

Shaw, George Bernard 1856-1950 TCLC 3, 9, 21; DA; DAB; DAC; DAM DRAM, MST; WLC
See also Shaw, Bernard
See also CA 104; 128; CDBLB 1914-1945; DLB 10, 57; MTCW

Shaw, Henry Wheeler 1818-1885 .. NCLC 15
See also DLB 11

Shaw, Irwin 1913-1984 CLC 7, 23, 34; DAM DRAM, POP
See also AITN 1; CA 13-16R; 112; CANR 21; CDALB 1941-1968; DLB 6, 102; DLBY 84; MTCW

Shaw, Robert 1927-1978 .... CLC 5
See also AITN 1; CA 1-4R; 81-84; CANR 4; DLB 13, 14

Shaw, T. E.
See Lawrence, T(homas) E(dward)

Shawn, Wallace 1943- .... CLC 41
See also CA 112

Shea, Lisa 1953- .... **CLC 86**
See also CA 147
Sheed, Wilfrid (John Joseph) 1930- **CLC 2, 4, 10, 53**
See also CA 65-68; CANR 30; DLB 6; MTCW
Sheldon, Alice Hastings Bradley 1915(?)-1987
See Tiptree, James, Jr.
See also CA 108; 122; CANR 34; INT 108; MTCW
Sheldon, John
See Bloch, Robert (Albert)
Shelley, Mary Wollstonecraft (Godwin) 1797-1851 **NCLC 14, 59; DA; DAB; DAC; DAM MST, NOV; WLC**
See also AAYA 20; CDBLB 1789-1832; DLB 110, 116, 159, 178; SATA 29
Shelley, Percy Bysshe 1792-1822 . **NCLC 18; DA; DAB; DAC; DAM MST, POET; PC 14; WLC**
See also CDBLB 1789-1832; DLB 96, 110, 158
Shepard, Jim 1956- .... **CLC 36**
See also CA 137; CANR 59; SATA 90
Shepard, Lucius 1947- .... **CLC 34**
See also CA 128; 141
Shepard, Sam 1943- **CLC 4, 6, 17, 34, 41, 44; DAM DRAM; DC 5**
See also AAYA 1; CA 69-72; CABS 3; CANR 22; DLB 7; MTCW
Shepherd, Michael
See Ludlum, Robert
Sherburne, Zoa (Morin) 1912- .... **CLC 30**
See also AAYA 13; CA 1-4R; CANR 3, 37; MAICYA; SAAS 18; SATA 3
Sheridan, Frances 1724-1766 .... **LC 7**
See also DLB 39, 84
Sheridan, Richard Brinsley 1751-1816 **NCLC 5; DA; DAB; DAC; DAM DRAM, MST; DC 1; WLC**
See also CDBLB 1660-1789; DLB 89
Sherman, Jonathan Marc .... **CLC 55**
Sherman, Martin 1941(?)- .... **CLC 19**
See also CA 116; 123
Sherwin, Judith Johnson 1936- ... **CLC 7, 15**
See also CA 25-28R; CANR 34
Sherwood, Frances 1940- .... **CLC 81**
See also CA 146
Sherwood, Robert E(mmet) 1896-1955 **TCLC 3; DAM DRAM**
See also CA 104; 153; DLB 7, 26
Shestov, Lev 1866-1938 .... **TCLC 56**
Shevchenko, Taras 1814-1861 .... **NCLC 54**
Shiel, M(atthew) P(hipps) 1865-1947 **TCLC 8**
See also Holmes, Gordon
See also CA 106; 160; DLB 153
Shields, Carol 1935- .... **CLC 91; DAC**
See also CA 81-84; CANR 51
Shields, David 1956- .... **CLC 97**
See also CA 124; CANR 48
Shiga, Naoya 1883-1971 ..... **CLC 33; SSC 23**
See also CA 101; 33-36R; DLB 180
Shilts, Randy 1951-1994 .... **CLC 85**
See also AAYA 19; CA 115; 127; 144; CANR 45; INT 127
Shimazaki, Haruki 1872-1943
See Shimazaki Toson
See also CA 105; 134
Shimazaki Toson 1872-1943 .... **TCLC 5**
See also Shimazaki, Haruki
See also DLB 180
Sholokhov, Mikhail (Aleksandrovich) 1905-1984 .... **CLC 7, 15**
See also CA 101; 112; MTCW; SATA-Obit 36
Shone, Patric
See Hanley, James
Shreve, Susan Richards 1939- .... **CLC 23**
See also CA 49-52; CAAS 5; CANR 5, 38; MAICYA; SATA 46, 95; SATA-Brief 41

Shue, Larry 1946-1985 **CLC 52; DAM DRAM**
See also CA 145; 117
Shu-Jen, Chou 1881-1936
See Lu Hsun
See also CA 104
Shulman, Alix Kates 1932- .... **CLC 2, 10**
See also CA 29-32R; CANR 43; SATA 7
Shuster, Joe 1914- .... **CLC 21**
Shute, Nevil .... **CLC 30**
See also Norway, Nevil Shute
Shuttle, Penelope (Diane) 1947- .... **CLC 7**
See also CA 93-96; CANR 39; DLB 14, 40
Sidney, Mary 1561-1621 .... **LC 19, 39**
Sidney, Sir Philip 1554-1586 **LC 19, 39; DA; DAB; DAC; DAM MST, POET**
See also CDBLB Before 1660; DLB 167
Siegel, Jerome 1914-1996 .... **CLC 21**
See also CA 116; 151
Siegel, Jerry
See Siegel, Jerome
Sienkiewicz, Henryk (Adam Alexander Pius) 1846-1916 .... **TCLC 3**
See also CA 104; 134
Sierra, Gregorio Martinez
See Martinez Sierra, Gregorio
Sierra, Maria (de la O'LeJarraga) Martinez
See Martinez Sierra, Maria (de la O'LeJarraga)
Sigal, Clancy 1926- .... **CLC 7**
See also CA 1-4R
Sigourney, Lydia Howard (Huntley) 1791-1865 **NCLC 21**
See also DLB 1, 42, 73
Siguenza y Gongora, Carlos de 1645-1700 **LC 8**
Sigurjonsson, Johann 1880-1919 ... **TCLC 27**
Sikelianos, Angelos 1884-1951 .... **TCLC 39**
Silkin, Jon 1930- .... **CLC 2, 6, 43**
See also CA 5-8R; CAAS 5; DLB 27
Silko, Leslie (Marmon) 1948- **CLC 23, 74; DA; DAC; DAM MST, MULT, POP; WLCS**
See also AAYA 14; CA 115; 122; CANR 45; DLB 143, 175; NNAL
Sillanpaa, Frans Eemil 1888-1964 .... **CLC 19**
See also CA 129; 93-96; MTCW
Sillitoe, Alan 1928- .... **CLC 1, 3, 6, 10, 19, 57**
See also AITN 1; CA 9-12R; CAAS 2; CANR 8, 26, 55; CDBLB 1960 to Present; DLB 14, 139; MTCW; SATA 61
Silone, Ignazio 1900-1978 .... **CLC 4**
See also CA 25-28; 81-84; CANR 34; CAP 2; MTCW
Silver, Joan Micklin 1935- .... **CLC 20**
See also CA 114; 121; INT 121
Silver, Nicholas
See Faust, Frederick (Schiller)
Silverberg, Robert 1935- **CLC 7; DAM POP**
See also CA 1-4R; CAAS 3; CANR 1, 20, 36; DLB 8; INT CANR-20; MAICYA; MTCW; SATA 13, 91
Silverstein, Alvin 1933- .... **CLC 17**
See also CA 49-52; CANR 2; CLR 25; JRDA; MAICYA; SATA 8, 69
Silverstein, Virginia B(arbara Opshelor) 1937- **CLC 17**
See also CA 49-52; CANR 2; CLR 25; JRDA; MAICYA; SATA 8, 69
Sim, Georges
See Simenon, Georges (Jacques Christian)
Simak, Clifford D(onald) 1904-1988 **CLC 1, 55**
See also CA 1-4R; 125; CANR 1, 35; DLB 8; MTCW; SATA-Obit 56
Simenon, Georges (Jacques Christian) 1903-1989 .. **CLC 1, 2, 3, 8, 18, 47; DAM POP**
See also CA 85-88; 129; CANR 35; DLB 72; DLBY 89; MTCW
Simic, Charles 1938- .... **CLC 6, 9, 22, 49, 68; DAM POET**

See also CA 29-32R; CAAS 4; CANR 12, 33, 52, 61; DLB 105
Simmel, Georg 1858-1918 .... **TCLC 64**
See also CA 157
Simmons, Charles (Paul) 1924- .... **CLC 57**
See also CA 89-92; INT 89-92
Simmons, Dan 1948- ..... **CLC 44; DAM POP**
See also AAYA 16; CA 138; CANR 53
Simmons, James (Stewart Alexander) 1933- **CLC 43**
See also CA 105; CAAS 21; DLB 40
Simms, William Gilmore 1806-1870 **NCLC 3**
See also DLB 3, 30, 59, 73
Simon, Carly 1945- .... **CLC 26**
See also CA 105
Simon, Claude 1913- **CLC 4, 9, 15, 39; DAM NOV**
See also CA 89-92; CANR 33; DLB 83; MTCW
Simon, (Marvin) Neil 1927- **CLC 6, 11, 31, 39, 70; DAM DRAM**
See also AITN 1; CA 21-24R; CANR 26, 54; DLB 7; MTCW
Simon, Paul (Frederick) 1941(?)- ..... **CLC 17**
See also CA 116; 153
Simonon, Paul 1956(?)- .... **CLC 30**
Simpson, Harriette
See Arnow, Harriette (Louisa) Simpson
Simpson, Louis (Aston Marantz) 1923- **CLC 4, 7, 9, 32; DAM POET**
See also CA 1-4R; CAAS 4; CANR 1, 61; DLB 5; MTCW
Simpson, Mona (Elizabeth) 1957- .... **CLC 44**
See also CA 122; 135
Simpson, N(orman) F(rederick) 1919- **CLC 29**
See also CA 13-16R; DLB 13
Sinclair, Andrew (Annandale) 1935- **CLC 2, 14**
See also CA 9-12R; CAAS 5; CANR 14, 38; DLB 14; MTCW
Sinclair, Emil
See Hesse, Hermann
Sinclair, Iain 1943- .... **CLC 76**
See also CA 132
Sinclair, Iain MacGregor
See Sinclair, Iain
Sinclair, Irene
See Griffith, D(avid Lewelyn) W(ark)
Sinclair, Mary Amelia St. Clair 1865(?)-1946
See Sinclair, May
See also CA 104
Sinclair, May .... **TCLC 3, 11**
See also Sinclair, Mary Amelia St. Clair
See also DLB 36, 135
Sinclair, Roy
See Griffith, D(avid Lewelyn) W(ark)
Sinclair, Upton (Beall) 1878-1968 **CLC 1, 11, 15, 63; DA; DAB; DAC; DAM MST, NOV; WLC**
See also CA 5-8R; 25-28R; CANR 7; CDALB 1929-1941; DLB 9; INT CANR-7; MTCW; SATA 9
Singer, Isaac
See Singer, Isaac Bashevis
Singer, Isaac Bashevis 1904-1991 **CLC 1, 3, 6, 9, 11, 15, 23, 38, 69; DA; DAB; DAC; DAM MST, NOV; SSC 3; WLC**
See also AITN 1, 2; CA 1-4R; 134; CANR 1, 39; CDALB 1941-1968; CLR 1; DLB 6, 28, 52; DLBY 91; JRDA; MAICYA; MTCW; SATA 3, 27; SATA-Obit 68
Singer, Israel Joshua 1893-1944 .... **TCLC 33**
Singh, Khushwant 1915- .... **CLC 11**
See also CA 9-12R; CANR 6
Singleton, Ann
See Benedict, Ruth (Fulton)
Sinjohn, John
See Galsworthy, John

Sinyavsky, Andrei (Donatevich) 1925-1997 CLC 8
See also CA 85-88; 159
Sirin, V.
See Nabokov, Vladimir (Vladimirovich)
Sissman, L(ouis) E(dward) 1928-1976 CLC 9, 18
See also CA 21-24R; 65-68; CANR 13; DLB 5
Sisson, C(harles) H(ubert) 1914- .... CLC 8
See also CA 1-4R; CAAS 3; CANR 3, 48; DLB 27
Sitwell, Dame Edith 1887-1964 CLC 2, 9, 67; **DAM POET; PC 3**
See also CA 9-12R; CANR 35; CDBLB 1945-1960; DLB 20; MTCW
Siwaarmill, H. P.
See Sharp, William
Sjoewall, Maj 1935- .... CLC 7
See also CA 65-68
Sjowall, Maj
See Sjoewall, Maj
Skelton, Robin 1925-1997 .... CLC 13
See also AITN 2; CA 5-8R; 160; CAAS 5; CANR 28; DLB 27, 53
Skolimowski, Jerzy 1938- .... CLC 20
See also CA 128
Skram, Amalie (Bertha) 1847-1905 TCLC 25
Skvorecky, Josef (Vaclav) 1924- CLC 15, 39, 69; DAC; **DAM NOV**
See also CA 61-64; CAAS 1; CANR 10, 34; MTCW
Slade, Bernard .... CLC 11, 46
See also Newbound, Bernard Slade
See also CAAS 9; DLB 53
Slaughter, Carolyn 1946- .... CLC 56
See also CA 85-88
Slaughter, Frank G(ill) 1908- .... CLC 29
See also AITN 2; CA 5-8R; CANR 5; INT CANR-5
Slavitt, David R(ytman) 1935- ..... CLC 5, 14
See also CA 21-24R; CAAS 3; CANR 41; DLB 5, 6
Slesinger, Tess 1905-1945 .... TCLC 10
See also CA 107; DLB 102
Slessor, Kenneth 1901-1971 .... CLC 14
See also CA 102; 89-92
Slowacki, Juliusz 1809-1849 .... NCLC 15
Smart, Christopher 1722-1771 .. LC 3; **DAM POET; PC 13**
See also DLB 109
Smart, Elizabeth 1913-1986 .... CLC 54
See also CA 81-84; 118; DLB 88
Smiley, Jane (Graves) 1949-CLC 53, 76; **DAM POP**
See also CA 104; CANR 30, 50; INT CANR-30
Smith, A(rthur) J(ames) M(arshall) 1902-1980 CLC 15; DAC
See also CA 1-4R; 102; CANR 4; DLB 88
Smith, Adam 1723-1790 .... LC 36
See also DLB 104
Smith, Alexander 1829-1867 .... NCLC 59
See also DLB 32, 55
Smith, Anna Deavere 1950- .... CLC 86
See also CA 133
Smith, Betty (Wehner) 1896-1972 ... CLC 19
See also CA 5-8R; 33-36R; DLBY 82; SATA 6
Smith, Charlotte (Turner) 1749-1806 NCLC 23
See also DLB 39, 109
Smith, Clark Ashton 1893-1961 .... CLC 43
See also CA 143
Smith, Dave .... CLC 22, 42
See also Smith, David (Jeddie)
See also CAAS 7; DLB 5
Smith, David (Jeddie) 1942-
See Smith, Dave
See also CA 49-52; CANR 1, 59; **DAM POET**
Smith, Florence Margaret 1902-1971
See Smith, Stevie
See also CA 17-18; 29-32R; CANR 35; CAP 2; **DAM POET**; MTCW
Smith, Iain Crichton 1928- .... CLC 64
See also CA 21-24R; DLB 40, 139
Smith, John 1580(?)-1631 .... LC 9
Smith, Johnston
See Crane, Stephen (Townley)
Smith, Joseph, Jr. 1805-1844 .... NCLC 53
Smith, Lee 1944- .... CLC 25, 73
See also CA 114; 119; CANR 46; DLB 143; DLBY 83; INT 119
Smith, Martin
See Smith, Martin Cruz
Smith, Martin Cruz 1942- ..... CLC 25; **DAM MULT, POP**
See also BEST 89:4; CA 85-88; CANR 6, 23, 43; INT CANR-23; NNAL
Smith, Mary-Ann Tirone 1944- .... CLC 39
See also CA 118; 136
Smith, Patti 1946- .... CLC 12
See also CA 93-96
Smith, Pauline (Urmson) 1882-1959 TCLC 25
Smith, Rosamond
See Oates, Joyce Carol
Smith, Sheila Kaye
See Kaye-Smith, Sheila
Smith, Stevie .... CLC 3, 8, 25, 44; PC 12
See also Smith, Florence Margaret
See also DLB 20
Smith, Wilbur (Addison) 1933- .... CLC 33
See also CA 13-16R; CANR 7, 46; MTCW
Smith, William Jay 1918- .... CLC 6
See also CA 5-8R; CANR 44; DLB 5; MAICYA; SAAS 22; SATA 2, 68
Smith, Woodrow Wilson
See Kuttner, Henry
Smolenskin, Peretz 1842-1885 .... NCLC 30
Smollett, Tobias (George) 1721-1771 ... LC 2
See also CDBLB 1660-1789; DLB 39, 104
Snodgrass, W(illiam) D(e Witt) 1926-CLC 2, 6, 10, 18, 68; **DAM POET**
See also CA 1-4R; CANR 6, 36; DLB 5; MTCW
Snow, C(harles) P(ercy) 1905-1980 CLC 1, 4, 6, 9, 13, 19; **DAM NOV**
See also CA 5-8R; 101; CANR 28; CDBLB 1945-1960; DLB 15, 77; MTCW
Snow, Frances Compton
See Adams, Henry (Brooks)
Snyder, Gary (Sherman) 1930-CLC 1, 2, 5, 9, 32; **DAM POET**
See also CA 17-20R; CANR 30, 60; DLB 5, 16, 165
Snyder, Zilpha Keatley 1927- .... CLC 17
See also AAYA 15; CA 9-12R; CANR 38; CLR 31; JRDA; MAICYA; SAAS 2; SATA 1, 28, 75
Soares, Bernardo
See Pessoa, Fernando (Antonio Nogueira)
Sobh, A.
See Shamlu, Ahmad
Sobol, Joshua .... CLC 60
Soderberg, Hjalmar 1869-1941 ..... TCLC 39
Sodergran, Edith (Irene)
See Soedergran, Edith (Irene)
Soedergran, Edith (Irene) 1892-1923. TCLC 31
Softly, Edgar
See Lovecraft, H(oward) P(hillips)
Softly, Edward
See Lovecraft, H(oward) P(hillips)
Sokolov, Raymond 1941- .... CLC 7
See also CA 85-88
Solo, Jay
See Ellison, Harlan (Jay)
Sologub, Fyodor .... TCLC 9
See also Teternikov, Fyodor Kuzmich
Solomons, Ikey Esquir
See Thackeray, William Makepeace
Solomos, Dionysios 1798-1857 .... NCLC 15
Solwoska, Mara
See French, Marilyn
Solzhenitsyn, Aleksandr I(sayevich) 1918- CLC 1, 2, 4, 7, 9, 10, 18, 26, 34, 78; DA; DAB; DAC; **DAM MST, NOV; WLC**
See also AITN 1; CA 69-72; CANR 40; MTCW
Somers, Jane
See Lessing, Doris (May)
Somerville, Edith 1858-1949 .... TCLC 51
See also DLB 135
Somerville & Ross
See Martin, Violet Florence; Somerville, Edith
Sommer, Scott 1951- .... CLC 25
See also CA 106
Sondheim, Stephen (Joshua) 1930- CLC 30, 39; **DAM DRAM**
See also AAYA 11; CA 103; CANR 47
Sontag, Susan 1933-CLC 1, 2, 10, 13, 31, 105; **DAM POP**
See also CA 17-20R; CANR 25, 51; DLB 2, 67; MTCW
Sophocles 496(?)B.C.-406(?)B.C. .. CMLC 2; DA; DAB; DAC; **DAM DRAM, MST; DC 1; WLCS**
See also DLB 176
Sordello 1189-1269 .... CMLC 15
Sorel, Julia
See Drexler, Rosalyn
Sorrentino, Gilbert 1929-CLC 3, 7, 14, 22, 40
See also CA 77-80; CANR 14, 33; DLB 5, 173; DLBY 80; INT CANR-14
Soto, Gary 1952- CLC 32, 80; **DAM MULT; HLC**
See also AAYA 10; CA 119; 125; CANR 50; CLR 38; DLB 82; HW; INT 125; JRDA; SATA 80
Soupault, Philippe 1897-1990 .... CLC 68
See also CA 116; 147; 131
Souster, (Holmes) Raymond 1921-CLC 5, 14; DAC; **DAM POET**
See also CA 13-16R; CAAS 14; CANR 13, 29, 53; DLB 88; SATA 63
Southern, Terry 1924(?)-1995 .... CLC 7
See also CA 1-4R; 150; CANR 1, 55; DLB 2
Southey, Robert 1774-1843 .... NCLC 8
See also DLB 93, 107, 142; SATA 54
Southworth, Emma Dorothy Eliza Nevitte 1819-1899 .... NCLC 26
Souza, Ernest
See Scott, Evelyn
Soyinka, Wole 1934- .... CLC 3, 5, 14, 36, 44; BLC; DA; DAB; DAC; **DAM DRAM, MST, MULT; DC 2; WLC**
See also BW 2; CA 13-16R; CANR 27, 39; DLB 125; MTCW
Spackman, W(illiam) M(ode) 1905-1990 CLC 46
See also CA 81-84; 132
Spacks, Barry (Bernard) 1931- .... CLC 14
See also CA 154; CANR 33; DLB 105
Spanidou, Irini 1946- .... CLC 44
Spark, Muriel (Sarah) 1918-CLC 2, 3, 5, 8, 13, 18, 40, 94; DAB; DAC; **DAM MST, NOV; SSC 10**
See also CA 5-8R; CANR 12, 36; CDBLB 1945-1960; DLB 15, 139; INT CANR-12; MTCW
Spaulding, Douglas
See Bradbury, Ray (Douglas)
Spaulding, Leonard
See Bradbury, Ray (Douglas)

Spence, J. A. D.
See Eliot, T(homas) S(tearns)

Spencer, Elizabeth 1921- .... **CLC 22**
See also CA 13-16R; CANR 32; DLB 6; MTCW; SATA 14

Spencer, Leonard G.
See Silverberg, Robert

Spencer, Scott 1945- .... **CLC 30**
See also CA 113; CANR 51; DLBY 86

Spender, Stephen (Harold) 1909-1995 **CLC 1, 2, 5, 10, 41, 91; DAM POET**
See also CA 9-12R; 149; CANR 31, 54; CDBLB 1945-1960; DLB 20; MTCW

Spengler, Oswald (Arnold Gottfried) 1880-1936 **TCLC 25**
See also CA 118

Spenser, Edmund 1552(?)-1599 **LC 5, 39; DA; DAB; DAC; DAM MST, POET; PC 8; WLC**
See also CDBLB Before 1660; DLB 167

Spicer, Jack 1925-1965 **CLC 8, 18, 72; DAM POET**
See also CA 85-88; DLB 5, 16

Spiegelman, Art 1948- .... **CLC 76**
See also AAYA 10; CA 125; CANR 41, 55

Spielberg, Peter 1929- .... **CLC 6**
See also CA 5-8R; CANR 4, 48; DLBY 81

Spielberg, Steven 1947- .... **CLC 20**
See also AAYA 8; CA 77-80; CANR 32; SATA 32

Spillane, Frank Morrison 1918-
See Spillane, Mickey
See also CA 25-28R; CANR 28; MTCW; SATA 66

Spillane, Mickey .... **CLC 3, 13**
See also Spillane, Frank Morrison

Spinoza, Benedictus de 1632-1677 .... **LC 9**

Spinrad, Norman (Richard) 1940- .. **CLC 46**
See also CA 37-40R; CAAS 19; CANR 20; DLB 8; INT CANR-20

Spitteler, Carl (Friedrich Georg) 1845-1924 **TCLC 12**
See also CA 109; DLB 129

Spivack, Kathleen (Romola Drucker) 1938- **CLC 6**
See also CA 49-52

Spoto, Donald 1941- .... **CLC 39**
See also CA 65-68; CANR 11, 57

Springsteen, Bruce (F.) 1949- .... **CLC 17**
See also CA 111

Spurling, Hilary 1940- .... **CLC 34**
See also CA 104; CANR 25, 52

Spyker, John Howland
See Elman, Richard

Squires, (James) Radcliffe 1917-1993 **CLC 51**
See also CA 1-4R; 140; CANR 6, 21

Srivastava, Dhanpat Rai 1880(?)-1936
See Premchand
See also CA 118

Stacy, Donald
See Pohl, Frederik

Stael, Germaine de
See Stael-Holstein, Anne Louise Germaine Necker Baronn
See also DLB 119

Stael-Holstein, Anne Louise Germaine Necker Baronn 1766-1817 .... **NCLC 3**
See also Stael, Germaine de

Stafford, Jean 1915-1979 **CLC 4, 7, 19, 68; SSC 26**
See also CA 1-4R; 85-88; CANR 3; DLB 2, 173; MTCW; SATA-Obit 22

Stafford, William (Edgar) 1914-1993 **CLC 4, 7, 29; DAM POET**
See also CA 5-8R; 142; CAAS 3; CANR 5, 22; DLB 5; INT CANR-22

Stagnelius, Eric Johan 1793-1823 . **NCLC 61**

Staines, Trevor
See Brunner, John (Kilian Houston)

Stairs, Gordon
See Austin, Mary (Hunter)

Stannard, Martin 1947- .... **CLC 44**
See also CA 142; DLB 155

Stanton, Elizabeth Cady 1815-1902 **TCLC 73**
See also DLB 79

Stanton, Maura 1946- .... **CLC 9**
See also CA 89-92; CANR 15; DLB 120

Stanton, Schuyler
See Baum, L(yman) Frank

Stapledon, (William) Olaf 1886-1950 **TCLC 22**
See also CA 111; DLB 15

Starbuck, George (Edwin) 1931-1996 **CLC 53; DAM POET**
See also CA 21-24R; 153; CANR 23

Stark, Richard
See Westlake, Donald E(dwin)

Staunton, Schuyler
See Baum, L(yman) Frank

Stead, Christina (Ellen) 1902-1983 **CLC 2, 5, 8, 32, 80**
See also CA 13-16R; 109; CANR 33, 40; MTCW

Stead, William Thomas 1849-1912 **TCLC 48**

Steele, Richard 1672-1729 .... **LC 18**
See also CDBLB 1660-1789; DLB 84, 101

Steele, Timothy (Reid) 1948- .... **CLC 45**
See also CA 93-96; CANR 16, 50; DLB 120

Steffens, (Joseph) Lincoln 1866-1936 . **TCLC 20**
See also CA 117

Stegner, Wallace (Earle) 1909-1993 .. **CLC 9, 49, 81; DAM NOV; SSC 11**
See also AITN 1; BEST 90:3; CA 1-4R; 141; CAAS 9; CANR 1, 21, 46; DLB 9; DLBY 93; MTCW

Stein, Gertrude 1874-1946 **TCLC 1, 6, 28, 48; DA; DAB; DAC; DAM MST, NOV, POET; PC 18; WLC**
See also CA 104; 132; CDALB 1917-1929; DLB 4, 54, 86; DLBD 15; MTCW

Steinbeck, John (Ernst) 1902-1968 **CLC 1, 5, 9, 13, 21, 34, 45, 75; DA; DAB; DAC; DAM DRAM, MST, NOV; SSC 11; WLC**
See also AAYA 12; CA 1-4R; 25-28R; CANR 1, 35; CDALB 1929-1941; DLB 7, 9; DLBD 2; MTCW; SATA 9

Steinem, Gloria 1934- .... **CLC 63**
See also CA 53-56; CANR 28, 51; MTCW

Steiner, George 1929- .. **CLC 24; DAM NOV**
See also CA 73-76; CANR 31; DLB 67; MTCW; SATA 62

Steiner, K. Leslie
See Delany, Samuel R(ay, Jr.)

Steiner, Rudolf 1861-1925 .... **TCLC 13**
See also CA 107

Stendhal 1783-1842 **NCLC 23, 46; DA; DAB; DAC; DAM MST, NOV; SSC 27; WLC**
See also DLB 119

Stephen, Leslie 1832-1904 .... **TCLC 23**
See also CA 123; DLB 57, 144

Stephen, Sir Leslie
See Stephen, Leslie

Stephen, Virginia
See Woolf, (Adeline) Virginia

Stephens, James 1882(?)-1950 .... **TCLC 4**
See also CA 104; DLB 19, 153, 162

Stephens, Reed
See Donaldson, Stephen R.

Steptoe, Lydia
See Barnes, Djuna

Sterchi, Beat 1949- .... **CLC 65**

Sterling, Brett
See Bradbury, Ray (Douglas); Hamilton, Edmond

Sterling, Bruce 1954- .... **CLC 72**
See also CA 119; CANR 44

Sterling, George 1869-1926 .... **TCLC 20**
See also CA 117; DLB 54

Stern, Gerald 1925- .... **CLC 40, 100**
See also CA 81-84; CANR 28; DLB 105

Stern, Richard (Gustave) 1928- ... **CLC 4, 39**
See also CA 1-4R; CANR 1, 25, 52; DLBY 87; INT CANR-25

Sternberg, Josef von 1894-1969 .... **CLC 20**
See also CA 81-84

Sterne, Laurence 1713-1768 **LC 2; DA; DAB; DAC; DAM MST, NOV; WLC**
See also CDBLB 1660-1789; DLB 39

Sternheim, (William Adolf) Carl 1878-1942 **TCLC 8**
See also CA 105; DLB 56, 118

Stevens, Mark 1951- .... **CLC 34**
See also CA 122

Stevens, Wallace 1879-1955 **TCLC 3, 12, 45; DA; DAB; DAC; DAM MST, POET; PC 6; WLC**
See also CA 104; 124; CDALB 1929-1941; DLB 54; MTCW

Stevenson, Anne (Katharine) 1933- **CLC 7, 33**
See also CA 17-20R; CAAS 9; CANR 9, 33; DLB 40; MTCW

Stevenson, Robert Louis (Balfour) 1850-1894 **NCLC 5, 14, 63; DA; DAB; DAC; DAM MST, NOV; SSC 11; WLC**
See also CDBLB 1890-1914; CLR 10, 11; DLB 18, 57, 141, 156, 174; DLBD 13; JRDA; MAICYA; YABC 2

Stewart, J(ohn) I(nnes) M(ackintosh) 1906-1994 .... **CLC 7, 14, 32**
See also CA 85-88; 147; CAAS 3; CANR 47; MTCW

Stewart, Mary (Florence Elinor) 1916- **CLC 7, 35; DAB**
See also CA 1-4R; CANR 1, 59; SATA 12

Stewart, Mary Rainbow
See Stewart, Mary (Florence Elinor)

Stifle, June
See Campbell, Maria

Stifter, Adalbert 1805-1868 **NCLC 41; SSC 28**
See also DLB 133

Still, James 1906- .... **CLC 49**
See also CA 65-68; CAAS 17; CANR 10, 26; DLB 9; SATA 29

Sting
See Sumner, Gordon Matthew

Stirling, Arthur
See Sinclair, Upton (Beall)

Stitt, Milan 1941- .... **CLC 29**
See also CA 69-72

Stockton, Francis Richard 1834-1902
See Stockton, Frank R.
See also CA 108; 137; MAICYA; SATA 44

Stockton, Frank R. .... **TCLC 47**
See also Stockton, Francis Richard
See also DLB 42, 74; DLBD 13; SATA-Brief 32

Stoddard, Charles
See Kuttner, Henry

Stoker, Abraham 1847-1912
See Stoker, Bram
See also CA 105; DA; DAC; DAM MST, NOV; SATA 29

Stoker, Bram 1847-1912 **TCLC 8; DAB; WLC**
See also Stoker, Abraham
See also CA 150; CDBLB 1890-1914; DLB 36, 70, 178

Stolz, Mary (Slattery) 1920- .... **CLC 12**
See also AAYA 8; AITN 1; CA 5-8R; CANR 13, 41; JRDA; MAICYA; SAAS 3; SATA 10, 71

Stone, Irving 1903-1989 .. **CLC 7; DAM POP**
See also AITN 1; CA 1-4R; 129; CAAS 3; CANR 1, 23; INT CANR-23; MTCW; SATA 3; SATA-Obit 64

Stone, Oliver (William) 1946- .... **CLC 73**
See also AAYA 15; CA 110; CANR 55

Stone, Robert (Anthony) 1937-**CLC 5, 23, 42**
See also CA 85-88; CANR 23; DLB 152; INT CANR-23; MTCW

Stone, Zachary
See Follett, Ken(neth Martin)

Stoppard, Tom 1937-**CLC 1, 3, 4, 5, 8, 15, 29, 34, 63, 91; DA; DAB; DAC; DAM DRAM, MST; DC 6; WLC**
See also CA 81-84; CANR 39; CDBLB 1960 to Present; DLB 13; DLBY 85; MTCW

Storey, David (Malcolm) 1933-**CLC 2, 4, 5, 8; DAM DRAM**
See also CA 81-84; CANR 36; DLB 13, 14; MTCW

Storm, Hyemeyohsts 1935- ...... **CLC 3; DAM MULT**
See also CA 81-84; CANR 45; NNAL

Storm, (Hans) Theodor (Woldsen) 1817-1888 **NCLC 1; SSC 27**

Storni, Alfonsina 1892-1938 . **TCLC 5; DAM MULT; HLC**
See also CA 104; 131; HW

Stoughton, William 1631-1701 .... **LC 38**
See also DLB 24

Stout, Rex (Todhunter) 1886-1975 ..... **CLC 3**
See also AITN 2; CA 61-64

Stow, (Julian) Randolph 1935- .. **CLC 23, 48**
See also CA 13-16R; CANR 33; MTCW

Stowe, Harriet (Elizabeth) Beecher 1811-1896 **NCLC 3, 50; DA; DAB; DAC; DAM MST, NOV; WLC**
See also CDALB 1865-1917; DLB 1, 12, 42, 74; JRDA; MAICYA; YABC 1

Strachey, (Giles) Lytton 1880-1932**TCLC 12**
See also CA 110; DLB 149; DLBD 10

Strand, Mark 1934- **CLC 6, 18, 41, 71; DAM POET**
See also CA 21-24R; CANR 40; DLB 5; SATA 41

Straub, Peter (Francis) 1943- **CLC 28; DAM POP**
See also BEST 89:1; CA 85-88; CANR 28; DLBY 84; MTCW

Strauss, Botho 1944- .... **CLC 22**
See also CA 157; DLB 124

Streatfeild, (Mary) Noel 1895(?)-1986**CLC 21**
See also CA 81-84; 120; CANR 31; CLR 17; DLB 160; MAICYA; SATA 20; SATA-Obit 48

Stribling, T(homas) S(igismund) 1881-1965 **CLC 23**
See also CA 107; DLB 9

Strindberg, (Johan) August 1849-1912**TCLC 1, 8, 21, 47; DA; DAB; DAC; DAM DRAM, MST; WLC**
See also CA 104; 135

Stringer, Arthur 1874-1950 .... **TCLC 37**
See also CA 161; DLB 92

Stringer, David
See Roberts, Keith (John Kingston)

Stroheim, Erich von 1885-1957 ..... **TCLC 71**

Strugatskii, Arkadii (Natanovich) 1925-1991 **CLC 27**
See also CA 106; 135

Strugatskii, Boris (Natanovich) 1933-**CLC 27**
See also CA 106

Strummer, Joe 1953(?)- .... **CLC 30**

Stuart, Don A.
See Campbell, John W(ood, Jr.)

Stuart, Ian
See MacLean, Alistair (Stuart)

Stuart, Jesse (Hilton) 1906-1984**CLC 1, 8, 11, 14, 34**
See also CA 5-8R; 112; CANR 31; DLB 9, 48, 102; DLBY 84; SATA 2; SATA-Obit 36

Sturgeon, Theodore (Hamilton) 1918-1985 **CLC 22, 39**
See also Queen, Ellery
See also CA 81-84; 116; CANR 32; DLB 8; DLBY 85; MTCW

Sturges, Preston 1898-1959 .... **TCLC 48**
See also CA 114; 149; DLB 26

Styron, William 1925-**CLC 1, 3, 5, 11, 15, 60; DAM NOV, POP; SSC 25**
See also BEST 90:4; CA 5-8R; CANR 6, 33; CDALB 1968-1988; DLB 2, 143; DLBY 80; INT CANR-6; MTCW

Suarez Lynch, B.
See Bioy Casares, Adolfo; Borges, Jorge Luis

Su Chien 1884-1918
See Su Man-shu
See also CA 123

Suckow, Ruth 1892-1960 .... **SSC 18**
See also CA 113; DLB 9, 102

Sudermann, Hermann 1857-1928 .. **TCLC 15**
See also CA 107; DLB 118

Sue, Eugene 1804-1857 .... **NCLC 1**
See also DLB 119

Sueskind, Patrick 1949- .... **CLC 44**
See also Suskind, Patrick

Sukenick, Ronald 1932- .... **CLC 3, 4, 6, 48**
See also CA 25-28R; CAAS 8; CANR 32; DLB 173; DLBY 81

Suknaski, Andrew 1942- .... **CLC 19**
See also CA 101; DLB 53

Sullivan, Vernon
See Vian, Boris

Sully Prudhomme 1839-1907 .... **TCLC 31**

Su Man-shu .... **TCLC 24**
See also Su Chien

Summerforest, Ivy B.
See Kirkup, James

Summers, Andrew James 1942- .... **CLC 26**

Summers, Andy
See Summers, Andrew James

Summers, Hollis (Spurgeon, Jr.) 1916- . **CLC 10**
See also CA 5-8R; CANR 3; DLB 6

Summers, (Alphonsus Joseph-Mary Augustus) Montague 1880-1948 .... **TCLC 16**
See also CA 118

Sumner, Gordon Matthew 1951- ...... **CLC 26**

Surtees, Robert Smith 1803-1864 .. **NCLC 14**
See also DLB 21

Susann, Jacqueline 1921-1974 .... **CLC 3**
See also AITN 1; CA 65-68; 53-56; MTCW

Su Shih 1036-1101 .... **CMLC 15**

Suskind, Patrick
See Sueskind, Patrick
See also CA 145

Sutcliff, Rosemary 1920-1992**CLC 26; DAB; DAC; DAM MST, POP**
See also AAYA 10; CA 5-8R; 139; CANR 37; CLR 1, 37; JRDA; MAICYA; SATA 6, 44, 78; SATA-Obit 73

Sutro, Alfred 1863-1933 .... **TCLC 6**
See also CA 105; DLB 10

Sutton, Henry
See Slavitt, David R(ytman)

Svevo, Italo 1861-1928 . **TCLC 2, 35; SSC 25**
See also Schmitz, Aron Hector

Swados, Elizabeth (A.) 1951- .... **CLC 12**
See also CA 97-100; CANR 49; INT 97-100

Swados, Harvey 1920-1972 .... **CLC 5**
See also CA 5-8R; 37-40R; CANR 6; DLB 2

Swan, Gladys 1934- .... **CLC 69**
See also CA 101; CANR 17, 39

Swarthout, Glendon (Fred) 1918-1992**CLC 35**
See also CA 1-4R; 139; CANR 1, 47; SATA 26

Sweet, Sarah C.
See Jewett, (Theodora) Sarah Orne

Swenson, May 1919-1989**CLC 4, 14, 61; DA; DAB; DAC; DAM MST, POET; PC 14**
See also CA 5-8R; 130; CANR 36, 61; DLB 5; MTCW; SATA 15

Swift, Augustus
See Lovecraft, H(oward) P(hillips)

Swift, Graham (Colin) 1949- ...... **CLC 41, 88**
See also CA 117; 122; CANR 46

Swift, Jonathan 1667-1745 **LC 1; DA; DAB; DAC; DAM MST, NOV, POET; PC 9; WLC**
See also CDBLB 1660-1789; DLB 39, 95, 101; SATA 19

Swinburne, Algernon Charles 1837-1909 **TCLC 8, 36; DA; DAB; DAC; DAM MST, POET; WLC**
See also CA 105; 140; CDBLB 1832-1890; DLB 35, 57

Swinfen, Ann .... **CLC 34**

Swinnerton, Frank Arthur 1884-1982**CLC 31**
See also CA 108; DLB 34

Swithen, John
See King, Stephen (Edwin)

Sylvia
See Ashton-Warner, Sylvia (Constance)

Symmes, Robert Edward
See Duncan, Robert (Edward)

Symonds, John Addington 1840-1893 **NCLC 34**
See also DLB 57, 144

Symons, Arthur 1865-1945 .... **TCLC 11**
See also CA 107; DLB 19, 57, 149

Symons, Julian (Gustave) 1912-1994 **CLC 2, 14, 32**
See also CA 49-52; 147; CAAS 3; CANR 3, 33, 59; DLB 87, 155; DLBY 92; MTCW

Synge, (Edmund) J(ohn) M(illington) 1871-1909 .. **TCLC 6, 37; DAM DRAM; DC 2**
See also CA 104; 141; CDBLB 1890-1914; DLB 10, 19

Syruc, J.
See Milosz, Czeslaw

Szirtes, George 1948- .... **CLC 46**
See also CA 109; CANR 27, 61

Szymborska, Wislawa 1923- .... **CLC 99**
See also CA 154; DLBY 96

T. O., Nik
See Annensky, Innokenty (Fyodorovich)

Tabori, George 1914- .... **CLC 19**
See also CA 49-52; CANR 4

Tagore, Rabindranath 1861-1941**TCLC 3, 53; DAM DRAM, POET; PC 8**
See also CA 104; 120; MTCW

Taine, Hippolyte Adolphe 1828-1893 . **NCLC 15**

Talese, Gay 1932- .... **CLC 37**
See also AITN 1; CA 1-4R; CANR 9, 58; INT CANR-9; MTCW

Tallent, Elizabeth (Ann) 1954- .... **CLC 45**
See also CA 117; DLB 130

Tally, Ted 1952- .... **CLC 42**
See also CA 120; 124; INT 124

Tamayo y Baus, Manuel 1829-1898 **NCLC 1**

Tammsaare, A(nton) H(ansen) 1878-1940 **TCLC 27**

Tam'si, Tchicaya U
See Tchicaya, Gerald Felix

Tan, Amy (Ruth) 1952-**CLC 59; DAM MULT, NOV, POP**
See also AAYA 9; BEST 89:3; CA 136; CANR 54; DLB 173; SATA 75

Tandem, Felix
See Spittler, Carl (Friedrich Georg)

Tanizaki, Jun'ichiro 1886-1965 CLC 8, 14, 28; SSC 21
See also CA 93-96; 25-28R; DLB 180
Tanner, William
See Amis, Kingsley (William)
Tao Lao
See Storni, Alfonsina
Tarassoff, Lev
See Troyat, Henri
Tarbell, Ida M(inerva) 1857-1944 . TCLC 40
See also CA 122; DLB 47
Tarkington, (Newton) Booth 1869-1946 TCLC 9
See also CA 110; 143; DLB 9, 102; SATA 17
Tarkovsky, Andrei (Arsenyevich) 1932-1986 CLC 75
See also CA 127
Tartt, Donna 1964(?)- .... CLC 76
See also CA 142
Tasso, Torquato 1544-1595 .... LC 5
Tate, (John Orley) Allen 1899-1979 CLC 2, 4, 6, 9, 11, 14, 24
See also CA 5-8R; 85-88; CANR 32; DLB 4, 45, 63; MTCW
Tate, Ellalice
See Hibbert, Eleanor Alice Burford
Tate, James (Vincent) 1943- ...... CLC 2, 6, 25
See also CA 21-24R; CANR 29, 57; DLB 5, 169
Tavel, Ronald 1940- .... CLC 6
See also CA 21-24R; CANR 33
Taylor, C(ecil) P(hilip) 1929-1981 ... CLC 27
See also CA 25-28R; 105; CANR 47
Taylor, Edward 1642(?)-1729 .... LC 11; DA; DAB; DAC; DAM MST, POET
See also DLB 24
Taylor, Eleanor Ross 1920- .... CLC 5
See also CA 81-84
Taylor, Elizabeth 1912-1975 .... CLC 2, 4, 29
See also CA 13-16R; CANR 9; DLB 139; MTCW; SATA 13
Taylor, Frederick Winslow 1856-1915 T C L C 76
Taylor, Henry (Splawn) 1942- .... CLC 44
See also CA 33-36R; CAAS 7; CANR 31; DLB 5
Taylor, Kamala (Purnaiya) 1924-
See Markandaya, Kamala
See also CA 77-80
Taylor, Mildred D. .... CLC 21
See also AAYA 10; BW 1; CA 85-88; CANR 25; CLR 9; DLB 52; JRDA; MAICYA; SAAS 5; SATA 15, 70
Taylor, Peter (Hillsman) 1917-1994 CLC 1, 4, 18, 37, 44, 50, 71; SSC 10
See also CA 13-16R; 147; CANR 9, 50; DLBY 81, 94; INT CANR-9; MTCW
Taylor, Robert Lewis 1912- .... CLC 14
See also CA 1-4R; CANR 3; SATA 10
Tchekhov, Anton
See Chekhov, Anton (Pavlovich)
Tchicaya, Gerald Felix 1931-1988 . CLC 101
See also CA 129; 125
Tchicaya U Tam'si
See Tchicaya, Gerald Felix
Teasdale, Sara 1884-1933 .... TCLC 4
See also CA 104; DLB 45; SATA 32
Tegner, Esaias 1782-1846 .... NCLC 2
Teilhard de Chardin, (Marie Joseph) Pierre 1881-1955 .... TCLC 9
See also CA 105
Temple, Ann
See Mortimer, Penelope (Ruth)
Tennant, Emma (Christina) 1937- CLC 13, 52
See also CA 65-68; CAAS 9; CANR 10, 38, 59; DLB 14
Tenneshaw, S. M.
See Silverberg, Robert
Tennyson, Alfred 1809-1892 .. NCLC 30, 65; DA; DAB; DAC; DAM MST, POET; PC 6; WLC
See also CDBLB 1832-1890; DLB 32
Teran, Lisa St. Aubin de .... CLC 36
See also St. Aubin de Teran, Lisa
Terence 195(?)B.C.-159B.C. CMLC 14; DC 7
Teresa de Jesus, St. 1515-1582 .... LC 18
Terkel, Louis 1912-
See Terkel, Studs
See also CA 57-60; CANR 18, 45; MTCW
Terkel, Studs .... CLC 38
See also Terkel, Louis
See also AITN 1
Terry, C. V.
See Slaughter, Frank G(ill)
Terry, Megan 1932- .... CLC 19
See also CA 77-80; CABS 3; CANR 43; DLB 7
Tertz, Abram
See Sinyavsky, Andrei (Donatevich)
Tesich, Steve 1943(?)-1996 .... CLC 40, 69
See also CA 105; 152; DLBY 83
Teternikov, Fyodor Kuzmich 1863-1927
See Sologub, Fyodor
See also CA 104
Tevis, Walter 1928-1984 .... CLC 42
See also CA 113
Tey, Josephine .... TCLC 14
See also Mackintosh, Elizabeth
See also DLB 77
Thackeray, William Makepeace 1811-1863 NCLC 5, 14, 22, 43; DA; DAB; DAC; DAM MST, NOV; WLC
See also CDBLB 1832-1890; DLB 21, 55, 159, 163; SATA 23
Thakura, Ravindranatha
See Tagore, Rabindranath
Tharoor, Shashi 1956- .... CLC 70
See also CA 141
Thelwell, Michael Miles 1939- .... CLC 22
See also BW 2; CA 101
Theobald, Lewis, Jr.
See Lovecraft, H(oward) P(hillips)
Theodorescu, Ion N. 1880-1967
See Arghezi, Tudor
See also CA 116
Theriault, Yves 1915-1983 ... CLC 79; DAC; DAM MST
See also CA 102; DLB 88
Theroux, Alexander (Louis) 1939- CLC 2, 25
See also CA 85-88; CANR 20
Theroux, Paul (Edward) 1941- CLC 5, 8, 11, 15, 28, 46; DAM POP
See also BEST 89:4; CA 33-36R; CANR 20, 45; DLB 2; MTCW; SATA 44
Thesen, Sharon 1946- .... CLC 56
Thevenin, Denis
See Duhamel, Georges
Thibault, Jacques Anatole Francois 1844-1924
See France, Anatole
See also CA 106; 127; DAM NOV; MTCW
Thiele, Colin (Milton) 1920- .... CLC 17
See also CA 29-32R; CANR 12, 28, 53; CLR 27; MAICYA; SAAS 2; SATA 14, 72
Thomas, Audrey (Callahan) 1935- CLC 7, 13, 37; SSC 20
See also AITN 2; CA 21-24R; CAAS 19; CANR 36, 58; DLB 60; MTCW
Thomas, D(onald) M(ichael) 1935- . CLC 13, 22, 31
See also CA 61-64; CAAS 11; CANR 17, 45; CDBLB 1960 to Present; DLB 40; INT CANR-17; MTCW
Thomas, Dylan (Marlais) 1914-1953 TCLC 1, 8, 45; DA; DAB; DAC; DAM DRAM, MST, POET; PC 2; SSC 3; WLC
See also CA 104; 120; CDBLB 1945-1960; DLB 13, 20, 139; MTCW; SATA 60
Thomas, (Philip) Edward 1878-1917 . T C L C 10; DAM POET
See also CA 106; 153; DLB 19
Thomas, Joyce Carol 1938- .... CLC 35
See also AAYA 12; BW 2; CA 113; CANR 48; CLR 19; DLB 33; INT 116; JRDA; MAICYA; MTCW; SAAS 7; SATA 40, 78
Thomas, Lewis 1913-1993 .... CLC 35
See also CA 85-88; 143; CANR 38, 60; MTCW
Thomas, Paul
See Mann, (Paul) Thomas
Thomas, Piri 1928- .... CLC 17
See also CA 73-76; HW
Thomas, R(onald) S(tuart) 1913- CLC 6, 13, 48; DAB; DAM POET
See also CA 89-92; CAAS 4; CANR 30; CDBLB 1960 to Present; DLB 27; MTCW
Thomas, Ross (Elmore) 1926-1995 ... CLC 39
See also CA 33-36R; 150; CANR 22
Thompson, Francis Clegg
See Mencken, H(enry) L(ouis)
Thompson, Francis Joseph 1859-1907 TCLC 4
See also CA 104; CDBLB 1890-1914; DLB 19
Thompson, Hunter S(tockton) 1939- . CLC 9, 17, 40, 104; DAM POP
See also BEST 89:1; CA 17-20R; CANR 23, 46; MTCW
Thompson, James Myers
See Thompson, Jim (Myers)
Thompson, Jim (Myers) 1906-1977(?) CLC 69
See also CA 140
Thompson, Judith .... CLC 39
Thomson, James 1700-1748 ... LC 16, 29, 40; DAM POET
See also DLB 95
Thomson, James 1834-1882 NCLC 18; DAM POET
See also DLB 35
Thoreau, Henry David 1817-1862 NCLC 7, 21, 61; DA; DAB; DAC; DAM MST; WLC
See also CDALB 1640-1865; DLB 1
Thornton, Hall
See Silverberg, Robert
Thucydides c. 455B.C.-399B.C. ...... CMLC 17
See also DLB 176
Thurber, James (Grover) 1894-1961 CLC 5, 11, 25; DA; DAB; DAC; DAM DRAM, MST, NOV; SSC 1
See also CA 73-76; CANR 17, 39; CDALB 1929-1941; DLB 4, 11, 22, 102; MAICYA; MTCW; SATA 13
Thurman, Wallace (Henry) 1902-1934 T C L C 6; BLC; DAM MULT
See also BW 1; CA 104; 124; DLB 51
Ticheburn, Cheviot
See Ainsworth, William Harrison
Tieck, (Johann) Ludwig 1773-1853 NCLC 5, 46
See also DLB 90
Tiger, Derry
See Ellison, Harlan (Jay)
Tilghman, Christopher 1948(?)- .... CLC 65
See also CA 159
Tillinghast, Richard (Williford) 1940- CLC 29
See also CA 29-32R; CAAS 23; CANR 26, 51
Timrod, Henry 1828-1867 .... NCLC 25
See also DLB 3
Tindall, Gillian 1938- .... CLC 7
See also CA 21-24R; CANR 11
Tiptree, James, Jr. .... CLC 48, 50
See also Sheldon, Alice Hastings Bradley
See also DLB 8
Titmarsh, Michael Angelo
See Thackeray, William Makepeace

Tocqueville, Alexis (Charles Henri Maurice Clerel Comte) 1805-1859 ... **NCLC 7, 63**

Tolkien, J(ohn) R(onald) R(euel) 1892-1973 **CLC 1, 2, 3, 8, 12, 38; DA; DAB; DAC; DAM MST, NOV, POP; WLC**
See also AAYA 10; AITN 1; CA 17-18; 45-48; CANR 36; CAP 2; CDBLB 1914-1945; DLB 15, 160; JRDA; MAICYA; MTCW; SATA 2, 32; SATA-Obit 24

Toller, Ernst 1893-1939 .... **TCLC 10**
See also CA 107; DLB 124

Tolson, M. B.
See Tolson, Melvin B(eaunorus)

Tolson, Melvin B(eaunorus) 1898(?)-1966 **CLC 36, 105; BLC; DAM MULT, POET**
See also BW 1; CA 124; 89-92; DLB 48, 76

Tolstoi, Aleksei Nikolaevich
See Tolstoy, Alexey Nikolaevich

Tolstoy, Alexey Nikolaevich 1882-1945 **TCLC 18**
See also CA 107; 158

Tolstoy, Count Leo
See Tolstoy, Leo (Nikolaevich)

Tolstoy, Leo (Nikolaevich) 1828-1910 **TCLC 4, 11, 17, 28, 44; DA; DAB; DAC; DAM MST, NOV; SSC 9; WLC**
See also CA 104; 123; SATA 26

Tomasi di Lampedusa, Giuseppe 1896-1957
See Lampedusa, Giuseppe (Tomasi) di
See also CA 111

Tomlin, Lily .... **CLC 17**
See also Tomlin, Mary Jean

Tomlin, Mary Jean 1939(?)-
See Tomlin, Lily
See also CA 117

Tomlinson, (Alfred) Charles 1927- **CLC 2, 4, 6, 13, 45; DAM POET; PC 17**
See also CA 5-8R; CANR 33; DLB 40

Tomlinson, H(enry) M(ajor) 1873-1958 **TCLC 71**
See also CA 118; 161; DLB 36, 100

Tonson, Jacob
See Bennett, (Enoch) Arnold

Toole, John Kennedy 1937-1969 **CLC 19, 64**
See also CA 104; DLBY 81

Toomer, Jean 1894-1967 ... **CLC 1, 4, 13, 22; BLC; DAM MULT; PC 7; SSC 1; WLCS**
See also BW 1; CA 85-88; CDALB 1917-1929; DLB 45, 51; MTCW

Torley, Luke
See Blish, James (Benjamin)

Tornimparte, Alessandra
See Ginzburg, Natalia

Torre, Raoul della
See Mencken, H(enry) L(ouis)

Torrey, E(dwin) Fuller 1937- .... **CLC 34**
See also CA 119

Torsvan, Ben Traven
See Traven, B.

Torsvan, Benno Traven
See Traven, B.

Torsvan, Berick Traven
See Traven, B.

Torsvan, Berwick Traven
See Traven, B.

Torsvan, Bruno Traven
See Traven, B.

Torsvan, Traven
See Traven, B.

Tournier, Michel (Edouard) 1924- **CLC 6, 23, 36, 95**
See also CA 49-52; CANR 3, 36; DLB 83; MTCW; SATA 23

Tournimparte, Alessandra
See Ginzburg, Natalia

Towers, Ivar
See Kornbluth, C(yril) M.

Towne, Robert (Burton) 1936(?)- ..... **CLC 87**
See also CA 108; DLB 44

Townsend, Sue 1946- ... **CLC 61; DAB; DAC**
See also CA 119; 127; INT 127; MTCW; SATA 55, 93; SATA-Brief 48

Townshend, Peter (Dennis Blandford) 1945- **CLC 17, 42**
See also CA 107

Tozzi, Federigo 1883-1920 .... **TCLC 31**
See also CA 160

Traill, Catharine Parr 1802-1899 . **NCLC 31**
See also DLB 99

Trakl, Georg 1887-1914 ...... **TCLC 5; PC 20**
See also CA 104

Transtroemer, Tomas (Goesta) 1931- **CLC 52, 65; DAM POET**
See also CA 117; 129; CAAS 17

Transtromer, Tomas Gosta
See Transtroemer, Tomas (Goesta)

Traven, B. (?)-1969 .... **CLC 8, 11**
See also CA 19-20; 25-28R; CAP 2; DLB 9, 56; MTCW

Treitel, Jonathan 1959- .... **CLC 70**

Tremain, Rose 1943- .... **CLC 42**
See also CA 97-100; CANR 44; DLB 14

Tremblay, Michel 1942- **CLC 29, 102; DAC; DAM MST**
See also CA 116; 128; DLB 60; MTCW

Trevanian .... **CLC 29**
See also Whitaker, Rod(ney)

Trevor, Glen
See Hilton, James

Trevor, William 1928- . **CLC 7, 9, 14, 25, 71; SSC 21**
See also Cox, William Trevor
See also DLB 14, 139

Trifonov, Yuri (Valentinovich) 1925-1981 **CLC 45**
See also CA 126; 103; MTCW

Trilling, Lionel 1905-1975 ...... **CLC 9, 11, 24**
See also CA 9-12R; 61-64; CANR 10; DLB 28, 63; INT CANR-10; MTCW

Trimball, W. H.
See Mencken, H(enry) L(ouis)

Tristan
See Gomez de la Serna, Ramon

Tristram
See Housman, A(lfred) E(dward)

Trogdon, William (Lewis) 1939-
See Heat-Moon, William Least
See also CA 115; 119; CANR 47; INT 119

Trollope, Anthony 1815-1882 .. **NCLC 6, 33; DA; DAB; DAC; DAM MST, NOV; SSC 28; WLC**
See also CDBLB 1832-1890; DLB 21, 57, 159; SATA 22

Trollope, Frances 1779-1863 .... **NCLC 30**
See also DLB 21, 166

Trotsky, Leon 1879-1940 .... **TCLC 22**
See also CA 118

Trotter (Cockburn), Catharine 1679-1749 **LC 8**
See also DLB 84

Trout, Kilgore
See Farmer, Philip Jose

Trow, George W. S. 1943- .... **CLC 52**
See also CA 126

Troyat, Henri 1911- .... **CLC 23**
See also CA 45-48; CANR 2, 33; MTCW

Trudeau, G(arretson) B(eekman) 1948-
See Trudeau, Garry B.
See also CA 81-84; CANR 31; SATA 35

Trudeau, Garry B. .... **CLC 12**
See also Trudeau, G(arretson) B(eekman)
See also AAYA 10; AITN 2

Truffaut, Francois 1932-1984 .. **CLC 20, 101**
See also CA 81-84; 113; CANR 34

Trumbo, Dalton 1905-1976 .... **CLC 19**
See also CA 21-24R; 69-72; CANR 10; DLB 26

Trumbull, John 1750-1831 .... **NCLC 30**
See also DLB 31

Trundlett, Helen B.
See Eliot, T(homas) S(tearns)

Tryon, Thomas 1926-1991 **CLC 3, 11; DAM POP**
See also AITN 1; CA 29-32R; 135; CANR 32; MTCW

Tryon, Tom
See Tryon, Thomas

Ts'ao Hsueh-ch'in 1715(?)-1763 .... **LC 1**

Tsushima, Shuji 1909-1948
See Dazai, Osamu
See also CA 107

Tsvetaeva (Efron), Marina (Ivanovna) 1892-1941 .... **TCLC 7, 35; PC 14**
See also CA 104; 128; MTCW

Tuck, Lily 1938- .... **CLC 70**
See also CA 139

Tu Fu 712-770 .... **PC 9**
See also DAM MULT

Tunis, John R(oberts) 1889-1975 .... **CLC 12**
See also CA 61-64; CANR 62; DLB 22, 171; JRDA; MAICYA; SATA 37; SATA-Brief 30

Tuohy, Frank .... **CLC 37**
See also Tuohy, John Francis
See also DLB 14, 139

Tuohy, John Francis 1925-
See Tuohy, Frank
See also CA 5-8R; CANR 3, 47

Turco, Lewis (Putnam) 1934- .... **CLC 11, 63**
See also CA 13-16R; CAAS 22; CANR 24, 51; DLBY 84

Turgenev, Ivan 1818-1883 .... **NCLC 21; DA; DAB; DAC; DAM MST, NOV; DC 7; SSC 7; WLC**

Turgot, Anne-Robert-Jacques 1727-1781 **LC 26**

Turner, Frederick 1943- .... **CLC 48**
See also CA 73-76; CAAS 10; CANR 12, 30, 56; DLB 40

Tutu, Desmond M(pilo) 1931- **CLC 80; BLC; DAM MULT**
See also BW 1; CA 125

Tutuola, Amos 1920-1997 **CLC 5, 14, 29; BLC; DAM MULT**
See also BW 2; CA 9-12R; 159; CANR 27; DLB 125; MTCW

Twain, Mark **TCLC 6, 12, 19, 36, 48, 59; SSC 26; WLC**
See also Clemens, Samuel Langhorne
See also AAYA 20; DLB 11, 12, 23, 64, 74

Tyler, Anne 1941- . **CLC 7, 11, 18, 28, 44, 59, 103; DAM NOV, POP**
See also AAYA 18; BEST 89:1; CA 9-12R; CANR 11, 33, 53; DLB 6, 143; DLBY 82; MTCW; SATA 7, 90

Tyler, Royall 1757-1826 .... **NCLC 3**
See also DLB 37

Tynan, Katharine 1861-1931 .... **TCLC 3**
See also CA 104; DLB 153

Tyutchev, Fyodor 1803-1873 .... **NCLC 34**

Tzara, Tristan 1896-1963 ...... **CLC 47; DAM POET**
See also Rosenfeld, Samuel; Rosenstock, Sami; Rosenstock, Samuel
See also CA 153

Uhry, Alfred 1936- .. **CLC 55; DAM DRAM, POP**
See also CA 127; 133; INT 133

Ulf, Haerved
See Strindberg, (Johan) August

Ulf, Harved
See Strindberg, (Johan) August

Ulibarri, Sabine R(eyes) 1919- CLC **83**; DAM MULT
See also CA 131; DLB 82; HW
Unamuno (y Jugo), Miguel de 1864-1936 TCLC **2, 9**; DAM MULT, NOV; HLC; SSC **11**
See also CA 104; 131; DLB 108; HW; MTCW
Undercliffe, Errol
See Campbell, (John) Ramsey
Underwood, Miles
See Glassco, John
Undset, Sigrid 1882-1949 TCLC **3**; DA; DAB; DAC; DAM MST, NOV; WLC
See also CA 104; 129; MTCW
Ungaretti, Giuseppe 1888-1970 CLC **7, 11, 15**
See also CA 19-20; 25-28R; CAP 2; DLB 114
Unger, Douglas 1952- .... CLC **34**
See also CA 130
Unsworth, Barry (Forster) 1930- ..... CLC **76**
See also CA 25-28R; CANR 30, 54
Updike, John (Hoyer) 1932- CLC **1, 2, 3, 5, 7, 9, 13, 15, 23, 34, 43, 70**; DA; DAB; DAC; DAM MST, NOV, POET, POP; SSC **13, 27**; WLC
See also CA 1-4R; CABS 1; CANR 4, 33, 51; CDALB 1968-1988; DLB 2, 5, 143; DLBD 3; DLBY 80, 82; MTCW
Upshaw, Margaret Mitchell
See Mitchell, Margaret (Munnerlyn)
Upton, Mark
See Sanders, Lawrence
Urdang, Constance (Henriette) 1922- CLC **47**
See also CA 21-24R; CANR 9, 24
Uriel, Henry
See Faust, Frederick (Schiller)
Uris, Leon (Marcus) 1924- CLC **7, 32**; DAM NOV, POP
See also AITN 1, 2; BEST 89:2; CA 1-4R; CANR 1, 40; MTCW; SATA 49
Urmuz
See Codrescu, Andrei
Urquhart, Jane 1949- .... CLC **90**; DAC
See also CA 113; CANR 32
Ustinov, Peter (Alexander) 1921- .... CLC **1**
See also AITN 1; CA 13-16R; CANR 25, 51; DLB 13
U Tam'si, Gerald Felix Tchicaya
See Tchicaya, Gerald Felix
U Tam'si, Tchicaya
See Tchicaya, Gerald Felix
Vaculik, Ludvik 1926- .... CLC **7**
See also CA 53-56
Vaihinger, Hans 1852-1933 .... TCLC **71**
See also CA 116
Valdez, Luis (Miguel) 1940- .. CLC **84**; DAM MULT; HLC
See also CA 101; CANR 32; DLB 122; HW
Valenzuela, Luisa 1938- CLC **31, 104**; DAM MULT; SSC **14**
See also CA 101; CANR 32; DLB 113; HW
Valera y Alcala-Galiano, Juan 1824-1905 TCLC **10**
See also CA 106
Valery, (Ambroise) Paul (Toussaint Jules) 1871-1945 TCLC **4, 15**; DAM POET; PC **9**
See also CA 104; 122; MTCW
Valle-Inclan, Ramon (Maria) del 1866-1936 TCLC **5**; DAM MULT; HLC
See also CA 106; 153; DLB 134
Vallejo, Antonio Buero
See Buero Vallejo, Antonio
Vallejo, Cesar (Abraham) 1892-1938 TCLC **3, 56**; DAM MULT; HLC
See also CA 105; 153; HW
Vallette, Marguerite Eymery
See Rachilde

Valle Y Pena, Ramon del
See Valle-Inclan, Ramon (Maria) del
Van Ash, Cay 1918- .... CLC **34**
Vanbrugh, Sir John 1664-1726 LC **21**; DAM DRAM
See also DLB 80
Van Campen, Karl
See Campbell, John W(ood, Jr.)
Vance, Gerald
See Silverberg, Robert
Vance, Jack .... CLC **35**
See also Kuttner, Henry; Vance, John Holbrook
See also DLB 8
Vance, John Holbrook 1916-
See Queen, Ellery; Vance, Jack
See also CA 29-32R; CANR 17; MTCW
Van Den Bogarde, Derek Jules Gaspard Ulric Niven 1921-
See Bogarde, Dirk
See also CA 77-80
Vandenburgh, Jane .... CLC **59**
Vanderhaeghe, Guy 1951- .... CLC **41**
See also CA 113
van der Post, Laurens (Jan) 1906-1996 CLC **5**
See also CA 5-8R; 155; CANR 35
van de Wetering, Janwillem 1931- ... CLC **47**
See also CA 49-52; CANR 4, 62
Van Dine, S. S. .... TCLC **23**
See also Wright, Willard Huntington
Van Doren, Carl (Clinton) 1885-1950 TCLC **18**
See also CA 111
Van Doren, Mark 1894-1972 .... CLC **6, 10**
See also CA 1-4R; 37-40R; CANR 3; DLB 45; MTCW
Van Druten, John (William) 1901-1957 TCLC **2**
See also CA 104; 161; DLB 10
Van Duyn, Mona (Jane) 1921- CLC **3, 7, 63**; DAM POET
See also CA 9-12R; CANR 7, 38, 60; DLB 5
Van Dyne, Edith
See Baum, L(yman) Frank
van Itallie, Jean-Claude 1936- .... CLC **3**
See also CA 45-48; CAAS 2; CANR 1, 48; DLB 7
van Ostaijen, Paul 1896-1928 .... TCLC **33**
Van Peebles, Melvin 1932- CLC **2, 20**; DAM MULT
See also BW 2; CA 85-88; CANR 27
Vansittart, Peter 1920- .... CLC **42**
See also CA 1-4R; CANR 3, 49
Van Vechten, Carl 1880-1964 .... CLC **33**
See also CA 89-92; DLB 4, 9, 51
Van Vogt, A(lfred) E(lton) 1912- .... CLC **1**
See also CA 21-24R; CANR 28; DLB 8; SATA 14
Varda, Agnes 1928- .... CLC **16**
See also CA 116; 122
Vargas Llosa, (Jorge) Mario (Pedro) 1936- CLC **3, 6, 9, 10, 15, 31, 42, 85**; DA; DAB; DAC; DAM MST, MULT, NOV; HLC
See also CA 73-76; CANR 18, 32, 42; DLB 145; HW; MTCW
Vasiliu, Gheorghe 1881-1957
See Bacovia, George
See also CA 123
Vassa, Gustavus
See Equiano, Olaudah
Vassilikos, Vassilis 1933- .... CLC **4, 8**
See also CA 81-84
Vaughan, Henry 1621-1695 .... LC **27**
See also DLB 131
Vaughn, Stephanie .... CLC **62**
Vazov, Ivan (Minchov) 1850-1921 . TCLC **25**
See also CA 121; DLB 147
Veblen, Thorstein (Bunde) 1857-1929 TCLC **31**
See also CA 115
Vega, Lope de 1562-1635 .... LC **23**
Venison, Alfred
See Pound, Ezra (Weston Loomis)
Verdi, Marie de
See Mencken, H(enry) L(ouis)
Verdu, Matilde
See Cela, Camilo Jose
Verga, Giovanni (Carmelo) 1840-1922 TCLC **3**; SSC **21**
See also CA 104; 123
Vergil 70B.C.-19B.C. ..... CMLC **9**; DA; DAB; DAC; DAM MST, POET; PC **12**; WLCS
Verhaeren, Emile (Adolphe Gustave) 1855-1916 .... TCLC **12**
See also CA 109
Verlaine, Paul (Marie) 1844-1896 NCLC **2, 51**; DAM POET; PC **2**
Verne, Jules (Gabriel) 1828-1905 TCLC **6, 52**
See also AAYA 16; CA 110; 131; DLB 123; JRDA; MAICYA; SATA 21
Very, Jones 1813-1880 .... NCLC **9**
See also DLB 1
Vesaas, Tarjei 1897-1970 .... CLC **48**
See also CA 29-32R
Vialis, Gaston
See Simenon, Georges (Jacques Christian)
Vian, Boris 1920-1959 .... TCLC **9**
See also CA 106; DLB 72
Viaud, (Louis Marie) Julien 1850-1923
See Loti, Pierre
See also CA 107
Vicar, Henry
See Felsen, Henry Gregor
Vicker, Angus
See Felsen, Henry Gregor
Vidal, Gore 1925- CLC **2, 4, 6, 8, 10, 22, 33, 72**; DAM NOV, POP
See also AITN 1; BEST 90:2; CA 5-8R; CANR 13, 45; DLB 6, 152; INT CANR-13; MTCW
Viereck, Peter (Robert Edwin) 1916- . CLC **4**
See also CA 1-4R; CANR 1, 47; DLB 5
Vigny, Alfred (Victor) de 1797-1863 NCLC **7**; DAM POET
See also DLB 119
Vilakazi, Benedict Wallet 1906-1947 TCLC **37**
Villiers de l'Isle Adam, Jean Marie Mathias Philippe Auguste Comte 1838-1889 NCLC **3**; SSC **14**
See also DLB 123
Villon, Francois 1431-1463(?) .... PC **13**
Vinci, Leonardo da 1452-1519 .... LC **12**
Vine, Barbara .... CLC **50**
See also Rendell, Ruth (Barbara)
See also BEST 90:4
Vinge, Joan D(ennison) 1948- CLC **30**; SSC **24**
See also CA 93-96; SATA 36
Violis, G.
See Simenon, Georges (Jacques Christian)
Visconti, Luchino 1906-1976 .... CLC **16**
See also CA 81-84; 65-68; CANR 39
Vittorini, Elio 1908-1966 .... CLC **6, 9, 14**
See also CA 133; 25-28R
Vizenor, Gerald Robert 1934- CLC **103**; DAM MULT
See also CA 13-16R; CAAS 22; CANR 5, 21, 44; DLB 175; NNAL
Vizinczey, Stephen 1933- .... CLC **40**
See also CA 128; INT 128
Vliet, R(ussell) G(ordon) 1929-1984 . CLC **22**
See also CA 37-40R; 112; CANR 18
Vogau, Boris Andreyevich 1894-1937(?)
See Pilnyak, Boris
See also CA 123
Vogel, Paula A(nne) 1951- .... CLC **76**
See also CA 108

Voight, Ellen Bryant 1943- .... **CLC 54**
See also CA 69-72; CANR 11, 29, 55; DLB 120
Voigt, Cynthia 1942- .... **CLC 30**
See also AAYA 3; CA 106; CANR 18, 37, 40; CLR 13; INT CANR-18; JRDA; MAICYA; SATA 48, 79; SATA-Brief 33
Voinovich, Vladimir (Nikolaevich) 1932-CLC 10, 49
See also CA 81-84; CAAS 12; CANR 33; MTCW
Vollmann, William T. 1959-.. **CLC 89; DAM NOV, POP**
See also CA 134
Voloshinov, V. N.
See Bakhtin, Mikhail Mikhailovich
Voltaire 1694-1778 **LC 14; DA; DAB; DAC; DAM DRAM, MST; SSC 12; WLC**
von Daeniken, Erich 1935- .... **CLC 30**
See also AITN 1; CA 37-40R; CANR 17, 44
von Daniken, Erich
See von Daeniken, Erich
von Heidenstam, (Carl Gustaf) Verner
See Heidenstam, (Carl Gustaf) Verner von
von Heyse, Paul (Johann Ludwig)
See Heyse, Paul (Johann Ludwig von)
von Hofmannsthal, Hugo
See Hofmannsthal, Hugo von
von Horvath, Odon
See Horvath, Oedoen von
von Horvath, Oedoen
See Horvath, Oedoen von
von Liliencron, (Friedrich Adolf Axel) Detlev
See Liliencron, (Friedrich Adolf Axel) Detlev von
Vonnegut, Kurt, Jr. 1922-CLC 1, 2, 3, 4, 5, 8, 12, 22, 40, 60; DA; DAB; DAC; DAM MST, NOV, POP; SSC 8; WLC
See also AAYA 6; AITN 1; BEST 90:4; CA 1-4R; CANR 1, 25, 49; CDALB 1968-1988; DLB 2, 8, 152; DLBD 3; DLBY 80; MTCW
Von Rachen, Kurt
See Hubbard, L(afayette) Ron(ald)
von Rezzori (d'Arezzo), Gregor
See Rezzori (d'Arezzo), Gregor von
von Sternberg, Josef
See Sternberg, Josef von
Vorster, Gordon 1924- .... **CLC 34**
See also CA 133
Vosce, Trudie
See Ozick, Cynthia
Voznesensky, Andrei (Andreievich) 1933- **CLC 1, 15, 57; DAM POET**
See also CA 89-92; CANR 37; MTCW
Waddington, Miriam 1917-............... **CLC 28**
See also CA 21-24R; CANR 12, 30; DLB 68
Wagman, Fredrica 1937-..................... **CLC 7**
See also CA 97-100; INT 97-100
Wagner, Linda W.
See Wagner-Martin, Linda (C.)
Wagner, Linda Welshimer
See Wagner-Martin, Linda (C.)
Wagner, Richard 1813-1883 .... **NCLC 9**
See also DLB 129
Wagner-Martin, Linda (C.) 1936-... **CLC 50**
See also CA 159
Wagoner, David (Russell) 1926-CLC 3, 5, 15
See also CA 1-4R; CAAS 3; CANR 2; DLB 5; SATA 14
Wah, Fred(erick James) 1939-......... **CLC 44**
See also CA 107; 141; DLB 60
Wahloo, Per 1926-1975 .... **CLC 7**
See also CA 61-64
Wahloo, Peter
See Wahloo, Per
Wain, John (Barrington) 1925-1994 **CLC 2, 11, 15, 46**

See also CA 5-8R; 145; CAAS 4; CANR 23, 54; CDBLB 1960 to Present; DLB 15, 27, 139, 155; MTCW
Wajda, Andrzej 1926-......................... **CLC 16**
See also CA 102
Wakefield, Dan 1932- .... **CLC 7**
See also CA 21-24R; CAAS 7
Wakoski, Diane 1937- **CLC 2, 4, 7, 9, 11, 40; DAM POET; PC 15**
See also CA 13-16R; CAAS 1; CANR 9, 60; DLB 5; INT CANR-9
Wakoski-Sherbell, Diane
See Wakoski, Diane
Walcott, Derek (Alton) 1930-CLC 2, 4, 9, 14, 25, 42, 67, 76; BLC; DAB; DAC; DAM MST, MULT, POET; DC 7
See also BW 2; CA 89-92; CANR 26, 47; DLB 117; DLBY 81; MTCW
Waldman, Anne 1945- .... **CLC 7**
See also CA 37-40R; CAAS 17; CANR 34; DLB 16
Waldo, E. Hunter
See Sturgeon, Theodore (Hamilton)
Waldo, Edward Hamilton
See Sturgeon, Theodore (Hamilton)
Walker, Alice (Malsenior) 1944-CLC 5, 6, 9, 19, 27, 46, 58, 103; BLC; DA; DAB; DAC; DAM MST, MULT, NOV, POET, POP; SSC 5; WLCS
See also AAYA 3; BEST 89:4; BW 2; CA 37-40R; CANR 9, 27, 49; CDALB 1968-1988; DLB 6, 33, 143; INT CANR-27; MTCW; SATA 31
Walker, David Harry 1911-1992 ...... **CLC 14**
See also CA 1-4R; 137; CANR 1; SATA 8; SATA-Obit 71
Walker, Edward Joseph 1934-
See Walker, Ted
See also CA 21-24R; CANR 12, 28, 53
Walker, George F. 1947- **CLC 44, 61; DAB; DAC; DAM MST**
See also CA 103; CANR 21, 43, 59; DLB 60
Walker, Joseph A. 1935- .... **CLC 19; DAM DRAM, MST**
See also BW 1; CA 89-92; CANR 26; DLB 38
Walker, Margaret (Abigail) 1915- **CLC 1, 6; BLC; DAM MULT; PC 20**
See also BW 2; CA 73-76; CANR 26, 54; DLB 76, 152; MTCW
Walker, Ted .... **CLC 13**
See also Walker, Edward Joseph
See also DLB 40
Wallace, David Foster 1962- .... **CLC 50**
See also CA 132; CANR 59
Wallace, Dexter
See Masters, Edgar Lee
Wallace, (Richard Horatio) Edgar 1875-1932 **TCLC 57**
See also CA 115; DLB 70
Wallace, Irving 1916-1990 **CLC 7, 13; DAM NOV, POP**
See also AITN 1; CA 1-4R; 132; CAAS 1; CANR 1, 27; INT CANR-27; MTCW
Wallant, Edward Lewis 1926-1962 CLC 5, 10
See also CA 1-4R; CANR 22; DLB 2, 28, 143; MTCW
Walley, Byron
See Card, Orson Scott
Walpole, Horace 1717-1797 .... **LC 2**
See also DLB 39, 104
Walpole, Hugh (Seymour) 1884-1941 **TCLC 5**
See also CA 104; DLB 34
Walser, Martin 1927- .... **CLC 27**
See also CA 57-60; CANR 8, 46; DLB 75, 124
Walser, Robert 1878-1956 **TCLC 18; SSC 20**
See also CA 118; DLB 66
Walsh, Jill Paton .... **CLC 35**

See also Paton Walsh, Gillian
See also AAYA 11; CLR 2; DLB 161; SAAS 3
Walter, Villiam Christian
See Andersen, Hans Christian
Wambaugh, Joseph (Aloysius, Jr.) 1937-CLC 3, 18; DAM NOV, POP
See also AITN 1; BEST 89:3; CA 33-36R; CANR 42; DLB 6; DLBY 83; MTCW
Wang Wei 699(?)-761(?) .... **PC 18**
Ward, Arthur Henry Sarsfield 1883-1959
See Rohmer, Sax
See also CA 108
Ward, Douglas Turner 1930- .... **CLC 19**
See also BW 1; CA 81-84; CANR 27; DLB 7, 38
Ward, Mary Augusta
See Ward, Mrs. Humphry
Ward, Mrs. Humphry 1851-1920 .. **TCLC 55**
See also DLB 18
Ward, Peter
See Faust, Frederick (Schiller)
Warhol, Andy 1928(?)-1987 .... **CLC 20**
See also AAYA 12; BEST 89:4; CA 89-92; 121; CANR 34
Warner, Francis (Robert le Plastrier) 1937- **CLC 14**
See also CA 53-56; CANR 11
Warner, Marina 1946- .... **CLC 59**
See also CA 65-68; CANR 21, 55
Warner, Rex (Ernest) 1905-1986 ...... **CLC 45**
See also CA 89-92; 119; DLB 15
Warner, Susan (Bogert) 1819-1885 **NCLC 31**
See also DLB 3, 42
Warner, Sylvia (Constance) Ashton
See Ashton-Warner, Sylvia (Constance)
Warner, Sylvia Townsend 1893-1978 CLC 7, 19; SSC 23
See also CA 61-64; 77-80; CANR 16, 60; DLB 34, 139; MTCW
Warren, Mercy Otis 1728-1814 ...... **NCLC 13**
See also DLB 31
Warren, Robert Penn 1905-1989 CLC 1, 4, 6, 8, 10, 13, 18, 39, 53, 59; DA; DAB; DAC; DAM MST, NOV, POET; SSC 4; WLC
See also AITN 1; CA 13-16R; 129; CANR 10, 47; CDALB 1968-1988; DLB 2, 48, 152; DLBY 80, 89; INT CANR-10; MTCW; SATA 46; SATA-Obit 63
Warshofsky, Isaac
See Singer, Isaac Bashevis
Warton, Thomas 1728-1790 ..... **LC 15; DAM POET**
See also DLB 104, 109
Waruk, Kona
See Harris, (Theodore) Wilson
Warung, Price 1855-1911 .... **TCLC 45**
Warwick, Jarvis
See Garner, Hugh
Washington, Alex
See Harris, Mark
Washington, Booker T(aliaferro) 1856-1915 **TCLC 10; BLC; DAM MULT**
See also BW 1; CA 114; 125; SATA 28
Washington, George 1732-1799 .... **LC 25**
See also DLB 31
Wassermann, (Karl) Jakob 1873-1934 **TCLC 6**
See also CA 104; DLB 66
Wasserstein, Wendy 1950- .. **CLC 32, 59, 90; DAM DRAM; DC 4**
See also CA 121; 129; CABS 3; CANR 53; INT 129; SATA 94
Waterhouse, Keith (Spencer) 1929- **CLC 47**
See also CA 5-8R; CANR 38; DLB 13, 15; MTCW
Waters, Frank (Joseph) 1902-1995 . **CLC 88**
See also CA 5-8R; 149; CAAS 13; CANR 3,

18; DLBY 86
Waters, Roger 1944- .... **CLC 35**
Watkins, Frances Ellen
 See Harper, Frances Ellen Watkins
Watkins, Gerrold
 See Malzberg, Barry N(athaniel)
Watkins, Gloria 1955(?)-
 See hooks, bell
 See also BW 2; CA 143
Watkins, Paul 1964- .... **CLC 55**
 See also CA 132; CANR 62
Watkins, Vernon Phillips 1906-1967 **CLC 43**
 See also CA 9-10; 25-28R; CAP 1; DLB 20
Watson, Irving S.
 See Mencken, H(enry) L(ouis)
Watson, John H.
 See Farmer, Philip Jose
Watson, Richard F.
 See Silverberg, Robert
Waugh, Auberon (Alexander) 1939- ...**CLC 7**
 See also CA 45-48; CANR 6, 22; DLB 14
Waugh, Evelyn (Arthur St. John) 1903-1966
 CLC 1, 3, 8, 13, 19, 27, 44; DA; DAB; DAC; DAM MST, NOV, POP; WLC
 See also CA 85-88; 25-28R; CANR 22; CDBLB 1914-1945; DLB 15, 162; MTCW
Waugh, Harriet 1944- .... **CLC 6**
 See also CA 85-88; CANR 22
Ways, C. R.
 See Blount, Roy (Alton), Jr.
Waystaff, Simon
 See Swift, Jonathan
Webb, (Martha) Beatrice (Potter) 1858-1943
 TCLC 22
 See also Potter, (Helen) Beatrix
 See also CA 117
Webb, Charles (Richard) 1939- .... **CLC 7**
 See also CA 25-28R
Webb, James H(enry), Jr. 1946- ...... **CLC 22**
 See also CA 81-84
Webb, Mary (Gladys Meredith) 1881-1927
 TCLC 24
 See also CA 123; DLB 34
Webb, Mrs. Sidney
 See Webb, (Martha) Beatrice (Potter)
Webb, Phyllis 1927- .... **CLC 18**
 See also CA 104; CANR 23; DLB 53
Webb, Sidney (James) 1859-1947 .. **TCLC 22**
 See also CA 117
Webber, Andrew Lloyd .... **CLC 21**
 See also Lloyd Webber, Andrew
Weber, Lenora Mattingly 1895-1971 **CLC 12**
 See also CA 19-20; 29-32R; CAP 1; SATA 2; SATA-Obit 26
Weber, Max 1864-1920 .... **TCLC 69**
 See also CA 109
Webster, John 1579(?)-1634(?) .. **LC 33; DA; DAB; DAC; DAM DRAM, MST; DC 2; WLC**
 See CDBLB Before 1660; DLB 58
Webster, Noah 1758-1843 .... **NCLC 30**
Wedekind, (Benjamin) Frank(lin) 1864-1918
 TCLC 7; DAM DRAM
 See also CA 104; 153; DLB 118
Weidman, Jerome 1913- .... **CLC 7**
 See also AITN 2; CA 1-4R; CANR 1; DLB 28
Weil, Simone (Adolphine) 1909-1943 . **T C L C 23**
 See also CA 117; 159
Weinstein, Nathan
 See West, Nathanael
Weinstein, Nathan von Wallenstein
 See West, Nathanael
Weir, Peter (Lindsay) 1944- .... **CLC 20**
 See also CA 113; 123
Weiss, Peter (Ulrich) 1916-1982 **CLC 3, 15, 51; DAM DRAM**

See also CA 45-48; 106; CANR 3; DLB 69, 124
Weiss, Theodore (Russell) 1916-**CLC 3, 8, 14**
 See also CA 9-12R; CAAS 2; CANR 46; DLB 5
Welch, (Maurice) Denton 1915-1948**TCLC 22**
 See also CA 121; 148
Welch, James 1940- ..... **CLC 6, 14, 52; DAM MULT, POP**
 See also CA 85-88; CANR 42; DLB 175; NNAL
Weldon, Fay 1933- **CLC 6, 9, 11, 19, 36, 59; DAM POP**
 See also CA 21-24R; CANR 16, 46; CDBLB 1960 to Present; DLB 14; INT CANR-16; MTCW
Wellek, Rene 1903-1995 .... **CLC 28**
 See also CA 5-8R; 150; CAAS 7; CANR 8; DLB 63; INT CANR-8
Weller, Michael 1942- .... **CLC 10, 53**
 See also CA 85-88
Weller, Paul 1958- .... **CLC 26**
Wellershoff, Dieter 1925- .... **CLC 46**
 See also CA 89-92; CANR 16, 37
Welles, (George) Orson 1915-1985**CLC 20, 80**
 See also CA 93-96; 117
Wellman, Mac 1945- .... **CLC 65**
Wellman, Manly Wade 1903-1986 ... **CLC 49**
 See also CA 1-4R; 118; CANR 6, 16, 44; SATA 6; SATA-Obit 47
Wells, Carolyn 1869(?)-1942 .... **TCLC 35**
 See also CA 113; DLB 11
Wells, H(erbert) G(eorge) 1866-1946**TCLC 6, 12, 19; DA; DAB; DAC; DAM MST, NOV; SSC 6; WLC**
 See also AAYA 18; CA 110; 121; CDBLB 1914-1945; DLB 34, 70, 156, 178; MTCW; SATA 20
Wells, Rosemary 1943- .... **CLC 12**
 See also AAYA 13; CA 85-88; CANR 48; CLR 16; MAICYA; SAAS 1; SATA 18, 69
Welty, Eudora 1909- **CLC 1, 2, 5, 14, 22, 33, 105; DA; DAB; DAC; DAM MST, NOV; SSC 1, 27; WLC**
 See also CA 9-12R; CABS 1; CANR 32; CDALB 1941-1968; DLB 2, 102, 143; DLBD 12; DLBY 87; MTCW
Wen I-to 1899-1946 .... **TCLC 28**
Wentworth, Robert
 See Hamilton, Edmond
Werfel, Franz (Viktor) 1890-1945 ... **TCLC 8**
 See also CA 104; 161; DLB 81, 124
Wergeland, Henrik Arnold 1808-1845**N C L C 5**
Wersba, Barbara 1932- .... **CLC 30**
 See also AAYA 2; CA 29-32R; CANR 16, 38; CLR 3; DLB 52; JRDA; MAICYA; SAAS 2; SATA 1, 58
Wertmueller, Lina 1928- .... **CLC 16**
 See also CA 97-100; CANR 39
Wescott, Glenway 1901-1987 .... **CLC 13**
 See also CA 13-16R; 121; CANR 23; DLB 4, 9, 102
Wesker, Arnold 1932- ... **CLC 3, 5, 42; DAB; DAM DRAM**
 See also CA 1-4R; CAAS 7; CANR 1, 33; CDBLB 1960 to Present; DLB 13; MTCW
Wesley, Richard (Errol) 1945- .... **CLC 7**
 See also BW 1; CA 57-60; CANR 27; DLB 38
Wessel, Johan Herman 1742-1785 .... **LC 7**
West, Anthony (Panther) 1914-1987 **CLC 50**
 See also CA 45-48; 124; CANR 3, 19; DLB 15
West, C. P.
 See Wodehouse, P(elham) G(renville)
West, (Mary) Jessamyn 1902-1984**CLC 7, 17**
 See also CA 9-12R; 112; CANR 27; DLB 6; DLBY 84; MTCW; SATA-Obit 37

West, Morris L(anglo) 1916-......... **CLC 6, 33**
 See also CA 5-8R; CANR 24, 49; MTCW
West, Nathanael 1903-1940 **TCLC 1, 14, 44; SSC 16**
 See also CA 104; 125; CDALB 1929-1941; DLB 4, 9, 28; MTCW
West, Owen
 See Koontz, Dean R(ay)
West, Paul 1930- .... **CLC 7, 14, 96**
 See also CA 13-16R; CAAS 7; CANR 22, 53; DLB 14; INT CANR-22
West, Rebecca 1892-1983 ... **CLC 7, 9, 31, 50**
 See also CA 5-8R; 109; CANR 19; DLB 36; DLBY 83; MTCW
Westall, Robert (Atkinson) 1929-1993**CLC 17**
 See also AAYA 12; CA 69-72; 141; CANR 18; CLR 13; JRDA; MAICYA; SAAS 2; SATA 23, 69; SATA-Obit 75
Westlake, Donald E(dwin) 1933- **CLC 7, 33; DAM POP**
 See also CA 17-20R; CAAS 13; CANR 16, 44; INT CANR-16
Westmacott, Mary
 See Christie, Agatha (Mary Clarissa)
Weston, Allen
 See Norton, Andre
Wetcheek, J. L.
 See Feuchtwanger, Lion
Wetering, Janwillem van de
 See van de Wetering, Janwillem
Wetherell, Elizabeth
 See Warner, Susan (Bogert)
Whale, James 1889-1957 .... **TCLC 63**
Whalen, Philip 1923- .... **CLC 6, 29**
 See also CA 9-12R; CANR 5, 39; DLB 16
Wharton, Edith (Newbold Jones) 1862-1937
 TCLC 3, 9, 27, 53; DA; DAB; DAC; DAM MST, NOV; SSC 6; WLC
 See also CA 104; 132; CDALB 1865-1917; DLB 4, 9, 12, 78; DLBD 13; MTCW
Wharton, James
 See Mencken, H(enry) L(ouis)
Wharton, William (a pseudonym)CLC **18, 37**
 See also CA 93-96; DLBY 80; INT 93-96
Wheatley (Peters), Phillis 1754(?)-1784**LC 3; BLC; DA; DAC; DAM MST, MULT, POET; PC 3; WLC**
 See also CDALB 1640-1865; DLB 31, 50
Wheelock, John Hall 1886-1978 .... **CLC 14**
 See also CA 13-16R; 77-80; CANR 14; DLB 45
White, E(lwyn) B(rooks) 1899-1985 **CLC 10, 34, 39; DAM POP**
 See also AITN 2; CA 13-16R; 116; CANR 16, 37; CLR 1, 21; DLB 11, 22; MAICYA; MTCW; SATA 2, 29; SATA-Obit 44
White, Edmund (Valentine III) 1940-**CLC 27; DAM POP**
 See also AAYA 7; CA 45-48; CANR 3, 19, 36, 62; MTCW
White, Patrick (Victor Martindale) 1912-1990
 CLC 3, 4, 5, 7, 9, 18, 65, 69
 See also CA 81-84; 132; CANR 43; MTCW
White, Phyllis Dorothy James 1920-
 See James, P. D.
 See also CA 21-24R; CANR 17, 43; DAM POP; MTCW
White, T(erence) H(anbury) 1906-1964 **C L C 30**
 See also AAYA 22; CA 73-76; CANR 37; DLB 160; JRDA; MAICYA; SATA 12
White, Terence de Vere 1912-1994 ..**CLC 49**
 See also CA 49-52; 145; CANR 3
White, Walter F(rancis) 1893-1955 **TCLC 15**
 See also White, Walter
 See also BW 1; CA 115; 124; DLB 51
White, William Hale 1831-1913

See Rutherford, Mark
See also CA 121
Whitehead, E(dward) A(nthony) 1933-CLC 5
See also CA 65-68; CANR 58
Whitemore, Hugh (John) 1936- .... CLC 37
See also CA 132; INT 132
Whitman, Sarah Helen (Power) 1803-1878 NCLC 19
See also DLB 1
Whitman, Walt(er) 1819-1892 . NCLC 4, 31; DA; DAB; DAC; DAM MST, POET; PC 3; WLC
See also CDALB 1640-1865; DLB 3, 64; SATA 20
Whitney, Phyllis A(yame) 1903- ..... CLC 42; DAM POP
See also AITN 2; BEST 90:3; CA 1-4R; CANR 3, 25, 38, 60; JRDA; MAICYA; SATA 1, 30
Whittemore, (Edward) Reed (Jr.) 1919-C L C 4
See also CA 9-12R; CAAS 8; CANR 4; DLB 5
Whittier, John Greenleaf 1807-1892 NCLC 8, 59
See also DLB 1
Whittlebot, Hernia
See Coward, Noel (Peirce)
Wicker, Thomas Grey 1926-
See Wicker, Tom
See also CA 65-68; CANR 21, 46
Wicker, Tom .... CLC 7
See also Wicker, Thomas Grey
Wideman, John Edgar 1941- CLC 5, 34, 36, 67; BLC; DAM MULT
See also BW 2; CA 85-88; CANR 14, 42; DLB 33, 143
Wiebe, Rudy (Henry) 1934- .. CLC 6, 11, 14; DAC; DAM MST
See also CA 37-40R; CANR 42; DLB 60
Wieland, Christoph Martin 1733-1813 NCLC 17
See also DLB 97
Wiene, Robert 1881-1938 .... TCLC 56
Wieners, John 1934- .... CLC 7
See also CA 13-16R; DLB 16
Wiesel, Elie(zer) 1928-CLC 3, 5, 11, 37; DA; DAB; DAC; DAM MST, NOV; WLCS 2
See also AAYA 7; AITN 1; CA 5-8R; CAAS 4; CANR 8, 40; DLB 83; DLBY 87; INT CANR-8; MTCW; SATA 56
Wiggins, Marianne 1947- .... CLC 57
See also BEST 89:3; CA 130; CANR 60
Wight, James Alfred 1916-
See Herriot, James
See also CA 77-80; SATA 55; SATA-Brief 44
Wilbur, Richard (Purdy) 1921- CLC 3, 6, 9, 14, 53; DA; DAB; DAC; DAM MST, POET
See also CA 1-4R; CABS 2; CANR 2, 29; DLB 5, 169; INT CANR-29; MTCW; SATA 9
Wild, Peter 1940- .... CLC 14
See also CA 37-40R; DLB 5
Wilde, Oscar (Fingal O'Flahertie Wills) 1854(?)-1900 TCLC 1, 8, 23, 41; DA; DAB; DAC; DAM DRAM, MST, NOV; SSC 11; WLC
See also CA 104; 119; CDBLB 1890-1914; DLB 10, 19, 34, 57, 141, 156; SATA 24
Wilder, Billy .... CLC 20
See also Wilder, Samuel
See also DLB 26
Wilder, Samuel 1906-
See Wilder, Billy
See also CA 89-92
Wilder, Thornton (Niven) 1897-1975 CLC 1, 5, 6, 10, 15, 35, 82; DA; DAB; DAC; DAM DRAM, MST, NOV; DC 1; WLC
See also AITN 2; CA 13-16R; 61-64; CANR 40; DLB 4, 7, 9; MTCW
Wilding, Michael 1942- .... CLC 73
See also CA 104; CANR 24, 49
Wiley, Richard 1944- .... CLC 44
See also CA 121; 129
Wilhelm, Kate .... CLC 7
See also Wilhelm, Katie Gertrude
See also AAYA 20; CAAS 5; DLB 8; INT CANR-17
Wilhelm, Katie Gertrude 1928-
See Wilhelm, Kate
See also CA 37-40R; CANR 17, 36, 60; MTCW
Wilkins, Mary
See Freeman, Mary Eleanor Wilkins
Willard, Nancy 1936- .... CLC 7, 37
See also CA 89-92; CANR 10, 39; CLR 5; DLB 5, 52; MAICYA; MTCW; SATA 37, 71; SATA-Brief 30
Williams, C(harles) K(enneth) 1936-CLC 33, 56; DAM POET
See also CA 37-40R; CAAS 26; CANR 57; DLB 5
Williams, Charles
See Collier, James L(incoln)
Williams, Charles (Walter Stansby) 1886-1945 TCLC 1, 11
See also CA 104; DLB 100, 153
Williams, (George) Emlyn 1905-1987 CLC 15; DAM DRAM
See also CA 104; 123; CANR 36; DLB 10, 77; MTCW
Williams, Hugo 1942- .... CLC 42
See also CA 17-20R; CANR 45; DLB 40
Williams, J. Walker
See Wodehouse, P(elham) G(renville)
Williams, John A(lfred) 1925- .... CLC 5, 13; BLC; DAM MULT
See also BW 2; CA 53-56; CAAS 3; CANR 6, 26, 51; DLB 2, 33; INT CANR-6
Williams, Jonathan (Chamberlain) 1929- CLC 13
See also CA 9-12R; CAAS 12; CANR 8; DLB 5
Williams, Joy 1944- .... CLC 31
See also CA 41-44R; CANR 22, 48
Williams, Norman 1952- .... CLC 39
See also CA 118
Williams, Sherley Anne 1944-CLC 89; BLC; DAM MULT, POET
See also BW 2; CA 73-76; CANR 25; DLB 41; INT CANR-25; SATA 78
Williams, Shirley
See Williams, Sherley Anne
Williams, Tennessee 1911-1983 CLC 1, 2, 5, 7, 8, 11, 15, 19, 30, 39, 45, 71; DA; DAB; DAC; DAM DRAM, MST; DC 4; WLC
See also AITN 1, 2; CA 5-8R; 108; CABS 3; CANR 31; CDALB 1941-1968; DLB 7; DLBD 4; DLBY 83; MTCW
Williams, Thomas (Alonzo) 1926-1990 . C L C 14
See also CA 1-4R; 132; CANR 2
Williams, William C.
See Williams, William Carlos
Williams, William Carlos 1883-1963 CLC 1, 2, 5, 9, 13, 22, 42, 67; DA; DAB; DAC; DAM MST, POET; PC 7
See also CA 89-92; CANR 34; CDALB 1917-1929; DLB 4, 16, 54, 86; MTCW
Williamson, David (Keith) 1942- ...... CLC 56
See also CA 103; CANR 41
Williamson, Ellen Douglas 1905-1984
See Douglas, Ellen
See also CA 17-20R; 114; CANR 39
Williamson, Jack .... CLC 29
See also Williamson, John Stewart
See also CAAS 8; DLB 8
Williamson, John Stewart 1908-
See Williamson, Jack
See also CA 17-20R; CANR 23
Willie, Frederick
See Lovecraft, H(oward) P(hillips)
Willingham, Calder (Baynard, Jr.) 1922-1995 CLC 5, 51
See also CA 5-8R; 147; CANR 3; DLB 2, 44; MTCW
Willis, Charles
See Clarke, Arthur C(harles)
Willy
See Colette, (Sidonie-Gabrielle)
Willy, Colette
See Colette, (Sidonie-Gabrielle)
Wilson, A(ndrew) N(orman) 1950- ... CLC 33
See also CA 112; 122; DLB 14, 155
Wilson, Angus (Frank Johnstone) 1913-1991 CLC 2, 3, 5, 25, 34; SSC 21
See also CA 5-8R; 134; CANR 21; DLB 15, 139, 155; MTCW
Wilson, August 1945- CLC 39, 50, 63; BLC; DA; DAB; DAC; DAM DRAM, MST, MULT; DC 2; WLCS
See also AAYA 16; BW 2; CA 115; 122; CANR 42, 54; MTCW
Wilson, Brian 1942- .... CLC 12
Wilson, Colin 1931- .... CLC 3, 14
See also CA 1-4R; CAAS 5; CANR 1, 22, 33; DLB 14; MTCW
Wilson, Dirk
See Pohl, Frederik
Wilson, Edmund 1895-1972 CLC 1, 2, 3, 8, 24
See also CA 1-4R; 37-40R; CANR 1, 46; DLB 63; MTCW
Wilson, Ethel Davis (Bryant) 1888(?)-1980 CLC 13; DAC; DAM POET
See also CA 102; DLB 68; MTCW
Wilson, John 1785-1854 .... NCLC 5
Wilson, John (Anthony) Burgess 1917-1993
See Burgess, Anthony
See also CA 1-4R; 143; CANR 2, 46; DAC; DAM NOV; MTCW
Wilson, Lanford 1937- CLC 7, 14, 36; DAM DRAM
See also CA 17-20R; CABS 3; CANR 45; DLB 7
Wilson, Robert M. 1944- .... CLC 7, 9
See also CA 49-52; CANR 2, 41; MTCW
Wilson, Robert McLiam 1964- .... CLC 59
See also CA 132
Wilson, Sloan 1920- .... CLC 32
See also CA 1-4R; CANR 1, 44
Wilson, Snoo 1948- .... CLC 33
See also CA 69-72
Wilson, William S(mith) 1932- .... CLC 49
See also CA 81-84
Wilson, Woodrow 1856-1924 .... TCLC 73
See also DLB 47
Winchilsea, Anne (Kingsmill) Finch Counte 1661-1720 .... LC 3
Windham, Basil
See Wodehouse, P(elham) G(renville)
Wingrove, David (John) 1954- .... CLC 68
See also CA 133
Wintergreen, Jane
See Duncan, Sara Jeannette
Winters, Janet Lewis .... CLC 41
See also Lewis, Janet
See also DLBY 87
Winters, (Arthur) Yvor 1900-1968 CLC 4, 8, 32
See also CA 11-12; 25-28R; CAP 1; DLB 48; MTCW
Winterson, Jeanette 1959-CLC 64; DAM POP
See also CA 136; CANR 58
Winthrop, John 1588-1649 .... LC 31

See also DLB 24, 30
Wiseman, Frederick 1930- .... **CLC 20**
See also CA 159
Wister, Owen 1860-1938 .... **TCLC 21**
See also CA 108; DLB 9, 78; SATA 62
Witkacy
See Witkiewicz, Stanislaw Ignacy
Witkiewicz, Stanislaw Ignacy 1885-1939
TCLC 8
See also CA 105
Wittgenstein, Ludwig (Josef Johann) 1889-1951
TCLC 59
See also CA 113
Wittig, Monique 1935(?)- .... **CLC 22**
See also CA 116; 135; DLB 83
Wittlin, Jozef 1896-1976 .... **CLC 25**
See also CA 49-52; 65-68; CANR 3
Wodehouse, P(elham) G(renville) 1881-1975
CLC 1, 2, 5, 10, 22; DAB; DAC; DAM NOV; SSC 2
See also AITN 2; CA 45-48; 57-60; CANR 3, 33; CDBLB 1914-1945; DLB 34, 162; MTCW; SATA 22
Woiwode, L.
See Woiwode, Larry (Alfred)
Woiwode, Larry (Alfred) 1941- ... **CLC 6, 10**
See also CA 73-76; CANR 16; DLB 6; INT CANR-16
Wojciechowska, Maia (Teresa) 1927-**CLC 26**
See also AAYA 8; CA 9-12R; CANR 4, 41; CLR 1; JRDA; MAICYA; SAAS 1; SATA 1, 28, 83
Wolf, Christa 1929- .... **CLC 14, 29, 58**
See also CA 85-88; CANR 45; DLB 75; MTCW
Wolfe, Gene (Rodman) 1931- **CLC 25; DAM POP**
See also CA 57-60; CAAS 9; CANR 6, 32, 60; DLB 8
Wolfe, George C. 1954- .... **CLC 49**
See also CA 149
Wolfe, Thomas (Clayton) 1900-1938**TCLC 4, 13, 29, 61; DA; DAB; DAC; DAM MST, NOV; WLC**
See also CA 104; 132; CDALB 1929-1941; DLB 9, 102; DLBD 2, 16; DLBY 85; MTCW
Wolfe, Thomas Kennerly, Jr. 1931-
See Wolfe, Tom
See also CA 13-16R; CANR 9, 33; DAM POP; INT CANR-9; MTCW
Wolfe, Tom .... **CLC 1, 2, 9, 15, 35, 51**
See also Wolfe, Thomas Kennerly, Jr.
See also AAYA 8; AITN 2; BEST 89:1; DLB 152
Wolff, Geoffrey (Ansell) 1937- .... **CLC 41**
See also CA 29-32R; CANR 29, 43
Wolff, Sonia
See Levitin, Sonia (Wolff)
Wolff, Tobias (Jonathan Ansell) 1945- . **C L C 39, 64**
See also AAYA 16; BEST 90:2; CA 114; 117; CAAS 22; CANR 54; DLB 130; INT 117
Wolfram von Eschenbach c. 1170-c. 1220
CMLC 5
See also DLB 138
Wolitzer, Hilma 1930- .... **CLC 17**
See also CA 65-68; CANR 18, 40; INT CANR-18; SATA 31
Wollstonecraft, Mary 1759-1797 .... **LC 5**
See also CDBLB 1789-1832; DLB 39, 104, 158
Wonder, Stevie .... **CLC 12**
See also Morris, Steveland Judkins
Wong, Jade Snow 1922- .... **CLC 17**
See also CA 109
Woodberry, George Edward 1855-1930
TCLC 73
See also DLB 71, 103
Woodcott, Keith

See Brunner, John (Kilian Houston)
Woodruff, Robert W.
See Mencken, H(enry) L(ouis)
Woolf, (Adeline) Virginia 1882-1941**TCLC 1, 5, 20, 43, 56; DA; DAB; DAC; DAM MST, NOV; SSC 7; WLC**
See also CA 104; 130; CDBLB 1914-1945; DLB 36, 100, 162; DLBD 10; MTCW
Woollcott, Alexander (Humphreys) 1887-1943
TCLC 5
See also CA 105; 161; DLB 29
Woolrich, Cornell 1903-1968 .... **CLC 77**
See also Hopley-Woolrich, Cornell George
Wordsworth, Dorothy 1771-1855 .. **NCLC 25**
See also DLB 107
Wordsworth, William 1770-1850 . **NCLC 12, 38; DA; DAB; DAC; DAM MST, POET; PC 4; WLC**
See also CDBLB 1789-1832; DLB 93, 107
Wouk, Herman 1915- .... **CLC 1, 9, 38; DAM NOV, POP**
See also CA 5-8R; CANR 6, 33; DLBY 82; INT CANR-6; MTCW
Wright, Charles (Penzel, Jr.) 1935-**CLC 6, 13, 28**
See also CA 29-32R; CAAS 7; CANR 23, 36, 62; DLB 165; DLBY 82; MTCW
Wright, Charles Stevenson 1932- ... **CLC 49; BLC 3; DAM MULT, POET**
See also BW 1; CA 9-12R; CANR 26; DLB 33
Wright, Jack R.
See Harris, Mark
Wright, James (Arlington) 1927-1980**CLC 3, 5, 10, 28; DAM POET**
See also AITN 2; CA 49-52; 97-100; CANR 4, 34; DLB 5, 169; MTCW
Wright, Judith (Arandell) 1915-**CLC 11, 53; PC 14**
See also CA 13-16R; CANR 31; MTCW; SATA 14
Wright, L(aurali) R. 1939- .... **CLC 44**
See also CA 138
Wright, Richard (Nathaniel) 1908-1960 **C L C 1, 3, 4, 9, 14, 21, 48, 74; BLC; DA; DAB; DAC; DAM MST, MULT, NOV; SSC 2; WLC**
See also AAYA 5; BW 1; CA 108; CDALB 1929-1941; DLB 76, 102; DLBD 2; MTCW
Wright, Richard B(ruce) 1937- .... **CLC 6**
See also CA 85-88; DLB 53
Wright, Rick 1945- .... **CLC 35**
Wright, Rowland
See Wells, Carolyn
Wright, Stephen Caldwell 1946- .... **CLC 33**
See also BW 2
Wright, Willard Huntington 1888-1939
See Van Dine, S. S.
See also CA 115; DLBD 16
Wright, William 1930- .... **CLC 44**
See also CA 53-56; CANR 7, 23
Wroth, LadyMary 1587-1653(?) .... **LC 30**
See also DLB 121
Wu Ch'eng-en 1500(?)-1582(?) .... **LC 7**
Wu Ching-tzu 1701-1754 .... **LC 2**
Wurlitzer, Rudolph 1938(?)- .... **CLC 2, 4, 15**
See also CA 85-88; DLB 173
Wycherley, William 1641-1715**LC 8, 21; DAM DRAM**
See also CDBLB 1660-1789; DLB 80
Wylie, Elinor (Morton Hoyt) 1885-1928
TCLC 8
See also CA 105; DLB 9, 45
Wylie, Philip (Gordon) 1902-1971 ... **CLC 43**
See also CA 21-22; 33-36R; CAP 2; DLB 9
Wyndham, John .... **CLC 19**
See also Harris, John (Wyndham Parkes Lucas) Beynon

Wyss, Johann David Von 1743-1818**NCLC 10**
See also JRDA; MAICYA; SATA 29; SATA-Brief 27
Xenophon c. 430B.C.-c. 354B.C. ... **CMLC 17**
See also DLB 176
Yakumo Koizumi
See Hearn, (Patricio) Lafcadio (Tessima Carlos)
Yanez, Jose Donoso
See Donoso (Yanez), Jose
Yanovsky, Basile S.
See Yanovsky, V(assily) S(emenovich)
Yanovsky, V(assily) S(emenovich) 1906-1989
CLC 2, 18
See also CA 97-100; 129
Yates, Richard 1926-1992 .... **CLC 7, 8, 23**
See also CA 5-8R; 139; CANR 10, 43; DLB 2; DLBY 81, 92; INT CANR-10
Yeats, W. B.
See Yeats, William Butler
Yeats, William Butler 1865-1939**TCLC 1, 11, 18, 31; DA; DAB; DAC; DAM DRAM, MST, POET; PC 20; WLC**
See also CA 104; 127; CANR 45; CDBLB 1890-1914; DLB 10, 19, 98, 156; MTCW
Yehoshua, A(braham) B. 1936- . **CLC 13, 31**
See also CA 33-36R; CANR 43
Yep, Laurence Michael 1948- .... **CLC 35**
See also AAYA 5; CA 49-52; CANR 1, 46; CLR 3, 17; DLB 52; JRDA; MAICYA; SATA 7, 69
Yerby, Frank G(arvin) 1916-1991 **CLC 1, 7, 22; BLC; DAM MULT**
See also BW 1; CA 9-12R; 136; CANR 16, 52; DLB 76; INT CANR-16; MTCW
Yesenin, Sergei Alexandrovich
See Esenin, Sergei (Alexandrovich)
Yevtushenko, Yevgeny (Alexandrovich) 1933-
CLC 1, 3, 13, 26, 51; DAM POET
See also CA 81-84; CANR 33, 54; MTCW
Yezierska, Anzia 1885(?)-1970 .... **CLC 46**
See also CA 126; 89-92; DLB 28; MTCW
Yglesias, Helen 1915- .... **CLC 7, 22**
See also CA 37-40R; CAAS 20; CANR 15; INT CANR-15; MTCW
Yokomitsu Riichi 1898-1947 .... **TCLC 47**
Yonge, Charlotte (Mary) 1823-1901**TCLC 48**
See also CA 109; DLB 18, 163; SATA 17
York, Jeremy
See Creasey, John
York, Simon
See Heinlein, Robert A(nson)
Yorke, Henry Vincent 1905-1974 ..... **CLC 13**
See also Green, Henry
See also CA 85-88; 49-52
Yosano Akiko 1878-1942 ... **TCLC 59; PC 11**
See also CA 161
Yoshimoto, Banana .... **CLC 84**
See also Yoshimoto, Mahoko
Yoshimoto, Mahoko 1964-
See Yoshimoto, Banana
See also CA 144
Young, Al(bert James) 1939- **CLC 19; BLC; DAM MULT**
See also BW 2; CA 29-32R; CANR 26; DLB 33
Young, Andrew (John) 1885-1971 ...... **CLC 5**
See also CA 5-8R; CANR 7, 29
Young, Collier
See Bloch, Robert (Albert)
Young, Edward 1683-1765 .... **LC 3, 40**
See also DLB 95
Young, Marguerite (Vivian) 1909-1995 **C L C 82**
See also CA 13-16; 150; CAP 1
Young, Neil 1945- .... **CLC 17**
See also CA 110
Young Bear, Ray A. 1950- ..... **CLC 94; DAM**

MULT
See also CA 146; DLB 175; NNAL
Yourcenar, Marguerite 1903-1987. **CLC 19, 38, 50, 87; DAM NOV**
See also CA 69-72; CANR 23, 60; DLB 72; DLBY 88; MTCW
Yurick, Sol 1925- .... **CLC 6**
See also CA 13-16R; CANR 25
Zabolotskii, Nikolai Alekseevich 1903-1958 **TCLC 52**
See also CA 116
Zamiatin, Yevgenii
See Zamyatin, Evgeny Ivanovich
Zamora, Bernice (B. Ortiz) 1938- .. **CLC 89; DAM MULT; HLC**
See also CA 151; DLB 82; HW
Zamyatin, Evgeny Ivanovich 1884-1937 **TCLC 8, 37**
See also CA 105
Zangwill, Israel 1864-1926 .... **TCLC 16**
See also CA 109; DLB 10, 135
Zappa, Francis Vincent, Jr. 1940-1993
See Zappa, Frank
See also CA 108; 143; CANR 57
Zappa, Frank .... **CLC 17**
See also Zappa, Francis Vincent, Jr.
Zaturenska, Marya 1902-1982 ..... **CLC 6, 11**
See also CA 13-16R; 105; CANR 22
Zeami 1363-1443 .... **DC 7**
Zelazny, Roger (Joseph) 1937-1995 **CLC 21**
See also AAYA 7; CA 21-24R; 148; CANR 26, 60; DLB 8; MTCW; SATA 57; SATA-Brief 39
Zhdanov, Andrei A(lexandrovich) 1896-1948 **TCLC 18**
See also CA 117
Zhukovsky, Vasily 1783-1852 .... **NCLC 35**
Ziegenhagen, Eric .... **CLC 55**
Zimmer, Jill Schary
See Robinson, Jill
Zimmerman, Robert
See Dylan, Bob
Zindel, Paul 1936- **CLC 6, 26; DA; DAB; DAC; DAM DRAM, MST, NOV; DC 5**
See also AAYA 2; CA 73-76; CANR 31; CLR 3, 45; DLB 7, 52; JRDA; MAICYA; MTCW; SATA 16, 58
Zinov'Ev, A. A.
See Zinoviev, Alexander (Aleksandrovich)
Zinoviev, Alexander (Aleksandrovich) 1922- **CLC 19**
See also CA 116; 133; CAAS 10
Zoilus
See Lovecraft, H(oward) P(hillips)
Zola, Emile (Edouard Charles Antoine) 1840-1902 **TCLC 1, 6, 21, 41; DA; DAB; DAC; DAM MST, NOV; WLC**
See also CA 104; 138; DLB 123
Zoline, Pamela 1941- .... **CLC 62**
See also CA 161
Zorrilla y Moral, Jose 1817-1893 .... **NCLC 6**
Zoshchenko, Mikhail (Mikhailovich) 1895-1958 .... **TCLC 15; SSC 15**
See also CA 115; 160
Zuckmayer, Carl 1896-1977 .... **CLC 18**
See also CA 69-72; DLB 56, 124
Zuk, Georges
See Skelton, Robin
Zukofsky, Louis 1904-1978 **CLC 1, 2, 4, 7, 11, 18; DAM POET; PC 11**
See also CA 9-12R; 77-80; CANR 39; DLB 5, 165; MTCW
Zweig, Paul 1935-1984 .... **CLC 34, 42**
See also CA 85-88; 113
Zweig, Stefan 1881-1942 .... **TCLC 17**
See also CA 112; DLB 81, 118
Zwingli, Huldreich 1484-1531 .... **LC 37**
See also DLB 179

Literary Criticism Series Cumulative Topic Index

This index lists all topic entries in Gale's *Classical and Medieval Literature Criticism, Contemporary Literary Criticism, Literature Criticism from 1400 to 1800, Nineteenth-Century Literature Criticism,* and *Twentieth-Century Literary Criticism.*

Age of Johnson LC 15: 1-87
  Johnson's London, 3-15
  aesthetics of neoclassicism, 15-36
  "age of prose and reason," 36-45
  clubmen and bluestockings, 45-56
  printing technology, 56-62
  periodicals: "a map of busy life," 62-74
  transition, 74-86

Age of Spenser LC 39: 1-70
  Overviews, 2-21
  Literary Style, 22-34
  Poets and the Crown, 34-70

AIDS in Literature CLC 81: 365-416

Alcohol and Literature TCLC 70: 1-58
  overview, 2-8
  fiction, 8-48
  poetry and drama, 48-58

American Abolitionism NCLC 44: 1-73
  overviews, 2-26
  abolitionist ideals, 26-46
  the literature of abolitionism, 46-72

American Black Humor Fiction TCLC 54: 1-85
  characteristics of black humor, 2-13
  origins and development, 13-38
  black humor distinguished from related literary trends, 38-60
  black humor and society, 60-75
  black humor reconsidered, 75-83

American Civil War in Literature NCLC 32: 1-109
  overviews, 2-20
  regional perspectives, 20-54
  fiction popular during the war, 54-79
  the historical novel, 79-108

American Frontier in Literature NCLC 28: 1-103
  definitions, 2-12
  development, 12-17
  nonfiction writing about the frontier, 17-30
  frontier fiction, 30-45
  frontier protagonists, 45-66
  portrayals of Native Americans, 66-86
  feminist readings, 86-98
  twentieth-century reaction against frontier literature, 98-100

American Humor Writing NCLC 52: 1-59
  overviews, 2-12
  the Old Southwest, 12-42
  broader impacts, 42-5
  women humorists, 45-58

***American Mercury,* The** TCLC 74: 1-80

American Popular Song, Golden Age of TCLC 42: 1-49
  background and major figures, 2-34
  the lyrics of popular songs, 34-47

American Proletarian Literature TCLC 54: 86-175
  overviews, 87-95
  American proletarian literature and the American Communist Party, 95-111
  ideology and literary merit, 111-7
  novels, 117-36
  Gastonia, 136-48
  drama, 148-54
  journalism, 154-9
  proletarian literature in the United States, 159-74

American Romanticism NCLC 44: 74-138
  overviews, 74-84
  sociopolitical influences, 84-104
  Romanticism and the American frontier, 104-15
  thematic concerns, 115-37

American Western Literature TCLC 46: 1-100
  definition and development of American Western literature, 2-7
  characteristics of the Western novel, 8-23
  Westerns as history and fiction, 23-34
  critical reception of American Western literature, 34-41
  the Western hero, 41-73
  women in Western fiction, 73-91
  later Western fiction, 91-9

Art and Literature TCLC 54: 176-248
  overviews, 176-93
  definitions, 193-219
  influence of visual arts on literature, 219-31
  spatial form in literature, 231-47

Arthurian Literature CMLC 10: 1-127
  historical context and literary beginnings, 2-27
  development of the legend through Malory, 27-64
  development of the legend from Malory to the Victorian Age, 65-81
  themes and motifs, 81-95
  principal characters, 95-125

Arthurian Revival NCLC 36: 1-77
  overviews, 2-12
  Tennyson and his influence, 12-43
  other leading figures, 43-73
  the Arthurian legend in the visual arts, 73-6

Australian Literature TCLC 50: 1-94
  origins and development, 2-21

characteristics of Australian literature, 21-33
historical and critical perspectives, 33-41
poetry, 41-58
fiction, 58-76
drama, 76-82
Aboriginal literature, 82-91

Beat Generation, Literature of the TCLC 42: 50-102
overviews, 51-9
the Beat generation as a social phenomenon, 59-62
development, 62-5
Beat literature, 66-96
influence, 97-100

The Bell Curve **Controversy** CLC 91: 281-330

Bildungsroman **in Nineteenth-Century Literature** NCLC 20: 92-168
surveys, 93-113
in Germany, 113-40
in England, 140-56
female *Bildungsroman*, 156-67

Bloomsbury Group TCLC 34: 1-73
history and major figures, 2-13
definitions, 13-7
influences, 17-27
thought, 27-40
prose, 40-52
and literary criticism, 52-4
political ideals, 54-61
response to, 61-71

Bly, Robert, *Iron John: A Book about Men and Men's Work* CLC 70: 414-62

The Book of J CLC 65: 289-311

Buddhism and Literature TCLC 70: 59-164
eastern literature, 60-113
western literature, 113-63

Businessman in American Literature TCLC 26: 1-48
portrayal of the businessman, 1-32
themes and techniques in business fiction, 32-47

Catholicism in Nineteenth-Century American Literature NCLC 64: 1-58
overviews, 3-14
polemical literature, 14-46
Catholicism in literature, 47-57

Celtic Twilight
See **Irish Literary Renaissance**

Chartist Movement and Literature, The NCLC 60: 1-84
overview: nineteenth-century working-class fiction, 2-19
Chartist fiction and poetry, 19-73
the Chartist press, 73-84

Children's Literature, Nineteenth-Century NCLC 52: 60-135
overviews, 61-72
moral tales, 72-89
fairy tales and fantasy, 90-119
making men/making women, 119-34

Civic Critics, Russian NCLC 20: 402-46
principal figures and background, 402-9
and Russian Nihilism, 410-6
aesthetic and critical views, 416-45

Colonial America: The Intellectual Background LC 25: 1-98
overviews, 2-17
philosophy and politics, 17-31
early religious influences in Colonial America, 31-60
consequences of the Revolution, 60-78
religious influences in post-revolutionary America, 78-87
colonial literary genres, 87-97

Colonialism in Victorian English Literature NCLC 56: 1-77
overviews, 2-34
colonialism and gender, 34-51
monsters and the occult, 51-76

Columbus, Christopher, Books on the Quincentennial of His Arrival in the New World CLC 70: 329-60

Comic Books TCLC 66: 1-139
historical and critical perspectives, 2-48
superheroes, 48-67
underground comix, 67-88
comic books and society, 88-122
adult comics and graphic novels, 122-36

Connecticut Wits NCLC 48: 1-95
general overviews, 2-40
major works, 40-76
intellectual context, 76-95

Crime in Literature TCLC 54: 249-307
evolution of the criminal figure in literature, 250-61
crime and society, 261-77
literary perspectives on crime and punishment, 277-88
writings by criminals, 288-306

Czechoslovakian Literature of the Twentieth Century TCLC 42: 103-96
through World War II, 104-35
de-Stalinization, the Prague Spring, and contemporary literature, 135-72
Slovak literature, 172-85
Czech science fiction, 185-93

Dadaism TCLC 46: 101-71
background and major figures, 102-16
definitions, 116-26
manifestos and commentary by Dadaists, 126-40
theater and film, 140-58
nature and characteristics of Dadaist writing, 158-70

Darwinism and Literature NCLC 32: 110-206
background, 110-31
direct responses to Darwin, 131-71
collateral effects of Darwinism, 171-205

de Man, Paul, Wartime Journalism of CLC 55: 382-424

Detective Fiction, Nineteenth-Century NCLC 36: 78-148
origins of the genre, 79-100
history of nineteenth-century detective fiction, 101-33
significance of nineteenth-century detective fiction, 133-46

Detective Fiction, Twentieth-Century
TCLC 38: 1-96
    genesis and history of the detective story, 3-22
    defining detective fiction, 22-32
    evolution and varieties, 32-77
    the appeal of detective fiction, 77-90

Disease and Literature TCLC 66: 140-283
    overviews, 141-65
    disease in nineteenth-century literature, 165-81
    tuberculosis and literature, 181-94
    women and disease in literature, 194-221
    plague literature, 221-53
    AIDS in literature, 253-82

The Double in Nineteenth-Century Literature NCLC 40: 1-95
    genesis and development of the theme, 2-15
    the double and Romanticism, 16-27
    sociological views, 27-52
    psychological interpretations, 52-87
    philosophical considerations, 87-95

Dramatic Realism NCLC 44: 139-202
    overviews, 140-50
    origins and definitions, 150-66
    impact and influence, 166-93
    realist drama and tragedy, 193-201

Electronic "Books": Hypertext and Hyperfiction CLC 86: 367-404
    books vs. CD-ROMS, 367-76
    hypertext and hyperfiction, 376-95
    implications for publishing, libraries, and the public, 395-403

Eliot, T. S., Centenary of Birth CLC 55: 345-75

Elizabethan Drama LC 22: 140-240
    origins and influences, 142-67
    characteristics and conventions, 167-83
    theatrical production, 184-200
    histories, 200-12
    comedy, 213-20
    tragedy, 220-30

The Encyclopedists LC 26: 172-253
    overviews, 173-210
    intellectual background, 210-32
    views on esthetics, 232-41
    views on women, 241-52

English Caroline Literature LC 13: 221-307
    background, 222-41
    evolution and varieties, 241-62
    the Cavalier mode, 262-75
    court and society, 275-91
    politics and religion, 291-306

English Decadent Literature of the 1890s NCLC 28: 104-200
    fin de siècle: the Decadent period, 105-19
    definitions, 120-37
    major figures: "the tragic generation," 137-50
    French literature and English literary Decadence, 150-7
    themes, 157-61
    poetry, 161-82
    periodicals, 182-96

English Essay, Rise of the LC 18: 238-308
    definitions and origins, 236-54
    influence on the essay, 254-69
    historical background, 269-78
    the essay in the seventeenth century, 279-93
    the essay in the eighteenth century, 293-307

English Mystery Cycle Dramas LC 34: 1-88
    overviews, 1-27
    the nature of dramatic performances, 27-42
    the medieval worldview and the mystery cycles, 43-67
    the doctrine of repentance and the mystery cycles, 67-76
    the fall from grace in the mystery cycles, 76-88

English Romantic Poetry NCLC 28: 201-327
    overviews and reputation, 202-37
    major subjects and themes, 237-67
    forms of Romantic poetry, 267-78
    politics, society, and Romantic poetry, 278-99
    philosophy, religion, and Romantic poetry, 299-324

Espionage Literature TCLC 50: 95-159
    overviews, 96-113
    espionage fiction/formula fiction, 113-26
    spies in fact and fiction, 126-38
    the female spy, 138-44
    social and psychological perspectives, 144-58

European Romanticism NCLC 36: 149-284
    definitions, 149-77
    origins of the movement, 177-82
    Romantic theory, 182-200
    themes and techniques, 200-23
    Romanticism in Germany, 223-39
    Romanticism in France, 240-61
    Romanticism in Italy, 261-4
    Romanticism in Spain, 264-8
    impact and legacy, 268-82

Existentialism and Literature TCLC 42: 197-268
    overviews and definitions, 198-209
    history and influences, 209-19
    Existentialism critiqued and defended, 220-35
    philosophical and religious perspectives, 235-41
    Existentialist fiction and drama, 241-67

Familiar Essay NCLC 48: 96-211
    definitions and origins, 97-130
    overview of the genre, 130-43
    elements of form and style, 143-59
    elements of content, 159-73
    the Cockneys: Hazlitt, Lamb, and Hunt, 173-91
    status of the genre, 191-210

Fear in Literature TCLC 74: 81-258
    overviews, 81
    pre-twentieth-century literature, 123
    twentieth-century literature, 182

Feminism in the 1990s: Commentary on Works by Naomi Wolf, Susan Faludi, and Camille Paglia CLC 76: 377-415

Feminist Criticism in 1990 CLC 65: 312-60

Fifteenth-Century English Literature LC 17: 248-334
    background, 249-72

poetry, 272-315
drama, 315-23
prose, 323-33

Film and Literature TCLC 38: 97-226
overviews, 97-119
film and theater, 119-34
film and the novel, 134-45
the art of the screenplay, 145-66
genre literature/genre film, 167-79
the writer and the film industry, 179-90
authors on film adaptations of their works, 190-200
fiction into film: comparative essays, 200-23

French Drama in the Age of Louis XIV
LC 28: 94-185
overview, 95-127
tragedy, 127-46
comedy, 146-66
tragicomedy, 166-84

French Enlightenment LC 14: 81-145
the question of definition, 82-9
Le siècle des lumières, 89-94
women and the salons, 94-105
censorship, 105-15
the philosophy of reason, 115-31
influence and legacy, 131-44

French Realism NCLC 52: 136-216
origins and definitions, 137-70
issues and influence, 170-98
realism and representation, 198-215

French Revolution and English Literature
NCLC 40: 96-195
history and theory, 96-123
romantic poetry, 123-50
the novel, 150-81
drama, 181-92
children's literature, 192-5

Futurism, Italian TCLC 42: 269-354
principles and formative influences, 271-9
manifestos, 279-88
literature, 288-303
theater, 303-19
art, 320-30
music, 330-6
architecture, 336-9
and politics, 339-46
reputation and significance, 346-51

Gaelic Revival
See **Irish Literary Renaissance**

Gates, Henry Louis, Jr., and African-American Literary Criticism CLC 65: 361-405

Gay and Lesbian Literature CLC 76: 416-39

German Exile Literature TCLC 30: 1-58
the writer and the Nazi state, 1-10
definition of, 10-4
life in exile, 14-32
surveys, 32-50
Austrian literature in exile, 50-2
German publishing in the United States, 52-7

German Expressionism TCLC 34: 74-160
history and major figures, 76-85
aesthetic theories, 85-109
drama, 109-26
poetry, 126-38
film, 138-42
painting, 142-7
music, 147-53
and politics, 153-8

***Glasnost* and Contemporary Soviet Literature** CLC 59: 355-97

Gothic Novel NCLC 28: 328-402
development and major works, 328-34
definitions, 334-50
themes and techniques, 350-78
in America, 378-85
in Scotland, 385-91
influence and legacy, 391-400

Graphic Narratives CLC 86: 405-32
history and overviews, 406-21
the "Classics Illustrated" series, 421-2
reviews of recent works, 422-32

Greek Historiography CMLC 17: 1-49

Harlem Renaissance TCLC 26: 49-125
principal issues and figures, 50-67
the literature and its audience, 67-74
theme and technique in poetry, fiction, and drama, 74-115
and American society, 115-21
achievement and influence, 121-2

Havel, Václav, Playwright and President
CLC 65: 406-63

Historical Fiction, Nineteenth-Century
NCLC 48: 212-307
definitions and characteristics, 213-36
Victorian historical fiction, 236-65
American historical fiction, 265-88
realism in historical fiction, 288-306

Holocaust and the Atomic Bomb: Fifty Years Later CLC 91: 331-82
the Holocaust remembered, 333-52
Anne Frank revisited, 352-62
the atomic bomb and American memory, 362-81

Holocaust Denial Literature TCLC 58: 1-110
overviews, 1-30
Robert Faurisson and Noam Chomsky, 30-52
Holocaust denial literature in America, 52-71
library access to Holocaust denial literature, 72-5
the authenticity of Anne Frank's diary, 76-90
David Irving and the "normalization" of Hitler, 90-109

Holocaust, Literature of the TCLC 42: 355-450
historical overview, 357-61
critical overview, 361-70
diaries and memoirs, 370-95
novels and short stories, 395-425
poetry, 425-41
drama, 441-8

Homosexuality in Nineteenth-Century Literature NCLC 56: 78-182
defining homosexuality, 80-111
Greek love, 111-44
trial and danger, 144-81

Hungarian Literature of the Twentieth Century TCLC 26: 126-88
surveys of, 126-47
Nyugat and early twentieth-century literature, 147-56

mid-century literature, 156-68
and politics, 168-78
since the 1956 revolt, 178-87

Hysteria in Nineteenth-Century Literature NCLC 64: 59-184
the history of hysteria, 60-75
the gender of hysteria, 75-103
hysteria and women's narratives, 103-57
hysteria in nineteenth-century poetry, 157-83

Imagism TCLC 74: 259-454
history and development, 260
major figures, 288
sources and influences, 352
Imagism and other movements, 397
influence and legacy, 431

Indian Literature in English TCLC 54: 308-406
overview, 309-13
origins and major figures, 313-25
the Indo-English novel, 325-55
Indo-English poetry, 355-67
Indo-English drama, 367-72
critical perspectives on Indo-English literature, 372-80
modern Indo-English literature, 380-9
Indo-English authors on their work, 389-404

Industrial Revolution in Literature, The NCLC 56: 183-273
historical and cultural perspectives, 184-201
contemporary reactions to the machine, 201-21
themes and symbols in literature, 221-73

The Irish Famine as Represented in Nineteenth-Century Literature NCLC 64: 185-261
overviews, 187-98
historical background, 198-212
famine novels, 212-34
famine poetry, 234-44
famine letters and eye-witness accounts, 245-61

Irish Literary Renaissance TCLC 46: 172-287
overview, 173-83

development and major figures, 184-202
influence of Irish folklore and mythology, 202-22
Irish poetry, 222-34
Irish drama and the Abbey Theatre, 234-56
Irish fiction, 256-86

Irish Nationalism and Literature NCLC 44: 203-73
the Celtic element in literature, 203-19
anti-Irish sentiment and the Celtic response, 219-34
literary ideals in Ireland, 234-45
literary expressions, 245-73

Italian Futurism
See **Futurism, Italian**

Italian Humanism LC 12: 205-77
origins and early development, 206-18
revival of classical letters, 218-23
humanism and other philosophies, 224-39
humanisms and humanists, 239-46
the plastic arts, 246-57
achievement and significance, 258-76

Italian Romanticism NCLC 60: 85-145
origins and overviews, 86-101
Italian Romantic theory, 101-25
the language of Romanticism, 125-45

Jacobean Drama LC 33: 1-37
the Jacobean worldview: an era of transition, 2-14
the moral vision of Jacobean drama, 14-22
Jacobean tragedy, 22-3
the Jacobean masque, 23-36

Jewish-American Fiction TCLC 62: 1-181
overviews, 2-24
major figures, 24-48
Jewish writers and American life, 48-78
Jewish characters in American fiction, 78-108
themes in Jewish-American fiction, 108-43
Jewish-American women writers, 143-59
the Holocaust and Jewish-American fiction, 159-81

Knickerbocker Group, The NCLC 56: 274-341
overviews, 276-314

Knickerbocker periodicals, 314-26
writers and artists, 326-40

Lake Poets, The NCLC 52: 217-304
characteristics of the Lake Poets and their works, 218-27
literary influences and collaborations, 227-66
defining and developing Romantic ideals, 266-84
embracing Conservatism, 284-303

Larkin, Philip, Controversy CLC 81: 417-64

Latin American Literature, Twentieth-Century TCLC 58: 111-98
historical and critical perspectives, 112-36
the novel, 136-45
the short story, 145-9
drama, 149-60
poetry, 160-7
the writer and society, 167-86
Native Americans in Latin American literature, 186-97

Madness in Twentieth-Century Literature TCLC 50: 160-225
overviews, 161-71
madness and the creative process, 171-86
suicide, 186-91
madness in American literature, 191-207
madness in German literature, 207-13
madness and feminist artists, 213-24

Metaphysical Poets LC 24: 356-439
early definitions, 358-67
surveys and overviews, 367-92
cultural and social influences, 392-406
stylistic and thematic variations, 407-38

Modern Essay, The TCLC 58: 199-273
overview, 200-7
the essay in the early twentieth century, 207-19
characteristics of the modern essay, 219-32
modern essayists, 232-45
the essay as a literary genre, 245-73

Modern Japanese Literature TCLC 66: 284-389
poetry, 285-305

drama, 305-29
fiction, 329-61
western influences, 361-87

Modernism TCLC 70: 165-275
definitions, 166-184
Modernism and earlier influences, 184-200
stylistic and thematic traits, 200-229
poetry and drama, 229-242
redefining Modernism, 242-275

Muckraking Movement in American Journalism TCLC 34: 161-242
development, principles, and major figures, 162-70
publications, 170-9
social and political ideas, 179-86
targets, 186-208
fiction, 208-19
decline, 219-29
impact and accomplishments, 229-40

Multiculturalism in Literature and Education CLC 70: 361-413

Music and Modern Literature TCLC 62: 182-329
overviews, 182-211
musical form/literary form, 211-32
music in literature, 232-50
the influence of music on literature, 250-73
literature and popular music, 273-303
jazz and poetry, 303-28

Native American Literature CLC 76: 440-76

Natural School, Russian NCLC 24: 205-40
history and characteristics, 205-25
contemporary criticism, 225-40

Naturalism NCLC 36: 285-382
definitions and theories, 286-305
critical debates on Naturalism, 305-16
Naturalism in theater, 316-32
European Naturalism, 332-61
American Naturalism, 361-72
the legacy of Naturalism, 372-81

Negritude TCLC 50: 226-361
origins and evolution, 227-56
definitions, 256-91
Negritude in literature, 291-343
Negritude reconsidered, 343-58

New Criticism TCLC 34: 243-318
development and ideas, 244-70
debate and defense, 270-99
influence and legacy, 299-315

The New World in Renaissance Literature LC 31: 1-51
overview, 1-18
utopia vs. terror, 18-31
explorers and Native Americans, 31-51

New York Intellectuals and *Partisan Review* TCLC 30: 117-98
development and major figures, 118-28
influence of Judaism, 128-39
Partisan Review, 139-57
literary philosophy and practice, 157-75
political philosophy, 175-87
achievement and significance, 187-97

The New Yorker TCLC 58: 274-357
overviews, 274-95
major figures, 295-304
New Yorker style, 304-33
fiction, journalism, and humor at *The New Yorker*, 333-48
the new *New Yorker*, 348-56

Newgate Novel NCLC 24: 166-204
development of Newgate literature, 166-73
Newgate Calendar, 173-7
Newgate fiction, 177-95
Newgate drama, 195-204

Nigerian Literature of the Twentieth Century TCLC 30: 199-265
surveys of, 199-227
English language and African life, 227-45
politics and the Nigerian writer, 245-54
Nigerian writers and society, 255-62

Nineteenth-Century Native American Autobiography NCLC 64: 262-389
overview, 263-8
problems of authorship, 268-81
the evolution of Native American autobiography, 281-304
political issues, 304-15
gender and autobiography, 316-62
autobiographical works during the turn of the century, 362-88

Northern Humanism LC 16: 281-356
background, 282-305
precursor of the Reformation, 305-14
the Brethren of the Common Life, the Devotio Moderna, and education, 314-40
the impact of printing, 340-56

Novel of Manners, The NCLC 56: 342-96
social and political order, 343-53
domestic order, 353-73
depictions of gender, 373-83
the American novel of manners, 383-95

Nuclear Literature: Writings and Criticism in the Nuclear Age TCLC 46: 288-390
overviews, 290-301
fiction, 301-35
poetry, 335-8
nuclear war in Russo-Japanese literature, 338-55
nuclear war and women writers, 355-67
the nuclear referent and literary criticism, 367-88

Occultism in Modern Literature TCLC 50: 362-406
influence of occultism on literature, 363-72
occultism, literature, and society, 372-87
fiction, 387-96
drama, 396-405

Opium and the Nineteenth-Century Literary Imagination NCLC 20: 250-301
original sources, 250-62
historical background, 262-71
and literary society, 271-9
and literary creativity, 279-300

Periodicals, Nineteenth-Century British NCLC 24: 100-65
overviews, 100-30
in the Romantic Age, 130-41
in the Victorian era, 142-54
and the reviewer, 154-64

Plath, Sylvia, and the Nature of Biography CLC 86: 433-62
- the nature of biography, 433-52
- reviews of *The Silent Woman*, 452-61

Political Theory from the 15th to the 18th Century LC 36: 1-55
- Overview, 1-26
- Natural Law, 26-42
- Empiricism, 42-55

Polish Romanticism NCLC 52: 305-71
- overviews, 306-26
- major figures, 326-40
- Polish Romantic drama, 340-62
- influences, 362-71

Popular Literature TCLC 70: 279-382
- overviews, 280-324
- "formula" fiction, 324-336
- readers of popular literature, 336-351
- evolution of popular literature, 351-382

Pre-Raphaelite Movement NCLC 20: 302-401
- overview, 302-4
- genesis, 304-12
- *Germ* and *Oxford and Cambridge Magazine,* 312-20
- Robert Buchanan and the "Fleshly School of Poetry," 320-31
- satires and parodies, 331-4
- surveys, 334-51
- aesthetics, 351-75
- sister arts of poetry and painting, 375-94
- influence, 394-9

Preromanticism LC 40: 1-56
- overviews, 2-14
- defining the period, 14-23
- new directions in poetry and prose, 23-45
- the focus on the self, 45-56

Presocratic Philosophy CMLC 22: 1-56
- overviews, 3-24
- the Ionians and the Pythagoreans, 25-35
- Heraclitus, the Eleatics, and the Atomists, 36-47
- the Sophists, 47-55

Protestant Reformation, Literature of the LC 37: 1-83
- overviews, 1-49
- humanism and scholasticism, 49-69
- the reformation and literature, 69-82

Psychoanalysis and Literature TCLC 38: 227-338
- overviews, 227-46
- Freud on literature, 246-51
- psychoanalytic views of the literary process, 251-61
- psychoanalytic theories of response to literature, 261-88
- psychoanalysis and literary criticism, 288-312
- psychoanalysis as literature/literature as psychoanalysis, 313-34

Rap Music CLC 76: 477-50

Renaissance Natural Philosophy LC 27: 201-87
- cosmology, 201-28
- astrology, 228-54
- magic, 254-86

Restoration Drama LC 21: 184-275
- general overviews, 185-230
- Jeremy Collier stage controversy, 230-9
- other critical interpretations, 240-75

Revising the Literary Canon CLC 81: 465-509

Robin Hood, Legend of LC 19: 205-58
- origins and development of the Robin Hood legend, 206-20
- representations of Robin Hood, 220-44
- Robin Hood as hero, 244-56

Rushdie, Salman, *Satanic Verses* Controversy CLC 55 214-63; 59: 404-56

Russian Nihilism NCLC 28: 403-47
- definitions and overviews, 404-17
- women and Nihilism, 417-27
- literature as reform: the Civic Critics, 427-33
- Nihilism and the Russian novel: Turgenev and Dostoevsky, 433-47

Russian Thaw TCLC 26: 189-247
- literary history of the period, 190-206
- theoretical debate of socialist realism, 206-11
- *Novy Mir,* 211-7
- *Literary Moscow,* 217-24
- Pasternak, *Zhivago,* and the Nobel Prize, 224-7
- poetry of liberation, 228-31
- Brodsky trial and the end of the Thaw, 231-6
- achievement and influence, 236-46

Salem Witch Trials LC-38: 1-145
- overviews, 2-30
- historical background, 30-65
- judicial background, 65-78
- the search for causes, 78-115
- the role of women in the trials, 115-44

Salinger, J. D., Controversy Surrounding *In Search of J. D. Salinger* CLC 55: 325-44

Science Fiction, Nineteenth-Century NCLC 24: 241-306
- background, 242-50
- definitions of the genre, 251-6
- representative works and writers, 256-75
- themes and conventions, 276-305

Scottish Chaucerians LC 20: 363-412

Scottish Poetry, Eighteenth-Century LC 29: 95-167
- overviews, 96-114
- the Scottish Augustans, 114-28
- the Scots Vernacular Revival, 132-63
- Scottish poetry after Burns, 163-6

Sentimental Novel, The NCLC 60: 146-245
- overviews, 147-58
- the politics of domestic fiction, 158-79
- a literature of resistance and repression, 179-212
- the reception of sentimental fiction, 213-44

Sherlock Holmes Centenary TCLC 26: 248-310
- Doyle's life and the composition of the Holmes stories, 248-59
- life and character of Holmes, 259-78

method, 278-9
Holmes and the Victorian world, 279-92
Sherlockian scholarship, 292-301
Doyle and the development of the detective story, 301-7
Holmes's continuing popularity, 307-9

Slave Narratives, American NCLC 20: 1-91
background, 2-9
overviews, 9-24
contemporary responses, 24-7
language, theme, and technique, 27-70
historical authenticity, 70-5
antecedents, 75-83
role in development of Black American literature, 83-8

Spanish Civil War Literature TCLC 26: 311-85
topics in, 312-33
British and American literature, 333-59
French literature, 359-62
Spanish literature, 362-73
German literature, 373-5
political idealism and war literature, 375-83

Spanish Golden Age Literature LC 23: 262-332
overviews, 263-81
verse drama, 281-304
prose fiction, 304-19
lyric poetry, 319-31

Spasmodic School of Poetry NCLC 24: 307-52
history and major figures, 307-21
the Spasmodics on poetry, 321-7
Firmilian and critical disfavor, 327-39
theme and technique, 339-47
influence, 347-51

Steinbeck, John, Fiftieth Anniversary of *The Grapes of Wrath* CLC 59: 311-54

Sturm und Drang NCLC 40: 196-276
definitions, 197-238
poetry and poetics, 238-58
drama, 258-75

Supernatural Fiction in the Nineteenth Century NCLC 32: 207-87
major figures and influences, 208-35
the Victorian ghost story, 236-54
the influence of science and occultism, 254-66
supernatural fiction and society, 266-86

Supernatural Fiction, Modern TCLC 30: 59-116
evolution and varieties, 60-74
"decline" of the ghost story, 74-86
as a literary genre, 86-92
technique, 92-101
nature and appeal, 101-15

Surrealism TCLC 30: 334-406
history and formative influences, 335-43
manifestos, 343-54
philosophic, aesthetic, and political principles, 354-75
poetry, 375-81
novel, 381-6
drama, 386-92
film, 392-8
painting and sculpture, 398-403
achievement, 403-5

Symbolism, Russian TCLC 30: 266-333
doctrines and major figures, 267-92
theories, 293-8
and French Symbolism, 298-310
themes in poetry, 310-4
theater, 314-20
and the fine arts, 320-32

Symbolist Movement, French NCLC 20: 169-249
background and characteristics, 170-86
principles, 186-91
attacked and defended, 191-7
influences and predecessors, 197-211
and Decadence, 211-6
theater, 216-26
prose, 226-33
decline and influence, 233-47

Theater of the Absurd TCLC 38: 339-415
"The Theater of the Absurd," 340-7
major plays and playwrights, 347-58
and the concept of the absurd, 358-86
theatrical techniques, 386-94
predecessors of, 394-402
influence of, 402-13

Tin Pan Alley
See **American Popular Song, Golden Age of**

Transcendentalism, American NCLC 24: 1-99
overviews, 3-23
contemporary documents, 23-41
theological aspects of, 42-52
and social issues, 52-74
literature of, 74-96

Travel Writing in the Nineteenth Century NCLC 44: 274-392
the European grand tour, 275-303
the Orient, 303-47
North America, 347-91

Travel Writing in the Twentieth Century TCLC 30: 407-56
conventions and traditions, 407-27
and fiction writing, 427-43
comparative essays on travel writers, 443-54

True-Crime Literature CLC 99: 333-433
history and analysis, 334-407
reviews of true-crime publications, 407-23
writing instruction, 424-29
author profiles, 429-33

***Ulysses* and the Process of Textual Reconstruction** TCLC 26: 386-416
evaluations of the new *Ulysses,* 386-94
editorial principles and procedures, 394-401
theoretical issues, 401-16

Utopian Literature, Nineteenth-Century NCLC 24: 353-473
definitions, 354-74
overviews, 374-88
theory, 388-408
communities, 409-26
fiction, 426-53
women and fiction, 454-71

Utopian Literature, Renaissance LC-32: 1-63
overviews, 2-25
classical background, 25-33
utopia and the social contract, 33-9
origins in mythology, 39-48
utopia and the Renaissance country house, 48-52
influence of millenarianism, 52-62

Vampire in Literature TCLC 46: 391-454
   origins and evolution, 392-412
   social and psychological perspectives, 413-44
   vampire fiction and science fiction, 445-53

Victorian Autobiography NCLC 40: 277-363
   development and major characteristics, 278-88
   themes and techniques, 289-313
   the autobiographical tendency in Victorian prose and poetry, 313-47
   Victorian women's autobiographies, 347-62

Victorian Fantasy Literature NCLC 60: 246-384
   overviews, 247-91
   major figures, 292-366
   women in Victorian fantasy literature, 366-83

Victorian Novel NCLC 32: 288-454
   development and major characteristics, 290-310
   themes and techniques, 310-58
   social criticism in the Victorian novel, 359-97
   urban and rural life in the Victorian novel, 397-406
   women in the Victorian novel, 406-25
   Mudie's Circulating Library, 425-34
   the late-Victorian novel, 434-51

Vietnam War in Literature and Film CLC 91: 383-437
   overview, 384-8
   prose, 388-412
   film and drama, 412-24
   poetry, 424-35

Vorticism TCLC 62: 330-426
   Wyndham Lewis and Vorticism, 330-8
   characteristics and principles of Vorticism, 338-65
   Lewis and Pound, 365-82
   Vorticist writing, 382-416
   Vorticist painting, 416-26

Women's Diaries, Nineteenth-Century NCLC 48: 308-54
   overview, 308-13
   diary as history, 314-25
   sociology of diaries, 325-34
   diaries as psychological scholarship, 334-43
   diary as autobiography, 343-8
   diary as literature, 348-53

Women Writers, Seventeenth-Century LC 30: 2-58
   overview, 2-15
   women and education, 15-9
   women and autobiography, 19-31
   women's diaries, 31-9
   early feminists, 39-58

World War I Literature TCLC 34: 392-486
   overview, 393-403
   English, 403-27
   German, 427-50
   American, 450-66
   French, 466-74
   and modern history, 474-82

Yellow Journalism NCLC 36: 383-456
   overviews, 384-96
   major figures, 396-413

Young Playwrights Festival
   1988—CLC 55: 376-81
   1989—CLC 59: 398-403
   1990—CLC 65: 444-8

NCLC Cumulative Nationality Index

AMERICAN
Alcott, Amos Bronson **1**
Alcott, Louisa May **6, 58**
Alger, Horatio **8**
Allston, Washington **2**
Audubon, John James **47**
Barlow, Joel **23**
Beecher, Catharine Esther **30**
Bellamy, Edward **4**
Bird, Robert Montgomery **1**
Brackenridge, Hugh Henry **7**
Brentano, Clemens (Maria) **1**
Brown, Charles Brockden **22**
Brown, William Wells **2**
Brownson, Orestes **50**
Bryant, William Cullen **6, 46**
Calhoun, John Caldwell **15**
Channing, William Ellery **17**
Child, Lydia Maria **6**
Chivers, Thomas Holley **49**
Cooke, John Esten **5**
Cooper, James Fenimore **1, 27, 54**
Crockett, David **8**
Dana, Richard Henry, Sr. **53**
Dickinson, Emily (Elizabeth) **21**
Douglass, Frederick **7, 55**
Dunlap, William **2**
Dwight, Timothy **13**
Emerson, Mary Moody **66**
Emerson, Ralph Waldo **1, 38**
Field, Eugene **3**
Foster, Stephen Collins **26**
Frederic, Harold **10**
Freneau, Philip Morin **1**
Fuller, Margaret **5, 50**
Halleck, Fitz-Greene **47**
Hamilton, Alexander **49**
Hammon, Jupiter **5**
Harris, George Washington **23**
Hawthorne, Nathaniel **2, 10, 17, 23, 39**
Holmes, Oliver Wendell **14**
Irving, Washington **2, 19**
James, Henry, Sr. **53**
Jefferson, Thomas **11**
Kennedy, John Pendleton **2**
Lanier, Sidney **6**
Lazarus, Emma **8**
Lincoln, Abraham **18**
Longfellow, Henry Wadsworth **2, 45**
Lowell, James Russell **2**
Melville, Herman **3, 12, 29, 45, 49**
Murray, Judith Sargent **63**
Parkman, Francis **12**
Paulding, James Kirke **2**
Pinkney, Edward **31**
Poe, Edgar Allan **1, 16, 55**
Rowson, Susanna Haswell **5**
Sand, George **57**
Sedgwick, Catharine Maria **19**
Shaw, Henry Wheeler **15**
Sheridan, Richard Brinsley **5**
Signourney, Lydia Howard (Huntley) **21**
Simms, William Gilmore **3**
Smith, Joseph, Jr. **53**
Southworth, Emma Dorothy Eliza Nevitte **26**
Stowe, Harriet (Elizabeth) Beecher **3, 50**
Thoreau, Henry David **7, 21**
Timrod, Henry **25**
Trumbull, John **30**
Tyler, Royall **3**
Very, Jones **9**
Warner, Susan (Bogert) **31**
Warren, Mercy Otis **13**
Webster, Noah **30**
Whitman, Sarah Helen (Power) **19**
Whitman, Walt(er) **4, 31**
Whittier, John Greenleaf **8**

ARGENTINIAN
Echeverria, (Jose) Esteban (Antonino) **18**
Hernandez, Jose **17**

AUSTRALIAN
Adams, Francis **33**
Clarke, Marcus (Andrew Hislop) **19**
Gordon, Adam Lindsay **21**
Kendall, Henry **12**

AUSTRIAN
Grillparzer, Franz **1**
Lenau, Nikolaus **16**
Nestroy, Johann **42**
Sacher-Masoch, Leopold von **31**
Stifter, Adalbert **41**

CANADIAN
Crawford, Isabella Valancy **12**
Haliburton, Thomas Chandler **15**
Lampman, Archibald **25**
Moodie, Susanna (Strickland) **14**
Richardson, John **55**
Traill, Catharine Parr **31**

CUBAN
Martí, José **63**

CZECH
Macha, Karel Hynek **46**

DANISH
Andersen, Hans Christian **7**
Grundtvig, Nicolai Frederik Severin **1**

Jacobsen, Jens Peter **34**
Kierkegaard, Soren **34**

ENGLISH
Ainsworth, William Harrison **13**
Arnold, Matthew **6, 29**
Arnold, Thomas **18**
Austen, Jane **1, 13, 19, 33, 51**
Bagehot, Walter **10**
Barbauld, Anna Laetitia **50**
Beardsley, Aubrey **6**
Beckford, William **16**
Beddoes, Thomas Lovell **3**
Bentham, Jeremy **38**
Blake, William **13, 37, 57**
Borrow, George (Henry) **9**
Bronte, Anne **4**
Bronte, Charlotte **3, 8, 33, 58**
Bronte, (Jane) Emily **16, 35**
Browning, Elizabeth Barrett **1, 16, 66**
Browning, Robert **19**
Bulwer-Lytton, Edward (George Earle Lytton) **1, 45**
Burney, Fanny **12, 54**
Burton, Richard F. **42**
Byron, George Gordon (Noel) **2, 12**
Carlyle, Thomas **22**
Carroll, Lewis **2, 53**
Clare, John **9**
Clough, Arthur Hugh **27**
Cobbett, William **49**
Coleridge, Samuel Taylor **9, 54**
Coleridge, Sara **31**
Collins, (William) Wilkie **1, 18**
Cowper, William **8**
Crabbe, George **26**
Craik, Dinah Maria (Mulock) **38**
Darwin, Charles **57**
De Quincey, Thomas **4**
Dickens, Charles (John Huffam) **3, 8, 18, 26, 37, 50**
Disraeli, Benjamin **2, 39**
Dobell, Sydney Thompson **43**
Eden, Emily **10**
Eliot, George **4, 13, 23, 41, 49**
FitzGerald, Edward **9**
Forster, John **11**
Froude, James Anthony **43**
Gaskell, Elizabeth Cleghorn **5**
Gilpin, William **30**
Godwin, William **14**
Gore, Catherine **65**
Hazlitt, William **29**
Hemans, Felicia **29**
Hood, Thomas **16**
Hopkins, Gerard Manley **17**
Hunt (James Henry) Leigh **1**
Inchbald, Elizabeth **62**
Ingelow, Jean **39**
Jefferies, (John) Richard **47**
Jerrold, Douglas William **2**
Jewsbury, Geraldine (Endsor) **22**
Keats, John **8**
Kemble, Fanny **18**
Kingsley, Charles **35**
Lamb, Charles **10**
Lamb, Lady Caroline **38**
Landon, Letitia Elizabeth **15**
Landor, Walter Savage **14**
Lear, Edward **3**
Lennox, Charlotte Ramsay **23**
Lewes, George Henry **25**
Lewis, Matthew Gregory **11, 62**
Linton, Eliza Lynn **41**
Macaulay, Thomas Babington **42**
Marryat, Frederick **3**
Martineau, Harriet **26**
Mayhew, Henry **31**
Mill, John Stuart **11, 58**
Mitford, Mary Russell **4**
Montagu, Elizabeth **7**
More, Hannah **27**
Morris, William **4**
Newman, John Henry **38**
Norton, Caroline **47**
Oliphant, Laurence **47**
Opie, Amelia **65**
Paine, Thomas **62**
Pater, Walter (Horatio) **7**
Patmore, Coventry **9**
Peacock, Thomas Love **22**
Piozzi, Hester **57**
Planche, James Robinson **42**
Polidori, John Willam **51**
Radcliffe, Ann (Ward) **6, 55**
Reade, Charles **2**
Reeve, Clara **19**
Robertson, Thomas William **35**
Robinson, Henry Crabb **15**
Rossetti, Christina (Georgina) **2, 50, 66**
Rossetti, Dante Gabriel **4**
Sala, George Augustus **46**
Shelley, Mary Wollstonecraft (Godwin) **14**
Shelley, Percy Bysshe **18**
Smith, Charlotte (Turner) **23**
Southey, Robert **8**
Surtees, Robert Smith **14**
Symonds, John Addington **34**
Tennyson, Alfred **30, 65**
Thackeray, William Makepeace **5, 14, 22, 43**
Trollope, Anthony **6, 33**
Trollope, Frances **30**
Wordsworth, Dorothy **25**
Wordsworth, William **12, 38**

FILIPINO
Rizal, Jose **27**

FINNISH
Kivi, Aleksis **30**
Lonnrot, Elias **53**
Runeberg, Johan **41**

FRENCH
Augier, Emile **31**
Balzac, Honore de **5, 35, 53**
Banville, Theodore (Faullain) de **9**
Barbey d'Aurevilly, Jules Amedee **1**
Baudelaire, Charles **6, 29, 55**
Becque, Henri **3**
Beranger, Pierre Jean de **34**
Bertrand, Aloysius **31**
Borel, Petrus **41**
Chateaubriand, Francois Rene de **3**
Comte, Auguste **54**
Constant (de Rebecque), (Henri) Benjamin **6**
Corbiere, Tristan **43**
Daudet, (Louis Marie) Alphonse **1**
Dumas, Alexandre **9**
Dumas, Alexandre (Davy de la Pailleterie) **11**
Feuillet, Octave **45**
Flaubert, Gustave **2, 10, 19, 62, 66**
Fourier, Charles **51**
Fromentin, Eugene (Samuel Auguste) **10**
Gaboriau, Emile **14**
Gautier, Theophile **1**
Gobineau, Joseph Arthur (Comte) de **17**
Goncourt, Edmond (Louis Antoine Huot) de **7**
Goncourt, Jules (Alfred Huot) de **7**
Hugo, Victor (Marie) **3, 10, 21**
Joubert, Joseph **9**
Kock, Charles Paul de **16**
Laclos, Pierre Ambroise Francois Choderlos de **4**
Laforgue, Jules **5, 53**
Lamartine, Alphonse (Marie Louis Prat) de **11**
Lautreamont, Comte de **12**
Leconte de Lisle, Charles-Marie-Rene **29**
Maistre, Joseph de **37**
Mallarme, Stephane **4, 41**
Maupassant, (Henri Rene Albert) Guy de **1, 42**
Merimee, Prosper **6, 65**
Michelet, Jules **31**
Musset, (Louis Charles) Alfred de **7**
Nerval, Gerard de **1**
Nodier, (Jean) Charles (Emmanuel) **19**
Pixerecourt, Guilbert de **39**
Renan, Joseph Ernest **26**
Rimbaud, (Jean Nicolas) Arthur **4, 35**
Sade, Donatien Alphonse Francois **3**
Sainte-Beuve, Charles Augustin **5**
Sand, George **2, 42, 57**
Scribe, (Augustin) Eugene **16**
Senancour, Etienne Pivert de **16**
Stael-Holstein, Anne Louise Germaine Necker **3**
Stendhal **23, 46**
Sue, Eugene **1**
Taine, Hippolyte Adolphe **15**
Tocqueville, Alexis (Charles Henri Maurice Clerel) **7, 63**
Verlaine, Paul (Marie) **2, 51**
Vigny, Alfred (Victor) de **7**
Villiers de l'Isle Adam, Jean Marie Mathias Philippe Auguste **3**

GERMAN
Arnim, Achim von (Ludwig Joachim von Arnim) **5**
Arnim, Bettina von **38**
Bonaventura **35**
Buchner, (Karl) Georg **26**
Droste-Hulshoff, Annette Freiin von **3**
Eichendorff, Joseph Freiherr von **8**
Fichte, Johann Gottlieb **62**
Fontane, Theodor **26**
Fouque, Friedrich (Heinrich Karl) de la Motte **2**
Goethe, Johann Wolfgang von **4, 22, 34**
Grabbe, Christian Dietrich **2**
Grimm, Jacob Ludwig Karl **3**
Grimm, Wilhelm Karl **3**
Hebbel, Friedrich **43**
Hegel, Georg Wilhelm Friedrich **46**
Heine, Heinrich **4, 54**
Hoffmann, E(rnst) T(heodor) A(madeus) **2**
Holderlin, (Johann Christian) Friedrich **16**
Immerman, Karl (Lebrecht) **4, 49**
Jean Paul **7**
Kant, Immanuel **27**
Kleist, Heinrich von **2, 37**
Klinger, Friedrich Maximilian von **1**
Klopstock, Friedrich Gottlieb **11**
Kotzebue, August (Friedrich Ferdinand) von **25**
Ludwig, Otto **4**
Marx, Karl (Heinrich) **17**
Morike, Eduard (Friedrich) **10**
Novalis **13**

Schelling, Friedrich Wilhelm Joseph von 30
Schiller, Friedrich 39
Schlegel, August Wilhelm von 15
Schlegel, Friedrich 45
Schopenhauer, Arthur 51
Storm, (Hans) Theodor (Woldsen) 1
Tieck, (Johann) Ludwig 5, 46
Wagner, Richard 9
Wieland, Christoph Martin 17

GREEK
Solomos, Dionysios 15

HUNGARIAN
Arany, Janos 34
Madach, Imre 19
Petofi, Sandor 21

INDIAN
Chatterji, Bankim Chandra 19
Dutt, Toru 29
Ghalib 39

IRISH
Allingham, William 25
Banim, John 13
Banim, Michael 13
Boucicault, Dion 41
Carleton, William 3
Croker, John Wilson 10
Darley, George 2
Edgeworth, Maria 1, 51
Ferguson, Samuel 33
Griffin, Gerald 7
Jameson, Anna 43
Le Fanu, Joseph Sheridan 9, 58
Lever, Charles (James) 23
Maginn, William 8
Mangan, James Clarence 27
Maturin, Charles Robert 6
Moore, Thomas 6
Morgan, Lady 29
O'Brien, Fitz-James 21

ITALIAN
Collodi, Carlo (Carlo Lorenzini) 54
Da Ponte, Lorenzo 50
Foscolo, Ugo 8
Gozzi, (Conte) Carlo 23

Leopardi, (Conte) Giacomo 22
Manzoni, Alessandro 29
Mazzini, Guiseppe 34
Nievo, Ippolito 22

JAPANESE
Higuchi Ichiyo 49
Motoori, Norinaga 45

LITHUANIAN
Mapu, Abraham (ben Jekutiel) 18

MEXICAN
Lizardi, Jose Joaquin Fernandez de 30

NORWEGIAN
Collett, (Jacobine) Camilla (Wergeland) 22
Wergeland, Henrik Arnold 5

POLISH
Fredro, Aleksander 8
Krasicki, Ignacy 8
Krasinski, Zygmunt 4
Mickiewicz, Adam 3
Norwid, Cyprian Kamil 17
Slowacki, Juliusz 15

ROMANIAN
Eminescu, Mihail 33

RUSSIAN
Aksakov, Sergei Timofeyvich 2
Bakunin, Mikhail (Alexandrovich) 25, 58
Bashkirtseff, Marie 27
Belinski, Vissarion Grigoryevich 5
Chernyshevsky, Nikolay Gavrilovich 1
Dobrolyubov, Nikolai Alexandrovich 5
Dostoevsky, Fedor Mikhailovich 2, 7, 21, 33, 43
Gogol, Nikolai (Vasilyevich) 5, 15, 31
Goncharov, Ivan Alexandrovich 1, 63
Herzen, Aleksandr Ivanovich 10
Karamzin, Nikolai Mikhailovich 3
Krylov, Ivan Andreevich 1
Lermontov, Mikhail Yuryevich 5
Leskov, Nikolai (Semyonovich) 25
Nekrasov, Nikolai Alekseevich 11
Ostrovsky, Alexander 30, 57

Pisarev, Dmitry Ivanovich 25
Pushkin, Alexander (Sergeyevich) 3, 27
Saltykov, Mikhail Evgrafovich 16
Smolenskin, Peretz 30
Turgenev, Ivan 21
Tyutchev, Fyodor 34
Zhukovsky, Vasily 35

SCOTTISH
Baillie, Joanna 2
Beattie, James 25
Campbell, Thomas 19
Ferrier, Susan (Edmonstone) 8
Galt, John 1
Hogg, James 4
Jeffrey, Francis 33
Lockhart, John Gibson 6
Mackenzie, Henry 41
Oliphant, Margaret (Oliphant Wilson) 11
Scott, Walter 15
Stevenson, Robert Louis (Balfour) 5, 14, 63
Thomson, James, 18
Wilson, John 5

SPANISH
Alarcon, Pedro Antonio de 1
Caballero, Fernan 10
Castro, Rosalia de 3
Espronceda, Jose de 39
Larra (y Sanchez de Castro), Mariano Jose de 17
Tamayo y Baus, Manuel 1
Zorrilla y Moral, Jose 6

SWEDISH
Almqvist, Carl Jonas Love 42
Bremer, Fredrika 11
Tegner, Esaias 2

SWISS
Amiel, Henri Frederic 4
Burckhardt, Jacob 49
Charriere, Isabelle de 66
Keller, Gottfried 2
Wyss, Johann David Von 10

UKRAINIAN
Taras Shevchenko 54

NCLC-66 Title Index

"Advent" (Rossetti) 66:330
"Advertisement to the First Edition" (Browning) 66:90
Almanacks (Emerson) 66:186-8, 190-5, 197, 221-2
"Amor mundi" (Rossetti) 66:305
Annus Domini: A Prayer for Every Day in the Year (Rossetti) 66:305
"Another Spring" (Rossetti) 66:382
"An Apple Gathering" (Rossetti) 66:351-4, 383
"At Home" (Rossetti) 66:307
Aurora Leigh (Browning) 66:1-118
The Battle of Marathon: A Poem (Browning) 66:44, 71
"A Better Resurrection" (Rossetti) 66:330
"A Birthday" (Rossetti) 66:311, 342, 344, 382
"Blessed Damozel" (Rossetti) 66:304
"The Book of the Poets" (Browning) 66:44
Bouvard et Pécuchet (Flaubert) 66:256, 263
"Brandons Both" (Rossetti) 66:352
"A Bruised Reed Shall He Not Break" (Rossetti) 66:330
Caliste; or, the Sequel to Letters [Written] from Lausanne (Charriere)
  See *Caliste; ou, Suite des lettres écrites de Lausanne*
Caliste; ou, Suite des lettres écrites de Lausanne (Charriere) 66:121, 123-6, 128, 135, 138, 142-3, 145-6, 160-1, 163-7, 169
Called to Be Saints (Rossetti) 66:344
Camille, ou le nouveau roman (Charriere) 66:180
Casa Guidi Windows: A Poem (Browning) 66:44-5, 52, 90-1, 95
Cheerfulness Taught by Reason (Browning) 66:44

"Cobwebs" (Rossetti) 66:341
Un coeur simple (Flaubert) 66:281
Collected Poems (Rossetti)
  See *The Poetical Works of Christina Georgina Rossetti*
Collected Works (Rossetti)
  See *The Poetical Works of Christina Georgina Rossetti*
Commonplace, and Other Short Tales (Rossetti) 66:328, 330
"Confessions" (Browning) 66:42
"Consider the Lilies of the Field" (Rossetti) 66:301
"The Convent Threshold" (Rossetti) 66:304-5, 308, 311-2, 341
Correspondance (Flaubert) 66:289
"Cousin Kate" (Rossetti) 66:329, 331, 350-3, 355
"Cowper's Grave" (Browning) 66:44
Crowned and Buried (Browning) 66:44
"The Cry of the Children" (Browning) 66:25, 42, 44
"Dead before Death" (Rossetti) 66:341
"The Dead City" (Rossetti) 66:306
"The Dead Pan" (Browning) 66:44
Dictionary of Received Ideas (Flaubert)
  See *Dictionnaire des idées recues*
Dictionnaire des idées recues (Flaubert) 66:263, 274
"A Drama of Exile" (Browning) 66:3, 44, 71
"Dream-Love" (Rossetti) 66:311
"Eden Bower" (Rossetti) 66:305
L'éducation sentimentale: Histoire d'un jeune homme (Flaubert) 66:256, 270, 293
L'émigré (Charriere) 66:136
Les Émigrés (Charriere) 66:124

"Essay on Mind" (Browning) 66:44
"Eve" (Rossetti) 66:330
The Face of the Deep: A Devotional Commentary on the Apocalypse (Rossetti) 66:306-9, 376
"Friends" (Rossetti) 66:307
"From House to Home" (Rossetti) 66:301, 304, 306-9, 312, 320-1, 329, 356, 382
"From Sunset to Star Rise" (Rossetti) 66:341, 372
"Goblin Market" (Rossetti) 66:297-390
Goblin Market, and Other Poems (Rossetti) 66:312-3
"He and She" (Rossetti) 66:341
"I Commend You" (Rossetti) 66:307
"In an Artist's Studio" (Rossetti) 66:350
"In the Round Tower at Jhansi, June 8, 1857" (Rossetti) 66:371, 377
"The Iniquity of the Fathers upon the Children" (Rossetti) 66:329
"Lady Geraldine's Courtship" (Browning) 66:44-5, 56, 71, 74, 87-91, 93, 101
"Laughing Life Cries at the Feast" (Rossetti) 66:307
"The Lay of the Brown Rosary" (Browning) 66:44
"The Legend of the Brown Rosarie" (Browning)
  See "The Lay of the Brown Rosary"
Letter and Spirit: Notes on the Commandments (Rossetti) 66:306-7, 342, 375
The Letters of Elizabeth Barrett Browning (Browning) 66:50-1, 70
Letters of Elizabeth Barrett Browning to Mary Russell Mitford 1836-1854 (Browning) 66:74
Letters of Mrs. Henley (Charriere)
  See *Lettres de Mistriss Henley publiées par son amie*

TITLE INDEX

The Letters of Robert Browning and Elizabeth Barrett 1845-1846 (Browning) **66**:69, 74, 76-7
Letters [written] from Lausanne (Charriere)
See *Lettres écrites de Lausanne*
Lettres de Mistriss Henley publiées par son amie (Charriere) **66**:121-3, 125, 128-9, 138-43, 146-54, 156-7, 176
Lettres écrites de Lausanne (Charriere) **66**:121, 123-5, 135, 138, 142-3, 145, 161, 165, 168-9, 172, 176
Lettres neuchâteloises (Charriere) **66**:122-6, 136, 138, 160, 165, 168, 176
Lettres trouvées dans des porte-feuilles d'émigrés (Charriere) **66**:125, 136, 172, 174-7
Lettres trouvées dans des porte-feuilles d'émigrés,sui (Charriere) **66**:176-7
"Life and Death" (Rossetti) **66**:341
"A Life's Parallels" (Rossetti) **66**:343
"Light Love" (Rossetti) **66**:329, 331, 352
"Listening" (Rossetti) **66**:307
"Lord Walter's Wife" (Browning) **66**:90
"The Lost Titian" (Rossetti) **66**:328
"Love from the North" (Rossetti) **66**:328
"The Love of Christ which Passeth Knowledge" (Rossetti) **66**:330
"The Lowest Place" (Rossetti) **66**:330-1, 352
"The Lowest Room" (Rossetti)
See "The Lowest Place"
"Maggie, a Lady" (Rossetti) **66**:302, 331
"Maiden Song" (Rossetti) **66**:302, 328
"Maude Clare" (Rossetti) **66**:330-1, 352-3, 355
Maude: Prose and Verse (Rossetti) **66**:317, 320-1, 331
"Meeting" (Rossetti) **66**:311
Memoires (Flaubert)
See *Les mémoires d'un fou*
Les mémoires d'un fou (Flaubert) **66**:269-72
Mistriss Henley (Charriere)
See *Lettres de Mistriss Henley publiées par son amie*

"A Musical Instrument" (Browning) **66**:85
La Nature et l'art (Charriere) **66**:126
"No, Thank You, John!" (Rossetti) **66**:331
Le Noble (Charriere) **66**:121-2, 172-6, 178
"Noble Sisters" (Rossetti) **66**:302, 312, 352
The Nobleman (Charriere)
See *Le Noble*
Novembre: Fragments de style quelconque (Flaubert) **66**:269-72
Oeuvres complètes (Charriere) **66**:134-5, 137, 141-2, 146, 161, 172
"An Old World Thicket" (Rossetti) **66**:342
"One Day" (Rossetti) **66**:307
"One Foot in Sea and One on Shore" (Rossetti) **66**:341
One Word More (Browning) **66**:52
"Parting After Parting" (Rossetti) **66**:311
"A Peal of Bells" (Rossetti) **66**:307
Pénélope (Charriere) **66**:127
Poems of 1844 (Browning) **66**:88
The Poetical Works of Christina Georgina Rossetti (Rossetti) **66**:304, 310
"The Poet's Vow" (Browning) **66**:56
"The Prince's Progress" (Rossetti) **66**:304, 328, 356
The Prince's Progress, and Other Poems (Rossetti) **66**:349
Prometheus Bound, and Miscellaneous Poems (Browning) **66**:44, 47
"Repining" (Rossetti) **66**:386
"Rest" (Rossetti) **66**:301
Le Roman de Charles Cecil (Charriere) **66**:126
"A Romance of the Age" (Browning)
See "Lady Geraldine's Courtship"
"The Romance of the Swan's Nest" (Browning) **66**:44
"The Romaunt of the Page" (Browning) **66**:56
"A Royal Princess" (Rossetti) **66**:331
Saint-Anne (Charriere) **66**:125, 172, 178
"Seek and Find" (Rossetti) **66**:331, 362
Sentimental Education: A Young Man's History (Flaubert)

See *L'éducation sentimentale: Histoire d'un jeune homme*
"The Seraphim" (Browning) **66**:71
The Seraphim, and Other Poems (Browning) **66**:44, 83
"Shadow of Dorothea" (Rossetti) **66**:307
A Simple Heart (Flaubert)
See *Un coeur simple*
Sing-Song: A Nursery Rhyme-Book (Rossetti) **66**:330, 341
Sir Walter Finch et son fils William (Charriere) **66**:124-5, 137, 161, 164
"Sister Louise de la Misericorde" (Rossetti) **66**:305
"Sister Maude" (Rossetti) **66**:312, 352
"Sleeping at Last" (Rossetti) **66**:343
Some Account of the Greek Christian Poets (Browning) **66**:44
Sonnets from the Portuguese (Browning) **66**:44, 90-1
"The Soul's Expression" (Browning) **66**:85
Speaking Likenesses (Rossetti) **66**:331
The Temptation of St. Anthony (Flaubert)
See *La tentation de Saint Antoine*
La tentation de Saint Antoine (Flaubert) **66**:262, 269-72
"The Three Enemies" (Rossetti) **66**:305
"Three Stages" (Rossetti) **66**:307, 311
Time Flies (Rossetti) **66**:305-6, 331, 341-2
"A Triad" (Rossetti) **66**:330
Les Trois Femmes (Charriere) **66**:124-6, 134, 136-7
"Troy Town" (Rossetti) **66**:305
"Twice" (Rossetti) **66**:342
"Two Charades" (Rossetti) **66**:341
"Two Enigmas" (Rossetti) **66**:341
"Two Pursuits" (Rossetti) **66**:305
"Up Hill" (Rossetti) **66**:301
"Vanna's Twins" (Rossetti) **66**:330
"The Way of the World" (Rossetti) **66**:342
Work (Browning) **66**:44
"The World" (Rossetti) **66**:305
"A Year's Spinning" (Browning) **66**:60